THE NEW OXFORD HISTORY
OF ENGLAND

General Editor · J. M. ROBERTS

Shaping the Nation

ENGLAND

1360–1461

GERALD HARRISS

CLARENDON PRESS · OXFORD

OXFORD

UNIVERSITY PRESS

Great Clarendon Street, Oxford OX2 6DP

Oxford University Press is a department of the University of Oxford.
It furthers the University's objective of excellence in research, scholarship,
and education by publishing worldwide in

Oxford New York

Auckland Bangkok Buenos Aires Cape Town Chennai
Dar es Salaam Delhi Hong Kong Istanbul Karachi Kolkata
Kuala Lumpur Madrid Melbourne Mexico City Mumbai Nairobi
São Paulo Shanghai Taipei Tokyo Toronto

Oxford is a registered trade mark of Oxford University Press
in the UK and in certain other countries

Published in the United States
by Oxford University Press Inc., New York

© Gerald Harriss 2005

The moral rights of the author have been asserted
Database right Oxford University Press (maker)

First published 2005

British Library Cataloguing in Publication Data

Data available

Library of Congress Cataloging in Publication Data

Data available

ISBN 0-19-822816-3

3 5 7 9 10 8 6 4 2

Typeset in Ehrhardt MT by
Jaycee, Trivandrum, India
Printed in Great Britain
on acid-free paper by
Biddles Ltd.
King's Lynn, Norfolk

TO ANNE AND OUR FAMILY

General Editor's Preface

The first volume of Sir George Clark's *Oxford History of England* was published in 1934. Undertaking the General Editorship of a *New Oxford History of England* forty-five years later it was hard not to feel overshadowed by its powerful influence and well-deserved status. Some of Clark's volumes (his own among them) were brilliant individual achievements, hard to rival and impossible to match. Of course, he and his readers shared a broad sense of the purpose and direction of such books. His successor can no longer be sure of doing that. The building-blocks of the story, its reasonable and meaningful demarcations and divisions, the continuities and discontinuities, the priorities of different varieties of history, the place of narrative—all these things are now much harder to agree upon. We now know much more about many things, and think about what we know in different ways. It is not surprising that historians now sometimes seem unsure about the audience to which their scholarship and writing are addressed.

In the end, authors should be left to write their own books. None the less, the *New Oxford History of England* is intended to be more than a collection of discrete or idiosyncratic histories in chronological order. Its aim is to give an account of the development of our country in time. It is hard to treat that development as just the history which unfolds within the precise boundaries of England, and a mistake to suggest that this implies a neglect of the histories of the Scots, Irish, and Welsh. Yet the institutional core of the story which runs from Anglo-Saxon times to our own is the story of a state-structure built round the English monarchy and its effective successor, the Crown in Parliament, and that provides the only continuous articulation of the history of peoples we today call British. It follows that there must be uneven and sometimes discontinuous treatment of much of the history of those peoples. The state story remains, nevertheless, an intelligible thread and to me appears still to justify the title both of this series and that of its predecessor.

If the attention given to the other kingdoms and the principality of Wales must reflect in this series their changing relationship to that central theme, this is not the only way in which the emphasis of individual volumes will be different. Each author has been asked to bring forward what he or she sees as the most important topics explaining the history under study, taking account of the present state of historical knowledge, drawing attention to areas of dispute and to matters on which final judgement is at present difficult (or, perhaps, impossible) and not merely recapitulating what has recently been the fashionable centre of professional debate. But each volume, allowing for its special approach and proportions, must also provide a comprehensive account, in which politics is always likely to be prominent. Volumes have to be demarcated chronologically but continuities must not be obscured; vestigially or not, copyhold survived into the 1920s and the Anglo-Saxon shires until the 1970s (some of which were to be resurrected in the 1990s, too). Any single volume should be an entry-point to the understanding of processes only slowly unfolding, sometimes across centuries. My hope is that in the end we shall have, as the outcome, a set of standard and authoritative histories, embodying the scholarship of a generation, and not mere compendia in which the determinants are lost to sight among the detail.

J. M. ROBERTS

Preface

The period treated in this volume has been the subject of half a century of scholarly revision and debate. From being seen as one of disorder and decline, it has emerged as one of crucial transformation, in which English society and government acquired the shape it was to retain until the Civil War. I have tried, first, to reflect the research that has produced this reassessment; secondly, to provide a serviceable guide for the study of the period at university level; and thirdly, to convey my own understanding of it. I have summarized that in the Conclusion, which can also serve as an Introduction.

Reading and writing history is always so enjoyable that this book has never seemed a burden, but had it been so I would have been sustained by the encouragement and helpfulness of many friends and colleagues. To the community of learning at Magdalen College, with which I have been connected at varying levels for over sixty years, I am deeply indebted in too many ways to specify here; but above all I wish to recall the inspiration of Bruce McFarlane, my teacher and friend for the first part of that time. I have profited, too, from the fresh intelligence which my own pupils, both undergraduate and postgraduate, have brought to the problems of medieval history. I recall in particular how Simon Walker's innovative thesis repeatedly yielded new insights, and my frequent citation of his work indicates how greatly he illuminated the study of late medieval England and how impoverished we are by his untimely death. I owe a specific debt to some colleagues for reading, and commenting critically on, particular chapters about which I felt unsure. In this respect Christine Carpenter, Jeremy Catto, Ian Doyle, and Simon Payling have all been most generous with their time and knowledge. Many others have unstintingly answered my appeals from deepest Dorset for factual and bibliographical references.

Academic commitments while in post meant that most of the book had to be written in retirement, and I have constantly marvelled at the unreproachful patience with which the Oxford University Press has waited for it, matched by the unwavering encouragement and assistance of my General Editor, John Roberts, to whom I would dearly have wished to deliver the final typescript. Above all I am grateful for the support and understanding of my wife, Anne, in my continuing preoccupation with matters historical.

GERALD HARRISS

Contents

PART II WORK AND WORSHIP

PART III MEN AND EVENTS

Plates

Figures, Maps, Tables

Abbreviations

Agr. Hist. Rev.	*Agricultural History Review*
AHEW	E. Miller (ed.), *The Agrarian History of England and Wales*, iii: *1348–1500* (Cambridge, 1991)
AHR	*American Historical Review*
Anon. Chron.	*The Anonimalle Chronicle, 1333–1381*, ed. V. H. Galbraith (Manchester, 1927)
Arch. Jnl.	*Archaeological Journal*
Bekynton, *Correspondence*	*The Official Correspondence of Thomas Bekynton*, ed. G. Williams, 2 vols., Rolls ser. (London, 1872)
Benet's Chron.	*John Benet's Chronicle*, ed. G. L. Harriss and M. A. Harriss, in *Camden Miscellany, XXIV*, Camden Society, 4th ser. 9 (London, 1972)
BIHR	*Bulletin of the Institute of Historical Research*
BJR[U]L	*Bulletin of John Rylands [University] Library*
BL	British Library
BRUO	A. B. Emden (ed.), *Biographical Register of the University of Oxford to 1500*, 3 vols. (Oxford, 1957)
Brut	*The Brut, or, Chronicles of England*, pt. 2, ed. F. W. Brie, 2 vols. EETS, old ser., 136 (1908)
CCR	*Calendar of the Close Rolls*
CFR	*Calendar of the Fine Rolls*
CHB	L. Hellinga and J. B. Trapp (eds.), *The Cambridge History of the Book*, iii (Cambridge, 1997)
CHMEL	D. Wallace (ed.), *The Cambridge History of Medieval English Literature* (Cambridge, 1999)
Chron. Angliae	*Chronicon Angliae*, ed. E. M. Thompson, Rolls ser., 64 (1874)
Chron. Lond.	C. L. Kingsford (ed.), *Chronicles of London* (Oxford, 1905)
Chron. Rev.	*Chronicles of the Revolution, 1397–1400*, ed. C. Given-Wilson (Manchester, 1993)

Complete Peerage	G. E. Cokayne, *The Complete Peerage*, ed. V. Gibbs *et al.*, 13 vols. (London, 1910–59)
CPR	*Calendar of the Patent Rolls*
CUH	D. Palliser (ed.), *The Cambridge Urban History of Britain*, i (Cambridge, 2000)
Davies (ed.), *Eng. Chron.*	*An English Chronicle*, ed. J. S. Davies, Camden Society, 64 (1855)
Davis (ed.), *Paston Letters*	N. Davis (ed.), *Paston Letters and Papers of the Fifteenth Century*, 2 vols. (Oxford, 1971, 1976)
Econ. HR	*Economic History Review*
EETS	Early English Text Society
EHD	A. R. Myers (ed.), *English Historical Documents, 1327–1485* (London, 1969)
EHR	*English Historical Review*
Eulog. Hist.	*Eulogium Historiarum sive Temporis*, ed. F. S. Haydon, 3 vols., Rolls ser., 9, vol. iii (London, 1863)
Gairdner (ed.), *Paston Letters*	J. Gairdner (ed.), *The Paston Letters* (Gloucester, 1986)
Gesta	*Gesta Henrici Quinti*, ed. F. Taylor and J. S. Roskell (Oxford, 1975)
Gregory, *Chron.*	*Gregory's Chronicle*, ed. J. Gairdner, Camden Society, new ser., 17 (1876)
Hardyng, *Chronicle*	John Hardyng, *Chronicle*, ed. H. Ellis (London, 1812)
Hist. Jnl.	*Historical Journal*
Hist. Res.	*Historical Research*
House of Commons	J. S. Roskell, L. Clark, and C. Rawcliffe (eds.), *The History of Parliament: The House of Commons, 1386–1421*, 4 vols. (Stroud, 1992)
JBAA	*Journal of the British Architectural Association*
JEH	*Journal of Ecclesiastical History*
Jnl. Brit. Stud.	*Journal of British Studies*
Jnl. Hist. Soc.	*Journal of Historical Sociology*
Jnl. Legal Hist.	*Journal of Legal History*
Jnl. Med. Hist.	*Journal of Medieval History*
Jnl. Relig. Hist.	*Journal of Religious History*
Kail (ed.), *Political Poems*	J. Kail (ed.), *Twenty Six Political Poems*, EETS, old ser., 124 (1904)
Knighton, *Chron.*	*Knighton's Chronicle, 1337–1396*, ed. G. H. Martin, Oxford Medieval Texts (Oxford, 1995)

Law and Hist. Rev.	*Law and History Review*
Med. Aevum	*Medium Aevum*
Mid. Hist.	*Midland History*
Mum and the Sothsegger	*Mum and the Sothsegger*, ed. M. Day and R. Steele, EETS, old ser., 199 (1936)
Northern Hist.	*Northern History*
Nott. Med. Stud.	*Nottingham Medieval Studies*
OHS	Oxford Historical Society
P & P	*Past and Present*
Parlty. Hist.	*Parliamentary History*
PBA	*Proceedings of the British Academy*
PMLA	*Proceedings of the Modern Languages Association*
PRO	Public Record Office
Proc. & Ord.	*Proceedings and Ordinances of the Privy Council of England*, ed. N. H. Nicolas, 6 vols. (London, 1834–7)
Reg. Chichele	*The Register of Henry Chichele, archbishop of Canterbury, 1414–1443*, ed. E. F. Jacob, 4 vols., Canterbury and York Society, 42, 45–7 (Oxford, 1938–47)
Robbins (ed.), *Hist. Poems*	R. H. Robbins (ed.), *Historical Poems of the XIVth and XVth Centuries* (New York, 1959)
Rot. Parl.	*Rotuli Parliamentorum*, ed. J. Strachey *et al.*, 6 vols., Record Commission (London, [1783], 1832)
Rymer (ed.), *Foedera*	T. Rymer (ed.), *Foedera, Conventiones, Litterae*, 20 vols. (London, 1704–35)
St Albans Chron.	*The St Albans Chronicle, 1406–1420*, ed. V. H. Galbraith (Oxford, 1937)
SCH	Studies in Church History
Select Docs.	A. Brown and S. Chrimes (eds.), *Select Documents of English Constitutional History, 1307–1485* (London, 1961)
SEWW	A. Hudson (ed.), *Selections from English Wycliffite Writings* (Cambridge, 1978)
Six Town Chron.	*Six Town Chronicles*, ed. R. Flenley (Oxford, 1911)
SR	*The Statutes of the Realm*, ed. A. Luders *et al.*, 11 vols. (London, 1810–28), i (1810), ii (1816)

Test. Vet.	*Testamenta Vetusta*, ed. N. H. Nicolas, 2 vols. (1826)
Tout, *Chapters*	T. F. Tout, *Chapters in the Administrative History of Mediaeval England*, 6 vols. (Manchester, 1920–33)
TRHS	*Transactions of the Royal Historical Society*
UH	*Urban History*
UHY	*Urban History Yearbook*
VCH	H. A. Doubleday, W. Page, L. F. Salzmann, and R. B. Pugh (eds.), *Victoria History of the Counties of England* (1900–)
Wals., *Hist. Anglicana*	*Thomae Walsingham, Historia Anglicana*, ed. H. T. Riley, 2 vols., Rolls ser., 28a (1863–4)
Wars of Eng.	J. Stevenson (ed.), *Letters and Papers Illustrative of the Wars of the English in France during the Reign of Henry the Sixth, King of England*, 2 vols. in 3, Rolls ser. (London, 1861–4)
West. Chron.	*The Westminster Chronicle, 1381–94*, ed. L. C. Hector and B. H. Harvey (Oxford, 1982)

PART I

Political Society

CHAPTER I

Concepts of Governance

1. THEORIES OF AUTHORITY

By 1461 Sir John Fortescue could present France and England as examples of absolute and mixed monarchy.[1] Yet both drew on a common fund of European political thought and their political destinies over many centuries had interlocked. Nor were these immutable forms. English governance rested on an unstable balance of theocratic (descending) and representational (ascending) authority which royal policy or political circumstances might at any time upset. This tension at the heart of the late medieval polity is best appreciated if we briefly review the derivation of these opposing principles and how they were manifested in English constitutional practice.

Early medieval kingship claimed authority from God, who had set the king above his subjects to protect and govern them for their common good in peace and justice. As God's deputy, the king's judgement and will were all-sufficient, the law was his alone to declare and enforce. To oppose him was disobedience to God, who alone could remove an errant ruler. The appeal and strength of absolutist theocracy was that of a closed system which simply negated all terrestrial authority, which St Augustine had judged to be intrinsically corrupted by man's fall. Monarchy, validated by God, reflected the unity and hierarchy of the divine order, to which human society should aspire. The king acquired sacerdotal qualities. In the English coronation rite the vesting of the monarch with priestly robes, the chanting of *Veni Creator Spiritus* as at ordinations, the mystic marriage of monarch and kingdom symbolized by the ring, and above all the anointing with holy oil as in the Old Testament, all set the monarch 'above the people whom God gave him to rule and govern'.[2] By 1300 the principle of hereditary succession reduced the approval of subjects to a ritualized acclamation.

Nevertheless, theocracy had an essential flaw: the king, like other men, was corruptible, and thus subject to the Church, whose power to bind and loose from

---

[1] Sir John Fortescue, *The Governance of England*, ed. C. Plummer (Oxford, 1885); id., *De Laudibus Legum Angliae*, ed. and trans. S. B. Chrimes (Cambridge, 1949).

[2] W. Ullmann, *Principles of Government and Politics in the Middle Ages* (London, 1961), 129, quoting the prayer text *Unguantur Istae Manus* from the coronation rite.

sin did not stop at the steps of the throne. Medieval kings accepted an admonitory papacy but repelled any papal claim to exercise ruling power within their realm. Their resistance had been fortified by the revived study of Roman Law in the twelfth century which vested the ruler with absolute power, asserting that the state was an emanation of his will. He was the law (*lex animata*), the source of his subjects' rights and liberties, which were thus revocable at his will. He was the state.

Both theocracy and Roman Law appealed to the medieval intellectual and ruling elite as safeguards against anarchy. But at a lower level society was being organized by forces to which such theories gave little recognition: feudal lordship and community. Feudal lordship expressed the relationship between a military leader and his followers: their fidelity, aid, and advice to him being matched by his trust, protection, and reward of them. It was a contractual relationship within society, the breaking of which by either party would dissolve it. This vitiated its application to state-building, but feudalism coexisted with monarchy at a subsidiary level. At the same time another form of local organization was appearing, principally in an urban and economic context: the commune. This was a horizontal, not hierarchic, society which itself validated the laws by which it was governed and the social and political obligations of its members. Both the contractual nature of military feudalism and the representational structure of the commune stood in stark contrast to the God-given authority of the monarch and the corporative authority of the prince. Yet the former remained simply modes of social organization, while the latter were theories of state power. Only in the thirteenth century did there appear a theory which located the source of authority in the state in its members rather than in the head.

The rediscovery of Aristotle's *Politics* presented a double challenge. Where St Augustine saw political society as a manifestation of man's sin, for Aristotle it expressed the fulfilment of man's nature as a social and rational animal. Secondly, rather than deriving the political order from divine precept, Aristotle established it from empirical observation and rational deduction, working upwards from cohabitation in families and villages to cooperation in a *polis*. The authority to regulate society for the common good came not from the ruler above but from the citizens below. Greek rationality thus inverted the hierarchic principles of both Christian theology and monarchy, making the ruler the officer of the community. It fell to St Thomas Aquinas to fashion a synthesis between the principles of order and reason. Aquinas sought to retain monarchical rule within a politically autonomous society, as figuring the hierarchy and unity of heaven. The king thus retained divine attributes in rendering justice and upholding the law, but it was now acknowledged that the common good to which society was directed was defined by the collective reason of the citizens, as also were the laws by which it was governed. In these respects the king was part of society, not over and above it; he administered the law but was not its source; he was the trustee not the owner of the kingdom. The kingdom was conceived as a body composed of head and members, and symbolized by the Crown, which gave it a perpetual identity. There were thus two types of rule: 'regal' as exercised by an absolute monarch, and 'political' when power was exercised in accordance with the laws of the realm.[3]

Mixed monarchy of this type accorded well with English political development. By 1300 the basic rights of subjects had been enshrined in Magna Carta, the king had accepted the need for counsel and consent from the magnates in making law, his public promise to uphold such laws was added to the coronation oath in 1308, and the need for the assent of the realm to extraordinary taxation had recently been vindicated. The establishment of parliament as a recurrent and hence normal element was extending political awareness and participation to an increasing number of landowners, to create a political society which bridged centre and locality. The structure of that society will be explored in Part I of this book, but two important points must be made in the light of the preceding discussion.

First, mixed monarchy did not simply displace or efface preceding forms of government; rather it was constructed out of them. Theocratic kingship remained embedded in the coronation ritual and the king retained an area of prerogative power and rights untouched by common law. He held his throne from God alone and there was no agreed procedure for his removal. Feudatories claimed a right to counsel the king and constrain an erring one; ultimately even to repudiate their allegiance. Parliament asserted its rights in taxation and lawmaking, but its assembly depended on royal will. Inconsistent legacies and uneasy compromises meant a constant tension between the elements of the polity—king, magnates, churchmen, commons—which could at times lurch into crisis. Thus Richard II revived the vocabulary of theocracy, taking Edward the Confessor as his model; his baronial opponents placed constraints on royal power as they had under Edward II and John; the middling classes claimed authority through parliament to reform government for the common good; the plebs revolted in the name of natural justice. The political system of late medieval England, because it was a historical amalgam, was essentially unstable, its tensions exposed by conflict and fuelled by precedents. So it was to remain until the seventeenth century.

Secondly, while mixed monarchy, as celebrated in Sir John Fortescue's writings, became characteristic of England, in France the same cultural traditions had been shaped by historical forces into a more absolutist monarchical system.

---

[3] R. Eccleshall, *Reason and Order in Politics* (Oxford, 1978), 61, quoting from Aquinas's *Commentary on Aristotle's 'Politics'*.

The dominance of Roman lawyers in the government of the late Capetian kings reinforced royal supremacy through the doctrine that the king was 'emperor within his kingdom'. By 1300 the French monarchy was significantly more theocratic in character than the English, and had secured an able apologist in Giles of Rome. In his *De Regimine Principum* (1277) he argued that purely regal authority accorded better with divine order and natural reason than mixed monarchy. The king must rule for his people's good, and the law must accord with reason and promote justice, but the ruler's right will, informed by God's grace, must be unconstrained. With the unity of France threatened and royal authority challenged in the Hundred Years War, men turned to the monarchy as the symbol of French identity. The government of Charles V consciously promoted 'une religion royale' in the tradition of St Louis: a holy king and a holy nation united in a *corpus mysticum*, a new Israel.

Thus two opposed theories of authority existed in north-west Europe. Both treated monarchy as divinely sanctioned, but one held that the monarch was infused with God's authority by which he ruled and gave being to the body politic; the other that the monarch held authority in trust from the people, God's children, to be exercised with their assent and for their good. Yet this was no ideological cold war, dividing Europe into opposing camps. There was much in their common inheritance that united; much indeed that particular English kings envied and sought to emulate in their rival's power. Richard II hoped to imitate Charles VI, Henry V hoped to succeed him. Other Englishmen were distrustful of the French political system and by the time of Fortescue condemned it by reference to the English. How a king should govern his people was intensively debated in the new vernacular literature of the age of Chaucer.

2. THE LITERARY MODEL OF GOVERNANCE

The literary discussion of governance was predominantly Aristotelian in tone, derived from Aquinas and from the *Secretum Secretorum*, a pseudo-Aristotelian work of oriental origin which circulated in England in Latin and English translation.[4] The literature was of broadly two types: systematic expositions of the duties of kingship as 'mirrors for princes', and occasional verses on political events and abuses. Of the former one of the first examples was the tract *De Quadripartita Regis Specie*, a free adaptation of the *Secretum*, presented to Richard II in 1391.[5] During Richard's minority John Gower had already, in *Vox Clamantis* (1378–81), called on the king to be guided by sound counsel, and

---

[4] *Secretum Secretorum: Nine English Versions*, ed. M. A. Manzalaoui, EETS, old ser., 276 (Oxford, 1977); A. H. Gilbert, 'Notes on the influence of the *Secreta Secretorum*', *Speculum*, 3 (1928), 84–98.

[5] J.-P. Genet (ed.), *Four English Political Tracts of the Later Middle Ages*, Camden Society, 4th ser., 18 (London, 1977).

in *Confessio Amantis*, begun in 1390 at Richard's invitation, he had appealed to the king to heal political divisions.[6] Subsequently his disapproval of Richard's rule made him an apologist for the Lancastrian regime, which promoted a programme of 'bone governance' to legitimize its rule. Thomas Hoccleve's *Regement of Princes*, written to support this in 1410–11, drew on both *De Regimine Principum* and *Secretum Secretorum*.[7] In 1412 Prince Henry also commissioned John Lydgate to write the *Troy Book*, and later the *Siege of Thebes*, which celebrated the king's triumph in 1420.[8] A further phase of advice books marked the troubled years of Henry VI's majority: the *Tractatus de Regimine Principum* of 1437–45 dwelt on the sacerdotal character of the monarch, but the Ashmole version of the *Secretum* in 1445, and the more original *Three Considerations* of the mid-century, were more secular.[9] Finally the experience of the 1450s is reflected in George Ashby's *Active Policy of a Prince*, written for Prince Edward in 1470,[10] and in the weightier *Governance of England* by Sir John Fortescue. Though often prompted by royal patronage, these works commanded a wide audience in political society, as did the shorter anonymous verses provoked by the recurrent political crises. They are evidence of lively debate on the expectations and shortcomings of kingly rule.

All affirm, if not the king's sacrality, certainly his status as God's vicegerent. He is *electus a Deo*, even usurpers like Henry IV and Edward IV being chosen by God to restore good governance. When guided by right reason his rule is God-like: in Hoccleve's words,[11]

> a king by wey of his office
> to God i-likened is . . .

This God-like power is most clearly displayed in his role as judge, with power over life and limb. For this he must be above both law and subjects, 'free to all other then God', as Gower says.[12] Though set above the law to enforce it, he must conform to it in his own acts. Indeed, as the channel for God's rule his personal life should be exemplary. As verses from the mid-fifteenth century put it,

---

[6] John Gower, *The Complete Works*, ed. G. C. Macaulay, 4 vols. (Oxford, 1899–1902).

[7] T. Hoccleve, *The Regement of Princes*, ed. F. J. Furnivall, EETS, extra ser., 72 (London, 1897). For differing views, see D. Pearsall, 'Hoccleve's *Regement of Princes*: The poetics of royal self-representation', *Speculum*, 69 (1994), 386–410, and N. Perkins, *Hoccleve's Regiment of Princes: Counsel and Constraint* (Woodbridge, 2001), esp. 50–7.

[8] John Lydgate, *Troy Book*, ed. H. Bergen, 4 vols., EETS, extra ser., 97–106 (London, 1906–12); id., *Siege of Thebes*, ed. A. Erdmann, EETS, extra ser., 108 (London, 1911).

[9] Genet (ed.), *Four English Political Tracts*, 40–210.

[10] George Ashby, *Poems*, ed. M. Bateson, EETS, extra ser., 76 (London, 1899).

[11] Hoccleve, *Regement*, 87; Perkins, *Hoccleve's 'Regiment of Princes'*, 132.

[12] Gower, *Confessio Amantis*, bk. 7, lines 2733–5, in id., *Works*, ed. Macaulay, iii. 307.

> so ought your lyfe be clennest from offence,
> and shyne en vertue above your subgectes all.
> a vycyous prynce es as a plage mortall
> and foule example to all his comonte.[13]

If kings sin their people perish, while their virtues infuse society with peace and order: a theme expounded by Hoccleve in verses addressed to Henry V at his accession.[14]

Second to governing himself the king had to rule his court, for it mirrored his government of the realm. A large and honourable entourage was a manifestation of royal 'magnificence', while unworthy courtiers and a bankrupt household brought disrepute. In *Vox Clamantis* Gower portrayed Richard II as led by young, vain courtiers and older, greedy ones, and later attributed his fall to their factious self-interest. The plundering of the Crown's wealth by courtiers was condemned by the author of *Richard the Redeles*, and in the mid-fifteenth century the greed of the courtiers of Henry VI had

> made the kyng so pore
> That now he beggeth from dore to dore.[15]

The *Secretum* recommended that the king's dress and carriage should reflect the royal dignity, that he cultivate taciturnity and gravity in speech, and distance himself from courtiers to avoid over-familiarity. A shrewd king could learn from his courtiers' talk how his rule was seen outside.

Beyond the court the king's government was channelled through his subjects and this made his choice of ministers and officials crucial. All the advice books insisted on his need for true and wise counsellors with whom any project should be thoroughly discussed. For Gower, 'Conseil . . . is the substance of all a king's governance' and the poem 'Truth, Reste and Peace' declares

> What king that wol have good name
> He wol be led by wys counsayle.[16]

Yet disinterested counsel was rare: the searcher for Truth in *Mum and the Sothsegger* did not expect to find him in the council; rather, it was among the poor that the king would learn of misgovernment.

Beyond the council lay the nobility, likened to the shoulders and backbone of the body politic and elsewhere to functioning parts of the ship of state.[17] They

---

[13] Robbins (ed.), *Hist. Poems*, 234.

[14] *Selections from Hoccleve*, ed. M. C. Seymour (Oxford, 1981), 58.

[15] *Mum and the Sothsegger*, 5–6; Robbins (ed.), *Hist. Poems*, no. 86.

[16] Gower, *Confessio Amantis*, bk. 7, lines 3890–4026, in id., *Works*, iii. 344–8; Kail (ed.), *Political Poems*, no. 3.

[17] Kail (ed.), *Political Poems*, no. 15; Robbins (ed.), *Hist. Poems*, no. 78.

were pledged to defend the throne and dynasty against its enemies while, conversely, the king should protect their honour and inheritance and strive to keep them in unity. Rivalry for the king's favour, mutual suspicion, and individual pride and honour bred faction and division which boded ill for king and kingdom:

> Lo, what meschef lyth in variaunce
> Amonge lordes, whan thei not acord.[18]

The king should lead them boldly and impartially:

> Thi peres in parlement pull hem togeders,
> Worche after wysdom, and worshipe wil folowe;
> For as a lord is a lord and ledeth the peple,
> So shuld prowesse in thi persone passe other mennes wittes.[19]

The king was the focus of service, the foremost patron in terms of honour and reward. Even the humblest Crown official was in some sense his representative, and his feed retainers wielded influence in their locality. He was thus urged to select his officers with care and enquiry, to reward only the deserving, and punish any who wronged or oppressed his subjects. Langland denounced the harshness of royal purveyors and the corruption of sheriffs; their oppressions if unredressed were tantamount to tyranny, and Richard's retainers, the poet claimed, lost him the hearts of his subjects because they had immunity for their misdeeds. Indeed the symbiosis of king and people is a constant theme in this literature. Kings existed for their people, not the people for kings; kings must love their subjects and win their hearts, for their subjects' love is their greatest treasure and security and without it the king is lost. Gower likened subjects to the soil which the king tills and fructifies with rain, and Ashby exhorted him to make them prosper. For their wealth and labour support the Crown; they are the mast of the ship of state. For Langland their moral support underpins the Crown, for from them alone will the king hear the truth.

The interdependence of all estates as members of the body politic is the theme of verses from 1413, 'God Keep our King and Save the Crown':

> What doth a kynges crowne signifye,
> Whan stones and floures on sercle is bent?
> Lordis, comouns, and clergye,
> To ben all at on assent,[20]

the theme of which is to exalt the commons:

> For comouns is the fayrest flour
> That evere god sette on erthely crown.

---

[18] Lydgate, *Troy Book*, bk. 3, line 2342, ed. Bergen, ii. 461.
[19] Robbins (ed.), *Hist. Poems*, no. 95.   [20] Ibid., no. 14.

Elsewhere knights, esquires, and yeomen are seen as the arms, hands, and fingers of the body politic.[21] As Gower insisted, when all members perform their proper functions the body is in a state of health, and the role of the king, like that of David the supreme harpist, is to tune their efforts to the common good. Discord and division ('disseverance') are a sure road to destruction:

> If we among our-self debate,
> Then endeth floure of chyvalrie
> Alle other londis that doth us hate
> Oure feblenes wole aspye.[22]

Advice to the king on how to rule himself, his court, and his subjects is followed by recommendations for governance. His subjects were concerned with four aspects: finance, justice, heresy, and war. Financial prudence was necessary for the king's own reputation and his subjects' welfare. It was axiomatic that he should avoid the extremes of prodigality and avarice, and follow the mean of liberality. True largesse meant rewarding the deserving 'in mesure', as against 'fool largesse' that 'giveth so moche away that it the king's cofres maketh bare'. This central message of the *Secretum* was expounded by Gower and Hoccleve and taken up in the mid-fifteenth-century writings on kingship. Equally commonplace was their insistence on balancing income and expenditure, echoed by George Ashby:

> Take you to live of youre own properte,
> Of your revenues, lyvelode and rent,
> Propornouning after the quantite
> Youre expenses by youre oune Jugement.[23]

That the king should live of his own from an inalienable estate—the central feature of Fortescue's blueprint—had a long history in both political and literary contexts. Even so, the viewpoints of subjects and monarch on financial rectitude did not necessarily coincide. For kings, expenditure was bound to be determined more by prestige, honour, and political need than by a canon of private domestic economy. A similarly blinkered appreciation of royal needs underlay writers' attitudes to taxation. While it was roundly asserted that kings should not seize the goods of subjects, the grounds for legitimate taxation were rarely acknowledged. Only Hoccleve allowed that 'in some case' aids 'been good and necessarie'.[24] Awareness of the principles of public taxation—sufficient cause, common assent, and public need—underlay this writing, but it lacked the sophistication of parliamentary debate.

That their discussion of law-keeping was equally generalized, much of it being a commentary on the king's coronation promise to do justice in mercy and truth.

---

[21] Kail (ed.), *Political Poems*, no. 15.   [22] Robbins (ed.), *Hist. Poems*, no. 14.
[23] Hoccleve, *Regement*, 174; Ashby, *Poems*, 21.   [24] Hoccleve, *Regement*, 159.

Law was seen as the essence of governance. A king who failed to uphold the law was, in Langland's view, a king only in name, and Gower asked:

> What king of lawe taketh no kepe,
> Be law he mai no regne kepe.
> Do lawe awey, what is a king?
> Wher is the riht of eny thing,
> If that ther be no lawe in londe?[25]

Most criticism centred on the corruption of the judicial system by bribery, fear and influence, and the failure of enforcement. The activities of Lady Meed in *Piers Plowman*, like the allegation in a poem of 1414 that

> In England, as all men wyten
> Law as best is solde and boghte,[26]

attest the anger at the venality of the law which could all too easily erupt in social unrest:

> Whanne lawe is put fro right assise
> and domes man made by mede
> For fawte of lawe if comouns rise
> Than is a kyngdom most in drede.[27]

Justice was the quality by which a king's rule was most readily judged; but it was also the area of government in which he was most dependent on his subjects.

The disarray in the Church at the end of the fourteenth century gave urgency to the king's coronation promise to protect its liberties and faith. Addressing Henry V, whom he likened to Constantine, Hoccleve acclaimed him as

> piler of our feith, and werreyour
> Ageyn the heresies bittir galle,[28]

exhorting him to

> Holde up Crystes Baner, lat it nat falle!
> This yle or this had been but hethenesse,
> Nad been of your feith the force and vigour.

Finally, as 'Swerd of Knyghthood', the king was the principal defender of the realm. Hoccleve was confident that Henry V would

> make many a knightly rode,
> And the pride of oure foos thristen adoun.[29]

---

[25] Gower, *Confessio Amantis*, bk. 7, lines 3070–7, in id., *Works*, iii. 317.
[26] Kail (ed.), *Political Poems*, no. 13.   [27] Ibid., no. 3.
[28] *Selections*, ed. Seymour, 59.   [29] Hoccleve, *Regement*, 143.

Success in war was the clearest testimony of a king's knightly quality and of God's favour. Yet many writers warned against the evil, futility, and waste of war. In his last English work, a poem in praise of peace, Gower denounced war as 'the moder of all wrongs'.[30] All acknowledged the doctrine of the just war: that kings had an obligation to pursue their rightful claims by arms if negotiations failed. Yet all major poets warned that war should not be undertaken lightly for in it there were no winners. It impoverished rulers, who ended in thrall to their subjects and generals, it brought suffering to non-combatants, and it often resulted in a peace to which both sides could have agreed at the outset. By the time Lydgate came to write the *Siege of Thebes* he had turned from the celebration of heroic feats of arms in the *Troy Book* to reflect on the tragedy and futility of fighting. The Anglo-French war engaged but also satiated the poets' patriotism, Gower finally urging Henry IV to

> lay to this old sore a new salve
> and do the war away, what so betide.[31]

For the purpose of war was a just peace, and when Henry V claimed to have secured this by the Treaty of Troyes, Lydgate was ecstatic in acclaiming him as 'sovereyn lord and prince of pes' who

> maken oon that longe hath be tweyne;
> I mene thus, that Yngelond and Fraunce
> May be al oon, withoute variaunce.[32]

It proved, alas, a chimera.

This apparently insatiable demand for writing on governance between *c*.1370 and 1460 is evidence of the political consciousness of the literate class. Yet it was not 'politicized' in the modern sense. Neither the polity itself nor its politics were conceived in the Aristotelian mode as rationally and morally autonomous. Both had their place in the cosmic framework, whose *raison d'être* was the fulfilment of God's purpose for mankind. Authority was instituted for this end and political action (policy) evaluated in these terms. The political destinies of individuals were likewise governed by God's will and judgement as much as by their own decisions. The cosmic penetrated the mundane, and men sought for the divine scheme in daily events. The king was the pivot of this relationship in secular matters, at once God's vicegerent and the officer of the people. The kingdom was his inheritance but not his property; rather was it held from God in trust for His people. Subjects were part of the immortal and inalienable crown of which the king was the present wearer. King and commons had mutual obligations for the common weal, the performance of which would ensure amity, unity, and stability in the kingdom. Conversely the crises which rent the political fabric

---

[30] Gower, *Works*, iii. 481.   [31] Ibid.   [32] Lydgate, *Troy Book*, iii. 870.

were attributed to the moral failure of each estate. A selfish or insouciant king, ambitious and factious nobles, venal judges, cowardly knights, dishonest officials, sycophantic clergy, and the destructive mob were all manifestations of society's moral failure and the cause of political discordance. There was no awareness of the science of politics, of where power was located, whence it was derived, how it was apportioned, through whom it was channelled. The court was idealized or denounced but not analysed; parliament was where wrongs were redressed and social ills cured, not where power was mobilized for sectional interests; its members were satirized for their moral failings, not presented as politicians.

The literary view of politics was thus stereotyped and blinkered, but it provided, in some respects at least, a workable model for political cooperation and the exercise of authority. A king ruling justly could be regarded as God's instrument and command obedience; one accused of injustice legitimized opposition. The belief that the proper end of government was the common good provided subjects with the grounds for both criticism and participation, and as members of the Crown they had a stake in the well-being of the kingdom. This accorded with their role in parliament and with their increasing participation in local office. In such matters political ideology was not divorced from practice but guided and nourished it.

CHAPTER 2

The King and the Court

The advice books presented the ideal of royal governance from the viewpoint of subjects. They postulated a ruler whose political will was attuned—through nurture and counsel—to the common good of the realm. Yet in practice the king had a will and interests of his own, which were not necessarily in harmony with those of his subjects. The tensions between the king's private and public capacities often came to the fore in the context of the royal household and court, which was at once his domestic environment, the arena for the display of majesty, and the channel for his political will.

In the broad perspective of state formation the late medieval court was in transition from the small, mobile, military household of the earlier Middle Ages to the hierarchical palace establishments of the later 'Court Society', which constituted the hub of the absolutist state. In our period such linear development is less discernible than the court's reflection, chameleon-like, of the character and policy of each monarch. While its prime purpose was to exalt the king's majesty through ritual and magnificence, it could at times epitomize chivalric prowess, religious piety, and political harmony, or indulgence, scandal, and faction. It both implemented and manipulated the king's will. I shall consider in turn its domestic organization and finance, its function as the source of royal governance, and its role as a religious and cultural centre.

1. THE COURT AS THE KING'S DOMESTIC ENVIRONMENT

No source enables us to picture or describe life at court in this period, and even our knowledge of its physical setting is sketchy. The pattern of court life was largely set by Edward III's great building programme of the 1350s and 1360s. This centred on the rebuilding of Windsor in 1357–68 as 'a new Camelot', a seat of chivalry to complement and outshine the old Palace of Westminster as the seat of government. The stark, uniform façade of Windsor, punctuated by crenellated towers, evoked an ideal of military austerity; yet in fact it had no defensive capacity and was built as a palace, not a fortress. Like Westminster, it could

accommodate the whole of the royal household, but unlike that of the old privy palace the layout of the royal chambers formed a long ceremonial sequence of increasing privacy, from hall and chapel to the great chamber, audience chamber, dining chamber, and bedchamber. Grandeur was achieved through lavish spaciousness rather than adornment: ceilings and walls were unpainted, though hung with textiles, but the queen had spacious apartments of her own and the hall could stage a tournament. Windsor was a showpiece for the martial eminence of the English Crown and nation, now firmly identified with 'Christ's most invincible athlete', St George, whose chapel formed the seat of the new Order of the Garter; but it was neither the only nor the preferred residence of the king. The more compact and architecturally innovative castle of Queenborough was built (at proportionate expense) for his consort, and a whole arc of residences around the capital were enlarged and made comfortable for Edward's declining years. Edward's successors made further improvements to whichever of these became their favourite residences. Richard II acquired Kennington and constructed a rustic retreat on an island at Sheen, Le Neyt, only to destroy it in his grief at Queen Anne's death. Henry V commenced the rebuilding of Sheen as a palace with attendant twin monasteries, 'almost an Escorial', but with his death the great period of rebuilding came to an end.[1]

Just as striking as the remodelling of these residences was the neglect of the Palace of Westminster. By 1360 it was indisputably the seat of government, where the courts and departments of state were permanently located, but as a royal residence it was in decline. To match Edward III's rebuilding of Windsor, Charles V remodelled the Louvre as a show castle to attest the majesty and legitimacy of the Valois monarchy at the heart of Paris, along with an equally imposing residence outside at Vincennes.[2] By contrast the piecemeal huddle of buildings forming the privy palace at Westminster were merely repaired and repainted. Richard II reconstructed the old Norman hall, but it housed courts and offices and was mostly used by lawyers, litigants, clerks, and hucksters.[3] Edward's preference for a monument to chivalry meant that the English monarchy continued to govern not from a palace in the capital but from a series of country houses between which it was in constant peregrination. The court moved between 50 and 100 times a year, on average every 3.5 to 7 days, covering

[1] C. Wilson, 'The royal lodgings of Edward III at Windsor Castle: Form, function, and representation', in L. Keen and E. Scarff (eds.), *Windsor: Medieval Art and Architecture of the Thames Valley*, British Archaeological Association Transactions, 25 (2002), 15–94.

[2] M. Fleury and V. Kruta, *The Medieval Castle of the Louvre* (Paris, 1989); M. Whiteley, 'The courts of Edward III of England and Charles V of France', in N. Saul (ed.), *Fourteenth Century England*, i (Woodbridge, 2000), 153–66.

[3] C. Wilson, 'Richard II's remodelling of Westminster Hall, 1393–99', in D. Gordon, L. Monnas, and C. Elam (eds.), *The Regal Image of Richard II and the Wilton Diptych* (London, 1997), 33–60.

a distance of between 10 and 20 miles each day. For almost one-third of the year it stayed for two weeks or longer at one of the great palaces, where the principal feasts—Christmas, Easter, St George's Day—were habitually celebrated. About the same amount of time was spent in travelling between them and staying in smaller royal residences within a 30-mile radius of London. Then during the summer months longer excursions were made westwards to Clarendon, to the Midlands for hunting, and to Walsingham or Canterbury for pilgrimages. Generally only military exigencies led the king to the far north or beyond the Severn. Windsor never became the king's habitual residence, for it was too remote from the centre of government. Only Henry VI spent much time there, his birthplace and home to his favoured foundation.[4]

Constant peregrination was a habit and a way of life, but as a mode of governance it was an uncomfortable compromise, and it certainly inhibited the development of any daily court ceremonial. The suite of chambers at Windsor was planned for such, and at other royal residences the provision of a basic three chambers allowed the king to receive and eat with dignity. The English court had a traditional ceremonial not inferior to those of France and Burgundy, but it was mostly displayed on great occasions when the king feasted in the hall under a canopy of estate and was ceremonially attended. Then, a ritual of magnificence underlined his distance from his subjects. But for much of the time the court must have presented itself as a train of wagons and horses, with its daily setting and ceremony closer to that of a magnate's household.

Although the sources are mostly uninformative about court life, they tell a great deal about the organization of the royal household.[5] Up to 1390 and again in the mid-fifteenth century the household totalled around 400 persons or slightly more, with another 120 or so for the queen. Enlarged during the years 1395–1405 mainly by a swollen retinue, it shrank during the illnesses of Edward III and Henry IV and the minority of Henry VI.[6] The household was divided into the upper *domus magnificencie* and the lower *domus providencie*. The centre of the former was the king's chamber, under the chamberlain, a noble high in the king's trust and favour. He controlled access to the royal presence and chose the chamber staff of knights and esquires ('of the body') who were the king's closest attendants and might be his confidants. Beyond the royal presence the ushers regulated the ceremonial for audiences and seating at meals, while the sewer and

---

[4] G. L. Harriss, 'The court of the Lancastrian kings', in J. Stratford (ed.), *The Lancastrian Court* (Donington, 2003), 1–18; C. M. Woolgar, *The Great Household in Late Medieval England* (New Haven, 1999), ch. 9.

[5] A. R. Myers, *The Household of Edward IV* (Manchester, 1959), for the household ordinances for 1445 and 1478 as well as the Black Book of 1472.

[6] C. Given-Wilson, *The Royal Household and the King's Affinity* (New Haven, 1986), app. III and 278; Myers, *Household of Edward IV*, 9.

surveyor controlled the serving of food. Yeomen, grooms, and pages attended to
the furnishing and cleaning of the royal apartments. A larger body of household
esquires, men of local standing, received fees and robes for attending court on a
rota basis—twenty or thirty at a time—to accompany the king and of an evening
to entertain visitors with music, tales, and talk. Finally there were a band of
minstrels, the chaplains and choristers of the chapel, trainee pages (henxmen),
and any sons of the nobility who were being educated at court—'the supreme
academy for the nobles of the realm' as Fortescue termed it.[7] In all, the upper
household numbered some 160 persons, of whom about one-third would be in
direct attendance on the king.

To service this was the task of the lower household, whose head, the steward,
was normally a lord. He had disciplinary jurisdiction within the bounds of the
court (the verge). Finance was under a treasurer, from 1406 onwards usually a
knight, whose active deputy, the cofferer, was a clerk, with a layman controller.
These were the upper echelons; provisioning was the task of five principal offices
each under a clerk: the kitchen, buttery, pantry, spicery, and stables and their sub-
departments. The household consumed staple foods in large quantities: every
year some 2,000 quarters of wheat, 300 tuns (1 tun = 252 gallons) of wine, 1,200
oxen, and 12,000 sheep. Supplies were organized in various ways. Purchases
were made in bulk from London merchants—grocers, fishmongers, vintners—
who developed profitable commercial and often political ties with the court.
London was also the source of specialized imports—spices, sugar, and dried
fruits—as well as silks and other luxury artefacts. Other foodstuffs like fish and
game could be bought direct from suppliers, and basic supplies acquired by purveyors as the household moved through the countryside. Following much outcry
against purveyance the king's rights had been carefully defined by the statute of
1362. Goods taken for the household were to be purchased at current market
rates under the supervision of village constables. But villagers remained vulnerable to heavy-handed action by royal officials and the goods taken were not usually paid for in cash but by debentures. Popular complaint over non-payment for
purveyances was endemic; for many rustics it was their sole contact with the
court and a defining experience of kingship. Royal exactions and conspicuous
consumption were both difficult to contain. Periodically there were attempts to
reduce its size or cost and to keep records of daily consumption.

In the years 1368–90 the normal cost of the household was around £16,000
per annum, by far the largest element being the consumption of victuals at a rate
of £30–5 per day. On the greater feast days this rose to £150–200, and even on
lesser ones to around £100. After Richard II's assertion of his rule in 1389 costs

[7] Sir John Fortescue, *De Laudibus Legum Angliae*, ed. and trans. S. B. Chrimes (Cambridge,
1949), 111.

began to rise: to £25,000 in 1395, and to over £34,000 in 1396–9, before returning to £25,000 until 1406 and thence to under £20,000. Under Henry V the domestic and military costs were merged, and only after 1430 did those of the young Henry VI begin to climb from a modest £10,000 per annum to around £13,000 from 1437 to 1453. To these must be added the charge of the great wardrobe, normally some £3,000 (though reaching over £8,000–11,000 in 1395–1403), and the chamber, which received a fixed sum of around £4,000, though sometimes more.[8]

While kings asserted their right and responsibility to ensure that the household adequately reflected the royal dignity, the problem of financing it raised questions of its (and their) public and private status. The generally accepted convention was that 'the king should live of his own', and the advice books made the avoidance of debts and of seizures of subjects' property prime tests of good kingship. They never defined what constituted his 'own', but in political parlance its kernel was undoubtedly the hereditary revenues of the Crown, the enduring 'fisc'.[9] These were handled through the exchequer, the controlling agency for all national revenue, and to this extent were considered public. The queen was endowed, on marriage, with an estate amounting to some £4,500 per annum under Richard II and £6,666 under the Lancastrian kings.[10] This too was drawn principally from the Crown revenues but was withdrawn from exchequer control and managed by the queen as a private estate. The Crown also had a patrimony, constituted in the thirteenth century, composed of great territorial blocs: the principality of Wales, the duchy of Cornwall, and the earldom of Chester. These formed an independent apanage for the prince of Wales, but otherwise could be used to support the queen or other members of the royal family. The other royal siblings had no such assurance of independence. However necessary they were to ensure the continuance of the dynasty, to endow them presented great difficulties. The king was unwilling to alienate royal lands, and preferred to find them an heiress to marry. Of the Black Prince's surviving brothers, Lionel of Antwerp married Elizabeth de Burgh, heiress of Ulster, in 1342, John of Gaunt acquired the whole of the Lancaster earldom through his marriage to Duke Henry's daughter and heiress Blanche in 1359, and Thomas of Woodstock a moiety of the Bohun inheritance by his marriage to the co-heiress Eleanor in 1376. Lacking such opportunities at home, they might have to look overseas, but Edmund of Langley's bid for the hand of Margaret of Flanders was frustrated by the pope in 1367.[11] Henry V required his younger brothers to support themselves largely by

[8] Given-Wilson, *Royal Household*, 82, 87, 94, and app. 1; Myers, *Household of Edward IV*, 46.

[9] i.e. excluding the king's patrimonial estates and the duchy of Lancaster.

[10] A. Crawford, 'The king's burden—the consequences of royal marriage in fifteenth century England', in R. A. Griffiths (ed.), *Patronage, the Crown, and the Provinces* (Gloucester, 1981), 41–5.

[11] W. M. Ormrod, 'Edward III and his family', *Jnl. Brit. Stud.* 26 (1987), 398–422.

service in France; not until after his death did John and Humphrey marry. In short the Crown did not have sufficient resources of its own to endow younger sons, who had to work for their living unless they could make the wealth of an heiress work for them.

In addition to the Crown revenues and the patrimonial lands, the Lancastrian kings enjoyed the revenues from their inherited duchy. On securing the throne in 1399, Henry IV had expressly kept his family lands legally and financially separate from Crown revenues. These provided the king with a sizeable income of some £11,000 per annum to spend on projects and policies of his choice. But the Crown also came under pressure to use it to support first its family and ultimately its household expenses. Revenue from the duchy formed part of the dower of all three Lancastrian queens; it was applied to discharge the debts of Henry IV and Henry V after their deaths; and finally under Henry VI it was for some years allocated to the expenses of the royal household before being used for the building of the royal colleges.[12] The very existence of this private revenue, and the pressure upon the king to use it for public charges, indicated how difficult it was to separate his feudal lordship from his headship of the state.

The king's household epitomized this ambiguity, for it provided the king's domestic environment, it embodied his own and the realm's honour, and it was the heaviest charge on Crown revenues. Since these also bore the costs of administration and were the principal source for royal largesse in the form of annuities to a variety of royal servants, they were rarely if ever sufficient to support the whole cost of the household. Thus it would either be forced to accumulate debts, or it would have to draw on other revenues, notably taxation. Either was likely to produce an outcry, the first from disappointed creditors, the second from the Commons in parliament. Having granted the taxes for the defence of the realm, their riposte was that the king should live of his own revenues. In the literary model of good kingship, the emphasis was upon 'live', signifying that the king should not get into debt; in parliament the emphasis was on 'own', signalling that the king should not draw on the taxes which his subjects had granted for their common defence. These principles and slogans became part of a prolonged debate between the monarchy and its subjects from the fourteenth to the seventeenth century.[13] Within our century there were two periods when this became politically contentious, from 1376 to 1406, and around 1450. The political circumstances of these will be more fully presented later, but the issues under debate can be briefly summarized here.

The king could rightly insist that the size and cost of his household, and indeed how he used the Crown revenues, was his prerogative; but excessive costs

---

[12] R. Somerville, *History of the Duchy of Lancaster* (London, 1953), 188.

[13] G. L. Harriss, 'Medieval doctrines in the debates on supply, 1610–1629', in K. Sharpe (ed.), *Faction and Parliament* (Oxford, 1978), 73–104.

or eroded revenues exposed him to criticism in parliament. Burdened by the unprecedented war taxation of 1371–81, the Commons demanded not only a reduction in the size and cost of the household but commissions to examine and reform royal government. These were ineffective, and in 1383 Richard set his face against such intervention, undertaking that he himself would 'set such rule and governance in the household as was best, saving his honour'.[14] Renewed demands for taxation in 1385 and 1386, and magnate hostility to Richard's favourites at court, made the household the focus for a combined attack by Lords and Commons in the parliament of 1386 and led to the setting up of a commission to remove government from the king's hands for a year. For Richard this was unacceptable; he famously refused to remove the lowest scullion from his kitchen at their bidding and withdrew his household from London.[15] The resultant military confrontation in 1388 exposed, without really resolving, these opposing viewpoints. The uneasy political compromise during the first part of the 1390s ended as Richard reasserted his prerogative in 1397. When a petition voiced criticism of the increasing size and cost of the household in the January parliament of 1397, Richard declared this to be 'against his regality, royal estate and liberty' and forbade subjects to make any ordinance relating to the governance of the king's person or household.[16]

These disputes were registered in the charge brought against Richard II in 1399 that 'whereas the king should have been able to live from the revenues of his patrimony in time of peace . . . he had burdened and impoverished subjects with taxes which were spent in vain display, and accumulated debts for the household despite the abundant wealth in his treasury'.[17] For the first six years of Henry IV's reign the Commons strove to enforce the principle that the king should live of his own, requiring the household to be supported from the Crown revenues while taxation was reserved for defence. The Commons' complaint was that Crown revenues had been eroded by the extensive annuities—estimated at £24,000 per annum—which Henry had granted to buy support for his regime. Their demands thus came to focus on a resumption, or at least a restraint, of royal grants and the reduction of household costs. Henry's response in 1404 was ostensibly positive, promising to put 'the household in good and moderate governance so that the costs can be met from the revenues of the realm'.[18] The council proposed an allocation from Crown revenues 'in order that the king can honourably sustain his estate and live without charge to his people'.[19] Both proved dead letters, and in a decisive confrontation in the parliament of 1406 Henry agreed to a reform of the household and the direction of royal finance by

---

[14] *Rot. Parl.* iii. 57, 73–5, 100–1, 147.   [15] Knighton, *Chron.* 354.
[16] *Rot. Parl.* iii. 339.   [17] Ibid. iii. 419.   [18] Ibid. iii. 433, 547, 528–9.
[19] Ibid. iii. 527–8; *Proc. & Ord.* i. 107.

the council. Thereafter the council was able to plan an annual allocation of money to the household to enable it to pay its way, helped by a decline of military expenditure and a reduction of annuities. Thus for thirty years the finance of the household had been the focus of conflict between the Crown and the Commons. Richard II had made it an issue of prerogative, and even for the more pragmatic and duplicitous Henry IV it became a test of his credentials as a ruler.

The problem only recurred at mid-century. During Henry VI's long minority the expenses of the household had been modest, and revenue from the duchy of Lancaster had been used for its support. But when, in 1445, Henry married, he began to use the duchy revenues to build his colleges, while the Crown revenues were depleted by his feckless generosity. In 1450 the insolvency of the exchequer, the indebtedness of the household, and military disaster in France produced a crisis for which a programme of draconian resumption of royal grants and strict allocation of Crown revenue to the household seemed to offer the only solution. From the resumed revenues a sum of £11,000 was set aside 'to provide for the contenting and payment of your household and other ordinary charges'.[20] This was accompanied by a political attack on the courtiers accused of reducing the Crown to poverty. Although this, the most ambitious programme of reform, suffered decreasing viability in the last decade of Lancastrian rule, it was adopted as the central proposal in Fortescue's blueprint for the restoration of kingship in *The Governance of England*.[21] Adherence to it was subsequently proclaimed by both Edward IV and Henry VII, to attest the legitimacy of their rule and to strengthen the resources of the Crown.

The finance of the royal household was thus a politically sensitive issue throughout this period. It was an area in which the interests of king and subjects demanded cooperation but which they approached from different standpoints. For the king the household visibly expressed his regality; for his subjects its solvency was a crucial test of his just rule. They could agree that it should be adequately funded, but should the king alone decide its size and costs and from what revenues it should be financed, as Richard II believed, or should it be provided with a fixed revenue to match its agreed cost, as prescribed by the council under Henry IV? Should it be financed solely from the Crown's hereditary revenue as the Commons repeatedly demanded, if necessary by restraining royal patronage and cancelling royal grants? Or would this not be to dishonour the king and encroach on his prerogative, reducing him to the position of a minister of the realm? Such issues engaged the very status and authority of the king.

---

[20] *Rot. Parl.* v. 185.

[21] G. L. Harriss, 'The finance of the royal household, 1437–1461', D.Phil. thesis (Oxford University, 1953); Fortescue, *Governance of England*, ch. 14.

2. THE COURT AS A CENTRE OF PATRONAGE
AND SERVICE

The court was the focal point of relations between the king and the political class. It was above all a relationship of loyalty, service, and reward. Service to the Crown was honourable, and carefully attuned to status. For the nobility it meant upholding the authority and dignity of the Crown by representing it in their 'countries', holding military commands, and giving counsel. For knights and gentry service was rendered through the exercise of magistracy and in war. Reward was expressed as the king's good lordship (*benevolentia*) and materially in gifts and privileges. This was not a commercial exchange: patronage did not buy service. Service was a duty and largesse a matter of grace, reciprocal elements of a political relationship.[22]

This relationship was most explicit at the court. The nobility's right of access to the king was fundamental to their status. Some were of the royal blood (to varying degrees), and all were his natural companions, with whom the king could hunt and joust, drink and feast, and from whom he could seek advice on matters of state. On state occasions their attendance at court was a symbol of political harmony, but very few apart from the steward and chamberlain were permanent residents. The greater nobility visited the king from their own houses in the capital, perhaps staying overnight, and at some royal houses guest rooms were reserved for the king's close relatives and favourites. At court the nobility also competed for royal favour. Although in later ages a monarch might use patronage to promote factions at court and manipulate his nobility, medieval advice literature encouraged him to practise 'franchise' (familiarity with respect) and even-handedness, as a means to unity. The nobility looked to the king to safeguard their lineage, inheritance, and local influence, to afford them opportunities for military prowess, and in general to validate their status within the hierarchy of honour.

In founding the Order of the Garter, Edward III had consciously set the court at the apex of chivalric society. Meeting annually on St George's Day at Windsor, it formed an elite company of twenty-six knights of different ranks, all elected for their martial prowess and honour. By evoking the image of King Arthur and the ideals of fidelity and service, the Order consolidated the nobility behind the Crown. Since its members were effectively chosen by the king, it provided 'a sophisticated instrument of royal patronage and control'. Edward III surrounded himself with his brothers in arms, Richard II with his trusted companions at court. Under Henry IV those elected were all committed supporters of the

---

[22] R. Horrox, *Richard III: A Study of Service* (Cambridge, 1989), 1–26.

Lancastrian dynasty, and under Henry V of the king's ambitions in France. Henry VI's pacific nature was alien to the Order's ideals, and its membership was manipulated by court factions. Yet in all reigns those elected were demonstrably outstanding in arms and in honour, giving the Order an esteem greater than that of any other in Christendom.[23]

For the nobility rank and precedence were of prime importance. Ducal titles, introduced by Edward III, were confined to the immediate royal kin until more widely awarded by Richard II. Earldoms had an order of precedence which the king might alter to advance or demote individuals.[24] Only very rarely did the king make direct grants of land to promote and endow a new peer, but he could use his right to dispose of the marriages of minors and widows with major dynastic consequences. In addition the king disposed of appointments to offices of responsibility and profit. As chief stewards of royal estates, justices of the forests, and constables of major castles the nobility could extend their local influence. They held military commands on strategic frontiers at Dover and Calais, in the northern marches, and overseas in Ireland, Gascony, and Normandy, all of which demanded some degree of active residence, while service in the field with the king was a mark of supreme honour and trust. They would also represent the king on important embassies to other courts. Such appointments were marks of favour, arousing competition, intrigue, and enmity.

The leading courtiers stood in a different relation to the king, being chosen by him for permanent attendance, as the nobility were not. They were men whose temperament and interests harmonized with the king's, generating at times a deep and lasting friendship. Many were also men of considerable ability in war, diplomacy, and administration, who undertook missions as representatives of royal authority. On embassies they were often the effective negotiators, even the king's private agents; they could be commissioned to investigate local administration, or resolve a dispute, or enforce an unpopular measure; they warned the king about local discontent or disloyalty; they got elected to parliament and sometimes sat in the council. Their personal proximity to the king and representative capacity gave them considerable political influence.

Since they were at the fount of patronage, they were richly rewarded. Chamber knights and esquires received no salary but were awarded annuities of between £40 and £100 often from royal manors. Beyond this all courtiers had access to the vast and varied reservoir of Crown patronage, comprising royal lands and offices, feudal profits, and fines. Leading courtiers could expect leases of the Crown's richest manors at a beneficial valuation, and to hold major local

---

[23] H. L. Collins, *The Order of the Garter, 1348–1461* (Oxford, 2000), 1 and *passim*.

[24] For an illuminating example, see R. Archer, 'Parliamentary restoration: John Mowbray and the dukedom of Norfolk in 1425', in R. Archer and S. K. Walker (eds.), *Rulers and Ruled in Late Medieval England* (London, 1995), 99–116.

positions like steward, constable, or forester for life. The esquires and yeomen of the upper household had lesser estate offices, which were occupied by deputy and mostly held during pleasure.

The Crown exploited its feudal rights by selling them to interested parties. Courtiers kept a keen watch for wardships and marriages of heirs and the custody of their lands but above all, perhaps, for marriage to widows, particularly any who brought not only their dower but property of their own. Sometimes they formed a consortium to farm the temporalities of a see or abbey, or even occasionally a magnate inheritance, though this met with disapproval. Small eschcats of land were quickly identified and petitioned for. Indeed the Crown could only exploit (and even discover) such feudal incidents by sharing their yield with the grantee. The same was partly true of the fines and forfeitures of many kinds for which the Crown depended on informers. The network of information through which the Crown was enabled to uncover and exploit its rights was also a network of influence and corruption which linked courtiers to agents in the localities whose malpractices they protected.

Courtiers were also the channel through which those outside submitted petitions to secure a beneficial grant. A king's accessibility to subjects was praiseworthy, and days were appointed—often Wednesdays and Fridays—when petitions were received. Both Henry IV and Henry V set aside an hour after dinner to answer them.[25] Petitions were handed to the steward in the hall but presented to the king by the chamberlain, whose endorsement signified the king's assent, though Henry VI personally initialled many. It was here, in the king's chamber, that courtiers interceded for themselves or others. Under Henry VI it was ordered that the names of those present were to be entered on the petitions, and surviving examples of these show who were at the king's side.[26] As the immediate beneficiaries and brokers of royal favour, the courtiers attracted envy and calumny. They were regularly accused of enriching themselves and denuding the Crown, and were denounced as an exclusive coterie just as the nobility were upbraided for being factious. In truth this was the nature of life at court, where devotion to the king was matched by competition for his favour; and favour provided the stimulus for loyal service, which the king needed.[27]

While the court reflected the personal favour and policy of each king, it also incurred the scrutiny and judgement of political society. In the decade after 1360 Edward III's court was the natural venue for the nobles and knights who had been his companions in arms, but in the years before his death their number had

---

[25] Harriss, 'Court of the Lancastrian kings', 10.

[26] Thus in the first half of 1445 the presence of John Hampton, Edmund Hungerford, Thomas Daniel, and John Trevelyan is noted on petitions: PRO, Council and Privy Seal, E 28/74, 75.

[27] R. Horrox, 'Caterpillars of the commonwealth? Courtiers in late medieval England', in Archer and Walker (eds.), *Rulers and Ruled*, 1–16.

dwindled and as the king came to be ruled by his mistress Alice Perrers the court became the centre of intrigue and enrichment rather than a company of chivalry and honour. In 1376 the attack in the Good Parliament on the 'covin' around the king focused political attention on it in a way that had not happened for thirty years and more.[28] To restore its reputation the Black Prince's knights were appointed to serve Richard II, and it was not until the early 1380s that he was able to choose and favour his own friends. In bestowing new dignities and lands on Robert de Vere, Michael de la Pole, Simon Burley, and John Beauchamp, Richard was consciously affirming his regality.[29] But the sense that royal favour was being concentrated on a small coterie of intimates, inferior in dignity and wealth to the established nobility, quickly bred distrust of the court. John of Gaunt even feared that the courtiers were plotting against his life.[30] Impatient and affronted by the king's 'enslavement' to his 'favourites', the greater magnates attempted to discipline Richard, only to find themselves locked in a battle with the prerogative and resorting to force. Essentially the quarrel represented opposing views of the court. For Richard it was an expression of his dignity and will, where his right to favour or disfavour, trust or mistrust, was pre-eminent. To the magnates the court should be a place of familiarity and opportunity, where their status and honour was validated by the king and their service rendered and accepted. But in 1386–8 it became a battleground of ins and outs, leading to the destruction of Richard's friends and the purge of his court.[31] By the mid-1390s Richard had successfully reconstituted a court circle of his choice among the nobility, but his purge of his enemies in 1397, and his distribution of their lands and titles to his 'dukelings', had a logic and momentum which carried the seeds of its own destruction. His further seizure of the Lancastrian inheritance in 1399 divided and alarmed the other nobility, winning their support for Richard's deposition by John of Gaunt's heir Henry.

The bloodletting of 1397–1400 had fundamentally imperilled the bond between the Crown and the upper nobility, and Henry IV had to rely on a band of courtiers of knightly rank, some of whom had been his companions in exile and who were now awarded major offices and commands normally held by magnates. At different times the offices of steward and chamberlain of the household, treasurer of England, and admiral, and the constableships of Calais, Dover, Windsor, and the Tower, were in the hands of non-noble courtiers. Henry's armed and vigilant household, perpetually on the move to anticipate rebellion, had the

---

[28] Given-Wilson, *Royal Household*, ch. 3. For the Commons' denunciation of 'Les privez entour le Roi et lour covyne', see *Rot. Parl.* ii. 323.

[29] For the ennoblement of Michael de la Pole, see *Rot. Parl.* iii. 206, and in general N. Saul, *Richard II* (New Haven, 1997), ch. 14.

[30] A. Goodman, *John of Gaunt* (London, 1992), 99–103.

[31] Discussed below, Ch. 12, sects. 4 and 5.

character more of a camp than a court. On this group of some dozen and a half non-noble confidants fell a shower of rewards which put some of them on a par with the baronage in wealth. Yet they did not incur the hatred and retribution that had attended Richard's courtiers. This was partly because of their reputations for valour and prowess in war, but principally because they were seen as supplementing, not supplanting, an upper nobility that had been eliminated by rebellion. Then, in 1406, the king's illness gave an opportunity for the magnates of Prince Henry's generation to take control of the council, the offices of state, and royal patronage, displacing the courtiers.[32]

Henry V's long apprenticeship in war and government meant that he was surrounded by close allies among the nobility and trusted household servants. He made it plain that the nobility must earn royal favour and reward by strenuous service in war, and the chivalric character of his household was personified in the chamberlains Lord Fitzhugh and Sir Lewis Robesart and the stewards Thomas Erpingham and Walter Hungerford, all of them knights of the Garter. Magnates and courtiers formed an entourage which acted as a headquarters staff on campaign, advising on political and military strategy, with some, like John Tiptoft and Thomas Chaucer, being entrusted with the king's secret business. Their rewards came mainly through a generous distribution of conquered lands and titles in France. After the plot on his life in 1415 Henry V faced no magnate dissent and, perhaps uniquely among medieval kings, his household escaped criticism.[33]

After Henry V's death his entourage formed the kernel of the royal council in his son's minority. Although partially reconstituted for Henry VI's coronation in France in 1430, the household only came to function as a court as he began to exercise kingship in his sixteenth year. Its ethos was no longer chivalric. The king was too young, and too pacific in temperament, to lead a nobility who were mostly middle-aged and weary of war. In this respect his position was akin to that of Richard II, but unlike Richard he made little attempt to elevate a peerage of his coevals. Those promoted in the 1440s were overwhelmingly those who had rendered service during his minority and had waited long for reward. Henry's generosity created some factional divisions, but in general the decade 1437–47 was a bonanza of enrichment and goodwill among the nobility. How many attended the court is difficult to judge, and certainly the devout king took no delight in its

[32] A. L. Brown, 'The reign of Henry IV: The establishment of the Lancastrian regime', in S. Chrimes, C. Ross, and R. Griffiths (eds.), *Fifteenth Century England, 1399–1509* (Manchester, 1972), 1–28; Given-Wilson, *Royal Household*, 188–98.

[33] In general G. L. Harriss (ed.), *Henry V: The Practice of Kingship* (Oxford 1985), chs. 2 and 4, and more specifically D. Morgan, 'The household retinue of Henry V and the ethos of English public life', in A. Curry and E. Matthew (eds.), *Concepts and Patterns of Service in the Late Middle Ages* (Woodbridge, 2001), 64–79.

size and ceremonial; but none were denied access and many came to seek favour. It was less Henry's insouciant generosity than his abdication of regal impartiality that destroyed the consensus in Lancastrian kingship. In 1447 Henry became persuaded of the duke of Gloucester's enmity and agreed to his gratuitous arrest and death, marking the first breach in the sense of security which the Lancastrian kings had been at pains to cultivate.

From 1433 the court was also a magnet for soldiers and gentry seeking wealth and advancement. The inner group who shared Henry's company and confidence are clearly defined: John Beauchamp, James Fiennes, John Hampton, and others appear as feoffees for the royal foundations, witnesses of royal warrants, and above all recipients of unprecedented largesse.[34] The heyday of their gains was in 1437–45. The most favoured received outright grants of land; they monopolized grants of wardships and marriages, forming syndicates to acquire them, while the flow of benefits reached down to yeomen of the household and country retainers. By 1450 Henry VI had made at least 192 grants of royal lands and properties, over half of which, with an annual value of £5,500, had been to members of his household.[35] Their identity, if not the precise extent of their rewards, was known far beyond the court, and in the maelstrom of 1450 they were lampooned and their expulsion from the court and the resumption of their gains were demanded. Yet it is difficult to be sure whether these were men of a different quality from the courtiers of other ages or whether their multiple rewards simply reflected the king's prodigality. As the dynastic challenge to Henry's throne unfolded over the following decade, the court became a political, and ultimately an armed, camp alternately triumphant and embattled, until its faithful remnant lost their lands and lives in the Lancastrian defeat.

While the court was in some respects self-contained, and even introverted, it also needed to be permeable, forming 'a bridge between the king and his subjects'.[36] The interaction of power elites at the centre and in the localities was part of the structure of politics, and the leading courtiers were major landowners on whom the king relied to rule the shires. Local offices could augment their personal standing. Thus Richard II built up the power of Simon Burley in Kent, of Sir John Beauchamp in Worcester, and of the Holland family in the West Country. Under Henry IV, Sir John Arundell as steward of the duchy of Cornwall, Sir Thomas Rempston in Nottinghamshire, Sir John Pelham in Sussex, and Sir Thomas Erpingham in Norfolk were effective brokers of royal power. James Fiennes, Lord Saye, in Kent, and Sir Thomas Tuddenham in Norfolk, were their equivalents under Henry VI. Secondly, the Crown's

[34] B. P. Wolffe, *Henry VI* (London, 1981), ch. 14.
[35] B. P. Wolffe, *The Royal Demesne in English History* (London, 1971), 128 and app. C.
[36] Horrox, 'Caterpillars of the commonwealth?', 9.

extensive properties provided a multitude of lesser offices whose holders drew
fees from the Crown and exercised some authority. Fortescue reckoned there
were more than a thousand of these—stewards and bailiffs of lands, gaolers and
porters of castles, rangers, parkers, and herbergers of forests—and emphasized
their potential for mobilizing political and military support.[37] Many were held as
non-resident sinecures by petty household officers, yet they represented a
network of royal authority and provided a channel of communication between
court and locality.

Beyond the court the Crown could seek to retain directly members of the local
gentry, on the model of the larger magnate affinities. Richard II was the first to
mobilize support in this way. Edward III had rewarded many of his war retinue
with local annuities, but from 1360 to 1385 the Crown ceased to be the focus for
military retaining, and the diminishing royal affinity became merely a list of pensioners. After freeing himself from baronial constraints in 1389 Richard began to
retain knights from the leading families in most counties, with annuities of £40
to £60. Over seventy knights were retained from 1389 to 1397 and, along with
those of the household, formed the core of the armies which Richard took to
Ireland in 1394 and 1399. After 1397 Richard retained more esquires, some 175
in the last two years of the reign. Over 100 of these were from Cheshire and
Lancashire, from which Richard also drew over 300 archers to form a permanent
bodyguard, organized into seven daily watches and led by esquires. By the end of
1398 the king's affinity comprised 760 Cheshire retainers and a further 250
knights and esquires, who wore the king's livery of the white hart.[38] Although it
gave Richard a sense of security, it had two drawbacks. First, it imposed a significant burden on royal finances (the archers alone costing £5,000 per annum), and
secondly, it was divisive. For the Cheshire guard became a byword for intimidation. The author of *Richard the Redeles* believed that for every livery of the white
hart Richard gave he lost ten score of his people's hearts.[39]

As it turned out, Richard II's affinity had no chance to defend him against
Henry's advance in 1399. It was the duchy of Lancaster affinity that was more
effectively mobilized, and after his usurpation Henry began to retain on an
extensive scale, including no less than forty-two of Richard's knights, half of
them within six months of his accession.[40] After 1401 this rapid enlargement of
the royal affinity eased and contracts for life ceased, but by 1406 Henry still had

---

[37] Fortescue, *Governance of England*, ch. 17; R. A. Griffiths, 'For the myght off the lande, aftir the
myght of the grete lordes theroff, stondith most in the kynges officers', in Curry and Matthew
(eds.), *Concepts and Patterns of Service*, 80–98.

[38] Given-Wilson, *Royal Household*, 214–23, 311 n. 88, app. v.

[39] *Mum and the Sothsegger*, 8; N. Saul, 'The Commons and the abolition of badges', *Parlty. Hist.*
9 (1990), 313.

[40] Given-Wilson, *Royal Household*, 231–2.

well over 100 knights in his retinue. The cost was ultimately unsupportable: £8,000 from the revenues of the duchy and over £20,000 from Crown resources were being paid out in annuities.[41] Its military value was demonstrated not only at the battle of Shrewsbury in 1403, when it withstood the Percy rebellion, but in frequent summonses to all retainers for service in Wales, the north, and overseas. Did it have a comparable political role, in spreading royal authority and controlling political society in the shires? Where royal or duchy of Lancaster lands were numerous, these provided patronage through which both courtiers and local gentry could be rewarded and linked to the Crown. Thus in Berkshire and Oxfordshire successive generations of courtier–gentry families like Golafre, Wilcotes, Chaucer, Rede, Norreys, and Hampden led the shire, and duchy estates provided a similar basis in the North Midlands. But elsewhere the local gentry had to be retained with annuities, and at £10–20 a head this was costly and could be seen as intrusive. In fact the royal affinity, like any other, could only effectively be built on the royal lands, and had to be integrated into local political networks.[42] Nor was it a normal accessory of kingly rule. It was the revolutionary situation in the decade either side of 1400 that impelled the creation of a large royal affinity. Normally the Crown commanded the loyalty of the political class without special payment or written indentures; indeed such devices, which committed it to favouring its own retainers against other liegemen, reduced the acceptance of its authority at large. Thus in the North Midlands under Henry IV the monopoly of influence exercised by royal-duchy retainers alienated other gentry who were excluded.[43]

Where an enlarged and costly affinity had been necessary to safeguard Henry IV's throne, under Henry V it was used to spearhead his military ambitions in France. Annuitants had a special duty to serve, and were comprehensively summoned for both the 1415 and 1417 expeditions on pain of losing their fees. Even so, Henry gave few new annuities and reduced those on the duchy revenues from over £8,000 under his father to less than £6,000. Moreover, on his death the duchy estates were divided in fulfilment of his will and no further annuities were granted under his infant son.[44] In these circumstances the royal affinity lost its cohesion, at best retaining a localized identity and at worst being absorbed into the affinities of local magnates. Thus in Derbyshire the duchy affinity was led by the Vernons as stewards of High Peak, and in Norfolk it was Sir William Philip and the earl of Suffolk, both household officers, who inherited and reorganized

[41] Ibid. 136; *Proc. & Ord.* i. 154. Some of these annuities were non-military and inheritable.

[42] For this, see below, Ch. 6, sect. 2.

[43] H. Castor, *The King, the Crown, and the Duchy of Lancaster, 1309–1461* (Oxford, 2000), esp. 3–31, 191–224; also S. J. Payling, *Political Society in Lancastrian England* (Oxford, 1991), ch. 5.

[44] Somerville, *Duchy of Lancaster*, 106, 187, 214; Castor, *The King, the Crown, and the Duchy of Lancaster*, 32–8.

the royal affinity after Sir Thomas Erpingham's death.[45] The new pattern of
localized control by greater magnates was formalized in 1436–7 by the appointment of curialist lords to the major duchy stewardships, while subsidiary offices
came to be held by local gentry who were also household esquires. The duchy
was thus closely linked into the household at both the highest and intermediary
levels as a potent channel for royal influence in the localities.[46] Where the royal
affinity was organized and exploited by magnates attached to the court to
serve their particular interests, as in East Anglia and Kent, it provoked a hostile
reaction.

The decline of the royal affinity from being a military force and a reservoir of
dynastic loyalty to become a channel of favour under Henry VI was matched by
an unprecedented expansion in the numbers of household esquires. In the
decade after 1438–9 those receiving fees and robes on the household roll rose
from the normal number of around 120 to 315.[47] These did not form a reconstituted affinity on the earlier pattern. Their retaining fee was a mere £2 per annum
and they attended court in rota, when summoned or at the five principal feasts.
No more than one-third were country gentry of some standing, and the remainder were merchants, soldiers, and sons of minor local families. Their attachment
to the court sprang from individual opportunism. Most were from the counties
of the south-east and areas controlled by the court nobility. They received little
local patronage, but even if their link to the court was occasional and honorific, it
added to their local standing and influence. Between 1437 and 1449 just under
one-third of those who served as sheriffs were household esquires, with a much
higher proportion in the shires where court influence was strong. Election to
parliament between 1439 and 1449 followed a similar pattern. Just over 35 per cent
of the shire knights returned were household esquires. For crucial parliaments
like that of 1447, staged for the arrest of Humphrey, duke of Gloucester, fifty-
eight MPs had court attachments, many of whom were sitting for the first time.[48]
Thus even a minimal link to the court could on occasion be utilized by the
Crown. This extended and diluted royal affinity of the mid-fifteenth century
was primarily political in character. In both commitment and cost it was a
long way removed from the military affinity through which Henry IV had won
and kept his throne. With few exceptions it proved a broken reed when the
Lancastrian dynasty looked for support to retain the throne in 1459–61.

[45] Castor, The King, the Crown, and the Duchy of Lancaster, 82–99, 234–52.

[46] J. Watts, Henry VI and the Politics of Kingship (Cambridge, 1996), 172–3; Castor, The King, the
Crown, and the Duchy of Lancaster, 100–16, 253 ff.

[47] PRO, Various Accounts, E 101/408/24, 409/9, 11, 16, 410/1, 3, Feoda et Robae section;
Myers, Household of Edward IV, 127, 246 n. 201.

[48] These figures are based on my own work on the household of Henry VI. Compare Payling,
Political Society in Lancastrian England, 109–85, 246–50.

In each of its aspects, as the epitome of chivalry, the focus for loyalty and service, 'an exchange and mart of royal patronage', a bridge between the king and the realm, and an instrument of political control, the court was a central and indispensable agency of royal rule, used by each king in different ways and for different purposes.

3. THE COURT AS A RELIGIOUS AND CULTURAL CENTRE

The religious life of the court centred on the royal chapel, a body of twenty or more chaplains and ten choristers under a dean, who accompanied the king as a kind of spiritual bodyguard. At Agincourt the chaplains sat at the rear of the battle fervently praying for victory.[49] Most kings took a direct interest in the ordering of the chapel: Henry IV, a talented musician, reorganized the choir, and Henry V is identified in the Old Hall manuscript with the group of composers associated with the chapel royal who were the leading exponents of the new polyphonic style, characterized by 'sprightly concord' and 'angelic sweetness'. Both in performance and in composition the music of the English court had an unrivalled reputation on the Continent up to 1450.[50] In prayer and ceremony the royal chapel affirmed the sacrality of kingship and the personal piety of the king.

In public terms Edward III generously fulfilled the religious role of the monarchy, establishing the collegiate foundations of St George's Windsor and St Stephen's Westminster, making regular pilgrimages to shrines at Walsingham and Canterbury, and providing intercessory masses for his own soul and those of his family. There is no indication of whether Edward's personal beliefs or practices went beyond these conventional forms. In his old age, while the liturgy of his chapel was elaborated, it was to Alice Perrers rather than to his Dominican confessors at King's Langley that he turned for consolation. National pride, epitomized in the cult of St George, and dynastic pride, depicted in the wall paintings of his family before the throne of God in St Stephen's Chapel, were the prime impulses behind his religious commitment.[51]

Young, vulnerable, and deeply affected by the indelible regality laid upon him at his coronation, Richard II turned for support to his chaplains and to the assurance of divine protection for his kingship. Richard's confessor, the Dominican

---

[49] Liber Regie Capelle, ed. W. Ullmann, Henry Bradshaw Society (London, 1961), 8, 15; Gesta, 88–9.

[50] M. Bent, 'Old Hall manuscript', in S. Sadie (ed.), The New Grove Dictionary of Music and Musicians, 2nd edn. (London, 2001); R. Bowers, 'The music and musical establishment of St George's Chapel in the fifteenth century', in C. Richmond and E. Scarff (eds.), St George's Chapel, Windsor in the Late Middle Ages (Windsor, 2001), 171–85.

[51] W. M. Ormrod, 'The personal religion of Edward III', Speculum, 64 (1989), 849–77.

Thomas Rushook, and some of his chaplains were expelled from the court by the Appellants, but all except Rushook returned in the 1390s and were joined by Alexander Bache and John Burghill as confessors and another group of chaplains; these formed an inner circle of royal advisers whom Richard promoted to bishoprics and named as his executors.[52] Richard's spiritual home was Westminster Abbey. It was there that he went to pray before meeting the rebels at Smithfield in 1381 and again in November 1387 as he faced the challenge from the Appellants. At dusk one evening in 1386 he took the king of Armenia there to show him the coronation regalia. He paid special devotion to the shrine of Edward the Confessor, taking him as the model for and protector of his own kingship. In 1394 he impaled the Confessor's mythical arms on his own, and commissioned the double tomb for himself and his wife in the last space in the Confessor's chapel. There, too, Richard had his special friends buried, and his own iconic painting, the first full-face royal portrait, was to manifest the king's symbolic presence, probably above the royal pew.[53]

Even more eloquent of Richard's sacral view of kingship is the beautiful Wilton Diptych, a portable altarpiece made for Richard's personal devotions probably around 1395–7. The king, depicted as a tender youth gorgeously arrayed, kneels on the earth attended by St Edward, St Edmund, and St John the Baptist. He gazes towards the Virgin and Christ child, surrounded by eleven angels in a flower-strewn heaven, one of whom holds the banner of St George, symbol of the realm of England. Richard's hands are held apart, not in prayer but to receive the banner blessed by the infant. Richard and the angels wear the king's badge of the white hart and the broomscod collar, the emblem of his father-in-law, Charles VI of France. The two halves, though related, are each self-contained, conveying the king's inward vision of heavenly protection for his rule of England. These associations are made explicit in the king's will. The painting is perhaps best interpreted as commemorating the divine commitment of England, known as the Virgin's dowry, to Richard at his coronation in his eleventh year.[54] Richard's religious experience was absorbed into his cult of kingship, as Christ's vicar. Although his own devotional practice is not known, there is no indication that he was attracted to either the spiritual introspection or the moral puritanism of his age. He identified less with the suffering Christ, or Christ the redeemer of mankind, than with Christ the king. When in the 1390s he

[52] Given-Wilson, *Royal Household*, 175–83.

[53] N. Saul, 'Richard II and Westminster Abbey', in J. Blair and B. Golding (eds.), *The Cloister and the World* (Oxford, 1996), 99, 191–211; J. Alexander, 'The portrait of Richard II in Westminster Abbey' in Gordon *et al.* (eds.), *Regal Image of Richard II*, 197–206.

[54] For an authoritative discussion, see Gordon *et al.* (eds.), *Regal Image of Richard II*. Richard's will opens with an invocation of the Virgin, John the Baptist, Edward the Confessor, and the whole court of heaven: J. Nichols (ed.), *Royal Wills* (1780), 191–201.

proclaimed himself the defender of the Church, it was because he had come to identify orthodoxy with obedience and heresy with treason.[55]

Richard II had predicted his successor's hostility to the Church, and at first the temper of Henry IV's court was lay and even anticlerical, and the royal chapel ceased to be either a centre of influence or a route to promotion.[56] Although Henry had been anointed with the newly rediscovered chrism of holy oil miraculously delivered to St Thomas Becket, he felt unable to exploit the religious mystique of monarchy. Politically, he needed the Church's support, and was ready to legalize the burning of convicted heretics and protect it against demands for disendowment. After 1406, afflicted by illness and guilt over the execution of Archbishop Scrope, he fell increasingly under Archbishop Arundel's influence. His will in English, made seemingly at the point of death in 1409, has more religious individuality than Richard's: in it he bequeaths his sinful soul to God, declares his life misspent, and puts himself wholly in God's grace and mercy.[57]

Whereas both Richard II and Henry IV had remained personally detached from the spiritual problems of their age, Henry V saw himself as the spiritual mentor of his people. Just as his own assumption of kingship was marked by his 'conversion', so he pressed the Church to renew its leadership through reformation. No less than Richard, Henry believed that he stood in a unique relationship to God—he was *verus electus Dei*—but, rather than setting him apart from his subjects, this identified him with them. He was the channel of God's mercy and favour to England, a theme expounded in the *Gesta Henrici Quinti*, produced at his command and in his chapel. Through God's grace and his own faith the king had survived, in turn, Oldcastle's rising, the baronial conspiracy of 1415, and seemingly inevitable defeat at Agincourt. The deliverance of his people from heresy, division, and invasion was testimony that God had chosen the king to bring justice and peace to England and France. This mission demanded ardent prayer from the king, his chaplains, and a Church spiritually alert and reformed. Henry's own prayerfulness was remarked by his chaplain: the night vigil at Westminster before his coronation, the concentration of his devotion at mass, his silent prayer on his triumphant entry into London in 1415. For his confessors he chose Carmelites, Stephen Patrington and Thomas Netter; in his chapel he reordered the liturgy; and among his bishops favoured those who, in the tradition of Hallum, were seeking to foster a climate for personal spirituality in public worship by incorporating meditative prayer into the new liturgical

---

[55] S. K. Walker, 'Richard II's views on kingship', in Archer and Walker (eds.), *Rulers and Ruled*, 49–64.

[56] Ibid. 50; P. McNiven, *Heresy and Politics in the Reign of Henry IV* (Woodbridge, 1987), 72–7; Given-Wilson, *Royal Household*, 197.

[57] McNiven, *Heresy and Politics*, 79–92; Nichols (ed.), *Royal Wills*, 203.

feasts.[58] Prayer was also to be a public affirmation of national destiny. The saints whose cults Henry promoted and to whom he appealed at Agincourt were England's special protectors: St John of Bridlington, St George, and the Virgin Mary.

Henry's vision was manifested above all in his new monastic foundations. Not disendowment but re-endowment of the Church was to be the means of reform, and this on an unprecedented scale. For his new foundations he chose Carthusians, Bridgettines, and Celestines, the most rigorous and austere of the new wave of monasticism. Their function was to produce a torrent of prayer, protecting him as he faced continual test and danger on behalf of his people. Sheen, with forty monks, reflected Henry's belief in solitary prayer; Syon with sixty nuns and twenty-five brethren, represented the attainment of heavenly peace on earth; the Celestine foundation, never achieved, invoked the ideals of renunciation, and rigorous adherence to the Rule, which Henry sought to rekindle in the Benedictines in 1421. As a monastic founder Henry V stands unmatched among English kings at a time when monasticism generally was in decline.[59] Like Richard, whose body he reinterred at Westminster, he saw the Abbey as a royal mausoleum, providing for his own tomb near the Confessor's shrine, where three daily masses were to be the focus for public devotion.

Inevitably this model of the king governing his people as God's elect lost its force under the infant Henry VI. Those who guided his upbringing certainly instilled a sense of responsibility for the *respublica Christiana*, impressed upon him by his double coronation in England and France at about the same age as Richard II. As he advanced towards manhood, Henry came under the influence of his confessors William Ayscough and the Carmelite John Stanbury, his almoner John de la Bere, and his secretary Thomas Bekynton. From 1437 the chapel grew in size: there were twenty-eight chaplains by 1443/4 and thirty-seven by 1448/9, and the court became the focus for churchmen seeking promotion.[60] Between 1437 and 1444 a book was produced from within this circle to inform and guide Henry on the duties of Christian kingship.[61] It was matched to the king's personal inclinations, prescribing a regular pattern of religious observance in daily life. It enjoined a strict sabbatarianism on the alleged model of King Edgar, the commemoration of the Five Wounds on rising, daily matins of the Virgin, silent repetition at the Mass, a lengthy catena of prayers said meaningfully, and the recital of a Carthusian hymn at compline. The high seriousness

[58] *Gesta*, esp. 150–5; J. I. Catto, 'Religious change under Henry V', in Harriss (ed.), *Henry V*, 97–116.

[59] D. Knowles, *The Religious Orders in England*, ii (Cambridge, 1955), 175–84.

[60] PRO, Various Accounts, E 101/409/11, 410/1.

[61] *Tractatus de Regimine Principum ad Regem Henricum Sextum*, in J.-P. Genet (ed.), *Four English Political Tracts of the Later Middle Ages*, Camden Society, 4th ser., 18 (London, 1977), 40–168.

of the royal chapel, established by Henry V, became the setting for the practice of the *devotio moderna* by the king himself. Henry's hagiographer John Blacman confirms the king's active participation in the liturgy, his immersion in private meditation, his use of a hair shirt at crown-wearings, his preference for reading scripture and chronicles, his veneration of the Holy Cross, his censoriousness of court manners.[62] Henry's devotion was centred on the pattern of Christ's manhood and sufferings, and on the adoration of the Real Presence to the point of visualization. Christ's kingship was signified by the crown of thorns, and the abnegation of worldly pomp, and dominion, and this was the model for his own.

Nonetheless, Henry held firmly to the indelible kingship to which he had been divinely called. He had a twofold mission for his people's salvation: to bring peace and an increase in faith. To end the war, which he believed un-Christian, was his 'souveraine and singuler desire', which he sought not by pursuing his just claims (as his father had) but, Christ-like, by embracing his ancient enemy with love and trust.[63] At the same time he marked the inception of his active rule by foundations at Eton and Cambridge for the increase of an educated clergy on the model of Wykeham's colleges at Winchester and Oxford. In this he was assisted by a group of keen educationalists at court, Thomas Bekynton, William Lyndwood, William Waynflete, and Richard Andrew, all Wykehamists.[64] Henry VI had a priestly, not a military, vocation: for the salvation of his people rather than their defence.

'Court culture' is a disputable concept. Scholarly attention has focused on the renaissance of English literature under Richard II, but the culture of the court was more material and visual than literary and intellectual. The records contain more references to jewels and goldsmiths than to books and writers. Likewise, as a patron the king was in equal measure the receiver and disburser of precious gifts—jewels, plate, apparel, books—and the last of these were more likely to be valued for their binding or illuminations than for their literary content. Intellectual patronage—the promotion of perceived talent or new ideas and techniques—was an idiosyncratic rather than a normal function of kingship. Nonetheless, the court did provide a focus for writing and ideas. It exemplified some of the themes of chivalric romance: the valour and loyalty of the Arthurian round table, hospitality and treachery, and courtly love and trial, as in *Sir Gawain and the Green Knight* or Chaucer's Knight's Tale.[65] It was the natural setting for stories of the Wheel of Fortune (the fall of princes) and of concealed identity (the prince as pauper) as illustrating innate nobility. In both their

[62] M. R. James (ed.), *Henry the Sixth: A Reprint of John Blacman's Memoir* (Cambridge, 1919).
[63] Bekynton, *Correspondence*, i. 189.
[64] Wolffe, *Henry VI*, 135–45; V. Davis, *William Waynflete* (Woodbridge, 1983), 35–56.
[65] A. C. Spearing, *The Gawain Poet* (Cambridge, 1970).

religious and secular manifestations princely courts, at least until 1400, shared a cosmopolitan and multilingual culture.[66]

It is more difficult to assess the literary interests and patronage of individual kings. Of the books specifically commissioned or owned by Richard II, the most intriguing is the composite volume Bodley MS 581, which includes a book of divination with tables giving 3,200 possible answers to twenty-five personal and political eventualities. Astrology was increasingly in vogue among the intellectual classes, as the many references in Chaucer's work show, and clearly engaged Richard's attention.[67] Two volumes of statutes on the royal power compiled for him in 1389, and Roger Dymoke's tract against the Lollards presented in 1396, addressed more mundane concerns, while in 1395 Philippe de Mézières adroitly flattered the king's self-image in the *Letter to King Richard*, urging his marriage with Charles VI's daughter Isabella as a means to peace with France and a joint crusade.[68] In the same year Froissart's claim to have presented the king with a book of love poems, which he took to his chamber, recalls Gower's account of Richard's request for 'som newe thing' which led him to write *Confessio Amantis* in 1387, described in its first recension as 'a book for King Richard's sake'.[69] All this suggests, if anything, that Richard was an eclectic patron.

With Gower we are on the fringe of the court and the literary coteries of which he and Chaucer were members. Chaucer had been an esquire in the household of Edward III and remained on the livery roll, serving on royal expeditions in 1359 and 1369 and as an envoy to France and Italy in 1377–81. He was controller of the customs in London from 1374 to 1386, with lodgings over Aldgate. All his work, from *The Romaunt of the Rose* and *The Book of the Duchess* in the late 1360s to *Troilus and Criseyde* in the mid-1380s, was for a court audience and used the traditional framework of courtly and chivalric romance. This had for its subject matter the legendary history of classical and Arthurian mythology, the heroes of which were invested with the chivalric qualities of military prowess and valour, fidelity to the brotherhood of arms, courtesy, endurance in adversity, and stoic acceptance of fate. The counterpart of this military ethic was the erotic code of courtly love, marked by fidelity and service to the beloved in both arms and love, the preservation of her honour and repute (not the same as her chastity) in a 'fantasy world of amorous play'.[70] Chaucer's ability to invest these stylized myths with dramatic tension between individual desire and social imperatives, freedom of choice and historical determinism, culminated in *Troilus and Criseyde*, a

    [66] M. Vale, *The Princely Court* (Oxford, 2001), 93–115, 169–200, 222–37, 282–98.
    [67] H. M. Carey, *Courting Disaster* (London, 1992), 98–106; D. Pearsall, *The Life of Geoffrey Chaucer* (Oxford, 1992), 216–20.
    [68] Philippe de Mézières, *Letter to King Richard II*, ed. G. W. Coopland (Liverpool, 1975).
    [69] Gower, *Confessio Amantis*, Prologue, lines 51–3.
    [70] Lee Patterson, *Chaucer and the Study of History* (London, 1991), 25.

daring story of sexual and personal discovery. This was dedicated to Gower and Ralph Strode, and had an appreciative audience among a circle of chamber knights, Clanvowe, Clifford, Stury, and Vache, whose intellectual and religious independence made them Lollard suspects. It has been suggested that the brilliance and joyousness of books II and III reflected the youthful Richard's court,[71] and in *The Legend of Good Women*, written in 1386–7 as reparation for his treatment of womanhood in Criseyde, Chaucer makes easy allusions to the fashionable court games, and promises the completed work to Queen Anne. These years witnessed the triumph of English as the medium for major literary works: Clanvowe's *The Book of Cupid* (mid-1380s), Thomas Usk's *Testament of Love* (1387), and Gower's commencement of *Confessio Amantis* (1387). All these were court-centred works, but direct evidence of royal patronage is lacking; even the famous frontispiece to *Troilus* (of between 1410 and 1420), showing Chaucer reading to a listening audience, must be regarded as a literary conceit.[72]

The Appellants' attack on the chamber knights broke up this coterie, and Chaucer lost his post in the customs and his London lodgings and retired to Kent. In the 1390s he found the divisive politics of the court uncongenial, and turned away from chivalric themes to the world of non-noble society in *The Canterbury Tales*. Similarly Gower's dismay at royal policies seems to have led him to seek the patronage of Henry of Derby, to whose children Chaucer's friend Henry Scogan was tutor.[73] Their writing took on a new tone, concerned with man's nature and destiny, his moral dilemmas and those of society. This was expressed in different ways. *Confessio Amantis* is the most politically engaged of Gower's works, with its extended discussion of 'Policie', or governance, in book VII. In contrast, Clanvowe in *The Two Ways* expressed his puritanical revulsion from worldly ambition and society. Chaucer's genius was now channelled into character portraits of his own contemporaries and the attitudes and relations of an increasingly commercialized and literate society.[74] The poetry of Chaucer and Gower had moved beyond the court to this wider commonwealth, distancing itself from the Francophile culture fostered by a king more concerned with fulfilling his divine kingship than governing a diverse political society.

Gower embraced the Lancastrian revolution more explicitly than Chaucer, supported by the remarkable outburst of political versification which, without any identifiable connection to the court, had the common good of the body

---

[71] Pearsall, *Life of Chaucer*, 131–2, 168–77, 181–5.   [72] Ibid. 178–81.

[73] In his presentation of the final recension of *Confessio Amantis* to Henry of Derby in 1393, Gower now described it as 'a bok for Engelondes sake' (Prologue, line 24; the dedication to Henry of Lancaster is at lines 81–93).

[74] J. H. Fisher, *John Gower: Moral Philosopher and Friend of Chaucer* (New York, 1964), 196–203; G. R. Coffman, 'John Gower, mentor for royalty', *PMLA* 69 (1954), 953–64; Sir John Clanvowe, *Works*, ed. V. J. Scattergood (1965), esp. 66–72.

politic as its central theme and London political society as its audience.[75] It was
in this context that, early in the century, the house of Lancaster began to be associated with major literary works, more particularly of a didactic and political
kind. The translations made for Thomas, Lord Berkeley, by John Trevisa and
John Walton, of *De Regimine Principum* and Vegetius, *De Re Militari*, may well
have prompted Prince Henry's patronage of Richard Ullerstone's *De Officio
Militari* and Thomas Hoccleve's *Regement of Princes*.[76] On becoming king,
Henry swiftly and explicitly promoted the use of English in personal and official
documents. Lydgate represented him as encouraging the retelling of the story of
Troy in the common tongue:

> Bycause he wolde that to hyghe and lowe
> The noble story openly were knowe
> In oure tonge, aboute in every age
> And y-writen as wel in oure langage
> As in latyn and frensche it is.[77]

The Troy saga legitimized kingship by identifying its origin in the transference
of authority from ancient Greece to the west, though whether to Britain or
France was a bone of contention. Henry V's ambition to challenge French hegemony in Christendom gave it a topical relevance.[78] Similarly, Lydgate's *Siege of
Thebes*, commenced in 1420, provided a moral commentary on Henry V's
campaign in France, presenting him as a history-making prince, able to bring
peace through war.[79] From Gower to Lydgate a whole generation of writing had
as its central theme the linked destinies of king and people, the moral integrity of
the ruler guaranteeing the harmony and prosperity of his realm.

Lydgate now became poet laureate for the aristocratic oligarchy of Henry VI's
minority, writing religious verses for Queen Catherine and the ladies of the
court, and translating *The Pilgrimage of the Life of Man* for the earl of
Salisbury. His Christmas Mummyngs, written for the court at Eltham in 1424, at
Hertford in 1427 and 1430, and at Windsor in 1429, were in a lighter vein, with
touches of rustic humour about shrewish wives, but he could turn his hand
equally to pageants to celebrate Henry VI's return to London in 1431, and act as

---

[75] Gower's *Cronica Tripertita* condemning Richard II is discussed by Fisher, *John Gower*,
109–15; for popular political verse, see J. Coleman, *Medieval Readers and Writers, 1350–1400*
(London, 1981), 98–113.

[76] R. Hanna, 'Sir Thomas Berkeley and his patronage', *Speculum*, 64 (1989), 878–916; Pearsall,
'Hoccleve's *Regement of Princes*', 386–410; cf. Perkins, *Hoccleve's Regiment of Princes*, esp. 50–60,
89–114.

[77] John Lydgate, *Troy Book*, ed. H. Bergen, 4 vols., EETS, extra ser., 97–106 (London,
1906–12), i. 4.

[78] Patterson, *Chaucer and History*, 91–8, 161.

[79] D. Pearsall, *John Lydgate* (London, 1970), 151–6; R. W. Ayers, 'Medieval History, Moral
Purpose, and the Structure of Lydgate's *Siege of Thebes*', *PMLA* 72 (1958), 463–74.

a propagandist for Gloucester's attack on Flanders in 1436. Gloucester was his foremost patron, commissioning and closely supervising the monumental *Fall of Princes*, at once a universal biography and mirror for princes. His 'moral earnestness, love of platitude and generalisations, and a sober preoccupation with practical and ethical issues' was 'the pattern of the new orthodoxy' of his Lancastrian patrons.[80] Lydgate had no successor as court poet and Henry VI, despite his love of reading, did not directly commission any work. Only after his deposition did George Ashby and Sir John Fortescue write their recommendations for governance.

Until his death in 1447 Humphrey, duke of Gloucester, was also the patron of John Capgrave, monk of Bury, who wrote his biography (not extant), while Abbot Whetehamstede was his close friend and literary adviser. But it is for his introduction of humanistic Latin that Duke Humphrey is justly famed. In commissioning Tito Livio to write the *Vita Henrici Quinti* soon after 1436 and the *Humfroidos* to celebrate his own attack on Flanders, he was promoting his own political and family interests; but his intellectual respect for Bruni and Decembrio, to whom he sent eager requests for classical texts, and his fostering of native humanists like his secretary Thomas Bekynton, established him as the only serious patron of humanism in Lancastrian England. Although his gift of 263 books to Oxford University was of major intellectual importance, it stood in the tradition of Lancastrian book-collecting. Henry IV and Henry V had initiated a royal library which, while in no way comparable to that of Charles V, was carefully maintained until dispersed by Henry VI to religious and academic houses.[81]

An intellectual diversion in most courts was an addiction to astrology. In the 1390s Richard II had commissioned a book of geomancy and had horoscopes cast, and under the Lancastrians astrologers became fashionable and influential. An extensive treatise on Henry V's nativity, the *Nativitas Nocturna*, forecasting his victories, marriage, and offspring, may have been presented to him by the famous French astrologer Jean de Fusoris, whom Bishop Courtenay invited to England in 1415. Henry later employed his chaplain, the Cambridge mathematician John Holbroke, to cast his son's horoscope at birth. Astrology held an inherent fascination for the world of chivalry, whose perennial hope of manipulating Fortune was intensified by the vicissitudes of fighting in France. In the 1430s Duke Humphrey's household at Greenwich included the highly reputable native astrologers Thomas Southwell and Roger Bultingbroke, whose fatal casting of Henry VI's horoscope for the duchess Eleanor in 1441, predicting his

---

[80] D. Forbes (ed.), *Lydgate's Disguising at Hertford Castle* (Hertford, 1998); J. A. Doig, 'Propaganda, public opinion and the siege of Calais in 1436', in R. E. Archer (ed.), *Crown, Government and People in the Fifteenth Century* (Stroud, 1995), 96–104.

[81] R. Weiss, *Humanism in England* (Oxford, 1957), chs. 3, 4, 5. For the royal libraries, see J. Stratford, 'The early royal collections and the royal library, to 1461', in *CHB* 255–67.

illness, brought their arrest and subsequent deaths on a charge of treasonable necromancy. Even this failed to diminish the popularity of astrology in court circles, where the fortunes of the great were matters of intrinsic interest and speculation.[82]

Yet literary patronage in any form was a less conspicuous element in the households of Bedford and Gloucester than wall-painting, illumination, tapestry, gold and silver work, jewellery, and the elaborate construction of pleasure gardens, water walks, dancing chambers, etc. which comprised the court culture of the Lancastrian monarchy. As regent of Henry VI in France, Bedford's court at the Hôtel des Tournelles in Paris was the symbol of the dual monarchy. He had acquired the tapestries, chapel and domestic furnishings, plate, and great library of Charles V and VI and had little need to commission more. His personal taste is best reflected in the illuminated liturgical works he commissioned: the Psalter illuminated by Herman Scheere, the Bedford Hours made in Paris in 1423–30 for his wife, Anne (given to Henry VI in 1430), the Salisbury Breviary, likewise with personal allusions commenced in 1424, and the Benedictional for use in his chapel. The sheer wealth of illumination in these represented an ambitious, long-term—and highly expensive—enterprise.[83] In panel-painting, by contrast, there was no fifteenth-century successor to the Wilton Diptych, nor any scheme of wall-painting of the scope and quality to match those at Westminster Palace.

[82] Carey, *Courting Disaster*, 128–53.
[83] J. Stratford, *The Bedford Inventories* (London, 1993), 55–126.

CHAPTER 3

Central Government

By 1360 the principal agencies of government were normally located within the Palace of Westminster, the administrative capital of the realm. This reflected the king's usual proximity to London, for government remained dependent on, and responsive to, the king's authority. It also reflected the huge accumulation of records by the executive offices and their need for continuous accessibility. Enrolment was the normal method: the chancery enrolled all royal charters and letters under the great seal; the exchequer enrolled its receipts and expenditure, accounts, and memorandums; each of the courts of law had a roll of the pleas it heard; and parliament kept a roll of its proceedings. Enrolment constituted a public legal record, available for either official or private reference. For the business transacted in these offices of state was in equal measure that of the king and his subjects. Government was the interaction of their interests, and its impetus came as often from below as from above. The physical setting emphasized this, for Westminster Hall was open and accessible to all who had business there: petitioners, litigants, those rendering accounts and seeking payment, and all who hoped to 'nobble' officials to seek a favour or make an excuse—a busy, noisy, chaotic place.[1]

In the century after 1360 the Westminster offices became the hub of national government. Awareness of its mechanism was spread among the thousands of subjects who had business with it. How was it organized? What did it embrace? Who were the officials who made it work? I shall consider, in the first place, the executive agencies: the secretariat, the courts of law, and the exchequer; then the consultative bodies of parliament and council; and finally the organization of diplomacy and defence.

I. THE SECRETARIAT

The three secretarial offices were the chancery, the privy seal, and the signet in descending order of seniority, size, and formality. The chancery issued letters

---

[1] See the vivid picture in 'London Lickpenny', printed in Robbins (ed.), *Hist. Poems*, 130–4.

granting land, money, offices, pardons, and releases. Each was an act of royal grace and a political decision, which reflected the quality of the king's rule and his reputation for even-handedness or favouritism. Virtually all requests for the king's grace were made by petition, and a king might expect to receive around 3,000 in a year. On each he made a decision which was conveyed to the chancellor in person if he was with the king, but more usually through the keeper of the privy seal, or exceptionally by a letter under the king's signet.[2] This emphasized both the king's personal involvement in government and the need for safeguards in the form of duly authorized warrants and formal enrolment of record. This tension between the personal and bureaucratic elements in government operated at all levels of medieval royal administration. Suppliants needed not only to know the correct procedures but to secure the goodwill of the officials who operated them.

In all some 2,500 letters under the great seal were issued each year, to a wide range of the king's subjects, virtually all of whom would be among the political nation. Beyond these was a steadily growing number of letters under the privy seal or signet, to individuals, officials, and corporations, which were administrative rather than dispositive documents. Many were commands or requests: to appear before the king or council, to keep the peace, to lend money, or to attend to some matter locally, while some dealt with diplomatic affairs abroad. No register of these was kept and how many were issued each year is impossible to say. Government thus generated a huge volume of letters of different kinds, and the writing offices were kept perpetually busy. Who staffed them, what qualifications did the clerks have, and under what conditions did they work?

The chancellor was normally a cleric and usually a bishop, although during 1371–7 and for six of the years between 1378 and 1386 lay lords held the post. Traditionally the chancellor was the king's public conscience, with a duty to conserve the royal estate. In 1382 Richard, Lord Scrope, refused to seal royal grants which he deemed imprudent, and in 1386 Michael de la Pole was impeached for sealing charters contrary to the Crown's interest.

Below the chancellor was the keeper of the rolls, the effective head of the office. His staff consisted of twenty-four clerks and twenty-four cursitors who drew up the standard (*de cursu*) writs.[3] The clerk of the parliaments and the clerk of the petty bag had responsibility for servicing parliament, and other senior clerks were allocated business on a territorial basis. The chancery clerks worked long hours, including Sundays and feast days, at least in term time, and though assisted by an army of sub-clerks, the pressure could be intense, with 300 documents being sealed in a day. All were trained in house, in a lifetime of service

---

[2] A. L. Brown, 'The authorisation of letters under the great seal', *BIHR* 37 (1964), 125–56.

[3] M. Richardson, *The Medieval Chancery under Henry V*, List and Index Society, special ser., 30 (London, 1999), 16, shows that the cursitors were reduced to twelve under Henry V's ordinance.

which could last for forty or even fifty years, and only at the very end of our period were university graduates in civil law appointed. It was a closed shop, insular and introspective, in which promotion was slow. The senior clerks were celibate, drawing their living partly from benefices in the gift of the chancellor, and partly from fees from clients. Perhaps more lucrative were the payments for their personal services as attorneys retained by the nobility, as mainpernours or sureties in legal proceedings, and as feoffees and witnesses in land transactions. In these respects they could become deeply implicated in gentry litigation, using their professional position to assist or impede the suit of a party through the issue of writs from the chancery.[4] They were also moneylenders, they invested in land and property, and some left considerable movable wealth.[5] In 1381 a Commons' petition denounced them as 'too fat in body and purse alike and too well clothed in fur', and when in 1388 parliament demanded a review of the offices, a resulting ordinance in 1389 pruned the establishment and regularized working practices. Its reissue in 1417 reflected a growing laicization of personnel in the second and lower grades, so that by Henry VI's reign about one-third of the clerks were married.[6]

The senior clerks who remained celibate did not live communally, but a number of them kept *hospitia*, or inns, in the Farringdon district in which the juniors lived and trained. In the 1390s Serjeants' Inn was leased to John Scarle, in 1407 Clement's Inn to John Wakering, John Franke, and John Rowland, and the Old Bell Inn to Simon Gaunstede. As schools for teaching the forms of writs required in the stages of legal process, they attracted apprentices at law as residents. Comparatively quickly these replaced the trainee clerks and by 1432 the Inns of Chancery were resembling preparatory schools for lawyers in which, by Fortescue's day, readings and possibly moots were held, as in the Inns of Court.[7]

By 1360 the privy seal office had ceased to accompany the king as part of his household (though the keeper sometimes did so) and had settled at Westminster next to the new Star Chamber of the council. Its recognition as one of the five principal offices of state was marked in 1386 when the Commons asked that the keeper be appointed in parliament. In practice the office was filled by men who enjoyed the personal confidence of the king. Some had trained as chancery clerks

---

[4] Ibid., ch. 2; for the flagrant manipulation of chancery procedure by the clerks in 1427–32 against Robert Armburgh, see C. Carpenter (ed.), *The Armburgh Papers* (Woodbridge, 1998), 8–9, 141–2.

[5] See the will of John Franke in *Reg. Chichele*, ii. 591–5, and *CPR, 1436–41*, 497, for his bequest of £1,000 to Oriel College.

[6] *Rot. Parl.* iii. 101. The text of the 1389/1417 ordinances is printed in B. Wilkinson, *The Chancery under Edward III* (Manchester, 1929), 214–23, and discussed also in Richardson, *Medieval Chancery*, 9–11.

[7] S. E. Thorne and J. H. Baker (eds.), *Readings and Moots at the Inns of Court in the Fifteenth Century*, ii, Selden Society (London, 1990), pp. xxx–xxxii; Richardson, *Medieval Chaucery*, ch. 3.

while others came up through the household, often as the king's secretary. Since the keeper was ex officio a member of the council, and often its link to the king, the privy seal also came to be used by the council to exercise its own executive and judicial authority.

The privy seal office was far smaller than the chancery, comprising half a dozen clerks who lived in a *hospitium*, in Hoccleve's day Chester's Inn near the Strand.[8] Although they were not university graduates (*magistri*), the clerks had to be well versed in French and Latin and may have had notarial training. They were salaried but, like the chancery clerks, they looked for benefices, remaining in minor orders and eventually marrying if none matured. They took fees for writing warrants and petitions and hoped for odd grants from the Crown of forfeitures or sinecure local offices, but unlike the chancery clerks they could not act as attorneys in the law courts. Hoccleve had entered the office in 1387 and remained there until his death in 1426, a lifetime's employment in a dead-end job. His contemporary Robert Frye was more successful, rising to become clerk of the council, secondary in the office, and MP for Wilton.[9]

Hoccleve gives a vivid autobiographical picture of the life of a privy seal clerk. The work was exacting, requiring continuous attention, yet repetitive and solitary: it strained the eyes and arms and produced writer's cramp. But out of hours there was the conviviality of city life among a dining, drinking, and literary circle, a 'court of good company' around his friend Henry Somer in the Paul's Head tavern. By the age of 40 fears of loneliness and poverty in old age and lack of a benefice induced him, in 1410, to marry. His life was now centred on his writing, completing his major work, *The Regement of Princes*, writing poems and 'balades' invoking patronage from the great. In 1416 he had suffered a mental breakdown, from which he only slowly recovered, and his poetic mood changed to moral and religious concerns. Though a conscientious and competent clerk, as his carefully indexed formulary reveals, his literary sensibilities and neuroses set him apart from his fellows.[10]

With the privy seal office established at Westminster and its keeper not regularly at court, Edward III began to use his signet as a personal seal of warranty, and Richard II from 1383 systematically extended this, using the signet to warrant grants directly under the great seal. The restrictions laid upon Richard II in 1386 prohibited this, requiring all grants under the signet to pass the scrutiny of the privy seal. Signet letters, headed 'By the King', continued to be the most personal expression of the king's will when writing to his officers, councillors,

---

[8] A. L. Brown, 'The privy seal clerks in the early fifteenth century', in D. A. Bullough and R. L. Storey (eds.), *The Study of Medieval Records* (Oxford, 1971), 260–81.

[9] *House of Commons*, iii. 143–5.

[10] Brown, 'The privy seal clerks'; *Selections from Hoccleve*, ed. M. C. Seymour (Oxford, 1980), pp. xi–xxxiii.

corporations, and other individual subjects. Henry V used the signet to send commands, instructions, and news from France. Most of these direct and occasional signet letters have disappeared, and no estimate can be made of their number; no register was kept, or storage provided for its records, until the reign of Richard III.

At the head of the signet office was the king's secretary. All royal secretaries were graduates, some were papal notaries and doctors of civil law, and for many their personal attendance on the king procured them a bishopric or deanery.[11] The clerks of the signet office had similar qualifications and rewards to those of the privy seal, though they were not salaried and depended on benefices. But after 1437 all were laymen, who used their influence at court to secure a modest wealth through farms, wardships, forfeitures, and sinecure offices on Crown estates. Such men were representative of the rapidly enlarging class of 'gentlemen bureaucrats', entitled to wear the livery of the king or lord whom they served and thereby to claim gentility. Hoccleve was gratified to be 'for a verray gentil man yholde' by the cooks and taverners at Westminster Gate.[12]

As laicization proceeded in the offices of state, so the civil servants became increasingly entangled in landed society, acquiring property, securing local offices, forging business connections, and utilizing their secretarial, legal, and financial skills and contacts for the benefit of their associates and clients. Their offices became sources of profit and perhaps began to be turned into freeholds, the reversion of which could be sold. The old clerical civil service supported by ecclesiastical revenues was rapidly disappearing in the fifteenth century, and with it much of the influence and prestige which the Church traditionally enjoyed with the Crown.[13]

As clerk of the royal works, Geoffrey Chaucer was the prototype of this new class, and it was the circle of London civil servants, lawyers, lesser courtiers, and merchants who formed the primary audience for *The Canterbury Tales*. Hoccleve was on the fringe of this circle and among his contemporaries two chancery clerks, Richard Southworth and John Stopyndon, were successive owners of the earliest recorded manuscript of the poem.[14] It was these multilingual and

[11] J. Otway-Ruthven, *The King's Secretary and the Signet Office in the XV Century* (Cambridge, 1939).

[12] R. L. Storey, 'Gentlemen-bureaucrats', in C. H. Clough (ed.), *Profession, Vocation, and Culture in Later Medieval England* (Liverpool, 1982), 90–129; 'La Male Regle de T. Hoccleve', in *Selections*, ed. Seymour, 16, line 184.

[13] No survey has been made of the political culture of the late medieval royal bureaucracy comparable to that of Gerald Aylmer for the 17th century. R. A. Griffiths, in *King and Country: England and Wales in the Fifteenth Century* (London, 1991), 137–60, indicates some of the important questions to be asked.

[14] D. Pearsall, *The Life of Geoffrey Chaucer* (Oxford, 1992), 181–5; M. Richardson, 'The earliest known owners of *Canterbury Tales* MSS and Chaucer's secondary audience', *Chaucer Review*, 25 (1990), 17–32.

cultured civil servants who presided over the adoption of English in government documents for the first time since the Anglo-Saxon writ. From the moment when Henry V landed in Normandy on 5 August 1417 all letters under the signet were written in English, and the first privy seal in English was issued from Vincennes on 22 August 1422, a week before Henry died. From 1422 English was increasingly used in the record of parliament's proceedings. Chancery written English introduced standard spelling, vocabulary, and style, a conscious and artificial development, independent of the spoken dialects and individual written usage current in London. That this revolution was prompted by the king himself, who, 'in his letters missive and divers affairs touching his own person . . . for the better understanding of his people hath . . . procured the common idiom to be commended by the exercise of writing', was acknowledged in the records of the Brewer's Guild. Moreover, many of the signet letters, dictated by Henry himself, in his 'direct, sinewy style', anticipate the spelling, verb forms, and pronoun usage of standard chancery English.[15] Henry's use of English to convey a direct and unambiguous message, as in his secret instructions to Sir John Tiptoft, was to become the mark of all signet letters. His letter starts without salutation:

Tiptoft. I charge you by the Feith that ye owe me, that ye kepe this Matere her after Writen, from al Men secre save from my Brother Th'Emperor owne Persone, that never Creature have Wittynge thereof, withowt my especial Commandement, of my owne Mouthe, or els Writen with myn owne Hand, and Seely'd with my Signet.[16]

The influence of chancery standard English quickly extended beyond government documents and beyond London to produce the first age of lay letter-writing. In fact writing ability was less common than reading, and most laymen dictated their letters to professional scribes.[17] It was they who fashioned the normative structure and language of private letters for the next century, drawing on the tradition of the Latin *dictamen* with its formal greeting, expression of goodwill, narration, request, and conclusion. It remains recognizable in their phraseology: 'Right trusty and welbeloved . . . I recommend me unto you . . . please you to understand that . . . desiring you of your goodwill to . . . may God keep you in his mercy'. English letter-writing thus acquired form, precision, and directness from the *dictamen* and became the accustomed form of communication among the political class for personal, business, and political matters.[18] In the letters of

---

[15] M. Richardson, 'Henry V, the English chancery, and chancery English', *Speculum*, 55 (1980), 726–50; J. H. and J. Fisher and M. Richardson (eds.), *An Anthology of Chancery English* (Knoxville, Tenn., 1984), 3–51.

[16] Rymer (ed.), *Foedera*, ix. 327–30. [17] Davis (ed.), *Paston Letters*, vol. i, pp. xxxvi–xxxix.

[18] M. Richardson, 'The *dictamen* and its influence on fifteenth century English prose', *Rhetorica*, 2 (1984), 207–26; id., 'Medieval English vernacular correspondence: Notes towards an alternative rhetoric', *Allegorica*, 10 (1989), 95–118.

the Pastons, Armburghs, Stonors, and Plumptons we have a lively picture of their material and emotional concerns, their social conventions and beliefs, daily routines, and notable events. The middle-class lay mentality and viewpoint is revealed for the first time as recognizably akin to our own, and their world is made real and immediate, not veiled or romanticized.

Letter-writing, habitual in personal and business matters, also developed a political dimension. Kings sent news bills describing their campaigns in Ireland or France; Londoners wrote accounts of particular events of national interest— a parliament, a battle, a political ritual, or a coup—for the benefit of a provincial audience; letters were issued as public manifestos by noble malcontents or plebeian rebels; well-reasoned letters upheld Lollard beliefs against ecclesiastical persecution. Such public and semi-public letters were passed round, read out, nailed on doors, retained in private collections, or copied into private journals and official registers. Ubiquitous literacy drew political society together in a web of information, rumour, warning, and advice. 'The intimacy of the governing class, its limited size, its interconnectedness, and its openness made the circulation of information within it easy'—nourishing a political mentality.[19]

2. LAW AND JUSTICE

In no respect was the king more conspicuously God's minister than in enforcing the law and rendering justice. He alone had God's authority to shed the blood of transgressors, while to his subjects he promised to do equal and rightful justice in mercy and truth. Law underpinned and validated royal governance.[20] King and subjects tended to view law and justice from different standpoints. For the king it was an instrument of punishment and control, part of his executive authority; for subjects it was the guarantor and adjudicator of their rights and the framework for social harmony. The interaction of these different and potentially conflicting approaches affected the development of legal institutions and procedures in this period. For the late Middle Ages saw an unprecedented enlargement of the legal system, with the growth of the Crown's criminal jurisdiction, the emergence of an equitable jurisdiction in chancery, the extension of the law to economic and social regulation, the institution of justices of the peace and quarter sessions linked to assizes, and the multiplication of new writs and actions. Accompanying this, there was an outburst of litigation, to claim and enforce individual rights, mainly in property. Increased litigation in turn stimulated the expansion of the legal profession, impelled not only by expertise in law

---

[19] C. Richmond, 'Hand and mouth: Information gathering and use in England in the later Middle Ages', *Jnl. Hist. Soc.* 1 (1988), 233–52.

[20] Above, Ch. 1; T. Hoccleve, *The Regement of Princes*, ed. F. J. Furnivall, EETS, extra ser., 72 (London, 1897), lines 2733–5.

but by the prospect of wealth and status. This produced tension between the concept of justice, embodied in the Crown, and the practice of law in the interests of subjects, generating criticism and complaint. We shall discuss each of these in turn.

At the apex of the judicial system were the three ancient courts of common law: the common pleas, the king's bench, and the exchequer. The first two, with the court of chancery, were (until 1884) located in Westminster Hall, with the court of chancery in an adjoining chamber. Judges sat on a raised bench against the wall, their clerks at a long table in front, and litigants and counsel on either side. Their business was conducted within earshot of each other, from eight to eleven o'clock each morning during the four law terms, at most a total of twenty weeks in the year. The function of each had largely been established in the thirteenth century. Common pleas, which heard litigation exclusively between subjects, had jurisdiction in actions over real estate and debt, and embraced civil trespass. Its accessibility to subjects generated a larger volume of litigation than any other court, and it was served by one chief justice and up to six junior or puisne justices. The king's bench had, in origin, followed the king, dealing with all cases touching his interests. From the mid-fourteenth century it was generally at Westminster, although the Crown on occasion could send it on itinerary to enforce order and review the work of lesser courts. As the foremost criminal court, it received indictments for felonies and breaches of the peace brought before the justices in the localities. King's bench was less busy and less profitable than common pleas, and its chief justice was assisted by up to four puisne judges. The court in the exchequer chamber was a meeting of senior judges for discussion of difficult cases referred from lesser courts, and thus dealt with technical points of law.[21]

The courts of common law had evolved an elaborate process for bringing the plaintiff and defendant into court before an impartial jury. Plaintiffs could purchase a writ from the chancery ordering the sheriff to summon the defendant into court, and if this proved ineffective further writs ('mesne process') ordered his repeated summons, arrest, and eventual outlawry. If he was brought to court the trial proceeded before a jury, which the parties could legitimately 'inform' about the facts of the case, but might also seek to 'labour' or pressure by bribery and threats. The jury's verdict might be challenged if corruption could be proved. Pleading was done by qualified attorneys, under rules which permitted objections to the form of the writ or technicalities in the legal process: not territory for laymen. The time taken, from the issue of the original writ until the trial and verdict, could be up to twelve months, and at every stage the defendant

[21] J. H. Baker, *An Introduction to English Legal History*, 3rd edn. (London, 1990), ch. 3; M. Hastings, *The Court of Common Pleas in Fifteenth Century England* (New York, 1947), ch. 2.

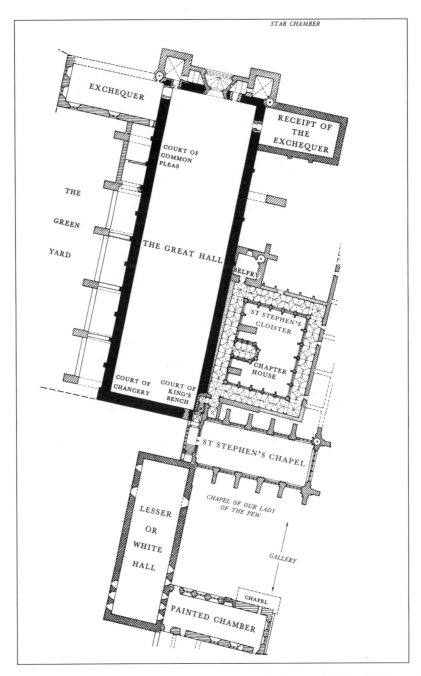

FIG. 3.1. The Palace of Westminster. Source: R. A. Brown, H. M. Colvin, and A. J. Taylor, *History of the King's Works* (London, 1963), iii. *Plans.*

might secure a royal pardon. Litigation at common law was lengthy and easily became bogged down in procedure. It was costly in both money and mental strain and only a small minority of cases reached judgement. Yet the courts were intensively used: some 3,000 new suits each year were coming to the central courts by 1460.

Alongside these common law courts was the court of chancery, which developed in the fourteenth century. The chancellor's jurisdiction derived from his presidency of the council, though by Richard II's reign it was exercised separately from it. He had a Christian duty to secure justice for those unable to obtain it at common law 'as law, reason, and conscience demand', a phrase first appearing in 1391. In 1419 Henry V ordered the chancellor to do 'right and equite' to parties in such a case and the chancellor's court came to be known as a 'court of conscience', administering an 'equitable' jurisdiction. It dealt with disputes over fiduciary arrangements not recognized at common law, like the investing of trustees with land for another's benefit or 'use'; or promises made in private and commercial undertakings; and it also took cognizance if intimidation or the perversion of justice was alleged. The plaintiff did not have to sue under the form of a Latin writ, but could make his petition in French or, by 1420, in English. The defendant could be compelled to appear within fifteen days under a fiscal penalty (*sub poena*), to answer unspecified allegations (*quibusdam certis de causis*), and be informally interrogated. There was no jury and for the most part no judgment, the parties being brought to a settlement. Both the court's power and its informality aroused mistrust, and from the end of the fourteenth century there were protests about the misuse of writs of *sub poena*, while a statute of 1352 excluded it from all judgments on freehold title. But the chancellor's court did afford the disadvantaged the opportunity, denied in the common law courts, to pursue their case against the mighty, and by the 1430s it was used by persons from the middling ranks of society for a wide range of causes. Even though the medieval court of chancery 'was a remedy more than a jurisdiction', it became the foundation of the equity jurisdiction and penal authority of the court of Star Chamber under the Tudors.[22]

In the localities the old system of sheriffs' courts controlled by visits of justices on eyre was radically transformed in the course of the fourteenth century. The eyres had become cumbersome and extortionate and new agencies had to be found more in touch with, and acceptable to, local society. The punitive commissions of trailbaston to deal with crime were equally disliked, and from early in Edward III's reign the gentry were asking, in parliament, for powers to keep the peace and then to act as local justices. Their undeniable claim to be better aware

---

[22] Baker, *Introduction to English Legal History*, ch. 6; T. S. Haskett, 'Conscience, justice, and authority in the late medieval court of chancery', in A. Musson (ed.), *Expectations of the Law* (Woodbridge, 2001), 151–64.

of local conditions was counterbalanced by the judiciary's distrust of their partiality and ignorance of law. Half a century of argument and experiment, in which at times (1338–44, 1361–4, 1380–2, 1389–94) gentry justices of the peace were empowered to try felonies, and at others the harsh visitation of central justices was revived, eventually resulted in the establishment of local commissions of the peace composed of magnates, professional lawyers, and local gentry. An essential element in this amalgam was the provision in 1394 that felonies were to be tried before a quorum of two local men of law and the justices appointed for gaol delivery. The record of wages paid for attendance at the peace sessions, after 1389, shows that the work was mostly done by a handful of JPs, including those of the quorum, in rapid two-day sessions around the county. In the main they punished the petty felonies and misdemeanours of the non-gentry, an exercise in social control, while also taking indictments for more serious felonies and breaches of the peace which were remanded to gaol delivery sessions at the assizes.[23]

The twice-yearly assizes were held by justices and serjeants-at-law from the central courts, who, in Lent and summer vacations, went on circuit for some twelve days. They could hear real and personal actions relating to the locality which were pending in the central courts (under the *nisi prius* system), thereby reducing congestion at Westminster; they also 'delivered' the county gaol, by trying those arrested for felonies; and they sat with other JPs of the quorum at quarter sessions to deal with the more serious felonies. Thus while the gentry exercised a local magistracy, professional lawyers and judges controlled the trial and punishment of the more serious crimes. This provided an integrated system of justice, the merits of which were attested by its survival as a permanent feature of the English legal system.

The structure of the late medieval system of justice raises important questions about the character of English government. Was it fashioned by the Crown and judiciary as an instrument of punishment, or did it evolve out of the demands for litigation and social control by the landed classes? Did it render effective and impartial justice, or did it serve the interests of those who used it? It has been argued that under Edward III the Crown's control over both law-making and law-keeping was diluted by deference to pressures from subjects. Legislation came to be made on the basis of ill-informed petitions by the Commons rather than by the judges, while the devolution of law-keeping to gentry justices of the peace was a surrender to local interests. This was a consequence of the financial strains of war and the social and economic crisis of the Black Death.

[23] For recent work on JPs, see E. Powell, 'The administration of criminal justice in late medieval England: Peace sessions and assizes', in R. Eales and D. Sullivan (eds.), *The Political Context of Law* (London, 1987), 49–59; S. K. Walker, 'Yorkshire justices of the peace, 1389–1413', *EHR* 108 (1993), 281–313.

A more persuasive formulation sees the Crown deliberately incorporating the middling landowning and mercantile class into a more inclusive ruling elite. The Crown did not abandon its responsibility for law-making; indeed it extended the authority and scope of statutes into social and economic life, with nationwide regulation of wages and prices, servile obligations, personal mobility, and social behaviour. In enforcing these, the gentry JPs came to see themselves as mediating the Crown's authority and upholding the public interest.[24] It has been further urged that the government extended the scope of the common law to the enforcement of occupational undertakings (like building contracts) through writs of assumpsit and trespass on the case, in order to 'compel the lower orders to stand to their obligations'; though whether the pressure for this came from the government or from consumers remains uncertain.[25] Actions for the recovery of debts saw a similar growth after the Statute of the Staple in 1354 provided penal bonds of conditional defeasance, which came to be sued in large numbers in the court of common pleas.

What all this signifies is a growing convergence of the interests of the Crown, the judiciary, and the political class in the business of legal regulation and enforcement. Resort to law by both government and subjects to regulate social relations became normal, and free men at all levels had to familiarize themselves with the rudiments of legal process and employ attorneys to prosecute their interests. How did this affect the function of the law in punishing crime and purveying justice?

At first sight the prosecution and punishment of crime seems woefully ineffective. Local crimes were presented by hundredal juries at the sheriff's tourn or before the JPs at peace sessions. Juries were expected to have knowledge of the crimes committed in their neighbourhood, though in practice accusations were often made by constables and bailiffs, the jury being asked to decide whether this was a 'true bill'. The process was open to malicious indictments framed by lords and their officials, and virtually all those indicted were of non-gentry status. Only about one-third of those indicted eventually stood trial—the remainder never appeared and were outlawed. Those brought before the justices of gaol delivery were swiftly dealt with, often in batches at the rate of twenty minutes each batch. The trial juries were composed of men drawn from the whole county who had £5 or more in landed income, only some of whom, if any, had

---

[24] For these interpretations, see R. W. Kaeuper, *War, Justice, and Public Order: England and France in the Late Middle Ages* (Oxford, 1988); A. Musson and W. M. Ormrod, *The Evolution of English Justice* (Basingstoke, 1999).

[25] R. C. Palmer, *English Law in the Age of the Black Death, 1348–81: A Transformation of Government and Law* (Chapel Hill, NC, 1993); criticized by A. Musson, 'New labour laws, new remedies? Legal reaction to the Black Death crisis', in Saul (ed.), *Fourteenth Century England*, 73–89.

knowledge of the case. The jury was generally presented with evidence by the prosecution, and witnesses called, but no defence counsel. If this gives the impression of summary process, in fact over 80 per cent of those tried at gaol delivery were acquitted, and only some 10 per cent were convicted and executed (the rest escaped).[26] This high rate of acquittal is explained by the reluctance of juries to apply the mandatory death penalty for all felonies to any but homicides. Judges seem to have accepted a large degree of discretion in juries' verdicts.[27] Indeed the majority of those who submitted themselves for trial (and did not flee) did so to secure acquittal and clear their name.

This ineffectiveness of the system was more apparent than real. Those acquitted after trial, or even pardoned before it, did not escape punishment. Most had spent weeks or months in prison awaiting trial and some were then remanded to the next sessions. Within their local community they had been stigmatized as suspect, and made to give sureties for their good behaviour. Appearance in court did therefore make a positive contribution to peacekeeping. But if it was so rarely applied, why was the death penalty retained? First, as a deterrent, but more practically because there was nothing to replace it. With only one gaol in a county, long custodial sentences were impracticable, and money penalties were reserved for non-felonious crimes. More serious was the high proportion of those who never appeared in court, either by purchasing a pardon, or by simply ignoring the summons. The Crown's readiness to pardon serious crime produced repeated complaint in parliament, but in fact the number producing pardons in court was always small and securities against further offence were always required.[28] In a wider context pardons which restored a criminal to the king's grace were often the prelude for his recruitment into the royal army. The most striking demonstration of this was the visitation of the king's bench to the West Midlands in 1414, which brought some 800 persons into court where, after perfunctory trial, the majority were pardoned and put under sureties, and many served next year in France. The operation had served not to punish serious crime but to bring it within the determination of the courts.[29]

Thus, in dealing with crime, late medieval society was largely non-retributive. On average only two men a year were hanged in each of the East Anglian counties in the years 1422–42. Mutilations too had declined since the thirteenth

[26] Based on the king's bench and gaol delivery records relating to East Anglia in the period 1422–42 in P. C. Maddern, *Violence and Social Order* (Oxford, 1992), ch. 2.

[27] T. A. Green, 'Societal concepts of criminal liability for homicide in medieval England', *Speculum*, 47 (1972), 669–94; id., 'The jury and the English law of homicide, 1200–1600', *Michigan Law Review*, 74 (1976), 413–99.

[28] J. G. Bellamy, *Crime and Public Order in England in the Later Middle Ages* (London, 1973), 191–8; E. Powell, *Kingship, Law, and Society* (Oxford, 1989), 83–5.

[29] Powell, *Kingship, Law, and Society*, chs. 7 and 9.

century, perhaps from reluctance to disable a man from working. Both hanging and mutilations were to increase under the Tudors.[30] Murderers and persistent criminals whom local society wanted punished were generally removed from it, but most criminal cases in the courts were non-violent, and a high rate of acquittal did not mean condoning violence. In fact the system of criminal justice served primarily as an instrument of social control. Not only did members of the gentry sit as JPs to deal with a range of social and economic offences, but it was their servants and clients who staffed the system as bailiffs, under-sheriffs, constables, and clerks, in arresting suspects, enforcing writs, and sitting as jurors. The appearance of the culprit in court, before the representatives of royal authority, served to reprobate his violation of the social code and return him to his local context.

While the felonies committed by the lower classes were principally heard at sessions of the peace and gaol delivery, crimes committed by the gentry were removed to king's bench. Some of these involved armed disorders, but the great majority were property actions under the guise of trespass *vi et armis* (by force and arms). This could be brought either by a plaintiff who had been forcibly ejected from occupancy of his property or by a claimant to it who alleged that he had been kept out by force. In either case mere verbal threats or ritual gestures were deemed to amount to the use of force. In the 1440s Friar Hauteyn, claiming title to Oxnead, was barred entry by Edmund Paston at the manor gateway with threatening words; thereupon he bent down, scooped up earth, and called on those with him to witness his taking possession. As in novel disseisin, which the action of trespass *vi et armis* superseded, the court in deciding who had committed the trespass was in fact declaring title.[31] While in form a criminal action, this was in fact tort (i.e. civil hurt).

The political class thus had a proprietary attitude to the law, using it to settle their disputes and to enforce social control. It was their servant, not their master. To what degree did this open the door to corruption and to the perversion of justice? At the centre, royal judges since the thirteenth century had succumbed readily to lordship, for in status and wealth they were the natural associates of the magnates, by whom they were retained. By 1350 this was arousing the concern of both the Crown and subjects. Petitions in parliament in the 1380s against judges taking bribes and fees eventually secured the cessation of the practice after 1390.[32]

---

[30] Maddern, *Violence*, 71–4; Bellamy, *Crime and Order*, 181 ff., says that mutilations were more common in towns than in the countryside.

[31] D. W. Sutherland, *The Assize of Novel Disseisin* (Oxford, 1973), 171–6; J. G. Bellamy, *Bastard Feudalism and the Law* (Portland, Ore., 1989), 39–52; Maddern, *Violence*, 31–5; Davis (ed.), *Paston Letters*, ii. 522.

[32] J. R. Maddicott, *Law and Lordship: Royal Justices as Retainers in Thirteenth and Fourteenth Century England, P & P*, suppl. 4 (1978).

Similarly by the later fourteenth century the ability of magnates to procure special commissions of oyer and terminer in their own suits, to which they named judges favourable to them, was curtailed by statute.[33] Even so few royal judges were impartial and incorruptible, for there were many channels through which lordship and favour flowed.

Lordship likewise pervaded the whole system of local justice. Sheriffs, JPs, and jurors could all be lords' retainers. The sheriff could impede or assist a plaintiff's suit, he could empanel a favourable jury, and jurors might be intimidated and bribed by the parties.[34] Nor was this surprising, for in naming an heir in an inquisition post mortem, or making an indictment for forcible entry, or giving a verdict in an assize of novel disseisin, a jury touched the vital interests of family and property. Whether through embracery, champerty, or maintenance, or more strictly legal devices like fraudulent indictment, men did not hesitate to bend the legal process. The line between legal chicanery and corruption was fine and easily breached, for litigants sought not justice but victory. There could never be equality at law between rich and poor, and to those without access to it the law was a weapon of lordship and oppression, the very antithesis of justice.

As a literary topos, the corruption of justice manifested the sense of crisis in society during the half century 1365–1415. God had ordained punishment for the wrongdoer, mercy for the penitent, and justice between rich and poor. But to Langland and his contemporaries man's mercenary nature was perverting God's design. Penance and absolution for sin was sold by the friars, while law was sold through wrongful verdicts and pardons, and used by the rich to oppress the poor. Money had corrupted men's sense of sin and their relation both to God and to each other; Christian society rested on justice and would fall apart if this was not upheld. The king, as God's minister, had prime responsibility for enforcing law and justice, and in Langland's narration of the trial between Wrong and Peace at Westminster, it is the king, guided by Reason, who sweeps aside the specious plea of Meed (wealth). Langland was ready to believe that a king guided by reason should be the source of laws and guarantor of justice, but to many others it seemed safer if the king were restrained by positive as well as divine law. Yet if the law, rather than the king, was to be supreme, those who administered it must be incorruptible. Manifestly that was not so, nor could be, for judges and lawyers served their clients' interests and their own pockets. Langland acknowledges this and hints at a utopian provision of legal aid, but his essential standpoint is moral: perfect kingship and perfect justice had been corrupted by man's venal nature.

---

[33] R. W. Kaeuper, 'Law and order in fourteenth century England: The evidence of special commissions of oyer and terminer', *Speculum*, 54 (1979), 734–84; Bellamy, *Bastard Feudalism and Law*, 53–6.

[34] Bellamy, *Crime and Order*, 21, 28.

Langland's *Visio* of Lady Meed and her retinue of corrupt sheriffs, pleaders, and jurors is an allegory of man's fallen state.[35]

The theme was echoed in the literature of complaint and satire that followed Langland. Gower, observing the cupidity of judges, the wealth of serjeants and apprentices, and the bribery of sheriffs and jurors, recalls them to their social obligations; Hoccleve denounces the maintenance practised by the great and the violence it breeds; and the Digby MS poems warn that where law is sold and lordship rules the commons will rise.[36] This literature speaks with one voice about the corruption of justice by money and favour and the failure of the king to correct this and uphold the law. The complaint had substance; yet its literary context, the rule of the perfect prince in a Christian society, made it ingenuous. For in practice the king had little, or limited, power to affect the operation of the law. What controlled it was rather the burgeoning legal profession and their moneyed clients.

At the top of the profession were eight or ten judges of the central courts and four or six serjeants-at-law, who pleaded on behalf of the king and from whom the judges were drawn. This identity of the bar and the bench was unique to England. Judges and serjeants were appointed by the Crown for life and were in general immune from political changes. Beneath this top echelon were fifty or so apprentices at law, authorized to plead in the courts, the king's attorneys in the principal courts, and senior court officers: in all some 120 men who stood at the head of, and regulated, the profession. Beyond the bench and the bar were the host of common lawyers, preparing briefs on behalf of a multitude of clients: a competitive and largely unregulated business. Here a man built up a practice through local connections, to a nobleman, monastery, town, or neighbours, and through personal familiarity with the Westminster pleaders and judges. Success in litigation demanded both technical expertise—in commencing, pursuing, and pleading actions—and also influence with the serjeants and justices.[37] Landowners retained counsel with an annual fee, usually £2 for a serjeant and a mark for a solicitor, and might employ more than one lawyer on a case.[38] After 1350 the number of lawyers increased strikingly, not merely at Westminster but in the localities, where quarter sessions, assizes, and the growth of arbitration procedures created a demand for local attorneys. Men with legal training were also

[35] M. Stokes, *Justice and Mercy in 'Piers Plowman'* (London, 1984), 1–3, 24–31, 71–6; Langland, *Piers Plowman*, passus ii–iv.

[36] Gower, *Mirour de l'omme*, lines 24, 349–54, 396; Gower, *Confessio Amantis*, bk. vii, lines 3068–77; Hoccleve, *Regement*, lines 2500ff., 2787–2808, 3032–3410; Kail (ed.), *Political Poems*, nos. 3, 13. See also Musson and Ormrod, *Evolution of Justice*, ch. 6.

[37] E. W. Ives, *The Common Lawyers of Pre-Reformation England* (Cambridge, 1983), 60–93; J. H. Baker, *The Order of Serjeants at Law*, Selden Society, suppl. ser., 5 (London, 1984), 3–132.

[38] N. Ramsay, 'Retained legal counsel, *c*.1275–*c*.1475', *TRHS*, 5th ser., 35 (1985), 95–112.

in demand as under-sheriffs and stewards and bailiffs of lords, and were often the most acquisitive and disliked element in local society.

In the earlier fourteenth century legal training had been acquired largely through attendance in court. Around mid-century the Inns of Court and Chancery appear as hostels for law students and by the early fifteenth century some ten Inns of Chancery can be identified, the most important of which were Clifford's and Clement's Inns. These *hospitia*, under a master of chancery, took students through the preliminary study of writs, though by 1408 moots and readings might be held there.[39] The Inns of Court were parallel but more prestigious institutions, not (as was once thought) merely hostels, but with an educational curriculum through lectures and disputations which followed a sequence of statutory texts. By 1388 three distinct Inns were in existence under their later names of the Inner Temple, Gray's Inn, and Middle Temple, while Lincoln's Inn is first mentioned in 1417, each drawing students from broadly different parts of England. Here the students lived, two to a chamber, paying a termly pension and weekly commons, for twenty-eight weeks in the year.[40]

Students continued to learn by attendance at court, but by 1408 learning vacations with readings had appeared and in 1436, in an attempt to organize them on a regular basis, nineteen fellows of Lincoln's Inn agreed to attend over the next four years. A reading on a particular statute would continue for two hours on four days of a week over three or four weeks, conducted by seniors. These were the 'benchers' and before them, at the bar, the 'barristers' argued in the moot. Being called to the bar marked a specific degree of attainment. Both readings and moots were still at an early stage by 1450, but already collections of moots were being made, and at the end of our period Thomas Littleton, justice of the common pleas, wrote the first legal textbook, *The Newe Tenures*, to make the principles and not just the procedures intelligible to his son Richard, a student at the Inner Temple. The education at the Inns was tough and exhausting. Many of the cases discussed at the moots were of horrendous complexity and demanded retentive memory and a clear mind. The system 'trained a small core of advocates to a high level of expertise'. Not surprisingly the drop-out rate was high: fewer than half the students became benchers of their Inns, from whom the serjeants were appointed; many retired to the provinces to use what law they had acquired as attorneys and pleaders, and many were sons of gentry sent to acquire a general familiarity with legal process to complete their education.[41]

[39] Ives, *The Common Lawyers*, 39–40.

[40] Ibid. 40–1; J. H. Baker, *The Third University of England*, Selden Society (London, 1990), 5–12.

[41] E. W. Ives, 'The common lawyers', in Clough (ed.), *Profession, Vocation, and Culture*, 181–208; Ives, *The Common Lawyers*, ch. 3; Baker, *Third University*, 12–18; J. H. Baker, *The Legal Profession and the Common Law* (London, 1986), 7–24.

The teaching and practice of law were closely related. The record of cases, collected in yearbooks, served not as precedents but as guides to previous arguments on an issue—the common learning or 'erudition' of the profession—for what was at issue was often interpretation. This produced 'a largely oral, systematic tradition which breathed sense and order into [the practice of] oral pleading'.[42] In both its institutional and intellectual aspects the system of legal training which evolved in the century after 1350 remained until the mid-seventeenth. The exploding demand by civil society for litigation had been channelled into arcane procedures and language which gave the legal profession a monopoly exercised for the benefit of its clients and itself. At least in the eyes of its own members (like Sir John Fortescue), it was one of the success stories of the later Middle Ages, peculiarly English, entirely pragmatic, and fiercely independent.[43] By the same token, he and his fellow judges chose not to see the corruption intrinsic to its blinkered concern with the interests of the propertied class.

3. STATE FINANCE

During the half-century from 1290 to 1340 the fiscal basis of the English state shifted from domainal to tax revenues. The tax state was also emerging in other European kingdoms, but England was notable for both the volume and proportion of its tax income and its sophisticated system of public finance.[44] We shall consider these in turn.

The old domainal and feudal revenues of the Crown which formed the regular basis of Crown finance in the thirteenth century still yielded some £10,000 per annum to the exchequer in the late fourteenth century. Revenue was also received from feudal 'casualties'—wardships, marriages, escheats, and temporalities—to around some £5,000 per annum.[45] The Crown's patrimonial estates acquired in the thirteenth century—Wales, Chester, and Cornwall—were also available to the exchequer when not held by a prince of Wales. From these revenues provision had, at most times, to be made for a queen and for annuities granted as rewards, but for much of the century they yielded between £10,000 and £18,000 per annum at the exchequer. The estates of the duchy of Lancaster remained the king's private possession and were only occasionally used for state finance, at his discretion.

---

[42] Ives, *The Common Lawyers*, 160; Baker, *Third University*, 19.

[43] Sir John Fortescue, *De Laudibus Legum Angliae*, ed. and trans. S. B. Chrimes (Cambridge, 1949).

[44] W. M. Ormrod, 'England in the Middle Ages', in R. Bonney (ed.), *The Rise of the Fiscal State in Europe, c.1200–1815* (Oxford, 1999), 19–52, provides an authoritative conspectus.

[45] Based on my own calculations from receipt rolls at periodic intervals.

The modest Crown revenues were overshadowed by those from taxation. Indirect taxation levied on overseas trade, principally exports of wool, comprised a small 'ancient' custom (6s. 8d. the sack for native, 10s. for alien, merchants) which was hereditary, and the much larger subsidy (40s. or more) granted for consecutive periods of years by parliament. This had first been granted in 1337, and from 1362, when Edward III persuaded parliament to renew the tax in peacetime, it became virtually permanent and was, at different points (1398, 1415, 1453), granted to the king for life. Its yield varied in the short term with small changes in the rate of the duties, and over the long term with fluctuations in the volume of wool exported. These could be affected by war and trade embargoes, but much more by the growing replacement of wool exports by those of finished cloth from the last decades of the fourteenth century. For cloth bore a very much lighter duty, imposed in 1347, which even when it was absorbed into grants of tunnage and poundage after 1386, represented only 8.76 per cent of its value compared with the far heavier custom on wool.[46] As the English cloth-making industry expanded, wool exports dropped from 32,000 sacks in 1350–60 to under 24,000 in the 1380s and under 18,000 after 1390; from 1400 to 1430 they stabilized at around 14,000 sacks and then plunged to 9,000 for the next thirty years. Cloth exports meanwhile surged in 1385–1410, made a further advance in the 1420s, and finally began to equal and overtake the volume of wool in the 1440s.[47]

This shift between commodities with very disparate rates of duty reduced the revenue from the customs and subsidies from an average of £70,000 per annum in 1360–75 to around £57,000 in 1375–1400, to £45,000 in 1400–25, and to under £30,000 after 1430. This represented a startling decline in taxable capacity, for whereas the total volume of wool exported (both raw and as cloth) dropped by one-third between 1350 and 1450, the tax collected fell from 23.5 per cent of the export value in 1350 to only 12 per cent a century later.[48]

Crown finance was thus trapped in the inexorable decline of its principal taxable commodity, raw wool, the profitability of which was being transferred to its subjects. Yet no proposal to raise the duty on cloth so as to bring it in line with that on wool was ever canvassed, for that would have destroyed the ability of English cloth producers to compete in the hostile market of the Low Countries.

Direct taxation on movable property had longer antecedents, and parliament's unique authority to grant it had been established under Edward I. It was rated at a tenth in urban and a fifteenth in rural communities. After 1334 this was levied

[46] For cloth, see W. M. Ormrod, 'Finance and trade under Richard II', in A. Goodman and J. L. Gillespie (eds.), *Richard II: The Art of Kingship* (Oxford, 1999), 175–6. The organization of the wool trade is discussed below, Ch. 8, sect. 1.

[47] Ormrod, 'Finance and trade', p. 160, fig. 8.1.

[48] Using Ormrod's figures (ibid., p. 177, fig. 8.7) incorporating tunnage and poundage. For tax ratio, ibid. 186.

as a fixed sum on each town and vill, the burden falling almost wholly on the working population. The value of a full fifteenth and tenth was about £37,500 with costs of collection of some £1,000. Despite changes in the level and the distribution of population and wealth consequent upon the Black Death, it remained unchanged until remissions for poverty reduced it by £4,000 in 1433 and by £6,000 in 1446. Fixed and familiar, it could be levied speedily and without friction. It was reckoned to be 'the moost easy, redy and prone payment of any charge to be borne within this Reaume'.[49] It was generally accepted that direct taxation should be granted only for a necessity of the king and kingdom, normally equated with war. That was not unduly inhibiting since a state of war existed between England and France for most of the period between 1337 and 1453. But in the periods of formal peace after the Treaty of Brétigny (1360–70), after the Treaty of Troyes (1422–8), and after the loss of English Gascony (1454–60), no direct taxes were granted. Each grant of taxation had to be specifically asked for and justified in parliament. At times of armed truce an annual half subsidy was generally granted for the maintenance of overseas and border garrisons, while for active hostilities a full subsidy and even more was granted to dispatch expeditions. Taxation at the full rate could not be sustained for more than a few years without provoking distress and discontent, but an annual half subsidy became a tolerable and normal levy.[50]

From time to time parliament experimented with other taxes. Poll taxes, in 1377, 1379, and 1380–1, were designed to remedy the inequalities of the obsolescent fifteenths, but the last attempted to double the yield of the fifteenth, and backfired in the revolt of 1381.[51] A tax on parishes in 1371 was heavier by one-third than the fifteenth, but another in 1428 yielded only one-third of a fifteenth.[52] All these were substitutes for the fifteenth, whereas taxes levied on the higher incomes of the propertied classes in 1404, 1411, 1435, and 1450 were supplementary and of varying effectiveness. Finally the clergy were subject to royal taxation on their income from temporalities, making grants in their convocations often at the same time as the Commons in parliament. Like the fifteenth, the tenth levied from the clergy yielded a stable sum of £15,000–16,000. The clergy contributed to the three poll taxes, and in the fifteenth century granted light supplementary taxes on non-beneficed clergy.

Direct taxation, as an item in the Crown's revenue, thus amounted to some £52,000 in a year when full lay and clerical subsidies were collected. However,

[49] *Rot. Parl.* vi. 151.

[50] In the November parliament of 1380 it was admitted that the fifteenth was 'in many ways oppressive to the poor commons' (*Rot. Parl.* iii. 90).

[51] E. B. Fryde, 'Peasant rebellion and peasant discontents', in *AHEW* 768–72.

[52] W. M. Ormrod, 'An experiment in taxation: The English parish subsidy of 1371', *Speculum*, 63 (1988), 58–82, shows that it yielded £49,600; id., 'England in the Middle Ages', p. 39, fig. I.14.

this occurred in only twenty-nine years of the century 1360–1460, notably in the periods of active war 1371–86 and 1414–20, and in eighteen years no taxes were collected. For about half the century, direct taxes were levied at the rate of half a subsidy a year. Over the whole period indirect taxation accounted for more than half of the exchequer's revenue,[53] although the decline of the customs enforced a greater reliance on direct taxes, notably to meet the war expenditure of Henry V. The exchequer's total income thus varied greatly over the whole century, with marked fluctuations depending on the Crown's political authority, its family commitments, the volume of trade and level of duties, and military activity. In the years 1371–2, with wool exports at their height and full lay and clerical subsidies granted for war, it could have exceeded £150,000, whereas in the 1420s and 1440s it attained a mere £60,000. But overall there was a structural decline, reflecting the ossification of the tax system and a failure to devise new levies.[54] The Crown never developed a tax on general sales, although this was briefly considered by parliament in 1380 and by Sir John Fortescue when he addressed the problem of the Crown's poverty in the 1460s.[55] By then the circumstances which had made England a precocious tax state had faded, and Fortescue's advocacy of a renewed exploitation of domainal revenues and feudal prerogatives was already being adopted by the Yorkist Crown.

An effective system of taxation generated, and was linked to, a pattern of high expenditure. This was mainly military, for late medieval England was a 'war state'. Expenditure is less easy to quantify than revenue, although some contemporary estimates of the main standing charges and allocations of revenue for them provide evidence of norms. The household departments could be reckoned as requiring around £24,000 per annum from the exchequer. That total fluctuated with royal needs: between 1390 and 1406 it rose by half as much again and even more, while in the minority of Henry VI it dropped to under £10,000. For the costs of administration estimates prepared for the council at different times between 1363 and 1433 show an order of £5,000–7,000. An allied charge was the annuities granted by the Crown, some as fees to officials, others as favours to members of the nobility and royal family. In the 1360s estimates put these at over £13,000, but the period 1390–1412 saw them increase to £20,000–24,000, dropping in the minority of Henry VI to under £12,000. If a total of £42,000 represented something like a norm for domestic charges (as in the period 1370–89), this increased in the two decades 1390–1410 to around £60,000 and dropped after 1422 to around £30,000.

The standing charges for defence in times of truce comprised the garrisons at Calais (c.£13,000), the northern marches (£5,000–6,000), Ireland

[53] Ormrod, 'An experiment in taxation', p. 42, fig. I.16.
[54] The decline is well illustrated in Ormrod's graphs: ibid., pp. 30–3, figs. I.9–I.11.
[55] *Rot. Parl.* iii. 89–90; Fortescue, *Governance of England*, 132–3.

(£6,000–8,000 from 1370–90 but thereafter progressively reduced to £2,000), and Gascony (c.£3,400). For a period in the late fourteenth century Brest and Cherbourg were also garrisoned at a cost of some £14,000. The permanent defensive charges thus stood at a minimum of £25,000, so that with a 'norm' of £42,000 on the domestic side the ordinary charges of state could be reckoned at not less than £67,000–70,000. Up to c.1400, therefore, the Crown might reckon to support these adequately from the Crown revenues (£15,000) and customs (£60,000). But just as the domestic charges in this equation could be abruptly increased by the individual extravagances of Richard II and Henry IV, so those for defence were enlarged by particular crises. The attempts by Edward III and Richard II to subdue Ireland, Henry IV's prolonged struggle to suppress the Welsh rebellion, the periodic need to check French incursions into Gascony, and the cost of fleets to keep the sea and coasts against raids and pirates, all made significant additions. Whether for domestic or defensive needs, these additional charges had to be met from direct taxation. The Commons were loath to acknowledge any obligation to meet such emergencies, but from 1386 they granted tunnage and poundage for defence of the sea and after 1391, along with the clergy, they began to grant half subsidies in most years during time of truce (amounting to c.£27,000) for standing military and naval charges, which partly offset the declining income from the wool custom.

For open war the Crown could claim direct taxation at the rate of an annual lay and clerical subsidy or even more, but even this was insufficient for a prolonged period of war. For a major expedition to France for six months, led by the king or his lieutenant, cost in the region of £60,000–75,000, well exceeding the yield of a lay and clerical subsidy.[56] Moreover, in war the costs of Calais and the northern marches were almost doubled and a fleet had to be maintained. In the two periods of intensive warfare, 1371–81 and 1416–21, naval and military costs overseas consumed all or nearly all the receipts from direct and indirect taxation, leaving insufficient for the domestic charges, and producing substantial debts. Sustained intervention in France was not only beyond the financial resources of the English state, it was beyond the capacity of the taxpayer. After both these periods there had to be a respite from taxation, the first precipitated by the Great Revolt, the second consequent on the ratification of the Treaty of Troyes.

A judgement on the viability of the English tax state might be that until 1430 the normal recurrent charges, both domestic and defensive, could be met from the revenues of the Crown and the customs, increasingly supported by grants of half subsidies in periods of truce; but that even in the 1370s and certainly by 1415 it could not sustain for more than short periods the huge costs of active war. After

---

[56] J. W. Sherborne, *War, Politics and Culture in Fourteenth Century England* (London, 1994), 55–70.

1430 the steep fall in indirect taxation left it dependent on a half subsidy each year to achieve a very precarious balance on its normal anticipated expenditure.[57] This framework shaped royal policy and set military and political parameters. It also conditioned the operation of the financial system.

This was centred on the exchequer, which, by 1360, was established as the sole receipt for national revenues and the sole channel for their disbursement. That was governed by royal warrants, those for recurrent payments like salaries and annuities being standing, but the majority for occasional payments being specifically authorized under the privy seal either by the king himself or by the council and treasurer on his behalf. These covered both the king's own concerns and the costs of state, military and civil. There was normally no attempt to control and coordinate this expenditure before these diverse warrants reached the treasurer. When they did he might complain, as Lord Cromwell did to the king in 1433, that

daily many warantis come to me of paiementz . . . of much more than all your revenuz wold come to . . . the which warrantes yf I shuld paye hem, youre Household, chambre and warderope and werkes shuld be unservid and unpaide, and yf I paye hem not, I renne in grete indignation of my lordes, and grete sclandre, noyse and maugre of all youre peple.[58]

Cromwell went on to ask 'who shuld be preferred in payment, and who shull not, and who shuld be paied and who shull not'. By 1433 the state was in the grip of endemic insolvency and all those with financial claims were using whatever influence they or their friends had to secure payment. As Cromwell hinted, the pressures of individual claimants could well jeopardize payment for the king's own household. A system of priorities was required, and this would be fashioned partly by need but partly by political influence. Under Henry VI the dilemma had become recurrent and acute, but it was far from new.

That was one consequence of a recurrent national deficit. The other was perennial debt, and this could take three forms. First, the Crown contracted short-term loans without interest from its subjects. A few individuals like Richard, earl of Arundel (d. 1376), under Edward III and Cardinal Beaufort under Henry V and VI lent large sums repeatedly, but mostly the loans were raised under parliamentary authority from a wide range of the political class on the security of future taxes.[59] The Crown could no longer borrow large sums at high rates

[57] J. L. Kirby, 'The issues of the Lancastrian exchequer and Lord Cromwell's estimates of 1433', *BIHR* 24 (1951), 133, and his concluding comments on pp. 147–8.

[58] *Rot. Parl.* iv. 439, cited by G. L. Harriss, 'Preference at the medieval exchequer', *BIHR* 30 (1957), 39.

[59] C. Given-Wilson, 'Wealth and credit, public and private: The earls of Arundel, 1306–1397', *EHR* 106 (1991), 1–26; G. L. Harriss, 'Cardinal Beaufort, patriot or usurer?', *TRHS*, 5th ser., 20 (1970), 129–48; H. Kleineke, 'The commission *de mutuo faciendo* in the reign of Henry VI', *EHR* 116 (2001), 1–30.

of interest from Italian merchant companies on the security of the customs revenue, as it had in the early fourteenth century. Secondly, those who served or supplied the Crown could find their payment hugely in arrears. At the end of a campaign commanders returned with claims for wages for themselves and their troops which might take years to clear, and the wages of those in garrisons—at Calais, the northern marches, and Ireland—were habitually overdue. On the domestic side the same was true: the household departments carried long lists of creditors awaiting (and often despairing of) payment. At the king's death such debts were charged on his estate, prolonging further their discharge. Thirdly, under pressure from such charges and creditors the exchequer had developed a means of making promissory payments in place of cash. This was by tallies of assignment. The tally, a wooden stick with its value notched on it, was issued by the exchequer to a payee for him to take to a specified revenue collector (e.g. a sheriff or tax collector) for direct payment, who would then produce it as a receipt when accounting at the exchequer. It provided quick access to payment—provided the money was available. For if the exchequer issued more tallies for payment than the collector had cash in hand to meet, the payee would have to join a queue of expectant payees. He could either wait (perhaps for as much as two years), or return the tally to the exchequer for payment on some other source.[60]

The exchequer was thus the focus of a continuing struggle for preferential payment between departments and individual payees. It meant that the king's subjects were as heavily engaged in manipulating its procedures as the king, his ministers, and officials. This had a political dimension, not only in the influence used by powerful creditors to secure warrants, and payment on those warrants, but in the credit of exchequer instruments which reflected that of royal government. A perennially insolvent monarchy lost credibility and respect with subjects by disappointing or defaulting on a myriad of payments to them. Both the advice literature written for kings and the literature of complaint written for their lesser subjects has, as one of its major themes, the king's responsibility to live within his revenue and not to burden his subjects by defaulting on payment.

Some kings took this to heart—or at least sought to impose order and priorities on exchequer finance in the interests of efficiency. The basic principle was to provide the major domestic and defence charges with either a particular revenue or a fixed annual sum from different revenues. This was first done on an ad hoc basis. Thus, first in 1390 and on occasions in 1403–5, a proportion of the wool customs was appropriated for Calais, and in 1404 an allocation of revenues was made for the support of the household.[61] Similar guarantees for their wages were

---

[60] Ormrod, 'England in the Middle Ages', p. 35, fig. I.12, gives a diagram of the volume of cash receipts, assignments, and failed assignments from 1378 to 1461.

[61] *CPR, 1388–92*, 227, 371; *CPR, 1401–5*, 413; *Proc. & Ord.* ii. 96; *Rot. Parl.* iii. 528; *CCR, 1402–5*, 343.

provided for the wardens of the marches and for Ireland. These became the building blocks for a sustained attempt from 1407 to 1411 to estimate the main items of government expenditure on the basis of previous years. Estimates of revenue were similarly based on the average of three previous years (in the case of the customs), the known yield of the lay and clerical subsidies, and the largely conventional figures for the revenues of the Crown. Comprehensive budgets for each forthcoming year were prepared and their implementation monitored by the council under Archbishop Arundel and Prince Henry.[62] The lessons were applied by Henry V to his war finances, and subsequent treasurers like Lord Cromwell in 1433 and Bishop Lumley in 1447 adopted similar measures when faced by financial breakdown.[63] Attempts to adhere to such budgetary planning were liable to be derailed by unforeseen circumstances and depended on the king's own resolve to adhere to its constraints against political pressures from creditors and his own desires. Most lacked Henry V's resolution. Even if such measures represented crisis management rather than consistent practice, they demonstrate the ability of the late medieval exchequer not merely to keep track of its operations, and provide information for budgetary exercises, but to fashion and implement a financial policy.

In this process subjects claimed a role, not merely as individual creditors, but as representatives of the common good. When they granted taxation the Commons often sought to ensure that it was spent on the particular military or naval projects for which it had been asked, even on occasion placing it under special treasurers of war, whose accounts they might inspect. They might also appropriate the wool subsidies and tunnage and poundage for the defence of the seas and of the Staple port of Calais.[64] These broadly coincided with the government's own priorities in time of war, even if controversy could erupt over how effectively they had been implemented. But in time of truce the Commons suspected (rightly) that direct taxes might be used to support the royal household. Although, as its suppliers, they had a direct interest in its finance, as taxpayers they repudiated any obligation to support it through their grants. They advocated an allocation of revenues for the household from the revenues of the Crown (and possibly the customs). If the treasurer reported that such revenues were insufficient, the Commons' response was to ask why the king had granted them away as favours and to demand that his liberality be restrained; ultimately,

---

[62] 'T. E. Wright, 'Royal Finance in the Latter Part of the Reign of Henry IV of England, 1406–13', D.Phil. thesis (Oxford University, 1984); id., 'Henry IV, the Commons and the recovery of royal finance in 1407', in Archer and Walker (eds.), *Rulers and Ruled*, 65–82.

[63] G. L. Harriss, 'Marmaduke Lumley and the exchequer crisis of 1446–9', in J. G. Rowe (ed.), *Aspects of Late Medieval Government and Society* (Toronto, 1986), 143–78; Kirby, 'Issues of the Lancastrian exchequer', 121–51.

[64] A. Rogers, 'Henry IV, the Commons and taxation', *Medieval Studies*, 31 (1969), 44–70.

indeed, that such grants should be resumed.[65] Thus the Crown's financial management and policies became a matter of parliamentary concern and intervention, often expressed in the demand that 'the king should live of his own' and taxes be spent on extraordinary needs.

Thus the common concern of Crown and subjects in state finance made it the subject of political debate. As creditors at the exchequer, the political class were intimately conversant with its procedures and the state of its credit. By the fifteenth century they were being informed of, and involved in, its macro financial policy formulated in budgets and allocations of revenues. In these respects the late medieval tax state had moved a considerable way towards a system of public finance. But because it had been grafted on to a feudal monarchy, the system of state finance still operated at the will and for the purposes of the king. It could never develop any procedure for public accountability nor establish a public debt. Indeed in the late fifteenth-century crisis of viability the war state largely ceased to be a tax state and fell back on the Crown's domainal and prerogative revenues.[66]

4. PARLIAMENT

By 1360 a body termed *parliamentum* had figured in royal records for 120 years. The second century of its existence was crucial both in defining it as an institution and in establishing its functions.[67] By its end parliament had emerged as recognizably the same body as that which challenged the sovereignty of the Stuarts. That perspective can distort our understanding of its medieval function, which was to act neither as an opponent of the Crown nor as an instrument of royal government. It had as yet no continuous identity or existence in the body politic, as had the court and the council, no part in the machinery of state like the great offices. What it did—as these did not—was to reflect and represent the political nation. From the first it had been summoned to deal with the great business of the realm, and by 1340 was fully representative of the political class through whom the Crown was learning to govern. This class was developing its own political agenda, and in our century parliaments provided for the interchange of views between the Crown and subjects.

Parliament met more frequently in this century than in that which preceded or followed. Eighty parliaments were summoned, with only three gaps of three years or more between them. Annual parliaments were considered the norm, and this was indeed the average between 1377 and 1422. In the fourteenth

[65] B. P. Wolffe, 'Acts of resumption in Lancastrian parliaments', *EHR* 74 (1958), 583–613. See above, Ch. 2, sect. 1.

[66] Ormrod, 'England in the Middle Ages', 47.

[67] J. G. Edwards, *The Second Century of the English Parliament* (Oxford, 1979).

century one session was normal, but after 1400 two-thirds of the parliaments lasted for two or more sessions. Their length was also increasing, from three weeks before 1360 to five weeks under Richard II, to nine weeks under Henry IV, and twelve weeks under Henry VI—though those of Henry V averaged only four weeks. Parliament was thus a habitual and familiar experience for the political class.

Parliament normally met at Westminster, and when on the fifteen occasions it met elsewhere this was generally for political reasons. At its opening the Lords met in the Painted Chamber of the Palace of Westminster, the Commons in Westminster Hall, from where they were called to the entrance of the Painted Chamber to hear the 'charge', or cause of summons, declared by the chancellor. The Lords and Commons then retired to their separate meeting places.[68] By 1460 the division of parliament into two 'houses' was recognized in both a corporate and locative sense.[69]

The king's presence at parliament was essential, it being 'the king's parliament of England' in which, as Henry VIII memorably declared, 'we as head and you as members are conjoined and knit together in one body politic'. The king could not negate its authority by refusing to attend, as Richard II attempted in 1386, though he had the right to dissolve it. In parliament laws were enacted in the king's name, taxes were granted to him, he accepted or refused petitions, and appointed and dismissed ministers, who were answerable to him alone. Moreover, the king determined parliament's agenda and order of business—the *regimen parliamenti*—to challenge which could be judged treasonable (1387). But conversely the king could not make law (though he could dispense with it), impose a tax, change the succession to the throne, and probably even declare war or peace, without parliament's assent. These matters concerned the body politic over which the king-in-parliament was sovereign.

The status and function of the Lords and the Commons differed. The Lords were summoned by individual writs, as of hereditary right. They sat in order of precedence, wearing special parliamentary robes, the lords spiritual to the right of the throne, the lords temporal to the left, with counsellors and judges to the front.[70] Along with some dozen earls and fifty barons were forty-six bishops and mitred abbots, giving a total of around one hundred. In practice only about half this number usually assembled. It was these men whose advice and support the king needed for his policies and governance, and whose wealth, power, and familiarity with affairs of state gave them the determining role in parliament.

[68] These were, for the Lords, the White Chamber; for the Commons either the Painted Chamber or Chapter House and, after 1395, the refectory: ibid. 4–7.

[69] S. B. Chrimes, *English Constitutional Ideas in the Fifteenth Century* (Cambridge, 1936), 126–30.

[70] J. E. Powell and K. Wallis, *The House of Lords in the Middle Ages* (London, 1968), 476, 555 (pls. xiv, xx).

The Commons were summoned through the sheriffs, to whom writs were sent forty days before the parliament ordering the election of two knights from each county and two burgesses from each borough within it. The Commons numbered 74 county and about 180 borough representatives. Virtually all attended. The county members were drawn from the magisterial class, though not all were knights, and were natural associates of the lords both in and outside parliament. The borough representatives were a more heterogeneous body, drawn from widely different communities. Wealthy merchants came from great international centres like London and Bristol; local traders and oligarchs from medium-sized ports and inland towns like Hull and Coventry; and from the smaller and already 'decayed' boroughs, ambitious lawyers, royal officials, and lords' retainers were, by the fifteenth century, being returned to parliament as 'carpet baggers'. This trend did much to erode the different character of the county and borough members and emphasize their corporate identity as 'the Lower House'. By 1410 the Speaker could describe knights and burgesses as constituting an 'estate' of parliament.[71]

The Speaker was the symbol of this unity, chosen by the Commons and expressing their opinions, not his own. The king formally accorded him liberty to speak saving the royal dignity—and some Speakers were forthright in their criticism of royal government. His ability to lead the house, mould opinion, and perhaps even order debate—by 1483 it could be claimed that 'in the Lower House all is directed by the Speaker'—gave the Crown an interest in who was selected; but he remained the servant of the House.[72]

No contemporary account of how parliament functioned was written in this period although the early fourteenth-century *Modus Tenendi Parliamentum* still circulated.[73] From 1339 an official record, or roll, of its decisions was kept by the clerk of parliament. This normally contains neither the debates that preceded decisions nor a narrative of proceedings; only rarely does it paraphrase speeches, and then only those made in full parliament, when both houses met together. The separate discussions of Lords and Commons, where their views and decisions were thrashed out, were not its concern. For the Commons we have what purports to be a unique eyewitness account, in 1376, of a debate in the chapter house; otherwise we are dependent on reports in chronicles and letters. So much of what made parliament a truly political assembly—the lobbying, bargaining, and bribery, the informal contacts between members of both houses, and the opportunities to press individual interests—emerges in only occasional and incidental references. All we can describe is its formal business.

[71] Roskell, in *House of Commons*, i. 47–50; *Rot. Parl.* iii. 623.

[72] J. S. Roskell, *The Commons and their Speakers in Medieval English Parliaments* (Manchester, 1965); Chrimes, *Constitutional Ideas*, 174.

[73] N. Pronay and J. Taylor (eds.), *Parliamentary Texts of the Later Middle Ages* (Oxford, 1980), 7.

This was reckoned to be threefold: that of the king, that of the realm, and that of individuals, in order of importance and precedence. The king's business touched his estate and that of the crown—his title, lands, rights, family, and succession. Such matters were dealt with in the Lords, the Commons merely rendering assent. The temporal lords also acted as a court for the trial of peers and ministers for treason and misdemeanours, whether on the information of the king, or on appeals by peers, or by impeachment by the Commons. More generally they saw themselves as responsible for upholding the king's estate and prerogative in the event of his incapacity, as in 1422–7, when they declared that 'thexecucion of the kinges said auctoritee . . . belongeth unto the lordes spirituel and temporel of his land at suche tyme as thei be assembled in parlement or in greet counsail'.[74] In general they upheld the king's rights against the Commons' attempts to make the king reform the household, render account for taxation, and restrain or resume royal gifts. When, exceptionally in 1386, they imposed a commission on the king and removed 'evil counsellors' whom they accused of enslaving the royal power, the Crown lawyers adjudged this treasonous.

As the king's natural counsellors the Lords expected to be consulted over, and sanction, decisions on the great business of the realm. Of prime concern were matters of foreign policy: war and peace, diplomatic relations including those with the papacy, and the condition of overseas dependencies like Gascony and Ireland.[75] They were briefed on the costs of foreign expeditions, and in general on the king's financial needs, receiving financial statements, and advising what taxation should be asked from the Commons—with whom they met for discussion. They often pitched the king's demands high, and in 1407 the Commons complained that the Lords had even pre-empted their own decision. On domestic issues they scrutinized the petitions of the Commons and, with the advice of the judges, advised the king on his answers. The Lords' leadership of the political community was thus reflected in parliament, where their responsibility for maintaining unity and upholding order and justice was forcefully stressed by the Commons.

If the Lords in parliament were the pillars of the realm, the Commons acted as its conscience. Placed midway between the divinely guided king and the brute plebs, their magistracy fitted them to make reasoned criticism of abuses in royal government so that popular grievances could be redressed before they provoked revolt. Although individual bishops, and preachers like Thomas Bromyard and Thomas Brinton, deplored the social evils of the age, from the time of the Good Parliament (1376), it was the Commons, through their common petition, who were authorized to 'shewe the sores of the royaulme';

---

[74] *Proc. & Ord.* iii. 231.
[75] Chrimes, *Constitutional Ideas*, 175; *Proc. & Ord.* i. 143–4.

authorized, because the chancellor invited and instructed them to do so in opening parliament.[76]

A glimpse of how the Commons formulated their common petition is provided by *The Anonimalle Chronicle* at the time of the Good Parliament. Meeting in the chapter House, individual members took the floor to express complaints and demands of general concern, which could be formulated into petitions. Written petitions, some framed in the shire court on behalf of communities, others presented by individuals, were also produced. The Commons thus acted as a conduit for the common concerns of the people but they evidently exercised minimal scrutiny over what petitions they included, for some could be contradictory, and in others private concerns were framed as matters of common interest.[77] Their common petition was framed as a set of articles, each beginning 'prie la Commune', and the whole petition was then sent by the clerk of parliament for consideration by the Lords and council and the royal response. At the end of parliament the petition, with the king's answer written in, was entered on the parliament roll. Such was the procedure from 1343 to 1423, when the consolidated petition in this form was discontinued. By then a different kind of petition was being favoured. This was the 'singular', or private, petition. From its early days parliament had been a place where subjects of all kinds could petition the king, and panels of lords and justices were named to 'try' these petitions and advise how they should be answered. Petition and answer were then returned to the individual and not enrolled, the Commons as such not being involved. But after 1375 a few of these were addressed not to the king but to 'the honorable and wise Commons' asking them to intercede with the king for the petitioner, and the Commons forwarded these to the Lords and council through the clerk of parliament, as with their common petition. Quite rapidly after 1400 this practice spread and by the reigns of Henry V and Henry VI almost half of these singular petitions followed this route. The petitioners included some of the greatest in the land—bishops, earls, ladies—and their private bills, having received the approval of all estates of parliament, were enrolled as part of its proceedings. They are the precursors of the great volume of private business it enacted in the seventeenth century.[78]

There were corresponding developments in the legislative process, with bills originating with the king and lords being sent to the Commons for their assent, while important pieces of royal legislation (e.g. the statutes on Truces, Riots, and

---

[76] G. R. Owst, *Literature and Pulpit in Medieval England* (Oxford, 1961), 579–80, 584; *The Sermons of Thomas Brinton*, ed. M. A. Devlin, Camden Society, 3rd ser., 85–6 (London, 1954), vol. i, p. xxv, vol. ii, pp. 316–17; *Mum and Sothsegger*, line 1120; *Rot. Parl.* iii. 257, 420.

[77] Edwards, *Second Century*, 44–55.

[78] Ibid. 56–65; G. Dodd, 'Parliament and the private petition in the fourteenth century', in Musson (ed.), *Expectations of the Law*, 135–50.

Lollards in 1414) were introduced as Commons' bills. Clearly the assent of all three estates of parliament was felt necessary. Nor was this assent a mere formality. We do not know how many bills were debated, but by the later fifteenth century, and possibly earlier, three readings were required and some were passed on a majority vote. Any subsequent amendment by the Lords which enlarged the terms had to be returned to the Commons for assent.[79]

Legislation had thus become a prime function of parliament and the Commons its principal initiators. Although in the fourteenth century there are signs that legislation based on petition could be indiscriminate, in the fifteenth century petitions became more closely related to legislation, perhaps reflecting greater selectivity in the Commons and a growing appreciation of the authority of statute. From the 1360s the superiority of statutes over ordinances by the king and council, and their universal authority over all men in the realm, was based on the lawyers' acceptance that parliament 'represents the body of the realm' (Thorpe CJ, 1366) and that 'every man is party to an act of parliament' (1463).[80]

Although the written petition, or bill, was essential in the Commons' procedures, much of their communication with the king and Lords was oral. This was primarily through their Speaker, but at times the Commons asked that a panel of members might—with the permission of the king—'intercommune' with the Lords. Twelve such occasions are recorded between 1352 and 1407 but more may have occurred. This was generally a sign of tension, with the Commons seeking support for measures of reform or questioning demands for taxation. Occasionally the Commons were asked their views on foreign policy, and in so far as alliances, wars, and peace touched their interests they might—as in 1383 in preferring an expedition to Flanders over one to Spain—make this plain. But normally their attitude was studiously non-committal, treating this as a matter for the king and Lords.[81] Yet dramatic failures of foreign policy were a potent ingredient of parliamentary crises.

If the Commons saw their role in parliament as being 'as well assentirs as peticioners' (1414), for the king and Lords their primary function was to grant taxes. Taxation was a politically sophisticated act. It had to be formally justified by a necessity which threatened the common good, normally a war in defence of the realm. This was usually spelled out by the chancellor at the opening of parliament. Subjects were thereby obliged to contribute, for common peril demanded common aid. They could only refuse to grant a tax by questioning the necessity for it, although the poverty of subjects might be pleaded in mitigation, as in 1382. Within these broad principles, conventions had developed about the level of taxation in different circumstances. A full fifteenth would be granted in time of

---

[79] Chrimes, *Constitutional Ideas*, 220–5; J. G. Edwards, 'The emergence of majority rule in the procedure of the House of Commons', *TRHS*, 5th ser., 15 (1965), 165–87.
[80] Chrimes, *Constitutional Ideas*, 76, 269.   [81] Roskell, in *House of Commons*, i. 103–16.

open war; an annual half fifteenth was seen as appropriate in periods of truce after 1389; while treaties of peace formally released subjects from any obligation. These did not cover all eventualities, and there were grey areas: the Commons regarded the suppression of rebels, as in Ireland in 1394 and Wales in 1401–8, as the king's responsibility, for which they were not obliged to contribute (though in fact they did).[82] What they strove to avoid was any commitment to a continuing charge which could jeopardize the principle that direct taxation was exceptional and occasional. In particular they were opposed to taxation for the ordinary domestic charges or for payment of royal debts. The principle that direct taxation should be confined to exceptional needs was an important part of the political legacy of the late Middle Ages.[83] That this could be sustained was largely due to the establishment of continuous indirect taxation to meet the Crown's recurrent costs. The renewable grants of wool subsidies for periods of years (on three occasions for the king's life) provided the Crown with a guaranteed revenue, albeit under parliament's ultimate sanction.

The representative authority of parliament thus empowered both its legislative and its fiscal functions, and these furnished the context for the Commons' role as critics of royal government. As such, they were not opponents of the king; indeed they looked to him for redress. Yet for thirty years after 1376 parliament was the scene, and often the instrument, of power struggles involving the king, the Lords, and the Commons. Did these fulfil or distort its role and did they affect how it was viewed by political society?

The Good Parliament (1376) achieved unprecedented prominence. Over the previous thirty years the king and nobility had treated parliament as a tax-granting body, while the Commons has used it to extend and establish their magistracy in the shires. Chroniclers virtually ignored it. In 1376 this dramatically changed when parliament became the instrument for an attack on court corruption. Under the leadership of their Speaker, Peter de la Mare, the Commons acquired a sense of mission to reform central government in the name of the common good. Detailed reports of parliament's proceedings from witnesses and participants, which were embodied in chronicles at St Albans and St Mary's, York, created a body of opinion favourable to the Commons' enlarged role and gave de la Mare the status of a popular hero.[84] But some had misgivings; Bishop Thomas Brinton had welcomed the Commons' protests but baulked at them taking the political initiative away from the Lords. Langland, in the B text of Piers Plowman, used the fable of the mice who feared to bell the cat to depict the Commons as subverting royal authority and hence divinely ordained hierarchy

---

[82] Rot. Parl. iii. 330; Wals., Hist. Anglicana ii. 216; Eulog. Hist. iii. 399.

[83] G. L. Harriss, 'Thomas Cromwell's "new principle" of taxation', EHR 93 (1978), 721–7.

[84] J. Taylor, 'The Good Parliament and its sources', in J. Taylor and W. Childs (eds.), Politics and Crisis in Fourteenth Century England (Gloucester, 1990), 81–96.

and order.[85] John of Gaunt's outrage at the Commons' presumption led him to reverse parliament's acts and exact retribution on its leaders.

If the Good Parliament split political society over the proper role of the Commons, their continuing pressure for commissions into financial and administrative abuses aligned them with the growing magnate opposition to Richard II's court. In 1386 the impeachment of the chancellor, Michael de la Pole, was followed by the appointment of a wide-ranging commission, not only to reform government but to remove it for a year from the king's hands. The magnates justified this usurpation of royal authority by parliament as being for the common weal and salvation of the realm, propelling the Commons to cross the Rubicon from critics to opponents of the Crown. Their embroilment in political controversy was compounded by the Appellants' remorseless purge of the king's friends in the parliament of February 1388. They were swept along on a tide of hatred of the court, strongly reflected in the partisan and well-informed accounts of the major chroniclers.[86] All reflected the standpoint of the opposition; none expressed doubts of the legality of the commission. But by the end of 1388 the Commons had begun to detach themselves from the magnates, alienated by their excesses and disillusioned by their indifference to reform. Nor had the crisis of 1386–8 changed the system of government or the status and powers of parliament.

Despite an attempt to normalize relations with the Crown, the Commons were comprised in Richard II's revenge on the former Appellants in 1397, being forced to purchase pardon for the 1386 commission with an unprecedented grant of taxation. This enabled Richard's supplanter to pose as the defender of parliament's rights and functions and to emphasize its active association in his usurpation, through the official account, the *Record and Process*, which was disseminated and absorbed into the chroniclers' narratives. Henry set out to manage parliament by a mixture of flattery, conciliation, and manipulation.[87] Yet the Commons were, if anything, more vociferous in demanding 'good governance', fed by suspicions of the misuse of taxes, the costs of the household, and the ineffectiveness of royal policy. It was the collapse of Henry's health in 1406 that finally procured from the council the financial reforms they had been seeking over the previous five years, but in contrast to 1386–8, this council was composed of Lancastrian nobles acceptable to the king and sympathetic to the Commons' demand for 'good governance'.

---

[85] Brinton, *Sermons*; W. Langland, *The Vision of Piers Plowman: The B Text*, ed. A. V. C. Schmidt (London, 1978), pp. xxv, 6–8; A. Gross, 'Langland's rats: A moralist's view of parliament', *Parlty. Hist.* 9 (1990), 286–301.

[86] See the introductions to *West. Chron.*; Knighton, *Chron.*; M. McKisack (ed.), *Historia sive Narracio Mirabilis Parliamenti . . . per Thomam Favent*, Camden Society, 3rd ser., 37 (London, 1926).

[87] For Lancastrian propaganda, see G. O. Sayles, 'The deposition of Richard II: Three Lancastrian narratives', *BIHR* 54 (1981), 257–70; *Chron. Rev.* 162–89.

How the Commons adjusted to their problematic role as critics following their dangerous involvement with the magnate opposition to Richard II is illustrated in two very different sources from early in Henry IV's reign. One is a newsletter sent by a clerk to the prior of Durham from the Hilary parliament of 1404. It contains the unique record of an outspoken and tense interchange over the demand for taxation between the king and the Commons' Speaker, Sir Arnold Savage, who detailed the abuses in royal government. The second is the polemical poem *Richard the Redeles*, ostensibly treating of Richard II's tyranny. When the king wrongly seeks a tax from parliament to cover his household debts, some members make a show of protest, but in fact all have been bribed or intimidated and the Commons cave in under pressure from the Lords. These apparently contradictory glimpses show the Commons maintaining their freedom to expose royal misgovernment but, lacking magnate support, accepting the need for political compromise if the ship of state is not to run aground. Similarly the duty of parliament both 'to show forth the sores of the realm' and to support the power of the Crown in peace and war are parallel themes in the popular verse of this decade.[88] Finally, with Henry V's commitment to a programme of 'bone governance' and the Commons' commitment to support the war in France, Crown and parliament were in harmony, and interest in the latter fades from the chronicles for a generation. Only at the end of our period did the cataclysm of 1450 again propel parliament into the political arena, first to express popular outrage and then as the instrument of contending baronial factions.

5. COUNCIL

The late medieval council has been the subject of debate between historians. On one view its emergence in the late fourteenth century in institutional form— with (at times) appointed and salaried members, a designated meeting place, its own clerk and occasional journal, and rules for the conduct of business—was a consequence of the growing complexity and sophistication of government. At different periods its prominence, powers, and composition varied, depending on the circumstances and character of royal government, and it might function with or without the king, with many or few in attendance; but it remained 'le conseil', 'with many common features over a long period'.[89] As an essential element in royal government it became the natural substitute for royal authority in the king's incapacity.

---

[88] *Mum and the Sothsegger*, lines 1118–32; Kail (ed.), *Political Poems*, no. 3: 'Truth, Rest and Peace' (1401); no. 13: 'Dede is Worchyng' (1414).

[89] J. F. Baldwin, *The King's Council in England during the Middle Ages* (Oxford, 1913); A. L. Brown, *The Governance of Late Medieval England, 1272–1461* (London, 1989), ch. 2 (quotation at p. 36).

From a different viewpoint there was neither a necessity nor a legitimate role for such a council in the context of late medieval monarchy. It was the king's prerogative to receive advice from whatever source he wished, and the privilege of the great lords to offer it as his natural counsellors. A formally appointed advisory council was incompatible with both. Royal government rested on the independent will of the king receiving 'a perpetual stream' of counsel from the nobility as representatives of political society, rendered informally at court rather than formally at Westminster. If that was the normative pattern, the institutionalizing of counsel appears 'specious', the result of 'a continuous series of emergency measures arising from a nearly continuous crisis in government' over the sixty years 1376–1436.[90]

These contrary interpretations thus have different starting points: the first in the recorded activities of the council, which it treats as normative, the second in the exercise of royal power, from which a formally constituted council was an abnormal deviation; likewise the first is mainly concerned with the council in its administrative aspect, the second as an advisory body. The two standpoints, that is, do not wholly confront each other, and an attempt to reassess the function of the council in royal government can best start by considering the forms of counsel and the matters dealt with, before evaluating the political legitimacy of 'the council'.

All medieval writers agreed that counsel was at the heart of royal governance. In Gower's words,

> for ther is nothing
> which mai be betre aboute a king
> Than conseil, which is the substance
> Of all a kinges governance.[91]

At the heart of kingship lay the tension between the ruler's personal will and power and his duty to exercise these for the common good of his subjects: his private and public capacities. Good counsel pointed him towards the common good; evil counsel pandered to his self-interest and set him on the path to tyranny. The king's responsibility for following good, rather than evil, counsel was matched by that of his counsellors to speak for the common profit, and not to further their private interests or flatter the king. Counsel was in this sense a public not a private function, to be given openly and not covertly, and in the interests of the king and realm. The king was therefore advised to draw his counsellors from men of standing and experience who were devoid of self-interest. If this pointed in the first place to his greater magnates, his 'natural counsellors', it might also include

---

[90] J. L. Watts, 'The counsels of King Henry VI, *c.*1435–1445', *EHR* 106 (1991), 270–98 (quotation at p. 283); id., *Henry VI and the Politics of Kingship*, 82–90 (quotations at pp. 84, 101).

[91] Gower, *Confessio Amantis*, bk. 7, lines 3944–4026, in id., *Works*, iii. 346–8.

the lords, knights, and esquires in daily attendance in his household. There was an inbuilt role for familial counsel in the king's answering of petitions for pardons, justice, and royal patronage: i.e. matters of grace. Such petitions formed an almost daily element in royal rule, and in answering them the king must have relied heavily on the personal knowledge of those at hand. Yet a wise king would also want to be informed of the larger political and financial implications of his decisions, and for this would turn to his chancellor and treasurer, who were part of the Westminster council.

Counsel was likewise offered in an informal and domestic aspect by individual magnates when they were at court. Evidence of this is sparse and indirect, for it generated no record (as did the answering of petitions), and its frequency and normality can only be guessed at.[92] The legitimacy of such individual counsel was unquestioned, but on matters of common interest, and even more for policy decisions on these, wider counsel was necessary, and other peers had a right to be heard. Thus in 1434 the young Henry VI was warned not to listen to 'mocions and sturrings apart' which some had made to him; in 1440 Humphrey, duke of Gloucester, complained of being excluded from counsel by Cardinals Beaufort and Kemp, and in 1450 the Kentish rebels claimed that lords of the royal blood were excluded from counsel by lesser men.[93] When, in 1399, Henry IV promised to act only with 'commune conseil et assent', he was reaffirming the basic principle of true counsel, and in fact neither of the first two Lancastrians were accused of listening to 'prive conseil'.

Common counsel could well be had by the king at court through a gathering of magnates and others broadly representative of interests and opinions. But weighty matters on which decisions were needed were often reserved for specially summoned meetings of the great council, two or three times a year. Some thirty or more peers spiritual and temporal would attend, often meeting in the king's presence before or after a parliament.[94] Regrettably no formal record of their proceedings was made, but the agenda of the council at this level was vividly characterized by Bishop Russell (1483):

What ys the bely or where ys the wombe of thys grete publick body of Englonde but that and there where the kyng ys hym self, hys court and hys counselle? Thidir be brought alle maters of weight, peax and were with outwarde londes, confederacions, ligues and alliances, receivynge and sendyng of embassades and messages, brekyng of treux, prises in the see, routes and riotts, and unlawfulle assemblees, oppressions, extorsions, contemptes and abusions of the lawe, and many moo surfettes than can be welle nombred.[95]

---

[92] See above, Ch. 2, sect. 2.

[93] *Proc. & Ord.* iv. 278; J. Stevenson (ed.), *The Wars of the English in France*, Rolls ser., 3 vols. (London, 1851–4), ii. 440–51; I. M. Harvey, *Jack Cade's Rebellion of 1450* (Oxford, 1991), 187.

[94] Brown, *Governance*, 40.

[95] Chrimes, *English Constitutional Ideas*, 175.

Russell's emphasis on the king as the source and centre of the council, and the council as a body dealing with public policy, defines the political role of the council in the late medieval state.

The council that figures most clearly in the surviving records, however, is that which met habitually in the Star Chamber in Westminster without the king. Its nucleus was the three officers of state with a handful of temporal and spiritual lords (often former officers) and sometimes knights from the royal household. In this way the Westminster council replicated the familial, magnate, and official elements of the counsel around the king. It met regularly on a daily basis during the legal and exchequer terms and attendance had to be in a measure obligatory to secure a quorum. But the average attendance was small—around seven. Its daily involvement in government generated records which were normally filed, though John Prophet, the first to bear the title of clerk of the council, kept a summary record in book form for some weeks in 1392–3, and a more official record was made during the minority of Henry VI.[96] From the reign of Richard II its executive documents were issued under the privy seal. It was a more continuous and thus more institutionalized body than others with whom the king held counsel. What kind of business did it deal with and what purpose did it serve?

The range of matters discussed was, in fact, as full as that in Bishop Russell's list. To characterize its business as 'mundane and politically insignificant' is to misread its function.[97] This was twofold. In relation to matters of state—diplomatic instructions and correspondence, financial and military planning, domestic disorder, and anything touching the king's estate and prerogatives—it provided advice and information on which the king could make a responsible decision. On some matters he then ordered the council to take action and these might be delegated to its individual members with appropriate expertise.[98] On debatable issues the king might well present the council with a series of options, or points for consideration, as Henry V did over his diplomatic strategy in 1418.[99] King and councillors were thus in constant interlocution on the great business of the realm. Secondly, the continual council did deal with mundane administrative matters, and it was precisely because it had at its fingertips both the current issues of policy and the daily mechanics of government, as the king and the lords did not, that its advice was indispensable. That advice was always offered deferentially—'if it pleases the king'—in what has been termed 'a close but unequal daily relationship'.[100] Thus in periods of adult and uncoerced

[96] Baldwin, *King's Council*, 489–504; A. L. Brown, *The Early History of the Clerkship of the Council* (Glasgow, 1969).

[97] Watts, *Henry VI and the Politics of Kingship*, 84.

[98] Brown, *Governance*, 37–9 (for 1392); *Proc. & Ord.* i. 102–300 (for Henry IV); J. I. Catto, 'The king's servants', in Harriss (ed.), *Henry V*, 82–3 (for 1415).

[99] *Proc. & Ord.* ii. 350–8.   [100] Brown, *Governance*, 38.

kingship, counsel came in different forms from bodies of different status, the membership of which overlapped. Familiar counsel mainly related to matters of grace; the Westminster council advised on matters of government; for decisions on the great business of the realm the king needed to take counsel from the political elite. In each of these the king was free to seek, accept, and reject counsel.

But at times either the natural deficiency of the king, or his perceived misgovernment, led to pressure for 'sad and substantial counsel' to be provided by the magnates. They saw this as their right and duty, for 'God ne reson ne wol that this land stande withoute governance.'[101] It could involve no more than afforcing the Westminster council with leading nobles, but more often certain lords spiritual and temporal, and occasionally knights also, were appointed for a limited term, either as an advisory body or with powers of government, as circumstances required. They were usually appointed at a parliament, often at the request of the Commons, so that their identity and role would be public knowledge. In such circumstances the council could acquire a politically contentious role.

I shall consider first the appointment of purely advisory counsellors to an adult and active ruler. Mostly this was prompted by financial and military failure. Thus in 1381 after the Great Revolt, the Commons expressed concern for the governance of the realm and asked that the young Richard II should have 'good and sufficient persons around his person and for his counsel'. Though not formally named, a council of magnates and officers appears to have operated over the next four years, but with gradually deepening divisions between it and Richard's familiar counsel at court.[102] In the October parliament of 1385 the Commons asked for a commission of lords to review the estate of the exchequer and household and for a restraint on royal grants to be operated by the council. The lords were reluctant to force such measures on the king, but as a body they offered formal 'Advice' on the right relationship between the young king and his council.[103] It asked him to trust their advice, not to countermand their acts, and to give time to listen to and attend council so that he could learn what pertains to the government of himself and his estate. The king undertook to heed these points but was clearly under no compulsion to do so; indeed it was his disregard of the Commons' proposals that led to the enforcement of reform on the king in 1386.

Twenty years later the Commons, critical of Henry IV's financial embarrassment and military weakness, asked in 1401 and 1404 for his council to be named and charged, preferably in parliament. Their particular complaint, which they made in every parliament of these years, was of the king's excessive liberality with Crown revenues, which it was hoped an appointed council would restrain.

---

[101] *Proc. & Ord.* vi. 312.   [102] *Rot. Parl.* iii. 100; *Select Docs.* 125; *West. Chron.* 54–5.

[103] *Proc. & Ord.* i. 84–6; *Select Docs.* 160–2; J. J. N. Palmer, 'The parliament of 1385 and the constitutional crisis of 1386', *Speculum*, 46 (1971), 480–3.

The king duly named his councillors, who had no wish to be answerable to parliament or in any way to control the king. They proved as reluctant and unable to enforce financial reform as those of 1385, and only in 1406, when the sick king empowered the council to assume government, was a measure of financial reform achieved.[104]

An advisory council was also formally named at the point of Henry VI's initiation into active kingship at the age of 16 in 1437.[105] Though continuing the membership of those who had governed during his minority, its terms of reference were changed. Matters of grace were left to the king and his familial advisers 'to do and dispose of hem as hym semeth good', but the largely magnate council was empowered to deal with all matters of governance which came before it, seeking the king's advice on matters of weight, and referring to his decision matters on which it was seriously divided. Its role was essentially that envisaged in 1385: to monitor and guide the young king to active rule.[106] The formal appointment of an advisory council to an adult king thus gave public status to its members and underlined their responsibility for providing common counsel for the good of the realm. They did not constrain the king, their counsel was not exclusive, and they answered to him alone; it is therefore not easy to see them as incompatible with the exercise of kingship.

More restrictive of the king's freedom to govern were the councils appointed in 1376–8 and 1422. The 'continual councils' of twelve lords commissioned in the Good Parliament and then in 1377 and 1378 during Richard II's minority were to deal with 'the business of the king and the realm during the king's tender age'. The Commons also asked for them to control the king's patronage. They were temporary expedients, empowered for one year at a time, and discontinued in 1380 when the Commons declared the king was of sufficient age to govern himself.[107] In 1422 on the death of Henry V the lords faced a far longer period of royal incapacity during the infancy of his son. Although full authority rested in his person, the exercise of it was deemed to devolve upon the lords spiritual and temporal meeting in parliament or great council, and otherwise on a restricted number of councillors, named and appointed in parliament as a continual council. They were to be responsible for 'the politique rule and governaille of his land' and in fact the council refrained from matters of grace, confining itself to necessary appointments to offices. This ruling council continued until replaced by the advisory council of 1437, though the king had begun to exercise an unfettered

---

[104] *Rot. Parl.* iii. 585–9; *Select Docs.* 220–5; A. L. Brown, 'The Commons and the council in the reign of Henry IV', *EHR* 79 (1964), 1–30. See below, Ch. 12, sect. 8.

[105] *Proc. & Ord.* vi. 312–15; Watts, *Henry VI and the Politics of Kingship*, 131–5.

[106] See in general Watts, *Henry VI and the Politics of Kingship*, ch. 5.

[107] *Rot. Parl.* ii. 322; *Select Docs.* 113, 115, 119; N. B. Lewis, 'The Continual Council in the early years of Richard II', *EHR* 41 (1926), 246–51.

patronage a year earlier. It was to this model that the lords returned in 1454, on the petition of the Commons, to provide 'a sadde and a wyse counsaill' during the prostration of Henry VI, and again in the parliament of 1455, though both proved to be interim measures.[108]

The councils that actually governed during 1377–80, 1422–37, and 1454–5 did so as a consequence of the declared natural incapacity of the monarch and by his explicit or implicit commission. Each was terminated when he was deemed able to govern. Until then their collective responsibility for government required them to be autonomous, exclusive, and united. They were surrogates for kingship, not challenges to it.

In 1386–8, however, a magnate council did replace the rule of an active king, and did so by force. The parliament of October 1386 empowered a commission of eleven spiritual and temporal lords, with the officers of state and household, to take control of government for a year and effect far-reaching reforms. It was prompted by the Commons' frustration at the failure to implement reforms promised in the previous year and the magnates' increasing hostility to Richard's courtiers. The preamble complained of 'non sufficieant conseil et mal governaille', but Richard resisted the claim of the Lords and Commons to reform royal government. He authorized the commission only under duress, formally reserving his prerogative, and in 1387 had it condemned as illegal and treasonous even though he was unable to sustain this verdict until 1397.[109] Despite the exoneration of the commission after Richard's deposition, the imposition of rule by a magnate council on a resistant king, even in the name of the common weal, was never again attempted. The magnates recognized its dubious legality and political hazards and when in 1406 the Commons demanded a credible commission of reform, a council of thirteen lords appointed by the king for one year insisted on its answerability to him alone.

The formally appointed magnate councils which operated during some thirty-six years in this century were all the response to royal incapacity or misgovernment. Some were advisory, guiding and monitoring an inexperienced king, some were surrogates for a king's natural incapacity, and some were attempts to reform and repair misgovernment. The Commons were generally more urgent in their demands for the last than the magnates, for whom it was an unwelcome and hazardous resort to which they committed themselves only with elaborate safeguards. Other than in 1386–8 they sought not to displace but to sustain the king's rightful power to govern, preferring to discharge their role as natural counsellors individually, and only perforce accepting a duty to maintain the 'politique rule and governance of the land'.

---

[108] *Select Docs.* 251–5, 256–9, 298–302, 305–8; *Rot. Parl.* v. 240, 286–90.
[109] *Select Docs.* 136–8; *Rot. Parl.* iii. 349.

6. DIPLOMACY

The agencies of government so far considered shared one significant characteristic: their development was stimulated and shaped by the concerns and pressures of subjects. This was more immediately true in the daily business of
chancery, the courts of law, and the exchequer; more indirectly so for the consultative bodies of parliament and council which served the common good. In a
word, late medieval government grew as much from the bottom up as from the
top down.[110] The same was not true for external affairs: the medieval English
state had no foreign office or ministry of defence, because the king himself
directed diplomacy and war. Medieval diplomacy was essentially communication between rulers. It was carried on in their name and involved their personal
decisions and participation. Yet through it the ruler represented the people of his
realm, binding them to friendship or enmity with their neighbours and regulating their commercial, religious, and military relations.

Some matters were the king's personal concern, above all his or his children's
marriage. Envoys were sent to view a prospective bride, report on her physical
and moral qualities, and perhaps have a portrait made.[111] The subsequent negotiation would be entrusted to a nobleman in high favour, an advocate of the
match, like William Scrope for the marriage of Richard II in 1396 and William,
earl of Suffolk, for that of Henry VI in 1444–5.[112] Of similar importance were
negotiations which involved the king's title or claims to lands, and binding
alliances with foreign rulers. These too the king would direct in person, framing
strategy in discussions with his councillors, in whose presence he would normally receive and consider proposals brought by foreign ambassadors.[113] Henry V
conducted his own diplomacy to an exceptional degree: negotiating personally
with John the Fearless and Sigismund at Calais in 1416, steering the tortuous
negotiations with the Dauphin in 1418, and himself determining the main
features of the Treaty of Troyes. Both Richard II and Henry IV personally
instructed the council about the terms of negotiations with foreign envoys.[114]

With the pope, the king had more regular contact: over provision to benefices
(in the case of bishoprics often involving prolonged bargaining), over papal

[110] G. Harriss, 'Political society and the growth of government in late medieval England', *P & P*
138 (1993), 28–57.

[111] P. Chaplais, *English Medieval Diplomatic Practice* (London, 1982), i. 89–93, ii. 733–5.

[112] P. Chaplais, 'English diplomatic documents, 1377–99', in F. R. Du Boulay and C. Barron
(eds.), *The Reign of Richard II* (London, 1971), 26–7; J. Ferguson, *English Diplomacy, 1422–1461*
(Oxford, 1972), 27.

[113] Chaplais, *Diplomatic Practice*, i. 126–35, ii. 706–7; *Proc. & Ord.* i. 6–7, 22–7, 222, 238–41;
R. A. Griffiths, *The Reign of King Henry VI* (London, 1981), 490–2.

[114] Chaplais, *Diplomatic Practice*, i. 192 (France), 299–300 (Flanders); *Proc. & Ord.* i. 176
(Bayonne), 225 (Cleves).

taxation of the Church, and over privileges for the king's religious foundations. Such matters would normally be handled by the king's proctors at the papal court. In the fourteenth century these had been nominated from among the English clergy at Rome, but after 1413 a succession of royal agents were appointed who were, in Henry V's phrase, 'promoters of his nation' at the Curia.[115] These men handled the normal themes of Anglo-papal relations, but on occasion much more contentious issues arose. The question of English allegiance during the papal Schism, and the schemes to restore unity, became entangled not only with the reform of the Church and curtailment of papal power, but with Anglo-French rivalry and eventual war. Then papal mediation for peace had to confront the English king's claim to the French Crown and this in turn brought into question the king's readiness to compromise his control over the English Church, signified by the Statutes of Provisors and Praemunire and the royal veto over papal taxation. Over and above all of this the papacy needed the support of the secular arm to eradicate heresy (the Lollards in England, the Hussites in Bohemia) and to launch a new crusade, while rulers needed the pope's spiritual authority to sanction crucial marriage alliances (e.g. of Lionel of Antwerp and Margaret of Flanders in 1362–8) or annul others (e.g. that of John of Brabant and Jacqueline of Hainault in 1424–6) on which far-reaching political ambitions were being built.[116]

To handle such matters of high policy professional and specialized diplomats were required; but much diplomacy was at a lower level, on matters such as the prolongation of truces, compensation for their infringement, and the rights of merchants and other nationals. Missions were broadly of two kinds: those conveying a message and those empowered to negotiate. Messengers—*nuncii*—were issued with safe conducts (though some were still arrested or killed) and with a letter of credence to the recipient which established their bona fides and authority to speak. For usually their message was delivered orally, though its substance was written down as a safeguard. Having delivered his message the envoy would be rewarded and return, though not usually with the response.[117]

More important than the *nuncius* was the *procurator*, empowered to negotiate and conclude an alliance, such as Lord John Neville did with the duke of Brittany in 1372. The procuration notifying his authority was presented at the start of negotiations, and he also carried a credence, or instructions for his own use. These would have been drawn up by the council as an aide-memoire, setting out the options, the limits of concessions, and any matters reserved.[118] The opposite party might request to see this if they suspected an offer to be unauthorized, or a

[115] M. Harvey, *England, Rome and the Papacy 1417–64* (Manchester, 1993), 8–24.

[116] E. Perroy, *L'Angleterre et le Grand Schisme d'Occident* (Paris, 1933); Harvey, *England, Rome and the Papacy*, 130–92; Chaplais, *Diplomatic Practice*, ii. 514, 452–6.

[117] Chaplais, *Diplomatic Practice*, i. 75–103, 346–50.   [118] Ibid. i. 191–5.

concession was being withheld, but normally it was kept private. Those who negotiated at the highest level on the king's personal business might also have oral instructions and discretionary powers, as Cardinal Beaufort did in 1439 and the earl of Suffolk in 1445.[119] If agreement was reached, this was embodied in articles and remitted to the king for ratification. They would be drawn up in the form of a treaty and copies exchanged with the other party, often in more than one language. Finally important treaties or military alliances or truces would be publicly proclaimed and copies circulated.[120]

The envoys who performed these missions varied in rank and qualifications. Single messengers were generally of lesser rank, an esquire, a lesser Church dignitary, or even a merchant, though those with confidential messages between rulers would be chamber knights. A summons to a conference or a declaration of alliance or war was often performed by a royal herald.[121] For the negotiation of border or commercial truces it was usual to name proctors with knowledge of local conditions. A major embassy, sent to negotiate an alliance, peace, or marriage, would be led by members of the upper nobility and include lords and bishops who could meet their opposites on equal terms at the foreign court. Such leaders would be accompanied by a retinue of up to fifty persons including an armed bodyguard. Those conducting English foreign policy, like John of Gaunt and Cardinal Beaufort, were experienced negotiators, but often the nobility were honorific figures and left matters to the active diplomats who accompanied them. The foremost of these would probably be a bishop, trained civil and canon lawyers, papal notaries, or royal secretaries.[122] Their working associates were household knights who enjoyed the royal confidence. Sir Nicholas Dagworth (d. 1402) spent the 1380s on almost permanent embassies to the Curia and other European courts, and under Henry IV, Sir John Cheyne and Sir William Esturmy became specialists, the one on France, the other on Germany and the Hanse.[123]

Their professionalism was based not only on personal experience but on an accumulated archive in the form of precedent books for diplomatic documents and protocol, and dossiers of evidences, treaties, letters, instructions, and memorandums. By the reign of Henry V these were copied into registers, or *libri recordorum*, relating to different countries for convenient reference, while the

[119] G. L. Harriss, *Cardinal Beaufort* (Oxford, 1989), 297, 345.

[120] Ratification: Chaplais, *Diplomatic Practice*, ii. 513 (1363); articles of agreement: ibid. ii. 576 (1376); proclamations of truces and treaties: ibid. ii. 657 (1410), 658–63 (1420).

[121] Ibid. ii. 810–11; Ferguson, *English Diplomacy*, 180, 189, 196.

[122] For the careers of Walter Skirlaw and Nicholas Rishton (under Richard II), John Stokes and Henry Chichele (under Henry IV and Henry V), and William Sprever and Thomas Beckington (under Henry VI), see entries in *BRUO*.

[123] Their careers are in *House of Commons*.

originals were kept in the treasury of receipt.[124] Diplomats required a detailed knowledge of previous negotiations. In the cat-and-mouse atmosphere of international conferences they had to be alert to the small print, the omitted clause, the techniques of delay and obstruction, if they were not to be hoodwinked. Some glimpse of these diplomatic tactics can be gained from the aide-memoires drawn up for the participants, and from their reports, in three major Anglo-French conferences: the peace negotiations at Bruges in 1375, the Congress of Arras in 1435, and the negotiations for a long truce at Oye in 1439. These reveal medieval diplomacy at work.[125]

On the first two of these occasions the conference met under the auspices of papal nuncios who acted as mediators. The numbers attending a major conference could be huge—calculated to have been 5,000 at Arras—and not only accommodation and victualling but effective security against fighting had to be provided. At Arras the negotiations took place in the hall of the abbey of St Vaast where the delegations also had separate conference rooms. At Oye the negotiations were in a large tent placed between the stockaded encampments of French and English, and similar stockades were built for the meeting of Henry V and Queen Isabella at Melun in 1419. At Montereau, later that year, the barriers made for the meeting of the Dauphin and John the Fearless on a bridge in midstream had been tampered with and did not prevent the latter's assassination.

The proceedings were usually conducted by mediators, who at Bruges and Arras were papal envoys. The mediators sat on thrones, the delegations on benches. Sessions began at 7 a.m. and again at 3 p.m. Proceedings opened with the reading aloud of the procurations of each embassy and the delivery of these to the other side for scrutiny. The preliminaries past, each side made its offer. These were set orations in Latin, an opportunity for each side to maximize its claims and seize the moral high ground, with professions of peace and demands for justice—which their opponents duly ridiculed. It was a rule that offers had to be made alternately, through the mediators, who attempted at each stage to narrow the gap between them, as well as judging whether each contained new matters of substance. The contending parties might thus never meet face to face. Offers were normally made orally, though the other side might ask for clarification in writing. Exceptionally a delegation might be asked to reveal its instructions if an offer was suspected of going beyond these. At some point the

---

[124] E. Perroy (ed.), *The Diplomatic Correspondence of Richard II*, Camden Society, 3rd ser., 48 (London, 1933), pp. xvii–xxvii; *Gesta*, pp. xxxix–xlviii; *Proc. & Ord.* i. 218.

[125] The following section is based on E. Perroy (ed.), *The Anglo-French Negotiations at Bruges, 1374–1377*, in *Camden Miscellany, XIX*, Camden Society, 3rd ser., 80 (London, 1952), 1–95; J. C. Dickinson, *The Congress of Arras, 1435* (Oxford, 1955); C. T. Allmand (ed.), *Documents Relating to the Anglo-French Negotiations of 1439*, in *Camden Miscellany, XXIV*, Camden Society, 4th ser., 9 (London, 1972), 79–150.

mediators would either admit failure or draft 'articles of agreement', which would be translated and referred back to the respective rulers for ratification and enactment.[126] All three of these peace conferences failed to reach a formal settlement. Those that did—at Brétigny and Troyes—were dictated by the military situation and were speedily concluded. That did not mean that the ensuing treaties were hurriedly or loosely drafted: considerable pains were taken to ensure that Troyes was legally watertight, and at Brétigny the removal from the main treaty of the legal renunciations to be made by each king (which eventually invalidated it) was by their conscious decision.[127]

Medieval diplomacy demanded professional training and skills, it had its own language and protocols for negotiating, and employed deceit, trickery, and obstruction as much as in later ages. Where the parties were of a mind, it could produce agreements which were honoured, alliances reinforced by marriage, and even transfers of territory. But it could not square the circle of competing claims of sovereignty which lay at the heart of the Anglo-French conflict, and at more than one of these conferences it was clear that neither party really desired a settlement. The diplomat's job was then a charade, conducted to gain time for his master or save his honour.

7. DEFENCE

War was an act of state. In legal terms, it had to be waged under the authority of a ruler, this distinguishing it from private banditry and bloodshed. Its moral justification was the redress of an injustice when other means had been exhausted, and its purpose was the establishment of a just peace. Before he embarked on war a ruler needed to secure a legal and moral judgement of his cause from civil and canon lawyers, and the acceptance of it by the nobility and people of his realm. The former attested the validity of his claims or title, the latter assessed it in terms of the common profit of the realm.[128] Such requirements were most evidently satisfied in defending the homeland against invading enemies, but war was also justified if waged to recover lands and rights wrongfully seized and withheld. On that ground the English invaded France—which the French defended as their native homeland. Both sides could thus claim to be in the right, and both invoked the protection and judgement of God in their cause. Victory attested the justice of one's cause and the favour of God to both ruler and

---

[126] Chaplais, *Diplomatic Practice*, ii. 527–36.

[127] P. Chaplais (ed.), *Documents Regarding the Fulfilment and Interpretation of the Treaty of Brétigny, 1361–1369*, in *Camden Miscellany, XIX*, Camden Society, 3rd ser., 80 (London, 1952), 1–84; M. H. Keen, 'Diplomacy', in Harriss (ed.), *Henry V*, 181–200.

[128] As in January 1397, when the Commons disclaimed any commitment to Richard II's proposed aid to Charles VI in Lombardy (*Rot. Parl.* iii. 338).

people; yet defeat did not (to the defeated) brand a cause as unjust, but rather indicated God's displeasure at a people's sins. Such responses were common to both French and English.[129]

Although the Hundred Years War had originated as a dispute over the feudal tenure of Aquitaine, its course was marked by a growing sense of nationhood and of the exclusive character of sovereignty. The Treaty of Brétigny (1360) acknowledged that the feudal relationship had become an anachronism and proposed the establishment of two sovereign rulers in a partitioned France. When that solution proved unacceptable it left their mutually exclusive claims to the Crown and territory of France to be resolved by war. This was accompanied by the development of an ideology of the monarchical state, uniting king and people as a sovereign body, answerable only to God and forging its own destiny. The king personified the identity and well-being of the realm, enhanced by the continuity of his dynasty and the myth of its descent from the remote past. His subjects were sanctified as a chosen people, defending a holy land and imbued with a sense of mission by a growing awareness of national history. War sharpened these attitudes by encouraging patriotism and directing it against the enemy of the nation. God and a chosen national saint as patron—St George in England, St Michael in France—was its protector, the defender of its rights and integrity, the overseer of its destiny. War became the instrument of that destiny.[130] But though in this sense war was an act of state, a matter of public policy and common involvement, it was waged on the personal initiative and for the personal ambitions of the king, and was fought by subjects on a voluntary basis and for their individual motives. This dichotomy between war as an act of state and war as personal gratification was manifested in the way it was fought and organized.

Up to 1360 Edward III's strategy had been to intervene in support of the opponents of the French Crown in Flanders, Normandy, and Brittany. Small expeditions of mounted men-at-arms and mounted archers were sent to ravage enemy-held countryside and undefended smaller towns, with the object of undermining the economy of a region, its ability to support taxation for war, and ultimately its loyalty to the French Crown. Eventually such tactics would impel the French king and nobility to offer battle which the English were confident of winning.[131] The two decisive victories at Crécy and Poitiers did appear to put the French Crown within Edward's reach, and his great army of 1359, 10,000 strong, was intended to enforce his claim. But its failure to breach the defences of either Reims or Paris demonstrated the logistical weakness of this type of campaigning: it lacked the staying power to reduce the main political centres. If Edward III's

---

[129] C. T. Allmand (ed.), *Society at War* (Edinburgh, 1973), ch. 1, pp. 16–43.

[130] C. Beaune, *The Birth of an Ideology*, trans. S. Ross (Berkeley, 1995).

[131] J. le Patourel, 'Edward III and the kingdom of France', *History*, 43 (1958), 173–89; C. J. Rogers, 'Edward III and the dialectics of strategy', *TRHS*, 6th ser., 4 (1994), 83–102.

strategy failed in its political objective, it yielded huge dividends to his soldiers in terms of both renown and material gains—booty, ransoms, *appatis* (protection money). War by *chevauchée* could thus be fought at the option of the English—who controlled the place, time, duration, and objective of expeditions. After war was renewed in 1369 this pattern of warfare yielded less success. The French Crown was able to reassert control over its dissident subjects and to neutralize the military operation of the *chevauchée*; slowly it recovered the lightly held lands and fortresses under English control. By 1389 the *chevauchée* had been discredited as both a political and a military strategy.

When Henry V reactivated the claim to the French throne he turned to a different kind of warfare: the systematic reduction by siege of major towns which controlled their *pays*, and their occupation by English garrisons. The piecemeal conquest of a whole region—Normandy—was designed to be permanent and to position the king for a political bid for the French throne, this time with temporary success. Victory in battle (at Agincourt and Verneuil) contributed little to this but brought renown and profit to the nobility and knights. *Chevauchées* were abandoned—the object was now to protect and exploit the land and people—and the soldiers were rewarded with lands and status as permanent colonists. Thus only in the latter phase of the war did the political objectives of the Crown correspond with the interests of those who fought.

Henry V's warfare demanded a change not only in tactics but in organization. Under Edward III non-royal armies would consist of 4,000–6,000 men under one or more commanders, who indented with captains to recruit men for six months' service at the Crown's wages. As the king's lieutenant the commander (often a nobleman) had strategic autonomy and often discretionary power to treat with the enemy, as well as full command in the field. The army was furnished with two months' supply of victuals until it could live off enemy territory, while each soldier provided his own weapons and equipment. These armies were manageable in size and cost and politically acceptable to parliament, which granted taxation for a limited campaign. It was within this political convention that Henry V conducted the Agincourt campaign in 1415 and raised an army in 1417. But although that army was contracted for one year, it remained in France for three, and an army of occupation (of varying size) was maintained for thirty years thereafter. This had two consequences: first, it meant that the army in Normandy had to be supported by recurrent taxation of the conquered territories. Secondly, it induced fundamental changes in military organization. The permanent army in Normandy, part in garrison and part in the field, developed an effective chain of command from the centre, with discipline enforced through regular musters linked to the payment of wages.[132] Had Henry V lived to become

---

[132] A. Curry and M. Hughes (eds.), *Arms, Armies, and Fortifications in the Hundred Years War* (Woodbridge, 1999), 21–68, 103–20 (contributions by A. Ayton, A. Curry, and M. Jones).

king of the Dual Monarchy, and continued to extend the conquest, further development towards a standing army supported by permanent taxation might have occurred in both countries. This indeed took place in France as part of Charles VII's military reforms designed to expel the English and consolidate royal power. The English Crown, by contrast, continued to fight the war with annual reinforcements paid for by parliamentary grants of the traditional kind. War continued to be a joint enterprise of king and subjects, with no possibility of a permanent army becoming an instrument of royal power.

Naval defence rested on a different tradition. Maritime security was vital both for England's wealth—derived from wool exports to the Low Countries—and for security from invasion by her larger continental neighbour, France. Edward III's aggressive military strategy established clients and bases along the French littoral, from Normandy to Aquitaine, through which the interior could be penetrated. Even when this policy collapsed after 1370, Cherbourg, St Malo, Brest, and La Rochelle were held for a time as 'barbicans', outposts of England and entry points into France. Henry V's conquest of Normandy turned the Channel into an English waterway. But if carrying the war into France safeguarded the English coast, that in turn depended on being 'maysteres of the narowe see' for both offensive and defensive operations. It seems the more surprising therefore that, apart for a few years under Henry V, the Crown made no attempt to create or maintain a regular navy. To understand why, we have to examine how fleets were assembled, how they operated, and what they could achieve.

Unlike the royal galleys of Castile, manned by a permanent body of professional oarsmen, English naval forces were mostly composed of ships owned by merchants and crewed by private sailors, serving for periods of three to six months at the Crown's wages—much as retinues were brought to the royal army by captains. But there was one important difference: a fleet was impressed by royal authority, not voluntarily raised. This was so ancient a right of the Crown that no constitutional objection was ever raised to it, though by the 1380s a measure of compensation (tontyght) was being paid to shipowners.

The most common types of ships impressed were cogs, hulks, and balingers. The cog was a broad-beamed, high-sided vessel, clinker-built with a straight keel and straight stern post, with a hung rudder. With one square sail she had a speed of 1 to 1.8 knots. For war service 'castles' could be erected at bow and stern to serve as shooting platforms and perhaps accommodation. Most cogs were under 100 tons. A variant on the cog was the hulk, having a crescent-shaped hull, built in reverse clinker, with planking parallel to the lower and upper edges, and finishing in platforms for castles fore and aft. By the early fifteenth century a ship more adaptable to war was becoming common, the balinger. These were also small, of less than 100 tons, with a shallow draught, mostly single-masted, but with thirty or more oars for use in sheltered waters or for close fighting. Also with oars were the larger and slower barges. Large cogs and balingers would have a crew of fifty to a hundred, and for military operations would carry an equivalent number of men-at-arms and archers.[133]

In addition the Crown possessed, from time to time, ships of its own. Edward III had claimed to be 'king of the sea', but his fleet was not maintained after 1360 and on the renewal of war in 1369 towns were ordered to build barges and balingers to meet the threat of Castilian raids.[134] But after 1380 no English army fought in France for thirty years and naval activity declined. No ships were added to the royal fleet, which in 1413 had once more to be expanded into a wartime force. A shipbuilding programme with an average budget of £5,000 per annum was sustained between 1415 and 1420. In particular four big ships were built, the chief of which was the royal flagship, the *Grace Dieu* of 1,400 tons, a huge, three-masted vessel, 125 feet in length and 48 in the beam. This was one of the largest vessels to be built before 1600 and was said to be 'the fairest that ever man saw'.[135] As the *Libelle* says, Henry's 'entente' in building these ships was

that he caste to be
Lorde rounde about environ of the see.[136]

His supremacy was sealed at the battle of the Seine in 1416 when Genoese and Castilian carracks were captured and added to the fleet, and by 1420 the whole of the north European seaboard from Middleburg to Brest was under Henry's overlordship. A fleet was now superfluous and after 1422 all but the four great ships were sold off. A royal fleet was thus an ephemeral measure mainly for the protection of military communications with France; it was a supplement to, not a replacement for, the normal assembly of a fleet by impressments, though it also served to counter or deter any immediate, unforeseen threat.[137]

Command of the sea—'to keep the sea', in contemporary parlance—served a variety of purposes: the transport of an army to France, the capture or sustenance of a port of disembarkation, and the safeguard of cross-Channel communications. Large armies were transported to Calais in multiple crossings. In 1369 Gaunt's army of 6,000 men was shipped in some 250 vessels, half of which were of 50 tons or less, as was his force for the great *chevauchée* of 1373.[138] To put ashore a sizeable army in hostile territory was more hazardous and required

---

[133] I. Friel, *The Good Ship* (London, 1995).

[134] Sherborne, *War, Politics, and Culture*, 29–40.

[135] S. Rose (ed.), *The Navy of the Lancastrian Kings*, Navy Records Society (London, 1982), 28–56; G. Hutchinson, *Medieval Ships and Shipping* (London, 1994), 30–7.

[136] *The Libelle of Englyshe Polycye*, ed. G. Warner (Oxford, 1926), p. 51, line 1019.

[137] *Libelle*, p. 24, lines 470–4; C. F. Richmond, 'English naval power in the fifteenth century', *History*, 52 (1967), 1–15.

[138] Sherborne, *War, Politics, and Culture*, 36–7.

larger vessels, for it involved the transport of numerous horses penned in the holds by hurdles and provided with special gangplanks for disembarkation. Henry V's fleet disembarked 10,000 men at Chef de Caux for the siege of Harfleur in 1415, and again in 1417 he effected a landing in similar strength at Touques. Even more hazardous was Gaunt's invasion of Galicia in 1386 with ninety ships, some of 300 tons, manned by nearly 2,800 seamen, and escorted by Portuguese galleys: in all a fleet of some 14,000 tons carrying perhaps 7,000 men. Armies bound for Spain shipped from Plymouth and did not carry horses.[139]

Most fraught with danger was the relief of a port under siege. Sir Hugh Calveley engaged the Castilian fleet to succour St Malo in 1379, but the earl of Pembroke's expedition to La Rochelle in 1372 was destroyed by the Castilian galleys. These were both small fleets, but the relief of Harfleur in 1416, besieged by French, Genoese, and Spanish carracks, involved a fleet of 300 ships and a sizeable army.[140]

At certain periods of the war fleets were assembled to 'keep the sea', sailing in relays for up to six months at a time. They carried complements of between 1,000 and 2,500 soldiers and had both a defensive and an offensive role. From 1369 to 1380 a series of such fleets put to sea to challenge the Franco-Castilian navies in the Channel.[141] During the English conquest of Normandy it became vital both to defend cross-Channel communications and to deny passage to hostile forces from Scotland. Fleets of a dozen or more vessels were commissioned each year, but they did not stop Scottish troops reaching France in some numbers from 1419 to 1424.[142]

Any such operation might result in a sea battle. The techniques of fighting, so vividly described in the *Morte Arthure*, were essentially those of land combat. To come to close quarters, the foreign carracks tried to ram the English ships, while the higher English cogs tried to come alongside and board the carracks. Hand-to-hand fighting ensued, in which the enemy was killed or thrown overboard, and the ships were fired. Small cannon might be mounted on deck and fired at close quarters but there were no artillery duels. Most engagements took place in coastal waters, the retreating ships being chased along the Channel.

At times the English were thrown on the defensive by attacks on coastal towns and shipping. During the 1370s Jean de Vienne reorganized the French navy, with a galley dock at Rouen, and with Castilian support launched devastating coastal raids from Rye to Plymouth. From 1383 to 1386 there were serious attempts to mount a massive invasion of England which only political and

[139] P. E. Russell, *The English Intervention in Spain and Portugal* (Oxford, 1955), 412–17.

[140] Sherborne, *War, Politics, and Culture*, 41–54; Rose, *Lancastrian Navy*, 49.

[141] Sherborne, *War, Politics, and Culture*, 37–8.

[142] R. A. Newhall, *The English Conquest of Normandy, 1416–24* (New York, 1924; repr. 1971), 196–9.

organizational difficulties frustrated. French and Spanish raids along the south and east coasts were resumed after 1400 and in 1406 penetrated to the mouth of the Thames. It was rarely possible to defend a coastline once a hostile fleet was at sea; the most effective defence was a pre-emptive strike. Command of the sea was gained and usually held by the fleet that first set sail.

The defence of commercial shipping was possibly of even greater importance, for on it depended the livelihood of numerous subjects and the wealth of the Crown. After war was resumed in 1369 the Commons responded to the threat by granting a new tax, tonnage and poundage, for the protection of shipping, initially for specific annual periods and recurrently after 1382, which underwrote the fleets commissioned in these years. In the years after 1400 English and French conducted wholesale war on each other's shipping by licensed piratical fleets.[143] Under Henry V the Crown undertook more effective policing, enforcing the Statute of Truces of 1414, and not until the 1440s did piracy again become rampant, with West Country captains and shipowners attacking Spanish and Flemish shipping. This culminated in the capture of the huge Bay fleet of over 100 Hanse, Flemish, and Dutch ships on its way up-channel in 1449, creating a major international incident and forcing the Crown to pay compensation.[144]

Naval activity was at least as common as military, and at certain periods—e.g. from 1369 to 1380—it involved as many men as those engaged in field operations in France, though voyages were shorter than military expeditions. The cost to the exchequer of naval operations in these years was £246,000, about two-thirds of that of military expeditions to northern France. But the real cost was greater, for the impressment of large numbers of merchant ships and their crews for periods of up to six months seriously disrupted commerce. Nevertheless, merchants and shipowners supported strong naval forces to safeguard them against war and piracy.[145] Chaucer's Merchant typically

> wolde the see were kept for any thing
> Bitwixe Middelburgh and Orewelle.

The war at sea had a more direct impact on English national life than that waged in France. For most Englishmen land war remained distant and opportunistic, while the war at sea was more immediate and threatening. Doubtless the seafarers of the southern and western ports, like Chaucer's Shipman, engaged in war and privateering as an ingrained way of life, but among the wider mercantile and political community a hundred years of naval warfare bred a more cautious

---

[143] C. J. Kingsford, *Prejudice and Promise in Fifteenth Century England* (Oxford, 1925), ch. 4; C. J. Ford, 'Piracy or policy: The crisis in the channel, 1400–1403', *TRHS*, 5th ser., 29 (1979), 63–78.

[144] *Rot. Parl.* v. 59–60; C. F. Richmond, 'The keeping of the seas during the Hundred Years War: 1422–1440', *History*, 49 (1964), 292–6.

[145] Sherborne, *War, Politics, and Culture*, 38–9, 69.

attitude. With them England's safety weighed more than its foreign enterprises, and as the Hundred Years War closed on a note of defeat and isolation, that safety was seen to depend on its defence of the sea. A fortress island became the last resort of national pride, a fortress mentality an ingrained element of national character:

> Kepe than the see abought in speciall,
> Whiche of England is the rounde wall,
> As thoughe England were lykened to a cite
> And the wall environ were the see.
> Kepe than the see, that is the wall of Englond
> And than is Englond kepte by Goddes honde.[146]

[146] *Libelle*, p. 55, lines 1092–7.

CHAPTER 4

The Nobility

The late medieval nobility enjoyed a position of political, social, economic, and military dominance unmatched in any later age. While the king was the head of the body politic, the lords formed the shoulders and backbone, and acted as arms for its defence.[1] Their fidelity to the Crown validated their own rule over lesser subjects, thus constituting a hierarchy of authority on which the social order rested. Bishop John Stafford likened them to mountains towering above the hills and undifferentiated plains of the lower classes.[2] Their status as a hereditary elite rested upon their lineage and lands, which furnished them with huge wealth and extensive lordship. As military leaders they epitomized the chivalric ideal of valour, prowess, and courtesy. In all these respects they provided the role model for a society of which they were the unquestioned leaders.

Yet the nobility did not form an autonomous and coherent estate. They held their lands and titles from the Crown, and their public service was a response to royal leadership and favour. It needed the king to make them an effective channel for royal rule:

> Thi peres in parlement pull hem to-geders,
> Worche after wisdom, and worshipe will folowe;
> For as a lord is a lord and ledeth the peple,
> So shuld prowesse in thi persone passe other mennes wittes.[3]

Further, the collective identity of the nobility embraced individual ties and enmities, with the solidarities of kinship, the rivalries of neighbours, and the constant competition for honour and advantage, making the peerage a volatile and fissiparous body, rarely united behind a political strategy.[4] Finally, both as major landowners and as military leaders the nobility were prone to see their service to the Crown and common weal as an extension of their own status and interests.

---

[1] Kail (ed.), *Political Poems*, no. 15; John Lydgate, *The Fall of Princes*, bk. ii, lines, 848–52.

[2] *Rot. Parl.* iv. 419.　　　[3] Robbins (ed.), *Historical Poems*, 230.

[4] M. A. Hicks, 'Cement or solvent? Kinship and politics in late medieval England: The case of the Nevilles', *History*, 83 (1998), 31–46.

Nor was this period in any sense a golden age for aristocratic fortunes. Population decline reduced the exploitation of their estates by villein labour and threatened their income. Their credibility as guardians of stability and order was shaken by the two worst outbreaks of popular revolt in the Middle Ages, in 1381 and 1450, and by criticism of the disorderly behaviour of their retainers. Their leadership of political society, both nationally and in the localities, was increasingly shared with the middling landowners as these grew in wealth and assumed responsibilities in government. The failure which dogged military and naval operations after 1370 discredited their military leadership, and later they were unable to halt the slow attrition of Henry V's conquests in France. Their assumption of constitutional responsibilities, whether to restrain Richard II's autocracy or to preserve the Lancastrian dynasty under Henry VI, imposed strains which destroyed the unity of the nobility and eventually that of the state. But if, in each of these spheres, by 1461 the leadership of the nobility had been brought in question, in no real sense was their position in crisis. They maintained their economic pre-eminence, they prescribed the values and objectives of political society, and government remained channelled through their hands. Late medieval society and its politics cannot be understood without a close examination of this small group. Who constituted the peerage and how coherent a body were they? What resources did they command and how well did they manage them? By what values did they live, and what did they believe in? How well did they fight and how well did they govern?

I. THE PEERAGE

Over the century preceding 1360 the greater tenants-in-chief, numbering some two to three hundred families, had narrowed to a peerage of at most sixty, identified by personal writs of summons to parliament where they formed the House of Lords. There they wore special robes, were allowed to carry arms, had the right to be tried by their peers, and themselves functioned as a high court. After about 1375 their titles became hereditary in the male line, and they formed an upper peerage of a dozen or so dukes and earls and a lower peerage of some forty or fifty barons.

Titles were attached to land as well as held by persons, and common law rules of inheritance were weighted towards preserving the integrity of the inheritance. Land descended to males as sole heirs in sequence of birth, and thereafter to females as co-parceners; thence to the lineal descendants of the last holder and thereafter to the collaterals of their blood. Titles could not, however, be inherited by females nor be divided, and went into abeyance if the estate descended to female heirs. The population decline in the century after the Black Death increased the likelihood of that. It has been shown that whereas before 1350 over

70 per cent of families in the upper landowning class left a direct male heir, in the following eighty years under 60 per cent did so, with corresponding rises in the proportions of sole and co-heiresses (from 10.5 to 15.5 per cent) and of those leaving no children (from 18 to 29 per cent). It was thus a period 'uniquely favourable to the transmission of land through heiresses' but also one in which new legal devices were evolved to preserve estates by strengthening the claims of direct descendants and male heirs. Entailing land to the heirs of the body of the original holder ('fee tail') limited its descent to the proximate family, barring heirs general and collaterals. A stronger version, the entail 'in tail male', excluded all female heirs so that in the second generation the male heirs of a junior branch would exclude the female heirs of the elder branch. These entails could be effected by passing the lands to a group of feoffees who would regrant them to the original holder and the heirs (male) of his body. Entails in tail male were indeed employed by some leading noblemen such as Thomas Beauchamp, earl of Warwick, in 1344 and Richard FitzAlan, earl of Arundel, at about the same date; but they were not adopted for the majority of estates. Natural affection held lords back from disinheriting their own daughters in favour of more remote male heirs, preferring to see the title descend to a son-in-law rather than a cousin or nephew. Not all were concerned for the long-term destiny of their family, and even tail male could never offer infallible insurance against a failure of males in all branches—a fate which overtook the Beauchamps in 1445.[5]

Similar legal devices also increased freedom to devise land, by enfeoffing it to trustees for specific purposes ('uses'), whether charitable bequests, or a jointure for their widow, or the endowment of a younger son, or even the disposal of the inheritance outside the family altogether. Such attempts to frustrate the normal rules of succession were exceptional and could be contentious, but they illustrate the conflicting pressures upon lords and the greater freedom which the law now offered them.

Demographic failure and this new legal flexibility made this a period of exceptional flux for aristocratic families. Two main tendencies can be observed. Families who survived in the male line had good chances of increasing their estates by the acquisition of an heiress, and this process of accumulation led to the emergence of some huge territorial complexes among the late medieval earldoms. But, secondly, these might in turn become divided among co-heiresses, while at a lower level the availability of heiresses offered a means of entry into the peerage from below. However, such heiresses rarely or never raised men from the dust; they were bestowed, or bestowed themselves, on families whose landed wealth already qualified them for entry into the peerage. That wealth had usually been acquired

---

[5] S. J. Payling, 'Social mobility, demographic change, and landed society in late medieval England', *Econ. HR* 45 (1992), 51–73, for this and the two following paragraphs.

in a previous generation, through service at court or, more rarely, from the profits of war, law, or trade. It was the sons of these entrepreneurs who reaped the fruits of their fathers' success: the first generation acquired lands through purchase, the second a title through marriage. Thus access to the peerage was conditioned by rules of inheritance and the possession of land.

To what extent could the Crown control the shape and size of the peerage? It could not interfere with the laws of inheritance and it perforce had to recognize the claim of the husband of an heiress to her family title, as when Alice Montagu brought the earldom of Salisbury to Richard Neville in 1429. Similarly, at a lower level, the Crown conferred baronies on the three younger sons of Ralph, earl of Westmoreland, William, Edward, and George Neville, on their marriage to heiresses.[6] But where the Crown had the wardship of an unmarried heiress it might give this to a favoured noble. William de la Pole, duke of Suffolk, secured the wardship of two infant heiresses to comital titles, those of Lady Margaret Beaufort in 1444 and Anne, countess of Warwick, in 1446. Such cases were exceptional, for most heiresses were already married at the time of their father's death, and in general the Crown's right of wardship was being eroded by entails and feoffments to use. Thus in conferring new titles the Crown often found itself merely endorsing family arrangements, while its attempts to create new titles independent of any inheritance proved contentious. In the mid-fourteenth century some of Edward III's distinguished captains received writs of summons as bannerets, a non-hereditary rank; but by 1400 this military subclass of the peerage had disappeared and Richard II's attempt in 1387 to confer a barony by letter patent on Sir John Beauchamp of Kidderminster, who had no hereditary claim to the land or title, aroused baronial opposition. The precedent was not followed for sixty years, until Henry VI's creation of at least ten new baronies by letters patent between 1441 and 1455 definitively established the Crown's right to ennoble in this way.[7]

Apart from hereditary succession, marriage, and royal service, there were few ways into the peerage. In the fourteenth century the baronial families of Scrope, Thorpe, and Bourchier had all sprung from successful chief justices, but none of the Lancastrian justices founded a baronial house. Even less auspicious was the practice of trade. Michael de la Pole was the only son of a merchant to attain the peerage, and though his father's outstanding wealth had laid the foundation, it was Richard II's favour which brought him the lands and title to the Ufford earldom of Suffolk. Despite his family's service in war, its mercantile origins were never forgotten.

---

[6] Hicks, 'Cement or solvent?', 33, 40.

[7] J. E. Powell and K. Wallis, *The House of Lords in the Middle Ages* (London, 1968), 402, 470, 481 ff.

In the century after 1350, therefore, demographic, legal, and political trends all helped to make the peerage a small and exclusive class. Demographic wastage reduced peerage families by roughly a quarter over each period of twenty-five years, except for 1400–24, when the proportion rose to 35 per cent. After 1360 this natural wastage was not offset by new creations, as in the preceding half-century, and the peerage shrank from 147 in 1350 to 73 in 1450.[8] Although the Crown's ability to enlarge and shape the peerage as a whole was constrained by rules of inheritance, the fact that earldoms survived on average for no more than two or three generations offered scope for the king to promote to its upper ranks. Promotions into the upper peerage were broadly of three kinds. There were the largely unexceptionable cases of peers who secured the title to an earldom by marriage to a sole heiress; there were the close relatives of the king himself, his brothers, uncles, or sons, the princes of the blood; and there were those whose companionship he valued either as military leaders or as courtiers. In 1337 Edward III had elevated his military captains, but in his middle years his primary concern was the provision of inheritances for his sons, and earldoms were created for Lionel, John, Edmund, and Thomas, mainly through marriage to heiresses.[9] By 1377 there were twelve earls, and Richard II, who had no sons, felt free to promote those he favoured from the ranks of the baronage, raising the upper peerage to a total of eighteen in 1399. The first Lancastrian kings restricted their promotions to members of the royal blood, and for the first forty years of the fifteenth century the upper peerage was usually not more than fourteen in number. But in the following two decades a range of baronial families received comital titles, raising the upper peerage to twenty. Whether by accident or design the upper peerage received an infusion of new titles roughly every half-century: in the 1330s, 1390s, and 1440s.

As well as controlling entry into the upper peerage the Crown, over this period, introduced a hierarchy of grades. Until 1385 ducal titles had been confined to royal offspring, but in the following year the creation of Robert de Vere as duke of Ireland extended the rank beyond the royal family, to be followed in 1397 by the creation of five new dukes (derisively termed 'dukelings'), mostly related to the king at some remove. Richard also introduced the rank of marquess. Henry IV annulled these creations, and ducal titles were again restricted to the blood royal, until Henry VI (who had no immediate kin) conferred ducal titles beyond the royal family and introduced the further rank of viscount. By the late 1440s the upper peerage comprised five dukes, two marquesses, nine earls, and two viscounts.

---

[8] K. B. McFarlane, *The Nobility of Later Medieval England* (Oxford, 1973), 172–6.

[9] Lionel by marriage to the heiress of Ulster and Clare (1342), John to the heiress of Lancaster (1359), Thomas to a Bohun co-heiress (1374), while Edmund acquired lands of the last Warenne earl of Surrey; W. M. Ormrod, 'Edward III and his family', *Jnl. Brit. Stud.* 26 (1987), 398–422.

Unless a new dignity was supported from hereditary lands the Crown was expected to endow it with a notional minimum of 1,000 marks per annum for an earl and £1,000 per annum for a duke. Most kings were reluctant to alienate Crown lands, even for the endowment of cadet branches of the royal family, and new titles had often to be supported from escheats, forfeitures, exchequer annuities, and—under Henry V—grants of conquered lands in France. Thus by the mid-fifteenth century the Crown's power to enlarge the peerage by letter patent and to introduce new grades had significantly grown, while its capacity to endow these had significantly shrunk. Provided they could maintain a succession in the male line, the older comital families tended to absorb extinct titles and lands, making it difficult for the Crown to endow its cadet and collateral branches. A gulf steadily opened within the upper peerage between the older families with huge landed inheritances, and the newer families, often of the royal blood, who remained dependent on office and Crown favours to supplement their slender lands and uncertain annuities, and this had important political implications.

2. THE INHERITANCE

The leading peerage was a far from homogeneous body. There were marked differences in their origins, wealth, and influence. By 1360 a handful of families had held their earldoms for a century or longer, like Oxford (de Vere), Warwick (Beauchamp), Arundel (FitzAlan), Hereford (Bohun), and Devon (Courtenay); others, like Pembroke (Hastings), Stafford (Stafford), Salisbury (Montague), Suffolk (Ufford), March (Mortimer), dated from earlier in that century, and those of Nottingham (Mowbray), Northumberland (Percy), Westmorland (Neville), and Somerset (Beaufort) were to be later creations. Some were of royal blood, like Lancaster, Clarence, York, and Gloucester, or of the half-blood, like Kent and Huntingdon (Holland).[10] The more ancient earldoms tended to be the wealthiest, having accumulated more extensive lands, though two—Oxford and Devon—were among the poorest. Others depended on income from offices and annuities given by the Crown. Patterns of landholding and local influence varied considerably: the intensive lordship exercised by the Nevilles and Percys in the north and FitzAlans and Mortimers in the Welsh marches contrasted with the more piecemeal landholding of Beauchamps, Staffords, and Mowbrays in lowland England; nor could any of these rival the vast, extended lordship of the house of Lancaster. There were thus huge disparities of wealth and territorial influence among these families, while their power and prestige depended not only on their estates, the abilities of the lord, and the favour of the Crown, but

[10] The higher nobility are listed by their titles in E. B. Fryde *et al.*, *Handbook of British Chronology*, 3rd edn. (London, 1986), 447–89.

on the vicissitudes of fertility and mortality which governed the extent and continuance of the inheritance. It is to these matters that we must now turn.

Any assessment of the wealth of the leading peerage must be in some degree artificial. Surviving estate accounts are rarely comprehensive and in various ways offer a notional, rather than actual, view of the financial position. Even so the wealth of most of the greater peerage can be ascertained within broad limits, although the size of a family's estates and income could change dramatically in the course of the century.[11] After 1360 the two wealthiest peers were Edward III's sons, the Black Prince with lands of almost £10,000 per annum in 1376 and John of Gaunt with an income of £11,750 in 1395. These princes of the blood towered over the rest of the peerage, their incomes reflecting their international standing. By 1400, however, both their dukedoms had been rejoined to the Crown. Below them the three wealthiest families were FitzAlan with estates of £4,500 to £5,000 per annum, and Mortimer and Bohun each with around £3,000 to £3,500. All three drew a significant proportion of their income from Welsh marcher lordships. The families of Beauchamp, Percy, and Montagu enjoyed between £2,000 and £3,000, with Mowbray, Courtenay, and Hastings in the bracket £1,000 to £2,000.

By 1430–50 the picture had changed considerably. Income from land had generally fallen as the economy contracted, and that from the marcher lordships had been severely reduced by Glyn Dŵr's revolt, but the accumulation of inheritances had made some families far wealthier. At the top were now Beauchamp (until 1439), Stafford (from 1438), and York (from 1432). Each of these enjoyed, at their peak, estates yielding £5,000 and more gross. The rest of the upper peerage fell well below this level. The Mowbrays never realized the full potential of their inheritance and fell into a group with incomes of £2,000 to £3,000 along with Percy, Neville (until 1425), and Courtenay, below which came the residue of the FitzAlan inheritance, and the families of de la Pole, Holland, Beaufort, and de Vere. We are less well informed about baronial incomes, for there are fewer surviving estate accounts. But the returns to the 1436 tax on incomes suggest that while a few, including Lords Cromwell and Tiptoft, enjoyed more than £1,000 per annum, the majority had between £750 and £350.

While some families were growing richer, the total income of what was a shrinking peerage may have diminished. This was a century of population decline and a contracting agrarian economy. By 1400 peasant holdings were vacant for lack of tenants, and attempts by landlords to enforce villein services and restrain the rising costs of wages precipitated flight from the manor or active opposition to estate officials and manorial courts. The collapse of grain prices in

[11] The following paragraphs are based on the studies of magnate estates listed in the Bibliography.

the mid-1370s intensified this confrontation between the legal authority of landlords and the economic power of the workforce, until the rising of 1381 administered a shock from which the system of direct management never recovered. The greater landlords switched from direct cultivation by serf labour to leasing the demesne, either collectively to peasants or, more usually, to individual farmers. On the comital estates of Beauchamp, Stafford, Courtenay, Mowbray, and Percy, as on the baronial estates of Berkeley and Talbot, virtually all agrarian manors had been leased by 1410, though some pasture remained in demesne. However, with shortage of tenants and accumulating arrears, the shift to rent did not necessarily increase or even stabilize income. For the first half of the fifteenth century there seems to be no consistent trend. Courtenay income rose by 5 per cent over the period 1400–30 and the English estates of both Beauchamp and Stafford enjoyed stability before 1440. But revenues on the Percy estates in both Sussex and Northumberland declined steeply over the period 1400–50. Much depended on active estate management. Landlords also sought to diversify their operations, notably by changing to pastoral farming to cut labour costs. Some had considerable flocks of sheep. On the Sussex downs and on their Welsh estates the earls of Arundel had some 25,000 sheep at the end of the century, and in 1376 drew some £2,722 from the sale of wool. On the eve of Glyn Dŵr's revolt the Beauchamp estates in Glamorgan yielded £1,000 from wool sales. Industry followed, with fulling mills making particular manors like Topsham in Devon and Stansted in Essex highly profitable.

Cattle-farming also increased, both for dairy products and for meat consumption. East Anglia saw the growth of vaccaries, and in the south and west the FitzAlan manors supported a thousand beef cattle at the end of the fourteenth century. The natural resources of other estates also yielded modest profits, though they were not always fully exploited. Timber sales were a regular feature in the Stafford lordship of Caus, the Beauchamps developed mining on a small scale in Gower, and lead was extracted on the FitzAlan lordship of Bromfield and Yale. However, the Percys seem to have ignored the coal deposits of Northumberland. A few lords are known to have owned ships or engaged in trade. Around 1400 Lord Berkeley owned a small fleet of ships based in Bristol, and four ships belonging to Lord Fitzwarin were trading with Iceland in 1451. Finally there were opportunities for those with reserves of capital to invest in loans, though few did so to the extent of Richard, earl of Arundel, who deposited over 60,000 marks with bankers 'to traffic therewith to his profit' between 1360 and 1370.[12]

From the marcher lordships of Wales a handful of the upper peerage drew a significant part of their incomes in the later fourteenth century. There they

---

[12] C. Given-Wilson, 'Wealth and credit, public and private: The earls of Arundel, 1306–1397', *EHR* 106 (1991), 19–20.

exercised the Crown's criminal jurisdiction at its widest extent in the eyre, holding 'Great Sessions' every three to five years which were 'redeemed' by payment of a communal fine, as at Brecon for £1,800 in 1375. Equally distinctive was the casual income from gifts, aids, and tallages, a substitute for parliamentary subsidies. In lordships like Brecon, Chirk, and Kidwelly between 42 and 58 per cent of revenue came from these two sources in the later fourteenth century. As these were rigorously, even mercilessly, exploited and as sheep-farming boomed, revenue from the marcher lordships formed an increasingly important element on the Bohun, FitzAlan, and Lancastrian lordships and most of it was sent direct to England for the lord's benefit. The Mortimer lordships yielded over £3,000 per annum, those of FitzAlan and Lancaster over £2,000, and those of Stafford, Despenser, and Beauchamp over £1,000. The solid financial basis which they provided for these leading families underlines the political importance of the marches in Richard II's reign. Glyn Dŵr's revolt brought a collapse of both seigniorial authority and the economy of the region, which drastically reduced their income. Only slowly was lordship reasserted and arrears recovered in the years after 1410, but by 1450 revenues on the Mortimer estates were fully restored. Elsewhere lordship was less effective. In Brecon and Newport the great fines could not be collected, rents had declined by 10 per cent from 1400, and a valor of 1447–8 for the Stafford lands in Wales shows that only £1,093 of the anticipated £1,508 had been received. Thereafter, absenteeism, local disorder, and the devolution of authority to native leaders, all contributed to a general disintegration of seigniorial control, which was not reasserted until the end of the century.

Since land was the basis for title, it was supremely important to preserve the integrity of the inheritance. The greatest single means of enlarging an estate was through marriage to an heiress. In practice this was less often the result of a conscious strategy—as when Maurice, Lord Berkeley, arranged for his son Thomas to marry the Lisle heiress in 1367 while both were still children[13]—than from an unforeseen failure of heirs, such as transferred the earldoms of Salisbury and Warwick to successive generations of Nevilles. Indeed it might be the unlooked-for consequence of a marriage made several generations earlier. Nevertheless, the marriage alliances of major families were carefully planned. The father of an heir would seek an alliance that extended his estates, while the father of the bride one that enlarged his political and social connections. The marriage of an heiress raised the stakes: since it brought an accretion of land to the groom's family, they would have to provide a correspondingly larger jointure, or be of a higher social standing, while the bride would bring no marriage portion. Thus the price of an heiress was high, and was a gamble that might not pay off, for she might die, or

[13] J. Smyth, *Lives of the Berkeleys* (London, 1885), ii. 1–2. Margaret Lisle was aged 7; her marriage portion was 1,100 marks.

fail to inherit if her father subsequently produced a son. Hence heiresses were more favoured for younger sons and by lesser baronial houses than for the heirs of the upper nobility.[14] Since the premature death of a father would deliver the wardship and marriage of his children to the Crown, betrothals were frequently contracted by the parents before puberty. Thomas Mowbray and Catherine Holland were betrothed in 1391 at the ages of 6 and 4 although they were not married until 1401. When the Crown had the custody and marriage of an heir it could act as a marriage broker among the higher nobility. In 1380 John of Gaunt purchased for 5,000 marks the marriage of the co-heiress Mary Bohun for his son Henry, aged 14, and in 1411 and again in 1423 Ralph, earl of Westmorland, paid sums of 3,000 marks to acquire the custody of John Mowbray and Richard of York, whom he married to his daughters.[15] Marriages served political and social as well as territorial interests.

Some heiresses were of mature years, the survivors of one or more husbands. Almost 70 per cent of the fifteenth-century peerage left widows and about 40 per cent of these remarried.[16] They might, like Isobel Despenser, the second wife of Richard Beauchamp, earl of Warwick, be both heiresses in their own right and have considerable lands as dower. Widows could carry their dower to successive husbands: Joan Holland, though only 24, brought her third husband, Henry, Lord Scrope, estates that trebled his income.[17] The principal lordships thus incorporated inheritances from a number of families. Much less frequently land was purchased, often to extend or consolidate lordship in a newly acquired area; thus the Greys of Ruthin steadily enlarged their new estate in Bedfordshire, buying Ampthill in 1454. Compared to the accretions from inheritance or purchase, those from royal favour were few and often precarious. Kings rarely alienated Crown lands, and grants of escheats or forfeitures were mostly to royal cadets or favourites.

The same means by which estates grew—marriage, purchase, favour—could also operate in reverse, to reduce them. Few inheritances were sold in their entirety and then only for lack of heirs. In 1376 Lady Mohun, the last of her line, sold the reversion of the whole estate to the Luttrells for 5,000 marks though she lived thirty years longer.[18] Occasional sales to meet a ransom or debt were more common. Heavy ransoms forced Lord Grey of Ruthin to part with some of his Hastings inheritance in 1402, and Lady Hungerford to mortgage the

---

[14] S. J. Payling, 'The politics of family: Late medieval marriage contracts', in R. H. Britnell and A. J. Pollard (eds.), *The McFarlane Legacy* (Stroud, 1995), 21–48, and id., 'The economics of marriage in late medieval England: The marriage of heiresses', in *Econ. HR* 54 (2001), 413–29.

[15] McFarlane, *Nobility*, 86–7.

[16] J. T. Rosenthal, *Patriarchy and Families of Privilege in Fifteenth Century England* (Philadelphia, 1991), 182.

[17] T. B. Pugh, *Henry V and the Southampton Plot of 1415* (Southampton, 1988), 112–13.

[18] H. C. Maxwell-Lyte, *Dunster and its Lords* (privately printed, 1882), 53.

Hungerford inheritance to pay the ransom of her son Lord Moleyns after 1453.[19] Family needs and vicissitudes also eroded estates. The settlement of a jointure, the creation of an estate for younger sons or a second family, or the endowment of a religious or charitable foundation could withdraw substantial portions of an estate for an appreciable period. The desire to accumulate and transmit the inheritance was always counterbalanced by the obligation to make provision for the family.

Often a widow was the greatest burden on an estate. She could claim as dower from her husband's estate an income of one-third its value, but it was increasingly common for a husband to make a jointure, supplementing or incorporating the dower, either at marriage or at the birth of issue. The purpose was not only to make better provision for his widow but to retain a larger proportion of the estate in her control during an heir's minority, rather than see it fall into the Crown's custody. The disadvantage was that the widow could carry both her dower and jointure to a second husband, who, if issue was born of this second marriage, could retain the jointure (though not dower) for his life 'by courtesy of England'. Jointures could thus subtract parts of an estate for considerable periods from an adult heir; indeed it has been calculated that in the fifteenth century 76 per cent of noble estates were reduced by at least one-third, for on average a period of seventeen years. Some renowned dowagers who outlived successive husbands, like Margaret of Brotherton, Anne, countess of Stafford, and Alice, duchess of Suffolk, were the wealthiest women of their age, enjoying incomes comparable to those of the upper nobility and managing their estates with the tenacity and acumen of businesswomen, unencumbered by military commitments or the maintenance of a lavish lifestyle. They often enjoyed a rare degree of independence and might exercise it in choosing husbands from a lower social rank and a younger generation. Their impatient heirs might try to wrest the lands by legal and other pressures, but mostly they just had to wait.[20] Yet dowagers could on occasion save an inheritance from extinction, for the Crown usually excepted their lands from the penalties of their husband's forfeiture; in this way the Percy estates survived after the family was attainted in 1461.

The provision of marriage portions for daughters generally had less effect on the inheritance, for most were in cash and were paid in instalments from income, which avoided the sale of land. The size of the bride's portion, which was paid to

[19] R. I. Jack, *The Grey of Ruthin Valor* (Sydney, 1965), 4; M. A. Hicks, 'Counting the cost of war: The Moleyns ransom and the Hungerford sales, 1453–87', *Southern History*, 8 (1986), 11–31.

[20] R. E. Archer, 'The estates and finances of Margaret of Brotherton, 1322–1390', *Hist. Res.* 60 (1987), 264–80; ead., 'Rich old ladies: The problem of late medieval dowagers', in A. Pollard (ed.), *Property and Politics* (Gloucester, 1984), 15–35; ead., 'Women as landholders and administrators in the later Middle Ages', in P. J. P. Goldberg (ed.), *Woman is a Worthy Wight* (Stroud, 1992), 149–81.

the groom's father, reflected the status of the groom and the size of the jointure with which his father would endow the couple. At baronial level they were mostly over 1,000 marks. The provision of a jointure for the couple by the groom's father involved considerably more outlay and a sizeable alienation of land in tail. In the contract for the marriage of Henry Holland to Anne of York in August 1445 the duke of York was to provide £1,000 for his daughter on the wedding day and a further £2,000 in instalments, while the duke of Exeter undertook to enfeoff the newly married couple with land to the annual value of 400 marks in (unusually) tail male, three-quarters of which she was to retain for life if widowed. To ensure that a daughter (and her son) retained a sufficient estate, restrictions might be imposed on any further alienation of land by the groom's father, e.g. in the event of his second marriage.[21] Marriage contracts thus incorporated complex conditions and required prolonged negotiation. Mortality in child marriages was a hazard against which families sought protection by contracting parallel marriages with pairs of brothers and sisters, as did the earls of Arundel and Northampton in 1359 and the Nevilles and Beauchamps in 1434, while some contracts provided for the further marriage of the surviving partner to a sibling of the deceased, as in the case of Anne of Woodstock's marriage to successive Stafford brothers.

The setting up of a new family thus involved both parents in considerable outlay, though for a male heir this did not constitute a permanent alienation. It was the provision for younger sons that tested most severely the conflicting claims of parental affection and obligation to maintain the inheritance. Some provision was essential; neither dignity nor prudence permitted a younger son to be left penniless, and though some could enter the Church, for others a modest landed endowment was necessary, if only to enable them to make a profitable marriage. Cadet lines provided some safeguard against demographic failure, though in this period few survived long. Of the eight sons of Hugh Courtenay, earl of Devon (d. 1377), only one established a cadet branch, the Courtenays of Powderham. Parental affection could, on occasion, override both family duty and convention by preferring a younger son or a second family over the heir. Before his death in 1414 William, Lord Roos, of Helmsley bestowed on his second son a considerable estate carved out of his elder brother's inheritance and left his three younger sons merely a share of his goods.[22] More frequently it was the stepmother who sought to disinherit the eldest son in favour of her own children, as notoriously did Joan, countess of Westmorland.[23] In such situations, when entails were used for the purposes of estate planning, they engendered devices to bar them,

---

[21] Payling, 'Politics of family', 31, 43 n. 22.   [22] *Reg. Chichele*, ii. 22–7.

[23] Similarly Margaret, countess of Shrewsbury, for her son John, Viscount Lisle; A. Pollard, 'The family of Talbot', Ph.D. thesis (Bristol University, 1968), 52–4.

first by collateral warranty and ultimately by the development of the common recovery.[24]

Family estates were thus in constant flux to meet different stages of the life-cycle. What imparted a degree of continuity was the administration. The distinctive administrative unit in a late medieval estate was the receivership, usually covering two or more counties, headed by a receiver responsible for collecting rents and a steward who maintained the properties and the lord's rights. The Beauchamps and Staffords grouped their central estates under a receiver-general with the outliers under local receivers, while on the extensive estates of the duchy of Lancaster the receiverships were grouped into northern and southern parts each under a receiver-general.[25] A balance had to be struck between local receivers who could best exploit the estate and a central receiver less prone to local influence.

At the manorial level reeves, bailiffs, and feodaries collected the rents and dues, or a farmer answered for a composite sum. The principal difficulty faced by the receiver was the collection of arrears, requiring much persistence and extensive travelling. Receivers were trusted and influential men, in the main professional and careerist managers, although in the fifteenth century many were local gentry for whom the office and its fee constituted attachment to a lord's affinity. Alongside the receiver was the steward, responsible for holding the manorial court, sanctioning leases, and maintaining repairs. But many of the steward's duties could be performed by bailiffs, so that stewardships likewise tended to fall into the hands of the local gentry. Stewards had the important responsibility of mobilizing the tenants for military service in an emergency, as on the Stafford estates during Jack Cade's rising.

At the centre of the estate the chief officers were the receiver-general, the chief steward, the surveyor, and the auditors, who, with legal advisers, formed the core of the lord's council. Normally, however, the receiver-general was itinerant, spending two-thirds of the year on the road in a ceaseless effort to get rents in, as did Simon Bennett on the Beauchamp and John Lewys on the Mowbray estates.[26] After discharging administrative expenses, the receiver-general paid the residue to the treasurer of the household or the lord himself. The chief steward was the most senior official, with responsibility for the efficiency of the whole estate. He

[24] S. J. Payling, 'Arbitration, perpetual entails, and collateral warranties in late medieval England', *Jnl. Legal Hist.* 13 (1992), 32–62; J. Biancalana, *The Fee Tail and the Common Recovery in Medieval England* (Cambridge, 2001), 185–260.

[25] A. Sinclair, 'The Beauchamp earls of Warwick in the later Middle Ages', Ph.D. thesis (London University, 1987), ch. 4; C. Rawcliffe, *The Stafford Earls of Stafford and Dukes of Buckingham, 1394–1521* (Cambridge, 1978), ch. 3; Somerville, *Duchy of Lancaster*, 98–102.

[26] Sinclair, 'The Beauchamp earls of Warwick'; R. E. Archer, 'The Mowbrays', D.Phil thesis (Oxford University, 1984); C. D. Ross, *The Estates and Finances of Richard Beauchamp, Earl of Warwick*, Dugdale Society Occasional Papers, 12 (Oxford, 1956).

was always a layman, often a knight or senior lawyer, like Sir Nicholas Lilling on the Beauchamp estates and Sir Thomas Hungerford on the duchy of Lancaster in the late fourteenth century. The chief steward conducted tourns of each lordship to bring local officers under detailed scrutiny, and periodically make a new rental, as on the Stafford estates in 1443. He spent long hours in the saddle. Lords needed to wage a ceaseless battle against corrupt officials at all levels. Local officials were wont to lease land at low rates to their own profit, intimidate tenants and demand bribes, pervert justice, and line their pockets at the lord's expense. Mounting arrears could reflect not economic difficulties but the inefficiency of a receiver or his embezzlement of money. To contend with all this was the task of the auditors, who were habitually clerks and needed to be vigilant and feared. By 1418 there were four auditors on the Beauchamp estates, assigned to different districts, with a central audit at Warwick. Finally, from the audited accounts of both local and general receivers was compiled a valor. This was a statement of the potential clear income from the estate, not a valuation of assets or gross yield, or even of what had been collected in the current year. A handful of such valors from the first half of the fourteenth century bear witness to the desire of lords to have an annual, accessible summary of the mass of local accounts and one which, unlike these, indicated the profitability of the estate. The shift from direct management to rent, and the mounting constraints on landlords, served to popularize the valor, which, by 1400, had attained a standard form. Occasionally an even more summary digest, a certificate of account, would be prepared for the lord's convenience.[27]

Auditors, surveyors, and valors provided a powerful check on embezzlement and inefficiency; yet it was still possible for a lord to be defrauded by his own receiver-general or be ignorant of the abuses of his local officials. The two guarantees against this were, first, the lord's council and, secondly, his personal vigilance. The council had as its core the handful of senior estate and household officers with one or two trusted knights of the lord's retinue and a regular legal adviser, rarely exceeding half a dozen members. For much of the time the officers, meeting by themselves, would appoint officials, settle disputes with tenants, review leases, receive petitions, and keep track of the lord's litigation in the courts. During a lord's minority the heir depended on the loyalty and efficiency of his councillors to preserve his inheritance in good shape, as did a lord absent for long periods in war. The council was particularly well suited to the tasks of negotiating with other landowners and arbitrating in internal disputes between tenants, retainers, and officials.[28] The prestige and authority of a great lord as peacemaker, whether in settling feuds or in resolving tangled property disputes, had to be backed by the legal expertise and records of his council. Registers of letters as well as cartularies of deeds were compiled in magnate chanceries, which were staffed by professional bureaucrats and housed in special buildings within the castle.[29]

Finally, what was the role of the lord himself? It was increasingly normal for him to have a private treasury and privy purse, held by the cofferer, into which surplus revenue was paid and from which his personal expenditure, whether on jewels, debts, or finery, were met. By 1446 Lord Grey of Ruthin was receiving half his income into his privy purse. Considerable sums in cash could be stored in the lord's treasuries, which could be at two or more castles of a large estate. The earl of Arundel's fortune of £60,000 and more in 1376 was exceptional, but even a lord with very modest estates like John, earl of Somerset, left £20,000 at his death in 1410. The expenditure of his wealth actively engaged the lord, but did its acquisition likewise? Lords undoubtedly attended their councils, and Humphrey, earl of Stafford took his on progress through his Welsh estates in 1425 and 1433. As we have seen, the production of valors and certificates apprised lords of their revenues, and some kept their officials under persistent scrutiny, putting queries, checking expenses, and binding them to pay arrears. Among the middle baronage the Berkeleys, Talbots, and Greys of Ruthin sought to improve the profitability of their estates. The horizons and duties of the upper nobility were often broader and they perforce relied more heavily on their chief officials, not always happily in the case of Richard Beauchamp, earl of Warwick, who was defrauded of £3,000 over six years.[30] Always the peerage numbered among them the weak, the feckless, the reckless, and the incompetent, who bequeathed debts to their heirs or mortgaged lands. But it is clear that every lord had the protection of trained and businesslike officers and advisers, and the means, if he were inclined, to control and oversee his inheritance.

3. DOMESTIC CULTURE

Just as the management of his estates depended ultimately on the lord, so to a more personal degree did the life and organization of the household. The household was first and foremost a statement of lordship, of the virtues of magnificence and largesse, and the vices of pride, extravagance, and oppression. Contemporaries read this statement with an informed and critical eye. Was a lord's household too numerous or too small? Did it contain men of repute or flatterers and adventurers? Was it economically run, and did it pay its debts? Noble

---

[29] For the duchy of Lancaster registers, see Somerville, *Duchy of Lancaster*, 115–17, and for the Stafford estates survey, Red Book of Caus, Rawcliffe, *Staffords*, 3.

[30] Ross, *Estates and Finances of Richard Beauchamp*.

households were becoming larger and acquiring a public dimension as lords increasingly made one principal residence their ancestral seat, and late medieval England witnessed a major programme of castle-building. The first phase, in the later fourteenth century, was largely concentrated in the north; the second, from c.1430 to c.1455, was exclusively in the south.

Castles had always fulfilled three functions: as defences against enemies, as statements of lordship, and as residences. The first was now of diminishing importance. Although after 1375 the truce on the northern border was punctuated by raids and skirmishes, the castles built there were not designed to withstand long sieges or heavily armoured assaults, but were refuges and centres for mobilizing resistance. Their more important *raison d'être* was to be symbols of the hegemony of the Percy and Neville families as the king's wardens of the marches. Alnwick and Warkworth for the Percys, Brancepeth and Raby for the Nevilles, were designed as palace fortresses. The seemingly impregnable keep at Warkworth, like the sequence of massive towers linked by a curtain wall at Brancepeth and Raby, crowned with battlemented parapets and machicolations, presented a heavily militarized aspect, but one more eloquent of chivalric lordship than military defence. The tower houses built by the lesser nobility who were clients of these leading families, at Hylton, Chipchase, Belsay, Edlingham, and Langley, similarly boasted octagonal turrets and bartisans, but their fortress aspect was belied by the generous windows of the residential apartments. At Raby the hall, solar, chapel, bedrooms, and accommodation for guests and officers extended along the walls and was incorporated into the towers, and at Warkworth and the smaller tower houses equally capacious accommodation was stacked in the keeps. These were emphatically family houses for the lord and his family, with ample amenities like private garderobes. Between the palaces and the tower houses were the castles built in the rectangular tradition with strong corner towers and sometimes a gatehouse, as at Lumley and Bolton, the latter built by John Lewyn in 1378–90 for Lord Scrope. This had an intricate and highly articulated plan on three floors, with the hall and kitchen at first-floor level and the lord's apartments on the second, in the south-west tower, linked to the chapel. Accommodation for family, guests, and retainers was graded in rooms of different sizes and location.[31]

In southern England there was no military justification for castles (apart from French coastal raids, which ostensibly prompted Dallingridge's erection of Bodiam in 1385). Neither the Crown nor the nobility had in mind the threat of civil war or baronial feuds. Here the pattern had been set by Lord Clinton's Maxstoke (1342–6), a rectangular fortified house with four corner towers and a huge three-storey gatehouse. Though enclosed by a moat, it had no defensive

[31] A. Emery, *Greater Medieval Houses of England and Wales, 1300–1500, i: Northern England* (Cambridge, 1996); for Bolton, M. Hislop, 'Bolton Castle and the practice of architecture in the Middle Ages', *JBAA* 149 (1996), 10–22.

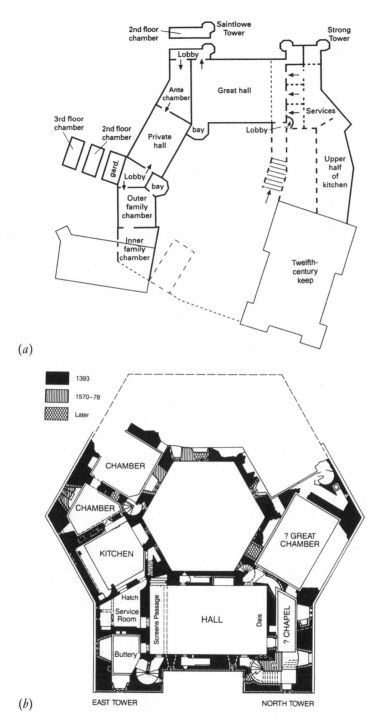

FIG. 4.1. Castle planning: courtyard and tower. (*a*) Kenilworth Castle: first-floor plan. Source: A. Emery, *Greater Medieval Houses of England and Wales*, ii (Cambridge, 2000), 400, fig. 97. (*b*) Old Wardour Castle: first-floor plan of the keep. *Source: Old Wardour Castle*, English Heritage guidebook, 9.

pretensions, with two-light windows on all sides. Its symmetrical formality set the tradition for Bodiam, Hampton, and Herstmonceux. A different tradition had been initiated at Goodrich, built by Aymer de Valence in the first quarter of the century as a rectangular towered enclosure with a closely integrated complex of hall and chamber blocks on three floors. This was developed at Nunney (1373) and Wardour (1393), as seemingly lofty fortress-towers but with compact court-yards and intricately planned accommodation within. This desire to combine maximum military effect with optimum residential comfort was achieved through a display of architectural virtuosity.[32]

On a far more ambitious scale were the palace fortresses of scions of the royal family at Kenilworth and Fotheringhay, which adopted the double courtyard, the outer for the retinue and services, the inner for the lord's apartments. At Kenilworth, Gaunt's great hall of six bays raised on an undercroft, its windows reaching to the roof line, and spanned by a majestic roof, provided the setting for his quasi-regal estate, while from it extended a sequence of rooms for the lord and his family. His brother's palace at Fotheringhay adopted a similar layout. The external aspect of these great palace fortresses was similarly contrived to impress. At Kenilworth, as at Bodiam and later Herstmonceux, the castle rose out of a sheet of water like a romantic vision. More self-consciously martial was Warwick, its residential range set strikingly above the river Avon, and its entrance gatehouse curtain-linked to the lofty Guy's and Caesar's towers, each fortified by a *chemin de ronde*, a frontage executed with spectacular verve.[33]

A new phase opened in the fifteenth century with major castles built on new sites by first-generation nobility. These have been termed 'trophy' castles, built to celebrate the wealth and status attained through the profits of office or war. Ampthill, built by Henry IV's supporter John Cornwaile, Lord Fanhope, was the first, a major, double-courtyard residence of which nothing remains. The 1430s and 1440s saw a spate of such houses, built by Lord Cromwell at Tattershall, Sir John Fastolf at Caister, Lord Hungerford at Farleigh, Lord Stourton at Stourton, Sir Roger Fiennes at Herstmonceux, and Lord Sudeley at Sudeley. All of these boasted two courts with the full range of seigniorial accommodation (Herstmonceux's great rectangle embraced four internal courts); some had encircling moats and all (in Leland's words of Stourton) were 'magnificent and high embateled castelle lyke', with the full apparatus of towers, battlements, machicoulis, portcullis, octagonal turrets, and even gun ports.

---

[32] P. Dixon and B. Lott, 'The courtyard and the tower', *JBAA* 146 (1993), 95; P. Faulkner, 'Castle planning in the fourteenth century', *Arch. Jnl.* 120 (1963). For Goodrich, see Woolgar, *Great Household*, 51–9.

[33] A. Emery, *Greater Medieval Houses, ii: Central England* (Cambridge, 2000). On Bodiam, see *Medieval Archaeology*, 35 (1991), 155–7 and C. Whittick, 'Dallingridge's bog and Bodiam Castle millpond', *Sussex Archaeological Collections*, 131 (1993), 119–23.

Yet the ingenuity required to marry a fortress with a palace imposed strains—vertical suites of rooms in towers and halls rising through two floors—and already a decisive break from the fortress tradition had been made by John Holland, duke of Exeter, at Dartington in 1388–1400.[34] Three features made it distinctive: it was approached through a gatehouse with no portcullis or drawbridge, leading into a large courtyard of domestic buildings, with the hall at the far side. Secondly, the other sides of the courtyard contained ranges of individual chambers for the retinue, some forty to fifty in all. Thirdly, behind the hall was a small courtyard containing, almost certainly, suites of rooms for the lord, his family, and guests. This plan of a central hall range separating inner and outer quadrangles was developed at South Wingfield (1440s), where the inner court lay behind a cross range with a gatehouse. Wingfield was on the grandest scale and of superb workmanship. Like Kenilworth, it had a raised hall (the largest to be built since that at Westminster), a lofty audience chamber lit by an eight-light window, a withdrawing room, and a suite of private apartments; yet it also included a five-storey tower with great chambers on each floor on the pattern of Cromwell's other great structure, at Tattershall, where each room occupied the whole area of the rectangular tower. Tattershall and Herstmonceux were built of brick, as was Caister and some smaller houses of the mid-century, like Hunsdon.

Whatever their size, all these houses were proud exemplars of noble status and dynastic pride. Many displayed the insignia of their owners: the Percy lion at Warkworth, the heraldry of family lineage at Maxstoke and Hylton, the arms of royal patrons at Dartington and Lumley, while at Tattershall and Wingfield Cromwell flaunted his success as lord treasurer with his badge of a purse and the motto 'N'ay je le droit' ('Do not I have the right?').[35] How much they cost is impossible to know, for complete building accounts do not survive. Tattershall and Caister probably cost around £6,000, and Bolton twice as much according to Leland.[36] Some were financed from the perquisites of office, others from the spoils of war. All those built by the new nobility in the fifteenth century represented extraneous profits or windfalls. Only the older comital families could build on this scale out of the surplus from their landed income, and after 1400 strikingly few chose to do so. It was the *arrivistes* who felt impelled to assert their presence with grandiose structures in an anachronistic military mode, their castellated walls and turrets, massive keeps, and broad moats underlining the isolation from the rest of society of an elite with a lifestyle as governors and paradigms of chivalry.

[34] A. Emery, *Dartington Hall* (Oxford, 1970). For Fastolf's Caister, see Woolgar, *Great Household*, 63–7.

[35] R. L. Friedrichs, 'Ralph Lord Cromwell and the politics of fifteenth century England', *Nottingham Med. Stud.* 32 (1988), 11–12.

[36] McFarlane, *Nobility*, 93–4, 196.

The lord's principal residence had to accommodate an ever enlarging household. Calculations of size are complicated by different types of sources and different definitions of the household. Livery rolls, like that of the earl of Devon for 1384–5, embrace non-resident retainers, while 'kalendars' of those fed daily in the household include visitors.[37] A baronial household like that of Lord Grey of Ruthin may have numbered some 50 persons, the major comital households of Devon and Warwick around 100, with those of Gaunt in the 1390s and Buckingham in 1450 rising to 150.[38] To estimate household costs is correspondingly difficult. Expenditure reflected the rank and circumstances of the individual lord: John of Gaunt's household cost over £5,750 in 1376 rising to £7,000 in 1392, and this was more than twice the level of the earl of Stafford's half a century later, which in turn was double the cost of the establishment maintained by Margaret of Brotherton, who, out of an income of £2,839, spent little more than £1,000 on her household. As a proportion of disposable income the household rarely cost less than 50 per cent and could rise towards 75 per cent.[39]

Like that of the king, a nobleman's household was organized into an upper part concerned with its ceremonial and a lower concerned with material provision. Contemporary treatises on household management, like the *Boke of Nurture* by John Russell, marshal of the hall to Humphrey, duke of Gloucester, prescribed in detail the rules for seating in hall according to degree, for serving and carving at the lord's table, and for table manners and conversation. The principal meal, at midday, might last two to three hours and was a ritual display of a lord's 'magnificence' and hospitality. The servants who attended the lord's person were all of gentle birth and all male; they included a variety of semi-specialized professionals such as apothecaries, physicians, minstrels, confessors, almoners, and the cofferer, or keeper of his privy purse. The lady had gentlewomen attendants and probably her own confessor. Household service at its higher levels was an honourable occupation which conferred gentility and was a ladder of opportunity for those with aptitude.[40]

Provisioning by the lower household was done by purveyance in the locality and increasingly by purchase at local market towns, like Warwick and Dunster; smaller households, such as that of Elizabeth de Burgh, drew proportionately more from their own local estates. Diet varied with the locality. Fish, both fresh and preserved, was a major element of diet and was transported from coastal

[37] McFarlane, *Nobility*, 110–13.

[38] C. Given-Wilson, *The English Nobility in the Late Middle Ages* (London, 1987), 88–9; Rawcliffe, *Staffords*, 69; Jack, *Grey of Ruthin*, 53; S. K. Walker, *The Lancastrian Affinity, 1361–1399* (Oxford, 1990), 11.

[39] Walker, *The Lancastrian Affinity*, 18; K. Mertes, *The English Noble Household, 1250–1600* (Oxford, 1988), chs. 2, 3; Given-Wilson, *English Nobility*, 93–4; Archer, 'Margaret of Brotherton', 274–5.   [40] Woolgar, *Great Household*, ch. 3 and 160–5.

areas. Over half the food expenditure in the Stafford household in 1452 was on fish and meat, fresh meat being increasingly available throughout the year as conversion to pasture gave a surplus of hay for winter feeding. Otherwise animals were killed for stock at Martinmas. Beef, pork, mutton, and poultry were most favoured, though game reserves and rabbit warrens added variety to the diet: in 1431–2 the earl of Oxford's household consumed thirty-six deer. Comital households consumed victuals in vast quantities: figures of 30,000–40,000 gallons of ale and of 32,372 lb of meat a year appear in the Stafford and Vere accounts of the fifteenth century. Gentle and non-gentle members of the household had different dietary regimes. At each meal the gentlemen were served with ¾ lb of fish, 1–1½ lb of meat, 2 pints of ale, and ½ lb of bread. There were two meals a day except on days of abstinence, providing a daily intake of some 6,800–7,800 kcal or even more—about three times the level of a modern diet. Lords generally ate less red meat and more poultry and delicacies, and the non-gentle members were served with less meat and fish in general. Roasted meat was served only to the gentlemen (for others it was boiled), while as much attention was given to the presentation of the food as to its taste.. Some food was purchased from urban suppliers, notably stockfish in bulk and delicacies like boar, swan, oysters, sturgeon, and lampreys if such were not locally available. Wine, too, was purchased, in pipes of 120 gallons, though its price at four to eight pence a gallon made it a strictly aristocratic drink. Households baked their bread and had their own cottage industries, notably making butter, cheese, and ale, but also using carcasses to make hides, candles, cooking fat, and rough clothing. Little would be wasted.[41]

Food had to be provided not only for members but for guests. Hospitality was both a virtue and an obligation, but this did not mean either keeping open house or inviting only personal friends. Hospitality was a social ritual emphasizing the integrity of the household against strangers but also the protection which the lord's authority provided. *The Boke of Curtasye* (1430–40) prescribes how the stranger, on his arrival at the gatehouse, must deliver his sword to the porter, and be conducted to the hall, where he doffs his hood and shoes, and stands at the screens until assigned his place by the marshal of the hall. The lord's equals dined in his chamber or at the dais in hall, the lesser men on tables with their equals. This graded ascent from the gatehouse to the inner chamber was reserved to few. Many visitors were there on business—the lord's estate officials, lawyers, or perhaps local gentry—while the poor and the wayfarers would be fed at the kitchen gate and given alms. Invited guests were likely to be local gentry

[41] C. Dyer, *Standards of Living in the Later Middle Ages* (Cambridge, 1989), 55–70; Woolgar, *Great Household*, ch. 6; id., 'Diet and consumption in noble and gentry households', in Archer and Walker (eds.), *Rulers and Ruled*, 17–34; id., 'Fast and feast', in M. Hicks (ed.), *Revolution and Consumption in Late Medieval England* (Woodbridge, 2001), 7–26.

and, on Sundays, clergy, the lord's social inferiors;[42] peers normally only visited each other by arrangement, as when journeying on business. No lord would arrive unannounced with his full riding household, expecting to be entertained.

If largesse was an aristocratic virtue, it could only be indulged by careful household management. All households tended to increase in size and cost. The feeding of unauthorized guests, the embezzlement of supplies by servants, and extravagance in personal consumption were habitual. How, and how far, could these be kept in check? Contemporaries saw the key in daily accounting, which had become widespread by 1400. George Ashby advised lords to

> Take you to live of youre own properte
> of youre revenues, lyvelode and rent,
> propornouning after the quantite
> youre expenses by youre oune jugement.[43]

Each night the total consumed was costed in cash and logged as *dieta* in a journal, to provide daily and weekly patterns of expenditure. The accounts of Gilbert, Lord Talbot, in 1417–18 give the total cost of the household, its average weekly cost, the total cost of each department, and the average cost of each portion served. The written accounts of the clerks of departments and of the treasurer of the household came under the scrutiny of the steward and auditors (of whom *The Boke of Curtasye* lamented that 'few are true, many false') and took their place alongside the receiver-general's account and the valor to give the lord an overview of his income and principal domestic charges. Some households did demonstrably take action to check or reduce rising costs.[44]

Food was relatively cheap, leaving money available for expenditure on costly furnishings and possessions. Surviving inventories, taken when a household was dispersed, rarely give the value of these, but Thomas of Woodstock's goods at Pleshey and London in 1397 were valued at £2,200 and Lord Scrope's movables (excluding money) at about £5,000 in 1415. Inventories provide a vivid and telling picture of aristocratic wealth and taste. Among the repetitious lists of rugs, cushions, basins, candlesticks, and salvers are mentioned such items as the large tapestry depicting the legend of Charlemagne at Pleshey, the arras in Fastolf's hall at Caister showing the siege of Falaise, and Scrope's tent of blue cord with six towers. In the personal wardrobe of the lord or lady were dresses, hoods, capes, and gowns, many lined with fur or worked with gold and silver thread, while the chapel was a veritable treasury of crucifixes, reliquaries, and

[42] As in V. B. Redstone (ed.), *The Household Book of Dame Alice de Bryene, 1412–13* (Ipswich, 1931).

[43] George Ashby, 'Active Policy of a Prince', lines 274–7, in id., *Poems*, ed. M. Bateson, EETS, extra ser., 76 (London, 1899), 21.

[44] Dyer, *Standards of Living*, 94–9; C. M. Woolgar (ed.), *Household Accounts from Medieval England*, i (Oxford, 1992), chs. 3, 4.

monstrances set with an abundance of precious stones, along with whole wardrobes of vestments—Lord Scrope's chapel containing ninety-two copes. All this reflected an increasingly residentiary and ceremonial style of living, coupled with a concern for personal comfort.[45]

But the household was more than meat and drink, a costly and sumptuous setting, and an administrative centre. It was a community with a daily framework of education, religion, and amusement, all expressive of the reciprocity of lordship and service. It was unusual for the resident family of the lord to comprise more than himself, his wife, and their under-age children. Dowagers, uncles, and nephews normally had their own estates, and there was no tradition of an extended household sheltering under the family roof. Even the lord's own children were not infrequently sent to another noble household at an early age. That did not mean that the lord and lady lived in splendid isolation. Guests and visitors were frequent, while the sons of other noble and gentle families might correspondingly board with them. In particular the custody of a ward made a significant addition to the household, extending into the first years of his marriage if, while still a minor, he married the lord's own daughter. Richard of York, who married the 9-year-old Cecily Neville in 1424, remained in the custody and household of her father and later mother until 1430. The ward's upbringing would be monitored by his custodian, who would not hesitate to impose a regimen, as Henry VI did on the young duke of Norfolk in 1435, to prohibit adolescent habits or undesirable associations that might become addictive. Corporal punishment was in general approved, but an overbearing guardian, such as York himself was to his son-in-law Henry Holland, provoked lasting resentment. Either at home or, quite frequently, as a guest elsewhere, a noble boy received his education within the household. What kind of education was it?

Childhood was conventionally divided into three phases: *infantia* up to the age of 7, *pueritia* from 7 to 14, and *adolescentia* from 14 to 21. During the first of these the children of the nobility would generally live in the parental home under the charge of their mother and nurses, one of whom of gentle stock would be governess, like Catherine Swynford for Gaunt's children. Children were cherished as heirs and carefully educated. At 6 or 7 the boy was given a governor, who would instruct him in *lettrure* and *nourritrure*. Book learning began at 4 with the alphabet, followed by reading and writing in English and French (*langage*), and at 7 he would begin Latin, learning the rules of composition and syntax from a primer and becoming familiar with liturgical texts. Normally, as in the Roos household, it was one of the chaplains who instructed the lord's sons.

More characteristic of aristocratic education was *nourritrure*, courtly etiquette. Though learnt primarily by example, short treatises in verse were written for the

[45] McFarlane, *Nobility*, 96–8; for the Caister inventory, see Woolgar, *Great Household*, 66–7.

young in the fifteenth century: *The Babees Boke*, *Stans Puer ad Mensam*, *The Boke of Curtasye*, all indicative of an increasingly literate culture. These set forth the rules not only for table manners but for decorous and disciplined behaviour in adult society, while the *Distichs of Cato* inculcated practical morality in the Stoic tradition. From his own observation the boy would learn to recognize gradations in rank, and he would be set to memorize heraldic arms. Fourteen or fifteen was the age for bearing arms, when his governor would instruct him in martial and equestrian arts: to use a sword and lance, to tilt at the quintrain and practise in the lists. It was in such practice that the young heir of the earl of Salisbury was accidentally killed by his father in 1382.[46]

Training in horsemanship, the management of weapons and knowledge of the terrain was also acquired in the hunt, which combined the pleasure of exercise with an element of danger. Hardyng extols its value in developing manliness:

> For dere to hunt and sla[y] and se thaym blede,
> Ane hardyment gyffith to his corage,
> And also in his wytte he taketh hede
> Ymagynynge to take theym at avauntage.[47]

Hunting, like the tournament, was the jealously guarded preserve of the aristocracy, with its own technical language, rules governing the chase, servants and dogs as functionaries, and rituals to be observed in the slaying and dismembering of the quarry. The hunt was an affirmation of social harmony and solidarity, provided as an act of hospitality, preceded by the brotherhood of the Mass, and followed by that of a great feast. It figured in literary culture, as the background for the trials of Gawain and as a manual for the aristocracy in *The Master of Game*, translated from the French of Gaston Phoebus by Edward, duke of York. Women could take part in the chase, though some held that they should not be present at the kill. Falconry had a similar status and appeal, hawks being costly to acquire and train, and hawking having its own language and complicated rituals. Here too women participated. Field sports linked man into the natural world, bonding with animals and managing wildlife. The culmination of the youth's education came when, after the age of 16, he served as an esquire in a lord's retinue, both in peace and in war. Hardyng, as a youth in Hotspur's household, fought in border skirmishes, and of the sixteen witnesses in the Grey versus Hastings armorial dispute, all but one had campaigned at the age of 16.

---

[46] N. Orme, *From Childhood to Chivalry* (London, 1984), chs. 1–3; *Complete Peerage*, xi. 391; J. Gillingham, 'From *civilitas* to civility: Codes of manners in medieval and early modern England', *TRHS*, 6th ser., 12 (2002), 267–90.

[47] Hardyng, *Chronicle*, ed. Ellis, pp. i–ii; N. Orme, 'Medieval hunting', in B. Hanawalt (ed.), *Chaucer's England* (Minneapolis, 1992), 133–53.

Far less is known about the education of the daughters of the nobility, and treatises confined themselves to counsel on marriage and household management. Daughters mainly learned embroidery, dancing, and singing, and rarely had their own tutors. Often reared at nunneries from 7 to 10 or 14, they were then sent to board in other noble households including that of their parents-in-law if they were already married, unless indeed they stayed on at the convent to become professed. Though many learned to read, and had more leisure and inclination to do so than men, few were taught Latin, and those devotees of saints' lives and devotional treatises, like Cecily Neville and Margaret Holland, had these translated for them.

All peers were literate to the extent of reading English and probably French and signing their name. Their reading of Latin was normally restricted to administrative and liturgical usage and their letters were usually written by secretaries, though when circumstances or secrecy required some could pen them with their own hand.[48] Few wrote anything more ambitious; Henry of Lancaster had no successor in this period, though William de la Pole and Thomas Montagu wrote poems. The literary culture of the nobility can only be discussed in terms of the books they owned and the works they patronized; it is virtually impossible to be certain of how much they read and absorbed. Evidence for book ownership is imperfect, coming almost wholly from inventories and wills. The 120 volumes forfeit by Thomas of Woodstock in 1397 and the 80 by Henry, Lord Scrope, in 1415 were probably exceptional, and many of the nobility may have owned less than two score. Bequests to individuals reflected more personal tastes, comprising primers, Mass books, books of hours, lives of saints, and the works of the English mystics Richard Rolle and Walter Hilton. Such books were clearly for private and silent reading, but lectern-type volumes, including most chivalric romances and histories, would be read aloud to the lord in his chamber or in public in the household. A lament for Sir John Berkeley, who died abroad in 1375, recalls how he enjoyed the

> Daliance of damisels to drive away tho day
> To rede him oright romance were redi on (ar)ay.[49]

More than half Simon Burley's books in 1387 and nineteen of Thomas of Woodstock's books in 1397 were of this kind, though Scrope's were all religious. From the middle of the fourteenth century works on political theory were increasingly popular, notably translations into French of Giles of Rome. Only with the humanist library of Duke Humphrey and the personal scholarship of

---

[48] McFarlane, *Nobility*, 241, for Lord Bourchier's letter written in captivity in 1374, and M. D. Legge (ed.), *Anglo-Norman Letters*, Anglo Norman Text Society (Oxford, 1941).

[49] T. Turville-Petre, 'The Lament for Sir John Berkeley', *Speculum*, 57 (1982), 332-9, lines 43-4.

John, Lord Tiptoft, do classical texts appear to any extent in noble collections. Taken across its whole range, from devotional works through romances to history and political theory, this literature could have provided a varied intellectual diet. But did the nobility read the books they owned? Books were treated as luxury furnishings, their bindings embossed and the pages heavily illuminated, and they were often exchanged as presents. Evidence of personal annotation of a book by any noble other than Duke Humphrey is virtually non-existent. Yet the nobility must have absorbed some of the content of the books they listened to or read.

The evidence for literary patronage is scarcely easier to interpret. Authors sought patrons for works both written and projected, and claims that the patron had commissioned the work and suggested the theme, like any praise of his discrimination, should be treated with reserve. Yet the numerous instances when noble patronage was invoked at least suggest that the nobility provided an audience for serious-minded poetry and prose about philosophy, love, political morality, and chivalric honour, and looked to history as a pattern for action in its own day.

Perhaps the best example of consistent patronage is provided by Thomas, Lord Berkeley, whose chaplain and secretary John Trevisa made major English translations at his behest. Trevisa's translation of Higden's *Polychronicon* (1387), the *De Regimine Principum*, and Bartholomeus Anglicus' *De Proprietatibus Rerum* (1398) provided a conspectus of world history, government, and the created world for the educated layman. His successor as chaplain, John Walton, translated Vegetius' *De Re Militari* for Lord Berkeley in 1408 and Boethius for his daughter Elizabeth.[50] After 1400 English rapidly gained ground for serious reading, actively promoted by Prince Henry's commissions to Lydgate and Hoccleve, and numerous surviving manuscripts of *The Fall of Princes* and *The Regement of Princes* demonstrate the popularity of this didactic, moralizing, and quasi-historical material. Lords looked to such works for practical guidance. The earl of Ormond had James Yonge translate the *Secretum* to assist him to rule Ireland, and the translation of Claudian's *De Consulatu Stiliconis*, made for the duke of York as Protector, had a contemporary political message, while Walter, Lord Hungerford, was said to have encouraged the production of *The Libelle of English Polycye*.[51] Chivalry was a firm favourite, whether as adaptations of Vegetius, as in *Knyghthode and Bataile*, sponsored by Viscount Beaumont for presentation to Henry VI, as family history in *The Life of Guy of Warwick*, commissioned by Margaret Beauchamp in 1425, or as the lessons to be learned from defeat in

[50] R. Hanna, 'Sir Thomas Berkeley and his patronage', *Speculum*, 64 (1989), 878–916; R. Waldron, 'John Trevisa and the use of English', *PBA* 74 (1988), 171–202; D. C. Fowler, *John Trevisa, Medieval Scholar* (Seattle, 1995), ch. 4.

[51] On *De Consulatu Stiliconis* compare J. Watts, 'Texts and politics in the reign of Henry VI', *Jnl. Med. Hist.* 16 (1990), 251–66, and S. Delany, 'Bokenham's Claudian as Yorkist propaganda', *Jnl. Med. Hist.* 22 (1996), 83–96.

The Boke of Noblesse. Although Hoccleve warned Sir John Oldcastle that Vegetius, Lancelot, and the *Siege of Troy* were more suitable reading for a knight than was theology, orthodox devotional works were commissioned and read by both sexes of the aristocracy. Hoccleve's *Complaint of the Virgin* was written for Joan, countess of Hereford, and Lady Bourchier suggested the life of Mary Magdalen as a suitable subject for the pen of Osbert Bokenham in 1445.

In the later fourteenth century the language of the court nobility was French and their literary tastes adhered to the tradition of courtly romance. Beyond the court was a regional culture and language with strong traditions in the West Country and the north-west. Experiments in the vernacular reflect this. Lord Berkeley's programme of English translations, the production of the Simeon and Vernon manuscripts from the same area, the alliterative tradition of *Gawain* and *Pearl* from the Cheshire–Derbyshire borders, all reveal an aristocratic culture centred on the castle and manor house, even if transmitted via its patrons to the court.[52] In the early fifteenth century this tradition of provincial aristocratic patronage was subsumed into the court-centred promotion of translations of works of practical relevance in the fields of politics, history, war, morality, and devotion.

4. RELIGION

Just as the rituals of the hall displayed the lord's political rule of his household, so those of the castle chapel marked his governance of its spiritual life. It provided the setting for daily worship and for the occasional rites of passage of the lord's family, at baptisms, marriages, and deaths, while his own devotional preferences might be expressed in the relics it housed, the feasts celebrated, and the sermons preached in it. The rich furnishings, with books, vestments, and chalices bearing the lord's arms, and its complement of chaplains and choristers, were a statement of his magistracy in the spiritual sphere. The religion of the nobility was conditioned both by contemporary patterns of devotion and by their social position. Late medieval piety focused on the Mass as an intercessory and expiatory penance for the burden of sin. The increasing emphasis on the individual's conscience and responsibility, on the one hand, and on the doctrine of purgatory with its requirement of continuing generational responsibility for the soul of an ancestor on the other, accorded with the nobility's sense of pre-eminence and patriarchy.[53] Hence, in this century the wealth of the nobility went far less into monastic foundations than into chantries and colleges of secular priests.

[52] A. I. Doyle, 'English books in and out of court', in V. Scattergood and J. Sherborne (eds.), *English Court Culture in the Late Middle Ages* (London, 1983), 163–81.

[53] Mertes, *Noble Household*, ch. 5; J. I. Catto, 'Religion and the English nobility in the later fourteenth century', in H. Lloyd Jones, V. Pearl, and B. Worden (eds.), *History and Imagination* (London, 1981), 43–55.

A perpetual chantry required an endowment in land sufficient to produce an income of 10 marks a year for each priest, and most of those founded by the nobility supported more than one. Cost was not the only problem. To procure a licence to alienate land to the Church in mortmain was a long and uncertain business, requiring much lobbying and the payment of a steep fine. Walter, Lord Hungerford, in 1423 and Richard, earl of Warwick, in 1437 only obtained permission to found chantries by undertaking service in France. Most chantries were established in local parish or collegiate churches, but some families who were long-standing patrons of a religious house made it their own mausoleum, as did the Montagus at Bisham Abbey, the Mowbrays at Axholme Priory, and the Veres at Earl's Colne Priory. Mendicant churches were generally popular, those in London like the Grey Friars in Newgate and the Black Friars becoming so crowded with chantry tombs that by 1436 Lord Fanhope had to erect his in the Blackfriars churchyard. Many fewer were erected by the nobility in cathedrals, except where there was a close local or family connection, like the Hungerfords at Salisbury and the Nevilles at Durham.[54]

The problem of how to prevent an endowment from being alienated was met by passing land to feoffees, who were charged to build and maintain a chantry and even to appoint the chantry priest. Yet such a permanent detraction from the inheritance might be unwelcome to the widow and next heir, producing a familial conflict between piety and prudence. Testators commonly invoked divine judgement on executors and feoffees, exhorting them, as did Humphrey Stafford in 1463, not to forget his soul, so that 'I have no cause to crye upon you at the dredefull day of Dome'.[55] Understandably, then, this was something which many attended to in their lifetime, like Lord Hungerford, who began his in Salisbury Cathedral in 1429, buried his first wife in it in 1438, and was himself buried there in 1449.[56] For his great chantry and chapel in Warwick church Richard Beauchamp conveyed lands to feoffees in 1425, leaving instructions for its construction in his will in 1439, and being eventually buried there in 1475 after it had cost at least £3,634.[57] Chantries might also be established as expiatory acts for those killed in a feud or quarrel, as was that at King's Langley in 1386 by John Holland for the murder of Ralph Stafford.

The most prestigious form of commemoration, characteristic of this period, was the foundation of a college of chantry priests and choristers. Such frequently originated in a plan to upgrade the castle chapel, as at Newark, Arundel, and

---

[54] J. T. Rosenthal, *The Purchase of Paradise* (London, 1972), chs. 3, 4, and below, Ch. 10, sect. 2.

[55] F. W. Weaver (ed.), *Somerset Medieval Wills*, Somerset Record Society, 16 (London, 1901), 197.

[56] M. A. Hicks, 'Walter, Lord Hungerford (d. 1449) and his chantry in Salisbury Cathedral', *Hatcher Review*, 28 (1989), 391–9.

[57] M. A. Hicks, 'The Beauchamp Trust, 1439–87', *BIHR* 54 (1981), 140.

Warkworth, and then, by extension, to convert or even reconstruct the adjacent parish church as a college. These successive stages marked the foundation of Fotheringhay between 1398 and 1415, which became a mausoleum for the house of York.[58] At Staindrop the Nevilles' chantry in the parish church was to be served from collegiate buildings alongside, and at Stoke by Clare, Edmund, earl of March, was able to refound the near-defunct alien priory of his ancestors in 1413 as a college of Augustinian canons. Many of these chantry colleges incorporated almshouses for the indigent and old servants of the lord. Tattershall supported twenty-six bedesmen and women, Staindrop eighteen pensioners, some of them gentlefolk, while similar hospital foundations by de la Pole at Ewelme (1437) and by Hungerford at Heytesbury (1442) had schools attached. Nevertheless, the almshouse served primarily to provide intercession for the soul of the founder, not social relief. All such foundations were physically or emotionally linked to the residence and burial place of the family, perpetuating the ties between the departed lord and his *familia*, by continuing intercession for his soul and the enjoyment of his endowment and spiritual protection. The only foundations of religious houses by the nobility were the Charterhouses at Hull by de la Pole, at Coventry by Zouche, at Axholme by Mowbray, and at Mountgrace by Holland, and all had occurred before 1400.

In addition to these new foundations, the nobility both in their lifetime and in their wills enriched their chapels and churches with vessels, vestments, service books, and relics. Lord Lovell commissioned for his own chapel a magnificent lectionary illustrated by John Siferwas. William Lord Botreaux, for lack of a male heir, left £1,000 for books and vestments for each of the parishes in his patronage, and Edmund, earl of March, bequeathed portions of the true cross and bones of English saints to the family abbey at Wigmore.[59] They enlarged and beautified the fabric of their parish churches, building not only their chantry chapels but bell towers and, as patrons, the chancel. They filled the windows with painted glass, as did the Roos family at York Minster, while at Trotton (Sussex) Lord Camoys commissioned a scheme of wall paintings depicting the seven works of mercy and deadly sins. The nobility fulfilled their obligation to use their wealth for the benefit of the Church, but in ways that advertised their worldly dignity and power as patrons. Their elaborate tombs, often fashioned according to their detailed instructions, carried their effigy in alabaster or stone, with weepers figuring relatives, companions, or penitents. Some, like Lord Camoys, figured with their wives on large monumental brasses, under elaborate canopies and with inscriptions asking for prayers for their souls. On these, as on much else that they built or commissioned, they placed their coat of arms to affirm their patronage and the continuity of their lineage.

[58] A. Hamilton Thompson, 'Fotheringhay', *Arch. Jnl.* 75 (1918).
[59] 'The Lovell Lectionary', BL, Harley MS 7026, fo. 4ᵛ; *Test. Vet.* i. 111, 191.

Great significance was attached to the rites of passage, which were prescribed in detail in wills. In the funeral procession the lord's warhorses, armour, and helm, emblems of his knightly status, preceded his *familia*, clad in black, and a suitable contingent of the poor, carrying torches and candles. Banners with the coat of arms would be displayed on the pillars of the church, and continuous intercession made at the tomb to fulfil the one, five, or ten thousand masses which men of the status of Richard Beauchamp (1439) or William, Lord Bergavenny (1408), desired in all haste for the safety of their souls. Yet not all subscribed to this public display. For some, a sense of spiritual unworthiness and the transitory character of temporal privilege found expression in their last rites. From 1359, when Henry of Lancaster desired nothing vain or extravagant at his funeral and in particular forbade armed men bearing his coat of arms, a significant number of the nobility before 1410 reacted against a costly and showy funeral. At this point the prayers of the poor were deemed of special value: Humphrey Bohun, earl of Hereford (d. 1361), ordered that no great men be invited, and Guichard d'Angle (d. 1380), a soldier of renown, would have no hearse, arms, or banners, and ordered the money saved to be given to the poor.[60] This puritanical element in the fourteenth-century conscience also, though less frequently, found expression in language denigrating the body and earthly renown. Under his copper-gilt effigy in full armour in Canterbury the Black Prince set an inscription describing himself as a poor caitiff, now deeply laid in earth, and reminding others that they would be as he. But such language was rarer in the wills of the nobility than the gentry, just as the placing of a cadaver beneath the sumptuously clothed figure on the tomb was confined to those of John, earl of Arundel (d. 1435), and Alice, duchess of Suffolk (d. 1475).[61] At one level this funerary austerity was a fashion, recognized and deplored as such by clerical writers. Did it also reflect the influence of contemporary penitential and contemplative writing on the individual?

Something may be gleaned from their books and wills about their devotions. None of the nobility in this century wrote of their spiritual life in terms comparable to Henry of Lancaster's *Livre de Seyntz Medicines*. Though hardly representative of his peers, his catalogue of the desires through which sin enters and corrupts the soul vividly illustrates the pleasures of the aristocratic lifestyle. The concern to accumulate property, to exact revenue, to over-indulge in feasting, to covet furs and fine clothes, to have women, to envy and emulate neighbours, to boast, to find excitement in hunting and fighting rather than in devotions, all served to alienate him from God. The honesty and intensity of his self-scrutiny

[60] *Test. Vet.* i. 109, 171; Warwick' s will, in T. Hearne (ed.), *Historia Vitae et Regni Ricardi Secundi* (1729), 242.

[61] P. King, 'Cadaver tombs and the commemoration of women in fifteenth century England', in L. Visser-Fuchs (ed.), *Tant d'emprises—So many Undertakings, The Ricardian*, xiii (2003), 294–314.

had clearly been developed through confession, just as the remedies which he applied as medicine are those popularized by the fourteenth-century Church: the intercession of the Virgin, and meditation upon the sufferings and sacrifice of Christ the Redeemer. The influence of the mystics is apparent in the personalized relation with Christ, the conflict between flesh and spirit, and the interpenetration of the divine and natural order.[62]

Some noblemen practised daily meditation and examination with their confessors and perhaps on their own. Henry Beauchamp, duke of Warwick, said every day 'unless he had great business' the entire psalter, which he knew by heart.[63] The works of the English mystics Hilton and Rolle, and penitential and catechetical literature like Waddington's *Manuel des Péchés*, all featured in noblemen's libraries. Doubtless no more than a handful had the 'sophisticated liturgical and theological understanding' displayed by members of the Hungerford family, whose detailed regulations for their chapels at Farleigh and Salisbury, like those of Thomas Montagu for his at Bisham, and Edward of York's at Fotheringhay, specified the cycle of masses and special collects, and a sequence of prayers for the chantry priest to say.[64] If more private and personal, how eclectic and idiosyncratic was the religion of the nobility? Did it ever stray into heterodoxy and Lollardy?

Only John Oldcastle (Lord Cobham) and John Montagu, earl of Salisbury, can be identified with any certainty as holding Lollard beliefs, and neither was typical of their class. Whatever the attractions of religious simplicity and austerity for some, their belief in purgatory was linked to their sense of lineage, while Wyclif's doctrine of dominion was anathema to them as landlords, and as rulers they treated Lollards as subversive. Nor is there any indication that they favoured disendowment of the Church and were greedy for its lands. Their rights of patronage were used for the benefit of their *familia* and even younger sons. In short, they were directly linked into the ecclesiastical system.

The religion of noblewomen was distinctive but not essentially different from that of their husbands. Whether as wives or, for a prolonged period, as widows, they were immersed in affairs of family, household, and estates, and few were able to conduct their life as a cycle of prayer, worship, and devotional reading such as that ascribed to Cecily, duchess of York, in her old age.[65] Their devotions

---

[62] E. J. F. Arnould (ed.), *Le Livre de Seyntz Medicines*, Anglo-Norman Text Society (Oxford, 1940); similarly the will of Edward, duke of York (1415), in *Reg. Chichele*, ii. 64.

[63] C. Ross (ed.), *The Rous Roll* (Gloucester, 1980), no. 54.

[64] Hicks, 'Walter, Lord Hungerford and his chantry'; id., 'Four studies in conventional piety', *Southern History*, 13 (1991), 1–21; *Reg. Chichele*, ii. 391.

[65] R. E. Archer, 'Piety in question: Noblewomen and religion in the later Middle Ages', in D. Wood (ed.), *Women and Religion in Medieval England* (Oxford, 2003), 118–40; C. A. J. Armstrong, 'The piety of Cecily duchess of York', in D. Woodruff (ed.), *For Hilaire Belloc* (London, 1942), 73–94.

tended to be focused on their books of hours, and in some which they commissioned they are depicted praying to the Virgin face to face, expressive of a visu-
alized sense of communion with the divine. Their personal devotions are also
indicated in the prayers which Mary Bohun inserted into her father's psalter, and
the spiritual exercises in the Simeon manuscript belonging to her sister Joan.
Some commissioned devotional works, like the life of St Jerome translated for
Margaret, duchess of Clarence, by Simon Wynter, monk of Syon, and an English
verse life of Saint Elisabeth of Hungary for Elizabeth, countess of Oxford.[66]
While the Bridgettine house at Syon was a focus for the instruction and piety of
these aristocratic women, none in fact surrendered their wealth and took the veil.
Nor did their favouring of the 'new devotion' abate their addiction to the traditional forms of commemoration. Like their husbands they provided masses for
their souls—Lady Cobham in 1369 wanted 7,000, to be said by mendicants—and
gave elaborate instructions for their funerals: Joan, Lady Bergavenny, required
hers to be conducted 'with alle the worship that ought to be don unto a woman of
myne estate. . . . not of no pompe or veynglory that I am sette ynne for my body,
but for a memorial and a remembraunce of my soule to my kyn, frendes, ser-
vantes and alle other'. Some founded chantries, or devoted themselves to building and enlarging that of their husband, as did Lady Margaret Hungerford at
Salisbury and Joan Cantilupe at Lincoln. Many made charitable bequests, like
Elizabeth, countess of Salisbury (1414), to the poor and bedridden.[67] Attended
by their chaplains and confessors, welcoming mendicants, and visiting shrines,
recluses, and anchorites, the overall impression of these noblewomen's religion
is of an instructed and self-contained pattern of devotional practice. Any conflict
or intensity in their spiritual life escapes us, unless in the prescription for her
effigy left by Isabel, countess of Warwick: 'all naked with my hair back . . . with
Mary Magdalen laying her hand across and St John the Evangelist on one
side and St Anthony on the other'.[68] Even here an element of exhibitionism,
inseparable from the aristocratic life, is present.

  A distinctive concern in female devotions was, of course, for the propagation of
an heir and the attendant dangers of maternity. The perpetuation of the lineage
laid an additional burden on noblewomen, encouraging devotion to the Virgin and
cult of the Holy Family. Most made a pilgrimage to the shrines of Our Lady at
Walsingham and St Margaret of Antioch (the patron saint of women in labour).[69]

[66] Test. Vet. i. 148; L. F. Sandler, 'Images of devotion', in D. Gordon, L. Monnas, and C. Elam
(eds.), The Regal Image of Richard II and the Wilton Diptych (London, 1997), 143 and pl. 74. G. R.
Keiser, 'Patronage and piety in fifteenth century England', Yale University Library Gazette (1985),
32–46.   [67] Test. Vet. i. 81, 127, 183, 239; Reg. Chichele, ii. 535.
    [68] King, 'Cadaver tombs', 309.
    [69] C. Rawcliffe, 'Women, childbirth, and religion in late medieval England', in Wood (ed.),
Women and Religion, 91–117.

For noblemen pilgrimage more often had a political or dynastic connotation. When that of St John of Bridlington was popularized by Lancastrian patronage, members of the court peerage like Thomas, earl of Arundel, vowed to visit it every year. Devotion to the place of Christ's birth and crucifixion was central to the chivalric ethic, and for every nobleman pilgrimage to the Holy Land was a supreme spiritual obligation. Some, like Lord Hungerford, undertook it in their youth; in the Pageant of Richard Beauchamp, earl of Warwick, it is depicted as a decorous diplomatic visit.[70] For others the opportunity came only with disgrace, as for Thomas Mowbray exiled in 1398, or was imposed as a penance for murder, as for Lord Clifford in 1391. The journey was always made from Venice, touching the coast and islands of the Aegean, but never without danger from pirates, shipwreck, and disease. For the earl of Stafford in 1386 and Lord Roos in 1393 it became a final resting place.

5. CHIVALRY AND WAR

Leadership in war was the principal function of the nobility both as commanders and as exponents of the chivalric ethic. Chivalry drew on old and deep traditions. It demanded skill in arms, ruthlessness in battle, courage, and endurance; and it brought worldly acclaim, wealth, and power. It celebrated individual prowess and reward, but also had political, social, and religious dimensions. The knight upheld the social order in enforcing law, protecting the weak, and, as a *miles Christi*, defending the faith and the Church. The very rituals of admission to knighthood had a religious connotation: purification by bathing, vestment in a white robe, girding with the belt and sword of justice, the taking of vows, the vigil, and testing. Conversely the knight's internal struggle against sin could be represented as 'dedes of armes spirituall' and his God 'the souverayn chevetun and knyght off all chevalrie'.[71] This fusion of a military and Christian ethic gave knighthood its distinctive and enduring character.

The military elite drew much of its inspiration from classical mythology and romance. The deeds of Greek and Roman heroes—Hector, Alexander, Caesar— the stories of the Nine Worthies, and the comparable feats of Charlemagne's Paladins, or even those of the already legendary Godfrey de Bouillon in the Crusades, provided an inexhaustible fount for emulation. Arthurian romance was an equally potent influence, receiving fresh currency in the fourteenth century from the Anglo-French war and through conscious promotion by the

[70] J. St John Hope (ed.), *Pageant of the Birth, Life and Death of Richard Beauchamp Earl of Warwick* (London, 1914), pls. 16, 17.

[71] M. H. Keen, *Chivalry* (New Haven, 1984), ch. 4; Christine de Pisan, *The Epistle of Othea to Hector (translated by Stephen Scrope)*, ed. C. F. Buhler, EETS, old ser., 264 (Oxford, 1970), quotation in Scrope's prologue for Fastolf, app. A, p. 121.

Crown. The Arthurian cycle was retold in the stanzaic *Le Morte Arthur* (*c*.1350), in the English alliterative *Morte Arthure* (*c*.1400), and finally in the English prose of Sir Thomas Malory (*c*.1470). Edward III developed the concept of a round table of 300 knights, sworn to a brotherhood of honour around the Crown, to consolidate support for his war in France.[72]

Imaginative literature, which exalted individual prowess and honour, reflected but did not influence the practice of war. But alongside it there developed a more technical war literature derived, again, partly from antiquity, partly from experience, and partly from law. Its emergence in the thirteenth century reflected growing interest in the science and techniques of war, the increasingly national character of war, and the concern that war fought for a just end should be governed by legal conventions. For military techniques this drew on the authority of Vegetius, whose *De Re Militari*, written in the late fourth century, was translated into French by 1300 and into English at the behest of Lord Berkeley in 1408, while a verse adaptation under the title *Knyghthode and Bataile* was made at Calais in 1458.[73] Although the structure, battle tactics, and armour of the Roman army made much of it inapplicable to medieval warfare, Vegetius was valued for his tactical principles, for his description of the devices and methods of siege warfare, and above all for his concept of an army as a disciplined and cohesive force, a model increasingly dictated by the national conflicts of the late Middle Ages. A further impetus came from the late medieval lawyers, the post-glossators, who sought to produce for their age a legal code of practice for war, combining Roman law and later custom. Here the influential work was that of John of Legnano, whose *Tractatus de Bello*, written in 1360 for Italian conditions, was quickly popularized in France. The importance of John's work was that it defined legitimate war not merely by natural and divine law but by the *jus gentium*, positive law; and though princes did not fight war by the rules, war fought under their authority was deemed legitimate while private war was banditry. Together the concept of military discipline and the concept of lawful authority facilitated the organization of royal armies in which the nobility served as the king's lieutenants, fighting for the defence of the common weal. Chivalry thus acquired a public and political dimension.

The popularization of these academic doctrines on war began with the appearance of Honoré Bonet's work *L'Arbre des Batailles* in 1387.[74] Bonet drew heavily on Vegetius and John of Legnano, but he wrote in the vernacular for a lay, knightly audience and he presented his subject in terms of their likely experience on campaign. He attempted to frame rules of behaviour governing the incidents of war: the capture of towns, the treatment of non-combatants, the ransoming of

[72] J. Vale, *Edward III and Chivalry* (Woodbridge, 1982).
[73] *Knyghthode and Bataile*, ed. R. Dyboski and Z. M. Arend, EETS, old ser., 201 (London, 1935).
[74] G. W. Coopland (ed. and trans.), *The Tree of Battles of Honoré Bonet* (Liverpool, 1949).

prisoners, the performance of contracts of service, the legitimacy of trial by battle, the use of coats of arms. It is easy to see why these pithy, practical discussions of experienced dilemmas proved so popular and influential. Christine de Pisan drew heavily on it and Vegetius for her *Livre des Faites d'Armes et de Chivalrie*, written in 1409, which like Bonet's work circulated widely in England in the fifteenth century and was translated in 1489 by Caxton. In setting out to convey 'in plain and entendible language' the learning of clerks on the rules of war, she was at the same time alive to contemporary developments, such as the use of gunpowder and cannon. Such innovations needed to be recorded, and not left to hearsay 'for scripture in books is a thing perpetual in the world'.[75] If warfare was coming to be regarded as a science about which its practitioners needed to be informed, this did not mean that such works determined actual practice. There was no law of war which was uniformly enforced nor any overall authority to enforce it; the treatment of prisoners and civilians, and the conduct of sieges, ultimately depended on the captain on the spot. The laws of war were conventions for a chivalric elite, but by setting personal prowess and honour within a theological and legal framework, and by emphasizing that war was a science requiring intelligence, training, and judgement, the nobility were made to see war within a broader framework and to assess their own experience on a comparative scale.

Among this new, informed chivalry Froissart's work found a ready audience, for it appealed to both the romantic and the scientific traditions. It did not perhaps even purport to present a historically accurate account, for Froissart wrote variant accounts of particular episodes; rather it was a celebration of heroes and heroic deeds within a narrative of campaigns which realistically detailed the rigours, cruelty, and destructiveness of contemporary conflict. Like a modern war correspondent, Froissart offered an apparently informed and rationalized picture of councils of war, battle plans, and tactics, which emphasized discipline and forethought as recipes for victory but left room for personal prowess and honour. Battles are described in a series of montages: the dispositions on each side, the challenges and harangues, the fracas, the panic, flight, and massacre or taking of prisoners. All this was recognizable to the nobility, though because his audience was international the chivalric elite is depicted as a brotherhood who, while they may be professional rivals, are rarely deadly enemies. There is little patriotism and equally little xenophobia.[76]

By contrast, *The Boke of Noblesse*, written initially around 1453 to explain the English defeat in Normandy and justify renewed war, derived from the experience of a distinguished captain, Sir John Fastolf, who in retirement had become an armchair pundit. Although examples are drawn from classical models, from

---

[75] Christine de Pisan, *The Book of Faytes of Armes and of Chyvalrye*, ed. A. T. P. Byles, EETS, old ser., 189 (London, 1932), 2, 153.

[76] J. J. N. Palmer (ed.), *Froissart: Historian* (Woodbridge, 1981).

Vegetius, and from the experience of war in France, the *Boke* is not, like Froissart's, either a narrative of campaigns or an evocation of chivalric valour. It is an analysis of military practice; of the causes of defeat and the requirements for victory. Even more striking, war is seen in terms of its political purpose; it is waged to fulfil national destiny and it reflects a nation's moral virtue. The English lost Normandy, which was rightfully theirs, because they exploited it for their own gain, not the common good, lacking self-discipline and abandoning true chivalry.[77] In the half-century since Froissart the individual valour of the knight has been subsumed into that of the nation.

If literature helps us to glimpse the mental world of chivalry, so also do its rituals and training. As noted, its religious character was explicit in the elaborate ceremonies when the king invested knights after his coronation or prior to a campaign. A commander might also dub knights on the eve of battle where the verdict of God would be rendered, as did the Black Prince at Najera and the earl of Salisbury at Verneuil. Knighthood was fulfilled in battle, but tournaments offered the next most honourable setting for feats of arms. Hastiludes (to use the generic term) had a long history, back to the twelfth century, but by 1350 they had entered a distinctive phase. The old indiscriminate mêlée had been replaced by a form of tourney where mounted knights, individually or in groups, fought with sword, mace, and club. But far more popular were jousts where two mounted knights armed with lances encountered each other in an enclosure, the lists. Usually these were urban settings: Smithfield, or even Westminster Hall, and were occasions for aristocratic display and popular excitement. Jousts were either 'of war' (*à l'outrance*) or of peace (*à plaisance*). The former tended to occur between traditional enemies, on frontiers or on the eve of battle, but they could also provide a duel during periods of truce. The most famous of such occasions took place at St Ingelvert in the Calais–Picardy borderland in the spring of 1390 when over one hundred English knights and esquires joined those from France and the Low Countries in a series of challenges which Froissart recounted with an eye for the finer points of skill and valour. By the late fourteenth century jousts were only held under royal licence, for they could inflame national rivalries, endangering truces and negotiations, and even be a cover for rebellion.[78]

Jousts of peace employed blunted or rebated lances, and the combatants were protected with heavy armour. From about 1420 a barrier of cloth or wood was erected to separate the horses and this increased the angle at which the lance would strike. Accurate selection of the point of impact was needed to unhorse an opponent, requiring skilled horsemanship. Such occasions gave full rein to the

[77] *The Boke of Noblesse*, ed. J. G. Nichols, Roxburghe Club (London, 1860), discussed by C. T. Allmand, in *La 'France Anglaise' Au Moyen Âge* (Paris, 1988), 103–11.

[78] Keen, *Chivalry*, ch. 6; id., *Nobles, Knights and Men at Arms in the Middle Ages* (London, 1996), 83–99; J. Barker, *The Tournament in England, 1100–1400* (Woodbridge, 1986).

theatrical and fashionable element of chivalry. Peers, and even the king, might engage under false names, or masked, to win acclaim for their own prowess independent of rank. Kings patronized tournaments, both to sanction them and to affirm their pre-eminence of honour in a military society. Certain families and individuals among the nobility won reputations for their skill in arms, which Bohuns, Uffords, de Veres, and Hollands all exhibited in the lists in France, Germany, and Spain. *The Pageant of Richard Beauchamp* depicts him as jousting on pilgrimage to Jerusalem, at the Council of Constance, and at Guines in 1414 when in the successive guise of three of his ancestors he challenged French knights.[79] But next year the renewal of the Anglo-French conflict brought to an end a period of thirty years during which the English nobility had been familiar figures in continental tournaments. War was a sterner matter; Henry V cut short the tourneys at his marriage in 1420, saying that they could display their prowess in real war at the siege of Sens. Nor did tournaments return to popularity under the clerkly Henry VI.

Given the cult of arms and the fame and honour to be won at hastiludes, their existence needs no other explanation; but did they have any military function and value? To tilt with a lance couched or to engage in swordplay on foot perfected fighting skills and demanded alertness and fitness.[80] Nevertheless, jousts were increasingly seen as artificial and socially exclusive diversions and attracted the censure of preachers. Bromyard poured scorn on those who apparisoned themselves for jousts but fled the field of battle. He also denounced them as occasions for immorality. Women were accorded an increasing prominence as tournaments became ritualized occasions within a confined setting. Stands could be erected for spectators, and ladies could select their own champion by giving items of their clothing—scarves, sleeves—to be attached to his helm or lance. Moreover, the jousts themselves were preceded by masques and dancing with prizes for the lady who danced best, or by a procession in which ladies would lead their knight's horse by the bridle. Ladies who attended without their husbands endangered their reputation, for they might be entrapped into liaisons with manly knights, or so the preachers thought. These also condemned the pride, extravagance, and indulgence, and the cost to the lords' labourers and tenants, from whom the money was wrung. But of the popularity of such occasions they left no doubt, Brinton complaining that many more would go to a tournament procession than to a procession of relics on a feast day.[81]

At the highest level late medieval chivalry found expression in a proliferation of knightly orders. Unlike the crusading orders these demanded no quasi-monastic vows, but were companies of honour, chosen for valour and prowess, and bound

[79] St John Hope (ed.), *Pageant of Richard Beauchamp*, pls. XIV, XXII, XXVII–XXXI, XXXIV.
[80] S. Anglo, 'The techniques of chivalric combat', *Antiquaries Journal*, 68 (1988), 248–64; M. Vale, *War and Chivalry* (London, 1981).
[81] G. R. Owst, *Literature and Pulpit in Medieval England* (Oxford, 1961), 334–8.

to a prince by special loyalty. Their corporate and visible identity was marked by a badge, insignia, or livery, and was focused on their own chapel where the rites of initiation were conducted. The only such order established in England was that of the Garter, founded by Edward III in 1348–9 as a celebration for victory at Crécy and an affirmation of the support of his nobility. The twenty-four stalls which faced each other in St George's Chapel, Windsor, like two tournament teams, were initially occupied by those in Edward's and the Black Prince's divisions at Crécy. Election to this exclusive order was a mark not of rank but of military prowess and royal favour. Garter knights represented England at international tournaments and their helm and sword above their chapel stall symbolized their commitment to the defence of Church and realm. The Order of the Garter thus fused the worlds of battle and tournament, of aristocratic pageantry and knightly prowess, of religious commitment and political loyalty.[82]

Was the chivalric code a charade, or did it influence military decisions? At the lowest level it provided knightly enemies with mutual expectations for their behaviour in battle and sieges which it was often convenient to observe. When critical military choices had to be made, however, it became one factor among others. The contrasting fate of two knights of the Garter make this point. In 1429 Sir John Fastolf fought his way out of the battle of Patay when the vanguard under Lords Talbot and Scales was surrounded, bringing his troops back to the defence of Paris but leaving his fellow commanders to be captured. For deserting the field of battle, contrary to the rules of the Order, he was suspended while his conduct was investigated. A year later Sir Lewis Robessart, Lord Bourchier, chose to stand his ground against overwhelming odds at Conty, thereby vindicating the vow not to flee the field but also by his death demonstrating the English commitment to the Burgundian alliance at a critical moment in its fortunes. Military and political considerations were paramount in each case, but chivalric honour was an important element in their decisions.[83]

The Church had always held that the primary function of knighthood was to fight the infidel, and even in this period, when crusades to the Holy Land had ceased, crusading was deemed the apex of chivalric endeavour. Between the Treaty of Brétigny and 1400, during the long periods of truce with France, the English nobility were prominent in crusading ventures. The liberation of the Holy Land continued to haunt men's imagination, though the Turkish advance, which by 1389 had reached Serbia and was threatening Prague, posed a more immediate threat. By that date the signing of a semi-permanent Anglo-French truce permitted knights from both countries to join the duke of Bourbon's

[82] Collins, *Order of the Garter*, ch. 1 and *passim*.

[83] D. A. L. Morgan, 'From a death to a view: Louis Robessart, Johan Huizinga, and the political significance of chivalry', in S. Anglo (ed.), *Chivalry in the Renaissance* (Woodbridge, 1990), 93–106; Collins, *Order of the Garter*, 274, 287.

Barbary crusade in 1390. From 1393 Philippe de Mézières, a counsellor of Charles VI, was enrolling the nobility of both realms in his crusading Order of the Passion. In the event English participation in the crusade which met defeat at Nicopolis in 1396 was minimal, and that disaster together with the madness of King Charles in the same year ended further crusading projects.[84]

At a different level the crusade appealed as an adventure and test of military skills, and west European chivalry found a not too distant outlet for their energies in Prussia. The *Reyse* against Lithuanian heathens brought spiritual benefits equivalent to those in the Holy Land; it required less organization since individual nobles could join their retinues to the army of the Teutonic knights, and it could be contained within a limited period, either the hot summer months or the frozen winter ones being suitable for campaigning in barren wilderness between Lithuania, Livonia, and Prussia. Campaigning was hard and raids rarely very profitable, but the venture was prestigious and the Teutonic Order—which depended on volunteers from the west—laid on a round of heavy feasting, drawing their guests into rituals of honour or leading them on expeditions and hunts if a *Reyse* was not possible. Generations of English nobility made the journey and did so at no small cost: Henry of Derby's expedition of 1390–1 cost him £4,438 though he took a particularly large and prestigious retinue. It remained a private venture for the rich, an opportunity to display and perfect military technique. The fashion ended abruptly with the revolution of 1399 and the commencement of the Welsh war in England, and with the conversion of Lithuania and defeat of the Teutonic Order at Tannenberg in 1410.[85]

The brotherhood of Christian chivalry expressed in the international tournament and the international crusade could not survive the mortal struggle for France which Henry V unleashed in 1415. The state itself appropriated the idea of the holy war, with the concept of the nation as God's chosen people, fulfilling an appointed mission. The red cross of the crusading banner was adopted for St George of England. Similarly, the bitter political feuds which engulfed the nobility of England and France from the 1380s undermined their community of honour. If chivalry faced 'a crisis of identity', it was less due to internal tensions between its ideals and practice (which, as in Christianity, had always existed without invalidating its claims) than to political imperatives displacing individual honour and prowess. Within a generation the world for which Froissart, Mézières, and Christine de Pisan wrote had passed away.

Even in war, where leadership remained the prerogative of the nobility, the commander of a royal army was increasingly answerable to the Crown for the

---

[84] J. J. N. Palmer, *England, France and Christendom, 1377–99* (London, 1972), ch. 11.

[85] N. Housley, *The Later Crusades* (Oxford, 1992), chs. 11, 12; Keen, *Nobles, Knights*, 101–20. For Henry of Derby, see L. Toulmin Smith (ed.), *Expeditions to Prussia and the Holy Land*, Camden Society, new ser., 52 (London, 1894).

achievement of its military and political objectives, and responsible for the good order and discipline of his troops. A number of permanent offices and commands involved active military responsibilities. The hereditary offices of constable and marshal were exercised on royal expeditions, the constable notionally deciding strategy and battle tactics, the marshal enforcing discipline and the rules of engagement. Together they exercised jurisdiction in the Court of Chivalry over disputes touching the law of arms.[86] The office of admiral of England was held after 1435 by the family of Holland, who were active seafarers. Calais, the largest garrison overseas, was always entrusted to a peer who enjoyed the king's special confidence. In the north members of the Percy and Neville families were normally appointed as wardens of the marches to Scotland, retaining permanent forces at the Crown's expense. In Ireland the office of king's lieutenant had vice-regal status and before 1412 was at times held by a royal duke or earl, though subsequently by the Anglo-Irish families of Talbot, Ormond, and Mortimer.

Lieutenants with vice-regal powers were also sent to the king's dominions in France: in Guyenne until 1453 and in Normandy from 1422 to 1450. The nobility were frequently summoned to join expeditions to France, with participation in a 'royal army' (i.e. one led by the king in person) being virtually obligatory for all able-bodied peers. Besides two of his sons, Edward III was accompanied on his last expedition in 1359 by ten earls and seventy bannerets, and in 1385 all the upper nobility except one, and fourteen major barons, were led by Richard II to Scotland.[87] Henry V got service in France from all the active peerage, while for his coronation in Paris in 1431 the boy Henry VI was protected by seven earls and twelve barons.

The nobility, and especially the upper nobility, were the principal military leaders of their age. In proportion to their numbers their experience of war was more frequent and varied than that of the gentry, and both as individuals and as a class war held a greater importance in their outlook and their lives. John of Gaunt participated in twelve major campaigns and prepared for several others, and Richard Beauchamp held commands in every decade of his life from 1403 to 1439.[88] Service in war was not only a duty but a personal venture with its tally of gains and losses. Military abilities varied; some nobles were acclaimed by contemporaries and attracted men to serve with them, while others did not. Thomas Beaufort's steadfastness, discipline, and loyalty to his men won him respect, as did the impetuous bravery displayed by Clarence at the assault on Caen in 1417, though it later led to disaster at Baugé; Talbot had an awesome reputation among the French for the speed and surprise of his attacks. Other commanders were

[86] Keen, *Nobles, Knights*, 135–48.

[87] A. E. Prince, 'The strength of English armies in the reign of Edward III', *EHR* 46 (1931), 353–71; N. B. Lewis, 'The last medieval summons of the feudal levy, 1385', *EHR* 73 (1958), 24.

[88] Walker, *Lancastrian Affinity*, 40–1.

downright failures, like Edmund, earl of Cambridge, in Portugal in 1381 and John Beaufort, earl of Somerset, who returned disgraced from France in 1443.

Was war profitable for the peerage? To attempt a balance sheet either for individuals or for the class as a whole is impracticable, but the areas in which the prizes and hazards of war could be anticipated are fairly clear. War was in the king's service and at his wages; did these cover a lord's costs and was there any margin of profit to be made? For his personal wage an earl received 6s. 8d. per day and a baron 4s. with an additional bonus ('regard') of 100 marks for every thirty men in his retinue. He would also be paid the wages of his retinue, to the number specified in his indenture, at fixed rates of pay. Against this the expense of equipping for a campaign, particularly for a royal expedition in which display was as important as weaponry, was very heavy. Tents, horses, armour, weapons, livery for his men, the additional support staff like armourers, cooks, surgeons, and priests, and the necessary victuals, all figure in the accounts for John Mowbray's preparation for the Agincourt campaign, which cost him £1,000 more than the wages he received.[89] Others, like Edward, duke of York, had to borrow heavily and mortgage estates to equip themselves. And if the Crown's cash ran out, royal jewels were delivered to be held as security for future payment, which might be considerably delayed. Ten years after Agincourt the exchequer was still redeeming jewels held for wages owed. Commanders in the field might have to dig into their own pocket to keep an army or garrison together if royal wages failed. From his extended *chevauchée* of 1373 Gaunt returned with a claim for additional wages of £9,462, half of which he was never paid.[90] Arrears of pay could be offset by licensing the army to plunder. This was William, Lord Latimer's defence when accused in 1376 of enriching himself to the sum of 145,000 francs from the ransoms levied around Bécherel.[91] Profits could also be made by retaining fewer men than specified in the indenture and pocketing the surplus wages. In his will of 1408 William, Lord Say, admitted that he had taken wages of war from Richard II 'peradventure more than my dessert' and ordered his executors to repay £80.[92] But overall any profits on royal wages were far outweighed by attendant costs and royal default. If the nobility served the Crown in war it was not because they were paid handsomely to do so.

Wages were never the main financial inducement for military service. That was the prospect of gain from prizes of war—the booty from a captured town or the spoils of battle. Richard Beauchamp, earl of Warwick, who had been present at the sieges of Caen, Pontoise, and Meaux, sent a rich haul of jewels and prisoners back to England in 1421 to finance the building of the south front of Warwick Castle, and Talbot's capture of Le Mans in 1428 yielded a rich haul of apparel,

[89] Archer, 'The Mowbrays', ch. 5.   [90] Walker, *Lancastrian Affinity*, 58–66.
[91] M. Jones, *Ducal Brittany, 1364–1399* (Oxford, 1970), 166–71.
[92] *Test. Vet.* i. 163.

horses, and armour.[93] But the profits of plunder are largely unrecorded; we know more about ransoms, where the sum fixed and the stages of its payment were set down in writing. The spectacular ransoms from the capture of the French higher nobility were unpredictable, for in the confusion of battle a noble surrendered to his nearest captor of knightly rank, who sold him on to a lord. The brisk trade in ransoms which followed victory provided entrepreneurs with handsome profits. Lord Fanhope bought large numbers of French prisoners from the earl of Norfolk in 1421 and from their ransoms built his new castle at Ampthill.[94] Even larger sums could be exacted from towns and regions which lay at the mercy of the army. Among the most spectacular of such payments was the £35,000 for which Clarence undertook to withdraw from central France in 1412, for the payment of which Count Jean of Angoulême became hostage. At a siege either side might compound to withdraw: in 1375 the English garrison at Saint-Sauveur accepted £9,000 to evacuate, while in 1428 the French garrison at Laval paid Talbot £3,000 under the terms of surrender.[95]

Conversely, however, personal and family fortunes were vulnerable to capture and death in battle. Chivalric convention set the limit of a ransom at one year's revenue of the captive's estates, but larger sums were extracted under duress, as Sir John Bourchier explained to his wife in 1374 when ill health persuaded him to pay £2,000 for release from a Breton prison.[96] Maintenance costs in captivity could legitimately be added to ransom money: Robert Hungerford, Lord Moleyns, who was ransomed for £6,000 in 1453, had to pay a further £3,800 for his sustenance before his release in 1459. Beyond the financial penalties was the effect on morale: the frustration at a lost manhood and the strains on family loyalty. After spending nine years 'in harde prison' Roger, Lord Camoys, took to freebooting on his release.[97] For some release never came: John, earl of Pembroke, captured at La Rochelle in 1372, was so harshly treated that he died in 1375 even as his ransom of 120,000 francs was being negotiated. A ransom was thus a serious setback for a family, likely to entail the mortgaging of estates, or even their sale. Death in battle was undoubtedly cheaper, though it might cost a family dear in long minorities or even terminate its male line. Families rarely suffered so grievously as the Lords Roos of Helmsley, losing three members between 1421 and 1430, but few were exempt from battle's steady toll.

[93] Sinclair, 'The Beauchamp earls of Warwick', 122; A. J. Pollard, *John Talbot and the War in France, 1427–53* (London, 1983), ch. 6.

[94] M. K. Jones, 'Ransom brokerage in the fifteenth century', in P. Contamine, C. Giry-Deloison, and M. H. Keen (eds.), *Guerre et société en France, en Angleterre et en Bourgogne XIV–XV siècle* (Lille, n.d.), 225.

[95] McFarlane, *Nobility*, 31; Pollard, *John Talbot*, 105.

[96] McFarlane, *Nobility*, 28, 45, 241; M. K. Jones, 'The fortunes of war: The military career of John, second Lord Bourchier (d. 1400)', *Essex Archaeology and History*, 26 (1995), 145–61.

[97] Hicks, 'Counting the cost of war', 11–31; Jones, 'Ransom brokerage', 224, 226.

The hazards of war were unpredictable, and it is unlikely that the nobility weighed these carefully when taking service, though most were conscious of their duty to the lineage and begat an heir before sailing. An amalgam of chivalry, fealty, and profit formed the proud tradition of a military elite, which identified its leadership of society with its military prowess. Service alongside the monarch afforded access to his grace, expressed in grants of wardships and marriages, lands and leases, licences and pardons, even the hand of an heiress or advancement in dignity. The close link between war service and political reward, between companionship in arms and baronial loyalty to the Crown, underlined the symbiosis of chivalry and good governance claimed by the author of *Knyghthode and Bataile:*

> Res publica right commendabil is,
> If chivalers and armys there abounde,
> For, they present, may nothing fare amys,
> And ther thei are absent, al goth to ground.[98]

That was how the nobility saw its role, but how did it appear to those beneath them? The peasantry voiced its detestation of lordship in the Great Revolt, desiring to have no other lord than the king. The gentry were perforce muted in criticism of the peerage; there was little overt complaint of their military ineptitude; rather more of their failure to uphold justice and order in the shires, where their retainers acted 'like second kings' and 'law goeth as lordship willeth'.[99] Further criticism of their shortcomings appears in clerical writing and sermons, though this follows the topos of estates satire, which ascribed social ills to the failure of each estate in its duty. Such criticism was mainly directed at the lifestyle of the lords: their extravagance in dress, numerous servants, costly furnishings, and feasts.[100] The old tradition of *noblesse oblige*, of compassion for the poor, graciousness to inferiors, and courtesy towards equals, had been replaced by harsh exploitation, contempt for servants, and bragging towards rivals. Bromyard warned that, at the day of judgement, the poor would cry out that the lords' tournaments were their torments, the lords' feasts their fasts. The predictable terms of such clerical criticism should not incline us to dismiss it too readily. Its volume was greater in the later fourteenth century than ever before, and it was popularized in the occasional political verse of the time. A strong anti-seigniorial current ran through these disastrous decades; yet it did not shake the political power and pre-eminence of the nobility. Indeed its very terms affirmed the role to which it sought to recall them.

---

[98] *Knyghthode and Bataile*, lines 404–7, and similarly lines 1622–8.
[99] *Rot. Parl.* iii. 5; Walker, *Lancastrian Affinity*, 117, 167, 255–60.
[100] Owst, *Literature and Pulpit*, 287–338.

CHAPTER 5

The Gentry

First what is gentylnes and what nobylyte
And who shulden be chose to hye auctoryte
Thys questions they be so large and soltell
Few dare presume to dyffyne them well.[1]

The existence of medium and small landlords between the baronage and peasantry with distinctive economic, military, and social functions can be traced for
at least two centuries prior to this period. But it was in the century following the
Black Death that they acquired a role in the polity which they were to retain as
long as land remained the basis of wealth and power. Moreover, within the broad
category of middling landowners there emerged a graded hierarchy of status
which substantially accorded with wealth and which entitled and obliged men to
undertake military or magisterial functions. Title, wealth, and function conferred social esteem and bred a class with recognizable social and political attitudes, making the emergence of the 'gentry' arguably the most momentous
development of this period; one which not only illuminates the economy, culture, and polity of late medieval England but distinguishes it from its continental neighbours.

I. STATUS, ECONOMY, AND INHERITANCE

In the late thirteenth century the term *gentil* encompassed all those of noble
blood. In the next half-century the formation of the parliamentary peerage drew
a line though this chivalric brotherhood, and though knights retained *noblesse* by
virtue of their military functions, by 1450 they shared gentility with the grades
of esquire and 'gentilman' who constituted the middle sector of society. By then
knighthood was the mark of the local landed elite, below whom the *armigeri*,
or esquires, first designated as a specific social grade in the sumptuary legislation
of 1363, were likewise of military origin and entitled to the use of family coats

---

[1] John Rastell,—'Gentylnes and Nobylyte', lines 1100–3, in R. Axton (ed.), *Three Rastell Plays*
(Cambridge, 1979), cited by P. W. Fleming, 'The Gentry of Kent in the Fifteenth Century', Ph.D.
thesis (University of Wales, 1985).

of arms.[2] These esquires fought alongside the knights, though their wages of war were at only half the level, and along with the knights they were permitted to receive livery of company as life retainers of a lord, under the 1390 ordinance of livery. In these respects the esquires were recognized as part of the chivalric class, and this they affirmed with pride when they ordered effigies in armour for their tombs. Yet over this century their identity as a group gradually became less military than magisterial, as their entitlement to occupy the principal shire offices, alongside the knights, was statutorily recognized on the basis of their income.[3] Military service, chivalric tradition, and civil responsibility had brought into being a local governing class which numbered some 4,000 families.

Beneath this compact and identifiable group the gradations of gentle society were fluid. In the 1379 poll tax 'franklins' were rated as lesser esquires, and by 1400 the line separating them from the *valettus*, or 'yeoman', was coming to be that which defined gentility. By the early fifteenth century the *generosus*, 'gentilman', has replaced the franklin as the lowest grade of gentility, a defining criterion for which was probably the exercise of lordship over land and men through the possession of a manor and court. Many of the village franklins recorded in the 1379 poll tax must (like Chaucer's figure) have been edging their way towards gentility over the next half-century, particularly in areas where small manors abounded and resident knights and esquires were few.[4] The term 'gentilman' was familiarized by the statutory requirement in 1413 for personal status to be recorded in actions at law, but not until mid-century was it much employed in private deeds and only in 1446 did a gentleman's family, that of Oxinden in Kent, receive a grant of arms from the heralds.

Attainment of these social and economic qualifications equipped gentlemen for the duties of lesser magistracy, such as coroners, tax collectors, and on the less important local commissions. As officers in royal and seigniorial service their household livery was a mark of gentility, as was service in arms, chivalric behaviour, and social bearing ('apport') in their lifestyle. Gentility was not precisely related to income, but from the income tax returns of 1436 it is possible to extrapolate the numbers in each income grade over the whole country, though the conclusions must be treated with caution on account of probable under-assessment

---

[2] N. Saul, *Knights and Esquires: The Gloucestershire Gentry in the Fourteenth Century* (Oxford, 1981), ch. 1; D. A. Morgan, 'The individual style of the English gentleman', in M. Jones (ed.), *Gentry and Lesser Nobility* (Gloucester, 1986), 15–35; P. R. Coss, 'The formation of the English gentry', *P & P* 147 (1995), 38–64.

[3] P. R. Coss, 'Knights, esquires and the origins of social gradation in England', *TRHS*, 6th ser., 5 (1995), 155–78; M. H. Keen, *Origins of the English Gentleman* (Stroud, 2002), chs. 6–8.

[4] M. C. Carpenter, *Locality and Polity* (Cambridge, 1992), 35–95, esp. 43–5; for Chaucer's Franklin, N. Saul, 'The social status of Chaucer's Franklin: A reconsideration', *Medium Aevum*, 52 (1983), 10–26.

and evasion.[5] The fifteenth-century gentry thus appear as a social class with sharply graded economic differentials. The average income of the greater knights (a few of whom had baronial-size incomes of over £400) was more than three times that of the lesser and they formed a small elite within every shire. A larger elite consisting of those with incomes of £20 and more (knights and esquires) were qualified to hold shire offices and constituted a magistracy, forming one-third of all those who had £5 and more in landed income. The relative proportions of these grades varied within individual counties, with fewer than ten families of knightly estate in some northern shires and twenty and more elsewhere.[6]

TABLE 5.1. *The gentry in 1436: social grade, number, and income*

Grade and wealth	Numbers	Total income £	Average income £ s.
Greater knights (£100+)	183	38,000	208 00
Lesser knights (£40–100)	750	45,000	60 00
Esquires (£20–39)	1,200	29,400	24 10
Gentleman (£10–19)	1,600	19,000	12 00
Yeoman (£5–9)	3,400	19,000	5 13

Source: Payling, *Political Society*, 2–3, based on H. L. Gray, 'Incomes from land in England in 1436', *EHR* 49 (1934), 607–39.

The gradations of income reflected the size of their estates. Esquires usually owned one or two manors, lesser knights three or more, and greater knights up to ten. The estates of the greater knights averaged approximately 8,000–9,000 acres, those of lesser knights 2,500–3,000 acres, and those of esquires 1,200 acres.[7] Knights were also likely to hold lands in more than one county, others far less so. The wealthier knights thus had wider political horizons and social contacts than the mass of the local gentry.[8] Within the county the manors of the older and greater knightly families tended to be situated in areas of primary settlement and were probably of larger size than those of the lesser esquires and mere gentry, which might represent subsequent settlement on marginal land. Thus in Nottinghamshire the major gentry families clustered thickly along the valley of

[5] Keen, *Origins of the English Gentleman*, chs. 7–8; T. B. Pugh, 'The magnates, knights and gentry', in S. Chrimes, C. Ross, and R. Griffiths (eds.), *Fifteenth Century England, 1399–1509* (Manchester, 1972), esp. 97–101, warns of the exaggeration of gentry wealth in 1436 by the inclusion of annuities, though cf. Payling, *Political Society*, 2–3.

[6] Payling, *Political Society*, 17 (cols. 1 and 2 of table I.6).

[7] Estimates of acreage from J. P. Cooper, 'The social distribution of land and men in England, 1436–1700', *Econ. HR* 20 (1967), 420–1.

[8] E. Acheson, *A Gentry Community* (Cambridge, 1992), 46–52; S. M. Wright, *The Derbyshire Gentry in the Fifteenth Century*, Derbyshire Record Society (Chesterfield, 1983), 17.

the Trent; in Warwickshire they occupied the valleys of the Avon, Leam, and Tame while smaller gentry lived in Arden; and in Leicestershire the area of Charnwood was devoid of major gentry families, as was the Vale of Belvoir.[9] To the extent that the greater and lesser gentry tended to inhabit different land-scapes as well as different social worlds, their gentility was of a different order and kind. The absence of greater gentry in some areas permitted the lesser to assume the trappings of lordship and status. This had important implications for the functioning of the shire as a political community and the exercise of magis-tracy within it, which will be considered later.

TABLE 5.2. *Distribution of Landholding by income grade, 1412*
(eight southern counties)

Distribution of holdings	No. of individual assessments within income grades (£)				
	20–39	40–99	100–99	200–99	300+
In 1 county	418	144	15	1	—
In 2 counties	24	54	10	—	—
In 3 counties	5	15	14	2	2
In 4 counties	—	—	5	1	1
In 5 counties	—	—	1	—	1

Source: J. M. W. Bean, 'Landlords', *AHEW* iii. 534 (table 6.4) based on the 1412 tax returns.

Social differentiation had also proceeded at the upper level within the grade of knights. Over the century before 1436 the numbers of belted knights had markedly declined from forty or fifty per county to under twenty or even less. This reflected not a decline in wealth but increasing selectivity in assuming knighthood. For this the reasons were both military and social. Between 1360 and 1415 war was intermittent and rarely successful so that military inducements to assume or maintain knighthood diminished. At the same time the heavy costs of chivalric display in tournaments, and of the expensive new plate armour and weapons, may have deterred many. While the military attractions of knighthood declined, it was increasingly seen as a mark of social distinction by local gentry elites.[10] Even so some, like Thomas Chaucer, five times Speaker in parliament, chose to remain esquires, underlining the growing equivalence in status between these grades.

[9] Payling, *Political Society*, p. xiii, fig. 1; Carpenter, *Locality and Polity*, p. 21, fig. 1, p. 54, fig. 3; Acheson, *A Gentry Community*, pp. 47–51, maps 4–7; A. F. Pollard, *North Eastern England during the Wars of the Roses* (Oxford, 1990), pp. 92–3, map 2.
[10] Payling, *Political Society*, 74–7.

The gentry as a whole lacked coherence as a class. Lordship was scarcely a common bond, for that exercised by the parish gentry was of a different order from that wielded by the greater knights. The entitlement to family arms was still unrestricted by the heralds and mere gentlemen had begun to assume them. Different grades exercised different kinds of magistracy. There were steep differentials in income, reflected in living standards and social pretensions. Knighthood itself was losing its cohesive force, as it became identified with a narrow elite. That elite had more in common with the baronage than with the gentlemen; indeed the prevailing climate of social aspiration, or snobbery, meant that each grade saw itself as a pale reflection of that above and sought to distance itself from that below. While as a class the gentry possessed a preponderance of landed wealth within the shire, the steeply graded economic and social differentiations within it reinforced the hierarchic structure of society.

Even if the emergence of the gentry represented a process of social definition rather than of economic rise, it also reflected ambitions to enter it and to advance to higher grades within it. How were these achieved? The key lay in the acquisition of land, more often by inheritance and marriage than by purchase. Only those without direct heirs, or who wished to endow pious trusts or were in debt, chose to sell. Normally families sought to transmit intact the inheritance which provided their identity and status. Quite a few succeeded in doing so, the survival rate in the male line over any twenty-five-year period (a notional generation) being well over 80 per cent before 1400 and just under in the next century, rather than 75 per cent as in the case of the peerage.[11] Yet entails in tail male were uncommon among the gentry and failure in the male line generally transmitted the estate through female heirs or heirs-general to related families. It has been calculated that in Warwickshire 80 per cent of the land changed hands between 1349 and 1520, and in Nottinghamshire 65 per cent of knights' fees changed between families over the course of three generations.[12] The heiress thus had a paramount role in the transference of land and family aggrandizement.

Wealthy and established families were well placed to pursue an aggressive policy of heiress-hunting. Substantial heiresses would look to marry at or above their own family level, reinforcing the position of elite families within the shire and extending it beyond. The Cheyne family in Kent had thereby established branches in Sussex and Berkshire by the mid-fifteenth century, and leading Warwickshire families set up cadet branches in and outside the shire.[13] The acquisition of a substantial inheritance through marriage could even impel a

---

[11] Payling, *Political Society*, 66–70, for survival rates of Nottinghamshire gentry, drawing comparative figures for Leicestershire and Derbyshire from the work of Astill and Wright. For Warwickshire, cf. Carpenter, *Locality and Polity*, 138–43.

[12] Carpenter, *Locality and Polity*, 150; Payling, *Political Society*, 66–70.

[13] Fleming, 'Gentry of Kent'; Carpenter, *Locality and Polity*, 97–8, 101, 116–19.

family to move its main residence, as did the Throgmorton, Littleton, and Chetwynd families in Warwickshire.[14] Marriage alliances beyond the bounds of the shire were characteristic only of greater families with regional status, being infrequent among the lesser knights and rare for the squirearchy.

The acquisition of lands through an heiress was the principal means by which middling families advanced into the elite, and was virtually the only way for an outsider to gain admission to the county gentry community. Yet first he needed to have property in his own right. With little land available for purchase, it was those with professional or political connections within landed society who stood the best chance of acquiring it, and pre-eminent among them were the lawyers. The salaries, fees, and perquisites of judges, their professional concern with land transactions, and their gentle birth enabled many to enter landed society. Even so it could be a slow ascent, for if the first stage was the purchase of a respectable estate, the second was often marriage to a widow, bringing status and connections which could be exploited for the marriage of the next generation. The phenomenon can be found in many counties: Bingham and Littleton in Warwickshire, Neele and Kebull in Leicestershire, Yelverton and Paston in East Anglia.[15] Nor was it confined to the top of the legal profession. Administrators and estate officials in royal and magnate service had similar financial and legal expertise and the patronage to facilitate the purchase of land and heiresses.[16] It was far less frequent for successful merchants to establish themselves among the landed gentry. Only a few had sufficient capital surplus to their trading requirements to invest in land, though some acquired estates by foreclosing on mortgages. In Nottinghamshire the family of Richard Stanhope (d. 1379), wool merchant of Newcastle, and in Kent the London merchant families of Pecche and Crowmer were among those which bought their way into the gentry elite.

At the lower end of gentry society those with additional incomes from fees and offices, like attorneys, minor estate officials, and Crown officers, likewise found it easier to marry upwards than did those dependent on agricultural profits in a sluggish economy. Though land was more available to lease, or even to buy piecemeal, possession of land alone did not qualify a family for gentility; it had to exercise lordship through the acquisition of manorial title and jurisdiction. This may have been easier in areas of small and fragmented manors like Arden in Warwickshire, where the families of Porter and Greswold were both of yeoman origin.[17] It was not until the enlargement of the wool market at the end

[14] Carpenter, *Locality and Polity*, 149.

[15] Payling, *Political Society*, 36–40; Carpenter, *Locality and Polity*, 123–5; Acheson, *Gentry Community*, 74–5; C. Richmond, *The Paston Family in the Fifteenth Century*, i (Cambridge, 1990), chs. 1 and 2.

[16] Carpenter, *Locality and Polity*, 101–4, 124, gives examples.

[17] Ibid. 125–7, 135–6.

of the fifteenth century that the rise into gentility from agricultural profits became at all usual.

   The degree of social mobility among the gentry underlay not only changes in social structure but the ethos and attitudes of the class. This century probably was 'a period of more restricted social mobility among the gentry' than either the thirteenth or sixteenth, in both of which more land changed hands with greater rapidity as the result of agrarian expansion or political change. Demographic crisis and decline, along with a sluggish economy, rendered biological and economic survival precarious and produced a constant rate of family failure. How unsettling this was is suggested by the desire to record the local gentry families who had failed in the main line, as in Sir Thomas Erpingham's armorial window in the Austin Friars church in Norwich and William Worcester's compilation of a similar list. At the same time the transference of land through the marriage of heiresses and widows provided opportunities to those with patronage and favour to enter the elite from outside.[18] Thus demographic failure induced some families to seek stability and concentrate on survival while tempting the more adventurous to turn it to their advantage. Hierarchy and mobility became twin obsessions, upward mobility more likely to be deplored than acclaimed, and downward mobility widely feared and anticipated. For both the Wheel of Fortune provided a monitory symbol.

Far less is known about the economic position of the gentry in the century following the Black Death than about that of either the magnates or the peasantry. Very few of their estate records survive, and their role as landlords must be deduced from the character of their estates and occasional evidence of individual activities. The estates of the upper gentry held by long-established families tended to be in the cultivated lowland areas, often with a high proportion of arable and nucleated settlements. Clusters of two or four manors within a 10-mile radius could give a degree of coherence to the estate. Well before the Black Death the knightly class had chosen to commute the labour services of their villeins and to work the manor with permanent and hired labour. Though they actively marketed their surplus produce, the smaller scale of their operations did not tie them to the economy of the market as much as the greater lay and ecclesiastical landlords. Like these they continued to benefit from the buoyancy of grain prices for a quarter of a century after the Black Death and perhaps even to limit wages and increase demesne production, but this was a short-lived Indian summer which defied the underlying crisis from the cumulative fall in population. By the last quarter of the century this was felt in demands for higher wages and in the lack of labour to work the demesne. There are indications from a few

---

[18] Walker, *Lancastrian Affinity*, 194; McFarlane, *England in the Fifteenth Century*, 219.

estates that the quality and frequency of ploughing was declining, and weeds were reducing crop yields. From the 1390s knightly landlords began to face the twin problems of holdings standing vacant for lack of tenants and of mounting arrears of rents and were following the example of lords in leasing the demesnes, at first for short terms and then for ten or twenty years, and ceasing to produce for the market.[19]

However, there were limits to wholesale leasing. Where manors had a mixture of arable, pasture, and wood, the latter were often retained in hand for animal husbandry. Secondly, the demesne was often kept in hand on one or more manors as a home farm to supply the lord's household. Thirdly, some landlords alternated between leasing and direct management on individual manors, according to changing circumstances. For leasing did not entirely avoid the difficulties of an economy in decline. Reliable tenant farmers were eagerly sought and not always easy to find, and landlords had to balance the need of a tenant for a livelihood against their own for rent. As James Gloys wrote to Sir John Paston, 'And lete your lond, that your ferrmour may leve and pay you, and than shall your lordshepes ben good and your lond wele teled; and if ye undo your tenauntes with overcharging of your fermes it shall distroy your tenauntes and lordshepes.'[20] Landlords were haunted by the problem of arrears and could face the dilemma that in distraining they might lose a tenant and not find a substitute. Rarely did they dare to evict. The ultimate disaster was if land stood untenanted and started to deteriorate; then, as a desperate measure, the lord would have to take it back into demesne. At the making of a new rental or a new lease arrears might have to be waived and the rent set at a lower level. Besides keeping the land farmed, the main concern of the gentry as landlords was to keep the property in repair, and this was specified in the lease, the apportioning of responsibility between landlord and tenant being carefully defined. There is scattered evidence of landlord investment in mills and farm buildings, with stock and equipment being the responsibility of the tenant. As Dr Carpenter has written, 'the record of investment and maintenance by the Warwickshire gentry is impressive'.[21]

If leasing the demesne signified, to some degree, a withdrawal from agrarian management, did the gentry show enterprise and adaptability in other uses for their estates? The compactness of many gentry estates made them amenable to rationalization and diversification. Besides retaining the demesne at the

---

[19] N. Saul, *Scenes from Provincial Life* (Oxford, 1986), 110–16, 120–8; C. Dyer, *Warwickshire Farming, 1349–c.1520*, Dugdale Society Occasional Paper, 27 (1981), 14–15; Acheson, *Gentry Community*, 52–9; J. B. Bean, 'Landlords', in *AHEW* iii. 579–86.

[20] Davis (ed.), *Paston Letters*, ii. 376, cited by C. Richmond, 'Landlord and tenant: The Paston evidence', in J. Kermode (ed.), *Enterprise and Individuals in Fifteenth Century England* (Stroud, 1991), 35.

[21] Carpenter, *Locality and Polity*, 168.

principal residence for domestic consumption, they might also introduce more
diverse cultivation, with different manors producing different cereals or
legumes. The easing of pressure on the land as population fell permitted annual
adjustments to the type of crops grown, with benefits from up and down husbandry, as fields were left fallow to recover. But the major shift was from tillage to
pasture. In many areas, like north Oxfordshire and Leicestershire, this could be
practised on the same estate, while in other areas, like Sussex, Yorkshire, or
Norfolk, contiguous lowland and upland supported a long tradition of both corn
and sheep. Within most regions the balance between the two had always taken
account of market variations, and over the century after 1380 pasture probably
increased by about one-third. Many landlords turned instinctively to sheep-
farming, which required small labour costs, though some capital investment for
enclosure. The upper gentry, like the Verneys in Warwickshire, the Vernons in
Derbyshire, and the Pelhams in Sussex, had flocks of three or four hundred
sheep, managed on an inter-manorial basis; a few, like the Catesbys at
Radbourne, turned a whole parish over to sheep with a flock of over 2,500 in
1447.[22] But there were drawbacks: sheep were liable to foot-rot and pasture had
to be well drained; wool prices remained low until the end of the fifteenth century; and small producers had to compete with the traditional large-scale graziers in the north and the Cotswolds, whose high-quality wool and flocks of
several thousands dominated the market. All these limited the scale of gentry
sheep-farming until the end of the fifteenth century when entrepreneurial families like the Spensers and Townshends followed the Catesby lead, enclosing
whole manors in lowland England for flocks of many thousands of animals.

Cattle were another alternative, and by the mid-fifteenth century numerous
vaccaries had been established, mainly for beef rather than dairy products. If
kept for purely domestic consumption, like the Mountfords' at Hampton, the
herd would be small. To fatten for the market depended on access to drove roads
and an adjacent town where cattle could be sold. In Warwickshire only William
Catesby and John Brome indisputably supplied a commercial market in the first
half of the fifteenth century, the latter using Baddesley Clinton to fatten 400 cattle
and supply meat to the royal household.[23] Land could also be used to make
parks and rabbit warrens for both sport and food, and a park was already a status
symbol which the upper gentry added to their principal residences in the fifteenth century. Others turned to exploit the mineral wealth on their lands: the
Shirleys had stone quarries at Barrow in Nottinghamshire, the Vernons

[22] Carpenter, *Locality and Polity*, 182–9; Wright, *Derbyshire Gentry*, 19–20; Saul, *Provincial Life*,
133; Dyer, *Warwickshire Farming*.
[23] Dyer, 'A small landowner in the fifteenth century', *Mid. Hist.* 1 (1972), 1–14; Carpenter,
Locality and Polity, 188–93.

extracted and sold lead from their Derbyshire manors, the Willoughbys coal from their estate at Wollaton. The felling of timber added significantly to receipts in any year, while weirs and fish pools supplied domestic needs.[24]

If diversification helped to keep gentry fortunes afloat in difficult times, so did good management. The more compact an estate was, the more easily and economically it could be run, with maximum use of manpower and minimal wastage of produce. Judicious purchase, sale, or exchange built up easily managed units.[25] Far-flung estates acquired by marriage or inheritance, which were a problem to manage, might be made over to a cadet or collateral branch, but the major gentry with estates in many shires had to follow the magnate model of local receiverships or a receiver-general.

The operations and the opportunities of the lesser gentry were more restricted, even if they were able to turn their own skills to advantage. They could personally supervise the management of their one or two manors, utilize the produce for the household, create a complementary economy from arable, pasture, and woodland, and limit dependence on hired labour. An estate could be consolidated by piecemeal acquisition and supplemented by leasing. By these means the Bullock family in Derbyshire and Roger Heritage in Warwickshire advanced in wealth and status in the fifteenth century. Secondly, if they belonged to the class of small lawyers, or household and estate officials, their income from fees and annuities provided an external source of income, and their professional expertise facilitated their purchase of land. The rise of Bartholomew Bolney from yeoman to esquire as seneschal of Battle Abbey was a copybook example.[26] Minor gentry without such advantages were likelier to face decline; many held manors not on the best land and found their position undermined by vacant tenancies and mounting arrears of rent. Overtaken in wealth by prospering yeomen and husbandmen, their sons found themselves compelled to 'follow the plough'. In general a combination of falling rents and expensive labour did not favour landlords, and it was only those who were ready to organize effectively and experiment audaciously who survived and prospered.

While the family's landed inheritance gave it identity and status, it also had to meet the needs and obligations of each generation. The head of the family had to

---

[24] Wright, *Derbyshire Gentry*, 21–2; Carpenter, *Locality and Polity*, 181; Acheson, *Gentry Community*, 60.

[25] S. K. Walker, 'Sir Richard Abberbury and his kinsmen: The rise and fall of a gentry family', *Nott. Med. Stud.* 34 (1990), 113–40; Wright, *Derbyshire Gentry*, 26–8; Carpenter, *Locality and Polity*, 184–6.

[26] Wright, *Derbyshire Gentry*, 26; C. Dyer, 'Were there any capitalists in fifteenth century England?', in Kermode (ed.), *Enterprise and Individuals*, 10–16; M. Clough (ed.), *The Book of Bartholomew Bolney*, Sussex Record Society, 63 (Lewes, 1964).

provide for his wife and children in this life and the rest of his soul in the next out of landed revenue. Birth, marriage, and death were nodal points of family fortunes.

Marriage was central to both the continuance of the family and its social status. The gentry arranged the marriages of their children with some care, most being between families of comparable status living within the shire.[27] Neighbourhood and kinship were the primary bonds of local society, and marriage linked families into kin networks which could be invoked for support in land transactions and disputes or in the search for patrons. The connections of the greater gentry extended beyond the shire and for them the marriage market operated, like the property market, by report, connections, and influence. Service in the larger world provided the opportunity: for William Haute to win the hand of Richard Woodville's daughter in 1429 while both were in garrison at Calais, while intermarriage among John of Gaunt's retainers 'turned the duke's affinity into a large and complex cousinage'. A lord's influence was often the means to acquire an heiress.[28]

The eldest son was generally married by the age of 20, before his father's death, to a woman of childbearing age. John Paston, at 19, married Margaret Mautby, 18, and was a father by 21 when he was still at Cambridge.[29] The marriage contract settled estates on the new family. Among the upper gentry the bride's marriage portion was frequently around 100 marks, though the wealthy Vernon and Hastings families could furnish £300 or £400 per daughter, for whom jointures of £100 per annum and more would be provided. Among middling gentry a marriage portion of £40 would secure a jointure of not much more than £5 per annum, and minor gentlemen might not afford more than £10 for a portion.[30] The jointure safeguarded a wife who was widowed, and preserved a significant part of the estate from wardship in the event of a minority. Marriage contracts also sought to safeguard the interests of the children should the wife die and the husband remarry, by limiting his power to alienate their inheritance. But a jointure could ultimately disadvantage the heir, who would be kept out of a large part of his inheritance while his mother lived. Moreover, if a widow remarried and carried her jointure along with her own lands to her second husband for his life, this could tie up over half an heir's inheritance and trigger a downward spiral in the family's fortunes. The families of Shirley in Leicestershire and Cokayn in Derbyshire both found it impossible to sustain knighthood in the fifteenth century on the remnant of the inheritance in their hands.[31]

---

[27] Acheson, *Gentry Community*, 158; Payling, *Political Society*, 77; M. J. Bennett, *Community, Class and Careerism* (Cambridge, 1983), 30; Carpenter, *Locality and Polity*, 99, 106.

[28] Fleming, 'Gentry of Kent', nn. 243–5; Acheson, *Gentry Community*, 158; Walker, *Lancastrian Affinity*, 153.   [29] Richmond, *Paston Family*, 210.

[30] Wright, *Derbyshire Gentry*, 45 and app. 4; Carpenter, *Locality and Polity*, 107–8.

[31] Wright, *Derbyshire Gentry*, 34; Acheson, *Gentry Community*, 153.

A different kind of threat to the elder son came from the remarriage of his father. Not only would the second wife demand a jointure for herself but she and her husband might seek to provide for their second family by enfeoffments which withdrew the inheritance from the first-born. Notorious instances occurred in the Willoughby family in 1362 and 1443 and in that of Mountford in 1452. But such action was reprobated by contemporary society as destabilizing, and efforts were made to restore the succession.[32]

Even when primogeniture was respected, the provision for younger siblings could woefully erode the heir's resources. Younger sons were the subject of earnest debate. They were a desirable insurance against failure in the elder line, but to fulfil this role they had to marry, and to marry had to be provided with a landed estate. Nor did paternal affection or pride like to think of them reduced to poverty and compelled, as Judge Paston put it, 'to hold the plowe be the tayle', like a peasant. In the event he left lands worth 25 marks to each of his two younger sons. Sons of the lesser gentry who received land worth a mere £2 to £8 per annum found themselves at the level of husbandmen. Even providing an annuity from income or a grant of lands for life made severe inroads on an estate, and an heir like John Paston burdened with his mother's jointure, his sister's marriage portion, and the endowments for his younger brothers faced severe financial constraints and was understandably resentful. Indeed a family could be rent asunder by the fury of an heir who saw his inheritance dismembered between his siblings, and some fathers did just that. Having made his family the richest in Nottinghamshire, Sir Richard Willoughby in 1362 condemned it to half a century of obscurity by substantial bequests to his younger sons.[33] Interestingly such generosity was often characteristic of the first generation of new families, eloquent of the successful founder's reluctance to see his offspring descend to the level from which he had risen. The dream solution was an heiress, but a younger son would not attract one if penniless, and had first to be given land. More usually younger sons supplemented their small inheritance with posts as bailiffs or farmers of outlying manors. Their lot was never easy, in either financial or emotional terms, and contemporary references in literature acknowledged their plight. The alternative to impoverishment and dependence at home was a career in the world outside. Few entered the Church, for this negated their role as surrogate heirs, nor did many enter the law, it being the eldest who was sent to the Inns of Court to learn how to defend the inheritance. A military career did not exclude marriage, but until the Lancastrian conquest of

---

[32] Payling, *Political Society*, 72–3; Carpenter, *Locality and Polity*, 110, 457 ff.; R. A. Griffiths, 'The hazards of civil war: The Mountford family and the Wars of the Roses', *Mid. Hist.* 5 (1980), 1–19.

[33] Richmond, *Paston Family*, 76, 172–3; Acheson, *Gentry Community*, 150–2; Payling, *Political Society*, 34, 72.

Normandy it rarely afforded the opportunity of permanent employment. In fact, their opportunities for establishing a cadet line tended to be limited, and this added to the demographic decline in male heirs.[34]

The likelihood of failure in the senior male line was ever present to families. Some sought insurance in an entail in tail male in order to preserve the family name, but mostly in exceptional circumstances. Whether from affection for daughters or pressure from their husbands, many left their estates to be divided among co-heiresses when male collaterals were available. Yet the failure of the direct male line was not often viewed with equanimity. Where a sole heiress took the estate to her husband it was easier for the father to regard him as a natural heir, as John Hotoft evidently did John Barre, and occasionally a father might try to devise the estate to one daughter and her husband, disinheriting her sisters, as did Thomas Palmer of Holt. A collateral heir might offer, or be required, to assume the family name, as in the cases of Thomas Littleton and Thomas Cokesey, or Hopton's son John in 1420–1. A bastard was the last resort of some heirless landowners, like Sir Andrew Sackville in Sussex and John Bradgates in Leicestershire.[35]

A landowner without direct issue would be likely to sell lands before his death, or order his executors to do so. Sir John Geney of Dilham in Norfolk died in 1423, having sold all his estate to Sir Henry Inglose, and for a similar reason Sir Thomas Erdington sold the reversion of his to Viscount Beaumont in 1444. Sales might also occur if a father fell out with his son and sold lands to spite him, as did Inglose later. Others indulged in conspicuous expenditure, building castles for their present security and providing chantries for their future, as did John, Lord Cobham (d. 1408), and Sir John Fastolf. In the sad case of Sir John Waleys, whose only son and heir failed to return from pilgrimage, not until three days before his death in 1376 did he commit his lands to feoffees to perform his will.[36]

Late medieval landowners had greater freedom than ever before both to determine the descent of their estates by entail and to dispose of them by feoffment and gift. But the majority respected social conventions and the rules of inheritance. For landowners saw their property as a generational trust, were linked to families in their neighbourhood, and were moved by affection and obligation to their immediate kin. These set important parameters to their actions and restrained the indulgence of their desires. Anxious as they were to uphold

[34] Carpenter, *Locality and Polity*, 211–22; Keen, *Origins of the English Gentleman*, 113–14; Morgan, 'Individual style', 16, 21.

[35] C. Richmond, *John Hopton* (Cambridge, 1981), 2, 5; Carpenter, *Locality and Polity*, 248–53; Wright, *Derbyshire Gentry*, 35–8; Acheson, *Gentry Community*, 160; Saul, *Provincial Life*, 26; J. T. Driver, 'Thomas Palmer of Holt', *Transactions of the Leicestershire Archaeological and Historical Society*, 69 (1993), 42–58.

[36] Richmond, *Paston Family*, 209, 212; Acheson, *Gentry Community*, 160; Saul, *Provincial Life*, 17–18; N. Saul, *Death, Art, and Memory in Medieval England* (Oxford, 2000), 54, 234–8.

primogeniture, from which they themselves had benefited, many were concerned to provide for their present family of wives, daughters, and younger sons. To do so, however, risked withdrawing significant portions of the estate or income from the heir for appreciable periods and even endangering his ability to sustain the family's inherited status. It could be a testing dilemma.

2. DOMESTIC CULTURE AND RELIGION

As with the nobility, the gentry household was an emanation of the nuclear family, consisting of the lord, his wife, and their children while under age. Children left the home on marriage, as did a widow, though an elderly parent might have a chamber assigned to them.[37] The presence of collateral relatives in the household was extremely rare.

The household was thus built around the marriage relationship with its social and personal obligations. In that marriage symbolized the union of Christ with his Church, canon law required it to be publicly entered into by free consent, informed by self-giving love, and lifelong. Clandestine marriage though valid was reprobated, while the dissolution of marriage other than for cruelty, disability, or crime was sanctioned only on grounds of technical invalidity.[38] Parents negotiated their children's marriages with some forethought, though betrothals before puberty were rare, and prospective partners were customarily introduced to establish a degree of acceptability and elicit their consent. Girls were advised to spare the make-up, not to fast to make themselves pale and thin, not to talk too much, and not to flaunt themselves, or they would lose their suitor. Suitors had an eye not only to the girl's dowry and capacity to breed, but to her looks, personality, and good sense. An ideal of ordered and harmonious married bliss, widely popularized in sermons and advice books, was voiced in almost identical terms by Chaucer's Merchant and by Peter Idley, who concluded that:

> To lieve in quyete it is a blissful lyffe
> Ever a good man maketh a good wyffe.[39]

This rested on the principle of male sovereignty, in both a social and a sexual context. A hierarchically ordered male society gave the husband control of his wife's lands, goods, and behaviour, while for the purpose of procreation the Church

[37] As did Sir John Camoys in that of his son-in-law: H. Le Strange, 'A roll of household accounts of Sir Hamon le Strange of Hunstanton, Norfolk, 1347–8', *Archaeologia*, 69 (1920), 111–20.

[38] R. H. Helmholz, *Marriage Litigation in Medieval England* (Cambridge, 1974), ch. 3, summarized in P. R. Coss, *The Lady in Medieval England* (Stroud, 1998), 125; H. Leyser, *Medieval Women* (London, 1995), 106–22.

[39] Chaucer, 'The Merchant's Tale', lines 1319–54; Idley's panegyric on marriage is in *Peter Idley's Instructions to his Son*, ed. C. D'Evelyn (Boston, 1953), lines 1226 ff. Idley was of the same social level as Chaucer.

allowed him sovereignty over her body. She could not refuse him, or take a unilateral vow of chastity, as Margery Kempe wished to do, but neither should he
abuse her in illicit practices, which confessors' manuals spelt out and forbade.
Popular didactic writing exhorted her to win his love by obedience to his wishes
and sufferance of his faults. For Chaucer it was precisely this social and sexual
'maistrye' of the male that frustrated the mutuality of the marriage relationship.
The Tales of the Miller and Manciple show wives tamed and caged, denied their
natural liberty; for the Merchant his wife is a possession to serve a sexual fantasy;
in the Clerk's Tale Griselda's abject submissiveness makes her husband a tyrant;
and when the Wife of Bath reverses roles and asserts a woman's 'maistrye', it is
equally disastrous. Even the domestic mutuality depicted in the Franklin's Tale
cannot be acknowledged in chivalric society.[40] This pathology of dominance in
marriage was observable in the world of the Pastons, whose enemies John
Heydon and Sir Thomas Tuddenham were both cuckolded.[41] Yet it is clear that
a companionate and loving relationship between spouses was not uncommon.
Affection and respect existed between John and Thomasin Hopton and even
John and Margaret Paston, and at the final separation the husband often paid
tribute to 'my entirely beloved wife', Sir Richard Poynings in 1430 describing his
as 'diligentissime et fidelissime'.[42]

   To their children some parents, as today, showed affection and others indifference. The experience of a fifteenth-century schoolboy was that 'when I come
home to my father and to my mother we wept for joy ych to other', though elsewhere a different situation is portrayed: 'When my father was in this worlde, he
loved me as hertely as eny father might do his childe. Notwithstandynge to my
mother I was as hatefull as enythynge . . . as menn say, whom the father loveth the
mother hateth.'[43] That the high rate of infant mortality inculcated indifference
in parents is belied in the same source: 'a great while after my brother diede, my
mother was wont to sytt wepynge every day'. While they were in the household
the children's upbringing was the prime responsibility of the mother, who, if
faced with disobedience, was recommended to 'take a smart rod and beat them
till they cry mercy and know their guilt'.[44]

---

[40] D. Traversi, *The Canterbury Tales* (London, 1983), 91–160; D. Pearsall, *The Life of Geoffrey Chaucer* (Oxford, 1992), 253–62; L. Patterson, *Chaucer and the Subject of History* (London, 1991), 307–17, 338–49.

[41] Richmond, *Paston Family*, i. 171 n. 16; R. Virgoe, 'The divorce of Sir Thomas Tuddenham', *Norfolk Archaeology*, 35 (1969), 406–18.

[42] K. Dockray, 'Why did fifteenth century English gentry marry?', in Jones (ed.), *Gentry and Lesser Nobility*, 61–80; Richmond, *John Hopton*, 117–20; Davis (ed.), *Paston Letters*, i. 218; Fleming, 'Kentish Gentry', n. 358.

[43] W. Nelson (ed.), *A Fifteenth Century School Book* (Oxford, 1956), 15, 17.

[44] B. Hanawalt, *Growing up in Medieval London* (Oxford, 1993), 72. For the beating of Elisabeth Paston, see Davis (ed.), *Paston Letters*, ii. 32.

But principally the wife had to run the household at a level which matched the family's standing, or 'apport', in society, affording her greater power and responsibility than her subordinate status would suggest. This meant the buying-in of victuals, the supply of clothing, the employment and organization of domestic staff, and the arrangement of hospitality for guests and visitors. In her husband's absence her responsibilities were extended to managing the estate, collecting debts, dealing with the steward and tenants, and even defending the property. It was here that the solid virtues of frugality and good sense came into their own.

The size of household appropriate for gentlemen of different degrees was defined in the *Liber Niger* of *c*.1471–2. That of a greater knight was to contain twenty-four servants and to cost £150 per annum, that of a lesser knight sixteen servants at a cost of £100, and that of an esquire seven servants at £50. This is borne out by the handful of household accounts that have survived. Those of Sir William Waleys at Glynde in 1382–3, Sir Hugh Luttrell at Dunster in 1425–6, and Sir William Mountford at Coleshill in 1443 all show fewer than twenty servants.[45] Higher up the social scale Dame Alice Bryene in Suffolk maintained a household of fifteen to twenty at a cost of £161 16s. in 1412–13.

Liberal hospitality, as practised by Chaucer's Franklin, was a mark of gentilesse, and this is well documented in Lady Bryene's accounts. The daily guests at table were mostly those on business from the estates and locality—bailiffs, local clergy, passing friars—and on occasion the lady's relatives and friends would stay overnight. Then special delicacies were provided—swan, heron, beef, goose, oysters—though the standard fare for the household was mutton, herring, and saltfish. Bread was baked once a week, some 250 loaves at a time, and 100 or so gallons of ale was brewed, though Lady Bryene herself drank wine each day. Much of the staple food came either from the home farm, which was kept in hand, or from local markets, while dried fruit and spices were bought at Colchester or Stourbridge. Of the total cost of Lady Bryene's household almost half was food, compared to 60 per cent in the notional budget for a knight and 71 per cent in the household of Gilbert, Lord Talbot, in 1417–18. By contrast food was a mere 12 per cent of the £110 spent by John Catesby on his household in 1392–3.[46] It looks as if hospitality (or perhaps wastage) became a significant burden as one moved up the social scale.

In fact a strict account was kept of daily, weekly, and monthly expenditure, a practice common to small gentry like Multon (1343–4) and elite families like

[45] Myers, *Household of Edward IV*, 89, 107–10; Dyer, *Standards of Living*, 51; Saul, *Provincial Life*, 162; Carpenter, *Locality and Polity*, 208.

[46] *The Household Book of Dame Alice de Bryene of Acton Hall, Suffolk, 1412–1413*, ed. M. K. Dale and V. B. Redstone (Ipswich, 1931); Acheson, *Gentry Community*, 141; J. T. Driver, 'The career of John Catesby', *Northamptonshire: Past and Present*, 51 (1998), 7–14; Dyer, *Warwickshire Farming*, 70, for table of household consumption.

Mountford and Luttrell.[47] Prudent budgeting, as recommended by John Paston to Sir John Fastolf, 'that my maister shuld be lerned whate hys housold standyth uppon yerlye . . . and that don, then to see by the revenues of hys yeerly lyfelode whate may be leyd and assigned owte for that cause to meynteyn hys seyd housold' was central to the moral economy of the gentry, designed to maintain a lifestyle appropriate to their station and avoid debt.[48] Nevertheless, there is plentiful evidence that credit was used in all kinds of transactions. The gentry borrowed from their fellows, from the local nobility, religious houses, and from London merchants like Gilbert Maghfeld, whose debtors included Sir Edward Dallingridge. Much of this was short-term, while awaiting the receipt of rents and agricultural revenues at particular times in the year, and many gentry kept a sizeable store of cash for current expenses.[49]

Conspicuous expenditure was most marked in building projects. Although the greatest knights asserted their equality with the peerage by erecting castles, as at Bodiam, Herstmonceux, and Caister, the unfortified manor house was more characteristic of the knightly class and the development of its plan and design mark this as the first major era in English house-building.[50] By the mid-fourteenth century the aisled hall had been superseded by a single-span roof. The hall retained its size and importance throughout this period, providing the focus of household life, where meals were taken, entertainment and ceremonies could be staged, and lordship was exercised in the manor court. At either end of the hall were cross wings containing domestic rooms on two floors. Frequently (though not invariably) that at the dais end contained the lord's solar, or great chamber, a spacious and pleasant room, with fireplace, serving for sleeping as well as living, and provided with a curtained bed for the lord and truckle beds for his attendants (seven in an inventory of the chamber at Appleby Magna in 1374). Adjoining it would be a small chapel. Beneath the chamber was a storeroom, originally for special purchases like wine and spices, but by the mid-fifteenth century this had sometimes been made into a parlour in which the lord might dine. By the late fourteenth century an oriel chamber linked the access to the lord's apartments from the hall, and in the fifteenth this blossomed into an oriel bay, which at Nevill Holt and Great Chalfield rose the full height of the hall, to balance the entrance porch at the lower end. Screens protected the hall from the entrance and from the doorways to the pantry and buttery in the domestic office wing. Over these service rooms chambers might be allocated to gentlemen servants or even for a

---

[47] Woolgar, *Household Accounts*, i. 38–40.   [48] Richmond, *Paston Family*, 252–3.
[49] M. K. James, 'A London merchant of the fourteenth century', *Econ. HR* 8 (1956), 372; Richmond, *Paston Family*, 155, 175.
[50] S. Pearson, *The Medieval Houses of Kent* (London, 1994), 128; Carpenter, *Locality and Polity*, 199–202; Acheson, *Gentry Community*, 137, 140; in general, M. Wood, *The English Medieval House* (London, 1965).

newly married son or aged parent. At this end, too, stood the kitchen, still in the fifteenth century detached as a safeguard against fire, and in the greater houses one of some height and elaboration, like that surviving at Stanton Harcourt. The lengthening of the cross wings and the joining of them by a range containing a gatehouse to form a quadrilateral, which could then be crenellated or sur-rounded by a moat like a miniature castle, was a prestige development among the wealthier gentry of southern England, like John Heydon at Baconsthorpe (1440s), John Brome at Baddesley Clinton (1440s), and Sir Thomas Brown at Tonford, Kent (1449).[51]

Through much of central and northern England gentry houses were solidly constructed of local stone or, in East Anglia, of brick, which by the fifteenth cen-tury had penetrated to the Home Counties and Thames Valley, as at Rye (Herts.), Stonor, and Ewelme. Where stone was not available half-timbering continued, and numerous timber houses of the lesser gentry dating from after 1370 survive in south-east England.[52] In these the roof line of the hall is carried over the cross wings, terminating with a hipped roof, to form the 'Wealden' type house. These were often the product of piecemeal enlargement as a family moved up the social ladder. Little other than the presence of a hall, the mark of lordship, distinguished these houses of the lesser gentry from those of bailiffs and yeomen farmers.

For internal decoration the gentry relied principally on furnishings, for most rooms were limewashed, though a few had wainscoting and the principal cham-ber would have ceramic floor tiles. By the late fourteenth century the hall and great chamber would be hung with tapestries or at least cloth painted in stripes of purple, red, and green. The will of Henry Inglose mentions one depicting the Nine Worthies, and hunting and allegorical scenes were also popular. In the remarkably full inventory of Sir Edmund Appleby's house at Appleby Magna (Leics.) in 1374 the lord's chattels represented 40.5 per cent of his wealth, and a comparable proportion has been deduced for the Kent gentry.[53] The houses of even the middling gentry were colourfully and comfortably furnished with one or two items of luxury. Soft furnishings relieved bare boards and hard settles, and plate gave a hint of opulence, though it also provided security for loans: at his death in 1445 John Throgmorton's silver plate was in pledge to the abbot of Northampton.[54]

What were the recreations of the gentry? For men a hunt lasting several days was the prime sport. The leisure and resources for hunting and knowledge of its rituals was a mark of gentility, and one of the principal occasions for hospitality.

---

[51] G. G. Astill, 'An early inventory of a Leicestershire knight', *Mid. Hist.* 2 (1974), 274–83; Emery, *Greater Medieval Houses*, ii. 49, 211, 282, 359.

[52] E. Mercer, *English Vernacular Houses* (London, 1975); Pearson, *Medieval Houses of Kent*.

[53] Richmond, *Paston Family*, 212; Astill, 'Early inventory of a Leicestershire knight', 279.

[54] Carpenter, *Locality and Polity*, 206.

The 'Lament for Sir John Berkeley' recalls his generosity in distributing the spoils of the hunt. The creation of parks became a status symbol for the wealthier gentry in this period, providing an exclusive right to hunt which echoed that of the king in the royal forests. To enclose an area of 300 acres, the size of Thomas Palmer's park at Holt (1448) with an earthen bank topped by a fence of cleft stakes and a ditch, was a huge physical operation. Poaching was almost as popular and skilled a diversion as hunting, both for the gentry who poached the deer of the nobility (as Sir Edward Dallingridge did in John of Gaunt's Ashdown Forest) and the lower orders who poached in the parks of the gentry.[55] Ladies might participate in hunting or, more frequently, hawking, but mainly took their recreation walking in the garden or indoors dancing and singing in the hall. While men played games of chess and backgammon, women occupied themselves with clothes-making and embroidery. At times the household as a whole would be entertained by visiting minstrels or players or the reading aloud of romances and histories. Pious ladies might gather as a circle to read devotional books in a chamber.

The gentry educated their children along the same lines as the nobility, though drawing more extensively on schools. Until 8 or 10, children were taught within the household by the chaplain or at a school run by the local vicar, like that at Kingston upon Thames in 1377. Children of both sexes would be taught to read from an ABC and thence to a primer containing the three basic prayers (Our Father, Hail Mary, and the Creed), matins, the hours of the Virgin, and some plainsong. By 7 they were ready to learn the rules of grammar, using the normal textbook, the *De Arte Grammatica* of Donatus, popularly known as the 'Donet', containing the parts of speech and elementary construction of sentences. This was the gateway to the next stage, the study of grammar, begun about the age of 10.[56]

At this point the sons of the upper gentry might either receive a chivalric upbringing as a page in a noble household, as was John Hardyng in that of the Percy family, or be placed under a schoolmaster, within the household, as in the Luttrell family in 1424. For those of the lesser gentry there were increasing opportunities to attend a local grammar school. These were generally attached to major churches and chantry colleges, with a resident schoolmaster who would charge 8*d*. a term for tuition (a total of 2*s*. 8*d*. per annum). Schools had to have around fifty pupils to be viable. With an additional boarding charge of 8*d*. a week, to educate a bright child was something that even a prosperous

[55] Turville-Petre, 'The Lament for Sir John Berkeley', *Speculum*, 57 (1982), 332–9; Pollard, *North Eastern England*, 198–208; N. Orme, 'Medieval hunting', in B. Hanawalt (ed.), *Chaucer's England* (Minneapolis, 1992), 133–53; Walker, *Lancastrian Affinity*, 127–41.

[56] N. Orme, *English Schools in the Middle Ages* (London, 1973), 59–69; Mertes, *Noble Household*, 172; Richmond, *John Hopton*, 130–6.

husbandman like Clement Paston found a struggle, and beginning with the foundation of Winchester in 1382 a number of schools or schoolmasters were endowed to provide free instruction. No other churchman followed Wykeham's lead, and most of these were appendages to chantries and colleges founded by the nobility and gentry, like that of Lady Katherine Berkeley at Wotton under Edge in 1381, that of Lady Isabel Pembridge at Tong in 1410, and that of the earl of Suffolk at Ewelme in 1440, though a few were initiated in towns. But overall the numbers were small, and the dearth of grammar schools in London prompted a petition to parliament in 1447.[57]

The late medieval gentry undoubtedly prized grammar schooling, for its discipline, for its techniques, and for its career opportunities. Pupils had an eight- or ten-hour day, beginning at 6 a.m. Teaching was mainly viva voce, learning by rote and rhyme, by question and answer, and was enforced by the generous use of the birch. Agnes Paston thought well of the master who 'belashed' her son Clement, and an entry in a fifteenth-century schoolbook vividly evokes the boy's shock at passing from the comforts at home to the harshness and discipline of boarding school.[58] Grammar teaching was based on the *Doctrinale* of Alexander de Villa Dei and reading the *Distichs of Cato*. The study of syntax, quantity and metre, and figures of speech led on to the highest achievement, the composition of Latin verse. The skills learnt were not purely academic, for the *dictamen* trained in letter-writing, and Latin was needed for deeds and charters, court rolls, and accounts. Indeed more practical matters, like accountancy and elementary legal procedures, crept into the grammar school curriculum, and formularies of business documents were produced by men like Thomas Sampson (1350–1409), who taught 'business studies' at Oxford. Late medieval schoolbooks reflected contemporary social attitudes: they emphasized piety, wisdom, and good manners, and drew examples from everyday life.[59]

This was reinforced by the change from French to English as the medium for teaching Latin. According to Trevisa (with probable exaggeration) by 1385 'in alle the gramere scholes of Engelonde, children leveth Frensshe and construethe and lerneth in Englisce'. Certainly by 1425–35 parallel English and Latin sentences were being used in the Accidence of John Leland and the *Parva Latinitates* of John Drury of Beccles, initiating a method of teaching through *vulgaria* which culminated in that of Stanbridge in the early sixteenth century. From the mid-fifteenth century, too, comes the first English–Latin dictionary, *Promptorium Parvulorum*. This growing use of English in schools came to threaten familiarity with French. French remained a vernacular for the court and

---

[57] Orme, *English Schools*, 183–98, 221.
[58] Davis (ed.), *Paston Letters*, i. 41; *Fifteenth Century Schoolbook*, 1, quoted in full in Orme, *English Schools*, 138–9.　　　　　　[59] Orme, *English Schools*, 76–7, 87–106.

peerage but from the mid-fourteenth century was ceasing to be so for the knightly class. Yet because, like Latin, it was essential for the world in which they were to move—in law, war, diplomacy, travel, and trade—it had to be learnt, using a French 'Donet'—*Le Donait français*.[60]

The teaching of young gentlemen at home and school was thus systematic, full-time, and comprehensive, aimed to equip them for the social, business, political, and religious activities of their station. Increasingly in the fifteenth century it was crowned by the study of law. There was a general consensus among the gentry on the advantages, indeed the necessity, for this. From school a few proceeded to university but many more to the Inns of Court, to acquire a general familiarity with legal process and complete their education. The Inns resembled small colleges in which the students lived as a community for twenty-eight weeks in a year. Fortescue called them an 'academy of all the manners that nobles learn', and the social life included singing, dancing, plays, and knightly sports, all set in the heady context of London society. But the education was arduous and serious. Many of the serjeants and judges were men of wide culture, while the law itself touched philosophy and theology and raised issues of political and social concern. It has been suggested that Fortescue's concept of mixed monarchy—of regal power limited by law enacted in parliament—reflected the common understanding of the legal profession of his day. Law had its arcane reaches, but education at the Inns of Court appealed to the gentry not only for its practicality and career prospects but because it inculcated an alert and informed approach to social and political developments.[61]

The spread of schooling and literacy among all grades of the gentry was paralleled by the development of English as a vehicle of literary expression. It has been strongly argued that these were connected: that Middle English alliterative verse was the peculiar medium of an emergent non-noble readership. Whereas the court and aristocracy continued to read and write French, and to favour French chivalric romance, those below them turned to English for instruction, literary expression, and political comment.[62] But the situation was more complex than this. In the mid-fourteenth century the literate population was effectively trilingual in its daily usage, and alliterative Middle English was developed principally as a literary form and in an oral context. Since very little alliterative verse

    [60] Orme, *English Schools*, 95–9; id., 'Schools and schoolbooks', in *CHB* 449–69.
    [61] Ives, 'The Common Lawyers', in C. H. Clough (ed.), *Profession, Vocation, and Culture in Later Medieval England* (Liverpool, 1982), 181–217; above, Ch. 3, sect. 2, for the Inns of Court and the legal profession.
    [62] E. Salter, *Fourteenth Century English Poetry* (Oxford, 1983), chs. 2, 4; T. Turville-Petre, *The Alliterative Revival* (Cambridge, 1977), ch. 2; R. Hanna, 'Alliterative poetry', in *CHMEL* 488–512; P. R. Coss, 'Aspects of cultural diffusion in medieval England', *P & P* 108 (1985), 35–79.

can be securely dated, and even less assigned a known authorship, analysis of it has focused on evidence of patronage and on local dialect and verse forms. The earliest collection to show a preference for English over French is the Auchinleck Manuscript, copied in London c.1330–40 for a non-aristocratic readership, while Harley MS 2253, a collection of about the same date, had a local audience in the West Midlands. Somewhat later the poem *William of Palerne* puts into English a French chivalric text for the benefit of the household retainers of Humphrey de Bohun, earl of Hereford (d. 1361). In the second half of the century it is from the north-west that come such different works as *Wynnere and Wastoure* (1352), a dialogue contrasting the chivalric and prudential ethos, and *Sir Gawain and the Green Knight*, which explores the moral dilemmas of knighthood in the context of the rituals and values of courtly life.[63] From the Midlands come *The Tale of Gamelyn* and the stanzaic *Le Morte Arthur* (1350), and London was the setting of the poem *St Erkenwald*, c.1380. Alliterative verse was produced and read all over midland and southern England, assisted by the fact that midland English was widely understood. The alliterative form was favoured because it lent itself both to high narrative and to aural presentation. Its subject matter was also eclectic. Arising initially from the demand for access in English to the French and Latin romances, it embraced a range of religious, chivalric, historical, and social themes. Such personal and contextual evidence as exists relates it to middling society rather than to courtiers and aristocracy, from whose wills and book collections such items are wholly absent.

Yet it was not the alliterative, midland form, but 'Chaucerian' London English that became the standard usage by 1400. How and why this happened has not been conclusively established. It was certainly not by natural development from Middle English, but was an artificial construct.[64] The initiative came from Chaucer and his literary circle, but its speedy adoption by the translators of the Wycliffite Bible and by spiritual writers like Hilton suggest that it was meeting a felt need. Chaucer's aim was to fashion a literary vernacular suitable for the translation (in the broadest sense) of the continental tradition of courtly romance into English upper-class culture. Then, after 1390, he turned to address the small but diverse group of lawyers, merchants, beneficed clergy, and members of the royal household and civil service whose focuses were the city, Westminster, and the royal palaces of Eltham and Sheen. Avoiding both the metre and rhetoric of the alliterative tradition, and jettisoning the artificiality of traditional romance, he framed a critique of his society drawn from its familiar types, whom he presented as real people in language both sophisticated and

---

[63] E. Salter, 'The timeliness of *Wynnere and Wastoure*', *Medium Aevum*, 47 (1970), 40–65, connects the poem to the household of Sir John Wingfield. The provenance of *Gawain* remains obscure; Bennett, *Community, Class and Careerism*, ch. 10.

[64] J. Catto, 'Written English: The making of the language, 1370–1400', *P & P* 179 (2003), 24–59.

colloquial, moral and detached. Langland, on the fringe of the same milieu though coming from the West Midlands and from a lower social level, had retained a modified alliterative style for his great poem describing an agonized search for a truly Christian life and his strictures on the disparity between the Christian ethic and contemporary society. Different again were the Wycliffite translators of the Bible, whose intention was to produce an authoritative and nuanced text for the dissemination of their reconstructed Christian message through the pulpit. Such widely differing yet contemporaneous projects were all responding to the need for a vernacular literature to engage directly with the problems of daily experience. Early in the new century political polemic revived the alliterative tradition in such works as *Richard the Redeles* and *Mum and the Sothsegger* and the poems of Digby MS 102. When that finally passed it was the Chaucerian style that emerged as the model for standard London English through the work of Hoccleve and Lydgate and the active patronage of the Lancastrian Crown.[65]

Henceforth the dominance of the Chaucerian tradition in the literary culture of the gentry is reflected in their libraries. Copies of *The Canterbury Tales* were owned by those serving the Lancastrian court and administration, like John Stopyndon, the king's secretary in 1422, John Leventhorpe, receiver of the duchy of Lancaster, and Sir John Stanley, usher of the chamber, who also possessed works by Lydgate. Indeed the Chaucerian poets could be expected to figure in the library of any provincial knight of culture. The Lincolnshire knight Thomas Cumberworth (d. 1451) left a copy of *The Canterbury Tales* to his niece, and a list of books associated with John Broughton of Toddington (Beds.) includes Chaucer and Hoccleve, law books, religious tracts, and courtesy books. Within the same social bracket, but enjoying closer connections with the court, were Sir Edmund Rede and Sir Thomas Charlton. Rede had an extensive and varied library at his house at Boarstall (Bucks.) and Charlton, a Speaker of the House of Commons, left a collection which included *Troilus and Criseyde*, *The Canterbury Tales*, and *Piers Plowman*.[66] By the time we reach the library of Sir John Paston, and those of judges like Littleton and Kebull, the majority of books, apart from legal works, are in English and cover a wide range of Chaucerian verse, chivalric literature, romances, and spiritual and philosophical discourses.

Such collections formed by personal choice were undoubtedly read. Indeed there was a vogue for collecting together in one volume an eclectic choice of

[65] Salter, *Fourteenth Century Poetry*, chs. 5, 6; G. Olson, 'Chaucer', in *CHMEL* 561–88; Strohm, 'Hoccleve and Lydgate', in *CHMEL* 638–58.
[66] A. I. Doyle, 'English books in and out of court', in V. Scattergood and J. Sherborne (eds.), *English Court Culture in the Late Middle Ages* (London, 1983), 173–6; H. E. Salter (ed.), *The Boarstall Cartulary*, OHS 88 (1930), 286–91; S. Thrupp, *The Merchant Class of Medieval London* (Chicago, 1948), 248.

reading matter. Robert Thornton of East Newton (Yorks.) made a composite volume which included the *Morte Arthure* and Richard Rolle; that of the MP John Whittocksmede embraced hunting, husbandry, politics, and religion, with a subject key; and John Paston II's *Grete Book*, compiled under his direction by William Ebesham, was 'a great manual of knightly practice'. Such volumes formed 'a library *in parvo*' of chosen texts.[67]

There is little evidence that the gentry themselves wrote much. A didactic purpose prompted Peter Idley of Drayton (Oxon.) to compile the largely derivative *Instructions for his Son* embodying the prudential moral economy of the lesser gentry. At a higher level Sir John Fastolf commissioned his amanuensis William Worcester to record his views and experience of the French wars. Worcester produced a brief chronicle, the (lost) *Acta Domini Fastolf* and *The Boke of Noblesse*.[68] The *Boke* was written around 1452–3 to exhort the English to avenge their defeat in Normandy and to regain the lost territories. This they would only do by recovering the valour and virtues of the Romans and by repairing the moral failings by which they had forfeited divine favour. They also had to repair the defects in military organization, tactics, and discipline which the English collapse had revealed. With its compound of Roman history, Christian theology, and practical observation, the *Boke* is a typical product of the intellectual equipment of Fastolf's class. If Fastolf was the epitome of the military adventurer who fought the Hundred Years War for his own profit, he was also, like Idley, someone who sought to commit his experience and convictions to writing, to explain the changes of fortune, and to draw on a range of intellectual traditions.

The culture of the knightly elite was thus still broadly chivalric in its concern with both the practice of arms and traditional romances, now read largely in translation. It extolled the ideals of fidelity and loyalty as underpinning the political and social order, and displayed an associated obsession with the mutability of fortune, with fate and free will, though with some ambivalence about how far this was determined or revealed by the stellar system. Politically their ideas were shaped by the Aristotelian doctrine of the common good and the emphasis on law as the foundation of the polity. They saw their role as that of defenders of the realm and as magistrates under the king, God's representative. They valued education, avidly collected or commissioned books, and digested manuals on all kinds of practical topics from manners and cookery to medicine and hunting. Yet their culture reflected neither recent social changes nor new intellectual trends; it remained orientated to hierarchic values and historical myths.[69]

---

[67] Davis (ed.), *Paston Letters*, i. 447; G. R. Keiser, 'Practical books for the gentleman', in *CHB* 470–94; G. A. Lester (ed.), *Sir John Paston's Grete Book* (Woodbridge, 1984).

[68] J. G. Nichols (ed.), *The Boke of Noblesse*, Roxburghe Club (London, 1860); K. B. McFarlane, 'William Worcester: A preliminary survey', in id., *England in the Fifteenth Century*, 199–230.

[69] H. Cooper, 'Romance after 1400', in *CHMEL* 690–716.

But at a lower stratum, that of the lesser 'parish' gentry, estate administrators, and rising professionals in the towns, literature from *The Simonie* to *Piers Plowman*, and *Mum and the Sothsegger* was concerned with moral and social reform. It tended to be anticlerical and anti-chivalric, and to place the responsibility for spiritual and political abuses on those with authority. Nurtured on the moral economy of the small household, it emphasized mutual (not courtly) love, prudence rather than ostentation, and the safeguarding of inheritance through law and justice. The alliterative tradition lent itself to impassioned and direct address to an audience represented as lay, committed, and concerned with the common profit. Such literature was the product of social and spiritual tensions, of social mobility and individual questioning, and its heyday in the last half of the fourteenth century is a good index of the times. Thereafter it was submerged by the Chaucerian mode and the new Lancastrian orthodoxy. No more major alliterative work was produced, but the polemic strain resurfaced in mid-century in the satires and ballads that excoriated the courtier regime. As a disparate class, the gentry embraced both these lifestyles and cultures, which coexisted uneasily and on occasion underlay conflicting political attitudes.

Did the gentry, as a literate and landowning magistracy, have a distinctive attitude to the Church and religious belief? Like others in this age they sought protection against worldly misfortune and the uncertainties of the afterlife in the Church's doctrines and sacraments. But their wealth and social eminence enabled them to display an individualism in externals, while literacy opened the door to personal devotions.

The gentry were the natural leaders of their local Christian community centred on the parish church. Some held the advowson, giving them valuable patronage which could be exercised for clerks who served them as chaplains and confessors. Yet in general their patronage was not extensive, and was actively directed towards those churches associated with their family and residence. Most surviving medieval churches contain work done post-1300 but this is rarely documented, and direct evidence for the contribution of the gentry comes either from their wills or from their armorials on the fabric. In a few instances members of the greater gentry undertook the rebuilding of the entire church, but more often of part of it: a new perpendicular tower, a clerestory and new timber roof, an additional aisle, or the glazing of enlarged windows. Equally they might pay for redecoration and furnishings: for a scheme of wall paintings as at Trotton (Sussex), for the rood loft, or reredos, or font.[70] They regularly furnished the

---

[70] Saul, *Provincial Life*, 143–4, 148; M. C. Carpenter, 'The religion of the gentry of fifteenth century England', in D. Williams (ed.), *England in the Fifteenth Century* (Woodbridge, 1987), 53–74; Saul, *Death, Art, and Memory*, 215.

church with altar vessels, service books, and vestments, although these were also the subject of donations and bequests from parishioners. Indeed it was in the size rather than the frequency of their donations that the gentry were distinctive, since many projects both for the fabric and for the furnishing of the church were communally supported. A munificent lord was thus affirming his patriarchal role in the Christian community as well as purchasing his ticket to paradise.

Most of the gentry chose to be buried in their parish church, either in the chancel or in an adjoining aisle, in which they might build a family chapel. A few took this appropriation of sacred space to excess, turning the chancel into a family mausoleum and even obstructing the altar.[71] The tomb chests they favoured were costly and elaborate. Often these supported recumbent effigies of the lord and his wife in stone or alabaster, with figures of weepers or family escutcheons in the side panels beneath. A latten band along the edge of the tomb recorded their names and lifespan and asked prayers for their souls. The style and detail of these tombs might well be specified in the will or instructions of the deceased, and even fashioned before his death. Although the details of arms, armour, and clothing were scrupulously accurate it is improbable that the faces were portraits, for the effigies were representations of status and were produced in provincial or London workshops. Brasses, as an alternative to tomb sculpture, were placed either on the chest or on the chancel floor. Their design reached high standards of artistry and individuality in this period and all were made in London workshops, although the inscriptions, armorials, armour, and even posture were specifically commissioned.[72] Both effigies and brasses have been vulnerable to loss and defacement over the centuries and those that survive are the remnants of a near-universal mode of commemoration among gentry families. Their dual function made them virtually obligatory, for they served both to affirm the family's status and to secure intercession for the departed soul.

For monumental tombs, with or without effigies, were endowed as chantries for long-term or even perpetual prayers, to mitigate the pains and duration of purgatory which were vividly anticipated. The wealth that had furnished the means for a comfortable and culpable lifestyle was now employed to multiply— into the thousands—the number of post mortem masses for their soul. They also, in their wills, left bequests to churches and clergy, the poor, and those to whom they owed (or whom they had defrauded of) money. This discharge of their consciences, like the erection of their tombs, fell as a solemn duty on their executors and heirs, making unwelcome inroads into the inheritance. The same

[71] P. W. Fleming, 'Charity, faith, and the gentry of Kent, 1422–1529', in Pollard (ed.), *Property and Politics*, 44; Saul, *Provincial Life*, 154–5; id., *Death, Art, and Memory*, 21–2, 243–4.

[72] Indenture for the tomb of Ralph Grene (d. 1418) at Lowick, Northants., with plates in F. H. Crossley, *English Church Monuments, 1250–1550* (London, 1921), 30; Saul, *Death, Art, and Memory*, chs. 4, 5.

fusion of family pride and placatory penance marked their funerals where the hearse, decked with the trappings of chivalry (horses, shields, the deceased's armour) was followed by a procession of poor men clothed in black and paid a funeral dole. A few marked their personal piety by insisting that their unworthiness should be reflected in austere funerals and even the depiction of a cadaver on their monument.[73]

The parish church, then, was the theatre in which the patriarchal role of the gentry was given a religious dimension. Was it also the focus for their personal belief and devotions? Did they attend its common worship, and were they nourished by its rituals? Here the evidence is less tangible and less plentiful. Many—perhaps most—had private chapels or oratories in their houses. These were authorized by special indults from Rome (which were not uncommon) for a portable altar and personal confessor, a recognition of the growing interest among the literate laity in personal religious experience.[74] One root of this lay in the contemplative writings of Richard Rolle and later Walter Hilton, but possession of these was fairly restricted, and a more pervasive influence was the practice of confession. This taught the penitent to examine his conscience and analyse his failings, and was supplemented by a catechetical literature on the elements of faith, like Walter Nassyngton's *Speculum Vitae* and *The Lay Folk's Catechism*. Didactic and devotional collections like *The Poor Caitif* and *The Prick of Conscience*, meditative works like Nicholas Love's *Mirror of the Blessed Life of Jesu*, and collections of saints' lives in prose or verse appeared in gentlemen's libraries. But most of the books bequeathed in gentry wills were service books used in their chapels.[75] Nevertheless, the domestic chapel and the household confessor could underpin a regime of daily mass, personal penance, individual prayer, and private reading or meditation. There are indications that some of the gentry followed this, like Sir John Depeden, who used his missal daily, and Sir John Heveningham, who had heard three masses in church and said 'a little devotion in his garden' before suddenly collapsing and dying in July 1453.[76] Some thereby acquired a familiarity with the liturgy comparable with that of the priesthood, detailing the forms and sequences of prayers to be used in their

---

[73] E. Duffy, *The Stripping of the Altars* (New Haven, 1992), 349–50, 358–60; C. Richmond, 'Religion and the fifteenth century English gentleman', in B. Dobson (ed.), *The Church, Politics and Patronage in the Fifteenth Century* (Gloucester, 1984), 195–6.

[74] Fleming, 'Charity', 42; J. A. F. Thomson, 'The well of grace: Englishmen and Rome in the fifteenth century', in Dobson (ed.), *Church, Politics and Patronage*, 109.

[75] For this, see below, Ch. 10, sect. 3. For book bequests, see M. Vale, *Piety, Literacy and Charity among the Yorkshire Gentry* (York, 1970); J. H. Moran, *The Growth of English Schooling* (Princeton, 1985), 152–6.

[76] Davis (ed.), *Paston Letters*, i. 39; Vale, *Piety, Literacy, and Charity* (for Depeden); Richmond, 'Religion and the fifteenth century gentleman', 197–8.

chantries and introducing votive masses and particular cults into the ritual of their chapel. They lavishly furnished it with altar vessels, vestments, and books, and even with prized relics like the pieces of the true cross owned by Richard Poynings, Sir William Yelverton, and William Haute.[77]

Could this cultivation of the private chapel and a personal religion devalue the gentry's commitment to the parish church and common worship? The author of *Dives and Pauper* feared so, warning them not to despise the parish church, for 'comoun preyere of a comonte in chirche is beter than synguler preyere' in their oratories, and recalling their obligation to attend church at the principal feasts.[78] For although the private chapel did facilitate devotion, the lord's withdrawal had often more to do with maintaining social distance, just as in the church he might sit in his own pew and even claim (as Judge Yelverton did) a patron's seat in the chancel.

If the gentry practised their religion to some degree at a different level and socially apart, was it a religion of a different kind from that of the parishioners? For the great majority there was, of course, no divergence in doctrine, but it has been suggested that education was inculcating a more mental and private approach, as against the sensory, magical, and communal practices of their villagers.[79] If this was true for a few, it was only partially so for the majority of the gentry in this period. Generally theirs was not a religion of the book or the mind, but one of reassuring ritual, incantatory repetition, and salvific invocation of the saints. These were the common media through which the power of the holy could be harnessed to daily needs. Only to a handful of 'Lollard knights' did the biblical fundamentalism of Wyclif make an appeal, either as a destructive critique of ecclesiastical hierarchy or as a puritanical observance of biblical precepts. But the few gentry who used their wealth and position to protect Lollard preachers and disseminate Lollard writings were a passing phenomenon.[80] As a whole the gentry were conditioned by their magistracy to uphold the hierarchy and orthodoxy of the Church.

3. MAGISTRACY

The gentry were the immediate governors of the localities, and acted there in three capacities. First, they served as officers of the Crown, as sheriffs, justices of the peace, and escheators. Secondly, many, and perhaps most, of those who held

---

[77] Saul, *Provincial Life*, 157–60; Richmond, 'Religion', in Horrox (ed.), *Fifteenth Century Attitudes*, 198.   [78] *Dives et Pauper*, ed. P. H. Barnum, 1/i, EETS, 275 (Oxford, 1976), 195–6.

[79] Richmond, 'Religion and the fifteenth century gentleman', 202–3; Carpenter, 'Religion of gentry', 58–9, 68–9.

[80] C. Richmond, 'Introduction', in C. Richmond and M. Aston (eds.), *Lollardy and the Gentry in the Later Middle Ages* (Stroud, 1997), 1–27, and below, Ch. 10, sects. 4, 5.

these offices would be feed retainers of a local magnate, the natural ruler of the locality, and thus channels of his lordship. Thirdly, they held manorial lordship and jurisdiction in their own right. Any local office to which the Crown appointed carried sufficient authority to require its occupant to possess some form of lordship of his own, and hence to have gentry status. The poem *Gentylnes and Nobylyte* expresses this essential magistracy:

> Myn Auncestors who have ever be
> Lordes, Knyghtes and in gret auctoryte
> Capteyns in warr and governors
> And also in tyme of peace gret rulers.[81]

This admixture of public and private authority was characteristic of, and essential to, the operation of late medieval government. As central government extended its reach, it tended to enlist traditional lordship into government, to the advantage of both. This was to remain characteristic of English government into modern times. Like any system it was exposed to strains and failures, either through the attempt by central government to override local power or by the temptation for a local power to turn royal authority to its own advantage. I shall consider its malfunction in due course, but first the role of the gentry as a magistracy must be outlined.

Although the ancient office of sheriff was of less importance than in earlier centuries it carried prestige and influence in a local context. The sheriff presided at the monthly county court as the king's officer but also as the symbol of the shire's identity. Financially he had to answer for the farm of the shire, though this had now become a vestigial sum. He was also personally chargeable for levying debts to the Crown and all judicial fines imposed by the courts. These financial burdens deterred some men from accepting the office. Additionally onerous was the execution of administrative orders from the Crown and servicing numerous special commissions. He was also empowered to deal with riots and breaches of the peace.

The judicial business of the county court had much diminished, being mainly confined to personal actions of trespass and debt detinue, and receiving some indictments for felonies. Yet while the sheriff's judicial functions were largely obsolete, his duties in policing and administering the judicial system grew as the amount of litigation in the central courts increased. He was responsible for the delivery of writs in mesne process; for taking pledges for appearance in court and distraining the recalcitrant; for proclaiming outlaws and seizing their goods, arresting suspected criminals, and empanelling juries; and ultimately for hanging convicted felons. His key role in the judicial system prompted attempts to influence him by bribery, favours, and threats. In 1451 Sir John Fastolf

---

[81] Above, p. 136 n. 1.

instructed his servant Thomas Howes to 'labour to the sheriff for the return of such panels as will speak for me, and not be shamed . . . entreat the sheriff as well as ye can by reasonable rewards, rather than fail'.[82] Finally, the sheriff had a political and military role. In the shire court he promulgated royal proclamations while outside it he could raise the *posse comitatus* to enforce the peace or muster support for the Crown in the face of magnate rebellion or popular insurrection.

The appointment of sheriffs rested with the king's council. From 1340 the Commons had secured statutes restricting the sheriff's tenure to one year and (in 1377) prohibiting reappointment within three years, but Richard II saw this as a limitation on the royal prerogative (1384) and in 1397 prolonged them in office on the ground that it took a year for an occupant to become versed in the job.[83] Against the Crown's need for experience and continuity in royal officials, the people of the shire pressed for accountability and redress against those who abused power. The Lancastrian kings accepted the principle of annual appointments, though men often served for repeated (but not consecutive) terms. In Buckinghamshire Sir John Aylesbury was sheriff for eleven years in 1365–87 and in Nottinghamshire Sir Thomas Chaworth served ten times between 1403 and 1424. The office was filled from an increasingly narrow elite of knights and wealthier esquires: it was, as Sir John Shynner said (1481), 'a presentabell office' sought by the 'worcheppefollyst yn ye sher', while those below, like James Gresham in the divided Norfolk of 1450, looked for 'a man of gret byrthe and lyflod' to 'lede the peple in most peas'.[84] It brought not only prestige but rewards from the Crown in the shape of farms of manors, wardships and marriages, and local offices of profit.

Undoubtedly magnates sought to influence the choice of sheriffs in the royal council, and during periods of a lord's dominance in a shire most sheriffs would be his retainers. Thus it was in Nottinghamshire in the 1430s while Lord Cromwell was treasurer, in Warwickshire under Earl Richard Beauchamp during Henry VI's minority, and in Staffordshire during the ascendancy of Humphrey, duke of Buckingham, in the 1450s.[85] Magnates exploited this connection for their own ends. In 1440 Lord Cromwell used John Cokfield as sheriff to empanel a favourable jury to indict Lord Grey of Codnor, on whose destruction he was bent.[86] The Crown likewise influenced the choice of sheriffs. Increasingly under Richard II and the Lancastrians it appointed its own retainers, amounting to

---

[82] Gairdner (ed.), *Paston Letters*, no. 154.   [83] *SR* i. 283, ii. 4; *Rot. Parl.* iii. 339.

[84] C. L. Kingsford (ed.), *Stonor Letters and Papers, 1290–1483*, Camden Society, 3rd ser., 30 (London, 1919), ii. 134; Gairdner (ed.), *Paston Letters*, nos. 117, 124–5; Payling, *Political Society*, app. 5; Acheson, *Gentry Community*, app. I.

[85] Payling, *Political Society*, 140–2; Carpenter, *Locality and Polity*, 276; I. D. Rowney, 'The Staffordshire political community, 1440–1500', Ph.D. thesis (Keele University, 1981), ch. II.

[86] Payling, *Political Society*, 196.

one-fifth of all those between 1437 and 1460.[87] But both magnates and the Crown depended on a sheriff's own intrinsic authority and acceptability to the shire establishment if his rule was not to be seen as factional or intrusive.

The office of escheator was of less consequence than that of sheriff and over the period suffered a perceptible decline in social status. A statute of 1368 had required the holder to have £20 per annum in landed income, but in the fifteenth century it was from the middling and lesser gentry, not the shire elite, that escheators were drawn. On the death of a tenant-in-chief he was responsible for declaring the true heir, taking proof of his age, declaring the value of the lands, making partition between heiresses, and assigning dower to the widow. For all this he empanelled a jury of twelve local men. Where the inheritance was in dispute, competing claimants might exert pressure on the jury and the escheator to return verdicts in their favour. So in 1431 Lord Cromwell got himself declared heir to the Heriz lands against the claims of Sir Henry Pierpoint; and in 1452 Edmund Mountford was recognized heir to his father, Sir William, in place of his elder half-brother, the right heir.[88] The escheator could thus be an important pawn in the chicanery of the landowning class, taking bribes for false returns, but also a petty tyrant to those below him, threatening to seize lands and goods illegally.

Below the sheriff and escheator were a range of lesser officials: the coroner, the sheriff's officers, constables, and tax collectors. The coroner's was a specialized post, generally held by lesser gentry. On the sheriff's staff were his under-sheriff, receiver, clerk, and the hundredal and itinerant bailiffs. Hundred bailiffs presided at the hundred court and empanelled the juries; itinerant bailiffs collected the king's rents, served writs, and made distraints in royal hundreds. Three points emerge about these lesser executive officials. First, there were sufficient posts at this level to provide opportunities for semi-specialized careerists among the minor gentry; secondly, their duties and careers compounded the private and public; thirdly, in consequence they could exercise their office to their own gain, not only in drawing fees but by bribery and intimidation. The tyranny of these petty officials when retained by lords who relied on them for revenue collection and social control was a constant fear and hazard in local society. Complaint against them was made repeatedly in private and parliamentary petitions (notably in 1376 and 1384), while in local and national uprisings, as in 1381 and 1450, they became the targets of violence and judicial indictment.[89] The

---

[87] Saul, *Knights and Esquires*, 113; R. M. Jeffs, 'The late medieval sheriff and the royal household', D.Phil. thesis (Oxford University, 1961), ch. 5.

[88] S. J. Payling, 'Inheritance and local politics in the later Middle Ages: The case of Ralph Lord Cromwell and the Heriz inheritance', *Nott. Med. Stud.* 30 (1986), 67–96; Carpenter, *Locality and Polity*, 464.

[89] Walker, *Lancastrian Affinity*, 163–7; A. J. Musson, 'Sub-keepers and constables: The role of local officials in peace keeping', *EHR* 117 (2002), 1–24; Harvey, *Jack Cade's Rebellion*, 41–4, 105–7.

extent of injustice and oppression at this level of society, the identity of its perpetrators, and the effects on social stability have never been adequately explored.

The stages by which peacekeeping in the shires was devolved to commissions
composed of magnates, professional lawyers, and local gentry has already been
outlined.[90] In practice many of the felonies and misdemeanours of the lower
classes were dealt with by pairs of JPs holding sessions throughout the county, an
exercise in social control, while the more serious felonies and breaches of the
peace were remanded to quarter sessions and assizes, where the more important
gentry participated.[91] While the criminal jurisdiction of JPs was circumscribed,
their role was extended in two other ways. First, in addition to their established
role in enforcing the statutes on labour and wages—consolidated in the Statute
of Cambridge (1388 and 1414)—they were made responsible for a range of economic regulations, and for statutes on purveyances (1441–2), sumptuary laws,
liveries, clipping and counterfeiting, and apprehending Lollards. In these matters they were more actively policing local society than exercising strictly criminal jurisdiction. Secondly, by a statute in 1411 they were empowered, with the
sheriff, to arrest those making a riot or forcible entry or report them to the council or king's bench. But they might also seek to avert a threatened riot or assault,
imposing recognizances to keep the peace or persuade the parties to mediation.
In these matters they were dealing primarily with the gentry as transgressors,
and very often their role had a political as well as a judicial dimension.[92]

The attitude of the gentry to the magnates on the commission was ambivalent.
Magnates lent a necessary weight, but in the last quarter of the century the parliamentary Commons repeatedly blamed them for disorder in the localities, condemning the inclusion of their stewards on the peace commission, their
perversion of justice through maintenance, and the activities of the lesser men
who wore their livery, all of which they saw as subverting their own magistracy
within the shire. Between July 1389 and December 1390 Richard II bowed to this
by temporarily excluding the magnates, but their local power and their close relationship with the king made them the preferred channels of royal authority, and
in the following century leading lay, and later ecclesiastical, magnates headed the
commissions as a matter of course.[93]

The proportion of a peace commission who were members of a noble
affinity and to what extent this affected its operation depended greatly on local

[90]   Above, Ch. 3, sect. 2.
[91]   Maddern, *Violence and Social Order*, 61–4, 249–54; Walker, 'Yorkshire Justices of the Peace',
281–313.
[92]   J. G. Bellamy, *Criminal Law and Society in Late Medieval and Tudor England* (Gloucester,
1984), 61–70.
[93]   R. L. Storey, 'Liveries and commissions of the peace, 1388–90', in Du Boulay and Barron
(eds.), *Reign of Richard II*, 131–52.

circumstances. In counties under the rule of a single great lord, like Lancashire and the West Riding under Gaunt, Devon under Courtenay, Warwickshire under Beauchamp, and East Anglia under de la Pole, the majority of the justices would be their retainers. In a county of multiple lordship, like Essex, no single lord dominated the bench through his followers.[94] Such ties strengthened the cooperation of gentry and nobility as a governing class, though attempts by rival lords to influence the membership of the commissions could disrupt the sessions, as in the Bedford 'riots' in 1437 and 1439 between the factions of Lord Fanhope and Lord Grey.[95]

The evolution of the peace commissions in the century after 1361 reconciled the Crown's concern for professional judicial standards with that of local communities to retain dispute settlement and peacekeeping in their own hands. They proved an enduring means of dealing with local crime and social control, to the satisfaction of both Crown and locality. By recognizing the gentry as local rulers, and making them royal officers, the Crown enhanced their political status and associated them in governance. Gradually this wrought a change in their attitude to the law: from seeing it as extraneous and hostile they became its custodians and manipulators. Their role as governors strengthened the growing hierarchy within the shire, so that a Justice of the Peace could take pride in being 'a capitaine or a ruler at a session or a shire day'.[96] The devolution of royal authority did, however, raise the danger of its appropriation and abuse by local interests. The checks on this were partly political, through the Crown's reliance on loyal magnates and its own retainers, and partly judicial, through the appointment of incorruptible central justices and the ultimate intervention of the king's bench or council.

Much of the work done later by Tudor JPs was undertaken in this period by gentry acting under ad hoc commissions. In Devon and Cornwall 399 such commissions were issued in the period 1377–1422, an average of eight a year; in Norfolk during the period 1437–61 there were 68, involving over a hundred different men.[97] They would often embrace a wide social range, from parish gentry with knowledge of local conditions to elite families known and trusted by the Crown. Particularly was this so in commissions of inquiry, often into matters of local concern, whereas on commissions enforcing royal authority or meeting royal needs the weightiest in the shire were named.

Inquiry commissions were numerous and varied. Some, like those into

---

[94] S. J. B. Endelman, 'Patronage and power: A social study of the Justices of the Peace in late medieval Essex', Ph.D. thesis (Brown University, 1977), 90.

[95] Maddern, *Violence and Social Order*, 206–25.

[96] *Boke of Noblesse*, 78.

[97] C. J. Tyldesley, 'The Crown and the local communities in Devon and Cornwall, 1377–1422', Ph.D. thesis (Exeter University, 1978), ch. 4; R. Virgoe, 'The Crown and local government: East Anglia under Richard II', in Du Boulay and Barron (eds.), *Reign of Richard II*, 218–41.

concealments of Crown rights, wastes, titles to property, necromancy, treasons, and Lollardy, were recurrent and perhaps unspecific; those to investigate piracy, smuggling, poaching, pollution of rivers, treasure trove, thefts, murders, and robberies usually addressed particular local circumstances. A group concerned the maintenance of the economic infrastructure, like sewers and weirs, ditches and dykes, highways and bridges. Many commissions sought to affirm and enforce royal authority: to issue proclamations, to warn malefactors of punishment, to administer oaths (e.g. against maintenance of lawbreakers in 1434), to detect and suppress confederacies and risings (in 1381–2 and 1414), and to array soldiers in times of war and rebellion. All these, and those that touched the fiscal dues of the Crown, like negotiating general loans (particularly under the Lancastrians), assessing novel taxes (in 1412, 1431, 1436, 1450–1), awarding tax rebates (1373), and supervising tax-collecting, needed to include the leading local gentry.

Men known and trusted by the central government could serve on twenty or thirty commissions in their lifetime as well as holding other shire offices and sitting on the bench. Not only were they the backbone of local government, but they formed a vital link between Westminster and the provinces. They were familiar with courts of all kinds: from that of the king and the central courts in Westminster Hall, to those of the assizes, the quarter sessions, and sheriff. They knew their procedures and persons, the thrust of royal policy and the instincts of the political class. Typical of the bustling, contentious, and versatile world of courts and country, they were the natural choice as the community's representatives in the high court of parliament.[98]

Since 1300 the status of those elected as knights of the shire had risen, as parliament grew in importance. By 1400 the shire elite—knights and greater esquires— monopolized shire representation. In Lancastrian Nottinghamshire only four of the thirty-eight MPs, and in Leicestershire only six, came from the lesser squirearchy; and a similar pattern characterized Kent and Bedfordshire. In 1445 a statute required those elected to be 'knights or suitable esquires or gentlemen capable of bearing knighthood'. In fact the proportion who were actual knights, from being a majority before 1399, dropped to a quarter under Henry V and to a fifth by mid-century before recovering to almost half by the end. This reflected a broader re-evaluation of knighthood. Whereas before 1375 the Crown had at times expressly desired the return of knights with military experience, between the 1380s and 1415 military needs declined and fewer assumed knighthood. Military knighthood survived more strongly in the north, but in the south it became a mark of social distinction for elite gentry families. Alongside the decline

---

[98] Biographies, *House of Commons*.

of knights went a steadily increasing proportion of lawyers (despite prohibitions in 1372–3 and 1404), rising from 8 per cent in 1388 to over 20 per cent under Henry V and Henry VI. This reflected partly the growth in the profession, but more specifically a change in the Crown's attitude from hostility to a need for their services. Some of the best lawyers now got elected to parliament and established themselves among the shire elite: men such as Roger Hunt, John Throgmorton, Robert Darcy, and Roger Flore, all of whom sat in the parliament of 1422.[99]

It was expected—and required by statutes of 1413 and 1430—that MPs should be 'resident and dwelling' in the county when the writs were issued. Virtually all were, though many held land in more than one shire. Most of those elected were in their vigorous middle years, between 30 and 45, and as he accumulated experience of shire administration, an MP acquired the respect of both his community and the Crown and might expect further election. On average, shire representatives sat in three or four parliaments; no more than one-fifth sat only once. Most of them thus acquired a modicum of experience of parliament. In more than half the parliaments of Edward III's reign members with experience were in a majority, and in the last quarter of the century this proportion rose to two-thirds before falling back to 60 per cent or under in the fifteenth century. The smaller proportion re-elected in consecutive parliaments followed a broadly similar curve, reaching an average of almost one quarter under Richard II but thereafter doing so only occasionally. For parliamentary business this meant a considerable degree of discontinuity, but in personal terms experience was more important than consecutive election. Virtually every county produced men who sat for ten or twelve parliaments—there were sixteen of such in the parliament of 1422—with the record held by William Burley for nineteen parliaments and Sir William Bonville for twenty. This meant not only that the collective memory of a parliament could be considerable (that of 1422 ranged back over every parliament since 1395) but that it was also available to local society. A wealthy local elite thus commanded a degree of familiarity with parliament and politics which gave them national stature. The frequency of parliaments linked centre and locality, and a long-serving member became a trusted channel of communication between them.[100]

The relationship between the member and his constituency may be gauged from the mode of election and from his representation of its interests. Elections were made in the county court 'by the common assent of the county'. Allegations

---

[99] *SR* ii. 342; Roskell, 'Introductory survey', in *House of Commons*, i. 55–7, apps. B1, B2; Acheson, *Gentry Community*, 122–4; Fleming, 'Kent gentry', ch. 3; S. J. Payling, 'The rise of lawyers in the lower house, 1395–1536', in L. Clark (ed.), *Parchment and People: Parliament in the Middle Ages* (Edinburgh, 2004), 103–20.

[100] *House of Commons*, i. 508, 666, apps. B3, D1, 2, 3, ii. 282, 432; J. S. Roskell, *The Commons in the parliament of 1422* (Manchester, 1954), 38–43.

that sheriffs had manipulated elections or made false returns under pressure
from the Crown or magnates may have prompted an important change to electoral procedure in 1406. Henceforth the sheriff was to return the names of the
two members elected in an indenture attested by all those present. This did not
define who the electors were or how the election should be conducted. That was
done in the famous statute of 1429 conferring the franchise on those with forty
shillings of freehold land in the shire. This extended the electorate well below
the gentry to include yeomen and even husbandmen, matching the requirement
for jury service in the shire court and embracing all those charged to pay the
wages of the elected member. The shire community was thereby defined as its
freeholders. Yet the intention was not to extend but to limit the franchise by
excluding those 'poor and without property' who, there is reason to believe, had
disrupted recent contested elections. Where that occurred, the statute laid down
that the candidate with the greater number of electors should be returned. The
sheriff was to examine the freeholders individually, eliminating any with insufficient property, and thereafter establish a numerical majority, either by voices, or
by a show of hands, or by physical division. He was then to record the names of
all the electors, irrespective of whom they had voted for, the election being
deemed to be 'by common assent'.[101]

Not all elections involved this sophisticated procedure, for in fact most were
pre-arranged among the magistracy, and uncontested. Where more than fifty
names were entered on an election return, a contested election may be presumed,
but even those named represented only a small proportion of the electorate,
which in a county of average wealth like Nottinghamshire probably numbered
around 625. Election procedures were thus too complex and the electorate too
large for general intimidation. Where elections were contested, rival factions
within the magistracy tried to mobilize the electors from their vicinity. If they
also enlisted a mob of other men to overawe or disrupt the proceedings, as happened in Derbyshire (1433), Cambridgeshire (1439), Suffolk (1453), and
Norfolk (1461), the sheriff might refuse to proceed with the election or to accept
those elected. Alternatively he might try to test the qualifications of the freeholders. In 1461 the under-sheriff of Norfolk 'tried' the electors and declared
that the duke of Norfolk's candidates had more of 'the sufficiency' than their
opponents, John Paston and John Berney, who tried to stop him by crying 'Nay
pleynly sheriff, ye shall trie no sufficient here for every man shall have his election and gif his voice.'[102] Parliamentary elections thus incorporated many below

---

[101] *House of Commons*, i. 55–68, 573; *Rot. Parl.* iii. 530, 601, iv. 350; *SR* ii. 156, 243–4; J. G.
Edwards, 'The emergence of majority rule in English parliamentary elections', *TRHS*, 5th ser., 14
(1964), 175–96.
[102] S. J. Payling, 'The widening franchise', in Williams (ed.), *England in the Fifteenth Century*,
167–85; id., 'County parliamentary elections in fifteenth century England', *Parlty. Hist.* 18 (1999),

even the minor gentry into the political life of the shire, extending political debate and the appraisal of government to the yeomen, husbandmen, and minor officers of hundred and vill. By the mid-fifteenth century it was at this level that the demand for 'free' elections was heard.

Nevertheless, the choice of shire representatives on most occasions was made within the magistracy itself. How this was done is largely obscure, but it embraced some unspoken assumptions. First, in a shire dominated by a single large magnate affinity one at least of the MPs would be likely to come from this circle.[103] A few letters survive from magnates to gentry and towns naming those whom they wish elected or would find unacceptable, though informal pressures were probably more usual. Secondly, however, a magnate would be unwise to try and impose a candidate unacceptable to the local elite. To do so was to put his authority and repute at risk. Thirdly, the candidates themselves felt their own prestige, or 'worship', to be at stake and for this reason were generally unwilling to contest an election if they risked defeat. For this reason John Paston withdrew in 1455 as his son did in 1472.[104] Much the same kind of management must have taken place where the county was dominated by an elite of gentry families. In Derbyshire, Vernon and Grey in the 1430s and later Vernon and Blount virtually divided the representation, each controlling one seat.[105] Where there was no controlling lordship, the gentry had to order matters themselves. Here repute, ability, experience, and perhaps contacts at court were likely to recommend a man for repeated election. John Wilcotes had connections to five different lords but it was probably his standing with Henry IV and V and personal qualities that led to his election for Oxfordshire to eleven parliaments between 1399 and 1421.[106] The selected candidates thus 'emerged' through informal soundings and direct canvassing among the magistracy; often there seems to have been a conscious effort to pair an experienced member with a novice. Only where this elite was already split and the election became an open trial of strength did a contest result, with possibly dire consequences. Contests represented a failure of the system, an opening for the serpent of division.

For the most part magnate influence was localized, but that of the duchy of Lancaster and the Crown was widespread. In at least fifteen counties over the

237–59; R. Virgoe, 'The Cambridgeshire election of 1439', *BIHR* 46 (1973), 95–101; C. H. Williams, 'A Norfolk parliamentary election, 1461', *EHR* 40 (1925), 79–86.

[103] For the Beauchamp, Fitzalan, and Courtenay affinities, see *House of Commons*, i. 669 (Warwickshire), 723 (Worcestershire), 645 (Sussex), 339 (Devon).

[104] McFarlane, *England in the Fifteenth Century*, 1–21.

[105] Wright, *Derbyshire Gentry*, 114–17. Similarly, Dorset was monopolized by the Stafford family (*House of Commons*, i. 361–2) and Somerset by the Bonville, Brooke, and Luttrell families (ibid. i. 585–6).

[106] *House of Commons*, iv. 860–3. Other counties of this type were Buckinghamshire, Berkshire, Middlesex, Northamptonshire, and Hampshire.

length and breadth of England the estates and officers of the duchy spawned a network of clientage. John of Gaunt exercised a major influence on elections in five counties and this was, if anything, increased when the duchy was annexed to the Crown.[107] The influence of the Crown lay mainly in the south-east, in counties adjacent to London and Windsor. Essex returned royal servants like John Doreward and Lewis John; in Surrey they were present in two-thirds of the parliaments of 1386–1421 and in Oxfordshire half. Here it was often royal confidants who managed the elections: Sir John Pelham in Sussex under Henry IV, Thomas Chaucer in Oxford and the adjoining counties, Sir John Tiptoft in Cambridgeshire and Huntingdonshire. Allegations of the Crown's direct intervention in elections through sheriffs or by writs were made from the end of the fourteenth to the middle of the fifteenth century and there is little doubt that for critical parliaments the Crown could and did secure the return of its supporters. How this was achieved is not in detail clear, but when controversy was anticipated informal pressures from Crown agents could make men stand or withdraw. There was also an element of individual decision, as some instinctively drew back from the dangers of partisan involvement, which others embraced for the favour they might win. The gentry needed to be alert to politics at national as well as local level. As John Jenney remarked in 1455 to John Paston, 'Sum men hold it right straunge to be in this parlement, and me thenkith they be wyse men that soo doo.'[108]

Broadly speaking, therefore, representatives were of four main types: the traditional magistracy for whom election was part of the *cursus honorum* of shire office; the men of business for whom it was a normal facet of their professional career at the centre; a few men who stood high in royal favour and were links between court and country; and other local gentry who served occasionally, for particular reasons.

Whatever their individual status and motives, their prime obligations as shire representatives were to present petitions and grant taxation. The knights' duty to present the grievances of their communities was affirmed in parliament and at their election in the shire court.[109] These were subsumed into the 'common petition' which was compiled by the Commons in parliament. In these some broad themes recur: the mechanics of trade, external and internal; legal loopholes and abuses; crime and disorder; remedies for abuses by royal officials in the localities; social evils like livery and maintenance; and excessive wages. For a wide spectrum of such problems parliament conscientiously sought remedies, mostly traditional but sometimes new. Yet by far the greater proportion concerned the interests of the magisterial class and of an electorate which amounted to

---

[107] Walker, *Lancastrian Affinity*, 238; *House of Commons*, i. 328–33.
[108] *House of Commons*, i. 60, 184–238 (sect. C); Davis (ed.), *Paston Letters*, ii. 120.
[109] *Rot Parl.* ii. 271, iii. 420.

less than 20,000 in a population of over 2 million. Representation effectively stopped at that level.[110]

Nevertheless, at times the shire knights saw themselves as having not merely a representational but a wider remedial role. In 1376 they asked for annual parliaments 'to make correction of the errors and faults in the realm', and for some, like Sir Thomas Hoo of Bedfordshire, these had a quasi-religious function, as voicing the realm's conscience.[111] Between the monarch, guided by divine grace, and the mob, instinctively resisting oppression, political society, guided by reason, had its own function. The Commons' role was to expound in reasoned terms what grievances required redress and thereby avert popular revolt. They could be saviours of both king and kingdom if they spoke fearlessly and honestly. Such was the view of a radical alliterative versifier around 1400. In the political society where none speak the truth parliament holds a special importance, for there the Commons are

> assembled to show the sores of the realm
> and spare no speech though they should perish.

In the imagined debate over the king's demand for a tax, an ostensibly principled member reminds them that,

> We be the servants and are paid wages
> and sent from the shires to show what grieves them
> and to speak for their profit and go no further,
> nor grant taxes to the great lords
> for wrongful cause, but only for war.
> And if we be false to those who sent us
> we shall be unworthy to receive our hire.

But it is the satirist's vivid caricature of the slothful, sycophantic, timid, and hired MPs that stays in mind:

> Then sat some as a cipher does in arithmetic
> that denotes a place but is worth nothing.
> And some had supped with Simon in the evening
> and the shire gained nothing from their presence.
> Some were tittle-tattlers and went to the King
> and warned him of foes who were really good friends.
> Some slumbered and slept and said but a little.
> Some mumbled and knew not what to say.
> Some had been hired and were bound therewith
> to venture no further for fear of their masters.[112]

---

[110] Payling, 'County parliamentary elections', 245.

[111] *Rot. Parl.* iii. 355; A. Goodman, 'Sir Thomas Hoo and the parliament of 1376', *BIHR* 41 (1968), 139–49.

[112] *Mum and the Sothsegger*, pp. 59–60, lines 1119–24; pp. 24–5, lines 46–65 (modernized).

In fact, if the knights of the shires saw themselves as mediators between the polarities of king and plebs it was more as the governors than the conscience of the realm. Their main concern was political stability and social control, and there was an underlying tension (even contradiction) between their magisterial and representative roles. For when oppressed, the common people looked to the gentry to procure redress from the lords and the king, even through revolt. Kings, however, expected the magistracy to control the people and suppress revolts when these occurred. In the popular risings of the sixteenth century some gentry were to find themselves trapped between these millstones. This was prefigured only in isolated incidents in the revolts of 1381 and 1450. But it was between these years that the character of the gentry's magisterial role was established.

4. WAR AND CHIVALRY

By 1360 the English had perfected a method of raiding into France which, in relation to its destructive effects, was economical in cost and manpower. Armies of not more than four to six thousand men, organized in companies of knights, mounted men-at-arms, and archers, were recruited under captains to serve for six months or a year. Their effectiveness as fighting units rested not merely on military skills but on a high degree of social cohesion, for they were drawn from a lord's retainers and from a pool of local landowning families who constituted 'a martial genteel community'. Edward III's wars had brought about a significant remilitarization of the middling landowners, who, as 'esquires' (*armigeri*), became entitled to use 'coat armour' as a means of identification in battle. Henry V's wars encouraged many more to claim gentility by virtue of serving as men-at-arms, eventually prompting regulation of family arms through the heralds. Military experience was thus a prime, even the primary, force in the formation of the gentry.[113] How widespread and frequent was it?

A broad correlation existed between military function and social status, determining whether a man served as a man-at-arms or archer. From the late fourteenth century the man-at-arms wore plated armour which protected the whole body, with a surcoat, or jupon, on which his heraldic arms could be depicted. He had a lance, 12 feet long, a sword, a dagger, and an axe or truncheon. All this was expensive and moderately weighty (about 66 lb), and in addition he would need at least two horses, probably coursers rather than the great warhorse or *destrier*. He was attended by a page. The archer wore an armoured jacket known as a brigantine or 'jack', with a sallet or helmet weighing in all about 30 lb. He had a 6-foot long bow, of yew, maple, or oak, a short sword or dagger, and an

---

[113] A. Ayton, *Knights and Warhorses* (Woodbridge, 1994), 9–25.

axe. Most, but not all, archers were mounted.[114] There was a marked disparity of esteem between the armigerous men-at-arms fighting under the banner of a knight, and the archers organized in companies of their own. The man-at-arms was trained to fight on horseback, with a premium on mobility and individual prowess, while the effectiveness of the archer depended on the rapid coordinated volleys of arrows delivered before the enemy was engaged.

In the century after 1360 the size and frequency of expeditions varied considerably, giving some generations greater war experience than others. Edward III's last expedition in 1359 had involved up to 3,500 men-at-arms, and when war was resumed ten years later the seven expeditions to northern France before 1383 involved some 10,000 indentures with knights and men-at-arms, while about the same number were made for those led by the Black Prince and John of Gaunt to Gascony and Spain between 1364 and 1386.[115] This points to a military element in society which, inclusive of archers, numbered some 10,000 men. But this represented a peak, for no English army was sent to the Continent for a quarter-century after 1386. A generation habituated to war had been succeeded by one that lacked any significant experience of it.

The Agincourt campaign opened another extended phase of gentry involvement in war. The two major expeditions of 1415 and 1417, together with reinforcements in 1418–22, involved over 6,000 indentures with knights and men-at-arms, a level of service comparable to 1369–80. Then in the twenty-two years from Henry V's death to the truce of 1444, twenty-four expeditions went to France. But despite continuous military activity in the thirty years 1414–44, only some 9,000 indentures were made, a very marked decrease over the years 1360–90. This reflected smaller armies, with a decreasing proportion of men-at-arms to archers, a development to which we shall return. The pool of men-at-arms was also diminishing. In 1419, out of a total of some 3,750 landowners with incomes over £10 per annum, there were 2,500 knights and men-at-arms serving in France, and this represented the effective limit of mobilization.[116] In fact the prolonged warfare of 1417–20 was wholly exceptional; normally the gentry could expect a royal summons to no more than two campaigns in a lifetime.

Those who served more frequently did so as indentured retainers of a lord. The backbone of a magnate's military company were the members of his household, life retainers, and annuitants, all of whom were bound to serve him under

[114] M. Bennett, *Agincourt 1415* (Botley, 1991), 20–8; Ayton, *Knights and Warhorses*, 209–50; R. A. Newhall, *Muster and Review* (Cambridge, Mass., 1940), 32–3.

[115] Sherborne, *War, Politics, and Culture*, 1–28; Russell, *English Intervention in Spain and Portugal*, 80, 187, 302, 418.

[116] M. R. Powicke, 'Lancastrian captains', in T. A. Sandquist and M. R. Powicke (eds.), *Essays in Medieval History Presented to Bertie Wilkinson* (Toronto, 1969), 371–82; A. Goodman, 'Responses to requests in Yorkshire for military service under Henry V', *Northern History*, 17 (1981), 240–52.

penalty of dismissal. John of Gaunt led his retinue on twelve campaigns, but most of its members served on only one or two. It was an inner core of trusted and experienced warriors who provided continuity, men such as Sir Walter Blount, Sir Hugh Hastings, and Sir Thomas Morieux, all from families with long military traditions.[117] Members of the high chivalric class like Sir John Chandos, Sir Walter Manny, and Sir Guy Brian spent a lifetime of service under royal and noble commanders. Equally professional were the esquires who made a career as men-at-arms, like Nicholas Sabraham, who claimed, like Chaucer's Knight, to have served in virtually every theatre of war over thirty-nine years.[118]

This pool of regular soldiers was fed from two sources, one social the other regional. Those with few or no lands, like heirs waiting to inherit, younger sons, debtors, and any attracted by the prospect of gain and adventure, needed only to equip themselves to offer service on a variety of expeditions. Beyond his own retainers, up to half a lord's contracted quota would be composed of captains, each bringing a small company or even a single archer. Some captains recruited through the armigerous families of their locality, many of whom had proud traditions of service stretching back generations, others through 'military enterprisers', like Jankyn Nowell, who enlisted men for Sir Hugh Hastings in 1380 from the unemployed soldiery in London.[119] There was normally no lack of volunteers.

One region in particular was a seedbed for recruits at this level. The north-western counties of Lancashire and Cheshire, lightly manorialized and with a high proportion of free tenures, supported large numbers of small landowners able to equip themselves as men-at-arms and archers. Orientated towards Wales and Ireland, and under the sole dominance of the dukes of Lancaster and earls of Chester, it was a militarized and cohesive society. Cheshire men from minor gentry and merchant families like Calverley, Knolles, and Norbury rose to knighthood, serving alongside those from established knightly families like Audley and Delves.[120] What rewards did war service bring? After 1370 it must have become obvious that the chances of spectacular victories and profitable freebooting had diminished. Only one major battle, Najera in 1367, brought in ransoms from some 2,000 prisoners, benefiting among others Sir Thomas Cheyne, who sold Bertrand du Guesclin to the king for £1,483.[121] But thereafter many more suffered capture themselves, their careers blighted or ruined by the ransom they

[117] Walker, *Lancastrian Affinity*, ch. 3 and app. 1.
[118] N. H. Nicolas (ed.), *The Scrope and Grosvenor Controversy* (London, 1832), i. 124–5.
[119] Keen, *Origins of the English Gentleman*, 56–7; Saul, *Knights and Esquires*, 52–4; A. Goodman, 'The military sub-contracts of Sir Hugh Hastings, 1380', *EHR* 95 (1980), 114–20.
[120] P. Morgan, *War and Society in Medieval Cheshire, 1277–1403* (Manchester, 1987); Walker, *Lancastrian Affinity*, 141–81 and app. 1.
[121] Russell, *English Intervention in Spain*, 106 n. 3; McFarlane, *English Nobility*, 31.

paid: Sir Hugh Hastings in 1367, Sir John Bourchier in 1374, Sir Richard Cradock in 1383.[122] Plunder, too, was scarce as the French learned to strip the enemy's route of march and harass his column, while town defences had been strengthened to resist any but a prolonged siege.

Wages of war were, in theory, adequate and even generous, and some captains, like Sir John Strother in 1374–5, made a profit by paying their men less than the standard wages which they drew from the Crown.[123] But payment of wages was all too often in arrears by many years. Even so, provided capture was avoided, war gave many opportunities for casual pickings, and soldiers who returned to spend their wealth on houses, chantries, and churches are not far to find. Moreover, their military experience and connections often served them well in a domestic context, winning them a place in a magnate retinue with a life annuity, the reward of a beneficial farm of land, or a local stewardship. Such benefits counterbalanced the expense and hazards of military service. Men returning from a successful military career, whether upstarts like Calverley and Norbury who purchased lands in Cheshire and Hertfordshire, or those like Sir John Waleys who returned to their inherited estates in Sussex, were absorbed into the shire elite, serving as sheriffs and JPs. Others exploited their foreign experience to serve the Crown in diplomacy and government, like Sir William Elmham and Sir Nicholas Dagworth.[124] Men who had campaigned in the company of princes and peers were easily absorbed into chivalric society which prized their loyalty and service.

The hiatus of thirty years between Gaunt's invasion of Spain in 1386 and Henry V's invasion of Normandy in 1415 marked a severe setback to this tradition. Among the armigerous class there was little incentive to assume knighthood, while for the lesser gentry the loss of livelihood and advancement generated discontent: as Gloucester protested in 1397, 'they can't live decently without war; peace is no good to them'.[125] Richard II's peace policy ruptured the continuum of service and loyalty binding king, magnates, and gentry into the prosecution of a consensual war. When Henry V reopened the war with France this chivalric tradition was merely a memory and there was no certainty that it could be revived.

Two things made possible its regeneration. The first was the existence of a huge royal retinue, embracing the old Lancastrian affinity and enlarged by Henry IV to stabilize his usurpation. The second was that, for the first time since 1359, the king in person led a royal army to France. War became again the prime

---

[122] Walker, *Lancastrian Affinity*, 73–5; McFarlane, *English Nobility*, 28, 45, 241.

[123] S. K. Walker, 'Profit and loss in the Hundred Years War: The subcontracts of Sir John Strother, 1374', *BIHR* 58 (1985), 104.

[124] Morgan, *War and Society in Medieval Cheshire*, 169–70, 174–6; Saul, *Provincial Life*, 16–17; *House of Commons*, ii. 733–5, iii. 13–17.

[125] Jean Froissart, *Chronicles*, trans. G. Brereton (Harmondsworth, 1968), 421.

expression of service to the Crown and the means to favour and reward. In both 1415 and 1417 most of the armigerous class served in France. As in the preceding century, the magnate retinue formed the backbone of the contracted following, drawing together the local gentry elite and through them their families and tenants in the region. These local networks gave cohesion and permanence to retinues throughout the ensuing campaign. They can be identified in the musters of troops in garrisons or at sieges, in grants of land, and in casualties suffered.[126] Yet the service to which this armigerous class found itself committed differed from that in the fourteenth century. Rather than a six-month *chevauchée*, they were caught up in four years of piecemeal conquest, in sieges, skirmishes, and castle guard. At its peak in 1421 the army numbered some 13,000 men, of whom perhaps 3,000 were men-at-arms. By 1421 the majority of gentry had acquired a professionalism in arms that far exceeded that of their fourteenth-century ancestors. War, rather than family, inheritance, or shire magistracy, had guided their careers, reinforcing the links between lords and retainers, forging bonds of brotherhood in arms, and fostering both discipline and opportunism. The English cause had engaged the pride and ambitions of a generation and might have been expected to generate a continuing commitment to service. Yet for many the conquest of Normandy and the Treaty of Troyes marked the limit of their service and they returned to England with Henry in 1421. The king's death next year precipitated the return of numbers of the nobility, with their retinues, and opened up a division in the armigerous class between a professional army remaining in France and a demilitarized gentry in England, which gradually deepened into a chasm.

Those who stayed in France did so because they had acquired lands and offices which substantially raised their status. Henry V had envisaged the permanent settlement in Normandy of a resident, militarized English gentry; fiefs were granted with obligations for service, and their disposal to any but Englishmen prohibited. Landholding was attractive to military careerists, not so much for its profits, which the ravages of war had reduced, as for the status it conferred. Areas of conquered Normandy were settled by lesser gentry families already linked by ties of neighbourhood and family in England who had fought as brothers in arms. The English military occupation, though regulated through indentures and wages, was essentially a cellular organization based on personal and territorial attachments. This new magistracy displayed all the brash arrogance and suppressed unease of typical *colons*.[127]

[126] Powicke, 'Lancastrian captains', 374–8. Almost half the shire knights in the parliament of 1422 had war experience; Roskell, *Parliament of 1422*, 94.

[127] R. Massey, 'The land settlement in Lancastrian Normandy', in Pollard (ed.), *Property and Politics*, 76–96; C. T. Allmand, *Lancastrian Normandy* (Oxford, 1983), ch. 3. Below, Ch. 14, sect. 2.

The military careers of those who remained in Normandy were clearly very different from those of Edward III's captains. How did their rewards compare? Fastolf enriched himself vastly from the war, so that by 1439 he had remitted to England sufficient to spend £14,000 in purchasing lands and a further £9,000 on building Caister Castle, and among Bedford's other captains Sir Andrew Ogard and Sir William Oldhall made almost comparable investments on their English estates.[128] We know less of the fortunes of those captains of the second rank, like Salvain, Nanfan, and Merbury, whose wealth may have been invested mainly in French lands, all of which they lost in 1450.[129] Beneath the captains, men-at-arms certainly went to war anticipating significant gains. An indenture of brotherhood sealed between two landless esquires at the start of their career in 1421, John Winter and Nicholas Molyneux, bound them to remit their individual profits to a common chest in England for investment in lands against their eventual return and marriage. Patronage and service provided others with advancement: as Clement Overton, Fastolf's receiver, acknowledged, he had been 'enriched in the service of the king, the regent and other lords, and raised in status'. Nicholas Upton observed in the 1440s 'how many poor men, labouring in the French wars, are become noble'.[130]

But the hazards were there, known and feared. Winter and Molyneux bound each to ransom the other even at the cost of dispersing their gains, and capture was all too likely for those actively engaged in a lifetime of sieges and skirmishes. All ranks shared the experience: Sir John Nanfan was 'ransomed at great cost', and Sir Thomas Rempston was captured first at Patay in 1429 and then in Gascony in 1442. Lesser ranks were equally accident-prone: Thomas Dring, who was declared in 1444 to 'have served in our wars of France this thirty years where five times he hath been taken prisoner and yet standeth to ransom for £300', was captured a sixth time at Formigny in 1450.[131] Even without such calamities the lifestyle of soldiers at this level must have been modest, particularly as agrarian profits and property values fell during the 1430s; yet their lands in Normandy brought them status and livelihood, if not profit.

The professional captains and militarized gentry of Normandy came to form a society detached from the those in England. After the royal expedition of 1430–2 it was mainly those with a stake in the war who raised and led the annual

---

[128] McFarlane, *England in the Fifteenth Century*, 178, 185; A. R. Smith, 'The acquisition of Sir John Fastolf's English estates', in Archer and Walker (eds.), *Rulers and Ruled*, 137–53.

[129] For Nanfan, see M. K. Jones, 'Ransom brokerage in the fifteenth century', in P. Contamine, C. Giry-Deloison, and M. H. Keen (eds.), *Guerre et société en France, en Angleterre et en Bourgogne XIV–XV siècle* (Lille, n.d.), 222; for Merbury, see Allmand, *Lancastrian Normandy*, 80.

[130] McFarlane, *England in the Fifteenth Century*, 151–74; C. T. Allmand and C. A. J. Armstrong (eds.), *English Suits before the Parlement of Paris*, Camden Society, 4th ser., 26 (London, 1982), 19.

[131] Jones, 'Ransom brokerage', 223–5.

expeditions which brought reinforcements to France. They were a dwindling band and found increasing difficulty in filling their quotas both with knights and with men-at-arms. The earl of Arundel's expedition of 1,168 men in 1434 had only one baron and three knights, and Lord Talbot's army of 2,000 in 1435 two lords and two knights. The ratio of men-at-arms to archers, which had stood at 1:3 under Henry V, declined in the 1430s to 1:6. There were financial and military grounds for this, but the overall effect was further to diminish gentry participation in war.[132]

The reasons for this are not far to seek. After Henry V's death royal leadership was lacking, and as the war turned against the English its inducements, even for the landless, decreased. The 1430s brought growing insecurity and disorder in some regions and were accompanied by acute economic downturn and a shortage of coin, leaving little surplus to expend on equipment. Some of the experienced but ageing captains in Normandy returned to England, but few had roots in English landed society and their attachment to royal or magnate households led them into the partisan politics of Henry VI's majority. York's retinue after 1446 harboured quite a number like the Mulso brothers who had served him in Normandy. In the divided England of the 1450s the military skills and experience of a few were put to the final test in civil war. Matthew Gough fell fighting Cade's peasants on London Bridge; Sir Bertrand Entwistle died at St Albans in 1455; Andrew Trollope betrayed Warwick at Ludford and won St Albans for Henry VI. Altogether one-third of the 135 captains serving in Normandy in the 1440s were directly involved in the civil wars, in which twenty-six met their death.[133]

Consideration of the gentry's experience in war leads naturally into how they viewed it. But this presents difficulties. Few articulated their impressions, and the perceptions of both individuals and society were conditioned by chivalric ideals. Chivalry provided an influential model for armigerous society, but it is its inner tensions that are most evident in the literature of the late fourteenth century. The heroic Germanic ideal of personal prowess and fidelity to companions in arms had been infused with the Christian and court culture of the high Middle Ages. French chivalry in particular acquired a religious and moral dimension, developed in Ramon Lull's treatise *The Book of the Order of Chivalry*, written *c.*1270, and echoed in the work of Geoffrey de Charny. Knighthood became a quasi-religious vocation for the defence of the faith, so that martial prowess had to be matched by moral rectitude.[134] Woven into this, also under French

[132] H. Ratcliffe, 'The military expenditure of the English Crown, 1422–35', M. Litt. thesis (Oxford University, 1979), 94, 101.

[133] A. E. Marshall, 'The role of English war captains in England and Normandy, 1436–61', MA thesis (University of Wales, 1974), 202 ff.

[134] Keen, *Chivalry*, 8–15, 23–30, 44–63.

influence, was the theme of courtly love, reaching its finest flowering in the work of Chrétien de Troyes at the end of the twelfth century. The knight now pledged fidelity to the lady by whose love he was inspired to seek adventure and perform deeds of arms. How this courtly love could conflict with, and indeed undermine, the fidelity to lord and brotherhood, as in the love of Lancelot for Arthur's wife, Guinevere, which brought division and destruction to the Round Table, was described in the stanzaic *Le Morte Arthure* of 1350. Similarly human love might conflict with the quest for spiritual perfection, which could ultimately be attained only by renunciation, as in the English romance *Guy of Warwick*. Romance thus dealt with dilemmas at the heart of chivalry inherent in the human condition: the tension between aspiration and fallibility, ideal and reality.[135] The two greatest English romances written in the late fourteenth century explored this on the personal and political level.

In *Sir Gawain and the Green Knight* it is the pretensions of chivalry itself that are challenged. The Green Knight, a giant with magical powers, invites the court at Camelot to a test of knighthood. Sir Gawain is chosen to accept, and on his way to meet the Green Knight in a duel he receives hospitality at the castle of Hautdesert, whose lord, Bertilak, presses him to stay for three days. During this time they shall each day exchange their winnings, Bertilak from the hunt and Gawain from residing in the castle with Bertilak's wife. Having successfully resisted the lady's attempts to seduce him, and dutifully keeping faith with his host by rendering to him the kisses he has each day received, Gawain on the third day is tempted to retain the magic girdle which she has given him as protection against violent death. He goes to meet the Green Knight and survives the duel but is challenged with his false retention of the girdle which he is wearing, and recognizes the Knight to be Bertilak. His 'untruth' confronts him with his moral failure as a knight and he returns to Arthur's court wearing the girdle sinister-wise as a badge of shame. The reaction of the knights of the Round Table, who condone Gawain's act by adopting the girdle as their emblem, is ambivalent: is this an acknowledgement that self-preservation is, after all, stronger than chivalric aspiration; is it demonstrating the absurdity of the high chivalric ideal? The sophistication of the poem, its composition in a north-western dialect, and its survival in a unique, plain copy have generally suggested that its audience was very restricted.

The stanzaic *Le Morte Arthure*, likewise surviving in a single manuscript from the North Midlands, is a highly individual treatment of part of the Arthurian canon. Arthur is the prototype of Christian kingship, his personal prowess valid-ated by his piety, and his rule directed to the protection of Christendom and the

---

[135] W. J. Barron, *English Medieval Romance* (London, 1967), 73–9, 166–73, 138–42; A. C. Spearing, *The Gawain Poet* (Cambridge, 1970).

upholding of justice. Challenged by the pagan emperor Lucius to become his vassal, Arthur leads his knights and army to Burgundy to do battle, on the way delivering Brittany from subjection to a tyrannical giant, whom he kills in mortal combat. Having defeated Lucius his ambition tempts him to conquer Lombardy and assume the imperial title, only to hear that back in Britain his kingdom and his wife have been seized by his lieutenant Modred. Warned in a dream that Fortune has deserted him, he returns to meet his death. Again, the verdict on chivalric aspiration is ambivalent: that even a just enterprise is flawed by sin and that military triumph is not proof against division and treachery. Thus beneath the swiftly moving narrative of bloody duels and heroic fights, and evocative descriptions of countryside, castle, and court, romance literature explores the moral ambivalence of the chivalric ideal.

To what degree do these works reflect the mood of their time? Clearly society at all levels in the fourteenth century was receptive to the lessons of legend and history, which were readily transposed into contemporary settings. Gawain's journey through the wild scenery of North Wales and the Wirrall, the comforts of Castle Hautdesert, and the descriptions of his host's hunting all have a verisimilitude, so that the story 'crosses and recrosses the border of romance and reality'. Similarly the warfare described in *Morte Arthure* is recognizably that of the fourteenth century while its themes of treachery, usurpation, and the destruction of political unity were acutely contemporary. In many other respects romance and reality interpenetrated. The knightly *aventure* was the paradigm of the *chevauchée*; prowess in the duel was replicated in the joust; the warrior band was recognizably an indentured retinue; while the Arthurian Round Table was consciously re-created in Edward III's Order of the Garter, whose members were to be 'sans peur et sans reproche'.[136] The knightly class went into battle mindful of the heroes of legend, as those on the Najera campaign recalled Roland and Oliver, and this heightened their anticipation of combat, their exaltation in battle, and the sacrificial call of brotherhood in arms extolled by Jean de Bueil:

When one feels that one's cause is just, and one's blood is ready for the fight, tears come to the eye. A warm feeling of loyalty and pity comes into the heart on seeing one's friend expose his body with such courage to carry out and accomplish the will of our Creator; and one makes up one's mind to go and die or live with him, and out of love not to abandon him. No man who has not experienced it knows how to speak of the satisfaction which comes from this sort of action.[137]

In its exploration of the eternal disjunction between human aspiration and performance, the chivalric ethic had the quality of religious belief, so that

---

[136] E. Porter, 'Chaucer's knight, the alliterative *Morte Arthure* and medieval laws of war', *Nott. Med. Stud.* 27 (1983), 56–78.

[137] *Le Jouvencel*, as trans. in C. T. Allmand, *Society at War* (Edinburgh, 1973), 27–8.

it was not easily discredited by personal shortcomings. Nevertheless, by the late fourteenth century it was facing criticism both as an ideal and in its individual manifestations. Its code of personal honour and prowess was overshadowed by doubts over the morality of war and by the overriding authority of the *respublica*.

The Thomist doctrine of the just war as one waged under due authority had been directed primarily against unlicensed warfare. It had acquired fresh relevance in the anarchy induced by the free companies in France after 1356, leading writers like Honoré Bonet to insist that war was a *chose publique*, waged under royal authority and regulated by laws.[138] In England, which escaped such anarchy, military failures and war-weariness produced a reaction after 1375 which questioned the morality and consequences of national wars. Philippe de Mézières in France and Chaucerian writers in England developed a topos which contrasted the ease and trivial pretexts with which kings went to war with its long and fruitless continuation. As they observed, it impoverished both victors and vanquished, benefited only the soldiery, and reduced rulers to dependence on their subjects. Gower, the most sensitive observer of contemporary society, voiced a heartfelt desire for peace—'that our deadly war cease'— and exhorted Henry IV to 'lay to this old sore a new salve and do the war awei'.[139]

In this reaction against war the chivalric ideal of individual prowess and adventure came under scrutiny. First, the corruption of knighthood was denounced: the greed for private gain, the addiction to courtly fashion, and the failure to defend Church and people. Others contrasted the old-fashioned knight who fought for fame, not gain, with the mercenary and courtier of the present, as in the poem *Mede and Much Thanke* (*c.*1400). Chaucer's Knight, with his tally of battles against the heathen, his war-stained armour, and lack of riches, is emblematic of good old knighthood, as his squire may stand for the dandified courtier.[140] Secondly, the concept of war as *chose publique*, waged for the common good, imposed on the knight a new role and new obligations. The ordinances regulating military discipline issued by Charles V in 1374 and by Richard II at Durham in 1385 were symptomatic.[141] Personal prowess and individual gain were to be subordinated to collective action and commands. The pillaging of churches and rape of women was forbidden, as was the unlicensed

[138] C. T. Allmand, 'Changing views of the soldier in late medieval France', in Contamine *et al.* (eds.), *Guerre et société en France*, 171–88.

[139] Mézières, *Letter to King Richard II*, 7–20, 51–3; Lydgate, *Siege of Thebes*, lines 4134 ff.; Keen, *Origins of the English Gentleman*, 89–90; and see note 142 below.

[140] Allmand (ed.), *Society at War*, 39; Kail (ed.), *Political Poems*, no. 2; Porter, 'Chaucer's knight'; Keen, *Nobles, Knights and Men at Arms*, 101–20.

[141] Allmand (ed.), *Society at War*, 55–9; M. H. Keen, 'Richard II's ordinances of war of 1385', in Archer and Walker (eds.), *Rulers and Ruled*, 33–48.

seizure of victuals and the commandeering of lodgings. To ensure the coherence of companies in battle no one was to go ahead of their captain's pennon or banner, to raise the cry 'havok' and break ranks to pillage, or to cry 'monte' to start a retreat. Disputes over prisoners were to be avoided by taking pledges from those surrendering in battle and guaranteeing their safety. This recognized that the greatest dissolvents of an army were pillage and ransom, and the greatest tactical mistakes arose from the pursuit of individual glory and honour.

The subordination of personal repute and prowess to public duty and army discipline inevitably changed men's perception of chivalry. In *Confessio Amantis* it is depicted as disrupting ordered civil society. Endeavour and self-sacrifice had to be focused on service to king and country; patriotism rather than personal adventure was the knight's vocation. Peter Idley exhorted his son,

> Also for thy king and for the Reawmes right
> To put thy body with due diligence,
> With alle thy power and thy hooll myght,
> Looke in thee be founde noo negligence
> To stande with thy kynge in the Reawme's defence,

and professional soldiers like Richard Handford and Robert Stafford spoke with pride of their service to the king.[142] If patriotism came to subsume chivalry, this owed much to the policy and person of Henry V. A poem in Digby MS 102 relating explicitly to Henry V's renewal of the war reaffirms the ideal of the knight militant, enduring hunger and fear, fighting for the common good, and proving himself God's knight by clean living.[143] But traditional knighthood, its reputation reinstated, had only a brief resurgence in fifteenth-century England. By mid-century it is its political function as the foundation of the *respublica* and guardian of the Crown that is uppermost in *Knyghthode and Bataile*, while Fastolf's threnody on the English venture in France, in *The Boke of Noblesse*, blamed defeat on the decay of military virtues and the addiction of the chivalric class to civil duties.[144]

The transformation of knighthood into civil and political rule reflected the priorities of a demilitarized society. Caxton might deplore how few in his day 'had the use and exercise of a knyght' and were 'redy to serve theyre prince when he shalle calle them', but civil knighthood retained the sense of elite leadership, with a duty and privilege to serve the king and realm. Heraldry might

---

[142] Gower, *Confessio Amantis*, bk. 4, lines 1635 ff., and 'In praise of peace', line 122; cf. W. Westerbee, 'Gower', in *CHMEL* 600–2; *Peter Idley's Instructions*, p. 95, lines 855–61.

[143] Kail (ed.), *Political Poems*, no. 13, pt. 2.

[144] *Knyghtood and Bataile*, ed. R. Dyboski and Z. M. Arend, EETS, old ser., 201 (London, 1935), lines 404–10, 1622–35; J. G. Nichols (ed.), *The Boke of Noblesse*, Roxburghe Club (London, 1860), 77–8.

have become distanced from chivalry, but for the knight and gentleman his entitlement to a coat of arms denoted his status as lord and governor, the upholder of hierarchy, authority, and justice. His qualities of courage, stoicism, fidelity, courtesy, and honesty, transposed from military to civil leadership, became those of the enduring English gentleman.[145]

---

[145] Allmand (ed.), *Society at War*, 29–30; Keen, *Origins of the English Gentleman*, 98–100.

CHAPTER 6

The Local Polity

In the preceding chapters the peerage and the gentry have been considered largely in isolation. Yet as major constituents of landed society, they displayed a continuum of wealth, exercised a complementary magistracy, and had a largely similar outlook. How did this society operate? What governed the relations of magnates and gentry? How was power distributed between them and for what was it used? Was the local polity stable and how could instability be corrected? How did local and national politics interconnect? There are no straightforward answers to these questions, partly because local conditions varied but more fundamentally because historians hold divergent views on how the local polity was organized. For some the shire was not merely an administrative unit but a political community with a historic identity and corporate existence. For others the magnate affinity provided the only true political structure in local society, for it alone was able to mobilize effective power.[1] I shall first assess these two viewpoints; then explore the interaction of community and affinity; thirdly, discuss the character of and remedies for instability; and finally examine the interaction of local and national politics and assess the political roles of magnates and gentry.

1. COUNTY COMMUNITY OR MAGNATE AFFINITY?

In asking whether the county functioned as a social and political community the starting point must be the associations formed by the gentry for their own concerns of family and inheritance. Gentry society, rooted as it was in landed power, was held in a volatile balance of cooperation and rivalry. A recognition that the preservation of property depended on respect for the law and the trustworthiness of neighbours and family went with an awareness that the law could be manipulated and that those who were closest were most likely to be in dispute. The complex rules of inheritance, the uncertainties of legal title, the sophistication of legal devices, and the incidence of personal misfortune all presented

---

[1] These viewpoints are discussed by C. Carpenter, 'Gentry and community in medieval England', *Jnl. Brit. Stud.* 33 (1994), 340–80.

hazards against which the gentry sought support from 'friends' (i.e. their circle of kinsmen, neighbours, associates) and lords. For the performance of their wills and family settlements they turned first to their immediate kin as executors, to the lords as supervisors, and to neighbours and associates as witnesses and feof-fees. For the conveyance of land it was desirable to involve neighbours of equiva-lent status with local knowledge, and those with legal skills. In 1366 Sir Robert Pashley assembled two knights, two local esquires, and a local sergeant-at-law, all neighbours, to witness a quitclaim of his feoffees.[2] In special circumstances a man might reach out to a wider circle. In 1446 Robert Sherard of Stapleford (Leics.) called on twenty leading Leicestershire gentry to attest the deaths of his wife and daughter in childbirth to validate his claim to the custody of her estates by courtesy of England.[3] The shire elite formed a network of their own, often bound together by kinship and association in county office, and pride in the num-ber and antiquity of the gentry families which a shire could boast.

Yet personal associations for private matters are not evidence of a sense of political community. Indeed in many shires geographical and historical divisions made it unlikely that the shire could function as a polity. The two parts of Kent, divided by the Weald, had a long-standing separateness, as did east and west Sussex, where the rape rather than the county was the basis of community. Midland counties like Warwickshire and Nottinghamshire had no geographical unity and both Yorkshire and Lincolnshire were too large to function as units of social organization, as their historical divisions testified. Yet even if most shires were artificial administrative units, their antiquity and that of their judicial insti-tutions and peacekeeping responsibilities must have inculcated a sense of cor-porate identity. Moreover as, from the thirteenth century, the more lawful and worthy men were delegated as representatives for governmental purposes, the shire developed a viewpoint of its own. In the fourteenth century they had won a large measure of control over shire offices and government which set real limits to central intervention.

Yet in only a few areas did the whole shire function routinely as a political institution. It did so most obviously for judicial business. We know little about the size and composition of the regular monthly meetings of the county court but the presence of the gentry elite seems unlikely. The quarterly peace sessions and assizes, however, could bring together some of the major gentry.[4] The county court functioned most conspicuously in a political capacity as the venue for parliamentary elections, which the major gentry attended regularly in some

---

[2] Saul, *Scenes from Provincial Life*, 1.   [3] Acheson, *Gentry Community*, 83–5, 89–92.

[4] Carpenter, 'Gentry and community', 347–8; R. C. Palmer, *The County Courts of Medieval England, 1150–1350* (Princeton, 1982), 81–6, 134–6; Maddern, *Violence and Social Order*, 54–64. However, cf. Bennett, *Community, Class and Careerism*, 23, 36, and Keen, *Origins of the English Gentleman*, 112.

counties (e.g. Cumberland), though infrequently in others (e.g. Warwickshire).[5] Although there was no regular occasion on which the shire manifested itself as a political entity, it has been suggested that it was given political unity by its ruling elite. Lords and knights formed a community of honour and governance, such as was visually realized in the armorial glass in Etchingham parish church, arranged in a hierarchic scheme with the arms of gentry families in the nave, those of magnates in the chancel, and the royal arms in the east window.[6]

Other historians have seen the magnate affinity, rather than the shire community, as giving form and identity to the shire, and absorbing the networks of the gentry to give the lord effective rule over it. The interdependence of the gentry as members of a shire community was complemented by their individual dependence on a lord for protection and favour, a dependence embodied in a quasi-legal contract, the indenture of retainer. The indenture was a contract for life, binding the retainer to serve his lord in peace and war (i.e. in his household and on campaign) in return for an annual fee and wages of war. Individual indentures specified the obligations in more detail and with variations: to ride with the lord at his summons to court, wearing his livery; to reside in his household at particular times, receiving sustenance ('bouche of court') for himself and his squire; to support the lord against all men save the king; in war to serve at specified wages with an entitlement to a proportion of the gains of war, the lord (before 1370) undertaking to replace horses lost on campaign or to ransom his retainer if he were captured. The lord might also promise his good lordship in his man's affairs 'as far as law and conscience allowed'.[7] This solemn and ostensibly permanent commitment was not lightly undertaken, and was often preceded by a period of probation. A less formal and exclusive mode of retaining was by the grant of an annuity, either for life or at pleasure, 'for service done or to be done'. With its less specific commitment this could serve both for those in administrative posts, and for those retained by other lords. Yet the annuity was not a casual bond; it could be suspended if service was refused, and payment was enforceable by distraint if the lord defaulted. Thirdly, there were those paid a fee at pleasure for specific services, such as domestic servants (cooks, chaplains, and physicians), legal counsel, and attorneys in the central courts and departments of state.

All these ways of retaining required some written document; but beyond these were other symbolic ways of attesting attachment to a lord. The wearing of a

---

    [5] S. J. Payling (personal communication), citing PRO, C 219/15/2, for Cumberland in 1442, and cf. id., 'County parliamentary elections in fifteenth century England', *Parlty. Hist.* 18 (1999), 237–59.

    [6] Saul, *Knights and Esquires*, 259; id., *Provincial Life*, 150.

    [7] J. M. Bean, *From Lord to Patron* (Pittsburgh, 1989), 13–22; S. K. Walker, Introduction, in Michael Jones and Simon Walker (eds.), *Private Indentures for Life Service in Peace and War, 1278–1476*, in *Camden Miscellany, XXXII*, Camden Society, 5th ser., 3 (London, 1994), 9–33.

lord's livery had very ancient antecedents and was paralleled in the late fourteenth century by the giving of badges, caps, or hoods, and in the case of the
Lancastrian affinity in the 1380s, a collar of esses. These symbols of a lord's protection and favour could embolden the wearers to intimidate and oppress with
impunity, and after 1390 legislation endeavoured to curb and regulate the giving
of livery. This became restricted to magnates, while only knights and esquires
retained by life indenture and resident household servants (later including estate
officials and councillors) were entitled to wear it. The new dynasty imposed more
drastic restrictions. Henry IV's first parliament prohibited all badges except
the king's, and though in 1401 the Commons sought to prohibit even the king's
use of badges, on the ground that they differentiated between his 'loyal subjects',
the Crown insisted on retaining its monopoly of livery of company, making the
collar of esses a special mark of loyalty.[8] No legislation limited retaining or the
giving of fees, and good lordship extended beyond the retinue to 'friends' and
'well-willers', who might undertake particular service to a lord on the promise of
his 'good lordship' in the future.

Did the affinity constituted by these different means have any corporate sense
or institutional form? It is difficult to claim that it did. Each member stood in an
individual relation to the lord, and occasions when the whole affinity assembled
must have been extremely rare. Life retainers, with their special relationship to
the lord and attendance upon him, administrative staff who met on the lord's
council, and his household servants did have opportunities to develop a corporate loyalty, as their association in legal and land transactions and in religious
functions testify. But for the affinity as a whole, only a sense of collective fidelity
and service gave it a sense of identity.

These varieties of association make it difficult to measure the size of any lord's
affinity, and even the number of indentured retainers and annuitants cannot now
be recovered other than in a handful of examples. In 1384–5 the earl of Devon
was giving his livery to 135 persons but of these the armigerous core of the retinue was formed by only 8 knights and 43 esquires. Thomas, earl of Warwick,
paid fees to 6 knights and 33 others in 1397, and his son, the last Beauchamp earl,
had a retinue of around 60 of whom a dozen were knights in the 1430s.
Humphrey, duke of Buckingham, had one of the largest comital retinues in the
mid-fifteenth century, with 10 knights and 26 esquires among a total of 84 annuitants, but it was dwarfed by those of the earls and dukes of Lancaster in the fourteenth. That of John of Gaunt rose from 173 bannerets, knights, and esquires in
1382 to almost 200 in the 1390s. The decline in the size of retinues was possibly
general. In the fifteenth century Lords Roos and Grey of Codnor had a mere

---

[8] Given-Wilson, *Royal Household*, 234–45; N. Saul, 'The Commons and the abolition of badges',
Parlty. Hist. 9 (1990), 302–15.

handful of armigerous retainers, and middling Yorkshire barons like Fitzhugh and Clifford of Skipton virtually none. Whether the reasons behind this trend were financial or reflect a reappraisal of the service they needed is not clear.[9]

Magnates were selective in whom they retained and only a fraction of the 3,000 or so armigerous families found a place in a retinue. Confirmation of this comes from the returns for the income tax of 1436, in which peers were allowed to deduct what they paid out in life annuities. These suggest that this represented about 10 per cent of their income.[10] Studies of the larger affinities broadly confirm this, e.g. those of Richard Beauchamp, earl of Warwick, in the 1430s and of Humphrey, duke of Buckingham, in the following decade. Among the lesser magnates only four in 1436 were paying annuities in excess of 10 per cent of their income.[11] Lords recruited retainers in a variety of ways. Those who were active campaigners could draw on a pool of soldiers of proven ability. A significant number of Gaunt's indentures were made at the end of campaigns as a reward for valour, a prime example being that of Sir John d'Ipre at the battle of Najera; similarly eleven of Warwick's forty-nine annuitants in 1431 had been recruited from his military retinue.[12] Members of the royal family like the Beauforts and Hollands, and nobility known to be in the king's favour like de Vere and de la Pole, were magnets for retainers from far afield. But for the most part a lord drew retainers from his own country and often from his own estates, men whose fathers and grandfathers had served his ancestors. One–third of those receiving the earl of Devon's livery were his tenants, while generations of Hungerfords, Swillingtons, and Leventhorpes were in Lancastrian service as were Hugfords and Throgmortons in that of the Beauchamp earls. Established retainers recruited others, while those brought up in a magnate's household, as wards or sons of local knights, stood a good chance of being retained as they came of age.

Membership of a noble household conferred status and opened wider horizons but it also brought material rewards. The most immediate was the retaining fee, usually £20 or 20 marks for a knight, £10 or 10 marks for an esquire. Though forming a small proportion of the income of those of knightly status, when combined with other offices or annuities from other lords, it could amount to a significant cash addition. Ten of Gaunt's leading retainers are known to have

[9] M. Cherry, 'The Courtenay earls of Devon: A late medieval aristocratic affinity', *Southern History*, 1 (1979), 71–97; Sinclair, 'The Beauchamp earls of Warwick in the late Middle Ages', Ph.D. thesis (London University, 1987) ch. 6; Rawcliffe, *The Staffords*, app. D, pp. 232–40; Walker, *Lancastrian Affinity*, 14, 21; T. B. Pugh, 'The magnates, knights and gentry', in S. Chrimes, C. Ross, and R. Griffiths (eds.), *Fifteenth Century England, 1399–1509* (Manchester, 1972), 101–4.

[10] Pugh, 'The magnates, knights and gentry', 97–8.

[11] Sinclair, 'The Beauchamp earls', ch. 6; Rawcliffe, *The Staffords*, 73. For lesser magnates, see Pugh, 'The magnates, knights and gentry', 101–5; J. M. Bean, *The Estates of the Percy Family, 1416–1537* (Oxford, 1958), 86–93.

[12] Walker, *Lancastrian Affinity*, 43; Sinclair, 'The Beauchamp earls', ch. 6.

netted more than 100 marks per annum in this way, sufficient to provide lands for younger sons or marriage portions for daughters. At lower levels even a single fee of £10 per annum could provide the extra capital for economic investment. Offices to which deputies could be appointed, like those of steward, forester, and parker, were further sources of profit and influence, and some leading gentry collected stewardships of the local estates of non-resident lords. The lord's favour brought further perquisites in the shape of beneficial leases, gifts of timber and game, the chattels and lands of felons, and, potentially more advantageous than any of these, the wardship or marriage of a tenant, which could provide a marriage for a younger son or an heiress for an elder. The lord might also exert his influence or pressure to secure an important match for his retainer. Through Gaunt's favour Sir Thomas Rempston secured the marriage of Margaret Foljambe, and Sir Walter Blount married his duchess's lady-in-waiting, Sancha Garcia.[13] Such 'good lordship' in family matters reflected the patriarchal relationship between a lord and his affinity.

A life indenture implied, and sometimes stipulated, an exclusive attachment, allegiance to the king alone being reserved. This was not thought incompatible with receiving annuities from other lords, and these might or might not be specified. Some of Gaunt's leading retainers received up to five from lords other than the duke himself.[14] This was no impediment to good service; indeed it provided valuable connections between lords at an informal level. Multiple lordship also provided an escape route for a retainer who fell out with his primary lord, as well as an opportunity to move to a more distinguished master. But attempts to play one lord off against another were dangerous and generally eschewed; and where a region was traditionally divided between potential rivals, as was Yorkshire between Percy and Neville, there was little overlap between their affinities. For the majority of lesser retainers, certainly, one lord at a time was the rule, unless they were retained for their professional skills, as were lawyers; for them the annuity was a contract of employment and had little or no chivalric content. The permanence implied by a life indenture was seriously regarded; indeed the lord's heir would normally confirm his father's indentures. Conversely, loyal retainers helped to maintain the lord's inheritance during minorities or periods of political disgrace.[15] Service to a great lord was sufficiently coveted to induce a high degree of fidelity, tempered always by self-preservation.

---

[13] Walker, *Lancastrian Affinity*, 89–90; Wright, *Derbyshire Gentry*, 63.

[14] Pollard, *North Eastern England*, 131–3; Walker, *Lancastrian Affinity*, 107

[15] R. E. Archer, 'The Mowbrays', D. Phil. thesis (Oxford University, 1984), ch. 2; Sinclair, 'The Beauchamp earls', ch. 5; also M. Hicks, 'Between majorities: The Beauchamp interregnum, 1439–49', *Hist. Res.*, 72 (1999), 27–43; A. Dunn, 'Exploitation and control: The royal administration of magnate estates, 1397–1405', in M. A. Hicks (ed.), *Revolution and Consumption* (Woodbridge, 2001), 27–44.

The mutual obligations and benefits of service and good lordship operated in a variety of ways. Actual attendance on a lord, whether in his household or progresses, might occupy up to half the time of an indentured retainer but was none the less valued for the access to a privileged world. A lord, for his part, needed intimate and trusted counsellors as negotiators, witnesses, feoffees, and ultimately executors for his own affairs. The Oxfordshire esquire Richard Quatremains recorded on his tomb that he 'with rial princes of Counsel was true and wise famed'.[16] Of even greater value was the service of those able and ambitious knights who moved confidently in the world of central politics, acting as diplomats, financial administrators, keepers of fortresses, and even as royal councillors. Some had entered royal service from that of a magnate and most had connections with many lords. Of such a type were Sir Richard Abberbury, Sir Gerard Braybrooke II, and John Pelham. It was for their experience and influence, rather than in expectation of their exclusive loyalty, that such men were retained.[17]

As well as household intimates and experienced advisers, a magnate needed to retain some at least of the gentry elite of his 'country' who could uphold his influence in the government of the shire. They served as conduits to lesser men, a role which brought them both honour and profit, and through them the lord was kept informed of opinion in the shire. Such men were lords in their own right, perhaps with affinities of their own among the lesser gentry and yeomen. In the fourteenth century Sir John Cokayne of Ashbourne could muster twenty-one of his own retainers and Sir Ralph Hastings of Slingsby distributed his own liveries and annuities; in the reign of Henry VI Sir Randle Mainwaring had Cheshire gentry and yeomen in his affinity, as did Sir Richard Vernon.[18]

Ultimately it was upon a magnate's power to mobilize his retinue that his authority rested and upon which the Crown relied to deal with rebellion and revolt. Indentures often required the retainer to come when summoned with a reasonable number of his own men defensibly arrayed. In 1450–2 the Stafford retinue was repeatedly summoned, both to deal with the attacks of Sir Thomas Malory and to provide a royal bodyguard during Cade's revolt and the duke of York's rebellion. Just as important was a lord's capacity to outface the challenge of a rival lord; and in all such situations it was upon the stewards of his estates and the local retainers that he relied.[19]

---

[16] J. T. Driver, 'Richard Quatremains: A 15th-century squire and knight of the shire for Oxfordshire', *Oxoniensia*, 51 (1986), 101.

[17] Walker, 'Sir Richard Abberbury and his kinsmen: The rise and fall of a gentry family', *Nott. Med. Stud.* 34 (1990), 113–40; *House of Commons*, ii. 346–8, iv. 37–43.

[18] Walker, *Lancastrian Affinity*, 222, 259; Bennett, *Community, Class and Careerism*, 41; Wright, *Derbyshire Gentry*, 24.

[19] Carpenter, *Locality and Polity*, 453, 335; Rawcliffe, *The Staffords*, 77–8.

Just as the lord depended on his retainers for support in war and peace and looked to the affinity to actualize his authority, so his lordship brought them advantage in their own affairs. Lordship was primarily sought and used in disputes and litigation. Although the expectation that a lord would maintain his friends and servants in their just quarrels was of immemorial antiquity, the growing sophistication of legal procedures and the widening scope of litigation raised questions of how much 'maintenance' was acceptable. A lord could do much to procure a favourable verdict. He commanded the best legal advice, retaining serjeants-at-law and rising lawyers. If a retainer was indicted or convicted his lord might well be able to procure him a pardon. He was also able to maintain his supporter's case by various illicit means. The offence of 'maintenance' encompassed influencing judges and jurors; persuading the sheriff to delay a suit or empanel a partial jury; bribery of the jury, witnesses, sheriff, or judge; and intimidating the court by the presence of supporters.[20] It was not easy either to detect or to suppress. As sheriffs or JPs, the gentry were well placed to practise maintenance both on their own and their lord's behalf; similarly the bribery, or packing, of a jury could be arranged through intermediaries. Both sides almost routinely offered inducements to the sheriff and the boundary between legitimately 'informing' the jury and illegally 'labouring' it was easily crossed. Yet the fact that lords generally practised maintenance discreetly and indirectly is significant. They constantly professed to proceed by due course of law and periodically took the oath to dismiss from their retinue all lawbreakers and maintainers. It did no good to their reputation that the Commons should complain, as they did of Sir Philip Courtenay in 1393 and 1402, or of Sir Richard Stanhope in 1414, that he was 'of so great lordship and maintenance that noone had remedy against him'.[21]

Beyond maintaining a retainer at law there lay the option of defending him by arms. To protect a retainer's possession of his lands was the litmus test of good lordship. William Worcester noted how, in a dispute with William Appulyerd over the manor of Beighton in 1416, Sir John Fastolf had 'kept the said manor with force by the help of the squires and household men of his master the duke of Clarence'.[22] Hence men often named a lord as a feoffee of any land liable to be disputed. Yet because it could entangle a lord in local quarrels, even the greatest lords often drew back from using force on behalf of their clients.[23] So

[20] A. Harding, 'The origin of the crime of conspiracy', *TRHS*, 5th ser., 33 (1983), 89–108; *West. Chron.* 358–9.

[21] *House of Commons*, ii. 672–3; *Rot. Parl.* iv. 29–31. For a jury allegedly wearing the livery of a lord, see Carpenter (ed.), *Armburgh Papers*, 65.

[22] A. R. Smith, 'Litigation and politics: Sir John Fastolf's defence of his English property', in Pollard (ed.), *Property and Politics*, 62.

[23] Walker, *Lancastrian Affinity*, 160–1 (Gaunt's support for Roger de Langley); Castor, *King*,

unpredictable were the consequences of supporting a retainer's quarrel that it was the more important for a lord to be able to restrain and discipline him. Household retainers could be suspended or dismissed, but control over their local officials, such as stewards, bailiffs, and receivers, was both remote and limited by dependence on their services. It was often such men who were petty tyrants in their locality, intimidating, exploiting, and dispossessing the lord's tenants in his name. Neither Gaunt in the fourteenth century nor Warwick and Buckingham in the fifteenth were wholly successful in restraining the oppressions and private feuds of their followers.[24] There were, then, limits to a lord's authority over his retainers. When powerful local gentry took fees from a lord they did not thereby renounce the pursuit of their quarrels and could well look to a lord to endorse them. To control his affinity a lord needed some of the qualities of a statesman.

An affinity was neither monolithic, nor a machine for the enforcement of the lord's will; it was a series of individual relationships, conditioned by the circumstances of both lord and retainer. Whether it achieved a degree of cohesion depended on the character of the lordship. If geographically restricted and long established, like the Beauchamp, Courtenay, and Percy affinities, the common vertical tie of loyalty to the lord and lateral ties of marriage and mutual support among retainers could give it considerable coherence. Of the thirty-three retainers on the Courtenay livery roll, twenty-one were directly related to other members of the affinity, who were also predominantly used as feoffees and sureties in their land transactions.[25] The more diffused Lancastrian and Mowbray affinities displayed fewer internal ties, and retainers found associates just as often among neighbours and kin as they did among fellow retainers. Nevertheless, an affinity was, by definition, bound to its lord by formal obligations and good lordship, and together by common service and shared expectations. It was part of, but apart from, the local community. How did this affect its role in society?

2. THE AFFINITY IN THE LOCAL COMMUNITY

No lord could retain more than a fraction of the gentry in his region. Overall the £7,000 per annum which the nobility spent on fees to life retainers could have sufficed to pay only five or six hundred of the 3,000 odd armigerous gentry, allowing for £20 for a knight and £10 for an esquire. Of the fifty to seventy armigerous families in any shire only a minority were permanently attached to a retinue; even in Lancashire, where he was undisputed lord, John of Gaunt never

Crown, and Duchy of Lancaster, 167–8 (York's support for Thomas Daniel); Carpenter, *Locality and Polity*, 377, 391 (Warwick's support for William Bermingham).

[24] Walker, *Lancastrian Affinity*, 227–8, 258; Carpenter, *Locality and Polity*, 416; Wright, *Derbyshire Gentry*, 125–7.   [25] Cherry, 'The Courtenay earls of Devon', 134.

managed to retain more than one-third of the gentry, and Richard Beauchamp did not command the allegiance of all the leading Warwickshire gentry.

That does not imply that lordship played a minor role in a society of predominantly independent gentry. In virtue both of their individual wealth and of their position at the apex of the social and political hierarchy, great lords were bound to bestride their locality. Moreover, gentry society was steeply graded, and a magnate who sought to 'rule' the shire needed the support of those 'greater' knights with incomes in excess of £100 per annum, in whose hands was concentrated almost one-third of the total wealth of the gentry. There was no sense in which a lord would either seek or be able to wrest control of the shire from this elite, for his own estates were often localized and his authority could only extend beyond them through the medium of his retainers. Rather he aimed to use and extend their networks of influence and authority for his own purposes. It was thus the quality rather than the quantity of his retainers that was important. Conversely an affinity could provide a channel of access to lordship for other local gentry, enabling a magnate to become the focus for the loyalty and service of all the gentry of his 'country'. But this harmony between affinity and country was not easily achieved. For, first, an affinity was a divisive influence in local society and, secondly, its own internal tensions could feed into the outside world.

Although an affinity could provide a channel to a lord it could also monopolize his favour and protection, cornering the shire offices and the fruits of patronage and alienating those excluded. The stranglehold of the earl of Arundel's affinity in Shropshire early in Henry V's reign thus provoked assault from those excluded, as did the monopoly of Suffolk's retainers in East Anglia in the 1440s. A lord needed to defuse such tensions by allowing other interests a proportionate share. In Lancashire, where he brooked no rival, Gaunt was yet careful not to exclude from the shire offices those outside his retinue; similarly Richard Beauchamp generally allowed the return of one of the parliamentary seats to go to a non-retainer as MP and his insistence on filling both in 1426 aroused resentment.[26] An affinity also generated instability when its members quarrelled; the feuding of John of Gaunt's North Midland retainers brought the king's bench into the area in 1392–6, a sharp rebuff to his lordship.[27] As Sir John Paston noted in his quarrel with Gilbert Debenham, 'it was dysworshep to my lord [the duke of Norfolk] that tweyn of hys men schold debat so ner hym', and Lord Cromwell forbade two of his retainers to pursue their quarrel until they had discussed the matter with him, warning 'faile not hereof, as I may do anything for you hereafter'.[28] A lord had to practise crisis management as much as directive command.

---

[26] Powell, *Kingship, Law and Society*, 216–24; Castor, *King, Crown, and Duchy of Lancaster*, ch. 4; Walker, *Lancastrian Affinity*, 179; Carpenter, *Locality and Polity*, 383.

[27] Walker, *Lancastrian Affinity*, 227–8

[28] Gairdner (ed.), *Paston Letters*, iv. 198; Payling, *Political Society*, 208.

Yet areas where a single lord could pretend to the control of an entire shire were exceptional, and in a county like Essex multiple lordship generated a web of overlapping and multi-layered loyalties and channels of patronage. This was not necessarily beneficial, for the gentry looked to lordship both to ensure the stability of society and to provide the opportunity for individual advancement. It was precisely the pursuit of these contradictory goals that fed the tensions in gentry society.

3. DISPUTE AND DISORDER IN GENTRY SOCIETY

Since the overriding concern of the gentry was the acquisition and defence of family property, most disputes arose from and focused on this. Social advancement depended on acquiring land, and its loss threatened the livelihood and identity of the family. Contests over it became economic and social imperatives. They also engaged a man's honour, for there was a duty to prosecute a just claim and to resist a wrongful one. Both sides in any dispute claimed that justice and right was on their side. To countenance loss was not only to incur dishonour but to invite further challenges. The high incidence of land disputes among the gentry arose from the complexity of common law inheritance and the uncertainties of title, while an armigerous class found it natural to defend its interests by force of arms. The containment of dispute was thus of prime importance if social unity among the landowning class was to be preserved.

Several means were available, of which the most obvious was the law. The gentry were indefatigable, even obsessive, litigators. In the years 1422–42 two medium-ranking East Anglian gentry, Sir Henry Inglose and Henry Sturmer, are known to have pursued respectively thirty-nine and thirty-seven suits in the king's bench, and in the decade after 1464 Sir William Plumpton was engaged in nine suits.[29] A legal verdict provided the most formal decision, but many cases in the courts never came to judgment and it is clear that men embarked on litigation less to settle a dispute than because it offered an honourable method of affirming and protecting their rights. With the support of 'lordship' and 'friendship', and by a series of legal actions and procedures, a litigant would seek to probe and exploit the weakness of an opponent's position. The arena for this highly sophisticated legal warfare was commonly the courts of common pleas and king's bench. Suits in the king's bench between parties were brought by actions of trespass, in some of which allegations of forcible entry and destruction of property sought to establish a felonious breach of the peace. Not all actions of this kind were between gentry (who often impleaded their social inferiors), while the allegations of violence were often procedural. They cannot therefore provide a

---

[29] Maddern, *Violence and Social Order*, 35–6; Pollard, *North Eastern England*, 118.

measurable index of the nature or incidence of gentry disorder. Plaintiffs brought actions in the common law courts not with the purpose of securing a favourable jury verdict but in the hope of pressuring the defendant into making an informal settlement. In a twenty-year sample of East Anglian cases in the court of king's bench 70 per cent were settled before the defendant was summoned to court and a jury appointed.[30]

For settling gentry disputes litigation had several disadvantages. All litigation was slow and costly; it was wide open to corruption and personal influence, and though this was usually practised by both sides it meant that the outcome might not accord with law and justice. Where descent of title was involved the issues and the law itself might be unclear, as might the facts, for title deeds and conveyances were not always forthcoming either through loss or detinue, leaving the case in suspense. Moreover, litigation was essentially adversarial and could exacerbate and perpetuate division in the local community. If it reached a verdict this would award the disputed property wholly to the victor, leaving the vanquished with nothing, a position which he might be tempted to remedy by force if his inheritance were at stake or his honour compromised. For all these reasons litigation was not the sole or even principal means for resolving a dispute. 'Plea' was therefore closely linked to 'treaty', litigation being employed to induce an opponent to settle out of court. This was often facilitated by some form of arbitration, involving both a man's lord and his community.[31]

A lord, as has been said, was traditionally expected to support his follower's just quarrel, whether by appearing with him in court, defending his property, or using his political influence to deflect legal penalties. Yet 'good lordship' of this kind placed a lord in an ambivalent position, for a lord could easily be compromised by his follower's quarrel and alienated from the community. Above all he had to be sure that those he supported were lawful and respected men and not social outcasts.[32] Good lordship was thus often employed to secure a peaceful settlement by treaty and arbitration. Like litigation this was an essentially honourable process; indeed its rituals consciously promoted the re-establishment of the social peace through compromise and the repair of any slights to honour. When parties agreed to arbitration each appointed arbiters who might, if they wished, choose an umpire. The parties would then enter bonds to follow their award, perhaps vacating the disputed property meanwhile. 'Treaty', or negotiation, between the arbiters was often conducted in a formal and public set-

[30] Maddern, *Violence and Social Order*, 35–6; P. Tucker, 'Historians' expectations of medieval legal records', in A. Musson (ed.), *Expectations of the Law* (Woodbridge, 2001), 191–202.

[31] E. Powell, 'Arbitration and the law in the late Middle Ages', *TRHS* 33 (1984), 49–67; id., 'The settlement of disputes by arbitration in fifteenth century England', *Law and Hist. Rev.* 2 (1984), 21–43.

[32] Maddern, *Violence aid Social Order*, 164–6, for the duke of Norfolk's protection of John Belsham.

ting, before lawyers and justices, with the production of evidences by both sides and the submission of proposal and counter-proposal. It was not solely focused on points of law, as in a court, but could take in all issues under dispute. When the terms had been agreed the award was published, both parties having given prior acceptance that they would not appeal against it, and a date set for the formal loveday between them. If there had been personal insult or injury some ritual reparation was made, in money or a form of words, and where a death had occurred intercession would be provided for the man's soul. By these means the social relationship was restored and formalized by embrace and perhaps a feast. An accepted arbitration was a bar to further legal proceedings and it could be sealed by taking out enforceable bonds, or by a collusive settlement. Arbitration was suited to disputes where parties were ready to compromise on claims; it was also speedier and cheaper than litigation. John Russe, deploring John Paston's 'exspense of good [i.e.money] so onprofitably in the lawe' told him that if he had proceeded 'be the meanys of trety, ye had made peace'.[33] But the parties needed to be convinced that an award was both equitable and honourable, through each receiving some recognition of their right and having the settlement validated by the participation of their neighbours.

The quarrel of two Cheshire notables, Sir Thomas Grosvenor and Robert Legh, was settled at a loveday at which more than sixty knights and gentlemen from all over Cheshire gathered at Macclesfield church in April 1412, and in 1409 thirteen middling gentlemen of Bassetlaw wapentake in Nottinghamshire subscribed to an award of eight arbitrators between the two heiresses of Hugh Cressy over their disputed inheritance.[34] At all ranks of the social hierarchy those of superior status and authority might be called on to settle their inferiors' quarrels. The inherent authority of a great lord was complemented by the representative weight of his counsellors, while bishops drew on the civil law expertise of their councils to provide a kind of equitable jurisdiction. Thus Archbishop Kemp was called on to settle the murderous Pierpoint–Foljambe feud in 1436 after arbitration by a panel of local gentry and lawyers had failed.[35] Yet not all arbitrations were impartial and not all were acceptable and permanent. Pressure was sometimes put upon the weaker party to accept an arbitration weighted against him: the Derbyshire family of Revell imprisoned Richard Page until he agreed to arbitration by persons they named.[36] A biased award could then provoke refusal or even an armed confrontation at a loveday.

[33] Davis (ed.), *Paston Letters*, ii. 306–8: a long and eloquent letter on the theme.
[34] Bennett, *Community, Class and Careerism*, 2; Payling, *Political Society*, 204.
[35] C. Rawcliffe, 'The great lord as peacekeeper: Arbitration by English noblemen and their councils in the late Middle Ages', in J. A. Guy and H. G. Beale (eds.), *Law and Social Change in British History* (London, 1984), 34–54; Payling, *Political Society*, 200; Wright, *Derbyshire Gentry*, 133.
[36] Wright, *Derbyshire Gentry*, 123; Rawcliffe, 'The great lord as peacekeeper', 49.

Where local mediation was suspect or had broken down, or where a party claimed he was being intimidated, resort could be made to the jurisdiction of the chancellor on the ground of default of justice. To this ascending hierarchy of authority to whom disputes could be referred must finally be added parliament and the king himself. Walter Aslak and John Paston both considered petitioning parliament as an alternative or addition to the chancellor. Parliament could not itself render an award but it was an excellent venue for preliminary discussions and arrangements, and it could authoritatively require parties to come to an arbitration. In 1404 parliament required Sir Robert Leyburn and Thomas Warcop under severe financial penalties to settle their quarrel, which was jeopardizing the defence of the northern border. Ultimately the king might intervene to enforce an award, as did Henry IV against Justice Tyrwhit in 1411, and Henry V in the Gerard–Standish dispute in 1414.[37]

By one method or another the magistracy were expected to resolve their quarrels peacefully, but where litigation, lordship, private treaty, or public authority failed, it was likely that one of the parties would resort to force. In a chivalric society the resort to arms had a significance which could not be dissociated from the knightly qualities of valour and honour. The right to bear arms implied the right to use them in defence of the status of oneself and one's family. The armigerous class did not regard this as criminal, and though the flouting of the king's authority and breach of the peace would be punished by fine or token imprisonment, they expected to be pardoned, even for homicides. Only for treason was the death penalty exacted, for that challenged the very authority which validated their status in society. If violence in defence of property and honour was in some degree condoned, acts of violence that subverted the social hierarchy had to be reprobated as well as suppressed. Broadly speaking we have to distinguish between four different types of gentry violence: those arising from property disputes; personal feuds; struggles for political control; and gangs. Clearly these were often linked and overlapping, but reaction to each tended to be different.

While some clashes over property represented opportunistic attempts to assert a dubious title, like Lord Moleyns's destruction of the Pastons' manor of Gresham, many arose out of inheritance disputes as those dispossessed attempted to regain their rights. The descent of an inheritance to a sole heiress might leave her exposed to attempts by other relatives to abduct her and seize the family lands, as in the case of the Lasborough estate in 1390 and the Peshale lands in 1394, which brought about the murder of Sir John Ipstones.[38] Such disputes were generally amenable to legal settlement, but murders could initiate a feud

---

[37] C. Rawcliffe, 'Parliament and the settlement of disputes by arbitration in the later Middle Ages', *Partly. Hist.* 9 (1990), 316–42.

[38] Saul, *Knights and Esquires*, 190–3; Walker, *Lancastrian Affinity*, 226–7.

between families, like that of the Harcourts and Staffords from 1450 to 1470. More often they were incidents in power struggles in a locality, such as that in east Derbyshire between Sir Henry Pierpoint and Thomas Foljambe, which culminated in the murder of Foljambe's brother-in-law Henry Longford in Chesterfield church in 1434. Arbitration at a political level was needed to heal such divisions.[39]

Lesser gentry pursued political aggrandizement by abusing their lord's protection and their office, terrorizing and blackmailing whole localities. Gaunt's officials Chadderton and Chorleigh in Lancashire, Arundel's officers Lacon and Wele in Shropshire, even the king's chamberlain of North Wales Thomas Barnby, perpetrated acts of oppression and cruelty which were only eventually brought to book.[40] It had been against such 'petty kings' that the Commons had complained in 1377 and that legislation restricting livery was aimed. Remote and impoverished areas like the Forest of Dean, the Cheshire–Staffordshire border, and the Welsh and Scottish marches were bandit country, harbouring gangs of outlaws like John de Aynesworth in Lancashire and Cheshire c.1377, Ralph Greyndour and John Poleyn in Gloucestershire c.1380–1400, and William Walwayn in 1416 in Herefordshire.[41] Often they were recruited from and led by dissidents and fall-outs from gentry families: younger sons, mortgagees, the disinherited and dispossessed with nothing to lose. But sometimes members of the upper gentry or even nobility sought to terrorize a neighbourhood, like John, Lord Fitzwalter, around Colchester in 1342–51, Sir Richard Stanhope in Nottinghamshire in 1410–13, and Sir Thomas and Nicholas Burdet in Warwickshire. Men such as Sir Thomas Malory and Robert Ardern in Warwickshire, John Cokayne in Derbyshire, and John Belsham in Norfolk, flawed in character or by misfortune, embarked on a downward spiral of violence which brought the withdrawal of lordly and neighbourhood protection.[42]

No realistic measurement can be made of the incidence of gentry violence either overall or at different times and places. Even discounting the token violence alleged in legal prosecutions, many individual acts of violence must have gone unrecorded, both from the reluctance of juries of yeomen to indict their superiors, and from victims too frightened to petition for redress. Yet the

[39] R. L. Storey, *The End of the House of Lancaster* (London, 1966), 57–8; Wright, *Derbyshire Gentry*, 128–30.

[40] Walker, *Lancastrian Affinity*, 163–6; Powell, *Kingship, Law, and Society*, 123–4, 217–21, 238–9.

[41] Walker, *Lancastrian Affinity*, 169–70; Saul, *Knights and Esquires*, 176–81; A. Herbert, 'Herefordshire, 1413–61: Some aspects of society and public order', in Griffiths (ed.), *Patronage, Crown, and Provinces*, 103–22. Also *Proc. & Ord.* iii. 327, 346, for gentry gangs in Lancashire and Cheshire in 1429.

[42] Carpenter, *Locality and Polity*, 492 ff., 432–3; Wright, *Derbyshire Gentry*, 134–7; Maddern, *Violence and Social Order*, 154–66.

surviving evidence suggests that it was sporadic and related to particular situations, personal and political. In general the property disputes of the gentry did not entail violence, but where they did, especially if it became endemic, it fell to the Crown and greater nobility to restore control.

This could only be done with the cooperation of the local community. The Crown's own retainers were an important link with the centre, conveying information about local tensions and able to invoke royal authority. Under the statutes of riots (1411 and 1414) JPs were empowered to arrest and imprison rioters or certify the offence to the council, which could summon the parties *sub poena* or issue a commission of oyer and terminer. In exceptional circumstances the Crown could give this additional weight by sending the court of king's bench into the locality as a superior eyre, as in the Midlands in 1414. Similarly a commission to deal with the Pierpoint–Foljambe feud in 1434 took indictments of the offenders from two grand juries of Derbyshire gentry. But if the local community regarded it as intrusive (as in Devon in 1414) or politically biased (as in Derbyshire in 1454) the gentry absented themselves and frustrated its work.[43] Until the mid-century descent into partisan feuds, the general oyer and terminer commission was respected as an instrument of royal authority, but it usually achieved its effect by removing the cause of dissension and persuading the parties that they stood to gain from restoration to the king's grace and goodwill. In general the magistracy supported intervention by royal authority, for they abhorred dissension and disorder, which jeopardized both individual security and that of the realm.

The restraint and correction of disorder in landed society was thus a highly complex process in which all its grades participated and had responsibilities. If, in the eyes of the Crown, the magnate had the prime responsibility for the 'rule' of his shire, the balance of wealth and property within it required that his 'control' be exercised in a 'political' rather than a 'regal' manner. The local polity was to this degree a microcosm of the national, and the connection between them was often causal and direct.[44]

4. CENTRAL POLITICS AND THE LOCAL POLITY

The disputes endemic in landed society could never be of merely personal and local concern. To prosecute or defend their interests the gentry needed access to political forces at the centre, while the Crown for its part needed to understand the pattern of authority at local level if it was to govern effectively. Although local and national politics for much of the time had their distinct agenda and dialectic, they interacted at both personal and political levels.

[43] Powell, *Kingship, Law and Society*, ch. 8; Wright, *Derbyshire Gentry*, ch. 9.
[44] Watts, *Henry VI and the Politics of Kingship*, 70.

A magnate who enjoyed royal favour quickly increased his local influence. Richard II's enlargement of Robert de Vere's power in Cheshire had, by 1387, attracted to him Lancashire knights disaffected with Gaunt's rule, and in the 1390s the king's support for Thomas Holland, earl of Kent, against Gaunt in the Midlands and for John Holland, earl of Huntingdon, in the West Country against Courtenay destabilized those areas by creating rivalry between their retainers.[45] By the mid-fifteenth century the factions at Henry VI's court had their followings in the regions. At every turn of the political wheel from 1441 to 1456 Sir William Bonville was able to use his influence at the centre to discredit and undermine the lordship of the earl of Devon, while in East Anglia the legal and political protection which William de la Pole could afford to his local affinity negated Mowbray lordship for a decade and more.[46]

Conversely, local quarrels—both personal disputes and contests for lordship—could manifest themselves in enmities at court. Gaunt's attempt to discipline Sir Edward Dallingridge deepened the hostility between him and Dallingridge's lord, Richard, earl of Arundel, a hostility revealed at Arundel's trial in 1397. Lord Cromwell's similar attempt to suppress and punish Sir William Taillboys in Lincolnshire brought him up against Taillboys' protector, the earl of Suffolk, whose impeachment in 1450 Cromwell allegedly abetted.[47] The alignment of magnates behind the court and the duke of York in the 1450s was greatly influenced by a series of territorial disputes. The very proliferation of such conflicts evinced the lack of impartial and authoritative regulation by the king, but they amply demonstrate the divisive effects of local issues on the central polity.

These tensions affected not merely the leaders of political society but those connected to them. Thus the revolution of 1399 blighted or advanced the fortunes of leading supporters of Plantagenet and Lancaster: in Norfolk Sir Simon Felbrigg was displaced by Sir Thomas Erpingham; in Sussex Dallingridge by Pelham.[48] In the mid-fifteenth century some local gentry sought support from magnate factions at the centre to bolster their local ambitions.[49]

---

[45] Walker, *Lancastrian Affinity*, 167–76, 231; C. J. Tyldesley, 'The Crown and the local communities in Devon and Cornwall, 1377–1422', Ph. D. thesis (Exeter University, 1978), ch. 6.

[46] M. Cherry, 'The struggle for power in mid-fifteenth century Devonshire', in Griffiths (ed.), *Patronage, Crown, and Provinces*, 123–44; Castor, *King, Crown, and Duchy of Lancaster*, chs. 4, 5.

[47] Walker, *Lancastrian Affinity*, 127–40; R. Virgoe, 'William Taillboys and Lord Cromwell: Crime and politics in Lancastrian England', *BJRL* 55 (1972–3), 459–82.

[48] E. L. T. John, 'Sir Thomas Erpingham, East Anglian society, and the dynastic revolution of 1399', *Norfolk Archaeology*, 35 (1970), 96–108; A. Curry (ed.), *Agincourt 1415* (Stroud, 2000), 53–110.

[49] For Walter Blount in Derbyshire and Edmund Mountford in Warwickshire, see H. Castor, 'Walter Blount is gone to serve traytours', *Mid. Hist.* 19 (1994), 21–39; C. Carpenter, 'Law, justice and landowners', *Law and Hist. Rev.* 1 (1983), 203–57.

Even more serious was the ability of a local elite linked to the court to monopolize shire offices and exclude other gentry from influence and patronage. Opposition to the dominance of Staffordshire by duchy of Lancaster retainers after 1403 produced a decade of violent disorder, and in the 1440s the rule of Kent by William Crowmer, Stephen Slegge, and William Isle under Lord Saye's protection, and of East Anglia by Tuddenham and Heydon under the earl of Suffolk's, all severely disrupted the local polity and threatened royal authority.[50]

While the direct interaction of the politics of the centre and the locality is indisputable in such instances, these were extreme manifestations of what was more normally a latent connection. Ambitious gentry who used influence at court for their own advancement encountered the caution and coherence of a shire elite resistant to political adventurism. And when faced with confrontation at national level retainers were likely to reconsider their allegiances. Thus the Nottinghamshire elite, though bound by tradition and material reward to the duchy of Lancaster, disengaged almost completely from the armed struggle in 1459–61 and survived intact, as did that of Warwickshire.[51] National rivalries were not automatically replicated at local level, for the gentry did not respond solely to the imperatives of lordship, but pursued their own interests and nourished their loyalties to family, neighbourhood, and Crown.

This survey of the local polity suggests a reassessment of the power structures within it. Rather than divide political society simply between peerage and gentry it is more helpful to separate four elements. At the top were families of comital rank and a small number of baronial families with comital-size incomes (i.e. £1,000 and more per annum). These could claim the political leadership of their country and exercise this from a great castle and through a retinue containing at least some of the leading baronial and knightly families of the area. This represented the classical model of the late medieval affinity. The group beneath, the lesser baronage and greater knights with incomes in excess of £100, were closely associated with them as leaders of their war retinues, counsellors, and companions; they also provided the channels for magnate lordship in the locality. They were lords of their own areas, leaders of the shire magistracy, with connections to central politics, and able to support their own modest retinue. Thirdly, the rest of the armigerous class, with incomes of less than £100, exercised lordship at manorial level and, though aspirants to the patronage of the great, primarily used a network of connections with neighbours and family to further their personal interests. Only a few were formally or permanently retained, though most

<hr />

[50] Castor, *King, Crown, and Duchy*, ch. 6; R. Virgoe, 'The crown, magnates, and local government in fifteenth century East Anglia', in R. Highfield and R. Jeffs (eds.), *The Crown and Local Communities* (Gloucester, 1981), 72–87; Harvey, *Jack Cade's Rebellion*, ch. 2.

[51] Payling, *Political Society*, 154–6; Carpenter, *Locality and Polity*, 485–6.

were eager to win good lordship by any service. Finally, operating within this landed society but from a different basis was another hierarchy, of those who directly served the Crown and the nobility. These included not merely the professionals and careerists—the lawyers, land agents, financial officials—but, at a higher level, those who had advanced their fortunes by war or membership of the royal household. Their influence in local society rested more on their connections and services than on their landlordship. Lordship and service thus provided the impulsion for this society.

When Bishop Russell declared that 'the polityk rule of every region wele ordeigned stondithe in the nobles', foremost in his mind were the comital families who were accepted in their 'country' as 'prynce and soverayne next owre sovereyne lord'.[52] But just how common were these? It has been emphasized that the 'rule'—if by that we mean the active direction—of the local gentry ideally required the lord's residence and certainly his continuous attention. Where this was exercised over a traditional and close-knit society with a strong regional identity, as by Courtenay in the south-west and by Neville and Percy in the north, the model was most nearly realized. It was somewhat harder for the Beauchamp earls to rule their slice of the amorphous Midlands, though earl Richard did so through an extended affinity and influence at the centre, as did William, duke of Suffolk, over the disparate regions of East Anglia.

Yet such successes must be set against an equal or greater record of failure. This could have many causes. Some complexes were too extended. Even in Gaunt's natural base, Lancashire, or in the heartland of his power in the North Midlands, his infrequent presence encouraged disobedience and detachment from the bonds of affinity. The same may have been true for other major families with widely scattered estates, like York, Mowbray, Stafford, and FitzAlan. Secondly, most of the upper nobility had political and military commitments which they pursued far away from their territorial base and which they almost certainly viewed as more honourable, rewarding, and obligatory than the affairs of their local polity. Such activities were by no means divorced from the rule of their affinity and locality; for war and political influence helped to enlarge the retinue and give it coherence. But when the local polity needed to be steered through a crisis, or a challenge directly countered, an absent lord was hampered in the speed and aptness of his response. Thirdly, there were, at any time, some among the upper peerage who lacked the personal capacity to rule effectively. The premature blindness of Edward Courtenay, earl of Devon, after 1390 and the indiscipline and ineptitude of his grandson Thomas, sent Courtenay influence into decline throughout the first half of the fifteenth century. Some, like

[52] Chrimes, *English Constitutional Ideas*, 172; Davis (ed.), *Paston Letters*, ii. 84; Watts, *Henry VI and the Politics of Kingship*, 74.

Henry Holland, duke of Exeter, allied a streak of criminal behaviour to a crippling poverty which deterred any but the disreputable from joining his retinue. Finally demographic hazards and political miscalculation as always took their toll of a system that depended on personal rule. Three successive minorities and the longevity of the Countess Anne removed Stafford lordship between 1392 and 1438, and the FitzAlan lordship disintegrated among co-heiresses on the death of Earl Richard in 1415. The Mortimers suffered a succession of early deaths and lived under a permanent cloud of royal distrust; and the Percys faced a long road to recover their standing after the failed revolts of 1403–5. In fact it was something of a rarity for comital rule to remain an active political force over two successive generations.

There were thus limitations—natural, circumstantial, and political—to a lord's 'comprehensive control' of his country. Moreover, there were counties, or localities within counties, where no lord of high rank held sufficient land to rule in this fashion or to embrace a significant number of leading gentry in his affinity. There the lesser baronage and greater knights might constitute an informal ruling elite in virtue of both their own lordship over lesser gentry and their virtual monopoly of shire office. Magnate leadership was generally welcomed as imparting honour, authority, and cohesion to gentry society, but it does not follow that the gentry depended on it to save themselves from feud and anarchy. The horizontal bonds of social intercourse and the settlement of disputes by neighbourhood mediation could usually afford sufficient mechanism for political society to operate. Networks at this level had a high degree of continuity drawing on family tradition and relationships. They provided the essential framework through which the shire was governed and through which magnate leadership could be exercised.

PART II

Work and Worship

CHAPTER 7

Agrarian Society

I. THE AGRICULTURAL FRAMEWORK

Late medieval England exhibited infinite variations in the use of the land, often within very localized areas. These were determined by the terrain and soil, economic location, and social and agrarian organization. I shall first survey the broad diversity of its regions, even if the range of their micro-economies can only be hinted at.[1]

A distinction is usually drawn between upland and lowland economies. The former, relying on rough pasture and woodland with little and poor arable, was mainly dependent on livestock, notably sheep and pigs, with timber and mineral extraction providing an industrial element. Settlement was dispersed in isolated farms and hamlets, held by free tenants and worked in severalty. Villages, located at long intervals in river valleys, were less units of agrarian organization than seigniorial and ecclesiastical centres. In lowland England, by contrast, nucleated villages had been formed over the four centuries preceding 1350 as centres of a predominantly arable economy. Many lay within 2 or 3 miles of each other, tightly surrounded by their open fields, which were communally cultivated. This broad contrast between the upland 'natural' countryside and the lowland 'planned' countryside was not absolute, for numerous individual farmsteads existed in lowland England and nucleated villages in the uplands.

Predictably, a map of population density, based on the 1377 poll tax returns, follows the contours. The areas of higher density, with upward of 20 persons per square mile (12 per square kilometre), lay generally to the south and east of a line between York and Bristol including East Anglia, with the highest density in the Midlands. But this area also contained pockets of sparse settlement, in the Weald and downland of the southern counties, the Fens and Breckland of Norfolk, and the forests of the Chilterns and Hampshire. Mapping the distribution of lay wealth on a county basis, from the tax assessment of 1334, produces a similar alignment. The poorest counties lay to the north and west of the York–Exmouth

---

[1] The discussion in this section is based upon A. R. H. Baker and R. A. Butlin (eds.), *Studies of Field Systems in the British Isles* (Cambridge, 1973); *AHEW*, chs. 1–3; B. M. S. Campbell, *English Seigniorial Agriculture, 1250–1450* (Cambridge, 2000).

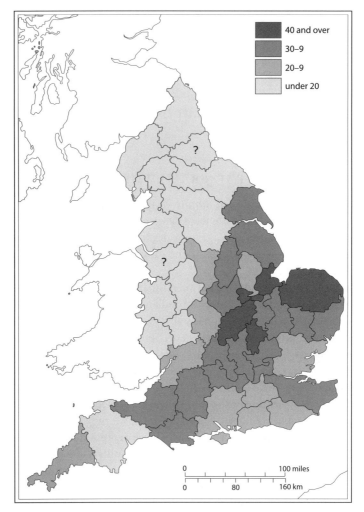

MAP 7.1. Distribution of rural population per square mile, 1377. Source: Based on the poll tax figures for the lay population over 14 years of age, taken from J. C. Russell, *British Medieval Population* (Albuquerque, N. Mex., 1948)

line, the wealthiest being in the midland belt from Lincoln to Gloucester and Yarmouth to Reading.[2] But wealthy and populous districts lay alongside marsh and moorland.

The terrain of each region determined its economy and agricultural techniques. North of the Tees lay a wild and incompletely tamed countryside of

[2] R. S. Schofield, 'The geographical distribution of wealth in England, 1334–1649', *Econ. HR* 18 (1965), p. 506, map 2.

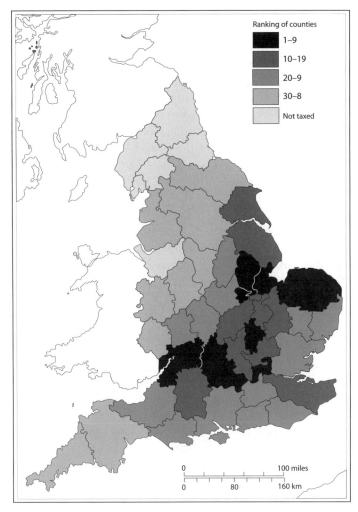

MAP 7.2. Distribution of lay wealth, 1334. Source: R. S. Schofield, *Economic History Review*, 18 (1968), 506

moor, marsh, and woodland which dictated a largely pastoral economy. Arable cultivation and nucleated villages were restricted to the coastal plains and the valleys of the Tyne, Wear, and Tees. Between the Tees and the Humber the rich lowlands of the North and East Ridings, with open-field husbandry, contrasted with the hillier west and south-west, where pasture and arable were interspersed in enclosed fields. In parts of Lancashire less than one-third of the land was arable. Much was given over to cattle- and sheep-rearing. In the Yorkshire lowlands wheat was the main crop; in Lancashire oats.

Midland England was the classic area of cultivation in two or three open fields, each upward of 100 acres. Fields were divided into furlongs comprising bundles of quarter-acre strips, distributed among the villagers. They ploughed with teams of six to eight oxen, moving from the circumference to the centre, the mould board creating ridge and furrow in the stiff clay soil. Villagers held strips distributed over each of the common fields, which were cultivated in annual rotation following a cycle of winter-sown wheat, spring-sown barley and oats, and fallow, though in some areas the furlong formed the unit of rotation 'according to the needs of the fields and of the village'.[3] After the harvest the stubble would be grazed by the villagers' stock, helping to enrich the soil with dung. Beyond the open fields lay areas of meadow, waste, and common on which the pasturing of beasts was regulated by the villagers or the manorial court. While the three-field system held sway in the valleys of the Trent, Nene, and Welland, to the west lay two different types of countryside. In the formerly wooded and more recently settled areas, such as Cannock, Arden, the Malvern Hills, and the Forest of Dean, hamlets and scattered farms, with fields of irregular sizes, reflected cumulative assarting by a predominantly free peasantry in the preceding two centuries. In southern Warwickshire, Worcestershire, and Gloucestershire older settlement under seigniorial authority had produced densely distributed villages along the valleys and tributaries of the Avon and Severn. Here corn was king, with 70–96 per cent of the land under the plough in 1350. In this area two-field rather than three-field systems predominated, providing greater intensity of cultivation, with wheat and oats the main demesne crop and barley, dredge, or legumes on peasant holdings.

Cambridgeshire formed a watershed between the midland pattern and that of East Anglia, which exhibited wide varieties of soil and land use. On the light, fertile soils to the north and east of Norwich, barley and wheat were the main crops, with rye in the centre and south of the county. Horses could be used for ploughing these soils on a scale equalled only in Kent, while dairy farming vied with sheep flocks. This larger element of animal husbandry was the basis for a system of mixed farming in which better fertilization, systematic weeding, and the replacement of fallow by nitrogenous legumes (pulse, beans, and peas) raised crop yields to levels not attained until the eighteenth century. Intensive cultivation rested on the cheap labour of numerous free smallholders, the main component of the peasantry. Manorial organization was weak and fragmented except to the north-west and on the large ecclesiastical estates; only there did manor and vill coincide. The Breckland evolved as a distinct economy based on sheep-grazing and rabbit warrens, with run-rig husbandry producing rye. The densely populated Fenlands provided fisheries and rough grazing, and peat extraction

---

[3] King, citing by-laws, in *AHEW* 211.

had filled the Broads with water. To the south, in Suffolk, Hertfordshire, and Essex, the boulder clay demanded a system of three-course rotation using oxen; while sheep and cattle were reared on the coastal and estuary marshes. The region was geared to the demands of the London market for wheat and oats, firewood, and meat.[4]

The midland system ran down to the Chiltern escarpment in Oxfordshire, Bedfordshire, and Buckinghamshire. There the lowlands had nucleated villages with common fields, while on higher and more wooded ground tenant closes of 5 or 10 acres included arable, wood, and heath, producing a mixed economy of sheep and corn. In the three south-eastern counties, Kent, Surrey and Sussex, the determinant was the contrast between the littoral and the Weald, reflecting distinct eras of colonization. In the coastal plain and river valleys great ecclesiastical landlords practised intensive husbandry. A threefold rotation based on the furlong provided the flexibility for a pattern of convertible husbandry. High sowing rates controlled weeds, and yields were among the highest achieved.[5] London provided a market for wheat and barley and also for cattle, which were grazed on Romney Marsh. Kent went over to the use of horses for ploughing, while Sussex continued with the traditional oxen. By contrast the forested Weald was similar to the Chilterns, a mosaic of small fields and farmsteads of about 15 acres with a pastoral economy, whose smallholders migrated to the coastal plain to work as shepherds, artificers, and ploughmen.

In the southern counties to the west, from Hampshire to Somerset, there was first-class grazing for sheep, with great flocks like the bishop of Winchester's of 22,000 on the downland. In the lowlands arable was dominant, comprising 80 per cent of demesne acreage even in the late fourteenth century. Two-course rotation was practised on the downland slopes, where oats and rye were grown, three-course on the more fertile lands growing wheat and barley. The eight-oxen team remained the norm. Finally, Devon and Cornwall formed a distinctive agricultural province. This was a land of contrasts, between the high central moors used for summer pasturage, the fertile area of the estuaries to the south, and the poor clay soils along the northern littoral. Yet before 1350 two-thirds of the land was under arable cultivation. This was never organized around nucleated villages, which served more as small market centres for their locality. Rather, it was a landscape of dispersed settlement and small, enclosed fields used for both arable and pasture. Mostly it was the coarser grains, of rye and oats, that were cropped, providing a diet of dark bread and potage and plentiful ale, though

[4] B. M. S. Campbell, 'Arable productivity in medieval England: Some evidence from Norfolk', *Journal of Economic History*, 43 (1983), 379–401; id. *Seigniorial Agriculture*, 121–9; M. Bailey, *A Marginal Economy? The East Anglian Breckland in the late Middle Ages* (Cambridge, 1989).

[5] P. F. Brandon, 'Demesne arable farming in coastal Sussex during the later Middle Ages', *Agr. Hist. Rev.* 19 (1971), 113–34.

much cider was also made. Some cattle-grazing and dairy farming was practised but the pastures were mainly used for sheep.

Given the variety of local conditions, it was in terms of the *pays* rather than the region that the agrarian economy functioned. Yet two overall generalizations can be made. First, in 1350 the economy bore the imprint of two centuries and more of population growth, with land of all types growing grain to feed the densely filled countryside, and with pasture under pressure in many areas. Arable accounted for 60 per cent of land use in terms of value. Secondly, in most areas productivity levels were 'strikingly low by the standards of later centuries', with crop yields of cereals often below 15 bushels per acre, and seed yielding on average not more than three and a half the amount sown.[6]

2. AGRAGARIAN STRUCTURES BEFORE THE BLACK DEATH

The growth of population from some 2 million in 1086 to 4.25 million (and possibly more) in 1300 affected the social structure of regions in different ways.[7] In lowland England open-field tillage was under manorial control. Lords' demesnes of up to 250 acres of arable, either consolidated or interspersed among the open-field strips, were worked by unfree villein tenants who owed labour services for two to four days a week and by the hired labour of free tenants. A villein's notional holding was a yardland, or virgate, of 20–30 acres, but population pressure had reduced the size of most holdings to no more than 10 acres, and while some 20 per cent had 1 virgate or more, 30 per cent had 5 acres or less. Even wider disparities existed among free tenants: while 8–10 per cent had holdings larger than a virgate, 47–50 per cent had less than 5 acres, many no more than 2. Beneath them lay the landless cottagers and the vagrant poor.[8] Thus between half and two-thirds of peasants' holdings were insufficient to support a family between harvests, and had to be supplemented by employment as agricultural labourers or rural craftsmen. In fact the great division in peasant society was less between the free and unfree than between those who had sufficient land to live upon and those who did not. Not merely the villein's land but his house and chattels belonged to his lord, though custom usually protected his family's succession to the property on his death by payment of an entry fine, and allowed him to

[6] Britnell, in *AHEW* 209; Dyer, in *AHEW* 230; Campbell, *Seigniorial Agriculture*, 65, 316–18.

[7] For the range of historians' estimates of between 4 million and 7 million in 1300, see J. Hatcher and M. Bailey, *Modelling the Middle Ages* (Oxford, 2001), 129.

[8] J. Hatcher and E. Miller, *Medieval England: Rural Society and Economic Change, 1086–1348* (London, 1978), 143–50. For regional variations, see B. M. S. Campbell, 'Population pressure, inheritance, and the land market in a fourteenth century peasant community', in R. M. Smith (ed.), *Land, Kinship, and Life Cycle* (Cambridge, 1984), 103–6.

devise his chattels by payment of a 'heriot', usually of livestock. The persons of those born unfree likewise belonged to the lord—they had to pay 'chevage' to live outside the manor, 'merchet' when a daughter married, and 'leyrwite' for her illicit intercourse before marriage. Such incidental financial rights were as profitable to the lord as their villeins' labour services.

Manorial obligations were regulated through the manor court, representing the lord's authority and presided over by his steward, but operating through the tenants, who acted as jurors and chief pledges to declare the 'custom' of the manor, which regulated the agricultural routine and services of the customary tenants. Since the unfree were debarred from the royal courts of common law, the manorial court registered their landholding and debts, resolved disputes, and punished disciplinary offences. The court rolls recorded the tenants' obligations, individual and communal. Manorial custom represented 'a shifting compromise between the lord and the community', reflecting the balance between the lord's need for service (to cultivate the land) and the peasant's need for land (to survive).[9] During these centuries of population growth, land hunger had reduced the size of peasant holdings while lords had strengthened and defined the apparatus of manorial control.

Even within this open-field system there were considerable varieties of agrarian structures. In the Hundred Rolls of 1279, covering southern midland counties, manorial vills accounted for no more than 75–80 per cent, and outside this area manorialized agriculture was very far from typical. East Anglia and Kent were populated by numerous small freeholders. North of the Tees labour services were rare except in eastern Durham, and across southern England areas of upland and forest, like the Weald, the Chilterns, the Warwickshire Arden, and the Norfolk Breckland, had been cleared and cultivated by individual peasant settlement as rent-paying freeholds. Overall, the proportions of villeins and freeholders cannot be established, but while in the counties covered by the Hundred Rolls there were 60 per cent villeins and 40 per cent freeholders, the latter accounted for 60 per cent in the northern Danelaw and 55–70 per cent in East Anglia.[10]

The attempts both to accommodate more people within the framework of the agricultural manor and to extend the area of cultivation by assarts were reaching a critical point by 1300. Subdivided holdings no longer afforded subsistence, and while some reclaimed lands could be highly productive, on others the soil was poor. It has been argued that the balance between agrarian and animal husbandry

    [9] R. H. Hilton, *Class Conflict and the Crisis of Feudalism* (London, 1985), 50 ff.; id. *The English Peasantry in the Later Middle Ages* (Oxford, 1975), 54.

    [10] Hatcher and Miller, *Medieval England*, 120; R. H. Hilton, *Bond Men Made Free* (London, 1976), 163–71; T. Lomas, 'South east Durham', in P. D. A. Harvey (ed.), *The Peasant Land Market in Medieval England* (Oxford, 1984), 269–79.

had swung too heavily to the former, overcropping and insufficient fertilization by animal dung reducing yields. The question thus raised is whether agricultural production had reached the limits of its technology and was now seriously unable to accommodate further increases of population.[11]

That medieval agriculture did have the capacity for improvement was shown by the higher yields achieved on some diverse estates in southern England. The key lay partly in the practice of intensive mixed farming—sheep and corn husbandry—and partly in the deliberate enrichment of the soil by manuring and marling, reducing weed growth, and intensive sowing. Yet such improved techniques were both cost- and labour-intensive, and never became widespread. Over England south of the Trent they were practised on no more than one-eighth of the land.

Not only production but marketing was improving. During the thirteenth century a network of small markets sprang up in towns and villages for the exchange of simple commodities. At these peasants sold their small surplus and local craftsmen their artefacts to procure money for their rents, and on these the near-landless depended to buy their food. Most markets lay within a range of 10 miles, easily accessible with a horse and two-wheeled cart, so that local shortages and surpluses could be adjusted. At a higher level more than a dozen towns had populations of over 10,000 drawing provisions from a 10- to 20-mile radius. Almost half of seigniorial agricultural output was marketed, and market demand bred a degree of regional specialization in agrarian products and an extended range of occupations among artisans. The growth of a 'commercialized' economy helps to explain how a region like East Anglia could contain a dense population of smallholders and how, in 1300, agriculture was supporting double the population of 1100 without a proportional increase in the cultivated area. Commercialization was facilitated by exports of wool and grain and an enlarged money supply, with £900,000 of coin in circulation.[12]

Nevertheless, the agrarian economy functioned within powerful systemic constraints. Direct management by large landlords, lay and ecclesiastical, tended to be conservative, retaining the communal structure of manorial agriculture which set limits to individual enterprise. Throughout the 'long' thirteenth century, from 1180 to 1315, high prices for cereals encouraged the management of the demesne for immediate returns. Production costs could be kept low by enforcing customary labour services, and while hired labour was increasingly

[11] For the debate initiated by B. Harvey's criticism of Postan in 'The population trend in England between 1300 and 1348', *TRHS*, 4th ser., 16 (1966), 23–42, see Hatcher and Bailey, *Modelling the Middle Ages*, 34–8, 44–5; Campbell, *Seigniorial Agriculture*, 17–19.

[12] R. H. Britnell and B. M. S. Campbell (eds.), *A Commercialising Economy: England, 1086–c.1300* (Manchester, 1995), 1–26; Bailey, *A Marginal Economy?*, 191–9; Campbell, *Seigniorial Agriculture*, 173–9, 188–228, 411–12.

used—as being more efficient—its surplus capacity ensured that wages remained low. The combination of favourable economic forces and increasing judicial power buttressed landlords' exploitation of their demesnes. The same forces pushed much of the peasantry into a subsistence economy. Even a half-virgate holding was barely sufficient to sustain a normal peasant family, providing little margin against a poor harvest. Yet almost half the villein holdings were smaller than this, while the majority of freeholders, with less than 10 acres—and many with 5 acres or less—were proportionately more dependent on wage employment. Though an expanding economy helped them to survive, the fall in the level of real wages after 1260, which persisted for the next seventy years, further tightened the screw. When struck by personal or natural disasters, the peasant sold his beast(s), if he had any, and then his land, generating a trend towards the emergence of a few wealthier peasants with 2 or 3 virgates and the steady depression of smallholders into the ranks of the landless. Some of these would migrate to the towns, but whether in an urban or rural context, the existence of a numerous sector living at subsistence level was a drag on the economy. Thus the thirteenth-century economy presents seemingly contradictory aspects, in some respects expansionist and innovative, in others stationary and overloaded.[13]

In the first half of the fourteenth century it was assailed by external shocks. Climatically the years 1315–45 were of exceptional harshness, with failed harvests and livestock disease generating famine conditions in 1315–22, exceptionally cold weather in the 1340s, and coastal inundation which submerged thousands of acres in East Anglia and Kent. War brought devastation to the northern shires before 1330, and lowland England was periodically subject to heavy war purveyance and taxation from 1297 to 1340. Whether these shocks checked expansion and precipitated the crisis of an over-exploited agrarian system has been much debated. Did it mark the nemesis of overpopulation, soil exhaustion, and seigniorial exploitation, or did the economy possess the resilience to absorb and recover from the catastrophes?[14] Evidence points both ways. Famine could have produced a mortality of 10 per cent, easing but not fundamentally altering the ratio of land and people; and in some areas population had recovered by 1348. Landlords at first profited from famine prices, but after 1325 demand and prices fell and in the 1330s real wages rose for the first time in seventy years. Many lords now felt the cost of having commuted labour services from the 1280s. None of this was sufficient to overturn the prevailing pattern of 'high farming'; only a few lords changed from direct management of the

[13] Campbell, *Seigniorial Agriculture*, 306–10, 357, 414–24; M. Bailey, 'Peasant welfare in England, 1290–1348', *Econ. HR* 51 (1998), 232–46; H. Kitsikopoulos, 'Standards of living and capital formation in pre-plague England: A peasant budget model', *Econ. HR*, 53 (2000), 251–4.

[14] B. M. S. Campbell (ed.), *Before the Black Death: Studies in the 'Crisis' of the Early Fourteenth Century* (Manchester, 1991).

demesne to leasing. Perhaps the greater effects were among the peasantry, where lands vacated by smallholders who had died or been forced to sell were bought by their wealthier neighbours, increasing the polarization of the class. If the economy, at this point, gives the impression of being in unstable equilibrium and balanced on a knife edge, it was soon to be completely subverted by the devastating outbreak of plague in 1348–9.

3. POPULATION DECLINE AND ECONOMIC CHANGE

For the next century and a half population stagnated or fell—for the longest period in English history. Evidence from different sources points to a mortality of between one-third and a half in 1348–9 in different localities.[15] The level of mortality in the subsequent epidemics of 1361–2, 1368–9, 1375, and 1390 is less certain, though it was certainly lower. Nevertheless, a cumulative reduction of the population of almost one-half seems plausible. The nature of the infection seems open to doubt. Recent studies have shown that it could not have been bubonic plague. Contemporary accounts indicate that it was haemorrhagic, transmitted by interpersonal contact, and usually fatal within three to four days. In some outbreaks it was noted that children and the elderly were most at risk, and men more vulnerable than women.[16] In the fifteenth century references to plague in the chronicles are less frequent and specific. Outbreaks were mostly localized, although thirteen of regional dimensions can be identified between 1400 and 1479.[17] Moreover, the generally low temperatures and wet weather, with some particularly severe winters in the late 1430s, spread influenza, dysentery, and tuberculosis. By 1390 an ageing population was beginning to find difficulty in replacing itself, so that the population which, on the evidence of the poll tax returns of 1377 then stood at around 2.5 million, may have declined further over the following century.[18] This was a level barely if at all higher than in 1086. If this suggests that plague had become endemic in the population, it still leaves uncertain how far it was responsible for the failure of population to recover.

Those who believe that the population was kept in check by plague can point

[15] J. Hatcher, *Plague, Population and the English Economy, 1348–1530* (London, 1977); L. R. Poos, 'The rural population of Essex in the later Middle Ages', *Econ. HR* 38 (1985), 515–30; M. K. McIntosh, *Autonomy and Community: The Royal Manor of Havering* (Cambridge, 1986), 126–9.

[16] S. Scott and C. J. Duncan, *Biology of Plagues: Evidence from Historical Populations* (Cambridge, 2001), 1–114, 353–94. For contemporary comment, see R. Horrox, *The Black Death* (Manchester, 1994), 85–92.

[17] Listed by J. M. W. Bean, 'Plague, population, and economic decline in England in the later Middle Ages', *Econ. HR* 15 (1963) 430.

[18] Hatcher, *Plague, Population and the English Economy*, 27; Poos, 'Rural Population of Essex', 529–30; M. Bailey, 'Demographic decline in late medieval England: Some thoughts on recent research', *Econ. HR* 49 (1996), 1; Campbell, *Seigniorial Agriculture*, 402–4.

to specific evidence of the level of mortality among two monastic communities, at Christ Church Priory, Canterbury, and at Westminster Abbey. At the former, crude deaths at a crisis level of 40+ per thousand per annum occurred in one year in every four during the period 1395–1505, more frequently before 1457 but more severely afterwards, the mean expectation of life at 20 years being 28.0 years.[19] At Westminster over the period 1390–1500 a similar level of mortality obtained, with eight years at crisis level and thirteen of above average. The year 1419–20 saw a major cull at the level of 150 per thousand per annum. Life expectancy here was strikingly similar to that at Canterbury.[20] While both communities were clearly experiencing an above-normal rate of mortality, such evidence has clear limitations. These are minuscule samples from conditions where plague could spread easily; nor do the years of high mortality always correlate with reported epidemics elsewhere. It has therefore been questioned whether the localized, albeit heavy, mortality occasioned by random occurrence of plague could have been sufficient to keep the replacement rate below zero in the population at large. This was, after all, a period in which the living standards of the peasantry were higher than at any other time in the Middle Ages. Land was abundant, rents low, wages remained high and foodstuffs relatively cheap. Such would generally be accounted ideal conditions for early marriage and the establishment of a new household, with a consequent rising birth rate.[21] High mortality—particularly infant mortality—might have held this in check; but so equally might a low rate of fertility. But before the commencement of parish registers in the sixteenth century statistical evidence on any scale for birth rates, age at marriage, and family size is lacking. Medieval historians have therefore had to exercise much ingenuity in interpreting localized sets of figures and the ambiguous evidence of social trends.

One apparently unique source of evidence for birth rates is provided by the record for the churching of women after childbirth in the Essex parish of Walden. Unfortunately the sample is both localized and fragmentary, covering only seventeen years over the period 1439–88. With a probable population of 1,500, the average 44 births each year gives a crude birth rate of 30 per thousand per annum, similar to that in the period of low population at the end of the seventeenth century.[22] On this evidence rising living standards were not producing a rising birth rate. Further, using data from Essex tithing musters, a

[19] J. Hatcher, 'Mortality in the fifteenth century: Some new evidence', *Econ. HR* 39 (1980), 19–38.

[20] B. Harvey, *Living and Dying in England, 1100–1540* (Oxford, 1993), 122–9. The eight years were 1399–1400, 1419–20, 1420–1, 1433–4, 1457–8, 1463–4, 1478–9, 1490–1.

[21] This is urged by Z. Razi, *Life, Marriage and Death in a Medieval Parish* (Cambridge, 1980), 135–7, and supported by M. Mate, *Daughters, Wives, and Widows after the Black Death* (Woodbridge, 1998), 23, 147, 181.

[22] L. R. Poos, *A Rural Society after the Black Death: Essex, 1350–1525* (Cambridge, 1991), 120–7.

life expectancy of 40 years at the age of 12 (equivalent to one of 32–4 years at birth) has been adduced, indicating a high but not crisis level of mortality.[23] The 'appallingly low' replacement rate may thus reflect a decline in births as much as excessive mortality. Another measure of the mortality level is the number of children mentioned as heirs or legatees in inquisitions post mortem and wills, though both sources are liable to omit women. For tenants-in-chief the male replacement rate was generally below parity in every decade from 1350 to 1450, while wills from the Norwich archdeaconry and elsewhere indicate a rate of 0.75 for all classes prior to 1470. More than half the testators had no surviving sons, half the families only one surviving child, and those with surviving sons and daughters formed only 19 per cent.[24] But we cannot be sure whether such a low level of replacement was the result of biological infertility, infant mortality, or conscious family limitation through contraception or deferred marriage.

For the first two of these there is no evidence. Family limitation by contraception (*coitus interruptus*) has generally been associated with times of economic hardship.[25] Alternatively, it has been argued that late medieval England exhibited a 'north-western European marriage pattern' of neolocality, lifecycle servanthood, high proportions never marrying, and high ages at first marriage for both sexes. Such a pattern obtained when parish registers commence in the mid-sixteenth century. Marriage at the age of 24–5 would leave ten to fifteen years for childbearing during which, with periods of lactation, and allowing for mortality in childbirth, an average family size of 3 to 5 children and a survival rate of 2.5 children might be predicated, bringing the population level to around parity. Attention has thus focused on the question of the age at marriage. Little reliable data on this exists before 1500. The imperfect poll tax returns of 1381, which note the marital status of taxpayers over the age of 15, suggest that 'a low proportion of both sexes were currently married in late fourteenth century Essex',while from the depositions in marriage litigation in the York consistory court, it has been deduced that the normal age of marriage for men was around 25 and for women the earlier twenties.[26] This pattern of relatively late marriage has been attributed to the increased opportunities for mobility among wage-earners and young women. Labourers seeking a niche in rural society would move in search of high wages in order to acquire capital to purchase a messuage, and women would enter servanthood at puberty, saving up a marriage portion

[23] Poos, *Rural Society*, 115–20. This is calculated on the Princeton Model West life tables.

[24] Hatcher, *Plague, Population and the English Economy*, p. 27, table 1.

[25] P. A. Biller, 'Birth control in the medieval West', *P & P* 94 (1982), 8–13.

[26] Poos, *Rural Society*, 149–56; P. J. Goldberg, 'Marriage, migration, and servanthood in the York cause paper evidence', in id. (ed.), *Woman is a Worthy Wight*, 1–15; id., *Women, Work, and Life Cycle in a Medieval Economy* (Oxford, 1992), ch. 8.

from their wages. Mobility gave them greater choice of both marriage partner and timing, making deferral until their mid-twenties more common. Servanthood, like apprenticeship, formed an important stage in the lifecycle.[27] Not all historians would accept that this admittedly very tenuous evidence of marriage deferral has general validity, nor that it represents a new phenomenon directly related to the post-plague economy. Indeed it could be said that for young women the low wages and annual contracts of domestic service might have less attraction than the higher wages paid for casual agricultural work at a time of labour shortage.[28]

Thus, while it seems to be certain that during the century after 1377 the population of England remained at a historic low of around 2.3 million, a rare period of stagnation, the reasons for this remain unclear. Since neither crude birth rates nor crude death rates (especially for infants) can be established, life expectancy can only be assessed at different life stages for small samples. The low replacement rate can be measured for some sectors of the population, though whether this resulted from low levels of fertility or high levels of mortality remains uncertain. If we look for psychological explanations, the daily imminence of death through plague, along with a sense of increased personal freedom and well-being, may have encouraged a degree of family limitation, though by what means or on what scale must remain speculative. Yet the very fact that even the upper levels of the landowning and mercantile classes, who enjoyed a higher standard of living, were more protected from epidemic disease, adhered to an early age for marriage, and had no interest in family limitation, exhibited a similar low replacement rate may suggest that biological rather than socio-economic factors were responsible.

Depopulation of this order changed the work and face of the countryside, almost literally overnight. The old ratio of land to labour was reversed. The survivors were left with a surplus of cultivated land and livestock for fewer mouths, and a stock of housing and equipment. Both the extension of cereal cultivation to marginal soils and the labour-intensive methods of improving yields were unneeded and uneconomic. Crops could be grown on the best-suited soils and elsewhere arable could be returned to pasture, a better balance with livestock improving productivity. This more relaxed and rational mode of agriculture had different consequences for lords and peasants. The decreased demand for cereal crops from a shrunken population spelt the end of the long period of assured profits for landlords from the sale of their surplus, and ultimately falling prices made direct cultivation of the demesnes uneconomic. As land values fell, so did rents, held down by the shortage of tenants. While the decline in seigniorial

---

[27] Poos, *Rural Society*, 179, 183–91. See further, below, Sect. 5.
[28] Bailey, 'Demographic decline', esp. 11–18.

incomes operated over a long period, the rise in peasant incomes was more immediate. Holdings could be enlarged by taking in vacated plots and in places leasing parts of the demesne; more recent assarts of marginal land were allowed to revert to pasture on which more animals could be kept, enriching the land and providing an improved diet. The benefits of commercialization in the form of improved techniques of cultivation, specialized production, and a matured marketing structure were there to be exploited by peasant initiatives. Once again, the nature and extent of the changes wrought by the Black Death differed between areas where nucleated villages were centres of agrarian production and marketing, and areas of dispersed settlement with a looser and more flexible framework. I shall consider these separately.

On most seigniorial estates the Black Death brought little immediate disruption of the agrarian economy. Despite a mortality of 40 per cent and even more in many villages, most vacated holdings were quickly filled by the survivors: widows, sons, relatives, neighbours, and local immigrants.[29] The subsequent outbreaks in 1361, 1369, and 1375 proved more destabilizing, for although less lethal they struck at children and adolescents, and men rather than women, thus undermining the next generations of the workforce and producing an acute shortage of labour. For a quarter of a century landlords struggled to maintain the old structure of manorial organization, sustained by legislation restricting wages and the continuance of good prices for cereals in a period of bad harvests. But when grain prices fell after 1375, large-scale arable cultivation began to be uneconomic and the retreat from it began in earnest. It has been estimated that whereas before 1350 some 6.23 million acres was sown each year (the largest area before the nineteenth century), by 1375 the figure was barely 4 million acres. In champion Warwickshire the acreage of arable, which stood at 96 per cent in 1350, had shrunk to 57 per cent by 1500. This reflected the pattern in the West Midlands as a whole.[30] In general—though not universally—it was the less fertile soils that were abandoned, though the proximity of markets was also an important factor. Corn continued to be grown in north-east Norfolk in the fifteenth century and was shipped to London, but to the south-east the land was turned over to cattle and sheep.[31]

Across central and southern England a new pattern of farming emerged as lords switched to pasture as less labour-intensive. On the Hampshire and Wiltshire chalklands a monoculture of sheep-rearing emerged with flocks of more than 4,000 belonging to the bishops of Winchester and Worcester and the earls of Warwick. Though small farmers and richer peasants followed suit,

---

[29] Razi, *Life, Marriage and Death*, 99–113; *AHEW* 71–2, 82–3, 120, 140.
[30] Campbell, *Seigniorial Agriculture*, 388–90; Dyer, in *AHEW* 78–9.
[31] Campbell, 'Arable productivity', 399–400; Bailey, *Marginal Economy?*, 237–44.

stocking their enlarged holdings with sheep or cattle, peasant flocks now formed a smaller proportion than those of lords. Yet in open-field husbandry the peasants' sheep helped to fertilize the land. A yardlander might have 60 sheep and 6 cattle, but larger peasant holdings of 40 to 60 acres supported 200 sheep and 20 or more cattle, providing a viable mixed husbandry and opportunities for individual experiment.[32] While sheep-farming was sustained by the growth of local cloth-making, dairy farming was limited by the continuing decline of population.

TABLE 7.1. *Changes in the proportion of arable and pasture in the West Midlands, 1345–1520* (%)

Region	Arable		Pasture	
	1345–53	1496–1500	1350	1520
Avon, War.	96	57	0	33
Arden, War.	71	34	7	38
Gloucestershire	83	46	2	34
Staffordshire	85	58	3	31
Bromsgrove, Worcs.	81	53	3	22

Source: Based on figures in C. Dyer, 'The Western Midlands', in *AHEW*, 79–81.

In only a few places did the decline of arable and the increase of pasture threaten the existence of the village. A handful, like Tusmore and Tilgarsley (Oxon.) and Hale (Northants.) were abandoned in the 1350s and are so recorded in subsequent tax lists; but even in the West Midlands most villages still had a tax-paying population in 1377–81.[33] Thereafter plague and increasing migration began to undermine the smaller and poorer communities, many of which had originated as satellite settlements from longer-established villages. Greater landlords generally tried to preserve the tenantry and buildings which represented capital assets, but too often a prolonged shrinkage prepared the way for desertion or depopulating enclosure in the mid-fifteenth century. The removal of the last tenants was generally the work of a gentleman or a yeoman farmer who had leased the demesne en bloc to form a sheep or cattle farm. Thus the Catesbys had made Radbourne and Westcote in Tysoe (War.) into 'a great pasture' for 2,000 sheep and 40 cattle by 1443–4. At Compton Verney, Richard Verney 'expelled' the tenants of the rectory in 1447. In all some 300 villages in the West Midlands region had been deserted by the early sixteenth century.[34] The

---

[32] Campbell, *Seigniorial Agriculture*, 151, 164–5, 179–81; *AHEW* 144, 233, 236, 265, 282.

[33] *AHEW* 73, 109; C. Dyer, *Everyday Life in Medieval England* (London, 1994), 37–8.

[34] R. Hilton, *The English Peasantry in the Later Middle Ages* (Oxford, 1975), 161–73; Dyer, *Everyday Life*, 33, 35; id. in *AHEW* 85–90.

chronology of depopulation can rarely be established, but John Rous had already drawn it to the attention of parliament in 1459, and in 1486 he listed sixty villages that had then disappeared. This was an area of old arable, where settlement had been dense, and the area to the east, from Buckinghamshire to Hertfordshire, was another where shrinkage took place from the early fifteenth century. Total desertion only came later, though the courtier Sir Robert Whittingham expelled the villagers from Pendley (Herts.) in the 1440s to create a park. Further north it was on the poorer soils of western Norfolk, on the Lincolnshire Wolds, and on the foothills of the Pennines that contraction and desertion set in, leaving small isolated churches as witness.[35]

Depopulation in the upland zone showed up less dramatically. Assarting ceased after 1350, not only along the Pennine foothills, as in the Forest of Knaresborough, but in the Weald of Kent. Marginal lands were abandoned, for pasture was already abundant, and the Lancashire and Yorkshire Pennines became 'a region of large open commons and small enclosed farms' given over to stock-rearing.[36] Even in south-west Lancashire arable declined. Likewise in north and mid-Devon the moorland reverted to its natural condition, increasing in size from 8 to 30 per cent of the area. Population migrated from the uplands, probably dropping by a half in the Kent and Sussex Weald by 1440. Sometimes weather as well as disease led to the abandonment of arable cultivation, as on the coastal plains of the Pevensey and Romney marshes, subjected to heavy rains and flooding in the 1420s.[37] Both the extent and the impact of this retreat from cultivation is more difficult to measure than in the regions of nucleated villages. The use of the land could be adjusted to local soils and market opportunities, as in the Warwickshire Arden, where cattle and sheep farms and rabbit warrens sprang up. In south and east Devon arable farming continued on two-thirds of the land while livestock prevailed in depopulated mid- and north Devon. There are therefore few traces of deserted villages in these areas, though downland settlements shrank and a general decline in rents spelled a contracting economy.

Two features of the changing economy of these upland areas were the enlargement of woods and parks and the growth of industries. By 1350 woodland had become a precious asset, to be carefully managed and conserved. It covered at most 10 per cent of the countryside. Woodland was coppiced at 4 to 8 years old, with selected trees allowed to mature for 60 to 100 years for use in building. Peasants were allowed to gather deadwood for fuel, but livestock-grazing was strictly excluded from the coppice. Parks provided timber, game reserves, and areas of sport if they were large enough. Before the Black Death there were more than 3,200 in England, many of them small. In some, wood and pasture were

---

[35] Harvey, in *AHEW* 110–14; M. Beresford and J. Hurst, *Wharram Percy* (London, 1990).
[36] *AHEW* 46, 119.   [37] *AHEW* 127, 158–63.

interspersed, in others they were separated. They were usually enclosed by a pale of wood and a ditch to restrain the deer, and might also contain rabbit warrens and fish ponds—all prime seigniorial assets which made them obvious targets for poachers. Because their maintenance was costly and labour-intensive, many were abandoned in the later fourteenth century, but in the fifteenth century the emparking of large areas became a status symbol for the upper nobility, absorbing former tenants' lands. Large new parks were created at Minster Lovell (Oxon.), Beaudesert (War.), Chalgrave (Beds.) and Olney (Bucks).[38]

Woodlands had always nurtured a charcoal industry, notably in the Forest of Dean, the Chilterns, and the Kentish Weald. Mineral extraction occurred in the north-east, where coal was used locally for heating and shipped from Newcastle to London, in the lead mines of Derbyshire, and in the extensive tin stannaries in Cornwall, which are said to have devastated 300 acres and more every year. Here and in the turbaries of the Norfolk Broads, created by the extraction of peat, industry dramatically changed the landscape.[39] But the most striking industrial development in the countryside after 1360 was the spread of rural cloth-making, which brought employment, expansion, and wealth to areas in the west, East Anglia, and Yorkshire. This will be considered in the next chapter.

In general, then, the retreat from arable brought both disruption and growth to the agrarian economy. Much of England remained champion country, with open fields and nucleated villages, but even in fertile landscapes pasture had replaced arable. A livestock industry became part of lowland England, not confined to the downs and the moors, with a growing proportion of cattle. Though occasioned by the decline of population, this represented a more beneficial and rational use of the land than mono-cereal cultivation.

4. LORDS AND PEASANTS, 1360–1381

From the revolution in agriculture flowed one in tenurial and social relations. For seventy years before 1350 lords had been commuting week work on their demesnes, finding that hired labour was more efficient and, while wages remained low, more economical. Labour services were probably exacted from no more than one-third of the households which owed them.[40] Even so, the regime of direct management rested on servile obligations. Lords retained the right to reimpose week work on customary tenants, had never abandoned the crucial boon works at harvest, and continued to exact servile dues. By reversing the ratio between land and labour, making the first abundant and the second scarce, the

[38] G. Astill and A. Grant (eds.), *The Countryside of Medieval England* (Oxford, 1988), 128–46.
[39] *AHEW* 161–2.
[40] D. Stone, 'The productivity of hired and customary labour: Evidence from Wisbech Bolton in the fourteenth century', *Econ. HR* 50 (1997), 640–56.

Black Death undermined the economic basis of these customary servile obligations. But at first the manorial routine suffered little disruption. Most vacated
holdings were reoccupied by the survivors, partly under seigniorial pressure and
partly to enlarge existing holdings or satisfy the hitherto landless. Some
lords offered inducements, remitting entry fines or customary services, and dis-
continuing tallage, but all regarded these concessions and the current situation
as temporary.[41]

More immediate was the impact on wages, which rose swiftly and steeply in
1350–1. The hurriedly enacted Ordinance of Labourers in 1349, given statutory
form in 1351, set wage rates for specific occupations at levels current in 1346–7,
gave lords the first claim on their villeins' labour, and enforced annual contracts
with their permanent workforce, the *famuli*. It imposed a general obligation on all
able-bodied men and women, free and unfree, to accept work on the terms
offered. Penalties were laid upon those paying as well as receiving inflated
wages—a measure aimed at the richer peasants who competed with the lords for
labour to work their holdings. Thus what had hitherto been regulated by manorial
custom and seigniorial authority was replaced by legislated norms on a national
scale. The Act protected the interests both of the few larger landlords who cultivated demesnes by labour services and of the many lesser lords who depended on
hired labour. It was the latter who, as Justices of Labourers (after 1361 Justices of
the Peace), enforced this legislation with vigour. The village hierarchy of jurors,
chief pledges, and constables were co-opted into the task of uncovering and presenting the offences of their neighbours. Most prosecutions were for receiving
excessive wages and for refusing work at the prescribed rates, and the counties
most heavily penalized were those where wage labour was in greatest demand. It
was a divisive exercise, uniting lords and the village elite as employers of labour
against the smallholders and landless who lived by their wages. Nor did the lords
act in unison, but used the statute as a weapon in their competition for labour,
themselves paying higher wages to their workers with extras like grain allowances
and expenses, while enforcing it against lesser employers.[42]

For a few years, while wage increases could be restrained and grain prices kept
rising, landlords were able to feel that the effects of the Black Death had been
contained and a course set for a return to pre-plague conditions. In the event the
plagues of 1361–2, 1369, and 1375, which devastated the next generation of the

---

[41] Razi, *Life, Marriage and Death*, 107–13; B. Harvey, *Westminster Abbey and its Estates in the
Middle Ages* (Oxford, 1977), 244, 262; C. Dyer, *Lords and Peasants in a Changing Society*
(Cambridge, 1980), 239.

[42] The text of the statute (*SR* i. 311–13) is printed in Horrox, *Black Death*, 312–25. For its
enforcement in Essex, see L. R. Poos, 'The social context of Statute of Labourers enforcement', *Law
and Hist. Rev.* 1 (1983), 27–52. For the level of wages, Farmer, in *AHEW* 471, 484, 489, and C. Dyer
and A. C. Penn, 'Wages and earnings in late medieval England', in Dyer, *Everyday Life*, esp. 179–86.

workforce, brought a cumulative shortage of labour which stretched the manor-ial economy to the breaking point. Wages for both agricultural and craft workers rose decisively in 1362–4, a 30 per cent increase over the years 1350–80, and registered a further less dramatic advance in the second quarter of the fifteenth century.[43] This accompanied a steep increase in the prices for agricultural prod-ucts in 1362–5 and 1369–70, generated by floods and harvest failures which induced famine conditions in 1370. Until the good harvests of 1375–6 grain prices in the preceding decade were the highest since the famine years at the beginning of the century.[44]

While this era of continued high grain prices perpetuated the traditional emphasis on grain production and guaranteed reasonable profits for landlords, it held down the real wages of the peasantry, who found themselves unable to profit from the scarcity of their labour. For labourers and smallholders their higher wages did not buy significantly more food: only with the fall of grain prices after 1375 did their real wages start to climb, to reach a plateau one-third higher from 1390 to 1440.[45] *Famuli*, who received a substantial proportion of their wages in kind, were shielded from higher prices, as were villeins with sufficient land to feed their family, while those who produced a marketable surplus benefited, though having to meet the cost of extra labour to cultivate it.

The thirty years following the Black Death were thus a time of confusing and contradictory trends in which lords and peasants were engaged in a kind of guer-rilla warfare over the terms of work and tenurial obligations. The lords invoked their legal powers as landlords and justices; the peasants sought to profit from the scarcity of their labour and the availability of land. On demesne manors, espe-cially those on ecclesiastical estates, lords began to enforce or extend servile tenure by reversing previous commutation and insisting on it from all new ten-ants, even free smallholders. Some compelled bond tenants, and even the whole *villata*, to take on the cultivation of vacated holdings. They sought to preserve villein status: manumissions were few and heavily charged for, chevage was enforced as a means of keeping track of villeins who migrated through marriage or otherwise, and attempts by villeins to send their sons to school or as apprentices were forbidden. While obsessively guarding their servile labour, great lords also exploited the incidental obligations. Where the peasant demand for land remained strong, as in Suffolk and Essex, entry fines were increased to £5 or £6 in the 1370s, merchet payments from 2s. to 4s. or 5s., and common fines and

---

[43] Dyer and Penn, 'Wages and earnings in late medieval England', 169–71; Farmer, in *AHEW* 471, 485, and app. I, pp. 520–2, 770; Poos, *Rural Society*, 207–9.

[44] Farmer, in *AHEW*, p. 444, table 5.1, and p. 502, app. D; M. Mate, 'Agricultural economy after the Black Death: The manors of Canterbury Cathedral Priory', *Econ. HR* 37 (1984), 341–54.

[45] Farmer, in *AHEW*, p. 491, table 5.11. A graph of real wages, plotted from Farmer's figures, is in Campbell, *Seigniorial Agriculture*, 5.

tallages were reintroduced.[46] Even so, such measures were individual and related to local conditions; there was no concerted reaction by the landlords as a class. Indeed while some lords racked up their demands, others relaxed them. Some lords remitted entry fines or improved their tenants' grazing rights, or gave them freer use of the lord's mill; others provided better food for their *famuli*, and hot meals 'at the lord's table' for harvest workers. Through pressure and cajolery lords strove to keep up their profits, and had a fair measure of success. By and large demesnes were still under direct management in 1380, and it has been reckoned that baronial incomes had not dropped by more than 10 per cent since the 1340s.[47]

Where lords attempted to perpetuate the demesne economy by reviving and intensifying customary obligations, they risked provoking unrest. The custom of the manor, declared by the suitors in the manor court, reflected the cooperation of lord and tenants in the agricultural routine, and afforded protection to villagers' traditional rights. If their rights were overridden, passive and communal resistance took the form of a refusal to perform some labour service, or to attend the manor court and register land transfers, or to pay merchet, chevage, or other fines. There was an increasing reluctance to undertake manorial offices like those of reeve, constable, and juror, which exposed a villager to penalties from the lord and vilification by his neighbours.[48] Underlying all was an implicit repudiation of villeinage. This could appear as an explicit quasi-legal challenge. Attempts by villeins to establish that their manor had been registered in Domesday Book as part of the royal demesne, and was thus under royal jurisdiction, had occurred in different places during the century preceding the Black Death. In 1376–8 a wave of such appeals spread across the southern counties, fanned by 'a Great Rumour' and orchestrated by local legal 'counsellors' who procured copies of extracts from Domesday. In the parliament of 1377 the Commons voiced fears that this heralded a rebellion against lords, as in the French Jacquerie. In fact the movements had seen little violence against property or persons, but articulated the deep-rooted affront felt by those excluded from royal justice.[49]

[46] Fryde, in *AHEW* 760–7; R. H. Britnell, 'The feudal reaction after the Black Death in the palatinate of Durham', *P & P* 128 (1990), 28–47; P. Hargreaves, 'Seigneurial reaction and peasant responses: Worcester priory and its peasants after the Black Death', *Mid. Hist.* 24 (1999), 53–78.

[47] Hargreaves, 'Seigneurial reaction and peasant responses'; Dyer and Penn, 'Wages and earnings in late Medieval England', 182–6; G. Holmes, *The Estates of the Higher Nobility in the Fourteenth Century* (Cambridge, 1957), 109–20.

[48] P. Franklin, 'Politics and manorial court rolls', in Z. Razi and R. M. Smith (eds.), *Medieval Society and the Manor Court* (Oxford, 1996), 162–98; Z. Razi, 'The struggles between the abbots of Halesowen and their tenants', in T. H. Aston, P. R. Coss, C. Dyer, and J. Thirsk (eds.), *Social Relations and Ideas: Essays in Honour of R. H. Hilton* (Cambridge, 1983), 151–68; R. H. Hilton, 'Peasant movements in England before 1381', in id., *Class Conflict*, 49–65.

[49] R. Faith, 'The Great Rumour of 1377 and peasant ideology', in R. H. Hilton and T. H. Aston (eds.), *The English Rising of 1381* (Cambridge, 1984), 43–73; Dyer, *Everyday Life*, 210–14, 225–30; *Rot. Parl.* iii. 21–2, printed in R. B. Dobson, *The Peasants' Revolt of 1381* (London, 1970), 76–7.

The lords' enforcement of servile obligations through the manorial courts went hand in hand with the resort to the machinery of the state to protect the rights of employers and criminalize free wage bargaining. The Statute of Labourers was designed to restrain wages, enforce contracts, and prosecute those who fled from their masters. Its application in the highly commercialized areas of the east and south-east, where freeholders predominated and seigniorial authority was fragmented, was bound to be complex. Here manorial lords, lesser gentry, and indeed substantial peasants all competed for labour, while opportunities for employment existed in the many small towns. Such conditions made it tempting to invoke legal sanctions to control socio-economic change, so that in Essex as many as one in seven of the population were fined in 1352.[50] Not only was this futile, it was socially divisive. The prosecutions generated deep resentment against the gentry JPs and local lawyers who were using the judicial machinery of the state in their own interests, and helped to align the village leaders with the labouring classes in a common grievance. Even so, neither the seigniorial reaction nor the enforcement of the labour laws were sufficient to transform local protest into national revolt. That was precipitated by the poll tax of 1381—or rather the attempt to enforce its collection in face of widespread resistance—and predictably it occurred in the commercial and political hinterland of London.

In February–March 1381 the preliminary returns of the collectors of the third poll tax revealed a nationwide shortfall. Overall about one-third of those who had paid the tax in 1377 were now missing, with even higher proportions in the shires of the south-west and north-west. In all 458,356 taxpayers had 'disappeared'; in London and the south-east these numbered 102,500. The majority were among the poorest, for whom the levy of 12*d*. per head (three times as high as in 1377) was a heavy burden. There is some evidence that the assessors had sought to spare them, as parliament had envisaged, by exacting more tax from their wealthier neighbours, but many of the poor simply fled.[51] The new forms of taxation—the tax on parishes in 1371, and the poll taxes of 1377, 1379, and 1380—were levied on people rather than on possessions and land, and fell disproportionately on the most populous region, East Anglia. The parish tax had increased the assessment of Norfolk by one-third above the traditional fifteenth,

---

[50] Poos, 'Social context', 44; J. Hatcher, 'England in the aftermath of the Black Death', *P & P* 144 (1994), 20–3; C. Given-Wilson, 'The problem of labour in the context of English government', in J. Bothwell, P. J. P. Goldberg, and W. M. Ormrod (eds.), *The Problem of Labour in Fourteenth Century England* (York, 2000), 85–100; id. 'Service, serfdom, and English labour legislation, 1350–1500', in Curry and Matthew (ed.), *Concepts and Patterns of Service*, 21–37.

[51] Fryde, in *AHEW* 771, and id. Introduction in C. Oman, *The Great Revolt of 1381*, new edn. (Oxford, 1969), pp. xvi–xxxii; W. M. Ormrod, 'The politics of pestilence', in W. Ormrod and P. Lindley (eds.), *The Black Death in England* (Stamford, 1996), 162–7.

and of Essex by one-fifth, while that of Suffolk had doubled. In the four years preceding the levy of 1381 national taxation had reached unprecedented levels, with three and a half fifteenths and three poll taxes. In 1381 the poll tax was designed to yield £66,666, almost twice that of a fifteenth, to be sent to the army under the duke of Buckingham in Brittany. Faced with a likely shortfall of one-third, the government ordered the collectors to return to the shires and on 16 March special commissions of inquiry were appointed in selected shires to check evasion and collect the arrears. Those appointed were local landowners and lawyers. At Brentwood on 30 May two Essex commissioners, John Gildesborough and Thomas Bampton, were set upon and put to flight by the men from the marshland village of Fobbing, who asserted that they had already paid the tax and would pay no more. Fearing reprisals, they began to gather local support and on 2 June, Whit Sunday, men from other villages gathered at Bocking swearing 'to destroy diverse lieges of the king, and his common laws, and all lordship . . . because they wished to have no other law in England but only those laws they themselves ordained'.[52] All subsequent risings were directed against different manifestations of law and lordship.

It was an apt time to revolt. Whitsun week opened the time of summer games in which the role of lords and peasants were ritually reversed, while the feast of Corpus Christi on 13 June provided a symbolic occasion to demonstrate the corporate solidarity of the rebels' *societas*.[53] In the three days since the confrontation at Brentwood the surrounding locality was mobilized and appeals for support were sent to Kent, where a rising had already occurred. As the rising spread to central Essex the houses of the treasurer, Sir Robert Hales, at Cressy Temple and the sheriff, Sir John Sewale, at Coggeshall were attacked and the escheator murdered. The sheriff's financial records—sealed with the exchequer's green wax—were burned at a great bonfire in Chelmsford on 11 June, and throughout the county manorial court rolls in over seventy places were seized and burned 'so that their lords would be completely unable to claim their rights over them in future'.[54] This targeted destruction of the records of lordship contrasted with the absence of indiscriminate violence against lords, who in general lay low, though some were compelled to ride with the rebels. It was those identified with the magistracy—sheriffs, escheators, JPs, tax assessors—who were selectively attacked and sometimes killed. By Wednesday 12 June bands from Essex had converged at Mile End and from Kent at Blackheath under Wat Tyler and Jack

---

[52] McIntosh, *Autonomy and Community*, 82; H. Eiden, 'The Peasants' Revolt in Essex and Norfolk', *History*, 83 (1998), 11.

[53] S. Justice, *Writing and Rebellion: England in 1381* (Berkeley, 1994), 156ff.

[54] H. E. O. Grieve, 'The rebellion and the county town', in W. H. Liddell and R. G. Wood (eds.), *Essex and the Great Revolt of 1381* (Chelmsford, 1981), 42–3; Dobson, *Peasants' Revolt*, 133–4.

Straw. Rebels on both sides of the Thames had thus coordinated their arrival at the gates of London on the eve of Corpus Christi.[55]

Their numbers are impossible to assess, but they may have been outnumbered by the poor who joined them from the suburbs and from within the city itself. Their progress was marked by the release of prisoners from the Marshalsea, the Fleet, and Newgate, the burning of John of Gaunt's Savoy Palace in the Strand, the murder of legal officials, and the execution of the chancellor, Archbishop Sudbury, and the treasurer, Sir Robert Hales, whom they extracted from the Tower. When they confronted the king at Mile End on Saturday 14 June their demands were for the abolition of serfdom and servile tenure, for the rent of servile land at 4*d*. per acre, for the ability to buy and sell freely in all boroughs and markets, and to enter contracts of service at their free will. For these men who had some property and hoped to improve their condition further, serfdom and its obligation stood as the great barrier to new economic opportunities. Wat Tyler's demands at Smithfield both endorsed and widened these, by proposing the abolition of all lordship other than the king's, the disendowment of the Church and the removal of its hierarchy, the annulment of all law 'except the law of Winchester' (local responsibility for peacekeeping), and free access to natural resources—the woods, fisheries, and parks under seigniorial control. This was a vision of an England of self-governing and self-legislating communities. Despite Tyler's dominant leadership and bravado, this vision evaporated with his death, but the Essex rebels returned with specific charters of freedom on the authority of which they continued for a time to challenge lordship. Richard's revocation of the charters, his arrival at Waltham on 23 June, and the suppression of the last resistance at Billericay on 28 June ended the revolt.[56]

The rising in Essex ignited rebellions against lordship in East Anglia and Hertfordshire and provoked acts of disobedience across southern and midland England, evidence of the ubiquitous discontent. In Hertfordshire and Suffolk these were principally directed against the lordship of the abbeys of St Albans and Bury St Edmund, both on their rural manors and in the monastic boroughs. Peasants and townsfolk had a broad unity of purpose—the removal of the status and disabilities of villeinage—and their actions were largely coordinated. Both abbeys were forced to grant the townsfolk charters confirming their ancient liberties, but whereas at St Albans the movement was controlled by the literate William Grindecobbe, in Suffolk under the vicious John Wrawe it was marked by

---

[55] A. J. Prescott, 'Essex rebel bands in London', in Liddell and Wood (eds.), *Essex and the Great Revolt*, 55–66; N. P. Brooks, 'The organisation and achievements of the peasants of Kent and Essex in 1381', in H. Mayr-Harting and R. I. Moore (eds.), *Studies in Medieval History Presented to R. H. C. Davis* (London, 1985), 247–70.

[56] Fryde, in *AHEW* 780. For the events in London, see below, Ch. 12, sect. 3, and Dobson, *Peasants' Revolt*, 161, 165 for the rebels' demands.

the murder of the chief justice, Sir John Cavendish, and the prior of Bury. Their heads were stuck on poles and, in a gruesome charade, made to 'whisper' in each others' ears to mock their connivance in perverting justice. On the following days, 16–18 June, there were widespread risings in the villages, with attacks on the magistracy and the burning of manorial records. As in Essex, these were often led and directed by the leading men of the village, the constables, jurors, and chief pledges.[57]

In north-east Norfolk widespread risings were organized under Geoffrey Lytster, a dyer, who secured support from some local gentry. Like Wrawe, Lytster and his company extorted protection money while attacking magistrates and estate officials and burning the records of the abbey of St Benet's Hulme. The rising was predominantly rural, and when the rebels entered Norwich and seized the castle on 17 June their actions were purely destructive. Ten days later the rebels' heavily staked camp at North Walsham was overrun by the knights of Bishop Despenser, and Lytster was killed. The rising had drawn support from some 240 places across the county, and among the thousand and more rebels named many were substantial tenants, with lands and livestock, alongside craftsmen, weavers, and labourers, all seeking 'to hold their tenements at their own will freely and not at the will of the lord'.[58] Disturbances in the Yorkshire towns of York, Beverley, and Scarborough occurred at broadly the same time. All reflected the existing tensions between a ruling oligarchy and the lower classes and apparently drew in no rural support. In each place the commons were able to replace the rule of the worthy citizens with councils of their own, but they had not envisaged any radical reordering of law and authority and their rule was short-lived. Even so, they had shown their capacity to articulate and enforce their demands for good government.[59]

A number of aspects of the revolt call for comment. First, although its outbreak had been unpremeditated, some among the landowning class had foreseen its likelihood. In parliament the Commons had expressed alarm at villein conspiracies and the boldness of vagrants, and Gower had warned of the impending rising, which he later portrayed as the unleashing of an irrational and bestial horde.[60] Secondly, within the manorial economy the peasants' anger had built up as the opportunities for acquiring land and money raised their hopes of

[57] Dobson, *Peasants' Revolt*, 243–5, 269–76 prints Walsingham's account; C. Dyer, 'The rising in Suffolk', in id., *Everyday Life*, 221–39, gives brief biographies of the leaders.

[58] Eiden, 'Peasants' Revolt', 27–9, with map; B. M. S. Campbell, 'Inheritance and the land market', in Smith (ed.), *Land, Kinship, and Life Cycle*, 90–1.

[59] R. B. Dobson, 'The risings in York, Beverley and Scarborough', in Hilton and Aston (eds.), *English Rising of 1381*, 112–42.

[60] Dobson, *Peasants' Revolt*, 72–6, 97, 388; J. H. Fisher, *John Gower* (London, 1965), 98–9, 106–7, 308.

economic and personal freedom, to which lordship barred their way. Here their primary target had been the legal records of servitude, the court rolls, and custumals of the manor. Both in destroying these and in securing charters of their rights and freedom, they showed an understanding of the importance of written evidence. In the commercialized society of East Anglia and Kent anger was directed against the Statute of Labourers, which, by strictly enforcing service on serfs and free alike and limiting wages, negated the legal status and economic opportunities of the free peasantry. It had provided landlords, as JPs, with a new public jurisdiction to bolster their manorial rights. Thirdly, the impact of the Black Death had changed the relations of town and countryside. Peasant immigration into the towns in search of freedom and better wages had been accompanied by burgess investment in vacant land outside; they were linked in a local economy. Where a town lay under direct seigniorial authority, as in the monastic boroughs, there was common opposition to its jurisdiction and control of access to mills, pasture, woods, etc. Revolt in the countryside thus immediately triggered revolt in the towns, where the sense of *communitas* was strong.[61] Fourthly, the regressive and ill-considered poll tax thrust the burden of military failure by the government and the nobility onto the peasantry. The tax also outraged local sentiment in being levied by external assessors and collectors, whereas the familiar fifteenth was apportioned within the village community, the rich often relieving the poor. It was seen as inquisitorial and open-ended, and in populous places might be paid by seven times more persons than the fifteenth. People were reported as saying that 'they would assent and acquiesce in no tax except the fifteenth which their fathers and ancestors had known and accepted'.[62] Fifthly, the vill provided a ready and familiar unit for opposition, a peasant and agrarian unit not a seigniorial and governmental one. Its officers—constables, beadles, etc.— were accustomed to represent its interests towards the lord, while the tithing was responsible for order, discipline, and policing, and the chief pledges joined those from other vills in the hundred court, with the sense of being part of a wider community. Royal officials, like the sheriff, escheator, and commissioners, were superimposed on this local framework, and these were systematically attacked. Sixthly, then, the vill provided the basis of the political economy of the peasantry, whose demand for the abolition of both manorial lordship and the whole legal superstructure of the common law would leave the vill to live under its own laws and maintain order, as under the Statute of Winchester.

The destruction of lordship did not mean the abolition of private property— no hint of common ownership emerged—but it did imply free access to and use

[61] Hilton, *Class Conflict*, 87–9.

[62] Dobson, *Peasants' Revolt*, 133; McIntosh, *Autonomy and Community*, 87; C. Dyer, 'Taxation and communities in late medieval England', in R. Britnell and J. Hatcher (eds.), *Progress and Problems in Medieval England* (Cambridge, 1996), 168–90.

of natural resources like rivers, woods, and pastures. This vision of a realm composed of village communities under a distant king is indicative of the restricted horizons of the villagers who led it. While destroying the legal claims of their lords, as enrolled on the court rolls, they looked to the king as the sole legal authority for the grant of their charters of manumission. From the viewpoint of the political classes they were guilty of conspiracy and treason against the Crown, of organizing a political revolt to usurp the royal power; but to the rebels it was the lords who were traitors and it was they—and not the JPs and the MPs—who formed the 'true commons', representing the real communities. In some aspects the peasant movement echoed the bastard feudal society it sought to overthrow: in the formation of sworn confederacies, the distribution of livery, the extortion of protection money, and the formation of bands or 'routs'. But their determination to eradicate law and lordship made them true radicals.[63]

5. A NEW AGRARIAN ORDER, 1381–1461

In the course of one generation, *c*.1380–1430, the legal and economic position of the manorial peasantry was transformed. With the end of demesne management, servile obligations were permanently replaced by rent tenancies, leaving villeinage to survive as no more than a ghostly presence. Larger holdings and the increase in real wages improved peasant living standards beyond recognition. The medieval manorial institutions gradually yielded to those of the parish, on which the life of England was based until the industrial revolution. Such a momentous change calls for explanation at different levels.

To attribute it to the Peasants' Revolt alone would be simplistic; at most that provided the catalyst for change. Yet political society had always lived in fear of social revolution, and in 1381 it peered into the abyss and took heed. While the court and the clergy denounced the rising as subverting divine and political order, lesser lords saw it for what it was, a protest against the enforcement of a doomed system. They had to accommodate to economic change. With few exceptions the devices for extracting revenue from seigniorial rights were dropped as entirely as the poll tax. The punitive measures of King Richard in Essex and of Bishop Despenser in Norfolk were not replicated by local lords, whose concern was to retain their workforce, not to alienate it by imprisonment, fines, and confiscations. Above all they were forced to recognize that the shortage of villein tenants and labourers spelt the end of seigniorial cultivation of the demesne lands. Villeins were prepared to flee their holdings rather than hold them by labour service, and labourers to refuse employment rather than accept the old wages. By the

---

[63] A. Harding, 'The revolt against the justices', in Hilton and Aston (eds.), *English Rising of 1381*, 165–93.

1390s there is widespread evidence that villein holdings were remaining vacant after the death or flight of tenants. The estates of Ramsey and Croyland abbeys saw a continuous seepage, which became a flood at the end of the century, many villeins fleeing to nearby manors in search of better tenurial conditions, others to the towns, which offered freedom and higher wages. Norwich attracted the tenants of Coltishall, Coventry those of Kibworth Harcourt, and Oxford those of Brookend.[64] Despite the re-enactment of the Statute of Labourers in 1388, many employers were ready to pay well over the fixed rates and, as corn prices dropped in the 1380s and the labourer's food became cheaper, his real wages rose to an all-time plateau. The smallholder with 5 acres could now pay his rent with ten days' wages, one with 10 acres with twenty working days. The landless labourer not tied by an annual contract could earn £2 8s. 4d. for 200 days' work in the year—more than that of a full-time ploughman—and could choose whether to enjoy his leisure for the rest. The able-bodied vagrant and the idle haunter of alehouses became stock figures of condemnation. The wages of craftsmen and building workers rose significantly in the early fifteenth century, particularly in the southeast. Slowest to improve was the position of the *famuli*, receiving payment in kind, whom lords increasingly relied on to work their demesnes.[65]

Even more compelling in forcing landlords to abandon demesne cultivation were the 'price scissors' of higher wages and falling profits. When in 1376–7 grain prices fell by one-third from the level which they had held since 1362–3, agricultural produce could no longer be marketed with profit. There followed a century in which overproduction in the face of reduced demand from a smaller population kept prices generally low and the currency famine slowed down market turnover.[66] The decade of the 1390s saw many major landlords, lay and ecclesiastical, abandoning direct management, and by 1420 there were few estates indeed on which more than a handful of manors were retained in the lord's hand. One after another the episcopal estates of Durham, Canterbury, and Worcester, the monastic lands of Leicester, Ramsey, and Westminster, and the aristocratic holdings of the families of Lancaster, FitzAlan, Percy, and Stafford were leased and their lords became rentiers rather than agriculturalists. For many the change was made slowly, piecemeal, and with reluctance—as a temporary adjustment 'until the better world returns'.[67] Local conditions determined each

[64] Fryde, *Peasants and Landlords*, 124–6; *AHEW* 620–1, 676, 788–90; J. C. Raftis, 'Peasants and the collapse of the manorial economy on some Ramsey Abbey estates', in Britaell and Hatcher (eds.), *Progress and Problems*, 196.

[65] Farmer, in *AHEW*, p. 494, table 5.13; Harvey, in *AHEW* 692–4; McIntosh, *Autonomy and Community*, 160; Dyer, *Everyday Life*, 183.

[66] Farmer, in *AHEW*, pp. 502–5, app. D; Mate, 'Agrarian economy after the Black Death', 353.

[67] *AHEW* 573–4, 587, 614; R. H. Hilton, *The Economic Development of Some Leicestershire Estates* (Oxford, 1947), 88, 145–7.

decision: manors close to important market centres or which supplied the lord's household, and those with valuable pastures, tended to be retained in hand longer. Nor did it necessarily entail financial loss, for it saved the costs of management. Lords had always been rentiers to some extent, and just as they had taken up direct management in response to increased population and productivity in *c.*1180–1250, so they reverted to a rentier economy in changed circumstances.

The leasing of the demesne followed no single pattern. In the first instance it was those with immediate experience in cultivating the land who took the lease. They might be manorial officers like reeves, or more substantial villeins who would add the lord's strips to their own. In some cases the whole homage, or *villata*, took a collective lease of the whole demesne, continuing the agricultural routine with little change. But the peasantry often lacked the capital to maintain the stock, the reserves to weather bad harvests, and the experience in marketing to meet the high rents. From the start some individuals were leasing substantial holdings of 50 to 80 acres, and the trend was towards replacing piecemeal renting with leases of large blocs to former estate officials, gentry, merchants, and clergy. But the pattern varied between localities: in the north demesnes were mostly leased to groups of tenants at will; in Wiltshire the lessees were mainly substantial village families, with some gentry, lords' stewards, and merchants from Salisbury. The monks of Westminster favoured working farmers or gentry with local connections, not peasant husbandmen, and on the Canterbury estates the lessees were thrifty franklins, substantial yeomen, and gentry, rather than small peasantry.[68]

In the first generation of leasing, the terms and conditions varied widely, evidence of the volatility of the land market and the landlords' need to keep the land in production and secure a regular rent. Leases stipulated for personal occupation by the farmer restricted sub-leasing (which could form a proto-manorial complex), and the upkeep of houses, barns, and mills. For small villein tenants these might be insupportable burdens, and landlords might have to stock and equip a farm, give compensation for repairs, and undertake rebuilding. Lords could distrain for arrears of rent, but at the risk of precipitating the flight of lesser tenants or defiance from those of gentry status. Initially some lords increased their income from leasing the demesne. Well-tended demesne arable might command up to 2*s.* per acre, compared to customary land at 6*d.* or at most 1*s.* per acre. Rents on good pasture were higher on the Sussex downs than arable in the lowland. But the shortage of tenants and low agricultural prices exerted a

[68] J. C. Hare, 'Demesne lessees of fifteenth century Wiltshire', *Agr. Hist. Rev.* 29 (1981), 1–15; F. R. H. Du Boulay, *The Lordship of Canterbury* (London, 1996) 218–37; B. H. Harvey, 'The leasing of the abbot of Westminster's demesnes in the late Middle Ages', *Econ. HR* 22 (1969), 17–27; Fryde, *Peasants and Landlords*, 77–83.

downward pressure which was unmistakable by the fifteenth century. The rent for the 400 acres of the prime Westminster Abbey manor of Islip fell from £15 to £12 over the first quarter of the century, and the Lincolnshire manor of Long Sutton leased for £162 in 1368 was farmed for £128 13s. 4d. in 1439. Landlords of all kinds anxiously sought farmers who would maintain rent payments without arrears. As the shortage of tenants continued, the terms of leases lengthened. In the late fourteenth century leases of one to five years were common, but these had lengthened to seven, twelve, or even thirty years on the Westminster and Canterbury estates by 1450, though both on the Durham Priory lands and in southern England ten or twelve years was standard. Alternatively leases were made for life, and renewable.[69]

The farming out of the demesne meant that the customary tenants were released from servile obligations and came to hold by payment of a fixed ('assise') rent with a moderate entry fine.[70] The terms began to be recorded on the manor court rolls in some detail, specifying the tenure, the land, the rent, and the services; and the copy of this which the tenant received became the basis of his title. His desire for hereditable tenure was met by him holding 'to himself and his heirs' (sibi et suis), and even his assigns—giving him a right of alienation like an estate in fee simple. By 1457, when Ramsey Abbey compiled a register of its customary holdings, tenure by copy was well established in eastern England, though Westminster Abbey did not acknowledge 'copyhold' as a form of tenure, and at this stage it was still just a convenience for tenant and landlord, having no status at common law or protection in the royal court. Thus by the late fifteenth century 'a handful of tenants held freely and under legal protection but the great majority held by customary titles'; in practice there was little difference, for the customary tenant paid his fixed rent, which guaranteed his tenure and he could pass on his holding to his heirs. Only in the following century was the weakness of his tenure at will exposed, when dispossessing landlords applied pressure by increasing entry fines or rents at the point of inheritance.[71] For most of the fifteenth century rents for customary holdings followed the downward trend, with arrears and refusals to pay becoming a landlord's nightmare by the middle of the century. Although a few ecclesiastical landlords optimistically compiled lists and genealogies of their serfs by blood, hoping for the former days to return, and some were occasionally able to exploit the servile status of a prosperous villein to mulct his widow of an entry fine or sell manumission at an extortionate fee, in

[69] T. Lomas, 'South-east Durham', in Harvey (ed.), Peasant Land Market, 306–7, 311; AHEW 598, 605–6, 639–40, 671, 687–8, 709–12.

[70] AHEW 629–31, 639–40; Fryde, Peasants and Landlords, 229–33; Harvey, Westminster Abbey, 244–67.

[71] Harvey, Westminster Abbey, 268–93; Fryde, Peasants and Landlords, 238–41; AHEW 597, 626, 711 (for the quotation).

general servile status, like its obligations, began to fade away as relics of a disappearing society.[72]

The release of land from servile tenure and obligations, and the peasants' opportunity for greater personal mobility, reshaped peasant landholding and society. Peasant landholding had never been static. For two centuries before 1360 small pieces of land, often less than 2 acres, were habitually transferred between kin and neighbours, but there is little evidence of a land market in larger holdings. Following the Black Death, much more land became available from vacated holdings and leases of the demesnes, and some peasants were able to accumulate sizeable properties. In a halmote court in Durham in 1373 it was said that whereas before the plague each tenant had a separate holding, now each had three, and both there and at Kibworth Harcourt (Leics.) in the late fourteenth century the average size of a holding had grown to 24 acres. This represented an increase in the number of full virgate holders and a decrease of the half virgaters. On the latter manor there were, in 1372, 14 full virgaters, 38 half virgaters, and 27 quarter virgaters, but a century later only 8 half virgaters survived between the full virgate holders and the landless labourers. Over much of England the virgate became the normal holding, and only in Essex and East Anglia did those with less than 10 acres remain a majority of the population.[73] By 1400 the full virgater's livelihood had improved from a century before. He could now direct his whole energies to the cultivation of his holding, though his family was likely to be smaller and he might have to hire labour. His surplus crops might realize less at market, but if he could use his additional land for grazing he would profit from the sale of wool or cattle meat. A half virgater's family able to cultivate and live off the holding could survive well enough, but would be vulnerable to external demands and misfortunes; the smallholder with less than 10 acres would need to supplement his livelihood with casual labour or a craft. Wages were high, and two and a half months' work might be sufficient to pay his rent; yet in a generally depressed economy casual work could be precarious and many smallholders had to struggle to survive. Ultimately the individual peasant's economy is impossible to measure. Cash was needed to pay rent, taxes, and fines, and formed an important element in wages, purchases, and sales at the market; but a significant exchange economy operated within the village in both goods and services, while the natural resources of both gardens and countryside contributed food and fuel to the family budget.[74]

Some indication of the improved diet of the peasantry is provided by the food allowances to harvest workers, although by definition these would be above

---

[72] *AHEW* 629, 639, 667.

[73] C. Howell, *Land, Family, and Inheritance in Transition* (Cambridge, 1983), 59, 148, 176, 243; McIntosh, *Autonomy and Community*, 85, 105–17; *AHEW* 600–1, 704–5, 724–5.

[74] Dyer, *Standards of Living*, 148–50, 185–6; Howell, *Land, Family, and Inheritance*, 236.

normal daily levels. With overall grain production exceeding demand, and prices falling after 1376, the value of bread corn supplied to harvest labourers fell in value from one-half to one-fifth of the total cost, while brewing malt rose from one-eighth to one-quarter, being equivalent to a daily allowance of 6 pints of the best ale to a worker or family group. Meat supplied rose from a tenth of the food budget to a quarter or third, with the allowance to each worker reaching nearly 1 lb a day by 1400. Such evidence from manorial accounts underpins the complaints of contemporary writers that labourers were demanding white bread, fresh meat, and strong, not weak, ale at their midday meals. In the last decades of the century wheat replaced barley or rye as the main bread corn, and beef in place of bacon, while barley was grown principally for brewing. Fish, which was always expensive, now began to figure more regularly in the peasant's diet, reflecting his increased purchasing power, with deepwater fish (herring and cod) sold at inland markets along with freshwater fish from local rivers. This revolutionary change from a cereal based diet to one of meat and fish was remarked on by writers from Langland to Fortescue. The poem 'How the Plowman Learned his Paternoster' depicts the abundance of bacon, dairy produce, salt beef, and onions in a peasant household. One consequence of this was an increase in life expectancy. Measured at the age of 20, this rose from 20–8 years in the early fourteenth century to just over 30 years around 1400 and to something like 35 years by 1450.[75] This indication of the improved health of the population throws into starker contrast the low level of population growth, held obstinately below zero by plague, infertility, or the limitation of live births.

Not only the diet but the dwellings of the virgater or husbandman improved. The survivors of the Black Death inherited a large stock of housing, much of it adequately built. Most houses were timber-framed, using either cruck construction or vertical posts resting on stone footings or cills. Walls were close-studded with wattle and daub infill, or cob; roofs generally thatched with barley straw. The standard unit was the bay of 15 feet, the majority of smaller peasant houses being of one or two bays. It would have a central hearth, but a separate room, or division, would be used for sleeping. The quarter-acre tofts along the village street would contain, in addition to the house, some outbuildings like a barn and byre, perhaps an oven and a separate kitchen, the whole plot forming a courtyard bounded by banks and ditches. In the countryside of the north and west the byre formed an extension of the house, to form a 'long house'. The collapse of population left many of these tofts unoccupied, a problem for landlords and an opportunity for peasants. Though landlords sought to maintain former dwellings in the hope of their reoccupation, many were plundered for their building materials. With more land for animal husbandry, the unoccupied barns and byres, and

---

[75] Dyer, *Standards of Living*, 85–6, 182, 210, 268.

even former houses, were used to shelter the animals, so that the 'long house' disappeared except in the far west. Probably the average size of peasant houses increased, most becoming of two or three bays, and costing £3 or £4 to build. In midland England the cruck house of three bays and a thatched roof was typical.[76] Furnishings were a little more plentiful but not essentially different, though some vessels were now of brass and copper and there was an increased range of brightly glazed pottery. Changes in the peasant's dress likewise reflected his increased well-being and aspirations. The loose, undyed woollen tunics of ankle length worn by both men and women gave place to more closely fitting clothes, shaped to the body. Men's tunics became shorter, requiring the wearing of hose or leggings, with a lined or padded doublet; women wore lined cloaks or hoods. Some brighter colours of blue and green dyes were introduced, and women adorned themselves with brooches, buckles, and rings. As lower-class dress began to ape upper-class fashions, legislation was passed in 1363 prescribing the clothes to be worn by each social grade, while clerical moralists inveighed against the sexual laxity that the new shapely fashions seemed to invite.[77]

Undoubtedly the most significant feature of the new economic order was the consolidation of a peasant aristocracy, which by the end of our period identified itself as a yeoman class. By the fifteenth century many villages could boast prosperous peasant families which, like the Cubbells of Coleshill (Berks.), had accumulated 60 to 80 acres of arable with pasture for 100 sheep. Some farms of the demesnes were even bigger. Thomas de Westhope in Yorkshire in 1366 had 240 acres under crop and extensive flocks of sheep; and a century later Roger Heritage of Warwickshire had 500 acres of land with a rabbit warren and 800 sheep.[78] Such yeomen families, who straddled the gap between the peasantry and the gentry, seemed destined to move upwards into the landowning county families of the sixteenth century. A few indeed laid the foundations of dynastic greatness: Clement Paston, who held 100 acres in Norfolk in 1419, the Goddards of Ogbourne in Hampshire, and the Harvests of Urchfont in Wiltshire, but often their fortunes failed to survive more than two generations. To some extent that reflected the transient and personal nature of their landholding, which they used to provide for younger sons, to form a jointure for a widow, or to purchase masses for their souls. Land had begun to be seen as a commodity for the satisfaction of personal status and ambitions, and not merely for the family's subsistence. Yet it also appears that such large enterprises might be only marginally profitable. Rent

---

[76] Peasant buildings are discussed by Dyer, ibid. 160–70 (with diagrams of cruck and wealden houses); id. *Everyday Life*, 133–66; H. E. J. le Patourel, 'Rural Building in England', in *AHEW* 820–93; Howell, *Land, Family, and Inheritance*, 55–7, 114–46.

[77] Dyer, *Standards of Living*, 175–7, with tabulated peasant inventories.

[78] R. Faith, 'Berkshire', in Harvey (ed.), *Peasant Land Market*, 157–9, 174; Miller, in *AHEW* 602; Dyer, *Everyday Life*, 315–21.

was a significant burden, capital investment in buildings and stock was essential, labour costs were high, and prices for agricultural products low. The large peasant farmer faced the same economic scissors as the lords and gentry, but without their capital resources and opportunities for acquiring wealth elsewhere. While for him 'agricultural production was a way of life', to which (unlike the gentry) he brought direct experience, 'he needed to live on his wits to make farming pay', and even then his own living style might remain frugal.[79] Even so, their houses, which in some areas have survived in quantity, set new standards of construction and comfort. In the north they were of stone, with roofs of king post construction able to support stone slates. In eastern England some timber-framed and thatched houses were provided with upper floors, and in the south-east 'wealden' houses were normal for yeomen and richer husbandmen with 60 acres or upward. These, with the open hall flanked by upper-storeyed cross bays at either end, used abundant timber framing under a tiled roof. The additional space provided not only bedrooms but a solar for private use and ground floor storerooms; the kitchen would normally be a separate building, though by the end of our period end-wall chimneys were beginning to replace the central hearth. Such houses enabled the yeomen to adopt something of the lifestyle of the lesser gentry in the rituals of eating and entertaining, in the use of pewter and even odd pieces of silver, instead of pottery and wooden utensils. Trestle tables, chests, and even a chair or two, carpets, pillows, feather beds, linen sheets, and coverlets provided a domestic ambience with a higher level of comfort than that of the normal peasant family.

The increased spending power of the peasantry at all levels provided a stimulus to artisan and cloth production in the towns and injected some buoyancy into a depressed agricultural economy. In respect of their personal freedom and improved living standards, the fifteenth century has been claimed as a golden age for the peasantry; yet it was overshadowed by death and economic uncertainty. The surplus currency after the Black Death, which had fed inflationary prices, gave way in the last decade to severe contraction, as the European silver famine reduced the volume in circulation. The stock of silver coins per head fell from 5–7s. in 1351 to 1–2s. in 1422, depressing internal markets and prices. By 1430 the effects of cumulative population decline were apparent in permanently vacant holdings, accumulating arrears, and 'rent strikes', which forced landlords to concede reductions and revise rentals downward. Extremely wet and cold weather in the 1430s, culminating in the failed harvests of 1438–40, brought the worst famine of the century to the north of England with widespread disease (murrain and foot rot) among livestock. Grain prices rose sharply for a time but then fell back to the lowest level for a century. From 1435 to 1450 war with Burgundy and France, followed by the political crisis of the Lancastrian regime,

---

[79] *AHEW* 616, 665, 713; Dyer, *Lords and Peasants*, 299–301, 312 (for the quotation).

severely disrupted wool and cloth exports, which the increased domestic demand could not compensate for. When the price of wool collapsed in 1450, wool remained unsold. The large producers, like the duchy of Lancaster and bishopric of Winchester, cut back or even abandoned production, but the peasants' income fell and with it their ability to pay the rents for their holdings.[80]

Thus the century between 1360 and 1460 cannot be represented as uniformly one of growth or decline. The economy exhibited both in different sectors and in the fortunes of different groups. More characteristically it was a century of fluidity and change, marked by the breaking of an old mould and the piecemeal formation of a new. Released from the constraints of manorial lordship, English society became a continuum within which the status of men and women would be ultimately determined by their economic circumstances.

6. THE VILLAGE COMMUNITY AND CULTURE

What were the consequences of this for the economy and communal identity of the vill? The old pattern of standardized holdings, with the village crofts linked to the strips in the open fields, gave each peasant his niche in the economy and his identity in the community. The cooperative agricultural routine enforced by lordship gave village society an integrated character, while the continuity of the family holding generated an emotive bond with its land.[81] After 1380 social and economic change began to dissolve and reshape the village community. First, the decline of serfdom and the availability of land provided the opportunity for larger holdings and greater independence in their cultivation. Secondly, the lord's withdrawal from agrarian management weakened the collective routine enforced by the manorial court. Thirdly, the peasants' greater mobility undermined the land–family bond and the leadership of the traditional village elite. How did each of these affect the peasant community?

The enlargement of holdings encouraged more flexible and individual management. Where there was an opportunity to consolidate and enclose holdings, as on the farms of the West Country and in East Anglia, individual sowing and cropping patterns could be followed and a measure of convertible husbandry could be practised. In midland England the continuing structure of open-field husbandry set limits to individual enterprise, creating tensions between the new

---

[80] M. Allen, 'The volume of the English currency, 1158–1470', *Econ. HR* 54 (2001), 606–7. For the 15th-century depression, see J. Hatcher, 'The great slump of the mid-fifteenth century', in Britnell and Hatcher (eds.), *Progress and Problems*, 237–72; Fryde, *Peasants and Landlords*, ch. 10, 11; A. Pollard, 'The north-eastern economy and the agrarian crisis of 1438–40', *Northern History*, 25 (1989), 88–105.

[81] These have been matters of debate: see Harvey (ed.), *Peasant Land Market*, 119–20, 238; J. Whittle, 'Individualism and the family–land bond', *P & P* 160 (1998), 30–48; M. Mate, 'The East Sussex land market and agrarian class structure in the late Middle Ages', *P & P* 139 (1993), 46–65.

entrepreneurs and lesser landholders, particularly over the pasturing of increased livestock on the common meadows. With the decline of manorial authority the village assembly increasingly took over the regulation of the agrarian routine. Such assemblies were sometimes of long standing: at Fountains the 'plebiscite' had always been distinct from the manorial court. Where the whole homage had taken a collective farm of the demesne, it could form a body with its own seal and with quasi-legal functions of recording sales of land and wills; or where the village contained multiple manors, as at Wymeswold, the *villata* framed by-laws by common assent and for the common good.[82] Where manor and vill coincided the manorial court became the vehicle of communal authority, regulating the seasonal routine of mowing, reaping, and gleaning, the pasturing of beasts on the stubble and fallow, the ringing of pigs, and the punishment of trespass on the growing crops. The maintenance of hedges, fences, and boundary marks, and the preservation of access roads, could be matters of contention as landholding became fluid and individual enterprise grew.[83]

Before the Black Death it had been the richer peasant families who habitually filled the manorial offices and acted as chief pledges; but during the period 1380–1420 this traditional elite was prone either to die out or to leave the village, the sons not waiting to inherit the family holding if opportunities to acquire land existed elsewhere. Before 1340 few families in Kibworth Harcourt had left the village or ceased to hold land, whereas by 1390 there were only sixteen families of long standing and by 1440 only eight.[84] Evidence from villages in Yorkshire, Warwickshire, and elsewhere confirms the unprecedented degree of mobility, which reflected not only the new attitude to land as a marketable commodity, but the intense desire for freedom from servile constraints.[85] Yet in some places, it seems, the familiarity and stability of the old order held men for longer. Zvi Razi has found that at Halesowen the sharp fall in established families only occurred around 1430, as the cumulative fall in population finally broke up the kin networks of the traditional community.[86]

It has been suggested that family discontinuity undermined 'the old cohesiveness . . . of village life, that social tensions and acts of violence increased, and that personal and social trust weakened'.[87] This has been challenged: Razi has thrown

---

[82] *AHEW* 610–11, 613, 725; W. O. Ault, *Open Field Farming in Medieval England* (London, 1972), 68–9, 75–6, document nos. 88–90, 97, 101, 107–8, 122.

[83] Ault, *Open Field Farming*, 24–34, 50–60; Dyer, *Everyday Life*, 1–6.

[84] Howell, *Land, Family, and Inheritance*, 240–9.

[85] *AHEW* 607–9, 647, 672, 717–18; Whittle, 'Individualism and the family–land bond'.

[86] Z. Razi, 'Family, land, and the village community in late medieval England', *P & P* 93 (1981), 3–36; id. 'The myth of the immutable English family', *P & P* 140 (1993), 3–44; id. *Life, Marriage and Death*, 117–24.

[87] J. A. Raftis, *Warboys* (Toronto, 1974), 216–24; E. B. De Windt, *Land and People in Holywell-cum-Needingworth* (Toronto, 1971), 274.

doubt on the evidence for increased disharmony and has argued that at Halesowen the village community maintained its coherence and vitality, with newcomers elected into village offices and the village assembly keeping the peace and resolving conflicts. Even in the more fluid society of East Anglia it has been shown that newcomers became servants in husbandry in order to acquire capital to establish themselves in the village community.[88] The village elite, accustomed to order the agrarian routine, became the natural governors of the community's social behaviour. Emphasis was placed on living in charity with neighbours whose help one might need, on parish unity, and on the resolution of conflicts which might endanger it. It was the first manifestation of that 'silent revolution by which the administrative initiative in the vill passed from the manor to the parish'.[89]

The formal system for identifying misbehaviour rested on the chief pledges of the tithings and the constable of the vill, on whose reports the jury of leading villagers presented offences to the hundred court and the Justices of the Peace. Criminal offences—burglary, theft, assault, wounding, conspiracy—formed a minority of the presentments, which mainly covered such antisocial behaviour as eavesdropping and nightwalking (male offences), and malicious gossip ('backbiting'), slander, and scolding (mainly female offences), all of which posed a threat to 'the peace of our lord king'. From around 1400 alehouses in the larger villages and small towns were the subject of regulation, both as centres of misbehaviour— gaming, dicing, all-night drinking, and prostitution—and for testing the quality of the ale by aletasters. Sexual misconduct was strictly a matter for the Church courts, though it might be punished by public shaming—the parading of the culprit to a cacophony of 'rough music', as well as by formal whipping and penance at church. Policing morality and misbehaviour had become the responsibility of the parish community, though at a less intensive level than in the sixteenth century.[90]

The problems of vagabondage and poor relief also came to involve the parish. Already in 1349 the royal council had alerted local officials not only to the excessive demands of wage labourers but to the accompanying prevalence of 'sturdy beggars', who refused work and took to crime. Following the biblical injunction that 'he who will not work neither shall he eat', it forbade giving them alms or charity. In the last quarter of the century petitions and legislation against vagrants and 'vagabonds' attempted to curb mobility, requiring all beggars to stay in their own vill and all vagabonds to return there.[91] Such men were both a

---

[88]   Razi, 'Family, land, and community', 29–35; P. R. Schofield, 'Tenurial developments and the availability of customary land in a later medieval community', *Econ. HR* 49 (1996), 250–67.

[89]   Britnell, in *AHEW* 622–3.

[90]   M. McIntosh, *Controlling Misbehaviour in England, 1370–1600* (Cambridge, 1998), 7–37, 57–73, 80, 113–15.

[91]   *SR* i. 308, ii. 56; texts in Horrox, *Black Death*, 289, 323.

physical menace and a threat to moral values, and entrenched Christian teaching on the duty to the poor had to accommodate itself to the new phenomenon. It was a basic theological tenet that the rich and the poor were complementary in God's order, the rich winning merit in purgatory by relieving the needs of the poor. But if the beggar's need was feigned, his prayers for the soul of his bene-factor would be valueless and the donor would be cheated of his reward. It was therefore essential to discern the truly needy from the pretended. Some were fairly evident: the old, the sick, the maimed, orphans, and widows. But then there were the unemployed, the alleged victims of misfortune or accidents, those beg-ging for their children or wives, and many with plausible tales. Indiscriminate giving was therefore discouraged, and people were advised to give in the first place to neighbours whose needs were verifiable. Charity should begin at home, and in 1391 a statute for the first time lay the onus for the support of the poor on the parish.[92] This was a personal and voluntary, not a legal, obligation, though it was to some degree institutionalized by providing a 'poor' or 'alms' box under the care of the churchwardens. In larger and wealthier parishes charitable guilds organized collections and distributions for the poor, even providing places for them at the annual guild feast. Public charity, controlled and supervised by the village elite, affirmed communal solidarity. More informally, the poor were allowed to glean in the common fields and gather firewood, and received doles at funerals and leftovers from the tables of the gentry.[93]

Because they figure so little and so selectively in the records, it is difficult to guess the numbers of the poor. Poverty is always relative, and at a time of general peasant well-being it was clearly not the major social problem which it became in the following century. But for those in its grip the level of organized charity was painfully inadequate, and Langland's exhortation to relieve the poor 'presents the inner life of those who live in powerlessness and poverty' with 'a voice [that] is not heard so clearly again for another four hundred years':

Poor people in cottages, burdened with children and with a quitrent to find. What they can make by spinning they spend on the house rent; what they can save up in milk and meal they use for porridge to fill the bellies of their children who cry out to be fed. They themselves endure sharp hunger and misery in winter time; they are kept awake at nights to get out of bed and rock the cradles along the wall. How they card and comb, patch and wash, scrape flax and wind it, and peel rushes, would be distressing to read about or put into verses—the misery of women who live in the cottages; and of many other people

[92] SR ii. 80 c. 6; M. Rubin, 'The Poor', in Horrox (ed.), *Fifteenth Century Attitudes*, 169–82; Dyer, *Standards of Living*, ch. 9; E. Clark, 'Social welfare and mutual aid in the medieval country-side', *Jnl. Brit. Stud.* 33 (1994), 381–406.
[93] Dyer, *Standards of Living*, 256; G. Rosser, 'Going to the fraternity feast: Commensality and social relations in late medieval England', *Jnl. Brit. Stud.* 33 (1994), 438–40.

suffering hardship, short of food and drink, who yet keep up appearances and are
ashamed to beg, and do not want to make known what they could well do with from their
neighbours for breakfast or supper.[94]

The role of peasant women, both in the family and in the community, was prescribed by Christian doctrine, tradition, and economic needs. The Virgin Mary
exemplified sexual purity, motherhood, and family life, so that on marriage a
woman's prime task was deemed to be the production and nurture of children
and management of the home, under the rule and authority of her husband. She
would also help to support the family economically, whether as a yeoman's wife
managing the domestic farm, or as the wife of a labourer working in it herself and
beyond it alongside her husband in the fields. Such work would be unpaid, but at
haymaking and harvest she would work with others on the demesne, reaping,
binding, and winnowing, for which she would be paid as a labourer. These were
the tasks deemed suitable for a woman's status, skill, and strength; they were varied and multiple, but all were essentially low-grade occupations, befitting her
designated role as helpmate and dependant. Did the distinctive economic conditions in the century after the Black Death change this pattern?

With labour scarce and wages high, were women a reserve workforce, and did
their ability to earn bring them greater independence? In agricultural work
women were disadvantaged by lack of physical strength, their lack of agricultural and artisan skills like thatching or carpentry, and their occupation in
domestic duties. Whether they formed a larger proportion of the agricultural
labourers, and how often they were employed, is impossible to say. Of those prosecuted for taking excessive wages in Somerset in 1358–60, 74 per cent were men
and 26 per cent were women, though women may have been discriminated
against.[95] Nor is it certain whether they were normally paid at the same rate as
men. Yorkshire prosecutions show a differential for harvest work of $4d.$ per day
for women as against $5\frac{1}{2}d.$ for men. Other evidence suggests that this was part of
a general stratification, with differential time rates for healthy males, boys and
women, and the old and disabled, though for piecework their remuneration may
have been the same. Women were part of the second-grade workforce, earning
three-quarters of the rate of able men. Overall their contribution was probably
neither sizeable enough nor consistent enough to erode the traditional male
structure of the workforce.[96]

[94] G. Shepherd, 'Poverty in *Piers Plowman*', in Aston *et al.* (eds.), *Social Relations and Ideas*,
169–89, with the passage modernized as above.

[95] S. A. C. Penn, 'Female wage earners in late fourteenth century England', *Agr. Hist. Rev.* 35
(1987), 1–14.

[96] Mate, *Daughters, Wives, and Widows*, 55–6; S. Bardsley, 'Women's work reconsidered: Gender
and wages differentiation in late medieval England', *P & P*, 165 (1999), 1–29; ead. and J. Hatcher,
'Debate', *P & P* 173 (2001), 191–202.

A pastoral economy provided more work suited to women's skills than an agricultural. In areas with a textile industry women undertook the preliminary processes of carding and spinning in a domestic context, though most weaving was done by men. Women had particular occupational niches in marketing and brewing. Both married women and single were prosecuted as 'tranters' or 'regrators', for buying produce cheaply and reselling it at markets—mostly produce of poor quality and in small quantities, to meet the needs of the poor.[97] Married women, often the wives of butchers and victuallers, brewed ale for sale, trading under their husband's name. Some might keep an alehouse—perhaps no more than the front room of their dwelling. During the fifteenth century this domestic ale-making was in decline as the brewing of beer with hops, essentially a male craft requiring capital, increased in popularity.[98] Baking, while also a domestic task, was undertaken for retail sale by both men and women, but butchering remained wholly a male preserve. In general, where women were able to exploit labour shortages in agricultural work, crafts, and trade, it was in low-status, non-capitalized occupations; nor could they always be assured of the continuous employment to ensure their independence. For the wives of the more prosperous peasants a larger holding might well increase their burden of work.

One opportunity for employment was open to the young and single, that of migration to a town. Probably the optimum period for this was 1370–1420, when the increased demand for commodities, generated by higher wages, was working through the economy, and the trade and population of some towns was expanding. Migration was probably greater from the agrarian than the pastoral areas, and it was mostly neo-local, from 10 to 20 miles. Some women brought, or acquired, skills in textile-working, but many—probably the majority of unmarried girls—entered service. Servanthood was a stage in their lifecycle—from upward of 12 years to their early twenties—during which they might accumulate money as a basis for marriage. Cash wages were low—not more than 2s. to 5s. a year for girls, compared to 13s. 4d. for males—but they would receive board and lodging and probably a gown or two. Servanthood was widespread, and in major towns like York and London could account for 20 to 30 per cent of the population. In the countryside it was far less, perhaps around 10 per cent. It embraced both men and women: the *famuli*, married and unmarried, and in craft households male apprentices and children.[99]

---

[97] H. Graham, 'Labour and gender in the late medieval countryside', in Goldberg (ed.), *Woman is a Worthy Wight*, 126–48; Goldberg, *Women, Work, and Life Cycle in a Medieval Economy*, 137–49.

[98] Goldberg, *Women, Work, and Life Cycle*, 111–14, 141–3; Mate, *Daughters, Wives, and Widows*, 59–66.

[99] Goldberg, *Women, Work, and Life Cycle*, 158–202, 280–304; id. 'Marriage, migration, and servanthood', and 'Marriage and economic opportunities for women in town and country', in id. (ed.) *Woman is a Worthy Wight*, 1–15, 108–25.

Moreover, servanthood away from home and village offered a greater choice of a marriage partner and greater freedom of social and sexual behaviour. Among the lesser peasantry marriages were often contracted by exchanging a verbal pledge of present or future intent, and if these were well attested they were held to be legally and canonically binding. But among the families of yeomen and husbandmen, who might pursue a strategy of land accumulation through marriage, parental selection and veto was more common, though canon law required the free consent of both parties. At this level marriage became more public and formalized, with families meeting to define the contract prior to a solemnization at the church door.[100] Similarly, the women who never married were nearly all of the lower class. They had either remained in servanthood or through misfortune or fecklessness had ended in prostitution. Unable to find a partner, they supported themselves by low-grade work in laundering, carding and spinning, child-minding, or as hucksters and tranters.

Many peasant women—probably the majority—became widows. While married they held no land independently of their husband, and on his death their claim to a part of the holding would depend on the arrangements made by him. In customary land the widow had a right of 'free bench', being one-third or a half of the holding, according to the custom of the manor. But by the mid-fourteenth century this traditional right was giving way to devices similar to those in the higher levels of society, which gave more freedom to devise land. Jointures, set up with the lord's consent during the husband's life, provided the widow with greater security and allowed her to retain control of a significant part of the estate to provide for her children's upbringing. A jointure expressed a husband's confidence in his wife's capabilities, though it risked withdrawing part of the heir's inheritance while his mother lived. The other device was a deathbed transfer— 'the villein's oral will'—made by the dying man before witnesses, which vested the widow with part of the holding for her support with reversion to the heir. In the 1420s in East Anglia it was common to assign one-third or one-quarter of the estate in this way.[101] Such arrangements were not always to the widow's advantage, for they might involve smaller portions than her traditional right to dower, and they might bring conflicts of interest between her and her children. In any case widowhood made her vulnerable. If she had land, she had either to manage it or lease it; if she was left unendowed, she had to earn her living by low-paid domestic skills. If she was young and endowed, she was more likely to

[100] Goldberg, *Women, Work, and Life Cycle*, 245–50, 259–62.

[101] Women's inheritance and widowhood is discussed in Mate, *Daughters, Wives, and Widows*, chs. 4, 5; also by R. M. Smith, 'Coping with uncertainty: Women's tenure of customary land in England, 1370–1430', in Kermode (ed.), *Enterprise and Individuals*, 43–67. Lloyd Bonfield and L. R. Poos, 'The development of death bed transfers in medieval English manor courts', in Razi and Smith (eds.), *Medieval Society and the Manor Court*, 117–42.

remarry: on some Sussex estates in the mid-fifteenth century one-third of the widows remarried, though among younger women the proportion was higher. For older women with little land widowhood was probably lifelong, and these numbered many of those who appear as sole tenants: amounting at Ombersley (Worcs.) in 1419 to one in seven of the homage. In general widowhood brought problems to all but the well endowed; in particular the aged, single relict of a labourer or craftsman was likely to have a precarious life in a cottage on the village edge, solitary, suspect, and dependent on charity.[102]

Thus the position of peasant women was largely constrained by their legal and economic dependence on their husbands, and in the village they were debarred from office or any public role. But though subordinate, they were not downtrodden. Within the home many doubtless achieved effective equality, and in the village they were likely to be collectively a separate force. Some of their domestic tasks, such as baking and laundering, as well as work in the fields and journeys to market, took them beyond the house, providing opportunities for companionship and rivalry, gossip and strictures. If they constructed for themselves a social space and a judgemental role, this lacked any peculiar locality. Some frequented the alehouse, but not those who valued their reputation. Only at communal dancing and the feasting of the ritual year did they publicly adorn and display themselves. For some the Church provided a focus for devotion, for the communication of hopes and fears, for penance and thanksgiving. It was generally allowed that women were more devout than men and that acts of charity to the needs of both neighbours and beggars were their proper role. Churchyards, and the cottages around them, could become the dwelling places of poor women, succoured by the distribution of church alms.

The communal life of the peasantry centred on work and worship, the first in the fields, the second at Mass in the parish church. The seasons of the Church and the agricultural year had similar rhythms of fast and feast, sowing and harvest, dying and resurrection. Bread was the common substance of the daily meal and the daily Mass. Throughout the ritual year ceremonies were scrupulously performed as precautionary and propitiatory acts against misfortune, while others celebrated in feast and thanksgiving the escape from it. Ritual externalized men's fears and anxieties, and promised safeguards against catastrophe: disease and famine in this world, and damnation in the next.[103]

Michaelmas marked the beginning of the agricultural year, not only in manorial accounts but in the fields which lay bare after the harvest, with the cattle on the stubble and the corn being winnowed and threshed in the barn. The shorter

---

[102] Mate, *Daughters, Wives, and Widows*, 127–8.

[103] For the following see G. C. Homans, *English Villagers of the Thirteenth Century* (New York, 1960), 353–418; R. Hutton, *The Rise and Fall of Merry England*, (Oxford, 1994), 5–68; Duffy, *Stripping of the Altars*, ch. 1.

and colder days of approaching winter anticipated the first great feast of the year, All Saints and All Souls (1–2 November), when intercession was made for souls in purgatory, accompanied by continuous tolling from the many new bell towers. Apart from the sowing of last year's fallow, this was a time for work on ditches and boundaries. At Martinmas (11 November) the cattle would be brought in for shelter or slaughter. At the end of November began the Advent fast for the four weeks to Christmas. The Christmas feast, lasting twelve days to Epiphany, was a time for eating and revelry, the drinking of one's neighbour's health with 'wassail'. Whether village society sanctioned the ritualized misrule which featured in noble households is unclear, but by the fifteenth century groups called Hogglers or Hogners, wearing disguises, collected money for the poor or for church funds. Immediately after Epiphany the opening up of the soil on which the community depended was symbolized by bringing the plough to church for blessing, a ceremony first mentioned in 1413. An immemorial pagan ritual, encircling the plough with fire or rolling wheels of fire down the hillside, invoked the rising strength of the sun. But inside the church burnt a plough light, and the ploughman was the symbol of honest labour and of Christ's humanity.

Spring began with the feast of the Purification, or Candlemas (2 February), with a procession of lighted candles to ward off the Devil and his works. Easter being a movable date, Shrove Tuesday could fall in February or March, a day not only for confession and absolution before Lent, but for sports, notably football and cockfighting, both recorded at this time. With Ash Wednesday commenced the long abstinence of Lent, with the altar stripped and the rood in the church veiled, while outside the spring-sown corn germinated in the sodden and still fields. Holy Week opened with Palm Sunday, as branches of yew and willow fashioned into crosses were carried with the sacrament in a procession of clergy and people around the church. On Maundy Thursday the altars would be stripped and the *tenebrae* sung; and on Friday the faithful would creep to the cross, which would then be placed in the Easter sepulchre, surrounded by tapers. Easter Day celebrated the liberation from death with the opening of the Easter sepulchre in the church, and the commencement of festivities which culminated in the traditional Hocktide revels of the villagers on the Monday and Tuesday. Here the practice of reversing roles, with women 'capturing' and 'ransoming' men, ritualized the urges of spring and raised money for church funds.

May Day introduced the three months of summer with secular celebrations: the gathering of flowers in the early morning, the crowning of a king or queen of the May, and the decoration of a maypole, as part of the 'May Games' or 'Robin Hood' games of licensed disorder. At least from 1450 Morris dancing was performed. But divine protection was also needed for the growing crops, and the Monday to Wednesday before Ascension were Rogation Days when a procession around the village boundaries blessed the fields. The now established feast of

Corpus Christi affirmed the unity of the Christian body, though how elaborately it was celebrated in the countryside is not clear. With the haymaking and sheep-shearing finished, there was time for 'summer games', days of high spirits and the loosened constraints among the young, and also of church ales, popular in the fifteenth century as a way of fund-raising. As much as 51s. was raised from a parish of 300 people at Tintinhull (Som.) in the 1430s.[104] Particular saints' days, some of them local, interspersed these summer months, notably that of St John Baptist, 24 June (midsummer), which was marked by bonfires of bones and wood to ward off the ill humours of the coming autumn when plague was rife. The games continued to the end of July when Lammas (1 August), or loaf mass (made from the new wheat), initiated the corn harvest. This was the beginning of autumn, and for the next five or six weeks there were prayers for fine weather to ensure the winter's food supply, and no time for festivities until the last cartload was brought in with traditional singing and wakes.

The festive calendar of the Church was thus interwoven with the natural cycle of the seasons and penetrated by the folklore and propitiatory rituals of trad-itional peasant mythology. At the same time there are indications that the impera-tives of work and worship were becoming less exacting. Feast days and Sundays now accounted for over one-third of the year, and work at other times was less than intense. As high wages enabled labourers to meet their needs with a limited amount of work, a leisure culture began to emerge among the lower orders. Poaching and illegal stalking with dogs were on the increase, as were communal games like football, handball, and tennis on Sundays and holy days.[105] Did greater freedom and higher living standards raise the political horizons of the peasantry? In 1381 the labouring classes not only rose but for the first time for-mulated their political demands in 'letters' under the names of John Ball and others.[106] These were couched in the secret, alliterative language of the peas-antry—a kind of slang cockney, 'full of obscurities' to the chroniclers—which drew on the world of work and worship. They had no chiliastic content; rather they looked back to the Fall and the Redemption: 'When Adam dalf and Eve span | W[h]o was thane a gentleman?' was not just a call for equality but a reminder that hard physical labour was the consequence of sin and the common burden of mankind, not of one class. Honest work was the basis of society. If 'Jack the Miller' set up his mill (an analogy for the common weal) to work prop-erly, with the four sails turning in the right order,

---

[104] Cited by Dyer, *Standards of Living*, 182–3.

[105] M. Bailey, 'Rural Society', in Horrox (ed.), *Fifteenth Century Attitudes*, 162–4.

[106] Printed in Dobson, *Peasants' Revolt*, 380–3, and discussed by Justice, *Writing and Rebellion*. See too M. E. Aston, 'Corpus Christi and Corpus Regni: Heresy and the Peasants' Revolt', *P & P* 143 (1994), 3–47.

With right and with might, with skyl and with wylle, lat might help right,
and skyl go before wille, and right before might, then goth oure mylne aright;
[But] if might go before right and wylle before skylle,

then the mill would be ruined.[107] It was also Langland's message: that power must support justice and truth if society was to be saved. In the letter 'Jack Carter' the honest Plowman is elided with the figure of Christ, so that the corn which the miller 'hath grounden small, small' becomes, in Christ's suffering and death, the bread of the eucharist through which 'the king's son of heaven he schall pay for [redeem] alle'. That of 'Jack Trewman's is a call for 'trewthe' to replace 'falsnes and gyle' in society, for justice is only accessible to those able to spend and bribe. Ball's letters are an epitome of these themes, and his unrecorded sermon to the rebels at Corpus Christi must have emphasized the equality and liberty bought by Christ's sacrifice. The symbolism of Christ as the ploughman, sowing the word, suffering, and bearing his cross (the plough) for humanity, was an existing tradition and no direct linkage with Langland's *Piers Plowman* can be assumed. Moreover, 'estates theory' had long recognized that the labours of the peasantry supported the rest of society. Langland did no more than echo this in writing that 'Might of the commones made hym [the king] to regne', but for the rebels their direct access to the king became part of a political programme. 'With whom do ye hold? With King Richard and the true [virtuous] commons' was their password. They marched under banners bearing the royal arms and the cross of St George, the slayer of injustice and defender of England.[108] Though naive and ill defined, and derived from Christian belief and mythology, their vision was of a free, just, and equal commonwealth.

The perspective of the village elite may have been rather different. The husbandmen and yeomen who served as officials, chief pledges, and presenting jurors had acquired pragmatic literacy and a familiarity with the working of the local courts and government. As such they found themselves drawn into the litigious world of political society. They could be caught up in gentry quarrels, presenting their superiors for trespass or forcible entry, or testifying to who was the rightful heir in an inquisition post mortem. They might be bribed or intimidated by one party, and indicted for embracery by the other. As small property holders they were vulnerable to the intimidation and corruption of the officers and retainers of lords—'petty kings' in league with shire officials—who could

---

[107] For readings of this passage, see Justice, *Writing and Rebellion*, 136–7, and Aston, 'Corpus Christi and Corpus Regni', 26–8.

[108] *Piers Plowman* (C text), Prologue, lines 112–22. For the perceived role of the peasant, see P. Freedman, *Images of the Medieval Peasant* (Stanford, Calif., 1999), 223–35. In Derbyshire the rebels similarly raised the banner of St George after capturing the castle at Horston; D. Crook, 'Derbyshire and the English rising of 1381', *Hist. Res.* 60 (1987), 12, 16. For a depiction of the rebels at Smithfield beneath the banner, see BL, MS. Royal 18 E. i, reproduced on the dust jacket.

exploit law and lordship. Thus they stood at the threshold of political society and were caught up in its tentacles, but were debarred from entering it in their own right as JPs or MPs.[109] They shared neither the lords' contempt for the peasantry nor the peasants' repudiation of all lordship.

Their sympathies may have been engaged by the tales of Robin Hood, whose hero, a free-born yeoman of the forest, devotes himself to redressing injustice.[110] The text of the central *Gest* derives from the last quarter of the fourteenth century, and the first literary reference to Robin Hood, in the B text of *Piers Plowman* (*c*.1377), reflects its origins in older oral tradition. The tales are a kind of bastard minstrelsy, incorporating elements of traditional romance for recital to a non-noble (but not peasant) audience. Further references in various contexts over the next century attest their continuing appeal for the literate middling strata. Robin is the defender of the honest and dispossessed—the 'gode felawes'—restoring their rights and meting out violent punishment to their oppressors. That should properly be the role of the king and the law, but since that has been corrupted, it falls to one outside the law and outside political society. For Robin and his band, all yeomen, live in the Greenwood, beyond the spheres of both the court and countryside, needing neither lands nor families. There he is king, exercising a distributive justice, and when he meets the political king his role is sanctioned. Thus the myth of a natural alliance between the honest folk and the king against the political corruption, as in 1381, is restated. The 'gode yoman', like the good ploughman, convicts the political order by his own honesty, and shames its spurious chivalry by his innate 'curtesye'. But unlike Tyler's rebels, he is no social revolutionary: he judges and redresses political society but does not reorder it.

Did political society's view of the peasantry change in the aftermath of the Peasants' Revolt? The traditional view of the peasant had been ambivalent. He was portrayed as bound to the earth and to physical toil, irrational, ignorant, and bestial in appearance, bearing the mark of Cain. Yet Christian doctrine insisted on his full humanity, while his poverty and suffering conferred a special virtue in God's sight. As labour acquired freedom and new economic power at the end of the century, political literature began to recognize its place in the common weal and its contribution to the common good. Both the king (in 'Love God and Drede') and the lords (in 'Dede is Worchyng') are reminded that the people

---

[109] R. B. Goheen, 'Peasant politics? Village, community, and the Crown in fifteenth century England', *AHR* 96 (1991), 46–62; Dyer, 'Taxation and communities', 168–90.

[110] For the following discussion, see R. B. Dobson and J. Taylor, *Rymes of Robyn Hood* (London, 1976), introd. and text; J. C. Holt, *Robin Hood* (London, 1982), 109–56; P. R. Coss, 'Aspects of cultural diffusion in medieval England', *P & P* 108 (1985), esp. 60–76; R. Almond and A. J. Pollard, 'The yeomanry of Robin Hood and social terminology in fifteenth century England', *P & P* 170 (2001), 52–77.

belong to God and provide their revenues.[111] Lords should not overburden their tenants, nor a king overtax his subjects, for his wars and regality depend on them:

> Thi povere peple with here ploghe pike out of the erthe,
> And they geve here goddes to governe hem even,
> And yit thi peple ben wel apaid to plese thee alone
>
> ('The Crowned King', lines 72–5)

The king must not ignore the people's complaints,

> For the swope [labour] and swete and swynke for they fode
> Much worship they wynne the in this worlde riche.
>
> (Ibid., lines 66–7[112])

If governed justly they will be loyal, but 'for fawte of law if commons rise | than is a kingdom most in drede' ('Treuth, Reste, and Pes'[113]). The inclusion of the peasantry in the common weal becomes explicit in a poem likening a kingdom to the human body which equates the martial knights and esquires with the arms and hands, the yeomen with the fingers, artisans with the legs, and finally the feet with

> all trewe tylers of landes
> the plough and all that dig in clay;
> alle the world on hem standes.
>
> ('The Descrying of Mannes Membres'[114])

Indeed the commons not only support the Crown and realm, but are part of it:

> The comouns is the fayrest flour
> That evere God sette on erthely crown,

and even more explicitly,

> The leste lygge-man with body and rent
> He is a parcel of the crowne.
>
> ('God save the King and Kepe the Crown'[115])

Such verse, directly linking the peasantry with the royal estate, stops short of endorsing the rebels' claim that royal power rests directly on them as the only true liegemen of the Crown. Indeed, over the following thirty years misgovernment weakened popular trust in the Crown as the redresser of wrongs. But until

---

[111] Freedman, *Images of the Medieval Peasant*, 17–105. See J. Coleman, *Medieval Readers and Writers, 1350–1400* (London, 1981), 98–113 for the genre and for a discussion of the poems in BL, Digby MS 102 printed in Kail (ed.), *Political Poems*, nos. 1, 13.

[112] Robbins (ed.), *Hist. Poems*, no. 95.   [113] Kail (ed.), Political Poems, no. 3.

[114] Ibid., no. 15.   [115] Ibid., no. 12.

1450 popular protest remained muted, and when it then erupted it was directed against political corruption and misrule, not as in 1381 against lordship. Indeed the rebels' articles declared that 'we blame not alle the lordes, nor all that beieth aboute the Kynges persone, nor alle gentilmene, nor alle men of lawe, nor alle byschoppes, nor all preestes . . .' but only those found guilty by process of law.[116] These are the words of the sub-gentry class, the yeomen, husbandmen, and farmers of Kent who organized and led the revolt. Their manifestos were no longer couched in private riddles, nor did they justify revolution by allusions to the scheme of salvation, but confidently used the language of parliamentary protest and endorsed the political reforms of the parliamentary Commons. The mob they led and vainly tried to control was less inhibited. It clung to its avenging role, but in doing so strikingly asserted its political legitimacy. The mariners who murdered the duke of Suffolk were said to have raised the banner of St George, proclaiming that all who held with the community of the realm should rally to it and that they would execute all traitors to the realm. That was the language of 1381; but then, repudiating the king's safe conduct for the duke, they said that 'they did not know the said king but they well knew the crown of England, and that the aforesaid crown was the community of the realm and that the community of the realm was the crown of that realm'.[117] From being part of the Crown, the commons had made the Crown part of the *communitas*.

After 1450 their discontent was enlisted by a factional nobility for political legitimacy and dynastic revolution. It was a far cry from the vision of Wat Tyler of a commonwealth devoid of lordship, based on justice, and blindly loyal to the figure of the boy king.

[116] Harvey, *Jack Cade's Rebellion*, 31–2, 103–6, 153, with the text of the manifestos on pp. 186–91.

[117] R. Virgoe, 'The Death of William de la Pole, duke of Suffolk', *BJRL* 47 (1964–5), 502. The words form part of the indictment.

CHAPTER 8

Trade, Industry, and Towns

I. OVERSEAS TRADE

If agriculture provided English society with its subsistence, trade provided much of its wealth. England lay on the great maritime artery from Scandinavia to the Atlantic and Mediterranean, but what made it a natural entrepôt—second only to the Low Countries—was its production of wool. From early in the twelfth century English wool fed the rapidly developing cloth industry of Flanders, reaching a peak of some 39,000 sacks a year around 1310. The trade brought wealth to the producers and to the companies of Italian merchants which had the resources to handle its export and advance huge loans to the English Crown on its security. The ruin of the Bardi and Peruzzi which followed Edward III's default on his debts in 1343, and the collapse of the syndicates of English merchants which sought to replace them, finally vested the monopoly of wool exports to Flanders in the Fellowship of English Merchants of the Staple at Calais.[1] Up to 1363 raw wool exports had stabilized at some 31,000 sacks per annum, but after the establishment of the Calais Staple they fell steadily to around 20,000 sacks by 1380 and to 17,000 by 1400. In part this was due to the growth of the English cloth industry, at first promoted by Edward III, which by 1360 was supplying both the domestic market and Gascony, and by 1380 was emerging as an effective challenge to the Flemish, with exports of 16,000 cloths a year. English cloth had been banned from Flanders since 1346, but it had a ready market in the Netherlands either for finishing or for onward sale to Cologne and distribution throughout Germany. In the last twenty years of the century cloth exports rose to 30,000 and then 40,000; then for the following twenty years both wool and cloth exports fell back in a general recession. Cloth exports recovered to 40,000 pieces in the 1420s and leaped ahead to the upper 50,000s in 1437–47. This marked the point where the volume of cloth exports finally exceeded those of raw wool, which after 1430 fell below 10,000 sacks annually for the remainder of the century.[2]

[1] The best survey is in T. H. Lloyd, *The English Wool Trade in the Middle Ages* (Cambridge, 1977).

[2] Figures from E. Carus-Wilson and O. Coleman, *England's Export Trade, 1275–1547* (Oxford, 1963), 122–3, 138–9; J. L. Bolton, *The Medieval English Economy, 1150–1550* (London, 1980), pp. 291–3, tables 9.1–9.3 (decennial averages for cloth and wool exports, 1421–51).

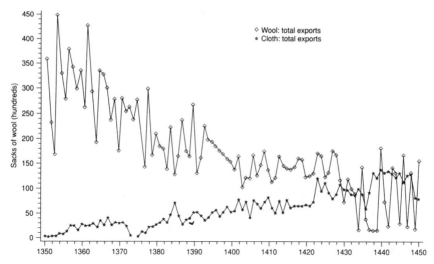

FIG. 8.1. Exports of English wool and cloth, 1350–1450 (expressed in sacks of wool). Source: W. M. Ormrod, 'Finance and Trade under Richard II', in A. Goodman and J. Gillespie (eds.), *Richard II: The Art of Kingship* (Oxford, 1999), 160

The prolonged shift in English exports from wool to cloth, while marking the emergence of a major industrial capacity, concealed an overall fall in exports and production. At an approximate conversion rate of one sack of wool to 4.3 cloths, the total volume of wool annually exported fell from the equivalent of 31,500 sacks in the early 1360s to 26,000 sacks up to 1400 and to 21,000 sacks in the first half of the fifteenth century. This reflected reduced demand as population contracted in late medieval Europe, and even allowing for domestic consumption of 10,000 cloths a year, English wool production was probably lower by about 30 per cent.[3] This was a lesser proportion than the fall in population, and reflected the heightened role of wool in the economy of the countryside; but the progressive conversion from arable to pasture produced periodic surpluses of wool and falls in price after 1380, most markedly in the mid-fifteenth century.

Wool thus remained the bedrock of England's trade and wealth, the more so as the added value of cloth meant that the value of total wool exports dropped less than their volume. On the basis of domestic market prices, the value of wool exports (in sacks and cloths) in the period 1360–80 was around £165,000 per annum. In the two following decades, after the domestic price and the quantity exported had dropped, the value had declined to some £110,000, but when cloth

---

[3] A. R. Bridbury, *Medieval English Clothmaking* (London, 1982), 115–16, apps. D, E; id., *Economic Growth* (Brighton, 1975), 25–38.

exports overtook wool in value and volume in the years 1428–48 the value of total exports rose to around £130,000 per annum.[4] Beyond the value of the product at the point of export, the Crown levied customs dues and the exporter took his profit. A huge differential existed between the rates of customs on wool and cloth. On the former the duty paid was 50s. the sack from 1370 to 1422 and 40s. thereafter, a levy of some 20 per cent on the market price at Calais. On cloth the export due, after 1386, was a mere 8.75 per cent of its value. This access to tax-free wool and a low export duty enabled English cloth to undercut the Flemish product in European markets, at least in the medium and cheaper ranges, and was undoubtedly one factor in the growth of cloth exports to the Netherlands markets and the decline of wool exports to Calais. But other factors were of equal importance, not least the fact that the wool trade became integrated with the Crown's political, military, and financial strategy whereas that in cloth remained purely commercial. The structure and problems of the two branches of the trade in wool will be considered separately.

The Trade in Wool and Cloth

England produced a wide range of different-quality wools which were finely graded by price: in a schedule of 1454 there were fifty-one grades.[5] The best were those from the Cotswolds, the Welsh borders, and Lincolnshire, followed by those from Yorkshire, the Midlands, and Somerset. Although Italian merchants might still buy up the year's clip on great lay and ecclesiastic estates, by the late fourteenth century much more production was in the hands of individual landowners of gentry status and below, and local negotiations with a multitude of graziers were usually conducted by middlemen—termed woolmen, or 'broggers'—who sold the wool either to exporters or to domestic clothiers. Woolmen might be in the trade themselves, as graziers, clothiers, drapers, and dyers, using their expertise to profit from the more entrepreneurial economy after the Black Death. Men like William and John Grevell of Chipping Camden in the 1390s, John Fortey of Northleach in the 1440s, and John Townshend of Lechlade in the 1450s rose from husbandmen status to the wealth and repute of merchants. Sales were negotiated locally, the price being agreed on the basis of a sample, and payment made in part at purchase and in part on delivery of the crop in London or some other port. After packing and weighing, the wool was ware-housed while awaiting shipment to Calais. After 1380 periodic surpluses of wool

---

[4] These figures are deduced, very broadly, from the graph constructed by W. M. Ormrod in Bonney (ed.) *The Rise of the Fiscal State*, p. 41, fig. I.15. See also, Bolton, *English Economy*, p. 293, table 9.1. For the effect on royal finances, see above, Ch. 3, sect. 3.

[5] For a map based on the 1336–7 prices, see J. Blair and N. Ramsay (eds.), *English Medieval Industries* (London, 1991), 321. The schedule of 1454 is in *Rot. Parl.* v. 274–5.

might delay its sale for eighteen months or more, in order to maintain the price at Calais. There the wool was again examined on being sold to clothiers from Flanders, Brabant, and Holland. After the payment of customs and port charges the exporter was left with a fairly narrow margin of profit, no more than £2 or £3 per sack. At all stages the process of sale involved a large element of credit, extending up to two years, within the relatively small and familiar circle of those engaged in the trade.[6]

Following the peace of 1360 Calais was chosen as the Staple for wool exports, being accessible to both London and Flanders, and guarded by a permanent garrison. It was placed under the government of a body of some 200 merchants who formed a fellowship, holding a monopoly and regulating the trade. Effectively this squeezed out the remaining foreign exporters, though the Italians retained an effective monopoly of exports to the Mediterranean. The boom years of the 1350s and 1360s ended when the war was resumed in 1370. Flemish buyers were prevented from reaching Calais and at times the Staple was removed to Middleburg or to England until it returned to Calais for good in 1392.[7]

The Fellowship of Merchants of the Staple became an instrument of royal finance in three ways: its trade financed the garrison, it made loans to the Crown, and it administered a bullion policy. These were interlinked. Thus when the Staple was set up in 1363 a mint was established at Calais and all foreign coinage had to be reminted there for transactions in English coin. When they sold their wool English merchants would pay their customs in this newly minted coin and this could be used to pay the garrison its wages. The system broke down during the removal of the Staple from Calais in the 1370s and 1380s, and a fixed proportion of the customs had to be allocated for the garrison. Even when the Staple returned to Calais after 1392, a European shortage of bullion reduced the operation of the mint, which closed in 1403, while a concurrent wave of piracy after the turn of the century imperilled trade, and royal finance slid into insolvency. The garrison faced mounting arrears of wages and finally mutinied early in 1407, seizing the Staplers' wool as security for what they were owed. Under this threat to the flow of trade and the safety of the town, the Crown underwrote a loan by the Staplers of £16,000 to pay the garrison and recover their wool. For the rest of the reign the garrison again received direct payment from the customs paid by exporters.[8] How far this continued under Henry V is not clear. Certainly

---

[6] E. Power, 'The wool trade in the fifteenth century', in E. Power and M. Postan (eds.), *Studies in English Trade in the Fifteenth Century* (London, 1933), 48–72; Lloyd, *English Wool Trade*, 313, citing *CPR, 1391–6*, 626–9; P. Nightingale, 'Knights and merchants: Trade, politics, and the gentry', *P & P* 169 (2000), 36–62.   [7] Lloyd, *English Wool Trade*, 217–33.

[8] D. Grummitt, 'The financial administration of Calais during the reign of Henry IV, 1399–1413', *EHR* 113 (1998), 277–99, though cf. J. L. Kirby, 'The financing of Calais under Henry V', *BIHR* 23 (1950), 173.

by the end of the reign the king's need for money for the war in France had led to the accumulation of further arrears in the garrison's pay of almost £29,000 and again, in 1423, the garrison impounded the Staplers' wool, which they had to redeem with a loan. As the customs fell and Crown revenues shrank, the situation was repeated in 1433, 1442, and 1448. The final occasion on which the garrison impounded the wool, in 1454, induced a serious and prolonged political crisis centred on the attempt by Richard, duke of York, to wrest control of Calais from his enemy Somerset.[9] The ability of the garrison to hold both the Crown and the Staplers to ransom induced Edward IV, by an act of retainer in 1466, to assign the whole of the customs and subsidies to the Staplers, who undertook to maintain the garrison.

As wealthy monopolists, the Fellowship of the Staple came under pressure to make loans to the Crown repayable from their own customs dues. On occasion, as we have seen, these were for the wages of the garrison; at other times—notably in the 1370s and 1450s—when a needy and venal king sold export licences to exempt Italian merchants and others from the Calais Staple, the Fellowship had to recover their monopoly by making a loan. Under Henry VI they lent substantial sums for the coronation expedition in 1429–31, for the defence of Calais in 1435–6, and for the defence of Normandy.[10]

The third area in which the interests of the Crown and the Staplers were linked was the enforcement of a bullion policy, but here it was usually the Crown that did the Staplers' bidding. Europe from the late fourteenth to the mid-fifteenth century suffered a general shortage of silver produced by the exhaustion and closure of the Bohemian silver mines at Kutna Hora. In the decades on either side of 1400 and 1450 this had a severe impact on trade, forcing governments into bullionist and mercantilist measures.[11] Accurate figures for the amount of money in circulation in England are not available, but one estimate gives a decline from £1.5 million in 1331 to £0.95 million by 1422. While this contraction was smaller than that of the population, the consequent rise in the per capita supply was counteracted by the shortage of silver coin available for domestic exchange.[12] Gold, as a less flexible currency for internal commerce, became subject to

[9] H. Ratcliffe, 'The military expenditure of the English Crown, 1422–35', M.Litt. thesis (Oxford University, 1975), 114; below, Ch. 15, sect. 6.

[10] A. Steel, *Receipt of the Exchequer, 1377–1485* (Cambridge, 1954), 175–6, 197, 208, 211; Harriss, *Cardinal Beaufort*, 206, 278.

[11] J. Day, 'The great bullion famine of the fifteenth century', *P & P* 79 (1978), 3–54; P. Spufford, *Money and its Use in Medieval Europe* (Cambridge, 1988), 339–62; J. H. Munro, *Wool, Cloth and Gold* (Toronto, 1972), *passim*.

[12] M. Allen, 'The volume of the English currency, 1158–1470', *Econ. HR* 54 (2000), 595–611; N. J. Mayhew, 'Population, money supply, and the velocity of circulation in England, 1300–1700', *Econ. HR* 48 (1995), 238–55.

clipping and forgery, and the demand for it in overseas trade generated a bullion war with the Burgundian Netherlands. In 1390 alien merchants were required to import one ounce of gold for every sack of wool exported. A more immediate threat was that English coin would be drained overseas by the debasement of the Flemish currency ordered by Philip the Bold in the 1380s. In the currency war that followed, stringent measures against foreign imports and foreign coins protected the value of English gold nobles, but by 1403 the acute shortage of both gold and silver forced the mints at Calais and Bruges to close. With the contraction of the money supply went a contraction of credit, so vital to the operation of the wool trade. This particularly hit the medium and smaller exporters and, along with the spate of piracy, brought a significant fall in exports of both wool and cloth after 1400. In 1411 Henry IV had to undertake 'a long overdue defensive debasement' to get trade moving again.[13]

By 1420 English supremacy in the Channel and the clientage of Burgundy opened the way for a revival of exports. It also encouraged the Staplers to press for the restoration of the mint at Calais and a larger proportion of payment in English coin. Ten years later, when the Crown was seeking a loan from the wealthier Staplers for the king's expedition, they secured the council's endorsement of their Bullion and Partition Ordinance. This provided for the entire price of all purchases of wool at Calais to be in cash, one-third in English coin; for all wools to be pooled for sale at different grades; and for the profits to be divided proportionately to the stock held by each Stapler after the shipment had been sold. Its purpose was to increase the flow of money to the Calais mint, to raise the price of the better grades of wool, and by deferring sales and restricting credit, to strengthen the position of the merchants with greater resources at the expense of their medium and smaller fellows. It evoked an immediate protest from the Flemish, who could no longer buy wool on credit, and from the duke of Burgundy, who retaliated by banning English wool and cloth from the Netherlands and forbidding the export of bullion to Calais. Although the Dutch refused to adhere to the ban, the wool trade to Calais went into irrecoverable decline as Flemish clothiers turned to Spanish wools: exports fell at once from 15,000 to 9,000 sacks, resulting in a loss of customs dues to the Crown of between £9,000 and £10,000 per annum. In this respect the scheme had backfired; yet it was renewed throughout the following decade and strictly enforced, with silver minted at Calais increasing to an average of £36,879 per annum.[14] When the bullion requirement was lifted, in 1442, it was probably due to divisions between the

[13] P. Nightingale, 'Monetary contraction and mercantile credit in later medieval England', *Econ. HR* 43 (1990), 560–74.

[14] Power, 'Wool trade in fifteenth century', 83–90; Lloyd, *English Wool Trade*, 259–62; Munro, *Wool, Cloth and Gold*, 84–92.

greater and smaller merchants of the Staple of which we are ill informed. But by now a second and more acute shortage of specie was intensifying the Anglo-Burgundian struggle. The duke strictly enforced the ban on English cloth imports and the parliament of 1449 retaliated by renewing the bullion laws and stringent restrictions on Burgundian imports. Neither could afford to maintain sanctions for long and by 1452–3 the ban on English cloth had been lifted, while in England the merchants opposed to partition seem to have won control in the Staple and secured the backing of the duke of York. By 1459 free trade to the Low Countries was temporarily restored, but further protectionist measures in the parliament of 1463, to which Burgundy responded with a third ban on English cloth, impeded trade until the alliance of Edward IV and Charles the Bold in 1467 inaugurated an era of friendly relations.[15]

The tangled story of the wool trade over the century from 1363 reflected the interplay of commercial and political factors. The shrinkage of wool exports, due to declining demand and a shift to cloth, brought a significant decrease in Crown revenues at a time when its military commitments were increasing. The establishment of the wool Staple at Calais under the control of a merchant fellowship ensured them a monopoly but also involved them in the payment of the garrison and safeguard of the town. With the Low Countries as their sole market, the Staplers also became involved in Anglo–Burgundian conflicts and diplomacy at a time when relations were exacerbated by a general shortage of bullion and commercial rivalry. This generated xenophobic feelings and mercantilist policies which in turn impeded trade.

The growth in the production and export of English cloth was one of the success stories of the late Middle Ages. From a minimal base of 10,000 cloths a year in 1356–64, exports increased by almost sixfold over eighty years, to supplant wool in volume and value.[16] The cloth trade was largely separate from that in wool, in its organization, merchants, and markets. Those who traded in cloth held no monopoly from the Crown, had no corporate organization, and were not locked into the Crown's military and financial commitments. Their trade was not channelled through a staple, and in their far-flung markets they competed with foreign importers. These conditions made it impossible for the Crown to impose a heavy export tariff on cloth for its own benefit, as it had on wool, for this would have made English cloth uncompetitive with that of Flanders. With English cloth banned from Flanders, it was in the Netherlands, as the entrepôt for Germany and central Europe, and to a lesser degree in the Baltic, that English clothiers captured the volume market for the medium and cheaper ranges. They

---

[15] The complex and often obscure history of the trade and bullion struggle in these years is discussed by Lloyd, *English Wool Trade*, ch. 8; Munro, *Wool, Cloth and Gold*, 127–80.

[16] Bridbury, *Medieval English Clothmaking*, app. F, pp. 118–22.

did so largely by producing good-quality cloths dyed and fashioned to the taste of the urban and landed classes below the nobility who could afford more than a basic local product. The finest wools for the luxury cloth trade still went to Italy, Flanders, and a few English centres, but it was English broadcloths that led the market in Middleburg, Dordrecht, and Cologne, while the cheaper worsteds, kerseys, and straits were sent in large numbers to Danzig, and to Riga for distribution to Lithuania, and to Novgorod in Russia.[17]

The growth of cloth exports was not gradual or continuous, but was helped and hindered by political contingencies. Broadly three periods can be distinguished. The first, from 1380 to 1400, was one of accelerating expansion; it was followed by twenty years of recession; then by thirty years when ground was recovered and further gains made, until halted by the general trade crisis of the mid-century. The renewal of war with France in 1369 probably reduced exports to Gascony, but the first major advance in the 1380s, to 19,000 cloths in 1381–3 and to around 25,000 in the rest of the decade, is likely to have resulted from the crisis in the Flemish industry during the civil war. It was this that caused Italian merchants to switch to the purchase of English cloth. From this base, cloth exports advanced to over 40,000 cloths in many years during the 1390s, though some of this represented the levy of duty for the first time on the lighter cloths, straits, and kerseys. Hanseatic merchants had been the first to export these in the 1370s but by the 1390s the English were pre-eminent in the Baltic trade, though mostly using Hanseatic ships. Exports to the Mediterranean remained firmly in Italian hands, but English merchants had achieved a dominant position in the Low Countries and handled almost 60 per cent of the total trade.[18]

From 1403 to 1422 English exporters saw trade decline and their share in it reduced. The bullion crisis and restriction of credit, along with the insecurity of the sea, brought cloth exports down to the level of the 1380s while, for the first time, exports by denizens dropped below 50 per cent to the advantage of their Hanseatic and Italian rivals.[19] The Treaty of Troyes brought security and a resurgence of trade to the Low Countries, and denizens regained their dominance of the Hanseatic trade, assisted by their exemption from tunnage and poundage after 1422. Cloth exports as a whole had returned to 40,000 per annum, the level in the 1390s, and from 1438 to 1445 achieved record totals in excess of

[17] N. J. Kerling, *The Commercial Relations of Holland and Zeeland with England* (Leiden, 1954), 73–80; E. Carus-Wilson, 'Trends in the exports of English woollens', in id., *Medieval Merchant Venturers* (London, 1954), 239–64; W. Childs, 'The English export trade in cloth in the fourteenth century', in Britnell and Hatcher (eds.), *Progress and Problems*, 121–47.

[18] T. H. Lloyd, *England and the German Hanse, 1157–1611* (Cambridge, 1991), 75–8, 96–100; Childs, 'English Export Trade', 137–47; A. Ruddock, *Italian Merchants and Shipping in Southampton, 1270–1600* (Southampton, 1951), 49–50.

[19] Nightingale, 'Monetary contraction', 562–4; Lloyd, *England and the German Hanse*, 156, 161–3.

50,000 cloths. The trade shrugged off Duke Philip's ban on English cloth from 1428 to 1434 during the bullion war, and was only briefly disrupted by his siege of Calais in 1436. In fact the Flemish industry suffered more from the suspension of English wool exports, making Dutch industry and traders even more dependent on English cloth. But in 1449 the boom suddenly ended, as England and France resumed the war, the English attack on the Bay fleet brought the Hanseatic trade to a stop, and Philip imposed a new and more effective ban on English cloth; only exports to Italy remained buoyant until 1452. There was some patchy recovery in 1455 but over all the cloth trade went into recession for twenty years, at no more than an average of 20,000 cloths per annum.[20]

Trade in Other Commodities

England exported little other than wool and cloth, but drew in a wide variety of imports from almost the whole of Europe. One principal centre of exchange was the fairs of the Low Countries, but Italians brought to England the produce of the Mediterranean and Levant, and direct trade links were established with Portugal, Castile, Gascony, and Iceland. Some tin and pewter, and at times some corn, were sent to these, but cloth was the principal export. Imports fell broadly into three categories: first, raw materials essential to the English economy; secondly, staple elements of food and drink; thirdly, luxury products for personal consumption.

The materials used in cloth production were among the bulkiest imports: alum from Genoa and Gascony, potash from Gascony and the Baltic, wool oil from Spain, and the crucial elements for dyeing cloth, woad, orchil, and brasil, and the prized kermes insect from the evergreen oaks of Castile and Portugal for scarlet grain. Iron came from the mines of Biscay and Guipuzcoa, salt from the Bay of Bourgneuf, timber and flax from Ireland and the Baltic lands.[21]

After 1350 England could normally feed its diminished population without foreign corn and its principal imports of comestibles were fish and wine. After 1370 the east coast fishing ports suffered a prolonged decline, as Flemish, Dutch, and Hanseatic fleets competed for the herring catch in the North Sea, but the south-western fisheries expanded, taking in Irish coastal waters, and supplying a wider variety of fish. In the fifteenth century English seamen opened up the Icelandic fisheries, using sturdier two-masted vessels with high prows to withstand the rougher seas of the north Atlantic. They sailed to Iceland every

[20] Lloyd, *England and the German Hanse*, 160–1, 217–18, 223–32; Kerling, *Commercial Relations*, 76–7, 84–5.

[21] W. Childs, *Anglo-Castilian Trade in the Later Middle Ages* (Manchester, 1978), ch. 4. pp. 104–48.

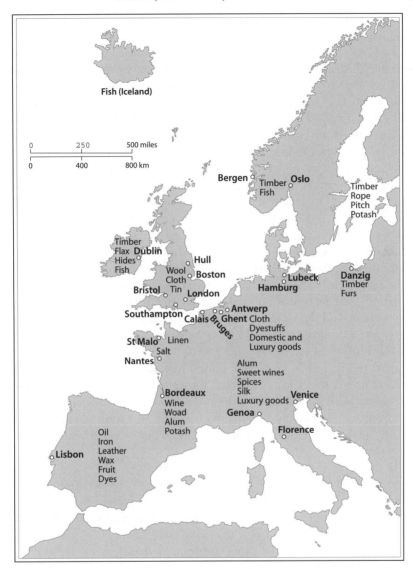

Fish (Iceland)

250 500 miles
0 400 800 km

Bergen Timber Oslo Timber
Fish Rope
Pitch
Potash

Timber
Flax Dublin Hull
Hides
Fish Wool Boston Lubeck Danzig
Cloth Hamburg Timber
Bristol Tin London Furs

Southampton Antwerp
Calais Ghent Cloth
Bruges Dyestuffs
St Malo Linen Domestic and
Salt Luxury goods
Nantes Alum
Sweet wines
Spices
Bordeaux Silk Venice
Wine Luxury goods
Woad Genoa
Alum
Oil Potash Florence
Iron
Lisbon Leather
Wax
Fruit
Dyes

MAP 8.1. English overseas trade

summer from both the east coast ports and Bristol, with barrels of salt, returning with stockfish, for which the market was almost unlimited. Nor did they shrink from violence and intimidation to wrest supremacy in the Iceland fisheries from native seamen and challenge the remote authority of the Danish kings. But after 1460 the exclusion of the English from the Baltic and the war with Denmark brought an end to the 'Iceland Venture', which had been virtually coterminous with Lancastrian England.[22]

This one-commodity trade with Iceland was paralleled by that in wine with Gascony. This, of course, dated from the twelfth century and by the early fourteenth century may have reached a level of almost 20,000 tuns (1 tun = 252 gallons) a year. From 1337 war disrupted both the production and the export of wine and by 1360 England's reduced population was consuming no more than half that amount. At this point Gascony was still England's chief market for cloth, taking half the total exports, mainly shipped from Bristol. That reciprocal trade continued, with wine imports surging to some 17,000 tuns a year in the last decade of the century. The general recession after 1400 reduced this to some 10,000 tuns, but Gascony remained largely immune from the renewed Anglo-French conflict and the trade returned to its fourteenth-century level before the final loss of Bordeaux in 1451–3 brought its total eclipse.[23]

Like wine, fur was a semi-luxury. It formed an integral part of clothing for all but the poorest, though only the gentle classes wore imported furs. Coats and outdoor cloaks, hats, shoes, bed coverlets, and nightgowns were all lined with fur for warmth, and the type of fur used was a register of rank. Red squirrel was the most common and abundant fur, and in the latter fourteenth century shipments of over 300,000 skins would arrive from the Baltic during the summer months. The Hanseatics had a monopoly of imports, purchasing skins at Novgorod for transport to Riga, while skins from central Europe came through Danzig and were sent on to Lubeck and Bruges and thence to London. But the thicker and more valued skins were those from the coldest climates, caught in mid-winter in the far north of Russia and Scandinavia: the grey-blue squirrel and soft white ermine, and the darker skins of sable, marten, and beaver which became fashionable in the fifteenth century.[24]

The trade in real luxuries was the prerogative of the Florentines and Venetians. They collected both raw and manufactured products from the ports of the eastern Mediterranean to accompany those of their own craftsmen in cargoes to Southampton, London, and Bruges. These comprised a rich variety of imports: all manner of spices (cardamom, cinnamon, cumin, ginger, cloves, nutmegs); medicinal plants for drugs and grain for dyes; lemons, oranges, dried figs, and exotic fruits; silks, satins, velvets, and cloth of gold; oriental carpets and hangings; pottery and glass; goldsmiths' work and jewellery. Sometimes animals

[22] M. Kowaleski, 'The expansion of the south western fisheries in late medieval England', *Econ. HR* 53 (2000), 429–54; Carus-Wilson, *Medieval Merchant Venturers*, 98–142.

[23] M. K. James, *Studies in the Medieval Wine Trade* (Oxford, 1971), chs. 1 and 2; Lloyd, 'Overseas trade', 121, enlarges James's figures for imports in 1386–99.

[24] E. M. Veale, *The English Fur Trade in the Later Middle Ages* (Oxford, 1966), chs. 4 and 8.

were imported—marmosets and monkeys, even an ostrich and a lion for
Henry VI. These were the 'nifles and trifles' sneered at in *The Libelle of Englyshe
Polycye*; but Italians also carried from Bruges the luxury products of northern
Europe, like tapestries made in Arras and Tournai, and household furnishings
such as cushions, linens, felt hats, and gloves, and Spanish leather and soap.[25]

Thus in one sense England was integrated into a huge network of European
trade, impressive in its variety, volume, and value. The demand for its exports
ensured it a consistently favourable balance of trade which underpinned the
basic agrarian economy and enriched the quality of life among the gentle
classes.[26] Yet from another viewpoint English trading remained undeveloped. It
depended on one basic commodity, wool, half of which continued to be exported
in its raw state, protected by a state monopoly but in terminal decline. Even cloth
exports remained essentially a transit trade, for English merchants never established retail outlets in the Baltic, northern Germany, and Italy. Compared to the
Italians, their trading techniques remained rudimentary and their capital
limited. In their credit dealings they depended on Italian banking and exchange
and their surplus wealth went into land or plate since there were no banking
institutions in which it could be productively invested. English commerce and
industry were thus starved of capital and kept in a medieval straitjacket.[27]

Alien Merchants and English Mercantilism

Trade with a far distant region usually required the residence abroad of a representative or factor of the trading nation. Thus small colonies of Hanseatic and
Italian merchants established themselves in London and Englishmen set up
trading posts in Baltic lands. Alien residents could arouse native hostility, and
needed protection by the sovereign authority in the host country; they could also
serve as agents of their own rulers in diplomatic and commercial negotiations.
Thus when, early in the fourteenth century, Hanseatic merchants established a
small *Kontor* of some twenty resident merchants and their families by the
Thames in London, later known as the 'Steelyard', they were granted jurisdiction over their members, a London alderman as their protector, and exemption
from further taxation. By the 1360s further smaller *Kontors* had been set up at
Hull, Boston, and Yarmouth and the Hanseatic towns had organized themselves
as a League, able to negotiate with the English Crown on behalf of its merchants.
Not for another decade did English merchants begin to trade in the Baltic ports

---

[25] Ruddock, *Italian Merchants*, 71–86.
[26] For the trade balance in 1386–99, see Lloyd, 'Overseas trade', 120, and in 1421–61, see Bolton,
English Economy, p. 307, table 9.3. Trade may not have been in balance in the intervening period.
[27] Here I follow the verdict of Bolton, *English Economy*, 344, 349.

to sell their exports of cloth, but when they did the question of them receiving reciprocal privileges to those of the Hanseatics in England became a diplomatic issue. Danzig and Prussia resisted this, seeing the English as intruders upon their markets, while back in England parliament's grant of a new tax on imports, tunnage and poundage, in 1371 had been fiercely but unsuccessfully opposed by the Hanseatic traders as contrary to their privileges. Relations became tense in 1385 when an English fleet attacked some Hanseatic ships in the Zwin, but a peace treaty in 1388, though asserting the principle of free trade, left unresolved both the status of English merchants and the Hanseatic's exemption from tax. These issues dominated diplomatic relations for the next fifty years, exacerbated by the spread of English trading settlements in Danzig and Prussia, intent on retailing English cloth in inland markets.

The bullion crisis at the turn of the century heightened tensions, with parliament imposing employment and hosting regulations on aliens in 1401–2 and the West Country pirate John Hawley capturing sixteen Hanseatic ships with the Bay fleet in 1404. These disputes were resolved by a new treaty in 1409 and relations remained amicable until the 1430s. In 1437 a treaty negotiated with the burgomeister of Danzig, Heinrich Vorrath, was envisaged as a final resolution of contentious issues. The Hanseatics were accorded exemption from tunnage and poundage, and the reparations promised in 1409 were paid, while the League formally recognized the principle of reciprocal privileges for English merchants. At this point, with cloth exports moving towards their peak, the advance of English merchants into the Baltic market seemed assured. In the event Prussia and Danzig refused to ratify the treaty or accord greater rights to English than to other foreign merchants. In England anti-alien feeling grew, with petitions in the parliaments of 1440–2 for the reintroduction of hosting laws and the revocation of the treaty. In 1449 relations deteriorated suddenly, with parliament introducing a new tax on aliens and in May the unprovoked seizure of the Bay fleet by Robert Wennington. While the Low Country ships were quickly released, those from Lübeck and the Wendish towns were plundered. Reprisals came quickly, with the arrest of all English settlers in Prussia. Protracted negotiations finally secured a truce in 1456, but in 1467 war with the Hanse flared up, the Danes attacked English ships in the Baltic Sound, and both sides impounded the goods of their resident alien merchants. In the settlement eventually reached in 1474 the principle of reciprocity was abandoned, and the English finally accepted their exclusion from the Baltic, as earlier they had the loss of the trade to Bergen and the Iceland fisheries. Thenceforward they were to concentrate on the major outlet for cloth through Antwerp.[28]

---

[28] M. Postan, in Power and Postan (eds.), *English Trade in the Fifteenth Century*, 91–153, and the more authoritative work by Lloyd, *England and the German Hanse*.

No issues of tax and reciprocity arose with Italian merchants. Although excluded from the wool trade via the Calais Staple, their monopoly over exports to the Mediterranean, on which they paid a higher rate of duty, was acknowledged in 1378. As they added cloth to wool, the value of their exports grew steadily in the 1380s and after 1390 reached one-fifth of all exports of wool and cloth. The Venetians used capacious galleys, manned by a crew of 200, which called at London and Bruges; for their bulkier cargoes the Genoese used carracks and favoured Southampton. Having lost their trading monopoly under Edward III, the Florentines exploited their financial expertise and banking facilities to service the credit transactions on which the wool trade depended. For all Italians, London was the principal business centre where some fifty or so merchants were resident as a unit for consular purposes. Though not covered by statutory privileges, as were the Hanseatics, they could generally count on the protection of the Crown, to which they made loans. English merchants regarded them with ambivalence, needing their financial services and valuing their trade, but remaining jealous of their wealth and influence. The Staplers were wary of their attempts to bypass the Calais Staple, while the Grocers and Mercers resented their dominance in luxury imports and their intrusion into the distributive trade. Both in London and in Southampton the ostentation of the Italians' houses and apparel aroused envy, but attacks on their property were rare. The most serious occurred in London in April 1456 and June 1457 when their houses in Lombard Street were looted and a massacre narrowly avoided.[29]

At the close of the fourteenth century a number of developments encouraged a mercantilist attitude among English merchants. As cloth markets expanded in the Netherlands and the Baltic they faced competition from alien traders; as the Mediterranean trade grew, the value of exports and imports by Italians increased; as a shortage of bullion restricted trade and credit, its export betokened a loss of national wealth; and as piracy flourished in the Channel after 1400, chauvinism impregnated economic rivalries. The first signs came with demands that alien importers 'employ' their profits on the purchase of English goods and conduct their business under the surveillance of English 'hosts', along with measures to conserve the quantity and quality of English coins. The military hegemony of Henry V, enshrined in the Treaty of Troyes, encouraged suggestions that English ships should police the Channel and check Flemish imports of non-English wool.[30] Henry had rejected these, but in 1436, when war with Burgundy had brought trade to a halt, the anonymous author of *The Libelle of Englyshe Polycye*

---

[29] G. A. Holmes, 'Florentine merchants in England 1346–1436', *Econ. HR* 13 (1960–1), 193–208; Ruddock, *Italian Merchants*, chs. 2, 5–7.

[30] *Rot. Parl.* iv. 126, nos. 15–17, 21.

vehemently urged the use of English sea power to force Burgundy to trade on English terms.[31] The theme proclaimed in the opening lines,

> Chershe marchandyse, kepe thamyralte
> That we bee maysteres of the narowe see,

re-echoed throughout the poem. By control of the straits of Dover, England could enforce an embargo on wool to Flanders, including shipments from Spain and Scotland; it could likewise hold the Hanseatic trade to ransom by intercepting the Bay fleet, and it could discipline the piracy of the Bretons. As for the other weapon in England's armoury, wool, it was outrageous that the Italians should purchase and export the finest, importing in return luxuries that we could well do without:

> All spicerye and other grocers ware,
> Wyth swete wynes, all manere of chaffare [merchandise],
> Apes and japes and marmusettes taylede,
> Nifles, trifles, that litell availed,
> And thynges with whiche they fetely blere our eye
> Wyth thynges not endurynge that we bye.   (lines 344–51)

Even worse was the Florentine stranglehold on credit and exchange; for by deferring payment on their purchase of wool in England, then using the cash from its sale in Flanders to service transfers of money by English merchants to London through letters of exchange, they were effectively charging their customers interest on their own money. So they 'wypen our nose with our owne sleve'. *The Libelle* vividly evokes the baffled resentment and growing isolationism in England as her continental conquests disintegrated in the middle years of the century. Addressed to three leading ministers of the Crown, it asserted that trade was a matter of national concern, of public policy, and an aspect of the Crown's responsibility for the common weal. In the event negotiations with Burgundy and the Hanse were preferred to *force majeure*. For while, in general, the English Crown pursued no commercial policy and was principally guided by military and political considerations, it appreciated that trade increased national wealth and royal resources, and it did not always bow to anti-alien prejudice or self-interested mercantilist demands. Yet in the climate of increasing insularity in late fifteenth-century England, the chauvinism of the *The Libelle* put down deep roots in the national psyche.[32]

---

[31] *The Libelle of Englyshe Polycye*, ed. G. Warner (Oxford, 1926); G. Holmes, 'The libel of English policy', *EHR* 76 (1961), 193–216

[32] An epitome of *The Libelle* written under Edward IV is headed 'Anglia, propter tuas naves et lanas omnia regna te salutare deberent'; T. Wright (ed.), *Political Poems and Songs*, Rolls ser. (London, 1861), ii. 282.

2. INTERNAL TRADE AND INDUSTRY

The Market Network

By 1350 a flourishing trade network linked the markets and towns of England. It had developed to meet the needs of an enlarged population. At village level more than 1,500 weekly markets supplied food and raw materials to labourers and artisans who lacked their own land, and basic artefacts like clothes and tools to peasants who brought their surplus produce for sale. Spaced generally at a distance of some 6 miles, these markets afforded a regular framework for local and low-level commercial dealings, facilitated by the £1.5 million of silver coinage estimated to have been in circulation in 1300–50.[33] Above this often unrecorded level were the 'small towns' with fewer than 2,000 inhabitants, the majority of whom were artisans, craftsmen, and victuallers engaged in non-agricultural occupations. They served as centres of exchange for a surrounding territory of 6 to 10 miles in depth and as collection centres for long-distance trade. Their distribution varied strikingly between regions, the heaviest concentrations being in the West Country, Suffolk, and Kent, and in the Midlands to the south of Watling Street. There were probably 400–500 towns of this size, containing half the urban population.[34] The next range of towns, with populations of between 2,000 and 5,000, were in some measure regional markets. Depending on their size and location, their economic hinterland, measured in terms of credit transactions and market exchange, might stretch up to 20 or 25 miles, though for bulky commodities like grain and fuel it would be considerably less. Such towns would have cattle markets to which animals might be driven from some distance, and their merchants would be wholesale traders bringing from larger centres both staple foods, like fish and wine, and specialist commodities, like wax, spices, and semi-luxury cloth, for sale to local gentry. Some might have specialist industries, like Nottingham's alabaster carvings, or act as collecting centres for cloth to be sent on for finishing; others, like Boston, were outports for their region. There were perhaps some fifty towns of this size, and above them another twenty with populations over 5,000 like Coventry and Salisbury, which were both industrial centres and linked to overseas trade. York, Norwich, Winchester, and Bristol, with populations of over 10,000, were regional centres. In all, well over 10 per cent of the population can be considered townsfolk.

---

[33] R. H. Britnell, 'The proliferation of markets in England, 1200–1349', *Econ. HR* 34 (1981), 209–21; J. Hatcher and M. Bailey, *Modelling the Middle Ages* (Oxford, 2001), 138–43.

[34] R. H. Hilton, *Class Conflict and the Crisis of Feudalism* (London, 1985), 102–42; id., 'Medieval market towns and simple commodity production', *P & P* 109 (1985), 3–23; J. Laughton and C. Dyer, 'Small towns in the East and West Midlands in the late Middle Ages: A comparison', *Mid. Hist.* 24 (1999), 24–52; C. Dyer, 'Small towns, 1270–1540', in *CUH* 505–35.

London, whose pre-plague population has been reckoned at 80,000–100,000, was surpassed north of the Alps only by Paris. Whereas even towns of 5,000 did not influence the economy of their region, London's demand for food and fuel was felt all over south-eastern England. Transport in bulk was largely confined to waterways, either by coastal shipments of fish and barley for brewing from East Anglia, and of corn from Kent and Sussex, or by river transport of grain from Kent and as far westwards as Henley. Livestock for slaughter were bred in East Anglia and driven from there and from the Midlands. Wood for fuel was brought from Essex and some coal from Newcastle. Both wool and cloth were brought to London in significant quantities for export and, conversely, London acted as the distributing centre to provincial capitals of wine and luxury products from the Mediterranean and Low Countries, with a virtual monopoly in the sale of gold and jewellery, tapestries, and precious furs. It also accommodated a vast number (over 100) of specialized crafts.[35]

London thus stood at the head of a hierarchy of markets, linked to regional capitals and county towns and these in turn to small towns and villages, but it must be stressed that England in the mid-fourteenth century was still a series of distinct economic regions, with local variations in supply and demand determining prices, and no pyramidal structure of distribution. Nevertheless, it exhibited an extensive trading network based on good communications. Roads were secure and generally well maintained, with bridges and causeways kept in repair; tolls and weirs were controlled, and many rivers were navigable to their higher reaches. Land transport by two-wheel cart and horse generally cost $1d$. to $1\frac{1}{2}d$. per ton-mile, travelling a distance of 15 to 20 miles a day. River transport was half that cost, at $0.7d$. per mile, and sea transport, used for bulky commodities like grain and fish, even cheaper—at $0.2d$. per mile. Most grain would be carried overland to the nearest river or port, usually not further than 10 miles. Only on the more difficult roads to the West Country and Wales were packhorses used, but on well-established routes like that from Southampton to the Midlands thousands of carts would travel each year taking woad, alum, and dyes to Salisbury and Coventry, and returning with cloth for export.[36] This well-integrated and much used network reflected the high level of commercialization in the internal economy which had taken place in the thirteenth century, spurred on by the growth of population to 6 million or more, which it helped to

[35] J. A. Galloway, 'One market or many? London and the grain trade of England', in J. Galloway (ed.), *Trade, Urban Hinterlands and Market Integration, c.1300–1600* (London, 2000), 23–42; D. Keene, 'Changes in London's economic hinterland', ibid. 59–82.

[36] J. Masschaele, 'Transport costs in medieval England', *Econ. HR* 46 (1993), 266–79; O. Coleman, 'Trade and prosperity in the fifteenth century: Some aspects of the trade of Southampton', *Econ. HR* 16 (1963), 9–22. B. P. Hindle, 'The road network of medieval England and Wales', *Journal of Historical Geography*, 2 (1976), 207–21.

sustain. If urban growth was the fruit of the commercialization of the economy, did the drastic cutback of population after 1348 produce recession and decline?

Urban mortality in 1348–9 was as heavy or even heavier than rural and no place of any size escaped, while in the following century plague tended to be more conspicuous in the towns. The initial loss of over 40 per cent of the population and its continuing erosion could not be replaced either by internal regeneration or by immigration. For the next two centuries towns remained much smaller. The poll tax returns of 1377 provide broadly reliable figures of the lay taxpaying population over the age of 14, and if a standard multiplier of 1.9 is applied for non-taxpayers, a new urban profile can be constructed. London now had a population of 40,000–45,000 and only two towns, York and Bristol, had in excess of 10,000. Another nine had populations of between 5,000 and 10,000 and a further twenty-five had between 2,000 and 5,000, giving a total of some 214,000.[37] This represented a severe contraction, but it did not amount to de-urbanization. In a population of 2.3 to 2.5 million, broadly the same proportion as before the Black Death lived in towns of more than 2,000. Secondly, among the towns with fewer than 2,000 were now many ancient civil and ecclesiastical centres: cathedral centres like Wells, Chichester, and Lichfield, fortified towns like Durham, and ports like Grimsby and Bridgwater, all specifically urban in character. No further series of figures for the calculation of population is available until the tax returns of the early 1520s, and these suggest no higher a level than in 1377, confirming the economic stagnation of the older and larger towns and a general shift in favour of smaller and newer towns. London, Norwich, and Exeter had grown, while York, Bristol, and Coventry had shrunk. Yet the span is too long for plotting urban fortunes within our period, since in many towns the full severity of the crisis was felt only after 1450. Even less helpful are attempts to chart changes in the taxable wealth of towns and the ratio of urban and rural wealth from the subsidy returns of 1334 and 1524. These show some marked changes in ranking, with Boston, Lincoln, Oxford, and Shrewsbury falling from among the leading ten towns to below the first twenty-five, while Exeter rose twenty places to sixth. But there were significant differences in the timing of these changes, determined by local circumstances. It is more helpful to examine the causes of urban prosperity or decline.[38]

[37] R. H. Britnell, 'The Black Death in English towns', *Urban History*, 21 (1994), 195–210.
[38] D. M. Palliser, 'Urban decay revisited', in J. A. F. Thomson (ed.), *Towns and Townspeople in the Fifteenth Century* (Stroud, 1988), 1–21; also A. Dyer, 'Urban decline in England, 1377–1525', in T. R. Slater (ed.), *Towns in Decline, 1000–1600* (Aldershot, 2000), 266–88.

TABLE 8.1. *Towns with recorded taxpaying population of over 1,000, 1377*

Town	Taxpaying population	Town	Taxpaying population
London	23,314	Hereford	1,903
York	7,248	Cambridge	1,902
Bristol	6,345	Exeter	1,666
Conventry	4,817	Hull	1,557
Norwich	3,952	Worcester	1,557
Lincoln	3,569	Plymouth	1,549
Salisbury	3,373	Ipswich	1,507
Lynn	3,127	Northampton	1,477
Colchester	2,951	Nottingham	1,447
Boston	2,871	Ely	1,394
Berverley	2,663	Scarborough	1,340
Newcastle upon Tyne	2,647	Stamford	1,393
Canterbury	2,574	Chester[a]	
Winchester	2,500	Newark	1,178
Bury St Edmunds	2,445	Ludlow	1,172
Oxford	2,357	Southampton	1,152
Leicester	2,302	Pontefract	1,085
Gloucester	2,239	Derby	1,046
Yarmouth	1,941	Lichfield	1,024
Shrewsbury	1,932		

Note: The figures show the recorded number of lay persons over the age of 14 paying the poll tax in 1377. A multiplier of 1.9 has been suggested to represent the actual population.

[a] No figures.

Source: J. C. Russell, *British Medieval Population* (Albuquerque, N. Mex., 1948), 142–3 (table 6.6).

Towns everywhere depended on immigration from the countryside to maintain their level of population, which at any time numbered at least one-third of first- or second-generation settlers. The majority of these came from within a radius of 6 to 10 miles of the lesser towns but from up to 20 miles around regional capitals. There is no direct measure of urban immigration; admissions of freemen, which rose dramatically in many towns in the late fourteenth century, had no fixed ratio to their overall population and were controlled by the governing oligarchy as a matter of policy. However, in the post-plague economy a number of factors favoured migration from the countryside. Although more land was now available and the numbers of cottars and underemployed had been reduced, the contraction of arable farming in favour of less labour-intensive animal husbandry produced some spare labour capacity. Secondly, mobility was stimulated among rural artisans and labourers by the attractions of high wages and cheap food in the towns and by the enforcement of labour legislation by local landlords. Thirdly, the greater purchasing power of the peasantry led to a demand

for artisan products, and membership of the urban craft guilds was swelled by artisans and apprentices from the countryside. Finally, many adolescent girls found
employment in domestic service and low-skilled occupations and were attracted
by the opportunities of town life. These factors were most potent in the period of
heightened mobility and rise in per capita wealth during the last three decades of
the fourteenth century; by the mid-fifteenth century immigration had generally
stabilized or declined, though continuing in a few towns like Exeter.[39]

With the contraction of population and production in the countryside after
1350 many village markets geared to simple commodity exchange became redundant, and facilities were consolidated into the market towns. The process went
largely unrecorded, but out of more than 2,000 markets with charters before
1348 fewer than 600 still existed in the sixteenth century. The shake-out was
most severe in areas of dense concentrations, like the West Midlands, Devon,
and East Anglia. Places like Brailes (War.), Broadway (Worcs.), Steeple Ashton
(Wilts.), and Writtle (Essex) lost their markets for ever. The fortunes of medium
and larger towns depended on their location and role in the regional economy.
Major towns like York, Norwich, Bristol, Coventry, and Salisbury which
regained population after 1360 (though never to their former size) were centres
of the booming cloth industry, as were smaller centres like Colchester and Exeter
where new expansion occurred. Medium-size towns in their hinterland like
Hull, Yarmouth, Ipswich, Worcester, and Reading acted as either outports or
collecting centres. Small towns on habitual transit routes, like those between
Southampton and Coventry, and others like Loughborough, Melton Mowbray,
and Gloucester which were interchange points between contrasting regional
economies, throve on medium-scale internal trade. Other places became entrepôts
for food supplies: Faversham for the grain from Kent which fed London,
and Knowle (War.) and Crediton (Devon) for the thriving cattle trade. A few
smaller towns developed specialized industries, like Droitwich for salt, Thaxted
for cutlery, and Bridport for ropes, and others became centres for professions,
like Oxford, Cambridge, and Bury. The purchasing power of the major ecclesiastical institutions, cathedrals and monasteries, provided a bedrock, though not
a basis, for prosperity. It did not stop the stagnation and decline of Lincoln and
Winchester among the larger and Beverley and Peterborough among the smaller
towns. The latter were the more vulnerable as prosperity shifted from north-east
to south-west, leaving Scarborough, Stamford, and Newark among the middling
towns and Doncaster, Louth, and Selby among the smaller to stagnate.[40]

---

[39] A. R. Bridbury, *Economic Growth: England in the Later Middle Ages* (London, 1962; Brighton,
1975), 65–9, has graphs showing freemen admissions in five towns; R. B. Dobson, 'Admissions to
the freedom of the city of York in the late Middle Ages', *Econ. HR* 26 (1973), 1–22.

[40] C. Dyer and T. R. Slater, 'The Midlands', in *CUH* 625–35; D. Keene, 'The south east of
England', ibid. 572–82; R. H. Britnell, 'Urban demand in the English economy, 1300–1600', in

For many towns the prosperity of *c*.1370–1430 proved an Indian summer. This was particularly true for those on the eastern seaboard like Boston, Hull, and Grimsby, and those in its hinterland like York and Colchester (but not Norwich). After 1400 they suffered not only from the interruption and eventual collapse of the Baltic trade and the Dutch challenge to the North Sea fisheries, but from London's increasing monopoly of trade to Calais and the Low Countries. Further, at Yarmouth and Grimsby the silting up of access channels diminished their viability as ports, just as it had that of Lincoln.[41] Moreover, by the mid-fifteenth century many of the major cloth towns were losing control of production to newer village centres in Gloucestershire, Wiltshire, Somerset, Suffolk, and the West Riding. When exports of cloth collapsed after 1450 many of these older towns went into long-term decline. To a large extent urban prosperity in the century after the Black Death thus rested on an infusion of wealth from external markets rather than on indigenous commerce, and was narrowly dependent on one product. Yet in the quantity, quality, and value of its products, late medieval English cloth-making was a triumph of craftsmanship, industry, and marketing.

The Cloth Industry

In trying to explain this extraordinary success story we are confronted by a baffling lack of evidence. Those who made and sold the cloth have left no accounts, and apart from the annual export figures, there are no indications of the volume of production. Aulnage accounts, which give the figures for cloth sealed for sale when it had been finished, exist only for five years in the 1350s and four years in the 1390s; nor do they indicate whether the cloth had been made in the centre where it was finished or in the surrounding villages. Thus, although some 6,000 cloths were sealed annually in Salisbury in 1394–8 it remains unclear how much of this represents the city's own industry. Since the expansion of rural cloth-making was a significant feature of the late Middle Ages, this is particularly frustrating. Similarly, there is a striking absence of detailed evidence of how this rural industry was organized.[42]

Galloway (ed.), *Trade, Urban Hinterlands and Market Integration*, 11–12; D. Postles, 'An English small town in the late Middle Ages: Loughborough', *UH* 20 (1993), 7–29; R. Holt, 'Gloucester in the century after the Black Death', in R. Holt and G. Rosser (eds.), *The Medieval Town* (London, 1999), 141–59.

    [41] S. H. Rigby, *Medieval Grimsby, Growth and Decline* (Hull, 1993), 113–46; id., 'Boston and urban decline in the late Middle Ages', *Mid. Hist.* 10 (1988), 47–61; J. Kermode, 'Merchants, overseas trade, and urban decline: York, Beverley, and Hull, 1380–1500', *Northern Hist.* 23 (1987), 51–76; id., 'Northern towns', in *CUH* 657–80.

    [42] Bridbury, *Medieval English Clothmaking*, 47–70, 114.

In general cloth production during the late Middle Ages remained in broadly the same areas as earlier: Yorkshire, Essex–Suffolk, Oxfordshire–Warwickshire, and Wiltshire–Somerset; though Lincolnshire declined and Devonshire developed. Expansion occurred at different times. In York, where cloth-making had been in recession in the early fourteenth century, it began in the 1350s and by 1377 the city's population had recovered to over 10,000 and freemen were being admitted from the cloth-making crafts in increased numbers. York passed its zenith shortly after 1400 as immigration fell and its exports of medium-grade cloths to the Baltic suffered setbacks; but the end of its prosperity came after the mid-century with the Hanseatic crisis and the emergence of cloth-making centres in the West Riding, notably Bradford and Halifax. By 1524 its ranking had sunk from second to eleventh. Coventry, which drew on wool from both Hereford and the West Midlands, expanded dramatically in the forty years before 1377, when it ranked fourth. It continued to grow into the early fifteenth century, but the trade crisis of the mid-century and a severe epidemic triggered its decay as a cloth-centre, although it retained its ranking in 1524 as an internal entrepôt. Salisbury, though smaller with 3,226 taxpayers in 1377, has been claimed as 'the most important cloth-making town of England', with perhaps 25 per cent of its population engaged in its industry which accounted for 11–16 per cent of English exports. Like Coventry it retained its position in 1524, though overtaken by Exeter. Colchester was different again. In 1300 it 'was not primarily a cloth town' and did not really emerge as such until the 1360s when its cheap russets began to find a market in the Baltic. Thereafter its growth was rapid, placing it ninth in the poll tax listing, with immigration swelling its population to perhaps 8,000 by 1400, but after 1450 the Hanseatic crisis and the emergence of rural cloth-making at Lavenham and Coggeshall brought stagnation and decline. Exeter's expansion came later, beginning in the 1390s and benefiting from the demand for its cheap, light cloths in the domestic market during the 1430s and 1440s; it retained its prosperity and that of its region into the sixteenth century.[43]

The industry in these major urban centres was linked to that in villages and small towns where the initial processes were undertaken and cloths were collected for finishing. Coggeshall, Hadleigh, and Lavenham within 20 miles of Colchester; Devizes, Trowbridge, and Warminster the same distance to the west of Salisbury; the villages that developed as cloth-making centres to the east of Bristol in the fifteenth century, like Nailsworth, Stroudwater, and, most famously, Castle Combe; and in Somerset small towns like Wells, Taunton, and

[43] J. N. Bartlett, 'The expansion and decline of York in the later Middle Ages', *Econ. HR* 12 (1959), 17–33; C. Phythian Adams, *Desolation of a City* (Cambridge, 1979), 33–50; R. H. Britnell, *Growth and Decline in Colchester, 1300–1525* (Cambridge, 1986), 14, 21, 53–71, 187–205; M. Kowaleski, *Local Markets and Regional Trade in Medieval Exeter* (Cambridge, 1995), 19–27, 148–55, 236–8.

Bridgwater by 1400, and the later growth villages like Croscombe and Mells, formed a commercial and industrial network. The emergence of rural centres of cloth-making was the product of rising demand and specialization rather than of direct competition with the towns. Each centre gave its name to cloths of a distinctive weave, quality, or colour. The 'russets' and later 'greys' of Colchester, the 'kerseys' of Suffolk, the 'rays' of Salisbury, the Coventry 'blues', the 'Stroudwaters' and 'Castle Combes', all added up to a diverse range which could be successfully marketed.[44]

Cloth-making was a laborious and labour-intensive process. The initial stages of washing, carding, and spinning the wool could be done by women in a domestic context. Dyeing and weaving were men's work and both demanded capital, a loom being valued at 18s. or £1. The cloth was woven in standard sizes, a broadcloth being 24 to 26 yards long and 1 foot 5 inches to 2 yards wide. The cloth was then fulled to thicken and felt it at a fulling mill with tilt hammers driven by water power. The fabric was then hung and stretched at tenter yards and finished to a fine velvet by carding and shearing.[45] While the preparatory stages could be done on a domestic and individual basis, each of the finishing stages was the work of a different craft in permanent workshops, using expensive plant or materials like alum and dyes.

In the old cloth towns where merchant clothiers were part of the ruling oligarchy, they would engage to supply the wool, put it out to be worked at different stages, and market the final product. But this was not a factory system; craftsmen at each stage worked in small independent units, often as a family workshop, and in many towns weavers, fullers, dyers, and shearers formed separate guilds. In the countryside much production remained small-scale, but in the new complexes which sprang up in Wiltshire, Suffolk, and later the West Riding in the fifteenth century the whole economy of the village was directed by the clothier–entrepreneur—men like William Haynes of Castle Combe, Thomas Spring of Lavenham, Thomas Paycocke of Coggeshall, and James Terumber (or Touker) of Bradford upon Avon. By using the local wool supplies and workforce, concentrating production more intensively, and marketing the produce directly to exporters, the rural clothiers challenged the monopoly of the urban merchants. Their investment in looms, fulling mills, and tenter yards created new industrial complexes in former centres of underemployment, in which they

[44] Britnell, *Colchester*, 187–92 (with map); Poos, *A Rural Society*, 58–72; J. N. Hare, 'Growth and recession in the fifteenth century economy: The Wiltshire textile industry and the countryside', *Econ. HR* 52 (1999), 1–26; E. M. Carus-Wilson, *Essays in Economic History*, ii (London, 1962), 151–67.

[45] P. Walton, 'Textiles', in J. Blair and N. Ramsay (eds.), *English Medieval Industries* (London, 1991), 319–55; H. Swanson, *Medieval Artisans* (Oxford, 1989), 30–6; Bolton, *English Economy*, 154–8.

regulated both work and society. In Castle Combe, where fifty new houses were built between 1409 and 1484, there were no craft guilds, and social policing was done by the court leet; and similar conditions existed in the cloth villages of northern Essex. Though not in the same league as the urban merchants, such clothiers were men of real substance who built houses and almshouses for their employees, and helped to raise the massive towers, lofty naves, and ornate roofs of their parish churches. As in the towns, this unparalleled expansion during the first half of the century was checked in 1450, with a slump in exports and prices for the next twenty years. The effects of boom and recession on these rural areas deserves further investigation.[46]

Other Industries

Besides cloth, two distinctive English exports were pewter and alabaster. Before 1340 Higden had remarked on the vogue for English pewter: 'Europa loveth and desirith the white metal of this lond,' which in Italy and the Low Countries was reckoned 'little inferior to silver'. Exports of up to 20 tonnes per annum in 1400 had more than doubled by 1450 and reached 90 tonnes by 1466–7. Pewterers' guilds were established in York, Bristol, Coventry, Norwich, and London, in the last of which alone some 60 tonnes of ware, equivalent to 200,000 separate items, were made in the early fifteenth century, mainly domestic utensils, church vessels, and badges.[47] It brought a revival of tin mining in the West Country, in decline in the late thirteenth century, and tin was also used in building, and in making guns and church bells. Mining required capital investment and this was provided by London merchants to the master tinners who owned the workings. One such, 'Abraham the tinner', was employing 300 men in seven different sites in 1357. But small independent tinners were traditionally the backbone of the industry, enjoying the right to prospect and open up seams, often in partnership. Operations were regulated by the Stannary courts, five in Cornwall and four in Devon, and the rural and mobile workforce precluded any guild organization. Although daily wage rates more than doubled from 1349 to 1420, tinners remained among the lowest-paid workers.[48]

Alabaster enjoyed a similar vogue both in England and on the Continent. A fine-grained gypsum, it was easier to carve than marble and particularly suitable

[46] Poos, *A Rural Society*, 58–72; Carus-Wilson, 'Evidence of industrial growth on some fifteenth century manors', in ead.; Hare, 'Growth and recession'; Britnell, *Colchester*, 192.

[47] Quoted in J. Hatcher, *English Tin Production and Trade before 1550* (Oxford, 1973), 9, 31, 89–117; R. F. Homer, 'Tin, lead, and pewter', in Blair and Ramsay (eds.), *English Medieval Industries*, 66–79.

[48] Hatcher, *English Tin Production*, 43–88; L. F. Salzman, *English Industries in the Middle Ages* (Oxford, 1923), 70–2.

for monumental effigies, and retables, which were widely distributed in France and Spain. It was found principally in Staffordshire and Derbyshire on manors owned by John of Gaunt, and was popularized by commissions (1358–74) for the tombs of Queens Isabella and Philippa and of Gaunt himself and for the Neville screen in Durham Cathedral. Much of the carving was done at workshops in York, Burton, and London, rather than at the quarry.[49] By the early fifteenth century the production of alabaster images on a very large scale had filled parish churches and private chapels.

The other extractive industries were coal- and-lead-mining, and stone-quarrying. Coal was mostly mined in the north-east, the North Midlands, and the Forest of Dean, mainly by open-cast extraction. A shaft was sunk to a shallow bed and extended as a bell pit as far as was safe. Mines were leased from local lords, and by the late fourteenth century coal was being shipped to the Low Countries and was used in London.[50] Lead was mined in Durham, Cumberland, Derbyshire, and the Mendips. As in the Stannaries the work was regulated by a miners' court which enforced discipline and penalties for stealing. Once extracted, the ore was broken up with a hammer, washed (by women), and taken to smelting furnaces which were powered by bellows.[51] Iron-smelting, earlier located in the Forest of Dean, was extensively practised in the Surrey and Sussex Weald, south Yorkshire, and Weardale in the fifteenth century, using bellows driven by water power. Even so, much iron was imported. Village blacksmiths were widespread, and some were women, but metal-working was primarily an urban industry, usually located in suburbs and environmentally noisome. All ore extraction was on a small scale, limited not only by technology but by the costs of transportation and, in the fifteenth century, a collapse of demand and consequent low prices.[52]

Unlike the extraction of ore, stone-quarrying was widely spread down the limestone belt from the Yorkshire coast to Dorset. Often quarries were opened up for particular building projects, like that at Thevesdale for York Minster from 1386 to 1466, and that at Huddleston for Eton from 1450. At 2d. per ton-mile cartage, stone could not be carried economically for long distances except by water, so that a local quarry on the lord's land was often preferred even if of inferior quality. Rough hewing of the stone was done by labourers, then rough dressing by masons at the quarry; the stone was then brought to the yard for skilled carving and setting. Although large institutions might carry a staff of masons

---

[49] N. Ramsay, 'Alabaster', in Blair and Ramsay (eds.), *English Medieval Industries*, 29–40.

[50] Salzman, *English Industries*, 12–16; J. B. Blake, 'The medieval coal trade of north-east England: Some fourteenth century evidence', *Northern Hist.* 2 (1967), 1–26; Pollard, *North Eastern England*, 75–7; Bolton, *English Economy*, 163–8.   [51] Salzman, *English Industries*, 50–7.

[52] Ibid., 30–40; J. Geddes, 'Iron', in Blair and Ramsay (eds.), *English Medieval Industries*, 167–88, which provides an excellent account of blacksmiths' techniques.

(York had eighteen), for any major project they were recruited—or for royal work conscripted—in large numbers. In 1359–62 William of Wykeham ordered sheriffs to impress 600 masons for work on Windsor Castle. Leading master masons might contract for all the work on a project with their own team of journeymen and in addition act as the architect. Such were John Spoule, chief mason at Windsor in 1362–4, John Lewyn for Bolton Castle in 1378, Henry Yevele for Westminster Hall in 1395, and John Marwe for the guildhall at Norwich in 1407–11. Since masons moved from job to job, they developed no guild framework but at each site set up a house or lodge as a workshop and residence under a master mason. Hours of work, from dawn to dusk except on feast days, were regulated by bells.[53]

Brick-making had commenced in the thirteenth century but it only became widespread for major buildings in the late fourteenth, in areas where stone was not readily available. It was used over a flint core at Cow Tower in Norwich (1398), on the walls, gates, and Holy Trinity Church at Hull before 1400 and at Beverley (1409), and contemporaneously on guildhalls at Lynn and Boston. By 1430–50 improvements in the quality of the bricks and the introduction of cusps and mouldings by Flemish workmen enabled them to be used for decorative detail in corbelling and archways. They were adopted for prestige royal buildings at Sheen and Eton, for major baronial houses at Herstmonceux (Sussex) and Tattershall (Lincs.), and for a cluster of gentry houses in the south-east. For major projects brickworks would be set up on site or up to 10 miles away to produce bricks in huge numbers—2½ million for Eton. Independent brickmasters took commissions for such major works: both William Vesey, appointed by Henry VI in 1437, and Baldwin 'Docheman', used by Lord Cromwell at Tattershall, were probably Low Country men.[54]

3. URBAN SOCIETY

Constitution and Government

As centres of commerce and industry, towns had in practice to be self-regulating communities, their government attuned to the interests of the merchants and artisans who generated their wealth. Yet relatively few towns were autonomous entities in law; most were under lay or ecclesiastical lordship. The impact of lordship varied in time and place, but in general it would be wrong to posit an intrinsic opposition between feudal and urban interests. Lords founded, developed,

---

[53] D. Knoop and G. P. Jones, *The Medieval Mason* (Manchester, 1949) contains a wealth of information; D. Parsons, 'Stone', in Blair and Ramsay (eds.), *English Medieval Industries*, 1–28; L. F. Salzman, *Building in England* (Oxford, 1952), 1–139.

[54] J. A. Wight, *Brick Building in England* (London, 1972), 17–60; N. J. Moore, 'Brick', in Blair and Ramsay (eds.), *English Medieval Industries*, 211–36; Salzman, *Building in England*, 140–8.

and protected towns as sources of wealth, even if they also taxed them. They entrusted them with maintaining order and regulating their economic and social life, even if the lord retained supreme judicial authority. Even so, the constitutional basis of a town's government was important because it determined the status of its ruling body and helped to shape its character.

Most of the major towns were royal boroughs, shire capitals with royal castles like Nottingham, Northampton, Lincoln, and York. Over the previous two centuries their right of self-government under a mayor and elected officers responsible for order and justice, on payment of a fee farm, had been granted and confirmed by royal charters. By the fourteenth century lawyers were defining their status as corporate bodies in terms of having a perpetual succession of officers and a common seal, with the capacity to hold lands, to sue and be sued, and to issue by-laws. The guild of leading citizens became the town's governing body, composed of the officers and aldermen. Beneath the mayor two bailiffs exercised judicial functions, a chamberlain answered for the town's finances (and fee farm), and by the mid-fourteenth century a common clerk or recorder acted as its legal officer. These officers were assisted by a council composed of twelve or twenty-four aldermen, usually the leading merchants. There were many variations on this model. In the fifteenth century a series of the greater towns added to their powers and prestige by becoming county boroughs, with the mayor acting as royal escheator, and their sheriffs as JPs, thus excluding royal justices. Bristol was the first to achieve this status in 1373 and was followed by York in 1397, Newcastle in 1400, Norwich in 1404, and Lincoln in 1409. In all cases the formal grant of incorporation as a legal principle defined the structure of government and strengthened the position of the ruling elite, which had actively sought it from the Crown. A second wave of incorporation charters followed in 1440–60, sold by the impecunious Henry VI, but only Hull and Southampton secured county status.[55] Many smaller boroughs possessed royal charters, from the thirteenth and early fourteenth centuries, which gave them self-government, civil jurisdiction, and the return of writs, on payment of a fee farm; indeed the fee farm by itself was a token of borough status.[56]

A few more important towns, like Leicester and Warwick, remained under direct lay lordship, which inhibited the development of their corporate status. Probably two-thirds of all medium and small market towns were owned by lords, ecclesiastics being less ready to acknowledge borough status than lay lords. Episcopal boroughs like Lynn and Beverley, situated at a distance from the

[55] J. Kermode, 'Obvious observations on the formation of oligarchies', in Thomson (ed.), *Towns and Townspeople*, 89–92; R. B. Dobson, 'The Crown, the charter, and the city, 1396–1467 ', in S. Rees Jones (ed.), *The Government of Medieval York* (York, 1997), 34–55; M. Weinbaum, *The Incorporation of Boroughs* (Manchester, 1937), 45–108.

[56] Rigby, *Medieval Grimsby*, 41–3.

bishop's see, secured a large measure of independence, but in towns which adjoined the monastery, like Bury and Evesham, there was an uneasy division of power between the lord's bailiff or steward and the burgesses.[57] Small towns under direct ecclesiastical lordship never acquired borough status or officers but remained technically manorial vills under the abbot's steward or bailiffs. Abingdon, Cirencester, Dunstable, and Westminster were among the larger of such small towns which remained in this position until the Reformation and beyond. This was a constant affront to their sense of civic identity but usually made little difference to their day-to-day government, which was regulated by the leading citizens through either the manorial court or their religious fraternity.[58] All towns were effectively oligarchies, if that is defined as the circulation of office among a narrow group of leading citizens, and the way this was organized did not differ significantly between the great chartered boroughs and the small monastic vills.

Town officers and councils were usually chosen through a mixture of indirect election and co-option, although the wider body of citizens, or part of it, were often accorded a nominating or confirmatory role. This tended to be greater in the larger cities. Thus in Norwich the choice of mayor was made by the freemen electing two aldermen at an open meeting, one of whom was then chosen mayor by the other aldermen in a secret ballot. At York, and at Hull, the retiring mayor and council of twelve nominated two or three aldermen from whom the burgesses selected one. Each town had its own peculiar and often complex mechanism, but most embodied the twin principles, that those selected to govern should be the most worthy citizens (*meliores*, *prudhommes*, *bones gentz*), able to support the burden of office, who were identified with the town's welfare and not factions, and that their rule should be validated by the endorsement of all citizens. Put in another way, this embodied the complementary beliefs in hierarchy as the guarantor of social order and of the common good as the purpose of government. Yet along with these ideals it was recognized that institutional checks were needed. These were provided by councils, on the principle that the wisdom of many was preferable to that of a single man.[59] The council of twelve, or twenty-four, which developed in most towns of any size from the thirteenth century, was intended to advise, but also to monitor, the rule of the mayor and officers on behalf of the community. Commonly the council had to approve all

[57] *House of Commons*, i. 474 (Leicester), 513 (Lynn), 670 (Warwick); Kermode, 'Observations on oligarchies', 93–6 (Beverley); Hilton, 'Medieval market towns', 13–20.

[58] S. H. Rigby and E. Ewan, 'Government, power, and authority', in *CUH* 293–7; D. G. Shaw, *The Creation of a Community* (Oxford, 1993), 104–6, 129–40 (Wells); G. Rosser, *Medieval Westminster* (Oxford, 1989), 226–50.

[59] J. Tait, *The Medieval English Borough* (Manchester, 1936), 270–85, with list; Britnell, *Colchester*, 115–20; Kowaleski, *Medieval Exeter*, 102; Rigby and Ewan, in *CUH* 304–5.

letters, bonds, and legal negotiations under the town seal, to control admissions to freedom, and view the chamberlains' accounts. Councils of twelve were composed of *meliores*, while those of twenty-four included some *mediocres*; they were co-opted to office by rotation or for life. This inbuilt tendency towards a closed oligarchy was countered in the fifteenth century by demands for a wider account-ability through the establishment of a larger 'common council' representing the body of citizens.

The model was that of London, where a common council elected by wards had developed out of the common assembly in the mid-fourteenth century, but elsewhere such councils were formally instituted. At Norwich an additional council of sixty, and at York a council of forty-eight selected by the crafts, was set up alongside the aldermanic council of twenty-four. At Lynn the establishment of a common council by Bishop Alnwick followed protests by the 'middling and lesser' citizens against a closed oligarchy. But in other places, like Shrewsbury (1433 and 1442), Exeter (1435–7 and 1450–9), and Colchester (1362), the existing council of aldermen was simply enlarged with the equivalent number of freemen, to form a 'common council'. Although such councils were often established by Act of parliament as safeguards against arbitrary rule and corruption, their role was limited. Meeting only once or twice a year to approve major decisions, particularly financial, and to take a prescribed part in the election of the mayor and officers, they did not formulate policy or take political initiatives. Thus they have been seen as a means to institutionalize the principle of common assent and defuse demands for popular representation. Indeed their meetings were often poorly attended and tended merely to rubber-stamp the decisions of the inner council. Neither did they entirely replace the occasional assembly of all citizens for major and controversial decisions.[60]

All these councils and assemblies were, of course, restricted to the citizens, those admitted to the freedom of the city. Traditionally this had been acquired by inheritance, by purchase, or after apprenticeship to a craft, the last becoming the normal route in the fifteenth century. The principal benefit of freedom was not the right to participate in town government but to trade retail, to be free of tolls, and to enjoy membership of a craft guild. Conversely, it brought liability to urban taxation and, for a few, to civic office. Citizens were thus full members of the town, set apart from the other inhabitants, who were regarded as 'foreigns' (*forinseci*), even if long resident. As the freemen of Grimsby complained in 1383, 'it is not lawful and reasonable that foreigners should be free to traffic [i.e. trade] unless they take up the freedom of the town and bear the charges of the burgesses'. The numbers admitted to freedom varied considerably as between

---

[60] Tait, *Medieval English Borough*, 303–37; Rigby, 'Urban oligarchy in late medieval England', in Thomson (ed.), *Towns and Townspeople*, 62–86.

towns and at different periods. At Grimsby with a population of about 1,500 they numbered only 70; York, at the height of its prosperity was admitting as many as 97 a year in the century 1350–1449, compared with an average of 40 at Norwich and 20 at Colchester. A town's admission policy was related to its economy, its financial obligations, and its social structure. Whereas at York freemen formed a quarter to a third of adult males and over half the householders, in Exeter they formed only one-fifth of householders in 1377, rising to one-third in the next century.[61]

Merchants and Crafts

Even in York, with its large proportion of burgesses, merchants—defined as those engaged in wholesale trade—were no more than 7 per cent of the population. The wealthiest of them, perhaps fewer than 1 per cent, formed the ruling oligarchy. Some members of the larger crafts might be aldermen and hold the lesser office of chamberlain, but mayors and sheriffs were almost exclusively merchants. In York nineteen of the twenty-six mayors in the latter fourteenth century were merchants. A normal *cursus honorum* would commence with election as alderman around the age of 30, followed within four years by appointment as chamberlain, then sheriff two years later, making a man eligible for the mayoralty in another six years. With a life expectancy of little over 50 years, they might hold office at most over a twenty-five-year period.[62] Below the offices of honour filled by great merchants were many others like bridge wardens, constables, market officials, and toll-collectors held by lesser merchants, craft masters, and other freemen. They were actively dissuaded from seeking higher office, and some tradespeople, like butchers, innkeepers, and tailors, might be specifically debarred. To serve as mayor or sheriff was demanding in both time and money. As the personage of the town, the mayor was official representative for the reception and entertainment of visiting dignitaries and at urban ceremonies and feasts. He had specific responsibility for peacekeeping and, along with the sheriffs, spent at least one day a week attending the borough court. The officers had direct financial responsibility for the fee farm, and for raising loans and gifts to the Crown, and might make a disproportionate contribution, as wealthy householders, to national taxes. Yet office also brought access to profits in the form of building contracts, or the farm of the town pastures, and the mercantile elite were likely to be connected into the royal administration as collectors of customs in the port, or serve with the local magistracy on shire commissions. At least in

[61] Rigby, 'Urban oligarchy', 71; Dobson, 'Admissions to the freedom of York', 23; Bridbury, *Economic Growth*, 61–9; Kowaleski, *Medieval Exeter*, 96–9.

[62] J. Kermode, 'The merchants of three northern towns', in Clough (ed.), *Profession, Vocation and Culture*, 8–9; id., 'Observations on oligarchies', 96–7.

the fourteenth century a town's representatives in parliament were largely drawn from its *probi homines*, and even in the fifteenth the major towns continued to return merchants as MPs, many of them former mayors. But over the whole range of towns the proportion of MPs who were resident burgesses fell from 77 per cent in 1422 to 42 per cent in 1478, as many towns chose local lawyers or royal and seigniorial servants. Often these had established connections with the town and could serve its interests, but this has been interpreted as marking a loss of urban self-confidence.[63]

Although wealthy enough to enjoy pre-eminence in their town, few provincial merchants were outstandingly rich. They had, necessarily, to keep a higher proportion of wealth in cash than did landowners; by the reckoning of the sumptuary legislation of 1363 a merchant with £500 in specie was equivalent to a landowner with £100 per annum in land. Leading Yorkshire merchants like Robert Holme left £400 in 1396 and Richard Wartre £333 in 1465, John Northe's fortune of £700 in 1432 and John Brompton's £900 in 1444 being exceptional. Mostly this represented their working capital. The humbler majority confined themselves to internal trade between local and regional markets; only the richer directly engaged in overseas trade, mainly exporting cloth and importing wine. For overseas ventures they formed financial partnerships, purchasing shipping for their cargoes in different vessels to spread the risk, so that a single ship might carry consignments from fifty or more merchants. The lack of their account books makes it difficult to speak in detail about their commercial methods or indeed to know what profit they made on their transactions, though 10 per cent on internal and 20 per cent on overseas ventures has been suggested. If a merchant netted £100 over a year he was doing well. Commercial transactions generally involved an element of credit, and credit networks were widespread. The rising prosperity of the late fourteenth century saw an upsurge of debt litigation, much of it for small amounts, but some involving direct moneylending. The wealthiest merchants were the shipowners. Although many might own part of, or even a whole, ship a very few owned small fleets of ten or more. The carrying trade was remunerative, and the prince of shipowners, William Canynge, owned nearly half of Bristol's ships and controlled one-quarter of its shipping. Commanding a total tonnage of 3,000, Canynge could have been receiving over £10,000 a year in freight charges. But he must have employed between 600 and 800 men, and besides the capital outlay the attendant risks were high. In

[63] J. Kermode, 'Urban decline and the flight from office in medieval York', *Econ. HR* 35 (1982), 179–98; M. Kowaleski, 'The commercial dominance of a medieval provincial oligarchy', in Holt and Rosser (eds.), *The Medieval Town*, 184–216; Roskell, *Commons in the parliament of 1422*, 125–44; R. Horrox, 'Urban patronage and patrons in the fifteenth century', in Griffiths (ed.), *Patronage, Crown, and Provinces*, 158–60.

addition to their commercial ventures merchants often invested in urban property, both for the income from rents and as collateral securities.[64]

Merchant dynasties rarely established themselves for longer than two generations. Recurrent plague reduced the likelihood of surviving male issue, a fact recognized in the language of wills, and sons might anyway lack the aptitude or interest in merchandising, preferring law or the Church. Borough inheritance law, which divided movable property between the widow, the eldest son, and the deceased's bequests, made it difficult to preserve working capital. A widow might convey her share to her son, but quite often would take it to another husband, a merchant. Nevertheless, a few notable dynasties survived, such as those of Coppendale, Tirwhit, and Holme in York and Beverley; of Baret and Drury in Bury; and of Canynge in Bristol. In all towns the merchant oligarchy was a continuously changing and permeable body; its strength lay in its collective identity as a ruling group, consolidated by civic and commercial obligations, and frequently bonded by intermarriage.[65]

Merchant society was separated hierarchically from the urban crafts and was distinct from, though often linked to, that of the country gentry. Some knights and esquires had houses within the town and might belong to its religious fraternities. Lawyers and officials practised in the town and the former filled town offices and built up urban property holdings. Merchants correspondingly acquired land outside the town, though more often as an investment than to relocate their family. Even when they married their children into armigerous families and themselves served alongside the shire magistracy on commissions or as escheators and under-sheriffs, they continued to live and die in the town. They were proud of their social standing as equivalent to gentlemen and, if officeholders, to that of esquire or even knight. When Henry VI visited Coventry in 1451 he sent a knight to summon the mayor and aldermen to audience.[66] They were equally alive to ranking among themselves. Town life gave many opportunities to assert this: in processions to church on Sundays and feast days, and in the order of seating, and at civic rituals where aldermen wore scarlet. Their wives likewise relished their status. Margery Kempe, who prided herself on being the daughter of a mayor, later repented of 'her cloaks . . . slashed and laid with divers colours between the slashes, so that they could be the more staring to men's sight, and herself the more worshipped'.[67]

[64] Kermode, 'Merchants of three northern towns', 25, 37; Kowaleski, 'Commercial dominance', 201–10; id., 'Port towns', in *CUH* 489–93; Carus-Wilson, *Medieval Merchant Venturers*, 80–92.

[65] R. S. Gottfried, *Bury St Edmunds and the Urban Crisis, 1290–1539* (Princeton, 1982), 150–66; Kermode, 'Merchants of three northern towns', 16–19.

[66] R. Horrox, 'The urban gentry in the fifteenth century', in Thomson (ed.), *Towns and Townspeople*, 22–44; id., 'Urban patronage', 150–1. For the town house of a lawyer, see W. N. Alcock, 'The Catesbys in Coventry', *Mid. Hist.* 15 (1990), 1–36.

[67] *The Book of Margery Kempe*, ch. 2.

Merchants generally had their houses in the centre of the town. The wealthiest might replicate a country manor, built round a small courtyard with an entrance gateway from the street. But the typical merchant house was smaller, with a narrow frontage to the street, the width of a single shop, and extending backwards with either a hall rising to the full height and an adjoining block of chambers, or with the hall and solar on the first floor, and additional chambers on the second, all accessed by an internal stair. Houses might rise to three storeys, with jettied overhang, but without the mouldings and carvings favoured on the Continent. Bequests in wills and inventories give evidence of feather beds, sheets, bed hangings, tapestries, and utensils of pewter, silver, and gold. Merchants also used their wealth to safeguard their souls. The wealthiest left enormous sums, of up to £400, to found perpetual chantries, and the less wealthy would endow a chantry priest for up to twenty years; all left money for obits and masses in a variety of churches and convents. Some provided for the poor at their funerals, for prisoners in the town gaol, and the sick in hospitals. There was rarely anything distinctive about their funeral instructions or their memorials. Many favoured a simple brass depicting them in merchant dress, or a stone slab, in their parish church. The richest could afford a canopied table tomb and effigies, like those of William Canynge and Philip Mede in St Mary Redcliffe, and William Soper in the friary at Southampton, but none seems to have wanted a cadaver memorial. The prevailing impression is that merchant culture was conventional and, unsurprisingly, 'bourgeois'. These were practical men, alive to what money could buy and determined to put their own to good use. They gave generously for building guildhalls, markets, bridges, and conduits, for paving streets and repairing roads. Their books, even their religious books, were practical manuals. Their world was tangible and confined, and beyond it they remained incurious and unspeculative.[68]

As well as directing town government, the greater merchants as wholesalers controlled the supply of raw materials for its manufactures. In every industry the different processes were in the hands of a multiplicity of crafts, or 'mysteries' (Old French: *mestier*): in cloth-making, weavers, fullers, dyers; in leather products, cordwainers, saddlers, skinners; in metal-working, armourers, pewterers, silversmiths; in victualling, bakers, brewers, and fishmongers. These and many others were typical of the range of specialized occupations, amounting to a hundred or more in towns the size of York and Coventry. Moreover, most industry was on a domestic scale, carried on in homes and shops. The craftsman, a freemen of the town, might employ a handful of 'journeymen' (day labourers) and take one or two apprentices. While the journeymen remained 'foreigns',

---

[68] D. Keene, *Survey of Medieval Winchester*, pt. 1 (Oxford, 1985), 172–6; Dyer, *Standards of Living*, 201–4.

apprentices after seven years might be admitted to the freedom and become craftsmen. Their working day occupied the daylight hours from 5 a.m. in summer and 6 a.m. in winter, with three short breaks for meals. Sundays were free, and so too were many saints' days. This fragmented but highly regulated workforce was organized by craft guilds. The major industries had guilds of their own; the lesser joined together. Thus in York there were over fifty guilds, and in Beverley some thirty-five. Some were in existence before 1350 but their rapid expansion in numbers and size came with the boom in the last quarter of the century. Their membership was confined to the craftsmen, and essentially they were employers' federations whose purpose was to regulate the industry and the workforce. Two views have been advanced about their origins and purpose. Some historians see them as spontaneous associations by those of a particular craft, centred on a religious guild dedicated to the patron saint of the craft in their parish church, their members framing regulations to protect and advance their economic interests. Other historians have seen them as instruments of social and political control, formed under pressure from the merchant oligarchs to contain wage demands and enforce labour discipline in a period of social instability. Direct evidence of how they functioned is scarce, and we are largely dependent on the ordinances drawn up by each craft setting out its aims and requirements.[69]

Many of these were submitted for inspection to the royal council pursuant to an order in November 1388. This reflected the unease over the rapid multiplication of such sworn associations, which could be used to press demands for higher wages and better terms of work, and which could accumulate property in mortmain. No guilds were suppressed, but in the major towns the mayor and council required craft guilds to register their ordinances for approval, and large numbers did so. In 1437 this was enforced by statute. Thus the authorities were clearly concerned to supervise the craft guilds and use them to control a workforce dispersed over individual masters and households. Yet the ordinances were drawn up by the craft masters themselves and embody their concerns. They limit work to members of the craft guild; detail hours of work and wages; forbid poaching of labour and price-cutting; regulate the number of apprentices, their terms and qualifications; and establish quality standards for products. The ordinances of the victualling guilds sought to enforce standard weights and measures, forbade forestalling and regrating, and required all produce to be sold in the market and

[69] For the two views of craft guilds, see (1) C. M. Barron, 'Parish fraternities in late medieval London', in C. M. Barron and C. Harper-Bill (eds.), *The Church in Pre-Reformation Society* (Woodbridge, 1985), 14–17; Goldberg, *Women, Work, and Life Cycle*, 34–5; M. Davies, 'Artisans, guilds, and government in London', in R. Britnell (ed.), *Daily Life in the Late Middle Ages* (Stroud, 1998), 140–3; (2) H. Swanson, 'The illusion of economic structure: Craft guilds in late medieval English towns', *P & P* 121 (1988), 29–48, and in ead., *Medieval Artisans* (Oxford, 1989), ch. 9, pp. 107–27.

not hawked around the streets. As with much medieval legislation, these ordin-ances were an attempt to make actual practice conform to an ideal and do not accurately reflect economic realities. Thus they wholly ignored the large female component in the workforce, they did not embrace service industries, and they inadequately distinguished the variety of processes involved in manufacture. They reflect the unending struggles of the urban oligarchy and the craft masters to regulate the fluid and opportunistic commerce of the late medieval town.[70]

Equally, they expressed the aspirations of the craft masters to a level of dignity and responsibility just below that of the merchant oligarchy. The very formation of a guild asserted the importance of the craft, its contribution to the prosperity ('the common good') of the town, and the status of its leaders as pillars of gov-ernment. The more important craftsmen in the major guilds wore livery and shaped themselves 'for to been an alderman'. Two or three craft masters might sit on the mayoral council of twelve, though only rarely did they attain to the may-oralty itself. The larger common council, where it existed, was often drawn from the crafts. The guild's corporate identity was expressed in the annual patronal service and feast, in the building of a guildhall, and in the purchase of a royal charter. All this gave the guild a recognized position of honour in the urban community, and this was visually proclaimed by its contribution to the town pageant and plays. This could be a heavy financial burden in times of recession, but it was also a chance to assert the repute of the craft in relation to others, and it is doubtful whether either the urban oligarchy or the crafts saw it as a penaliz-ing obligation. Despite their distinct economic interests and disparities of wealth, merchant oligarchs and craft masters shared the common standpoint of city freemen, identifying its well-being with their interests as wealth creators and employers. The greater social division, at times generating antagonism, was between masters and employees. In resisting attempts by journeymen to com-bine in pursuit of higher wages, to trade on their own, or to form their own 'yeomen's guild', the craft guilds looked to the town council for backing. Correspondingly, the oligarchy used the authority exercised by the crafts to limit admissions to the freedom, collect urban taxes, and control misbehaviour.[71] But this mutual dependence was not always proof against jealousy and dissension, carrying the threat of disorder.

[70] J. T. Smith (ed.), *English Guilds*, EETS, old ser., 40 (London, 1870) gives the writs and guild certificates in 1388–9; other guild ordinances are in M. Sellars (ed.), *York Memorandum Book*, i, Surtees Society, 120 (York, 1912). For ordinances at Coventry in 1421 and Norwich in 1449, see Salzman, *English Industries*, 115–16, 208, 217.

[71] Davies, 'Artisans, guilds, and goverment', 125–30, 141; Swanson, *Medieval Artisans*, 40–5, 107, 121.

Dispute and Disorder

How significant were the tensions between the elements of urban society—lords, the merchant oligarchy, the craftsmen, the journeymen, and 'the common people'? Some historians see these as at best precariously balanced and always liable to erupt into open and violent confrontation. Others believe that they were generally contained by the concept of the town as an organic community, bound together by its commercial welfare and religious fraternities. Attention has focused on the acceptability of rule by a merchant oligarchy. It has been argued that government by the *superiores*, whose wealth enabled them to shoulder the burden of office and gave them an interest in the prosperity of the town, was accepted as natural and only evoked opposition if it was inefficient or corrupt, and contrary to the 'common good'. Others have insisted that a principle of 'descending authority' by the rule of the best had to be endorsed by the 'ascending authority' of the people, expressed in their critical assent.[72] The participation of citizens both in the election of officers and in a common council gave a constitutional channel for the expression of discontent with oligarchic rule. Yet to explain the absence of recurrent organized riots against the rich—which, lacking a military force, they were powerless to suppress—we have to go beyond constitutional rules and concepts. In practical terms the dispersed and tightly supervised wage labourers had little time and opportunity for disruptive congregations, and the citizen–householders discountenanced disorder which put the liberties and material framework of the city at risk.

Where organized violence occurred, as it did in the late fourteenth century, it was mostly in 'external' quarrels between the town and its lord, particularly where this was a monastic landlord. At Bury St Edmunds continual friction between the abbey and burgesses over market tolls, taxes, and jurisdiction twice erupted into assaults on the abbey buildings and monks, at times of national disorder in 1327–8 and 1381. In the fifteenth century the citizens turned to legal arguments to win independence, as also at Reading and Cirencester, but found that judgment was habitually given for the monastery. In practice a modus vivendi was established, in which the townsfolk enjoyed a large measure of self-regulation through their guild while the nominal lordship of the abbey remained intact until the Reformation. Conflict could also occur in cathedral towns over the jurisdictional immunity of the cathedral close. Prolonged disputes at Lincoln from 1375 to 1390 and at Exeter and Hereford in the fifteenth century were settled by arbitration, often through the local nobility. There was an element of ritual in such incidents, as both sides sought to test the limits of

---

[72] S. Reynolds, 'Medieval urban history and the history of political thought', *UHY* 9 (1982), 14–23; Rigby, 'Urban oligarchy', 62–86; Rigby and Ewan, in *CUH* 304–11.

their jurisdictions and both cited precedents in historical documents. Such conflicts were a powerful stimulus to civic unity and the sense of corporate identity.[73]

Elsewhere there were internal discords when oligarchic councils were
attacked by *mediocres* and *inferiores* for misgovernment or electoral malpractice.
This occurred at Beverley, Scarborough, and York in 1381, and shortly afterwards, at Lincoln, the oligarchs expelled four leaders of the *mediocres* who had
been making 'fraudulent claims of liberties'. A settlement was arbitrated by John
of Gaunt which reaffirmed customary process in the mayoral election: 'custom'
embodied the tacit assent of the citizens and was equated with legality. Similar
disputes on this issue between the citizens and the ruling elite occurred at Lynn
early in the fifteenth century, at Colchester in 1430, and at Beverley between 1423
and 1465. Ill-informed as we are about the circumstances of these disputes, they
indicate that confrontation between citizens and ruling elites was sufficiently
disruptive to require settlement by external authorities.[74]

The better-documented and more persistent disputes at Norwich reveal how
personal ambitions, constitutional procedures, internal factions, and external
relations could all become intertwined.[75] The disputes centred first on the
authority of the aldermanic council to make ordinances for the commonalty
without its assent and secondly on the participation of the citizens in the election
of the mayor and sheriffs. In 1414 Sir Thomas Erpingham arbitrated an award
setting up a common council of sixty which would endorse the election of the
mayor by the aldermen from two names proposed by the citizens. His award was
accepted in a ritual display of amity and city unity on St Valentine's Day: 'to
make pees, unite and accorde, poore and ryche to ben oon in herte love and
charite'. It was personally inspected and approved by Henry V. The dispute
reignited in 1433 when the retiring mayor, Thomas Wetherby, procured the election of his ally William Grey by excluding the citizens' nominees. This produced
a division between pro- and anti-Wetherby factions within the aldermanry, the
former seeking support from the earl of Suffolk, the latter organizing a vigorous
'demonstration' at the election in 1437 which brought royal intervention. Six
years later the factions were again at war over the priory's attempt to remove the

[73] Gottfried, *Bury St Edmunds*, 215–36; Hill, *Medieval Lincoln*, 259–68; L. Attreed, 'Arbitration
and the growth of liberties in late medieval England', *Jnl. Brit. Stud.* 31 (1992), 205–35; G. Rosser,
'Conflict and political community in the medieval town' (Hereford), in G. Rosser and T. R. Slater
(eds.), *The Church in the Medieval Town* (Aldershot, 1998), 20–42.

[74] R. B. Dobson, 'The risings in York, Beverley, and Scarborough' in R. H. Hilton and T. H.
Aston (eds.), *The English Rising of 1381* (Cambridge, 1984), 112–42; Tait, *Medieval English Borough*,
319–21.

[75] Maddern, *Violence and Social Order*, 175–205; B. R. McRee, 'Peace making and its limits in late
medieval Norwich', *EHR* 109 (1994), 831–66; N. Tanner, *The Church in Late Medieval Norwich,
1370–1532* (Toronto, 1984), 141–52; C. Humphrey, *The Politics of Carnival* (Manchester, 2001),
63–82.

citizens' mills on the river Wensum. The Wetherby group supported the priory and the earl of Suffolk, but a popular demonstration in January 1443 led by a citizen, Robert Gladman, bearing a sword and supported by armed riders, provoked a riot and once again brought a suspension of the city's constitution and the imposition of a fine of £2,000.

The fissures in the polity of late medieval Norwich were not between rich and poor, merchants and crafts, crafts and journeymen, nor even between oligarchy and commonalty; they were between rival factions in the elite, over both power and policy, and they reached down to the wards where the power base of each side lay. What inflamed them was the identification of one faction with external interests, the priory and the earl, allowing their rivals to present them as betraying the common good. For individual views and interests had to be subordinated to the unity and well-being of the city. Urban life in the fifteenth century was compounded of structural tensions and personal rivalries, but it was also acquiring the sense of being, and acting as, a political community.

Civic Religion and Ritual

The dissensions in fifteenth-century Norwich were laid to rest when both the aldermen and the members of the common council were integrated with the Guild of St George, the major fraternity in the town. Guildsmen were required to attend the annual guild Mass and feast, led in dignified procession by the liveried brethren, and were enjoined to fraternal harmony, submitting their disputes to internal arbitration. The ideal of collective town government was thus strengthened by religious prescription. In these respects the Guild of St George was typical of major town guilds like that of Holy Trinity in Coventry, of St George in Chichester, of Corpus Christi in York and Boston, and of Holy Cross in Stratford, all of which embodied civic identity. Indeed in monastic boroughs like Bury, Cirencester, Abingdon, and Westminster the town guild functioned as a de facto governing council, its guildhall being the emblem of desired self-rule. A high entrance fee, of 1 mark to £5, confined membership to the urban patriciate, but also extended it to aristocratic and gentry families of the region, bridging city and shire.[76]

At a lower level parish fraternities had similar functions. Primarily formed to provide intercession for the souls of the departed at smaller cost than endowing an individual chantry or Mass priest, they provided a focus for social and religious activities within the parish. The annual patronal procession, Mass, and

---

[76] McRee, 'Peace making and its limits', 865; id., 'Religious guilds and civic order: The case of Norwich in the late Middle Ages', *Speculum*, 67 (1992), 69–97; M. Grace (ed.), *Records of the Gild of St George in Norwich*, Norfolk Record Society, 9 (1937), 39–43; Gottfried, *Bury St Edmunds*, 184–5.

feast affirmed fraternal harmony, and members were sworn to eschew quarrels and anger, subversive behaviour like nightwalking and eavesdropping, and moral and sexual misconduct. For their modest subscription—of 3s. to 5s. a year—they could not only draw on the accumulated 'treasury of grace' to discharge the penalty of sin in purgatory, but be assured of a worthy funeral even if they had fallen into poverty. Fraternities were largely a post-Black Death phenomenon, reflecting both the obsession with purgatory and concern at unceremonious burial after plague. The latter faded in the fifteenth century, but fraternities continued to flourish though founded in decreasing numbers. Some were small and impermanent but others numbered a membership in hundreds and acquired a hall of their own, urban property, and a hierarchy of officers. They appointed and paid a salaried priest and might not only build their own chapel in the parish church but contribute to the fabric or the interior embellishment. Thus they breathed life into the religious and social life of the parish, strengthening the participation of the laity, and affirming the community of the living and the dead. Urban parishes varied greatly in size. Norwich had 50 and York 41, with perhaps double that number of fraternities, but more recent towns like Coventry and Hull were divided into two large parishes each of which might contain a dozen fraternities. Their social composition was often mixed, though the town guilds tended to be exclusive while some of the smaller fraternities 'founded by common and middling folks' explicitly restricted membership to those of that rank. Women could join them on equal terms to men and not just as wives or widows.[77]

Craft guilds, which had grown out of parochial fraternities, retained a similar religious function, with requirements for procession and worship on their patronal saint's day and the cherishing of fraternal amity written into their ordinances. Their disputes were often settled by arbitration, sealed on the Gospels in church.[78] But the main contribution of the craft guilds to religious life, in the major towns, was the staging of the pageant and plays on the feast of Corpus Christi. The Christian community, made one by sharing in the sacrifice of Christ's body at Mass, affirmed its social unity by a procession in which first the craft guilds, then the aldermen and town officers, all in livery, traversed the town. This manifestation of hierarchy and authority within the body politic impressed both onlookers and participants, reminding them of the scriptural injunction of amity, unity, and peace in the community. The procession was followed by plays,

---

[77] C. M. Barron, 'Parish fraternities', *passim*; G. Rosser, 'Communities of parish and guild in the late Middle Ages', in S. Wright (ed.), *Parish, Church and People* (London, 1988), 29–55; D. J. F. Crouch, *Piety, Fraternity and Power* (Woodbridge, 2000), 255–6, 262–4; C. Burgess, 'London parishes: Development in context', in R. H. Britnell (ed.), *Daily Life in the Late Middle Ages* (Stroud, 1998), 151–74.

[78] C. Rawcliffe, 'The settlement of commercial disputes by arbitration in later medieval England', in Kermode (ed.), *Enterprise and Individuals*, 106–10.

each craft being assigned an episode in the Christian mythology of world history, from the creation to the crucifixion. In the York cycle fifty-four pageants involved more than a hundred crafts; at Beverley there were thirty-six pageants, at Chester twenty-five. Some guilds were traditionally associated with particular stories, either by virtue of their occupation (e.g. bakers with the Last Supper; shipwrights with building the ark), or by virtue of their patron saint. While the plays themselves were based on the biblical story, and scripted by the clergy, their idiom was essentially popular and gave plentiful opportunity for the expression of social attitudes. As burgess productions, the householder was the prototype of figures like Noah and Joseph, and the subordination of women, children, servants, and rustics was underlined. Civic and personal morality was upheld, yet symbolic figures of authority might be ridiculed and denigrated. While in one sense they asserted the laity's role in expounding the scriptural story, for the Lollard minority it was a scandal that the truths of religion should be made into stage illusions. The plays at York, Norwich, Chester, and Coventry were sufficiently renowned to attract visits from the nobility and even royalty, so that civic leaders were anxious to ensure that the performance was to the credit of the town. It has been argued that the heavy financial burden on the crafts was used by the oligarchy to emasculate their wealth and power; but for the craft guilds participation was a means of asserting civic dignity and of honouring their patron saint. The Corpus Christi processions and pageants formed the most prominent expression of the city as an inclusive social and religious community under its symbolic head, the mayor; they also offered a liberating pause in the routine of town life at the height of the summer.[79]

The ritual year of the city was structured around the same religious festivals as that of rural communities, though lacking the dimension of agrarian seasonal routine. It has been argued, in respect of Coventry, that it fell into two halves, from Christmas to midsummer, and thence to Christmas Eve; that the first embracing the major festivals was religious, and the second secular. The typology is not exact, for the first half contained the pagan festivities of May Day and Hocktide, and the second the intercessionary celebration of All Saints and All Souls. Indeed feasting and drinking accompanied most religious events, like Whitsun ales, while Christmas, Hocktide, Midsummer, and St Peter's Day (19 June) saw the ritual inversion of hierarchy. At Christmas a 'Lord of Misrule' (chosen from the city oligarchy) displaced the mayor; at Hocktide married women fought and 'conquered' their husbands in a mock historical battle; and at midsummer branches and blossoms from the country were brought into the city,

[79] M. E. James, 'Ritual, drama, and the social body in late medieval English towns', *P & P* 98 (1983), 3–29; J. Goldberg, 'Craft guilds, the Corpus Christi play, and civic government', in Rees Jones (ed.), *The Government of Medieval York*, 141–63.

bonfires lit, and masters served ale to their journeymen. Many of these rituals seem to have been elaborated in the fifteenth century. It is difficult to know whether, in relaxing tension, they 're-affirmed the social hierarchy and thus the structured wholeness of society'. Like the mystery plays, they were an opportunity for ordinary people to set the agenda and organize their society.[80]

Craft guilds and parish fraternities not only contributed to urban religion and rituals but provided charitable relief to the sick and needy. Although charity was enjoined on all parish priests, there was no requirement for the parish to support the poor, and no mechanism for it to do so. Such measures depended on individual and corporate initiatives. Provision was often made in wills for a number of poor men to be clothed and fed at the funeral and at annual commemoration of the deceased, and sums were left to relieve debtors in prison and provide dowries for poor girls. How much was habitually given to beggars by way of alms is unknown, but attitudes to poverty and the poor were highly ambivalent. As a spiritual ideal poverty had become unfashionable, discredited by the theological controversies of the early fourteenth century and by vernacular criticism of the mendicants. In the new economic order after the Black Death, in which labour was scarce, wages high, and rents had decreased, the able-bodied vagrant received not sympathy but vilification, as at best an idler and at worst a social menace. More deserving were the *pauperes verecundi*, the 'shamefaced poor', who through no fault of their own had suffered misfortune by fate or physical incapacity. Yet it was not always possible to distinguish these from the false beggars with tragic stories and feigned mutilations. And here the whole psychology and theology of almsgiving came into play, since it sprang less from pity for the victim than from the merit it would earn for the giver. In particular it was hoped that the recipient, rewarded for his poverty in the afterlife, would intercede for his benefactor. Yet if he were practising deceit his prayers would be valueless and the donor would acquire no benefit from his generosity. It was often impossible to be sure of a beggar's bona fides. A few churchmen advocated indiscriminate generosity, on the ground that it was impossible and even improper to judge the merit of the poor; but this was unacceptable both to individuals and to society at large.

The difficulties involved in an individual response could be largely avoided if almsgiving was channelled through corporate bodies. The ordinances of many guilds made provision for small pensions to indigent men and women. At Beverley and Lincoln these were no more than 3*d*. or 4*d*. a week, less than the minimum for subsistence, but others provided 10*d*. or even 20*d*. However, such

---

[80] C. Phythian Adams, *Desolation of a City* (Cambridge, 1970), 170–6; id., 'Ceremony and the citizen: The communal year at Coventry, 1450–1550', in Holt and Rosser (eds.), *The Medieval Town*, 238–64.

pensions were intended only for their members who had suffered misfortune, not as large-scale relief for the improvident, unemployed, and chronically poor. Fraternities also fed a token number of the poor at their annual feast. Additionally charity might be channelled into hospitals and almshouses. Most hospitals, which were clerical foundations served by priests, had come into existence before 1300; they provided spiritual rather than medical services and excluded the incurable and the insane. After 1360 many became impoverished and shrank or disappeared. Benefactions went instead to almshouses, or 'maisons Dieu'. Langland exhorted merchants to bestow their wealth on such foundations, housing the aged and infirm who were to pray for the founder's soul. There were usually no more than a dozen inmates, worthy local residents, not vagrants or beggars, living under a master. Some were endowed by merchants like William Canynge in Bristol and John Hosier in Ludlow, while others were run by guilds like those of the Holy Cross in Stratford and Colchester, and some simply by voluntary subscription among the townsfolk, as at Sherborne (Dorset). Yet provision for the needy remained woefully insufficient. Even in a small ecclesiastical town like Wells it was available for less than 5 per cent of the population.[81]

Urban Environment and Identity

The town's identity was defined by the boundaries of its jurisdiction, and in about half of the chartered towns this was marked by walls and gates. In virtually every case the line of the walls had been defined by 1300, and though some were simply earth and ditch ramparts, in all the larger towns they were of stone. The renewal of war in 1369 inaugurated a period of repair and fortification culminating in the sophisticated defences of the gateway flanked by round towers built by Henry Yevele at Canterbury in 1380 and in the Bargate at Southampton. The fifteenth century saw a relaxation of military defence, with gates and walls becoming symbols of urban prestige and security, as figured on town seals and in illuminated manuscripts. Among provincial towns, Norwich had the longest circle of walls, of 2½ miles, including twelve gates and forty towers; the 2 miles of Newcastle's walls had twenty-four towers. The town's walls would be linked to those of the adjoining castle, cathedral, or monastery, marking out the separate jurisdictions. From an early date settlements formed beyond the walls along the approach roads coalescing into suburban communities which remained outside the town's jurisdiction. These provided a large open place for markets

---

[81] M. Rubin, *Charity and Community in Medieval Cambridge* (Cambridge, 1987), 14–98, 123–7, 250–3, 289–99; id., 'The poor', in Horrox (ed.), *Fifteenth Century Attitudes*, 169–82; B. R. McRee, 'Charity and guild solidarity in late medieval England', *Jnl. Brit. Stud.* 32 (1993), 195–225; N. I. Orme and M. Webster, *The English Hospital, 1070–1570* (London, 1995), ch. 7.

and fairs, as at St Giles', Oxford, and inns for travellers, and acquired their own parish churches.[82]

Within the walls the landscape was one of intensive and crowded building alongside open spaces. Apart from the main thoroughfares, the streets were a network of lanes and alleys, constricted by shop stalls, entrances to cellars, and display signs overhead, while above ground-floor level jettied storeys narrowed the aperture. The building line was generally continuous except where tenements had decayed. In towns where loss of population was compounded by economic decline the consequences for the urban landscape could be dramatic. The mid-fifteenth century petitions for relief from taxation recite a litany of decay: and those listing the seventeen churches, eleven streets, and almost 1,000 houses that had decayed in Winchester over the preceding century were not fanciful. Larger houses that fell vacant might be colonized by the poor, living in single rooms or abandoned outbuildings, though in a prosperous town like Wells depopulation enabled houses to be extended into vacant plots.[83] At Winchester population density within the whole urban area was 18.6 per acre, but considerable variations existed between streets, and in the central High Street it rose to 80.6, uncomfortably high by modern standards. Although in the larger towns trades and occupations tended to occupy distinct areas, all districts contained both rich and poor. Most houses except the grandest were timber-framed, with oak shingle or clay tile roofs, thatch being generally forbidden. The houses of master craftsmen or small traders would have a workshop on the street, with a hall behind and two chambers on each floor, rising perhaps to three storeys. Costing some £10–£15 to build, and rented at about 12s. to £1 a year, they provided very reasonable accommodation. Wage-earners and the poorer population occupied rows of two-roomed, single-storey cottages with a frontage of only 5 to 8 feet, rented at 5s. or less. Furnishings were in general of a higher standard than in the country, reflecting partly the level of artisans' wages and partly the greater variety in the urban market, notably in metal and earthenware vessels and the quality of soft furnishings. Food, on the other hand, tended to be more expensive and more varied, though hucksters purveyed low-quality victuals on the cheap. Town councils tried to keep food prices down to restrain demands for higher wages, while also controlling trading standards.[84]

Councils also tried to control environmental and behavioural nuisance.

[82] H. L. Turner, *Town Defences in England and Wales* (London, 1971), 40–92; J. Schofield and G. Stell, 'The built environment', in *CUH* 372–3; D. J. Keene, 'Suburban growth', in Holt and Rosser (eds.), *The Medieval Town*, 97–118.

[83] Keene, *Medieval Winchester*, 96–100, 370; K. D. Lilley, 'Decline or decay? Urban landscape in late medieval England', in Slater (ed.), *Towns in Decline*, 235–65.

[84] Keene, *Medieval Winchester*, 172–7; Dyer, *Standards of Living*, 196–208; Schofield and Stell, in *CUH* 385–7; Phythian Adams, *Desolation*, 163–5.

Polluting traders like butchers were segregated in 'shambles', and noxious industries like blacksmithing and tanning were relegated to the suburbs. Householders were generally responsible for disposing of their garbage and for preventing accumulated dung and waste blocking the street channels. Some municipalities employed 'rakyers' to clean the streets and scavengers to clear cesspits and public latrines. Animals, too, had to be kept under control: dogs were supposed to be kept on a leash but pigs—kept in back yards—were the greater menace if they were free to forage in piles of waste. Most towns bordered a river, in which clothes were washed, waste disposed of, and from which water was drawn for drinking. Some towns (like Winchester) had a common well, while in the fifteenth century cities like Bristol (1400), Coventry (1426), and Exeter (1441) had water piped to conduits, for which householders paid a quarterly charge. Many towns were also concerned to improve the streets by 'paving', each householder being made responsible for the part of the street in front of his property. But 'paving' was done by ramming cobbles into a mixture of sand and gravel, and the passage of shod carts with studded wheels quickly broke it up.[85]

Controlling misbehaviour was a constant preoccupation of the authorities, for towns were magnets for immigrants, vagrants, and petty criminals. They also contained a high proportion of alehouses, which could be centres of disturbance. Policing was done by beadles and constables in each ward under a town sergeant. In Coventry there were twenty-four constables in 1422 and in Norwich sixteen. They organized the watch during the hours of curfew, formed from a roster of householders in each ward, checking on nightwalkers and eavesdroppers and prosecuting any carrying offensive weapons. There was a good deal of theft from persons and property; doors and windows were bolted at night, but thieves could break through wattle and daub walls to enter. Brawls occurred in streets and alehouses leading to injury and often death from knife wounds, but most homicides were unpremeditated. Rarely do series of coroners' rolls survive from which to measure the homicide rate. One series from Oxford in the 1340s has been thought to indicate a rate of 60–80 per 100,000, which would be exceptionally high even by medieval standards, but this assessment is fragile. It is probable that the level of interpersonal violence was higher than in the countryside.[86] Prostitutes were present in towns of any size, often working from home but sometimes from a brothel run as a family enterprise. Licensed urban brothels were unknown in English towns, where prostitutes were periodically fined and expelled beyond the walls; procurers were pilloried, and at times their establishments were literally opened up by removing the doors and windows. But much

---

[85] Keene, 'Suburban growth', 116; G. F. Salusbury, *Street Life in Medieval England* (Oxford, 1939), 13–125.
[86] Salusbury, *Street Life*, 126–62; C. L. Hammer, 'Patterns of homicide in fourteenth century Oxford', *P & P* 78 (1978), 3–12; cf. Maddern, *Violence and Social Order*, 8.

prostitution was casual and occasional, a means of supplementing earnings by the low-paid or unemployed.[87]

Urban society was both regulated by the authorities and self-regulating through the communal disciplines necessary in closely packed neighbourhoods. Although there was much interchange with the countryside, in which perhaps one-third of the population at any time had been born, town life had a distinctive character. To the countryman it appeared more treacherous, more 'streetwise'; John Ball warned his followers, 'beware guile in boroughs'. Did townsfolk see the town as an entity with which they could identify, and which commanded their loyalty? Did they form a community? Such questions are easier to answer for the larger towns and the upper social levels. From the end of the fourteenth century oligarchies show signs of pride in their town. The pressure for incorporation as a county borough, the enhanced dignity of the mayor and aldermen, and the civic processions were paralleled by the building of a city guildhall and clock tower, and the rebuilding of dignified entrance gates emblazoned with a coat of arms and symbolic figures. Towns proclaimed their antiquity, not only pointing to their Roman remains but claiming mythical historical figures as founders: King Coel at Colchester, King Lear at Leicester, the emperor Vespasian at Exeter. In the 1370s towns began to keep a systematic register of civic business—the Memorandum Books at York and the Red Paper Book and Oath Book at Colchester—and the town clerk of York from 1405 to 1436, Roger Burton, began the writing of its history. Some towns helped to promote the cult of their local saint, as Salisbury did that of St Osmund and York that of St William. There is thus no doubt that the ruling oligarchies had, and promoted, a conscious ideology of town identity.[88]

Among the *mediocres*, craftsmen and petty traders, the twin pressures for deference to magistracy and brotherhood among equals must have moulded their social consciousness. In their fraternities they were enjoined not to be proud, greedy, violent, or malicious and to bow to the common will and good. Their sense of community was thus bounded by their craft, ward, and parish, rather than the city. Only in their participation in civic and religious rituals did they absorb a sense of the city's identity. Among the poor, amounting to between a third and one-half of the population, any sense of 'urbanity' registered more in the markets and streets than through the guildhalls, churches, and processions of the bourgeoisie. Theirs was a gossiping, quarrelling, working, and dying community, for which the perambulation of ward constables, the hourly chiming of

---

[87] Salusbury, *Street Life*, 148–55; Keene, *Medieval Winchester*, 390–1; Goldberg, *Women, Work, and Life Cycle*, 148–52; R. M. Karras, *Common Women* (Oxford, 1996), 13–47.

[88] G. Rosser, 'Myth, image, and the social process in English medieval towns', *UH* 23 (1996), 5–25; id., 'Urban culture and the Church', in *CUH* 335–47, 368; Dobson, 'General survey', in *CUH* 283–9; Rees Jones, *Government of Medieval York*, 108–12.

the town clock, and the ritual ringing of church bells formed a background reminder of the town as an entity and authority, which nominally governed but actually rarely impinged on their daily life.

London and its Suburbs

In 1400 London was still mostly contained within its Roman and medieval walls, enclosing an area of less than 1 square mile from the Tower to the Fleet River and northwards to Bishopsgate, Moorgate, and Aldersgate. Development to the west had created the new ward of Farringdon Without, containing the Inns of Court, but to the north and east were fields —Moorfields, Smithfield, Fickett's Field— in which important monastic houses like the priories of St Bartholomew, St John at Clerkenwell, and the Charterhouse were established. Across the Thames to Southwark ran London Bridge, 900 feet in length, carried on nineteen narrowly spaced arches, and lined with 129 shops and houses.[89]

The population in 1377 was around 40,000–45,000. Having reached perhaps 80,000–100,000 in 1300, it had been reduced by the famines of the second decade and the severe mortality of 1348–9. Mass graves in Smithfield and beyond the Charterhouse had been dug and filled with victims, and London continued to suffer in the subsequent outbreaks and in general from a high incidence of infant mortality. The city needed constant immigration, and drew this from a range of up to 120 miles, twice as far as any other town. The social groups were well defined, though the numbers in each can only be estimated. At the top were the 'more sufficient', the *potentiores*, and below them about the same number of master craftsmen and lesser merchants, substantial middling men, the *mediocres*, while the smaller masters and artificers, the *inferiores*, were the more numerous. All these members of guilds or crafts were the citizens, who, as elsewhere, formed about one in four of the adult male population. Beyond these were the non-citizens, the *forinseci*, or 'foreigns', wage labourers and petty traders, and also the alien population of varying wealth who had the same legal position. Finally at the bottom were the poor and marginals.[90]

Just as London sucked in people, so it likewise did trade. Where the thirteenth century had seen the rise of the great wool-exporting ports of the east coast, in the century after 1360 the wool trade, while declining, became the monopoly of the Merchants of the Staple and the Italian merchants exporting from Southampton. London merchants never enjoyed a similar monopoly over cloth exports, in which they competed both with Italians in London and Southampton

[89] A. R. Myers, *London in the Age of Chaucer* (Norman, Okla., 1972), ch. 1; C. M. Barron, 'London, 1300–1540', in *CUH* 395–7.
[90] S. Thrupp, *The Merchant Class of Medieval London* (Chicago, 1948), 41–52; Barron, 'London, 1300–1540', 395–400.

and with native merchants in Bristol. London accounted for between 30 and
40 per cent of wool exports and 45 per cent of cloth. Its dominance should not be
overstated: Hull and Boston as wool ports, and Bristol and Southampton as cloth,
could still hold a candle to London. Where exports led, imports followed. Here the
Italians held the advantage, not merely in being able to supply wine, spices, and
luxury goods from the Mediterranean in demand in the capital, but in importing
raw materials like alum and dyes for cloth-making and a huge variety of manufactures from their trading entrepôts in the Low Countries. In this they directly competed with English importers and retailers, mercers and drapers, who tried to
preserve their monopoly of sale in the city. For London was the premier emporium
for southern England, to which provincial merchants brought wares and where
they bought native and foreign manufactures for distribution. Not only in size, but
as a trading, marketing, and manufacturing centre, London was way ahead of any
other English town, even if it was not quite yet the motor of the English economy.

London was governed by a council of twenty-four aldermen headed by a
mayor. Peacekeeping was enforced through two sheriffs and the mayor's court.
The council administered the city's property including London Bridge, which
was financially self-supporting; it supervised the guilds, and appointed wards
and trustees for the citizens' orphans. Beneath the aldermanic council was the
common council, which had developed out of the common assemblies of the
citizens and was formally constituted in 1376 with a membership of 96 citizens,
elected by the wards, increased to 187 by 1460. It met once a quarter in the
guildhall and regulated the life of the city 'for the common profit'. Since all citizens were taxpayers, it had some muscle in overseeing city finances, but it was
not really a political counterpoise to the power of the aldermen, who formed a
narrow mercantile oligarchy. In general this aroused little opposition, for only
the wealthy could support the costs of aldermanic and mayoral office, and they
alone possessed the political, financial, and commercial experience to run the
city. For a brief period between 1376 and 1384 the draper John of Northampton
led a movement to make the common council the instrument of the craft guilds,
who were to elect its members; he also tried to limit aldermanic office to one year.
The strife of these years produced a reaction: after 1394 aldermen could hold
office for life; their election was removed from the wards to the court of aldermen; and mayoral elections, traditionally held openly in the guildhall before all
the citizens, henceforth took place behind closed doors. Fifteenth-century
London was governed by an oligarchy in no way accountable to the citizens.[91]

Alongside this constitutional structure were the merchant and craft guilds
which controlled much of the commercial and industrial life of the city and were

[91] Tait, *Medieval English Borough*, 311–14; H. T. Riley (ed.), *Liber Albus* (London, 1861), 36;
House of Commons, i. 492–502; Davies, 'Artisans, guilds, and government', 130–5.

not without political influence. Many of these had formed over the century before 1360, as particular trades identified themselves with religious fraternities attached to parish churches or the protection of a patron saint. The merchant or victualling guilds—mercers, grocers, vintners, fishmongers—were the wealthier, and by the end of the fourteenth century many had secured incorporation by royal charter and developed their own internal hierarchy, headed by an elite who wore the guild livery and formed a ruling council. Sometimes these alone constituted the fraternity. The response of the ordinary freemen in the guild was to form their own 'yeomen' or 'bachelors' fraternity with a different patron saint. At first viewed with suspicion, these yeomen fraternities were largely accepted in the fifteenth century, and by the sixteenth century the typical livery company had two levels, liverymen and freemen. Some craft guilds, like those of the haberdashers, brewers, armourers, and cutlers, followed in securing incorporation, but among almost one hundred listed in 1389 many lesser ones could not afford a royal charter. In relations with the city government the incorporated guilds enjoyed a degree of autonomy in regulating their working practices, but the lesser craft guilds fell under aldermanic supervision.[92] This huge proliferation of trade associations at different levels provided the framework for the citizens' social life. Guilds amassed capital from the fees and bequests of their members; they acquired property which brought in rent, and they built guildhalls for feasts and meetings. The tailors, whose hall was in Threadneedle Street, had an annual income of £110 by 1400, which had doubled by 1453. Some of this was spent on religious and charitable functions: they maintained five perpetual chantries and twelve obits and built almshouses for seven persons. From their financial resources the guilds supported the city's religious and political processions, and the pageants at royal entries; they contributed to its corporate loans to the Crown, and could be called on to repair sections of the wall or furnish a quota of defencibles.[93]

The latent hostility between the craft and the merchant guilds could be incited for political ends. In procuring for the crafts the right to elect the common council, John of Northampton was seeking to mobilize the craftsmen and artisans— 'the smale people that konne non skylle and governance ne of gode conseyl'—as a political base against the mercantile elite. Even so, it was less his demagoguery than his ability to exploit the political divisions of Richard II's minority, and import these into city politics by securing the support of John of Gaunt, that made his vendetta with the grocers' leader, Nicholas Brembre, so destabilizing. Brembre's own ties with Richard II's court provoked his execution by the

[92] E. M. Veale, 'The craftsmen and the economy of London in the fourteenth century', in A. Hollaender and W. Kellaway (eds.), *Studies in London History* (London, 1969), 137–41; Myers, *London in the Age of Chaucer*, 108–15.

[93] M. Davies, 'The tailors of London: Corporate charity in the late medieval town', in Archer (ed.), *Crown, Government and People*, 161–90; id., 'Artisans, guilds and government', 137–49.

Appellants in 1388, and it was in recognition of the depth of the division within the city that the mayor, Adam Bamme, proscribed further mention of their names in 1391. Not for another fifty years did factions rend the city elite, and the merchant and craft guilds come into open conflict. Then again, in 1439–43, the tailors' leader, Ralph Holland, ranged himself against the aldermen in successive bids to be elected mayor, invoking the support of the middling and lesser citizens, who chose him by acclamation. Although in origin a demarcation dispute between the drapers and tailors, it quickly aroused class animosities, evident in the remark of one tailor that 'the prosperity of the city of London depends not on the merchants but on the artisans'. Tensions of this kind were always latent, but only became disruptive when a dissident among the elite invoked support either from the aristocracy or from the lower ranks.[94]

For the most part the merchant elite formed a coherent and exclusive body, though one with little dynastic continuity. No family produced aldermen in successive generations or lasted more than three as merchants. Replenishment came from the rise of successful traders, but mostly through apprenticeship. Merchants and gentry apprenticed their sons with liveried merchants for a fee, usually £2–£5, but the lesser crafts recruited the sons of yeomen and husband-men who would repay the entrance fee from their wages. Apprenticeship com-menced at the age of 12, rising to 15 in the fifteenth century as educational requirements increased; it lasted at least seven years, during which the appren-tice lived single in the home, and under the governance, of his master. He would then be formally admitted to the craft or guild, but to start trading as a merchant he would need a working capital of at least £20 and preferably of £100. This might be loaned him by his master, who would eventually sponsor him for the livery. This familial training, combined with membership of the fraternity, gave the merchant guild its strong *esprit de corps*.[95]

The leading merchants were men of considerable wealth. Richard Whittington left £5,000 and more in cash and jewels, as well as property, and John Hende similarly. Most others left estates of £100–£400, in both cash and property. Northampton had seventy properties, worth £120. Although all lived within the city, many bought property in the surrounding counties, partly as investments and partly (as the register of John Lawney makes clear) to entail the land on their family. A few, like John Pyel, retired to live in and endow their native village. Their wealth put them on a social level with gentlemen and esquires, with

[94] For Northampton, see R. Bird, *The Turbulent London of Richard II* (London, 1949), 1–85; P. Nightingale, *A Medieval Mercantile Community* (London, 1995), ch. 11. For Holland, C. M. Barron, 'Ralph Holland and the London radicals, 1438–1444', repr. in Holt and Rosser (eds.), *The Medieval Town*, 160–83.

[95] Thrupp, *Merchant Class*, 102–6, 214–23; B. Hanawalt, *Growing up in Medieval London* (Oxford, 1993), chs. 8 and 9 on apprenticeship.

whom they had commercial dealings. There was some interpenetration of cultures, for some gentry had town houses and some merchants enjoyed hunting. There was a steady trickle of intermarriage, with gentry marrying merchants' daughters, rather than vice versa. By the fifteenth century some aldermen acquired armorial bearings and a few were knighted. But the mercantile ethic differed markedly from that of chivalric society. Lacking ancestral genealogies, inherited property and wealth, and a tradition of magistracy, they had little concern for class and family honour, or for dynastic aggrandizement. Instead their guild ordinances enjoined fair dealing, mutual assistance, respect for verbal bonds, compromise, and self-discipline. Their compelling motivation, as Chaucer observed, was financial profit. Education was essential for the merchant class, and from the 1430s schooling was in demand at both elementary and grammar level; but apart from Whittington and Simon Eyre it was the London clergy, rather than the merchants, who promoted new foundations.[96]

The young merchant had perforce to defer marriage, and his wife was usually younger than himself. Unless she died in childbirth she was likely to be widowed, and possibly with children. London custom, known as 'legitim', gave the widow a life interest in the house and reserved one-third of the husband's estate for her, one-third for her children, and one-third for his funeral and bequests. This made it difficult for an adult heir to continue the business on his own, but where the children were under age the widow had effective custody of two-thirds of the estate. A few chose to run the business themselves, but more often she would— if there was an opportunity—marry an associate of her husband, amalgamating their business, and providing upbringing for her family. Inherited wealth thus reinforced the mercantile class rather than the patrilineal family. At the highest level the case of Margaret Stodeye illustrates this well. Her father, the wealthy John Stodeye, died in 1376 and she married (as her second husband) John Philpot, the associate of Nicholas Brembre. On his death in 1384 she married Brembre's colleague John Fitznichol, and when he died in 1391 her fourth husband was the mayor Adam Bamme, the former associate of John of Northampton. After she was again widowed in 1397, and by now a very wealthy woman, she took a vow of chastity to protect herself and lived until 1431.[97]

[96] C. M. Barron, 'Richard Whittington, the man behind the myth', in Hollaender and Kellaway (eds.), *Studies in London History*, 197–250; ead., 'The expansion of education in fifteenth century London', in J. Blair and B. Golding (eds.), *The Cloister and the World* (Oxford, 1996), 217–45; Thrupp, *Merchant Class*, 110, 118–25, 312; S. O'Connor, 'Adam Franceys and John Pyel', in D. J. Clayton, R. G. Davies, and P. McNiven (eds.), *Trade, Devotion and Governance* (Stroud, 1994), 17–35.

[97] C. M. Barron, 'The widow's world in late medieval London', and C. Rawcliffe, 'Margaret Stodeye, Lady Philipot', both in C. M. Barron and A. F. Sutton (eds.), *Medieval London Widows, 1300–1500* (London, 1994), pp. xv–xxxiii, 86–97; Hanawalt, *Growing up in Medieval London*, 91–110.

As well as providing for his business and family, the merchant took thought for his soul. The wealthiest, like Pulteney, Walworth, and Whittington, could afford to found colleges of priests; otherwise they endowed perpetual chantries or left money for numbers of masses. No London merchant followed William Canynge's example in entering the priesthood, though some asked for burial in monastic houses. Some left money for the poor, the sick, and those in prison; Thomas Knolles for water to be piped to the rebuilt Newgate and Ludgate prisons, and Whittington for a public latrine. A number of corporate projects attracted munificence: the new Guildhall in 1411, the water conduits at Cheapside and Cornhill, the public library at the Guildhall established by John Carpenter in 1423–5, and the granary store built at Leadenhall during the famine of 1439.[98]

Only under Richard II did the Crown intervene in London's government. The city's failure to assist the king against the Appellants and thereafter to lend money aroused Richard's enmity. In 1392, on the pretext of misgovernment, the city's liberties were suspended and its officers imprisoned, and it was forced into a humiliating submission and the payment of a £10,000 fine. Although for the rest of the reign London placated the king with large loans (not all repaid), its loyalty remained suspect: Richard exacted blank charters of submission from it and the surrounding counties in 1398 and largely withdrew the court to the north-west. Not until Henry IV had made Richard prisoner did London welcome him and acclaim his usurpation. The two leading citizens, Richard Whittington and John Hende, had already made large fortunes supplying the court of Richard II, and succeeded in maintaining strictly commercial relations with Henry IV. The new king borrowed frequently from them, but mostly for small sums, and all were repaid. They were not royal creditors on the scale of Edward III's merchants, nor did they receive the commercial benefits and political favours that had brought their predecessors to disaster.[99] Crown loans were now construed as public rather than private operations, and with the reopening of the war by Henry V it was the city which came under pressure to contribute to the national emergency with corporate loans from the citizens. It lent 10,000 marks in 1415, £10,000 in 1417, and £2,000 in 1421. In the first decade of Henry VI's reign it lent £15,000 and in the second £16,852 for the war; but following the truce in 1444 its corporate loans were few and small.[100] Despite the Crown's

---

[98]	Burgess, 'London parishes', 154; Barron, 'Richard Whittington', 229; id., in *CUH* 598; Thrupp, *Merchant Class*, 162, 176–90.

[99]	C. M. Barron, 'The quarrel of Richard II with London', in Du Boulay and Barron (eds.), *Reign of Richard II*, 173–201; id., 'Richard Whittington', 236–45; Steel, *Receipt of the Exchequer*, 142.

[100]	Steel, *Receipt of the Exchequer*, 152–3, 195, 219, 230, 232–7, 261–2; C. M. Barron, 'London and the Crown, 1451–61', in J. R. Highfield and R. Jeffs (eds.), *The Crown and Local Communities* (Gloucester, 1981), 88–109.

disastrous military and commercial policies after 1444, London maintained a careful loyalty to Henry VI. It refused to admit the duke of York in 1452, and maintained a studied neutrality from 1454 to 1460. Yet it must have felt deserted and dishonoured when Henry fled the city in the face of Cade's rebels in 1450 and when the court transferred to Coventry after 1456. If it bowed to *force majeure* in admitting the Yorkist lords in 1460 it was also because the aldermen were deeply divided. Thereafter Londoners' loyalties remained with York: Queen Margaret could not get supplies from the city in 1461 and dared not assault it, even after she had recaptured the king.

Did the 40,000 Londoners have a sense of community or see the city as 'an organic and knowable entity'?[101] It can be argued that neighbourhood divisions and social tensions inhibited this. London was, indeed, a collection of parishes if not villages, and the parish church was the immediate focus of social and religious identity. Structural tensions between social classes and between merchants and crafts surfaced in times of crisis; youth cultures clashed in riots of journeymen and servants with the students at the Inns of Court; aliens, who formed 4 per cent of London's population, were open to xenophobic attack. In the revolt of 1381 hundreds of Flemish immigrant textile workers and their families were murdered in the Vintry and outside Blackfriars, and they were again endangered at times of war with Flanders in 1424 and 1436. It is easy to believe that this fluid and heterogeneous population, even if confined within a small geographical area, felt no common identity. Yet there were occasions when the city's persona was manifested in communal experience: the sermons and proclamations at St Paul's Cross, the royal and municipal processions, and those of the religious year. The procession for the feast of London's patron saint, St Thomas Becket, took place on All Saints' Day. Further processions of the mayor and guilds took place at Easter, Whitsun, and Corpus Christi, and on 28 October the procession for the election of the mayor went to the exchequer at Westminster, a journey made by barge from 1452. Even more impressive were the processions and pageantry for royal entries and coronations. Less formal but more participatory was the marching for the Midsummer Watch on 24–9 June, when the watches from each ward made a great circuit from Cheapside, carrying lights on long poles. Bonfires were lit in the streets, the doorways adorned with branches and flowers, and tables set in the streets with meat and drink provided by the merchants. Cheapside also provided the setting for tournaments until these were transferred to Smithfield in 1391.[102]

[101] D. Wallace, 'Chaucer and the absent city', in B. Hanawalt (ed.), *Chaucer's England* (Minneapolis, 1992), 84.

[102] S. L. Thrupp, 'Aliens in and around London in the fifteenth century', in Hollaender and Kellaway (eds.), *Studies in London History*, 251–7; Myers, *London in the Age of Chaucer*, 82–4, 165–71; Hanawalt, *Growing up in Medieval London*, 125–7.

If popular attendance at such events promoted a sense of communal identity, at the higher level the ruling elite viewed the city as a legal and historical entity. A great register of the customs and liberties of the city, *Liber Albus*, was compiled by the city clerk John Carpenter in 1419. Individual merchants kept their own commonplace books, in which they entered historical memoranda relating to the city, such as an updated version of William FitzStephen's description of London in the twelfth century and the legend of its foundation by Brutus as a 'New Troy', a title favoured by Nicholas Brembre. The commonplace books were also the context for the development of the vernacular London Chronicles of the fifteenth century. The series of individual continuations of these begin in 1414. One such, ending in 1452, can be ascribed to the mayor William Gregory; another from 1437 to 1461 was probably the work of the notary Robert Bale. The Chronicles are written from a London standpoint, reflecting the views of the city leaders, and incorporate city documents and newsletters. They reveal a historically conscious and politically articulate, if blinkered, society.[103]

Beyond the city's walls and jurisdiction lay three suburbs, each with a population of just over 2,000, the size of a small town. They were very different in character. Westminster had grown up around the royal abbey and palace, where by 1360 the principal administrative offices of state were definitively established and parliaments habitually met. Comfortable inns were built to cater for the continual stream (and sometimes flood) of business visitors and pilgrims from all over England, and fashionable shops sprang up to sell them the sophisticated products of the capital. Tailors charged twice as much, and delectable cooked food was always available. It was to the courts at Westminster that the poor plaintiff in *London Lickpenny* came first, before pressing on to find sustenance in the city. But he could afford neither the fees of the lawyers nor the 'hot shepes feete' and 'rybbs of befe and many a pye' of the street vendors. In the prosperous, bustling years from 1360 to 1410 the abbey developed its property with shops, houses, and inns, but it never accorded the townsfolk borough status or legal independence. Westminster remained a manorial vill, yet it became in practice a self-regulating community, its twelve chief pledges forming an unofficial council, to which the abbey devolved responsibility. It was a thriving community, centred on the parish church of St Margaret.[104]

Across London Bridge, Southwark had some of Westminster's characteristics but was much more mixed. Here too, along High Street and Tooley Street, were large courtyard inns like Chaucer's Tabard, built to accommodate well-to-do visitors, and also town houses of the aristocracy and gentry. To the west lay the

---

[103] H. Kleineke, 'Carleton's book: William FitzStephen's "Description of London" in a late fourteenth century commonplace book', *Hist. Res.* 74 (2001), 117–26; A. Gransden, *Historical Writing in England*, ii (London, 1982), 220–48.

[104] Rosser, *Medieval Westminster*; *London Lickpenny*, in Robbins (ed.), *Hist. Poems*, 130–4.

palace of the bishops of Winchester, forming one of five jurisdictional entities which never coalesced to form a borough. If Southwark failed to develop into a community like Westminster, it was also because it contained disparate social groups. Indeed it has been described as 'London's scrap heap', for 'excluded occupations and rejected residents'. Among the former were the noisome trades and industries, dyeing, fulling, lime-burning, tanning, and brewing, which demanded water and open spaces. Among the latter were not only the small traders escaping from the craft and guild restrictions of London, but the main community of Low Country or 'Doche' aliens. In general they lived harmoniously alongside their English neighbours, though maintaining their discrete communities and not intermarrying. Mainly skilled in the leather and textile trades, they also specialized in brewing beer and making felt hats, clocks, spectacles, and bricks. 'Doche' women formed a significant proportion of the prostitutes who congregated in the 'stews' in the bishop of Winchester's liberty, and in the area of St Thomas's Hospital lived the highest proportion of single men and women in London. In addition Southwark housed two royal prisons, of the king's bench and the marshalsea.[105]

Beyond Aldgate and the Tower, London's east end had already developed into the industrial zone it was to remain until the twentieth century. Along the river front was St Katherine's dockyard, for the repair of ships, and further along the lime works at Limehouse. Development here stretched to Poplar and Bromley. Outside Aldgate was an area for metal-working, the bell foundry which had cast the bell 'Edward' for the king's clock tower at Westminster, and iron foundries where

Smoke-blackened smiths, begrimed with smoke, drive me to death with the din of their blows; such noise by night no man ever heard ... Heavy hammers they have that are handled hard, strong blows they strike on an anvil of steel. 'Lus, bus, las, das', they crash in turn. May the devil put an end to so miserable a racket.

At Whitechapel there were brickworks, and thence to Stratford ran a new road on causeways and bridges to cross the Lea Valley and connect the city with Essex. At Stratford grain brought on barges down the Lea from Hertfordshire was unloaded, and in the meadows and marshes cattle were fattened for slaughter. All this formed part of the bishop of London's Stepney manor, regulated by its bailiff. Its labouring population, while thriving, had no communal rights or institutions.[106]

---

[105] M. Carlin, *Medieval Southwark* (London, 1996); Wallace, 'Chaucer and the absent city', 60.
[106] K. McDonnell, *Medieval London Suburbs* (Chichester, 1978); 'Smoke Blackened Smiths', modernized in R. T. Davies (ed.), *Medieval English Lyrics* (London, 1963), 213.

CHAPTER 9

The Institutional Church

Ecclesia Anglicana was an integral part of both the Catholic Church and the English nation. All who lived within the realm owed allegiance to the king and spiritual obedience to the bishops and pope, and were subject to royal and ecclesiastical jurisdiction. That there was any incompatibility in this was inconceivable. The superiority of spiritual to temporal power had ceased to be a concept with any practical application. Since the twelfth century royal authority had achieved de facto independence, not as head of an autonomous secular state but by establishing itself as the Church's protector. This had enabled it to arrogate to itself indistinct notions of sacrality and divine right which the Church was prepared to endorse through coronation. By the late Middle Ages the mutual recognition of the interdependence of Church and Crown provided the basis for harmony and cooperation. The Church exalted royal authority; the Crown defended the Church's property, jurisdiction, and faith. Each gave support against the other's enemies. Where their interests conflicted—as over benefices as property and the Church's temporal wealth as a source of taxation—the Church largely bowed to the Crown's demands. Their dealings with each other were conducted within accepted parameters and in recurring situations, employing a wary familiarity and avoiding provocation. Nor did they inhabit separate worlds, for the Church penetrated lay society at every level. We can easily have the impression of a static, unchanging relationship in this period. There are no dramatic confrontations or conspicuous crises. Yet in fact behind the surface stability, profound change was taking place with the emergence of an articulate and moneyed lay society. For the Crown it meant taking account of an enlarged political class, demanding representation, critical of government, and susceptible to patriotism. For the Church it meant the loss of its monopoly of literacy, the emergence of individual belief and dissent, and the opportunity for extending its pastoral field. A widening segment of society began to re-evaluate its own religious expectations and to voice its concern over the role of the Church in society and in the realm.

I. THE BISHOPS IN CHURCH AND STATE

The Church was led by its bishops, occupying seventeen English and four Welsh sees. These were of unequal prestige and value. The Welsh sees, and that of Rochester, were all valued at under £500 per annum and usually were either held by monks and royal confessors or were stepping stones for the ambitious. A further four sees of less than £900 in value had similar status. Effectively that left one dozen sees ranging from Norwich (£1,051) to Winchester (over £4,000) occupied by those who led the Church. Although appointments were made through a mechanism of royal nomination, election by the cathedral chapter, and papal provision—which did not always work harmoniously—in practice the episcopate was largely self-selecting. It was, very largely, a meritocracy, drawn from those who had distinguished themselves in royal service as administrators, diplomats, or court chaplains. To these were added a sprinkling of scions of aristocratic families who commended themselves not only by birth but by ability.

Up to the mid-fourteenth century the principal route to a bishopric was through service in one of the offices of state or household. The great majority of Edward III's bishops were 'king's clerks', promoted through the offices of the wardrobe, privy seal, and chancery, some of whom continued to serve as treasurers and chancellors when bishops. Although trained in the royal administration, already two-thirds were university *magistri*, and over the period 1375–1461 among the 128 bishops only 27 had not attended a university.[1] The reign of Richard II marked another watershed, for whereas many of those reaching senior bishoprics, whether *magistri* or not, had made careers as civil servants (men like Waltham, Bubwith, and Langley), by the fifteenth century an increasing proportion chose to remain at university for the further ten years required for a higher degree. This rigorous and sustained training produced an intellectual elite bound by a common discipline and a common ethic of service to Crown and Church. Most were canon and civil lawyers whose skills were first employed in diocesan administration as chancellors and notaries, and in the bishops' consistory courts, advancing to the royal service as diplomats and proctors at the papal court. The prerogative court of Canterbury (the 'Court of Arches') had become a veritable nursery for high fliers around 1400, best epitomized by Archbishop Henry Chichele. Those with degrees in theology were less serviceable in royal government, but found their way into the royal court as chaplains and confessors, roles universally filled by regular clergy in the fourteenth century but increasingly taken by those with doctorates in the fifteenth. Moreover, where lawyers had come to dominate the episcopate in the half-century after *c*.1380,

---

[1] W. A. Pantin, *The English Church in the Fourteenth Century* (Cambridge, 1955), 10, 15; R. G. Davies, 'The Episcopate', in Clough (ed.), *Profession, Vocation and Culture*, 51–89.

during the majority of Henry VI they were replaced by theologians—a change
reflecting both the personal preferences of the king and the transition from war
to peace. Once Oxford had been purged of Lollardy, its theologians were in
demand as apologists and preachers of a reinvigorated orthodoxy and instructors
in the *devotio moderna*. Over the period 1375–1461 as a whole, theologians
formed one-third of the episcopate, gradually progressing from the poorer and
middling sees, which were their traditional lot, to occupy a few of the major sees
like Norwich (1446), Lincoln (1450), Lichfield (1452), and Ely (1454).[2]

The pool of men with ability to lead the Church was not only replenished
through an educational ladder which allowed men like Hallum and Bekynton
to rise to positions of the highest spiritual and political influence, but by the
material rewards which sustained their prolonged ascent. Whether as king's
clerks in royal government or as officials and advocates in the archdioceses, each
amassed multiple offices and sinecure benefices before surrendering them on
elevation to a see.[3] Few or none attained Wykeham's level of income (estimated
at £873 per annum), but Crown and Church ensured that their services were
amply recompensed. Such proven careerists generally became eligible for a bishopric at the age of 35 to 45. At that point some felt released to spend the remainder of their lives in the care and rule of their diocese, and the late medieval
episcopate numbered a few renowned for their piety, learning, and pastoral care;
but for others the Crown regarded episcopal rank as giving additional weight and
dignity to a political role. All bishops had seats in parliament though not all
attended; normally some were royal councillors; and one or two might serve as
officers of state or ambassadors, or be in personal attendance at court. The archbishop of Canterbury had a pre-eminent and personal role as 'keeper of the
king's conscience'. Thomas Arundel is said to have told Henry IV, 'I am your
spiritual father and second to none after you in the realm, and you should accept
the advice of no one before me if it be good.'[4] This close identification of the
Church's leaders with royal government reflected the king's own role as the head
and protector of the Christian polity.

To this general pattern of an episcopate recruited from a long-serving intellectual and administrative elite, there were two exceptions. A handful or less of
regulars, either abbots of major monasteries or royal confessors from the unen-
closed orders, held Welsh and minor English sees. The days had passed when
Franciscans held Canterbury under Edward I. Secondly, towards the end of the
fourteenth century scions from some of the greater aristocratic families filled

[2] P. Heath, *Church and Realm* (London, 1988), 138–9, 335; Davies, 'Episcopate', 64–5; J. M.
George, 'The English episcopate and the Crown, 1437–1450', Ph. D. thesis (Columbia University,
University Microfilms, 1976), 37, 51–2.

[3] Pantin, *English Church*, 36–8; George, 'English episcopate', 38–40; *BRUO* 894, 157.

[4] Heath, *Church and Realm*, 230, quoting *Eulog. Hist.* iii. 407.

major sees. They were normally appointed through the personal influence of their father or relatives, often in their early twenties (requiring papal dispensation) when they were still in minor orders. To a careerist episcopate drawn mainly from the middling to lower social levels, their birth brought dignity and a measure of independence. While most had minimal academic training, they comprised men of outstanding ability who shaped and led the Church of their day, like Courtenay, Arundel, and Bourchier at Canterbury, and Beaufort at Winchester. If they figured more as politicians than as saints, they were prominent defenders of the Church's rights.[5]

Bishops were successors to the Apostles, and both their suitability and their service were of direct concern to the pope. From the thirteenth century the papacy had asserted the right to override election by the cathedral chapter by 'providing' a candidate of its own choice. While this afforded a safeguard against local pressures, in practice papal choice was largely restricted to the available field. Opposition to foreigners, especially to any who held the see *in commendam* and were absentees, became particularly strong after the removal of the papacy to Avignon; certainly the Crown could not contemplate having aliens among its bishops in the era of the Hundred Years War. While the king had perforce to recognize the papal power to provide, which none of the bishops could dispute, what mattered was how the choice was made and the outcome determined. Ideally (from the royal standpoint) the chapter should elect the royal nominee, whom the pope would then provide. But if the pope had his own preference, or wished to exact a price for his compliance, the process became a muddied competition between royal and papal candidates which could open the door to a *tertium gaudens*. English officials at the papal Curia often secured bishoprics in this way. The principal casualty was the independent wishes of the chapter. Both sides recognized the limits of their powers: the pope could not provide a candidate unacceptable to the king (who could withhold the temporal revenues of the see) nor the king insist on one deemed unsuitable by the pope (who would refuse provision). Any prolonged vacancy was a scandal, and if an impasse arose it could usually be resolved as further sees were vacated by death and translation. The variety of sees and the abundance of candidates allowed plenty of room for adjustment. Nonetheless, episcopal appointments were an important strand in the complex web of English politics and Anglo-papal relations, and shaped the fortunes of the Church at the highest level.

Throughout the 1360s Edward III had little difficulty in securing the bishops he wanted. King's clerks like Langham, Barnet, Brantingham, and Wykeham filled the offices of state and were provided to the principal sees. When the pope frustrated the proposed marriage of Edmund of Cambridge and Margaret of

---

[5] Pantin, *English Church*, 18–23; George, 'English episcopate', 26–31, for their social origins.

Flanders, Edward vented his displeasure by re-enacting the Statutes of Provisors and Praemunire in 1365 and repudiating the notional arrears of King John's tribute money. The renewal of war in 1369 further excited hostility to the Avignon papacy, and Gregory XI's demand in 1372 for a charitable subsidy of 100,000 florins produced a wave of strident anticlericalism. The parliament of 1371 had seen proposals for disendowment, the dismissal of clerical officers of state, and demands for the curb of papal provision. From 1373 the deadlock of pope and king over taxation spread to appointments, with Canterbury remaining vacant from 1374. The impasse was resolved in 1375 when John of Gaunt licensed the levy of the subsidy (for 60,000 florins) forbidden in 1372 in return for Gregory making a series of provisions to Canterbury, London, Salisbury and Worcester to accord with Gaunt's wishes—including the compliant Sudbury. The deal aroused the wrath of the Commons in the Good Parliament, who saw Gaunt and the pope as conniving to mulct the English Church.[6]

During the first years of Richard II's reign the leading bishops were called on not only to fill the offices of state but to serve on both the continual council and successive commissions to reform the administration. The council's financial incompetence provoked the rising of 1381, in which Archbishop Sudbury was murdered, to be replaced by the more resolute Courtenay. Thereafter the growing distrust between Richard's courtiers and the leading magnates inclined most bishops to occupy themselves in their sees rather than meddle at court. Only Courtenay attempted to reprove Richard for his government and his complicity in plots on Gaunt's life, thereby endangering his own. Courtenay also tried to mitigate the Crown's unremitting demands for taxation. Throughout the 1370s the clergy had, almost annually, granted tenths and poll taxes, and continued to do so throughout the next decade. But in 1383 and 1384 the archbishop repulsed attempts by the Commons to make their grant dependent on a matching contribution from the clergy. Courtenay thus continued to be a robust defender of the Church's interests.[7]

Neither from conviction nor constitutionally were most English bishops anxious to align themselves behind the king or the magnates in the crisis of 1386. Yet they could not escape involvement. Courtenay, Wykeham, and Brantingham formed a trio of elder statesmen on the parliamentary commission, while Alexander Neville of York stood by the king. It was the young Thomas Arundel of Ely, propelled by his brother, who emerged as the most partisan and vocal of the bench, occupying the chancellorship on the dismissal of Michael de la Pole. Fordham of Durham and Skirlaw of Wells were dismissed and replaced by

---

[6] Pantin, *English Church*, 84–91; Heath, *Church and Realm*, 124–7; G. Holmes, *The Good Parliament* (London, 1975), 7–20, 40–56, 139–49; *Rot. Parl.* ii. 337–40.

[7] J. Dahmus, *William Courtenay, archbishop of Canterbury, 1381–1396* (London, 1966); Heath, *Church and Realm*, 114–16, 190–2, 197–200, gives details of taxation.

Gilbert of Hereford as treasurer and Waltham as privy seal. When the king removed himself from London in 1387 Neville, Fordham, and his confessor Rushook of Chichester accompanied him. In November, as befitted their birth, Courtenay and Arundel attempted to mediate between the now hostile camps, but the rebellion and triumph of the Appellants sidelined the episcopate. Courtenay and his colleagues absolved themselves from participation in the treason trials, but could do nothing to save Archbishop Neville, who had fled, and Bishop Rushook, who was condemned to exile. The pope met the Appellants' wishes in removing them from their sees as part of a widespread shuffle which rewarded Arundel with York. Thus apart from the victims and the conspicuous beneficiary Arundel, the episcopate had sought to remain detached from political feuding.[8]

Richard's concern, after the events of 1388, was to strengthen royal control over appointments against internal and external pressures. Empowered by the Commons' protests, new enactments of the Statutes of Provisors (1390) and Praemunire (1393) imposed draconian penalties on those who obtained bulls of provision to bishoprics and benefices and who procured translations against the king's will. While acknowledging the papal power of provision and translation, convocation endorsed the king's protest against any infringement of the rights of his 'imperial crown'. In practice Richard was seeking to reassert his grand-father's disposal of sees for the Crown's servants, and in 1395–6 he was able to procure two series of translations—the second occasioned by Courtenay's death and Arundel's succession to Canterbury—which placed some household clerks (Tideman of Worcester, Merks, and Rede) in lesser sees and promoted his sup-porters, Medford, Stafford, and Waldby, to more important ones.

When, in 1397, Richard took revenge on the Appellants, Archbishop Arundel was the only bishop to be forcibly translated. The colourless Walden, the king's secretary, was provided in his place, but it was the translation of Richard Scrope from Lichfield to York while he was at the papal Curia on royal business, and of the aged Bishop Buckingham to Lichfield to make way for Gaunt's legitimized son Henry Beaufort, that reignited Richard's alarm. In both cases the king was presented with a fait accompli. On 27 May Richard wrote to the royal council to advise him on 'the translations which are now made in our realm'. The issue was to figure among the proposals for a concordat with the papacy agreed in November 1398. The pope undertook in future to provide those whom cathedral chapters elected if they had the king's approval; should the king reject the elect, the pope would provide some other liegeman whom the king could approve (but not choose). Thus, if he could overawe the chapter, the king could secure whom he wished; however, his wishes could be bypassed if the chapter connived with the pope to elect another candidate, though even then the king had a veto. All foreigners (e.g. cardinals and papal *curiales*) were excluded. In fact the concordat was not ratified by parliament before Richard was deposed.[9]

Richard's relations with his episcopate were generally distant. Although some of his confessors were confidants, he had little personal contact with the leading churchmen or concern with their problems of heresy and schism. Waltham (Salisbury), Stafford (Exeter), and Mone (St David's) served latterly in the offices of state, but royal policy was managed by laymen. Richard's revenge on Thomas Arundel was personal and did not extend to his colleagues. Apart from his financial exactions in 1397–9, when he secured three and a half tenths without the justification of wartime needs, Richard did not oppress the Church. After 1390 his principal concern was to control the choice of bishops, and from 1395 he filled at least seven sees, including Canterbury and York, with members of his *familia*. But virtually all the other senior sees (Bath and Wells, Durham, Ely, London, Norwich, and Winchester) were occupied by those appointed before 1389. Had his reign continued until 1406 five of these would have been vacated and he would have secured an episcopate of his choice. As it was, he counted on their acquiescence. But that made it easier for the Church to accommodate to the revolution of 1399.[10]

Arundel's personal fortunes were identified with the success of Henry of Lancaster, in whose company he returned in 1399 and whose seizure of the throne he was ready to justify. Papal support for his restoration to the archbishopric and the removal of Walden had already been assured, and on 13 October he crowned Henry and anointed him with the Holy Oil of St Thomas. Undoubtedly Arundel helped to frame the charges against Richard's kingship and the 'Record and Process' which recited his renunciation of the Crown. In this, and more extensively in the gravamina of convocation, Richard was represented as having oppressed the Church and compromised the Crown's regality by invoking papal authority to enforce the judgments against the Appellants. Henry now presented himself as the protector both of the Church's liberties and of its faith. Any expectations that Gaunt's son would support its critics were swiftly discountenanced, and the statutory penalty of burning for relapsed heretics was enacted in line with continental practice. King and archbishop thus joined forces to reassert the sanctified authority of Crown and Church as the basis for legitimate rule.[11]

[9] E. Perroy, *L'Angleterre et le Grand Schisme d'Occident* (Paris, 1933), 336–51, 419; R. G. Davies, 'Richard II and the Church in the years of tyranny', *Jnl. Med. Hist.* 1 (1975), 329–62; M. Harvey, 'The power of the Crown in the English Church during the Great Schism', in S. Mears (ed.), *Religion and National Identity*, SCH 18 (1982), 229–43.

[10] R. G. Davies, 'Richard II and the Church', in A. Goodman and J. L. Gillespie (eds.), *Richard II: The Art of Kingship* (Oxford, 1999), 83–106.

[11] R. L. Storey, 'Episcopal kingmakers in the fifteenth century', in Dobson (ed.), *Church, Politics and Patronage*, 82–98; Heath, *Church and Realm*, 224–32.

Yet Arundel had never been closely identified with the house of Lancaster, which had connived in the judgments of 1397 against him and his brother. Nor until 1404 did Henry have much opportunity to secure bishops of his choice. In 1401 he insisted that his companion in exile, Henry Bowet, should have Bath and Wells, and on Wykeham's death in 1404 Henry Beaufort, already chancellor, received Winchester and vacated Lincoln for the king's confessor Philip Repingdon. With the next vacancy, at London, royal interests were checked, for although Henry got Thomas Langley elected, the new pope, Innocent VII, insisted on providing Walden in compensation for his removal in 1399. For nine months the king refused him the temporalities; only after the execution of Archbishop Scrope in June 1405 did Arundel persuade the king to relent. Henry regarded Scrope as having forfeited ecclesiastical immunity by taking up arms, while Arundel, with his own case in mind, and foreseeing the scandal it would cause, strove to deflect the king. When that failed he sought to mitigate its effects, suppressing the excommunication of the perpetrators and eventually procuring the king's exoneration. But Henry's position was weakened, and the breakdown in his health increased his dependence on the archbishop.

During the years of emergency, to 1405, Henry's *familia* had been mainly military, while in the council he had relied on churchmen: Stafford and Beaufort as chancellors, Bowet and Mone as treasurers, and Clifford and Langley as keepers of the privy seal, with other bishops from minor sees. Arundel himself did not figure much before 1403. A series of vacancies in major sees in 1405–6 led to a fencing match with the new pope, Gregory XII, in which some sees remained unfilled for two years. Eventually Henry got York for Bowet, Bath and Wells for Bubwith, Durham for Langley, and London for Clifford, while Hallum was suitably placed at Salisbury. That filled the major sees for the remainder of the reign. Ultimately Henry had got the men he wanted, but more than once the royal fiat had been checked. His principal candidates revealed his preference for career administrators guaranteed to have a safe pair of hands. Beaufort and Arundel, though from a different background, had the same reliability.[12]

Up to 1407 Henry had needed to call on the Church not only to maintain his government but for money. In 1399 he had promised not to tax except in emergencies, but in the following years these multiplied, and in each year from 1401 to 1406 and again in 1408 the clergy paid a full tenth with halves in the other years. Magnates were repeatedly sent to inform convocation of the Crown's needs, while Lollard proposals to resume the Church's wealth were laid before parliament in 1410. Although Henry did not countenance such, they made the clergy more amenable.[13] Yet Arundel was as robust as Courtenay had been in defending

[12] R. G. Davies, 'After the execution of Archbishop Scrope', *BJRL* 59 (1976–7), 40–74; R. L. Storey, *Thomas Langley and the bishopric of Durham* (London, 1961), 14–20.

[13] Details in A. Rogers, 'Clerical taxation under Henry IV, 1399–1413', *BIHR* 44 (1973), 123–44.

the clergy's independence in granting taxation and its privileged status. From 1407 to 1410 he was the king's first minister and confidant, and used his position to promote the concerns of the Church. His high-profile campaign against Lollardy will be considered later; of perhaps greater significance was his commitment of the English Church to conciliar reform. In 1408 Henry was persuaded, with Arundel's advice, to abandon support for Gregory XII and in 1409 to dispatch an English delegation to the Council of Pisa. Apart from its leader, Thomas Langley, this was drawn primarily from Arundel's circle and included Bishops Hallum and Chichele, Prior Chillenden of Canterbury, and Abbot Spofford of St Mary's, York. All these were zealous reformers, with a programme of measures entitled 'Petitions for the Reform of the Church Militant' drawn up by Richard Ullerstone of Oxford, which was dedicated to Henry IV. The main emphasis of these was on reform in the diocese and parish, where episcopal authority had been overruled by papal intervention in granting dispensations, privileges, and exemptions, permitting the appropriation of parish churches, and promoting the trade in indulgences. The reformers sought a return to right order in the Church, enhancing the authority of the metropolitan. Although the council achieved no more than the election of a further pope, the English Crown and Church remained committed to reform through a general council.[14]

While a new generation of churchmen was forming around Arundel, many of whom were practising advocates in the Court of Arches, others like John Catrik and Thomas Polton were attached to Beaufort, the key figure in Henry's secular diplomacy.[15] As political issues divided the council and the king's health worsened, Arundel and Beaufort moved to opposite poles, the archbishop resigning the chancellorship in 1410 when Prince Henry and his Beaufort associates secured control of the council. Under Arundel the Church had an unusually prominent role in high politics, but he was also a pugnacious defender of its rights and an inspirational promoter of its spiritual and pastoral life.[16]

Despite having distanced himself from Prince Henry, Arundel in his final year won the new king's support for his two concerns, the suppression of Lollardy and English participation in a general council. Henry V was a rare phenomenon, a king ready to take a personal and directive role in the life of the Church. He himself believed fervently in the efficacy of prayer, and sought to mobilize the Church's resources—its patron saints, its monastic orders old and new, and its bishops with their flocks—in ceaseless intercession. It was to be a national effort, embracing all subjects and directed to fulfilling the spiritual and temporal

[14] E. F. Jacob, *Henry Chichele* (London, 1967), 6–13, 72–9.
[15] Harriss, *Cardinal Beaufort*, 65–6.
[16] For Arundel's career up to 1396, M. Aston, *Thomas Arundel* (Oxford, 1967); thereafter R. G. Davies, 'Thomas Arundel as archbishop of Canterbury', *Journal of Ecclesiastical History*, 24 (1973), 9–21. His spiritual leadership is discussed below, Ch. 10, sects. 4–5.

destiny of England. Within their dioceses bishops were ordered to call the faithful to pray 'for our victorious king of England, Henry V, faithful soldier of Christ and strongest striver after peace'.[17] The king as *miles Christi*, and the English as God's chosen people, were to assume the leadership of Christendom. Secular and religious service were fused in this enterprise: military victories were supported on a wave of prayer, and orthodoxy encouraged and enforced by royal authority. Hearts and minds were to be reclaimed for the Church by preaching, processions, and the incorporation of affective devotion into liturgical worship. To a remarkable degree Henry's bishops absorbed his vision: none more so than Henry Chichele, who founded All Souls College to train future generations of priests in making 'the famous kingdom of England formidable to its enemies and renowned among foreign nations'.[18]

If the Church was enabled to recover its nerve, it was also required to put its resources at the king's disposal. In material terms it granted Henry V as many tenths in nine years as it had to Henry IV in thirteen, though the burden on the laity was as heavy. Many of the bishops found their lives consumed by the pressures of war, diplomacy, and administration. Henry's special friend Richard Courtenay, bishop of Norwich, died at the siege of Harfleur, Hallum, and later Catrik, at the Council of Constance. No less than seven bishops and seven heads of religious houses were numbered among the English nation at the council.[19] Bishops like Kemp, Alnwick, and even Chichele remained for long periods with the king in France, and those aspiring to bishoprics like Morgan, Polton, and Fleming knew that service as royal envoys or proctors at the papal court would best recommend them. All these were now men with higher degrees in law, the product of the quiet revolution which Arundel had helped to foster. Those who held the fort at home, Beaufort and Langley as chancellors, Wakering and Ware as keepers of the privy seal, were more often administrators, but were worked as hard and similarly rewarded.

So central was the Church in royal policy that Henry insisted on having the bishops of his choice. The vacancy of the papacy until the end of 1417 had given the Crown a free hand in appointments, those elected being confirmed by the metropolitans. But the newly elected pope, Martin V, was determined to stem the tide of autonomy in national churches and gave notice that he would press for

---

[17] From Hallum's sermon at the chapter for the canonization of St Osmund in 1416, cited by E. F. Jacob, *Essays in the Conciliar Epoch* (Manchester, 1943), 79.

[18] J. I. Catto, 'Religious change under Henry V', in Harriss (ed.), *Henry V*, 97–115; id., 'The world of Henry Chichele and the foundation of All Souls', in id., *Unarmed Soldiery* (Oxford, 1996), 1–13; Jacob, *Chichele*, 17, for a quotation from the preamble to the statutes of All Souls College.

[19] Some appointed in October 1414, others in July 1416; Rymer (ed.), *Foedera*, ix. 162, 167, 369, 370; C. M. Crowder, 'Some aspects of the English nation at the Council of Constance', D.Phil. thesis (Oxford University, 1953), 110–63.

the repeal of the obnoxious anti-papal statutes, to restore 'the pristine liberty of the Church in England'. For the moment this issue was set aside. The English concordat signed in 1418 omitted all reference to papal rights of provision, confining itself to restricting indulgences, papal dispensations, and the appropriation of churches, matters close to the hearts of the English reformers.[20] Martin had perhaps too precipitately shown his hand by nominating Henry Beaufort as cardinal and legate *a latere* in England, hoping to install a papal agent at the heart of the English Church. This displayed an ignorance of Henry's character and of the historical situation in England. The king backed Chichele's defence of the primate's legatine authority and forced Beaufort to renounce the dignity and powers by the threat of praemunire.[21] Henry and Martin could cooperate in promoting those who had served their mutual interests. In an extensive series of promotions of royal clerks and papal *curiales* to sees during 1418–21, the only disagreement arose from Martin's refusal to provide Thomas Polton (whom he disliked) to London, insisting on Kemp. It produced a sharp exchange, Henry protesting that his request was reasonable, Martin that he could not be expected to do everything the king wanted. What Henry wanted above all was papal recognition of his claim to the crown of France. For that alone he might have been prepared to meet Martin's demand for the repeal of the anti-papal statutes; indeed before the king's final departure to France in 1421 he undertook to bring the question before the next parliament after his return.[22]

If Martin thought that Henry V's death would make his task easier he was mistaken, for the council of regency had neither the authority nor the inclination to make concessions over the statutes. On that council Henry V's bishops formed a powerful group. Chichele, Beaufort, Kemp, Morgan, and Wakering, with Langley as chancellor, were committed to his legacy and determined to keep the episcopate under their own control. Even the factions that developed, as between Beaufort and Gloucester, complicated rather than served the pope's plans. He might believe that Beaufort and Kemp were his allies, but they had their own agenda. Nonetheless, Martin pushed ahead, in August 1423 reminding the council of Henry V's promise and making some translations in minor Welsh sees. The vacancy of York on Bowet's death in October gave him his chance. In January the council signified its choice of their colleague Morgan, with the treasurer, John Stafford, replacing him at Worcester. Martin ignored this and translated Fleming from Lincoln. Whether this was a calculated challenge and a bid

---

[20] Jacob, *Chichele*, 36–8; id., 'A note on the English Concordat of 1418', in J. A. Watt, J. B. Morrall, and F.-X. Martin (eds.), *Medieval Studies Presented to Aubrey Gwynn* (Dublin, 1961), 349–58.

[21] McFarlane, *England in the Fifteenth Century*, 79–114; Harriss, *Cardinal Beaufort*, 91–100.

[22] R. G. Davies, 'Martin V and the English episcopate', *EHR* 92 (1977), 309–44; M. Harvey, 'Martin V and Henry V', *Archivum Historiae Pontificiae*, 24 (1986), 49–70.

to break up the patronage network, or whether he was simply repaying Fleming for his valued support at the Council of Pavia–Siena, is not clear. The council stuck to its guns, forbidding Fleming to accept his bull of provision under pain of praemunire. By October he had agreed to decline York and seek the recovery of his see at Lincoln. Martin could not so easily retract, without loss of face. Not until July 1425 was an acceptable solution found. Through Bedford's influence his chancellor in Normandy, Kemp, was translated from London to York, and the learned and aristocratic William Gray provided to London. Vacancies at Norwich and Ely enabled the council to reward Alnwick, the privy seal, and Morgan. These moves were only finalized in 1426 in the course of Bedford's visit to England to compose the Beaufort–Gloucester quarrel, and as part of an attempt to place relations with the pope on a new footing. Beaufort was removed from the chancellorship and made a cardinal. He was to leave England (though retaining the see of Winchester) and enter papal service abroad.

Martin saw the settlement of 1425–6 as marking a new era of compromise and cooperation, but again he was mistaken. When he forced Chichele to lay his demand for the repeal of the statutes before parliament in January 1428, he predictably gained no satisfaction. Effectually that brought papal attempts to an end. Chichele won sympathy from the peers, and Martin's grudging recognition of his fidelity to the Holy See, but he was no longer able to serve papal policy in England, for he had no power base in the council. Martin's distance from, and ignorance of, the political scene in England meant that he was always one step behind, and dependent on those who (like Kemp) were opportunists or (like Beaufort) were deliberately deceiving him.[23]

Beaufort's attainment of the cardinalate, along with permission to retain the see of Winchester, brought no objections from Chichele or the council. It was his political rival Gloucester who sought to bring charges against him under the 1393 Statute of Praemunire in 1429 and 1431–2. Having narrowly survived these attacks, Beaufort in 1433–4 secured parliamentary endorsement of his status, becoming the first of a succession of national cardinals that was to culminate with Wolsey. As 'cardinal of England', he steered the diplomatic search for a peace with France that would safeguard English claims, enlisting support from both the papacy and the Council of Basel. Even when the papal legates refused recognition of Henry VI at the Congress of Arras in 1435, English policy remained loyal to Eugenius IV and never endorsed the Basel *monitorium* to the pope in 1437 and its subsequent 'deposition' of him. Chichele's staunch papalism, and latterly that of Henry VI, ensured English fidelity to Rome. It also ensured papal compliance with the Crown's wishes in the matter of appointments. Bedford and Beaufort procured the election of the aristocratic Thomas

---

[23] Davies, 'Martin V and the English episcopate', esp. 333–44; Harriss, *Cardinal Beaufort*, 153–6.

Bourchier, canonically under age, to the see of Worcester in 1434, and of Louis of Luxembourg, the chancellor of Normandy, to that of Ely in 1436 to hold *in commendam* with that of Rouen, much to Chichele's disgust.[24]

After 1437 a marked change occurred in episcopal appointments. Throughout Henry VI's minority it had been highly trained lawyers who had filled the embassies to France, Germany, the Curia, and the Council of Basel, and whose patrons like Bedford and Beaufort had secured their promotion to bishoprics and the king's council. By 1440 the era of England's continental engagement was ending and the Crown's authority once more had a single source. The royal court now became a channel for advancement as the devout king sought to reward his confessors and chaplains, and these were theologians, rather than lawyers. From 1443 to 1450 eleven English sees were vacated, marking the passing of all but two (Kemp and Lacy) of those promoted before 1420, including Beaufort and Chichele. A new generation took their place. Secondly, there were many fewer translations between the middling sees. Only Bourchier occupied more than two sees between 1437 and 1460. In part this reflected a decline in papal intervention, but also more decisive control on behalf of the Crown, which likewise reduced the number of contested appointments. Up to 1450 this probably reflected Suffolk's control. In the 1450s open political faction determined the promotion of Bourchier to Canterbury in 1454, and in 1455 on Lacy's death John Hales, Queen Margaret's chaplain, secured provision to the see of Exeter, only to be supplanted in February 1456 by the duke of York's nominee, George Neville.

During the 1440s a series of appointments were smoothly handled, particularly where an incumbent's death could be anticipated and the Crown acted swiftly. The most remarkable instance was at Winchester in 1447 where, following Beaufort's death on 11 April, the king on the same day instructed the chapter to elect William Waynflete, who received papal provision on 10 May. In six other cases the interval between the election and provision of a new bishop was under five weeks, with neither the chapter nor the pope dissenting from the king's choice. The contrast with the preceding decades could not be more telling. Most had attachments to the court as preachers, confessors, and chaplains: Ayscough, Praty, Lowe, Lyhert, Kemp, Close, Boulers, Carpenter, and Pecock were all of this kind. Virtually all were theologians, though Booth was that rare exception a common lawyer, and Waynflete and Chedworth academics. Although fewer in number, the canon and civil lawyers like Moleyns and Bekynton continued to occupy the most prominent offices of state and diplomacy. From 1444 the changing character of the episcopate was reflected in membership of the council, where Ayscough, Boulers, Lowe, Lyhert, and Waynflete began to figure. It is

---

[24] M. Harvey, *England, Rome and the Papacy 1417–64* (Manchester, 1993), 158–63; Jacob, *Chichele*, 51–60.

arguable that these pious and academic men were political lightweights who lacked the legal training and international experience of their predecessors, though they were only tangentially implicated in the court's disastrous policies.[25]

In each reign the pattern of the episcopate can be seen to reflect the preference and policy of the monarch. These men constituted an intellectual, administrative, and, in a few cases, spiritual elite. To the making of royal policy they brought trained minds and a traditional ethic which viewed royal government in the context of Christian kingship. Nor did they forget that as members of the Apostolate they were subject to the pope, and although major confrontations between the two powers were avoided, over the century under review the verdict must be that royal control over the bishops steadily and inexorably increased. Kings as devout as Henry V and Henry VI, aspiring to the title of 'the most Christian king', promoted the vision of an English Church with its national saints, its distinctive rituals, its native bishops, and its pre-eminence in Christendom. The Crown was the symbol of its orthodoxy and piety, the protector of the Christian commonwealth against schism, heresy, and the infidel. For all this the bishops were its instruments, while papal authority was harnessed to this purpose yet at the same time marginalized. Martin V had sensed this enough to make a stand, but neither before nor after him could the see of St Peter stem the tide.

Their political functions meant that most bishops for some of the time, and some bishops for most of the time, were absent from their diocese. That did not affect its normal administration, which was directed by a vicar-general, who exercised the bishop's jurisdiction in the consistory court, and a sequestrator, who oversaw the legal rights and dues of the benefices. The local clergy came under the regional jurisdiction of the archdeacons, normally two or three within a diocese. The bishop's sacramental functions—ordination, confirmation, consecration—could be performed in his absence by a suffragan, frequently from one of the mendicant orders, who nominally held a see *in partibus infidelibus*. Neither did the bishop generally intervene in the cathedral church, which was administered by the dean and chapter of canons in secular cathedrals and the prior and convent where it was part of a Benedictine monastery. Even where his palace was close to the cathedral, most bishops chose to reside at castles and manor houses some distance away, to avoid friction over their respective rights. It meant that, parallel to the diocesan administration, the bishop had his own officials, a chancellor who presided over the bishop's own court, the 'court of audience', and a secretary or registrar.[26]

---

[25] George, 'English episcopate', 68–97; V. Davis, *William Waynflete* (Woodbridge, 1993), 15–16; Heath, *Church and Realm*, 335–7.

[26] A. Hamilton Thompson, *The English Clergy and their Organisation in the Late Middle Ages* (Oxford, 1947), 40–71; R. L. Storey, *Diocesan Administration in the Fifteenth Century*, St Anthony's Hall Publications, 16 (York, 1959); id., *Langley*, 167–76.

Historians have become wary of accepting contemporary complaint about absentee bishops neglecting their flocks. It is now agreed that many did reside, but since episcopal registers mainly record routine administration, the bishop's personal activity is often lost to sight. Even in the years of most intensive service to the Crown, say from 1409 to 1449, not more than half of the seventeen bishops were involved in government. High office certainly implied non-residence: long-serving chancellors like both Arundel and Kemp, who were archbishops of York, Langley as bishop of Durham, and John Stafford as bishop of Bath and Wells, barely found it possible to spend more than a couple of months during the summer recess in their dioceses. Yet before or after their periods in office each of these were assiduous diocesans. Some, like Edmund Lacy, shook off royal service with relief and rarely left their dioceses even to attend parliament.[27]

Of the bishop's diocesan functions, that with the highest profile was a visitation. This was essentially a disciplinary procedure, though it offered opportunities for exercising pastoral care. Canonically it was supposed to be undertaken every three years, though this was not observed, and to commence with the cathedral chapter. The bishop would then proceed to visit the non-exempt religious houses, collegiate churches, and hospitals in the diocese, leaving the parishes to the archdeacon's visitation. In practice full-scale episcopal visitations were rare: Arundel, though resident for most of his time as bishop of Ely, conducted only one visitation, and likewise Langley one during his thirty years as bishop of Durham. More often bishops delegated them to their commissaries, as too did archdeacons.[28] Metropolitical visitations by archbishops were much more likely to produce conflict because they suspended the ordinary jurisdiction of the bishop and took over all the diocesan administration. Neither Islip nor Sudbury had dared to conduct one, but on becoming archbishop Courtenay embarked on a vigorous and sustained programme to visit every see in the southern province. He began with that of Exeter in 1384, whose bishop, Thomas Brantingham, was a personal friend. Nevertheless, this developed into a prolonged and acrimonious confrontation from which neither emerged with credit. Courtenay conducted his visitation of other sees without incident until at Salisbury in 1390, finding himself openly challenged by Bishop Waltham, former keeper of the privy seal, the archbishop excommunicated him, and the rift was only healed by the mediation of the king and higher nobility. Both the formidable Arundel and the emollient Chichele restricted their visitations and aroused no opposition, but in the York province Kemp asserted his authority

---

[27] Aston, *Arundel*, 37, 287 ff.; J. A. Nigota, 'John Kempe: A political prelate of the fifteenth century', Ph. D. thesis (Emory University, 1973), 319 ff.; Storey, *Langley*, 21, 167, 211; E. F. Jacob, *Essays in Later Medieval History* (Manchester, 1968), 43.

[28] Aston, *Arundel*, 46; Storey, *Langley*, 182.

over the chapter in 1428 and attempted to override the immunity of the arch-deaconry of Richmond.[29]

The pastoral activity of bishops is often obscure. In its formal aspect it consisted of issuing pastoral letters, which often ordered prayers for a specific purpose—half of them for a royal army—and offered indulgences. Bishops were not bound to preach, though many did, or appointed theologians as diocesan preachers. Many, like Thoresby, Brantingham, and Chichele, made a point of conducting ordinations in person, though others left them to their suffragans. Bekynton examined candidates, to make sure they understood scripture, and at times prescribed additional study. Frequently they acted in a personal context, dealing with reprobate clergy, examining suspect Lollards, and interrogating fringe recluses and charismatics like Margery Kempe, or the soothsayer brought before John Stafford in Somerset. The bishop's court of audience was relatively informal and was used for composing quarrels between persons and rival ecclesiastical bodies. Bishops like Thoresby and Chichele had a reputation as mediators, not least in the family and matrimonial quarrels of the gentry and nobility: Courtenay imposed a penance on Reginald, Lord Cobham, for his irregular marriage with Eleanor, widow of Sir John Arundel.[30]

Because they were great territorial lords, bishops were also involved in local disputes over land, revenues, and rights with their lay neighbours, and the protection of their own tenants and officials and Church property. These could lead to violent confrontations, as in Yorkshire in the early 1440s when Archbishop Kemp employed mercenaries to defend Ripon 'like a town at war' against the men of Knaresborough in a quarrel with Sir William Plumpton and the earl of Northumberland. Bishops, like other lords, had their household knights and fee'd retainers, whose menacing behaviour and language shocked Margery Kempe. But their households could also be centres of piety, education, and learning in which clerks were nurtured. Archbishop Thoresby's provided the environment for the northern spirituality of the late fourteenth century and Bishop Hallum's for the liturgical revival of the early fifteenth. A few bishops of the wealthiest sees endowed a college at Oxford to stiffen the ranks of the clergy with highly trained priests, theologians, and legal administrators. Others endowed and built choir schools, colleges of priests, hospitals, and almshouses. They made bequests of money and books to individual colleges in both universities, and were also benefactors to their own cathedrals. Thoresby built the Lady Chapel at York, Langley renovated the Galilee and built the monk's dormitory at

---

[29] Dahmus, *Courtenay*, 107–60; Davies, 'Arundel as archbishop', 9–21; Jacob, *Chichele*, 23; Nigota, 'Kempe', 355–78, 476–82.

[30] Aston, *Arundel*, 45; Jacob, *Chichele*, 22; J. Hughes, *Pastors and Visionaries* (Woodbridge, 1988), 138; A. K. McHardy, 'Liturgy and propaganda in the diocese of Lincoln during the Hundred Years War', in Mears (ed.), *Religion and National Identity*, 215–27; Dahmus, *Courtenay*, 190–1.

Durham, and Chichele erected the south porch at Canterbury as a memorial to the generation who fought at Agincourt.[31]

The Church was thus ruled by a meritocratic elite, some of whom had humble and others aristocratic backgrounds. They included lawyers, theologians, administrators, and a few monks. What bound them together was fidelity to the Church's doctrine and discipline and service to the Crown. They defended the Church against anticlericalism and heresy and generally sought to distance themselves from opposition to the Crown and political partisanship. They were moderate and responsible men. A few, like Thoresby, Hallum, and Repingdon, were men of piety, and others like Rede, Lyndwood, and Pecock, men of learning. Bekynton, Gray, and Holes took note of humanism. As a body they did not waver in allegiance to the Roman see, but the best combined this with a belief in the local episcopate as the immediate authority for reform and governance, with minimum papal interference. This 'episcopalism', 'a sort of English Gallicanism', had strong historical roots, and was actively promoted by the Lancastrian kings.[32]

2. CATHEDRALS AND RELIGIOUS HOUSES

The secular cathedrals were governed by a chapter of canons headed by the dean. They formed an autonomous body, controlling lands and benefices which were separate from those of the bishop, and exercising jurisdiction within the precinct. Bishops were rarely present except on major liturgical feasts, and services were ordered by the dean. Canons held other offices: the chancellor, who kept the common seal, had responsibility for the cathedral school and was normally a man of some learning; the treasurer had charge of the vessels, vestments, and reliquaries in the cathedral treasury; and the precentor trained and led the choir. The cathedral fabric fund was managed by one or more chamberlains.[33]

The number of canons differed widely among cathedrals. Lincoln, Salisbury, and Wells each had over fifty; others had between twenty-four and thirty-six. Each canon was supported by a prebend, the revenue from either a cathedral manor or a parish church of which the prebendary was titular rector. Prebends varied greatly in value: the richest by far were at York, where that of Masham was worth £120 per annum, and numbers in the dioceses of Salisbury and Lincoln yielded £30 or £40, but many were a mere £3 or less. Only at Exeter were they all

---

[31] Nigota, 'Kempe', 509–17; Heath, *Church and Realm*, 326; H. Jewell, 'English bishops as educational benefactors in the late fifteenth century', in Dobson (ed.), *Church, Politics, and Patronage*, 146–68; Jacob, *Chichele*, 20, 96; Hughes, *Pastors and Visionaries*, 142.

[32] Harvey, *England, Rome, and Papacy*, 229; Jacob, *Essays in the Conciliar Epoch*, 81–2.

[33] Two works on the secular cathedrals are by K. Edwards, *The English Secular Cathedrals in the Middle Ages*, 2nd edn. (Manchester, 1967) and D. Lepine, *A Brotherhood of Canons Serving God* (Woodbridge, 1995). See also Hamilton Thompson, *English Clergy*, 72–100.

of equal value. Those canons who were resident were also supported by a common fund, which at Salisbury provided each with £10 or more per annum, though substantially more at York. They could also supplement their income from the fees for obits and anniversaries. From these various sources, and provided with a spacious house in the cathedral close, a resident canon could enjoy a comfortable lifestyle. Their obligations of hospitality were heavy, but some of those at York built up notable libraries and left substantial bequests in their wills.[34]

Only a minority of the canons were resident. After their initial 'greater residence' for a year, 'normal residence' occupied only half the year. Canonries did not have cure of souls and could be used to support clerks serving in the royal administration and papal Curia. At York well over half of the cathedral's income of £2,000 per annum was in the hands of absentees. Prebends were formally in the gift of the bishop, who used them to provide for his own officials and *familia*; but bishops found it impossible to resist papal provisions or royal nomination, exercised especially during the vacancy of the see. Competition for prebends was intense and the turnover rapid, most being held for not more than ten years. Papal provisions had reached a height in the mid-fourteenth century. Under Pope Clement VI (1342–52) provisions had numbered some 1,600, while the significant proportion of prebends held by foreigners, amounting to half in the dioceses of Lincoln, Salisbury, and York, fuelled vociferous complaints in parliament. Yet the statutes against provision in 1351, 1353, and 1365 did little to reduce the number, for Edward III continued to license some hundred provisors a year for the benefit of royal servants as well as papal officials. In fact provisors for English clerks greatly outnumbered those for foreigners, with the latter decreasing towards the end of the century. The Schism drastically reduced the number of provisions by Urban VI and his successors, and the terms of the proposed concordat of 1398 signalled the end of papal provision to prebends. By the fifteenth century most prebends were held by officials of the bishop and clerks in the royal service, 70 per cent of them being *magistri*.[35]

The permanent staff of the cathedral formed a self-contained community, devoted to the daily performance of the liturgical cycle, the *Opus Dei*. This was the same in both secular and monastic cathedrals, consisting of the seven canonical hours from matins to vespers and compline, interspersed with the celebration of Mass. The burden of this cycle fell less on the few resident canons than on the vicars choral, one for each of the canons, who numbered between twenty

[34] For York, see B. Dobson, 'The late Middle Ages, 1215–1500', in G. Aylmer and R. Cant (eds.), *A History of York Minster* (Oxford, 1977), 44–110; id., 'Residentiary canons of York in the fifteenth century', *JEH* 30 (1979), 145–73.

[35] For the effect of provisions on cathedral chapters, see Pantin, *English Church*, 59–64, 81–98; Perroy, *L'Angleterre et le Grand Schisme*, 328–9, 417–20; Heath, *Church and Realm*, 262–3, 348; Lepine, *Brotherhood of Canons*, 20–40.

and thirty at most cathedrals, though fifty at Salisbury. In the course of the fourteenth century this numerous and essential body was in many cathedrals constituted as a college, with a common hall, chapel, and individual rooms, as in the
Vicars' Close at Wells. This aimed to provide a framework for discipline and control, although at York it did little either to remove the celibate clerks from the
immoral temptations of the city or to improve their standard of performance in
the choir. As well as vicars choral, the cathedral was served by priests attached to
the many perpetual chantries, known as cantarists. The major secular cathedrals—Lincoln, St Paul's, York, Salisbury, Wells—each housed some sixty or
more chantries by the fifteenth century. Although separately endowed, the
priests who served them were brought within the jurisdiction of the dean and
chapter and assisted in the cathedral masses and commemorations. They too
came to be provided with a common lodging, the most notable of which was
St William's College at York, founded in 1461.[36]

Changes in the mode of singing in the late Middle Ages introduced a further
group, the lay clerks. Plainsong had traditionally furnished all liturgical needs,
but in the later fourteenth century English musicians, already acquainted with
the French isorhythmic motet, began to use polyphonic settings in parts of the
Mass and for votive antiphons. The liturgical use of polyphony was pioneered in
the cathedral and collegiate churches and private chapels, although the enthusi-
asts who trained themselves in it were few in number—perhaps no more than 200
in England as a whole. As, after 1400, polyphonic settings for High Mass, Lady
Mass, and the Marian antiphon came to demand a balanced choir, vicars choral
were supplemented by lay clerks who occupied the second or middle form, while
increasing emphasis was also placed on the role of boy choristers, notably in the
Lady Mass. It became the practice to appoint a permanent and professional
informator to train the choristers, rather than a vicar choral. English choirs, with
their 'sprightly concordance and angelic sweetness', acquired an outstanding
reputation on the Continent in the early fifteenth century, and a series of notable
composers like John Plummer, Lionel Power, and above all John Dunstable gave
liturgical unity to the ordinary of the Mass through a cyclic tenor. Royal and aristocratic chapels were the leaders, but at Lincoln Cathedral in the 1430s polyphonic music had become part of the regular repertoire, providing a constant
stimulus towards professionalism. The new polyphony was also welcomed as
moving away from abstract intellectualism towards a more personal devotion,
particularly in the Lady Mass and Jesus Mass and extra-liturgical Mary
antiphon. Yet not all welcomed it: regulars were instructed to sing 'with the
utmost gravity and in a sweet and tranquil style', rather than 'wanton melodies',

---

[36] Edwards, *English Secular Cathedrals*, ch. 4, pp. 56–7, 251–302; Dobson, 'Late Middle Ages',
89–97, for the 'Bedern' and St William's College at York.

and the nuns of Syon were told that their singing should be 'sadde, sober, and simple with all mekenes and devotion; organs shal they never have none'. Organs were becoming common by the mid-fourteenth century, and were used not for solo repertory or for accompaniment but for improvised fanfares. They were usually situated on the pulpitum, or in a gallery on the north side of the choir.[37]

By its nature the liturgical life of the cathedral was measured, repetitive, and self-contained. What degree of devotion informed its worship, and what religious fervour inspired its clergy, can only be guessed at. The laity could attend the offices, but beyond the choir it is not easy to gauge how these great buildings were used. Certainly pilgrims came to the shrines of the cathedral saint— St Osmund at Salisbury, St Hugh at Lincoln—and casual visitors could usually find a Mass being celebrated at one of the altars, while on Sunday afternoons public sermons were becoming popular. At the principal feasts there were impressive processions in which the local guilds and fraternities might participate. But how and whether in other respects the cathedrals provided a focus for the religious life of the diocese it is hard to know.[38]

In the religious life of late medieval England the monasteries had a traditional but not vital role. The regular service of God in the *Opus Dei* was no longer seen as the sole path to salvation, and no new orders and few new houses were established. Most still enjoyed the respect and patronage of the laity but only the Carthusians offered spiritual inspiration. Monastic houses were densely distributed over every county of England and Wales, and by 1300 numbered some 650. A few were large and wealthy but many were small, poor, and undermanned. The Black Death severely reduced the numbers of monks, perhaps from 9,000 to 4,500, and though this number had recovered to almost 7,000 by 1377, it then remained static until the dissolution. There were wide variations in the size and wealth of individual houses. The half-dozen largest Benedictine houses contained some fifty monks, and a second tier, along with those of the Cistercians, twenty to thirty. The houses of the Augustinian (or Austin) and Premonstratensian canons had generally fewer than twenty, but a large number of small priories and cells of all orders had fewer than a dozen.[39] In the *Valor Ecclesiasticus* (1535) the landed

---

[37] F. L. Harrison, *Music in Medieval Britain*, 2nd edn. (London, 1963), 147–77, 193, 210–19; M. F. Bukofzer, 'English church music of the fifteenth century', in A. Hughes and G. Abraham (eds.), *Ars Nova and the Renaissance, 1300–1540, New Oxford History of Music*, iii (Oxford, 1974), 165–213; R. Bowers, 'The music and musical establishment in the late Middle Ages', in C. Richmond and E. Scarff (eds.), *St George's Chapel Windsor in the Late Middle Ages* (Windsor, 2001), 177–90; Edwards, *English Secular Cathedral*, 303–17; Barnum (ed.), *Dives and Pauper*, i. 266–7.

[38] R. B. Dobson, *Durham Priory, 1400–1450* (Cambridge, 1973), ch. 1.

[39] D. Knowles and R. N. Hadcock, *Medieval Religious Houses: England and Wales* (London, 1953), 359–62; D. Knowles, *The Religious Orders in England*, ii (Cambridge, 1955), 255–62; J. A. Moran, 'Clerical recruitment in the diocese of York, 1340–1530', *JEH* 34 (1983), 19–54.

income of the monasteries was put at £100,700. Twenty-eight houses each had a gross annual income of over £1,000, half of them in the range £1,700–4,000, ranking them with comital and ducal estates. All except six were Benedictine houses, part of the first wave of monastic foundations in the tenth and eleventh centuries. At the other extreme 168 houses had an income of less than £50 per annum, and 79 (14 per cent) of less than £20.[40] If in one sense this mirrored the gradations of wealth in landowning society, in another it underlined the anomaly of their role. They were worldly 'possessioners' on a vast scale, but their vows of poverty, chastity, and obedience ostensibly set them apart from secular wealth and power. In this dilemma two courses were open to them: to distance themselves from lay society by practising stricter observance and seclusion, a course followed by the Carthusians, or to accommodate the monastic life to the rising material standards of the world around. To varying degrees, as far as their resources enabled them, the rest of the monastic orders chose the latter.

Taking the orders in turn, the Benedictines were the oldest and largest, with some hundred abbeys and conventual priories. Each house was autonomous, with its abbot solely responsible for maintaining its observance. The order enjoyed exemption from episcopal visitation, but had been subject to regulation and reform by successive popes from Innocent III in 1215 to Benedict XII in 1336, when the English houses had been organized as a province with triennial meetings of its chapter to monitor observance and discipline in each house—though there is little evidence of active intervention. Cluniac priories, established in the twelfth century, were directly dependent on the mother house in France, as were, in different degrees, the second wave of foundations, the Cistercians, Carthusians, and Premonstratensians. These links were first strained and then severed by the Hundred Years War and the Great Schism. The Cluniacs suffered worst. Their major houses were organized as a separated English chapter, but the Crown seized the smaller priories and cells along with other alien priories, and eventually their revenues were mostly transferred to royal monastic and collegiate foundations in the fifteenth century. The Cistercians, whose life of simplicity and manual toil had originally attracted large numbers of lay brothers (*conversi*), now followed a claustral life like the black monks, their lands leased to farmers and their *conversi* a vestigial remnant. After the Schism their seventy-five houses renewed contact with Cîteaux, but on an intermittent basis. The Premonstratensian canons, with similar ideals to the Cistercians but holding some 150 appropriated parish churches which they served as rectors and vicars, reacted to the Schism by organizing an English chapter for their thirty abbeys in

[40] D. Knowles, *The Religious Orders in England*, iii (Cambridge, 1959), 473–4; A. Savine, *English Monasteries on the Eve of the Dissolution*, Oxford Studies in Social and Legal History (Oxford, 1909), 270–88.

1. The Court of King's Bench c.1460

The principal criminal court presided over by the chief justice and four puisne judges. Clerks write up the rolls while one prisoner stands trial and others await their turn.

2. Warkworth Castle, Northumberland
Tower house, built by Henry Percy, 1st earl of Northumberland, *c.*1390–1405. The foundations of the unbuilt collegiate church are in the foreground.

3. Nunney Castle, Somerset
Built by Sir John de la Mare after 1373.

4. Silver Collar of SS
Worn by Lancastrian
retainers of armigerous
rank (*c.*1400–1450).

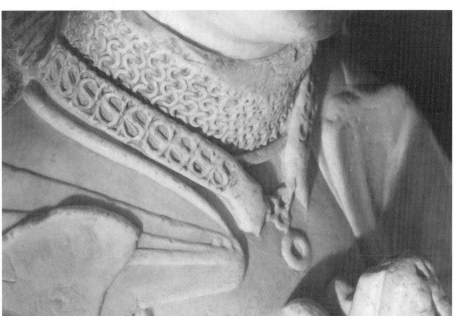

5. Effigy of Robert, Lord Hungerford (d. 1459), Salisbury Cathedral
Detail, showing the silver esses mounted on a leather or velvet strap which terminates in
buckles, linked by an ornamental trefoil and annulet, from which a badge could be suspended.

6. John, Duke of Bedford before St George

The Bedford Book of Hours was made to commemorate the duke's marriage to
Anne of Burgundy in 1423. John is depicted as Regent of France; he is making
obeisance to St George who, as patron saint of England and of the Order of the
Garter, wears the blue robe of the Garter.

7. Portrait by Jan Van Eyck
Painted in the 1430s, this has traditionally been identified as Cardinal Nicolo Albergati, but there are good grounds for supposing it to represent Cardinal Henry Beaufort (Malcolm Vale, 'Cardinal Henry Beaufort and the "Albergati" Portrait', *English Historical Review*, 105 (1990), 337–54).

8. Knightly Patronage of the Church (i)

The font in Blickling church (Norfolk) is adorned by lions similar to the one at the feet of Sir Nicholas Dagworth (d. 1402) on his nearby brass.

9. Knightly Patronage of the Church (ii)

The gateway to Norwich Cathedral Close commissioned by Sir Thomas Erpingham (d. 1429). In 1419 he had erected the window in the church of the Austin Friars, Norwich, commemorating the eighty-two noble families of Norfolk and Suffolk who had died without male issue since 1327.

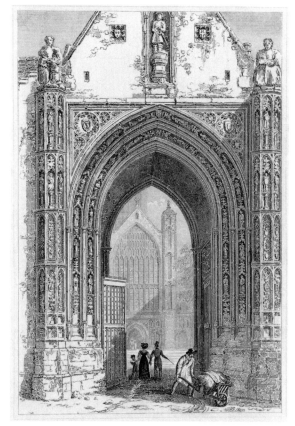

10. 'John Wyclif'
Initial at the beginning of a copy (*c.*1410) of *De Veritate Sacre Scripture*, made in Bohemia.

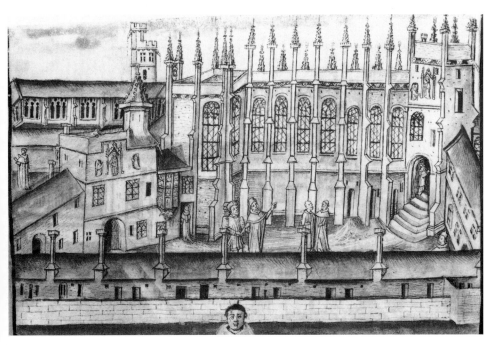

11. New College, Oxford, in the Fifteenth Century
Drawing in Warden Thomas Chaundler's manuscript (*c.*1461–5).

12. Sherborne Abbey, Dorset
The mid-fifteenth century fan vault in the choir is the earliest in existence in a major church.

1387, separated from Prémontré. The Austin canons numbered some 200 houses, mostly small though a few, like Leicester and Dunstable, were sizeable. Their economic and cultural life closely followed that of the black monks, and they had no ties with overseas houses. The Carthusian order, by far the smallest, was the only one to add to its houses by new foundations. Before 1370 it had only two, but in the next half-century six more were established, all by royal and aristocratic benefactors who were attracted by the brothers' pristine austerity. Carthusians lived as solitaries in cells around a cloister, observing strict silence and devoting themselves to prayer, contemplation, and individual labour. When Sir Walter Mauny founded the London Charterhouse in 1376 nobles, soldiers, courtiers, and London merchants all vied to build and endow the monks' cells. Over the following twenty years members of the nobility founded Charterhouses at Hull, Coventry, Epworth, and Mountgrace, and in 1415 Henry V established the largest, for forty monks, at Sheen. If this wave of aristocratic patronage had something of the whiff of fashion, it also made the order the prime source for the diffusion of new devotions, contemplative writing, and spiritual disciplines among the secular clergy and literate laity. English monasteries in the late Middle Ages were almost wholly native communities, organized and regulated by their national chapter, with minimal intervention from the Crown, the papacy, and their mother houses in France.[41]

After 1200 religious vocation passed to the mendicants. Theirs was an evangelizing mission, particularly to the urban laity. The Franciscans, embracing an ideal of complete poverty, converted by example, the Dominicans by new techniques of popular preaching; but in practice each borrowed from the other and both sought alms for sustenance. By the early fourteenth century the ideal of poverty had become a divisive issue, embroiling the Franciscans and the papacy in theological disputes over the absolute poverty of Christ and the Apostles as a model for the true Church. The Franciscans were able to adhere to their vow of corporate poverty by vesting their accumulated property in the papacy, while themselves enjoying the usufruct. But their popularity and growing wealth provoked outbursts of hostility among the secular clergy. One such had occurred in 1356–7 when Archbishop Fitzralph of Armagh had denounced their hypocrisy in fiery sermons at St Paul's Cross. The Austin friars responded vigorously with attacks on monastic possessioners in the 1360s, even advocating a partial confiscation of ecclesiastical wealth in the parliament of 1371 as a contribution to the

---

[41] Knowles, *Religious Orders*, ii. 3–13, 125–74. For Premonstratensians, see H. M. Colvin, *The White Canons in England* (Oxford, 1951), 232, 383–7; for Carthusians, E. M. Thompson, *The Carthusian Order in England* (London, 1930), 167–262. On the denization of the alien priories, see B. Thompson, 'Habendum et tenendum', in C. Harper-Bill (ed.), *Religious Beliefs and Ecclesiastical Careers* (Woodbridge, 1991), 197–238.

war. But when Wyclif urged the wholesale disendowment of the Church, the Austin friars joined the Dominicans in attacking his heresy. The Dominicans, under the influence of their greatest theologian, St Thomas Aquinas (c.1225–1274), had become the principal defenders of orthodoxy. Dominicans were foremost as royal confessors and chaplains, briefly giving place to the Carmelite friars favoured by the first two Lancastrian kings, an order originally eremitic but then similarly urban and academic. Yet while the mendicants enjoyed an influential position at court and in the universities, their greatest influence was over ordinary lay men and women. By 1350 the four orders had established 185 houses in England, probably containing some 5,000 friars. From these pairs of them travelled through the region preaching, hearing confessions, and soliciting alms. Their sermons were professional and persuasive, combining theological exposition with illustrative stories from daily life. Their readiness to mix with all social levels, to meet the spiritual needs of worldly men and women, to provide human comfort and promise prayers, all served to make religion part of the daily experience of the laity. Testimony to their success is provided by the bequests to them in numerous wills and in the size and enrichment of their churches, though of these virtually nothing remains. Yet their proselytizing and poverty made them butts for anticlerical satire and denunciations, exemplified in Langland and Chaucer and in the vitriolic attacks of Wyclif and the Lollards: as wolves in sheep's clothing, greedy in extracting money, adept at exploiting women's weakness, and complaisant as confessors. But direct evidence of their activity is scarce and the true measure of their influence escapes us.[42]

As with the friars, so with the smaller monastic houses whose internal records and buildings have mostly perished, there is insufficient evidence to assess their daily life. For this the historian is confined to a handful of major Benedictine monasteries whose conversion into cathedral chapters at the dissolution left their records largely intact. Those principally studied have been Christ Church Canterbury, Durham, and Westminster, flagship houses where, if anywhere, the vitality of late medieval monasticism can be assessed. Episcopal visitations of some lesser houses, particularly those of the diocese of Lincoln in the first half of the fifteenth century, afford a supplementary, though possibly less objective, insight.[43]

---

[42] A. Gwynn, *The English Austin Friars in the Time of Wyclif* (Oxford, 1940), 75–90, 211–16; Knowles, *Religious Orders*, ii. 61–73, 90–114; J. Rohrkasten, 'Londoners and London mendicants in the later Middle Ages', *JEH* 47 (1996), 446–77; W. Scase, *'Piers Plowman' and the New Anti-Clericalism* (Cambridge, 1989).

[43] R. A. Smith, *Canterbury Cathedral Priory* (Cambridge, 1943); Dobson, *Durham Priory*; id., 'The English monastic cathedrals in the fifteenth century', *TRHS* 1 (1991), 151–72; id., *Church and Society in the Medieval North of England* (London, 1996), 47–82; Knowles, *Religious Orders*, ii. 204–18.

By the late Middle Ages the larger houses were regulating their size to correspond with their largely stable incomes. Novices entered between the ages of 18 and 21—child oblations had long ceased—often having attended the almonry school. Most were drawn from the villages of the abbey's estates, although Westminster received numbers from London. The great majority came from the middling ranks of rural and urban society, all being freemen's sons; very few came from chivalric society, perhaps reflecting the worrying dearth of male heirs at this level. There was no tradition, as in Germany, of closed aristocratic communities, and English monks were in general of non-noble birth. Their novitiate lasted six to seven years, during which they learned the liturgical usages of the house, studied grammar, read the Bible and commentaries, and perhaps learned illumination, but had no specific spiritual training. On ordination they entered into the full life of the house as a cloister monk, attending the daily cycle of offices in the choir. A select few who showed aptitude would be sent to university. The lifespan of a monk was generally thirty-four to thirty-eight years from profession, i.e. to their middle to late fifties.

The life of the cloister monk was framed around the Divine Office, a cycle of psalms, prayers, and Bible readings at fixed hours. This began with matins and lauds at midnight or before dawn, resumed with prime between 6 a.m. and 7 a.m., followed by terce, sext, and nones at the appropriate intervals; then vespers at 4 p.m. and compline after supper at 7 p.m. or 8 p.m. Within this non-sacramental liturgy Mass was celebrated at the daily chapter at 9. 30 a.m., a High Mass at 11 a.m., and the Mass of Our Lady with professional cantors and choristers and increasing polyphonic elaboration. By the late fourteenth century mechanical clocks, first introduced at Durham and Salisbury, regulated the timing with precision. The afternoon interval might be occupied with reading and copying, taking communal walks for recreation, or even forms of sport. At the morning chapter common business was decided, largely by a committee of seniors, and defects in the daily life reported and reproved. Throughout the day cloister monks would also be saying Mass at numerous altars, some dedicated to various saints, others being chantries, though many of the latter would be served by secular priests. Perhaps only two-thirds of the community were present at the choir offices, those in charge of the administrative offices—the obedientiaries—being partially excused. At Durham and Canterbury there were twenty-five major officers, some with subordinates; at Westminster 60 per cent of the monks held office of some kind. Such were the sacrist, cellarer, precentor, refectorer, infirmarer, master of the novices, and many more. These were the more senior monks, appointed by the abbot, accountable to him, and forming a kind of ruling council. In the thirteenth century those in charge of the spending departments had been given the management of particular estates, acting—like the monk in Chaucer's Shipman's Tale—as bailiffs away from the monastery on business.

When, in common with other landlords, the monasteries abandoned direct management and turned to leasing, over the period 1380–1420, the obedientiaries
became merely rent receivers with less cause for absence. But in most houses the
system continued until the dissolution, the privileges of office and status being
hard to relinquish.

The abandonment of direct management was determined by the individual
needs and regional economy of each house. The period of manorial stability and
continuing profits after the Black Death had ended with the fall in grain prices in
1375, demands for higher wages, and a surge in peasant mobility, which pushed
monastic landlords reluctantly towards leasing. This change was generally initiated on the furthest, cash-producing manors, with the home farms which provided the monastery's food being retained in hand well into the fifteenth century.
At Battle Abbey twenty-eight manors were at farm by 1382–3, and at Christ
Church Canterbury, Prior Chillenden carried through a wholesale changeover
between 1391 and 1396. At Durham the crucial years for leasing were from 1408
to 1416, and Westminster had leased most of its demesnes by 1420. But on the
Wessex chalklands the large sheep farms of Winchester and Lacock were kept in
hand until the collapse of wool prices in the mid-fifteenth century. The effect on
monastic finances was variable: at Ramsey and Leicester it produced a steep
decline, but at Canterbury, Durham, and Westminster the demesnes were let at
good rents on short leases, administrative costs were reduced, and the monasteries enjoyed a period of stable income and prices. Many of the lessees were experienced local farmers, and the abbeys employed lay stewards and auditors who
answered directly to the abbot or bursar. The obedientiaries would now receive
their revenues from the central receipt, and though incompetence or dishonesty
could imperil the finances of a department or even of the monastery itself, as at
Durham in 1438, in general financial administration was competent.[44]

What was lacking was new sources of revenue. Over the preceding centuries
the revenues of numerous parish churches had been appropriated to religious
houses. The greater tithe (two-thirds of the value) went to the monastery, the
lesser tithe and offerings provided for a vicar who was instituted by the monks.
Already by 1291 some 1,500 of the 8,100 parish churches were served by vicars,
and a new wave of appropriation by papal licence occurred in the early fourteenth
century. By 1400 Durham was drawing at least £400 from its appropriated
churches, and Westminster a comparable sum. By then most of the wealthier
parish churches had been appropriated, and further endowment (as at

---

[44] Knowles, *Religious Orders*, ii. 309–30; Smith, *Canterbury Priory*, 192–200; Dobson, *Durham Priory*, 272–300; B. Harvey, 'The leasing of the abbot of Westminster's demesnes in the late Middle Ages', *Econ. HR* 22 (1969), 17–27; F. R. Du Boulay, *The Lordship of Canterbury* (London, 1966), 218–32; J. Raftis, *The Estates of Ramsey Abbey* (Toronto, 1967), 259–91.

Westminster and Sheen) could only come by royal grants of revenues from suppressed alien priories.[45] Gifts of land by the aristocracy had already dried up before 1350. Another source of external funding was the offerings at the shrine of a patronal saint. At Canterbury the shrine of St Thomas received an average of £545 per annum during the years 1370–83, although by 1436 this had fallen to £66 and by 1444 to £25. In the fourteenth century Gloucester had benefited from pilgrims to the shrine of Edward II, and at Durham that of St Cuthbert attracted pilgrims from all over the north, as did York after the martyrdom of Archbishop Scrope in 1405. At Westminster, the Confessor's shrine, though richly furnished with relics of great value, never attracted such popular devotion: offerings reached a height of £120 in 1372–3 but had declined to £23 in 1397–8. All monasteries derived a steady modest income from the endowment of obits, anniversaries, and chantries, but in general the laity were directing their donations for commemorative masses elsewhere.[46] With a relatively stable income and a ceiling on the number admitted, the late medieval monastery provided a standard of living comparable to that of the gentry, while the greater abbots lived in baronial style. In an age of personal prosperity this might be thought unexceptionable; even so, by the fifteenth century relaxations of the monastic regime had become institutionalized, fundamentally changing its character.

Meat-eating had a central significance, for it affected the communal life. The Rule prohibited it in the refectory, but Benedict XII had permitted it in an additional chamber, the misericord, so long as at least half the community were eating in the refectory. By the early fourteenth century the refectory was generally depleted at many of the major Benedictine houses except at the major feasts, and at Westminster it was actually partitioned to provide a separate room for meat-eating. There, two meals were served each day, a dinner at 11 a.m. and a lighter supper, though the latter was prohibited from Advent to Easter and during Fridays and fasts. In the refectory the dishes were of two kinds, 'generals' and 'pittances', the former often being a pottage of pieces of meat or fish and root vegetables, with bread and ale, the latter consisting of fish or fowl (not regarded as meat). Fish was served on three days of the week, normally cod, and some of it salted (stockfish). On the other four days the monks could eat flesh meat in the misericord on alternate days, in rota; it was generally freshly bought and was roasted, stewed, or boiled. The portions served were generous, 2 to 3 lb in weight, mutton being more often served than beef, pork, and veal. Fresh fruit and leaf vegetables seem to have been rarely eaten, but dairy products—milk, cheese, and eggs—were consumed in large quantities, often made into puddings.

[45] Colvin, *White Canons*, 276–87; Knowles, *Religious Orders*, ii. 290–1; Harvey, *Westminster Abbey*, 49–53; Dobson, *Durham Priory*, 268; Smith, *Canterbury Priory*, 11.
[46] Smith, *Canterbury Priory*, 12; Dobson, *Durham Priory*, 29; Harvey, *Westminster Abbey*, 34–5, 42–3.

Averaged over seven dinners and five suppers eaten in both refectory and misericord, the monk was served with just under 2 lb of meat a day, and his food intake
averaged c.6,210 kcal, a level considerably higher than normal today. Such a diet,
with its high protein content and marked deficiency in Vitamin C, was similar to
that eaten in an aristocratic household. His liquid intake was also considerable,
with a daily allowance of 1 gallon of ale and, on feast days, 2 to 3 pints of wine.
The cost was correspondingly high, an annual average for each monk for food of
£11, or 7d. per day, i.e. double the wages of a labourer. Such figures relate to the
portions of food and drink provided, and the question remains what proportion
if any was left over for servants and charitable distribution. It has been suggested
that this may have amounted to as much as 25 per cent on fast days and
40 per cent on other days, reducing his energy intake to more normal proportions,
but on this point evidence fails. Moreover, the Westminster monks were at the
top of the league; in the smaller and poorer monasteries there were continual
complaints about the quality of the food. Nonetheless, Chaucer's robust and
virile monk may well have been typical.[47]

It was also customary from the thirteenth century for the monk to receive a
wage allowance for clothes and spices, and payment for chantry duties, obits, and
funerals, amounting in all to some £2 or £3 per annum. This enabled him to own
a few books, or keep a boy servant, or be fined for breaches of discipline. Along
with personal possessions went the desire for privacy. Some obedientiaries,
elderly monks, and university graduates might be provided with carrels for study
or even rooms in which to take their meals. These could also be used for conviviality in the recreational space after compline, before bed, and even to entertain
women. The presence of women in the cloister was evidence of the collapse of
the enclosed life, so frequently noted in the visitation records of lesser houses.
But in the larger, urban monasteries too, the life of the town invaded the precinct
(nowhere more so than in Westminster) and monks freely visited friends,
taverns, and even brothels in the town. Durham, under the rule of Prior
Wessington, was an honourable exception. Holidays were taken at the abbot's
rural manors, or at a daughter house like Finchale near Durham, and four or five
times each year each monk retired to the infirmary for the institutionalized
bloodletting, or 'seyney', while some visited their families. The monastery
employed a body of servants, at least equal in number to the monks. Although
episcopal visitations of the non-exempt houses in Hereford, Lincoln, and Wells
dioceses provide evidence of apostasy, sexual immorality, factions, disorders,

---

[47] Knowles, *Religious Orders*, ii. 4; B. Harvey, *Living and Dying in England, 1100–1540* (Oxford,
1993), 34–71; M. Threlfall Holmes, 'Durham Cathedral Priory's consumption of imported goods',
in Hicks (ed.), *Revolution and Consumption*, 147; C. Harper-Bill, 'Complaints about diet in late
medieval English monasteries', in id., *The Church in Pre-Reformation Society* (Woodbridge, 1985),
95–107.

debt, and the neglect of liturgical observance, in the larger abbeys and cathedral priories the steady round of canonical hours and the ceremonial of the great feasts was conducted with professional solemnity.[48] Although the books written and copied in the Benedictine houses were almost wholly for internal use, some Carmelites and regular canons (like John Mirk) produced works of pastoral instruction while the Carthusians disseminated a growing devotional literature.[49] To the question whether the monasteries as institutions were meeting the expectations of lay society no easy answer is possible. Only Wycliffites attacked monasticism itself, and disendowment was never more than a threat; but there persisted an undercurrent of detachment from, and disillusion with, these great monuments to the unquestioning piety of a former age.

Although the validity of clerical possessions had first been questioned during the controversy over Apostolic poverty, it was the concurrence of heavy war taxation and Wyclif's denunciation of 'possessioners' that made it a lively issue in the years from 1370 to 1410. Thereafter Henry V's eradication of support for Lollardy among the political class lifted the threat of disendowment from this quarter, despite his own heavy taxation. Discussion of this is best left to later. At the same time Henry raised the other spectre, of reform. He wanted a monasticism of pristine holiness and discipline, to provide effective and unceasing prayer for his kingship. Such was the role of his own Carthusian foundation at Sheen, and it was partly on the prompting of the prior of Mountgrace that he ordered the chapter of the Benedictines to convene during the parliament of 1421 on his final brief visit. Sixty prelates and more than three hundred proctors and theologians heard the king chide them for their negligence and recall them to the ancient devotion which had earned them benefactions from his ancestors. With the king desperate to raise money for the next phase of the war, and parliament reluctant to grant it, the abbots were made to feel that they enjoyed their endowments on royal sufferance. Characteristically, Henry specified in detail the reforms he wanted on the basis of Benedict XII's constitution of 1336: in meat-eating, dress, the abolition of wages and private rooms, the curtailment of extra-claustral visits, and many other entrenched abuses. In the event the king's providential death spared the monks further pressure for reform until Thomas Cromwell's later, similar injunctions prefaced their suppression.[50]

Despite the separation of the estates and finances of abbot and convent, and

---

[48] For these aspects, see Knowles, *Religions Orders*, ii, ch. 18; Dobson, *Durham Priory*, 79, 121, 234–8; Harvey, *Living and Dying*, 78–80, 97–8, 150–2. For visitations, see Knowles, *Religious Orders*, ii. 204–18; C. Harper-Bill, 'Cistercian visitations in the late Middle Ages', *BIHR* 53 (1980), 103–13; and id., 'Monastic apostasy in late medieval England', *JEH* 32 (1981), 1–18.

[49] A. I. Doyle, 'Publications by members of religious orders', in J. Griffiths and D. Pearsall (eds.), *Book Production and Publishing in Britain, 1375–1475* (Cambridge, 1989), 109–23.

[50] Knowles, *Religious Orders*, ii. 175–84; *EHD* iv. 787–90.

the physical removal of the abbot to a separate house, the abbot remained its legal persona, and commanded the absolute obedience of the monks. The leading abbots and priors formed a group of twenty-seven parliamentary prelates, and although collectively their political influence was negligible, individuals acted as royal counsellors and even confidants: Thomas Chillenden of Canterbury with Richard II, Philip Repingdon of Leicester with Henry IV, Thomas Spofford of York to Henry V, and Reginald Boulers of Gloucester to Henry VI. But the Crown rarely sought to influence the election of an abbot, and the papacy abandoned the attempt to provide. The election was left to the convent, which usually chose one of the more senior office-holders who was likely to be in his forties, although John Whetehamstede was only 27. An abbot set the tone of the whole community, though he was often resident for less than half the year in the abbey. His lodging formed a large, detached complex, built to the highest standards of comfort and architectural refinement. In addition he had manor houses on his estates, one or more of which were often his habitual residence, where groups of monks might be invited for periods of refreshment. The abbot maintained his own household of esquires, yeomen, and grooms; he had his own receiver and auditor, and drew his counsellors from the local gentry and lawyers. His prominent position involved him in expensive hospitality. Great houses like Canterbury, St Albans, and St Swithun's, Winchester, on the main routes were accustomed to a stream of visits from the king and aristocracy, and from justices, royal officials, and military captains, but even the smaller houses found themselves offering hospitality, sometimes prolonged, to the nobility of their region. The Premonstratensian abbey of Halesowen entertained Lord Dudley and his wife for a week in 1361. The reception of all save the humblest guests fell to the abbot, and the rebuilding of many abbatial lodgings, as at Durham between 1424 and 1436, provided 'a style of living not easily matched elsewhere'.[51] Doubtless prelates like de la Mare and Wessington took such quasi-baronial status in their stride without compromising their integrity and vocation, but at smaller houses the abbot's self-indulgence, hunting, and keeping of women reveal the corrosive effects of his wealth and independence.

Inevitably abbots were involved in the bastard feudal politics of their region. Land disputes either with the abbey's own tenants or with local landowners protected by a lord could embroil the abbot in a confrontation at the highest level. If this resulted more often in expensive litigation than open violence, the community and its tenants were inherently vulnerable, as in Sir William Claxton's unofficial siege of Durham Priory in 1419 and Sir Henry Hussey's attack on the small Premonstratensian house of Durford under Henry VI. Lesser monasteries sought the protection of great magnates, as did Welbeck that of John of

---

[51] Dobson, *Durham Priory*, 102 (for quotation); Colvin, *White Canons*, 311 (for Halesowen).

Lancaster in 1411, while a major figure like the prior of Durham sufficiently commanded the respect and trust of local magnates to act as mediator in the quarrels of the Neville family in the 1430s and between the violent border families of Heron of Ford and Manners of Etal. Despite their own inferior birth, the wealth, power, and spiritual dignity of the abbot of a major house, supplemented by his own personal charm (like that of Abbot Clown of Leicester, the friend of John of Gaunt) or conspicuous ability (as with de la Mare), gave them natural influence at the highest level.[52] As the monasteries became increasingly integrated into the social world of the landowning class, their *raison d'être* as witnesses to the ideal of spiritual withdrawal began to fade. But they continued to fill a role in the social and ecclesiastical landscape which few thought to challenge for another century.

Their poorer sisters, the nunneries, numbered some 140 in all, with a total population of over 2,000, though almost half of them contained ten or fewer inmates, and only four had over thirty. There was a similar contrast in wealth, the top seven having incomes of £450 per annum and more, while at least half the remainder counted on less than £100 and some only half that. This largely reflected their historical origins and location. Of the wealthiest seven, five were Benedictine houses in the Anglo-Saxon kingdom of Wessex, the other two being royal foundations, Dartford by Edward III and Syon by Henry V. A second wave of foundations in the twelfth century spread houses of all orders over central and northern England, most of them small and founded by local lords. This made for major differences in their lifestyles. The large, wealthy, southern houses attracted women of high social rank or from prosperous merchant families; they were in general well run and some like Syon and Dartford became intellectual and spiritual centres. Since they were exempt from visitation there is little direct evidence of their daily life. Visitation records of the smaller, non-exempt houses in the Midlands show them facing many of the same problems as the monasteries. These included the substitution of the misericord for the frater and the grouping of nuns into 'familiae' for meals, the increase of privacy in rooms, and the growth of possessions including some personal wealth from gifts and annuities. Likewise the abbess now occupied a separate establishment with a freer lifestyle matched to the demands of hospitality and administration, while in some houses aristocratic widows became paying guests for longer or shorter periods. Gender induced differences in two respects. First, the nuns were overwhelmingly of gentle birth, often from local families who had paid a dowry of some £12 to £20 at their profession. Secondly, as a consequence, there was persistent tension over the ideal of enclosure. The Church's deep unease over

---

[52] Dobson, *Durham Priory*, 188–9, 194, 197–201; Colvin, *White Canons*, 299–301; Knowles, *Religious Orders*, ii. 39, 186.

female sexuality had produced, in the bull *Periculoso* (1299), a rigorous prohibition against going beyond the convent walls and of any but the most limited
visits of laity from outside. In practice the nuns largely refused to apply this, and
by the fifteenth century episcopal injunctions were content to set limits on visits
to relatives, and within the convent to place certain areas out of bounds to
visitors. Clearly in some houses a good deal more freedom than this was usual,
the more so if the house was a social and spiritual centre in a local community.

What can be said of their spiritual and intellectual life? Most of the nuns were,
of course, *illitteratae*; they had no Latin and sang the offices by rote, and they could
not read or copy Latin works of theology. Where they formed part of a double
house, as at Dartford and Syon, they were well instructed by the lay brethren, but
in smaller houses much time must have been passed in reading, clothes-making,
embroidery, and the nurture of their small school of young children. It might have
been supposed that the emergence of works of meditative piety in the vernacular
like those of Rolle and Hilton, and the translations of those of St Bridget,
St Catherine of Siena, and others, would have stimulated female devotional
practice and writing. Undoubtedly in some convents these works were read and
owned, and a few devotional works like Gascoigne's *Myrrour of Our Lady* were
specifically written for nuns; yet those for whom Rolle and Hilton wrote were
anchoresses, not conventuals, as was Julian of Norwich herself. We cannot point to
any conventual who had a similar role as spiritual model or mentor. It is possible
that the intellectual freedom, the exploration of the inner self, and even the opportunity for private meditative prayer from which mystical experience sprang were
only truly available outside the routine of the choir and the society of the convent.[53]

3. PERPENDICULAR REBUILDING, 1360–1461

No cathedral or abbey was rebuilt in its entirety in this century, and of the new
religious foundations—from St Mary Graces and the London Charterhouse
under Edward III to Henry V's Sheen and Syon—nothing now remains. The
ubiquity of Perpendicular, 'the first truly national style', is manifested in innumerable parish churches rather than in major ecclesiastical buildings. In the
latter it was mostly employed to replace—or more often to reconstruct—the surviving Romanesque parts of the main church, to enlarge the profile with towers,
or to add subsidiary elements in the monastic precinct. Rebuilding was less often
prompted by fashion than by necessity. Nowhere was the Gothic work of the

---

[53] E. Power, *Medieval English Nunneries* (Cambridge, 1922) is still essential for their internal
organization in this period. Recent studies have focused on the spiritual and conventual life; see P.
Lee, *Nunneries, Learning and Spirituality in Late Medieval English Society* (Woodbridge, 2000); M.
Olivas, *The Convent and the Community in Late Medieval England* (Woodbridge, 1998); H. Leyser,
Medieval Women (London, 1995), chs. 9, 10.

preceding century and a half destroyed, the new work being consciously adapted (as at Canterbury and York) to match its proportions or even (at Westminster) to reproduce its style. Often (as at Gloucester and Winchester) a Perpendicular interior encased older masonry or rested on pre-existing foundations. So too in its style, Perpendicular might be claimed to be a pragmatic development from the French Rayonnant of the later thirteenth century, of which the nave at York (1291–1360) represents the best English example. Even so, it was manifestly a total reaction from Decorated and uniquely English.[54]

The earliest extant building in the new style is the south transept and choir at Gloucester, the former constructed 1331–5, the latter completed in 1351–60. There not only the defining architectural features but the total experience of Perpendicular is immediately recognizable. The old Romanesque gallery was clothed in a veneer of rectangular panelling formed by mullions carried down from the heightened clerestory windows to the top of the arcade. In the great east window, the largest in medieval Europe, the dominance of the principal mullions of the central section, reaching to the curve of the arch, is similarly offset by multiple horizontal transoms to produce a rectangular grid (some have termed the style 'rectilinear' rather than 'perpendicular'). The vault, with its dense network of ribs, carries the upward thrust of the shafts to the apex of the roof where a longitudinal lattice of ribs and bosses runs the length of the choir. The total effect is one of stateliness and tranquillity, and of exaltation in the enclosure of a vast light-filled space.[55] Even if it be deemed functional, repetitive, and at times mechanical, such an architectural form which harmonized both length and height was well suited to late medieval cathedrals. Where did it originate and why was it so rapidly and universally adopted?

The first indications of the new style have been discerned in the window tracery of the cloister and the buttresses of the chapter house at old St Paul's and the panelling at St Stephen's Chapel, Westminster, around 1331–2 (both destroyed but recorded in later engravings). These were under royal patronage, and it must have been masons from this workshop who carried the style to Gloucester, which had become the resting place and shrine of Edward II.[56] That the style was favoured by the manly and martial Edward III, who used it at Windsor, is perhaps sufficient explanation for its adoption and diffusion by the king's masons, who in

---

[54] J. H. Harvey, *The Perpendicular Style, 1330–1485* (London, 1978). For its derivation from Rayonnant, see F. Woodman, *The Architectural History of King's College Chapel* (London, 1980), 9–12, 163–73, and C. Wilson, *The Gothic Cathedral* (London, 1992), 184–7, 210.

[55] On Gloucester, see Harvey, *Perpendicular Style*, 78–9, 85, 90–1; Wilson, *Gothic Cathedral*, 201–8, 212.

[56] J. M. Hastings, *St Stephen's Chapel* (Cambridge, 1955), 53–9, 76–86; Woodman, *King's College*, 9–12, and Wilson, *Gothic Cathedral*, 192–3, 205–8, emphasize the Kent school of masons. Cf. Harvey, 'The origins of the Perpendicular style', in E. M. Jope (ed.), *Studies in Building History* (London, 1978), 134–65, and id., *Perpendicular Style*, 16–17, 44–5, 50–8, and pl. 10, fig. 5.

1378 were formally constituted as a royal office of works. Yet its popularity may also reflect the temper of late medieval Catholicism. The authority and doctrine of the Church, linked to the celestial hierarchy, promised salvation earned (and purchased) through good works and intercessions. In the great perpendicular windows this ordered framework for man's spiritual destiny was represented through the panels of saints and biblical scenes set between soaring mullions like rungs in the ladder from earth to heaven. It was an architecture which expressed order, humanity, and aspiration.

What was built was determined by patrons rather than architects, and by the money available. Broadly, the period falls into two phases. The first, from 1360 to 1410, was dominated by interior rebuilding of major churches under architects of the first rank; the second, from c. 1420 to 1460, saw fewer and mainly smaller projects, apart from some imposing towers. Stylistic developments helped also to differentiate them. By 1365 the shortage of masons occasioned by the Black Death and Edward III's impressments for the royal works had begun to ease, and the way was open for a surge of ecclesiastical building in the last quarter of the century. This provided commissions for Henry Yevele, appointed the king's chief mason in 1378, and promoted the spread of the new style throughout the southeast. Yevele had already built the Clock Tower and Jewel House in Westminster Palace and rebuilt the west cloister of the abbey, and from 1375 he oversaw the resumption of work on the nave to the existing design, encouraged by Simon Langham's bequest in 1374. At that point Archbishop Sudbury decided on the demolition of the old Romanesque nave at Canterbury, and its replacement from 1378 to 1405 became Yevele's *chef d'œuvre*. Although the new nave was no longer than the old, its lofty arcades, slender piers, and unbroken shafts supporting a soaring vault produced a perfect equipoise between height and length; its proportions, moreover, tuned in with those of the earlier choir. This was a work of genius. Canterbury's estates had been reorganized by Prior Chillenden and, like Gloucester, it could fund a continuous building programme from offerings at a popular shrine. At Winchester it was the wealth of a single patron, William of Wykeham, that underpinned the reconstruction of the nave by Yevele's contemporary and peer William Wynford. But Wykeham baulked at demolition, and Wynford faced the challenge of cutting back the Norman piers, remoulding the arcade, enlarging the clerestory, and enhancing the verticality of the new design with strong shafts and a steeply pitched (and intricately ribbed) vault. Though lower and longer than Canterbury, Wynford's nave at Winchester achieved a synthesis as convincing and inspiring as Yevele's. Wynford's genius was also demonstrated in his planning and building of Wykeham's colleges at Winchester and Oxford and his completion of the south-western tower at Wells.[57]

[57] J. H. Harvey, *Henry Yevele* (London, 1944); id., *Perpendicular Style*, ch. 4; R. A. Brown, H. M. Colvin, and A. J. Taylor, *The History of the King's Works*, 3 vols. (London, 1963), ch. 5.

Powerful as was the example and appeal of the London style, it did not wholly efface the individual character of some provincial schools. At Worcester the central tower, built between 1357 and 1374, was a harmonious fusion of Perpendicular proportion and Decorated detail. At Gloucester the construction of the cloisters and lavatorium in different phases from 1364 first introduced the elaborate fan vault which was to reach its apogee a century later. About the architect and style of one other major monastic project, the rebuilding of the nave at Glastonbury (c.1343–c.1374), sadly nothing is recoverable. To East Anglia, Robert de Wodehirst brought the London style in 1385 but left his individual mark on the Norwich cloister and presbytery windows and perhaps at Ely in the Decorated tracery of the Lady Chapel (1371–4). Another area where London Perpendicular fused with regional traditions was Yorkshire. At York Minster, following the completion of the nave in 1360, the reconstruction of the Lady Chapel and choir (1361–1404) was undertaken by local architects, William Hoton and Robert Patrington. Although unmistakably Perpendicular, the work was consciously attuned to the proportions of the nave and indulged some eccentricity in the treatment of the clerestory windows. The great east window, glazed in 1405, rivalled that at Gloucester. At Beverley, too, Hoton's west façade (from 1380) was 'rich and vigorous', with the great west window and somewhat later towers forming a carefully balanced composition.[58] Finally at Durham, where John Lewyn had built the Prior's Kitchen in 1360–70, London influence arrived in the form of the superb Neville screen (1376–9), probably from Yevele's workshop.

In the hands of the generation of Yevele (d. 1400) and Wynford (d. 1405) the first phase of Perpendicular had an elegance, austerity, and spirituality which were best exemplified in the enclosure of space and the introduction of light. In its second phase, of the mid-fifteenth century, large-scale work on interiors gave way to the construction of towers and gateways and a multitude of miniature works like tombs and chantry chapels. There was a greater elaboration of surface ornament, with bosses, canopies, panelling, and parapets, and a recrudescence of the ogee in tracery. Whether or not this derived from the exposure of English architects to continental Flamboyant during the occupation of Normandy and Paris, it was a portent of the introduction of Burgundian forms in the final, late fifteenth-century phase. Not all patrons welcomed it: in Oxford the architect of the Divinity School, Richard Winchcombe, was warned in 1439 that 'numerous magnates of the realm and other knowledgeable men do not approve, but reprehend, the over curiosity of the . . . work already begun', and he was required 'to restrain the superfluous curiosity of the . . . work, as in niches for statues, bowtels, casements and fillets, and other foolish curiosities'. At Cambridge

---

[58] Harvey, *Perpendicular Style*, 105–7; id. 'Architectural history from 1291 to 1558', in Aylmer and Cant (eds.), *History of York Minster*, 149–92; Wilson, *Gothic Cathedral*, 216.

Henry VI in 1448 ordered the building of King's College Chapel to be 'in large form, clean and substantial, setting aside superfluity of too great curious work of entail [i.e. carving] and busy moulding'.[59]

The masterpieces in this phase were towers. At York the rebuilding of the central tower which had collapsed in 1407 and the completion of the two western towers to designs of 1430 proceeded until 1473. At Canterbury under Archbishop Chichele the south-west tower was built (1423–34) by Thomas Mapilton along with the porch as a memorial to the Agincourt generation. At Wells the central tower was remodelled in 1440 to a noble and satisfying design, and the finest of the central towers, at Gloucester (1450–60), achieved grandeur through simplicity. Finally, at Durham the first stage of the massive central tower, which had collapsed in 1436, was commenced in 1465. These towers apart (the only spires were at Chichester in 1400 and Norwich in 1362), the central years of the fifteenth century were unambitious, perhaps constrained by economic recession. The rebuilding of the west front at Gloucester (1420–37) halted at the second bay of the Romanesque nave, which was destined to remain. There was a spate of interior rebuilding in the minor houses of the west, at Malvern, Lacock, Forde, and Sherborne, the last noteworthy for the beautifully proportioned panelling and shafting in the choir, rising to support the first fan-vaulted church interior (1445–59). It leads into the last phase of Perpendicular, with its glasshouse chapels, pendant vaults, and Flamboyant decoration.

4. THE UNIVERSITIES

The universities of Oxford and Cambridge were part of the Church. As centres of learning they were to explore and uphold its doctrine; as centres of advanced teaching they were to produce an educated clergy. Yet they had their own *raison d'être*. They had sprung not from cathedral schools or the king's court, but from spontaneous gatherings of scholars. Although at first placed under the jurisdiction of the bishops of Lincoln and Ely, they elected their own chancellors and in the fifteenth century freed themselves from episcopal control. As corporations of masters with apprenticed scholars, they had legal identity, a common seal, and a governing body of regent masters known as Congregation. Oxford was the larger, with around 1,500 members c.1370, growing to some 1,700 by 1450; Cambridge over the same period grew (more rapidly) from some 400–700 to 1,300.[60] Such figures are no more than broad deductions from the notional

[59] For continental influence, see Woodman, *King's College*, 79–84; Harvey, *Perpendicular Style*, 183 (for quotations).

[60] Calculations in T. H. Aston, 'Oxford's medieval alumni', *P & P* 74 (1977), 6–7, and T. H. Aston, G. Duncan, and T. A. R. Evans, 'The medieval alumni of the University of Cambridge', *P & P* 86 (1980), 12–19. See too A. B. Cobban, *The Medieval English Universities* (Aldershot, 1988), 121–2.

complement of colleges, the number of halls, the number of regular clergy, and the record of those proceeding to degrees. The university kept no register of matriculation, it applied no formal test for admission, and kept no record of those who left before graduating. Although the regular orders selected and sent some of their members to university, for most other students it was an individual decision, governed by their academic capacity to pursue the course of study and the financial means to support this. Boys came from schools where they were expected to have acquired sufficient Latin grammar to read texts, understand lectures, and engage in disputations, though some initial assistance was provided for the less accomplished.

If, in 1360, the recruitment of the next generation of church leaders was to this extent haphazard, the rigour and length of the degree courses attested the intellectual capacity and stamina of those who completed them. Arts, the first degree, was taken by all except the regular clergy and those embarking on law. The bachelor's degree took four years and the master's another three. Its traditional structure encompassed the seven liberal arts: Grammar, Rhetoric, and Logic in the Trivium, Arithmetic, Music, Geometry, and Astronomy in the Quadrivium; followed by the study of the three Philosophies, natural, moral, and metaphysical, for the master's degree. The core of the baccalaureate was an intensive training in logic and linguistic analysis. Grammar focused on how words were used to signify objects, leading directly into the nominalist–realist controversy over the nature and validity of universal terms (e.g. 'men'). Logic embraced the 'old logic' embodied in Porphyry's *Isagoge* and the new Aristotelian logic received in the thirteenth century. Here again the nominalist critique by William of Ockham of the scholastic constructs of Thomas Aquinas and Duns Scotus gave contemporary relevance to old problems of how God could be known and men could be saved. Rhetoric, drawing mainly on Cicero, Aristotle, and Quintilian, also embraced epistolary training (from Seneca) and helped to develop the techniques of disputation, which qualified the student as a 'sophister' in his third year. Little time was spent on the Quadrivium, apart from the use of astronomy in plotting horoscopes for bodily health and personal fortunes.[61]

Quite a few—perhaps one-quarter to one-third—left after the BA. Those who continued to the master's degree used their training in logic in disputations over 'questions', taking it in turn to advance and respond to propositions in natural and moral philosophy. In this emphasis on the Arts course English universities had begun to diverge from those on the Continent, where it came to be considerably abbreviated to enable the commencement of higher degrees. Its rigorous and sustained training in linguistic logic was thus unique, and was of immediate

[61] For a useful survey of the subjects taught on the Arts course, see D. R. Leader, *A History of the University of Cambridge*, i (Cambridge, 1988), chs. 4, 5, 6; J. M. Fletcher, 'Developments in the Faculty of Arts, 1370–1520', in Catto and Evans (eds.), *Late Medieval Oxford*, 315–46.

service in the outside world. The dominance of the Arts curriculum was also reflected in the government of the university. As the largest faculty, the masters of arts effectively controlled Congregation and its business, chose the two proctors (second in importance to the chancellor) and lesser officials, and appointed preachers. In the hands of a transient, youthful, and numerous body, the government of the medieval English universities was never controlled by the senior and salaried members of the higher faculties as on the Continent. Until the later sixteenth century they remained democratic rather than oligarchic.[62]

Among the higher faculties theology was pre-eminent in both status and numbers. In the thirteenth century it had been dominated by the friars, who continued to form its largest component, but from the second quarter of the fourteenth century a new wave of secular masters took the lead in the intensive debate over Ockham's critique of Thomism. Ockham's insistence on the omnipotence and omniscience of God, and His inaccessibility to human reason, provoked responses from Fitzralph, Bradwardine, Buckingham, and others in the moderate realist and Scotist tradition. Although continental *studia* were more receptive to Ockham's thought, the works of Oxford theologians were sought after in German and Italian universities, culminating in the reception of Wyclif's writings in Prague. Both the preliminary training in Arts, and the emphasis on teaching by lectures and disputation, gave considerable opportunities for a critical and individual approach, which reached an extreme with Wyclif's attack on the entire structure and doctrine of the Catholic Church. This incurred ecclesiastical censure and the curtailment of Oxford's liberties, and brought it into disrepute as a centre of heresy. There followed a reaction from speculative to pastoral and systematic theology.[63]

The bachelor's degree in theology took seven years, with a further three for the doctorate. The study of Civil and Canon Law took even longer, though it could be started without the preliminary degree in Arts. In either it took fifteen years to complete a doctorate, or a combined degree ('in both Laws') in parts of each. Civil Law centred on the study of the *corpus juris civilis*, principally Justinian's *Code* and the *Digest*; Canon Law on Gratian's *Decretum* and subsequent Decretals. Medicine required five years' study after graduation in Arts and two years of medical practice. While only an elite proceeded to the higher faculties, it was a sizeable elite. At Oxford it represented almost one-third of the university, and at Cambridge, with a

---

[62] Fletcher, 'Developments in the Faculty of Arts', 318–19, 323–45; Leader, *History of the University of Cambridge*, 125–34, 157–69.

[63] W. A. Courtenay, 'Theology and theologians from Ockham to Wyclif', in Catto and Evans (eds.), *Late Medieval Oxford*, 1–34; Leader, *History of the University of Cambridge*, 170–91; J. I. Catto, 'Wyclif and Wycliffism at Oxford, 1356–1430' and 'Theology after Wycliffism', in J. I. Catto and R. Evans (eds.), *The History of the University of Oxford*, ii: *Late Medieval Oxford* (Oxford, 1992), 175–270. For Wyclif, see below, Ch. 10, sect. 4.

large law faculty, over one-third. At Oxford, Theology was the largest of the higher faculties, swollen by the presence of the regular clergy, who made it their principal study; it was closely followed by Civil Law, and was outnumbered by students of both Law faculties together, who formed 68 per cent of recorded graduate students. At Cambridge likewise legists were more numerous in the higher faculties over the period as a whole, though Theology had a revival in the fifteenth century. While Arts remained the largest faculty in both universities, with over half of recorded graduates, Law was a real rival, particularly at Cambridge.[64]

Teaching was through lectures and disputations, with very limited access to written texts at the Arts level. Ordinary lectures, delivered by regent masters of arts on prescribed days from 6 a.m. to 9 a.m., covered the glosses and commentaries on the prescribed texts. The extraordinary lectures which followed widened the area of study beyond these, while cursory lectures by bachelors amounted to a straightforward reading or paraphrase of the text. Regent masters also staged disputations in the schools as part of their year's 'necessary regency' after graduation. They were poorly remunerated from student fees, and by the fifteenth century the system was failing, as many chose to go into more remunerative employment. In practice teaching was already being organized in halls (especially those for legists) by the principals, acting as tutors with both disciplinary and academic functions, and similar provision came to be organized where colleges had undergraduates.[65]

In the fourteenth century all but a small fraction of undergraduates in both universities lived in halls or lodgings. This presented serious disciplinary problems, since most arrived in their teens, and in 1420 they were required by statute to swear obedience to the chancellor within one month of their arrival. Halls were essentially private hostels, leased for short periods by a graduate who acted as the principal and assumed responsibility for the behaviour of the students, their payment of fees, and even their attendance at lectures. In Cambridge the chancellor's official made a twice-yearly inspection. Halls could have a continuous existence under a series of principals and become associated with particular faculties. Of nearly seventy halls in Oxford in 1444, six were for Grammar, twenty-five for Arts, and thirty-three for Law, and some developed regional connections. They housed an average of 18.5 students, in all some 1,300. At Cambridge the halls were fewer and larger, seventeen halls containing in total 700–900 students.[66]

---

[64] Aston, 'Oxford's alumni', 16–22; Aston et al., 'Medieval alumni of Cambridge', 58–9; Cobban, English Universities, 213–15, 227–8.

[65] Leader, History of the University of Cambridge, 30–2; Fletcher, 'Developments in the Faculty of Arts', 333–8; Cobban, English Univesities, 162–71; id., 'Colleges and halls, 1380–1500', in Catto and Evans (eds.), Late Medieval Oxford, 618–19, 624–6.

[66] Aston, 'Oxford's alumni', 7, 36–40; Cobban, English Universities, 146–56. For the location of the halls at Oxford, see map 2 in Catto and Evans (eds.), Late Medieval Oxford.

Both universities at this date were thus still aularian rather than collegiate, but the preceding sixty years had seen a wave of college foundations. Unlike the transient halls, colleges were perpetual corporations of fellows, with endowments and a seal, and governed by statutes. Prior to 1379 Oxford had six colleges and Cambridge seven, all of them fairly small; by 1460 each had acquired four more, including the major foundations of New College (1379) and King's College (1441–5). Colleges were mainly for graduates reading for higher degrees and by 1460 they provided a statutory complement of 225 fellows in Cambridge and 150 to 200 in Oxford.[67] Only at King's Hall, Cambridge (1317, 1337), had scholars from the royal chapel been admitted to the foundation as undergraduates, but in founding New College in 1379 William of Wykeham provided for scholars from his school at Winchester to be eligible for fellowships after two years' probation. In its size, buildings, and constitution New College set the model for collegiate foundations for the rest of the Middle Ages. It had a warden, seventy fellows, ten priests, and sixteen choristers and was to serve the dual purpose of replenishing the Church with well-educated clergy and praying for the soul of the founder. This concept of an enclosed community of learning was reflected in the architecturally innovative grouping of chapel and hall as a single range of a residential quadrangle. Over the next century three further Oxford colleges were founded, all by bishops, though only one consciously followed Wykeham's pattern. In 1427 Richard Fleming of Lincoln established a small college of a rector and seven fellows expressly to combat Lollard heresies, though he died before he could give it statutes or buildings. More ambitious was Archbishop Henry Chichele's foundation of All Souls in 1437, which was to train the 'unarmed soldiery' of the Church militant and to be a chantry commemorating the generation who had fought under Henry V. Its forty fellows studying Theology and Law were to form a *corps d'élite* dedicated to the service of temporal and ecclesiastical government in the tradition of Henry V. Finally at Oxford, William of Waynflete initiated the foundation of Magdalen in 1448, though twenty-five years were to elapse before it became operative. As it eventually emerged, Magdalen was a close imitation of New College, with forty fellows and thirty undergraduate half-fellows ('demies'), built around an integrated cloister and provided with a similar feeder school to ensure competence in grammar. Its broader educational commitment was marked first by the acceptance of lay commoners as part of the college (though not on the foundation), and secondly by the endowment of public lectureships in moral and natural philosophy.[68]

At Cambridge, William Bingham, likewise concerned over the decline of grammar teaching, had founded Godshouse in 1439, later to develop into

---

[67] Aston, 'Oxford's alumni', 14.

[68] Cobban, 'Colleges and halls', 581–620; R. L. Storey, 'The foundation of the medieval college, 1379–1530', in J. Buxton and P. H. Williams (eds.), *New College Oxford, 1379–1979* (Oxford, 1979), 3–43; J. I. Catto, 'The world of Henry Chichele', in id., *Unarmed Soldiery*, 1–13.

Christ's College. Ten years later its site was appropriated by Henry VI for his foundation of King's College, for which Eton was to serve as a feeder school. It was to have seventy fellows, restricted to Eton scholars, and like the Oxford foundations was to train secular clergy. Henry's strict orthodoxy and unrestricted liberality made their mark in the choice of Cambridge (rather than Wycliffite Oxford) and the vast scale of the project. Two years later (in 1446–7) his queen established a smaller foundation 'for the extirpation of heresies and errors and the increase of faith', later refounded by Elizabeth Woodville as Queens' College. The second quarter of the fifteenth century, though a period of economic depression, thus brought a notable advance towards establishing both universities as collegiate. This was not accidental, but reflected the belief, at the highest level, that education in a small but exclusive intellectual community best trained an elite for service in the Church and commonwealth.[69]

The quasi-monastic life of a university college was clearly modelled on that of the regular clergy, with the provision of a common refectory, church, and cloister though not a dormitory. In the twelfth century regular houses had been established in Oxford by the Augustinians at St Frideswide's and Osney and by the Cistercians at Rewley, while in the thirteenth century the four mendicant orders, Dominicans, Franciscans, Austins, and Carmelites, built large convents and directly contributed to the intellectual vigour of the university. None of these were primarily intended as *studia*, but by 1300 the Benedictines had recognized the benefits which their own monks could obtain from university education and Christ Church, Canterbury, and Durham both set up eponymous daughter houses while a third, Gloucester College, housed monks from other major Benedictine abbeys. It was only by the latter fourteenth century that all these were firmly established as colleges, while much smaller colleges for the Cistercians (St Bernard's) and the Austin canons (St Mary's) were tardily founded in the 1430s. Over the whole period up to 1500 a total of 2,568 regular clergy are known to have studied at Oxford, three-fifths of whom were mendicants. They were neither wholly integrated into the university nor entirely separate from it. The large friary churches were used for sermons, disputations, and meetings; some secular students lodged in their convents; and some regulars held university offices, four of them as chancellor. Since the regular clergy were sent to Oxford in their early twenties after having studied in their mother houses, they were exempt from the Arts course, and almost all engaged in the study of theology. The friars were particularly prominent in disputations, notably as opponents of Wyclif. At Cambridge the friars were almost as numerous and equally prominent in the faculty of theology, but the only monastic house was

[69] Leader, *History of the University of Cambridge*, 228; Wolffe, *Henry VI*, 135–45; J. Saltmarsh, 'King's College', in *VCH Cambridge*, iii (1959), 376.

that for Benedictines established after 1470. For the monastic orders university study helped to revitalize the intellectual life of the cloister and became a sine qua non for the holding of high office in cathedral priories: all the late medieval priors of Durham were graduates in theology.[70]

The wave of college foundations, with a high proportion of fellowships allocated to theology, did not always translate into the production of more theologians. At Oxford both New College and All Souls, in defiance of their statutes, came to have a majority of legists, most of them civil lawyers. Indeed the proportion of theologians in Oxford colleges shrank from 81 per cent in the thirteenth century to 57 per cent in the fourteenth and to 44 per cent in the fifteenth. At Cambridge, however, the position was different. In the fourteenth century the Cambridge colleges 'had greater prominence as legal institutions' than at Oxford, with King's Hall, Peterhouse, and Clare the leading centres; but in the fifteenth century 'the production of lawyers was noticeably curtailed . . . and the theological element was increased dramatically'. Most colleges now showed a majority of theologians. This has been seen as 'a collective collegiate response to the encroaching tide of legal studies . . . and a positive affirmation of theological orthodoxy'.[71]

While royal and episcopal benefactors fostered the production of an elite, there was little or no support for those at the outset of their studies. Little is known in detail about the cost of university study. There were fees for lectures, for graces, and for admission to degrees; but board and lodging was certainly the heaviest charge, and this could vary widely as between college, hall, and lodgings. For undergraduates £2 10s. a year was a bare minimum, with £4 being often provided by patrons or legacies. Halls for legists were in general more expensive, and in the higher faculties students would have to find some £6 or £7 per annum. These charges largely determined the social intake, for parental support provided the principal funding although a few had charitable bequests. It is thus likely (for there is little direct evidence) that the lowest class from which an able boy would come was that of the husbandman or manorial official, and in the towns that of master craftsman or small merchant. Among recorded New College scholars before 1500, 61.4 per cent were from families of smallholders, 27.7 per cent from the middle to upper ranks of urban society, and 12.5 per cent from the gentry. Only 0.1 per cent were from lower levels. Even so, this was a broader social range than at any time before the twentieth century, and a university education provided an important means of upward mobility. The growth of university numbers from 2,000 to 3,000 in a century of declining population and

---

[70] For the regulars, see R. B. Dobson, 'The religious orders, 1370–1540', in Catto and Evans (eds.), *Late Medieval Oxford*, 539–80; Cobban, *English Universities*, 318–19.

[71] Cobban, *English Universities*, 214–31 (quotations from 224–30); id., 'Colleges and halls', 602–3.

rising living standards suggests that education was seen as an avenue for advancement.[72]

Nevertheless, these expectations were often sadly disabused, for 'almost certainly ... a very large proportion of students (very possibly more than half) never took a degree'. Even among the pre-selected New College students that proportion was one-third. Numbers of them died, lacked money, or found study too difficult.[73] Those who made a start, hoping to underpin their study with employment or patronage, faced a difficult time in the early fifteenth century. The lists of those seeking benefices to support their study which universities had sent to the papal Curia since the thirteenth century ceased shortly after 1400 as papal provision came under attack. Over that period the number of benefices worth more than 10 marks (the minimum required to support a vicar as well as a student) had also been eroded by their appropriation to monastic houses. That there was a perceived crisis is evident from petitions in convocation and parliament over the period 1392–1422, and attempts to negotiate for a proportion of benefices to be reserved for university scholars. The patronage available to graduates was ampler. In the fifteenth century 72 per cent of all episcopal appointments went to Oxford men and 19 per cent to Cambridge, and over 80 per cent of cathedral deans and officers were university graduates. They also filled a high proportion of prebends. At parish level the impact of university-trained men was another matter, and something much more difficult to measure. It has been estimated that an average of 450 benefices a year fell vacant, well over twice the number of graduates produced by both universities; moreover, if allowance is made for the falling numbers of clergy and the increasing attractions of a non-clerical career, it is probable that not more than one-quarter of parochial benefices would be filled by graduates. These were likely to be the wealthier benefices, as those with the presentation to them sought to attract graduates into their service. Probably few graduates ended up unbeneficed or in the poorer livings. Whether a period of university study, even for those who failed to graduate, made a priest better able to instruct and rule his flock can only be a matter of speculation.[74]

[72] T. A. Evans, 'The numbers, origins and careers of scholars', in Catto and Evans (eds.), *Late Medieval Oxford*, 500–15, reviews the evidence of social origins including Lytle's study of those of New College students (G. Lytle, 'Oxford students and English society, c.1300–c.1510', Ph. D. thesis (Princeton University, 1975); Cobban, *English Universities*, 304–13.

[73] Aston *et al.*, 'Medieval alumni of Cambridge', 27; Evans, 'The numbers, origins and careers', 497. At New College one in ten died in their first four years, before the age of 20 (Storey, 'The foundation of the medieval college', 17).

[74] The debate over whether there was a 'crisis of patronage' in 1340–1430, first suggested by G. F. Lytle, 'Patronage patterns and Oxford colleges, c.1300–1530', in L. Stone (ed.), *The University in Society*, i (Princeton, 1975), 111 ff., has been carried forward in Aston *et al.*, 'Medieval alumni of Cambridge', 68–80, 83–4; Cobban, *English Universities*, 357–60; Evans, 'Numbers, origins, and careers', 526–38; R. N. Swanson, 'University graduates and benefices in later medieval England', *P & P* 106 (1985), 28–61.

CHAPTER 10

Religion, Devotion, and Dissent

In the last quarter of the fourteenth century the English Church faced a multiple crisis of authority. Schism in the papacy, talk in parliament of disendowment, and the emergence of heresy at both learned and popular levels threatened its structure and faith, so firmly established in the preceding century. Traditionally the Church had been identified with the priesthood, as the essential mediators of divine grace through the sacraments, with the laity in a subordinate and passive role. The thirteenth century had seen this consolidated and extended. The formulation of the doctrine of transubstantiation, the obligation of annual confession and communion for the laity, and the drive to enforce clerical celibacy reinforced the status of the clergy as a sacred and separate order. They were set new standards of morals and learning through the surveillance of archdeacons, visitations, and church courts, while the friars began the evangelization of the urban laity. The apparatus of centralization extended hierarchical control from the papacy down through the dioceses, and in the universities scholastic theology provided greater intellectual coherence in the synthesis of faith and reason propounded by Thomism. The integrated character thus given to western Catholicism began to dissolve in the fourteenth century. William of Ockham insisted that God could not be known through human intellect, nor was His omnipotence and omniscience limited by the natural order; faith and reason were divorced. At the same time a doctrine of Christ's absolute poverty, propounded by the Spiritual Franciscans, called in question the legitimacy of the Church's temporal wealth. Royal power laid claim to that wealth on grounds of national necessity, and the papacy's removal from Rome to Avignon made it vulnerable to national pressures. These were all matters of doctrine and jurisdiction; a more fundamental problem would be the Church's response to the advance of lay literacy and the growing wealth, magistracy, and political sophistication of the upper and middle ranks of lay society.

The challenge was fundamental because the Church's authority rested on a long and rich tradition of Latin theology and canon law; its liturgy was exclusively in Latin, as were its administrative procedures and much of its preaching. From all this the laity—even most of the literate laity—were *ipso facto* excluded.

Nor was the gulf between lay and clerical status simply a matter of learning and language, for the priesthood controlled the means of salvation. Only the properly ordained priest could pronounce the Latin formula which miraculously transformed the sacramental bread and wine into the body and blood of Christ. How far did vernacular literacy represent any kind of threat to the Church's control of theology and faith? None at all in respect of academic theology, which was the preserve of the universities, except that controversial issues like predestination and freewill, poverty and possessions under debate in learned circles, would be popularized. A more direct challenge lay in the translation of sacred texts, notably the Bible, but also the Creed and the Lord's Prayer, for this invaded clerical control of their interpretation and charismatic authority. Thirdly, however, the translation of the store of devotional writing, of saints' lives and legends, and works of meditation, could fortify and extend religious awareness among the laity, opening up opportunities for evangelization.

In short, by the latter fourteenth century the Church could no longer be equated with the priesthood and an exclusively Latinized culture. It had to accommodate the laity and the vernacular, but to what extent it could do so while preserving its control of the faith was problematic. Essentially this was a problem at parochial level and I shall therefore begin by examining the relations between priests and their parishioners, before considering the nature of late medieval devotion, public and private, and the emergence of heresy.

I. PAROCHIAL STRUCTURES AND RELIGION

Around 1400 there were probably some 9,000 parishes in England, a slight reduction from a century earlier. Both in town and in country they varied greatly in size. In Hull and Coventry there were only two parishes, while in York and Norwich there were forty and more. In upland areas with dispersed settlement they covered many square miles, while in old settled river valleys churches might be no more than a mile apart. Their location and agrarian economy might well influence their religious temper, though this needs further research. In each a single priest, whether rector or vicar, exercised spiritual authority over all parishioners. Though instituted by the bishop, he was nominated by the patron of the benefice, who could be either a lay or an ecclesiastical lord, or an institution like a cathedral chapter, a college, or a monastery. If given the freehold, the rector would enjoy the emoluments, temporal and spiritual, but by the fifteenth century approximately one-third of all parish benefices (and in some dioceses over half) had been appropriated to religious houses. Where this happened the religious house became the rector and instituted a vicar to exercise the cure of souls. The monastery retained the greater tithes (of grain), leaving the glebe lands and lesser tithes (of wool and animals) to the vicar, who also received the fees for baptisms, marriages, churchings, funerals, and mortuary dues as well as voluntary offerings at the principal feasts.[1]

What kind of men secured a benefice, and how? Those presenting themselves for ordination had to be free-born, legitimate, without physical defects, and *litterati*. They did not have to demonstrate any spiritual vocation, but by the time they had attained the priesthood most would have spent time in minor orders in liturgical duties. Their training was through practical apprenticeship rather than a theological curriculum. They needed the capacity to read and construe liturgical Latin and most would have acquired this by attending an almonry or cathedral school, and then a local grammar school. Only a small proportion would have gone to university. How they had acquired schooling depended on their social class. Technically the sons of serfs were debarred by law, and those of lesser peasants would be by the cost; but there are plenty of examples of children from these ranks being selected and supported by local rectors, lords, or a religious house. The Church had an informal network of talent scouts. Mostly, however, the clergy were drawn from the middling social levels in town and country: artisans and small merchants, husbandmen and yeomen. Finally the ordinand had to establish that he was financially self-supporting, normally by producing a 'title' or certification from a religious house. By the fifteenth century this was a formality and implied no secure income.[2]

About 15 per cent of ordinands already had a benefice, having attracted a patron by their birth or ability, and being destined for high office in the Church. Some others could hope for a benefice within a short time through connections with a patron. Around 10 to 15 per cent of benefices were under lay patronage, but most lords had only a handful of advowsons which they used for their chaplains and officials. Monastic and episcopal patronage was more extensive, but demand far outran the number of benefices available. Many never received a benefice and had small hope of doing so from the moment of ordination. They were destined to spend their lives as stipendiary priests, either assisting the incumbent of the parish at an annual wage, or serving a chantry, or attached to a religious guild, or as a jobbing priest meeting the demand for votive masses at a penny a time. Even stable employment as a stipendiary in a prosperous urban

---

[1] Hamilton Thompson, *English Clergy*, ch. 4, esp. pp. 115–19; R. N. Swanson, *Church and Society in Late Medieval England* (Oxford, 1989), 44, 206–17; id., 'Standards of livings: Parochial revenues in pre-Reformation England', in C. Harper-Bill (ed.), *Religious Belief and Ecclesiastical Careers* (Woodbridge, 1991), 151–96; P. Heath, *The English Parish Clergy on the Eve of the Reformation* (London, 1969), 147–63.

[2] Swanson, *Church and Society*, 36–40; id., 'Problems of the priesthood in pre-Reformation England, *EHR* 105 (1990), 845–69; N. Tanner, *The Church in Late Medieval Norwich, 1370–1532* (Toronto, 1984), 24–32; R. W. Dunning, 'Patronage and promotion in the late medieval Church', in Griffiths (ed.), *Patronage, Crown, and Provinces*, 167–80.

parish offered little prospect of attaining a benefice. Thus of eight chaplains in the parish of St Mary Magdalene in Taunton *c.*1450 only two eventually secured local benefices. Nevertheless, the unbeneficed were by no means a clerical proletariat. Their earnings were probably about two-thirds of those of the average resident incumbent, and unlike him they had no extrinsic charges such as the maintenance of the priest's house, or procurations. In an expanding market for requiem masses, there was work for all.[3]

It is in this context that trends in numbers become important. There are no figures for the total number of priests before the Black Death but surviving ordination lists show as high a level as in the early sixteenth century. The mortality of parochial clergy in 1348–9 was around 40 per cent and the crisis of vacancies was met by a surge in institutions as bishops strove to maintain stability. The improved opportunities for securing a benefice also brought a surge in ordinations. As in the secular world, an excess clerical population filled the immediate gap in the workforce. Even so, the shortage of stipendiary priests produced an increase in wages which Archbishops Islip in 1350 and Sudbury in 1378 tried to fix at 6 and then 8 marks a year. Up to 1375 the numbers ordained showed large and inexplicable annual variations, perhaps reflecting visitation of plague, but from the last quarter of the century a significant and prolonged drop in ordinations set in, continuing until about 1460. In the poor diocese of Hereford the numbers slumped by two-thirds, and although in York the drop occurred only after 1390, thereafter ordinations were 34 per cent lower than before the Black Death. Everywhere bishops reduced ordination ceremonies from four or five to two a year, and in some years held none at all.[4]

How serious a problem did this pose for parochial life? Except in the north the drop in clerical recruitment was apparently greater than the fall in national population: there was a real shortage of clergy. The poll tax returns of 1377 and 1381 give a total of some 30,000 clergy, of whom perhaps 23,000 would have been secular priests. Thirty years later this figure may have fallen to little over 17,000. Unbeneficed chaplains and cantarists tended to congregate in the towns and larger ecclesiastical centres, where they were often supported by endowments and lay contributions. London, in particular, offered profitable employment and was a magnet for priests from other dioceses, a fact deplored by both Langland and Chaucer. It was in the poorer and rural parishes that a real shortage of clergy and the money to pay them had serious effects. Visitation records show

---

[3] V. Davis, 'Preparation for service in the late medieval English Church', in Curry and Matthew (eds.), *Concepts and Patterns of Service*, 38–51.

[4] J. H. Moran, 'Clerical recruitment in the diocese of York, 1345–1530: Data and commentary', *JEH* 34 (1983), 19–54; W. J. Dohar, *The Black Death and Pastoral Leadership* (Philadelphia, 1995), chs. 2–4; R. L. Storey, 'The recruitment of English clergy in the period of the Conciliar Movement', *Annuarium Historiae Conciliorum*, 7 (1975), 290–313.

insufficient assistant priests to maintain services in outlying chapels, and even the daily office in the parish church. And it was probably at the lower levels that improved opportunities of employment in lay society deflected men from the priesthood. It is not necessary to postulate either a climate of anticlericalism in society or a spiritual malaise in the Church to explain the deficit in clerical vocations. At a higher level it became easier to exchange and trade benefices, so that by the 1390s professional brokers had emerged to arrange profitable deals between these careerist priests ('chop-churches') denounced by Archbishop Courtenay. The Church could not remain immune from the fluidity and commercialism of late fourteenth-century society, especially when its services were in increasing demand.[5]

What duties did the priest perform and what were his relations with his parishioners? His principal function was his daily recital of the divine office and the celebration of Mass. His other ministrations and powers sprang from this central function. Thus before Easter he was to hear the confession of every parishioner and impose an appropriate penance in preparation for their annual communion. He also took the Host to the dying, receiving their confession and administering the last rites. He performed the other Christian rites of passage: baptism, marriage, churching, and burial, and in each of these he followed a prescribed ritual in Latin with which his parishioners must have become familiar, even if the full meaning of the words and actions was only partly comprehended. His was a sacramental ministry, for though he was encouraged to preach, this was only an occasional part of his canonical duties. The priest was thus a unique and charismatic figure, guiding the spiritual pilgrimage of his flock and literally holding in his hands the key to their salvation. How satisfactorily did he perform his pastoral duties?

Ultimately the parish priest was under the jurisdiction of his bishop, but more immediate surveillance rested with the archdeacon and his ears and eyes, the rural deans. Little is known about archdiaconal visitations, which could be perfunctory and principally concerned the maintenance of the church fabric; but by 1300 presentments were being made by the laity, summoned as 'questmen', on information from the churchwardens.[6] One of the most informative records for our period comes from the register of John Chandler, dean of Salisbury, covering his personal visitation of prebendal parishes in Dorset, Wiltshire, and Berkshire in 1405, 1408–9, and 1412. On average one-quarter of the presentments were of the

---

[5] Storey, 'Recruitment of English clergy', 291, 298; Dohar, *The Black Death*, 118–19; C. Harper-Bill, 'The English Church and English religion after the Black Death', in Ormrod and Lindley (eds.), *The Black Death in England*, 84–96; J. C. Russell, 'The clerical population of England, 1377–81', *Traditio*, 2 (1944), 177–212.

[6] R. W. Dunning, 'Rural deans in England in the fifteenth century', *BIHR* 40 (1967), 207–12; Dohar, *The Black Death*, ch. 5.

clergy themselves. The most common charge was of sexual misconduct, which was alleged against 16 per cent of the parish clergy in 1405 and 8 per cent in 1412, chaplains being more culpable than incumbents. This probably understates the prevailing level of clerical incontinence, and is eloquent of the strains of the priestly vocation in a rural parish. It is difficult to gauge the attitude of the laity to this. Prolonged cohabitation in the parsonage was rarely alleged, and while adultery was seen as seriously disrupting social relations, casual fornication might be overlooked for it did not invalidate the priest's sacramental ministrations. It was the failure to perform these adequately that was the other major complaint.

Prolonged absences from the parish for up to eight weeks, the failure to provide services at distant chapels, to say matins and vespers, to hold a weekday Mass, to administer to the sick and dying, and occasionally the failure to preach, were all matters of complaint. There were more serious allegations against priests, of betraying the confessional, of charging for sacramentals, of saying Mass twice a day to earn money, and of drunkenness, quarrels, and even violence. It has been rightly pointed out that these are evidence not of anticlericalism but of lay expectations of acceptable standards in the priesthood. Moreover, such allegations might represent parishioners' attempts to rid themselves of an unpopular priest. They occur in only a small minority of parishes. The priest could offer to purge himself in the bishop's consistory court or, if the sin was admitted, do penance; but to deprive him of his benefice was a protracted and difficult process.[7] Beyond these moral and pastoral failings, clergy might be indicted before lay justices for felonies and treason. Most of the charges were for housebreaking, theft, and rape, the last being the commonest. Nearly one hundred clergy were arraigned for rape in the Norwich diocese between 1423 and 1441, half of them incumbents and half chaplains. There is no doubt that, as convocation complained on several occasions (1402, 1421, 1439), a proportion of these accusations were malicious, intended to secure the priest's removal from the parish. Generally they pleaded not guilty, and four-fifths were acquitted. Only if found guilty did they plead benefit of clergy, being then conveyed to an episcopal prison to await (for an indefinite period) compurgation before an ecclesiastical court. This was almost invariably successful, but the delinquent had been named and shamed. In civil suits the clergy were also judiciable in lay courts, English law being in this respect at variance with canon law, but legitimized as a local custom.[8]

---

[7] *The Register of John Chandler, Dean of Salisbury, 1407–17*, ed. T. C. B. Timmins, Wiltshire Record Society, 39 (Devizes, 1984); R. N. Swanson (trans. and annot.), *Catholic England* (Manchester, 1993), 261; A. D. Brown, *Popular Piety in Late Medieval England* (Oxford, 1995), 78–83.

[8] A. K. McHardy, 'Church courts and criminous clerks in the late Middle Ages', in M. J. Franklin and C. Harper-Bill (eds.), *Medieval Ecclesiastical Studies* (Woodbridge, 1995), 165–84; R. L. Storey, 'Malicious indictments of the clergy in the fifteenth century', ibid. 221–40; Swanson, *Church and Society*, 149–52.

The judicial machinery of the Church was used more regularly and extensively in matters involving the laity. The consistory court heard cases of two kinds: 'office' cases brought to it by the archdeacon and churchwardens from visitations, and 'instance' cases brought by individual suit. The former mainly touched public morals. Half the charges brought in Chandler's visitation were of fornication or adultery (in equal proportions). Some long-standing liaisons were presented, and some amateur prostitution, but much probably represented extramarital sex arising from the deferred age of marriage. It is difficult to know whether the laity regarded these, in priestly fashion, as pollutant, or treated them as socially disruptive. The social code was also endangered by tavern-haunting and gaming, plotting, gossiping, and backbiting, all of which could fall under the sins of sloth, gluttony, and envy. Second to moral offences were charges of detinue of Church goods, concerning bequests, rents, and tithes. In the consistory court those who confessed received a penance of public humiliation, e.g. by ritual beating; more commonly penances were commuted to a fine, which might be regarded as a licence to sin, although a shilling fine represented three days' wages. Those who denied their offence had to find five local compurgators to attest their innocence. Either way, the punishment was exemplary and paved the way for the social reintegration of the accused. Those failing to appear before the court were excommunicated and a few chose to remain so, but most were eventually reconciled. The laity also brought their own cases to the consistory court, mostly of debt, defamation, and matrimony. Proceedings were formal and exhaustive and a case took three days, even when collusive. Matrimonial cases mostly centred on the attempt to enforce marriage after troth-plighting, in the context of premarital pregnancy or breach of contract.[9] Thus the daily life of the parish was subject to the surveillance of the Church, operating a system of mutual accusation by clergy and laity.

Priest and people also had mutual obligations for the upkeep of the church. Two-thirds of the churches visited by Chandler needed repair. The chancel was the responsibility of the rector, but in the thirteenth century canon law had made the parishioners responsible for the fabric of the nave and the provision of service books, altar vessels, and vestments. To manage this two churchwardens were elected from the upper stratum of the villagers to serve for two years. Some of their accounts surviving from the mid-fourteenth century show that they collected funds partly from customary dues at marriages, burials, etc., partly by annual fund-raising events like church ales, but above all from lands and money given and bequeathed to the church. Such gifts appear as normal, almost routine, in wills. In fifteenth-century Norwich 85 per cent of the clergy and 95 per cent of

    [9] *Register of Chandler*, *passim*; L. R. Poos, *Lower Ecclesiastical Jurisdictions in Late Medieval England* (Oxford, 2001).

the laity made bequests to at least one church, many for specific needs or objects. There can be no doubt that much communal effort went into the fabric and adornment of the parish church, but for more ambitious projects 'it would be wise not to overstate the contribution of the whole community'. Most parishioners were too poor to contribute significantly to a major project such as the rebuilding of the nave or tower. Then a separate building fund would be set up and appeals made to those with real wealth. In areas of wool and cloth production the extensive rebuilding of churches on an extravagant scale reflected the buoyancy of the local economy. Wealthy graziers and clothiers can be identified as paying for specified parts of the new fabric: a complete bay, or the clerestory, or an aisle; a stained-glass window, a rood-screen, or benches. The building of a western bell tower, the most characteristic late medieval addition, often—perhaps usually—had the support of a local lord, supplying either money or material. Virtually no building accounts for parish churches survive, and dating by surviving architectural detail is often imprecise, given local variations and time lags in style. But an analysis of church building in the diocese of Salisbury suggests that while enlargement was continuous from the thirteenth to the fifteenth century, the latter saw more complete rebuilding, and in particular the addition of towers and chapels.[10]

The parishioners were also responsible for the upkeep of the churchyard, and this could be more contentious. As hallowed ground, it was an extension of the church and under ecclesiastical discipline, while for the community it was occupied by those whose souls were in purgatory. Yet it was also the natural setting for village gatherings, for Sunday markets, and for recreational games, like wrestling, dancing, and as a 'camping close' for a form of football. A parliamentary statute of 1388 banned such games, but only from the mid-fifteenth century were such activities moved elsewhere. For their part parishioners might object to the priest grazing his sheep and pigs over the graves, or felling the trees.[11] In all the above respects the pastoral relationship between priest and people was subject to economic, social, and disciplinary tensions, but it would be wrong to let the record of these obscure the pastoral and consensual authority he exercised over the small flock whose problems and personalities were his daily concern.

In cities and small towns, and even in larger villages, lay involvement was

---

[10] C. Burgess, 'Pre-Reformation churchwardens' accounts and parish government', *EHR* 117 (2002), 306–32; B. A. Kumin, *The Shaping of a Community: The Rise and Reformation of the English Parish, c.1400–1500* (Aldershot, 1996), 20–42; Tanner, *Church in Norwich*, 113–40; P. Northeast (ed.), *Wills of the Archdeaconry of Sudbury, 1439–74*, Suffolk Record Society, 44 (2001), p. xlvii and text; Brown, *Popular Piety*, ch. 5, esp. pp. 113, 120. From the building contracts for parish churches in L. F. Salzman, *Building in England* (Oxford, 1952), 413–584, ten are with lay or ecclesiastical patrons, eleven with parishioners.

[11] D. Dymond, 'God's disputed acre', *JEH* 50 (1999), 464–97.

channelled through religious guilds or fraternities. These were voluntary associations with the complementary functions of providing mutual support for their members while alive and praying for their souls at and after their death. A high proportion of the parishioners might be members, each paying an annual fee which might range from as little as 4d. to 2s. or half a mark. Their ordinances enjoined fraternal behaviour: charitable assistance to members in need, the avoidance of quarrels and litigation, and above all attendance at the annual fraternity feast, where the kiss of peace and passing of a loving cup had religious symbolism. The fraternity provided full funeral rites for its members, with a procession, hearse, banners, candles, the tolling bell, and doles to the poor, and an obit light and anniversary commemoration. At the annual patronal service the recital of the names of deceased members in the fraternity's 'Book of Life' emphasized the community of the living and the dead. They established chapels dedicated to their patron saint or cult, either within the parish church or outside, and employed their own chaplains. Many fraternities were dedicated to Corpus Christi, underlining their corporate unity; others to one of the new cults of the fifteenth century.

Fraternities had existed before the Black Death but multiplied considerably after it; indeed over one-third of those in existence in 1389 had been formed after 1377. They continued to flourish until, at the end of the fifteenth century, there may have been some 30,000, over three times the number of parishes. London had some 150 to 200 between 1350 and 1550 though many were short-lived; in mid-fifteenth century Norwich there were 48, in Great Yarmouth 19, and in Bodmin 40. Rural parishes might have only a single fraternity: Northamptonshire had a total of 100, Lincolnshire 120. Were they a rival to the parish, or even a subversive force? Organizationally they had the marks of a sect, and their proprietary control over revenues, buildings, priests, and devotions has been seen as a lay invasion of the clerical magisterium. Yet doctrinally they remained orthodox, and although they siphoned off money in gifts and bequests, they used their financial resources not only on their own chapels but to contribute to the fabric and embellishment of the church and to its rituals, e.g. by supporting an organ and choir. Their chaplains often assisted the parish priest in the liturgical and pastoral work, and he himself might be a member of the fraternity. Lay fraternities brought vitality and resources into parish life at a time when revenues and numbers of clergy were in decline and gave the laity an active and responsible role in its religious life.[12]

---

[12] Fraternities are discussed in Kumin, *Shaping of a Community*, 145–60; Tanner, *Church in Norwich*, 73–81; Brown, *Popular Piety*, 132–58. Yorkshire religious guilds are discussed by D. J. F. Crouch, *Piety, Fraternity and Power* (York, 2000); those in London by C. Barron, 'The parish fraternities of medieval London', in Harper-Bill (ed.), *The Church in Pre-Reformation Society*, 13–37, and G. Rosser, 'Communities of parish and guild', in S. Wright (ed.) *Parish, Church and People* (London, 1988), 29–55; M. Rubin, *Corpus Christi* (Cambridge, 1991), 232–87.

Among the wealthier laity the same, and perhaps more compelling, urge to reduce the pains of purgatory prompted the foundation of chantries. By the fifteenth century the annual cost of maintaining a priest to say masses for one's soul in perpetuity was 10 marks, which required the alienation of 200 marks ($£133$ 6s. 8d.) of land. Financial provision for a chantry was often made before death, rather than by will, for executors could not be wholly trusted, and many preferred to vest the endowment in a corporation which acted as trustee, appointing, paying, and dismissing the priest and overseeing his performance. Some chantries were thus founded in monasteries and cathedrals and administered by the convent and chapter, but these were a minority. More were established in parish churches or guild chapels, with lay officers to appoint and control the chantry priest. Such a chantry would be sited in a chancel aisle or chapel of a parish church, or even on the north side of the chancel, where it would serve as an altar for the chantry priest.[13]

Chantries were characteristic of late medieval religion in at least three ways. First, they reflect the laity's concern with the mechanics of salvation. Foundation deeds might specify the daily duties of the chantry priest ('cantarist'), his moral character, holidays, and pension. Where the Church laid down a cycle of votive masses for the liturgical week, founders might vary it to introduce their favoured saints or cults and specific prayers and devotions, seeking intercession and forgiveness for their particular sins. Although such instructions were doubtless drawn up with the advice and approval of a priest, they can reflect the testator's own close familiarity with the liturgy. The furnishing of their chantries with images of saints, devotional emblems, and texts all formed a scheme of intercession for the soul's pilgrimage. Secondly, however, the chantry was not solely for the founder's benefit, but commemorated his family, living and dead, his friends and patrons, and, indeed, all who came to hear the votive Mass. Thus those who went to the tomb of William Carent in Henstridge church (Dorset) were promised forty days' indulgence. On the anniversary, provision was often made for a distribution of alms. Chantries thus had a social and not merely individual role. Thirdly, chantries contributed to the religious life of a church, providing additional priests and masses, and in some cases acting as chapels of ease in outlying parts of the parish. Despite being closely woven into the religious life of the family and the parish, most chantries had a limited life. The number of new foundations slackened after $c.1450$ and by the time of their suppression the memory and intentions of many founders had been lost.[14]

[13] K. L. Wood-Legh, *Perpetual Chantries in Britain* (Cambridge, 1965), 8–92; G. Burgess, '"By quick and by dead": Wills and pious provision in late medieval Bristol', *EHR* 102 (1987), 837–58; id., 'For the increase of divine service', *JEH* 36 (1985), 46–68; Rosenthal, *Purchase of Paradise*, 31–52; Hamilton Thompson, *English Clergy*, 132–60.

[14] M. A. Hicks, 'Chantries, obits, and almshouses: The Hungerford foundations, 1325–1478', in Barron and Harper-Bill (eds.), *The Church in Pre-Reformation Society*, 123–42; id., 'The piety of Margaret, Lady Hungerford (d. 1478)', *JEH* 38 (1987), 19–38.

In the late Middle Ages the parish, much more than the cathedral or monastery, was the vital unit of religious life because it afforded greater involvement to the laity, who contributed their wealth and energy to an unparalleled degree. We have now to examine how this affected its devotional life.

2. PUBLIC WORSHIP

The extension of spiritual disciplines and devotion beyond the regular and higher clergy to the life of the parishes had begun in the thirteenth century. First, the Lateran Council of 1215 had set in motion a diocesan programme of visitation and legislation designed to raise standards among parish priests, and secondly the friars vigorously evangelized the laity by preaching which mixed the castigation of sin with the affective piety of the Cistercian tradition. By the mid-fourteenth century these measures were bearing evident fruit in the emergence of a lay element who were doctrinally informed and spiritually aware. The question was, would they become critical and alienated or orthodox and involved?

From the late thirteenth century the ecclesiastical authorities had begun to ensure that the parish clergy could instruct their congregations in both their obligations and the faith. The code issued by Archbishop Pecham in 1281 known as *Ignorantia Sacerdotum* focused on confession (required annually by Innocent III in 1215) both to define and correct sin and to instruct on the central articles of the faith, the ten commandments, the creed, and the seven sacraments. The two were complementary, for penitents could be examined on their sins, and set the task of memorizing the commandments as penance. Writings like William of Pagula's *Oculus Sacerdotis* (1320–30) and its digest, the *Pupilla Oculi* of 1385, drew heavily on canon law to categorize sins, and on moral theology to guide the priest's interrogation and response in confession. An important advance came when Archbishop Thoresby commissioned the translation into the vernacular of a summary of *Ignorantia Sacerdotum* so that parish priests throughout the province of York could expound it to their flocks. This *Lay Folks' Catechism* (1357) set out all the articles of the faith, while a similar vernacular treatise, versified for memorizing, was produced by John Mirk, prior of the Augustinian house at Lilleshall (Salop.) around 1400 under the title *Instructions for Parish Priests*. This provided a complete vade mecum for the unlearned parish priest, covering his duties and behaviour, his hearing of confession, and examination of the laity's knowledge of the faith. It should be emphasized that none of these manuals were addressed to the laity; they were designed to equip the clergy to instruct the ignorant layman and respond to the more critical.[15]

---

[15] This literature is well surveyed in Pantin, *English Church*, 189–219; R. N. Swanson, *Religion and Devotion in Europe, c.1215–c.1515* (Cambridge, 1995), ch. 2 and pp. 59–64.

Sin, and the necessity for confession and absolution to secure salvation, lay at the heart of medieval religion. The nobility were allowed their own confessors, and all the laity could choose friars as confessors provided their annual pre-Easter confession was made to their parish priest. Although confessors' manuals detail the technique of questioning and the imposition of penance, the gradations between mortal and venial sins, sins of intention and those of deed, and those against God and neighbour, it is impossible to assess how closely these approximated to practice. Certainly the annual confession by all parishioners at the Easter vigil must have been more of a ritual than a personal examination, with the emphasis placed on purging the Christian community of the socially disruptive sins of pride, envy, and anger.[16]

Sin likewise formed the subject matter of much preaching. How much preaching there was is not easy to assess. Its nature and quality covered a wide range. At the higher end were Latin sermons preached in monasteries, colleges, and cathedrals to fellow priests, or at a public venue like St Paul's Cross. These might deal with theological controversies over poverty or grace and the corruption of contemporary society, and those who denounced most unsparingly (like Thomas Brinton, John Bromyard, and Thomas Wimbledon) were those who drew the largest audiences. Dominicans and Carmelites continued to enjoy a deserved ascendancy both at this level and as itinerant preachers in urban centres. Collections of sermons, mainly in Latin, survive in large numbers, though in what form and in what proportion they were preached cannot be known. Sermons preached in English were probably more common than the Latin texts (on which they drew) suggest. From archbishops down, prelates did preach *ad populum*, e.g. on a visitation. The sermons of the friars followed an academic construction but also employed ear-catching stories drawn from daily life, while itinerant Wycliffite preachers favoured the older homily on a biblical text. The normal parish sermon is better represented in Mirk's *Festial*, a vernacular collection for use by parish priests. Sermons were only obligatory on four occasions in the year and during Lent, and although a brief address might follow the offertory at High Mass, the lengthy discourses in the *Festial* would have been more suited to the extra-liturgical sermons delivered on Sunday afternoons. Mirk's homilies do interpret the gospel parables, but the main burden was always the detailing of sins and their personal and social consequences. At this level, preaching was closely allied to confession, and both were directed towards social harmony, the love of one's neighbour, more than to a searching examination of the individual conscience.[17]

[16] J. Bossy, *Christianity in the West, 1400–1700* (Oxford, 1985), 45–56; id., 'The social history of confession in the age of the Reformation', *TRHS*, 5th ser., 25 (1975), 21–38; Duffy, *Stripping of the Altars*, 58–60.

[17] G. R. Owst, *Preaching in Medieval England* (Cambridge, 1926) remains a valuable, if disordered, survey. For English sermons, see H. L. Spencer, *English Preaching in the Late Middle Ages*

In the Mass the emphasis was necessarily somewhat different. Although it did have a social content and significance, when those present received the *pax* and exchanged the kiss of peace and, as the body of Christ, were restored to wholeness by the priestly communion, it centred on the hurt done to God by individual sin and the unique satisfaction for this brought by Christ's sacrifice of himself. The re-enactment of that sacrifice on the altar, where Christ's body under the form of bread was again broken and consumed by the priest to procure salvation for the faithful, was the central act of the Christian faith. At its heart lay a miracle, indeed a double miracle: that the bread and wine became the actual body and blood of Christ and that they nevertheless, as a concession to human frailty, retained the appearance of elements. It was not surprising that the Church should shield this miracle from lay involvement by performing it at the altar, out of view and earshot, and in Latin. Nor that it took effect through words correctly said, *ex opere operato*, independent of the priest's own worthiness. This embodied 'an enormously high doctrine of priesthood'. Normally only the priests officiating received communion on behalf of the laity present; for the laity it was obligatory at Easter, recommended at the great feasts, and permitted at other times by personal dispensation.

The ritual of the Mass reflected the traditional gulf between the clergy, as guardians of mysteries defined and performed in a learned language, and the laity, as ignorant and largely passive observers. By the fourteenth century this gulf was being narrowed by the growth of literacy and lay devotion. But since the laity had no role in the liturgy, how could they participate? One answer was to make the Mass intelligible, so that the onlooker could follow its stages. Thus Mirk's *Instructions* and the *Lay Folks' Mass Book* (1375) taught the laity to follow the choreography of the Mass, the priest's movements and gestures, through the sequence of confession, gospel, offertory, and the canon of the Mass, culminating in the consecration and elevation of the Host and priest's communion. Secondly, the congregation was encouraged to echo these stages by private prayers in the vernacular, using a rhymed confession and version of the Gloria, repeating privately the Lord's Prayer and creed, making intercession at the offertory for grace, mercy, and safety, and at the *pax* for amity. Finally, at particular points they were told to stand for the gospel, sit for the sermon, and kneel and raise their hands at the elevation. The words of the Mass itself were not translated, but were to remain inaudible and incomprehensible. It is difficult to judge how satisfying was this encouragement of private devotion as a substitute for active participation. Clearly not all took pains to follow and understand. Since fixed seating was only being introduced in the fifteenth century, there was

(Oxford, 1993), 1–78, 109–19; Swanson (trans. and annot.), *Catholic England*, 51–77; A. J. Fletcher, 'John Mirk and the Lollards', *Med. Aevum*, 56 (1987), 217–24.

constant movement and talking in the body of the church while the liturgy continued in the chancel. For much of the time most people probably remained
mentally spectators. What is undoubted is that the elevation of the Host became
not merely the climax but the essence of the Mass, providing a kind of spiritual
infusion as a substitute for reception. For some it had a magical significance, safeguarding them that day against misfortune and sudden death, and they would go
from one mass to another to be present at the elevation. For the devout it could
release emotions nurtured by meditation. For the incredulous it was said
that God might strip away the veil to reveal the bleeding Christ and cure them of
their unbelief.[18]

Perhaps because it remained remote and inexplicable, the mystery of the Mass
captured and obsessed the lay mind, notably in the context of sin, death, and Last
Judgement which confession, sermons, and wall-paintings held constantly
before them. The canon of the Mass contained only a brief and impersonal commemoration of the souls of the departed, but its salvific power was seized on to
mitigate the pains of purgatory. Although not finally defined until the Councils
of Lyons (1274) and Florence (1439), the doctrine of purgatory had been developed in the twelfth century. Following death, the souls of those dying in a state of
grace needed to be purged of the remaining guilt (*culpa*) of their venial sins and
the penalty (*poena*) for man's original sin, in preparation for the Beatific Vision.
Although, unlike the souls in hell, those in purgatory could look forward to eternal salvation, purgation by fire was extremely painful and prolonged, and was
envisaged as lasting thousands of years. It could, however, be shortened by the
prayers of the living and especially by offering Christ's propitiatory sacrifice in
the Mass. At the risk of devaluing the plenary and complete nature of this, the
Church bowed to the demand for multiple masses by those who could afford
them. The richer went in for overkill: Archbishop Courtenay purchased 10,000
masses for his soul, and the wealthy merchant William Setman of Norwich paid
for 4,000 to be said immediately after his death. Almost half the Norwich wills
provide for masses for up to four years, costing £5 and over, but more modest testators had to be satisfied with a 'trental' covering the thirty days after death, and
an anniversary celebration. Benefactions to churches both for the fabric and for
the furnishings, like pulpits, fonts, and chalices, could likewise be pleaded as
good works for the remission of sins, and carry an inscription asking for prayers
for the donor's soul. Thus the communion of living and dead was constantly
manifest through the visible furniture of the church, the lights before altars and

---

[18] On the Mass, see Duffy, *Stripping of the Altars*, 91–130; Rubin, *Corpus Christi*, chs. 1, 2, esp.
p. 109; J. Bossy, 'The Mass as a social institution', *P & P* 100 (1983), 29–61; Swanson, *Religion
and Devotion*, 137–41; id., (trans. and annot.), *Catholic England*, 79–91; for behaviour in church,
M. Aston, 'Segregation in church', in W. J. Shields and D. Woods (eds.), *Women in Church*, SCH
27 (Oxford, 1990), 237–94.

shrines, and the sequence of votive masses at chantries and altars. Intercession was the predominant activity within the medieval parish church.[19]

The pains of purgatory could also be mitigated through an indulgence. Indulgences were based on a scholastic construct which was extrapolated to meet popular needs. Christ's sacrifice, being sufficient satisfaction for the sins of mankind throughout all ages, constituted an infinite treasury, or store, of grace or merit, which His successors in the chair of St Peter had power to administer. Since the penances to be undergone in purgatory were measured in terms of days and years, indulgences would remit specific lengths of time to those who performed meritorious acts on earth. These took many forms. Pilgrimages were undertaken both individually and in company as meritorious and penitential acts and for the relief of illness. They were made not only to the great shrines of Canterbury, Hailes, and Walsingham, but to innumerable small churches harbouring relics of local saints. Most carried an indulgence of variable length. Indulgences were often issued for new projects such as the establishment of a new shrine or repairs and additions to the cathedral fabric. The popes delegated a limited authority to bishops to issue such, which were hawked by licensed pardoners at established rates. Plenary indulgences were issued by the popes themselves.[20]

The purchase of indulgences by the living and the endowment of requiem masses for the departed both manifested the laity's determination to harness the power of the priesthood for personal salvation. While the Church inculcated guilt for sin and the fear of hell, the laity responded by reducing this to largely contractual terms. Contrition was, of course, requisite, but the penalties of sin could be traded against gifts and good works. Thus William Nesfield established his chantry at Scotton (Yorks.) 'for the establishment of celebrations of masses, which are the more profitable to Christ's faithful people unto salvation, inasmuch as in the same the King of Heaven is placated by mystic gifts, and remedies for sin are more easily obtained by asking'.[21] The doctrine of purgatory thus generated the flow of lay wealth not only into the building and adornment of churches but into the support of numerous priests who, as stipendiaries and cantarists, ensured the continual performance of masses, especially in urban churches. Yet if 'masses with a guaranteed power to relieve the dead were a felt need', a demand-led religion carried its own dangers. When man could purchase

[19] C. Burgess, '"A fond thing vainly invented": An essay on Purgatory and pious motive', in Wright (ed.), *Parish, Church, and People*, 56–84; Duffy, *Stripping of the Altars*, 338–56.

[20] Swanson, *Religion and Devotion*, 217–27; id., 'Indulgences at Norwich Cathedral Priory in the later Middle Ages', *Hist. Res.* 76 (2003), 18–29; Duffy, *Stripping of the Altars*, 287–90; N. Vincent, 'Some pardoners' tales: The earliest English indulgences', *TRHS*, 6th ser., 12 (2002), 23–58; G. W. Bernard, 'Vitality and vulnerability in the late medieval Church', in J. L. Watts (ed.), *The End of the Middle Ages?* (Stroud, 1998), 199–233.

[21] Hamilton Thompson, *English Clergy*, 141.

salvation, making God a party to the contract, the road to Pelagianism lay open. Some contemporaries deplored it: the author of *Dives and Pauper* castigated the bargaining for prayers and masses as 'much simony, much hypocrisy, much folly'.[22]

If the ordinary layman learnt to sanitize and accommodate the 'sin culture' of the medieval Church, he also drew comfort and strength from its corollary, the emotive or affective tradition. This, too, was centred on the figure of Christ, supported by that of His Virgin Mother and other saints. Within a church it was most vividly presented through the figures of the Rood, often below a depiction of the Last Judgement on the chancel arch. Crucifixion devotion in the late Middle Ages emphasized Christ's humanity, to arouse compassion for, and identification with, the torn and bleeding body on the cross. Christ was depicted as vulnerable and broken, and the wounds on brow, hands, feet, and side were subjects for particular devotions. Mary's own grief evoked corresponding devotion, her figure being the most frequent of any at shrines and altars. The images of other saints, in innumerable niches both within and outside the church, or depicted with reference to their miracles on walls and the panels of screens and pulpits, were all designed to give help and comfort to the viewer. Beset by the harshness, injustices, and tragedies of life, it was to Christ and the saints that men turned for support and the promise of a better world. Above all the Blessed Virgin, as a privileged mediatrix, could implore mercy for souls poised in the balance at the Last Judgement. Thus was she depicted in many dooms.[23] What emotions were evoked by these public images are only occasionally revealed, and the intensity of Margery Kempe's was probably not typical.

Public worship was elaborated and revitalized in the first half of the fifteenth century in response partly to the challenge of Lollardy, and partly to royal and episcopal initiative. By 1430 the general adoption of the Sarum Use imparted greater uniformity to common worship while it also afforded opportunities for liturgical elaboration and the burgeoning fashion for polyphonic settings. New feasts were inaugurated to express popular cults, and votive masses incorporated private devotions. Laymen figured alongside clergy in public processions accompanying the Host, and within the church icons multiplied on altars, furnishings, and walls. Much in this 'Theatre of Devotion' represented the external manifestations of piety, but it undeniably reflected a recovery of nerve and a sense of identity in the English Church.[24]

[22] Duffy, *Stripping of the Altars*, 373–5; Swanson, *Religion and Devotion*, 226.
[23] Duffy, *Stripping of the Altars*, ch. 5; Swanson, *Religion and Devotion*, 142–71.
[24] Catto, 'Religious change under Henry V', 97–116.

3. PRIVATE DEVOTION

The affective piety of the age is most clearly discerned in the books of hours and the writings of the mystics. Meditative and contemplative prayer had been by tradition the preserve of the regular clergy. When the literate laity sought to undertake the discipline of private devotion they understandably turned first to the divine office recited daily in religious houses. The breviary was too long and complex for their purpose, and from the fourteenth century a selection from the offices was adapted and abbreviated for devotional use. This 'book of hours', or 'primer', contained the hours of the Blessed Virgin Mary, the seven penitential and fifteen gradual psalms, the litany of the saints, the office for the dead, and the commendations (Psalms 119 and 139). Even in Latin much of this would be familiar to anyone hearing the daily offices, and from the end of the century it was available in translation as *The Lay Folks' Prayer Book*. Further, around this traditional core could be added petitionary prayers and affective devotions to be used in preparation for, and during the course of, the Mass. For these books were small and portable, and the more expensive of them had illuminations depicting the sequence of the crucifixion and resurrection, and scenes from the life of the Virgin.[25]

Late medieval devotion was Christocentric. It focused on the miracle of transubstantiation and developed the cult of Corpus Christi, both to honour it and to identify it with the body of the faithful. Fractures in the Christian society, by political and social disputes, or even worse through heresies, were violations to Christ's body, a message expounded in the processions and plays which celebrated the feast day. Accompanying this was a shift in devotion from the ascended and triumphant Christ of earlier centuries to the crucified figure evoking pity and love. St Bernard's famous exhortation to 'take note and see his head bowed to greet you, his mouth to kiss you, his arms spread to clasp you, his hands trembling to hold you, his side open to love you, his body stretched taut to give himself wholly to you'[26] had epitomized Cistercian devotion, and this theme of physical identification was elaborated in the affective meditations of the later Middle Ages. The prayer of adoration, *Adoro Te*, attributed to Aquinas and the *Ave Verum Corpus Natum*, written by Innocent VI (1352–62), were included in books of hours and translated into the vernacular. From the early fourteenth century the Five Wounds became one of the most popular votive masses, the wounds being associated with particular sins and the sources of corresponding graces. They were depicted in gory detail on statues, wall-paintings, and

[25] H. Littlehales (ed.), *The Prymer, or, Lay Folks' Prayer Book*, 2 vols., EETS, orig. ser., 105, 109 (London, 1895, 1897); Duffy, *Stripping of the Altars*, ch. 6; J. Bossy, 'Prayers', *TRHS*, 6th ser., 1 (1991), 137–50; J. Backhouse, *Books of Hours* (London, 1985).

[26] Swanson (trans. and annot.), *Catholic England*, 130; id., *Religion and Devotion*, 181.

illuminations, and emblematically on fonts and furnishings as heraldic supporters on the shield of Christ. The wound in Christ's side invited particular devotion as the source of the Eucharistic Blood and access to His heart, although the
cult of Christ's blood was never as developed in England as on the Continent.
The revelation to St Bridget of the exact number of Christ's wounds was developed into a meditation on stages of the crucifixion known as the fifteen 'Oes'
which came to form part of the primer, and was later refashioned as the Stations
of the Cross. This sustained imaginative attempt to visualize Christ's suffering
and experience the pain, besides arousing outrage and compassion, sought to
impress on worshippers the love for mankind which inspired His self-sacrifice.[27]

This emphasis on the humanity, rather than the divinity, of Christ was a
response to the growth of lay devotion. If it produced 'a pullulation of macabre
fictions', it generated others of a more tender and feminine character, in the
myths of a Holy Family and those associated with the Virgin Mary. These were
essentially attempts to domesticize the Incarnation, the mystery of God made
man, and make it graspable in human terms.[28] This was most conspicuous in the
mystery plays, where the whole cycle of Christian salvation was presented, but it
also generated devotional cults and literature. The *Golden Legend* fleshed out
Jesus's genealogy, emphasizing the matrilineal connections, fitting in his brothers Simon and Jude and making John the Baptist a cousin. St Anne assumed
greater prominence and popularity when her feast was promulgated by Urban
VI in 1386. The cult of the Virgin had an ever increasing appeal. On the one hand
her experience as a mother made her accessible to human emotions, with her
wonder and joy at the annunciation and nativity celebrated in paintings and
carols and her grief as the *Mater Dolorosa* in the *Pietà* with the body of her son.
These were elaborated into the Five Joys and Five Sorrows of the Virgin,
included in the primers, especially in the prayer *Obsecro Te*, imploring her aid.
On the other, her unique status was increasingly affirmed. Her Immaculate
Conception, which had been a matter of dispute between the two orders of
friars in the thirteenth century, was promulgated by Sixtus IV in 1476. St Bridget
had revelations of the physical details of the painless and unassisted virgin birth.
She was entitled Queen of Heaven and the *Salve Regina* was sung regularly after
compline. Where meditation on Christ's passion fed the desire for mystical
union with Him, Mary was implored as a mediator, with a natural understanding
of human sorrow, a bridge towards the Godhead.[29]

---

[27] Rubin, *Corpus Christi*, 156–9, 168, 264, 302–16; S. Beckwith, *Christ's Body* (London, 1993),
chs. 1, 2; Duffy, *Stripping of the Altars*, ch. 7; J. C. Hirsh, 'Prayer and meditation in late medieval
England: MS Bodley 789', *Med. Aevum*, 48 (1979), 55–71.
[28] Bossy, *Christianity in the West*, 7–11; Swanson, *Religion and Devotion*, 144–5; D. Aers and
L. Staley, *The Powers of the Holy* (University Park, Pa., 1996), ch. 1.
[29] Duffy, *Stripping of the Altars*, 256–66, 318–20; Rubin, *Corpus Christi*, 145.

The concentration of late medieval spirituality on an 'affectionate, penitential intimacy with Christ and his Mother' found expression not only in books of hours but in other writings used in lay instruction and devotion. These fall into three broad categories, though with much overlap between them.[30] The first, which I have already noted, were the manuals in the vernacular on the faith and religious practice addressed to the clergy but designed to be read to a lay audience. Such were *The Lay Folks' Catechism*, Mirk's *Instructions*, and *The Lay Folks' Mass Book*. In a second category were writings to instruct the individual in holy living and dying. A major part of these centred on the penitential system, analysing the seven deadly sins and the temptations to them through the five senses. This had an ancestry in the thirteenth-century *Manuel des Péchés*, versified in Robert Mannyng of Brunne's *Handlyng Synne* (1303), and underlay Henry of Lancaster's *Livre de Seyntz Medicines* (1354). A very popular tract written *c*.1360, which survives in 115 manuscripts, was *The Prick of Conscience*, calling for self-examination in terms of the four last things, death, judgement, hell, and heaven. Others, like *The Book of Vices and Virtues* (*c*.1375), a translation from French, *Dives and Pauper* (*c*.1410), and the long *Speculum Vitae* (1384) of William of Nassyngton, in verse and prose, were structured on the Decalogue or the Lord's Prayer. This catechetical and confessional literature for the laity undoubtedly reinforced the obligations of medieval society, both social (*caritas*, almsgiving, and sexual morality) and magisterial (work, tithe-paying, law-keeping, obedience). As a class, literate laymen had no taste for a more radical Christianity. Yet the priestly authors, as confessors and preachers, were not indifferent to social abuses and did not shrink from exhortations to social justice. They encouraged penitents to recall (as did Henry of Lancaster) occasions when they had oppressed the poor, defrauded the weak, and indulged in gluttony while others starved. Such sins had especially to be recalled at the point of death, a social drama at which friends and family anxiously judged whether the dying man's confession and absolution had won the final struggle between angels and devils for the possession of his soul. The art of dying well developed a literature and iconography of its own.[31]

In a third category of writings were those specifically addressed to the devout and literate laity, advising them how they might follow spiritual disciplines in a worldly and domestic context. This was a new genre. Hitherto the contemplative life had been the preserve of the regular clergy, at the other pole to the active life

---

[30] These are well surveyed in Pantin, *English Church*, ch. 10, in slightly different categories. See also, Hicks, 'Lord Hungerford's chantry', 394; M. C. Woods and R. Copeland, 'Classroom and confession', in *CMHEL* 376–406 (quotation at 400).

[31] Swanson (trans. and annot.), *Catholic England*, 125–49; V. Gillespie, 'Vernacular books of religion', in *CHB* 317–44; Woods and Copeland, 'Classroom and confession'; M. Aston, 'Death', in Horrox (ed.), *Fifteenth Century Attitudes*, 202–28.

of the secular clergy and laity. The latter could achieve salvation by loving God and their neighbour, undertaking good works, and honestly fulfilling their worldly obligations. The concept of a 'mixed life' embodying daily spiritual exercises met the desires of the educated laity, attracted by the meditative and mystical writing of the later fourteenth century. Its most influential exponent was Walter Hilton, whose own guide to mystical experience was written in the vernacular. His *Epistle on the Mixed Life* was addressed to lords and prelates who exercise worldly rule but also seek communion with God in meditation. They should not abandon the *negotium* of their office, but through meditation on Christ's passion and love their minds will be loosened from worldly concerns, and prepared for contemplation.[32] In the same spirit the anonymous *Instructions*, probably drawn up by his confessor for a town-dwelling lawyer, official, or merchant, set out a daily discipline.[33] He is first to hear Mass at his local church, then throughout his daily business he is to cultivate the habit of mental prayer, and even at home at family mealtime he is to keep his thoughts fixed on Christ's passion, silently arranging the bread on the table to represent the Five Wounds, before withdrawing to his oratory to pray. A more general exhortation to follow a programme of moral and spiritual development was the tract for married or widowed women with worldly responsibilities, entitled *The Abbey of the Holy Ghost*. None of these specifically set out the disciplines of meditation, but other treatises, often given the title of 'mirrors', present the impediments and aids to spiritual progress and themselves contain elaborate meditations on the life and passion of Christ: whereby 'a man or woman may be stirred to true devocion and have . . . great compuncion and sorwe for his synes'.[34] Many of these were native products, but others were translations from European mystical writings like *The Boke of Gostely Grace* from St Mechtild of Hackeborn (d. 1299) and *The Orcherd of Syon* from the *Dialogo* of St Catherine of Siena. Other works of instruction present man's life as a pilgrimage, encountering diversions and temptations in the quest for salvation, a theme treated imaginatively by William Langland and didactically by Guillaume de Deguileville (1330–1). Such devotional writings in the vernacular reflected the burgeoning piety of the era which sought to sacramentalize daily life. It brought the accompanying danger that individual experience could confront the deposit of the faith. This was greatest among those who carried affective devotion to its limits, the English mystics.

[32] Printed in Swanson (trans. and annot.), *Catholic England*, 104–24; H. M. Carey, 'Devout literate lay people and the pursuit of the mixed life in late medieval England', *Jnl. Relig. Hist.* 14 (1987), 361–81; J. Hughes, *Pastors and Visionaries* (Woodbridge, 1988), 251–69.

[33] W. A. Pantin, 'Instructions for a devout and literate layman', in J. G. Alexander and M. T. Gibson (eds.), *Medieval Learning and Literature* (Oxford, 1976), 398–422.

[34] Swanson (trans. and annot.), *Catholic England*, 96–103, for 'The Abbey'. For the 'Mirrors', see Pantin, 'Instructions', 403, and D. Gray (ed.), *The Oxford Book of Later Medieval Verse and Prose* (Oxford, 1985), 94–112; Hirsh, 'Prayer and meditation'; Gillespie, 'Vernacular books of religion'.

The mystical moment of direct communion with God had traditionally been the preserve of saints or the professed religious, and described in Latin. In the fourteenth century it was claimed by a handful of English people of very disparate background and capacities, who sought to communicate their experience to fellow Christians. Two of them, Walter Hilton and the *Cloud* author, were priests, drawing on theological training and language. Richard Rolle and Julian of Norwich were recluses, but Rolle had an Oxford background and Julian was not as unlettered as she claimed. Margery Kempe alone was unable to read and write, but had absorbed much from her priestly mentors. Rolle and Hilton wrote in both Latin and English, and the *Cloud* author used English by choice, though aware of its theological limitations. The movement had a strong feminine orientation, for as well as Julian and Margery as authors, both Hilton and Rolle wrote specifically for professed women or anchoresses. All write with a sense of striving to present a new spiritual dimension to a new audience in a new medium.[35]

Richard Rolle was the earliest of these and remained the most influential. Over 400 manuscripts of his work survive and he was still being recommended by Thomas More after two centuries. He was born near Pickering (Yorks.) around 1300, the son of a smallholder, by whose efforts and those of local clerical patrons, he was sent to Oxford. Reacting against scholastic thought, he returned to Yorkshire, adopted a hermit's dress, and won a reputation for holiness among the secular clergy and educated laity of the region. For this audience, until his death in 1349, he wrote a series of works in Latin and English describing his own mystical experiences and encouraging others in the practice of contemplation. In *Melos Contemplativorum* (1330) and *Incendium Amoris* (1340) he insisted that God could only be apprehended by love, and not through learning, and described his own sensations of heat, sweetness, and song when conscious of the divine presence. In *Emendatio Vitae* he set out the steps of spiritual ascent to mystical experience, and for Margaret Kirkby, a recluse at Hampole, he wrote *The Form of Living*, expounding the love of God as 'light and burning'. Here and elsewhere he proved himself 'the first master of Middle English prose', writing with clarity, lyricism, and balance.[36]

By 1380 mystics of a different temper were viewing Rolle's work with reservations. Walter Hilton was one of those academically trained administrators whom

---

[35] For the English mystics in general, see D. Knowles, *The English Mystical Tradition* (London, 1961); M. Glasscoe, *English Medieval Mystics: Games of Faith* (London, 1993); N. Watson, 'The medieval English mystics', in *CHMEL* 541–66; S. S. Hussey, 'The audience for the Middle English mystics', in M. G. Sargent (ed.), *De Cella in Seculum* (Cambridge, 1989), 109–22.

[36] Knowles, *English Mystical Tradition*, 48–66 (quotation at 63); *English Writings of Richard Rolle*, ed. H. E. Allen (Oxford, 1931); N. Watson, 'Richard Rolle as elitist and popularist: The case of *Judica Me*', in Sargent (ed.), *De Cella in Seculum*, 123–44. For Rolle's influence in Yorkshire and among the Carthusians, Hughes, *Pastors and Visionaries*, 64–126, 222–7, should be used with caution.

Rolle disliked, but spiritual dissatisfaction with his life led him, in 1384, to leave Cambridge to become first a hermit, then an Austin canon, and eventually prior of Thurgarton (Notts.) until his death in 1396. His own experience impelled him to seek a place for contemplation within the life of the secular Church, and his most influential works, the *Scale [or Ladder] of Perfection* and the *Epistle on the Mixed Life*, map out the practice of this, the one for an anchoress (but also for a wider audience), the other for those with secular authority. Hilton insisted that mystical experience must be grounded in a rigorous discipline of prayer and devotional persistence and must not discard objective faith for subjective feeling. While agreeing that God can only be approached through love, by meditation on the passion, he explicitly warns that bodily sensations of heat, sweetness, and song must not be mistaken for divine illumination. At the same time Hilton displays a humane common sense, cautioning against excesses of both exultation and depression. His work deservedly won acclaim across the spectrum from solitary religious to devout laymen.[37]

Hilton wrote as a churchman, conscious that lay individualism had already begun to infect vernacular theology with heresy. His contemporary, the unidentified author of *The Cloud of Unknowing*, was also a priest from the East Midlands, who wrote to advise a young solitary, possibly a Carthusian novice. He wrote with a higher level of aspiration and experience. For him the love of God was to be attained through mental and inward contemplation, not through visual and affective devotion to Christ's passion. That, and all other earthly matters, must be banished from the mind by an act of will, leaving the postulant in a vacant darkness, a 'cloud of unknowing'. God is obscured by this, until 'the sharp dart of love' pierces the cloud, and the human soul momentarily knows the presence of God, as before the Fall. His is an intellectual and austere work, perhaps influenced by Carthusian spirituality, yet avowedly stretching English to new limits to encompass mystical theology.[38]

Only the writings of Rolle and Hilton were widely disseminated, and those of the other two, Julian of Norwich and Margery Kempe, survive in single contemporary manuscripts. Both women were East Anglians and met each other at least once, but their worlds and lives were otherwise totally dissimilar. For most of her long life, from 1342 to *c.*1416, Julian was an anchoress at Carrow, near Norwich. In the course of a near-fatal illness in 1373—for which she had prayed—she had a series of visions, or 'showings', centred on a dialogue with the Godhead. The

---

[37] Hilton's works accessible in translation are *The Ladder of Perfection*, ed. L. Shirley Price (Harmondsworth, 1957) and *Epistle on the Mixed Life*, in Swanson (trans. and annot.), *Catholic England*, 104–24. G. R. Keiser, '"Noght how long man's life but how wele": The laity and the *Ladder of Perfection*', in Sargent (ed.), *De Cella in Seculum*, 145–59.

[38] *The Cloud of Unknowing*, ed. P. Hodgson, EETS, old ser., 218 (London, 1944) is available in *The Cloud of Unknowing and Other Works*, ed. A. C. Spearing (Harmondsworth, 2001).

exploration and interpretation of these became the subject of her meditations and writing. Her central preoccupation was the tension between God's omnipotence and benevolence and the existence of sin. Although her access to divine love had been through visualization of, and meditation on, the passion, her language and thought was not affective but rational. The originality of her vision lies in the intensity of her conviction that evil was essentially a negation, to be ultimately subsumed into God's goodness in the promise that 'all shall be well and all manner of things shall be well'. Her belief in God's mercy made her recoil from the notion of eternal damnation for those in mortal sin, and her sense of God's foreknowledge inclined her to predestination. She was probably aware that in these respects she was treading along the borderline of Catholic faith. Further, as a woman she did not presume to instruct, but merely recounted her experience for the benefit of 'even [other] Christians'. Her *Revelations of Divine Love* was the first book on the spiritual life to be written by an English woman for 200 years.[39]

Margery Kempe was born around 1373, the daughter of a mayor of Lynn, and married to a burgess, by whom she bore fourteen children before persuading him, in 1413, to live in chastity. Using her own financial resources she was able to make pilgrimages to the Holy Land and Italy in 1413–15, to Compostela in 1417–18 and, after the death of her husband, through Danzig, Germany, and Holland in 1433–4. Her autobiography, dictated to an amanuensis since she could neither read nor write, is a frank and detailed narrative of her spiritual experiences on these journeys, on visits to shrines in England, and on occasions in Lynn. It is the picture of an uninhibited religious ecstatic, moved regularly and readily to copious tears and loud lamentations at sermons, the sight of the Host, and images of the passion. These outpourings of affective piety aroused wonder and admiration in some, impatience and censure from others, both clerical and lay. Nor did she refrain from open rebukes to worldly and tepid clergy, and harangues to neighbours and strangers. Like Julian, she pursued an internal dialogue with the Godhead, though on a personal rather than transcendental level. An element of physical, indeed erotic, intimacy marked her visions of Christ, whose mouthpiece she proclaimed herself to be; but there is little sign of inner discipline or perhaps true mystical insights. Her assiduous observance of religious rites, her orthodoxy, and her social standing protected her from charges of Lollardy and won a measure of authorization from both prelates and local clergy, but it is clear that she aroused embarrassment and suspicion. It is easy to dismiss her naivety and doubt the quality of her religious ecstasy, but her *Book* attests the emotive hold of crucifixion piety over fifteenth-century society.[40]

[39] *A Book of the Showings to the Anchoress Julian of Norwich*, ed. E. Colledge and J. Walsh (Toronto, 1978). See also Aers and Staley, *The Powers of the Holy*, 77–104, 107–78.

[40] *The Book of Margery Kempe*, ed. S. B. Meech and H. E. Allen, EETS, old ser., 212, (London, 1940) is available in a modernized version, ed. B. L. Windeatt (Harmondsworth, 1985). Among the

In a historical, rather than spiritual, perspective the fourteenth-century English mystics are significant for their development of a vernacular theology. The Cistercian–Franciscan mystical tradition was now taken up by secular clerks, recluses, and literate laity for an audience of their own kind. That could only accentuate the challenge to ecclesiastical structures inherent in the mystical experience. Scholastic theology acknowledged the distinction between God's absolute and ordained power. The former could operate directly on the 'ground' or heart of the human soul, the latter through the normative channels of salvation, namely the sacraments of the Church. The former transcended sense and reason through the spark of love; the latter rested on a conferred authority. The former had the certitude of experience or feeling, the latter was embodied in carefully defined articles of faith.[41] Both churchmen and mystics were alive to this problem of individual revelation. Thus Hilton emphasized that, not feeling, but 'the Faith of Holy Church is what you believe, though you neither see it nor feel it', and others carefully affirmed their commitment to orthodoxy.[42] Yet in different ways all came to the brink: Rolle over the necessity of sacramental confession, Julian over God's tolerance of evil, and Margery Kempe over Jesus' direct authorization of her acts. That only Margery Kempe came under threat of investigation was partly because the others wrote before the persecution of Lollardy, and partly because of their personal and literary obscurity.

Nevertheless, in a period when the wealth of the Church and the careerism of the higher clergy were devastatingly criticized, its sacramental authority denied, and the individual's interpretation of the Bible asserted, the nervousness of the ecclesiastical authorities over the influence of mystical writing was understandable. While the 'negative' mysticism of the *Cloud* author was for the few, the affective piety of Rolle, echoed in numerous devotional treatises and meditations, excited a potentially anarchic religiosity. Hilton had warned of its dangers, and Archbishop Arundel took steps to bring vernacular theology under the Church's control. Particularly effective was the official approval he conferred on Nicholas Love's work the *Mirror of the Blessed Life of Jesus Christ* (1410), which presented the story of Christ's life and passion as a basis for affective meditations in the Carthusian spiritual tradition. Text and interpretation were elided to present 'fructuose' spiritual instruction. The laity were offered 'the milk of doctrine', without having to chew over hard theological problems. Love's work proved both popular and influential, helping to foster lay devotion in the rest of

extensive literature on Margery Kempe, see C. Atkinson, *Margery Kempe: Mystic and Pilgrim* (Ithaca, NY, 1983); Beckwith, *Christ's Body*, ch. 4; D. Aers, *Community, Gender, and Individual Identity* (London, 1988), 76–115.

[41] S. E. Ozment, *Mysticism and Dissent* (London, 1973), 1–13.
[42] Hilton, *Ladder of Perfection*, bk. I, ch. 21, bk. II, ch. 17.

the century.[43] For although the English mystics had no successors, the Carthusian houses of London, Mountgrace, and Sheen, and the Bridgettines of Syon, became centres for the dissemination among regular and secular clergy and devout laymen of the works of English and continental mystics, meditative studies, and private prayer sequences. These helped to shape a religious culture shared by the Latinate intellectual elite of John Blacman's circle within the royal court and colleges, busy professionals like the exchequer teller William Baron, who made an anthology of devotional treatises for his niece, a nun at Dartford, and those 'simple men and wymmen of goodwill' who relied on *The Poor Caitif* to guide them to heaven 'without multiplicacion of many books'.[44]

The vitality and exuberance of late medieval religion, both public and private, exemplified the Church's success in absorbing the aspirations of a newly literate laity to participate in its corporate and liturgical life. By the second quarter of the fifteenth century the challenge from anticlericalism and heresy had passed, and a wave of orthodoxy marked the convergence of lay and priestly piety. Dissent had been all but eradicated. Did this represent a triumph or a failure for religious faith?

4. WYCLIF AND WYCLIFFISM

As the great heresiarch of the late Middle Ages and the prophet of sixteenth-century Protestantism, John Wyclif seems a figure of seminal importance. Yet in the context of his times, he has been depicted simply as a scholastic philosopher, a disappointed careerist, and an anticlerical polemicist. There are disparities between what he attempted and what he achieved. Thus, although his writings systematically dismantled the institutions, authority, and practices of the medieval Church, their influence was greater in Bohemia than in England. While their tone was contentious, irascible, and negative, it was their appeal to individual faith that provided his most influential spiritual legacy. Here it is proposed to discuss his thought and career in tandem and then assess the influence of Wycliffism in the years following his death.[45]

---

[43] N. Watson, 'Censorship and cultural change in late medieval England', *Speculum*, 70 (1995), 822–59; K. Ghosh, *The Wycliffite Heresy* (Cambridge, 2002), ch. 5.

[44] Gillespie, 'Vernacular books of religion', in *CHB* 352; M. C. Erler, 'Devotional literature', in *CHB* 495–525; on William Baron's compilation (Bodleian Library, MS Douce 322), see A. I. Doyle, 'De Vere family books and Barking Abbey', *Essex Archaeological Society*, 25 (1958), 228–9; for Carthusian influence, R. Lovatt, 'The *Imitation of Christ* in late medieval England', *TRHS*, 5th ser., 18 (1968), 97–122; id., 'The library of John Blacman and contemporary Carthusian spirituality', *JEH* 43 (1992), 195–230.

[45] For a summary of Wyclif's career and writings, see *BRUO* iii. 2130–6. The most readable account is that by K. B. McFarlane, *John Wycliffe and the Beginnings of English Nonconformity* (London, 1952), 12–120.

Wyclif was born in Yorkshire around 1330 and was probably sent to Oxford by a noble or ecclesiastical patron. He held a fellowship at Merton in 1356, was master of Balliol in 1360–1, and was made warden of Canterbury College by Archbishop Islip in 1365, only to be removed when the Benedictine monks were reinstated by Archbishop Langham. Despite a growing academic reputation he had received only a couple of minor benefices, and by the age of 40 his career had still failed to take off. From 1365 he was propounding the metaphysical system which was to underpin his subsequent writings on the Church, the Bible, and the faith. Like most Oxford philosophers he was a realist, but one who took the extreme view that universals subsisted as real entities—'intelligible beings'— outside their material forms, and were located beyond time and space in the mind of God. All created matter thus derived from God's will and love, eternally and indestructibly. He regarded the opposing view, that particulars were discrete entities and universals mere names or categories, as sinful and anarchic, a denial of God as the source of being and knowledge.[46] By 1370 Wyclif had moved, both intellectually and formally, into theological discourse. He incepted as a bachelor of theology in 1369 and a doctor in 1372–3. At precisely this point the world beyond Oxford changed. War with France was renewed, and military defeats and crippling costs precipitated a political crisis. In the parliament of 1371 the episcopal ministers of the peace years, Wykeham and Brantingham, were dismissed, and heavy taxation was demanded from the Church to the accompaniment of orchestrated demands for its wealth to be confiscated to pay for the war. Suddenly the academic debates which had engaged Wyclif—Ockham's nominalism, Bradwardine's predestination, Fitzralph's theories of dominion— acquired a different significance. Wyclif set himself to answer the question: by what right did the Church enjoy its possessions, and could these be removed from it and by whom?

He set out his views in lectures on ecclesiastical and civil lordship which were subsequently published in 1375–6. It was traditional teaching that wealth and rule legitimately rested not on mere power, but on God's delegation to those who were in a state of grace. From it Giles of Rome had argued for the right of the Church, and the pope as God's vicar, to confer authority on temporal rulers. More recently Archbishop Fitzralph had deployed it against the friars, denying their right to privileges because they exercised them unjustly. Wyclif now extended this to the Church as a whole, claiming that its corruption through the

---

[46] His realist logic, contained in the *Summa de Ente* (1365–72), is lucidly presented by G. Leff, *Heresy in the Later Middle Ages* (Manchester, 1967), ii. 500–11, and by A. Kenny, *Wyclif* (Oxford, 1985), 18–41, and in J. I. Catto, 'Wyclif and Wycliffism at Oxford, 1356–1430', in Catto and Evans (eds.), *Late Medieval Oxford*, 187–93. For a distinctive view of Wyclif's realism, see M. Wilks, 'The early Oxford Wyclif: Papalist or nominalist?', repr. in id., *Wyclif: Political Ideas and Practice* (Oxford, 2000), 33–62.

pursuit of wealth and privilege had deprived it of the rightful enjoyment of lordship and possessions. Since it had been given these by previous kings to perform spiritual services, the Crown should now resume them, as being forfeited by sin. Wyclif was later to extend this argument to embrace the Church's spiritual jurisdiction, and to buttress it by confining true lordship to God's elect. Civil rule did not fall under the same condemnation, for kings were stewards of the nation's wealth, and (as Christ had commanded) temporal power should be obeyed even if it were abused.[47] Wyclif's real target was the institutional Church, and his arguments marked him out as a useful apologist for the anticlerical lobby, led by Gaunt and the Black Prince, who were seeking to tax clerical wealth and resist papal demands.

In 1371 and 1373 the friars had been their most vocal allies, and there is no record of Wyclif's direct voice; but he was now a king's clerk and in 1374 received the valuable living of Lutterworth by Crown patronage and was employed in ongoing negotiations with papal mediators at Bruges. These promising openings were not fulfilled, for in 1375 Gaunt's diplomatic volte-face, sanctioning papal taxation in order to secure a truce, provoked the attack on him and his court allies in the Good Parliament. When Gaunt regained influence, annulled the work of the Good Parliament, and prosecuted its leaders including Wykeham, he brought Wyclif to London to whip up anticlerical feeling from the pulpits. Bishop Courtenay of London was provoked into summoning him to appear before the bishops in convocation at St Paul's. There, on 19 February 1377, a trial of strength took place when Wyclif came, accompanied by Gaunt and Henry, Lord Percy, and four friars. Insults were traded between Courtenay and the lords and the proceedings broke up as the crowd which had gathered became restive. Next day Gaunt and Percy hastily retired from London and Wyclif returned to Oxford. There his lectures on dominion had already come under attack from the Benedictines, who had sent a list of his conclusions to the papal court at Avignon. In May 1377 Gregory XI condemned eighteen propositions as erroneous and deeply subversive of Church government and ordered his imprisonment. At the end of the year he was again summoned to appear, this time before Archbishop Sudbury at Lambeth, but not until March 1378 did he obey and then came protected by a safe conduct from the Black Prince's widow. The bishops enjoined him to silence, but at Oxford he was neither suspended nor his opinions condemned.

Though he had escaped virtually unscathed, the winter of 1377–8 marked the end of Wyclif's flirtation with political anticlericalism. With the new reign that became a fading issue, and Gaunt himself had less influence. Then, in 1378, on

---

[47] A. Gwynn, *The English Austin Friars in the Time of Wyclif* (Oxford, 1940), 59–60, 66–71, 80–9; Leff, *Heresy*, 546–9; Kenny, *Wyclif*, 142–55; Wilks, *Wyclif*, 16–32, 182–3; Catto, 'Wyclif and Wycliffism', 182–4.

the death of Gregory XI the papacy and Christendom itself fell into schism, with England supporting the Roman pope Urban VI and France the Avignon pope Clement VII. The weakening of papal authority favoured Wyclif's personal immunity but it also reduced anti-papalism and the government's need for Wyclif's polemical skills. He could return to his academic milieu, secure in Gaunt's protection, but he had not notably advanced himself, while the hierarchy had marked him as an enemy. Further promotion was unlikely.

Wyclif was now free to construct a theological *Summa* on the basis of his metaphysical, biblical, and historical studies, one which would overturn existing Church order and doctrine in favour of a return to first principles and apostolic practice. The two treatises which he wrote in 1378, *On the Church* and *On the Truth of Holy Scripture*, were interdependent. In the first, already foreshadowed in his work on dominion, he developed St Augustine's metaphor of the two cities, heavenly and earthly, into metaphysical entities of the elect, who constituted the Church, and the damned, who were outside it. Each subsisted eternally distinct in God's mind, but their physical forms, or identities, could not be known on earth. As the community of the elect, living and dead, the true Church was a mental concept, which deprived the institutional Church of any intrinsic identity and spiritual rationale. Its priests were not necessarily among the elect and were superfluous as a channel of grace, since all men were predestined to either salvation or damnation. This has been described as 'the single most destructive and heretical feature of his teaching'.[48] Having already undermined the Church's claim to temporal lordship, Wyclif had now denied it spiritual authority.

He applied the same metaphysical reasoning to the Bible. This was God's word, as made available to human understanding. It contained all truth and all knowledge, it regulated all Christian living, and its authority was paramount. He insisted that biblical truth could be rightly interpreted by the elect in conformity with apostolic and patristic authority. This was the true *sensus catholicus*, as against the papacy's use of sacred text in decretals to justify the enlargement of its powers. Historically, Wyclif believed that the Bible depicted the Church in the apostolic age and should be the mirror and touchstone for its priesthood in his own time. It mentioned no popes, cardinals, and bishops; no property, lordship, and jurisdiction; and all these should be dispensed with. Following Marsiglio of Padua, he denied that the Petrine commission conferred a continuing primacy and jurisdiction on the see of Rome. To claim spiritual authority, a pope should be chosen by God and live on the model of Christ. As the word of God, the Bible was not only the touchstone of faith and conduct but the principal channel of salvation. Preaching the word was thus of greater importance than the sacraments.[49]

[48] Leff, *Heresy*, 516–45 (quotation at 520); Kenny, *Wyclif*, 68–79; Gwynn, *English Austin Friars*, 250–2; A. Hudson, *The Premature Reformation* (Oxford, 1988), 314–25.

[49] Leff, *Heresy*, 511–16, 520–5; Catto, 'Wyclif and Wycliffism', 195–6, 208–9.

In two further tracts in 1379 Wyclif defined the limits of spiritual and lay authority. *On the Papal Power* largely elaborated what he had already said: the papacy was of human, not divine, institution; it had no jurisdiction and could command obedience only through love, on the model of Christ; it should embrace poverty. Just as he reduced the Church to a purely spiritual role, so in his other treatise, *On the Office of King*, he invested the monarch with supreme temporal power. Wealth and lordship derived from God, and kings were the first and natural stewards on earth. Further, the king was God's vicar, the image of Christ's Godhead, where the priest was that of Christ's manhood. Thus the king was guardian of the spiritual welfare of the realm, and it was his duty to restore the Church to a condition of apostolic poverty and primitive simplicity of living in which it could rightfully exercise spiritual, but not temporal, jurisdiction.

Wyclif's ecclesiology and his views on the relationship of the two powers have been reckoned his 'most explosive legacy'. In their incipient form they had incurred papal condemnation in 1377, yet between 1378 and 1381 he was left free to develop and publish them in Oxford. Although some mendicant doctors, like William Woodford and Stephen Patrington, rejected his metaphysics and his views on biblical authority, many were ready to welcome his arguments against Church wealth and papal power. From 1350 to 1380 these were important and divisive issues, and Wyclif's radical and compelling arguments would be sympathetically heeded among the laity and the friars. It seems clear that at Oxford Wyclif was respected and feared as an original thinker, a formidable disputant, and a charismatic teacher, with 'the dangerous gift of inspiring discipleship'. Fellow academics were prepared to countenance heterodoxy in order to see where and how far an argument would lead.[50] It is in such terms that we must explain the tolerance of Wyclif's views on the Church and the Bible in contrast to the immediate outcry against his doctrine on the Eucharist.

Wyclif developed his denial of transubstantiation in 1379–80 although, as many have pointed out, it was inherent in his realist metaphysic and had been troubling him since the early 1370s. The doctrine that the bread and wine were changed into the body and blood of Christ by the priest's words of consecration had been defined in the Lateran Council of 1215. Scholastic dispute about how this occurred had continued for the rest of the century.[51] It could be held that the body and blood were added to, and coexisted with, the bread and wine; or that the bread and wine were annihilated and replaced by Christ's very body; or that

---

[50] Catto, 'Wyclif and Wycliffism'; Wilks, *Wyclif*, 117–78; McFarlane, *John Wycliffe*, 55–6 (quotation).

[51] For this, see G. Macy, 'The dogma of transubstantiation in the Middle Ages', *JEH* 45 (1994), 11–41.

the substance of the elements was changed while their appearance as bread and wine remained. The two latter explanations both involved a divorce between appearance and reality—that the bread and wine had become in fact Christ's actual body—or, in scholastic terminology, between the accidents (bread and wine) and substance (flesh and blood). Wyclif held such a divorce to be logically impossible. He could not accept that the substance or essence of a thing could be changed while its accidents or appearance remained the same. It was also impossible for its substance to be annihilated, for that inhered in God. In any case an accident without substance was nothing, a mere shadow, a simulacrum, and to venerate the consecrated bread in the Mass as such would be blasphemy. Wyclif found himself forced towards explaining the real presence of Christ in the Eucharist (which he affirmed) by a theory of coexistence. The substance of the bread and wine remained after consecration but Christ's body was also present, not physically but figuratively and sacramentally. He argued that such a view was consistent with both scripture and the Fathers, notably St Augustine, and that it had only comparatively recently come to be seen as heretical, by Aquinas and Albert the Great. A modern historian has pronounced Wyclif's eucharistic doctrine as 'comparatively innocuous'. Why then did it arouse instant condemnation and terminate his career at Oxford?[52]

On the intellectual level Wyclif's logic was unanswerable. An accident without substance contradicted the natural order. Transubstantiation had therefore to be accepted by faith, as a miracle wrought by God's absolute power, and for Wyclif it strained credibility that this was daily repeated at every Mass. And it was at the level of everyday practice that the consequences of Wyclif's doctrine would have been devastating. For the central act of making and eating Christ's body was the essence of priestly authority. It was a rite performed at a distance from the laity, who were shown the consecrated Host but only occasionally admitted to communion. Moreover, over the previous century the Mass had developed as the vehicle of intercession for the dead in many forms, while the Host had become an object with salvific power, and the centre of the new cult of Corpus Christi. For Wyclif all this represented a recent and unscriptural accretion of sacerdotal power, which his own eucharistic doctrine discounted. For Christ's figurative, instead of carnal, presence depended less on a miraculous act by the priest than on a reception of the elements with faith, bringing an infusion of grace by direct contact with God. This implied—though unlike Hus, Wyclif did not make this specific—that the laity should receive communion more frequently. Even so, the Eucharist as a sacrament remained less important as a means of salvation than

---

[52] Leff, *Heresy*, 497, 545 ('too academic to be of any practical importance'), 549–58; Kenny, *Wyclif*, 80–90; M. Keen, 'Wyclif, the Bible, and transubstantiation', in A. Kenny (ed.), *Wyclif in his Times* (Oxford, 1986), 1–16.

the direct reception of God's word by preaching. All this represented a direct assault on the priestly role in the central mystery of the Christian faith.[53]

The enormity of Wyclif's offence was soon brought home to him. At Oxford his long-standing opponent William Barton, now chancellor, appointed a commission of twelve doctors to examine his treatise *On the Eucharist*. Reporting at the end of 1380, it found—by the narrowest majority of seven to five—that its doctrines were erroneous and that those holding them (Wyclif himself was not named) should be banned from teaching and excommunicated. In May 1381 he defiantly affirmed his beliefs in his *Confession*. Then one month later came the outbreak of the Great Revolt against lordship. It was at once attributed to his influence and made the Crown ready to support ecclesiastical measures against him. His old enemy William Courtenay, who had succeeded the murdered Sudbury as archbishop, convened a council at Blackfriars on 17 May 1382 to condemn Wyclif's teaching. Ten propositions were pronounced heretical and fourteen erroneous. Among the former were those on transubstantiation, the scriptural authority for the Mass, the sacrament of penance, and papal authority. From his rectory at Lutterworth, Wyclif took up his pen to defend and reiterate his opinions. A trilogy written in 1381 and 1382, *On Simony*, *On Apostasy*, and *On Blasphemy*, was filled with vituperative attacks on the friars who had deserted him and obsessive denunciation of the papacy as Antichrist. The 'private religion' of the regular orders should be annulled, the worship of the early Church restored, and sacramental practices and devotions should cease . In his last completed work restating his beliefs, the *Trialogus*, he affirmed that 'the sacrament of the altar is very God's body in form of bread', for which he claimed the authority of St Augustine.[54] Slowed by a stroke in 1382, Wyclif continued to work on his *Opus Evangelicum*, left uncompleted at his death on 31 December 1384. Though his heresies had been condemned, he had not been deprived, unfrocked, or excommunicated, and had suffered no physical harm. For the moment Courtenay was intent on eradicating Wycliffism from Oxford and Wyclif could be left to die in obscurity at Lutterworth.

Wyclif's writings constituted the most sustained and revolutionary attack on the structure and doctrine of the Catholic Church in the Middle Ages. What impelled him into heresy, and was his an idiosyncratic voice or did it resonate with his age? It should be emphasized that virtually nothing is known about Wyclif's personality. His contemporaries made the barest mention of his slight physique, abstemious habits, and personal magnetism. The rest we have to

[53] See the important article by J. I. Catto, 'Wyclif and the cult of the eucharist', in K. Walsh (ed.), *The Bible in the Medieval World*, SCH Subsidia, 4 (1985), 269–86. Late medieval eucharistic practice is discussed above, Ch. 9, sect. 2. See also M. Rubin, 'Corpus Christi, fraternities, and late medieval piety', in W. J. Shields and D. Wood (eds.), *Voluntary Religions*, SCH 23 (1986), 97–110.

[54] Printed in *SEWW* 17–18, and, for a discussion of its authenticity, 141–4.

deduce from his academic writings and his career. Broadly, three views have been taken of what drove Wyclif to heresy. First, a long tradition has treated him as an archetypal religious prophet castigating the abuses of his age and calling for a return to primitive simplicity. Commonplace this may be, but his sincerity was not less than that of Brinton and Langland, and in some recent scholarship his evangelism has been freshly stressed. Secondly, he can be seen as essentially a scholastic, who applied his extreme realism to theology with inexorable logic. His mind was powerful but inflexible, and he could not resist following its reasoning to the furthest conclusions. Thirdly, Wyclif has been portrayed as a disappointed careerist. Expecting reward for his talents, he exploited the anticlerical politics of the 1370s by justifying disendowment and reform, only to find that he had alienated the hierarchy without advancing his career or achieving his programme. He had the misfortune to live at a time when the royal power to which he appealed was in abeyance, and his frustration was vented on the hierarchy and doctrine of the Church.[55]

What seems clear is that neither his call to return to the age of the Apostles nor his realist metaphysic were likely to generate a widespread movement of spiritual reform, while political conditions afforded scant prospect of the overthrow of the Church from either above or below. If Wyclif appeared as the morning star of a reformation, it was not one for which his world was ready. But in one respect he did attune with the mind of his generation. Wycliffism was nourished by the emergence of lay literacy, access to scripture, and individual interpretation, the seedbed of religious nonconformity.

There is no clear evidence that Wyclif, in his final years, instigated or directed a movement to propagate his beliefs. Yet such had begun within months of his leaving Oxford, and its agents were initially his Oxford disciples. It was mainly academic in inspiration, although it acquired political and popular dimensions. Defiance was first shown in Oxford. With the support of the current chancellor, Robert Rigg, the Oxford masters Nicholas Hereford and Philip Repingdon preached university sermons on Ascension Day and Corpus Christi 1382, the former urging forcible dispossession of the Church, the latter supporting Wyclif's teaching on the Eucharist. There were also preaching tours outside Oxford: in May, Hereford, Laurence Bedeman, and Robert Alington were at Odiham, and Repingdon at Brackley. Other immediate followers of Wyclif, William Swinderby, John Aston, and John Purvey, attracted a following in Leicester and Bristol. It was against these academic dissidents that William

---

[55] For Wyclif's reputation, see Hudson, *Premature Reformation*, 60–2; M. Aston, 'John Wycliffe's Reformation reputation', in id., *Lollards and Reformers* (London, 1984), 243–72; Leff, *Heresy*, 494–9 (as a philosopher); McFarlane, *John Wycliffe*, 95–6 (as a disappointed careerist).

Courtenay directed his attack. When Rigg failed to promulgate the Blackfriars condemnation of Wyclif in Oxford he was summoned to London and was ordered to suspend Hereford, Repingdon, Bedeman, and Aston. They were examined at the council and by the autumn all except Hereford had recanted and he, after a fruitless appeal to Rome and a brief imprisonment on his return, did likewise. By showing firmness and forbearance Courtenay had decapitated Wycliffism at Oxford, and in November the university formally accepted his visitation and submitted.[56]

In fact academic Wycliffism was not so easily eradicated. Over the next twenty-five years its activities can be traced in three areas: in providing preachers, as the probable base for translating the Bible, and as the likely source of a vigorous polemical literature. Since all were, in some degree, covert and illicit, the evidence for them is imperfect and often oblique, as will be apparent in briefly surveying each in turn. The primacy of the Word of God in Wycliffite belief made preaching the priest's most important function. The text of Wyclif's own sermons preached between 1376 and 1379 is preserved in Latin, but a complete liturgical cycle of 294 sermons in English, produced in a Wycliffite scriptorium some time before 1401 and surviving in no less than thirty-one manuscripts, indicates the importance attached to preaching the gospel. These were serious expositions of biblical passages, eschewing both the use of popular fabliaux favoured by the friars and the divisions and distinctions derived from academic disputations. They may have been intended less for delivery than for guidance and material for preachers, or as homilies to be left as further reading after a more lively discourse. That Wycliffite preaching retained its academic base is suggested by the warnings issued by bishops in the late 1380s about itinerant preachers, some of whom can be identified as *magistri*. Most of their preaching was probably done from churchyards and market crosses and other local landmarks, though on occasion an incumbent sympathetic to the new ideas might offer them his pulpit. They seem mainly to have operated in the Midlands and in counties bordering the Thames.[57]

Within Oxford itself there is only intermittent evidence of continuing Wycliffite influence. Some texts of Wyclif continued to be copied, studied, and cited in disputations. Some infected *magistri* were from time to time expelled, like William James, Henry Crumpe, and Robert Lychlade in the 1390s, but others openly survived, like William Taylor and Peter Payne, principals of

[56] A. Hudson, 'Wycliffism in Oxford, 1381–1411', in Kenny (ed.), *Wyclif in his Times*, 68–73; ead., *Premature Reformation*, 70–80; McFarlane, *John Wycliffe*, 101–14; J. I. Catto, 'A radical preacher's handbook, *c*.1383', *EHR* 115 (2000), 893–904 (on Bedeman); J. Dahmus, *William Courtenay, archbishop of Canterbury, 1381–1396* (London, 1966), 85–110.

[57] Hudson, *Premature Reformation*, 64–5, 78–81, 196–7, 268–72; *SEWW* 11; Ghosh, *Wycliffite Heresy*, ch. 4.

St Edmund Hall in 1405–6 and 1411–13. The latter pulled off a propaganda prank in 1406, when he procured the university seal to attest the orthodoxy of Wyclif's opinions in a letter to the university of Prague. Next year scholars from Prague were in the locality of Oxford seeking copies of Wyclif's writings, which must have existed in some numbers before they were burnt in 1411. At a more scholastic level William Woodford continued to dispute Wyclif's eucharistic heresy in 1383–4 and in 1390 his *Four Determinations* defended the Church's authority to interpret scripture and the legitimacy of 'private religions'. Wycliffite views continued to get a hearing and command a measure of informed support.[58]

A more sustained and systematic endeavour was the Wycliffite translation of the Bible into English. The Catholic Church used the Bible liturgically in Latin and as texts for sermons in English, but for Wyclif's followers the Word of God was too important to be 'clasped up, ne closed in no cloyster', and had to be accessible to all Christians. A translation had therefore to be authoritative, complete, and comprehensible. The immense task, which undoubtedly owed its inspiration to Wyclif himself, was probably undertaken by a group of scholars at Queen's College who had been his followers, including Hereford, Repingdon, John Trevisa, and Robert Alington. Not only the size of the book but the large number of copies made indicate the scale of the venture. Despite the subsequent proscription and prosecution of those who had it, no less than 250 copies of the Wycliffite Bible survive either whole or in part, some as large, ornate 'lectern' Bibles for reading aloud; others (often of parts of the Gospels alone) small and for personal use. A remarkable preface, added by an individual as it neared completion, gives an insight into the problems faced and the principles which guided it. First, a reliable Latin text ('somdel trewe') had to be established, using the *Glossa Ordinaria*, Jerome, and Augustine; then a word-by-word translation was made which had been done by 1397, constituting an early version (EV). This was quickly seen to be clumsy and unintelligible and replaced by a more idiomatic version (LV), translated by the meaning of the sentence. Separate glosses were provided which, like the text, were both scholarly and unbiased. The Wycliffite Bible was in fact substantially orthodox and came to be used by those whose status and credentials put them beyond suspicion.[59]

The translators had defended their aim of making God's Word accessible to all, thereby opening up a debate on Bible translation in which learned opinion

[58] Hudson, *Premature Reformation*, 86–97; ead., *Lollards and their Books*, 77–84; J. I. Catto, 'Fellows and helpers: The religious identity of the followers of Wyclif', in P. Biller and B. Dobson (eds.), *The Medieval Church: Universities, Heresy, and the Religious Life* (Woodbridge, 1999), 141–61.

[59] Watson, 'Censorship and cultural change', 835; Hudson, *Premature Reformation*, 238–47; *SEWW* 67–72; Catto, 'Wyclif and Wycliffism', 221–39.

was sharply divided. The arguments are summarized in documents from 1401 in which two mendicant doctors, Thomas Palmer and William Butler, were opposed by the secular master Richard Ullerstone. Butler took the traditional view that theology was solely for priests and the laity should receive the faith through sermons and liturgy. Palmer questioned the advisability of translating Latin theological concepts into the unstructured grammar of English, through which errors of faith might creep in. Ullerstone, urging the more liberal view, protested that English was not a barbarous tongue and that a laity directly responding to the scriptures would form a harmonious Christian society. Even so, he reserved interpretation to priestly learning. Over the last half-century the Church had accorded a tentative welcome to the vernacular as enabling lay participation in worship, but the Wycliffite heresy brought this to an end. The Church's monopoly of the Bible had rested on the Latin of the Vulgate and the exegesis of scholars. The Wycliffite Bible with its text and glosses in English assaulted this directly. The laity were being invited to read and interpret, guided by the Holy Spirit, thereby encroaching on the learning of the Schools. Hoccleve sought to ridicule amateur biblical exegesis by women who asked,

> Why stant this word here; why this word there
> Why spak God thus, and seith this elleswhere
> Why dide he this wyse, and mighte han do this?

It was becoming clear that an English Bible could be far more subversive than an English sermon.[60]

While the Wycliffite Bible provided the bedrock of vernacular theology, a spate of short treatises and broadsheets publicized debate on Wycliffite tenets. Most were polemical, attacking the structure, doctrine, and practice of the Catholic Church; they were directed to a literate but non-academic audience, and though anonymous must have been written by graduates conversant with theological terms. Some of these were treatises on a single theme, such as the primacy of scripture, images and pilgrimages, or the Eucharist; others embraced the full range of the Wycliffite creed. Some confronted Catholic and Wycliffite doctrine and practice point by point, as in debate; others sought to prime a suspect under interrogation with equivocal answers. Some were vitriolic on Catholic abuses; others preached personal humility and charity. In not a few passages the English language was confidently used in invective, peroration, and irony.

The Lanterne of Light, from the beginning of the fifteenth century, is a carefully constructed statement of Wycliffite belief contrasting Christ's church of

[60] Watson, 'Censorship and cultural change', 840–7; Hudson, *Lollards and their Books*, 67–84; ead., *Premature Reformation*, 228–64; Ghosh, *Wycliffite Heresy*, 1, 3; M. Aston, 'Wycliffe and the vernacular', in id., *Faith and Fire* (London, 1993), 27–72 (quotations cited in nn. 52, 56).

the saved with the Fiend's church of the pope and hierarchy and the 'new orders' (i.e. the religious). The argument is liberally supported by citations of scripture and from the Church Fathers. This was a work procured for the well-to-do London skinner John Claydon, who had absorbed its message even though he was not himself literate. At a different level the *Twelve Conclusions* of 1395 crudely denounced Catholic practices and provoked a studied response from the Dominican Roger Dymoke. Satire in the well-practised genre of a *Letter from Satan* praised the clergy for departing from the model of Christ's priesthood, while the somewhat less effective polemic of *Jack Upland* listing their delinquencies elicited a scornful riposte entitled *Friar Daw's Reply*. Wycliffite sermons routinely attacked the wealth and corruption of the endowed clergy and the greed of the friars, contrasting it with the preaching and poverty of the 'true priests'. The relation between the two powers was similarly debated in the lively and colloquial *Dialogue between a Knight and a Clerk*, which concluded in favour of the Wycliffite view that the Church had a purely spiritual authority and should not claim temporal dominion. A more academic treatment of the same theme was the *Tractatus de Regibus*, a free translation of Wyclif's *De Officio Regis*, while the *Thirty-Seven Conclusions of the Lollards* drew on his *De Potestate Papae*.[61] Hostility to liturgical elaboration, the adornment of churches, and above all to the veneration of images and pilgrimages acquired greater prominence in Wycliffite writing than in that of the heresiarch. Wyclif had been prepared to accept images as books for the laity and condemn only their veneration as idolatrous, but among his followers the increasing emphasis on the first commandment, and on the offensiveness of intercession through saints, soon led to iconomachy and individual acts of iconoclasm. Man as God's image, particularly in the persons of the poor, was contrasted with the painted and adorned images in shrines to which pilgrimages were made. The scorn poured on relics and the denunciation of pilgrimages as covers for tourism and sin by William Thorpe fully anticipated that of the sixteenth-century humanists. In general, objection was stronger to three-dimensional images than those painted, and in particular to the conventional representation of the Trinity depicting God as an old man with the Son between his knees. The cross itself was respected but decorated portrayals of the crucified Christ fiercely condemned. All this castigation of the externals of worship reflected the development of Wycliffism out of an academic system into a living faith.[62]

---

[61] Hudson, *Premature Reformation*, 208–27; *SEWW*, sect. I, III, IV; ead., *Lollards and their Books*, 193–200; L. M. Swinburne (ed.), *The Lantern of Light*, EETS, old ser., 151 (London, 1917); P. L. Heyworth (ed.), *Jack Upland, Friar Daw's Reply and Upland's Rejoinder* (Oxford, 1968).

[62] M. Aston, 'Lollards and images', in id., *Lollards and Reformers*, 135–92, and likewise in id., *England's Iconoclasts*, i (Oxford, 1988), 96–159. Thorpe's picture of a pilgrimage crowd is unforgettable: 'men and wymmen that kunnen wel synge rowtinge songis, and also summe of these pilgrims

In the quarter-century following Wyclif's death his followers had opened up academic scholarship and argument to the world of vernacular reading. The translation of the Bible, a liturgical cycle of vernacular sermons, a Wycliffite dictionary of biblical and patristic texts (the *Floretum*), and popular instructional and polemical literature had furnished Wycliffism with an armoury of its own vernacular theology. In a literary context it forms part of the outburst of writing in English alongside the heartfelt denunciation and exhortation of Langland, Gower, and the author of *Mum and the Sothsegger* on moral, social, and political issues. Yet inasmuch as this literary programme had sought to make the Word of God accessible to all, it had invited departures from the canon of Wyclif's own beliefs. There was never an authorized Wycliffite creed. Indeed in an age of acute religious awareness Wycliffism was not always distinguishable from the radicalism of Langland's search for an uncorrupted faith and the mystical pietism of Rolle. Thus the history of Wycliffism in these years is one of both proliferation and dilution.

Among the inner core of Wyclif's disciples there had been some notable defections. Repingdon, Hereford, and Alington had quickly repented of their youthful radicalism and found a channel for their personal piety and evangelical zeal in a new reform movement within the Church. The rest remained Wycliffite in varying degrees of constancy, though none had to face the ultimate test, for the prevailing anticlericalism at both parliamentary and local level frustrated any general prosecution of Wycliffism. At the personal instigation of Archbishop Arundel the introduction of the death penalty for relapsed heretics in 1401 brought England into line with continental practice, but for the moment claimed only one victim, William Sawtre. In 1406 a statute ordered local magistrates to arrest suspect dissidents for interrogation before the chancellor and parliament, but that could prove double-edged. Under interrogation Wycliffites insisted on answering in English, thereby securing an audience for their views, as in the case of John Aston at the Blackfriars Council in 1382. It also enabled them to exploit the imprecision and ambiguities in transposing Latin theology and terminology into a Wycliffite context in which even common terms like 'Church' and 'priest' carried different connotations. Attempts to pin them down on eucharistic theology often foundered among such ambiguities. Wycliffite suspects anticipated interrogation by preparing statements of belief in innocuous terms, they were furnished with specimen questions through which the authorities hoped to entrap them, and warned never to admit a false proposition when coupled with a

wolen have with hem baggepipis so that in eche toun that thei comen thorugh, what with the ginge-lynge of her Cantirbirie bellis, and with the berkynge out of dogges aftir hem, these maken more noyse than if the king came there awey with his clarioneris and many other mynystrals' (A. Hudson (ed.), *Two Wycliffite Texts*, EETS, old ser., 301, (Oxford, 1993), 64; and see also *SEWW* 83–8).

true one.[63] The record of their defence at such trials made propaganda for the Wycliffite cause. The most notable was that of William Thorpe before Archbishop Arundel in 1407. Thorpe's account describes his interrogation on the Eucharist, the duty of confession, the adoration of images, pilgrimages, tithe, and the permissibility of oaths. He responds with verve and humour, parrying Arundel's questions and occasionally turning the tables on him. He is given the lengthiest speeches and the best arguments, being sustained like St Paul by the Holy Spirit. An undoubtedly historical occasion was thus turned into a highly effective piece of propaganda with hagiographical undertones, to sustain the faithful.[64]

Beyond the ranks of the Wycliffite priests and their converts the movement is known to have attracted the sympathies of some in chivalric and court society. Their proximity to, and influence over, the king alarmed the chroniclers, who named seven 'Lollard knights': Sir John Cheyne, Sir John Clanvowe, Sir Lewis Clifford, Sir Thomas Latimer, Sir John Montagu, Sir William Nevill, and Sir Richard Stury. Since royal protection guaranteed their immunity, none of them was ever subject to examination and the exact nature of their beliefs is uncertain. Their sympathies have been inferred from their protection of known Wycliffite priests, their patronage of Wycliffite writings, and the wording of their wills. These suggest that their religion was puritanical, biblical, and grounded in an immediate relationship with God. One of them, Sir John Clanvowe, wrote a pietistic treatise which pilloried the 'goode felawes' whom the world acclaimed: those who spent their lives indulging the lusts of the flesh and pursuing the 'foule stynkyng muk of this false faillynge world'. Their wills likewise reject the fashionable ostentation of funeral rites, express contempt for the body, and often make provision for the poor. None of this provides indubitable evidence that they subscribed to Wyclif's heretical beliefs like his ecclesiology and rejection of transubstantiation. Much of their language was common to both the Wycliffite and the devotional traditions.[65]

How representative were these Lollard knights at this level, and did their presence at court encourage political action? The only occasion under Richard II when Wycliffite views were voiced in a political context was the posting of the *Twelve Conclusions of the Lollards* on the doors of Westminster Hall and St Paul's during the parliament of 1395. Walsingham attributed this to the agency

---

[63] 'The sixteen points in which the bishops accuse the Lollards', in *SEWW* 19–23.

[64] Hudson (ed.), *Two Wycliffite Texts*, pp. xxvi–lix, 24–93; Hudson, *Premature Reformation*, 220–2; M. Jurkowski, 'The arrest of William Thorpe in Shrewsbury and the anti-Lollard statute of 1406', *Hist. Res.* 75 (2002), 273–95.

[65] K. B. McFarlane, *Lancastrian Kings and Lollard Knights* (Oxford, 1972), 139–232; Catto, 'Fellows and helpers', 154–6; Sir John Clanvowe, *Works*, ed. V. J. Scattergood (Cambridge, 1975), 67, 70, 72; Aston, *Faith and Fear*, 128–31.

of four named Lollard knights but none were in fact sitting in this parliament. Calling on the Lords and Commons of parliament to reform the English Church, the *Twelve Conclusions* detailed the moral corruption of the clergy by a sacramentalism which invested the priesthood with a spurious authority and misled the people. If its uninhibited polemic was designed to undermine support for the Church among the political class, it had the opposite effect.[66] It provoked Richard II to clamp down on known Lollards on his return from Ireland. Some were imprisoned, others were expelled from Oxford, and among those at court Sir Richard Stury and an esquire, John Croft, were cautioned. But by now their numbers had diminished. Clanvowe and Nevill were dead, Stury and Clifford had reached their sixties, and Cheyne had fallen out of favour. Richard had a new set of confidants, of whom only John Montagu, now earl of Salisbury, and perhaps Sir Philip Vache held suspect views.[67]

Whatever the grounds for Richard II's expressed view that Henry IV had no love for the Church, from the beginning of the new reign Archbishop Arundel sounded the alarm over the presence of its enemies in parliament and the court. He prevented Cheyne from becoming Speaker in the parliament of 1399 and throughout the first half of the reign constantly complained about the infidels at Henry's side. As the Crown's financial difficulties deepened, the cry for disendowment was revived as counterpart to the Commons' call for a resumption of Crown gifts. The archbishop successfully fended this off in 1404, but the threat reappeared in 1406. With the king and the Commons deadlocked over a grant of taxation conditional on the reform of royal government, the Wycliffite William Taylor secured the pulpit at St Paul's to rouse the Londoners against the temporal lordship of the Church. Answered the next day on the Church's behalf by Mr Richard Alkerton, he was in turn ridiculed by Henry IV's esquire Robert Waterton, who presented him with a curry-comb for currying favour with the bishops. The king protected Waterton from Arundel's fury and Taylor ignored the ecclesiastical censure.[68]

A full quarter of a century after Wyclif's departure from Oxford his influence was evidently still pervasive. Arundel, now aged 53, resolved to devote his last years to its eradication. He first directed his attack at its fount, in Oxford. In 1407 he issued Constitutions regulating the preaching and reading of Wycliffite beliefs. Within the university no MA was to teach theological matter, and all

---

[66] The *Twelve Conclusions* are printed in *SEWW* 24–9. For a discussion of some issues raised by them, see M. Aston and C. Richmond (eds.), *Lollardy and the Gentry in the Later Middle Ages* (Stroud, 1997), notably the contributions by C. Richmond, A. Hudson, and F. Somerset.

[67] For Cheyne, see *House of Commons*, ii. 549–52; for Vache, ibid. iv. 700–5. For Richard II's 'growing obsession with orthodoxy', see Saul, *Richard II*, 301–2.

[68] Aston, *Faith and Fire*, 107–31; Hudson (ed.), *Two Wycliffite Texts*, pp. xi–xxv, 3–23; P. McNiven, *Heresy and Politics in the Reign of Henry IV* (Woodbridge, 1987), 104–6.

proposition of, or disputation on, articles contrary to the Catholic faith and decrees was forbidden. No Wycliffite text was to be used in the Schools, and students were to be examined monthly on their orthodoxy. Beyond the university, all preaching had to be licensed, the matter to be orthodox, and criticism confined to sermons to clerical audiences. Finally, any translation of scripture had to be approved by the diocesan. These Constitutions struck at scholars' traditional liberty to test the bounds of heterodoxy in disputation within the walls of the lecture room. In Arundel's view that had been abused in two respects: by Wyclif's advocacy of heresies so fundamental that they inculcated mortal sin, and by his followers' propagation of these in secular society. In effect the university was being challenged to rethink its role: was it to be a centre of intellectual exploration and possible dissent, or was it to underpin the established order?[69]

This assertion of episcopal authority understandably aroused the scholars' opposition. They dragged their feet when ordered to review and proscribe Wyclif's heretical books, and only after renewed pressure from the archbishop was a bonfire of them made at Carfax in March 1411. In June, Arundel imposed an oath of orthodoxy on all members of the university, repulsed the university's attempt to escape his jurisdiction, and finally conducted a visitation to root out those who held heretical views. A number of these who had been sustained by the general opposition to Arundel now left; others conformed, among them Richard Fleming, later to become bishop of Lincoln. The last one of note to depart was probably Peter Payne, who fled to Prague in 1413. The university may have experienced this forceful disciplining with suppressed relief. It had already begun to move away from treating theology as a subject for scholastic disputation towards seeing it as 'a practical science which could be applied and diffused through sermons'. Ironically it had been Wyclif himself, the supreme scholastic of his age, who had initially signalled the change of direction. His insistence on the Bible's literal meaning and evangelical message placed greater weight on historical exegesis and pastoral diffusion through preaching. His followers had translated this into a programme of vernacular theology, but Arundel's measures to destroy this were seconded by the efforts of Oxford masters to recapture theology for orthodoxy. Greater attention was henceforth paid to the study of the Fathers than to the arguments of the Schoolmen; the propagation of received wisdom was set higher than specious originality; and a new form of preaching, less dialectic and more instructional, was introduced into the Schools.[70]

This change in the academic climate reflected a new era in the western Church. As the prospect of ending the Schism became a reality, so minds turned

[69] The Constitutions are summarized in Hudson, *Lollards and Books*, 146–7. For a discussion, see Watson, 'Censorship and cultural change', 822–32, and Spencer, *English Preaching*, 163–82.

[70] Catto, 'Wyclif and Wycliffism', 244–61; id., 'Theology after Wycliffism', in Catto and Evans (eds.), *Later Medieval Oxford*, 265 (for the quotation).

towards reforming the abuses associated with a papacy enslaved to political interests. Here again the excoriation of worldly clergy by Wyclif and others had prepared the ground for reform; not by the return to apostolic poverty which he had
demanded, but at least by curbing excesses and emphasizing pastoral responsibility, as in Ullerstone's proposals, which, on Henry V's command, were forwarded to the Council of Constance as an Oxford programme.

If Wycliffism had thus conditioned the reinvigorated Church of Henry V and
Archbishop Chichele, there is no escaping the scale of its defeat at Arundel's
hands. The proscription of translation and reading of the Bible brought vernacular theology to an abrupt halt. The provision of an 'open' Bible, in which the
meaning and intention of God's word could be directly apprehended by all men
through textual accuracy and scholarly glosses, charitable reading, and holy living, was outlawed for all but a privileged few. The barrier was thus restored
between theology as the preserve of a clerical Latinate elite and devotion and
worship to be practised by the laity. Sermons warned the 'lewd' (i.e. unlearned)
man that 'it is inowgh to thee to beleven as Holychurche techeth thee and lat the
clerks alone with the argumentes', or in Hoccleve's admonition to Sir John
Oldcastle:

> Lete holy chirche medle of the doctrine
> Of Crystes lawes and of his byleeve,
> And lete all other folk therto enclyne
> And of our feithe noon arguments meeve.[71]

The final, direct assault on Wyclif's theology was made by the Carmelite
Thomas Netter in the *Doctrinale Fidei Catholice*, undertaken at the request of
Henry V in order to demonstrate the recovery of English orthodoxy and completed in 1427–30. Netter read all of Wyclif's works, and adopted his historical
and exegetical approach to biblical texts, but whereas for Wyclif this had been the
basis for individual interpretation, Netter bowed to the tradition of the Church.
Netter saw historical development not as a corruption of revealed truth, to be
stripped away, but as a continuing interpretation of it. It is a debate that has continued ever since.[72]

Between 1409 and 1411 Arundel had exterminated Wycliffism at Oxford and
totally outlawed its literature, but its political influence remained untouched.
When, in December 1409, he was ousted from the chancellorship and succeeded
by one of Henry IV's household knights, Sir Thomas Beaufort, under the aegis
of Prince Henry's administration, it was the signal for the boldest political initiative by Lollard knights. This was a parliamentary petition to the king and

---

[71] J. Coleman, *Medieval Readers and Writers, 1350–1400* (London, 1981), 207; Hoccleve,
'Remonstrance against Oldcastle', lines 137–41.

[72] Catto, 'Wyclif and Wycliffism', 259–60; Ghosh, *Wycliffite Heresy*, chs. 6, 7.

Lords from 'alle the trewe comeners' proposing the confiscation of the temporalities of all bishoprics and the principal monastic houses. It was calculated that from these revenues the Crown could be endowed with an income of £20,000 per annum, and that fifteen new earls, 1,500 knights, and 6,200 esquires could be supported, along with 100 new almshouses, fifteen universities, and 1,500 Wycliffite priests for pastoral duties, leaving Catholic priests and prelates to live off spiritual resources. The institutional Church would thus be forcibly reformed in its apostolic state, its wealth returned to the laity, who had originally endowed it, and to the poor, from whom it had been extracted by deceit. While this formulated a long-matured Wycliffite vision, its chances of enactment were nil. It was vetoed by the king probably before it could be adopted by the Commons; it does not appear on the parliament roll, although another petition, for the virtual nullification of the statute *De Heretico Comburendo*, does and was formally rejected.[73]

Despite its far-fetched proposals, the political context of the bill makes its presentation comprehensible. Prince Henry had ousted Arundel in order to implement a reform of government with the support of the Commons, from whom he was seeking a guaranteed annual tax. Their unwillingness to authorize this provided an opportunity to revive the cry for the confiscation of the Church's wealth, raised intermittently since 1371. The proposals were designed to attract the widest support. Although the re-endowment of the Crown was modest, the largesse to be distributed to the political class anticipated that to the Bohemian nobility in the Hussite revolution and to the English after the Reformation. It was rather the vacuum of political authority that doomed it to remain a paper scheme. Whatever his own religious convictions—which were seemingly towards a puritanical orthodoxy—Prince Henry's position was too fragile for him to support such a contentious proposal. Even if some were sympathetic to a reduction of the Church's wealth, there would be strong opposition from Arundel, who showed that he was ready to raise the stakes by initiating the trial and burning of the heretic John Badby towards the close of the first session.[74] What support was there in parliament? In the Upper House Sir John Oldcastle, who had been summoned as Lord Cobham, was a committed Wycliffite and the likely sponsor of the bill. Among the Commons, for whom fewer than half the returns survive, only Sir Thomas Broke, the regular member for Somerset and Oldcastle's close ally, can be so identified. Others, like Sir William Stourton and John Golafre, who combined orthodoxy with an austere piety, may have favoured a degree of disendowment. Thus it is easy to see how the fluidity of the political scene could have both encouraged Lollard expectations and deterred Prince Henry. In the event neither side could claim victory: even though Arundel had

[73] Text and notes in *SEWW* 135–7, 203–7.   [74] McNiven, *Heresy and Politics*, 199–219.

defeated the most serious threat of confiscation to date, the Lollards had articulated and publicized a comprehensive plan at the highest political level.[75]

Beyond parliament it is impossible to assess how much support Wycliffism commanded among the gentry. Some small nests have been discovered, linked by locality, kinship, and business. One cluster in Herefordshire and Shropshire encompassed Thomas Clanvowe and his wife's family of Whitney, Sir Roger Acton, constable of Ludlow; and Sir John Oldcastle at Elmley. Another formed in the North Midlands around a group of local lawyer–administrators including Thomas Tickhill, Henry Booth, and John Findern. Tickhill was a local official of the prince of Wales and all had London connections. It has been suggested that the training and aptitudes of common lawyers provided fertile soil for heterodoxy.[76]

Archbishop Arundel now set his sights on Sir John Oldcastle, whose sympathies were ill concealed. As the Lollards' leader he had written letters to the Hussite nobleman Wok of Waldstein in 1410 and to King Wenzel in 1411 exhorting him to reform the Church, and was himself openly maintaining Wycliffite chaplains around Cooling. In 1411 Prince Henry, who valued his services as a soldier, sent him with the earl of Arundel to assist John the Fearless against the Armagnacs. Before the expedition finished, the prince had lost power and Archbishop Arundel returned as chancellor. When Henry IV's last parliament met in March 1413, as the king lay dying, Oldcastle was named in convocation as a maintainer of Lollards, and when it reassembled under the new king, incriminating evidence was produced and formal charges of heresy were laid against him. Arundel was fully aware of the problems and risks in directly attacking a courtier under royal protection, and agreed to a long suspension of proceedings while Henry attempted to persuade Oldcastle to recant. Only in August, when the accused abruptly left for Cooling, was the archbishop allowed to issue a summons which eventually brought his arrest and trial on 23 September. At the end of two days Oldcastle openly denounced and defied the authority of the pope and hierarchy, but even then was sent to the Tower for forty days to allow him to reconsider. Before that expired, on 19 October, he had escaped and gone to ground in London.[77]

To this point the facts are reasonably certain, but thereafter until his capture in 1417 Oldcastle remained a fugitive for whose acts and intentions we have only

[75] For the composition of the 1410 parliament, see the appendix by L. Clark in *House of Commons*, i. 218–24, and the biographies of Broke (ibid. ii. 377–9), Golafre (ibid. iii. 199–202), Oldcastle (ibid. iii. 866–70), Stourton (ibid. iv. 996–9).

[76] Ibid. ii. 576–8 (on Clanvowe); M. Jurkowski, 'Lawyers and Lollardy in the early fifteenth century', in Aston and Richmond (eds.), *Lollardy and the Gentry*, 155–82.

[77] For Oldcastle's career and revolt, see W. T. Waugh, 'Sir John Oldcastle', *EHR* 20 (1905), 434–56, 637–58; McFarlane, *John Wycliffe*, 160–85.

the official indictments. These allege that, from his hiding place, he summoned adherents to assemble at St Giles' Fields, outside the city walls, on the night of 9–10 January. Having planned to seize the king and his brothers at Eltham on Twelfth Night, Oldcastle and his force were to take control of London and the government. Whatever kernel of fact lay behind this improbable scenario, it formed the basis for charges of treason and heresy against the hundred or so persons captured or killed in St Giles and also for the exaggerated accounts in the chronicles about the thousands who had flocked to London in response to Oldcastle's summons. The commissions under which the rebels were tried, hanged, and burnt, and suspects rounded up, effectively conceal the intentions of the accused and the inducements which made them rebel, though they show that the numbers were pitifully small.[78] But if the event itself proved insignificant, its consequences were huge. First, it eliminated the last outlet of articulate Wycliffism among the political class. In challenging the immunity it had hitherto enjoyed, Arundel faced a considerable risk of failure. Henry V was in no hurry to abandon the tradition of royal protection for his servants and intimates, and a recantation of the most nominal kind would have saved Oldcastle his position in royal service and as the protector of Lollards. Arundel probably guessed that he would prove obdurate, and by demonstrating that any affiliation to Wycliffism forfeited royal favour, he killed support for it among the political class. Secondly, it provided propaganda for royal authority. The king was portrayed as God's chosen minister, delivered by His grace from personal danger and charged with protecting the orthodox faith of the realm. Finally, Lollardy would henceforth be identified with lower-class sedition and subject to systematic persecution. Thereby the way was cleared for the Lancastrian obsession with royal piety and national orthodoxy as twin guarantors of God's continuing favour to the dynasty, the realm, and its foreign conquests.

5. THE PERSECUTION OF LOLLARDY

Even before Wyclif died, Lollardy as a popular faith was being preached by chaplains and unbeneficed priests whose rustic dress and personal austerity made them the rivals and enemies of the friars. Already by 1382 one of the most persuasive, William Swinderby, who had won adherents in Leicester, was investigated by Bishop Buckingham. Having moved to Coventry and then to Herefordshire, where he was again examined, he eventually disappeared into Wales. In Bristol, too, Lollardy perhaps imported by Aston and Purvey in 1383, won support and protection from the urban authorities, as it did notoriously at

---

[78] Powell, *Kingship, Law, and Society*, 141–67; P. Strohm, *England's Empty Throne* (New Haven, 1992), 63–86.

Northampton a decade later through the favour of the mayor, Thomas Fox. It provoked episcopal attention in Worcestershire, Wiltshire, and Herefordshire, where the legendary Walter Brut, 'husbandman', engaged a panel of theologians in disputation; and further afield in Northumberland at the end of the century, Richard Wyche and William Thorpe were arrested, Thorpe in 1397 and Wyche by 1403. Both escaped punishment and resumed their missions elsewhere. John Purvey, who was in custody in 1401, was forced to make a public abjuration to escape the fate of William Sawtre, the first English Lollard to be burnt.[79]

These names, and others, figure prominently among those individually examined, but there is no systematic record of what local investigations took place or what these detected. How assiduous was the search for Lollards in the thirty years after 1382? After the Great Revolt, bishops were enabled to invoke the aid of the sheriffs; and in 1388 social and political disturbances led the council to issue commissions to search for and seize Lollard preachers and writings. In 1401 the statute De Heretico Comburendo stressed the 'dissensions and divisions' in the realm engendered by heresy, and empowered bishops to arrest and imprison suspects and deliver them to the secular arm after their conviction, while that of 1406 linked Lollards with adherents of Richard II. Such recurrent alarms thus brought a convergence of lay and ecclesiastical hostility to Lollardy as a seditious force. But were such measures more than a ritualized response?[80] They did not yet amount to a witch-hunt. The political class and some academics continued to enjoy immunity. Even the Lollard evangelists, like Swinderby, Purvey, Wyche, Crumpe, and Thorpe, not to mention the layman Walter Brut, were listened to at length by their interrogators, who sought both to elicit the extent of their errors and to pave the way for an abjuration which could be given maximum publicity. Abjuration might even be rewarded with the offer of a benefice, allowing the authorities to monitor the penitent's preaching. Wyche, Purvey, and Crumpe all availed themselves of this for a time, although Thorpe rejected it. While they sought patiently to reclaim the leaders, the bishops dealt more summarily with the unlettered. Long imprisonment served to bring the London skinner John Claydon and many more nameless heretics to abjure, though escape from episcopal gaols was none too difficult. But only those who relapsed were publicly burnt, and the trials of both Sawtre in 1401 and Badby in 1410 were staged for political ends. It was the Crown, rather than the Church, that set the level of persecution, and up to 1414 this was less than full-blooded.

---

[79] McFarlane, John Wycliffe, 121–59; Hudson, Premature Reformation, 145, 158–69. See also G. Martin, 'Knighton's Lollards', in Aston and Richmond (eds.), Lollardy and the Gentry, 28–40; Hudson, 'John Purvey', in Hudson, Lollards and their Books, 85–110, and ead., 'Laicus litteratus', in P. Biller and A. Hudson (eds.), Heresy and Literacy (Cambridge, 1994), 222–36 (on Walter Brut).

[80] H. G. Richardson, 'Heresy and the lay power under Richard II', EHR 51 (1936), 1–28; Aston, Lollards and Reformers, 1–48; Strohm, England's Empty Throne, 32–62; A. K. McHardy, 'De

Hitherto Lollardy, of itself, had posed no direct threat to the Crown; it was not a political movement, and though rhetorically linked to sedition it had not been involved in revolt. It had even served as a stick to induce the Church to grant taxation. Now, under Henry V, Lollards were accused of subverting both Church and Crown and a harsher campaign of persecution began. The immediate occasion was, of course, Oldcastle's rising and the conviction of the rebels for both heresy and treason. Even more influential was the new international significance it had acquired through the burning of Hus at Constance and the revolution in Bohemia, and through Henry V's bid to displace the French monarchy from the leadership of Christendom. It became his duty and aim to eradicate the 'English heresy' which threatened God's favour to himself and the English nation. Lollards could now be hunted and demonized: a statute of 1414 ordered all royal officers to arrest them on suspicion and deliver them to the diocesan authorities, and in 1416 the Church followed by ordering the presentment of suspects twice-yearly in every rural deanery and their imprisonment in episcopal gaols. The returns made of their numbers and names at each convocation gradually built up a central register of Lollards so that their movement between dioceses could be checked. The discursive and arbitrary interrogation of suspects was replaced by standard lists of questions, drawn up by jurists and theologians and circulated for entry in bishops' registers. Torture was not used to extract confessions, but abjurations were often procured by long terms of imprisonment, and suspects were required to inform on their associates. Persecution inculcated fear of Lollardy. Margery Kempe's ostentatious pietism led not only to her arrest and questioning by lay and church officials but to popular clamour for her to be burnt. Anti-Lollard hysteria was fed by some high-profile trials and burnings: Richard Gurmyn and John Claydon in 1415, Benedict Wolman in 1416, William Taylor in 1423. With Oldcastle at large until 1417, the king and many of the nobility in France, and Scottish raids in the north, the authorities were edgy.[81]

Another wave of anti-Lollard phobia erupted in 1428–31, associated with the papacy's crusade against the Hussites led by Cardinal Beaufort, which Lollards opposed. Pope Martin V ordered the exhumation and burning of Wyclif's bones, and in July 1428 convocation was warned that Lollardy was on the increase. An alleged rising at midsummer prompted Archbishop Chichele to ride round his diocese rounding up suspects. That seems to have brought a diaspora of the leaders to East Anglia, where Bishop Alnwick conducted a systematic investigation of Lollard communities to the east and south of Norwich. The principal evangelists, William White, Hugh Pye, William Caleys (priests), and

Heretico Comburendo, 1401', in Aston and Richmond (eds.), Lollardy and the Gentry, 112–26; C. van Nolcken, 'Richard Wyche, a certain knight and the beginning of the end', in ibid. 127–54.

[81] J. A. F. Thomson, The Later Lollards (Oxford, 1965), 99, 195, 220ff.; Hudson, Lollards and their Books, 125–40.

John Waddon (a skinner), were burnt and well over sixty lay men and women (perhaps double that number) were imprisoned and examined over the next two and a half years, the most part of whom abjured. Alnwick's investigations were not entered in his register and it is possible that similar purges took place in other dioceses where no more than a scatter of individual arrests are known during these years.[82] The best-publicized 'Lollard plot' occurred in May 1431, when bills were posted calling for the destruction of lords, some kind of attack was made on Salisbury Cathedral, and two weavers of Abingdon were arrested and executed. With the king and lords absent in France, Humphrey, duke of Gloucester, 'suppressed' the rising, and extensive investigations netted a few more suspects. It triggered alarm in London, where a wool-packer was executed for treason and Lollard books were burnt.[83]

Lollardy as sedition thus remained in political awareness, but in what form did it survive as a faith, and what were its beliefs a half-century after Wyclif's death? The first thing to note is that it lacked any support from the gentry, not merely in active leadership but in affording protection and employment in benefices and as household chaplains. Secondly, Arundel's prohibition of unlicensed preaching seems to have been sufficiently effective for it to draw the attention of local magistrates, and expose preachers to delation by unsympathetic audiences. In short, England after 1414 was no longer fertile ground for Wycliffite evangelists. To survive, Lollards had to become less conspicuous, to abandon public preaching and polemical argument, and restrict their activities to known sympathizers and safe environments. Lollardy came to be based on local communities, groups of neighbouring villages like those along the rivers Yare and Waveney in Norfolk, and in the Chiltern Hills, and within them on households like that of the Mone family in Loddon. Reliance was placed on domestic and familial bonds—on children, relatives, and servants who could be discreet—and women gained a more prominent role. Within the household a Lollard pattern of life was followed: meat-eating on Fridays, Bible readings, and secret 'schools' in Lollard doctrine. Phrases and turns of speech identified members of the sect to each other, and while some maintained the badge of russet dress and sanctimonious solemnity, others practised outward conformity, even attending Mass.

With the outlawing of the English Bible and the drying-up of Wycliffite writing, Lollardy retreated from literacy into oral instruction and memorizing, and from theology into dogmatic assertion. A valuable glimpse of rural Lollard beliefs is provided by the abjurations arising from Bishop Alnwick's

---

[82] Thomson, *The Later Lollards*, 52, 147–50, 175; Hudson, *Premature Reformation*, 32–42, 121–6. For Alnwick's investigation, see N. Tanner (ed.), *Heresy Trials in the Diocese of Norwich, 1428–31*, Camden ser., 4th ser., 20 (London, 1977); M. Aston, 'William White's Lollard followers', in id., *Lollards and Reformers*, 71–100.

[83] Thomson, *The Later Lollards*, 57–61; Aston, *Lollards and Reformers*, 31–8.

investigations in 1428–31. A degree of uniformity was imposed by the process of interrogation, as also by the memorized formulas of William White, although some held views which were extreme and distorted. There is little indication that laymen had read or learnt from books. The main thrust of the interrogation was on the sacraments, all of which the accused in some measure repudiated as superfluous and instruments of priestly power and exploitation. The assertion that material bread alone—'a cake of bread'—existed after consecration showed incomprehension of Wyclif's doctrine. The conspicuous manifestations of late medieval religiosity—the images of saints used for intercession, pilgrimages to shrines, and processions—were rejected, and the Church's regulatory power to enforce tithes, fasting, and confession was repudiated. Sacerdotal and papal authority and wealth were condemned as unbiblical, and contrasted with the biblical injunction to give to the poor and live in charity and fraternity. In fact dissent rested on biblical literalism and the belief in immediate access to God.[84]

There is no comparable evidence for the existence and nature of Lollardy in urban centres in the mid-century. It appears to have persisted in London, where the burning of the charismatic and elderly Richard Wyche in 1440 produced disturbances and an attempt to set up a shrine. More ambiguous evidence is provided in the writings of Reginald Pecock, designed to win over Lollards by force of reason. Pecock was above all a pedagogue. An Oxford theologian who had been master of Whittington College in London from 1431 to 1444 and then successively bishop of St Asaph and Chichester (though still largely residing in London), he claimed a first-hand knowledge of Lollards, having 'spoke oft tyme and bi long leiser with the wittiest and kunnyngist men of thilk seid sort' and 'patiently here her evydencis and her motives without exprobacioun'. The claim is unusual and the context obscure. Were these meetings in secret, or were they with Lollards in prison? How educated—and how numerous—were they? Pecock observed that the failure of sixty years of persecution justified his attempt 'bi cleer wit to drawe men into consente of trewe faithe otherwise than bi fier and swerd and hangement'.[85] His attempt to convince Lollards of the illogicality of their heresies by writing in English was as unique as it was hazardous. His work *The Repressor* (written by 1449, published 1455), directed to 'the lay party' in London, was a defence of the same devotional practices, hierarchy, and 'governances' of the Church which the Norfolk rustics had rejected. Pecock's concern was pastoral rather than (as with Netter) theological. He complains that the biggest barrier he encountered in arguing with Lollards was their biblical literalism—their assertion that no practice or belief was justified that was not in

[84] See Tanner's valuable introduction to *Heresy Trials*; also Aston, ibid. 49–101, 193–218; Hudson, *Premature Reformation*, ch. 3; Thomson, *The Later Lollards*, 239–50; R. G. Davies, 'Lollardy and locality', *TRHS*, 6th ser., 1 (1991), 191–212.

[85] Reginald Pecock, *The Book of Faith*, ed. J. L. Morison (Glasgow, 1909), 139, 202.

the Bible. He pinned his faith on the power of reason and the multiplication and diffusion of his writings, which he urged them to read.

Pecock's naive self-confidence extended beyond converting Lollards to a reconstruction of Catholic catechesis and dogma. He deplored the prohibition on a vernacular Bible and theology, arguing that the lawyers and merchants whom he daily met in London were as capable of grasping theological concepts as they were of dealing with litigation and negotiating commercial contracts. The Church's teaching should be accessible in a form and language that people could understand. He therefore drew up (in English) a new scheme of 'Seven Matters of Religious Knowledge and Four Tables of Moral Virtues' to replace the Decalogue and the seven cardinal virtues. These were summarized in a series of manuals of descending sophistication, from *The Boke of Faith* and *The Reule of Chrysten Religioun* to *The Donet* and *The Pore Mennis Mirror*, designed for daily study. Both in conception and in practicality the programme was overambitious. Even worse, Pecock's intoxication with his own reasoning led him to give to natural reason the primacy traditionally accorded to scripture and revelation as the source of moral commands. Further, his insistence on reading credal texts in their historical context led him to omit from the Apostles' Creed, as being a later addition, the article on Christ's descent into hell, and to doubt the authenticity of the Donation of Constantine. This made him an easy prey to his enemies, who numbered a group of Cambridge theologians who dominated the London pulpits as advocates of devotional orthodoxy. He was arraigned before the king's council on charges of subverting royal and priestly authority. Convicted of heresy before a panel of theologians, he was forced to resign his see and burn his writings, and was confined to a cell in Thorney Abbey deprived of books and writing materials. Essentially Pecock was restating Catholic doctrine, but he was both an old-fashioned Thomist, believing in the synthesis of faith and reason, and a modern demystifier, who wanted liturgy to be comprehensible and religious truth to be convincing. In both respects he was out of tune with the religious climate of his time. Far inferior in intellect to Wyclif, but as blindly opinionated, his vindictive punishment was a measure of the descent from scholastic freedom to repressive orthodoxy that separated their ages.[86]

Wycliffism faces the historian with two questions: first, why did it fail to displace Catholicism as in Bohemia, and secondly, has it attracted disproportionate attention?

---

[86] C. W. Brockwell presents a study of Pecock's thought in *Bishop Reginald Pecock and the Lancastrian Church* (Lewiston, NY, 1985); see also, Catto, 'Theology after Wycliffism', 275–8, and id., 'The king's government and the fall of Pecock', in Archer and Walker (eds.), *Rulers and Ruled*, 201–22; Aston, *Faith and Fire*, 86–92; E. F. Jacob, 'Reynold Pecock, bishop of Chichester', in Jacob (ed.), *Essays in Later Medieval History* (Manchester, 1968), 1–34.

The first is a complex problem, with both religious and political dimensions.[87] In religious terms it originated as, and remained, a movement of dissent, strongly negative in emphasis. Wyclif had dismantled medieval Catholicism intellectually, and his followers vigorously attacked its outward forms. Wycliffism did hold the seeds of an alternative Christianity—doctrinally in the apprehension of God's will through the Bible, ecclesiologically as a Church of the elect and a priesthood of true believers, structurally in favouring individual rather than hierarchic authority, evangelically through the primacy of preaching, and socially in its domestic and cellular context. But this remained largely embryonic, inhibited by persecution and resort to polemic, and it never developed its religious potential. In contrast, Catholicism by long tradition and adaptation was deeply integrated with communal beliefs and behaviour. Catholic rituals of worship in the Mass, the rites of passage, and the natural cycle knit together social relations; its intercessory role lifted the burden of sin and misfortune from the individual; its hierarchical structure derived from the divine and political order. Moreover, its doctrines and authority were conveyed through the senses rather than through the mind, by visual symbols and elaborate ceremonies, not as intellectual concepts. Intellection was an elite activity, confined to theological and devotional matters. In Wycliffism, by contrast, the Word of God made its impact on the individual conscience through the Bible, by unaided interpretation and belief. But in a period when levels of literacy and book production were low, this was premature: its influence was bound to be limited and could be easily contained.

In political terms the odds were likewise weighted against Wycliffism. At this period, and for some time afterwards, religion was integral to the state, the soul of the body politic. Religion was not a matter of individual choice or belief but of common membership of the Church. The Church, in turn, invoked God's blessing on the king and his subjects, on whom it imposed spiritual and moral disciplines in God's name. By the late Middle Ages royal rather than papal power crowned this edifice, the king being the guardian of the realm's orthodoxy and the channel for God's favour to the nation. Wycliffism had likewise exalted the authority of the temporal power, imputing to the king a duty to purify the Church of abuses and confine it to a purely spiritual role, notably by depriving it of lands and secular magistracy. But at the same time Wycliffite belief in the primacy of individual conscience made it too anarchic to serve the Crown's need for a controlling spiritual authority. The only circumstances in which the Crown might have supported Wycliffite demands to denude the Church would have been if its own control over the English Church had been threatened by the papacy, or if the Church had forfeited widespread support. Although at points in

---

[87] See the perceptive conclusion in Hudson, *Premature Reformation*, 508–17.

this period such possibilities were imaginable and alarming, there was little danger of them being realized, especially after Henry V threw the Crown's weight
behind a reinvigorated national Church as a bulwark of orthodoxy, order, and the
mystique of kingship.

Does Wycliffism, then, deserve to be studied?[88] Barely so in terms of the numbers of its adherents and its limited duration as a movement. Rather more so as
an element in the surge of individual questioning and dissent at the close of the
fourteenth century that heralded a more articulate and self-conscious society.
Indubitably so as an intellectual and puritanical critique of sacerdotalism which
strikingly foreshadowed the nonconformity of a later age.

[88] Duffy, *Stripping of the Altars*, 2.

PART III

Men and Events

CHAPTER 11

England, France, and Christendom, 1360–1413

1. LOSING THE PEACE, 1360–1369

While the capture of King John of France at Poitiers in 1356 dictated an eventual suspension of hostilities, peace was not achieved until 1360, the only peace of the Hundred Years War acknowledged by both sides. Yet the ensuing decade was not one of real peace or even of the absence of war. Neither side wanted a final peace; both treated it as a suspension of hostilities in which they manoeuvred for allies, contested spheres of influence, and even fought war by proxy. Edward III sought to open up further areas for military intervention by his sons, while Charles V, who succeeded on the death of John in 1364, set his mind to expel the English from the territories his father had conceded.

Although when the Treaty of Brétigny was agreed in April 1360 Edward had passed the peak of his military success, it reflected the commanding position he held. In May 1358 and in March 1359 he had forced the captive King John to sign humiliating 'ransom' treaties surrendering sovereignty not only over Aquitaine but over Touraine, Anjou, Maine, Normandy, and Boulonnais—in effect just under half of France—in return for Edward's surrender of his claim to the French crown. The rejection of the treaty by the Dauphin Charles gave Edward the excuse to attempt to wrest the crown by force; but his march to Reims was ineffectual and on his retreat via Paris he was advised to accept the French offers lest—as John of Gaunt warned—'we lose in a day all that we have gained over twenty years'.[1] Although Edward reluctantly agreed to renounce his claims to the French crown and to the lands of the Angevin Empire in northern France, he was to receive Calais, Ponthieu, and a widely defined Aquitaine in full sovereignty. The treaty thus reversed Henry III's acceptance of French suzerainty, the *casus belli* of the Hundred Years War, and by eliminating further dispute over feudal tenure and obligations earned its soubriquet of 'the Great Peace'. Yet it resolved

---

[1] J. le Patourel, 'The Treaty of Brétigny, 1360', *TRHS*, 5th ser., 10 (1960), 19–39; J. Sumption, *Trial by Fire* (London, 1999), 424–45.

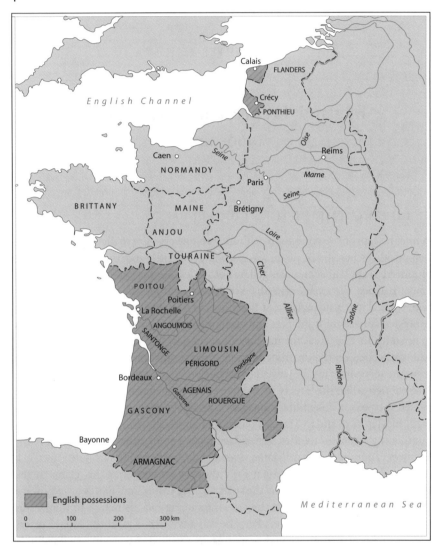

MAP 11.1. Lands ceded to Edward III by the Treaty of Brétigny, 1360 (shaded)

past feudal disputes at the cost of provoking new ones over sovereignty. The sense of the identity and sanctity of France which developed so powerfully under Charles V made a partition of France intolerable, something at which the French baulked in future negotiations. Edward, too, was reluctant to abandon his claim to the French crown, which had been the basis for his intervention in northern France. Each side had surrendered too much. This became apparent when the

delays in transferring lands by the appointed date of November 1361, to implement the treaty, allowed both kings to evade the renunciations of title which had
been consigned to a separate instrument. They thus retained their legal claims
intact, with the capacity to renew them when it seemed advantageous.

In north-western France the treaty had acknowledged French overlordship of
Normandy and Brittany, but English influence for a time remained strong in
both. When England's volatile ally Charles of Navarre, duke of Normandy,
rebelled against Charles V and was defeated at the battle of Cocherel in May
1364, he forfeited the duchy, which thereafter ceased to be a viable area of
Plantagenet influence.[2] The English presence was far greater in Brittany, where
in 1362 Edward restored the Anglophile claimant, his son-in-law Jean de
Montfort. In 1364, at the battle of Auray, Jean defeated and killed his rival,
Charles de Blois, and English influence was firmly established through the occupation of castles and lands by English mercenary captains. Although Duke Jean
legitimized his relations with Charles V, to whom he performed homage at the
Treaty of Guérande in 1365, in 1369 the English still retained a military presence
which could be activated when the war was renewed.[3]

In south-western France the treaty delivered to the English Crown in full sovereignty the vast area of Aquitaine, which in July 1362 Edward III bestowed on
his eldest son, the Black Prince, with authority over its finances, justice, and officers.[4] Ostensibly this was a rich and powerful principality, the fulcrum between
northern and southern Europe. To organize and exploit it politically, economically, and militarily was a huge challenge, a test of imperial government. For
Aquitaine was totally unlike England: it had no identity or political unity; it was
a society of large and small independent lords, fiercely and perpetually warlike,
of fortified castles and towns jealous of their privileges and exemptions, of a
variety of feudal tenures and a complex pattern of local jurisdictions. All this was
hardly compatible with the exercise of the sovereign power needed to rule and
exploit it as an entity in the way the Black Prince had his English lands. In fact
there is no indication that he harboured long-term plans for state-building. His
object became solely to extract military and financial support for his immediate
military objectives in Spain.

For three years after his arrival in June 1363 the Black Prince held court in
style at Bordeaux and toured the regions to receive the homage of towns
and lords. But English officials accustomed to operating within the restricted

[2] W. M. Ormrod, 'England, Normandy and the beginnings of the Hundred Years War,
1259–1360', in D. Bates and A. Curry (eds.), *England and Normandy in the Middle Ages* (London,
1994), 197–213.

[3] M. Jones, *Ducal Brittany, 1364–1399* (Oxford, 1970), 1–56.

[4] It comprised Poitou, Saintonge, Angoumois, Périgord, Limousin, Quercy, Rouergue,
Armagnac, Bigorre, and Agenais; see Map 11.1.

boundaries of English Gascony were too few and too foreign to enforce the prince's rule in areas traditionally loyal to the French Crown or to confront the great independent lordships of Albret, Armagnac, and Foix, petty kingdoms in all but name. In fact little is known about the prince's administration beyond the levy of a series of *fouages* in 1364, 1365, and 1367, a hearth tax newly introduced in France to support a standing army. Only a period of stable government and consistent pressure for recognition of his rights could have won respect for his authority.

Instead the prince was quickly drawn into the proxy war in Spain which opened in 1366 when the bastard Henry of Trastamara, with Franco-Aragonese backing, challenged the capricious and harsh rule of his half-brother Pedro the Cruel in Castile. For Charles V this was both an opportunity to rid France of the mercenaries and to oust Pedro, who had switched alliance to the English in 1362. A mainly French force (though with some English adventurers) invaded Castile in March 1366, forcing Pedro to flee to Bayonne and appeal to the Black Prince for aid. This was welcomed both as an opportunity for fighting and as an attractive way to raise money by taxation and from the spoils of war. Despite warnings from Sir John Chandos that these expectations were chimerical, the prince (with Edward III's backing) defrayed the whole cost of the invasion of Castile to the sum of £276,000, for the repayment of which, once he recovered his throne, Pedro sealed obligations and delivered his daughters as hostages.[5]

Although militarily successful (see below), Pedro's predictable failure to discharge his obligations left the Black Prince heavily indebted to the English captains and Aquitaine nobility who had accompanied him. On his return in January 1368 he again summoned the Estates to grant a *fouage* for five years. Jean, count of Armagnac, laid a formal appeal against it to Charles V, who at the end of 1368 summoned the Black Prince to answer it in Paris. On his defiant refusal, the duchy was declared forfeit and the war recommenced. The six years of the prince's rule had done nothing to habituate the towns and nobility of Aquitaine to his authority, and the English hold on the duchy proved tenuous.

The establishment of the Black Prince in Aquitaine presaged direct English involvement in the Iberian peninsula. Edward III had welcomed Pedro the Cruel's reversal of Castile's traditional alliance with France, which had endangered the English coasts, and was ready to provide financial and military backing for the Black Prince's invasion in 1367 to restore Pedro to the Spanish throne. Essentially an Anglo-French struggle for the control of Castile, it was largely fought by the professional captains of both sides: Bertrand du Guesclin and Arnoud d' Audrehem in the army of Henry of Trastamara; Hugh Calveley and

---

[5] Treaty of Libourne, 23 Sept. 1366; P. E. Russell, *The English Intervention in Spain and Portugal* (Oxford, 1955), 66 n. 2 and, in general, ch. 3.

Sir John Chandos in that of the Black Prince. The prince was supported by his Gascon feudatories and a company of 1,200 under his brother John of Gaunt, in all some 6,000 men. Given passage by his old ally Charles of Navarre, who was party to the treaty, his army crossed the Pyrenees via Roncesvalles in February 1367 and made for Burgos. The prince had reached Logrono by 1 April, and Navarrete next day, where Henry had prepared a strong defensive position at Najera. Charles V had warned him against fighting a pitched battle with the English, yet he chose to do so, and—fatally—with the river Najerilla at his rear. As predicted, English battle tactics proved superior; Henry's army was out-flanked and took to flight and many were slaughtered and drowned in the Najerilla, while the nobles were made prisoner.[6]

Pedro wanted his enemies put to the sword, but for the prince and the Gascon nobility their ransoms were a tangible pledge of the massive sum which Pedro owed them. At Burgos the prince, backed by the English army, pressed for pay-ment, but Pedro's attempts to levy a tax provoked discontent, and with the advent of the summer heat, malaria and dysentery dictated an English with-drawal. The prince, himself a victim, reached Bordeaux in September 1367, where the demands of the Gascon lords for wages forced him to order the levy of the *fouage* which was to precipitate their appeal to Charles V. In Castile, Pedro remained increasingly insecure, and in March 1369 he was captured and mur-dered by Henry of Trastamara, who recovered the throne. The Black Prince had no chance to reverse this outcome; a sick man and facing widespread revolt in Aquitaine, he returned to England at the end of 1370. Najera had been a spec-tacular victory, enhancing the prince's military reputation, but the outcome of his Spanish venture was to confirm the commitment of Castile to the French alliance with dire consequences for England as war was resumed. It left a further legacy, in the claims to the throne of Castile of John of Gaunt and Edmund of Cambridge through their marriages to Pedro's two daughters.

In the Low Countries, another area of traditional rivalry between the English and French kings, the struggle was conducted diplomatically. Here it was through an earlier proposal of marriage for his son Edmund that Edward III hoped to extend English hegemony.[7] The death of Philip de Rouvre, duke of Burgundy, in November 1361 left as his widow Margaret, the 12-year-old daugh-ter of Louis de Mâle, count of Flanders. She was heiress to the counties of Nevers, Flanders, and Rethel from her father, Burgundy and Artois from her grandmother, and the duchies of Brabant and Limbourg from her aunt. Immediately Edward opened secret negotiations for her marriage to his son

---

[6] The campaign is well described in Russell, *English Intervention*, ch. 4; Sumption, *Trial by Fire*, ch. 12.

[7] For what follows, see J. J. N. Palmer, 'England, France, the papacy and the Flemish succes-sion', *Jnl. Med. Hist.* 2 (1976), 339–64.

Edmund, created earl of Cambridge, followed by a formal embassy in 1362 and an application to the papal Curia for a dispensation from consanguinity. Louis de Mâle was favourably inclined, seeing it as a guarantee of Flemish independence from France, while Edward could apply commercial pressures and inducements, moving the staple for English wools from England to Calais in 1363. The full scale of Edward's project became apparent in October 1364 when he agreed to settle on Edmund all the English territories in north-eastern France (Ponthieu, Calais, and Guines), with the English Crown retaining overlordship. Along with his wife's inheritance this would have constituted a major power on France's north-eastern frontier under a new Anglo-Flemish dynasty, thus ensuring English ascendancy for the foreseeable future.

Up to this point Edward had been able to override resistance from King John of France, captive in England, but when John died in 1364, Charles V set himself to prevent the marriage by every possible means. The new Francophile pope, Urban V, was persuaded to refuse a dispensation and threaten Edward III with excommunication if he persisted. Edward in turn used diplomatic pressure and military threats to make Urban change his mind, but the pope held firm and in March 1367 he issued a dispensation for the marriage of Margaret to Charles V's brother Philip, duke of Burgundy. By then Louis de Mâle was becoming alarmed at French hostility, though also under increasing pressure from Edward to defy the pope, with English-led companies ravaging Nevers and Rethel in the autumn of 1367. Only in April 1369 did he finally accept Duke Philip as husband for Margaret de Mâle. Charles had frustrated Edward's great project, and paved the way for the emergence of the Burgundian Low Countries.

By 1369 the dominating influence which Edward III had exerted over north-western Europe in 1360 had vanished. His attempts to establish English hegemony in areas of traditional French influence, Flanders and Spain, had been defeated; even Normandy was now firmly attached to the French Crown, and Brittany a fragile client. The greatest material gain, the huge duchy of Aquitaine, had proved too large, amorphous, and independent to submit to English rule and exploitation. On each of these projects Edward had lavished the profits of his victories, to advance the prospects of his sons. But by 1369 the Black Prince was sick and confronting failure, and the ineffective Edmund, disappointed of greater prospects, had become the tool for John of Gaunt's own further ambitions in Spain.[8] To Gaunt, and his younger brother Thomas of Woodstock, it fell to uphold the residue of Edward's empire, against a king of France planning its destruction.

---

[8] For Edward III's dynastic ambitions, see W. M. Ormrod, 'Edward III and his family', *Jnl. Brit. Stud.* 26 (1987), 398–422.

2. LOSING THE WAR, 1369–1389

During the years of peace English policy had sought to encircle the French heartlands with a ring of clients and allies, from Flanders in the north-east, through Brittany in the north-west, to the enlarged duchy of Aquitaine in the south-west. The defeat of English influence in both Spain and Flanders not only nullified this hegemony but crucially exposed English vulnerability to Castilian sea power. At the same time the revival of the French monarchy under Charles V forced England's continental allies and clients onto the defensive. This presented a problem for England's military strategy, since the most effective weapon, the *chevauchée*, could not be used defensively or in friendly territory. Although the English could launch raids into the heartlands of France, designed to tempt the French to battle, Charles V and his able commander, Bertrand du Guesclin, deliberately chose to endure English devastation and avoid battle while pressing ahead with the reduction of English fortresses and the suborning of English allies.

The War in Northern France

Charles V was fully prepared for war in the spring of 1369, taking Ponthieu and Abbeville in April–May. John of Gaunt was hastily sent to safeguard Calais but Edward III's intention to follow with a substantial force was prevented by Queen Philippa's death of the plague. Gaunt's march down the coast to Harfleur may have deterred a French sea invasion, but it yielded no military gains either of territory or in battle.[9]

To counter the French in the north-west, a force of 4,000 men under the mercenary Sir Robert Knolles was commissioned in 1370 for two years' service. This was licensed freebooting, for Knolles was paid for only six months and allowed to deploy his force at will. He followed the favourite *chevauchée* route from Calais to the Île de France and Champagne, before heading westwards towards Brittany; but his force was badly mauled by the French near Le Mans and he disbanded it after six months. Disappointed of his support, Charles of Navarre then abandoned the English alliance and retired from Normandy. In Brittany, Duke Jean's alliance with Edward III in 1372 aroused the hostility of his subjects, and despite the arrival of English troops in the winter of 1372–3, the duke's position had become untenable and he fled to England.[10] English influence all but disappeared in the north-west. A fresh army assembled by John of Gaunt for the recovery of Brittany was diverted from Plymouth and landed at Calais in July. Gaunt

---

[9] Sherborne, *War, Politics and Culture*, 77–98.   [10] Jones, *Ducal Brittany*, 60–76

intended a *chevauchée* along the routes of Edward III in 1359 and Knolles in 1370, via Troyes and Sens, but once more found that the French refused battle and the major towns had been refortified and had to be bypassed. With the French closely shadowing his progress and denuding the countryside of provisions, Gaunt chose to bear south-west rather than make for Brittany. His route lay across the barren plâteau of Millevaches and the valley of the Dordogne to Bergerac and Bordeaux, which he reached only after Christmas. Desperately short of supplies for men and horses, having lost much of his wagon train, the march turned into an epic of endurance rather than military glory. Though it had temporarily drawn off the French from other areas, it had done nothing to reverse English fortunes in Brittany, Poitou, or Limousin.[11]

On his return to England in 1374 Gaunt came under pressure to bring effective relief to the last English garrisons in Brest, Bécherel, and Auray, but an expedition under Jean, duke of Brittany and the earls of Cambridge and March was too late to save Bécherel, and after failing to take St Brieuc the duke moved south to besiege Quimperlé. At about the same time Gaunt was opening negotiations for peace with the French at Bruges. There a truce for one year was signed on 17 June which provided for the last English-held fortress in the Cotentin, Saint-Sauveur le Vicomte, then under siege, to be put in the hands of papal mediators until the end of the truce. In fact it had already surrendered to the French, even while in Brittany, Duke Jean was induced to lift the siege of Quimperlé on the eve of its surrender. The Anglo-Montfortian commanders, angered by the loss of both fortresses through trickery, blamed Gaunt for agreeing to the terms in ignorance of the local position and being indifferent to their interests. Gaunt's enemies made capital out of this in the crisis of 1376.[12]

When war was resumed in 1377 it followed the same pattern, with somewhat better fortune for the English. Charles V's ill-advised attempt to confiscate and annex the duchy provoked a wave of support for Breton independence and led to Duke Jean's return in his own right, rather than as an English client. For the English the restored alliance was an opportunity to revive the traditional pattern of war, and in June 1380 Buckingham led an ambitious *chevauchée* along the route from Calais to Troyes, then westwards along the Loire to join the siege of French-held Nantes. At this point Charles V's death paved the way for Duke Jean to make peace with the new king, Charles VI, in the second treaty of Guérande (April 1381). Buckingham returned ingloriously, if with profit. Duke Jean had safeguarded Breton independence, but remained under pressure from both France and England. In France he relied on the dukes of Berry and Burgundy, who now controlled the government, to protect him against his

---

[11] Goodman, *John of Gaunt*, 232–4, reviews historians' verdicts on the campaign.
[12] Holmes, *The Good Parliament*, 37–45, gives the most modern account of these events.

inveterate enemy Olivier de Clisson, who supported the Penthièvre claimant Jean de Blois. Brittany, in fact, no longer provided an entry into France even though the English retained Brest and leased Cherbourg from Charles of Navarre as 'barbicans'.[13]

These had been of some use against the French and Castilian fleets, which carried out devastating raids on the south coast and Isle of Wight as Edward III lay dying. A further assault by land and sea on Calais briefly endangered it, provoking the English into a massive demonstration of naval power in which fleets under Buckingham, Arundel, and Gaunt, with no fewer than 17,000 soldiers and sailors, were at sea for up to eight months in 1378.[14] Again, in 1385 and 1386, the French assembly of a massive armada at Sluys for an invasion of England prompted the Appellants to take the counter-offensive, attacking the French fleet in the Zwin and aggressively 'keeping the sea' with combined military and naval forces of five to six thousand men in 1387–8. But such operations were exceptional. After 1381 England relapsed into a defensive posture, deprived of the opportunity to attack through northern France, and ruled by a king whose disinclination for war became yearly more influential. With the prolonged truce of 1389, twenty years of warfare had left the English with only the most vestigial presence and influence in north-western France. The 'barbicans' now lost their relevance, Cherbourg being relinquished in 1394 and Brest in 1397.

The War in Aquitaine

Here too the English were always on the defensive and dependent on local loyalties. It was a society of petty lords, whose private feuds were subsumed into the rivalries of the greater families such as Armagnac and Foix.[15] English rule maintained a precarious stability by arbitrating and composing these quarrels; it lacked the military power to suppress revolt and prevent Aquitaine beyond the area of English Guyenne from seceding to Charles V. Both the logistics of transport and the threat of Castilian sea power made it impossible to dispatch a major army for its defence; nor could the *chevauchée* be practised in areas whose loyalty it was hoped to retain. Yet little had been done to cultivate attachments to English rule in the years of the Black Prince's administration.

On the resumption of war large areas of southern Aquitaine under Armagnac influence quickly resumed their allegiance to the French Crown. Rouergue, Quercy, part of Périgord, Agenais, Bazas, and much of Limousin had been lost by the end of 1370. In July 1370 Gaunt arrived with 700 men and joined the Black

[13] Jones, *Ducal Brittany*, 83–92.
[14] Saul, *Richard II*, 32–3; Sherborne, *War, Politics and Culture*, 29–40.
[15] M. G. Vale, *English Gascony, 1399–1453* (Oxford, 1970), ch. 5.

Prince in the punitive sack of Limoges, remaining for the rest of the year as lieutenant when the prince returned to England in January 1371. In 1372 the English
planned to succour Poitou and Saintonge by dispatching the earl of Pembroke to
La Rochelle in advance of a royal expedition from the north. But Pembroke's
small force was intercepted and destroyed by Castilian galleys under Simon
Bocanegra at the entrance to La Rochelle on 22 June 1372, and he himself was
captured. The king's army embarked at Calais on 27 August but was forced by
contrary winds to return to port in October.[16] La Rochelle surrendered and in
1372–3 du Guesclin cleared English garrisons out of Poitou, Saintonge, and
Angoumois. By the time Gaunt reached Bordeaux at the end of his long march
in December 1373 nothing was left to the English of the territory ceded in 1360
and the confines of English Gascony were under threat.

    With the ending of the two-year truce in June 1377 the French made a deter-
mined attempt to eliminate the English presence. But the seneschal of Bordeaux,
Lord Neville of Raby, brought the French advance to a halt and by the time of
Charles V's death in 1380 the narrow confines of English Gascony for the rest of
the century had been stabilized. This comprised the Bordelais with a northward
extension into the Médoc peninsula, Blaye and Bourg on the right bank of the
Garonne, Landes, Labourt including Bayonne, and isolated outposts to the east.
Despite the status accorded it in the Treaty of Brétigny, Aquitaine remained a
secondary theatre of war for the English nobility. It denied them the opportunity
for plunder and profit, it brought little leverage on the French Crown, and it was
difficult to reach in force. Only for Gaunt did it have a particular value, as a bridge
towards the coveted crown of Castile.

'The Way of Spain'

For campaigning, Spain had some of the advantages of France. As a hostile and
largely defenceless land, it could be plundered and the English could exploit
their fearsome reputation. The enmities of Navarre, Aragon, Castile, and
Portugal afforded opportunities for alliances, with fiscal and military support.
Politically the weakening, or even replacement, of the Trastamaran dynasty
would remove the menace of the Castilian galleys and negate its long clientage to
France. To these was added after 1378 the cloak of a crusade in the Urbanist
cause. But the difficulties and disadvantages were as great. The transport of an
army of any size by sea was hazardous; horses were not easily shipped and those
in Spain, though fine and spirited mounts, were in short supply. On the march
provender was scarce and distances huge; the English found the summer heat
enervating while winter could be harsh. Dysentery was the great killer. Too few

---

[16] Sherborne, *War, Politics and Culture*, 41–54.

to be an effective force themselves, they were dependent on their allies and thus liable to become pawns in the endless shifts of Iberian politics.

On his return to England in January 1372 Gaunt formally claimed the crown of Castile in right of his wife, Constanza, King Pedro's daughter, and this remained an enduring element in his policy and military plans. Little could be done to realize it during the rest of the decade, for Henry of Trastamara was securely established as an ally of France.[17] But Henry's sudden death in May 1379, leaving the young and introspective Juan I as successor, was seized upon by Fernando of Portugal to strike a blow at Castile by offering an alliance to England in July 1380. Edmund of Cambridge was to bring 2,000 (later 3,000) men to Portugal, to be retained at Portuguese expense, for an invasion of Castile designed to put Lancaster on the throne. No word of this was given to the parliament at Northampton in November 1380, but £160,000 raised by the fateful poll tax was designed to cover not only Buckingham's fruitless siege of Nantes, and Cambridge's expedition, but possibly a subsequent invasion by Gaunt from Aquitaine.[18] Cambridge's force left Plymouth in June 1381 shortly after the Peasants' Revolt erupted.

By the time he arrived, the Castilian navy had overcome the Portuguese fleet and Cambridge's own transports remained blockaded in the Tagus. His lack of horses frustrated military action and mounting arrears of pay prompted the English to seize provisions at will and conduct unofficial raids into Castile. When at length the Portuguese and Castilian royal armies confronted each other near Badajoz in July 1382, it was to sign a treaty of peace, the main clause of which was to provide a Castilian fleet to reship Cambridge's men to England. The English fury at this betrayal was ineffectual. Cambridge returned in December discredited and deeply in debt to his troops. His failure enraged Gaunt and strengthened parliament's support for 'the way of Flanders' as against Gaunt's advocacy of 'the way of Portugal'.

It was three years before Gaunt could revive the Castilian project. The death of Fernando of Portugal in 1383 prompted King Juan to claim his throne in right of his marriage to Beatriz, Fernando's daughter. He was opposed by Fernando's illegitimate brother João, master of Aviz, who assumed the crown in April 1385, reorganized the army, and, adopting English tactics, won a complete victory over Castilian forces at Aljubarotta in August. To ward off Castilian revenge, he appealed to Gaunt, who, this time with financial support from both Richard II and parliament, raised an army of perhaps 4,000 men over the winter.[19] The

---

[17] For the minor English intervention in Navarre in 1378–9, see Russell, *English Intervention*, ch. 12.   [18] Ibid. 301 and, in general, ch. 14, for this phase.

[19] Goodman, *John of Gaunt*, 116–17, and, in general, ch. 7, for the expedition of 1386–8. Russell, *English Intervention*, 17, 18, provides an extended account, and Froissart a very vivid one: Froissart, *Chronicles*, trans. G. Brereton (Harmondsworth, 1968), 328–34.

alliance was sealed in the Treaty of Windsor in May 1386 and Gaunt sailed in July, the Portuguese undertaking to send galleys to transport his army (this time including horses) and to patrol the channel for six months against the threat of French invasion. Gaunt's venture was essentially dynastic: he was accompanied by his wife, Constanza, and daughters, and his force was Lancastrian in character, centred on his own retinue with no participation by other magnates. Proclaiming himself king of Castile, he landed not in Portugal but in Galicia, taking Santiago de Compostela and making Orense his winter base. The Anglo-Portuguese alliance was sealed by the marriage of João to Gaunt's daughter Philippa, but when the combined armies finally entered Castile late in March 1387 it was not long before the acute shortage of supplies and unnerving mortality from disease provoked mutiny and desertion among Gaunt's depleted force; nor had there been any native support for his legitimist claims. The enemy steadfastly refused open battle and could expect shortly to be reinforced by French troops. Gaunt now readily concurred in João's proposal to abandon the campaign, in the knowledge that King Juan was prepared for an honourable compromise. Gaunt's daughter Catherine was to marry Juan's son and heir Enrique, and Gaunt would relinquish his claim to the Castilian crown on receiving the sum of 600,000 francs (£100,000) as an indemnity and an annuity of 40,000 francs (£600) for life. At the end of a campaign in which his army had disintegrated and his generalship was discredited, Gaunt could hardly have expected such generous terms.

The Spanish imbroglio from 1367 to 1387 was essentially an expression of the buccaneering instincts of Edward III's sons. No national interest was involved apart from the Castilian naval threat, itself more the product than the cause of English hostility. The parliamentary Commons showed no enthusiasm for Gaunt's schemes, and his final treaty with King Juan, at Bayonne in 1388, won for England neither compensation for the Castilian raids nor a formal peace and alliance with Castile, such as Gaunt had promised. Lacking support from either the Spanish nobility or the people, Gaunt was never a credible claimant. He barely understood Spanish, had no sympathy for Spanish culture, and his pretensions to a crown bespoke his own self-esteem rather than loyalty to his wife's family.[20] Despite his fraternity with King Juan, Castile was not detached from her alliance with France or reconciled with Portugal, and after Juan's death (1390) English influence was minimal. The most far-reaching consequence was one which Gaunt probably rated least, the alliance with Portugal embodied in the Treaty of Windsor.

---

[20] Different verdicts on Gaunt's Spanish policy are given in Russell, *English Intervention*, 524–5, and Goodman, *John of Gaunt*, 137–8.

'The Way of Flanders'

From 1369 to 1379 the Flanders which Philip of Burgundy looked to inherit was a quiet and prosperous land under the rule of its count, Louis de Mâle. Its wealth was generated by the three industrial towns of Ghent, Bruges, and Ypres, importing raw wool from England and manufacturing cloth for export to Germany and Italy. Despite the renewal of the war with France in 1369 English wool exports remained at the level of some 27,000 sacks a year; nor did the incipient English cloth industry present any threat to Flanders until after 1380. Louis was under no pressure to become actively engaged in the Anglo-French conflict.

It was the papal Schism in 1378 that first reactivated the old fault lines in the Flemish polity between the Francophile count, Church, and nobility, who endorsed Clement VII, and the townsfolk, who supported Urban VI. Socially the industrial workers—the weavers and fullers—were an exploited and potentially revolutionary force, particularly in Ghent and Ypres. The revolt of Ghent in September 1379, led by the weavers, was also directed against the count's policy of centralization. Louis besieged Ghent in 1380 and again in 1381, but failed to reduce it and by 1382 the town had found a leader in Philip van Artevelde, son of the James who had led the revolt of 1338–45 and rendered allegiance to Edward III. His seizure of Bruges provoked Louis to appeal for French aid, to be countered by Artevelde's appeal to Richard II. But the English Crown hesitated to support a popular revolt and Charles VI won a decisive victory over the Flemish town levies at Roosebecke in November 1382 in which Artevelde was killed. Bruges, Ypres, and the rest of Flanders submitted, except for Ghent, saved by the onset of winter. This opened a prolonged struggle in which the town looked for English support.[21]

English policy was hesitant and divided, Gaunt pressing for an invasion of Castile, while the parliamentary Commons favoured intervention in Flanders. Wool exports had plummeted to under 11,000 sacks in 1382–3, and military intervention might undermine Philip of Burgundy's influence and perhaps offer the chance of engaging Charles VI in battle; ecclesiastically it could be represented as a crusade to support the Urbanist cause. Nor could the Crown ignore the historical precedent for aiding its oldest ally and most valued customer. The council advocated a royal expedition, but the Commons preferred to accept the more modest offer by Bishop Despenser of Norwich to lead an Urbanist expedition to aid Ghent. That at first achieved success, but the bishop had spurned the assistance of professional soldiers and after failing to take Ypres his force progressively disintegrated, while news came of a French counter-offensive under Charles VI. Despite the chance of a battle royal, it was too late to mount a

[21] R. Vaughan, *Philip the Bold* (London, 1962), 19–28.

full-scale royal expedition and Gaunt backed off, seeing no reason to save the bishop or mitigate his disgrace.[22]

Ironically it was the renewed resistance of Ghent to Duke Philip which, in the next two years, ensured the safety of England. In July 1385 the Ghentois surprised and captured Damme, securing access to the Zwin and communications with England. This aborted the planned French invasion of England, the army being diverted to the siege of Damme, which capitulated in August. In the winter of 1385–6 Philip came to terms with Ghent, paving the way for a renewed invasion of England on an even larger scale. By July 'a veritable forest of masts' had been assembled at Sluys. An army of 30,000 men 'was to deal a knock out blow', to end the war on French terms. The measures taken in England to resist it were ill coordinated, panic-stricken, and ultimately badly timed. The English fleets to keep the sea and the army to defend London had both been disbanded for lack of money when Charles VI finally embarked on 26 October. But at that point the deteriorating weather, shortage of money, and a loss of nerve decided the French council to abandon the enterprise.[23] The puny and half-hearted aid which England had given to Ghent could in no way match French power or impede French influence. By 1385 Duke Philip had secured a marriage alliance with Albert of Bavaria and had maintained his claim to Brabant and Limbourg against England's ally William, count of Guelders. Richard II's marriage to the half-sister of Wenzel of Bohemia in 1382 had failed to counteract French influence.[24] Flanders had become a French fiefdom, albeit one destined by both its commercial ties and ducal aspirations for an intermediary role between France and England.

By 1389 England's continental possessions were confined to Calais and Guyenne, and its pretensions to be a continental power had been abandoned. These had been based first on its clients and allies and secondly on its military superiority. It could be argued that the English failure in this phase of the war was due to the unreliability of its allies: that Charles of Navarre in Normandy, Jean de Montfort in Brittany, King Pedro in Spain, and King Fernando in Portugal had each reneged on their undertakings, forcing the English to withdraw. English military intervention had been negated by political betrayal, and Richard II's advocacy of withdrawal from Europe was based on the realistic

---

[22] M. Aston, 'The impeachment of Bishop Despenser', *BIHR* 38 (1965), 127–48; Goodman, *John of Gaunt*, 94–8.

[23] Vaughan, *Philip the Bold*, 35–8; for the projected invasion, J. J. N. Palmer, *England, France and Christendom, 1377–99* (London, 1972), 74–80; J. W. Sherborne, 'The defence of the realm and the impeachment of Michael de la Pole in 1386', in Taylor and Childs (eds.), *Politics and Crisis*, 97–116.

[24] Vaughan, *Philip the Bold*, 86–7, 96–102; J. A. Tuck, 'Richard II and the house of Luxembourg', in Goodman and Gillespie (eds.), *Richard II*, 205–30.

assessment that England lacked reliable allies. Yet that was only half the story. For militarily the English had ceased to carry conviction. Their reputation for invincibility, sustained by the victories at Auray and Najera in the 1360s, had crumbled with the futile *chevauchées* of 1370, 1373, and 1380, the defeat at La Rochelle, the expulsion from greater Aquitaine, and the disintegration of the armies of 1380–1 and 1386–8 sent to Spain. Too many expeditions had been aborted or delayed, like those of Edward III in 1369 and 1372, that of 1374–5 to Brittany, and that to Flanders in 1382. Allies who had appealed for support had been let down: Jean de Montfort in 1372 and 1373, Ghent in 1383, even King João in 1387. If this showed the incompetence and the self-interestedness of the English commanders, it also reflected the lack of any overall military strategy and planning. The English had no clear military objective other than to bring the French to battle, nor any political objective other than to support opponents of the French Crown. They had no interest in territorial conquest. Militarily and politically their attitude was defensive and reactive, lacking consistency of purpose and persistency in execution. It was prodigal of men and money, to no avail. It is hard to resist the conclusion that war had become not an instrument of policy but an end in itself, an indulgence for the nobility and professional soldiers.

3. THE SEARCH FOR A SETTLEMENT, 1374–1396

From the beginning of his pontificate in 1371 Pope Gregory XI had made repeated efforts to halt the conflict and mediate between the parties, but it was not until late in 1374 that agreement was reached for a peace conference at Bruges in 1375 under papal nuncios. Edward III's claim to the throne had become no more than a legal fiction, and in practical terms what had to be resolved was the limits and status of Aquitaine. Various propositions were considered: for it to become an independent duchy for Gaunt and his heirs; for it to be partitioned; and for a long truce during which Edward's title would be put in abeyance. No agreement could be reached on any of these and the truce was temporarily extended.[25]

The death of Charles V in 1380 brought a lull in the war, and the reluctance of parliament in England to finance further expeditions gave the opportunity for the young Richard II's desire for peace to assume tangible form. At the end of 1383 Gaunt and Buckingham were commissioned to negotiate a truce with France, which was subsequently extended to the winter of 1384, though with the expectation of resuming hostilities in 1385. At this point the royal council was divided. Richard's uncles Gaunt, Buckingham, and Cambridge urged him to

[25] E. Perroy (ed.), *The Anglo-French Negotiations at Bruges, 1374–1377*, in *Camden Miscellany, XIX*, Camden Society, 3rd ser., 80 (London, 1952).

lead an expedition to France like his father and grandfather; others argued that it would be hazardous for the king to leave the realm. The debate was heated and the royal uncles were left defeated. Richard's own disinclination for war added a personal twist to the dispute, even though England's lack of allies and lack of money were sound arguments for a defensive posture. Unable and unwilling to attack in northern France and Flanders, the council were able to agree on an expedition to Scotland, in which the king could lead the nobility. It proved fruitless, and exacerbated rather than healed the internal quarrels while preventing the dispatch of aid to Ghent. By 1386 Ghent had made peace with Duke Philip and a fresh invasion of England was being organized. When this in turn was abandoned, the ancient rivals France and England faced each other across the Channel in impotent stalemate.

Yet it was two years and more before the first advance could be made towards a settlement. This had to wait upon Gaunt's return from Spain and upon the failure of the Appellants' untimely attempt to reignite the war. In the spring of 1387 Arundel caught and destroyed a large part of the Franco-Flemish fleet, which was returning from La Rochelle with the wine harvest. To exploit this triumph, attempts were made to bolster opposition to Burgundy in the Low Countries by retaining William of Jülich and to woo Jean in Brittany by restoring to him the duchy of Richmond. But William and Jean were each forcefully dissuaded by French pressure, and in neither Flanders nor Brittany was there support for English intervention. The failure of the Appellants' war policy on both these fronts, at considerable expense, was compounded by the defeat of Henry Percy at Otterburn in August 1388 and the reaction against their regime in the Cambridge parliament in September. The war party had shot its bolt and both France and England were ready for negotiations.[26] Following Charles VI's dismissal of his uncles in November 1388 and Richard's corresponding assertion of his authority in May 1389, these were now undertaken by the two kings, who, professing fervent amity, quickly concluded a truce (18 June 1389) which was to be extended until peace was achieved.

The conditions for peace were auspicious. With the conflicts in Spain, Brittany, and Flanders settled, attention could focus on the lands held by the English in France, the *fons et origo* of the war. The English made it plain that they intended to retain Calais in sovereignty and by 1393 the French had implicitly accepted this.[27] The status of Gascony was to prove, as ever, insoluble; but both sides wanted to avoid further war as each had a different agenda to pursue. At the court of Charles VI the dukes of Orléans and Anjou had territorial ambitions in

[26] Palmer, *England, France and Christendom*, ch. 5.

[27] *Proc. & Ord.* i. 390; J. J. N. Palmer, 'Articles for a final peace between England and France, 16 June 1393', *BIHR* 39 (1966), 182–5.

Italy and the duke of Burgundy was anxious to restore Anglo-Flemish commerce; in England, Richard II was bent on reasserting his authority, while Gaunt, after his failure in Spain, saw a second chance to acquire princely rank in Aquitaine. Richard's grant of the duchy to him for life in March 1390 placed the question of its status at the centre of the peace negotiations, in which Gaunt was to have a leading role. Exceptionally, Richard conferred it on Gaunt using solely his title as king of France. The significance of this has been much disputed. Did it foreshadow a surrender of the claim to the French Crown, to enable Gaunt to hold Aquitaine as a French apanage similar to those of his friends the dukes of Burgundy and Berry?[28] To establish the line of an English royal duke as a hereditary peer of France might thus resolve the old problem of Aquitaine, preserving its integrity as part of France while maintaining its historic connection with England. This was what the peace negotiations in 1392–5 between the uncles of Richard II and Charles VI set out to explore.

Both sides accepted that the reconstituted duchy, with boundaries little less than those defined in 1360, should be held from the French Crown, and this marked an important surrender by the English of its sovereign status. At the same time they proposed that it should be held in simple, not liege, homage. This would limit the French king's right to hear appeals, summon the duke to Paris, and confiscate the duchy, as had happened in 1368. However, at Amiens in March 1392 the French were adamant that nothing less than liege homage was acceptable if Aquitaine was to be a constituent part of the French state. Gaunt and Richard II put these terms before a great council at Stamford in May. There they were firmly rejected, and the negotiators were sent back to France to find a new formula to regulate its status.[29] In the early summer of 1393, at Leulingham, the French proposed some modification of liege homage designed to remove the risk of the confiscation of the duchy, coupled with a large indemnity for the abandonment of the English claim to the French throne.[30] This seemed acceptable to both monarchs, but plans for their meeting to ratify the treaty were halted when Charles VI suffered a bout of insanity. However, when a draft treaty was submitted to parliament in January 1394 for formal approval, the Commons made plain their vehement opposition to any surrender of the Crown's rights, insisting that only simple homage be rendered, that Aquitaine should be immune from confiscation, and that the king be free to resume his title if the peace were broken. As they said, it was insupportable for the king and every Englishman to pass under

---

[28] Palmer, *England, France and Christendom*, 32–42, supported by Goodman, *John of Gaunt*, 195; for a critical discussion, see Saul, *Richard II*, 211–15.

[29] Palmer, *England, France and Christendom*, 145; Goodman, *John of Gaunt*, 150–1; *West. Chron.* 490.

[30] Palmer, *England, France and Christendom*, 147 (with map); Saul, *Richard II*, 215–17; Palmer, 'Articles for a final peace', nos. iii, xvi, xviii.

the heel of the French king, and they could not see how liege homage could be modified to make it acceptable.[31] Returning to Leulingham with this message, Gaunt and Gloucester must have been prepared for the suspension of negotiations early in June, when a four-year truce was signed.

Queen Anne's death and Richard's departure for Ireland in October deflected his concern with Gaunt's project, and the sense that the proposed solutions were unworkable was strengthened as political opposition to them spread. Not only had pointed language been used against Gaunt in parliament but in May 1393 a rebellion had broken out in Cheshire, a major recruiting ground for soldiers, in protest against both peace itself and the alleged intention of Gaunt and Gloucester to surrender the king's title to France. The dukes had to return hurriedly from Leulingham to pacify the rebels and offer them service. Arundel's outspoken opposition to the 1393 proposals aroused suspicions that he may have been behind the rebellion. Richard's apparent readiness to connive at Gaunt's ambitions in Aquitaine also bred renewed fears in Gascony for its direct attachment to the English Crown. In April 1394 the archbishop and some feudal lords formally repudiated the authority of the duke and complained that his officers had infringed their rights. Stung by their rebellion, Gaunt undertook a military expedition to Bordeaux to reassert his authority and redress injuries. In July 1395 the political future of the duchy came under discussion at a council in London. The Gascons had never fully accepted the legality of the 1390 grant of the duchy to Gaunt and now, despite the king's renewed confirmation of it, legal opinion was heard and accepted by most of those present that the duchy was annexed to the Crown of England, and could not be granted to any other than the king's eldest son and heir.[32] The grant to Gaunt was not formally revoked, but his authority thereafter became nominal. Once the prospect of holding an enlarged principality from the French Crown in perpetuity had faded, he had little interest in the lordship of a restricted and recalcitrant territory.

Gaunt's scheme for a peace treaty which would define the status and boundaries of Aquitaine had seemed to meet his own political ambitions for a hereditary apanage, Charles VI's concern to ensure the integrity of France into which the duchy might eventually be absorbed, and Richard II's yearning for a final peace and the removal of the *casus belli*. But to the English chivalric class it represented a betrayal of their history and their *raison d'être*, and the mounting opposition to peace was to receive leadership from first Arundel, and ultimately Gloucester. From 1390 the Gascons saw Gaunt's ambitions as a threat to the

[31] *Rot. Parl.* iii. 315–16; *West. Chron.* 518.

[32] For a review of the different interpretations of these events, see C. J. Phillpotts, 'John of Gaunt and English policy towards France, 1389–95', *Jnl. Med. Hist.* 16 (1990), 363–87; also R. Tuck, 'Richard II and the Hundred Years War', in Taylor and Childs (eds.), *Politics and Crisis*, esp. 117–22 and 127–8.

connection to England which gave them de facto independence. The negotiations had demonstrated conclusively that there could be no political compromise between feudal lordship and sovereignty.

Richard had been ready to concur in Gaunt's direction of the negotiations, and connive at his ambitions, but as the opposition to the scheme gathered in different quarters the duke became a political liability, and when he left for Bordeaux the king's advisers took charge of foreign policy. A settlement with France was still the aim, and a means of putting pressure on the French was identified in Richard's plans for a second marriage. At the beginning of 1395 when the king was in Ireland two of his confidential servants, Bishop John Gilbert and Sir William Elmham, were dispatched via France to Aragon with a proposal for the hand of Yolande, daughter of the ageing King John, an alliance which would neatly complement those of Gaunt's daughters to the kings of Castile and Portugal. Yolande, however, had since 1390 been betrothed to Louis of Anjou, titular king of Naples. It thus represented a direct challenge to French influence, and Charles VI reacted in alarm, halting the embassy in Paris and sending his own envoy to Richard with proposals for a French marriage. This was none other than Robert the Hermit, who bore a presentation copy from his master, Philippe de Mézières, of his *Epistre au Roi Richart*, along with a letter from Charles VI. In these Richard was urged not to endanger the friendship and will to peace between the two monarchs by seeking an Aragonese marriage, but to work together for the healing of the Schism, as the preliminary to a crusade for the recovery of the Holy Land. Peace would be facilitated and confirmed by Richard's marriage to Isabella, Charles VI's 6-year-old daughter.[33] Richard readily agreed to the marriage and after further negotiation a truce for twenty-eight years was signed in Paris on 9 March 1396, the dowry being set at £133,333. The amicable meeting of the two kings prior to the marriage was held at Ardres on 26 October, each outbidding the other in the richness of their personal dress, the number of attendants, and the lavishness of their gifts and hospitality.[34] The young bride was delivered and married to Richard on 4 November. The two kings sealed their amity with promises of mutual assistance and a pledge to make a final peace and end the Schism.

In contrast to the peace negotiations of the preceding years, the truce of 1396 ignored both the English king's title to the French Crown and the status of the lands he held in France; and it accepted the present territorial boundaries. It was a simple suspension of hostilities, guaranteed by the genuine if precarious

[33] J. J. N. Palmer, 'The background to Richard II's marriage to Isabel of France (1396)', *BIHR* 44 (1971), 1–17.

[34] Palmer, *England, France and Christendom*, 166–7; Saul, *Richard II*, 230–1; J. Stratford, 'Gold and diplomacy: England and France in the reign of Richard II', in J. Mitchell and M. Moran (eds.), *England and the Continent in the Middle Ages* (Stamford, 2000), 221–37.

friendship of the two monarchs. It had been fashioned less by diplomacy than by military stalemate and the recognition that French influence had triumphed in Flanders, Brittany, and Castile. It acknowledged, rather than brought, the termination of this phase of the war. Richard had effectively wound up the war, which he had always disliked and declined to participate in. Though he admired and imitated the French cult of kingship, he had no continental ambitions, and his political horizons—uniquely in his family—remained wholly insular. He recoiled from the risks and waste of war, from the leadership and comradeship it demanded, and the tests which it imposed. His efforts were concentrated on enforcing the obedience of his own subjects. Nor did he display any enthusiasm, as did other rulers, for the cause of Christendom and the crusade.

4. SCHISM, SECESSION, AND CRUSADE

Pope Urban V's decision against the proposed marriage of Edmund of Cambridge and Margaret of Flanders had strengthened Edward's detachment from the Avignon papacy and only at Bruges in 1375 was papal mediation in the war welcomed. When Pope Gregory XI returned to Rome early in 1377 and died a year later, the choice of Urban VI, an austere Italian, became the signal for the election of a French rival, Robert of Geneva, as Clement VII and the commencement of the Great Schism. The papacy thereafter ceased to act as the mediator and arbiter of Christendom as each pope became tied to, and dependent on, national support. The pontificate of Urban VI (1378–89) was marked by wrangles with the English Crown over provisions and taxation, as was that of his successor, Boniface IX (1389–1404). These culminated in parliament's re-enactment of the Statute of Praemunire (1393), outlawing the publication of bulls of provision and excommunication.[35] That marked the limits of confrontation, for Boniface could not risk alienating England at the moment when Anglo-French proposals were emerging to end the Schism through a common withdrawal of obedience ('the way of cession'). This was the brainchild of the university of Paris. The two current popes were simultaneously to resign and support the election of another, but this would depend on the cooperation of their principal supporters. It was first broached at the Anglo-French negotiations in March 1392, and by 1395 it had been adopted by the French, who pressed Richard to pledge his support in the context of his marriage to Isabella in 1396. Joint embassies were dispatched to Rome and Avignon in April 1397 to require the popes to resign by February 1398, but both refused, and in the summer of 1398 the French unilaterally withdrew obedience from Benedict XIII on the understanding that Richard would likewise abandon Boniface IX. Richard was

---

[35] See above, Ch. 9, sect. 1.

in no hurry to comply, for he was still negotiating a concordat with Boniface over provisions, and saw no advantage in replacing a tamed Boniface with an almost certainly more independent or even Francophile pope.[36] Probably he had only agreed to the 'way of cession' to procure the marriage and long truce.

If the peace process had not ended the Schism, neither did it check the menace of the Turkish advance into the Balkans. The Greeks suffered the fall of Thessalonika in 1387, Bulgaria was conquered in 1388–93, Christian Serbia was crushed at the battle of Kosovo in 1389, Morea was ravaged in 1395, and Constantinople besieged in 1394. Already in 1389 Charles VI's tutor, Philippe de Mézières, in *Le Songe du Vieil Pèlerin* had urged the cooperation of France and England to halt the infidel. Mézières's vision, presented with compelling eloquence in his *Epistre au Roi Richart*, was of a Christendom transformed by peace. The cessation of internal warfare, which shed Christian blood, enslaved rulers to the demands of generals and financiers, impoverished subjects by taxation, and brought the fear of plunder and rapine by soldiery, would be followed by the establishment of justice, order, solvency, trade, and prosperity under the effective rule of the king, as God's minister, for the common good. The Orchard of War, where tyranny and chaos ruled, was contrasted with the Orchard of Peace, of freedom and order.[37] This message made a powerful appeal to Richard II, for whom peace meant the chance to be truly 'emperor in his own kingdom'. But Mézières's call was also to international chivalry, whose task was now to turn their swords on the infidel.

Mézières had recruited the elite of European chivalry into his crusading Order of the Passion and, urged on by Sigismund, the leaders of Europe—the king of France and the dukes of Burgundy, Lancaster, and Orléans—began to shape plans, raise money, and organize armies in the winter of 1394–5. But in the course of 1395 other commitments prevented their participation, and it was a force led predominantly by Franco-Burgundian captains under John of Nevers which sailed from Regensburg down the Danube to Buda in the summer of 1396. Disregarding the defensive strategy advocated by Sigismund, it marched into Bulgaria to besiege the key fortress of Nicopolis—though lacking siege engines—and was a prey to the advancing army of the sultan Bayazid and, ultimately, the folly of a chivalric assault on the Turkish defences. The slaughter or capture of almost the whole force in September 1396 not only established the Turks in Europe for centuries to come but dealt a mortal blow to European

[36] Perroy, *L'Angleterre et le Grand Schisme*, 361–90; M. Harvey, 'Solutions to the Schism: A study of some English attitudes, 1378 to 1409', *Kirchengeschichtliche Quellen und Studien*, 12 (1983), 97–113.

[37] Philippe de Mézières, *Letter to King Richard II*, ed. and trans. G. W. Coopland (Liverpool, 1975).

crusading. The royal armies planned for the following year were abandoned and French leadership of Christendom was discredited.[38]

The collapse of common initiatives on the Schism and crusade, and the absence of any further negotiations for a final peace, reflected the divergence of French and English policies after 1397. None of this reflected any real estrangement between the two kings; merely the fact that their interests and priorities were not the same.[39] Richard II's policy since 1394–5 had been essentially to free himself from entanglements in France. His desire for a permanent end to hostilities reflected no corresponding wish for closer cooperation. Lacking all interest in military and territorial aggrandizement, and equally indifferent to the idealism and adventurism of the crusade, his concern was solely to establish mastery in his own kingdom. Yet in both countries the truce and marriage had aroused opposition: Louis d'Orléans was increasingly at odds with Burgundy's direction of royal policy, which frustrated his ambitions in Italy; in England, Gloucester's opposition to the truce had led to his brutal removal. Richard's subsequent exiling of Bolingbroke, and the confiscation of his lands on Gaunt's death in March 1399, won Bolingbroke sympathy abroad. Orléans gave him a cordial welcome in Paris, hoping to use his grievance as a lever against Burgundy's Anglophile policy. In the summer of 1399, while Duke Philip was in the Low Countries, Orléans permitted Henry of Bolingbroke to assemble an expedition for the recovery of his inheritance in England.[40] Henry landed in Yorkshire early in July and within a month had won control of England. By October, Richard had been deposed and imprisoned.

5. ENEMIES AND ALLIES, 1399–1413

Orléans could have had no inkling of the momentous consequences of his action for he was shocked by Richard's deposition and at once became the sworn enemy of the usurper. By the same token Duke Philip, who had moved rapidly to re-establish his control in Paris, was readier to accept King Henry, if only because the prosperity of Flanders and his own revenues depended on the flow of English wool. Over the next thirteen years English foreign policy had continually to adjust to the balance of power in France as the rivalry of the dukes swung the attitude of the French Crown between neutrality and enmity. Fortunately for Henry this internal struggle for power blunted French aggression, producing

---

[38] Palmer, *England, France and Christendom*, ch. 11, esp. pp. 200–7; N. Housley, *The Later Crusades* (Oxford, 1992), 73–9.

[39] Palmer, *England, France and Christendom*, ch. 12, argues for their continuing amity; C. Given-Wilson (ed.), *Chronicles of the Revolution* (Manchester, 1993), 25–31, emphasizes their increasing hostility.

[40] Given-Wilson (ed.), *Chronicles of the Revolution*, 28–30; Saul, *Richard II*, 405–8.

indecision and ultimately internal conflict. Henry was able to survive, maintaining almost to the end of the reign a defensive stance. In this context the pattern of English foreign policy was determined by the deaths of Duke Philip in 1404 and of Louis d'Orléans in 1407, each of which signalled a major shift of political influence.

The horror produced in France by the overthrow of sacral kingship and the accompanying affront to Charles VI's daughter was temporarily contained by fears for her safety and uncertainty about Henry's warlike intentions. In fact his internal difficulties dictated a conciliatory policy: he formally confirmed the truce in June 1400, and the return of Isabella (in effect a hostage) was protracted until May 1401. This breathing space had enabled Henry to secure recognition in Germany, where the marriage of his daughter Blanche to Ludwig, son of Rupert, Count Palatine and emperor elect, was arranged in March 1401, while in 1402 King Eric of Denmark agreed to marry Henry's youngest daughter, Philippa.[41] The need for this assiduous search for allies was underlined when, following the return of Isabella, he faced the determined enmity of Louis d'Orléans, who in August 1402 and March 1403 issued personal challenges to Henry. More dangerous was the offensive mounted against English-held Gascony when in October 1403 Orléans himself advanced into the duchy with the aim of encircling Bordeaux. Winter intervened, but the war was resumed in the spring under Bernard, count of Armagnac.[42]

Anglo-French warfare also developed in the Channel, with licensed reprisals by both sides. In 1402–3 unofficial fleets from the West Country under John Hawley and Mark Mixto were encouraged to seize French ships and those of neutrals carrying French cargoes. Anglo-Flemish relations were put under strain despite the renewal of a commercial truce in March 1403. Then, under the direction of Orléans, licensed piracy gave place to open war, with Breton and French attacks on Plymouth and the Channel Isles in September and an invasion of the Isle of Wight in December.[43]

English influence was also in retreat among its former clients in the Low Countries, Brittany, and Spain. During the 1390s Richard II had sought to check Burgundian influence by giving annual pensions of £1,000 to Rupert, Count Palatine, and William of Jülich, duke of Guelders. Henry had little money or incentive to maintain these and ineluctably ceded place to Orléans, who was intent on bolstering opposition to Duke Philip in his back yard. In Brittany, Duke Jean had remained under the influence of the dukes of Burgundy and Berry, but

[41] A. Tuck, 'Henry IV and Europe: A dynasty's search for recognition', in R. H. Britnell and A. J. Pollard (eds.), *The McFarlane Legacy* (Stroud, 1995), 107–26.

[42] Vale, *English Gascony*, 27–55.

[43] C. J. Ford, 'Piracy or policy: The crisis in the Channel, 1400–1403', *TRHS*, 5th ser., 29 (1979), 63–77.

his death in November 1399 leaving his son a minor posed the whole question of Breton loyalties. If Henry IV hoped to attach these by his marriage to Jean's widow, Joan of Navarre, in February 1403, he miscalculated. It lost her what little support she had in Brittany, where anti-English sentiment was inflamed by the sea war, and she was forced to deliver her son to the custody of Philip of Burgundy, to be brought up in Paris.[44] As in Brittany, so in Castile, marriage ties proved too weak to offset the historical alliance with France. The resumption of war in the Channel saw Castilian galleys under Don Pedro de Niño raid the south coast in 1405. To offset Castilian hostility Henry reinforced the Lancastrian connection with Portugal, making his brother-in-law King João a knight of the Garter, while Queen Philippa fostered English influence at the royal court.

Where Richard's disengagement from Europe had been largely a matter of choice, Henry's isolation was a reflection of his weakness. But though the French might treat him as a pariah, and their clients in Brittany and Spain follow suit, their own internal divisions set limits to their hostility, while Henry painstakingly cultivated support elsewhere. In particular Henry had been able to count on Duke Philip's interest in avoiding war with England, but when he died in 1404 the hostility of Orléans could not be so surely contained.

Philip the Bold died on 27 April 1404 and Margaret de Mâle the following year. During that period, while John the Fearless was consolidating his inheritance, Louis d'Orléans as regent was extending his control over the French state. In August 1405 John mounted an open challenge, marching to Paris and seizing the Dauphin from Queen Isabella; he denounced the 'absolutism' of Orléans and proposed a constitutional sharing of power. The mediation of the dukes of Berry and Bourbon defused the crisis but left Orléans essentially in control of the council and policy. He now developed a two-pronged attack on English territories. Against the remnant of English Gascony, Orléans himself led a large-scale invasion in the autumn of 1406, threatening Blaye, Bourg, and Saint-Émilion; but the siege of Bourg became mired in winter and was eventually abandoned. Bordeaux was once more saved, and this proved to be the last threat for thirty years.

Equally serious was that to Calais. In October 1406 Duke John, on royal orders, assembled an army at Saint-Omer to besiege Calais in parallel with Orléans's campaign in the south-west. John would have been glad enough to snatch Calais, but his underlying interest was to maintain trade with England and to defend his territories. Charles VI's inexplicable cancellation of the project in mid-November left Duke John ostensibly furious but was perhaps not unwelcome, for he had become alarmed at the intrusion of Orléans into the Low Countries in support of the duke of Guelders and the Luxembourg claim to Brabant. This pressure close to home, combined with his exclusion from power

---

[44] G. A. Knowlson, *Jean V, duc de Bretagne et l'Angleterre* (Cambridge, 1964), 32–49.

and money in Paris, determined John the Fearless to remove Orléans by assassination in November 1407.[45] The mortal feud of Burgundy and Orléans had thus brought about a reorientation of English policy. Richard II had maintained his grandfather's hostility to Philip of Burgundy, seeking to contain his territorial expansion by alliances with the bordering princes. But the emergence of Orléans as Burgundy's rival and Henry IV's enemy produced a convergence of Anglo-Flemish political interests which confirmed existing commercial ties. However, Henry IV's wary, defensive stance continued; no one in England desired or contemplated a renewal of war in France.

After a year in which John the Fearless brazenly justified the murder of Louis d'Orléans as being in the public interest, his formal reconciliation with Orléans's son Charles at Chartres in March 1409 confirmed the re-establishment of Burgundian control over the court and government. Once again royal revenue flowed into Burgundian coffers and the Dauphin Louis, married to John's daughter Margaret, was empowered as regent in the king's illness. The inevitable reaction of Charles d'Orléans to this, forcibly backed by Bernard of Armagnac, found expression in their alliance at Gien in April 1410. Both sides mustered troops around Paris; but it was not until July 1411 that the Orléanists declared war at Jargeau. Hesitating between attacking John in Paris or in Flanders–Artois, they finally in October seized Saint-Cloud and Saint-Denis, the keys to Paris. By then John had already appealed to England for aid.

Throughout the first half of 1411 the policy of the council in England under Prince Henry had been to strengthen the truces covering Gascony, the sea, and Flanders. But during July–September 1411 negotiations for a military alliance with John the Fearless gave the first indication that the English Crown was ready to exploit the internal divisions of France and revive its old claims. In fact it was only a small unofficial expedition under the prince's retainer the earl of Arundel that gave crucial assistance to Duke John in expelling Orléanist troops from Saint-Cloud on 9 November and relieving Paris.[46] The immediate object was to buttress the ascendancy of the duke of Burgundy, on which English security was thought to depend, but this was quickly to change. Even while the news of Saint-Cloud was reported in England, Henry IV had roused himself to discharge the prince's council and resume the direction of policy.

In the spring of 1412, as Burgundy carried the war into the Orléanists' territory with the siege of Bourges, they appealed to Henry IV for assistance on an even larger scale. By the Treaty of Bourges of 18 May the Orléanist lords undertook to deliver to Henry IV in sovereignty extensive lands in Aquitaine and to

---

[45] M. Nordberg, *Les Ducs et la royauté* (Uppsala, 1964), ch. VII; R. Vaughan, *John the Fearless* (London, 1966), 33–51.

[46] C. Philpotts, 'The fate of the truce of Paris, 1396–1415', *Jnl. Med. Hist.* 24 (1998), 74; Vaughan, *John the Fearless*, 82–92.

hold their own lands there (including Poitou) from him in homage, if he would join them with an army of 4,000 men to fight Burgundy. No reference was made in the treaty to Henry's claim to the French throne. Even though it was endorsed by the greatest peers of France—Orléans, Berry, Bourbon, Armagnac—Henry cannot have been unaware that such sweeping concessions were unsustainable. Indeed it was almost immediately abrogated by Charles VI in a lucid moment on 21 July. But Henry was impatient to recover Aquitaine for English rule, and the warlike and impetuous Clarence was bent on reviving the *chevauchée*. Had the expedition been able to sail earlier and confront the Burgundian army at Bourges, its political gains could have been significant. As it was, by the time it landed at Cherbourg on 10 August, Burgundians and Orléanists had already come to terms at Auxerre, agreeing to renounce foreign alliances. A devastating *chevauchée* was all that was left to Clarence, York, and Dorset, from which they exacted a ransom of 210,000 gold *écus*. On 14 November at Buzançais the Orléanists delivered hostages and much costly jewellery as pledge for payment. English intervention had yielded no political rewards commensurate with these material gains. Clarence, at Bordeaux, found himself unable to assert English sovereignty beyond the pale, and an alliance made with Armagnac and Albret recognized their right of *ressort* (appeal) to Charles VI.[47] The promise of Bourges had thus been deceptive, and though the vulnerability of France had again, after a long interval, been demonstrated, so had the illusory prospect of exercising sovereignty over Aquitaine. It was a lesson which Henry V took to heart.

The English intervention had been carefully assessed by Jean, duke of Brittany, who in 1411 entered a long truce with England for ten years, with provision for reparations for piracy. This signalled not merely the restoration of peace on the seas but the determination of Jean V to maintain Breton neutrality in the impending French civil war. John the Fearless was also looking ahead. The *bouleversement* of alliances in 1412 might have provoked him to attack Calais or take reprisals against English trade. He did neither, careful to maintain the friendship of Henry V. Commercial relations had been wholly cordial during the prince's administration in 1410–11, both sides suppressing piracy and renewing the truce in July 1411. The most contentious issue was the duke's policy of debasement and the minting of counterfeit English nobles, which eventually forced Henry IV into a like debasement in 1411. Breton neutrality and Burgundian friendship were to provide the essential protection for Henry V's invasion of Normandy.

The 1412 expedition ended thirty years of English non-intervention in France. The independent power of the dukes of Burgundy, the caution of the

---

[47] Vale, *English Gascony*, 59–68; J. D. Milner, 'The English enterprise in France, 1412–13', in Clayton *et al.* (eds.), *Trade, Devotion and Governance*, 80–101.

dukes of Brittany, and the repulse of English claims in Castile had together closed off potential allies through whom the French Crown could be destabilized. Latterly the disinclination of Richard II, and the domestic preoccupations of Henry IV precluded military intervention across the Channel. But when in 1410–12 Burgundians and Orléanists each in turn appealed for English aid, the scene was set for a prolonged period of English involvement in Europe.

Ecclesiastical developments likewise impelled Henry IV towards more positive involvement in healing the Schism. The French advocacy of 'the way of cession' had received little English support. No withdrawal of obedience from either Boniface IX or his successor, Innocent VII, had taken place and meanwhile, in 1403, Orléans secured the restoration of French obedience to Benedict XIII. On Innocent's death in November 1406 the division between the two obediences, reflecting national enmities, appeared as entrenched as at any time in the last thirty years. These were, in fact, to soften over the next three years, but of greater importance was the current of intellectual opinion within the Church and universities in favour of a new solution to the Schism through the summoning of a general council. Although this had been under active discussion in both England and France since 1395, the failure of the way of cession left this as the only serious alternative. It was espoused reluctantly by the leading Paris theologians Jean Gerson and Pierre d'Ailly, and the Italian Francesco Zabarella, because it raised fundamental questions about the nature of authority within the Church, indeed of the nature of the Church itself. Papal plenitude of power had somehow to be mitigated if the rival popes were to be forcibly replaced. Their obduracy could be represented as heresy, justifying their removal, but how was a universally recognized successor to be chosen? The cardinals of the rival allegiances were unlikely to agree, though d'Ailly and Zabarella insisted on their historic role. History offered the solution of a general council, as in the early Church, representing the *congregatio fidelium*. But this was a body without a head (except for Christ himself) and the councils of the Latin Church had always been summoned by the pope and acted conjointly with him. Some were prepared to assert that a council's authority was autonomous and superior to that of the pope in matters of faith, while to many, schism within the Church and heresy outside were symptomatic of the materialism and corruption for which they held the papacy primarily responsible. A general council should thus not only restore unity but carry through sweeping reforms in head and members. By 1406 a consensus in favour of a council had emerged, at least among the Paris doctors, and this forced it onto the agenda of European rulers.[48]

---

[48] On conciliar theory, consult B. Tierney, *The Foundations of Conciliar Theory* (Cambridge, 1955); R. N. Swanson, *Universities, Academics, and the Great Schism* (Cambridge, 1979).

A last attempt was made to persuade both popes to reach agreement on mutual resignation and submission to a council, and when in April 1408 this had failed, their supporters on both sides summoned a council to meet at Pisa in March 1409. In November 1408 Cardinal Uguccione, archbishop of Bordeaux, arrived in England to secure the support of Henry IV, who appointed a powerful delegation to act 'in the name the king, the lords, and the prelates of the English church', the most notable of whom were Bishops Chichele, Hallum, and Langley. The council was, in effect, 'a legal process against the *contendentes* for the crime of schism' at the end of which, on 5 June, they were both deposed.[49] A new pope, a Franciscan and ethnic Greek, was chosen as Alexander V, to whom in October 1409 Henry IV gave official recognition. English support for a conciliar solution to the Schism was paralleled by the fervour of its delegation for reform. Protected against papal provisions by the statutes which Henry IV had warned Alexander V to respect, it was the papal licensing of abuses at diocesan level that concerned Hallum and the Oxford reformer Richard Ullerstone.

Consideration of reform had to be deferred until the next council in 1412; nor were the judgements at Pisa universally accepted. Indeed there were now three popes, each with lay backing. Another general council was needed to break the impasse, and on the death of Rupert in 1410 the new emperor elect, Sigismund of Hungary, reasserted the imperial leadership of Christendom with a proposal for a council at Constance in 1414. Sigismund already had friendly relations with Henry IV and was personally committed to Church reform; the English Crown and conciliarists thus readily gave him support. The major influence which the English had acquired over the last five years ensured them a central role at the greatest international gathering of the Middle Ages.

England's involvement in Europe in the half-century after 1360 barely justifies the term 'foreign policy'. Particularly after Edward III's dynastic schemes proved chimerical and his direction of affairs faltered, there was no overall policy for furthering English interests or containing French influence. The piecemeal response to French recovery, whether by military intervention or by negotiation over the status of Aquitaine, both led to an impasse formalized in the twenty-eight-year truce. English policy was governed by the particular dynastic, military, and political interests of those who guided it, notably John of Gaunt. Richard II can be credited with abandoning the obsession with France as 'our ancient enemy', and seeking an enduring peace, but this reflected more his detachment from continental commitments than his identification with the schemes for a new crusade and an end to the Schism, to which the French monarchy and churchmen were pledged. Only at the end of the first decade of the new century did England begin to develop a new vision of its role in Christendom.

---

[49] E. F. Jacob, *Essays in Later Medieval History* (Manchester, 1968), 107.

CHAPTER 12

Ruling England, 1360–1413

1. PEACE AND PLENTY, 1360–1369

No one would have doubted, in 1360, that the 'Great Peace' marked the commencement of a new era. Although France's prostration exposed her to English and Gascon routiers, the Commons in parliament saw it as marking their 'deliverance from the bondage of other lands and the many charges they had sustained in times past'.[1] For thirty years the king had pressed them hard, securing their partnership in war with the promise of ruling with 'lenience and gentleness', when peace came. King and subjects could now look forward to the fruits of victory.

While the court replaced the camp as the focus of Edward's life, its tone was consciously chivalric. Still vigorous at 50, Edward indulged a passion for hunting and falconry, feasts and tournaments. Windsor was reconstructed as the ceremonial centre of the monarchy, with the Order of the Garter established in St George's Chapel. Some of those who had served Edward in arms, like Alan Buxhull and Richard Pembridge, now attended him as knights of his chamber; many others were granted substantial life annuities from the customs revenues. Though not large, his household was costly, drawing some £35,000 a year from the exchequer in 1360–7. Ostentation and largesse were part of the image of chivalric honour and loyal service which the royal court promoted, and in this both the royal family and the magnates had a role.[2]

In November 1362 the conferring of dukedoms on the king's sons Lionel and John, and an earldom on Edmund, placed them, along with the Black Prince, at the head of the nobility. Each was (or was to be) enriched by marriage to an heiress and given major territorial responsibilities: the Black Prince in Aquitaine; Lionel of Clarence as Lieutenant of Ireland; John of Gaunt in the north of England as potential successor to the childless David II of Scotland; and Edmund of Langley, predicated to marry Margaret de Mâle, heiress to Flanders. The danger of 'a brood of redundant and bickering princes' was avoided by

---

[1] *Rot. Parl.* ii. 276 (1363).

[2] Given-Wilson, *Royal Household*, 280 and ch. 2, for household costs; for the court at Windsor, see above, Ch. 2, sect. 1.

encouraging them to use their energies and resources in carrying forward the
next wave of Plantagenet imperialism.[3] But whereas in the first half of the
decade the royal family gave the appearance of conducting a united and dynamic
operation, by the end it had been blighted by death and disarray. English rule was
disintegrating in Ireland and Aquitaine, and English influence had been
excluded from Castile and Flanders; the king had suffered the loss of his wife and
second son, and faced the mortal illness of his heir apparent.

Although death was also thinning the circle of his leading commanders—
Lancaster, Northampton, Hereford, and Oxford all died in 1360–1—for much of
the decade Edward could enjoy the support of some favourite companions.
Robert, earl of Suffolk, and Ralph, earl of Stafford, had both campaigned with
Edward from 1346 to 1360, as had William, earl of Salisbury, while Thomas, earl
of Warwick, had the most distinguished record of all. Richard, earl of Arundel,
though not a soldier, had underpinned royal expeditions in the 1350s with his
loans. Edward could rely on the deeply ingrained loyalty of these senior earls.
Just as there is no evidence of friction with the Crown, so there is no record of
quarrels between them. Like the king himself they were using their gains of war
to embellish their castles, buy land, perhaps trade prisoners, and certainly in
Arundel's case multiply his treasure.[4] From the perspective of the king and his
immediate circle, England was a land at peace, of abundant wealth and political
stability. The 1360s were the golden evening of a generation of old soldiers, all
of whom joined the king in arms for the last time in 1369. It was a static peerage.
Outside the royal family Edward created no new earls and did nothing to promote a new generation into the baronage.[5]

In the 1360s Edward's political authority rested on his reputation and his
wealth. The ransoms from the royal captives, from the prisoners he purchased,
and from the spoils of the 1360 campaign made Edward far richer than previous
kings. From it he financed the military ventures of his sons, his building projects,
and his costly display. Though the expenditure of his treasure was recorded on
the exchequer rolls, so that the recipients could be held to account, the money
itself was held in the Tower treasury under the king's personal control. This
bred confusion in the exchequer, and following a retrospective review in 1364,
which found that the king had spent up to £170,000 (much of it fruitlessly on
war), the unspent balance of £47,000 was deposited in the king's chamber.
Edward now took alarm and decided on retrenchment. By 1368 building had

[3] W. M. Ormrod, 'Edward III and his family', *Jnl. Brit. Stud.* 26 (1987), 398–422.

[4] C. Given-Wilson, 'Royal charter witness lists, 1327–1399', *Medieval Prosopography*, 12 (1991),
35–93.

[5] In 1362 only twenty-nine barons were summoned to parliament and no significant enlargement
of the baronage occurred until 1371; J. E. Powell and K. Wallis, *The House of Lords in the Middle Ages*
(London, 1968) 363, 368.

ceased and his household expenses were reduced. After renegotiating the French and Scottish ransoms, from which another £84,000 was received before 1369, Edward managed to accumulate a war chest of well over £100,000 against the impending resumption of hostilities with France. He was still a rich king.[6]

The highly personal and proprietary view of government which this episode reveals was characteristic of Edward's rule in the 1360s. This was the decade of William of Wykeham's rise and rule: from clerk of the chamber with control of the king's treasure in 1361, to keeper of the privy seal in 1363, to bishop of Winchester in 1366, and as chancellor in the following year. What impressed contemporaries was Edward's reliance upon him and his own omnicompetence. First as 'the king's secretary who stays by his side', later as 'chief of the privy council and governor of the great council', 'all things were done by him and without him nothing was done'. Wykeham commended himself to Edward as being unhampered by routines, someone who would get things done and meet his wishes. Yet it is impossible at present to assess Wykeham's role in day-to-day government, for little is known about how policy was formulated, who author-ized its execution, and who composed the council. The impression is that Wykeham exploited Edward's detachment from detail to establish his own con-trol. Not that Edward was manipulated by his ministers; he could dismiss a chief justice and a baron of the exchequer in 1365 'for their enormous infidelities', but what he valued was their devotion to his interests rather than to standards of justice or even efficiency.[7]

Beyond the circle of his family, magnates, and officials Edward had to adapt his relations with his subjects to the conditions of peace. For thirty years the inexorable logic of common danger had required the Commons in parliament to grant taxation for the king's war. The peace treaty of 1360 removed this obliga-tion and no direct taxes were sought in the ensuing decade. The more productive subsidy on wool had been levied since 1353 at the rate of 50s. the sack, with a boom in wool exports producing an average of £87,500 per annum up to 1362. When it then came up for renewal the Commons secured a sharp reduction to 20s. for the next three years. Then in 1365, on the basis of a full statement of the king's revenues and expenditure designed to demonstrate a permanent deficit in Crown finance, they restored the subsidy to 40s. 'in salvation of the king's estate and honour'. It was again renewed in 1368 and increased to a wartime rate in 1369.[8] How had the Commons been persuaded to do this by a king demonstrably

---

[6] G. L. Harriss, *King, Parliament and Public Finance* (Oxford, 1975), ch. 20; W. M. Ormrod, 'The protecolla rolls and English government finance, 1353–1364', *EHR* 102 (1987), 623–32.

[7] *CPR, 1361–4*, 444; *Chron. Angliae*, pp. lxxv–vi; P. Partner, 'William of Wykeham and the his-torians', in R. Custance (ed.), *Winchester College* (Winchester, 1968), 1–36.

[8] W. M. Ormrod, 'The English Crown and the customs, 1349–1363', *Econ. HR*, 2nd ser., 40 (1987), 27–40; Harriss, *King, Parliament*, 467–9. After 1367 wool exports fell below 30,000 sacks.

rich and spending freely? Edward had insisted on separating his personal wealth from national finance: the royal treasure was abundant, but the national budget was in deficit. By demonstrating the latter in parliament he was acknowledging the Commons' claim to be informed of financial policy and their exclusive right to grant the wool subsidy. He also made some timely concessions, respiting the king's bench eyre, restricting royal purveyance, and establishing the Staple at Calais (in February 1363). Moreover, a growing crisis of social stability dictated a common front with those who ruled in the localities.

By 1360 the social consequences of the Black Death were apparent in demands for higher wages and the abolition of servile status. The recurrence of plague in 1361 and 1369 accentuated this, and the ending of war brought a mounting volume of banditry and local disorder.[9] In 1361, after a decade of enforcing labour legislation, the local gentry were granted power to determine felonies on their own, and by stages were integrated into the judicial system. Their complaints of aristocratic perversion of judicial process, in nominating to private commissions of oyer and terminer and in the retaining of royal justices, had begun to be heeded, and their increasingly lengthy common petitions in five parliaments during the decade were the basis for statutes which addressed their own social concerns—notably the sumptuary regulations of 1363 enforcing a strict hierarchy in dress. The Commons' active participation in the work of parliament was acknowledged in the opening charge (in English in 1362) and by their presence at dinner with the king and Lords at the end of parliament in 1368.[10]

Knights of the shire were drawn from the county elite and legislation reflected their viewpoint. They used the labour laws to reinforce their own seigniorial and economic power, while the smaller landlords—the petty gentry, yeomen, and husbandmen—found the day labourers' demands for higher wages undermining their livelihood. As a petition in 1368 complained, 'the commons who live by cultivation of their lands, or by trade, and who have no lordship or villeins to serve them' were being ruined by high prices and wages. The social cleavage in the countryside belied the political harmony at the centre. And at a lower level the 'ease and prosperity' of those who could extract the full price for their labour was matched by the resentment of those prevented from doing so. The peace rolls of the East Riding of Yorkshire in 1363–4 show how large an element labour offences formed in the work of the justices: 93 cases of excess wages, 57 of unlicensed departure, and 42 of refusal to work at legal wages.[11] Those ruling England at local level faced problems of which King Edward at Windsor was perhaps only dimly aware.

[9] Rot. Parl. ii. 268; Bellamy, Crime and Public Order, 6.

[10] Above, Ch. 3, sects. 2, 4. Sumptuary ordinance in SR i. 380–2; the charge in English, Rot. Parl. ii. 268; dinner with the king, ibid. ii. 297.

[11] Rot. Parl. ii. 296; H. Jewell, 'Piers Plowman—a poem of crisis: An analysis of political instability in Langland's England', in Taylor and Childs (eds.), Politics and Crisis, 59–66.

At the beginning of 1369 Edward's reputation was at its height. While the glow of his victories still dazzled, his rule also offered a model of kingship. His apotheosis in his later epitaph recalled him as 'the flower of kings past, the pattern for kings to come, a merciful king, the bringer of peace to his people . . . who revived sound rule, and reigned valiantly'.[12] Peace had indeed brought security, a release from direct taxation, and the confirmation of rights and liberties. Loyally supported by his older nobility and dutiful sons, he had acknowledged the parliamentary Commons and shire gentry as accessories to royal government. Harmony and cooperation knit the political classes; neither contentious policies nor personal rivalries disturbed the polity. His own demands were met from his prodigious wealth while an expanding economy and booming wool exports enabled the king to reward his old soldiers. If, at lower levels of society, structures were cracking and class tensions rising, as yet only ripples of these disturbed the political scene. Overseas, it is true, the clouds were gathering, with English power in retreat and war impending; and Edward's style of kingship was ill fitted for the tensions and divisions engendered by a losing war. His temper was regal and imperious, his world circumscribed by his nobles, war captains, judges, and bishops. He saw no call to engage in political dialogue with lesser subjects, or bow to public opinion. The Commons had learned to defend their interests but had yet to show themselves determined and devastating critics. Pragmatic in meeting their demands, Edward was never prepared to diminish his prerogative or belittle the royal dignity.

The general impression of the 1360s remains one of suspended animation, almost of a political vacuum, in which events were on a minor rather than a major scale. That impression is probably accurate, but there are large areas of which we are at present ignorant. The active operation of the king's will—in consultation, delegation, intervention—remains unexplored. We are in almost total ignorance of the politics of the nobility—their local rule, affinities, dynastic schemes, and quarrels. Finally the problems of law-keeping—the extent of disorder and the volume of litigation—are still obscure. Until areas such as these are explored the picture of Edward III's government in this decade will remain one-dimensional.

2. THE COURT AND THE COMMONS, 1369–1377

The last phase of Edward III's rule has a dismal unity: an unrelieved tale of military retreat, financial corruption, court faction, and parliamentary opposition. At first the king had met the challenge of war with some vigour, but after a series of failures culminating in the abandonment of his own voyage in 1372 he

---

[12] D. A. Morgan, 'The political after-life of Edward III: The apotheosis of a warmonger', *EHR* 112 (1997), 861.

withdrew to enfeebled seclusion, as did his dying heir. Similarly, although support for the war among the magnates and in parliament remained buoyant for three years, thereafter it became increasingly critical.

Edward spent freely in this opening phase of the war; some £200,000 on operations in northern France, Gascony, and on the sea, of which perhaps half came from his own accumulated treasure.[13] But by February 1371 he was turning to parliament and convocation for taxation. The huge sum of £100,000 needed for the next offensive was to be met equally by the laity and clergy. The Commons agreed to a novel tax on parishes while the Black Prince and other magnates bullied convocation for its contribution with hints of lay support for the arguments in favour of disendowment and apostolic poverty advanced by two Austin friars.[14]

The return of John of Gaunt in November 1371 and the appointment of John, Lord Neville, as steward and William, Lord Latimer, as chamberlain of the household, both vigorous and experienced soldiers, promised a more determined military effort. Despite the disasters which overtook the ambitious offensive strategy of 1372, the Commons in November were still prepared to grant a fifteenth, renew the wool subsidy, and add tunnage and poundage for the urgent support of the navy. Military expenditure, which again in 1373 and 1374 reached some £200,000, combined with mounting frustration at the failure to stem the French recovery, intensified the pressure on the Church. Pope Gregory XI's demand for a papal subsidy from the English Church for his war against the Visconti was strongly rebuffed under pressure from the Black Prince, and in December 1373, when parliament was again asked for taxation, a delegation of royal councillors pressured convocation into granting a further tenth. This time the Commons likewise needed convincing, and their grant of taxation for the following two years (1374 and 1375) was conditional on the continuance of the war.[15]

The war was putting heavy, but not insupportable, strains on Crown finances. From 1371 to 1375 wool exports remained relatively buoyant, at 25,000 sacks and more per annum, producing an average yield of around £70,000. Taxation roughly covered the costs of war though not normal expenditure as well.[16] Short-term loans (which might become long-term) were always needed in wartime, and in his heyday Edward had borrowed freely from Italian and later native

[13] Sherborne, *War, Politics and Culture*, 55–70.

[14] Tout, *Chapters*, iii. 266–81; W. M. Ormrod, 'An experiment in taxation: The English parish subsidy of 1371', *Speculum*, 63 (1988), 58–82; Aston, *Faith and Fire*, 105–6.

[15] J. I. Catto, 'An alleged great council of 1374', *EHR* 82 (1967), 764–71; McFarlane, *John Wycliffe*, 55–7; *Rot. Parl*. ii. 316–17.

[16] W. M. Ormrod, 'Finance and trade under Richard II', in Goodman and Gillespie (eds.), *Richard II*, 176, revising upward Sherborne's figures.

merchants. With the wool trade now regulated by the Company of the Staple, such merchant capitalists were no longer available; and there were few indeed with comparable resources. The earl of Arundel had lent large sums on the security of the customs in 1369–70 and was to make further loans in 1372–4 before his death in 1376.[17] Now three men came to the fore who proved able to raise liquid capital on a large scale. Two of these, John Pyel and Richard Francis, were already known to the court as occasional lenders and brokers to the Crown, the former being mayor of London in 1372. Their associate, Richard Lyons had emerged more recently as alderman and sheriff (1374), a man of considerable wealth and property.[18] Between July 1372 and August 1374 these three were advancing large sums which they had evidently raised elsewhere: 10,000 marks in July 1372, £6,000 in July 1373, and over £21,000 in three loans in 1374. In each case, as well as being repaid from the customs, they were enabled to cash in bonds and tallies representing ancient debts of the Crown to the value of half their loan. Some of these dated back thirty years and more, and most were in the names of Edward III's creditors, particularly the Italian merchant firm of Bardi. Evidently these bonds were being bought up at a discount and cashed at face value, thus bringing considerable profit. There was no secret about this; the arrangement was openly sanctioned by the greatest lords of the council and formally recorded on the exchequer and chancery rolls.[19]

For the Bardi it was a chance to clear a proportion of their bad debts, debentures to the value of £13,197 being now settled in this way, though at what discount is unclear. Certainly those who traded these must have made a considerable profit. The unpopularity of the Italians made it advisable to conceal their role. For since 1365 the Crown had been selling them licences exempting them from exporting via the Calais Staple. There had already been anti-alien riots in London in 1371, instigated by the draper demagogues John of Northampton and William Essex, and there were protests against the sale of such licences in the parliament of 1373. The threat of French coastal raids had galvanized the major wool merchants Nicholas Brembre, John Philpot, and William Walworth to raise a fleet to protect their trade, and they now organized themselves as a Company of Grocers to defend their monopoly at Calais. A deepening division opened between them and those like Pyel, Lyons, John Pecche, and Adam Bury with ties to the Italians and the court. In October 1375 the grocers secured the mayoralty and, with the support of John of Northampton's

[17] C. Given-Wilson, 'Wealth and credit, the earls of Arundel, 1306–1397', *EHR* 106 (1991), 1–27.

[18] S. O'Connor, 'Finance, diplomacy and politics: Royal service by two London merchants in the reign of Edward III', *Hist. Res.* 67 (1994), 18–40; A. R. Myers, 'The wealth of Richard Lyons', in T. A. Sandquist and M. R. Powick (eds.), *Essays in Medieval History Presented to Bertie Wilkinson* (Toronto, 1969), 301–4.   [19] Holmes, *Good Parliament*, 69–79.

group in the court of aldermen, initiated the prosecution of aliens accused of acting as brokers for usurious loans. When parliament was summoned in March 1376 this was carried forward into the impeachment of Lyons, Bury, and Pecche by the two London MPs, Walworth and Essex.[20]

By then John of Gaunt had procured a truce with the French, dictated by military failure and financial exhaustion. In relation to the immediate situation in Brittany, the timing was (as we have seen) misjudged, with the English forced both to hand over Saint-Sauveur and to raise the siege of Quimperlé. But what particularly enraged opinion was Gaunt's volte-face in allowing Gregory XI to levy a subsidy of £9,000 on the English Church during 1375–6—only the second such concession since 1336. Through it Gaunt secured the provision of Simon Sudbury to Canterbury instead of the uncompromising William Courtenay.[21]

John of Gaunt had managed a difficult situation with authority and flexibility and resented the obloquy later heaped upon him. He had tried to offset the paralysis of the Crown by assuming the direction of policy militarily in 1373–4 and diplomatically in 1374–5. For both he had secured the assent and support of the magnates. It was far more difficult for him to assume the direction of government and wield executive authority. For, first, he was out of England for much of the time, in France or at Bruges, and more importantly the king and court remained the source of authority. Though fast losing his mental grip, Edward III never ceased to exercise his royal will. The Black Prince was too sick to take control and Gaunt dared not displace the boy Richard as ultimate heir. In this vacuum it was those in close proximity to the king who manipulated his authority, Lords Latimer and Neville, his chamber knights like Alan Buxhull, Richard Stury, and Philip Vache, and above all his mistress Alice Perrers—who controlled access to him and the patronage he still delighted to distribute. They formed a tight-knit circle, using each other for their dealings in land and money, to procure favours for themselves and their clients, to manipulate legal process, and to extend their influence into the merchant community.[22] With the leading earls abroad on military and diplomatic assignments, Latimer, Neville, Stury, and Lyons, with the three officers of state, formed the nucleus of the continual council. Yet there is little to indicate that Gaunt or other lords felt that this was amiss, and many had recently received liberal grants from the king.[23] Gaunt himself was disinclined to mount a challenge to his father's servants, with many of whom he was connected. Probably he counted on seeing the reign to its close with the least disturbance. But that was not to be.

[20] Holmes, *Good Parliament*, 80–90; Nightingale, *Medieval Mercantile Community*, 228–44.

[21] Holmes, *Good Parliament*, 46–56.

[22] Given-Wilson, *Royal Household*, 142–54, 304 n. 24, gives references for their association, and numerous grants to them will be found in *CPR*, *1374–7*, 72–305.

[23] *CPR*, *1374–7*, 17, 20, 22–4, 29–30, 33, 42–4, 72, 188.

The Good Parliament

Parliament met at Westminster on 28 April 1376 to be told that the truce had been extended for a year but that taxation was needed for when it expired. More magnates than usual attended, and the air of expectancy was quickly confirmed as the Commons, meeting in the chapter house, took oaths of mutual support and secrecy and launched into complaints about corruption and misgovernment.[24] To press these further they would need evidence from officials, support from magnates, and the king's acquiescence. Their choice of the earl of March's steward, Sir Peter de la Mare, to present their demands, and the king's agreement for a committee of twelve lords to meet with the Commons, opened the way for formal accusations against Latimer, Lyons, and Alice Perrers before John of Gaunt in full parliament. The allegations of contriving evasions of the Staple, arranging a loan of 20,000 marks in August 1374 at an exorbitant and unnecessary rate of interest, and profiting from cashing discounted debentures were dramatically confirmed by the testimony of the former treasurer Sir Richard Scrope. On 24 May de la Mare refused to proceed with further business until the 'evil counsellors' had been removed and a new council appointed, demands to which the king agreed. This opened the way for charges to be brought not only against the three principals but against Lord Neville and the merchants William Ellis, John Pecche, and Adam Bury, who had fled. When Latimer demanded to know what person accused him, the Commons answered that they did so 'in common'— thus 'stumbling on' the process of impeachment by a prosecution before the Lords.[25] The trials lasted many days, with pointed and persistent questioning by de la Mare, ending with the conviction and imprisonment of Latimer, the forfeiture of Lyons, Bury, and Alice Perrers, and the dismissal of Lord Neville. Further charges against their lesser associates were brought and the circumstances of the surrender of Saint-Sauveur by Thomas Catterton, Latimer's captain, were the subject of an appeal at arms.[26] Then on 25 June, following the death of the Black Prince, the Commons asked that his son Richard should be brought into parliament and made prince of Wales. They renewed the wool subsidy but refused to grant direct taxation.

These proceedings brought parliament a new prominence and prefigured its role over the next thirty years. Claiming to represent and act for the common good, the Commons occupied the moral high ground. This directly reflected the

---

[24] J. Taylor, 'The Good Parliament and its sources', in Taylor and Childs (eds.), *Politics and Crisis*, 81–96; for the main accusations, see Holmes, *Good Parliament*, ch. 5; Tout, *Chapters*, iii. 291ff., provides an excellent narrative.

[25] T. F. T. Plucknett, 'The impeachments of 1376', *TRHS*, 5th ser., 1 (1951), 161.

[26] Holmes, *Good Parliament*, 126–34; J. G. Bellamy, 'Appeal and impeachment in the Good Parliament', *BIHR* 39 (1966), 35–46.

political circumstances of 1376. Royal leadership was in abeyance, the magnates were divided, and some were identified with corruption; the bishops, with exceptions like Wykeham and Courtenay, were cowed by threats; only the Commons had the confidence and conviction to demand the reform of the court. Their provision of taxation for common defence furnished the justification for denouncing a court where chivalry had been displaced by merchandising and private gain. They were not radicals: they sought to proceed with the king's assent and the support of the lords; they remained petitioners if also accusers, conscious that criticism, even on behalf of the Crown, trod close to treason. Their only prescription for central government was a council of nine to guide the king, which they asked him to nominate.[27] The Good Parliament thus dealt with an exceptional and temporary crisis in government, the product of the king's senility, the Black Prince's mortal illness, and Gaunt's absences. That its specific remedies were likewise temporary should not occasion surprise. But before considering the reaction we must attend to the Commons' wider grievances.

The common petition of 141 articles was the longest presented to any medieval parliament. A number related to aspects of royal policy already mentioned, demanding the expulsion of Italian brokers and usurers and the cessation of licences to evade the Staple; condemning papal tax collectors, provisions, and translations; asking for the restoration of the London franchise and the curtailment of the jurisdiction of the marshalsea. A heightened awareness of the gentry's political role was reflected in petitions for annual parliaments to correct the faults of the realm: for the election of shire knights, not their nomination by sheriffs; for sheriffs to be chosen each year and not appointed by brocage; for justices of the peace to be elected in parliament. Lesser landowners concerned for honest local administration protested against hundreds being farmed to profit-making bailiffs, against extortionate escheators, and fines exacted in the hundred courts. A crisis of law and order was developing, with armed bands in certain shires, which the sheriffs were told to confront. All these reflected the discontent with local administration by those who regulated order and socio-economic relations in the shires. Specific complaints related to fiscal administration. The royal lands were being farmed at a fraction of their true value and the king's fiscal prerogatives distributed as favours rather than being exploited to maintain his estate; tallies given for the payment of wages of war had been countermanded, and loans raised by the treasurer Brantingham still remained unpaid. In all these and other matters the Commons, 'who have come to parliament on behalf of the community of the realm', wanted 'to make correction of the errors and faults of

---

[27] For the twelve lords with whom the Commons chose to intercommune and for the Black Prince's tacit support, see Tout, *Chapters*, iii. 294–6. The earl of March and Bishop Wykeham were most closely identified with them.

the realm if such are found to exist'. Thus they affirmed the role which they believed this parliament had given them; but on their visit to the old king at Eltham such petitions as were not covered by existing statutes were referred to the council and no statutes were made upon them.[28]

The dissolution of parliament on 10 July, the earlier death of the Black Prince, and the king's severe deterioration left John of Gaunt free to reassert royal authority. He appointed a new steward and chamberlain and summoned a great council for October–December. The council of nine disappeared, and those who had supported and led the Commons—the earl of March, Bishop Wykeham, and Peter de la Mare—were vindictively pursued and punished. Latimer and Alice Perrers were pardoned in October, the impeached merchants not until the following spring. On 2 November Richard was invested as prince of Wales, and the succession settled thereafter on Gaunt and his descendants to the exclusion of Lionel of Clarence's heir Philippa, wife of the earl of March.[29] By the end of the year Gaunt was said to be *regni gubernator et rector* and was in a position to call another parliament. Probably some effort was made to ensure the return of amenable knights, but more important was the choice of Thomas Hungerford, Gaunt's steward, as speaker. The king's jubilee, celebrated by a general pardon (from which Wykeham was excepted), created a mood of loyalty in which the chancellor could point to the immediacy of war and the need for all to contribute. After discussion with the Lords, the Commons granted a novel poll tax of 4*d*. per head on adult males, in which the clergy perforce agreed to be included.[30]

Gaunt's political strategy had been strikingly successful; the court had been reinstated, the royal dignity affirmed, the nobility were arming for war, the Commons had granted a tax. It was not enough; he desired a more specific humiliation of the Church and the Staplers. Wyclif was brought from Oxford to popularize his attacks on clerical property and jurisdiction in the London pulpits, and on 19 February was cited to answer before Bishop Courtenay at St Paul's. He appeared flanked by Gaunt himself and Henry Percy as marshal, who openly defied and threatened Courtenay, provoking a fracas and their hasty retreat. On the following day rumours of their planned revenge, inflamed by the marshal's arrest of a citizen, brought a howling mob to the doors of the Savoy Palace, from which Gaunt and Percy escaped down the Thames to Kennington. In the city Gaunt's coats of arms were insulted and scurrilous libels posted on doors, while his retainers hurriedly concealed the livery collars which had been

---

[28] *Rot. Parl.* iii. 331–60, nos. 45, 128, for quotations.

[29] M. Bennett, 'Edward III's entail and the succession to the Crown, 1376–1471', *EHR* 113 (1998), 580–609. Dr Bennett argues that this was Edward's decision, uninfluenced by Gaunt. The charter survives in a 15th-century copy and may be a draft.

[30] Wals., *Hist. Anglicana*, i. 322; Roskell, *The Commons and their Speakers*, 120–1; *Rot. Parl.* iii. 362–4.

their proudest boast. The ferocity of Gaunt's anger at this 'insult to the king, his sons, and his lineage' was vented on the mayor and aldermen, who were removed from office and humiliated.[31]

The crisis of 1376 had shown Gaunt's strength and limitations. He had kept his nerve, waiting until he could recover the initiative and reassert his rightful authority. He regarded the Good Parliament as a challenge to the political and chivalric hierarchy which had to be reversed. From the perspective of his royal rank, merchants were moneyers, the Commons plebs,[32] bishops (especially non-aristocrats like Wykeham) upstarts, while even barons were among his retainers. But while he professed to live above the world of politics he could not refrain from exploiting its factions, nor did he understand the offence he gave in supporting opponents of the urban oligarchy and the episcopate. His alienation of the Church and Londoners, the two foremost moulders of public opinion, proved a big political blunder.

Like Gaunt the Commons wanted to restore the proper functioning of political society, but for them disorder had sprung from the failure of those in power to act honestly and responsibly for the common good, by procuring their own profit at the king's expense. They projected themselves as moral reformers, believing themselves to be infused by the Holy Ghost with wisdom to perceive the ills of the realm and expound them to the peers.[33] They saw their role as purgative—to name and shame—and had established a procedure for this which gave parliament a new function and status. But it did not enlarge their constitutional rights or political power. Moreover, by 1377 the political consensus had re-formed, with Gaunt himself, the young prince, and the leading earls indenting for a massive invasion of France. Only Edward's death in June prevented it from sailing. Yet the Good Parliament cast a long shadow over and beyond the coming reign, for it had revealed the tension between the principles of obedience to authority and pursuit of the common good which were at the heart of the late medieval polity.

3. UNEASY CONSENSUS, 1377–1383

Within ten years of succeeding his grandfather, Richard II faced a challenge to royal authority, his response to which set the course of royal policy for the rest of the reign. But if the crisis of 1386–8 is a turning point, its seeds lay in the political situation of the preceding years.

[31] McFarlane, *John Wycliffe*, 74–7; *Anon. Chron.* 105.
[32] Gaunt's derisive remarks about the knights of the shire, for which his retainers rebuked him, are retailed by Walsingham, *Chron. Angliae*, 74.
[33] *Chron. Angliae*, 70–2; A. Goodman, 'Sir Thomas Hoo and the parliament of 1376', *BIHR* 41 (1968), 139–49 (above, Ch. 5, sect. 3).

Richard was aged 10 in 1377. Already out of his mother's care, he had been given a governor, first Sir Simon Burley in 1377, then in 1379 Lord John Cobham. The household had been purged and reconstructed after the scandals of 1376, and in 1381 the earl of Arundel and Sir Michael de la Pole were appointed in parliament to oversee it. Richard's solitary and unwarlike temperament responded to the guidance of the elderly Burley and de la Pole and to the friendship of two companions of his own age, Robert de Vere and Thomas Mowbray. His chamber knights were men of proven service and experience, many having been his father's retainers. With the household clerks Richard perhaps felt greater intimacy: his confessor, the Dominican Thomas Rushook, his chaplains, Richard Clifford and Richard Medford, and his secretary, John Bacon. The household was not the source of policy, its members were not accused of corruption or greed, and its size and cost remained moderate.[34]

The question of who should rule England while the king was under age was not easily resolved. In terms of seniority, wealth, and influence it should have been John of Gaunt, acting as regent. But successful as his restoration of royal authority had been in 1377, the hostility and suspicion he had aroused left him exposed and wary. In the first parliament of the new reign he even sought a public vindication of his loyalty.[35] Government had therefore to be committed to a council, the Commons (once more led by Sir Peter de la Mare) asking for its appointment in parliament on the model of that of 1376. Nine councillors drawn from different estates were chosen by the magnates, along with the officers of state. They were to be 'continually resident', serving for a year, and 'ordering the war and all matters touching the estate of the realm' including the Crown's major patronage. They were duly changed in 1378, but in January 1380 the Commons, doubting their competence, asked for them to be discharged and for the king to govern with his five principal officers, who were named in parliament.[36] This collective effort to restore the reputation and authority of royal government in the aftermath of the Good Parliament had the support of the higher nobility, some of whom served as councillors while others engaged in military and naval operations.

The Commons for their part repeatedly granted taxation: three poll taxes and three and a half fifteenths were levied before the eruption of the Great Revolt. This was the equivalent of an annual burden of almost £43,000. They were spent on a series of military expeditions rendered ineffectual by the failure of allies,

---

[34] For the household personnel, see Tout, *Chapters*, iv. 187 ff., 341–6; Given-Wilson, *Royal Household*, 160–2, 282–3.

[35] *Rot. Parl.* iii. 5. Rumours had been spread that he had designs on Richard's throne.

[36] Ibid. iii. 5–6, 14; Tout, *Chapters*, iii. 332–46; A. Goodman, 'Richard II's councils', in Goodman and Gillespie (eds.), *Richard II*, 65–6.

bad organization (notably lack of shipping), weather, and indifferent leadership.[37] That, despite the poor results, the Commons were so generous up to 1381 expressed partly their commitment to the war and sense of participation in government and partly their difficulty in denying the Crown's legitimate needs. The French coastal raids with which the reign opened underlined that, as the Commons were reminded, 'the defence of the realm touches not only the king but all and each of you'.[38] Expeditions to France were represented as the best means of keeping the war overseas. The Commons attempted to contain their obligations by arguing that the defence of Calais and the sea should be met from indirect taxation, restricting fifteenths to particular expeditions.[39] But over the period 1377–81 total war expenditure was met from direct and indirect taxes which were paid out to military commanders without significant default.[40]

If a grudging consensus was reached on the need and terms for taxation, more contentious issues were opened up when the Commons switched their attention to the Crown revenues and expenses. While subjects were using their wealth for war, should not the king also contribute his? As one of the shire knights is reported to have said in 1376, 'it would be good to consider how the king could live and govern the realm and maintain the war from his own goods and not exploit his liege people'.[41] Debate was joined on this in the October parliament 1377. The Commons argued that the old Crown revenues should maintain the royal household, and when in 1378 it was reported that these now yielded little owing to the annuities granted on them by Edward III, they countered by asking for commissions to examine all the revenues and their administration. The first two of these, in 1379 and 1380, were primarily financial, with the purpose of increasing royal resources, but that of 1381, prompted by the Great Revolt, was to investigate abuses in the royal household, the departments of state, and the courts of law. In the event such 'reform in head and members' proved to be a dead letter. Along with their suggestions for improving Crown revenues, the Commons from 1377 to 1383 repeatedly asked for 'bon governaill' by wise and honest men around the king, so that his household expenses could be reduced. In fact both the cost and size of the household remained moderate.[42] But though the Commons' campaign was ill-informed and driven by the pressures upon themselves, their persistent harrying of ministers had some unintended effects. First,

---

[37] Above, Ch. 11, sect. 2.   [38] In 1377 and again in 1378: *Rot. Parl.* iii. 4, 36.

[39] Ibid. iii. 75, 90.

[40] Sherborne, *War, Politics and Culture*, 66–9; Steel, *Receipt of the Exchequer*, 436, 455.

[41] *Anon. Chron.* 81.

[42] *Rot. Parl.* iii. 14, 139 (42), 147 (18); Given-Wilson, *Royal Household*, 89, and app. 1 for household costs; W. M. Ormrod, 'The Peasants' Revolt and the government of England', *Jnl. Brit. Stud.* 29 (1990), 2–28, for the Commons' reform programme. See too G. Dodd, 'The Lords, taxation, and the community of parliament', *Parlty. Hist.* 20 (2001), 287–310.

it may have contributed towards the rising in 1381, in which the principal officers and the justices were the rebels' prime targets. Secondly, their pressure for commissions of reform set precedents for the opposition programme of 1385–6. Thirdly, although the council had consistently evaded taking action on household reform as touching the royal honour and prerogative, the Commons' demands had outraged and alarmed the young king. In March 1383 he rebuffed their petition, declaring that he would surround himself with such men as seemed to him profitable and regulate his household by the advice of his council.[43]

The Commons' claim to speak for the common good made them above all the mouthpiece for their shires. From 1377 to October 1383 they repeatedly warned of mounting disorder, of 'routs' and armed companies organized by men of lesser estate, riding and robbing, who were often protected by lords in the courts. At a lower level there was complaint about disobedience and resistance among the unfree, and of the demands for high wages by day labourers. Rumour and slander spread by vagrants was destabilizing society, with the infectious contagion of the French *Jacquerie*. In the parliament of March 1380 the Commons asked for greater powers for the JPs to deal with disorders, though for their pains these became particular targets of the rebels.

Nevertheless, it was the Commons' grant in December 1380 of a poll tax three times heavier than that of 1377 that stirred revolt. Faced with evidence of widespread evasion, the government dispatched further commissioners in March to gather the arrears, provoking the eruption of riots over the whole of East Anglia. Violence was directed primarily at royal and seigniorial officials and the local justices: in a word the agents of authority. Even more, perhaps, than the men it was the records, the symbols and evidence of servitude, that were destroyed: charters and court rolls. When the rebels entered London on 13 June their foremost target became the Savoy Palace, the symbol of Gaunt's wealth and arrogance, which they incinerated rather than plunder.[44]

While vowing the destruction of lordship, the rebels professed their loyalty to the king. How did he react? On Wednesday 11 June Richard rode swiftly from Windsor and entered the Tower with his bodyguard and the earls of Salisbury, Warwick, and Oxford.[45] To its shelter fled the queen mother, the chancellor, treasurer, and mayor, William Walworth. Next day Richard showed his mettle in going down the Thames to Greenwich to meet the rebels before they reached London. That proved too hazardous, and on Friday the London mob admitted

[43] *Rot. Parl.* iii. 147 (18).

[44] For the agrarian discontent, see above, Ch. 7, sect. 4; also Ormrod, 'Peasants' revolt'; *Justice, Writing and Rebellion*, 37–51, 90–3.

[45] For the events in London, see B. Wilkinson, 'The Peasants' Revolt of 1381', *Speculum*, 15 (1940), 12–34; Dobson, *The Peasants' Revolt*, 155–235.

those from Kent and thereafter those from Essex. As the burning, plunder, and slaughter of Flemish and Italians engulfed the city, the predicament of the royal party became clear. Though impregnable to assault, the Tower was a trap. Neither royal nor magnate forces could reach London quickly—most were at the remotest points of the realm.[46] Had Richard remained at Windsor he could have assembled an army in the Midlands and marched on London. As it was he had too few with him to attack the rebels from the Tower itself—in any case a dangerous operation. Conciliation was the only option. Relying on the rebels' proclaimed respect for the king, Richard prepared to meet them at Mile End on 14 June, guarded by his lords and knights, but leaving those in the Tower as hostages for his safety. When he was forced to concede pardons and charters of freedom to the rebels and promise the punishment of traitors, their fate was sealed: the treasurer, Hales, and the chancellor, Sudbury, were dragged out and executed. But hungry and exhausted and clutching their charters, the rebels began to go home; only a sizeable body of the more irreconcilable remained, heady with success. Using the same tactics, Richard appointed to meet them at Smithfield at 3 p.m. on Saturday. Beforehand he visited the shrine of St Edward at Westminster while Walworth, Philpot, and Brembre mustered the London militia. The rebels had armed themselves and were boldly displaying the royal standard and banner of St George in defiance of the king. Richard and his immediate retinue advanced to meet their leader, Wat Tyler, in the intervening space. Faced with demands for social revolution—the abolition of serfdom, an end to lordship, the disendowment of the Church—Richard readily conceded all, saving his regality, and ordered the rebels to disperse.[47] Tyler prevaricated, was provoked by the royal party to insult or threaten the king, and then struck down by Walworth. Richard rode towards the rebels, offering to be their captain while the aldermen summoned up the militia. The revolt collapsed into docility and the *rustici* were sent home under guard. The narrative sources differ in details but the sequence strongly suggests that the coup had been planned. Whether the king's intervention was rehearsed or improvised, Richard had displayed courage and assurance.

Despite the rebels' loyalty to him, the encounter cannot have endeared the *rustici* to the king. He was angered and affronted that his 'heritage and realm of England were near lost'. Within a week he was leading a strong force of the nobility into Essex, with chief justice Tresilian conducting a 'bloody assize'. The charters of manumission were revoked (2 July), with the king declaring, 'rustics you were and rustics you are still; you will remain in bondage, not as before but

---

[46] Gaunt was on the Scottish border negotiating a truce, Buckingham had landed at Falmouth on 2 May and disbanded his army, Cambridge was at Plymouth about to depart for Spain; a small force under Sir Peter de Veel at Dartmouth was summoned to London but arrived too late; G. O. Sayles, 'Richard II in 1381 and 1399', *EHR* 94 (1979), 820–9.

[47] Dobson, *The Peasants' Revolt*, 164–5, 193; Justice, *Writing and Rebellion*, 68 n. 4.

incomparably harsher'. In this Richard and his councillors were out of touch with those who ruled the shires. In Kent and Hertfordshire there was less enthusiasm for a harvest of heads; the gentry had an ingrained distrust of judicial visitations, which usurped the community's own role in upholding authority and did nothing to heal the rifts in local society. In the October parliament it was the Speaker, Richard Waldegrave, himself a tax commissioner in Essex, who put their view. Lordship over villeins must be reasserted, the charters of freedom revoked, and the rebel leaders must be punished, but leniency should be shown to their followers, for their revolt had demonstrated the need for reform in the realm. Justice was being perverted by maintenance and embracery, oppressions were committed by purveyors and seigniorial officers, taxation had been too heavy. This view prevailed; the rebels were punished by legal process, and with fines rather than executions. Although they had little comprehension of the peasants' hatred of servitude, the local magistracy had a more practical and humane approach than the king and the court, to whom *rustici* remained feared and incomprehensible.[48]

If fear and contempt for his lesser subjects and belief in the immunity afforded by kingship were two lessons that Richard drew from the revolt, it also affected his relations with London and with John of Gaunt. From the beginning of the reign the Staplers, led by Walworth and Philpot, had worked to restore the city's favour with John of Gaunt both by a formal reconciliation and by advancing loans and raising a fleet to deal with piracy. But the duke remained hostile, revoking the city's franchise and permitting licences of exemption from the Staple, while the destruction of his palace by the mob reinforced his estrangement from the city. Richard, too, could feel that he had found not safety in the city—'his own chamber'—but a trap, where his ministers had been lynched. Yet ultimately he had owed his safety and victory to Walworth and his colleagues, who thereby hoped to heal relations with the Crown. Throughout 1381–2 Gaunt gave his backing to the leader of the craft and victualling guilds, John of Northampton, in an effort to break the power of the Staplers (the grocers and fishmongers), but by 1383 under Nicholas Brembre the grocers had begun to reorganize. They declined to advance the loans which Gaunt sought in 1382 for an expedition to Spain, and in February 1383 they supported the intervention in Flanders favoured by the Commons and the court. In October, Northampton was defeated by Brembre in a bitterly contested mayoral election, for Brembre now had the Crown's support, and it was henceforth Richard who looked to control the politics of London.[49]

[48] For Waldegrave, *House of Commons*, iv. 735–9; for the Commons' attitude, *Rot. Parl.* iii. 99–100; also J. A. Tuck, 'Nobles, Commons and the Great Revolt of 1381', in Hilton and Aston (eds.), *The English Rising of 1381*, 194–212; N. Saul, *Richard II*, 61–82.
[49] These years are covered by Nightingale, *Medieval Mercantile Community*, chs. 10, 11. See also C. M. Barron, 'Richard II and London', in Goodman and Gillespie (eds.), *Richard II*, 128–48.

Gaunt's pressure for reactivating the war in 1382 won steadily increasing support among some lords who chafed at inactivity, notably Buckingham and Arundel. Proposals for a royal expedition to mark the king's manhood were adopted enthusiastically at great councils at the beginning and end of 1382, and when the parliament of February 1383 finally endorsed the bishop of Norwich's 'crusade' in Flanders, strongly supported by the court, Gaunt withdrew in outrage. Its ignominious failure, and the king's disinclination to go to his assistance, confirmed the militant earls in their contempt for the court and implicitly for Richard's reluctance to bear arms.[50] These tensions came into the open in the October parliament of 1383. In the new chancellor, Michael de la Pole, Richard found a vigorous protagonist of royal authority. The Commons were starkly recalled to their obligations: in the face of Scottish and French threats 'common defence demands common charge', for the king had not chosen war but inherited it, and had already spent his own money. Even so they granted only a half fifteenth, making a further half conditional on the continuance of war. Yet the Commons' refusal to grant more than minimal taxation largely nullified their pressure for the accountability of royal government just as Richard was beginning to impress his authority on it.

From 1382–3 men of Richard's own choice and generation entered the household. Robert de Vere, earl of Oxford, as chamberlain, Ralph, son and heir of the earl of Stafford, Thomas Mowbray, earl of Nottingham, and Thomas, brother of Lord Clifford, were all in their early twenties. Among the chamber knights Peter Courtenay, John Montagu, William Nevill, and John Beauchamp were marked out for Richard's personal favours. Lands and offices granted to Burley in South Wales, to Beauchamp in North Wales, and to Nevill in Nottinghamshire gave them positions of considerable local power.[51] But there was no great flood of patronage, for Richard had little to give. Most of the Crown's properties were in the hands of the older generation; the use of casual windfalls was closely watched by the council and parliament; above all in 1382 Richard had to provide both his queen's dowry and dower lands, using initially the escheated Ufford inheritance and the Burstwick estate of his aunt Isabella.[52]

Up to the end of 1383 there is slight evidence either of Richard's active involvement in government or of the influence of a courtier group. The major decisions were still being taken in great councils and parliaments where the directive force was not the king's will but that of Gaunt and the political

[50] *Rot. Parl.* iii. 122, 144; *West. Chron.* 36–7, 54–5.

[51] Given-Wilson, *Royal Household*, 282–3; for grants to courtiers from the earl of March's estates, see *CPR, 1381–5*, 93, 95, 107, 118, 122, 160–1, 164, 166, 176, 183, 206; also, J. A. Tuck, 'Richard II's system of patronage', in Du Boulay and Barron (eds.), *Reign of Richard II*, 7, for Richard's grant of Beauchamp's petition for Conwy Castle.

[52] Saul, *Richard II*, 90–2; Tout, *Chapters*, v. 280; *CPR, 1381–5*, 123, 125–6.

community. The individual voice of Richard is heard saving and asserting his prerogative,[53] and in favour of his selected companions, but the prevailing doctrine as he reached adolescence was that ruling England was a task he should share with the Lords in council and the Commons in parliament: i.e. the body of the realm of which he, as head, was part. In fact the consensus for this was rapidly falling apart. The Commons wanted the reform of government with an end to war and taxation; the Lords wanted a relaunching of the war with France, though Gaunt had his eyes on Spain; the court wanted peace and the release of royal patronage; above all Richard was determined to assert his regality untrammelled by accountability to parliament or constraints by magnates.

4. THE ASSERTION OF REGALITY, 1384–1386

In the course of the winter of 1383–4 the political climate changed markedly. The agenda was no longer set by the magnates and parliament but by the king and the court. At 17 Richard felt ready to exercise his royal will. His household contained men of experience on whose advice he could rely and friends of his own age whom he was anxious to honour and reward. He had his own priorities: to replace enmity to France with peace and friendship and, as a corollary, to replace the partnership of Crown and subjects engendered by war with a renewed emphasis on regality. The court, not the council or parliament, was to be at the centre of politics, not only as the arena of royal majesty and the source of patronage, but as the vehicle of the royal will and hence the source of policy. Pole's emphasis in parliament on the prime duty of obedience to the king and his ministers carried an implied rebuke to the Commons for their critical appraisal of government.[54] If all this amounted to a reversal of current conventions, it represented less a political programme than a new perspective. Even for Burley and Pole it marked the restoration of traditional royal rule, rather than an application of academic absolutism.[55] As to Richard, his immature and self-centred personality found identity in sacral kingship. But though regality was for him a state of mind, the royal will was an actual and vital element of the political system, and its exercise conditioned the working of the state at all levels. Richard's rule thus had consequences of which he had barely taken account. Beginning with its operation in the intimate circle of the court, and then among the wider circle of the magnates, the assertion of regality would ultimately have to confront the community of the realm in parliament.

By the beginning of 1384 most of those who were to attract censure in 1386 as favoured courtiers were already in the household. Notable recruits in the next

---

[53] *Rot. Parl.* iii. 165.   [54] Ibid. iii. 150.
[55] As argued by R. H. Jones, *The Royal Policy of Richard II* (Oxford, 1968).

two years were James Berners in 1383–4, Thomas Blount in 1384, and John Golafre and John Salisbury in 1385. The dignities, lands, offices, and financial perquisites with which Richard rewarded those whom he trusted were seen as evidence of their influence upon him and aroused criticism on several grounds. The elevation of Robert de Vere, first as marquess of Dublin in December 1385, a new rank in the peerage, and then as duke of Ireland in October 1386, a rank hitherto confined to the royal family, was condemned as revealing 'so great an appetite for promotion in so mediocre a man'. The creation of Michael de la Pole, son of a successful wool merchant, as earl of Suffolk in August 1385 affronted the ancient nobility. At the end of that year Richard seemed to be intent on similarly elevating Simon Burley by reviving the earldom of Huntingdon, while in October 1387 his creation of a barony for Sir John Beauchamp simply by letters patent asserted the king's right to enlarge the baronage at will. Not merely did these flout the conventions and offend the susceptibilities of the peerage, they expressed Richard's own view of its role. This was, as he said, to reflect the majesty of kingship through the honours they received from it, as satellites around the sun.[56]

Accompanying these dignities were more material benefits. In July 1385 the grant to de Vere of Queenborough Castle, newly built by Edward III, invoked the curse 'of God, St Edward and the king' on any who challenged it. For his lieutenancy of Ireland he was invested with quasi-regal power and in March 1386 was granted the £20,000 ransom from Jean de Blois to support his army. Both in rank and power, if not in resources, he had been raised to parity with John of Gaunt. Michael de la Pole was enabled to use his position as chancellor to obtain escheated lands, for which he was subsequently convicted of impoverishing the Crown.[57] Even more culpable in the eyes of the nobility was the royal generosity to Sir Simon Burley, to whom in 1384–5 Richard granted in tail male certain lands in Kent which Edward III had acquired for the endowment of religious houses. In January 1384 Burley was made constable of Dover and warden of the Cinque Ports and in May constable of Windsor Castle, two posts of immense strategic importance and trust. These and other grants were believed to have increased his income to 2,000 marks, in expectation of an earldom.[58] Richard's favour shown to his half-brothers Thomas and John Holland was less contentious. Thomas after an active military career with Gaunt had been made earl of Kent in 1380–1 at the age of 30 and in September 1385 inherited the dower

[56] Wals., *Hist. Anglicana*, ii. 148, for quotation; A. Tuck, *Richard II and the English Nobility* (London, 1973), 84; *Rot. Parl.* iii. 205–10; *CPR, 1385–9*, 78.

[57] Tuck, *Richard II and the Nobility*, 80–3, 85; J. S. Roskell, *The Impeachment of Michael de la Pole* (Manchester, 1984) for a full examination of the charges.

[58] C. Given-Wilson, 'Richard II and his grandfather's will', *EHR* 93 (1978), 320–37; Tuck, *Richard II and the Nobility*, 74–6.

lands of his mother, Joan of Kent. His brother John, five years his junior, was marked out for greater favour, until his killing of the king's favoured companion Ralph Stafford in a fracas in May 1385 brought him immediate disgrace and the loss of all his rewards. In 1386 he joined Gaunt's expedition to Spain, having seduced and married the duke's daughter Elisabeth.

Beyond this circle of the court elite several knights of the chamber were Richard's intimates and trusted agents. The Scottish expedition was the occasion for knighting and rewarding many of these with large annuities, in addition to their multiple grants of profit. Some of them were entrusted with important royal castles: John Devereux with Leeds, John Beauchamp with Conwy and Bridgnorth. Other chamber knights performed important military and diplomatic missions: Richard Abberbury, John Clanvowe, Lewis Clifford, Peter Courtenay, and Nicholas Dagworth mostly of an older generation.[59]

Richard was thus surrounded by a group of nobility and knights whom he had chosen and favoured, whose loyalty and services were both personal and political. That itself was in no way exceptional; such was the role expected of the entourage of an active king. What provoked criticism and mistrust was the sense that they formed an exclusive and manipulative clique. Several things contributed to this. The chroniclers noted Richard's personal attachment to de Vere, and there were stories of his special affection for Berners. The courtiers were suspected of exploiting Richard's friendship, for many of the grants to them were made under the signet at royal manors, probably in their presence and at their own petition. They acted for each other, and procured pardons and promoted petitions for their clients.[60] Patronage was being internalized among a closed circle, it was in some cases excessive, and it was not the reward for military service.

If such became the view of the wider political community, some members and sections of it had their own specific grievances. The king's uncles Gaunt and Cambridge, with the earls of Arundel, Stafford, and Warwick, were all in their forties, Buckingham and Kent being ten years younger. They were bound together not merely by age but by shared military service, which set them apart from both the older and younger elements of the court circle. They still expected active military careers. For Gaunt and Cambridge this meant the pursuit of their political and dynastic ambitions in Spain, though Cambridge lacked both ambition and competence in warfare. Their younger brother Buckingham was warlike in temperament, chafing at being engaged in warfare on the Scottish border after his great *chevauchée* of 1380 in France. As constable of England, and deeply chivalric in outlook, he attracted captains looking for further campaigning. He

[59] Given-Wilson, *Royal Household*, 160–74; *CPR, 1381–5* and *CFR, 1383–91*, see indexes under surname; and some longer biographies in *House of Commons*.

[60] Wals., *Hist. Anglicana*; A. Tuck, 'Richard II's system of patronage', in Du Boulay and Barron (eds.), *Reign of Richard II*, 1–20, esp. 7.

had other grounds for discontent, for he was dependent on Richard's generosity to maintain his dignities, first as earl in 1377 and then as duke in 1385, but on both occasions was awarded an annuity from the exchequer rather than land, in contrast to the lavish endowment of de Vere, de la Pole, and Burley. Richard, earl of Arundel, with estates in the Welsh marches and Sussex yielding an income of some £3,700, had no such financial worries and little need of royal patronage. More a man of business than a soldier, he brought the harsh efficiency of his own estate management to his view of government. Austere in temperament and brusque in speech, his appointment with de la Pole as overseer of Richard's household in 1381 had done little except provoke his disapproval of the court. Thomas Beauchamp, earl of Warwick, had a similar background and status, his family estates in the Midlands yielding some £3,000 per annum. Not as eagerly military as his father, he was proud of his family's chivalric traditions. He neither sought nor received royal patronage and was rarely at court.[61]

Although the established nobility had no need or expectation of grants of land for themselves, those made to the royal favourites could challenge their lordship in their own region. There has been little investigation of this, though there are some indications of tension. Disaffected members of John of Gaunt's affinity in Lancashire, notably Sir Thomas Molyneux, found support in Chester from first John Holland and later de Vere. The creation of Sir John Beauchamp's barony of Kidderminster angered the earl of Warwick, who secured it after Beauchamp's fall, while Gloucester must have resented the growing influence of de la Pole and de Vere as his neighbours in Essex. None of this amounts to very much, but when aggravated by royal partiality, local quarrels between rival lords could breed estrangement between the king and the nobles.[62]

Richard's relations with John of Gaunt certainly deteriorated in these years. As Richard's senior uncle, of quasi-regal status, and possessing lands which yielded an income three times larger than that of any other earl, John of Gaunt could well have sought to dominate the young king, had he not been preoccupied with his own ambitions in Castile. Yet his power and position, and overbearing personality, understandably aroused Richard's fears and those of his courtiers. For Gaunt bestrode the political world, and the key to his power was his affinity. In 1382 he had 173 indentured retainers, a number which had risen to nearly 300 by the time he sailed for Spain in 1386. This retinue reflected Gaunt's territorial power over a broad swathe of the north and North Midlands, where it numbered some of the principal lords and many knightly families. Up to 1381 the function

---

[61] For Buckingham, Arundel, and Warwick, see A. Goodman, *The Loyal Conspiracy* (London, 1971). For presence at court, see Given-Wilson, 'Royal charter witness lists', table 6.

[62] Goodman, *Loyal Conspiracy*, 113; Tuck, *Richard II and the Nobility*, 73–86; Walker, *Lancastrian Affinity*, 167–70.

of his retinue had been primarily military but thereafter he may have begun retaining for political support.[63] With Gaunt at their head the established nobility commanded territorial and military resources too strong to be assailed or ignored. It was their very impunity, along with their disdain for the courtiers, that provoked a series of incidents which poisoned relations between Richard and his magnates.

For most of these we are dependent on the Westminster chronicler, whose unique proximity to the court did not deter him from detached and sometimes hostile comment.[64] At the Salisbury parliament of April 1384 Arundel denounced the *malum regimen* which had brought the realm to the point of collapse. The king, white with anger, responded that if he imputed misgovernment to him he lied and could go to the devil. In the shocked and silent assembly Gaunt tried to gloss Arundel's words and placate Richard's wrath. In the course of the parliament a Carmelite friar, who had been saying Mass before the king in Robert de Vere's apartment, made allegations against Gaunt of treachery. Richard is said to have believed these and impulsively vowed his uncle's death, but was persuaded to investigate the charges. When the friar implicated members of the court he was removed and tortured to death.[65]

Gaunt's relations with the king and court deteriorated further in 1385. At a council at the end of January he and Buckingham advocated a royal expedition to France when the truce expired. This was rejected by Richard's advisers, who insisted on the king remaining in England, and both dukes walked out of the council in protest. Those around the king then plotted to have Gaunt assassinated during a tournament in Westminster Hall on 13–14 February. Warned in time, Gaunt withdrew to Pontefract. Ten days later he and the king were reconciled by the king's mother, but at a subsequent council Archbishop Courtenay denounced the instigators of such plots as ruinous to the peace of the kingdom; later, when he reproached the king to his face, Richard drew his sword and had to be restrained by his own chamber knights.[66] At the start of the king's first expedition, to Scotland in July–August 1385, Gaunt was formally reconciled with the court. The lowlands were ravaged, and when Edinburgh was reached on 11 August the duke advocated an advance to the highlands to complete the conquest, but Richard refused to cross the Forth, arguing that the army would not be able to support itself. His speedy withdrawal to England without fighting, amidst rumours that he feared Gaunt's treachery, brought his first leadership of the nobility in arms to an ignominious conclusion.[67]

[63] Walker, *Lancastrian Affinity*, ch. 2, app. 1; Goodman, *John of Gaunt*, ch. 12.

[64] From the beginning of 1384 the chronicle is the work of a new author, writing after 1388, both hostile to the court and at a distance from these events; *West. Chron.*, pp. xxii–xxxi.

[65] Ibid. 66–81.   [66] Ibid. 110–17.

[67] Ibid. 120–31; for another interpretation, see Goodman, *John of Gaunt*, 104.

Anecdotal and unsupported as much of this evidence is, it presents a widely credited and credible picture of the climate of suspicion, intrigue, and fear around the king. Richard's mistrust of Gaunt and his failure to command the respect of his greater lords produced growing unease about his rule. He was perceived to be susceptible to favourites, impetuous, wilful, and acutely sensitive to his regality. Even if some of this could be ascribed to his youth and bad advice, it was a dismaying prospect for the greater nobility, who faced the king across a gulf of misunderstanding.

Nevertheless, it was over the practice of government and in the context of parliament that Richard's rule provoked a crisis. This reflected not his autocracy but his indecision and insouciance. At its root was a division over policy within the political nation. The king and the court sought peace; the leading nobility wanted war—though in differing theatres; the Commons favoured peace to save themselves from being taxed, but even more demanded security on the coasts and borders, on the sea, and at Calais, to safeguard export markets in the Low Countries. For this they were prepared to pay, but were determined to avoid the combination of heavy taxation and military failure of pre-1381.

Taxation focused these divisions in three ways. First, with foreign policy being framed merely in response to external events, taxation was sought for a series of differing and inconsistent purposes. In May 1384 it was for a 'summit' meeting of the kings to seal a peace; by November, when the French were plainly intent on war, it was to finance the king's first expedition, though this eventually was to Scotland; in 1385 Ghent's seizure of Damme and the Portuguese victory at Aljubarotta presented differing opportunities for intervention, and consequent indecision; in October 1386, with the French invasion fleet assembled at Sluys, the chancellor advocated a royal expedition, but asked for the unprecedented sum of four fifteenths. Small wonder that the Commons regarded these proposals with scepticism, making part of each grant in 1384 conditional on an actual expedition, and placing that of 1385 under appointed treasurers of war.[68] Secondly, despite their attempts to limit and control their grants, the Commons and the clergy found themselves taxed at wartime levels. A full subsidy was paid in each of 1384 and 1385, with a subsidy and a half in 1386: the heaviest tax in a single year since 1381. Yet military expenditure was relatively light, and the total defence budget over the years 1383–6 was perhaps not more than £220,000, which was more than covered by taxation.[69] The Commons had thus good reason to feel that they were unjustifiably burdened. Thirdly, there are indications that, despite this, the exchequer was facing a monetary crisis in 1384–6, marked by the highest proportion (7.2 per cent) of failed tallies in the reign. At the same time borrowing, which since 1377 had never exceeded £10,000 in any year, mounted

---

[68] *Rot. Parl.* iii. 167, 185, 203–4.   [69] This is an estimate based on my own calculations.

progressively, producing an average of over £23,000 per annum.[70] Evidently expenditure was running well ahead of income, straining confidence in exchequer credit.

The Commons' dissatisfaction with royal government thus arose from the vacillation of royal policy, renewed taxation at wartime levels without significant military activity, and a deficit which was undermining exchequer credit and drawing attention to royal liberality. In the parliament of October 1385 they demanded retrenchment and reform, beginning with a resumption of royal grants from Crown revenues, a proposal denounced by Gaunt as dishonouring the king. But other lords (perhaps including Gloucester and Arundel) then produced articles of 'Advice' to the king about his conduct of government; they urged him to attend the council more often in order to learn 'what pertains to the government of him and his estate', not to countermand its decisions, to follow its advice in making appointments and restraining grants of revenue, and to appoint lords to review the estate of the exchequer and household. No constraints were imposed on the king, but the practices of good government were spelled out.[71]

Richard accepted the 'Advice' and agreed to a body of nine lords, some with financial expertise, who were to 'view and examine the estate of the king and realm'. Their tentative recommendations for restraint, economy, and accountability, to be implemented at the king's pleasure, revealed a nervous awareness of Richard's sensitivity on any measures touching his estate and regality.[72] They made it plain that the responsibility for retrenchment and reform rested with the king, and it was on his behalf that the chancellor undertook to put it into execution. However, the Commons stood out for more specific measures. Although their demands for an annual review of the household and the names of the officers of state were rejected, they secured a moratorium on grants from royal revenues of any kind for the following year, to be underwritten by the lords of the council. This was the price Richard had to pay for the grant of the subsidy and a half, along with its detailed appropriation under treasurers of war. Thus, although Richard had resisted any accountability for his household and ministers, he had been left in no doubt of the dissatisfaction of the political community with his rule, the Lords urging him to govern with their counsel and consent, the Commons enforcing fiscal restraint through their power to grant taxation. He was being told that government had to heed the interests of

---

[70] Steel, *Receipt of the Exchequer*, p. 436, table B1, p. 446, table C1 (real receipts), p. 455, table D1 (genuine and fictitious loans).

[71] The text is in *Select Docs.* 160–2; J. J. N. Palmer, 'The parliament of 1385 and the constitutional crisis of 1386', *Speculum*, 46 (1971), 477–8, reads it (at pp. 481–2) as restraining the king's patronage.

[72] Printed and discussed by J. J. N. Palmer, 'The impeachment of Michael de la Pole in 1386', *BIHR* 42 (1969), 96–101.

subjects, and not merely those of the king. This had some effect: in the following year grants from Crown revenues ceased, household costs were stabilized, and those of overseas garrisons slightly reduced; but no general overhaul of financial administration took place.

On 9 July 1386 John of Gaunt, with the king's encouragement, sailed from Plymouth with some 7,000 men, ridding the court of its feared critic. Yet his departure was overshadowed by the threat of a renewed French invasion, following the capitulation of Ghent on 21 December 1385. The Commons had earmarked taxes to furnish a fleet for three months from 1 July, the period of maximum danger. In fact it only proved possible to finance it for two months and with a much smaller complement. Had the French invaded, this token fleet would have been swept aside, for the French army assembled at Sluys was immense, probably some 30,000 strong, equipped with pre-constructed stockades to secure their landing.[73] Not until early August did the council address the need to defend the realm, and then the proposal to forestall the invasion by a royal expedition to France required the summoning of parliament (for 1 October) and the demand for further taxation. By the time parliament met, reports from Sluys had panicked the council into mobilizing troops on a large scale. By the end of September more than 10,000 men were under arms in the vicinity of London; but with insufficient money to pay them they plundered and intimidated the Kent countryside. Londoners prepared for a siege, stockpiling food and pulling down houses in the suburbs.[74] This atmosphere of military emergency and confusion lasted throughout October, while parliament was sitting; it was heightened by the well-founded report on the 15th that the invasion was fixed for 1 November, by which time most of the levies had returned home and only a small fleet in the Thames remained. Charles VI's decision to call off the invasion, and his departure from Sluys on 16 November, removed the military danger but came too late to save Richard from capitulation to parliament.

The invasion threat exposed Richard's appeasement of France as gullible and ineffectual, while his continued addiction to the counsel of de Vere and the courtiers, and his failure to implement the promised financial reforms, showed his indifference to the warnings of 1385. United in their frustrations, magnates and Commons sought to impose on the king policies and practices of government which they believed to be traditional and right. This had to be done through parliament and in the name of the common weal; in particular by recalling the king and his ministers to the undertakings given in the preceding parliament. Hence the attack focused on the chancellor, Michael de la Pole, and the treasurer, John Fordham, rather than on de Vere, Burley, and the court, who were more odious to the magnates.

[73] Sherborne, *War, Politics and Culture*, 106–8.   [74] Ibid. 108–13; Saul, *Richard II*, 153–5.

The proceedings had broadly two phases: the impeachment of de la Pole in October and the setting-up of the commission in November. The chancellor's requirement of four subsidies to mount a royal expedition and discharge royal debts was greeted with incredulity and outrage. Lords and Commons refused to proceed further until the king removed the chancellor and treasurer. Richard declined, dissolved parliament, and left Westminster, protesting that ministers were answerable to him, not to parliament. Parliament refused to disperse and delegated the duke of Gloucester and Bishop Arundel of Ely to visit the king and remind him that parliament represented the body of the realm, and of his duty to attend. The chroniclers report that Richard was only persuaded to return on 23 October, and remove his ministers, when threatened with the precedent of Edward II's deposition in 1327.[75]

The Commons' charges against de la Pole fell into two parts.[76] First, he had defaulted on his undertakings in the last parliament to reform finances, maintain the guard of the sea, and send assistance to Ghent. On these he acknowledged default but claimed that he shared the blame with other members of the council, and was acquitted. He was also exculpated from sealing grants and charters of pardon to the king's loss, pleading that he had merely obeyed royal warrants. The difficulty of convicting a minister who had the king's confidence on matters of policy was thus apparent. Ultimately it was on three counts of procuring grants for his own enrichment, to the king's loss, that he was found guilty. De la Pole was made the scapegoat for Richard's misrule, and his forfeitures were measured and not vindictive. But the Commons had reasserted their right—in abeyance since 1376—to initiate impeachment and had done this against the king's will.

These proceedings had been completed by the end of the first week of November, and parliament now turned to measures to ensure better government in the future. These brought it into deeper confrontation with the royal prerogative. By 19 November the king had agreed to name a commission for one year to conduct a wholesale and radical review of all offices of government, redress faults, and punish offences. This echoed the terms of the 1381 commission, while five of those named had been on the commission of 1385. They were now headed by the two royal dukes, York and Gloucester, both archbishops, and the earl of Arundel, giving it the political weight to overawe the king and induce his cooperation. For Richard was to be no longer just advised but constrained and taught to govern along the lines approved by the nobility. The court itself was left unscathed. The possibility that after the end of parliament the king could

---

[75] Knighton, *Chron.* 354–61, fabricates the dialogue at the interview but probably conveys its essence. *Eulog. Hist.* iii. 359–60 says they produced 'a statute by which Edward II was judged', which C. Valente, 'The deposition and abdication of Edward II', *EHR* 113 (1998), 857 n. 4, identifies with the 1327 articles of deposition; though see n. 77 below.

[76] Exhaustively and authoritatively examined by Roskell, *Impeachment of Michael de la Pole*.

rescind the commission, issued simply under letters patent, now led to the ultimate violation of the prerogative, the establishment of the commission by act of
parliament. There was a precedent for this—a very dangerous precedent, as the
lords must have been aware—in the ordinance forced upon Edward II in March
1310, and this may have been invoked, along with a renewed reminder of
Edward's fate, for Richard later said he conceded in fear of his life.[77] If it took the
magnates to intimidate the king, it took the Commons to give the commission
statutory authority, which they reinforced by making their grant of taxation
conditional on its operation.

The statute was promulgated on 1 December and subjects were commanded
to obey the commission, whose authority was now independent of the king's. Its
purpose was to institute and inculcate a new practice of government in which the
king should be guided by his magnate counsellors, and the departments of state
and household scrutinized to eliminate corruption, waste, and extravagance.[78]
But though intending to reform rather than subvert royal power, the magnates
had seriously misjudged the king's reaction. Although he could do no more than
protest that nothing done should prejudice him or his crown, he was outraged
that subjects had invaded the royal prerogative, the unique authority to rule.
Beside this, political considerations were unimportant: neither the complaints of
the Commons on his fiscal improvidence and their suggested remedies, nor the
reproaches of the lords for his spurning of counsel and distaste for war, nor even
the unanimity of both, made any impression. Richard scorned political compromise, for kingship stood above politics, deriving both its right to rule and its mission from God. That separated the king from all others, even the peerage. Both
derived their status from inheritance, but the king inherited by divine grace, the
peerage by common law. The peerage lived in a world of infinite social and political gradations which linked them to their inferiors; the king's 'estate' was
unique and separated from all other. The business of the peerage was with the
daily leadership of political society by force, manipulation, and compromise;
that of the king with effecting God's will for his people. The peerage thus
attempted to answer the problem of Richard's misrule by taking measures to
restore good government. But for Richard the essence of good government lay in
the king's will and subjects' obedience to it. Richard's view of government was
king-centred; that of his opponents subject-centred. It was the emergence of
this political chasm between king and subjects which made 1386 the turning
point of the reign. Their irreconcilable attitudes brought first the magnate
opposition and then the king himself to destruction.

[77] D. Clementi, 'Richard II's ninth question to the judges', EHR 86 (1971), 96–113, argues that,
in the context of establishing the commission by statute, Richard's reference to 'the statute by which
Edward II was adjudged' identifies it as the commission of 10 March 1310. Compare n. 75 above.
[78] The text is in SR ii. 44–6; West. Chron. 167–74; Knighton, Chron. 372–80.

It had equal significance for the political community. Under Edward III royal policy had provided an agreed framework of government, resting on military venture and political partnership. Complaint sought either to protect subjects' rights or (as in 1376) to condemn ministers' dereliction. But by 1386 subjects found themselves formulating an agenda of government in opposition to that of the Crown, an agenda which in many respects looked back to the kingship of Edward III, and which they expected his successor to follow. This involved the formulation of political concepts and policies: of the common weal of the realm of which the Crown was the embodiment; of a chauvinistic assertion of national sovereignty; of consultation with the political class and attention to its interests; of economy, solvency, and efficiency in national finance and the use of revenues for the common profit; of justice and respect for law by the Crown, its judges and officers; of honesty and accountability in royal officials. All this was subsumed in the words 'good governance', and its premiss was that the king was the minister of the community of the realm, with a duty to govern in its interests. How regality came to terms with this programme forms the major political theme of the ensuing thirty-five years.

5. THE MAGNATE BACKLASH, 1387–1389

In the Commons' eyes, if not the king's, the commission would be judged on whether it delivered financial retrenchment and reform. The level of taxation was sharply reduced, with only half subsidies being collected in 1387, 1388, and 1389. However, from 1386 tunnage and poundage was levied annually, offsetting the decline of the tax on raw wool exports, and the level of revenue available at the exchequer only dropped by some £10,000 per annum. That implied an increase in the yield of Crown revenues and casualties, probably resulting from measures taken by the commission early in 1387 and the forfeitures imposed by the Merciless Parliament. Revenue and expenditure were brought more nearly into balance, with both failed tallies and borrowing returning to pre-1383 levels.[79] Predictably the new regime now took an axe to wardrobe costs, which fell to an average of £12,800 per annum in 1386–9. Thus the commission did effect a material improvement in Crown finance, though at the same time both Gloucester and Arundel secured settlements of their annuities and claims against the Crown.[80]

---

[79] Ormrod, 'Finance and trade', p. 177, fig. 8.7; Steel, *Receipt of the Exchequer*, p. 436, table B1, p. 446, table C1 (real receipts), pp. 455–6, table D1. For the commission's revenue measures, see Given-Wilson, *Royal Household*, 118–19; *CPR, 1385–9*, 317–18, 320, 371; *CCR, 1385–9*, 222, 308, 647; *CFR, 1383–91*, 182–3.

[80] Given-Wilson, *Royal Household*, 105 and app. 1, p. 270; cf. p. 301 n. 73. For Gloucester, see *CPR, 1385–9*, 233, 479; Tuck, *Richard II and the Nobility*, 127–8.

Control of the exchequer was thus used to reshape financial priorities, and these now included provision for aggressive action against France. Late in March, Arundel sailed to intercept the French fleet returning to Sluys from La Rochelle laden with the year's wine harvest. At Cadzand he captured over fifty ships, and landed 8,000 tuns of wine in London at knock-down prices. As well as enhancing his popularity it finally removed the threat of further invasion. Less successful was the endeavour to exploit his victory by activating contacts with the duke of Guelders and Duke Jean in Brittany. Though Jean was regranted the earldom of Richmond as a bait, neither was prepared for a military alliance and the commission was forced to acknowledge that there was no scope for intervention in France and no financial support for anything more than keeping the sea.

Its greatest problem, however, was with the king. The commission rested on the assumption that it would govern under cover of the king's formal authority, and a degree of cooperation between them seems initially to have obtained. But early in February 1387 Richard moved the court to the Midlands to prevent the commission from meddling in the household. Although liaison between them continued on military and diplomatic matters, with the king's instructions conveyed under the signet, government was effectively taken out of his hands.[81] Richard could only exercise his regality in a personal and territorial context, in the court and countryside, rather than at the political centre. His 'gyration' took him to Yorkshire and Lincolnshire in March, to Stafford and Cheshire in June–July, to Shropshire and Worcester in August, and back to Leicestershire and Nottingham in September. In May he summoned a great council to Reading but few lords attended. Essentially he took counsel from those at court, notably de Vere, Burley, the reinstated de la Pole, Sir John Beauchamp, newly appointed steward, Sir James Berners, and Sir John Salisbury. He won over some local magnates: Archbishop Neville of York, Lords Beaumont and Ferrers of Groby in Leicestershire; and encouraged de Vere to build up support among the gentry of Cheshire, where dissident Lancastrians like Sir Thomas Molyneux, Sir Ralph Radcliffe, and Sir Gilbert Halsall were offered rival lordship.[82]

Richard was not planning an armed challenge to the commission. He was waiting for its expiry on 19 November, when his restored authority would enable him to put its members on trial. In August verdicts were secured in advance by secretly putting questions to a panel of judges on the legality of the recent proceedings in parliament. They pronounced the commission to be derogatory to the regality, adjudging worthy of death those who had procured the statute

---

[81] The last instrument warranted 'by king and council' was on 13 February 1387 (*CPR, 1385–9*, 277); for their further relations, see Saul, *Richard II*, 169–72.

[82] Walker, *Lancastrian Affinity*, 167–70.

and compelled the king to accept it. Illegal, likewise, were the proceedings of parliament contrary to the king's will and command, including the impeachment of de la Pole.[83] With this attested judgment in hand, the king planned to return to London in November and summon a parliament for the trial and sentence. His personal safety was to be ensured by the mobilization of soldiers under de Vere, appointed justice of Chester and North Wales in September–October, and his honoured reception into London was guaranteed by the mayor, Nicholas Brembre, his staunch supporter. The king had openly made preparations for negotiations with Charles VI, to secure whose support, it was rumoured, he was preparing to surrender Calais, Cherbourg, and Brest. Reports of the judges' verdict had already reached Gloucester, Arundel, and Warwick, and when Richard summoned them to meet him they refused to come, assembling their retinues at Harringay and Waltham Cross. The strength and swiftness of their reaction caught the king unprepared and uncertain how to respond. The three lords, pressing their advantage, now formally appealed de Vere, de la Pole, Archbishop Neville, Brembre, and Chief Justice Tresilian of treason, and repeated this in the king's presence three days later in Westminster Hall. Richard assigned them a day in the next parliament, hoping to buy time and turn a private appeal of arms into a state trial which he would adjudicate. To secure his position in London against the Appellants' retinues, Richard now summoned de Vere, who began moving south from Chester with some 3,000 or more men around 8–10 December, probably with the intention of joining the king at Windsor. But on Warwick's advice the three Appellants, now joined by the earls of Derby and Nottingham, moved to intercept him before he had the king's protection, and in a confused running battle in the upper Thames Valley, routed and dispersed his army at Radcot Bridge. De Vere managed to escape, first to Queenborough Castle and then to the Continent, while Richard retreated to the Tower.

Richard was now the prisoner of the Appellants, but on how to treat him they differed. Their resentment and contempt for Richard's favourites had been turned to fear and they were set on revenge; but would their removal be sufficient to change Richard's kingship and end the hostility, treachery, and misgovernment for which they now reproached him? What happened behind closed doors in the Tower on 30 December–1 January cannot be known with certainty. Gloucester favoured deposing Richard, while Derby and Nottingham were opposed to it; perhaps a formal deposition and re-coronation were contemplated, but in the end no action was taken. The consequences were too momentous and the likelihood of dividing political society, which was still firmly in their support, too great. For the moment Richard remained king and at their bidding, even

[83] Text in *West. Chron.* 196–202; Knighton, *Chron.* 394–8; discussed by S. B. Chrimes, 'Richard II's questions to the judges, 1387', *Law Quarterly Review*, 72 (1956), 356–90.

though they knew that this ultimate affront to his regality was never likely to be forgiven.[84]

Richard had issued writs for a parliament on 17 December while de Vere was still moving south, ordering that only men of non-partisan views should be elected. The Appellants had that clause removed and secured the return of a substantial number of their associates and retainers—certainly not less than thirty-four whose sole or main allegiance was to them. Further, no less than sixty-five members had sat in the preceding parliament and hence stood condemned under the judges' verdict, though most of these were borough representatives.[85] Beyond these personally committed, there was general support in the lower house for the attack on the court. The Appellants' propaganda, as reflected in the major chronicles and the parliament roll, was for the moment dominant.[86] Yet as the attack proceeded it was bound to disturb and divide political opinion.

Early in January the Appellants ordered widespread arrests of the chamber knights and the king's leading supporters. De Vere, Burley, and Beauchamp were deprived of their offices, as were six justices. De Vere, de la Pole, and Archbishop Neville had fled and Tresilian was in hiding, but Brembre was taken. Parliament met on 3 February 1388 in the White Hall with the king present. The five Appellants, with arms linked and wearing golden coats, presented their appeal in thirty-nine articles, read out for two hours to a tense assembly. The accused were charged with accroaching the royal power, alienating the king from his lords and people, leading him astray by their counsel, and impoverishing the realm. The king's withdrawal from London, the questions to the judges, and the raising of an army were ascribed to their advice. A hitch occurred when legal experts declared that an appeal of treason could not be brought under common law in the absence of the accused, leaving the Lords to decide that the trial should proceed 'under the law and course of parliament', thus asserting its supremacy as a court without clarifying the procedure. Condemnation was quickly pronounced on all those who had fled, but the trial in person of Nicholas Brembre revealed the fragility of the prosecution. Brembre unsuccessfully challenged the Lords' jurisdiction, but when 'tried' for treason by a committee, no evidence was produced that warranted his death. At this point (19 February) Chief Justice Tresilian was discovered in sanctuary at Westminster; he was forcibly removed and brought to parliament with cries of 'We have him'. Having been already

[84] Saul, *Richard II*, 185–90, gives a full account. Many details are supplied by *West. Chron.* and Knighton, *Chron.*, and, for the events in the Tower, the Whalley Abbey Chronicle discussed by M. V. Clarke, *Fourteenth Century Studies* (Oxford, 1937), 91–5.

[85] *House of Commons*, pp. 185–91, app. C1.

[86] See the introductions to *West. Chron.*, pp. xliii–lxvi; Knighton, *Chron.*, pp. xlvi–lxxi; Thomas Favent, *Historia Mirabilis Parliamenti, Camden Miscellany, XIV*, Camden Society, 3rd ser., 27 (London, 1926), pp. vi–viii.

condemned, he was summarily executed. Brembre was now convicted of misprision of treason on the evidence of some London aldermen and was sent for execution.[87] That completed the proceedings under the appeal, except for a formal declaration of the king's innocence of all the matters comprised in it, he having been led astray 'through his tender age and innocence'.

The parliament now turned to deal with the justices, clerks, and chamber knights arrested in January. Whereas the appeal had been conducted solely before the Lords, these were now impeached by the Commons. The judges pleaded that they had delivered their verdicts under duress, but were adjudged guilty and exiled to Ireland. Their agents, Thomas Usk and John Blake, who had framed the questions, were executed. The king's confessor, Bishop Thomas Rushook, was also sent into exile. The trial of the four leading chamber knights, Beauchamp, Berners, Burley, and Salisbury, was deferred until after the Easter recess during which a solemn oath to uphold the acts of the parliament was to be administered to the leading gentry and officials in every shire.

The parliament resumed on 12 April with the trial of the chamber knights. The case of the elderly Burley split the Lords. The king himself protested Burley's innocence, as did the duke of York, to the fury of Gloucester. The queen pleaded for Burley's life, and Derby and Nottingham may also have supported him. All in vain, as the 'undivided trinity' of the three senior Appellants insisted on his death, vigorously supported by the Commons. Disturbances in Kent, where his rule had made him unpopular, helped to seal his fate. His hurried execution on Tower Green on 5 May more than anything else determined Richard on revenge: in 1397 he would reject Arundel's plea for mercy, reminding him how little he had shown to Burley. For not only was Burley Richard's old and loved tutor but as a knight of the Garter and the confidant of the Black Prince he epitomized the chivalric tradition of loyal service to the royal house which was the common aspiration of the knightly class. That Richard could not protect his senior household servants was not merely an affront to his kingship but a matter of profound political concern. The sense that a boundary had been breached led to the release of the lesser knights and clerks of the chamber under caution. A new household establishment was named, to control the king, but no new council was appointed, nor was the commission renewed. However, the Appellants remained effectively in charge.

The ruthlessness of the Appellants revealed their frustration and fear. The attempt to change Richard's mode of government, first by counsel, then in 1386 by a controlling commission, had been branded as illegal and frustrated by Richard's refusal of cooperation; but it was his plan for their judicial destruction

---

[87] Saul, *Richard II*, 191–6. For Brembre's trial and London politics, see Nightingale, *Medieval Mercantile Community*, ch. 12.

that impelled them to remove their 'enemies' at court who had 'incited' the king. Richard's own enmity was clear enough, but having recoiled from his deposition, the Appellants' only hope of saving themselves was to isolate him. Even this offered no permanent guarantee; the king could not be kept a prisoner indefinitely. If the Appellants had driven themselves into a political cul-de-sac, so too had the king. In refusing to countenance parliamentary intervention he had 'saved' his regality but at the cost of divorcing it from political reality. Regality as the expression of the king's will to govern as he thought best, and parliament as an instrument to give legal force to his decisions, with its existence and procedures determined by the king, might accord with legal theory but had become politically unacceptable. For his subjects parliament was 'the highest court of the land . . . where the errors of the kingdom can be corrected and the state and governance of the king and kingdom can be considered . . . to the relief and benefit of the community'.[88] Regality could not be exercised in isolation from the political community, without its trust and against its interests.

Although the Merciless Parliament had evoked expressions of both savage hatred and apocalyptic hope, its close brought attempts to draw a line under the past and plan for the future. At a solemn Mass on 3 June, in recognition that the compact between king and community had broken down, Richard renewed his coronation oath and the lords rendered homage afresh. The Commons' petitions, to virtually all of which the king assented, showed a similar anxiety. While oaths were taken to uphold parliament's acts, the commission was not to be a precedent and neither were the judgments of treason; those not already punished were given immunity, and a general pardon sought to quieten and heal the divisions. They were no less anxious to pursue the reforms which the conflict had interrupted: they asked for a further parliament at Michaelmas, for a reform of the household to ensure 'sufficient counsel' around the king, for the goods of the condemned to be used to support Crown expenses, and for the restoration of Crown revenues. Once more they asked for the courts of law to be 'surveyed', and the course of law not to be perverted. As a mark of their gratitude and support, they granted the Appellants £20,000 for their costs.[89] Behind these enrolled petitions may have lain a wider-ranging, if diffuse, complaint about misgovernment in the localities, where royal and seigneurial officials acted like 'second kings', protected by their masters, who corrupted local justice. For the moment this went unanswered but these issues were to figure large in the following parliament.[90]

This met at Cambridge on 9 September.[91] The Commons were disappointed

---

[88] Knighton, *Chron.* 356–7.   [89] *Rot. Parl.* iii. 246, nos. 22–4, 34–8, 40, 46.

[90] Knighton, *Chron.* 442–51. There is little to date the petition with certainty; the editor assigns it to the session of May 1388.

[91] No roll survives for this parliament; its proceedings have been interpreted from the statutes and chronicles by J. A. Tuck, 'The Cambridge Parliament, 1388', *EHR* 84 (1969), 225–43.

with the progress of reform and blamed the lords for the crisis of order and just-ice in the country. The Merciless Parliament had divided political society. Not only within the royal household, but even in the chancery and exchequer, career officials had been dismissed and imprisoned for their unacceptable links to courtier magnates,[92] and a fortiori the local polity had been polarized between affinities. This local dimension has yet to be investigated, but instances of judicial persecution and violence are known to have occurred—in Leicestershire between Sir John Beaumont and Sir Thomas Erdington and between Sir John Walcote and William Lodbroke; in Cambridgeshire by John Pelham, the earl of Derby's retainer; and in Gloucestershire by John Poleyn, Lord Berkeley's.[93] Retinues had certainly been expanded, perhaps with less responsible elements and by casual attachments. The Commons now demanded that all liveries given by badges and hoods be abolished, but the Lords resisted any general proscription, offering only to discipline their own men. Their angry exchanges prompted the king to inter-vene with an offer to cease distributing badges himself if the lords would do like-wise. They did not take the bait—they had far more to lose—and yielded the moral high ground. Possibly a compromise was achieved along the lines of the ordinance promulgated in the next parliament, limiting the wearing of badges to those retained by life indenture, of the rank of esquire and above, with an excep-tion for domestic servants.[94] But no measures for enforcement were provided and it remained a subject for complaint for the rest of the decade. The Commons pressed their assault on the abuses of local justice, asking for justices of the peace and assize to be empowered to determine cases of maintenance, but this was ignored. Their major achievement was a comprehensive review and re-enactment of labour legislation, embodied in the thirteen chapters of a new Statute of Labourers. But the lords gave no ground to other petitions which touched their local interests, and the two houses ceased to act with a unity of purpose.[95]

By the end of the parliament Gloucester and Arundel had accepted that fur-ther attacks on France were out of the question and the initiative which Richard had taken for negotiating a truce in November 1388 was resurrected. Significantly this was entrusted to some of the more senior and experienced chamber knights—Devereux, Dagworth, and Clanvowe. At the same time others like Blount, Elmham, and Golafre recovered offices and returned to court, as did the clerks Clifford, Lincoln, Medford, and Slake. Gloucester and Arundel ceased to dominate the workaday council, whose low-key cooperation with the

[92] D. Biggs, 'The appellant and the clerk: The assault on Richard II's friends in government, 1387–9', in G. Dodd (ed.), *The Reign of Richard II* (Stroud, 2000), 57–70.

[93] R. L. Storey, 'Liveries and commissions of the peace, 1388–90', in Du Boulay and Barron (eds.), *Reign of Richard II*, 133–4; Saul, 'The Commons and the abolition of badges', *Parlty. Hist.* 9 (1990), 311–12.   [94] As suggested by Given-Wilson, *Royal Household*, 238–9.

[95] Tuck, 'Cambridge Parliament', 236–40.

king prepared the way for Richard's declaration at the beginning of May 1389 that, being of full age, he now intended to rule in person.

6. UNEASY EQUILIBRIUM, 1389–1396

> For the twelve years since I became king, I and the entire kingdom have been under the control of others and my people burdened year by year with taxes. Now it is fitting that I should assume the conduct of affairs since I have reached the age of maturity. I shall work tirelessly so that my subjects shall live in peace and the realm prosper.

With some such words to the great council on 3 May 1389 Richard II initiated a new phase of his reign.[96] The existing officers of state were dismissed and the justices purged, Gloucester and Warwick were removed from the council, and Arundel lost his military commands. Proclamations in the shires promised subjects better governance, lower taxation, and speedier access to justice and were followed on 16 May by the remission of the second part of the subsidy. For the next eight years the political harmony between the king and his former enemies enabled him to build up support until he could strike them down in the coup of July 1397.

Historians have been divided in interpreting Richard's motives and policy. Most have been disinclined to believe that Richard was plotting revenge under a cloak of dissimulation, preferring to accept that he was 'sincerely anxious to let bygones be bygones' and ready to engage in constructive compromise with conciliar government. Steel characterized the period as one of 'appeasement', in which Richard relapsed into indolent and perhaps neurotic passivity which lulled his enemies into a false sense of security. By contrast, Nigel Saul has described Richard's kingship as entering a more active and creative phase. Having 'recovered the political initiative', he 'shed the brittle and inflexible behaviour' of the adolescent and assumed 'the character of a mature and reasonable young ruler'. It has also been argued that in these years Richard was elaborating an ideology of kingship as the basis for the reassertion of royal authority, and formulating a new political consensus in which the king, as the fount of law and justice, would ensure peace and order among subjects who owed him absolute obedience.[97] In part these varied interpretations reflect the difficulty of identifying the personal will of the king during a period of conciliar cooperation, and it may be more helpful to approach this phase of Richard's kingship through

---

[96] *West. Chron.* 392–3; Wals., *Hist. Anglicana*, ii. 181.

[97] Tout, *Chapters*, iii. 456–8; Jones, *Royal Policy*, 64–70; Tuck, *Richard II and the Nobility*, 138–9, 152–6; Steel, *Richard II*, 181–4, 192–213; Saul, *Richard II*, 201–3, 235–69; M. Bennett, *Richard II and the Revolution of 1399* (Stroud, 1999), 41–4.

its political context. We can do this in respect of the magnates, his household, the council, and parliament.

The Magnates

Richard's dramatic and well-publicized act of emancipation on 3 May 1389 has generally been seen as setting the tone and agenda for his personal rule. He had freed his kingship, recaptured the political initiative, and proclaimed a programme. The magnates could not demur, for their reforms had prepared the way for the right exercise of kingly rule. However, the manner of its doing had alarmed and estranged the three older Appellants and it required the return of John of Gaunt to effect their reconciliation with the king at a great council on 10 December.[98] Gaunt now became the architect and guarantor of a new consensus, interposing his authority between Richard's regality and the Appellants' apprehensions. For this he was uniquely qualified. His own sense of regality was outraged by the king's abasement at the hands of his brother, yet he himself had experienced Richard's treachery and his son had become embroiled in the magnate opposition. His status and power, which guaranteed his own immunity, could also shield Richard from further humiliation and protect his son and brother from the king's revenge. Gaunt believed deeply in the unity and inviolability of the royal family. He also cherished the ambition of establishing himself and his family in an enlarged duchy of Aquitaine through a final peace. It was a project which the king, emotionally and politically ardent for peace, was only too ready to endorse.

Gaunt's dominance was quickly displayed. In January 1390 he and Gloucester were appointed to the council, in February his palatine powers in the duchy of Lancaster were extended to his heirs, and in March he was created duke of Aquitaine. His rapport with the king was manifested in magnificent and reciprocal hospitality, and at spectacular jousts at Smithfield, where Richard distributed his livery of the White Hart. Gloucester, too, began to reap the rewards of his brother's influence, with the grant of Holderness, in reversion from Queen Anne, and the promise of lands to replace his annuities.[99] Gaunt now harnessed his brother's support for the peace negotiations at Leulingham in March 1393 and for his plan to make Aquitaine a Lancastrian principality.[100] Although Gaunt had protected and supported his younger brother, he felt no similar obligation towards Arundel, with whom his relations worsened. The rising in Cheshire early in 1393 provided a flashpoint for these. Ostensibly a protest by the lesser gentry against the negotiations for a peace which threatened their livelihoods, its

---

[98] *Proc. & Ord.* i. 12; *West. Chron.* 406–9.   [99] *CPR, 1391–6*, 255; *Rot. Parl.* iii. 278.
[100] *West. Chron.* 486–7; Saul, *Richard II*, 276 n. 15; above, Ch. 11, sect. 3.

roots lay among the competing followings of Arundel (in Shropshire), Gaunt (in Lancashire), and the king (as earl of Chester). Richard's retainers Sir Thomas Talbot and Sir John Mascy were among the leaders of the revolt and both were enemies of Gaunt's affinity. Gaunt and Gloucester, returning from Leulingham, suppressed the rising, while Arundel stood aloof, and the king publicly disowned the rebels' plan 'to destroy the magnates of the realm'. But Talbot and Mascy were never punished.[101] Gaunt and Arundel engaged in bitter recriminations in the parliament of January 1394, Gaunt levelling charges of treachery and Arundel denouncing Gaunt's familiarity and favour with the king and dominance of the council. Forced by the king to make a public apology, Arundel next year provoked Richard's fury by his unfeeling and insulting behaviour at Queen Anne's funeral and was sent to the Tower.

Gaunt's dominance thus provoked tensions as well as containing them. This was so not only at the highest level but in the localities. In Yorkshire the Lancastrian affinity was locked in a bitter conflict with Sir William Beckwith and in Derbyshire with the retainers of the earl of Stafford, left leaderless after his death in July 1392. Here, as in Cheshire, Sir Nicholas Clifton, a retainer of Thomas Holland, earl of Kent, led the opposition to Gaunt's affinity. In 1392–3 the king intervened, sending the court of king's bench to Nottingham and Derby, the heart of Lancastrian lordship, to deal with disorders, while also recruiting those alienated from Gaunt into the royal affinity.[102] The events of 1387–8 had impressed on Richard the need for a royal following to counterbalance the magnate affinities, and from 1389 to 1397 he retained more than seventy knights and thirty-nine esquires among the leading local gentry, half of them in the years 1391–3. Up to one-third of these were drawn from the south-east, the area of the king's normal itinerary, but the remainder were distributed fairly evenly over other regions, including Yorkshire and the north-west, dominated by Gaunt. The king's affinity was the resort of those at odds with their existing lords or those attracted by a larger fee (£40 or 40 marks) and greater prospects; both Arundel and Warwick thus lost important retainers to royal service. Warwick's control of the West Midlands was undermined by the Crown's support for his enemies Sir John Russell in Worcestershire and Sir William Bagot in Warwickshire. However, the royal affinity differed in character and function from those of the magnates, for it lacked the density and family tradition which enabled a magnate to permeate and control an area of lordship. Thus the proportion of royal retainers among JPs remained minimal before 1397. It was rather the strong

---

[101] J. G. Bellamy, 'The northern rebellions in the later years of Richard II', *BJRL* 47 (1965), 254–74; P. Morgan, *War and Society in Medieval Cheshire, 1277–1403*, Chetham Society (Manchester, 1987), 193–8; Walker, *Lancastrian Affinity*, 171–4.

[102] Bellamy, 'Northern rebellions'; Walker, *Lancastrian Affinity*, 209–34.

vertical connections of royal retainers to the court and centre that made them conduits of royal influence and pathways to royal favour, while their status as royal representatives and watchdogs spread a sense of the king's surveillance.[103]

At the same time Richard was seeking supporters of his own age among the nobility to replace those whom the Appellants had removed. By 1395 Richard had won Nottingham (aged 29), York's son Rutland (22), and possibly March (21) to his side, though with Gaunt's son Derby his relations remained distant. Beyond these his two Holland half-brothers, Kent (45) and Huntingdon (43), provided the extended family which Richard, as an only child, lacked. Richard's ability to reward them with lands and revenues was closely controlled by the council, but he had more freedom to appoint to offices and commands. His former companion Nottingham was the first to recover favour, being made warden of the East March in 1389, then captain of Calais in February 1391 and justice of Chester and North Wales. In June 1389 Huntingdon replaced Arundel as admiral and captain of Brest and was made chamberlain of England in February 1390. Rutland succeeded him as admiral in 1391 and the two Hollands were made constables of a string of royal castles. For the king's expedition to Ireland in 1394–5, Huntingdon, March, Nottingham, and Rutland brought large retinues, demonstrating their brotherhood in arms, and were rewarded with Irish titles. By 1395–6 Richard had thus grouped around him a small number of the upper nobility who, in contrast to his favourites before 1388, had neither been promoted from lower status nor rewarded with extensive lands. Even so, by 1395 the nobility was becoming polarized into the king's friends at court and the older Appellants estranged from his presence and ensconced in their castles. When Gaunt returned from Aquitaine at Christmas 1395 he could no longer bridge the gap.

If the Irish expedition had forged a bond between Richard's new aristocracy and identified them with his leadership, it was in the negotiations for his second marriage that they emerged as the chosen instruments of his policy. The embassy appointed on 8 July 1395 named as principals the earls of Nottingham and Rutland, Lord Beaumont, Sir William Scrope, and Bishop Gilbert. In January 1396 they were empowered to conclude a twenty-eight year truce, accept a dowry of 800,000 francs, and arrange for the king's marriage at a meeting with Charles VI in October. Peace with France had been secured without Gaunt's participation, and against the declared opposition of Gloucester. Gaunt's ability to protect his brother was rapidly diminishing; he himself was ageing, he was not ready to oppose the king, and he was preoccupied with plans for marriage to his mistress, Catherine Swynford, and the legitimization of their

---

[103] Given-Wilson, *Royal Household*, 217–23; Saul, *Richard II*, 265–7; A. Gundy, 'The earl of Warwick and the royal affinity in the politics of the West Midlands, 1389–99', in Hicks (ed.), *Revolution and Consumption*, 57–70; S. Mitchell, 'The knightly household of Richard II in the peace commissions', ibid. 45–56, esp. 53.

children, and for the transmission of his vast duchy and wealth to his heir. For all these he needed Richard's favour.

The Household

The household provided the most intimate arena for regality and had thus been the focus of the Appellants' attack in 1388. The chamber knights whom they subsequently restored as the king's attendants were mainly senior men of proven ability and good repute like the chamberlain Peter Courtenay, the steward John Devereux, and William Nevill, Lewis Clifford, John Clanvowe, Richard Stury, and Nicholas Dagworth. Chastened by their experience, and beholden to the Appellants for mercy, they had little taste for any further flaunting of the prerogative by the youthful king and must have been a sobering influence. But death and retirement thinned their ranks after 1391, and by 1395 all had been replaced by a new generation. Sir William Scrope as chamberlain and Sir Thomas Percy as steward were scions of northern baronial families, with military experience, while Edward Dallingridge and John Russell had been tempted from the service of the Appellants. An even greater influence was exercised by the group of chaplains headed by Alexander Bache and John Burghill, the king's confessors.[104]

Between 1389 and 1395–6 the household grew significantly in size and cost. By 1395–6 it was larger by 150 persons and its costs rose to £26,000, for the king's marriage. The splendour of this occasion, designed to impress and outclass Charles VI, was only the most ostentatious of many celebrations noted for their extravagance by the chroniclers.[105] The annual expenditure of the great wardrobe had more than doubled, to reach almost £8,000 in 1392–4, and rose by a further £4,000 in the following years. The accounts provide details of the costly clothes, furs, and luxury objects purchased from the mercers and drapers of London. For his personal expenses Richard after 1392 doubled the sum drawn from the exchequer for the chamber. Put together, the total costs of the household departments show an increase from c.£21,000 per annum in 1377–89 to almost £34,000 per annum in 1392–5, representing a scale of expenditure not seen since the 1360s. If Richard sought to emulate the splendour of his grandfather's court, the background to his kingship was markedly different. He did not head a nobility united in loyalty to the Crown, nor command the private wealth of war ransoms, while France was not a beaten foe but a potential threat. Richard's household could again express his regality, but it was a fragile façade while his authority remained insecure.

[104] Given-Wilson, *Royal Household*, 164–6, 179–81, 282–3.

[105] Ibid. 79–94, 270, 278; *West. Chron.* 432–53, 455, 489, 511, 517; J. Stratford, 'Gold and diplomacy: England and France in the reign of Richard II', in J. Mitchell and M. Moran (eds.), *England and the Continent in the Middle Ages* (Stamford, 2000).

The Council

Far from Richard's declaration of May 1389 inaugurating the free exercise of his regality, the records show that his rule was for a period closely monitored by the council.[106] A council may have been formally appointed, for its members met virtually every month to deal with major affairs of state, internal and external. Though in 1390 Richard affirmed his right to appoint and remove councillors at his pleasure, he was not under constraint; rather the council's role was that envisaged in 1385, to guide him by advice which he should not disregard. The new chancellor, Wykeham, and the treasurer, Brantingham, were men of great seniority and experience, and the veteran chamber knights restored in 1389, along with curial lords like Beaumont, Lovell, and Cobham, ensured that there was no divorce between court and council. From the first, emphasis was laid upon the prudent and profitable management of Crown resources. In March 1390, when Gaunt, Gloucester, and Arundel had rejoined it, their assent was required to any grant by the king with financial implications, and all his signet warrants had to pass scrutiny by the privy seal. The council saw its prime function as being to harmonize the interests of the king and the political community, as a contribution to political stability. It was on this ground that in 1392 it refused Richard's request for the return of de Vere and Archbishop Neville from exile.[107] By the beginning of 1392 the council was ready to confirm Richard's full power to rule but probably retained its character and role up to the Irish expedition in 1394–5. With Gaunt's departure to Bordeaux, the retirement of the older chamber knights, and the influence of the new courtier nobility, the character of the council became perceptibly more curial.

In the offices of state, Bishop Arundel as chancellor, Bishop Waltham as treasurer, and Edmund Stafford, keeper of the privy seal, maintained efficient and responsible government up to 1395–6. Testimony to this is provided by the adequacy and stability of exchequer finances. The pattern was largely determined by the grants of direct taxation, which over the whole period averaged less than half a lay subsidy and little over a quarter clerical subsidy a year, though the incidence was heavier from 1393. The yield of indirect taxation was variable but averaged £60,000 per annum. Notional available revenue stood at about £85,000 per annum for 1389–92 and £116,000 per annum for 1392–6. After the first years there were few failed assignments, and not until 1394–5 did the Crown resort to short-term borrowing on a large scale, for the Irish expedition. Moreover, over the period as a whole revenue was predominantly received in cash, even from the

---

[106] The minutes kept by the council's clerk John Prophet for 1389–90 and 1392–3 are in *Proc. & Ord.* i. 6–63 and Baldwin, *King's Council*, 489–504; Goodman, 'Councils of Richard II', in Gillespie and Goodman (eds.), *Richard II*, 59–82.

[107] *Rot. Parl.* iii. 258; *West. Chron.* 484–7.

customs.[108] It suggests prudent and efficient revenue management on the lines adopted by the council in 1389. The prolongation of the truce enabled the costs of garrisoning Calais and the northern marches to be reduced. The steady increase in costs in the household produced a current deficit in 1389–92, but this was followed by three years of surplus, which cleared its debts. There are indications that Crown revenues were increased by the restraint of royal grants and the exploitation of fiscal casualties, as the council had recommended.[109] Low taxation, stable exchequer and household credit, and attentive management of the royal fisc all made for political harmony and absence of complaint about royal governance. They set the tone for relations with parliament in these years.

Parliament

With king and the nobility in outward harmony, parliament reverted to it traditional role as an agent of royal government rather than of magnate opposition. Both sides recognized the need to restore cooperation. The king promised relief from war taxation and measures of law enforcement in the localities; Lords and Commons jointly petitioned in 1390 and 1391 that the king should be 'as free in his regality' as his predecessors, implicitly acknowledging the illegality of the 1386 commission. The petition was certainly instigated by the king, but parliament was clearly anxious to erase the offence and allay his fears.[110]

Over taxation, the grant of effectively just under half a fifteenth a year was an acceptable level in time of truce when defences had to be maintained, though it was the product of political fencing on both sides. The king used the threat of issuing trailbaston commissions in 1391 and 1393, and on both occasions the Commons' grant fulsomely acknowledged his goodwill and was made for his 'costs and charges' and 'to honour his person'. From 1391 they renewed the wool subsidy and tunnage and poundage at the full rate. At the same time they set stringent conditions, making their supplementary grants for a royal voyage dependent on its taking place, and in granting a full fifteenth for the royal expedition to Ireland they were disclaiming any further obligation for its defence.[111]

The chancellors' opening addresses, both by Wykeham in 1390 and by Arundel in 1391, echoed Richard's own proclamation of 1389, promising law, justice, and tranquillity in the realm and inviting the Commons' cooperation. Large numbers of petitions were submitted in every parliament up to 1395. For

[108] Steel, *Receipt of the Exchequer*, 447, 456, 437; Ormrod, 'Finance and trade', 177.

[109] Given-Wilson, *Royal Household*, pp. 105–6, app. I; Saul, *Richard II*, 256–8; Steel, *Receipt of the Exchequer*, 60–72; *Proc. & Ord.* i. 8–10, 18b.

[110] *Rot. Parl.* iii. 279, 286. For other matters on which the king reserved his prerogative, see ibid. iii. 258 (no. 7), 265 (no. 26), 267 (no. 36).

[111] *Rot. Parl.* iii. 262, 285–6, 301–2, 314, 330; Wals., *Hist Anglicana*, ii. 216.

the Commons this was the real purpose of parliament, enabling them to press their interests both individual and communal. They complained of the pardons for felonies which lords obtained for their followers, of abuses by royal serjeants-at-arms, and of the encroachments of prerogative courts and procedures on the common law. Three matters raised in the Cambridge parliament continued to claim their attention: the enforcement and tightening of the Statute of Labourers, the implementation of the ordinance of 1390 restricting livery of company, and greater recognition of the status of JPs.[112] Thus from 1389 to 1395 the Crown and the Commons were each pursuing their respective objectives: the king was seeking taxation in the context of negotiations for peace, the Commons were setting the conditions for their assent while petitioning for their own interests. They were not intruding into high politics. The presence of magnates' retainers in the Commons was now matched by those of the Crown, and there was a degree of give and take. In this respect the situation was normal; what gave it a sense of artificiality was the ghost of 1386–8. The Commons strove to lay it, but could never be sure that Richard had forgiven and forgotten.[113]

The King

It is evident that up to 1394 policy and government were not fashioned by the sole will of the king. A council dominated by his three uncles, an administration headed by former appointees of the Appellants, and a parliament demanding economical and responsible government formed a trinity intent on containing, though not constraining, the king. Richard's reinvigorated kingship is evident in other areas. His efforts after 1389 to reconstitute a group of nobility as his personal friends, to attract to his household and service a new generation of knights, and to retain prominent local gentry to form a royal affinity were all attempts to repair the isolation inflicted on him in 1388. Likewise the greater style and cost of the royal household reflected his promotion of the court as the focus of loyalty and service among a specific circle. Yet before the Irish expedition this had little political impact.

Richard's own political interventions were occasional, the most dramatic being his systematic humiliation of London for supporting the Appellants after pledging loyalty to the king. Disorders in the city provided the opportunity to intervene. On 13 May 1392 all the courts and offices were ordered to move to

[112] *Rot. Parl.* iii. 265–73 (Jan. 1390); 280–3 (Nov. 1390); 290–6 (1391); 305–8 (1393); 318–23 (1394).
[113] G. Dodd, 'Richard II and the transformation of parliament', in id. (ed.), *Reign of Richard II*, 71–84. For retainers, see Clark, in *House of Commons*, i. 139, and Given-Wilson, *Royal Household*, 247–8.

York, in a calculated blow to the city's prosperity and prestige. Then 'a terrible and truly horrible writ' summoned the mayor and leading citizens to appear before the council at Nottingham. There they were detained, the city placed under a royal warden, and a commission of investigation appointed; in July the council suspended London's liberties and imposed a fine of £100,000. In the next months the city negotiated humbly under duress for the king's grace, with the queen and leading magnates interceding. In August the fine was reduced to £10,000, the liberties were conditionally restored, and the king and queen staged a triumphal entry in which the extravagance of the city's gifts was only matched by the language of its submission.[114] While some of the council lords were glad to teach the citizens a lesson, Richard's use of the incident to articulate his absolutist vision must have caused alarm.

The indications of Richard's view of regality reflected his own exploration of its historical and religious roots. Shortly after 1388 he had a book of statutes compiled relating to the royal power which included the 1311 ordinances, and to vindicate the deposed Edward II he visited his shrine at Gloucester and renewed pressure at Rome for his canonization. In 1390–1 a *Liber Regius* compiled at Bury listed his descent from Brutus, and the theme of dynastic continuity and legitimacy was developed in the rebuilding of Westminster Hall, commenced in 1393. There white harts lined the internal string course while thirteen statues of kings from the Confessor to Richard II were commissioned, possibly for niches on the end wall above the dais and throne, and two greater statues of Richard and the Confessor surmounted the entrance doorway. Westminster Hall was to orchestrate the message of majesty restored. Richard's conviction of the inviolability of his kingship also rested on the protection accorded by God and the saints, particularly those of the Anglo-Saxon royal house. This derived from his coronation and was nourished by his intimate connection with Westminster Abbey, to which he resorted at crises in his reign. That the coronation regalia had a special importance for Richard is clear from the treatise on them compiled in 1387–9 by William Sudbury, a monk of Westminster, and by his proud display of them to the King of Armenia on an evening visit to the abbey in 1386. His own kingship was manifested in the hieratic frontal portrait, which he commissioned around 1395 to hang in the abbey, perhaps over the royal pew, while in the same year he ordered the double tomb, adjacent to and stylistically linked with that of Edward III, and in close proximity to the shrine of the Confessor. In 1394–5 he impaled the arms of the Confessor on the royal arms.[115]

---

[114] *West. Chron.* 492–3; C. Barron, 'The quarrel of Richard II with London, 1392–1397', in and Du Boulay and Barron (eds.), *Reign of Richard II*, 173–201; also ead., 'Richard II and London', in Goodman and Gillespie (eds.), *Richard II*, 129–54.

[115] P. J. Eberle, 'Richard II and the literary arts', in Goodman and Gillespie (eds.), *Richard II*, 231–53; E. Scheifele, 'Richard II and the visual arts', ibid. 255–71.

In these years, then, Richard was exploring and proclaiming the historical and religious bases of his kingship. He believed himself to be protected and guided by the divine commission to rule his realm as his ancestors had done. He was impelled to express this in literary and visual forms, yet he had not been able to translate it into a political programme. To outsiders his addiction to the forms of majesty in a variety of individual statements might appear merely idiosyncratic if the sense of outrage which underlay them was ignored. But by 1395 Richard was acquiring the power to give his vision of kingship political content.

The death of Queen Anne in 1394 had provided the catalyst. For although Richard was for a time overwhelmed with grief, it bound him more closely to the younger nobility who had accompanied him to Ireland, and provided the occasion for them to seize the political initiative by masterminding the negotiations for his remarriage. Yet while this provided the bridge to his unfettered rule, it also highlighted the hollowness of his Crown, namely his childlessness. When in June 1394 both he and Henry of Bolingbroke suddenly found themselves widowers after respectively twelve and thirteen years of marriage, the king was still without issue while Henry had sired four sons, all living. Whether the cause was impotence in Richard, infertility in his wife, or even distaste for sexual intercourse must remain a matter of speculation. The implications were profound. Although he might view his childlessness as replicating that of the celibate Confessor, it would spell the end of the Plantagenet line, and it seemed to call in question God's blessing upon his marriage and dynasty. Politically it was equally destabilizing. Although he resisted designating an heir, it portended a struggle for the succession from which the house of Lancaster was bound to emerge the victor—a prospect Richard could not bear to contemplate. Nor, as might have been expected, did he use his remarriage to resolve the problem, for Isabella was a child of 6. Richard's unconcern baffled contemporaries.[116]

By the end of 1396 Richard was ready to give substance to his vision of *regimen regale* and re-establish true monarchy, the task he now saw as his life's destiny. Two obstacles remained: a challenge from the former Appellants, and the succession of Lancaster were he to die. The removal of these formed the political agenda of his final years.

7. KING RICHARD'S RULE, 1397–1399

The temper of Richard's rule was manifested in the parliament of January 1397. Fresh from his marriage and the sealing of a permanent truce with Charles VI,

---

[116] Bennett, *Richard II and the Revolution of 1399*, 61, 71–2; for Richard's view of the succession and his own destiny, see S. K. Walker, 'Richard II's views on kingship', in Archer and Walker (eds.), *Rulers and Ruled*, 49–63; for current doubts on his second marriage, see Mézières, *Letter to Richard II*, p. xx n. 35, and p. 67.

the king looked for goodwill and generosity from the Commons, who again elected as Speaker his councillor Sir John Bussy.[117] Yet within days they were at issue over Richard's commitment (probably given at Calais) to assist Charles VI to invade Italy. The Commons refused to be bound to grant money except for the defence of the realm; the king affirmed his right to aid his allies, and suspected that dissident magnates, like Gloucester, were inciting opposition. The dispute quickly subsided, and Charles VI anyway abandoned the expedition. How it related to the more open clash of king and Commons a week later is not clear.

On Friday 2 February the chancellor told the king that the Commons were considering petitions which touched his regality. One of these had been framed by a clerk, Thomas Haxey, a proctor in parliament. Haxey's bill complained of the great costs of the royal household arising from the numbers of bishops and ladies maintained at the king's court. Richard, in defence of 'his regality and the royal liberty of the crown', took 'offence and grief' that the Commons should make any ordinance for the governance of his person or household or attendants.[118] Next day the Commons, probably through Bussy, humbly excused themselves for the offence to his 'royal majesty, royal estate and liberty'. The matter did not rest there, either for the Commons or for Haxey. On 5 February the Lords gave judgment that if anyone should incite the Commons to anything which touched the king's person, regality, or rule (*regimen*) he should be held a traitor. On 7 February Haxey, in full parliament, admitted that he had made his bill to the Commons, 'for the honour and profit of the king and the whole community of the realm'. He was adjudged a traitor but spared the penalty on the intercession of the bishops, and in fact suffered little loss. What or who prompted Haxey's bill is unclear, but Richard seized upon it as an opportunity to cow the Commons by reviving the spectre of the 1387 judgment on their role in the commission. Reform of government in the name of the common profit was now outlawed. In the king's view parliament served to give effect to the royal will; he himself would make 'statutes and ordinances for the quiet and tranquillity of the people'. He showed his benevolence by undertaking not to tax them in future for his personal use, and in return the Commons renewed the wool subsidy for five years.

Richard's new tone of authority reflected the support of a core of nobles at court: Huntingdon, Nottingham, Rutland, and the recent successors to the earldoms of Kent and Salisbury. The appointment of Bishop Stafford as chancellor and Roger Walden (Richard's former secretary) as treasurer put government firmly under his control. In June Nottingham procured a judgment against the earl of Warwick to recover the lordship of Gower with the payment of £5,333 in

---

[117] For Bussy's career, see Roskell, *Parliament and Politics*, ii. 45–63; *House of Commons*, ii. 449–54.

[118] *Rot. Parl.* iii. 338–9, 341, 345, 407–8. The most reliable account of the incident is by Roskell in *House of Commons*, i. 80–3.

damages.[119] Gloucester retired to his castle at Pleshey, freely and dangerously voicing his opposition to the peace and his contempt for the unwarlike king; Arundel had likewise withdrawn, engaged in building 'Castle Philipp' at Shrawardine for his new wife. Nor did they look to Gaunt for leadership. Gaunt had long since quarrelled with Arundel and had outraged Gloucester by marrying his mistress, Catherine Swynford. His position was delicate. His own sense of regality debarred him from any action against the king, whose favour in any case he needed for legitimizing and promoting the Beauforts. And as he advanced in age it was the succession of his sole heir, the hard-living and adventurous Henry of Bolingbroke, earl of Derby, that filled his thoughts. But second only to his loyalty to the king and his own children was that to the Plantagenet family. Since 1390 he had sought to reconcile Richard to Gloucester and protect him; his brother's arrest was to shock and distress Gaunt profoundly.

What prompted Richard to destroy the three older Appellants was not a plot or even the suspicion of a plot, but first, personal revenge and secondly, the belief that they were impediments to his regality. This belief was rooted in the events of 1387–8; it did not reflect the situation in 1397, when they lacked the unity and political will to present a challenge.[120] Perhaps Richard's fear was less of them than of their territorial and military resources, which far exceeded those of the king and his circle. Lancaster, Gloucester, March, Arundel, and Warwick all had male heirs to perpetuate their great inheritances, in comparison to which those of the Hollands, Rutland, and Montagu were insignificant, with only Mowbray potentially in the same league. The king and his supporters needed to match their political authority with territorial power, and this could only be done by confiscation.

In the second week of July the three older Appellants were suddenly arrested after being summoned to the king. To disarm opposition Richard dissembled his reasons and brought troops from Cheshire for his protection. This was the critical moment when Gaunt and York might have intervened; in fact their compliance was bought by financial concessions, and in August their presence at Nottingham endorsed a new appeal by the court nobility charging the old Appellants with treason. This was to be heard in parliament, summoned for 17 September. Two days beforehand all royal annuitants were assembled in arms at Kingston upon Thames, and when parliament met it was in an open-sided structure in Westminster Yard (since the hall was being rebuilt), surrounded by the archers of Richard's Cheshire guard. Bishop Stafford's opening sermon was a carefully framed statement of regality: the power to rule lay wholly and solely with the king, to whom all owed obedience; it could not be alienated to subjects

---

[119] *Rot. Parl.* iii. 341–2; Saul, *Richard II*, 372–3.
[120] Saul, *Richard II*, 371–5, discusses the existence of a plot.

and any such act must be revoked and punished, so that the king should have the liberty and power of his forefathers. Sir John Bussy, once again Speaker, guided the proceedings, reciting the commission and acts of 1386–8, which were now condemned as treasonous, and any pardons issued for them were revoked. On impeachment by the Commons, Archbishop Arundel was convicted and sentenced to forfeiture and exile. The appeal was then heard before the Lords. The earl of Arundel put up a spirited defence, pleading his pardon and engaging in angry exchanges with Gaunt and Derby; Richard, showing him the same measure of mercy that the earl had to Simon Burley, ordered his immediate execution on Tower Hill. Gloucester had been taken to Calais after his arrest, and Nottingham, his gaoler there, now reported that he was already dead. A doctored transcript of his confession, made shortly before his death, was read to parliament; in it he acknowledged and regretted his actions in 1386–8 but denied any recent plot against the king. Suspicion of his murder centred on Nottingham and Rutland, acting at the king's wish. On 28 September Warwick was arraigned in person on the same charges and adjudged guilty; an old and broken man, he pleaded for his life and was sentenced to perpetual imprisonment on the Isle of Man. A new definition of treason was formally adopted embracing the Appellants' crimes, and the total forfeiture of their lands, both entailed and in fee simple, was pronounced. Their heirs were dispossessed. Gaunt's reward for compliance was the exoneration of Derby for his part in 1387–8, along with that of Nottingham, pronounced by the king himself.[121]

Richard's reversal of 1386–8 had been carefully choreographed not only to take a personal revenge on the Appellants but to reclaim impeachment and appeal for the royal prerogative and outlaw any restraint of royal rule by subjects in the name of the common good. These measures were definitive: all the Lords were to swear on St Edward's shrine to uphold the judgments, and the oath was to be administered to their successors; the shire knights swore likewise, and the bishops undertook to excommunicate any who became forsworn. An official account of the parliament was circulated, based on the parliament roll, which portrayed the king acting with justice and mercy. Contemporary chroniclers used it to celebrate the recovery of the royal liberty and extol the bursting forth of royal majesty like the sun from behind the clouds.[122]

While the coup was presented as the triumph of the royal prerogative, in reality it was purchased by a redistribution of the forfeited lands among the court nobility. The king was indeed a beneficiary: Arundel's lordships in the march of Wales were annexed to the Crown and united with Chester, which was raised to

---

[121] Accounts of the trials are in *Rot. Parl.* iii. 377–80, and *Vita Ricardi Secundi*, trans. C. Given-Wilson (ed.), *Chron. Rev.* 58–60.

[122] *Rot. Parl.* iii. 356; C. Given-Wilson, 'Adam Usk, the Monk of Evesham and the parliament of 1397–8', *Hist. Res.* 66 (1993), 329–35; *Chron. Rev.* 94–6.

the status of a principality. Nottingham was granted the Arundel estate at Lewes and twenty manors in tail male; Huntingdon got Reigate and thirty-three manors; Kent got Warwick Castle and nine manors; Rutland had Gloucester's lordship of Holderness and lands to the value of £800. All were raised to duke-doms, as were Nottingham and Derby. Somerset became a marquess, while Thomas, Lord Despenser, Ralph, Lord Neville, Sir Richard Scrope, and Sir Thomas Percy were rewarded with earldoms and other confiscated lands. This effected, in the space of a few days, the most sweeping territorial redistribution in the Middle Ages, creating not only a new aristocracy but new consolidations of land, men, and power.[123] On 30 September, less than a fortnight after it had assembled, parliament was adjourned to meet at Shrewsbury on 21 January. There had been no time for petitions.

Richard's coup aroused fears that the courtier group would encourage the king's further destruction of families of ancient lineage. Three were most obvi-ously at risk: Lancaster, Mowbray, and March. Richard's continued favours to Gaunt did not allay the old man's unease about his son Hereford's succession and pardon for his role in 1387–8. Norfolk, who daily expected to inherit the lands of Margaret of Brotherton, had similar fears. These he confided to Hereford in December 1397 as they rode between Brentford and London. He spoke of a plot by Surrey, Wiltshire, and Salisbury to seize or kill Gaunt and his family, and to persuade the king to annul the pardon of Thomas of Lancaster in 1327 and reinstate the forfeiture pronounced upon him in 1322, thus resuming the Lancastrian inheritance, a huge prize for the Crown and its supporters.[124]

Both the credibility of Norfolk's story and his motives have been questioned. That there was a plot against Lancaster to which Norfolk was privy emerged later; but was Norfolk tempting Hereford into a provocative act or was he genu-inely seeking mutual support from a former ally? Though highly favoured by Richard, Norfolk felt exposed. He was widely suspected of having been instru-mental in Gloucester's murder, and could inculpate the king himself. His des-perate attempt to seek Lancastrian protection was fatally misjudged. Gaunt held him responsible for his brother's death, and ordered his son to report Norfolk's words to the king. Richard told him to make formal charges in the parliament at

---

[123] R. A. K. Mott, 'A study in the distribution of patronage, 1389–99', *Leeds Philosophical and Literary Society*, 15 (1974), 124–30; A. Dunn, 'Exploitation and control: The royal administration of magnate estates, 1397–1405', in Hicks (ed.), *Revolution and Consumption*, 27–44. The titles of the new dukes and earls created in this parliament were: Henry of Bolingbroke, earl of Derby = duke of Hereford; Edward of York, earl of Rutland = duke of Aumale; John Holland, earl of Huntingdon = duke of Exeter; Thomas Mowbray, earl of Nottingham = duke of Norfolk; Thomas Holland, earl of Kent = duke of Surrey; Thomas Percy = earl of Worcester; William Scrope = earl of Wiltshire; Thomas Despenser = earl of Gloucester.

[124] C. Given-Wilson, 'Richard II, Edward II, and the Lancastrian inheritance', *EHR* 109 (1994), 553–71.

Shrewsbury. Norfolk panicked and refused to attend; he was stripped of his offices and ordered to appear before the king. When he denied Hereford's accusation both were ordered to prepare for trial by battle at Coventry on 16 September. Norfolk remained in prison while Hereford armed and trained himself for the duel.

The Shrewsbury parliament, according to one observer, was like a gathering for war. The earl of March, threatened with the loss of Denbigh to the earl of Salisbury, came in fear and quickly returned to Ireland, where he met his death in July. The custody of his estates was divided between the king and others. The truncated session closed with the Commons' grant of three half fifteenths to be levied over the next two years, 'for their great fondness and entire love of the king', and of the subsidy on wool for the rest of his life. These taxes were no longer associated with the needs of defence or the answering of their petitions; Richard extracted this unprecedented grant by withholding the general pardon for which the Commons asked and then making it conditional on the continuance of the tax. The docility of the Commons in this parliament was achieved both by intimidation and through the manipulation of elections to secure the return of members favourable to the court, including at least twenty-nine royal retainers.[125]

The Coventry duel took place in an atmosphere of extreme nervousness about the king's intentions and the intrigues of the court nobility. Large numbers of spectators had gathered but before it could commence Richard had taken the dispute into his own hands, as was his right, and pronounced sentence of banishment on both men, Hereford for ten years, Norfolk for life. He did so to safeguard the peace of the realm. Not only was Norfolk's exile longer, he was also degraded from the rank of duke and his lands were taken into the king's custody. He left England to make a pilgrimage to Jerusalem and died in Venice from plague on 22 September. Thomas Mowbray had acquired a reputation for intrigue and rumour-mongering, borne out by the inconstancy of his attachments. Essentially a courtier, it was jealousy of de Vere that detached him from the king in 1387 and led him to join the Appellants. Richard had little difficulty in regaining his support in 1389 and little compunction in assisting in his self-destruction when his loyalty again wavered. Hereford, on his father's advice, went to Paris and was honourably received at Charles VI's court, where his banishment was felt to be undeserved. For Gaunt the exile of his son was an unforeseen and devastating blow, which placed the succession to the duchy in untold jeopardy.

Richard's territorial revolution was now a year old. Between them the king and the new aristocracy held the lands and castles of Warwick, Gloucester, Arundel, March, and Norfolk and in their hands were not only the major offices of the household and the major commands in Calais, the north, and Ireland (where Surrey had replaced the earl of March) but numerous castellanships in England and Wales. At its heart was the king's new and enlarged principality of Chester and the adjoining principality of Wales. This came under the authority of William Scrope, earl of Wiltshire, as justice of North Wales, with command of the great castles of the northern coast. Salisbury now had possession of Denbigh, and the Mortimer estates in mid-Wales were in the king's custody. A huge bloc of territory from the Mersey to Cardigan Bay lay under royal control.[126]

The consequence of this was a shift of the political fulcrum to the north-west. Cheshire was promoted as the basis for Richard's personal power, and this generated a territorial confrontation with the duchy of Lancaster. Following the parliament of September 1397 Richard formed a Cheshire bodyguard composed of seven squadrons of forty-six men with two reserves, in all some 750 men who guarded him wherever he went—their motto being 'Dycun slep sicury quile we wake'. In fact Richard's main itinerary was now bounded by the West Midlands and Cheshire. The background to this was mounting competition for retainers between Richard and Gaunt. Richard provided an alternative patronage for those outside the Lancastrian affinity: in March 1398 five knights and twenty-two esquires from Lancashire became royal retainers, most of them already Gaunt's local opponents. Gaunt's response was to build up his affinity, granting additional fees to those who agreed to remain in his son's service after his death. In the North Midlands the king pursued a similar policy of retaining those hostile to the Lancastrian affinity, while the power of Thomas Holland, now duke of Surrey, augmented by the grant of Warwick's estates, began to rival that of Lancaster and Stafford. In these and other areas local society was riven between those with loyalties to traditional families and those who attached themselves to the new lords.[127]

This growing confrontation between the royal and Lancastrian power paved the way for the confiscation of Gaunt's duchy after his death in March 1399. Henry of Bolingbroke's licence to inherit, issued when he went into exile, was now annulled and he was sentenced to perpetual banishment. Richard had always feared and resented his contemporary, and detested the thought that he might succeed him. But his animosity was more than personal. The Lancastrian inheritance represented the subjection of royal to baronial power in the person of Thomas of Lancaster, the arch-rebel against Edward II. If kingship was to be restored it had to be freed from the control of old magnate families and their place

[126] R. R. Davies, 'Richard II and the principality of Chester, 1397–9', in Du Boulay and Barron (eds.), *Reign of Richard II*, 256–79; T. Thornton, 'Cheshire: The inner citadel of Richard II's kingdom', in Dodd (ed.), *Reign of Richard II*, 85–96.

[127] Walker, *Lancastrian Affinity*, 36–7, 174–9, 228–32. For the similar challenge to the Berkeley lordship in Gloucestershire by Despenser, see Saul, *Richard II*, 442–3.

taken by those who owed their position solely to the king's will and favour.[128] To make and break the higher nobility was the ultimate mark of regality.

This was the root of Richard's perpetual hostility to John of Gaunt. It was based on a selective view of history and a misreading of Gaunt's character. Kingship was bred into John of Gaunt and was the focus of his life. He believed in the unique and unassailable nature of regality, in obedience to and reverence for it, and in its capacity for leading and unifying political society. His model was his father, whose style of governance he wished to see continued, but he had to face a painful adjustment to the decay of Edward's person and rule and to the duplicity and wilfulness of Richard's kingship. He never won acceptance for himself as a national leader: he was denied the role of regent, and his titular kingship of Castile made his position ambivalent. Loyalty to the throne was his guiding principle, but a loyalty tempered by pride in his own ancestry and by a quest for recognition of his princely status in the courts of Europe. Superior to and semi-detached from the English nobility, his overbearing and imperious personality won few allies and made many enemies. Those below the nobility he treated with disdain: the knights of the shires, the citizens of London, the upstart bishops, and the courtiers, all felt the lash of his tongue and the penalties of his anger. He scorned their politics, their conspiracies, their grievances, their belief in law and justice, their prescriptions for good government. For him government belonged to the king and nobility. There was much that linked him to the young king, and despite the frequent plots at court against him, he—unlike Thomas of Lancaster—shunned rebellion. His own wealth and status gave him a vested interest in the status quo, underpinned by his deep loyalty to the house of Plantagenet and the monarchy of Edward III. Had Richard been willing to trust Gaunt more, his reign could have been less tumultuous.[129]

The custody of the Lancastrian estates was parcelled out among the court nobility, making an immense aggregation of land in the hands of the king and his followers.[130] But their lordship represented a series of legal decisions; how it was exercised on the ground was another matter. It was bound to be fragile, for so drastic a revolution was a recipe for local instability. This may account for the exceptional measures which Richard took to enforce the loyalty of subjects. The sheriffs appointed in November 1397 numbered many who were royal retainers and were continued in office the following year; all were put under fresh oaths to arrest those speaking ill of the king. Oaths to uphold the acts of the Westminster and Shrewsbury parliaments and the later banishments were administered to ecclesiastics and officers of the major cities. In 1398 charters were extracted from

---

[128] Given-Wilson, 'Richard II, Edward II', 567; cf. *Rot. Parl.* iii. 355–6.

[129] Goodman, *John of Gaunt*, presents a more favourable verdict.

[130] *CPR, 1396–9*, 293–4, 296–7.

London and sixteen south-eastern counties which incorporated admissions of guilt for treason with carte blanche submissions to the king's grace; these could be used to extract large sums as fines or sureties (called La Pleasaunce) when Richard passed through. The king also sought to instil insecurity among those implicated in the events of 1386–8. In the 1397 parliament he gave notice of a secret list of fifty names from whom his pardon was withheld, and the general pardon purchased by the Commons' grant of 1398 had to be individually secured through payment of a heavy fine. The pardon rolls of 1397–9 contain almost 600 names of those who paid, while the men of Essex and Hertfordshire compounded for £2,000. In all the pardon could have yielded some £30,000.[131]

These financial penalties reflected the shortage of revenue occasioned by the absence of lay taxation since 1395. In August 1397 loans were demanded from numbers of subjects; these were not compulsory and most of those who lent did so to purchase the king's goodwill. By advancing the sum of 10,000 marks London received final confirmation of the liberties conditionally restored to it in 1392. In all some £22,000 was received by December, but no repayment was made at Easter 1398 as promised and the loan figured among the charges of tyranny brought after Richard's deposition. The balance of expenditure had now swung away from defence towards domestic costs. In the last three years of the reign the household departments were requiring £55,000 per annum, one-third higher even than under Edward III in 1360–9 and at least double the level in 1388–92. Richard's household had attained a new level of size and magnificence. More was also spent on the enlarged affinity, with a further twenty-five knights and a larger number of esquires retained in 1397–8. The total cost of annuities including those of the Cheshire guard was around £20,000. To sustain these levels of domestic costs Richard would need to secure an annual half fifteenth from parliament or intimidate it into granting a direct tax for his life.[132]

Yet the exchequer finances tell only half the story, for in these years Richard was accumulating a personal treasure of significant dimensions in his chamber. From Isabel's dowry, £83,333 out of a total of £133,333 had been received by 1399. The fines for pardons in 1398, perhaps amounting to £30,000, were paid into a special bag, and Richard, like his courtiers, indulged in asset-stripping the Appellants' estates. Arundel's treasure at Holt became the basis of Richard's reserve, heavily guarded by John Ikelyngton. In his will Richard mentions 65,000 marks (£44,000) in Ikelyngton's care and a further £16,000 in Thomas Holland's. An inventory of his jewels and plate, forty membranes long, includes crowns valued at £50,000. Richard's private treasure was about as large as that of

[131] C. Barron, 'The tyranny of Richard II', *BIHR* 41 (1968), 1–18; Saul, *Richard II*, 383–4, 388.

[132] Barron, 'Tyranny of Richard II'; Steel, *Receipt of the Exchequer*, p. 437, table B20, p. 447, table C2, p. 456, table D2; Given-Wilson, *Royal Household*, p. 94, table 3, and for the size and cost of the affinity, pp. 136, 214–15, 223, 310–11 nn. 48, 88.

Edward II though not so great as Edward III's. It was kept apart from the exchequer, for abnormal expenses.[133]

Surrounded by a nobility of his own creation, protected by a devoted body-guard and a swollen affinity, and controlling a substantial treasure, Richard's position appeared impregnable. Of his mode of government in these last two years we know little. He relied on a small and active group of counsellors: Aumale, Exeter, and Wiltshire among the nobility, with John Bussy, William Bagot, Henry Green, John Russell, knights, and two lawyers, Lawrence Dru and Ralph Selby, being later identified as the agents of his 'tyranny'. They met in council with the great officers in London, but in the last two years it was the court, with its large retinue, elaborate ritual, and numerous chaplains and bishops that provided the environment for Richard's rule. It is tempting to believe that its sycophantic atmosphere shielded Richard from an increasingly alienated and divided political community.[134]

In this context Richard's decision to take many of his favoured nobility and the greater part of his affinity to Ireland at the end of May 1399 revealed a fatal over-confidence in his regality. The Irish submissions of 1395 had proved hollow and his presence was now required to tread down the rebels. What he failed to appreciate was that his absence from England could equally call in question the paper settlement of 1397–9. The king's household formed the largest contingent, with those of Aumale, Exeter, Gloucester, Salisbury, Surrey, and Worcester making up the total force of around 5,000. It thus removed precisely those who had been invested with the forfeited estates and would have to mobilize their resources to face a challenge.

York had been left as regent with Wiltshire and the rest of the council, but there was no force under arms to oppose Henry of Lancaster, who, with the con-nivance of the duke of Orléans, sailed from Boulogne at the end of June with a small body of companions to recover his inheritance. He landed at Ravenspur (Spurn Head), hoping to raise his tenants on the duchy estates in Yorkshire. At that point Gaunt's old rival Northumberland could have intercepted him, but Richard had shown him no favours and on 16 July he, with the earl of Westmorland and Lord Willoughby (both Gaunt's supporters), joined him at Doncaster. It was here, with a sizeable force composed of Lancastrian retainers, that he proclaimed that he had come to claim his inheritance and establish sound counsel and good government. By 20 July he had reached Leicester, where he had to decide whether to make for London, Bristol, or Chester. The duke of York with perhaps some 3,300 men had moved westwards to where the king was

---

[133] *Royal Wills*, ed. J. Nichols (1780), 191–202; Rymer (ed.), *Foedera*, viii. 162–3; Saul, *Richard II*, 430; Stratford, 'Gold and diplomacy', 220–2.

[134] Baldwin, *King's Council*, 140–3; Given-Wilson, *Royal Household*, 180–7; *Eulog. Hist.* iii. 380.

expected from Milford Haven. Henry followed, catching up with him at Berkeley, where on 28 July he negotiated York's surrender along with that of his own half-brother Somerset. Next day Wiltshire, Bussy, and Green were extracted from Bristol and executed. Henry thus signalled his purpose: to purge Richard's government but to accept submission from any of the nobility.

News of Henry's landing had reached Richard in Ireland on 10 July. He had immediately dispatched Salisbury to Conwy to raise troops in North Wales and Cheshire but it took another ten days for his army to assemble and cross to Milford Haven around 20–4 July. There he ordered Gloucester to raise South Wales on his behalf, but this failed and news arrived of York's submission and Wiltshire's execution. Lacking sufficient force to confront Henry, Richard with his bodyguard made a cross-country dash to join Salisbury's army in the north. He arrived at Conwy on 4–5 August to find that rumours of his death had caused Salisbury's army to desert. His only remaining source of support was among the Cheshire gentry who had not accompanied him to Ireland, but by 5 August Henry had reached Shrewsbury and Cheshire sought his protection. When Henry entered Chester on 9 August Richard, at Conwy, had either to flee by ship—to Ireland or Bordeaux—or to negotiate. Henry now sent Northumberland to Richard with his terms: the restoration of his lands and the trial of Richard's supporters in parliament, including Exeter, Surrey, and Salisbury. Richard was to retain his crown but with Henry as the effective ruler. Richard accepted these terms and transferred himself to Northumberland's custody at Flint. Both sides were dissimulating, Richard planning to turn the tables on his captor, Henry certainly prepared for deposition.[135] Richard found himself kept closely captive as they moved south from Chester on 20 August, and his attempt to escape en route was foiled. London was reached on 1 September, the king was imprisoned in the Tower, and in the next fortnight a commission of lawyers was appointed to establish the grounds for his deposition and how it could be legally carried through.

Henry's success had depended on two things. First, Richard's delay in bringing his forces from Ireland and through Wales allowed Henry's advance across England to gather momentum and attract popular support. Secondly, Henry was leading a counter-revolution on behalf of the old retinue structures and could count on all who had been, or feared to be, dispossessed. Thus he was joined not only by the northern earls and his own duchy retainers but in the Midlands by those of the earl of Stafford and in Gloucestershire by Lord Berkeley. His return represented the victory of the Lancastrian (and baronial) over the royal affinity, even though battle was not joined. Parliament had been summoned, in Richard's

---

[135] For the sequence of Richard's return from Ireland, see Sherborne, *War, Politics and Culture*, 119–53, and the extracts from document nos. 11–15 in *Chron. Rev.*

name, to meet on 30 September, though the procedure of divesting him of the crown remained unsettled. An official account on the parliament roll, 'The Record and Process', subsequently produced a bland and sanitized picture of Richard transferring the crown and rule to Henry with a cheerful countenance, but other sources reveal his dogged insistence on the indelible nature of his kingship. On 28 September he was shown the charges brought against him of crimes against his subjects, and next day was asked to resign the crown. After some protest he did this, signing the deed with his own hand. But then, and after his resignation had been reported to parliament, he protested that he neither wished to nor could divest himself of 'the special dignities of a spiritual nature that had been bestowed upon him' through the sacred unction. He was claiming what he believed had been offered at Conwy: the retention of his kingship even while the rule of the kingdom was transferred to Henry. Next day the drama moved to parliament. The throne stood vacant, and indeed Richard's resignation had invalidated the parliament, which was now described as a meeting of the estates. Richard's resignation was read out and the assent of all present given. 'For greater security' they were asked to agree to his deposition, which they did. Sentence of this was read out and proctors from each estate next day renounced their homage and fealty. Richard spiritedly seized the last chance to affirm the indelibility of his kingship, and denied that he was unfit to rule. He had not been allowed any public opportunity to challenge the proceedings or be heard in his own defence, but of his belief in the divine sanction for his kingship and in the incapacity of subjects to judge or depose him he left no doubt. Yet whatever he might protest, most of Richard's subjects accepted that he had resigned and that they had passed sentence of deposition.[136]

Richard II's Kingship

Richard II's kingship has been the subject of much historical debate. How far did his emphasis on the sacral character and unfettered authority of royal rule stem from his own personality, and how far did it represent a valid and viable political system? What does it reveal about the late medieval polity and what was its effect upon it?

Let us start with Richard's personality, which certainly shaped his rule. The majority of chroniclers, writing after the deposition, are eloquent on his personal failings: his addiction to flattery, display, and extravagance; his impetuosity, volatility, temper, and deceit; his immaturity and possible sexual

---

[136] See extracts 15–18 in *Chron. Rev.*; with G. O. Sayles, 'The deposition of Richard II: Three Lancastrian narratives', *BIHR* 54 (1981), 257–70; C. Given-Wilson, 'The manner of King Richard's renunciation: A Lancastrian narrative?', *EHR* 108 (1993), 365–71.

ambivalence. On all of these evidence can be produced from his lifetime, but other qualities are also in evidence. Physically he was tall, and is described and portrayed as having golden hair, a round feminine face, with a long nose, heavy eyelids and flared nostrils. When not in full control of himself he was apt to stammer, speak abruptly, and flush easily. He was intelligent and read attentively, and was a connoisseur of artistic workmanship and architecture. Though unmilitary in temperament and probably not proficient in arms, he enjoyed presiding at tournaments. He combined a degree of political dexterity with courage and obstinacy in adversity. He had a mocking humour. Above all he fiercely defended his royal status and was unforgiving to those who affronted or invaded it.

This last was the defining element in his kingship, and it is reasonable to discern behind it a deep personal insecurity. On the roots of this one can only speculate: but his father's great reputation and early death had propelled him into a role for which he was ill equipped, and his isolation as a boy among an older generation of different outlook could have reinforced a consciousness of his different nature. His coronation gave him a sacral identity, protected by God and the saints, and infused his person and rule with a sense of mission and destiny. This is deliberately conveyed in the *Imago Christi* iconography of the Westminster portrait and in the multi-layered symbolism of the Wilton Diptych, depicting Richard receiving the divine commission to rule England. Though dating from the 1390s, both portraits represent the youthful king of his coronation. He is said to have wanted this re-enacted in 1398 with the rediscovered chrism reputed to have been delivered by the Virgin to St Thomas Becket.

The sacral quality of kingship defined his relations with his subjects and his political mission. Although some historians have seen the principles of Roman law as inspiring Richard's view of monarchy, it was more the Augustinian view of a world ordered and set at peace by obedience to God the Father that informed Richard's vision. Subjects were bound by obedience to him as God's surrogate, and on that obedience depended their individual and common good.[137] That was the condition of their rights and their political action. The religious quality of the obedience Richard demanded was manifested in the ritual of courtiers prostrating themselves at his gaze, in Speaker Bussy 'ascribing not human but divine honour to the king', and in the abject submission and adulation of the Londoners on his entry in 1392.

If Richard 'embraced a political theology', was this developed into a political programme? Richard saw his mission as restorative. As he told Bagot, he wished to be remembered as having 'recovered his dignity, regality and honourable estate' and to see it 'so lowly obeyed ... as it had been in any other king's

---

[137] This is the tenor of Bishop Stafford's sermon on obedience to the parliament of 1397 in which the king is described as a good father to his people; *Rot. Parl.* iii. 347.

time'.[138] To reverse the assault on the prerogative in 1386–8 was his political purpose for the next ten years, and he celebrated its accomplishment in exultant letters to foreign rulers in 1398.[139] Yet there are indications that this formed part of a wider and longer-term view of political structures. Richard had a clear if selective historical perspective, seeing his kingship in the context of both Edward II and Edward the Confessor. The former had likewise defended the Crown against rebellious magnates, and Richard looked to vindicate him by procuring his canonization. The latter had invested royal rule with sanctity and had sought peace and justice for his subjects. He saw these reigns as offering a prescription for the problems of his own day.[140]

Richard had hardly defined his political attitudes before 1386, but he believed that the magnates of his father's generation who surrounded him had, over the previous ten years and more, misruled his kingdom. They had perpetuated a war with France with no success, inflating their retinues and burdening the community with heavy taxation, which provoked popular insurrection. At times, as in 1376 and during his minority, they had accepted criticism from, and conceded royal rights to, the Commons in the name of accountability. Finally, they had abased the Crown in the name of reform in 1386 and defeated it through their retinues in 1387. Instead of being pillars of its authority they had sought to pull it down. Their rebellion called not merely for revenge on them but for the reshaping of the whole political culture. In Richard's eyes his grandfather's partnership with the chivalric class, based on the plunder of France, was discredited both by its military failure and by its political consequences. Warfare of this kind had no attraction for him; it brought no political rewards, it impoverished the Crown and realm, and strengthened the independence of the magnates. The cessation of war would free the Crown from military dependence on the greater magnates and financial dependence on parliament. When the moment came (in 1397–9) royal power could replace the old magnate inheritances and remodel the peerage. With that went the dissolution of their retinues, whose settled loyalties gave them influence over local government, the creation of a royal affinity, and the assertion of control over sheriffs and JPs as royal agents. The new order, having ended baronial rebellion, could bring internal peace, order, and justice to subjects—though this for the present remained an aspiration. The cessation of war taxation in turn deprived the parliamentary Commons of opportunities for criticism or control of royal government in the name of the common profit. As

---

[138] *Chron. Lond.* 52, cited and discussed by S. K. Walker, 'Richard II's view on kingship', in Archer and Walker (eds.), *Rulers and Ruled*, 49–63.

[139] To Manuel Paleologus and William of Bavaria; see Myers (ed.), *EHD* 174; Saul, *Richard II*, 386–7; Walker, 'Richard II's view on kingship', 60.

[140] W. M. Ormrod, 'Richard II's sense of English history', in Dodd (ed.), *Reign of Richard II*, 97–110.

Richard made clear to Bagot, parliament was to do his will or he would dissolve it and execute its leaders. If taxes were needed they would be procured by intimidation, not concessions.

In sum, this was a programme for replacing the old 'war culture', which had bonded the Crown and the chivalric class in a common purpose, with a 'peace culture', in which the royal will stood above the political order and regulated it as God's vicegerent. It is, perhaps, doubtful whether Richard formulated this as a historical analysis or a political programme. Although he extolled wisdom (*sapientia*) in a ruler, he had neither the intellectual range of Charles V nor the political pragmatism of Henry VII or Louis XI. His policies were driven by his quest for personal fulfilment in a kingship restored to a theoretical and mythical plenitude. Richard was an ideologue, but one who saw clearly the way to realize his vision in the political circumstances of his time. And the fact that the Edwardian war culture was, by the 1380s, discredited provided him with the opportunity to replace it. Although his new kingship was soon to be swept away, it did not lack support. Richard's theology of kingship clearly attracted some clerics and writers, who saw it as the channel and model of divine order, and some of these later became martyrs for their belief. It also attracted the ambitious, the able, and the sycophants at all levels of political society for whom royal service and favour was the swiftest ladder to the top. Some of these were subsequently ready to adjust to a different king. Thirdly, Richard's policy could have won support from the parliamentary Commons with the prospect of greatly decreased taxation for defence and the promise of law enforcement and containment of the abuses of retaining. Given a further decade, his model of kingship might have acquired political acceptance and constitutional legitimacy, but in 1399 it commanded neither. His dominance rested on factionalism among the nobility and autocratic control of an emasculated parliament. In both these respects the royal power had become isolated from its political roots.[141]

8. LEGITIMATION AND CONSENT, 1399–1406

The deposition of Richard II changed the character of the English polity in at least four respects. It changed the practice of kingship and the basis for royal rule. It restored the old magnate families, their inheritances, and their political culture. It affirmed the political role acquired by parliament over the last quarter-century. It jeopardized the culture of peace. In none of these respects could Henry IV's counter-revolution simply revert to the position preceding Richard's personal rule. That had engendered division and distrust of which Henry was

[141] For a fuller exploration of the character of Richard's kingship, see Saul, *Richard II*, 439 ff., and id., 'The kingship of Richard II', in Goodman and Gillespie (eds.), *Richard II*, 37–57.

ineluctably the heir. It took the first six years of Henry's reign for the legacy of 1397–9 to be dissolved, for Lancastrian kingship to be validated, and relations with the magnates and parliament normalized.

Richard II's abdication and deposition had been framed as a judgement on his rule—a judgement by subjects, even if sanctioned by natural law. His insistence that he retained his indelible, sacral kingship had been ignored, but could even his death transfer this to his usurper? Henry IV was not Richard's natural heir, nor even his designated or legal one. Although he could assert his descent from Henry III in the male line, that drew attention to the claim of the earl of March, descended in the female line from Gaunt's elder brother Lionel of Clarence. Edward III had indeed preferred Gaunt's right of succession, but England acknowledged no 'Salic law' debarring women from the Crown, as in France, and any attempt to introduce one would vitiate the Plantagenet claim to the French Crown.[142] But if Henry was unable to establish a watertight claim by lineal descent, in practical terms his case was unchallengeable. For the earl of March was a mere 8 years old, and only in subsequent years did he emerge as the focus for conspiracies.

In default of a decisive lineal right, Henry claimed divine sanction for the overthrow of tyranny. Chief Justice Thirning deflected him from talk of conquest, which might be taken to jeopardize subjects' rights, and in the outcome Henry 'challenged' (against any other claimant) the vacant throne,

as I that am descended by right line of the blood coming from the good lord King Henry the Third and through that right that God of his grace has sent me with the help of my kin and of my friends to recover it; the which realm was in point to be undone for default of governance and undoing of the good laws,

and explicitly affirmed that his 'conquest' would not abrogate property rights.[143] The fact that Henry's claim was acknowledged by acclamation and sanctified by the ritual of coronation, in which the Holy Oil of the Virgin was now used, could not obscure its uncertain basis. Both Henry and Archbishop Arundel, who masterminded the formulation of Henry's title, were determined to avoid debate on it in or by parliament. But in practice Henry had been formally accepted by the peers, who individually swore allegiance, and on at least two subsequent occasions he justified his kingship in terms of his 'election'. All these elements of Henry's title were embodied in the carefully formulated parliamentary 'Record and Process', which was echoed by Lancastrian apologists like Usk, Gower, and Chaucer:[144]

---

[142] P. McNiven, 'Legitimacy and consent: Henry IV and the Lancastrian title, 1399–1406', *Medieval Studies*, 44 (1982), 470–88; Bennett, 'Edward III's entail and the succession to the crown'.

[143] *Rot. Parl.* iii. 415–24; *Chron. Rev.* 172–86.

[144] P. Strohm, 'Chaucer's Purse and the fabrication of the Lancastrian claim', in Hanawalt (ed.), *Chaucer's England*, 21–40.

O conquerour of Brutes Albyon
Which that by lyne and free eleccion
Been verray king, this song to you I sende.

(Chaucer, 'To his Purse')

Similarly the full justification for Richard's deposition was set out in the detailed list of his unjust acts: the destruction of his greater nobility (arts. 2–4, 11–12, 23, 33), the oppression of other subjects (arts. 4–5, 7, 13–14, 18, 20, 26–8), the perversion of government (arts. 13, 18–19), prodigality with the Crown estate (arts. 1, 15), the oppression of the Church (arts. 22, 30, 33), placing himself above the law (arts. 16–17), and acting deceitfully (art. 25). As the deliverer of the realm from Richard's tyranny, Henry sought to legitimate his rule by good government. Archbishop Arundel underlined this by contrasting Richard's immature and wilful rule with the wisdom and reason with which Henry would uphold justice, the law, and individual liberties. At the opening of parliament a week later he affirmed that Henry wished 'not to be governed by his own will or purpose or private opinion but by common advice, counsel and assent'.

Although Henry denigrated and distanced himself from Richard's kingship, he could not ignore its legitimacy. While Richard lived, there was the threat that he might be rescued and reinstated, but even after his death at Pontefract in February 1400, probably by starvation, and his burial obscurely at King's Langley, his suppressed kingship provided an alternative image and focus for loyalty. Impostors might have little credibility and even the rumour that Richard lived soon faded, but from 1402 to 1405 adherence to Richard as true king persisted among lesser folk, including priests and friars, and was punished as treason.[145] Yet generally it was not so much the flaws in Henry's title as the flaws in his rule which generated discontent, and these reflected the political instability bequeathed by Richard's revolution.

Only with difficulty did Henry contain the welter of accusations and recriminations brought against the remnant of Richard's nobility in the parliament of October 1399. He sought to pacify, not inflame, the hatreds of 1397–9, and though the Counter-Appellants were stripped of the titles and lands they had acquired, no blood was shed. Yet they were now political outcasts, dishonoured, impoverished, and exiled from royal favour. Their only hope lay in the restoration of Richard II, and as Christmas approached Huntingdon, Kent, Rutland, Salisbury, and Despenser met under the roof of the abbot of Westminster to plot the seizure of Henry and his sons under cover of the Twelfth Night festivities at

[145] P. McNiven, 'Rebellion, sedition and the legend of Richard II's survival', *BJRL* 76 (1994), 93–117; S. K. Walker, 'Rumour, sedition, and popular protest in the reign of Henry IV', *P & P* 166 (2000), 31–65; P. Morgan, 'Henry IV and the shadow of Richard II', in Archer (ed.), *Crown, Government and People*, 1–31.

Windsor. That was to signal the raising of their own tenants, along with risings in Cheshire, Derbyshire, and the West Country.[146] Only on the night of 4 January was their plot betrayed, probably by Rutland, Henry making his escape to London, where he hired troops. The rebel earls then retreated to the west hoping to meet the forces they had summoned. At Cirencester the earls of Kent and Salisbury were seized and beheaded by the townsfolk; Despenser, trying to escape via Bristol, suffered a similar fate; while Huntingdon was summarily executed at Pleshey on the orders of Arundel's sister Joan, countess of Hereford. The failure of the plot sealed Richard's fate, but it showed that numbers of his supporters remained unreconciled to Henry's usurpation.

The deaths of the Ricardian earls strengthened Henry's position but left him with a depleted nobility. For the heirs of Holland, Montague, Despenser, Mortimer, and Mowbray were all minors, while those of the earls of Arundel, Warwick, and Stafford were only just coming of age. Among the active and adult upper nobility York and his son Rutland were suspect, and Henry was dependent on his half-brother John Beaufort, earl of Somerset, his brother-in-law Ralph Neville, earl of Westmorland, and the might of the Percys. Their control of the northern marches and North Wales and Chester was complemented by their frequent attendance at court and council and participation in the king's personal diplomacy. For a time Percy influence was excluded from the household, where Somerset was chamberlain, until in March 1401 Thomas Percy, earl of Worcester, was appointed its steward.[147]

The lack of a numerous, established, and loyal upper nobility distorted the working of the polity. At the centre it concentrated military and political influence in too few hands; in the localities—particularly over wide areas of central and southern England—the absence of adult magnates deprived political society of its natural leaders, able to exercise control and act as channels of communication to the king. With gentry affinities divided and destabilized by Richard's revolution, seditious rumours rife, and conspiracies at all levels, the danger of a collapse of royal authority was real. Henry's single answer to these problems was a massive enlargement of the royal affinity. Following the advice of his council, he began to recruit the leading gentry in each shire, so that by 1406 he had retained 110 knights and more than 100 esquires. The wearing of the Lancastrian collar of esses now became a sign of loyalty to the dynasty and of royal favour to the wearer. The kernel was a group of Lancastrian baronial families: Grey of Codnor, Grey of Ruthin, Greystoke, Roos, Heron of Say, Willoughby, and Berkeley. They served at court, on council, as ambassadors, and

---

[146] P. McNiven, 'The Cheshire rising of 1400', *BJRL* 52 (1969–70), 375–96; D. Crook, 'Central England and the revolt of the earls, January 1400', *Hist. Res.* 64 (1991), 403–10; *Chron. Rev.* 224–39.

[147] A. L. Brown, 'The reign of Henry IV', in Chrimes *et al.* (eds.), *Fifteenth Century England*, 6–12.

as soldiers. Leading household knights were the focuses of loyalty in their shires: Thomas Erpingham in Norfolk, Thomas Rempston in Nottinghamshire, John Pelham in Sussex, and Walter Blount in Derbyshire. Yorkshire had a particularly heavy concentration of king's knights—seventeen by 1403—and the grant of the lordship of Richmond to the earl of Westmorland facilitated an interweaving of the Lancastrian and Neville affinities. The financial cost was high, annuities from exchequer revenues being estimated in 1401 as £24,000 per annum, with another £8,000 from the duchy of Lancaster estates. While Henry was purchasing loyalty, he was also calming fears by offering a pardon to all but a few individuals. To make his own usurpation acceptable it was necessary to confirm the property and inheritances of his subjects on an extensive scale.[148]

In military terms the huge royal affinity provided a reserve which could be mobilized for emergencies. Its potential was demonstrated in the expedition to Scotland in August 1400, and over the next five years it was called on to deal with revolt and conspiracy in Wales and the north. It was also used to lead and control political society in lowland England. Thus in East Anglia, where minorities in the comital families of March, Mowbray, and de Vere created a vacuum, a newly fledged affinity under Sir Thomas Erpingham assumed leadership.[149] In many shires it took control of the shire offices, effecting a wholesale shift of power in local elites. Even before Henry entered London in August 1399 he had replaced Richard's sheriffs in seven counties with Lancastrian retainers, and at least a dozen royal retainers held shrievalties in both 1400–1 and 1401–2. On the peace commissions issued in November 1399 over 90 per cent of the knights and esquires appointed were loyal Lancastrians, half of them for the first time.[150] The returns to Henry's first parliament, in October 1399, present a similar picture. A mere 11 per cent were re-elected from the parliament of 1397; indeed over half the members of that parliament were never to sit under Henry IV. While former Ricardians were excluded, twenty-two Lancastrian retainers and a further seventeen adherents of the old Appellants were returned in 1399. The shire establishments thus bore witness to the cleavage in the political class.[151] Henry depended on his affinity not only for military security and local control but also in government, where they occupied important offices: John Norbury as treasurer, Thomas Rempston as steward of the household and constable of the Tower, Thomas Erpingham as under-chamberlain and constable of Dover.

[148] Given-Wilson, *Royal Household*, 226–34; Brown, 'Reign of Henry IV', 5, 19–20.

[149] The effect of the usurpation at county level which Brown, in 1972, noted as being 'a large subject for investigation' ('The reign of Henry IV'), has still barely begun to be studied, except by S. J. Payling for Nottinghamshire and H. Castor for Staffordshire–Derbyshire and Norfolk.

[150] D. Biggs, 'Sheriffs and justices of the peace: The pattern of Lancastrian governance, 1399–1401', *Nott. Med. Stud.* 40 (1996), 149–66.

[151] *House of Commons*, i. 209.

Others, notably Sir John Cheyne, John Curson, John Doreward, and John Frome, were working members of the council.[152] Some, but not all, were members of Henry's household, whose thirty-five chamber knights gave it a predominantly military character, with fewer clerks and chaplains than in Richard II's.

If Henry's nervous reliance on his affinity was understandable in the aftermath of the usurpation, by 1401 there was a growing reaction against the partisan character of his rule and the accumulation of rewards by his retainers. There were vivid and recent memories of the oppressions committed by wearers of Richard's livery of the white hart which, in the poet's conceit, had lost him the hearts of the people. A petition to the parliament of 1401 complained that the distribution of badges and livery provoked divisions among loyal subjects who should be governed equally under the king as 'one nation' (*entier comyn*), and called for a complete abolition of the practice.[153] The growing disillusion with Henry's rule, voiced by Philip Repingdon in a somewhat apocalyptic open letter to the king, was fuelled by the revolt in Wales and disagreements with the Percys. In November 1401 Henry had appointed Thomas Percy, earl of Worcester, lieutenant in South Wales and governor of Prince Henry's household. But by 1402 Henry was becoming distrustful of the Percys' wish to negotiate with Glyn Dŵr and suspected they were conniving with him. To offset their dominance he invested the young earls of Arundel and Stafford and Lord Grey of Codnor with commands in the Welsh marches, and in the spring of 1403 capped this by making Prince Henry his lieutenant in Wales with his own retinue. By then his relations with Northumberland in the north were moving towards crisis. Henry was frustrating Northumberland's ambition to secure the lowland estates of the earl of Douglas, forbidding the ransoming of Douglas, and refusing his demand for £20,000 owed him for the wardenship of the marches.[154] In mid-July, as Henry with an army was marching northwards, Hotspur and Worcester came out in revolt in Wales. Had they been able to raise Wales and Cheshire, capture the prince, and trap the king between their forces and Northumberland's, they might have been successful. As it was, Henry with his North Midlands affinity was able to join Prince Henry at Shrewsbury with a sizeable army. Hotspur's appeal to the Ricardian loyalties of Cheshire, his endorsement of the earl of March's claim to the throne, and the size and severity of the battle marked it as the decisive challenge to Henry's usurpation. It was the battle which Richard's Cheshire retinue had not been given the chance to fight in 1399.[155] After his

---

[152] A. L. Brown, 'The Commons and council in the reign of Henry IV', *EHR* 79 (1964), 1–30.

[153] Saul, 'The Commons and the abolition of badges', 302–15; *Mum and the Sothsegger*, 8.

[154] J. M. W. Bean, 'Henry IV and the Percies', *History*, 44 (1959), 212–27; see also below, Ch. 13, sect. 3.

[155] For the battle, Morgan, *War and Society in Medieval Cheshire*, 207–18; see also below, Ch. 13, sect. 2.

victory Henry was urged to take revenge, to 'slay and burn'; but he preferred to pardon, fine the county £2,000, and recruit Cheshire men into Prince Henry's retinue. He had broken the power of the Percys, who had brought him to the throne. Hotspur had perished, Worcester was captured and executed, and Northumberland submitted, surrendering his castles and offices, though he was later pardoned. A further abortive coup in 1405 finally precipitated his forfeiture and flight to Scotland. The Neville–Lancastrian affinities now controlled the north.

After 1403 Henry's rule was not seriously threatened in England. His sons were achieving manhood and assisting in his rule; Somerset, his younger brother Thomas Beaufort, and Westmorland were soldiers of courage and resource, as were the young earls of Warwick and Arundel, all forming a new peerage wholly committed to the Lancastrian dynasty. Henry was also promoting outstanding administrators to the offices of state: Henry Beaufort, bishop of Winchester, as chancellor, Thomas Langley as keeper of the privy seal and then chancellor, Thomas Neville, Lord Furnival, as treasurer. Only in his relations with the Church was there a degree of tension and ambivalence. Archbishop Arundel had wholeheartedly supported his usurpation and in 1401 Church and Crown joined to pass a statute to burn relapsed heretics, Lollardy and sedition being seen as closely linked, at least at the lower levels of society. Among the knights of the household it was perhaps otherwise, for a vehement anticlericalism flourished among the hard-bitten soldiers who cast covetous eyes on the wealth and comfort of the clergy when their own wages and supplies ran short during the slog of the Welsh campaigns. At Worcester in 1403 they suggested seizing the bishops' horses and sending them home on foot when they refused to lend money. A year later there was a demand in parliament for the resumption of the Church's wealth, and there were incidents when household knights openly mocked its spiritual authority. It was they, too, who insisted on the execution of Archbishop Scrope as a rebel in 1405 against Arundel's desperate plea to the king to respect clerical immunity. Although Scrope's rising posed no military threat, it high-lighted the persisting complaints against Lancastrian rule: over the level of tax-ation, the hostility to the Church, the greed of the royal entourage, the partisanship provoked by the rise of Neville. These were not easily discounted, for they closely echoed the charges brought against Richard II's tyranny. The archbishop believed he was acting for the common good.[156] This discontent formed the background to Henry's relations with parliament.

[156] For anticlericalism and Lollardy, see above, Ch. 10, sects. 4, 5; for Archbishop Scrope's rising, see S. K. Walker, 'The Yorkshire risings of 1405: Texts and contexts', in G. Dodd and D. Biggs (eds.), *Henry IV: The Establishment of the Regime, 1399–1406* (Woodbridge, 2003), 161–84; Strohm, 'Chaucer's Purse', 32–62.

Both king and Commons began the new reign with high expectations. Half the members of the 1399 parliament had sat before 1397, a solid core before 1389, and these looked to restore parliament's function as the critical monitor of royal government. In the first three parliaments they used the instrument of the common petition to present no fewer than 180 bills. They likewise expected the king to seek taxation only for a common necessity, as Henry had promised, and not as Richard had done for his own use.[157] Henry was seen as the reformer and restorer of good governance and individual rights. The king, for his part, was determined not to treat criticism as a challenge to the prerogative, as Richard had, but as a constructive dialogue, and was alert to the danger of uniting the Lords and the Commons against him. Yet in the years following all these intentions were frustrated.

The root cause of Henry's problems was an immediate and steep plunge into insolvency. The evidence of this is clear in the exchequer records. Its effective revenue in 1399–1402 was £26,000 per annum lower than in 1392–8, and comparable with that in 1388–92. This reflected the initial suspension of direct taxation and tunnage and poundage until 1401 and a steep decline in wool exports from 17,500 sacks per annum in 1395–8 to 15,000 sacks per annum in 1398–1402 and to 12,000 sacks per annum in 1402–7.[158] For this there were a number of causes: privateering in the Channel and the threat to Calais, the acute bullion shortage which restricted credit, and the growth of cloth exports. In 1401, faced with escalating military costs in Wales and for the defence of Gascony, Calais, and the coasts, Henry asked for direct taxation; tunnage and poundage was restored, and in four of the following five years taxes were levied. That did something to counter the decline of the customs, but with expenditure increasing, the exchequer was forced into issuing tallies against future revenue, producing an unprecedented surge of failed tallies and a consequent collapse of exchequer credit in the years 1401–4.[159] Huge arrears of wages built up to garrisons at Calais, in the northern marches, and the Welsh castles.

As well as the decline in taxation, Crown revenues had been depleted by grants of annuities to royal retainers and the transfer of receipts from Wales, Chester, and Cornwall to the prince of Wales; then in 1403 Henry's new queen was provided with a dower of 10,000 marks. The household therefore had less to draw on, yet it was almost as large as that of Richard II and it was serving as an immediate treasury for a king facing recurrent emergencies. The cost of all the domestic departments, at £41,700 per annum in 1399–1403 and £32,300 per annum in 1403–6, was only a little less than in 1395–9, and the Commons were convinced

---

[157] *House of Commons*, i. 209–17; *Rot. Parl.* iii. 439–46, 468–79, 494–511.

[158] Steel, *Receipt of the Exchequer*, pp. 447–8, tables C2–3; Carus-Wilson and Coleman, *England's Export Trade*, 54–6, 122.

[159] Steel, *Receipt of the Exchequer*, 457. Henry also borrowed heavily in 1400 and 1402.

that it was run neither economically nor honestly.[160] Above all they were angered by the failure to pay for the goods which purveyors took from ordinary people and which merchants supplied on credit, when the exchequer was unable to honour the wardrobe's debentures. The accumulated debt of successive keepers had reached around £30,000 by 1405, and because the wardrobe's insolvency impacted on a wide range of people it became a symbol of the discredit and disarray of Henry's rule.[161]

The king's demand for taxation and the Commons' demand for economical government in the household involved important constitutional principles. The Commons tried to insist on the occasional nature of direct taxation by reserving it for particular emergencies. They protested that the cost of suppressing rebellion in Wales should fall on the marcher lords, who held their lands and privileges for this purpose, while the customs should be used for the defence of the sea and garrisons. The costs of the household should be reduced and met not from the customs and direct taxes but from the revenues of the Crown—its lands and fiscal profits. These had been too lavishly granted away, in annuities and rents, and needed to be harboured and if necessary resumed. In response to the king's demands, the Commons sought to impose this programme on Crown finance. They placed the land tax granted in March 1404, and both direct and indirect taxes granted in October 1404, under special treasurers accountable to the next parliament. They repeatedly urged the king to restrain his grants, won the promise of a year's moratorium on the payment of annuities in March 1404, and vainly demanded a resumption of all grants in 1399 and October 1404. They were promised a reduction of the household in March 1404 and tried to limit it to a fixed sum from certain sources of revenue. The Commons were not uninformed critics: members of the king's household and council sat in parliament and three of them were Speaker. In 1401 and 1404 the Commons asked for the council to be named and if possible charged in the parliament so that it could be brought to answer next time. They hoped that, through sound council, the king would provide 'good governance'. But all this was mostly ineffective. Henry was ready with promises—to live of his own and limit his gifts—but broke them repeatedly. Household costs fell slightly after 1403 but it continued to amass huge debts, Crown revenues were not restored, royal patronage was not limited, and the king retained effective control over the spending of the subsidies. Above all he had secured the grant of four fifteenths and a land tax in five years.

The parliament of 1406 proved a watershed.[162] When it met on 1 March it

---

[160] Given-Wilson, *Royal Household*, p. 94, table 3, apps. I, III.

[161] For this and the following paragraph, see A. Rogers, 'Henry IV, the Commons and taxation', *Medieval Studies*, 31 (1969), 44–70; Given-Wilson, *Royal Household*, ch. 2.

[162] *Rot. Parl.* iii. 567–91; *Select Docs.* 217–25. Differing interpretations are given by A. L. Brown, 'The Commons and the council', esp. 12–24; by A. J. Pollard, 'The Lancastrian constitutional

contained a core of royal annuitants—some thirty-five have been identified—
and it elected a household knight, Sir John Tiptoft, as Speaker. Neglecting the
chancellor's plea for a general tax, the Commons allocated money for a fleet
under merchant control to protect shipping. During the Easter recess Henry suffered what was probably a premonitory stroke which made him unable to open,
or probably even attend, the second session. Without the presence of an active
king ministers did not have the weight and authority to press for taxation. Even
when, on 22 May, the king acknowledged his inability to rule as he wished and
named a council with control over all financial warrants, this did not win the confidence of the Commons, who at the end of the session were still asking for 'good
governance' through a reduction of the household, a cessation of grants, and
measures to increase Crown revenue. Henry spent the summer visiting shrines
and doctors in East Anglia, and when parliament resumed in October it
embarked on the lengthy and obscure process of establishing a form of government during the king's incapacity and one which would command confidence in
parliament and beyond in its ability to provide 'good governance'. In this the
phalanx of royal retainers was vital in bridging the gap between a new aristocratic
ruling council, to whom the king entrusted authority, and the representatives of
the ruled, who were seeking firm guarantees. These were eventually provided in
thirty-one articles, presented by the Speaker on behalf of the king, Lords, and
Commons. Two of the Commons' central demands were accepted: for a complete moratorium on all grants from Crown revenues and a verifiable reduction
in the cost of the household, for which Tiptoft's appointment as its treasurer
provided some assurance. It only remained to ensure the reservation of the subsidy for defence, and in the last days of parliament the Commons tried to bind the
councillors to refund it if it was misspent. For the king that was too much; he
exploded in anger and the Commons gave way.

The parliament marked a political watershed in three ways. First, it set the
pattern of government for most of Henry's remaining years, during which he
relinquished rule to an aristocratic council. Secondly, this council publicly
adopted a programme of good governance which gradually achieved political
and financial stability and restored confidence. Thirdly, the settlement validated
the Commons' role as loyal critics and reformers and laid to rest the spectre of
parliament as a treasonous opposition to the Crown manipulated by a factious
nobility, raised by the events of 1386–8. The Commons perforce looked to the
Lords to secure reforms from the Crown, but in 1406 the Lords distanced themselves from a political alliance with the Commons, so that Henry was able to

experiment revisited: Henry IV, Sir John Tiptoft and the parliament of 1406', *Parlty. Hist.* 14
(1995), 103–19; and by D. Biggs, 'The politics of health: Henry IV and the long parliament of 1406',
in Dodd and Biggs (eds.), *Henry IV*, 185–205.

surrender authority to a commission–council of loyal magnates who remained answerable to him. Freed from any imputation of treason, they could endorse the reforms sought by the Commons as purely financial and administrative measures, detached from prerogative and high politics. The Commons, equally, had not sought to determine the membership of the king's household and council. They had emerged as custodians of the common profit, underpinning the governing process by their representative assent.

9. THE KING AND THE PRINCE, 1407–1413

The removal of government from the king's hands to those of the council solved some problems but raised others. Henry's generosity was curtailed and household costs were reduced. If Henry accepted his displacement grudgingly, his resentment was directed more at the Commons, whom he distrusted for the rest of the reign, than at the council, whose leader, Archbishop Arundel, had his entire confidence. The council wished to sustain the royal dignity and prerogative; it did not want to be the instrument of parliament, and at its request the king released it from the oath to the thirty-one articles in 1407. The prospects for its government were good. The gradual mastery of the revolt in Wales, the subsiding of domestic opposition, and the preoccupation of foreign enemies with their own quarrels, all permitted greater concentration on domestic matters. The decrease in the costs of both defence and the household enabled the council to tackle the perennial insolvency by planning expenditure in relation to revenue and gradually to re-establish exchequer credit. Likewise, a better political balance emerged as the depleted ranks of the upper nobility were filled by a new generation reaching maturity. Seven earls were summoned to the parliament of 1406, and their natural leader was Prince Henry. There were elements of instability in this situation, for the king's inability to be the focus for unity induced increasing division in the council between followers of the archbishop and the prince, aggravated by the sick king's fear of being supplanted by his heir.

In 1407 the council was a unified and determined body, with indisputable authority and a mandate to restore royal finance and public confidence in government. It 'set about its task in four ways. The paths through which royal financed flowed were rationalized and conciliar control over them strengthened; priorities were established among spending areas; both the costs of the household and provision for them were reduced; and allocations for defence were planned with meticulous care.'[163] It could now give priority to military expenditure, and in March 1407 authorized payments for the main military charges,

[163] E. Wright, 'Henry IV, the Commons, and the recovery of royal finance in 1407', in Archer and Walker (eds.), *Rulers and Ruled*, 65–82, esp. 71 ff.

totalling £20,000, from the lay fifteenth. The household was now reduced, its costs cut by 10 per cent, and over half of its receipts were now drawn from the Crown revenues. The council was able to face the Commons in the October parliament at Gloucester and proclaim its good stewardship, outflanking the Speaker's demand to account for the previous subsidy. The council had decided it needed one fifteenth and a half, and although the Commons protested that they had the sole right to decide and grant a tax, yet that is what they granted, spread over the next three years. The council could now plan its financial strategy until 1410.[164]

The practice of holding a budgetary review at the beginning of the year, on the basis of which allocations were made from specified revenues for the charges of defence and the household, was repeated in 1408 and 1409 with increasing sophistication.[165] Estimates of revenue and expenditure were based on an average over previous years, and allocations made by detailed assignments on particular sources, indicating a close coordination between the council and the exchequer. Though in 1408 the largest sum was still assigned for operations in Wales, the council had begun to draw on direct taxes for household costs. In 1408 £7,000 and in 1409 £10,000 were formally approved by the council as part of the £16,000 allocated to the household. That flouted the Commons' principle that the household should be supported solely from Crown revenues, but it brought its finances into balance and enabled it to repay some of its debts. It is not clear who should be credited with the experiment in financial planning in the years 1407–9. The techniques were all familiar to the exchequer; the vital element was conciliar direction, and for this the credit probably rests with Archbishop Arundel.

For eighteen months after the parliament of 1407 Arundel remained effective head of the council, with the king increasingly dependent on his political and spiritual guidance. It was Arundel, with the duke of York, Bishop Langley, and Tiptoft, who witnessed Henry's will at the height of his illness in January 1409, an illness which brought both Prince Henry and his brother Thomas to the king's bedside.[166] By the summer of 1409 Prince Henry was regularly attending council and asserting his own financial priorities. The mounting divisions within it came into the open when, on 11 December, Tiptoft resigned as treasurer to be followed ten days later by Archbishop Arundel as chancellor. This marked the displacement of the king's friends, including Langley, by the group of younger nobility

[164] *Rot. Parl.* iii. 608–12. For comment, Roskell, *House of Commons*, 132–3; McNiven, *Heresy and Politics*, 179–84.

[165] For what follows I have used T. E. F. Wright, 'Royal finance in the latter part of the reign of Henry IV of England, 1406–1413', D.Phil. thesis (Oxford University, 1984).

[166] *Royal Wills*, 203; P. McNiven, 'The problem of Henry IV's health, 1405–13', *EHR* 100 (1985), 747–72.

who had been the companions of Prince Henry in Wales: the earls of Arundel and Warwick, and Lords Charlton of Powys, Grey of Codnor, and Grey of Ruthin. The Beauforts formed a bridge between the two, for one brother—Bishop Henry of Winchester—was a close adviser to the prince, while another—Thomas—was in the king's household.[167] On 6 January the prince's friend Lord Scrope of Masham was appointed treasurer, and when parliament assembled on 27 January the Beauforts' cousin Thomas Chaucer was again chosen to be Speaker. Later in the session Thomas Beaufort was made chancellor, probably as a compromise. The fact that the king had been unable to sustain his personal friends in office was indicative of his political and physical weakness, but the prince was not mounting a challenge to his father. As heir apparent, he wanted to lead the council.

The prince's administration was thus installed and faced its first test in dealing with the Commons. The high proportion of members attached to the prince and his associates reflected their local influence, but the management of the assembled parliament proved more difficult. It may have been the prince's demand for taxation—reported as being an annual subsidy—that provoked the presentation of a Lollard bill to confiscate the Church's temporalities in order to fund new peerages, endow almshouses and universities, and provide the king with £20,000. It was not endorsed by Prince Henry, nor is it certain that it was adopted by the Commons, for all record of it was removed from the rolls. Arundel counter-attacked by staging a show trial of an obscure Lollard tailor called John Badby. The prince used it to demonstrate his own orthodoxy.[168]

With the first session ending on this note of high drama, the second got down to business. The Commons presented eighteen articles on the theme of good governance and asked for a council to be named and sworn in parliament, those so named on 2 May being the prince's associates. They granted three half fifteenths over the next three years, and tacitly endorsed the council's use of taxes for household costs by reserving 20,000 marks for the king's use. Though they had granted less than the prince wanted, they had given a cautious welcome to his rule.[169]

The prince could now implement his financial priorities, notably the reservation of three-quarters of the wool subsidy for the Calais garrison, of which he was captain. The household was again to be provided with £16,000, much of it from taxation, and other defence costs trimmed to ensure a balanced budget. In March 1411 a further financial review confirmed this pattern and reaffirmed the emphasis on solvency. Assignments were now generally effective and exchequer credit was sound. The corollary of this was to reduce defence spending by

---

[167] Harriss, *Cardinal Beaufort*, 48–9.
[168] *House of Commons*, i. 218–24; *St Albans Chron.* 53–5; above, Ch. 10, sect. 4.
[169] *Rot. Parl.* iii. 623–7, 635.

negotiating long-term truces with hostile powers, namely Burgundy (to 1413), Scotland (to 1418), and Brittany (to 1420). A vigorous campaign against the English pirates John Prendergast and William Longe underpinned a maritime truce. Only in Gascony and Picardy did the truce remain temporary. At this point, midsummer 1411, the prince's rule seemed to fulfil the Commons' demands for 'bone governance' in terms of economy, solvency, firm conciliar control over expenditure, and effective defence of England's frontiers and trade. That this was a conscious attempt to improve the image of royal government and win the confidence of the political class for Lancastrian kingship is confirmed by his specific commission to Hoccleve to popularize the treatise on government, the *Secretum Secretorum*, in the English of *The Regement of Princes*.[170] Yet even as this was being penned, the twenty years of English abstention from continental warfare was coming to an end.

In France the rivalry of Orléans and Burgundy for control over Charles VI erupted into armed confrontation in July 1411. Duke John the Fearless invoked his alliances—including that with England. On 1 September the prince's councillors drew up terms for a military alliance coupled with an offer of the prince's marriage. The former had the king's support, for in mid-August he called the royal affinity to arms, though in fact no muster took place. The prince, however, went ahead with a private expedition under his principal retainer, the earl of Arundel. Arundel's small but effective force parried the Orléanist threat to Paris at Saint-Cloud, demonstrating the value of English arms. But on 21 September, as Arundel sailed, Henry IV summoned parliament. No taxes were needed; the purpose was political. Whether this was the king's determination to reassert his authority or that of the prince to force his father's abdication is unclear.[171] Though the elections had returned many of the prince's supporters, and Thomas Chaucer again became Speaker, the king seized the initiative, warning that he would tolerate no 'novelties'. An obscure struggle ensued in which the Commons expressed support for the prince's government, but by 30 November the king was able to dismiss the prince's council, browbeat the Commons into an assurance of their loyalty, and extract a novel tax for his own disposal.[172] Archbishop Arundel returned as chancellor and his follower Sir John Pelham as treasurer. No council was named and the programme of financial planning was abandoned. For the rest of the reign the king ruled on his own authority.

This was a conflict not over policies but for political control. The prince was impatient of his ailing father and determined to rule; the king refused to be relegated. Burgundy's appeal was a catalyst, reviving the king's dream of

---

[170] Harriss (ed.), *Henry V*, 8–9; above, Ch. 1, sect. 2.

[171] The proposal for the king's abdication is found in *Chron. Angliae*, 63; *Eulog. Hist.* iii. 421; Davies (ed.), *Eng. Chron.* 37.

[172] *House of Commons*, i. 225–9; *Rot. Parl.* iii. 647–8, 658.

campaigning in France and opening up for the prince a prevision of his life's mission. But their open conflict revealed and hardened fissures in Lancastrian rule, with the earls of Arundel and Warwick and Bishop Beaufort behind the prince, and Thomas of Lancaster, the duke of York, and Archbishop Arundel behind the king. These divisions now manifested themselves in the plan for an expedition in May 1412 to support the Orléanists. Their beguiling offers for the restoration of the duchy of Aquitaine in return for a force of 4,000 English were accepted by the king at the Treaty of Bourges. All four of his sons endorsed the treaty, the king again summoned the royal affinity to arms, and the prince began to raise money and troops in Cheshire. But early in June the king's health forced him to withdraw, and he passed the command to his favourite son, Thomas. The prince reacted with fury, alarmed that this might portend a threat to his succession to the throne. He led his assembled retinue to London, demanding an interview with the king and the production of his detractors at the next parliament. The expedition under Thomas, now created duke of Clarence, sailed early in August. By then Orléanists and Burgundians had been reconciled, and Clarence was bought off with a 'ransom treaty' at Buzançais. Profitable as this was to the commanders, the only political result of English intervention had been to draw the French together. It might seem that the English had learned no lesson about war on the Continent since Edward III's last invasion of 1360.[173]

Even with Clarence in Guyenne, Prince Henry remained highly suspicious of those around the king. On 23 September he appeared in London 'with an huge pepyll' to answer allegations that he had retained large sums for the payment of the Calais garrison. He cleared himself, but remained isolated from the court. At Christmas, Henry IV's health collapsed and by February official business had ground to a halt. Before or during his final illness the chronicles embody a story of the king's deathbed reconciliation with his son, to whom he gave advice on how to govern.[174] Henry died on 20 March 1413 at the age of 46.

Henry IV has been something of an enigma to historians, as he probably was to his subjects. Before he became king, at the age of 33, he was strong, well-built, full of vigour, the very embodiment of the chivalric qualities of prowess in arms, adventure, and *courtoisie*. He had won acclaim at tournaments and on crusade, and was well received in the courts of Europe. In England he was a lord of extensive lands with a large retinue. In all this he was his father's son, and had been instructed and protected by Gaunt in the dangerous politics of Richard II's latter years. Unlike Gaunt he had acquired—had, perhaps, cultivated—a broader popularity, and possessed an ease of manner (*franchise*) which could bridge the

[173] Above, Ch. 11, sect. 5; P. McNiven, 'Prince Henry and the English political crisis of 1412', *History*, 65 (1980), 1–16; Harriss, *Cardinal Beaufort*, 59–60.

[174] Monstrelet has the story of the prince trying on the crown while his father lay dying.

social gulf. Feared and disliked by Richard II, Henry of Derby was well equipped to become his supplanter.

In his first six years as king Henry displayed energy and decisiveness in meeting the military challenge from the Ricardian nobility, the Percys, and the Welsh. In the absence of a numerous nobility, he buttressed his rule by enlarging the Lancastrian affinity to form a body of loyal and favoured supporters in the shires. Though this helped to secure his throne, it distorted his relationship with the political community and strained royal finances. His insolvency and indebtedness soured his relations with parliament, which he strove to placate with specious promises, knowing that he could not let it become a vehicle for political opposition. These years were an exercise in crisis management of the political community, the more pressing because both the circumstances of Henry's usurpation and his own secular cast of mind foreclosed any appeal to sacral kingship. Henry had perforce to speak to his subjects; he could not address himself to God alone, as had Richard II. But when his health collapsed in 1406, support was forthcoming among the political community both for Lancastrian rule and for the restoration of the 'bone governance' which had been promised at the usurpation and frustrated by the years of emergency. In 1399 circumstances left him little choice but to take Richard's crown, and pride in his own rights and lineage stifled any qualms. When asked on his deathbed whether he repented his usurpation, he merely observed—with his usual sardonic humour—that his sons would not permit him to surrender the kingdom now.

CHAPTER 13

England and her Neighbours

Edward III's prospective renunciation of the French crown in 1360 might have diverted his ambitions towards creating a multiple kingdom of Great Britain, with Scotland added to Wales, Ireland, and the Channel Islands. Like other such conglomerates, its sole bond would have been the king's lordship; it would not have been envisaged or realized as a unitary state, with common institutions and citizenship.[1] For Welsh, Irish, and Scots were distinct peoples, with different languages, laws or customs, social structures, and identities, who lived in defined territories. In each a sense of ethnic nationhood had been fostered by resistance to, and hatred of, the English.[2]

Over the past two centuries English national identity had been nurtured on the one hand through precocious and centralized institutions of government, and on the other by attempts to subdue their neighbours and impose English kingship, law, and government. In fact the indigenous structures of the subjugated peoples set limits to this. For neither the Welsh nor the Irish expressed their ethnic identity in 'regnal solidarity', i.e through a unitary kingship. Native lordship in both societies was tribal and based on lineage and kindred, offering no basis for the control of men and land through feudal lordship. Alien in language and manner, and unamenable to control, native society was bypassed by the English conquerors, who occupied land in sufficient numbers to form a colonial elite. This elite was linked to the English Crown as vassals, regulated by common law and parliamentary legislation, and ruled by a replica of English administration. The creation of a strong nexus between homeland and colonists reinforced the gulf between them and the indigenous population. Each dependency became a land inhabited by two peoples.

---

[1] See, in general, Griffiths, *King and Country*, 33–54; J. Wormald, 'The creation of Britain: Multiple kingdoms or core and colonies?', *TRHS*, 6th ser., 2 (1992), 175–94. Wales and Ireland were 'parcel of the crown of England' (*Rot. Parl.* iii. 231).

[2] The subject is explored in four lectures by R. R. Davies, 'The peoples of Britain and Ireland, 1100–1400', *TRHS*, 6th ser., 4–7 (1994–7), on which the following discussion draws.

I. IRELAND

By 1250 English conquest and settlement extended to most parts of Ireland except the extreme west and north. Settlement was densest in the fertile plains of the south and east, where manorial organization was introduced, and in the seaboard towns from which Gaels were excluded. Ireland was in general peaceful, but beyond the area of Meath, Louth, Leinster, and Kildare colonization was sparse and did not encompass the hills and forests. The fourteenth century witnessed a Gaelic resurgence. Edward Bruce's invasion of 1315 brought in Scottish mercenaries—'gallowglasses'—who helped Gaelic chiefs reclaim large areas of Ulster, Connacht, and south-west Munster from English rule. Native lordships like those of McMurrough, O'Byrne, and O'Toole were established even in Leinster. The growing insecurity impelled many English landlords to leave Ireland, while the Black Death ravaged English settlements which were not replenished from the depleted population of the homeland.[3] By the mid-fourteenth century four great Anglo-Irish earldoms had been created which were to survive for the rest of the Middle Ages. Three of these were held by the Geraldine earls of Desmond, the Butler earls of Ormond, and the Geraldine of Offaly earls of Kildare, while the earldom of Ulster had passed through the marriage of Elisabeth de Burgh to Lionel of Clarence. Lesser Anglo-Irish families held baronies, while some of the English peerage, such as Mowbray, Stafford, Despenser, and Talbot, were absentee landlords. The Anglo-Irish lords were summoned to the Irish parliament in Dublin and locally they served as sheriffs and commissioners. But their energies were heavily engaged in defending their lands, tenants, and livestock from Gaelic incursions, for which they had to maintain a permanent fighting retinue.

Over the space of two centuries the Anglo-Irish adopted elements of Gaelic lifestyle and culture, and most spoke Gaelic, learned in youth from the widespread practice of fosterage by Gaelic families. But there was little intermarriage except at the lowest level and the Anglo-Irish regarded the Gaels not only as enemies but as inferiors, 'degenerates'. The two peoples never integrated; the Anglo-Irish remained colonists, exercising a governing authority from which even the Gaelic lords were excluded. In political terms they saw themselves as English, not as a 'middle nation'. At the same time their 'Hibernicized' speech, dress, manners, and above all their viewpoint distinguished them from true English. Their pragmatic policy of both fighting and buying off the Gaelic

---

[3] R. Frame, *English Lordship in Ireland, 1318–1361* (Oxford, 1982), and J. F. Lydon, *The Lordship of Ireland in the Middle Ages* (Dublin, 1972), ch. 5.

chiefs was distrusted in England, and they in turn were affronted by the Crown's patent indifference to Ireland.[4]

The English administration at Dublin formed another element in Ireland's politics. There the Westminster offices were replicated, the chancellor, treasurer, and judges being appointed by the Crown, with staffs trained in English procedures. The Crown's immediate representative in the province was the chief governor or lieutenant, with the justiciar as deputy, appointed for a period of years from among the English or Anglo-Irish nobility. Much of his time was spent moving around the four counties with an armed escort enforcing English justice and collecting revenue. The normal yield was small and decreasing: hardly more than £2,000 in 1360, it had halved by the fifteenth century. Taxes to meet the Gaelic resurgence were habitually levied on a local basis, though from 1346 these were reinforced by parliaments meeting in Kilkenny which acted as the mouthpiece of the Anglo-Irish political community.[5] Yet the permanent absence of the Crown left political life without a natural focus, and its delegated authority was constantly questioned. Like all colonies Ireland remained politically stunted, and became increasingly beleaguered. The Crown's indifference was a compound of ignorance, suspicion of the Dublin administration as corrupt and of the Anglo-Irish as accomplices of the Gaels, uncertainty between their conflicting viewpoints, and a lack of urgency since Ireland posed no threat to England. Ireland came a bad third to France and Scotland in the Crown's priorities.

But although by 1360 the Irish settlement seemed to be doomed to permanent decline, it was not in danger of imminent collapse. Gaelic Ireland had never developed that 'regnal solidarity' under a 'high king' which would have inspired and coordinated resistance to the English; locked in their internecine wars, the chiefs could not match in battle the military resources of the Anglo-Irish lords, backed by the Crown. The English Crown never contemplated withdrawal from Ireland, nor did the Anglo-Irish envisage a declaration of independence. Indeed they jealously guarded their role as royal vassals which they were determined to deny to the Gaelic chiefs. While these political positions remained immobile, the progressive erosion of English settlement beyond and within the four counties demanded a strategic decision. The Crown either had to make a major military effort to subjugate Gaelic Ireland and make it pay or it had to face ultimate

---

[4] For the Anglo-Irish and their relations with Gaels, see A. Cosgrove, *Late Medieval Ireland, 1370–1541* (Dublin, 1981), 78–80; R. Frame, 'Les Engleys nees en Irlande: The English political identity in medieval Ireland', *TRHS*, 6th ser., 3 (1993), 83–104; J. F. Lydon, 'The middle nation', in id. (ed.), *The English in Medieval Ireland* (Dublin, 1984), 1–26.

[5] Frame, *English Lordship*, ch. 3; J. A. Watt, 'The Anglo-Irish colony under strain, 1327–1399', in A. Cosgrove (ed.), *A New History of Ireland*, ii: *1169–1534* (Oxford, 1987; 2nd impression 1993), 352–82; H. G. Richardson and G. O. Sayles, *The Irish Parliament in the Middle Ages* (Philadelphia, 1952), 101–12.

withdrawal to a seaboard 'pale' leaving the remainder of Ireland to be ruled by Gaelic and Anglo-Irish lords. The first was attempted in the later fourteenth century, its failure leading logically to the second in the fifteenth.

The appointment of Lionel of Clarence as king's lieutenant in Ireland in July 1361 was both a response to a dangerous Gaelic offensive in Leinster under Art McMurrough and a declaration of policy by Edward III. The earl of Ormond had come to parliament at Westminster to appeal for aid, and Edward was ready to use his war chest, replenished with French ransoms, to establish his second son in his wife's inheritance. Clarence was able to reassert English control in Leinster, capturing McMurrough and receiving the submission of O'Byrne and O'More in 1364, but he made no attempt to recover his own lordship of Ulster. Over the five years of his lieutenancy it had cost the English exchequer £37,724, with a further £5,852 from Irish revenues.[6] At his last parliament in Ireland, Lionel enacted the famous Statute of Kilkenny, which sought to check 'Hibernicization' and institutionalize the separation of Gaels and Anglo-Irish. Intermarriage, fosterage, and the adoption of Gaelic speech, dress, and customs by the English in Ireland were forbidden; they were recognizably to form a colonial elite.[7]

For the rest of the century the English Crown pursued its aim of reasserting English lordship. In March 1369 a new phase was marked by dispatching William of Windsor, an experienced soldier and follower of John of Gaunt, to recover the lands lost after Clarence's departure. He set about subduing Leinster, but by 1371 the £20,000 provided by the English exchequer was exhausted and the war in France was taking priority; Windsor had to support his army from Irish taxation, while his attempt to confiscate the lands of absentees brought local protests and his temporary recall. He was reappointed in 1374 but his further demands from the parliament at Kilkenny and reluctance to take the field against rebels produced protests in Ireland which were taken up in the Good Parliament, where his connections with Gaunt and Alice Perrers were used to denigrate the court. He was charged with extortion and oppression and dismissed, though he was never brought to trial. Windsor's failure was simply that of the English Crown, which between 1361 and 1376 had spent some £182,000 on the army in Ireland without remotely achieving the degree of security needed to exploit it.[8] The

---

[6] P. Conolly, 'The financing of English expeditions to Ireland, 1361–1376', in J. F. Lydon (ed.), *England and Ireland in the Later Middle Ages* (Dublin, 1981), 104–21.

[7] Text in H. F. Berry (ed.), *Statutes, Ordinances, and Acts of the Parliament of Ireland, King John to Henry V* (Dublin, 1907), 430–69, discussed in Watt, 'The Anglo-Irish colony under strain', 386–90; J. Otway-Ruthven, *A History of Medieval Ireland* (London, 1968), 291–3.

[8] S. Harbison, 'William of Windsor, the court party, and the administration of Ireland', in Lydon (ed.), *England and Ireland in the Later Middle Ages*, 153–74; Conolly, 'The financing of English expeditions'; J. F. Lydon, 'William of Windsor and the Irish parliament', *EHR* 80 (1965), 252–67;

Anglo-Irish lacked the numbers, will, and military presence to rule Ireland as conquerors and colonists; they might look to England for military support, but their circumstances dictated pragmatic cohabitation.

By 1385 Richard II had formed the intention of bringing England's western dependencies more directly under royal authority by constructing a royal seigniory through Cheshire and North Wales under the control of his favourite Robert de Vere. He was created marquess of Dublin and then duke of Ireland, to hold Ireland for life, exercising royal authority and receiving all revenues. But in 1387 de Vere fell victim to the baronial opposition and never reached Ireland. By 1393 the deteriorating position of English rule impelled the parliament of Kilkenny to appeal to England, and Richard II resolved to lead an expedition in person the following year. As befitted the first visit of an English king since 1210, Richard brought an army which, when reinforced in Ireland, numbered upward of 8,000 and was by far the largest to operate there in the later Middle Ages.[9] Its core was his own household and affinity, and it included the curial lords whom he trusted and those with lands in Ireland. Richard may have envisaged a long-term military occupation, for all absentee landlords were ordered to return on pain of forfeiture. Richard viewed the problem of Ireland from the perspective of Westminster and Dublin, rather than of the Anglo-Irish. Distinguishing between the 'wild Irish' as 'enemies', and the Gaelic chiefs as 'rebels', he aimed to bring the latter to submission, redress their grievances, and establish 'good government and just rule' on the basis of their feudal ligeance and the common obedience of all subjects to his kingship.[10] This application of his doctrine of kingship to the Irish situation was to achieve a striking, if superficial, success.

Richard's military strategy was equally novel and ambitious: to re-establish Leinster as an English land by expelling Art McMurrough and his Gaelic allies, and recolonize it with English settlers. He penned McMurrough into the Wicklow Mountains, blockading the coast, and by the end of the year had received his submission. The next stage was to subdue the 'rebel Irish' as the campaign moved westward into Cork, distributing their lands to the loyal Irish and royal followers. But this was anticipated by the Gaelic chiefs from Ulster, Connacht, Munster, and Clare, who voluntarily submitted in order to protect their lordships. Froissart gives a vivid if apocryphal account of how 'four Gaelic

M. V. Clarke, 'William of Windsor in Ireland, 1369–76', in id., *Fourteenth Century Studies*, 146–241; Holmes, *The Good Parliament*, 90–9.

[9] M. J. Bennett, 'Richard II and the wider realm', in Goodman and Gillespie (eds.), *Richard II*, 187–204; Saul, *Richard II*, 270; J. F. Lydon, 'Richard II's expeditions to Ireland', *Journal of the Royal Society of the Antiquaries of Ireland*, 93 (1963), 135–49.

[10] His views are contained in letters to the duke of Burgundy written at Haverfordwest in September 1394 (M. D. Legge (ed.), *Anglo-Norman Letters*, Anglo-Norman Text Society (Oxford, 1941), 47–8) and to the English council in February 1395 (*Proc. & Ord.* i. 55–7, 61–3).

MAP 13.1. Ireland: the Anglo-Irish and Gaelic lordships, *c*.1390

kings' were schooled in the rituals and ideals of chivalry in preparation for a
solemn ceremony of dubbing to knighthood and rendering of liege homage.[11]
Despite these feudal forms, their status in Richard's eyes was that of obedient
subjects, their acknowledgement of his kingship often being couched in terms of
abject humility. By accepting their allegiance and according them feudal status,
Richard had sought to incorporate the actual power of the Gaelic chiefs within
the political system. They were thus placed on a common footing with other subjects and this had two consequences: as his vassals Richard had to confirm the
Gaelic lords in their lands and, further, they now looked to the king for justice

[11] D. Johnston, 'Richard II and the submission of Gaelic Ireland', *Irish Historical Studies*, 22
(1980), 1–20.

and protection against their Anglo–Irish neighbours, whose status as a colonial elite was thus abrogated. Nowhere were the consequences more acute than in Ulster. There O'Neill had extended his lordship over Gaelic chiefs and had usurped the military and other service which they owed to the earls of Ulster, aiming to be recognized as a tenant-in-chief of the Crown. Thus, when faced with the earl of March's demand for his homage, O'Neill appealed to Richard II to be 'shield and helmet of justice between my lord of Ulster and me'. Richard could not abrogate March's feudal rights, but strove to retain the allegiance of O'Neill. He left their quarrel unresolved and primed to erupt on his departure. Left as chief governor, the earl of March soon came into conflict with O'Neill over the lordship of Trim, and in Leinster McMurrough reneged on his allegiance. By 1398 Richard's settlement had unravelled; the earl of March incurred his suspicion, and was dismissed as governor shortly before being ambushed and killed on 20 July 1398.[12]

In June 1399 Richard returned. His intentions are not easy to discern. He led a smaller army, of not more than 5,000, but the attendance of his closest magnates and bishops, with the full panoply of court ritual, gave the impression to contemporaries of his planning to exercise his kingship in Ireland for a prolonged period. That was not to be. A month later the news of Henry's landing in England compelled the king to organize a hurried return, sending Salisbury ahead on 17 July and himself following from Waterford the following week. His departure and the news of his overthrow dissolved Ireland into anarchy, as Gaelic and Anglo-Irish alike pursued their feuds and ambitions: Desmond allied with McMurrough against Ormond, O'Neill made war in Ulster, Dublin disbanded its defence force for lack of pay, and reported that the Gaels were everywhere 'strong and arrogant and of great power'.[13] After forty years the Crown's attempt to rule Ireland as a colony had ended in failure. The area of English control had continued to shrink, it had proved impossible to raise taxes for its defence, and the divisions between Gaelic, Anglo-Irish, and English prevented it from being ruled as an integral political society. If it could not be ruled from above, it would have to be left to rule itself by localized agreements. Their weakness and indifference recommended this solution to the Lancastrian kings.

There was little sympathy in Ireland for either Richard II or the earl of March, but with the eruption of the Welsh revolt it became both a potential ally for Owain Glyn Dŵr (to which he appealed in November 1401) and a place for intervention by foreign enemies. Henry IV's decision in June 1401 to appoint his

[12] K. Sims, 'The king's friend: O'Neill, the Crown and the earldom of Ulster', in Lydon (ed.), *England and Ireland in the Later Middle Ages*, 214–36; D. Johnston, 'The interim years: Richard II and Ireland, 1395–99', ibid. 175–95.

[13] D. Johnston, 'Richard II's departure from Ireland, July 1399', *EHR* 98 (1983), 785–805 (quotation at 804).

second son, Thomas, though only 13, as lieutenant for six years at a salary of £8,000 appeared to renew the policy of conquest initiated forty years before. In fact this was neither intended nor practicable. The dire financial crisis meant that Thomas's salary fell quickly into arrears—by June 1403 he was owed £9,000— and his military operations beyond Leinster ground to a halt.[14] Thomas returned to England in November and for the next four years the military emergency in England and Wales left only minimal sums for Ireland, where the English-held lands were defended by the earl of Ormond as lieutenant and Sir Stephen Scrope as justiciar.

Although Thomas was reappointed in March 1406, and again in 1408 when he made a brief visit, there was no expectation that he would or could mount a campaign; it was simply an attempt by the council to provide an unendowed royal sibling with a salary and remove him from the king's household. In fact he remained with the king until given the more congenial task of campaigning in France in 1412. Meanwhile the council reduced the annual 'charge' for Ireland to 4,000 marks per annum—putting it on a kind of care and maintenance basis— and at this level it remained for the duration of Lancastrian rule.[15] By then Ireland was no longer a potential threat to the security of England and the English kings had learnt the folly of pouring money into the hopeless task of reconquest. Without active English leadership, the Anglo-Irish increasingly accommodated themselves to the pattern of localized war in Gaelic society, governed by its own rules of family connections and feuds. Politically it constituted a kind of formalized anarchy, independent of the rule of the constricted Dublin government; socially it led to a perceptible increase in Hibernicization. There were exceptions to this, notably the young earl of Ormond, the 'White Earl', who succeeded his father in 1405; he moved between Gaelic, Anglo-Irish, and English society and was to be the principal link with England and the dominant influence in Ireland in the first half of the fifteenth century.

With his ambitions centred on France, Henry V was not ready to devote more than minimal attention and resources to Ireland. Yet he was not content to surrender royal authority to the Anglo-Irish, and he expected the English governors he appointed—Sir John Stanley (1413–14) and Lord Talbot (1414–20)—to pursue active operations at minimum cost. Talbot, a harsh, self-seeking, and aggressive soldier, quickly showed his mettle in a series of devastating raids on the Gaelic chieftains, capturing Donagh McMurrough and exacting submission from O'Neill, taking hostages, and securing the frontier. But his meagre salary of 3,000 marks a year (even though paid promptly and in full) set limits to his

[14] Otway-Ruthven, *A History of Medieval Ireland*, 342–4; PRO, E 404/16/728.
[15] *Proc. & Ord*. i. 313–18; Wright, 'Royal finance in the latter part of the reign of Henry IV of England, 1406–13', D.Phil. thesis (Oxford University, 1984), 166, 178, 247–8, 259, 269.

objectives and compelled him to revive the practice of 'coign and livery' (quartering his army on the population) and exploit his fiscal rights in Ireland to the full.[16] He thereby alienated the Anglo-Irish lords, notably Ormond, who accused him of seizing his lands while he was campaigning with Henry V in France in 1417. Their quarrel was to bedevil the government of Ireland for the next quarter-century.

When Talbot, in turn, was called to serve in France in 1420, Ormond made a determined bid to secure the governorship, by taking it at a reduced charge and increasing Irish revenue by one-third. The council of the minority found itself beset by charges and counter-charges as the Talbot and Ormond factions struggled for control of the Dublin administration.[17] The decision to appoint the young Edmund Mortimer, earl of March, as someone who would stand above these feuds was made in May 1423, his salary being increased to 5,000 marks. Having arrived in the autumn of 1424, he conducted a campaign in Connacht and Ulster which procured some Gaelic submissions, but his death in January 1425 revived the Talbot–Ormond contest for control. Under a series of short-term governors, the Dublin government became debilitated and unable to give backing to the Anglo-Irish lords, who increasingly resorted to buying off the Gaelic chiefs. By 1446 the area of direct English control had narrowed to a 'Pale' 30 miles long and 20 miles wide. Nor was the feud between the supporters of Talbot and Ormond quietened. The reinstatement of Ormond as governor in 1442 brought the conflict to a head. Archbishop Talbot objected to him as being too old—'unwieldly and unlustie'—and charges of corruption and maladministration were brought against him in 1443–4. On Lord Talbot's return from France in 1444 the council effected a reconciliation, followed by the appointment of Talbot as governor for two years in 1445. For a quarter of a century their competition for leadership had paralysed and eroded English authority, though either alone could have been effective.

As in 1423, it was to a Mortimer that the Crown turned to resume the task of stabilizing and recovering English authority. Richard, duke of York, was appointed on 30 July 1447. Disappointed of his expectation for a second term as lieutenant in Normandy, and already owed a massive sum from his five years in France, he could expect further debt to accrue in Ireland as the English exchequer descended into acute insolvency. When he finally reached Dublin in June 1449 with a force of perhaps no more than 600 men, his name and rank won him immediate submission from Eoghan O'Neill in Ulster and from O'Byrne and McMurrough in Leinster, replicating the success of Richard II. He reported

[16] E. Matthews, 'The financing of the lordship of Ireland under Henry V and Henry VI', in Pollard (ed.) *Property and Politics*, 97–115.

[17] M. C. Griffiths, 'The Talbot–Ormond struggle for control of the Anglo-Irish government, 1414–1447', *Irish Historical Studies*, 2 (1940–1), 376–97.

these triumphs by letter to the English council even as Charles VII's armies were invading Normandy. But by June 1450, with McMurrough again in revolt, he was seeking to exonerate himself from failure and declaring that the lack of payment from England (he was owed £3,000) would force him to return. In fact it was the political crisis centred on Suffolk's fall, the loss of Normandy, and Cade's rising that brought him back in August. English politics now fully claimed his attention, yet he saw his Irish lieutenancy as a continuing reality. He had accepted that Ireland could only be governed by investing the great lordships, Gaelic as much as Anglo-Irish, with authority. Enri O'Neill was left to control Ulster, as a vassal, and York made the old Ormond his deputy, supported by Desmond and Kildare. Beyond the now constricted Pale, York relied on the FitzGerald earl of Kildare, Thomas FitzMaurice, to control Leinster.[18]

The disturbed state of English politics in the 1450s prevented York from returning to Ireland until he arrived as a proscribed exile after the rout of Ludford in October 1459. His priority was not military operations in Ireland (though he undertook some) but to provide himself with a firm military and political base. A parliament meeting first at Drogheda and then at Dublin from February to May 1460 confirmed him as lieutenant-governor, declared opposition to him to be treason, and made a striking affirmation of the legislative and judicial autonomy of the Irish parliament, forbidding appeals beyond Ireland without its authority. It raised a force of archers, passed an Act of resumption, and created an independent Irish currency. These measures, perhaps framed by William Shirwood, bishop of Meath, provided York's rule in Ireland with a constitutional basis of sorts in defiance of the English Crown—though stopping short of a declaration of independence.[19] Even so, it was an indication of the alienation felt by both the Dublin government and the Anglo-Irish lords as a result of the prolonged indifference of the English Crown. Their viewpoints differed: the Anglo-Irish lords looked for greater recognition and responsibility, the English administration for greater protection and financial support; for the moment they exploited York's dependence on them to make a specious assertion of independence.

One may doubt whether York had a greater commitment to Ireland, or understanding of Irish society, than any other English nobleman. But his rank and ancestry conferred an authority over the different elements which no other could claim. That no attempt had been made before 1447 to send York to Ireland says

[18] P. A. Johnson, *Duke Richard of York, 1411–1460* (Oxford, 1988), 74–7. For York's rule, see E. Curtis, 'The duke of York as viceroy of Ireland, 1447–60', *Journal of the Royal Society of the Antiquaries of Ireland*, 62 (1932), 157–86.

[19] A. Cosgrove, 'Parliament and the Anglo-Irish community: The declaration of 1460', in A. Cosgrove and J. McGuire (eds.), *Parliament and Community*, Historical Studies, 14 (Belfast, 1983), 25–41; Johnson, *Duke Richard of York*, 198–9.

much for the primacy of England and Normandy in his and the Crown's eyes. Ireland claimed the least attention of all frontiers under English dominion. The fear expressed in *The Libelle of Englyshe Polycye* that it could be used as a base by England's enemies, like the warning that the 'wild Irish' might erect a king to challenge English rule, were—and could be—discounted. Similarly, though Ormond might urge that what was spent annually in France

> myght wynne Ireland to a fynall conquest
> in one soole yere to sette us all in rest,

the English council turned a deaf ear.[20] With the lesson of Richard II in mind, no Lancastrian king was going to venture to Ireland. Only intermittently did the shrinking Pale, the corrupt and factious administration, and the interminable feuding of Gaelic and Anglo-Irish claim the attention of the English Crown. Left to itself Ireland developed a pastoral economy with a thriving trade in hides and wool which brought a measure of prosperity in the late fourteenth century. But trade, like government, took place within the interstices of war; never a war of liberation, mounted by native Gaels against English rule; but a war of family feuds, temporary ascendancies, and changing alliances, which negated the reality of colonial rule while perpetuating its shadowy form.

2. WALES

Wales, like Ireland, had initially been conquered and settled by Anglo-Norman lords, and only after Edward I had defeated Llywelyn ap Gruffudd in 1282 did the Crown exercise direct rule in the confiscated principality of Gwynedd. The principality became the apanage of the heir apparent, while the marcher lordships to the south and east were virtually autonomous areas in which their lords exercised royal jurisdiction, raised troops and taxes, built castles, and enjoyed all the economic and feudal profits. By 1380 these were held by fifteen families, which included the great English comital titles of Arundel, Lancaster, March, Stafford, and Warwick.[21] Though not normally resident, all of these drew a significant part—in the cases of March and Arundel, the major part—of their income from their Welsh lordships, and used their military resources for expeditions, and the local offices and benefices for patronage. The wealth and power of these lordships made them important not only in Wales but in English politics. The principality was divided into a northern part of three shires (Caernarfon, Anglesey, and Merioneth) and a southern part of two (Carmarthen and Cardigan), administered separately under two justiciars. In the 1370s the Black

---

[20] *The Libelle of Englyshe Polycye*, 36–7, 39.
[21] R. R. Davies, *The Age of Conquest: Wales, 1063–1415* (Oxford, 1987), 466–72, supplies a useful list of the Anglo-Norman lordships.

Prince had extracted some £5,000 per annum from it and Flintshire, and its castles and local offices provided a pool of patronage.[22] Wales was thus a collection
of lordships, without even a royal lieutenant or a parliament, as in Ireland, to give
it political identity.

In contrast to Ireland, English lordship had all but dissolved native ties and
loyalties. By 1300 the lowlands had been extensively settled by English and
Flemish tenantry, while the Welsh had been expropriated from the best lands,
excluded from office and burgage status in the towns, and debarred from English
law. In lowland Wales demesne agriculture and cattle-farming, in upland Wales
vast flocks of sheep and some mineral extraction, provided a basically productive
economy for which England was an easily accessible market. But it was the profits from judicial lordship that provided the largest and easiest gains through periodic inquiries into crime and infringements of seigniorial rights conducted by
justices of eyre every three to five years. Communities might compound for
these, as did Brecon in 1375 for £1,800.[23] For the exaction of economic and judicial dues the lords relied on settled English families of petty gentry status—the
advenae—who served as stewards, bailiffs, and local justiciars, and were
rewarded with profitable leases and the opportunity to buy land. Most densely
settled in the lowland south, families like Devereux, Carew, Wogan, and
Stradling saw Wales as their homeland.[24] Though some married native Welsh
and used a Welsh alias name, they remained wholly English in their own esteem
and in the eyes of the law, and never adopted native language and customs.
Similarly in the eighty or so small market boroughs which acted as administrative and mercantile centres, the English burgesses were a property-owning and
governing elite.

Just as the English never became a 'middle race', so the Welsh aristocracy
never Anglicized. Certain families of princely descent engaged the respect of
the bards and retained the loyalty of their extended kin. The family head, or
'high man' (*uchelwr*), might manage to live in modest style in a small manor
house, maintain traditional hospitality, and act as patron of Welsh culture.
A handful among this native squirearchy entered the service of the English lords
in an administrative or military capacity; they acquired lands at lease and sought
to free themselves from the native custom of partible inheritance, in order
to build up family estates. In the north the families of Gruffudd, Tudur, and
Glyn Dŵr were marked out in this respect in the late fourteenth century. But
though valued by the English as channels of local influence, it was only
the Welsh who held them in esteem for their ancestry. English and Welsh

---

[22] Davies, *Age of Conquest*, 403, citing a valor of 1372–5.

[23] R. R. Davies, *Lordship and Society in the March of Wales, 1282–1400* (Oxford, 1978), 176–84.

[24] R. R. Davies, *The Revolt of Owain Glyn Dŵr* (Oxford, 1995), 45.

remained separate peoples in speech, dress, and culture, divided by the hostility of rulers and ruled.[25]

In the thinly populated and poorer soils of the upland zone English settlement was sparse and communications poor, and native speech and traditions were dominant. Livestock were the principal source of wealth and cattle-rustling common. The lowland economy was more affected by the Black Death. Depopulation led to a drastic decline in demesne farming and the disappearance of serfdom. The plentiful availability of land stimulated leases and sales to English as yeomen copyholders and to the lesser Welsh squirearchy. Depopulation also encouraged the change from arable to pasture, with large herds of cattle reared in eastern Wales and driven long distances into England.[26] But for landlords arrears of rent, vacant holdings, and remitted services threatened their income. They responded by intensifying the exploitation of seigniorial rights. They abrogated communal rights of pasture, leased escheated land on harsher terms, and increased personal and communal amercements. Baronial councils and officials were thus able to maintain seigniorial revenues into the last quarter of the century, so that Adam of Usk's belief that the Crown and marcher lords drew no less than £60,000 each year from Wales may not have been too gross an exaggeration. Verifiably Richard, earl of Arundel, had £30,000 stored in Holt Castle in 1376 and Roger, earl of March, had £2,775 sent from his marcher lordships in 1393.[27] But the intensification of lordship inevitably bred discontent.

Yet if Wales in this period saw social and economic changes, it remained firmly under English rule. The risings of 1381 found no echo within its borders nor, despite the pleas of Owain Lawgoch, did Charles V risk sending French troops to enter England by the back door. The Welsh nourished their identity through language, lineage, and prophecy, but the military power of the marcher lords and the Crown denied them liberty or nationhood. It was only an unforeseen crisis in English rule that provided the impulse and opportunity for revolt.

Ironically it was the displacement of marcher lordship by royal power that proved destabilizing. In 1389 the Crown gained the Hastings earldom of Pembroke by escheat and in 1398 the custody of the Mortimer estates on the death of Earl Roger. With the forfeitures of 1397 Arundel's lordships of Bromfield and Yale, Chirk, and Oswestry could be added to the new principality of Chester, while the confiscation of Gower and Chepstow from Mowbray in 1398 and the Lancastrian lands in February 1399 brought virtually all the marcher lordships into the Crown's hands. Royal power now stretched in the north from Anglesey and Merioneth through Denbigh to Chester and Oswestry, and in the south from Monmouth through Brecon and Kidwelly to Pembroke.[28]

---

[25] Ibid. 49–56.   [26] Davies, *Lordship and Society*, 107–19; id., *Age of Conquest*, 425–30.

[27] Davies, *Age of Conquest*, 439; id., *Owain Glyn Dŵr*, 70–4.

[28] Davies, *Age of Conquest*, 430–43; id., *Owain Glyn Dŵr*, 76–93.

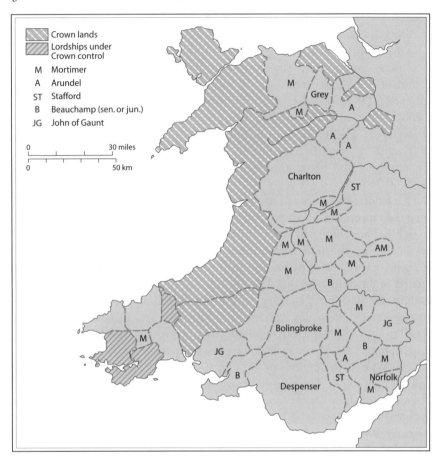

MAP 13.2. Wales: the principality and marcher lordships, *c.*1390. Source: R. R. Davies, *Owain Glyn Dŵr* (Oxford, 1995), 84

Such an agglomeration of territory could have been used to anticipate the Tudor integration of Wales with England. But with Richard II's ill-advised expedition in June 1399 his authority in Wales unravelled. Richard's displacement of the marcher lords had dissolved loyalties, and Despenser could not raise South Wales on his behalf nor Salisbury command the loyalties of the north. Further, the overthrow of legitimate kingship encouraged the Welsh to revolt against English rule.

The proclamation of Owain Glyn Dŵr as prince of Wales on 16 September 1400, followed by attacks on the English marcher boroughs, was seen at first as a local rising, which Henry IV sought to punish by a three-week expedition to Caernarfon. It was only after the daring, if brief, seizure of Conwy Castle by

Gwilym and Rhys ap Tudur in April 1401 that risings spread to the whole of North and mid-Wales, calling for a royal expedition in October to strengthen South and west Wales. Then, after a winter's lull, revolt flared again in April 1402 bringing the capture of Lord Grey of Ruthin, followed by Glyn Dŵr's slaughter of the Herefordshire levy under Sir Edmund Mortimer at Pilleth in June. By the summer Welsh forces were operating down in Gwent and Glamorgan, threatening Abergavenny, Usk, Caerleon, and Cardiff, while over much of North and mid-Wales the English were confined to castles and boroughs. The rebel forces were small and mobile, fierce and cunning, and versed in guerrilla warfare. But their capacity for inflicting damage was limited, for the upland area in which they operated was poor and sparsely populated. Only if the castles and lowland settlements were attacked would the English hold be endangered.

Yet the revolt posed a political threat to Henry IV, for in Wales and Cheshire loyalties to him were weakest. He had done much to bolster his position by restoring their marcher lordships to the heirs of Arundel and Warwick, recovering his own Lancastrian lands, and investing Prince Henry with the principality and Chester. But as the reward for their support in 1399 the Percys were put in charge of both North and South Wales: Hotspur as justiciar in North Wales and his uncle Thomas Percy, earl of Worcester, as lieutenant in South Wales and governor of Prince Henry. Further, they had the custody of the estates of the young Edmund Mortimer, earl of March. Their championship of Mortimer interests became suspect when, after his capture, Sir Edmund Mortimer married Glyn Dŵr's daughter, and Hotspur urged the king to negotiate a settlement with the rebels.[29] Just as the revolt empowered the latent Percy–Mortimer challenge to Henry's title, so it also in 1401 invited support from the Gaelic and Scottish enemies of the Crown. Financially, too, the revolt weakened Henry IV, for not only was revenue from the principality and the duchy of Lancaster estates lost for years on end, but the Crown faced a costly war of attrition.

The revolt and its ramifications thus endangered Henry IV's survival, but it was not easily dealt with in either military or political terms. In July 1402 armies under the prince went to relieve Harlech and Caernarfon and under the king (unsuccessfully) to bring Glyn Dŵr to battle.[30] That strategy came too late to prevent the revolt from spreading to the south, and in March 1403 the king determined to give Prince Henry sole command with an army of 500 men-at-arms and 2,500 archers. The displacement of the Percys in Wales and the frustration of Northumberland's ambitions in Scotland brought them into revolt in the second week of July, when Hotspur raised Cheshire in the name of Richard II and

---

[29] *Proc. & Ord.* ii. 60; Davies, *Owain Glyn Dŵr*, 183. Henry IV recovered the Mortimer lordships in mid-Wales from the Percys in November 1401 but Denbigh remained under their control.

[30] Davies, *Owain Glyn Dŵr*, 109.

Mortimer. Thomas Percy, as the prince's steward, suborned over a thousand men from his army to join Hotspur at the bloody battle at Shrewsbury. Had he been able to seize the prince while the king was in the north (as was probably intended), the Lancastrian dynasty might well have been destroyed. The combined forces of the king and prince were barely victorious in a struggle which left 2,000 dead and in which the prince was wounded.[31]

Glyn Dŵr had distanced himself from the battle and he had lost his principal ally, but it virtually paralysed the Crown's offensive for eighteen months, during which Glyn Dŵr was able to advance into south-west and south-east Wales, triggering a sea change of loyalties in which dozens of Anglicized native officials like Henry Dŵn went over to his cause. By the end of 1403 the northern castles of Aberystwyth, Harlech, and Beaumaris were isolated; next year the first two fell in the summer, Kidwelly was taken in August, and in November Caernarfon was attacked and Cardiff was captured.[32]

Owain Glyn Dŵr now won recognition for Welsh independence. In July 1404 he signed a military alliance with France; probably in February 1405 the infamous 'tripartite indenture' between Glyn Dŵr, Edmund Mortimer, and the earl of Northumberland proposed the division of England into three, with the borders of Wales at the Severn. In August 1405 the long-awaited French arrived in strength, taking Carmarthen and other castles on their progress to the English border. Within its now established bounds Glyn Dŵr started to furnish his principality with institutions. He held his first parliament at Machynlleth in 1404, his second at Harlech in July 1405. His chancellor, Gruffudd Yonge, issued documents in his name, dated by his regnal year as prince of Wales. He was supported by many senior churchmen, led by John Trefor, bishop of St Asaph, and Lewis Byford, bishop of Bangor, and by important Cistercian, Franciscan, and Augustinian houses. Recognition for an independent Welsh Church under the metropolitan see of St David's was sought from the Clementist pope, and two Welsh universities were to be founded. This hasty clothing of the new principality with the trappings of late medieval sovereignty could not conceal its vulnerability to the power of the English state.

A new offensive into Wales under the prince was planned in March 1405, only to be frustrated by the northern rising of Archbishop Scrope in May. It was the marcher lords, Arundel, Warwick, York, and Lords Grey of Codnor and Charlton of Powys, who conducted operations against the Welsh from a network of strongly garrisoned castles. Compared to the 2,400 men in garrison the field army was small, a mere 860; but it was from the garrisons that mounted men-at-arms and archers went out to defend and reduce the surrounding areas,

---

[31] Morgan, *War and Society in Medieval Cheshire*, 213–16.

[32] Davies, *Owain Glyn Dŵr*, 112, 200–1. The following three paragraphs are drawn from his account.

gradually reclaiming control over South Wales. In 1406 Prince Henry resumed command, though only intermittently in Wales himself, and by the end of the year the English advance had confined Glyn Dŵr to the upland zone. In November, Anglesey was retaken and the 'Edwardian' strategy of encircling and starving out the north could be applied. But it was another two and a half years before first Aberystwyth and finally Harlech, where Glyn Dŵr's family had taken refuge, were captured. Guerrilla activity continued alongside submissions of local communities in the piecemeal reduction of Merioneth, Caernarfon, and Denbigh in 1408–9.

Glyn Dŵr's bid for independence was doomed, for the English Crown had both the power and determination to retain Wales. The revolt had brought devastation and impoverishment to many areas, both English and Welsh; it had ruined Glyn Dŵr and other native *uchelwr* who had supported him, and created deep rifts between them and others, like Dafydd Gam, who had stayed loyal. Welsh hatred of English lordship had deepened and the yearning for independence, long sustained by prophecy and mythology, had been frustrated. The English distrust of the Welsh as fickle and treacherous was confirmed, and discriminatory legislation reinforced native disabilities in landownership, office-holding, burgess status, marriage, and fosterage. Both the Crown and the marcher lords attempted to recoup some of the losses of war from personal and communal fines on those who submitted. Yet there was to be no return to the profitable lordship of the fourteenth century. English lordship waned, settlement further declined, and a new pattern of government emerged in which the Welsh achieved greater prominence.

With the Lancaster and Bohun lordships added to the principality, the Crown was now the largest landowner in Wales and Henry V was determined that English rule should be both secure and profitable. Large garrisons were maintained in the principality until 1415 under soldiers from his own retinue, while sheriffs were all from resident *advenae* families. The administration was entrusted to royal agents like Hugh Huls and Thomas Walton in the north, John Scudamore, John Merbury, and Sir John Greyndour in the south. No more than a handful of Welshmen held offices above the local administrative divisions of *rhaglaw* and *rhingyll*.[33] Henry's determination to extract revenue for his war brought a steady restoration of the receipts from the principality, to £1,800 from South Wales and £1,300 from North Wales, though this remained well below the level of the fourteenth century. On the duchy of Lancaster estates arrears were steadily collected and three-quarters of current revenue was received on time; their annual yield was on average £2,666. Communal fines were levied at the

---

[33] Griffiths, *King and Country*, 168–9; id., *The Principality of Wales in the Later Middle Ages*, i: *South Wales, 1277–1536* (Cardiff, 1972), pt. II (Calendar of Royal Officers), *passim*.

Great Sessions both in the principality and in the marcher lordships of Brecon, Chepstow, and Gower in 1415.[34] But the death of Arundel in 1415, the long minority of Humphrey, earl of Stafford (1403–23), and the absence of March, Warwick, and Mowbray with the king in France weakened seigniorial authority.

At the same time the war in France offered the native Welsh the chance to demonstrate their loyalty and win advancement through service. English gentry like Edward Stradling and John Merbury and loyal Welsh like Dafydd Gam, Rhys ap Thomas, and Gruffudd Dŵn acted as recruiting agents for companies of Welsh who formed a distinctive component of armies in France from Agincourt to Formigny. Some became notable captains, spending all their lives in France like Matthew Gough and Fulk Eyton, and holding important captaincies like John Scudamore at Harfleur and Gruffudd Dŵn at Tancarville. These men had strong ties of loyalty and service to the English nobility under whom they served while their exploits were celebrated by native poets, notably Guto'r Glyn. For the ordinary archer service abroad, with good pay, the prospect of plunder, and the escape from poverty and subjection, was welcome. It also assisted the pacification of Wales and the reconciliation of Welsh and English. By 1430 Welshmen were being accepted as both traders and residents in all the border towns from Chester to Bristol despite some lingering mistrust.[35]

On Henry V's death the council chose as justiciars Humphrey, duke of Gloucester, in the north, and James, Lord Audley, in the south. In general, in the southern principality and the duchy lordships, those whom Henry V had appointed as stewards and constables (like Scudamore, Stradling, and Dŵn) continued for the decade after his death. But increasingly they chose their active deputies from the Welsh squirearchy, men like Gruffudd ap Nicholas, Gwilym ap Thomas, and Mareddud ap Owain. That was unusual in the north where Gwilym ap Gruffudd, as deputy sheriff of Anglesey, was the exception, he being the son-in-law of Sir William Stanley.[36] The slight improvement of receipts from the principality under Henry V was not maintained; by 1433 Lord Cromwell's estimates put the gross yield from both parts at not much more than £2,200. In Carmarthen and Cardigan it became the regular practice to redeem the sessions in advance by a communal fine; it was a convenience to free tenants, who were

[34] *Proc. & Ord.* ii. 172 gives net estimates for 1415. R. R. Davies, 'Baronial accounts, incomes, and arrears in the later Middle Ages', *Econ. HR* 21 (1968), 225–7; R. E. Archer, 'The Mowbrays', D.Phil. thesis (Oxford University, 1984), 155–7; C. Rawcliffe, *The Staffords 1394–1521* (Cambridge, 1978), 107.

[35] G. Williams, *Renewal and Reformation: Wales 1415–1642* (Oxford, 1993), 166–72; A. D. Carr, 'Welshmen and the Hundred Years War', *Welsh History Review*, 4 (1968–9), 21–46; R. A. Griffiths, 'After Glyn Dŵr: An age of reconciliation?', *PBA* 117 (2002), 139–64.

[36] Griffiths, *King and Country*, 171–4; A. D. Carr, 'Gwilym ap Gruffydd and the rise of the Penrhyn estate', *Welsh History Review*, 15 (1990), 1–20.

excused attendance, but it impeded the prosecution of criminals and redress against officials, thereby reducing the barriers to lawlessness and corruption.[37]

With the commencement of Henry VI's personal rule English administration in the principality underwent a fundamental change. It provided a pool of patronage, with magnate courtiers taking the principal offices and household servants the lesser ones, both being absentees. The two justiciarships came to be held by the earl of Suffolk in the north and the duke of Gloucester in the south, and the lesser offices colonized by their clients. It has been calculated that twenty-three grants of such offices in North Wales and seventeen in South Wales were made in 1437–40 alone. Half of these were for life.[38]

This large-scale absenteeism of the nominal office-holders opened up the actual government of the principality and duchy lordships to local men, some of them English but increasingly from the Welsh squirearchy. Gruffudd ap Nicholas was the most prominent of these: as deputy justiciar first to the duke of Gloucester and then to his successor, Lord Beauchamp, 'by the late 1440s he had virtually supreme control of the government of the principality in the south'. He exploited his powers as justiciar, chamberlain, and escheator to build up his own estate through leases of the royal lands, grants of wardships and escheats, and purchases. He extended his influence into Cardiganshire, where his son Thomas's struggle to establish himself against the rival families of Mareddud ap Owain and John Rhys led to riots in 1439.[39]

The emergence of the Welsh squirearchy owed much to the availability of land, which they avidly accumulated either on long leases of twenty to thirty years or by purchase. They recolonized English-settled areas like the Vale of Glamorgan, and began to acquire property in towns despite repeated re-enactment of laws debarring them; they intermarried with English families like Perrot, Stradling, and Scudamore. These now ceded local office to the Welsh squire-archy, who exploited it to establish their 'sovereignty of the countryside' through a web of influence and intimidation. Their feuds produced a succession of 'ambushes, assaults, killings and burnings'; law enforcement became impossible as the Welsh deputies perverted the petty sessions. There was growing com-plaint in parliament of misgovernance in the southern principality.[40]

The marcher lordships further to the east escaped the appropriation of office by magnates and courtiers, and active lordship continued to be exercised through seigniorial officials. Indeed the Staffords in Caus and Brecon, the Beauchamps in Glamorgan, and York in Denbigh, Montgomery, and Radnor brought in their

[37] *Rot. Parl.* iv. 433; Griffiths, *Principality*, 28–30; Williams, *Renewal and Reformation*, 40–1; T. B. Pugh, *The Marcher Lordships of South Wales, 1415–1536* (Cardiff, 1963), 36–9.

[38] Griffiths, *King and Country*, 174–8.   [39] Ibid. 181–99.

[40] Williams, *Renewal and Reformation*, 107–10, 175, with quotation at 108 from Sir John Wynn, *History of the Gwydir Family*, ed. T. Gwynfor Jones (Llandysul, 1990).

receivers and stewards from their English lordships, men like Thomas Arblaster, John Milewater, and William Burley.[41] An important, if unusual, exception was Sir Gwilym ap Thomas, 'the Blue Knight of Gwent', councillor of the duke of York and chief steward in the duchy of Lancaster and Mortimer lordships, and sheriff of Glamorgan. Having acquired Raglan through his first wife he, or more probably his son William Herbert, constructed its great and innovative castle.[42] Revenue from these marcher lordships was falling gradually rather than steeply in the years before 1450. Newport, which had produced £537 in 1400, yielded £400 in 1434 and the same in 1447–8; the Stafford lordships valued at £1,508 were producing £1,095 in 1447; on York's estates in Wales and the border, the estimated clear revenue of £2,879 in 1443 was boosted to almost £3,500 by the collection of arrears—a higher figure than before 1400.[43]

From 1450 political rivalries in England began to affect the Welsh lordships and involve the Welsh squirearchy. York's feud with Edmund Beaufort, duke of Somerset, was broadened when, in June 1453, the latter used his ascendancy at court to challenge the lordship of the new earl of Warwick, Richard Neville, in Glamorgan.[44] This brought York and Warwick together, making the Mortimer and Neville lordships in eastern Wales a power base against Somerset in west Wales. There the major figure was Gruffudd ap Nicholas, as deputy to both the justiciar and the chamberlain, and supported by Somerset as constable of Carmarthen and Aberystwyth. The creation of Jasper Tudur as earl of Pembroke in November 1452 further consolidated the Lancastrian position in west Wales, while east Wales was held for York by William Herbert at Raglan, Walter Devereux at Wigmore, and William Burley at Montgomery.[45] Even after York's flight to Ireland in October 1459 the Lancastrian Crown could not displace his officers, and when York returned in August 1460 he progressed down the border from Chester, drawing support from his own lordships. But Jasper Tudur maintained the Lancastrian cause in west Wales and, following York's defeat and execution at Wakefield in December, he assembled a force of Welsh, Irish, and Bretons and moved eastwards to join Queen Margaret as she came down from the north. At Mortimer's Cross near Wigmore on 3 February 1461

[41] Rawcliffe, *The Staffords*, 207, 213; Johnson, *Duke Richard of York*, app. III; T. B. Pugh, *Glamorgan County History*, iii: *The Middle Ages* (Cardiff, 1971), 190.
[42] A brief biography is in Griffiths, *Principality*, 147–8; for Raglan Castle, see Emery, *Greater Medieval Houses*, ii. 197–9, 631–5.
[43] Pugh, *Marcher Lordships*, 152; id., 'The estates, finances, and regal aspirations of Richard Plantagenet, duke of York', in Hicks (ed.), *Revolution and Consumption*, 71–88; Rawcliffe, *The Staffords*, 113–14.
[44] Their respective claims, and the complexities of the Beauchamp inheritance, are discussed in Pugh, *Glamorgan County History*, 188–96; Storey, *End of the House of Lancaster*, 238–41; Carpenter, *Locality and Polity*, 442–4, 466; M. A. Hicks, *Warwick the Kingmaker* (Oxford, 1998), 59, 84–5.
[45] Griffiths, *King and Country*, 206–19.

York's son Edward, earl of March, with the aid of Herbert and Dŵn, intercepted and defeated Jasper's army, executing Owain Tudur. The battle was significant, for it saved the Yorkist cause from extinction after Warwick's defeat at St Albans.

Not surprisingly this decade saw the financial collapse of English lordship. Both judicial and manorial profits plummeted. In Newport payments from the great sessions fell heavily into arrears after 1450 and those of 1453–4 were cancelled; in Brecon the fine of 2,000 marks set in 1450 had not been levied by Michaelmas 1454, when the arrears had reached £2,453. In the Mortimer lordships there was a similar failure to hold the great sessions in 1452–3. Outbreaks of lawlessness made it difficult to collect rents from tenants beset by robbery and pillage and led to progressive depopulation. As Stafford lordship weakened, it handed over estate offices to native Welsh and even hired Welsh mercenaries to protect its tenants. 'The crisis in seigniorial revenues in the Welsh marches was permanent and catastrophic ... and marked the ending of the middle ages in Wales.'[46]

Throughout the 1450s North Wales remained part of the fiefdom of Sir Thomas Stanley, which extended over Cheshire, Lancashire, and the Isle of Man. As chamberlain of the household the loyalty of Sir Thomas was beyond doubt, but on his death in 1459 his offices of justiciar and chamberlain in North Wales and Chester were not conferred on his son Thomas, who was married to a daughter of Richard Neville, earl of Salisbury. Thomas conspicuously absented himself from the Lancastrian forces under Lord Audley which were defeated by Salisbury at Bloreheath in September 1459, narrowly escaping attainder for his 'treachery'. North Wales had submitted to Edward IV by the end of 1461 with the exception of Harlech, which remained a Lancastrian refuge until 1468.

The half-century that followed the collapse of Owain Glyn Dŵr's revolt brought an escalating withdrawal of English settlement and lordship from Wales and the attendant rise of a native squirearchy which came to occupy the offices and lands of their former masters. While this process of decolonization reflected demographic and economic changes, it also sprang from a failure of will by the Crown and magnates. Neither Richard II nor Henry V had attempted to integrate the government of Wales with that of England. Henry VI largely abandoned it to his magnates. The narrowing group of absentees who held the marcher lordships valued them only as a source of income. As the settlement declined they tried to safeguard revenues by relinquishing the administration of their estates to the native gentry, thereby creating a landed and governing class on which the integration of Wales into the English polity would eventually be based.

[46] Pugh, *Marcher Lordships*, 175–8, and id., 'Estates, finances, of York', 77 (for quotation); Rawcliffe, *The Staffords*, 48–50, 113, 207, 213–14.

3. THE ANGLO-SCOTTISH BORDER

Across its northern frontier England faced a kingdom which English kings had twice made strenuous efforts to conquer in the century before 1360. Had these been successful some form of colonial rule would have been imposed, at least in the English-speaking, feudalized lowlands. In fact, Edward I's invasion had provoked an insurgent nationalism which turned a neighbour into a determined enemy and empowered the Scottish monarchy. Despite continuing to claim suzerainty, the English Crown had in practice to deal with the Scottish kingdom on equal terms, not least because the greater enemy, France, extended it protection to keep the back door into England open. English and Scottish kings thus faced each other across a militarized frontier running from Solway to the Tweed. In the first half of the fourteenth century this became a war zone, studded with castles, towerlets, and pele towers. In Cumbria alone there were 138 castles and towers. It was a society organized to launch and resist raids. Clan and kin, identified by patronymic, afforded protective solidarity in a world of restless feuding. Livestock was the principal form of wealth and the normal object of raiding. Districts and individuals were held to ransom, and the peasantry learned to survive by flight to the woods, the removal of livestock to barmkins, and the dismantling of houses. Though raids were temporary and the basic economy resilient, a pervading sense of insecurity isolated these border counties from those south of the Tyne. Royal lordship, authority, and justice were remote and nominal.[47]

The stability of the border was regulated by truces negotiated between the two Crowns for periods of years, but these were constantly under threat from local raiding and retaliation, from clashes between the baronage of both sides, and from royal invasions. To deal with the first, a system of border tribunals was evolved in the later fourteenth century, with conservators of the truce from both sides adjudicating blame and compensation at 'days of march'. These depended on the great border magnates enforcing their decisions, but gradually a code of border law was established which provided a working framework for dispute settlement. It was based on civil law principles, employing both arbitration and judicial combat.[48]

The territorial ambitions of the great border families, notably Percy and Douglas, centred mainly on the English enclaves in Scottish territory at Lochmaben in Annandale and Roxburgh in Teviotdale. The Percy family had

[47] R. L. Storey, 'The north of England', in Chrimes *et al.* (eds.), *Fifteenth Century England*, 129–44; A. Goodman, 'The Anglo-Scottish marches in the fifteenth century: A frontier society', in R. Mason (ed.), *Scotland and England, 1281–1815* (Edinburgh, 1987), 6–22.

[48] C. J. Neville, *Violence, Custom and Law* (Edinburgh, 1998).

been established at Alnwick and Warkworth from early in the century and their acquisition of the Lucy and Umfraville inheritances in the 1370s had led to their creation as earls of Northumberland in 1377. Their later rivals, the Nevilles, were at this point no more than a baronial family with castles at Raby and Brancepeth in Co. Durham and Middleham in Yorkshire. Lesser baronial families like Clifford, Dacre, Greystoke, and Ogle, and such knightly families as Grey, Heron, and Conyers, all of whom had strongly fortified castles along the border, were mostly clients of the Percys.[49] The Crown had to rely on them to defend the border, for the only royal fortresses were those at Carlisle and Berwick, at Bamborough on the coast, and at Roxburgh and Lochmaben. Yet they did not enjoy regalian powers, financial, judicial, and military, comparable to those of the Welsh marcher lords. The wardens of the northern marches were appointed by the Crown for limited periods, under indentures which detailed and limited their authority and set their salary. At times they were even subject to the superior authority of a royal lieutenant. Nevertheless, it was their own territorial power which gave force to their public office.[50] The English kings, having abandoned any thought of conquering Scotland, generally desired peace on the border, not least when they were fighting France. The Scottish kings, too, generally favoured peace: some (like Robert II) were notably pacific and others (David II and James I) were for long periods prisoners in England. But with French prompting, or to take advantage of English weakness, they might embark on war.

During the second half of the fourteenth century the captivity of David II from 1346 to 1357 and his subsequent liberation under a ransom treaty produced a continuous truce to 1371, which his successor, Robert II, renewed until 1384. After the Treaty of Brétigny, Edward III had toyed with the possibility of securing the succession to the childless King David for himself or for John of Gaunt but the Scottish parliament rejected this and after 1371 Gaunt's ambitions came to centre on Spain. Following the death of Edward III, hostility grew between the earls of Douglas and Northumberland over their rival claims to Jedburgh, and from 1379 to 1384 John of Gaunt was appointed as king's lieutenant in the march to ensure its stability. Gaunt held no land north of Yorkshire and Lancashire and his intrusion into the march was resented by Henry Percy, earl of Northumberland. In June 1381, while Gaunt was at Berwick, news of the peasants' rising in London and their burning of the Savoy led him to seek refuge at Alnwick. Percy refused him admittance, opening a breach between them which was never wholly healed. Gaunt temporarily removed Percy from the wardenship of the east march and promoted his own retainer John, Lord Neville, for the

[49] J. A. Tuck, 'The emergence of a northern nobility', *Northern Hist.* 22 (1986), 1–17; Emery, *Greater Medieval Houses*, i. 13–17, 20–9, 164–7

[50] Storey, 'The Wardens of the marches of England towards Scotland', *EHR* 72 (1957), 595–8, 609–10.

next three years. In February 1384 the earls of Douglas and Dunbar overran Annandale and captured Lochmaben, leaving Roxburgh the only isolated English outpost across the border. Gaunt conducted a retaliatory raid into the lowlands but the Scots admitted a French force under Jean de Vienne in July 1385, provoking an invasion by Richard II in August at the head of an army of 12,000–14,000 men. This met no resistance and occupied Edinburgh, where Gaunt is said to have urged the king to advance into the highlands to force a battle. Richard prudently refused, and Gaunt shortly afterwards withdrew, to make preparations for his voyage to Spain. The English invasion was followed by short truces, until in August 1388 the Scots launched a simultaneous attack in both east and west. Northumberland's son Henry Hotspur brought the smaller force to battle at Otterburn in Redesdale, where he was defeated and captured, though Douglas himself was killed.[51]

Since the summer of 1384 the multiple commissions of border lords who had monitored the truce under Gaunt had been replaced by a sole wardenship in the east march, held for two-year periods by Percy and Neville, while Neville, Clifford, and Greystoke jointly held the west. If the war thus confirmed the role of Percy and Neville as the principal defenders of the north, the challenge to Richard's kingship by the Appellants helped to draw them into English politics. In 1387–9 Northumberland played a mediatory role between Richard and the Appellants and in the early 1390s the king conferred the wardenship of both marches on him and his son Hotspur (whom the Crown had helped to ransom). They each held these for terms of five years, until in June 1396 Hotspur was given the east march for the unprecedented term of ten years. The terms of payment were also stabilized: for the east march £3,000 per annum in truce and £12,000 in time of war, with the west march at half these rates. Not merely was this monopoly of the wardenship for long periods under indenture unprecedented, but the Percys had successfully excluded their rival. John, Lord Neville, had died in 1388 and his son Ralph was given no command on the border during the 1390s, though he was created earl of Westmorland in 1397 and married to Gaunt's daughter Joan, receiving also the barony of Penrith.[52]

The twenty-eight-year truce with France in 1396 gave Richard the opportunity to end the Percys' monopoly of border defence. From 1395 he placed the west march under a sequence of courtier lords—Beaumont, Huntingdon, Aumale—removed Roxburgh from Hotspur's charge, and brought back Gaunt briefly as king's lieutenant. This alienated Northumberland, while Richard's serial destruction of the Appellants, Mowbray, and Lancaster in 1397–9 left him

[51] Goodman, *John of Gaunt*, 73–84, 98, 104, 177; A. Goodman and A. Tuck (eds.), *War and Border Societies in the Middle Ages* (London, 1992), 1–29.

[52] Storey, 'Wardens of the marches', 598–602, 610–13.

isolated and nervous. The landing of Henry of Lancaster at Ravenspur in 1399 presented him with both a dilemma and an opportunity.[53] The East Riding estates of the Percys lay across Henry's route to Pontefract, affording the chance to intercept him before he could gather support. Northumberland had no love for Gaunt's son but his distrust of Richard II ran deeper. His price for rallying to Henry was high: on 2 August by a grant under the duchy of Lancaster seal Henry restored him to the wardenship of the west march, and in October as king he confirmed Northumberland and Hotspur in both marches for ten years at the established rates, along with Roxburgh, Bamborough, and the Isle of Man. With Hotspur controlling Chester and North Wales, the Percys by 1400 had command of all the major garrisons apart from Calais.[54]

Even while the Percys' power was being entrenched in the north, Henry reopened the Scottish war. There was no compelling reason for his invasion in August 1400 with an army of 15,000–20,000. Although Robert III had refused to recognize Henry's title, there was little danger from Scotland either of support for Richard II's cause or through French intervention. The expedition has thus been judged 'futile' and 'unnecessary'.[55] From another perspective, however, it enabled Henry IV to assert his sovereign power on the border. Composed of retinues which the loyal nobility raised at their own cost, along with the newly enlarged royal affinity, it was a reminder to the Percys that the king intended to control policy towards Scotland.[56] On 6 August Henry summoned Robert III to do homage in Edinburgh; then marching across the lowlands he occupied the city without sacking it, and within two weeks had returned to Durham. It had been a symbolic demonstration rather than an act of war, and was designed not to provoke reprisals.

Henry IV's difficulties in Wales and England during the next two years perpetuated his dependence on the Percys, though he cautiously extended the power of the Nevilles and recruited some border families into his affinity. By 1402 events in Scotland threatened the truce on the border which Henry had striven to maintain. In January, King Robert's heir and lieutenant the duke of Rothesay was overthrown and died, and the duke of Albany and the new earl of Douglas seized power. A devastating foray into Northumberland by the earls of

---

[53] J. A. Tuck, 'Richard II and the border magnates', *Northern Hist.* 3 (1968), 27–52; id., *Richard II and the English Nobility*, 163–5, 201–2. Northumberland ceased to attend the court after July 1398 (PRO, C53/167).

[54] J. M. W. Bean, 'Henry IV and the Percies', *History*, 44 (1959), 212–27.

[55] A. L. Brown, 'The English campaign in Scotland, 1400', in H. Hearder and H. R. Loyn (eds.), *British Government and Administration* (Cardiff, 1974), 40–54.

[56] C. J. Neville, 'Scotland, the Percies, and the law in 1400', in G. Dodd and D. Biggs (eds.), *Henry IV: The Establishment of the Regime, 1399–1406* (Woodbridge, 2003), 73–94; cf. P. McNiven, 'The Scottish policy of the Percies and the strategy of the Shrewsbury campaign', *BJRUL* 62 (1980), 498–530.

Douglas, Angus, and Moray was intercepted by Hotspur and crushingly defeated at Homildon Hill in September. All three earls were captured along with Albany's son and heir Murdach of Fife.[57] Northumberland was now bent on annexing the Douglas lands in Annandale and Teviotdale, and in March 1403 Henry IV formally granted him the greater part of the Douglas possessions, opening up the prospect of a vast cross-border fiefdom. Shortly afterwards Hotspur entered Teviotdale while Northumberland insistently demanded from Henry the money owed to him as warden, which he set at £20,000, to hire troops for his offensive.[58] Neither financially nor politically could Henry afford to underwrite the Percys' empire-building; he wanted peace rather than war on his northern frontier, and needed the money for Prince Henry's coming offensive in Wales. He decided to lead his own army to the north—whether to assist the Percys in arms or to impose a truce on the border is not clear. On 16 July he had reached Burton upon Trent, where he heard news of Hotspur's revolt in Wales. Before Northumberland could move south, Henry IV had joined the prince and defeated Hotspur at Shrewsbury. Their overwhelming defeat destroyed the Percys' political pretensions.

The Nevilles now commenced their long tenure of the west march, while the king's son John held the east march for the next eleven years. This sudden replacement of Percy ascendancy with that of Neville–Lancaster introduced a period of turbulence in northern society, which culminated in the rebellions of Northumberland, Mowbray, and Archbishop Scrope in 1405 and the forfeiture of the Percy lands. The previous twenty years had thus seen the growth of the power and rivalry of the two great marcher families who were said to 'have the hertes of the people by north and ever had'.[59] Their wealth is attested by the size and quality of the palace fortresses they erected between 1377 and 1400: Percy at Warkworth, Cockermouth, and Wressle; Neville at Raby, Sheriff Hutton, and Penrith and large elements of Brancepeth and Middleham.[60] Yet it remains unclear how much they derived their resources from their own lands and how much from the Crown's wages. Similarly, virtually nothing is known about the size and composition of the Percy and Neville affinities at this date: how many they retained at the Crown's wages and whether these were from their own retainers, and how far they commanded the loyalties of other lords of the region.[61]

---

[57] R. Nicholson, *Scotland: The Later Middle Ages* (Edinburgh, 1974), 216–25; A. King, 'Northumberland, the Percies, and Henry IV, 1399–1408', in Dodd and Biggs (eds.), *Henry IV*, 139–60.

[58] Bean, 'Henry IV and the Percies', 223. Northumberland's letters are in *Proc. & Ord.* i. 203–5.

[59] Storey, 'North of England', 131–4 (quotation at 132).

[60] Emery, *Great Medieval Houses*, for descriptions of individual castles.

[61] J. A. Tuck, 'War and society in the medieval north', *Northern Hist.* 21 (1985), 33–52.

In March 1406 the uneasy relations between the two kingdoms were brought to resolution by the English capture of King Robert's 12-year-old heir James, who was being shipped to France for fear of the designs of the regent Albany. The news killed his father and Henry IV found himself in possession of the new Scottish king. It ensured that for the rest of the reign the truce was maintained and regularly renewed. With Henry V's invasion of France the captive king became a guarantee of crucial Scottish neutrality. Further, Henry negotiated the release of the regent Albany's son Murdach, in exchange for Hotspur's son, calculating that the restoration of a Percy to the earldom of Northumberland would guarantee the stability and defence of the march. When this was finalized in 1416 the new earl of Northumberland and the earl of Westmorland, Ralph Neville, held the north, repulsing the only Scottish incursion in 1417. Henry V was less successful in preventing the Scots from taking service in French armies. In 1419 a force under the earls of Buchan and Douglas was conveyed in Castilian ships to La Rochelle and helped to defeat Clarence at Baugé in 1421. But at Cravant in 1423, and decisively at Verneuil in 1424, Bedford defeated the Franco-Scottish army, leaving both earls dead on the field.

On Henry V's death the council decided that Scottish neutrality would be best guaranteed by the return of James I. His long captivity had Anglicized the king, who was a man of intelligence and sensibility, and he had won the heart of Somerset's daughter Joan Beaufort, whom he now married.[62] He bound himself to pay a ransom of £40,000 in annual instalments and signed a seven-year truce. The stability of the northern frontier thus rested externally on a Stewart–Beaufort marriage alliance and domestically on Neville–Lancastrian political hegemony, but its best guarantee remained English success in France. By 1435 English reverses in France and Bedford's death persuaded James to a more Francophile policy. He sent his daughter Margaret to France to marry the Dauphin and marked the end of the truce in May 1436 with an attack on Roxburgh. He thereby hoped to outface opposition to his rule from the nobility, whose independence he had set out to curb. But the garrison had been increased and its defences repaired and James had to retire from the siege. His enemies seized on his defeat to have him murdered at Perth in February 1437.

The minority of his son the 7-year-old James II was the signal for the emergence of factions which supplanted the regent mother, Joan Beaufort, and further strengthened ties with France. Charles VII helped to arrange the marriage of James's elder sister Isabella to Francis I, duke of Brittany, in 1442, and James's own marriage to a niece of Philip the Good, Mary of Guelders, in 1449. Yet the truce with England was renewed throughout the 1440s, and though briefly broken

<hr>

[62] James recorded his love for Joan and release from captivity in his poem 'The King's Quair', discussed in Nicholson, *Scotland*, 279–80.

by a cross-border clash at Sark in October 1448, it held throughout the months of 1449–50, when Charles and Francis launched their attack on Normandy and Henry VI faced revolt at home. After 1450 the growth of the opposing factions of York and Beaufort in England was echoed at the Scottish court, where James II inclined to his mother's family of Beaufort, and his opponents the Black Douglases supported the protectorate of the duke of York. The dismissal of York in February 1455 prompted James to advance against the Douglas castles, proscribe them, and seize their lands. Earl Douglas fled to England.[63]

James now hoped to crown his domestic triumph by taking advantage of the developing civil strife in England to recover Roxburgh and Berwick, but his incursions in July 1456 and February 1457 were both repulsed. The open war between York and the Crown in 1459–60 presented him with the opportunity he had planned for. As the Yorkists advanced from Kent in June 1460 he brought up the artillery he had been gathering to besiege Roxburgh. This time the siege was successful; it surrendered in August, ending the English occupation of Teviotdale. James, however, did not live to see this; he was killed when one of his own cannons exploded on 3 August. Thus, despite thirty-five years of war with France, and a further ten of internal turmoil, England escaped serious invasion from Scotland and lost only one outpost. The periods of open war (1417, 1436–8, 1448–9, 1455–6, 1460) amounted to only five years in all. That did not mean that peace reigned on the border. Raiding, ransoming, burning, and cattle-thieving were endemic, but after a hiatus in the first quarter of the century the border tribunals and days of march were revived to provide a practical measure of cohabitation.[64]

In committing the guard of the marches to Neville and Percy, Henry V had initiated almost forty years of near-continuous occupancy by them. At the same time he and his father had curtailed their inflated pretensions as kingmakers which Richard II's patronage had bolstered. The rates of pay were drastically reduced, set in 1411 at £2,500 for the east march, £1,250 for the west march, and £1,000 for Roxburgh in time of truce, with double in war. This was not sufficient to support more than a small body of troops, being in all hardly more than one-third the cost of the Calais garrison.[65] With peace on the border, no larger force was needed, and in time of war they would perforce mobilize their own affinities. But Henry VI's minority helped to exacerbate their rivalry. The Nevilles' tradition of service to the house of Lancaster had been strengthened by the second marriage of Ralph, first earl of Westmorland, to Joan Beaufort, daughter of John of Gaunt. After his death Joan secured the Neville lands in Middleham,

---

[63] Nicholson, *Scotland*, 347–73; R. Vaughan, *Philip the Good* (London, 1962), 110–12; Griffiths, *Henry VI*, 402–11.

[64] Neville, *Violence, Custom, and Law*, chs. 5, 6.

[65] These rates would pay 55 men-at-arms and 165 mounted archers in the east march and 28 men-at-arms and 84 archers in the west march for a year.

Sheriff Hutton, and Penrith for her eldest son, Richard, while leaving Westmorland's son and heir by his first wife only the Durham lands. In 1429 Richard Neville became earl of Salisbury through his marriage to the Montague heiress, and during the 1430s he could count on the support of his kinsman Cardinal Beaufort in the council to uphold this division of the Neville inheritance in his favour. His brother Robert's tenure of the bishopric of Durham from 1438 to 1457 further extended the Neville interest into the palatinate. In 1436 Salisbury also forged links, through the marriage of his children, to the Beauchamp earldom of Warwick, to which his son Richard succeeded in 1446.[66] As Neville influence expanded, that of Percy shrank. Northumberland had no place on the council during Henry VI's minority, and only in the 1440s did the family begin to regain its wealth and influence with the accession of the Poynings inheritance in Sussex.[67] Salisbury's territorial influence was also extending in these years. In Northumberland, Percy lordship had traditionally embraced the quasi-baronial families of Heron of Ford, Grey of Wark, Ogle of Bothal, and others, but by the 1450s some of these were at least temporarily attached to the Nevilles. Likewise, in the west march the baronial families of Clifford and Dacre had been old Percy adherents, but in the 1430s and 1440s Dacre, Greystoke, and some gentry families came under Salisbury's influence and numbers of his retainers were sheriffs and JPs. Further south at Middleham, Salisbury had more than twenty retainers among the Richmondshire gentry.[68]

Despite the mutual hostility of Neville and Percy, by 1450 the two families had cooperated in the defence of the border for thirty years. It was among their sons that discord now arose. Thomas Percy, Lord Egremont, 'a wild and belligerent young man', had established himself at the head of the Percy following in Cumberland in 1450 to counter Neville influence, but it was in Yorkshire that the first open confrontation occurred. Here the Neville lordships of Middleham and Sheriff Hutton lay cheek by jowl with those of Percy at Leconfield, Spofforth, and Topcliffe. Why conflict arose here in 1453 is not certain, but it seems to have centred on the castle of Wressle near Leconfield, a former Percy lordship which Lord Cromwell was promising to confer on Salisbury's son Thomas Neville, who was about to marry his niece Maud Willoughby.[69]

---

[66] Harriss, *Cardinal Beaufort*, 267–70; Storey, *End of the House of Lancaster*, 105–23; Pollard, *North Eastern England*, 249–53.

[67] J. M. W. Bean, *The Estates of the Percy Family, 1416–1537* (Oxford, 1958), 82–5.

[68] The evidence for retaining is scarce; this paragraph is based on Storey, *End of the House of Lancaster*, 120–3; A. J. Pollard, 'The northern retainers of Richard Neville, earl of Salisbury', *Northern Hist.* 11 (1976), 52–66; id., *North Eastern England*, 245–65.

[69] This explanation, advanced by Griffiths, *King and Country*, 325–50, and supported by S. J. Payling, 'The Ampthill dispute: A study in aristocratic lawlessness and the breakdown of Lancastrian government', *EHR* 104 (1989) 895, and by Pollard, *North Eastern England*, 255–7, is discountenanced by Hicks, *Warwick the Kingmaker*, 88–9.

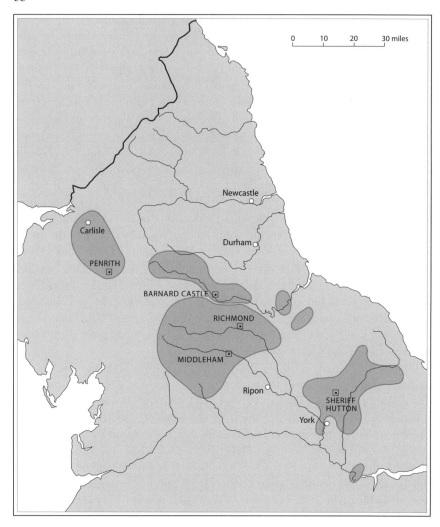

MAP 13.3. Estates of the Neville and Percy families in the north of England. Source:
A. J. Pollard, *North Eastern England during the Wars of the Roses* (Oxford, 1990), 95–6
(*a*) Neville of Middleham estates

Early in 1453 there were violent clashes between Lord Egremont and Sir John
Neville near Topcliffe, and in August and October confrontations in strength at
Heworth Moor outside York and at Topcliffe, though mediation prevented a
clash of arms. Serious as was this quarrel, it was at this stage local and dynastic
rather than political, something that the Crown and the council should have been
able to settle. But at this point Henry VI fell into a coma and the exercise of the

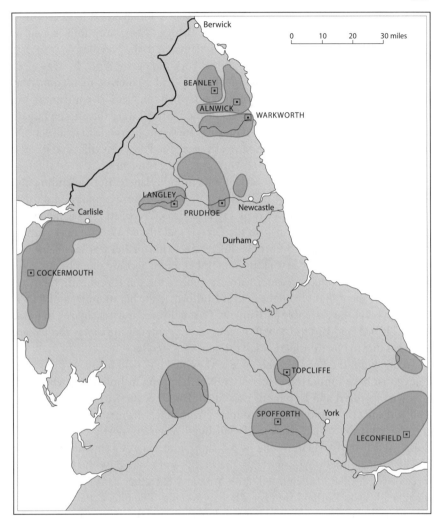

MAP 13.3 (*b*) Percy estates

royal authority was contested between the dukes of York and Somerset. The two
marcher earls were drawn in, with Salisbury supporting York's protectorate as
chancellor in April 1454, while Northumberland joined the duke of Exeter in
defying York's authority. This line-up, which reversed their traditional loyalties,
was determined more by the opposing ambitions of Warwick and Somerset in
South Wales than by the northern conflict.[70] In May 1454 York came northwards

[70] For the dispute over the Beauchamp–Despenser inheritance, see below, Ch. 15, sect. 5.

and Exeter submitted. In October, Salisbury's sons Thomas and John captured Egremont and Richard Percy at Stamford Bridge. They were imprisoned in London and condemned to pay £11,200 in damages to the Nevilles.

The two earls were now locked into the York–Somerset feud. In May 1455 Northumberland was accompanying the king and Somerset to a council at Leicester for the proscription of the Yorkists when the Nevilles confronted the royal force at St Albans. Northumberland and Clifford were the chosen targets of the Nevilles, as Somerset was that of York. It was the first time that border retinues had fought in the south. These deaths gave the Percy–Neville feud its own momentum. By 1456 the failure of York's second protectorate revived the fortunes of the Percys. The new earl of Northumberland, after defending the march against James II's siege of Roxburgh in 1455–7, was reappointed warden for ten years in 1457. The loveday of 1458 prescribed reparations for the deaths at St Albans, remitted the fines on the Percys, and placed Wressle in the king's hands. But soon both sides were enlisting retainers for further warfare. Salisbury marched south to join Warwick in September 1459, accompanied by his sons Thomas and John. His encounter with the queen's force at Bloreheath, followed by his subsequent flight from the field at Ludford, led to his attainder and that of his followers at the Coventry parliament. That delivered the west march to John, Lord Clifford, and laid the Neville estates under contribution to pay the arrears of wages due to Northumberland to the sum of £16,985.

To this point the Percys' adherence to the court had paid handsome rewards. They must have supported Henry VI at Northampton in June 1460, where the king was captured and Egremont was killed. But after the battle they still controlled the north, plundering the estates of York and Salisbury and their followers. To confront them York and Salisbury marched north in December. Supported from Durham by the new bishop, Laurence Booth, and the senior Neville branch under Westmorland, the Percys were joined by the Lancastrian forces assembled at Hull and fell upon York and Salisbury at Wakefield, killing them, York's son Rutland, and Sir Thomas Neville. The queen, having secured the neutrality of the Scots, led a large and vengeful northern army to London in the depth of winter.[71] It spread terror in the south and routed Warwick's Kentish army at St Albans. But provisions were short, and resistance in the capital forced it to retired to the north to fight the decisive battle. The immensely costly engagement at Towton on 28 March 1461 involved all the northern nobility and their retinues. On the Lancastrian side Northumberland and Lord Dacre fell in battle and a large number of Percy retainers were captured and executed. Even after his victory Edward IV did not venture beyond Newcastle and left the

---

[71] M. A. Hicks, 'A minute of the Lancastrian council at York, 20 January 1461', *Northern Hist.* 35 (1999), 214–21.

reduction of Northumbria to Sir Robert Ogle and the earl of Warwick. It was to be another three years before that was achieved.

The conspicuous part played by the marcher lords of Wales and the north in the Wars of the Roses has been seen as indicating a structural imbalance between the centre and the periphery in the late medieval English state. It is argued that the 'dominions and provinces' were too large, too distant, too amorphous, and too costly to be governed effectively. The Crown's authority was overextended, and was surrendered to nobles who commanded local loyalties and pursued their own dynastic rivalries.[72] As a commentary on the descent into civil war, this clearly has force, but a longer perspective suggests some qualification. The expansion of English lordship into Wales and Ireland had been undertaken by feudal lords rather than the Crown, and although in the thirteenth century the Crown claimed legal sovereignty over both countries, its own areas of rule remained restricted and the greater part was controlled by lords wielding quasi-regal powers. This pattern of devolved government largely determined the character of the Crown's rule for the rest of the Middle Ages. After futile and expensive attempts to extend the conquest over both Ireland and Scotland, by 1400 it had realistically accepted defeat. In Wales, once the revolt had been suppressed, government was gradually devolved to a native squirearchy. In the fifteenth century the Crown sought to stabilize the periphery by disengagement with the Irish and Scots, thereby reducing the military and financial burden. This proved viable up to 1450, enabling the Crown to concentrate on its greater ambitions in France, but it brought its own dangers. First, the unchecked freedom of the marcher lords to exploit (or neglect) their lands could generate discontent and even revolt, as in Wales. Secondly, their rivalries, like those of Ormond and Talbot, Beauchamp and Mowbray, and Percy and Neville, could destabilize their regions. Thirdly, any extension of their rivalries into the English peerage, as in 1459–61, could endanger the Crown. But this was exceptional and sprang from a personal and circumstantial deficit of royal authority rather than a structural opposition of centre and periphery. Generally the marcher nobility saw themselves as the Crown's servants and allies in defending and ruling the borders of the realm; only in 1403 and 1457–60 did they give primacy to their family ambitions and honour.

[72] R. A. Griffiths, 'The provinces and the dominions in the age of the Wars of the Roses', in S. D. Michalove and A. C. Reeves (eds.), *Estrangement, Enterprise and Education in Fifteenth Century England* (Stroud, 1998), 1–26 (quotation at 14).

CHAPTER 14

The English in France, 1413–1453

1. THE LANCASTRIAN CONQUEST IN FRANCE, 1413–1429

Conditions in 1413 appeared favourable for Henry V to renew war in France. Charles VI's feeble kingship and the feud of Burgundy and Orléans had already invited Lancastrian intervention. In England the dynasty's uncertain credentials would be fortified by consciously reviving the legal claims and chivalric tradition of Edward III on which Richard II had reneged. Henry's leadership of a nobility of his own generation would reaffirm the role of the Crown and heal the political divisions of the last fifteen years. Lastly, with the Welsh revolt subdued and the Scottish king a prisoner, foreign war was again feasible, while Henry's dedication to a programme of good governance had won the approval of political society.

But while the preconditions for war were in place, the prospects for a successful war were less promising. Henry V knew well enough that in the fourteenth century English intervention had ended in utter failure. The strategy of exploiting internal quarrels—in Flanders, Normandy, Brittany, and Castile—had been self-defeating, for whether their allies were victorious or defeated the English were eventually sent home. Similarly the chosen tactic, the *chevauchée*, designed to terrorize and to disrupt economic life, brought no permanent gain to the invader in terms of land or political authority. By the 1380s not only had the huge expenditure of wealth, prowess, and ambition ended in contention and impoverishment, but a reaction had set in against the chivalric exploitation of war. Literate opinion warned of its futility, deplored its moral corruption, and denounced it as a scandal among Christians. The lessons of recent history thus warned Henry V of almost certain disaster if he went to war with France: of unreliable allies, of evanescent gains, of burdensome taxation, and of mortal sin. Henry's response to this was twofold. On the ideological plane he insistently proclaimed the justice of his cause, while in practical terms he transformed the objectives and methods of warfare.

Henry could justify either a claim to sovereignty over the lands conceded in the unfulfilled treaty of Brétigny (and the unpaid portion of King John's ransom) or the crown of France which Edward III had never renounced. He knew that the Orléanist faction who controlled Charles VI would concede little if any of this in negotiation, but for two years he pressed these demands, while preparing to attack. His first envoys, in August 1414, had put his territorial demands at their widest: the whole of Aquitaine, and all the lands of the old Angevin empire, along with the balance of King John's ransom and a dowry with the hand of the princess Catherine. The Orléanists were prepared to negotiate a peace or truce linked to a marriage, similar to that of 1396, which would extend the bounds of English Aquitaine though not in sovereignty. When talks were resumed early in 1415 Henry seemed tacitly to have accepted this, but in fact the negotiations were a sham, pursued only to enable him to proclaim the unreasonableness of the French. News of Henry's preparations brought a final French embassy to Winchester at the end of June, where the king was assembling the invasion army. Their marginal concessions were swept aside and negotiations finally collapsed when Henry's assertion of his right to the French crown was met by the taunt that he was not even the rightful king of England.

While these negotiations for a peace were plainly a charade, Henry was conducting others with John the Fearless, duke of Burgundy, for an alliance. Burgundy's hope was to recover Paris and the control of Charles VI; his fear was of an agreement between his Orléanist enemies and the emperor-elect, Sigismund, to dismember his territories. In either case England would be a natural and traditional ally. But when Henry V tried to probe how ready the duke would be to defy Charles VI and recognize Henry as king of France, John backed away and came to terms with Orléans. Henry can scarcely have been surprised; for Duke John was the premier peer of France, and was not going to ally openly with France's ancient enemy. But Henry's diplomacy had established two facts of importance: first, that Burgundy and Orléans were unlikely to make common cause against him, and secondly, that Burgundy would be an unreliable ally. The same was true of the duke of Brittany, who wanted no more alliances with the English and was determined to maintain his independence. All he would agree to in 1413–14 was a ten-year truce. Henry thus knew that he would have to fight his own battles; something he probably welcomed.

He was thus free to choose his objective. Gascony was not an option: it was too far to transport a large army, the local nobility were unreliable, and he would be dangerously distant from England. The choice lay between Calais and the coast of Normandy. His decision showed how his concept of war had changed. Calais had been the launching pad for the plundering *chevauchées* of Edward III and his sons. Henry's purpose was not destruction but conquest. He saw war as a political rather than a purely military exercise, as a means to assert sovereignty. Harfleur was the chosen objective, for it 'was a noble and hereditary portion of his crown of England and of his duchy of Normandy'.[1] Henry's perspective had thus leaped back, past the treaties of Brétigny in 1360 and Paris in 1259, to 1066 and John's loss of Normandy in 1204. Such an appeal to history was beyond the purview of diplomacy, and could only be enforced by arms.

It also demanded warfare of a wholly new character: siege warfare. No major town in France had been captured by the English since Calais in 1347. But Henry had taken the measure of the challenge, and a full two years beforehand bows and arrows were being stockpiled in the Tower, guns were forged at Bristol, siege engines, scaling ladders, battering rams, and 100,000 gunstones were ordered. Alongside Nicholas Merbury, master of the ordnance, William Catton, clerk of the king's ships, worked to construct fifteen warships to be led by the flagship, the Trinity Royal of 540 tons, to guard the crossing. Transport was provided in a fleet of 1,500 ships, half of them hired from the Low Countries. Towards the end of July 1415 Henry moved to Portchester, and on 11 August the whole armada, carrying an army of over 10,000 men, sailed from Southampton. To the last its destination was not publicized, but its character and purpose appeared when it touched shore at the Chef de Caux near Harfleur.

The landing had been unopposed, but the garrison had been strengthened and the town was strongly walled. Henry ceaselessly directed the siege, concentrating on the barbican defending the main gate which was hammered by his artillery. Its destruction brought the surrender of the town on 22 September. Harfleur was 'the key to the sea of all Normandie',[2] commanding the mouth of the Seine and passage along the English Channel. Henry saw it as a permanent conquest, another Calais, and planned 'to stuff the town with Englishmen'.[3] It was the first step to his larger design. But in the eyes of contemporary chivalry it was a mediocre reward for a royal expedition, lacking even the glamour and profit of an assault. Moreover, many died from sickness, including the earls of Arundel and Suffolk and Henry's friend Bishop Courtenay of Norwich; almost one-third of the army had to be sent home, among them Clarence and the earls of March and Norfolk. His captains advised the king to recross the Channel, but Henry 'greatly desired to see those lands whereof he ought to be lord' and determined to march 'through his duchy of Normandy' to Calais.[4]

A garrison under the earl of Dorset was left at Harfleur, and on 8 October an army of almost 6,000, mostly archers, set off along the coast, aiming to cover the 150 miles to Calais in eight days. It was not a *chevauchée*; Henry forbade plunder, though he ransomed towns en route to supplement his provisions. Nor, probably, was he seeking to bring the French to battle. Their main army of some 14,000

[1] *Gesta*, 35.
[2] *The First English Life of King Henry the Fifth*, ed. C. L. Kingsford (Oxford, 1911), 35.
[3] *Brut*, ii. 377.   [4] *First English Life*, 42; *Gesta*, 59.

men lay at Rouen, too far away to catch him up, though smaller detachments shadowed his right flank and lay ahead at Abbeville. It was these that seized the ford at Blanchetacque by which Henry, like Edward III in 1346, looked to cross the Somme. With their direct route blocked, the English were forced to follow the river inland to find a crossing, while the French under the constable Albret shadowed them on the other bank. After five days' march an unguarded ford near Nesle allowed the army to cross and turn northwards to Calais. It was now clear that they would have to fight, for the main French army had moved ahead to cross the Somme at Abbeville and block their route to Calais. On 24 October the two armies faced each other at Agincourt.[5] The English were near-demoralized; they had marched 250 miles in seventeen days, were desperately hungry, and were outnumbered by three to one. The French army was overwhelmingly composed of men-at-arms; the English had scarcely 1,000, the rest being archers. One captain, Sir Walter Hungerford, told the king to his face that they needed 10,000 to fight such a battle. Henry cut him short: 'I would not have a single man more than I do; for these I have here with me are God's people.'[6] Darkness fell, and with it a heavy rain; and the army, enjoined to strict silence, snatched a few hours' rest.

The English men-at-arms held a line of 1,000 yards between two woods with the archers at either flank. In front stretched a recently ploughed field which the rain had turned to mud. The French had a broader front, where the woods opened out, and were drawn up in three 'battles' one behind the other. Their plan was for their cavalry on the wings to ride down the English archers before their men-at-arms advanced on the English centre. Yet they hesitated to attack across the muddy field. When neither side moved and English courage was ebbing, Henry ordered a slow advance in formation to within bowshot of the enemy— some 250 yards.[7] The archers fortified their new position with sharpened stakes driven into the ground, and stood among them. They opened fire with a volley of arrows, which provoked the French to charge their positions. Encountering a hail of arrows at deadly close range, and fearing to impale their horses on the stakes, they started to back away in confusion, only to meet their own men-at-arms advancing on foot towards the English line. In the hand-to-hand fighting that ensued, the restricted space became a killing field, as heavily armoured men and horses lost their balance and fell in the mud, to be dispatched by the knives and clubs of the English archers. The piles of bodies began to grow. This failure

[5] I have mainly relied on Bennett, *Agincourt 1415*, and A. Curry (ed.), *Agincourt 1415* (Stroud, 2000). See too C. Philpotts, 'The French plan of battle during the Agincourt campaign', *EHR* 99 (1984), 59–66, and the eyewitness description in *Gesta*, 60–99.

[6] *Gesta*, 79.

[7] For Henry's cry to advance 'In the name of Almighty God and St George, avaunt baner' or, in another more laconic version, 'Fellas, let's go', see C. T. Allmand, *Henry V* (London, 1992), 91, which has the best description of the battle.

of the main French attack left the English in possession of the field, but the third French 'battle' was seen gathering at a distance. Fearing encirclement, Henry ordered the prisoners, who had been only partially disarmed, to be killed. It is difficult to assess the circumstances—of the king's stretched nerves, of the need to keep control, of the perceived danger. The order was contrary to both the chivalric–Christian ethic and the self-interest of the captors, and when the knights refused to obey, the archers were ordered to shoot. To what effect is not certain, perhaps to cow rather than dispatch the prisoners, for more than 1,000 were brought back to England. These included the dukes of Orléans and Bourbon, and the counts of Eu, Richemont, and Vendôme.

Agincourt had momentous consequences for Henry's kingship. It established him overnight as a superb captain in the field. The strategic blunder which had trapped his small army, 'like sheep in a fold', to face a superior force was forgotten; it was his coolness, discipline, and confidence that held it together on the march and in the battle. Henry knew how to speak in their own terms to his predominantly non-noble troops, but he had also proved himself in the hand-to-hand combat that the nobility trained for. A king who feared to take his life in his hands and lead from the front, like Richard II and Henry VI, did well to avoid battle. In consequence, Agincourt established Henry as the true heir of Edward III, ending decisively any further challenge to the Lancastrian title. Further, and of even greater consequence, it established in English eyes his right to the crown of France. Agincourt became the centrepiece of a carefully constructed myth: that God had deliberately stacked the odds against the English, reducing their numbers through sickness and their self-confidence by the long march, in order to demonstrate His support in their divinely ordained mission. Already adumbrated in a letter to the king from his chancellor, Henry Beaufort, when the news reached London, it was elaborated by the clerks of the royal chapel to proclaim Henry's destiny as one 'chosen by God' and, by extension, the destiny of the nation he led.[8] That the author of *Gesta Henrici Quinti* selected and interpreted his evidence to formulate the legend hardly matters, for once born it acquired its own reality and potency. Agincourt changed men's vision. Finally it changed Henry himself. It convinced him of the justice of his claims, of his destiny, and of God's protection. But the narrowness of his escape also induced humility and caution, a resolve not to exult in his victory and not to presume on God's favour by taking unacceptable risks. Henceforth he planned his campaigns with care.

Yet the campaign had done little to advance Henry's ambitions. It left him with a single town, precariously held and soon to come under siege by the French. It had elicited no new negotiations or improved offers from the Orléanists, now led by the intransigent count of Armagnac. Nor was the duke of Burgundy any more

---

[8] Harriss, *Cardinal Beaufort*, 84–5.

eager to ally with the successful enemy of France, preferring to make his own bid (which failed) to oust Armagnac from Paris in November. Henry's mind was set on a further expedition, but that could not be organized until 1417, and in the meantime Harfleur had to be defended and the Armagnacs isolated, so that resistance to him would be reduced.

Harfleur was reinforced in February 1416, but in March it came under siege and by the end of May was closely invested on land, while the French hired Genoese carracks and galleys to blockade the mouth of the Seine. An initial attempt to relieve it failed, and preparations for a larger expedition under Bedford, and perhaps the king himself, began to be made for the end of June. Yet not until 14 August did it finally arrive off the mouth of the Seine, where, after a six-hour-long fight, the capture of three Genoese carracks put the rest to flight and Harfleur was relieved. The garrison was on the verge of starvation and surrender. The inadequacy of the victualling and the long delay in sending relief showed a misjudgement of the situation which had nearly proved fatal.

This may have been due to Henry's negotiations with the emperor Sigismund which took place during the summer. Sigismund's main attention was focused on the Council of Constance, convened in 1414 for the reform of the Church and ending of the Schism. Rivalry between the French and English 'nations' at the council was impeding a solution, prompting Sigismund to intervene in their quarrel as a peacemaker. After visiting Paris in March 1416, he arrived in England on 1 May. He was received with the utmost courtesy and honour, for Henry was angling for Sigismund's public endorsement of his claims at Constance and for the recruitment of military support in Germany. The king initially gave credence to Sigismund's proposals for a truce with France, and only when negotiations over this had failed did he order the relief expedition to Harfleur to sail. Sigismund, discredited as a peacemaker, was now cajoled into a treaty of alliance with Henry at Canterbury on 15 August, the very day on which the battle of the Seine was being fought.

Armed with his victory and his new ally, the king now sought to bring John the Fearless into their alliance and proposed a tripartite meeting at Calais in September. John was wary, fearing at worst a trap, at the least to lose face by consorting with France's enemies. Yet he had to know what the alliance of Henry and Sigismund portended, whether it was directed against himself, and how it would affect his own projected advance on Paris. When it took place early in October, amidst tight security, reconciliation was effected between Sigismund and John. What Henry V hoped to get from Duke John was probably an agreement on the lines of the Treaty of Canterbury, with the promise of recognition for Henry's claim to the French crown when the time was right. But John promised nothing. In the chronicler's opinion, 'the duke detained our king all this time with evasions and ambiguities . . . in the end he would be found a double dealer, one person in public and another in private'.[9] So was Henry, who perhaps expected nothing better. What each had gained was an understanding of the other's plans, and an assurance that they would not conflict. That was a good enough basis for Henry's projected invasion to go ahead.

On 1 August 1417 Henry landed for a second time in Normandy, at Touques, to the west of Honfleur. His army was broadly similar in size and structure (10,000–12,000 men, with a proportion of 1 man-at-arms to 3.5 archers) as in 1415, but its purpose was quite different: the conquest and occupation of Normandy. That meant the reduction of a series of large and well-fortified towns—Caen, Falaise, Cherbourg, Rouen. It meant, too, that the countryside could not be ravaged, but had to be pacified and protected to sustain the occupying army. This new pattern of warfare—the reverse of the old *chevauchée*—required a rethink not just of strategy but of logistics. To supply a large army in France for a prolonged period with victuals, armament, and horses, a regular sea crossing had to be established. This was done when the earl of Huntingdon won a second victory over Genoese carracks at the mouth of the Seine on 29 June 1417.

The Armagnacs knew of Henry's preparations but could not send an army into Normandy, for in April 1417 John the Fearless proclaimed war, though he delayed his advance on Paris until Henry's landing in August. Taking Amiens, Beauvais, and Reims without opposition, he had almost encircled Paris by mid-October. John thus pinned the Armagnacs down, leaving Henry with a clear field in lower Normandy. But Caen, impregnably situated and stoutly defended, had to be taken by assault, led by Clarence. Though not plundered with such ferocity as in 1345, its fate induced the surrender of neighbouring smaller towns like Lisieux and Argentan, and in January Falaise. Caen provided winter quarters for the army, with a *pays* to forage. In the spring of 1418 the offensive was resumed westward into the Cotentin, where Gloucester captured Cherbourg while Warwick pushed to the southern border of Normandy at Domfront. To the east Clarence with fresh troops from England under the duke of Exeter, took Louviers and Pont de l'Arche above Rouen, which itself came under siege in July.

By the autumn of 1418 events had opened a gulf between Henry V and Duke John and brought Henry closer to the Armagnacs. In May, Burgundy finally secured Paris, killing the count of Armagnac and capturing Charles VI though, crucially, the Dauphin escaped. John thereby incurred responsibility for the defence of Paris against the English. At the same time Henry's siege of Rouen posed a direct challenge to him, for Rouen was under a Burgundian garrison. Consequently, John sought to make common cause with the Dauphin against

---

[9] *Gesta*, 175. The draft treaty which Henry V failed to get Duke John to sign is discussed by Vaughan, *John the Fearless*, 213–15.

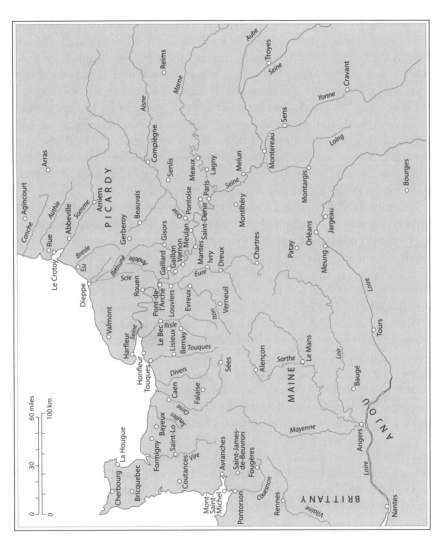

MAP 14.1. Northern France, 1415–1450. *Source:* C. T. Allmand, *Lancastrian Normandy* (Oxford, 1983), pp. x–xi

Henry, but their negotiations at Saint-Maur-des-Fossés came to nothing. The Dauphin then turned to Henry for support against Burgundy, but was unwilling to concede Henry's demand for a partition of France between them. Henry's priority was now the capture of Rouen. The siege, prolonged into the intense cold of mid-winter, became a test of endurance for the English. But the defenders were in a worse plight: as the influx of refugees reduced the inhabitants to starvation, it was decided to expel the non-combatants, women, children, and the old being forced into the town ditches between the walls and the English lines. Refused food by the English, they perished in large numbers. No relief came from Duke John, who feared an Armagnac assault on Paris if he moved. In January, Rouen surrendered, paying a huge indemnity. Its capture had important military and political consequences. It demonstrated Henry's invincibility in siege warfare and it confirmed that the English were in Normandy to stay. Resistance crumbled before the English advance into the Pays de Caux and Picardy and up the Seine to Vernon and Mantes. Individual landowners submitted in large numbers. Rouen could now replace Caen as the administrative capital of Normandy and a structure of government for the province could be introduced.

The capture of Rouen also initiated a new phase of negotiations between the three contestants. At this point Henry had to decide whether to confine himself to Normandy or extend his ambitions to Paris. He did not have the force to capture it, but could he reach an agreement with John the Fearless which would confirm his conquest and isolate the Dauphin? Their negotiations at Mantes in February and at Meulan in June 1419 came close to succeeding. Henry demanded full sovereignty over Normandy and the lands conceded in the Treaty of Brétigny as the price of peace and a marriage with the princess Catherine, whom he now first set eyes on. He refused to surrender his claim to the crown of France, though pressed to do so. This was asking more than Burgundy could deliver, for he dared not be seen to be partitioning France with her ancient enemy. With both the English and the Dauphinists menacing Paris, John reopened negotiations with the Dauphin at Pouilly. A personal meeting between them was arranged at Montereau for 10 September. They were to meet on a bridge over the river Yonne, guarded at each end by their respective followers, and divided into sections by palisades to limit the numbers accompanying each. When the two met, Duke John kneeled, but before he could rise he was struck and killed by the Dauphin's guard and his attendants disarmed and taken captive. The murder was premeditated and probably done with the Dauphin's connivance. It was represented as vengeance for the murder of the duke of Orléans in 1407 and it made Burgundians and Armagnacs irreconcilable enemies.[10]

---

[10] Vaughan, *John the Fearless*, 274–86, reviews the circumstances and evidence of culpability for the murder.

Henry saw at once the advantage to himself. The Burgundian garrison in Paris immediately sought his protection and by October envoys from the new duke, Philip, were crossing with his own. But whereas Philip was now ready to accept the terms set by Henry at Meulan, Henry's plan was more far-reaching. The Dauphin's crime having debarred him from the succession, Henry would become Charles VI's heir, marry his daughter, and when he became king rule France jointly with England. France would not be partitioned nor Charles VI deposed. The two crowns would be united but one nation would not be subjected to the other. Each would be governed by its own laws and institutions and through its own officials. The duke's advisers at Arras took some time to digest and discuss this audacious proposal, for which nothing had prepared them. Judging it in terms of what would be best for Burgundy, they concluded they had no choice but to accept. The alternative could well be an alliance of Henry and the Dauphin to make war on the Burgundian state. It would be better to have Henry V as king of France, and an ally, than to have the Dauphin their sworn enemy. Burgundians would retain control in Paris, where Henry would need them as administrators. In short it was the lesser of two evils, and the alliance between Henry and Philip was sealed at Rouen on 24 December. The agreement had to be endorsed by the constituted authorities: Charles VI and his queen, Isabel, whose son was to be disinherited; the *parlement* of Paris; the university of Paris; and the Church. The final text of the treaty was carefully drafted, and at Troyes on 21–2 May 1420 was solemnly ratified. On 2 June Henry and Catherine were married.[11]

The Treaty of Troyes purported to bring peace between England and France, and to respect the integrity of France and the sacrosanctity of the monarchy. But it did all this by omitting any reference to the Dauphin, who in public law and divine right could not be arbitrarily disinherited and who controlled a large and wealthy area of France. Henry's undertaking to subdue the Dauphinist territories, 'especially north of the Loire', pointed to continuing war. For some Frenchmen the alliance with the English was unnatural, but others were prepared to accept Henry V for the order and government he could bring. The English were equally ambivalent. Some suspected that English interests would be subordinated to French; others viewed it with apprehension as an indefinite commitment. The English were satisfied to have conquered Normandy but there was an uneasy feeling that beyond it was a step too far. In 1418 Henry had shared this unease, but the logic of his conquest—perhaps even more than his ambitions—had driven him on. Like Burgundy, he was left with little choice, for

---

[11] The making of the Treaty of Troyes has been examined by P. Bonenfant, *Du meurtre de Montereau au Traité de Troyes* (Brussels, 1958); for a perceptive discussion of its terms, see M. H. Keen, 'Diplomacy', in Harriss (ed.), *Henry V*, 193–9.

Normandy would be vulnerable to a Burgundian–Armagnac alliance. Moreover, his conquest lacked any legal basis, for neither of his opponents had been prepared to countenance a treaty with him to divide France. Only possession of the crown of France could entitle him to hold the duchy of Normandy, which was to be reintegrated in France when he succeeded Charles VI. Henry was thus forced to acknowledge the legal integrity of France and in practical terms his dependence on the duke of Burgundy for the government of France. He had become inescapably mired in French politics.

Immediately following his marriage Henry set out to secure the area to the south-east of Paris by taking Melun, Montereau, and Sens in a joint operation with the Burgundians. Melun held out until November, defying the authority of the puppet Charles VI. With the king in his train Henry V entered Paris on 1 December, rendering thanks at Notre-Dame and placing English garrisons in the Bastille and Vincennes. Then he and Catherine moved to Rouen to receive the homage of the Estates of Normandy, and so to England for the queen's coronation. Clarence was left as lieutenant-general, with Exeter as captain of Paris. In March news of the gathering of French and Scottish forces in Maine prompted Clarence to draw troops from the Norman garrisons for a pre-emptive strike. He and Salisbury had perhaps 4,000 men, enough to do battle. Returning from Angers, they had reports of the French to the east at Baugé. Clarence, impetuous as he was brave, and eager for a victory of his own (he had missed Agincourt), set out with a small body of men-at-arms, leaving the main army to follow. He surprised the French army but was soon overwhelmed by their numbers, meeting his death in the mêlée while his commanders were killed or captured. But the Franco-Scottish force failed to exploit their spectacular victory. Salisbury with the remainder of the army conducted an orderly retreat and refortified the garrisons; in Paris, Exeter imposed martial law. Normandy did not rise to throw off English rule and Salisbury could report to Henry V that 'it stood in good plight'.[12]

By June 1421 the Dauphinists were again on the offensive, near Chartres, and Henry V, returning via Paris, countered by taking Dreux. He then led the army of some 6,000 on an extended march to the borders of the Loire at Beaugency and Orléans, turning eastwards to reach the Yonne at Sens and then northwards to Meaux on the Marne. The long campaign in high summer, from July to September, wasted the army by disease and failed of its prime purpose, to bring the Dauphin to battle. But it was an impressive display of English power. Once again Henry settled down to a prolonged winter siege. Meaux was now the most important Dauphinist stronghold north of the Loire, and the key to Dauphinist

---

[12] Rymer, *Foedera*, x. 131. Salisbury's letter is quoted at some length in McFarlane, *Lancastrian Kings*, 132. For his military career, see M. Warner, 'Chivalry in action: Thomas Montagu and the war in France, 1417–1428', *Nott. Med. Stud.* 42 (1998), 146–73.

Champagne to the east. It was encircled by water, strongly fortified, and held by a garrison 1,000 strong. Henry's besieging army probably numbered some 2,500 men. Heavy rain and flooding before Christmas added to the difficulties of the siege and spread disease. The king and his leading nobility remained throughout the winter, directing the siege and maintaining morale. The town fell in March 1422, the adjoining suburb known as 'the market' resisted assault until May. Its fall gave the Anglo-Burgundian forces control of most of Champagne, leaving only lower Picardy under Dauphinist control. Henry planned to continue his subjugation of this area, the key to which was Compiègne, but a disease he had contracted at Meaux soon made him incapable of riding and by 13 August he had retired to Vincennes, where the terminal nature of his illness became apparent. On 30 August he made his last verbal dispositions, committing the regency of France to Bedford unless the duke of Burgundy desired it, and enjoining him to retain Normandy in any treaty with the Dauphin. He forbade the release of his major prisoners until his son was of age.

Henry V's death gave heart to the French, who in 1423 launched an offensive to the south-east of Paris designed to detach Burgundy from the alliance. Bedford responded with vigour, sending Salisbury to assist the Burgundians to repel a Franco-Scottish army at Cravant, while next year Picardy was made secure by the capture of Compiègne and Crotoy. In the summer of 1424 the French mounted a major challenge on the south-western border of Normandy with an army containing a large Scottish contingent and a squadron of Lombard heavy cavalry. Bedford with an army drawn from England and Normandy met the French in battle on the plain outside Verneuil, terrain which favoured cavalry. The Lombard horsemen rode straight at and through the English front line which, with remarkable discipline, re-formed to meet the oncoming French. In a long and fierce combat the English gradually achieved mastery, giving no quarter to the Scots, who were regarded as traitors. Verneuil was rightly seen to be a victory comparable to Agincourt, for it consolidated the English conquest of Normandy and undermined the French confidence in seeking battle. Henry V's mantle had descended to Bedford, who as regent of France represented the dual monarchy, and as the embodiment of chivalry stood as surrogate for St George.[13] Next year an offensive under Salisbury and Suffolk with another 1,400 men from England took Le Mans, Mayenne, and La Flèche and pushed the frontier of the English conquest to the Loir. A further advance to the valley of the Loire could not be long delayed.

Bedford had thus extended the conquest almost as far as Henry V had envisaged. Such a conquest and occupation of the major part of a neighbouring

---

[13] I have followed the excellent analysis of the battle by M. K. Jones, 'The battle of Verneuil (17 August 1424): Towards a history of courage', *War in History*, 9 (2000), 375–411. The portrait of Bedford kneeling before St George is in 'The Bedford Hours' (Pl. 6).

kingdom was without parallel in northern Europe since 1066. It was testimony, in the first place, to Henry's qualities as a military commander. In the initial phase he had held together an army for three years when the normal period of service was six months or a year. He had undertaken sieges of a length and complexity without precedent in European warfare at a time when town defences had been improved. His campaigns had been triumphs of strategic and logistical planning, their momentum had not flagged, and he had exercised a pervasive scrutiny over operations. But undoubtedly the secret of English success lay in the military discipline at company level. This was inherent in the retinue structures of companies under captains and bannerets which trained and fought as units under noble commanders. The battlefield integration of archers and men-at-arms likewise demanded a measure of social rapport unknown among the French, who feared to arm their peasantry. Henry was himself the product of this system. First in Wales and subsequently in France, he remained close to his men, communicating at their level and concerned for their welfare. The whole army participated in the honour and fruits of victory: those who fought at Agincourt were permitted to assume coat armour; all who fought at Verneuil were rewarded with grants of land. Individual honour and prowess were subsumed within that won for England and St George. Even so, for Henry V war was an instrument, not an end; it served a political vision as radical and far-reaching as his military strategy. It was interwoven with diplomacy and underpinned by government, in both of which he displayed an originality and fixity of purpose transforming the assumptions of his followers and confounding those of his opponents. We must shortly turn to consider how realizable was his vision in its political context; but first the English conquest must be followed to its denouement at Orléans in 1429.

Between December 1425 and March 1427 Bedford was in England resolving the problems of the minority council, in particular the feud between Gloucester and Bishop Beaufort. No French attack was mounted in his absence, but the earls of Salisbury and Suffolk raided Brittany, whose duke had reneged on his alliance. In 1427 fighting was confined to two areas, to the north and east of Orléans, and to the north of Angers. In both an advance to the Loire was the next stage. But more men were needed, and in the winter of 1427–8 Salisbury returned to England to raise an army of 2,700 men, the largest since 1421. His command was to be independent of Bedford, and on his return in June 1428 he revealed his intention of laying siege to Orléans, for which he had brought an impressive artillery train.[14] Yet Bedford, in May, had secured the agreement of the *grand conseil* for an attack on Angers. Behind these alternative and conflicting strategies lay personal interests. Bedford had been granted Maine and Anjou as Crown fiefs

---

[14] H. Ratcliffe, 'The military expenditure of the English Crown, 1422–35', M.Litt. thesis (Oxford University, 1975), 25–34.

and was anxious to enlarge his possessions there. Salisbury wanted to conquer land for himself in Orléannais which he could hold directly of the Crown. In political terms the capture of Orléans would complete the demoralization at Charles VII's court and confirm the belief that his cause was lost, while strategically it could be more quickly reinforced from Paris, and Burgundian help could be expected.[15]

Salisbury began by taking the Loire towns either side of Orléans, Meung, and Beaugency below and Jargeau above. By 12 October 1428 the English were on the south of the city and soon captured the castle Les Tourelles, guarding the bridge. It was from here that Salisbury was surveying the town and planning the assault when, on 24 October, he was struck in the face by a cannon ball, dying soon after. His lieutenants, the earl of Suffolk and Lords Talbot and Scales, abandoned an assault in favour of a prolonged siege. By April the siege had reached stalemate, and the defenders produced a proposal to cede the city to the duke of Burgundy with the English allowed access. When Bedford rejected this, the 500-strong Burgundian contingent withdrew, weakening the defences and enabling a relief force with Jeanne d'Arc to bring in supplies along the river, which the English had failed to impede. The French then attacked the besiegers, recapturing Les Tourelles and forcing them to retreat.[16] Still hoping to retain the Loire towns, the English commanders divided their forces, thereby enabling the French to take Jargeau and capture Suffolk on 12 June. Talbot and Scales now withdrew from Beaugency to meet Fastolf, who was approaching with a relieving force from Janville. But with the French close on their heels retreat became imperative, until a battle was forced on them at Patay. Fastolf held a ridge of ground, which Talbot covered with a body of archers. This time the French cavalry swept aside the archers, capturing Talbot and Scales; Fastolf, seeing the turn of the battle, managed to fight clear and retreat to Janville and Étampes with the remnant.[17] This completed the destruction of the army sent to Orléans and the road to Paris lay open to the French. The spell of English invincibility had been broken and the week of 12–18 June marked the turning point of the war.

The fate of Paris now lay in the balance. Jeanne d'Arc was confident that its inhabitants would rise, but on 10 July Duke Philip brought in 800 Burgundian troops and by 20 July Bedford had mustered 4,000 men, including Cardinal Beaufort's crusading force from England, to hold the capital. After a half-hearted assault on 8 September, Paris was not itself endangered; instead the French army swept into Vermandois, taking Senlis and Compiègne and forcing Burgundy into a truce. Paris was no longer secure and in October Bedford

[15] Report of Jacques Gelu to Charles VII, May 1429, cited by P. Contamine, 'La "France anglaise" au XV siècle: Mythe ou réalité?', in *La 'France Anglaise' au Moyen Âge* (Paris, 1988), 18–19.

[16] R. G. Little, *The Parlement of Poitiers* (London, 1984), 90ff.

[17] A. J. Pollard, *John Talbot and the War in France, 1427–53* (London, 1983), 17.

handed over control of it to Duke Philip, along with Champagne and Brie. Bedford moved all his personal treasures—books, tapestries, plate, and vestments—to Rouen, which became the headquarters of the regent. He was fulfilling Henry V's last injunction to keep Normandy secure. Henceforth that was to be the prime English concern; the vision of a Lancastrian France had disappeared. Orléans had demonstrated its fatal weakness: the lack of sufficient manpower both to garrison the towns and to field an army of conquest. Yet if the defeats of 1429 showed that the conquest was overstretched and unviable, the threat which the siege of Orléans had presented to Charles VII had been real enough. If, eight years after Henry V's death, the English seemed to be on the point of winning the war, one must ask whether Henry, had he lived, would not have brought it to a successful conclusion.

2. LANCASTRIAN RULE IN FRANCE, 1417–1435

Parallel with his military conquest in France, Henry V had conducted a diplomatic campaign to isolate the French monarch and secure recognition of his claim to the crown from both the emperor and the pope. The Council of Constance, through which the secular princes set out to reform the Church and end the Schism in the papacy, provided the ideal arena for this. The English delegation in November 1414 led by Bishop Hallum joined with Sigismund in giving priority to the reform of the Church ahead of the election of a new pope. After signing the Treaty of Canterbury in 1416, Sigismund returned to Constance as Henry's ally, believing that he had the support of the English delegation for reform. But Henry V, preparing to invade France, wanted the election of a pope sympathetic to his cause, and in no circumstances French or Spanish. In July 1417 he sent his chancellor, Henry Beaufort, to Constance to procure the immediate election of a pope, with the promise that reforms would follow. Henry's volte-face enabled the election of Martin V, an Italian, who showed his gratitude by naming Bishop Beaufort a cardinal, intending to use him to reassert papal control over the English Church, which he saw as too much under royal influence. Henry would not tolerate that; he forbade Beaufort's promotion and virtually suspended relations with Martin V.[18]

Throughout 1418–20 Martin maintained a strict neutrality in the Anglo-Dauphinist war, but the Treaty of Troyes brought Henry's claims to the top of the agenda. Henry now wanted papal approval for his succession to the crown of France and thus a judgment of disinheritance on the Dauphin for the crime at Montereau. Martin, on his side, asked for the repeal of the statutes restricting papal provision to benefices in England. Henry deferred his answer, and Martin

---

[18] Harriss, *Cardinal Beaufort*, 90–9.

refused to commit himself on the validity of the Treaty of Troyes. The reign ended on this impasse.[19]

Bedford had neither the influence in England to procure the repeal of the Statute of Provisors nor the power in France to enforce the Treaty of Troyes. He confined himself to securing papal cooperation for appointments to English and Norman sees and kept Anglo-papal relations on a steady keel during the consolidation of Lancastrian France. Then in 1428 an opportunity for bringing pressure on Martin V to give a favourable verdict on the Treaty of Troyes seemed to present itself. In March 1427 Martin V had elevated Bishop Beaufort to the cardinalate and commissioned him as legate for a crusade against the Hussites, whose extirpation had become his last aim. Martin had explicitly entrusted this task to the English nation not merely as valiant warriors but as penance for nurturing the heresiarch John Wyclif. It must have been in the mind of Bedford and Beaufort that a successful crusade in Bohemia would affirm Lancastrian leadership of Christendom and win Martin V's recognition of this. Moreover the crusade was timed to follow hard upon Salisbury's major offensive at Orléans in 1428–9, designed to compel Charles VII to sue for peace. For a brief moment Henry V's dream appeared realizable.

This congruence of opportunities never materialized. By the time Cardinal Beaufort had assembled a small force of crusaders in England in the spring of 1429, the siege of Orléans was already in trouble, and at the news of disaster at Patay the council required him to divert his army to the defence of Paris. Beaufort delivered his men to Bedford in mid-July. Martin V's fury at the betrayal of his trust doomed all hope of securing papal recognition of Henry VI as king of France, a title now rightfully asserted by Charles VII through coronation at Reims on 17 July.[20]

Though the pope was supreme judge, it was from the peers and feudatories of France that Lancastrian kingship needed recognition. Burgundy's subscription to it carried weight among some of his neighbours, but he had little desire to engage in active war against the Valois kingdom , nor did he wish to involve himself in the government of France, as had his father and grandfather. Burgundians ruled Paris, but the duke himself rarely went there. Even so Burgundian support underpinned the Lancastrian regime in the 1420s, being strengthened by Bedford's marriage to Philip's sister Anne in 1423. Bedford provided military and financial assistance for Burgundian campaigns in Picardy and discountenanced his brother Humphrey of Gloucester's pursuit of his wife Jacqueline's claim to Hainault in 1424–5.

If the alliance with Burgundy was the foundation of Lancastrian rule, that

[19] Harvey, *England, Rome and the Papacy*, 130–8.
[20] Harriss, *Cardinal Beaufort*, 174–90.

with the duke of Brittany was almost equally important for the defence of
the conquest. Duke Jean V faced internal opposition to his truce with Henry V
and he constantly adjusted his position in relation to English fortunes. He
had accepted the Treaty of Troyes in 1422 and had joined in a triple alliance
with Bedford and Burgundy in April 1423, but continued to be pulled towards
the court of Charles VII, where his brother Arthur of Richemont was constable.
In contrast to the fourteenth century, south-western France did not become
a major theatre of war. Although the count of Foix went over to Charles VII in
1424, he entered a local truce with the English in Gascony which was to last
until 1439.

By 1429, therefore, the English presence in France had acquired a degree of
stability in terms of both the territory held and the political acceptance accorded
it. The English had held Normandy for ten years, Paris for eight. Over half of
France, Henry VI's title was acknowledged. But this was deceptive, for not only
did it hang upon Burgundian self-interest and a military equipoise, but many
feudatories accorded it no more than reluctant recognition. The Lancastrian
monarchy evoked no deep loyalty, for it had no natural roots. Its appeal lay in
being the lesser of two evils, an alternative to Dauphinist domination or the
anarchy of civil war. Lacking any intrinsic legitimacy, Lancastrian rule had to
acquire it through the quality of government which it provided. For this Henry V
was well equipped. He had made 'bone governance' the foundation of his kingship in England; he was now to import the same principles and some of the same
methods into his conquests, first in Normandy and later in Lancastrian France.

The Rule of Normandy

War had brought economic ruin to Normandy, already weakened by the years of
Burgundian–Orléanist feuding. Landowners and peasants fled before the
English armies leaving lands depopulated and waste. In April 1418 Henry V
offered pardon and restitution to all who submitted, but few did so until after the
fall of Rouen. Then, as Henry started investing English lords, knights, and
esquires with forfeited lands, native landowners likewise accepted his rule. By
the end of 1420 some 5,000 grants of properties had been made, amounting to a
wholesale restructuring of Norman landholding.[21] One result of the disruption
of seigniorial authority in rural society was a surge of brigandage, as the dispossessed and disaffected took to the woods. In 1418–19 a task force was set up to
suppress brigands and a price put on their heads, but throughout the English

---

[21] R. A. Newhall, 'Henry V's policy of conciliation in Normandy, 1417–1422', in C. H. Taylor
(ed.), *Haskins' Anniversary Essays* (Boston, 1929), 205–30; C. T. Allmand, 'The Lancastrian land
settlement in Normandy, 1417–20', *Econ. HR* 31 (1968), 463.

occupation whole areas remained unsafe, such as the *bocage* between Bayeux and Caen, around Lisieux, and the Forest of Lyons near Rouen.[22]

At a higher level, central and local administration had to be restored. The financial offices remained at Caen, but following the capture of Rouen that once more became the administrative capital. This was the signal for a revival of traditional Norman government. A new ducal palace was built in Rouen as the seat of the chancery and the ducal *grand conseil*. The ancient office of seneschal, long suppressed, was restored, as was the *échiquier*, a judicial body to deal with Norman suits. Finally in January 1421 Henry assembled the Norman Estates, suspended since 1382, which granted a *taille* of 400,000 *livres tournois*. By 1421 Normandy was not only an autonomous financial unit, but was self-sufficient to the point of paying for the garrisons guarding it. Locally, the civil administration was eventually organized into eight *baillages* and thirty *vicomtés*, the latter under native Normans.[23] The establishment of civil administration in Normandy, even while the conquest was in progress, showed that Henry was intending a long-term occupation and had grasped the problem of ruling a different people and society. His government combined a respect for native institutions and methods with a new rigour and efficiency drawn from his English experience. In this Normandy was to be the model for the government of Lancastrian France. I shall consider in turn the military and civil organization and the character of English settlement in the countryside and towns.

On becoming regent Bedford took over an experienced and confident army of some 12,000 English troops, 4,500 of whom were garrisoned in some thirty-seven towns. Up to 1425 all garrisons were under the control of the seneschal of Normandy. The garrison comprised men-at-arms and archers in the ratio 1:3 and was mustered, and its equipment reviewed, on a quarterly or half-yearly basis, by the seneschal. The garrison's wages came from local taxation and were subject to certification that there had been no oppression of the local population. The garrison bought local goods and services, and protected the town's trade through its operations against the local brigands. The integration of the garrison with the local community was further strengthened when its members married and bought property in the town. At Château Gaillard they 'lived like simple persons of the country, paying their way without seizing or exacting anything from the people'.[24] This subordination of military to civil authority was well advised,

---

[22] Newhall, 'Henry V's policy of conciliation'; B. J. Rowe, 'John, duke of Bedford and the Norman brigands', *EHR* 47 (1932), 583–600; C. T. Allmand, *Lancastrian Normandy, 1415–1450* (Oxford, 1983), 229–35; R. Jouet, *La résistance à l'occupation anglaise en Basse-Normandie (1418–1450)* (Caen, 1969), for the argument that this was a patriotic resistance movement.

[23] J. H. Wylie and W. T. Waugh, *The Reign of Henry the Fifth*, iii (Cambridge, 1929), ch. 67.

[24] R. A. Newhall, *The English Conquest of Normandy, 1416–24* (New York, 1924; repr. 1971), 201–46; A. Curry, 'English armies in the fifteenth century', in Curry and Hughes (eds.), *Arms,*

for ultimately the safety of the town depended on the townsfolk. Every burgess had the duty of 'watch and ward' on the walls and gates, and every town was vulnerable to betrayal from within by Dauphinist sympathizers. In fact during the 1420s the 'bonnes villes' remained loyal. Bedford's achievement in winning acceptance for an alien occupation in conquered territory was remarkable.

The position in Paris was different. Its Burgundian sympathies meant that the English were there on sufferance. Henry V, taking no chances, strongly garrisoned the two great fortresses, the Bastille and Vincennes, and appointed the duke of Exeter as its military governor. Once again it was Bedford who had the confidence to commit the defence of Paris to the citizens under a Burgundian governor and *prévôt*. The English garrison was reduced, and in 1429 it was the townsfolk who defended the city against Jeanne d'Arc.[25]

No standing army was kept in the field; for campaigns, troops were drawn from the garrisons and from expeditionary forces sent each year from England. These were generally under 2,000 strong and were retained for six months or a year and paid from the English exchequer. Of the 12,000 men who crossed between 1421 and 1429 the majority returned after their period of indented service, but the prospect of receiving lands or joining a garrison tempted numbers to remain. Each campaigning season these fresh troops made a vital contribution to the forward movement of the conquest.[26]

In theory the defence of Lancastrian France rested on those who had received fiefs which carried specific military obligations, like the three men-at-arms and seven archers whom Lord Willoughby furnished for his lordship of Beaumesnil. This was an adaptation of the traditional *semonce des nobles*, and should have provided a force of some 1,400 men. In the twenty years after 1422 it was summoned on some fifty occasions, though with diminishing effect, for already by 1427–9 holders of fiefs had become absentee landlords. Instead, the professional captains who were given lands, men like Sir John Fastolf, Lord Scales, and Sir William Oldhall, had their own retinues. Armies were formed through personal rather than territorial bonds and the retinue was the unit of discipline, loyalty, and command.[27]

The backbone of the field army was in fact the garrison retinues, up to half of whose complement could be called out for short-term campaigning. With English reinforcements an army of some 4,000 could be mobilized at short

Armies and Fortifications, 48–60; B. J. Rowe, 'Discipline in the Norman garrisons under the duke of Bedford, 1422–35', *EHR* 46 (1931), 201, for quotation.

[25] G. L. Thompson, *Paris and its People under English Rule* (Oxford, 1991), ch. 4.

[26] Curry, 'English armies', 40–8; Ratcliffe, 'Military expenditure', chs. 1–3; Allmand, *Lancastrian Normandy*, 194–7.

[27] Allmand, *Lancastrian Normandy*, 53, 192, 203–5; Curry, 'English armies', 60–5; ead., 'Le Service féodal en Normandie pendant l'occupation anglaise', in *La 'France anglaise'*, 233–57.

notice, and for a major battle like Verneuil up to 8,000. In this sense the English lacked the manpower for a continual expansion of the conquest, and faced the consequences of this in 1429. The only source of reserves was soldiers who had detached themselves from expeditions or garrisons to live off the countryside. Some of these had been discharged and some had deserted; not all were criminal, but they lay outside disciplinary control. Yet they could be recruited and re-engaged in an emergency, as after the defeat at Patay. Finally there were the Irish, Welsh, Flemish, Germans, and French, for whom the continuing fighting was a magnet; many were ready to spend from ten to twenty years fighting for pay.[28]

Whereas in Normandy the English ruled as conquerors, in Paris they depended on an entrenched and experienced Burgundian administration. Bedford governed through his *grand conseil*, the members of which were mainly Burgundian servants of John the Fearless. Second in importance to the *conseil* was the *parlement*, a supreme court staffed by Burgundian lawyers and some churchmen. It was jealous of its jurisdiction, which covered the whole of France, and English landowners—including the earls of Salisbury and Suffolk and Bedford himself—appealed to its judgments in their private litigation.[29] Finally, the Estates General of France met twice in Paris, summoned by Henry V in December 1420 to approve the Treaty of Troyes and by Bedford in 1424 after Verneuil. By contrast, the Estates of Normandy met regularly in the 1420s to grant taxation and allocate expenditure, to hear complaints on the condition of the duchy, and to issue ordinances for its government.

In December 1420 Henry V entered a Paris menaced by Dauphinist forces, suffering acute shortage of food after a bad harvest, and a prey to inflation produced by currency debasement. With characteristic vigour and foresight he used his fleeting visit to initiate far-reaching financial reforms. He obtained from the Estates a subsidy in unminted metal to provide a new coinage, while reintroducing the *gabelle* and a sales tax on luxuries. This was followed in July 1421 by a sharp devaluation in preparation for the introduction of the new currency in November. Henry countered the unpopularity of these measures with an ordinance insisting 'that an essential element of a stable society was a stable currency'.[30] To increase domainal revenues he ordered surveys of confiscated lands, the resumption of grants, and the restraint of new ones. Annual assessments

---

[28] A. Curry, 'Les "Gens vivans sur le pais" pendant l'occupation anglaise de la Normandie', in P. Contamine and O. Guyotjeannin (eds.), *Guerre et violence au moyen âge* (Paris, 1996), 209–21.

[29] For the *conseil*, see B. Rowe, 'The *grand conseil* under the duke of Bedford, 1422–35', in *Oxford Essays in Medieval History Presented to H. E. Salter* (Oxford, 1934), 207–34; for the *parlement*, see C. T. Allmand and C. A. J. Armstrong (eds.), *English Suits before the Parlement of Paris, 1420–1436*, Camden Society, 4th ser., 26 (London, 1982); Allmand, *Lancastrian Normandy*, ch. 5.

[30] Thompson, *Paris under English Rule*, 26–34; Wylie and Waugh, *Henry the Fifth*, iii. 227; Allmand, *Henry V*, 402.

were to establish what the government had and how it could be exploited. Such measures breathed the spirit of Henry's rule in England, but were also in the tradition of the 'bone governance' of Charles V and the Cabochian ordinance. Essentially the financial system remained French. It was Normandy that bore the burden of the conquest. Here, 'some form of meeting of the Estates took place every year of the occupation' and most granted taxation. Bedford was forced into a heavy and relentless mulcting of Normandy by being unable to draw on either the king's personal and prerogative revenues in England (notably the duchy of Lancaster) as Henry V had done, or the exchequer. The conquest had to be self-sustaining.[31]

The English came not only to conquer and govern Normandy but also to settle there. Henry V envisaged a permanent colonization, granting properties to merchants, artisans, and officials in towns like Harfleur and Caen, and lands to knights, esquires, and archers according to their rank. Almost without exception grants were in fee tail; all lands were charges with military service and could only be sold to other Englishmen. Groups of soldiers from particular English regions—Cheshire, Yorkshire, East Anglia—settled and maintained their cohesion by intermarriage, exchange, and consolidation of their estates. Some areas were heavily colonized: the Cotentin, the Pays de Caux, the Caen–Bayeux district. Service and settlement in Normandy was particularly attractive to younger sons and any excluded from their inheritance. Their lands provided them with status and income rather than large profits, for initially many properties were deserted and had to be made productive. As aliens and expropriators, English landlords were viewed with hostility, but it was in their interest to conciliate the local population.[32]

In the towns the principal English residents were connected with the garrison and administration and probably formed an enclave around the castle. The settlement attracted very few merchants. Harfleur and Caen contained the largest English colonies, Rouen somewhat smaller. Caen was exceptional; the initial expulsion of the citizens and its role as the administrative capital attracted an English community which remained throughout the occupation. John Convers, a soldier, had married a Frenchwoman within weeks of its capture and his son was still there in 1450. Soldiers and officials bought property, became burgesses, and even held civic office as *échevins*. They came to regard Normandy as their

[31] Allmand, *Lancastrian Normandy*, 174–6; E. F. Jacob, *The Fifteenth Century* (Oxford, 1961), 205–8, has a long note on Norman finances.

[32] There are excellent discussions by Allmand, 'Lancastrian land settlement', and id., *Lancastrian Normandy*, chs. 3, 4; and by R. Massey, 'The land settlement in Lancastrian Normandy', in Pollard (ed.), *Property and Politics*, 76–96. See too N. Jamieson, 'The recruitment of northerners for service in English armies in France', in Clayton *et al.* (eds.), *Trade, Devotion and Governance*, 102–15.

home, knowing that 'there was no return ticket to England'. In Paris the situation was different. There the Burgundians had seized all Armagnac properties, and although Bedford secured substantial properties for himself and his lieutenants, the English were too few in number to impinge much on the life of the capital. What won acceptance for this rule by a military elite was above all the presence and lifestyle of John, duke of Bedford, and his duchess, Anne.[33]

Bedford's Rule

When Bedford entered Paris as regent on 5 November 1422, he was comparatively unknown there. Nor was he familiar with France, having spent most of the war governing England. His marriage to Philip of Burgundy's sister Anne in May 1423 helped to cement Anglo-Burgundian relations and to make him acceptable in Paris. Duke Philip's relations with Henry V, as Charles VI's heir, had been strained; with Bedford, his equal in status, there developed greater mutual trust. Bedford lacked Henry V's magnetism, but was more accessible. Parisians warmed to the pious and charitable Anne and came to respect the justice, efficiency, and dependability of Bedford's rule. Basin says that 'he greatly loved the French lords who adhered to him and honoured them'.[34]

Bedford set himself to affirm the status and authority of Lancastrian kingship. He made the palace of Les Tournelles his official residence and furnished it with the trappings of a royal court. From the estate of Charles VI he acquired the great library of 843 volumes collected by Charles V, many sets of tapestries worth over 9,000 *livres tournois*, thirty-seven sets of liturgical vestments, and the best pieces of the royal plate and jewellery including the royal gold cup, all being valued at 29,563 *livres tournois* or £3,284. He continued to add to this storehouse of costly and artistic treasures from prizes of war (notably the jewels and plate of the duke of Alençon captured at Verneuil), purchase, and commissions for finely illuminated liturgical volumes. By the time of his death he had valuables well in excess of £6,400. His chapel was renowned both for its visual splendour and for the quality of its musicianship. Bedford and Anne were munificent patrons to Notre-Dame, Saint-Denis, and the cathedral and the house of Carmelites at Rouen. Religious patronage strengthened political support: processions were held to celebrate victories, or to intercede in time of danger; ducal piety was displayed at the traditional royal veneration of relics in Sainte-Chapelle on Good Friday. Anne's piety was expressed in her visits to the hôtel-Dieu, where she caught the fever that brought her death in 1432.[35]

---

[33] Thompson, *Paris under English Rule*, ch. 5.

[34] T. Basin, *Histoire de Charles VII*, ed. S. Samaran (Paris, 1933), i. 89.

[35] Thompson, *Paris under English Rule*, 138–40, 184, 192–6; J. Stratford, *The Bedford Inventories* (London, 1993), 8–9, 66–7, 94–6, 105–27.

When he arrived in France, Bedford possessed no lands there and it was only after his victory at Verneuil that he was granted an apanage including the counties of Alençon, Maine, Mortain, and Beaumont, and the lordship of Mantes. In Paris he had no fewer than six houses. If his retention of royal fiefs was controversial, they provided him with a personal treasure which he employed to pay for his retinue and serve as a war reserve in the crisis of 1429. Thus Bedford endeavoured to govern as a Frenchman, using Burgundian officials and Burgundian councillors, and upholding the authority of the *parlement*. His rule conferred solid benefits of security, prosperity, and justice; but could it claim the legitimacy and sacral authority of the Valois monarchy?

Legitimacy could be asserted in many ways. Henry V had circumvented the old issue of Valois legitimacy by being designated Charles VI's heir, and having the Dauphin disinherited at a *lit de justice* in 1420; indeed a genealogy of Henry VI's descent from St Louis—through Isabella, wife of Edward II—was later displayed in churches and set forth in verse.[36] On the death of Charles VI the Dauphin immediately adopted the title of Charles VII as his blood right, without waiting for coronation; yet his uncertain legitimacy sapped his cause and perhaps even his will until his coronation at Reims. Burgundian propaganda harped on this with dramatized re-enactments of the murder at Montereau. Henry's propagandists construed his victories as divine recognition of his right to the French throne, but French patriots like Alain Chartier saw them as God's scourge for France's sins. Many symbols of sacrality attested the traditional role of the kings of France as the defenders of Christendom and protectors of the faith: the chrism of Holy Oil brought to Clovis and used for consecration at the coronation; the banner of Clovis, the 'Oriflamme', used in battle against France's enemies; the protection of the Virgin symbolized by the white lily on a ground of royal blue in the personal arms of the French monarch; and their descent from St Louis. In the competition between Paris and Bourges to appropriate these symbols of special holiness the Lancastrians had the advantage of holding both Notre-Dame and Saint-Denis with their relics and regalia. Each side engaged its patron saint. Charles VII promoted the cult of St Michael as the archangel of the resistance, slaying the dragon representing the invader. St Michael inspired the vision of Jeanne d'Arc and figured on her banner. His white cross confronted the red cross of St George.[37]

The Lancastrians were in the weaker position of trying to appropriate a

---

[36] B. J. Rowe, 'King Henry VI's claim to France in picture and poem', *The Library*, 4th ser., 13 (1932–3), 77–88; J. W. McKenna, 'Henry VI of England and the dual monarchy: Aspects of royal political propaganda, 1422–32', *Journal of the Warburg and Courtauld Institutes*, 28 (1965), 145–62.

[37] See the extended discussion of this in C. Beaune, *The Birth of an Ideology* (Berkeley, 1991), 152–71; also B. Bedos Rezak, 'Idéologie royale, ambitions princières, et rivalités politiques', in *La 'France anglaise'*, 493–5, 506–8.

monarchical tradition which was rooted in French consciousness as the symbol of French unity and identity. Of this Henry V was well aware, and his challenge for the French crown was presented as much in terms of good government as right descent. He came to restore order, unity, and justice to a France ruined, like Troy, by her divisions. This, and his stern piety and confidence in God's favour, made him the embodiment of Christian kingship which, had he received consecration at Reims, could possibly have secured him recognition as heir to St Louis. As it was, after the deaths of Henry V and Charles VI the undercurrents of French national feeling began to flow towards Bourges, even while the military and political tide flowed with Lancaster.

With Charles VII's coronation at Reims and his edict of Compiègne promising the restoration of all whom the English had expropriated, Valois kingship asserted its legitimacy and became the symbol of French unity. The English and Burgundians were forced to reassess their position. Abandoning any hope of a final victory over the kingdom of Bourges, the English tried to recover the initiative by a military offensive to safeguard Paris and a political riposte through the coronation of Henry VI. Both were designed to bind Duke Philip to the alliance, from which Charles VII was attempting to detach him. The young Henry VI, in his ninth year, landed at Calais on St George's Day 1430, protected by an army of his leading nobility almost 5,000 strong. The Anglo-Burgundian offensive aimed at clearing the way to Reims had already been blocked at Compiègne, succoured by Jeanne d'Arc. Even her capture could not secure its surrender and in November Philip abandoned the campaign. Paris now replaced Reims as the venue for the coronation, but first the passage of the Seine had to be secured by the recapture of Louviers, lost in December 1429, and Cardinal Beaufort was sent back to England to raise more money and a further 2,650 troops. When he returned to Rouen on 24 May 1431, it was to the penultimate act in the drama of Jeanne d'Arc. Already tried and condemned as heretical before Pierre Cauchon, bishop of Beauvais, in March, she was persuaded to make a public recantation before Cardinal Beaufort. Then following her predictable relapse immediate sentence of execution was passed. She was publicly burnt in the Old Market on 30 June. Neither Pope Eugenius IV nor Charles VII attempted to intervene. The trial had portrayed her as a woman of loose morals and an envoy of the devil whose victories had been gained by sorcery, a view acceptable for different reasons to Charles VII, his military commanders, and the English.

Louviers capitulated after a prolonged siege on 28 October, opening the way to Paris. Henry VI arrived there on 2 December and two weeks later was crowned by Cardinal Beaufort in Notre-Dame. Although this publicly asserted the validity of the dual monarchy, it brought little immediate relief to Paris nor any long-term commitment to its defence. The ceremony was in some respects novel and unseemly and the ensuing banquet an undignified scramble. The English distributed no favours or largesse to the citizens and seemed anxious to be gone. Having been hastily crowned, Henry VI quickly returned to England.[38] His sojourn in France had also occasioned disputes over Bedford's powers. The *grand conseil* under Cardinal Beaufort had not only exercised full civil and military authority but now called in question Bedford's claim to a prescriptive right to the regency by virtue of his birth and the dying wish of Henry V. It proposed that after the king's return Bedford should hold his title under royal commission. Bedford reacted angrily to this and a violent altercation with Cardinal Beaufort created a breach between them, with serious political repercussions in England.[39] The expedition had done little to reinforce the Anglo-Burgundian alliance. Duke Philip had neither attended the coronation nor even met Henry VI. Following his check at Compiègne he had signed a truce with Charles VII, protecting his lands from further attack. The English had been able to recover some towns lost in 1429 and strengthen garrisons with new troops; yet the French advance had merely been stemmed, not reversed.

By January 1432 there were upward of 4,000 soldiers in Normandy. A review of the Norman garrisons in 1433 showed a total strength of 3,400, while a significant number of soldiers were not in garrisons but 'living on the land', not subject to captains. Many of these were now recruited into *creues* supplementary to a garrison, mustered on a monthly basis and paid for whatever service they undertook. Before his visit to England in 1433–4 Bedford had organized the defence of Normandy into three sectors, with the earl of Arundel and Lords Talbot and Willoughby each having up to 1,600 men under their command. Bedford had also proposed the creation of a field army to be financed partly from the duchy of Lancaster and partly from his own resources, but though agreed in principle, it was not realized before his death. The underlying problem was a shortage of manpower.[40]

The crisis of 1429 had forced both England and Normandy to contribute large sums to the war. Having granted three fifteenths (£111,000) for the coronation expedition, the English parliament granted no more than £63,000 in the four years 1432–5. This furnished annual reinforcements averaging 1,600 men, and beyond this the exchequer paid some £46,000 towards the wages of the garrisons. The Norman Estates bore a comparable burden, 747,000 *livres tournois* (£83,000) being granted in 1429–31 and 804,000 *livres tournois* (£89,333) from

[38] Thompson, *Paris under English Rule*, 199–205; Wolffe, *Henry VI*, 60–3. For a contemporary account, see *A Parisian Journal, 1405–1449*, trans. J. Shirley (Oxford, 1968), 269–73.

[39] Harriss, *Cardinal Beaufort*, 208–9, and below, Ch. 15, sect. 2.

[40] J. Stevenson (ed.), *The Wars of the English in France*, Rolls ser., 3 vols. (London, 1851–4), ii. 540–3, 257; Curry, 'English armies', 50–65; ead., 'Les "Gens vivans sur le pais"', 213; ead. 'The first English standing army?', in Ross (ed.), *Patronage, Pedigree and Power*, 197–204; *Proc. & Ord.* iv. 222–32.

November 1432 to May 1435.[41] But while England was accepting an ongoing financial commitment to the defence of Normandy, fewer wished to serve there. Several of the lords who had accompanied Henry VI to Normandy never again returned. Increasingly the leadership was left to a handful of captains. Defensive campaigning was unattractive and hazardous for those seeking their fortunes in war.

Native disaffection began to present a serious military threat. Towns were more vulnerable to betrayal than to assault. Chartres was lost by trickery on Palm Sunday 1432 and the castle at Rouen temporarily betrayed in March. Restrictions on non-English serving in garrisons were introduced. But the greatest headache for the English was increasing brigandage, which rendered travel between the towns hazardous. To deal with this Bedford organized the local peasantry into bands of fifty or a hundred under English captains. This was to prove disastrous in 1435. Disbanded soldiery could also terrorize the country-side, like the gang under Richard Venables who slaughtered a thousand peasants at Saint-Pierre-sur-Dives in 1434, displaying a combination of chauvinism and class hatred. That triggered peasant risings at Avranches, Bayeux, and Caen.[42] Under the impact of taxation, hard winters, and insecurity, the economic revival of the 1420s was reversed. But this should not be exaggerated. The war and the most disturbed areas still lay beyond the borders of Normandy; agricultural pro-duction in the granary lands of Caux remained good, the *bonnes villes* were well governed and loyal. Nor were the English landlords pulling out. Their incomes were stable, property was still worth acquiring. Sir John Fastolf only began to sell his after 1435. In 1432 John Milcent was leasing his house in Caen for thirty years at a fixed rent. Caen was at the centre of a grain district and far removed from the war; the settled English community was reproducing itself, purchasing property, holding civic office, and even securing a university for their children, founded in January 1432 for the study of civil and canon law.[43]

Paris was in a far less comfortable position. The loss of the upper Seine made it dependent on supplies from the north, seriously impeded while Louviers was in French hands. Grain prices reached famine levels in 1433–4 and the increas-ing fear and despondency after Henry VI's departure is palpable in the *Journal* of a Paris citizen. It began to feel like a front-line city, as brigands raided to its walls, and the convoys of grain, meat, and vegetables on which it depended sometimes did not get through. Freak frosts and rains destroyed crops, the Seine froze over

[41] Ratcliffe, 'Military expenditure', 89, 100–1; B. J. Rowe, 'The estates of Normandy under the duke of Bedford, 1422–1435', *EHR* 46 (1931), 557–8; Allmand, *Lancastrian Normandy*, 176–7. The conversion is at 9 *livres tournois* to £1 current in 1429–30.

[42] R. A. Newhall, *Muster and Review* (Cambridge, Mass., 1940), 119–29; A. Curry, 'Le Service féodal', 255–6; *Parisian Journal*, 290, 292.

[43] Allmand, *Lancastrian Normandy*, 95, 105–20.

every winter from 1431 to 1434, while the hot summer of 1432 brought an epidemic in which Anne, duchess of Bedford, died. Little revenue was collected from the *baillages* to the south, the wages of the administration fell into arrears, and the business of the *parlement* declined. Bedford had moved to Rouen, returning only briefly in December 1434, and Duke Philip remained absent; Louis de Luxembourg remained as chancellor, but Parisians had the sense of having been abandoned.[44]

The Decline of the Alliance

In May 1433 Bedford decided to return to England to reorganize the government and revive its commitment to the war. His lieutenants, Lord Talbot and Willoughby, joined forces with the Burgundians to recover ground in Picardy and to the south-east of Paris, while in 1434 the earl of Arundel cleared the Valois from Maine, 'the last systematic effort of the English in this area'. In military terms the dual monarchy was able to hold its own against Valois France, which had made no significant advance since 1430. Yet though Duke Philip received both military and financial support from England, he was unwilling to attack Charles VII and was moving ever closer to an accommodation with him. In December 1434 he once again signed a truce, leaving the English to bear the full weight of the Valois offensive on the Somme in the new year. Étaples and Le Crotoy were lost, and in June the earl of Arundel was killed at Gerberoi. Near Paris, Saint-Denis was taken by surprise and not recovered until October. As the military balance swung towards the Valois, a conference was held at Nevers in February 1435, where terms of peace between Philip and Charles were outlined. Ever since 1429 Duke Philip's counsellors had endlessly evaluated the benefits and losses from the English alliance, and now those who argued that it was ceasing to be viable and that the English were exhausted won the day. It was time for Burgundy to come in from the cold. Beyond this political evaluation lay the problem that the duke was in honour bound to avenge his father's death, and had legal and religious obligations through his oath to the Treaty of Troyes. To resolve these questions was the task of the congress summoned by papal mediation to Arras in August 1435.

The English delegation to the Congress of Arras was led by Archbishop Kemp, with two bishops, two earls, and Cardinal Beaufort; Lancastrian France was represented by Bishop Cauchon and members of the *grand conseil*. Their staffs and retinues numbered 500–800 persons. French and Burgundian delegations of similar size, along with those of the papal mediators, made this one of the largest diplomatic gatherings of the Middle Ages. The English delegation

---

[44] *Parisian Journal*, 274–96; Thompson, *Paris under English Rule*, 226–7.

was housed in the *cité*, some ten minutes from the *ville* where the French and Burgundians lodged, and where the proceedings took place in the nearby abbey of St Vaast. The delegations did not negotiate directly with each other but submitted their offers to the papal mediators, Cardinals Albergati and Hugh de Lusignan. Despite the well-rehearsed—if at times ill-tempered—arguments over the Lancastrian claims, the English and French were not seeking a peace, or even a truce, but contending for the allegiance of Burgundy. The crucial decision to release Duke Philip from the Treaty of Troyes rested with the papal mediators, who finally sanctioned this, judging the treaty to be inherently flawed through the disinheritance of the Dauphin, and as having conduced to war rather than peace. Albergati expressed his own view that the crown of England should suffice for Henry VI, whose claim to that of France could not match that of Charles VII. Despite the incredulous protests of Kemp and an impassioned personal appeal to Duke Philip by Beaufort, the duke renounced the alliance and renewed his allegiance to Charles VII on beneficial terms. The English delegation defiantly left Arras on 6 September and a week later Bedford died at Rouen.[45]

Bedford's sole aim had been to uphold and, if possible, fulfil the vision of Henry V. He could not claim, and perhaps could not feel, his brother's messianic sense of destiny, but he never doubted the justice of the English conquest, nor questioned its feasibility. His commitment to it, as an honourable enterprise shared with his companions in arms, living and dead, was essentially chivalric. As he told the council in 1434, its loss 'should cause me a perpetual hert's hevynesse and sorrow'. He commanded respect as a fearless soldier, a stern and just commander, and a humane and enlightened military governor. Sir John Fastolf was to extol his memory in these terms.[46] As heir to Henry VI, he insisted on his pre-eminence and authority in confrontations with his brother Gloucester, Cardinal Beaufort, and the earl of Salisbury, though with Philip of Burgundy he worked on equal terms. His accumulation of lands and wealth had something of the obsessive acquisitiveness of a younger son, though his position demanded that the magnificence of his court should not be overshadowed by that of Burgundy. In short, Bedford bent his energies to sustaining the pretensions of Lancastrian kingship in circumstances which from the first were adverse and later became impossible. Though lacking the charisma of his brother, he would have made a worthy successor, under whom the fortunes of the Lancastrian monarchy would have been different not only in England but in France.

[45] Dickinson, *Congress of Arras*, gives a full account of its proceedings. For Beaufort's role, Harriss, *Cardinal Beaufort*, 249–51.

[46] *Proc. & Ord.* iv. 225–6; *Boke of Noblesse*, ed. J. G. Nichols, Roxburghe Club (London, 1860), 30–1, 72.

3. THE DEFENCE OF NORMANDY, 1435–1444

The withdrawal of Burgundy and the death of Bedford compelled a reassessment of the English position in France. Could Henry VI's title to the crown of France be maintained after the Treaty of Troyes had been pronounced invalid by papal authority? If Henry VI were to renounce it in the context of a general peace, what safeguards would the French give for the English to retain Normandy? These were problems for diplomacy, and so in a measure were future relations with Duke Philip. Was he now an enemy, or should he be cultivated as a neutral? In military terms Burgundy's withdrawal left the English position exposed not merely in Paris but along the whole eastern border of Normandy. What strategy should now be adopted for its defence? Already in 1434 Gloucester had criticized Bedford's policy of piecemeal defence and urged the dispatch of a large army to launch a major counter-offensive. Sir John Fastolf now argued for an offensive strategy in a memorandum to the *grand conseil*: two armies should be sent from England, the one to make 'sharp and cruelle war' in the east, from Picardy and Artois to Champagne and Burgundy, the other to do likewise towards Chartres and Anjou. Repeated for three years this would reduce these areas to 'an extreme famyn', creating a cordon sanitaire of devastation around Normandy. Both schemes were beyond English resources, and that of Fastolf abandoned any pretension to rule justly in France; the fight now was to retain a conquered province by whatever means.[47] It was an admission that Charles VII now stood for *une France entière* against *une France des divisions*. This was to be made explicit in the peace negotiations of the following years, but it also began to condition English rule in Normandy, which, faced with an insurgent patriotism, became increasingly militarized, repressive, and unnerved. Finally, Bedford's death forced a re-evaluation of the command structure. It broke the direct link with Henry V, necessitating a new basis for the authority of his successors, and it dissolved the nexus of personal service through which Bedford had exercised command. In all these respects, therefore, the history of the English occupation enters a new phase in 1435–6, centring on the defence of Normandy, by arms and by diplomacy.

The English were left no time to ponder these problems, for within weeks of Burgundy's withdrawal Normandy was on the point of being lost. On 29 October 1435 Dieppe was betrayed to marshal de Rieux and the news incited the peasantry of the Pays de Caux, recently armed by Bedford against 'brigands', to rise. The English were caught completely off guard: Dieppe had been garrisoned by only sixteen men and there were no more than 400 in the whole area. In the last days of

---

[47] *Wars of Eng.* ii. 575–85. Fastolf denied 'any noote of tirannye' in this, since the French had opted for all-out war; M. G. Vale, 'Sir John Fastolf's "Report" of 1435: A new interpretation reconsidered', *Nott. Med. Stud.* 17 (1973), 78–84.

1435 Arthur of Richemont captured all the coastal fortresses down to and including Harfleur, and overran the Pays de Caux. Rouen, the very heart of Normandy,
was now exposed to the north-east and cut off from reinforcement by sea. Lord
Talbot, in command, put 1,000 men into the city, and repelled an attack by
La Hire and Xaintrailles in February 1436. Rouen was safe, but Paris could no
longer be held. Throughout the winter of 1435–6 the surrounding fortresses
were captured or betrayed, and on 13 April the Burgundian governor in Paris,
L'Isle Adam, opened the gates. The English garrison retreated to the Bastille,
and four days later made an ignominious withdrawal from the city.[48]

At the end of 1435 the estates of Normandy had appealed urgently to Henry
VI for a great army to be sent under a prince of the blood—they probably had
Gloucester in mind. The king's reply promised an army of 11,000 strong, but
neither the money nor the troops could be found for this and it was not until
31 May that an army of 4,200 men sailed under the duke of York—a delay which
the desperate and exasperated council in Normandy found inexplicable. The
English council was by then facing a double threat, for in mid-March the duke of
Burgundy prepared to attack Calais. A force of 2,000 men under Edmund
Beaufort (financed by his uncle Cardinal Beaufort and intended for Maine) was
sent to reinforce the garrison early in April, while a general appeal was made for
loans to save this 'preciouse jueull . . . to this reaume . . . a bolewark and defense
to this londe'. This was envisaged as a 'royal army', 7,500 strong, under the
command of the duke of Gloucester as surrogate for the king. But even while
he was mustering at Dover, Edmund Beaufort and Lord Camoys had routed the
besieging Burgundian army on 28 April, depriving Gloucester of that honour
but allowing him to ravage Burgundian territory.[49]

Calais and Normandy had been saved, but the question of who should replace
Bedford and under what terms now had to be faced. With Henry VI commencing his formal rule, Bedford's powers to make appointments and grants of land
were reclaimed by the Crown (which meant in effect the council) as were his fiefs.
York was commissioned, as 'lieutenant and governor', for a single year and at a
fixed salary. At 25 he was still untried as a soldier and this was his first command.
Suffolk, a veteran of Agincourt, and Richard Neville, earl of Salisbury, ten years
his senior, were his minders. His replacement in November 1437 was the veteran
earl of Warwick, persuaded to accept the commission for eighteen months
despite his protest that it was 'full farre from the ease of my years'.[50] Warwick's
stopgap appointment had reflected the lack of a suitable candidate, but at his

[48] Thompson, *Paris under English Rule*, 232–40.
[49] Harriss, *Cardinal Beaufort*, 256–8, 263; A. Doig, 'A new source for the siege of Calais in 1436',
EHR 110 (1995), 404–16.
[50] *Wars of Eng.*, vol. ii, p. lxvi. Warwick was aged 56. In fact field operations were in the hands of
Richard Neville, earl of Salisbury.

death in April 1439 there were two. John Beaufort, earl of Somerset, was Warwick's lieutenant and well placed to succeed him. He had recently been ransomed after seventeen years of captivity in France and was anxious (though not well equipped) to resume his military career. The appointment became a trial of strength between his uncle, Cardinal Beaufort, and Humphrey, duke of Gloucester, who seems at first to have pressed his own claim to the post, but in July 1440 it was the duke of York who, with Gloucester's backing, secured the appointment for five years.

The short-term appointments between 1436 and 1440 had two consequences for Normandy. First, the *conseil* under the chancellor, Louis de Luxembourg, assumed greater responsibilities for defence, its members now including the principal captains like Lord Scales, Faucomberg, and Talbot. Secondly, the command structure which had stemmed from Bedford became fragmented. Bedford had used his supreme power and extensive patronage to create a clientage of lords and captains centred on his household, among them Lords Beauchamp, Willoughby, Talbot, Scales, and Sudeley, and knights like William Ogard, William Oldhall, John Fastolf, Thomas Rempston, John Handford, and John Montgomery.[51] These long-serving professionals, endowed with lands and offices, were the core of the Lancastrian occupation. Their own retainers constituted both their personal companies and the garrisons of which they were captains. The army defending Normandy was thus a collection of bastard feudal affinities stemming from Bedford. His death removed the keystone of this structure not only in terms of personal loyalty but in the power to appoint and remove captains. Many of the major captaincies appointed were now held for terms of years by nobility who placed their own lieutenants in them; these became islands of patronage effectively withdrawn from the control of the lieutenant-general. By the 1440s a unified command embracing all garrisons had disappeared, and York had limited power to remove absentee captains.

But if the growth of entrenched interests and loyalties made it difficult to exercise discipline, it did produce continuity at a time when many were reassessing the viability of the occupation. A small group of veteran peers like Willoughby, Scales, and Talbot had experience from the time of Henry V and Bedford. Others, like Dorset, Faucomberg, and Camoys, came to France in the 1430s hoping to secure permanent fiefs, and some young lords like Grey of Heton and Bourchier came as late as 1439–41 to recover baronies which their predecessors had been granted. Lordship was still prized even if its economic value had decreased.[52] Yet, significantly, all the newcomers were heirs or younger

---

[51] *Wars of Eng.*, ii. 434–7; A. Marshall, 'The role of English war captains in England and France, 1436–1461', MA thesis (University of Wales, 1974).

[52] M. K. Jones, 'War on the frontier: The Lancastrian land settlement in eastern Normandy, 1435–50', *Nott. Med. Stud.* 33 (1989), 115.

sons. For the established nobility in England a defensive war in France held no attractions, especially in the absence of royal leadership. For the professional captains who were the backbone of the army there were opportunities, even after 1429, to purchase fiefs from English holders. Bedford's captains like Ogard and Oldhall built up estates by these means, and after 1435 York, Warwick, and Somerset brought their own retainers. There was still a career to be made serving in different retinues though the hazards from death or capture were undeniably greater.[53]

The strength of Normandy lay in the garrisons in some forty-five towns, and in 1436 these were dramatically reinforced.[54] The fortifications of the great citadels of Rouen, Caen, Alençon, and Evreux were improved, *maisons fortes* were constructed or modernized in the countryside, while untenable fortresses were destroyed. But life in garrison was one of increasing uncertainty. With the Valois now on the borders of Normandy surprise attacks were more frequent and could receive support from disaffected peasantry, patriot–brigands, or a fifth column within the town. Plots to deliver Pontoise and Cherbourg in 1436, Rouen in 1439–40, and Argentan in 1441 all had native support. Captains were warned to stay alert, to enrol only English for watch and ward (the *guet*), to guard town gates, and to increase their armoury. The English garrisons came increasingly to resemble an army of occupation. By 1437 their pay was often in arrears and they took to levying *appatis* on their region. The countryside beyond the walls was becoming hostile territory. The Estates of Normandy repeatedly complained that brigands infested the forests and menaced the roads, and voted money for their suppression. And to the native 'patriots' were now added disbanded English soldiery, who terrorized a *pays* but also constituted a reserve on which captains drew in emergencies: almost 45 per cent of Talbot's troops in April 1440 and 20 per cent of those employed in his operations at Louviers and Conches in December 1440 were 'irregulars'.[55]

In 1439 a memorandum for Henry VI's council painted a discouraging picture of the state of Normandy. The misgovernment of English captains had alienated the local population, fortresses were ruinous, the economy was collapsing as the Seine became unsafe for traffic, and the burden of defence was increasing.[56] These conditions obtained notably in eastern Normandy. The Pays de Caux, once the granary of the north-east and a wealthy area, had been devastated by war and further depopulated when the harvest failures of 1436 and 1437 forced

---

[53] Allmand, *Lancastrian Normandy*, 77.

[54] A. Curry, 'English armies', 48–60, esp. fig. 3.7; Pollard, *John Talbot*, 33.

[55] Allmand, *Lancastrian Normandy*, 235–7; Curry, 'Les "Gens vivans sur le pais"', 217–18; Pollard, *John Talbot*, 72–3, 86–8.

[56] C. T. Allmand (ed.), *Documents Relating to the Anglo-French Negotiations of 1439*, in *Camden Miscellany, XXIV*, Camden Society, 4th ser., 9 (London, 1972), 79–149.

many into bankruptcy and flight to Picardy or to the forests. Disease took hold and weeds and scrub invaded the deserted lands. Insecurity also afflicted the area west of the Seine around Louviers–Evreux. The value of the *prévôté* of Elbeuf fell by a half, and rents on the barony of Neubourg were reduced to one-third of their value in 1400. Here English lords attempted to protect the peasantry on whom they depended.[57] However, western Normandy, the Cotentin, and the Bayeux–Caen country remained unscathed, and land in the south-west, pro-tected by Maine, was still prized and profitable. There the English occupation remained credible.

It was on these areas that the ever increasing burden of taxation fell. In the six years 1435–40 the Norman Estates granted subsidies to an annual average of 344,000 *livres tournois*, though this fell to 176,000 *livres tournois* in 1442–5 when a sales tax of 10 per cent was added. But increasingly the burden fell dispropor-tionately on the secure *baillages* of Caen and Cotentin, fragmenting the political unity of the duchy. Individual *baillages* 'came to regard local defence, rather than defence of the whole duchy, as paramount'.[58] Normandy could no longer sup-port its own defence and reinforcements had to be sent annually from England in increasing numbers. The nine expeditions from 1436 to 1443 inclusive totalled 21,339 men, an average of 2,667. The rising proportion of archers to men-at-arms made them less costly, but indicated the waning commitment of the landed classes to the war, and very probably resulted in their declining effectiveness as a fighting force. This seems to have been the case with Somerset's force in February 1440 and Talbot's in 1442.[59] In addition to the six months' wages for these expeditions, the English exchequer was paying quarterly subventions for the standing army which Bedford had initiated in 1435. On York's appointment in 1440 the council decided to pay him £20,000 per annum for the defence of Normandy, though for only one year did he receive this in full. Thus in both Normandy and England the Estates were required to meet the escalating cost of defending a beleaguered colony. Could it be justified in terms of the king's hon-our, military viability, and the interest of those with lands there?

From 1435 a twin-track policy of war and diplomacy was designed to secure a long truce in which the English occupation could be consolidated. The decade divides at the abortive peace negotiations of 1439, which marked the first attempt, and concludes with the truce achieved at Tours in 1444. By 1439 the English had stabilized the Norman frontier after the crisis of 1436. York's sub-stantial force was used by Talbot in a forceful counter-attack. In a dawn raid on

---

[57] Jones, 'War on the frontier', 105–11; A. Baume, 'Les Opérations militaires anglaises . . . 1436–1437', in *La 'France anglaise'*, 393–400; G. Bois, *The Crisis of Feudalism* (Cambridge, 1984), 333–45.   [58] Allmand, *Lancastrian Normandy*, 178–82.
[59] Curry, 'English armies', 45–7; Jones, 'War on the frontier', 108; Pollard, *John Talbot*, 59–60.

13 February 1437 he seized Pontoise and followed it up with the recovery of the Norman Vexin. Talbot and Scales drove La Hire and Xantrailles from the vicinity of Rouen and in the autumn recovered much of the devastated Pays de Caux. In 1438, having strengthened Meaux and Creil, he returned to the Seine Valley to capture Saint-Germain-en-Laye. Not until July 1439 was the increasingly convincing English recovery checked by the loss of Meaux.

The diplomatic offensive took longer to get under way. Duke Philip's desertion and siege of Calais had inflamed anti-Burgundian feeling in England, but by 1438 both sides were looking to restore commercial and diplomatic links. Burgundy now offered to mediate in the Anglo-French quarrel and negotiations were arranged to take place at Calais in mid-1439 with a French delegation in attendance and the captive duke of Orléans present nearby. Duke Philip kept himself at arm's length, commissioning his wife, Isabel, to act, along with Cardinal Beaufort, as 'mediators and sterers to peace'. Beaufort pinned his hopes on Burgundy persuading Charles VII to accept a long truce. He wanted no further meddling by papal envoys, whom the English now mistrusted.[60]

The conference opened at Oye, near Calais, on 10 July 1439. The English and Franco-Burgundian delegations occupied large tents, between which was a third for the conference meetings. Beaufort had power to compromise on Henry VI's title to the crown of France if he could obtain firm guarantees for the English to retain their territories in full sovereignty. His proposal was for each king to use his title only within their respective territories: there should be two kings in France, as in ancient times. The French showed no interest, asserting that the English must hold their lands as vassals of Charles VII; the legal integrity of France could not be compromised. Even more discouraging was their readiness to consider a long truce only if the French landowners expelled in the conquest of Normandy were restored and the duke of Orléans released without ransom. Thus two days into the conference the familiar impasse had been reached. At this point Orléans and Isabel suggested a different approach, for a truce of fifteen or twenty years during which Henry VI would refrain from using his title and Charles VII would waive his demand for homage. This recognized the military stalemate and mutual exhaustion and saved the honour of both kings. It seemed to offer security for Lancastrian Normandy—until it was discovered that the French were still insisting on the restoration of French landowners and Orléans's release. Nevertheless, Beaufort agreed to remit the proposal to the English council.

The debate that took place before the king at Windsor has not been recorded, but memorandums on the arguments, for and against, show the terms in which

---

[60] Harriss, *Cardinal Beaufort*, 295–305.

it was conducted.[61] The Norman *conseil* stressed the imperative need for peace if Normandy was not to be ruined, and openly asked whether the king and nobility had the will and capacity to defend it. The English council weighed the legal and political arguments: that Henry VI could not suspend using his title without losing credibility and honour and the right to rule; that the restoration of Norman landowners amounted to a de facto surrender and huge sums would have to be paid in compensation to the English who were extruded. These powerful objections carried the day; the terms were rejected, but even before the delegation had returned to Calais the French had decamped. Charles VII was resolved to accept peace only on his terms, and saw no benefit in prolonging the English occupation for another generation.

In England, Gloucester must have pressed for rejection in order to discomfort his rival Beaufort, whose policy and influence over the past twenty years he now denounced. He successfully deflected the appointment of the cardinal's nephew Somerset as lieutenant in France, and he advanced cogent arguments against the release of the duke of Orléans. This was advocated by Orléans's friend and keeper William de la Pole, earl of Suffolk, who saw it as a means of countering the influence on Charles VII of the anti-English house of Anjou. It had the enthusiastic support of the young Henry VI, who, in taking responsibility for it, voiced his 'souveraine and singuler desire . . . that the good paix might be had' between England and France. Gloucester's objection that, once released, Orléans would become Charles's tool, and his ransom money would be lost, proved realistic, but henceforth Henry's fervent pacifism was to be a factor in English policy.[62]

In 1440–2 the war was prosecuted with some vigour and varying success along the border of Normandy. Before York's arrival Somerset had recaptured Harfleur and restored English control in the Pays de Caux; in 1441 Talbot broke the French siege of Pontoise and himself laid siege to Dieppe; in 1442 the English lost, and then recovered, Conches. This cat-and-mouse game of siege and counter-siege showed that both sides were reaching the limits of their fighting capacity. The French were still trying to break into Normandy while the English lacked the resources to break out. Yet the French retained the initiative to strike at will and this eroded morale in Normandy. The English council, critical of York's defensive strategy, believed 'it behovefull and necessaire that the maner and conduit of the werre be changed' towards an aggressive strike at the army of Charles VII.[63]

This was also prompted by the renewal of war in Gascony. A French offensive to the mouth of the Gironde in 1438 had been met by the dispatch of an army of

[61] Allmand (ed.), *Documents Relating to the Anglo-French Negotiations, passim*; id., 'The Anglo-French negotiations, 1439', *BIHR* 40 (1967), 1–33.

[62] *Wars of Eng.* ii. 451–60 (quotation at 452).

[63] *Proc. & Ord.* v. 259. Criticism was already being expressed in October 1441; ibid. 178.

300 men-at-arms and 2,000 archers (the largest since 1412) under the earl of Huntingdon in August 1439. Its operations encouraged the count of Armagnac, one of the dissident princes, to offer an alliance, coupled with the marriage of one of his daughters to Henry VI. Charles VII acted swiftly to bring Armagnac to heel: advancing from Toulouse in June 1442, he seized the count and confiscated his lands. The year 1442 thus closed with both Normandy and Guyenne under threat from French armies.[64]

The council's response to this threat emerged only gradually over the winter, involving as it did the choice of commander, the size of the army, its finance, and its destination. Already by the autumn Somerset had been offered the command of a force to go to Gascony; but by the new year the evident need for an equivalent force for Normandy faced the council with a dilemma, for two such armies could not be afforded. Indeed for either a loan would have to be negotiated from Cardinal Beaufort, who was thus in a position to dictate the army's size and destination. By the end of March 1443 the decision had been taken for Somerset to lead an army of 4,200 men—as large as in 1436—to conduct an offensive campaign against Valois France, landing at Cherbourg, passing through western Normandy, and crossing the Loire to 'make moost cruel and mortel werre that he can and may', and if possible bring Charles VII to battle. The concept had a sound military rationale, for it would force the French to divert their attack from both Normandy and Gascony, take war into a hitherto untouched area where supplies could be seized, and lead Charles of Anjou to persuade Charles VII to sue for peace. Yet its political purpose was clear enough. The massive cost of the expedition was to be wholly met by a loan of £21,666 from the cardinal, who thereby secured revenge for the displacement of his nephew by York in 1440. Somerset was given equivalent military rank and authority with York outside Normandy, raised to a dukedom, and awarded all lands that he should conquer. The establishment of a Beaufort apanage in Maine and Anjou was put within his grasp.[65] By the time York and his commanders knew of the plan and realized its implications for Normandy it was too late. A powerful delegation led by Lord Talbot and Sir Andrew Ogard was sent to make representations to the council on 21 June. These are not recorded, but York's objections are clear enough: the plan infringed his overall authority as lieutenant governor, it implied lack of confidence in himself, and it denied him crucial money and reinforcements for the defence of the duchy.

The assembly of Somerset's army was protracted and it only arrived at Cherbourg in August. It moved down the western border of Normandy reaching

[64] Vale, *English Gascony*, 108–12, 114 ff., and 251–2 (maps).

[65] M. K. Jones, 'John Beaufort, duke of Somerset and the French expedition of 1443', in Griffiths (ed.), *Patronage, the Crown, and the Provinces*, 79–102; also, Harriss, *Cardinal Beaufort*, 332–44.

Angers, then pointlessly took La Guerche on the border of Brittany, and Beaumont le Vicomte in Maine. All the time Charles VII remained at Saumur avoiding battle, and with winter approaching Somerset disbanded the army in Normandy and himself returned to England to die in disgrace. The last supreme effort of the English in France simply ran into the sand. It would have needed a commander of far greater ability and self-confidence to have led an army of this size into territory dominated by a resurgent French monarchy and with the expectation of a major battle. Measured against what such an army could have done in Normandy under Talbot, its failure was a verdict on the war leadership in England: the abnegation by the king, the factions in the council, and the indifference of the nobility.

Neither had the council followed a clear diplomatic strategy after the failure of the Oye negotiations. In 1440 a caucus of the French nobility led by the dukes of Bourbon and Alençon and the count of Armagnac had openly revolted against Charles VII and sought to reopen peace negotiations through the duke of York. Charles consistently refused to secure peace through the mediation of the princes but in August 1443 offered Henry VI direct negotiations for peace even while Somerset's army was ending its pointless *chevauchée*.[66] These negotiations were to be wholly different in character from those of the preceding decade. As Henry VI made clear in council on 1 February 1444, Suffolk was to go as his personal emissary, not as part of a formal and aristocratic embassy, and was to proceed straight to the court of Charles VII to negotiate a perpetual peace or a general truce, to be sealed by the king's marriage. His commission echoed Henry's own conviction of his duty to seek peace and extinguish discord between the two realms, in accordance with God's will.[67]

Suffolk landed at Harfleur on 15 March and was at Tours a month later. He had probably little foreknowledge of the terms that Charles VII would offer. These were a two-year truce linked to a marriage to Margaret, daughter of René, duke of Anjou. Though not a blood relationship with the royal house—which might have further strengthened Lancastrian pretensions—it would forge a link with the most powerful family at Charles's court, who had hitherto opposed peace. For Charles the marriage removed any danger of an alliance between Henry VI and one of the dissident princely families, while the truce would enable him to disband the princely armies and introduce his reforms. Suffolk saw it as a guarantee of negotiations for a permanent peace, and Henry VI welcomed it as creating a bond of amity between two Christian monarchs. Agreement was rapidly achieved: a cash dowry was settled, an embassy from René of Anjou

---

[66] For the French background, see M. G. Vale, *Charles VII* (London, 1974), ch. 4; G. du Fresne de Beaucourt, *Histoire de Charles VII*, iii (Paris, 1885), chs. 5–10.

[67] *Proc. & Ord.* vi. 32–5; Beaucourt, *Histoire de Charles VII*, iii. 274; Rymer, *Foedera*, xi. 49.

promised, on 24 May the betrothal took place, and four days later a truce until 1 April 1446 was signed.

Although the truce was with Charles VII, it was the Angevin–Lancastrian marriage that provided the cement of the accord. For a twenty-year truce was envisaged between the two houses linked, it would seem, to an undertaking to restore the county of Maine, the hereditament of Margaret's uncle Charles of Anjou. This was not in the formal marriage agreement, for Suffolk was not empowered to surrender territory, but the French later claimed that some undertaking had been given, and as part of a family accord designed to stabilize the south-west frontier of Normandy it had an obvious place.[68] If, at Tours, Suffolk gave a verbal undertaking on Henry VI's behalf, it was probably with the king's agreement to it that he returned to Nancy in November 1444 for the proxy marriage and the conduct of Henry's bride to England in April 1445.

In England the truce of Tours was widely welcomed. The very ease and swiftness with which it had been achieved, instead of engendering doubts, swept these aside in a wave of euphoria. Even in Normandy it was welcomed as bringing security and relief from the burden of taxation. For Suffolk and others it seemed a reasonable assumption that the marriage would guarantee extensions of the truce during which professional negotiators could hammer out the terms for a final peace or at least a prolonged truce. It is tempting to believe that Charles VII saw it as simply a well-timed pause in his long-term campaign to recover Normandy and tame his nobility, but the truth may be that he too had bowed to pressure from those at court eager to divert their martial energies from the ravaged fields of Picardy to the spoils of Lorraine or Lombardy. Both sides were heartily sick of the struggle. The question was which would turn the breathing space to its advantage.

4. THE LOSS OF NORMANDY, 1445–1450

By 1444 Lancastrian Normandy was exhibiting the classic symptoms of a colony collapsing under the weight of its own defence. The truce of Tours was then hailed as its salvation, whereas five years later it was seen as the source of its destruction. What went wrong? The military dangers inherent in a short truce were appreciated, Suffolk both advising York and urging parliament 'to stuffe the castelles, tounes and alle maner forteresses . . . in Normandie and Fraunce' in readiness for renewal of the war.[69] At the same time Suffolk expected that the truce and marriage which he negotiated would lead to a permanent settlement. In fact they contained the seeds of further conflict.

---

[68] Harriss, *Cardinal Beaufort*, 345–6.   [69] *Rot. Parl.* v. 74.

The Diplomatic Failure

Suffolk made two crucial concessions at Tours. First, the secret promise to cede Maine to René of Anjou was detached from the projected peace negotiations and linked to the king's marriage as a gesture of Henry's goodwill; it was not, as in 1439, to be consequential on an agreed peace. Secondly, in the text of the truce of Tours the new duke of Brittany, Francis, was listed as an ally and subject of the French king, rather than of the English as his father had been. Brittany's allegiance was historically contentious, and if Suffolk knowingly accepted the change, it must have been from fear of jeopardizing the negotiations, reckoning that it would have little significance if peace were secured.[70] He was to pay dearly for both mistakes.

The consequence of the first of these appeared when peace negotiations opened in London in July 1445. These centred on the traditional issues of Henry VI's title to the crown of France and the lands he held there. Suffolk clearly assumed that Henry's marriage and the promise to cede Maine, for which a date of 1 October seems now to have been given, would persuade the French to greater flexibility than in 1439. In fact they remained adamant that even should Henry relinquish the title he could hold no lands in France in sovereignty, and that in any case he had no claim to Normandy. When it was clear that the French had no new proposals for a negotiated peace, a face-saving suggestion for a personal meeting of the two kings was readily agreed, the truce being extended from April to November 1446.[71] Suffolk was now in a quandary. He needed French concessions on the terms of peace to palliate the surrender of Maine when this became public knowledge. But Charles had decoupled the two, refusing to move on peace but pressing the cession of Maine in fulfilment of Henry's personal promise and as the price of extending the truce. In the context of a further extension to April 1447 Henry VI wrote in his own hand to Charles on 22 December 1445 explicitly promising to cede Maine by 30 April 1446. Thus from being a family settlement between the houses of Lancaster and Anjou the issue had become one of personal honour between the two kings on which the continued peace between their realms hung.[72]

Over the next two years Charles VII insistently pressed Henry VI to fulfil his promise, coupling personal reproaches and appeals to their friendship with ever shortening extensions of the truce. As the promise over Maine began to emerge, Suffolk's room for manoeuvre narrowed. Either the territory had indeed to be handed over or preparations had to be made for the truce to end and the war to

[70] Wolffe, *Henry VI*, 174–6.

[71] The journal of the French ambassadors is printed in *Wars of Eng.* i. 87–152, esp. 132–42. A full account is in Beaucourt, *Histoire de Charles VII*, iv. 142–68.

[72] As pointed out by Watts, *Henry VI and the Politics of Kingship*, 228.

resume. In the latter event large reinforcements would have to be sent, but (as will be seen) the exchequer was at this moment bankrupt and no money was available. Nor could Suffolk or Henry face the collapse of their peace policy. Yet to cede Maine was not a straightforward matter. Maine was a royal fief and only the earl of Somerset among the higher nobility held lands there, but the principal landowners and defenders of Normandy—York, Shrewsbury, Scales, and Faucomberg—would only endorse it as the price of a guaranteed peace. To circumvent this it was decided to replace York, who had ended his five-year term as lieutenant governor in September 1445. York was expecting to be reappointed and had returned to England to negotiate the arrears of his salary. His accounts were examined and in April 1446 he accepted a settlement of £26,000. He was still styling himself lieutenant and was expecting to accompany the king to his meeting with Charles VII.[73] But in the autumn a campaign to denigrate his conduct in Normandy was launched from within the court, and though he successfully confronted its author, Adam Moleyns, it became clear that he was to be replaced by Edmund Beaufort, earl of Somerset.[74] Although Somerset stood to lose most from the surrender of Maine, having been granted the county in 1438, his cooperation was secured by massive compensation and his appointment (on 24 December 1446) as lieutenant governor for three years from March 1447. York made no open protest though his captains in Normandy did. Nor did Somerset make any move throughout 1447 either to take up his commission or to order his captains in Maine to effect the surrender.

With the approach of the next deadline for the delivery of Maine, on 1 November 1447, Henry angrily ordered Somerset to implement his commands, but the earl continued to drag his feet with the object of procuring maximum compensation. On 13 November, Somerset was granted 10,000 *livres tournois* per annum for life from taxation in Normandy, and with this in hand he began to assemble his retinue.[75] But in Maine his captains stood out for compensation for all English landowners in confirmation of the twenty-year truce with Anjou. By February 1448 Charles VII had assembled 6,000 troops before Le Mans and an assault was only avoided when Henry's own envoys, Adam Moleyns and Sir Robert Roos, agreed to deliver the city on 11 March.[76] Henry VI saw this as manifesting his desire for peace; while for the English captains and landowners in Maine (among them Sir John Fastolf) it amounted to a shameful betrayal. The peace policy was generating political dissensions which Suffolk's influence over the king could barely contain.

[73] Johnson, *Duke Richard of York*, 51–62, 77.

[74] M. L. Kekewich *et al.* (eds.), *The Politics of Fifteenth Century England: John Vale's Book* (Stroud, 1995), 180–3.

[75] M. K. Jones, 'Somerset, York and the Wars of the Roses', *EHR* 104 (1989), 292–3.

[76] Wolffe, *Henry VI*, 193–203.

The terms of surrender, drawn up by the English, had deliberately included the duke of Brittany as an ally of Henry VI, belatedly rectifying the truce of Tours. The French appear to have overlooked this, and the issue was now to acquire practical significance. For Duke Francis's younger brother Gilles, a close boyhood friend of Henry VI, championed a pro-English against his brother's pro-French policy. This was seen as a threat by Charles VII, for whom Brittany's allegiance was of prime importance, and at his instigation the duke arrested and imprisoned Gilles in June 1446. Henry VI saw this as a personal insult, and in political terms it extinguished English hopes of detaching Brittany and prompted plans to rescue Gilles. Towards the end of 1447 an Aragonese captain, François de Surienne, who had fought on the English side since 1435, was recruited for a plan to seize the Breton frontier town of Fougères and bargain it for the release of Gilles. The project had Suffolk's personal support and in Normandy the logistics were organized by Talbot, now earl of Shrewsbury. A body of troops was secretly assembled, and on 23–4 March 1449 the town and castle were taken by surprise, plundered, and garrisoned. By 10 April Francis had appealed to Charles VII and two months later formally entered an alliance with him. Suddenly the prospect of a Franco-Breton attack on Normandy was a reality.[77]

As Duke Francis's ally and overlord, Charles VII opened negotiations with Somerset for the return of Fougères in June and July. But the issue was now not so much the town as the status of Brittany, Somerset insisting that the duke was an English vassal and refusing to acknowledge Charles's intervention. It was thus to assert his sovereignty over both Normandy and Brittany that Charles declared war on 31 July 1449. The attempt to safeguard Normandy by diplomacy thus ended catastrophically. For this Suffolk and Moleyns incurred blame, paying for it with their lives. However, arguments have been put for ascribing as much responsibility either to Henry VI, who constitutionally could not be held accountable, or to the lords of the council who had endorsed Suffolk's policies.[78] Evidently Suffolk had the king's authority for the truce, the marriage, the cession of Maine, and probably even the seizure of Fougères, and demonstrably for all of these he sought the approval (if sometimes retrospective) of council or parliament. Henry's correspondence with Charles VII and his encounters with the French ambassadors show him actively participating in this policy. He ardently desired peace as his Christian duty and sought it through a relationship of amity

---

[77] M. H. Keen and M. J. Daniel, 'English diplomacy and the sack of Fougères in 1449', *History*, 59 (1974), 375–91; Wolffe, *Henry VI*, 204–9. The monograph by A. Bossuat, *Perrinet Gressart et François de Surienne, agents de l'Angleterre* (Paris 1936), 301–52, gives the fullest account.

[78] These are the viewpoints of, respectively, Wolffe in *Henry VI* and Watts in *Henry VI and the Politics of Kingship*.

and trust with his 'uncle' which should transcend politics. Charles deliberately played on his gullibility with reproaches and affection to secure concessions. Yet it seems clear that it was Suffolk, not Henry, who conceived and controlled the diplomatic strategy. Similarly, from Tours right through to Fougères it was Suffolk and Moleyns who initiated and managed the negotiations, even if Suffolk's position required the endorsement of his peers. Public opinion was not wrong in placing the blame—however crudely—on Suffolk.

Was the policy inherently flawed? At the outset Suffolk made a basic mis-judgement. He interpreted Charles VII's readiness for a truce as offering the prospect of a long respite from war, rather than merely the breathing space which Charles needed. When only a short truce was offered Suffolk treated it as the start of an ongoing peace process, for which he could win the support of the house of Anjou through Henry's marriage and the cession of Maine. Such a pol-icy required diplomatic skills greater than Suffolk possessed. Charles outflanked this by decoupling the question of peace from the cession of Maine, refusing the former and insisting on the latter. Even so it was not the surrender of Maine but the issue of Brittany's allegiance on which Suffolk's policy broke. For this Suffolk's carelessness at Tours paved the way, but it was Gilles's intemperate ambitions and Suffolk's adventurism that played into Charles's hands—the more culpably in that Suffolk was well aware of the vulnerability of Normandy by 1448–9. In his belief that the truce would be prolonged, he may have become the prisoner of Henrys VI's invincible pacifism.

The Military Collapse

Despite Suffolk's exhortation to maintain the garrisons, their size was cut dras-tically after the truce of Tours: from 3,500 before 1444 to 2,100 by 1448.[79] This was dictated by the refusal of the Norman Estates to grant more than half the taxation needed in both 1446 and 1447 though granting the full sum in 1448.[80] Regular wages, the principal instrument of discipline, were the more essential as the spoils of war became unavailable, but by 1448 Somerset was able to pay only two-thirds of the garrisons' wages, and these were increasingly drawn from local sources or, even worse, levied as *appatis*. When he reached Normandy in 1448 Somerset took steps to tighten discipline, ordering a simultaneous muster of all garrisons. Even so, the Estates' complaint was less of the indiscipline of the gar-risons than of the discharged soldiery. After the surrender of Maine in 1448 some were assembled on the Breton frontier for the coup at Fougères, while others

---

[79] Curry, 'English armies', 51–2, 58; id., 'Les "Gens vivans sur le pais"', 213.
[80] Allmand, *Lancastrian Normandy*, 185–6.

were rounded up and marched to the ports to be sent home.[81] In the absence of an effective commander between York and Somerset, and of financial support from England, the defence structure of Normandy began to fall apart. Crucially the opportunity was lost to reconstitute the disbanded troops as a permanent force on the model of Charles VII's *compagnies d'ordonnance*. As a result Normandy lacked a field army when the crisis broke.

The appearance of a French army of 6,000 before Le Mans in March 1448 set alarm bells ringing and a force of 2,000 archers was mobilized, only to be disbanded when the crisis passed.[82] When he arrived Somerset took some measures to remedy the critical state of Normandy's defences. Disbanded soldiers were recruited into *creues*, new bastilles were erected, and some fortifications repaired. He undertook a *réformation générale* of the financial system, and by reviving the Norman *échiquier* as a supreme court he collected fines and fees from its proceedings.[83] These measures were scraping the barrel; Somerset found himself starved of resources, not only from within Normandy but from the English exchequer. Fastolf's advice to Somerset on taking up his command in March 1448, to victual and garrison the frontier towns, make troops pay for victuals taken, and keep men in reserve for a field army, betrayed an ignorance of the situation which Somerset may have shared.[84] A year later, in February 1449, he sent his personal envoys to report the true position to parliament: Charles was preparing for war with an army of considerable size, while English defences were ruinous and lacked artillery; the cost of refortifying these could not be borne by Normandy alone. If war came it would be lost irrecoverably.[85] His appeal went unheeded. The assumption was that, as in the past, the war would be one of piecemeal defence for which seasonal reinforcements could be dispatched. It was only as war began that urgent discussion took place in the June–July session at Winchester about how to raise money and troops. Before 1444 that would still have been feasible at even so late a stage, for there was a pool of soldiers to be recruited, experienced captains to lead them, and loans from Cardinal Beaufort to pay them. Virtually none of these obtained by 1449; it took a month to raise enough loans even for the token force of 400 men sent on 27 September.[86] In Normandy the Estates were summoned in May to grant 188,000 *lives tournois* but events quickly overtook its collection. On both sides of the Channel an air of defeatism prevailed.

[81] Allmand, *Lancastrian Normandy*, 209; Johnson, *Richard of York*, 48; Jouet, *Résistance à l'occupation anglaise*, 151–4.

[82] *Wars of Eng.* i. 479–82; Jones, 'Somerset, York', 294.

[83] Jones, 'Somerset, York', 299–300, and the full discussion in id., 'The Beaufort family and the war in France, 1421–50', Ph.D. thesis (Bristol University, 1982), ch. 5.

[84] *Wars of Eng.* ii. 592–4.   [85] *Rot. Parl.* v. 147.

[86] G. L. Harriss, 'Marmaduke Lumley and the exchequer crisis of 1446–9', in J. G. Rowe (ed.), *Aspects of Late Medieval Government and Society* (Toronto, 1986), 166–8.

Charles VII effectively reopened hostilities by taking Pont de l'Arche and capturing Lord Faucomberg as a reprisal for Fougères in May 1449. After he declared war on 27 July three armies advanced into Normandy, one from Beauvais taking Pont Audemer and Lisieux; another from the south taking Verneuil, Mantes, Vernon, and Argentan; and the third from the west taking Coutances, Carentan, Saint-Lô, and Fougères. There was little coordination between them and a skilful commander with 5,000 men might have defeated one and turned on the others. But with no field army, the towns surrendered one by one to a largely bloodless conquest. In most cases it was the inhabitants who effected the entry of the French troops, either by betraying the defences or by persuading the English garrison to withdraw. They were moved less by patriotism than by the desire to avoid damage to the town from Charles's artillery and punishment for their resistance; there was no confidence that the English could defend them. Even at Rouen, while the archbishop negotiated with the French, it was the rebellion of the townsfolk that forced the garrison to retreat to the castle. Somerset had then no choice but to negotiate his withdrawal by surrendering Harfleur and other towns in the Caux and leaving Shrewsbury as hostage.[87] No relief could now be sent from England to eastern Normandy, the only remaining ports being Cherbourg and Caen, to which Somerset had retired.

It was to relieve Somerset that an army of almost 3,000 men, mainly archers, was assembled at Portsmouth in December under Sir Thomas Kyriell. Delay in paying its wages turned it mutinous, and on 9 January Bishop Adam Moleyns, who arrived with the money, was accused of betraying Normandy and lynched. Kyriell eventually landed at Cherbourg on 15 March 1450 with orders to make for Caen, but he was intercepted by a French army at Formigny, 10 miles short of Bayeux. Most of the army perished, Kyriell being captured, and Bayeux fell on 16 May. After a fierce defence at Caen, Somerset surrendered on 24 June and was allowed to leave for Calais. The last English strongholds, Falaise and Cherbourg, had fallen by early August, at the news of which James Gresham wrote to John Paston that 'we have not now a foote of lond in Normandie'.[88]

To those English who had made Normandy their home for the last thirty or so years the collapse was as unexpected as it was swift and complete. The relative security of the truce and the easing of taxation had produced a modest economic recovery. The nobility were still acquiring and investing in land and sending the profits to England; a French reconquest was not anticipated.[89] For the artisans

---

[87] A. Curry, 'Towns at war: Relations between the towns of Normandy and their English rulers, 1417–50', in J. A. F. Thomson (ed.), *Towns and Townspeople in the Fifteenth Century* (Stroud, 1988), 148–72. For contemporary judgement on Somerset's actions, see Jones, 'Somerset, York', 302–4.

[88] Davis (ed.), *Paston Letters*, ii. 42.

[89] Jones, 'Somerset, York', 117–18; Johnson, *Duke Richard of York*, 47; Allmand, *Lancastrian Normandy*, 91–4.

and petty landowners who formed the backbone of the English occupation, their holdings of 20 to 60 *livres tournois* per annum furnished a respectable livelihood. They now lost their lands, houses, and possessions and returned to England destitute. Their numbers, experiences, and fate went largely unrecorded, but throughout August a stream of refugees, men, women, and children, on carts piled high with bedding and household goods, passed day after day through Cheapside 'in right pouer array pitewus to see dryven out of normandy'. They could look only for charity, but the mood in England was of indifference or hostility; for they were seen as having exploited the conquest for a lifetime and then failing to defend it.[90]

It was expected in England that the French would shortly lay siege to Calais, but in fact the French commanders Dunois and Xantrailles had already switched their attack to Gascony, taking Bazas. During the winter an army of 7,000 was built up to resume the offensive in May 1451, leading to the rapid capture of Blaye and Bourg and the surrender of Bordeaux on 12 June. In England, Somerset, having survived the challenge from York, began to assemble an army for a descent on northern France in 1452, causing Charles VII to strengthen the garrisons of Normandy while leaving Bordeaux lightly defended. The earl of Shrewsbury and Sir Edward Hull seized it in October, and in March 1453 Viscount Lisle and Lord Moleyns brought out an army of 2,325 men with a force of similar size planned to follow in August. This was preparing to sail when the news of Castillon arrived. In July 1453 the French army advanced in three parts, and Shrewsbury's strategy was to attack the smallest of these, under Jean Bureau, as it was besieging Castillon. He surprised and routed part of the French army beneath the walls of the town and pressed on to attack the well-defended camp. As his men fell before Bureau's close-range artillery he, his son Viscount Lisle, and his principal captains perished. This left the duchy indefensible, and Bordeaux surrendered on 20 October. Despite 300 years of attachment to England, there was little native support for English rule, at least beyond Bordeaux.[91]

The loss of Gascony, compounding that of Normandy, confirmed English inability to finance, organize, and fight war on the Continent after 1444. The French had achieved decisive superiority in military organization and discipline, in number and quality of troops, and above all in the use of artillery. The English defeat both exposed and exacerbated political divisions while the French monarchy emerged as the symbol of patriotism and unity. Yet Charles VII never secured the final prize, Calais, and Castillon became the last engagement of

---

[90] *Six Town Chron.* 134; Allmand, *Lancastrian Normandy*, 262.
[91] M. G. Vale, 'The last years of English Gascony', *TRHS*, 5th ser., 19 (1969), 119–38; Pollard, *John Talbot*, 129, 136–9.

French and English armies for the remainder of the century. The problems of re-establishing royal power and the social peace in Normandy and Gascony, his deepening quarrel with the Dauphin Louis, who fled to Philip of Burgundy in 1456, and his declining health, all dissuaded Charles from pursuing the war. As England moved towards civil war rival factions aligned with those abroad, Lancastrians with Charles VII, and Yorkists with Philip of Burgundy. Warwick's control of Calais, financed by attacks on French and Castilian ships, was supported by Duke Philip on both political and economic grounds, and the Yorkist invasion of 1460 and eventual victory at Towton in 1461 confirmed the Burgundian alliance as the bedrock of Edward IV's foreign policy, while Margaret of Anjou sought safety and support in France.

The Inquest

The explosion of anger at the loss of Normandy claimed the lives of Moleyns and Suffolk and precipitated a deadly feud between Somerset and York. Yet these violent political reactions contrast both with the signs of growing disengagement from the war in the preceding decade, and with the prevailing insularity of England in the following half-century. This suggests that the fall of Normandy was the catalyst for a seismic shift in English attitudes to war overseas. From being the test of military valour and source of national pride, the war in France became a nostalgic charade.

In March 1450 the Commons impeached Suffolk of treason for the loss of Normandy, seeking to establish his personal guilt for the release of Orléans in 1440, the abandonment of the count of Armagnac in 1442, the promise to surrender Maine in 1444, the failure to name Brittany as an ally at Tours, and the disclosure of English counsels and military secrets to the French ambassadors. Suffolk's detailed defence has not survived but it is clear from some further replications by the Commons that he derided and denied the more personal allegations and adduced the collective responsibility of the council for the major policy decisions. He did not shelter behind the king's authority.[92] Although Henry VI could dismiss the treason charges as unproven, the duke's ensuing murder on his way to exile attested the popular belief in his guilt. Suffolk was made the scapegoat for a multi-layered and predictable catastrophe, but he had been the principal architect and executor of policy at every stage and was identified with it. The Commons were right to sense this, though wrong to ascribe it to Suffolk's calculated treachery.

[92] The impeachment charges, mainly relating to Normandy, are in *Rot. Parl.* v. 177–9, with some in the further bill of misprisions on pp. 179–81. The (unofficial) replication to his defence is in Historical Manuscripts Commission, *Third Report* (London, 1872), 279–80.

Somerset, too, was charged with treason for his part in the loss of Normandy but on military grounds and by the duke of York. The charge came first, and predictably, from the disbanded soldiers who had returned in August 1450. York supported their outcry but he only brought specific charges against Somerset in February 1452 as part of his campaign to remove him. These were of financial malfeasance in the Norman administration and of treasonous capitulation in Rouen, the latter involving the honour and interests of York himself as its captain.[93] This detailed indictment of Somerset's acts in Normandy reflected the outrage and desire for revenge of those who had held command and lands there—men like Fastolf, Ogard, and Oldhall. However, the fact that it formed part of a political vendetta meant that it was set aside when York's bid to displace Somerset failed in 1452.

Although political feuds focused the blame on individuals, both the military and the civil weaknesses of Normandy were well understood. Before the crisis both Fastolf and Somerset had drawn attention to the vulnerability of the garrisons in numbers, victuals, fortifications, and artillery, and it was realized that the French army was now larger, better disciplined, and with greater striking power than before 1444. But the English still chose to depend on short-term reinforcements, the quality and quantity of which had steeply declined since 1443. The weaknesses of the civil structure in Normandy were equally apparent to contemporaries. The reluctance of the Normandy Estates to grant taxation during the truce jeopardized the pay of the garrisons, with a consequent decline of discipline, the resort to pillage and oppression, the alienation of the native population, and the encouragement to brigandage. To this vicious sequence Fastolf returned time and again in his analysis of the English occupation. To him the root cause of the decline was the 'feigned truce' proffered by the French, which had induced a false sense of security and encouraged the English to relax their discipline and lower their guard.[94] In *The Boke of Noblesse* he set out to recall the standards of English rule in Normandy under Henry V and Bedford. Fastolf firmly believed that the English had an ancient and indefeasible right to Normandy, deriving from 1066–1214. God would not suffer this right to be overthrown and would restore it in due course—when the English returned to the traditional chivalric ideal. Fastolf's mindset was that of the 1420s and 1430s, and perhaps not typical among those still engaged in war, but it revealed the gulf that had opened up between those steeped in the vision of Henry V and those who had attuned themselves to the patronage culture of the 1440s.

---

[93] *Wars of Eng.* ii. 718–22; Gairdner (ed.), *Paston Letters*, i. 103–8. For comment, see Jones, 'Somerset, York', 304–6.

[94] *Wars of Eng.* ii. 592, 718; *Boke of Noblesse*, 5, 30–3, 39–40, 71–4; C. T. Allmand, 'Le *Boke of Noblesse* de William Worcester', in *La 'France anglaise'*, 103–12.

Yet this was not just a crisis for the chivalric class and its lifestyle. The conquest of Normandy had brought proportionately greater benefit to the lower-ranking men-at-arms, archers, officials, and artisans who had formed themselves into a colonial class. The conquest and settlement had been national, not just aristocratic, in character, and the victories and gains of war had been celebrated as matters of patriotic pride. As the ebbing tide of success turned to defeat it brought recrimination between the ageing expatriates and those at home, to whom they looked in vain for support. By 1449 England was prepared to disown its colonization of Normandy as it had already that of Ireland and Wales.

The English enterprise in France thus ended in military defeat and dishonour, and political and social divisions. It evidently deepened the antipathy between English and French and after the euphoric triumph of 1415 Englishmen had to nurse their humiliating defeat in 1450 throughout a prolonged estrangement from military adventures abroad. Some welcomed this, declaring, 'we have England and do not need external possessions, and so we can remain at peace', though as a people the English remained conquerors and colonizers at heart.[95] For the myth of Agincourt was never forgotten, nor was Henry V's vision ever condemned. That has been left to historians, who have judged the whole enterprise flawed and to have left a *damnosa hereditas* for his successor.[96] In military terms, as we have seen, this is justified: England did not have the resources to conquer and hold part of northern France indefinitely. However, Henry's *imperium* was predicated not on holding a conquered territory but on securing a legal peace. Having failed to win this in 1418 from either the Dauphin or John the Fearless, he extended his design to encompass the kingdom of France. In the Treaty of Troyes, Henry envisaged England and France brought to a mutual peace through a common kingship and promoting internal order and justice through their own institutions and laws. Multiple kingdoms of this kind were both conceivable and feasible in this and the following century, and though it aroused some distrust many English and French accepted it in 1420. Had Henry V lived to establish this new order and embody it in his kingship, it might have acquired political legitimacy. But with his death it was a vision that quickly faded. The peace that was meant to knit English and French together became a war that inflamed their old enmity and reinforced their separate identities.

---

[95] *Wars of Eng.* ii. 726.   [96] Jacob, *The Fifteenth Century*, 202.

CHAPTER 15

Ruling England, 1413–1461

1. HENRY V, THE MODEL KING

Historians have come to see the crises in social and political relations from *c.* 1371 to *c.* 1406 as expressions of a more liberated and assertive society, produced by the better equilibrium between population and resources. But to contemporary moralists, from Langland to Gower, the demands of labourers for freedom and money, the political aspirations of men of middling degree, and the factious quarrels of the nobility were symptoms of the pride and greed which threatened to subvert the social hierarchy. At the head of society, protecting and controlling it, stood the Church and the Crown; yet they too had been engulfed by disorder. The Church was rent by schism, threatened by heresy, and corrupted by wealth; kingship had descended into tyranny and its sacral legitimacy had been violated by usurpation. Nevertheless, Gower, who voiced this sense of crisis, directed his call for moral regeneration to the king, for 'the king and his people are like the head and the body. Where the head is infirm the body is infirm. Where a virtuous king does not rule, the people are unsound and lack good morals.'[1]

Henry V's outlook was shaped both by this crisis, into which he was born, and by the remedy prescribed by his father's retainer and apologist. While still in his teens he had seen his father exiled and dispossessed, then return to seize the throne; thereafter he himself faced treachery in battle and gruelling, non-chivalric fighting against Welsh rebels. His political apprenticeship was shaped by membership of the council which governed for his ailing father. For two years in his early twenties he controlled government and stamped his own policy on its conduct, surrounding himself with advisers and servants who in effect constituted a ministry in waiting. Henry thus came to the throne with a far wider knowledge of the people and problems of the country he was to govern than any

---

[1] Gower, 'O deus immense', lines 83–6, in *The Complete Works*, ed. G. C. Macaulay, 4 vols. (Oxford, 1899–1902); F. Grady, 'The Lancastrian Gower and the limits of exemplarity', *Speculum*, 70 (1995), 532–75. Gower was a Lancastrian retainer; his effigy in Southwark Cathedral has the collar of esses.

king since Edward I. And as the tensions eased he became a symbol for the vigour and optimism of a new generation.

Believing, with Gower, that the king was the cornerstone of society's well-being, Henry sought to fulfil his coronation promises, which, for Hoccleve, provided the measure of a king's rule:

> Tho othes that at your creacioun
> Shul thurgh your tonge passe, hem wel observe.[2]

As much as Richard II, Henry saw his consecration as indelible and trans-forming, but where for Richard it was self-referential, conferring a personal inviolability, for Henry sacral kingship also embraced his kingdom: it was private and personal but also public and political. For the king mediated God's favour and protection to his people. God's purpose was for the English nation, and this concept of a holy nation, God's chosen people, was to be progressively developed by royal propagandists. This was to be formulated most explicitly in the context of war against the national enemy, France, in which Henry saw himself fulfilling his own and his people's destiny, as the instruments of God's justice.[3]

Henry V brought to English kingship not only political experience and belief in a divine commission, but high intelligence and disciplined vigour. He was brisk, decisive, and indefatigable, demanding of others and not sparing himself. The clipped phrases of his letters and commands reveal a controlled and analyt-ical mind. He could make courageous decisions with a cool head, thinking through a problem to possible solutions. Save for his lean and perhaps slight stature, he was every inch a king, holding himself with dignity, reserve, and inner confidence. He was a shrewd judge of men, with an instinct for the weakness of those he wished to bend to his will, but also a generous appreciation of courage and loyalty in others. He commanded respect, fidelity, and devotion. Such was the man who had waited impatiently for his father to die for his chance to lead and shape the English nation.

Although Henry's concept of kingship and of his own mission were fully formed in 1413, the first two years of his reign saw old discords surface which he used to define the quality of his rule. These involved his relations with the Church, the magnates, and the political community. The first centred on the Lollard plot to seize the king and his brothers and the subsequent rising of January 1414. It is not necessary to credit Henry with staging these events, but it is true that the king exploited his efficient and almost bloodless defeat of a hand-ful of rustics to claim divine protection and approval for his kingship.[4] Henry was

---

[2] Harriss, in *Henry V*, 1–29; Powell, *Kingship, Law, and Society*, 125–34. Quotation from Hoccleve, *The Regement of Princes*, lines 2192–3.

[3] Above, Ch. 14, sect. 1.

[4] Cf. Strohm, *England's Empty Throne*, 65–85. The rising is discussed above, Ch. 10, sects. 4, 5.

resolved to suppress Lollardy, not only out of personal conviction but as being inimical to his monarchical role. For while the Lollards appealed to the king to destroy the Church, Henry believed that the Church could empower his kingship through its prayers, its power over opinion, and its wealth. Moreover, he needed to demonstrate Lancastrian orthodoxy in an international as well as a domestic context: for the resolution of the Schism, and for his challenge to the crown of France, perhaps ultimately for his leadership of a crusade. He could not be seen to be soft on Lollardy like his father and grandfather, and he therefore used the Oldcastle incident to project himself as the hammer of heretics, the defender of both the Church and the faith, a new Constantine:

> To holy chirche a verray sustenour
> And piler of our feith, and werreyour
> Ageyn the heresies bitter galle.[5]

Henry's bishops shared his conviction of the need for spiritual discipline and reform if the Church was to fulfil its role, and Archbishop Henry Chichele provided the model for many other bishops, as a devout and conscientious diocesan and a loyal servant of the Crown. The royal chapel was itself a centre of spirituality and the source of works of edification, while Henry's twin foundations of Carthusians at Sheen and of Bridgettines at Syon were to be, the one a house of prayer for himself and the kingdom, the other a place of heavenly peace on earth.[6] Henry measured the efficacy of prayer by the virtue of those who prayed—himself, his clergy, and his subjects. His spirituality was thus directed both inward to his conscience and outward to his governance of the English Church and nation.

While a Lollard rising could not have been predicted, among the magnates the divisions of 1397–1403 still dangerously resonated. In his first two years Henry relied exclusively on old Lancastrian allies: the earls of Warwick and Arundel, his brother Bedford, and his Beaufort-related uncles, Dorset and Westmorland. They were given the principal offices and military commands and formed an inner group in his counsels.[7] The heirs of families who had rebelled against his father—Thomas Montagu, earl of Salisbury, John Mowbray, Earl Marshal, John Holland, earl of Huntingdon, and Henry Percy—were all younger than the king and anxious to recover forfeited lands and titles and restore their families' honour. Henry's policy was to encourage their aspirations but insist that restoration had to be earned by loyal service and received by royal grace. The old Ricardian families were to purge their rebellion, and hopefully restore their fortunes, by fighting in France. Henry Percy was to be exchanged for the Murdach of Fife, captured by his father at Homildon Hill in 1402, and

---

[5] Hoccleve, *The Minor Poems*, ed. F. J. Furnivall, EETS, extra ser., 61 (London, 1892), 41.

[6] Above, Ch. 2, sect. 3; Ch. 9, sect. 1.

[7] For a fuller discussion, see Harriss, *Henry V*, ch. 2.

re-created earl of Northumberland under heavy sureties. There remained the problem of Edmund, earl of March, whose latent claim to be Richard II's true heir had already made him the focus for magnate conspiracies. Since 1409 he had been kept under surveillance in Prince Henry's household, who had taken the measure of his mediocre abilities; but when in 1413 he entered his inheritance Henry imposed on him the huge fine of 10,000 marks, forcing him to mortgage part of his estates.

Other nobles, like the duke of York, Richard, earl of Cambridge, Lord Scrope of Masham, and Sir Thomas Grey of Heton were also in financial difficulties. Resentment and desperation led the last three to plot some kind of coup to remove the king and frustrate the royal expedition to France in 1415. The earl of March was to be its figurehead and to recruit Mortimer supporters in Wales, Henry Percy was to be brought from Scotland to raise the north, and the remnants of the Lollards mobilized. As the army gathered at Southampton, Henry was probably alerted by his spies, and on 31 July the earl of March lost his nerve and betrayed the conspirators, who, when seized, confessed before being executed.[8] Their plans had never been credible, but the fact that the conspiracy was a fiasco should not mask its significance. This lay both in its potentiality for rekindling old enmities to the house of Lancaster and (like the Lollard rising) in providing further evidence of God's providential guidance and protection of the king. When it came to be placed in the context of the far greater test and delivery of Henry and his people at Agincourt, Lancastrian kingship was finally vindicated and accepted. Henry's rule of his nobility was never again challenged, and those who fought under him won the honour and riches which would have been the reward of Cambridge, Scrope, and Grey had they been patient.

It was in parliament that the king and the larger political community, through its representatives, came face to face. Henry V's frequent, if short, parliaments were indicative of his tight and purposive control. In 1413 the Speaker called on him to provide the 'bone governance' which his father had failed to do: economical government, effective defence, the enforcement of law and order, and the redress of injustices. Five parliaments later Bishop Beaufort, as chancellor, claimed that Henry had implemented a programme of just government at home, in fulfilment of his coronation promise and as a prelude to asserting his just claims in France.[9]

Under his leadership of the council in 1410–11 a start had been made on limiting household expenses, curtailing grants, reducing the burden of annuities, and ensuring payment for household purveyances. When he became king these were continued as part of a drive for solvency on the ordinary account: the

[8] Pugh, *Henry V and the Southampton Plot*, 64–136.
[9] *Rot. Parl.* iv. 4, 94; Harriss, *Henry V*, ch. 7; Allmand, *Henry V*, ch. 17.

permanent defence costs were stabilized, revenue from royal lands and fiscal prerogatives increased, and the honesty and efficiency of revenue collectors scrutinized. While much effort was put into exploiting the king's own resources, war
could only be financed from taxation. The anchor of royal finance was the wool
subsidy which, exceptionally, the king was granted for life following the news of
Agincourt. Direct taxation was always more contentious and the incidence of
taxation was unprecedented, five full subsidies being paid within the three years
1415–17. Over the whole reign of nine years he received ten and one-third fifteenths. Yet not merely was there no opposition but the grants were not hedged
by conditions or removed from royal control. By straining all resources the
exchequer mobilized £131,000 for the Agincourt campaign and £161,000 for the
invasion of 1417. Henry had to push the financial system to its limits at a period
of shrinking revenues, disruption of trade, and shortage of bullion. Yet there was
no collapse of exchequer credit and his war debts remained far less than those of
Edward I and Edward III.[10]

Second only to the Commons' complaints of Henry IV's insolvency had been
their reiterated demands for law enforcement. The crisis of order sprang in
general from the crisis of lordship, particularly in the Welsh border counties
during Glyn Dŵr's revolt and in the north following the Percy rebellions. Both
contained 'liberties' and 'avowries', areas of immunity where criminal gangs
could take refuge. Further, as treason limited the number of peers on whom
Henry IV could rely, he gave over the rule of some shires to royal retainers, in
particular the Lancastrian affinity in the North Midlands and the earl of
Arundel's affinity in the Welsh borderlands. Opposition from local lords and
gentry had, by 1413, led to a series of violent feuds. Having assembled a parliament at Leicester in May 1414 to legislate on Lollardy, Henry launched a judicial
visitation of the Midlands and Welsh border using the court of king's bench as a
superior eyre. Under the king's eye and that of the duke of York, juries indicted
nobles and gentry, including followers of the king and Arundel, for illegal distribution of livery, assault, and extortion over the preceding years.[11] Henry's aim
was to pacify rather than to punish: to demonstrate his intolerance of disorder
and the abuse of power but to pardon and reinstate those who submitted. While
lordship must be exercised under royal authority, violence could be channelled
into service under the king in France. Drawing off criminals to war was a well-
recognized solution and one with a long future; nonetheless, the king had administered a short, sharp shock to bastard feudal society which was not forgotten.

---

[10]   For the financial position, see Harriss, *Henry V*, ch. 8; Allmand, *Henry V*, ch. 18.
[11]   For abuses by the royal affinity in the North Midlands, see Castor, *King, Crown, and Duchy of
Lancaster*, chs. 3 and 6; for the judicial proceedings, Powell, *Kingship, Law, and Society*, 117–268,
and p. 278, table A2.

The four years from March 1413 to July 1417 during which Henry V ruled England saw the restoration of effective kingship and government. Henry cultivated the traditional image of kingship to make it the focus of unity. He met the need of the nobility for loyal service and stability, of the Church for support against its critics, of the gentry for order and solvency, and of traders for secure markets. Because his programme was conservative it was welcomed readily and could be achieved speedily. Yet good governance went hand in hand with preparation for a major war, and their common theme was justice. Henry V saw the attainment of his rightful claims in France as integral to his restoration of the kingship of Edward III.

During Henry's absences in France a keeper and a council were appointed to govern England. John, duke of Bedford, who normally occupied the office, had vice-regal powers, but the king reserved to himself matters of prerogative and grace (petitions, rewards, and pardons), higher appointments, and decisions taken in parliament, sending warrants and signet letters from France. Henry also kept London informed of his campaign and victories, writing in English. Parliaments became summary affairs, although the short parliament of 1420 voiced its suspicion of the Treaty of Troyes, seeking assurances that Englishmen would not be subject to Henry V as king of France, and demanding his speedy return.[12] Opinion was turning against Henry's wider ambitions in France; the conquest and exploitation of Normandy had been popular, but to go beyond was to incur unlimited obligations. There were signs of this feeling in the country at large, many showing reluctance to lend money or serve in France.[13] Thus in February 1421 Henry returned to a war-weary land, if also to a victory pageant organized by London and with his new queen as the pledge of Lancastrian succession to the crown of France.

With characteristic briskness Henry left London immediately after the queen's coronation to tour the length and breadth of the kingdom, from North Wales to Yorkshire and East Anglia. It was both an exercise in self-presentation— visiting shrines, feeding the poor, and addressing the people—and a determined effort to wring money and service from the propertied classes.[14] By May he had a force of over 4,000 men under muster and had raised over £18,000 in loans, to be repaid from taxation granted by the clergy. The Commons made no grant, for their ratifying of the Treaty of Troyes marked the formal end of the war. Instead, Henry relieved Bishop Beaufort of most of his wealth by a loan of £17,666, with

[12] *Rot. Parl.* iv. 125–7; R. W. Chambers and M. Daunt (eds.), *A Book of London English* (Oxford, 1931), 64–85.

[13] A. E. Goodman, 'Responses to requests in Yorkshire for military service under Henry V', *Northern Hist.* 17 (1981), 240–52.

[14] J. Doig, 'Propaganda and truth: Henry V's royal progress in 1421', *Nott. Med. Stud.* 40 (1996), 167–79, which provides a map.

which he purchased his restoration to the king's grace after renouncing his cardinal's hat.[15] Despite parliament's brevity—less than four weeks—numerous petitions were answered and major measures enacted including the issue of a new coinage of good weight to counteract clipped and counterfeited coins and the influx of debased money from Burgundy; it was the first measure of Henry's rule common to both France and England.[16] Henry had handled a restive and critical nation with some success, the brevity of his five-month visit being offset by the intensity of his activity.

Henry left England for the last time on 10 June, Queen Catherine remaining at Windsor for the birth of Henry VI in December. Parliament, summoned to coincide with this, gratefully voted a full fifteenth. The king, as before, kept close control over appointments and rewards through a stream of warrants. Henry had made a will on leaving England in 1415 and another, which replaced it, on 10 June 1421.[17] In that he laid down the order of his funeral and the intercessions for his soul. He directed that his chantry tomb should be erected adjoining the Confessor's in Westminster Abbey, with the altar on an upper level visible to the people below who could share in the intercessionary Mass. Built of Caen stone and figuring the Trinity and the saints to whom he looked for protection— the Virgin, SS Edward, Edmund, and George, along with the French royal saint St Denis—it features scenes from his life depicting his coronation and campaigns.[18] His will, and the codicil he dictated with a clear mind four days before his death, contained his personal dispositions. He made bequests to his wife and infant son and gave directions for the latter's care and upbringing. Chroniclers report his oral instructions—that Bedford, who was in Normandy, should exercise the regency in France for Henry VI—and his intention, had he lived, 'to rebuild the walls of Jerusalem'.

Henry died firm in the conviction of his destiny as God's instrument to restore peace to Christendom by the union of the two traditional enemies France and England—rather as the architects of the European Union sought to end the historical enmity of France and Germany. His new order was based on the justice of the English claim to France and would be expressed in the justice of his own rule—as a Christian king, not a conqueror. In England his rule did indeed restore legitimacy to kingship, making it the keystone of the social order. Whether Frenchmen could have been persuaded to accept rule by their ancient enemy in these terms is doubtful, though for a time some were prepared to do so.

---

[15] Above, Ch. 9, sect. 1.

[16] Powell, *Kingship, Law, and Society*, 259–65; Allmand, *Henry V*, 400–3.

[17] P. and F. Strong, 'The last will and codicils of Henry V', *EHR* 96 (1981), 79–102.

[18] W. H. St John Hope, 'The funeral monument and chantry chapel of King Henry the Fifth', *Archaeologia*, 65 (1913–14), 153–83, with illus.; Allmand, *Henry V*, 171–81, for Henry's deathbed and funeral rites.

2. THE MINORITY OF HENRY VI, 1422–1435

The unexpected death of Henry V faced the monarchy with a crisis potentially even more serious than that of 1399. Suddenly there was no adult king to rule, as there had been for the last forty years. The unspoken choice had to be made between the principle of hereditary succession by an infant and his replacement by the eldest of the late king's brothers. But another usurpation would have destroyed Lancastrian legitimacy in England and the basis of English rule in France. The baby Henry was thus immediately acclaimed, and Bedford's loyalty underpinned his long minority. In Bedford's eyes his regency derived not only from Henry V's last wishes but from his blood relationship to Henry VI; not at all from authorization or recognition by the lords of the council. Bedford formally used the title only in respect of France, and Gloucester claimed a similar title in England on the same grounds. But the lords of the council would not accept that the guardianship (*tutela*) of his son, which Henry V had given Gloucester in the codicil to his will, extended to the kingdom itself; nor would Bedford countenance the partition of his pre-eminence, which he was determined to retain when visiting England. When the mode of government during the minority was decided in the parliament of 1422, Gloucester was given the title of 'Protector and Defender' of the king and realm, but the execution of the royal authority was deemed to lie in the lords of the council and parliament.[19] Although justified in constitutional terms, it was a decision dictated by personal and political considerations. The lords found the prospect of Gloucester's rule unacceptable; and judged that their interests would be better safeguarded by a corporate body. Yet monarchical government operated through the personal will of one man, and in endeavouring to replace it the council had to adopt rules for its constitution and procedures to make itself adequately representative, able to take unanimous decisions, and as far as possible suppress particular and competing interests. What saved this artificial form of government from dissolving into faction and anarchy were the constraints imposed by fighting a war in France and by its ultimate accountability when the king reached his majority. Even so, its survival and achievements owed much to the character and abilities of a group of men dedicated to the spirit and legacy of Henry V.

The minority divides naturally into two periods, the first up to the king's coronation and departure for France in 1429–30, the second until the death of Bedford in 1435, marked respectively by advance and retreat in France.

[19] Strong and Strong, 'The last will of Henry V', 99–100; Roskell, *Parliament and Politics*, i. 193–234. For the documents, see, *Select Docs.* 248–52, 258–62.

Henry VI's Childhood, 1422–1429

The council appointed in 1422 comprised the royal dukes, Gloucester and Exeter, the three officers of state, five earls, five prelates, and five barons or knights. There was a good age spread, six being over 50 and five under 30. It appointed the principal officers, controlled the crown's prerogative patronage, directed national finance, conducted foreign policy, answered petitions, supervised the whole range of local judicial and financial officials, and had authority to punish and compose breaches of the peace.[20] The three officers of state and four other councillors formed a quorum, and decisions were by a majority vote. Gloucester presided, but with very restricted powers to act alone. He made attempts to reclaim authority in January 1427, March 1428, and January 1432, asserting that he was answerable only to the king when he came of age, and denying in effect the collective authority of the council to exercise the royal authority.[21] Gloucester had supporters in the council but they were outweighed in ability and assiduity by the group who formed around Bishop Beaufort and liaised with Bedford. These included Bishops Kemp, Stafford, and Alnwick and Sir Walter Hungerford, who served as officers of state, the duke of Exeter and earl of Warwick, and Lords Cromwell and Tiptoft.

While the self-accredited authority of the council enabled it to govern, it could not invoke the royal power to command. It had to seek consensus and appeal for cooperation. This became evident in dealing with parliament, which took a consciously independent line over taxation. The wool subsidy granted in 1415 to Henry V for life had lapsed; it was now granted for short periods, and reduced to an unprecedented low rate (33s. 4d.) for denizens who were also exempt from tunnage and poundage. In 1425 tunnage and poundage was reimposed for denizens but the subsidies paid by aliens were reduced. Moreover, in each of the parliaments from 1422 to 1427 the Commons declined to grant direct taxation, despite pressure from the council, holding themselves absolved by the formal peace treaty of Troyes. Parliaments were no longer the short, businesslike, and tightly managed occasions of Henry V's reign; they now invariably extended to two sessions and lasted over two months. Their authority was invoked for political matters that would normally have involved the king, including the settlement of disputes among the magnates, and for the granting of many individual petitions, including numbers from the nobility.[22] The scope of parliament's activity thus widened to supply the deficiency of royal authority.

---

[20] *Select Docs.* 251–7.   [21] Watts, *Henry VI and the Politics of Kingship*, 113–17.

[22] Among the magnates' disputes were those of Fitzhugh v. Scrope (1423), Talbot v. Ormond (1423 and 1426), Norfolk v. Warwick (1425), Beaufort v. Gloucester (1426). R. A. Archer, 'Parliamentary restoration: John Mowbray and the dukedom of Norfolk in 1425', in Archer and Walker (eds.), *Rulers and Ruled*, 99–116.

To discharge his and his father's considerable debts, Henry V had placed a large part of the duchy of Lancaster in trust, naming Beaufort, Chichele, and other members of the council as senior feoffees. Relieved of this burden, the council could concentrate on stabilizing normal expenditure. Savings on the infant king's household went to pay the salaries of the Protector and council, the frontier garrisons were maintained at peacetime levels, the king's ships sold off, all grants of royal patronage were suspended during the minority, and the council undertook to exploit the fiscal prerogatives for profit rather than favour. But the treasurer had to meet Bedford's demands for annual expeditions for the campaigning season in France. Not only had direct taxation been suspended and the rates of customs reduced, but the receipts from two major ports, London and Southampton, had been pledged to Bishop Beaufort for the repayment of £20,000 loaned to Henry V. In February 1424, and again in 1425, the council was forced to contract further loans from Beaufort, thereby extending his repayment from the customs until April 1426.[23]

To this stranglehold over royal finance and growing influence on the council, Beaufort added high office on becoming chancellor in July 1424. By then Gloucester was already at loggerheads with the council and Bedford over his marriage to Jacqueline of Hainault and a projected expedition to recover her inheritance in Holland and Zeeland, which would bring him into direct conflict with Philip of Burgundy. Gloucester invaded Hainault in October 1424, but the expedition quickly lost momentum and he returned in April 1425, leaving Jacqueline to continue the struggle. But though discredited, Gloucester had support in London, where the duke of Burgundy was seen as a threat to the expanding market for English cloth and where popular hostility to the Flemish colony was easily excited. Beaufort's policy was pro-Burgundian and, as chancellor, it was his duty to protect alien minorities. The developing confrontation came to a head at the end of October when Gloucester proposed to ride to the king at Eltham. Beaufort interpreted this as an attempt to seize the infant and closed London Bridge with his retainers. Mediation eventually prevailed; but Beaufort had put himself in the wrong by challenging the Protector's authority, and to save himself he now appealed to Bedford, urging him to return and bring his brother under control. He was on sure ground, for Bedford's own dignity and Beaufort's financial support for the war were at stake. Bedford's arrival on 20 December immediately suspended Gloucester's authority; Beaufort had played the trump card.

Bedford came not to take sides but to compose the quarrel which threatened the unity of the government. Beaufort was forced to make a humiliating

---

[23] Details in Harriss, *Cardinal Beaufort*, 124–5, 138–9, 402.

submission and resign as chancellor in March 1426.[24] It was the first of many duels over the next twenty years in which Gloucester expressed his resentment at the bishop's dominance in council and over the young king, his influence with the dukes of Bedford and Burgundy, and his wealth, ability, and pride. Believing that Beaufort had usurped his natural pre-eminence, he sought to discredit and ruin him. On this occasion Bedford saved Beaufort, returning with him to France in March 1427 and securing for him the cardinal's hat which Henry V had denied him. Bishop Kemp replaced Beaufort as chancellor and Sir Walter Hungerford, one of Henry V's executors, became treasurer; both were closely attached to Bedford, who decided to remain in England for a year to stabilize the administration.

Despite bullying the clergy into granting a half tenth, Bedford was unable to extract a fifteenth from parliament. He was now planning his return to France with a sizeable army, and in the absence of taxation the new treasurer set about enforcing the Crown's fiscal rights and gathering in the customs to accumulate the cash needed. Bedford had seen at first hand how straitened were the Crown's finances and how little enthusiasm there was for the war in France. He had also been a witness to Gloucester's avowed intention 'to govern as me semeth good' on his departure, holding himself answerable only to the king and not the collective authority of the council. That had prompted the council to reaffirm its powers and require their endorsement by both Bedford and Gloucester. Nevertheless, freed from Beaufort's presence, Gloucester was able to build up support on the council and, in March 1428, propose an extension of his powers as Protector. The peers unanimously refused this, requiring him to accept the terms of 1422–3.[25]

Yet Gloucester was able to turn the tables on Bedford through the earl of Salisbury's expedition in 1428. Salisbury had returned to England in July 1427, he was in dispute with Bedford over his lordship of Perche, and Gloucester found him a natural ally. By March 1428 Gloucester had finally extracted from the Commons a graduated tax on parishes and knights' fees, and a half tenth from the clergy, sufficient to dispatch an army of some 2,400 men. Yet this was not to be for Bedford's planned conquest of Anjou, for Salisbury was given an independent command, enabling him to follow his own strategy of besieging Orléans.

Two months after Salisbury left for France in early July 1428, Cardinal Beaufort arrived in England as papal legate, to raise money and troops for the crusade against the Hussites. The council was unenthusiastic, but by April 1429

---

[24] The whole affair is well narrated in *Chron. Lond.* 89–94; for the context, see Harriss, *Cardinal Beaufort*, chs. 7, 8; Griffiths, *Reign of Henry VI*, 76–80.

[25] The interchanges between the council and the dukes of Bedford and Gloucester, November 1426–March 1428, are printed in *Select Docs.* 256–62. For comment, see Watts, *Henry VI and the Politics of Kingship*, 117.

he was starting to gather recruits when his plans were jeopardized by two crises. Gloucester accused him of procuring a papal licence to retain the see of Winchester as a cardinal, thereby incurring the penalties of praemunire. In France the imminent collapse of the siege of Orléans impelled Bedford to appeal urgently to the council for reinforcements and for Henry VI to be crowned in France. On the same day (17 April) on which the council discussed, inconclusively, the legality of Beaufort's retention of Winchester, it agreed to dispatch a small force to France, and a month later Beaufort himself indented with the council to contribute his crusading army to meet the deepening military emergency. His money, too, would be needed if a royal army was to safeguard Henry VI's passage to Reims. Thus, while Beaufort forfeited the trust and favour of the outraged pope, his indispensability to the council safeguarded his position in England, burying for a time Gloucester's charge of praemunire.

Henry VI's Boyhood, 1429–1435

The coronation of Henry VI at Westminster on 6 November 1429, on the eve of his eighth birthday, was adapted to conform to the French *ordo* with its greater stress on theocratic kingship.[26] Henry was perhaps not quite old enough to be impressed in the way the 10-year-old Richard II had been; his coronation in Paris two years later made a greater impact. In June 1428 the chivalric stage in his education was marked by the appointment of the earl of Warwick as his governor, and his household was constituted, with knights and esquires in attendance. For the most part he moved between the royal palaces in the Thames Valley or stayed with his mother at Hertford and Waltham. The bond between them was probably not intimate but the boy must have been conscious from his earliest days of his maternal descent from the kings of France and his relationship to his uncle Charles VII.

Henry's coronation terminated Gloucester's protectorship, but during the king's absence in France from April 1430 to February 1432 he acted as Custos Angliae with powers virtually unchanged. His rival Cardinal Beaufort became Henry's chief councillor in France, where he began to rebuild his influence with the king and lords. Nineteen lords accompanied the king to France with an army which included the royal household and totalled nearly 5,000. For a royal army of this size and purpose the Commons could no longer refuse taxation. On 12 December 1429 they granted a whole subsidy immediately, and a week later a further subsidy payable a year later, to provide security for loans. The largest of these (£8,333) was from Beaufort, whose indispensability was acknowledged by his formal readmission to the council, despite his position as cardinal. The crisis

---

[26] Wolffe, *Henry VI*, 48–51.

in France thus secured his reinstatement in English politics; though he knew that Gloucester's enmity had not abated.

The task of securing Henry's coronation in France was to prove more hazardous and costly than anticipated. By July 1430 the court was stuck at Rouen and it was becoming clear not only that Reims was inaccessible but that, even to reach Paris in safety, the French-held town of Louviers would have to be taken. But if the king had to winter in France the costs of his household and three-quarters of the wages of the army would have to be met from England. A further appeal to parliament was inevitable and Cardinal Beaufort returned at Christmas to meet one summoned for 12 January 1431. Both it and convocation again proved generous, granting subsidies as security for a massive loan-raising operation. The cardinal himself lent £12,758, and with loans from other bodies and individuals raised the unprecedented total of almost £46,000. That provided not only for the army in France but for reinforcements numbering 3,400 men under the cardinal's nephews Edmund Beaufort and Richard Neville, the new earl of Salisbury. Although in his four-month visit Beaufort had galvanized the English war effort, it was clear that this could not be sustained. Parliament authorized negotiations for peace 'considering the burden of war and how grievous it is to this land', and Beaufort was told that the army could only be supported for a further six months. He returned to France to bend his energies and resources to getting the king crowned, accompanied by three of his closest supporters on the council, Lords Cromwell and Tiptoft, and Bishop Alnwick. Clearly apprehensive of leaving Gloucester unchecked, the council re-enacted the ordinances of 1426 limiting the Protector's power.

Since Bedford's departure in March 1427 Gloucester, as Protector, had faced a rising level of crime and disorder. Some aristocratic quarrels were pacified by the council; special commissions under assize justices dealt with violence between landowners; and a notorious gang operating in Hampshire under a William Wawe was rounded up and executed in 1427. All this was reflected in the petitions of the Commons in the 1429 parliament complaining of criminal gangs and illegal liveries, and demanding 'good and sadde governance in every part of your realm'. The absence of the nobility in France increased the nervousness of Gloucester and the council over social discontent, and his swift and stern repression of a 'Lollard' rising in Oxfordshire in May 1431 won the approval of political society.[27]

The capture of Louviers on 28 October 1431 cleared the way for the king's coronation at Paris in December and thereafter his return to England. That would entail a reappraisal of the position of those who had hitherto exercised

---

[27] Griffiths, *Reign of Henry VI*, 129–31, 139–42; *Proc. & Ord.* iii. 276, 279, 327, 347. Discussed above, Ch. 10, sect. 5.

power in his name. In France, Bedford expected to resume governing as regent and was outraged by Beaufort's insistence that he should now exercise authority under royal commission and not by right of blood. Their quarrel may have emboldened Gloucester to revive the charge of praemunire against Beaufort for his retention of the see of Winchester as cardinal. Gloucester had decided that, with Henry VI's return, Beaufort and the council should no longer stand between him and the king.

Henry landed in England on 9 February 1432 and on 25th, when he had reached London, Gloucester had all Beaufort's supporters in the offices of state dismissed (Kemp as chancellor, Hungerford as treasurer, Alnwick as privy seal, Tiptoft as steward of the household, and Cromwell as chamberlain) and many of the clerks in the household removed. They were replaced by Gloucester's nominees. Gloucester's coup marked the end of the 1422 settlement which had made the exercise of the king's authority the collective responsibility of the council. He now claimed the position of chief minister answerable only to the king, with the officers and council advising and assisting him.[28]

For the moment Gloucester's flagrantly partisan action could not be challenged. Beaufort, fearing his own ruin by praemunire, had planned to remove his treasure from Gloucester's grasp by exporting his money and plate secretly at night from Sandwich on 6 February, but Gloucester discovered this and had it impounded. That left the cardinal with no option but to fight back, and he returned to England for the parliament on 12 May, at which Gloucester was preparing to charge him with treason. He had support from his dismissed followers Kemp and Cromwell, and had been mobilizing opinion in London; but his strongest card, as always, was his readiness to use his wealth and ability in the king's service. Thus when he asked who accused him of treason no one answered and, on the petition of the Commons, he was absolved from any penalties of praemunire and recovered part of his treasure, although he was still owed £20,000 by the Crown.[29]

Insolvency haunted and finally doomed Gloucester's government. Impoverished by their grants for the coronation expedition, the Commons would grant only half fifteenths, while there had been a sharp fall in revenue from the customs consequent on the Partition Ordinance of 1429. Wool exports from England suddenly dropped by some 5,000 sacks per annum, and revenue by £10,000, losses which were never made good.[30] Following on the reduction of the customs rates in 1422, it meant that ten years later revenue was some £20,000 below the level of Henry V's reign. By Easter 1433 the treasurer acknowledged that there was insufficient money to send reinforcements to France and an

---

[28] *Rot. Parl.* iv. 388; Watts, *Henry VI and the Politics of Kingship*, 155–8.
[29] Harriss, *Cardinal Beaufort*, 215–21.   [30] See above, Ch. 8, sect. 1.

embassy to the Council of Basel. That was the signal for Bedford to summon
Gloucester and Beaufort to Calais, where he announced his return to England to
rekindle the war effort and to answer his detractors. Beaufort and his allies were
reinstated on the council and Bedford summoned parliament.

Drastic financial measures were needed and Lord Cromwell was appointed
treasurer to carry them out. He put an immediate stop on the exchequer,
imposed rigorous controls on expenditure, and gathered in all available revenue.
For the resumed session of parliament in October his clerks had compiled a
detailed state of the exchequer, with projected estimates which showed an annual
deficit of £21,447 and a total debt of £108,500.[31] Yet even this failed to persuade
either the Commons or convocation to grant more than a single subsidy over two
years. Bedford had to accept that in a deteriorating economic climate the country had neither the will nor the wealth for wartime taxation. Indeed it was the situation in England rather than France that was the Commons' foremost concern.
The chancellor called for unity and concord among the lords, for justice to be
practised in political society, and obedience without murmuring by the people.
The Commons asked Bedford to stay in England 'for the good and restfull rule
and governaile of this land'. On 18 December he set out his terms, which effectively placed the government in his hands, reducing the council to an advisory
body in the way that Gloucester's rule in 1432 had foreshadowed.[32]

While Cromwell began to rebuild Crown finances, Bedford took measures for
law enforcement, using the council to prosecute riot and retaining, and early in
1434 administering a nationwide oath to lords and gentry of every rank to uphold
law and justice. That, and the absence of serious quarrels among the lords, seems
to have reduced the level of disorder. But Bedford's overriding purpose was to
revitalize the war effort in France. On 24 April 1434 he assembled a great council of lords, knights, and esquires to review the conduct of the war. Gloucester
seized the chance to advance his own strategy and leadership against that of
Bedford, proposing the dispatch of a mighty army to end the war by a decisive
victory. Thereby, he claimed, 'the people of the realm would be discharged of
any taille or tallage for many years to come'. Challenged to say how the money for
this great army (some £50,000) could be found, Gloucester made no recorded
answer but he probably had in mind the confiscation of Cardinal Beaufort's
wealth. It was not a bait to which Bedford was likely to rise, stung as he had been
by Gloucester's criticism of his defensive strategy. But while he protected
Beaufort's wealth, he extracted a further loan of £8,666 in May and June to
finance his return with an army under the earl of Arundel. More than that, in a
moving plea to the assembled great council to sustain the conquests for which

---

[31] *Rot Parl.* iv. 432–8; summarized in J. L. Kirby, 'Lord Cromwell's estimates of 1433', *BIHR* 24
(1951), 121–51.   [32] *Select Docs.* 268–70.

Henry V and many others had fought and died, Bedford asked the duchy of Lancaster feoffees (of whom Beaufort was the chief) to surrender their lands for the support of a permanent force in France. The feoffees agreed, though in the event they preferred to make further loans. But Bedford had procured a continuing commitment to the defence of Normandy for as long as the war continued.[33]

Bedford had taken power until Henry could 'exercise the governaunce of this his reaume in his owen persone'. In February 1433 the council arranged for the king to be informed of its major business, but the question was who would influence his impressionable years. In November 1432 Warwick, his governor, reported that Henry had advanced 'in conceit and knowledge of his high and royal authority' but that some persons had stirred the boy from his learning and told him things he ought not to hear.[34] Access to his presence was to be restricted, and it was arranged for him to spend the winter of 1433–4 at the abbey of Bury St Edmund. If the boy found such clerical company congenial, he came straight back to the great council of 24 April 1434 to witness the open quarrel of Gloucester and Bedford, which was only pacified when he took the matter into his own hands. Henry was being schooled to exercise royal authority, and before long he was being encouraged by Gloucester to rid himself of constraints and govern in person. Alarmed by this, members of the council rode to the king at Cirencester in November 1434 to remind him that he was still too young to decide between good and ill counsel and should endure patiently their advice. But the king's free will was implicitly acknowledged.

On Bedford's return to France he left Beaufort, Kemp, and Cromwell to shoulder the task of government. No parliament was summoned, and to meet its new commitment to support a standing army in Normandy the council had to find £11,741 between July 1434 and July 1435 from existing revenues. This was only possible at the cost of mounting arrears for Calais, Gascony, and Ireland. The campaigning season in 1434 had been remarkably successful, but the spring of 1435 saw the war turn against the English with the death of Arundel and the French seizure of Saint-Denis. An intensive series of council meetings in May and June 1435, attended by both Beaufort and Gloucester, organized the dispatch of 2,000 men under Lords Talbot and Willoughby in July. Despite the lack of hard security, nearly £22,000 was raised in loans, Beaufort contributing 10,000 marks. Soon afterwards the cardinal left for the Congress of Arras and when he returned early in September the dream of Lancastrian France lay shattered. Burgundy had repudiated the Treaty of Troyes and Bedford lay dying in Rouen. That heralded a new political era in England. It freed the young king from political control, and in May 1436 Warwick discharged himself from acting

---

[33] *Proc. & Ord.* iv. 210–32; comment in Harriss, *Cardinal Beaufort*, 236–8.
[34] Wolffe, *Henry VI*, 69.

as Henry's governor. It also deprived the council of Bedford's authority and removed his protection from Beaufort, Kemp, and Cromwell.

In 1422 a lay patron, probably Gloucester, commissioned from Lydgate a prose work, *The Serpent of Division*, which used the rivalry of Pompey and Caesar to argue that the safety of the state depended upon government being 'hooly undevided'.[35] The lords of the council had nonetheless preferred a collective consensus to the rule of one man. That by 1435 the young king's inheritance in England and France was still intact, if threatened, was a tribute to their political discipline, military commitment, and personal loyalty to the king and his father. Despite individual and factional rivalries, and the furthering of private interests, kingship had been protected, civil war avoided, and the resources of the Crown and state had not been plundered; in all of this England's experience was better than that of France. Bedford's authority had overshadowed England, restraining Gloucester and protecting Beaufort, but it was also others like the earls of Salisbury, Warwick, and Huntingdon, Lords Hungerford, Tiptoft, and Cromwell, and Bishops Alnwick, Kemp, and Stafford, who had used their abilities to keep the state functioning in the absence of active royal rule. That was striking testimony to the stability and maturity of English political society.

3. KING AND COUNCIL, 1435–1443

The immediate preoccupation of the English council in the winter of 1435–6 was to send reinforcements to Normandy and to meet the anticipated threat to Calais from the duke of Burgundy. Grants of taxation from parliament and convocation in December 1435 provided security for borrowing the huge sum of £48,000, half of which came from Cardinal Beaufort and the feoffees of the duchy of Lancaster. An army of 4,000 under the young duke of York and the veterans Suffolk and Salisbury was at last dispatched to Normandy in May 1436.[36] By then Duke Philip had invested Calais, and in July all lords and Crown retainers were summoned to form a 'royal army' of over 7,000 strong, which Gloucester, in the king's name, led to relieve the town and devastate Flanders. This was Gloucester's riposte for his ignominious withdrawal in 1425, and he may also at this time have sponsored the strident anti-alien *Libelle of Englyshe Polycye* with its demand for an aggressive trade war, including a blockade of the Straits of Dover, to force open the Flemish market. The council took a different view. With wool exports to Flanders virtually suspended in the years 1436–9 and tax revenue reduced almost to zero, Beaufort was striving to repair the breach by diplomacy, and by late 1438 a mercantile truce had been tacitly agreed and trade began to revive.

---

[35] W. F. Schirmer, *John Lydgate* (London, 1952), 81–8.
[36] Harriss, *Cardinal Beaufort*, 257, 404; Steel, *Receipt of the Exchequer*, 460.

Beyond these immediate concerns, Bedford's death had raised two longer-term problems. At the end of the year for which York had indented to serve, the question would arise of who would be appointed as the king's lieutenant in Normandy. Gloucester apart, three lords of the royal blood had claims: York, Huntingdon, and Beaufort's nephew John, earl of Somerset, though the last was still a prisoner in France. In February 1436 negotiations were opened for his release. It was the first indication of the cardinal's long-term plan to establish his nephews in Bedford's French lands. Until then the ageing earl of Warwick was persuaded to hold the lieutenancy in Normandy for eighteen months. Thus the direction of military and foreign policy had remained in the hands of Cardinal Beaufort and his allies in the council.

The exercise of the king's authority at home was a more difficult matter. This was the moment when Gloucester should have been able to assert his pre-eminent right to protect and counsel the boy king. But the divisiveness of his feud with Beaufort and the general distrust of his judgement nullified his expect-ations. The only solution was for the king to exercise his authority in person but under supervision. From October 1435, when he was almost 14, he began to attend meetings of council and parliament and send letters of state in his own name. To the nobility who answered the royal summons to arms in August 1436 he gave rewards and privileges, and in the autumn, after a solemn crown-wearing, he began to make gifts to members of his household and chapel. From early in 1437 these were made under Henry's signet or initials, and included many life grants of offices and lands. Henry's pliant generosity caused the council unease, but it had no power to restrain the royal grace; what it tried to do was to ensure that it retained control over policy.[37]

The ordinances drawn up in October 1437 defined the respective roles of the king and the council during Henry's adolescence. No restriction was placed on the king in matters of grace—pardons, rewards, and appointment to offices. But the council was to handle all business of state, referring to the king only matters which touched his rights and those on which they were divided.[38] This polarity between the household as the focus for patronage, and the council handling pol-icy, provided a misleading model of government and restricted the young king's experience of political matters. However, it was likely to be temporary, for some councillors were also members of Henry's household, notably the earl of Suffolk as steward and Sir William Philip as chamberlain, and from 1438 Adam Moleyns, who became clerk of the council, provided an additional link between court and council. The court indeed contained men of great political experience to whom

[37] Watts, *Henry VI and the Politics of Kingship*, 130ff.; Griffiths, *Reign of Henry VI*, 232–4.

[38] *Proc. & Ord.* vi. 64–6; *Select Docs.* 274–6; Watts, *Henry VI and the Politics of Kingship*, 133–5; Griffiths, *Reign of Henry VI*, 275ff.

the king could turn for advice and, as Henry matured, political decisions would naturally gravitate towards it.

Parallel with the formal renaming of the council, the local hegemony of its members was confirmed by their appointment as stewards of the duchy of Lancaster estates: Richard, earl of Salisbury, in Richmond and the forests beyond Trent; John, Viscount Beaumont, in Leicester and Bolingbroke; Humphrey, earl of Stafford, in Tutbury; and William, earl of Suffolk, in the northern parts. Ralph, Lord Cromwell, was made constable of Nottingham, the earl of Devon steward of the duchy of Cornwall, and Lord Tiptoft had lands of the honour of Richmond. This effort to strengthen royal authority in the regions through the loyalty of the leading nobility was complemented by Henry's own perambulations of the North Midlands in 1437, of the West Country in 1438, and to Canterbury in 1439. At a slightly lower level the custody of many royal castles was given to household knights or serjeants, while about one-third of the sheriffs named in 1437–44 had attachments to the royal household. But there was no systematic attempt to build up a royal affinity among the local gentry by the widespread distribution of annuities. Those already attached to the Crown were its principal local instruments.[39]

The young king seems to have passively endorsed this distribution of power. He was, as Piero del Monte had reported, of mild and gentle disposition, monastic in his self-discipline, and devoted to the Church.[40] In 1437 both the death of his mother and the departure of Warwick removed those who had guided his boyhood, and his companions and attendants were the natural focus for his affection. He could most directly express this through generosity, and for a time he had much to give. With no family to support, he held the apanage of the prince of Wales, while the dower lands of Queen Joan and Queen Catherine, and Bedford's honour of Richmond, had reverted to the Crown. Beyond these were the vast duchy of Lancaster estates, part of which still remained vested in Henry V's feoffees for the discharge of his debts. Most of this was strictly inalienable, but what Henry could distribute freely was the keeping for life of royal manors, forests, and hundreds, at beneficial or minimal rents, and the offices attached to them. This was a vast pool of patronage, accumulated during the restrictive years of the minority. The knights and esquires in attendance were the principal beneficiaries: the king's carvers, John and William Beauchamp, Edmund Hungerford, and Robert Roos; the esquires of the body, John St Loo, John Hampton, and James Fiennes; the ushers of the chamber, John Norris, John Stanley, and Edmund Hampden; and many of lesser status. From 1438 to 1441

---

[39] Griffiths, *Reign of Henry VI*, 334–8; Watts, *Henry VI and the Politics of Kingship*, 172–6; Castor, *King, Crown, and Duchy of Lancaster, passim.*

[40] J. Haller, *Piero del Monte* (Rome, 1941), 43–5; for other contemporary observations, see Griffiths, *Reign of Henry VI*, 240–2.

Henry made around seventy grants a year to members of the household, with the more prominent receiving two or three apiece, and this continued at only a slightly lower level up to 1445.[41] From being a well-endowed king whose estates should properly support his household, Henry was by then well on the way to being impoverished and heavily in debt. In this respect his unconstrained generosity had major consequences for political governance; on the other hand his open-handedness gave no ground for faction or discontent among the nobility, for whom the court as a centre of patronage became increasingly attractive.

While the king was left to distribute patronage, his youth and temperament made it advisable for another kingly function, the adjudication and reconciliation of political quarrels, to be handled by the council. As a matter of prudence the council generally threw its weight behind the more powerful, especially its own members. Thus in two long-running inheritance disputes it supported Salisbury against Westmorland from 1438 to 1443 over the Neville inheritance, and in 1439–41 Lord Talbot and Edmund Beaufort (who were serving in France) against Lord Berkeley over the Lisle lands. In contests over local influence it backed Lord Fanhope against Lord Grey of Ruthin in 1437 and 1439 in Bedfordshire, Lord Cromwell against Lord Grey of Codnor in Nottinghamshire in 1440, and Lord Tiptoft against the challenge of the earl of Ormond in Cambridgeshire in 1439. Two members of the upper nobility were briefly imprisoned in the Tower, Norfolk in 1440 and Northumberland in 1443, when their quarrels with their powerful neighbours Suffolk and Archbishop Kemp led to clashes between their respective retainers; and in each case the council imposed a settlement heavily weighted in favour of the latter. The only dispute arbitrated in the king's presence was that between the earl of Devon and Lord Bonville in 1441 over the office of steward of the duchy of Cornwall which Henry VI had inadvertently granted to both men. As an exercise in realpolitik, the council's settlement of these disputes was successful, but the concept of the king as the fount of impartial justice was seriously diminished.

Whereas in domestic politics the king's will was successfully confined to the distribution of patronage, in foreign policy it came to be enlisted in factional rivalries. A council of lords at Eltham in the spring of 1439 had approved Cardinal Beaufort's mission to Calais for peace negotiations, but when these took place in August at Oye–Calais all that could be obtained from the French was a long truce on terms which would ultimately undermine Lancastrian rule in Normandy. When they were debated in a council at Windsor the terms were rejected; Gloucester had probably opposed them.[42] Although Beaufort had secured a three-year commercial truce with Flanders which reopened the wool trade, his direction of English foreign policy was effectively discredited. The

---

[41] *CPR, 1436–41, 1441–6, passim.*   [42] Above, Ch. 14, sect. 3.

parliament of November to February 1439–40 saw a further weakening of his position. The agenda was framed to outflank him: on the Commons complaining that the household was not paying for its purveyances, the Crown offered to use revenues from the duchies of Cornwall and Lancaster for its support. Henry V's remaining feoffees in the duchy lands (Cardinal Beaufort and Lord Hungerford) were then pressed to surrender their trust, and within two years their effective control over these royal revenues was brought to an end. An even greater blow was aimed at him in the second session in January. Gloucester once again brought a series of detailed charges against his rival, designed to show Henry VI how his great-uncle had acted 'in derogation of your noble estate and the hurt of both your realms'. He accused the cardinal of defrauding the king, enriching himself, and estranging Gloucester and others from the king. Gloucester's last attempt to ruin his enemy proved a damp squib; Henry VI received his articles but took no action.[43] The old animosities of the minority had lost their relevance for the circle of courtier lords centred on the earl of Suffolk, who increasingly controlled policy in the king's name.

More immediately Gloucester's attack frustrated Beaufort's ambitions for his nephews, for at midsummer 1440 it was the duke of York, not Somerset, who was appointed for five years as Warwick's successor. Almost certainly York was Gloucester's choice, but it signified no revival of his influence. His strenuous objections to the release of the duke of Orléans as part of a new peace initiative were answered in a public memorandum issued in Henry VI's name in which the decision was said to have been made by the king 'hymself and of his owen advis and courrage . . . not of symplesse ne of self wille', but for good reasons, and to end the long and costly war.[44] Suffolk was Orléans's friend and keeper; he hoped that Orléans would persuade Charles VII to accept a truce, and for the next two years this became the basis of English policy.

All these controversial matters—the terms of peace, the finance of the household, the Beaufort–Gloucester quarrel, the appointment of York, and the release of Orléans—touched the king's rights and had to be referred to him. Henry's personal contribution must remain uncertain, but in each case the outcome favoured neither Beaufort nor Gloucester but reflected and enhanced the growing influence of the earl of Suffolk. At the same time all the decisions were congruent with the king's own desires. The effect of this was to transfer political decision-making to the court, as the king's will became operative and could be best manipulated by those at his side. It aroused little contention. The displacement of Beaufort and Gloucester had been assisted by their mutual enmity, by the cardinal's age, and by

---

[43] *Rot. Parl.* v. 7–8; Harriss, *Cardinal Beaufort*, 306–11; *Wars of Eng.* ii. 440–51.

[44] *Wars of Eng.* ii. 451–60; for differing views of Henry VI's authorship, see Griffiths, *Reign of Henry VI*, 451–4; Harriss, *Cardinal Beaufort*, 315–17; Watts, *Henry VI and the Politics of Kingship*, 106–7, 143–4; Wolffe, *Henry VI*, 157–9.

the lords' distaste for Gloucester's disruptive populism. And the fact that the nobility—the earls of Stafford and Salisbury and Lords Beauchamp, Beaumont, Dudley, Stourton, and Sudeley—now focused their political aspirations on the court maintained the consensus on which Henry VI's kingship continued to rest. Quite as important was the influence of Henry's clerical advisers, who enthused and guided Henry in the foundation of colleges at Eton and Cambridge to mark the attainment of his majority in 1440–2. For Henry the colleges became 'the primer notable work' of his kingship and proclaimed the court's priorities as domestic and religious rather than imperial and military.[45]

During 1440 the king had mostly remained in Windsor, at a distance from the council, but in the summer and autumn of 1441 a crisis shifted the focus to London. Since 1435 Gloucester had been heir presumptive to Henry VI, whose fragile health prompted the duke's wife, Eleanor, to commission a horoscope of the king which identified the summer of 1441 as a time when he was liable to fall into bodily or mental infirmity. When this became known Eleanor was brought before ecclesiastical and lay tribunals and charged with treasonable necromancy, for conspiring the king's death. She was pronounced divorced from Duke Humphrey and sentenced to perpetual imprisonment in the Isle of Man.[46] Though Duke Humphrey was not inculpated in his wife's crime, the fear which the accusations aroused in the melancholic king rendered the duke permanently suspect. It underlined the need for Henry to marry and produce an heir.

While Beaufort must have welcomed his rival's eclipse, there is no evidence that he had engineered it. Nor, similarly, did Gloucester have any role in the catastrophe that became the cardinal's swansong. By the winter of 1442–3 the council faced French threats to both Normandy and Gascony and turned once more to the cardinal to finance an army. The project that now took shape under his direction was for a large army under his nephew John, earl (and later duke) of Somerset, to invade Maine–Anjou to deflect Charles VII and perhaps bring him to battle. Somerset was given a status comparable to that of York and any lands that he could conquer. This naked aggrandizement of the Beaufort family seems to have had the personal compliance of the pacific king. Henry must have been conscious that he was now of an age to lead a royal army in person to recover his inheritance; but he shrank from 'cruel and mortal war', commissioning his kinsman as his lieutenant. His trust was tragically misplaced, for Somerset's incompetence and cowardice brought the venture and his own life to an inglorious end.[47] It marked the end of the cardinal's political career and of the council's

[45] Wolffe, *Henry VI*, 135–45; Watts, *Henry VI and the Politics of Kingship*, 167–71; Bekynton, *Correspondence*, ii. 279–85.   [46] Carey, *Courting Disaster*, 138–53.

[47] Above, Ch. 14, sect. 3; Harriss, *Cardinal Beaufort*, 332–43; M. K. Jones, 'John Beaufort, duke of Somerset and the French expedition of 1443', in Griffiths (ed.), *Patronage, Crown and Provinces*, 79–102.

remaining responsibility for foreign policy. Suffolk had held aloof from the project, but was quick to capitalize on its failure, by responding to an invitation from Charles VII to negotiate a truce. If the war could be ended Cardinal Beaufort's wealth would no longer be needed and he would be unable to determine policy to his own advantage.

Beaufort's retirement closed a political era. His life had been dedicated to the Lancastrian monarchy, its establishment, its military hegemony, and its survival. His considerable gifts as a politician, a diplomat, and an organizer were used in its service. The ambiguities of his position as the illegitimate half-blood of the royal house, and a cardinal with a Roman see, debarred him from political leadership and made it necessary for him to wield influence through consensus. To the establishment of conciliar authority during Henry VI's minority he made a decisive contribution. Thereafter he used his great wealth to sustain the military enterprise in France, to protect his own political position, and to advance the fortunes of his nephews. His legacy was both constructive and divisive.

The period from 1436 to 1443 was marked by a major shift in the character of public life, from a war culture to one of peace. The discipline and sense of national purpose inculcated by Henry V and enforced by the maintenance of English hegemony in France seeped away as his commanders and councillors one by one disappeared. Confidence in English superiority in arms and in the right to rule, with the conviction of divine support, all crumbled after 1435, as did the political coherence of the council which had sustained royal authority throughout the minority. Gradually that gave place to rule from within the royal household. That it was a long, confused, but also largely uncontentious process reflected the king's temperament and his prolonged adolescence. His docile nature, his preference for domesticity and religious routine, and his boundless generosity created a benign ambience far removed from the exacting service and measured rewards of his father. The court was inclusive and, as the hazards of war multiplied and its rewards shrank, all but the natural soldiers among the nobility preferred it to the camp. If Suffolk's was the guiding and moving hand in this, it was because he bridged both court and council, both the older and the newer political generation, the military tradition and the search for peace. He was trusted and favoured by the king without arousing envy or fear among his peers. Yet the seeds of deep divisions had been sown. Gloucester and Cardinal Beaufort would soon be in their graves, but their last clash had engendered a personal rivalry between York and the cardinal's nephews which could become politically charged. War had lost its appeal, but the honour and self-interest of those who had devoted their lives to the conquest of Normandy would not brook surrender. Finally, while the court provided a consensus among those who benefited from royal patronage, it formed only part of the political nation and was not identified with the common weal. In all these matters royal leadership could alone provide direction and unity; would Suffolk's surrogate model prove inadequate?

4. SUFFOLK'S RULE, 1444–1449

In political terms the shift of power from the council to the king marked a return to the traditional structure of royal rule. But it was already clear that Henry, though now adult, was incapable of a sustained political role. In two matters he did not lack views of his own or a measure of wilfulness. First, he abhorred war and felt a personal mission to heal the great wound in Christendom reopened by his father. To restore amity with his uncle Charles VII he was ready to meet him, receive his ambassadors, and give promises in writing. Indeed he probably saw his marriage not in terms of sexual satisfaction or even of the procreation of the needed heir, but as a sacramental pledge of peace. Secondly, the prime endeavour of his kingship was to promote holiness and learning in the Church. In all other matters his detachment from worldly concerns, and his responsiveness to the more ascetic and contemplative strains in current religious devotion, made him incapable of exercising the directive will which was the essential function of a king. Henry's gentle and retiring nature warmed to certain aristocratic companions like Gilles de Bretagne and Henry, duke of Warwick, but for the most part his prodigal patronage reflected his impatience with the importunities of courtiers and the problems of government—it was simply easier to say yes than no. Nervous, introspective, and vacillating, he depended heavily on the guidance of his mentors, notably the earl of Suffolk.

Suffolk saw his task as filling the vacuum of Henry's directive will by himself representing the king's public authority.[48] This was both difficult and dangerous; difficult because in other matters than peace and his colleges, Henry's will was rarely manifested, and dangerous because it could arouse the jealousy of his peers. Suffolk protected himself both by procuring the king's formal endorsement of his actions and by securing the consensus and cooperation of the lords and the court. Of the higher nobility only Buckingham, Salisbury, and Somerset besides Suffolk were prominent, but Viscount Beaumont, Lords Sudeley, Beauchamp, Dudley, Stourton, St Amand, Saye and Sele, and the circumspect Cromwell formed a favoured entourage. All these, apart from Cromwell, were to endorse Suffolk's policy, benefit from Henry's largesse, and support Suffolk in his hour of trial. Suffolk had equally warm relations with the clerical entourage, comprising bishops Ayscough, Bekynton, Boulers, Lowe, Lyhert, and Moleyns. His other constituency were the courtiers proper: the knights and esquires of the

---

[48] I have broadly followed the interpretation of Watts, *Henry VI and the Politics of Kingship*, ch. 6.

chamber and aspirants of lower rank. Many of these had entered the household during Suffolk's stewardship since 1433, but their careers and rewards did not depend on his patronage. Their daily attendance on the pliable king enabled them to obtain profitable offices and grants. Suffolk could influence but could not control the intense competition for favours among the more senior courtiers.

Suffolk's attempt to represent royal authority in Henry's default therefore embodied a fatal contradiction. Whereas true regal authority had to transcend subjects' particular interests, Suffolk could only exercise its simulacrum with the collusion of the leading nobility, churchmen, and courtiers whose expectations he had to gratify. He had also to further the king's own plans for peace and his colleges. Equally, this consensus rested on the absence of contentious political issues. Until the end of 1446 Suffolk's position looked secure; thereafter it progressively disintegrated. I shall examine these phases in turn.

The flaw in Suffolk's foreign policy was brutally exposed when the French 'peace' embassy in July 1445 ruled out any recognition of English sovereignty in Normandy. Suffolk had then either to reopen the war or become the prisoner of the French terms for peace. Neither the king and nobility nor parliament was prepared for the former; instead, the issue was deferred by a proposal for Henry to meet Charles VII and subsequently by his personal promise (in December 1445) to cede Maine. The projected royal 'summit' persuaded a reluctant parliament early in 1446 to grant half fifteenths for the next three years, but Suffolk now had to reckon on the political repercussions when the unilateral surrender of Maine became known. To carry this through Suffolk first engineered the replacement of York as lieutenant governor in Normandy with the more amenable Edmund Beaufort, earl of Somerset. York's five-year term had indeed ended, but he construed this as a dismissal, deepening the existing rivalry between them.[49]

Following this direct rebuff to York, Suffolk moved to an even more drastic step, the removal of Gloucester. Duke Humphrey had kept a low profile since his wife's disgrace, but he had always been ready to appeal beyond the court and council to political society at large, and his public exposure of the cession of Maine would threaten Suffolk and the peace process. The grounds for his destruction had been well prepared. Since 1441 Henry VI's fears that his uncle had designs on the throne had been worked up to the point where the king now surrounded himself with extra guards. The courtiers' appetites had been whetted by grants of the reversion of the duke's many lands and offices. A parliament was summoned to Bury St Edmunds to meet on 10 February. Twice the normal number of household retainers were returned as MPs, and the court nobility had rehearsed their roles.[50] When Gloucester reached Bury on 18 February he was

[49] See above, Ch. 14, sect. 4.
[50] Wolffe, *Henry VI*, 217; Watts, *Henry VI and the Politics of Kingship*, 227–31.

arrested by Viscount Beaumont, as steward of England, and other magnates. The intention was to charge him with treason, but the shock precipitated his death, probably through a stroke, on 23 February. In the event the manner of Gloucester's death proved more damaging to the court than any populist appeal he might have made over Maine. Its ruthlessness, in striking down the heir apparent and former Protector, bred not only popular outrage but a climate of fear and mistrust at the highest level.[51] None would feel this more acutely than York, whose detachment from the courtier group was underlined and whose dynastic claims were given unwelcome prominence by Henry's continued childlessness.

If, by the beginning of 1447, the search for peace had begun to destabilize domestic politics, so, in a different way, had court expenditure. Up to 1444 the cooperation of the Crown and the Commons had provided the royal household with an assured income from the duchy of Lancaster and taxation. But from 1445 the duchy revenues were divided between the king's foundations and the queen's dower while the additional cost of the queen's household and rising levels of court consumption left the exchequer to find some £27,000 per annum for domestic expenditure. This should eventually have been furnished by the 'peace dividend' from the reduction of military expenditure in Normandy, but in July 1446 the exchequer attempted to pay the arrears on York's salary (£26,000), the costs of the household (£14,670), and the wages due to the permanent garrisons (£7,000). The attempt to issue tallies to the sum of £56,787 to meet these and other charges proved to be vastly in excess of available revenue, as much as £30,578 being returned as uncashable.[52] From the exchequer's viewpoint it was a short-term cash flow problem, but for its creditors the failure of exchequer tallies on this unprecedented scale was traumatic. It destroyed the cooperation between the Crown and the Commons to finance the household, bringing protests in parliament and generating hostility to the king's foundations. The mounting evidence of the Crown's debt and insolvency began to focus popular criticism on the gains of the courtiers which had denuded the king's estate.

In the eighteen months following his marriage Henry VI's liberality knew no bounds. With the setting up of the queen's household the number of grants to royal servants on the patent rolls leaped from 59 in 1444–5 to 123 in 1445–6. Among the greater nobility Huntingdon and Stafford had been raised to the dukedoms of Exeter and Buckingham in 1444, to be followed by Warwick in 1445, while Suffolk was made a marquess. Henry VI's favour to Warwick, his boyhood companion, could have created tensions with the elder nobility, but on

[51] Public opinion already construed it as judicial murder in 1447 and by 1450 the responsibility was generally laid on Suffolk, Moleyns, and Lord Saye; Harvey, *Jack Cade's Rebellion*, 50.

[52] Steel, *Receipt of the Exchequer*, 442, 461 (tables B7 and D7); Harriss, 'Marmaduke Lumley and the exchequer crisis of 1446–9', in J. G. Rowe (ed.), *Aspects of Late Medieval Government and Society* (Toronto, 1986), 143–78.

his premature death in June 1446 the custody of the Beauchamp estates was granted to Salisbury (his father-in-law), Suffolk, and Lords Sudeley and Beauchamp. These lords strove to preserve the Beauchamp inheritance against a swarm of courtiers who procured grants of farms and offices from the disconsolate king. Suffolk, who had purchased the marriage of Warwick's 2-year-old daughter and heiress, wanted the inheritance for his son.[53] The fate of the Beauchamp lands and influence in the West Midlands and Wales thus hung in the balance, involving the potentially competing interests of Suffolk and Salisbury, and beyond them the husbands of the late earl Richard's elder daughters, Shrewsbury and Dorset.[54]

From the end of 1446 Suffolk struggled to retain control over developments in both foreign and domestic affairs, only to be overwhelmed in the multiple crisis of 1450. When the removal of Gloucester intensified rumours about the promised surrender of Maine, Suffolk sought to deflect blame from himself by securing Henry VI's formal endorsement of it in May 1447.[55] Somerset likewise evaded implementing it, and it was Henry's own envoys, Moleyns and Roos, who finally surrendered Le Mans in March 1448, with the French army at the gates. By then the train of events which was to result in the renewal of war had been started, with Suffolk's connivance in the plot to seize the castle and town of Fougères. François de Surienne had Suffolk's personal authority and was even enrolled as a knight of the Garter in 1448.[56] The surprise and capture of Fougères on the night of 23–4 March 1449 momentarily boosted Suffolk's popularity, but as the wholesale collapse of the English position unfolded in the latter part of 1449 he realized that he would be held responsible. Adam Moleyns paid the price when he was lynched by soldiers at Portsmouth in the last days of 1449 and Suffolk was sent to the Tower at the Commons' demand when parliament reassembled next month.

In his pursuit of peace Suffolk had the support of both Henry VI and the political establishment. But should he still have prepared for war? Here the difficulty lay in the continuing financial constraints as the crisis of assignments in 1446 worked its way through the system in 1447 and 1448.[57] The new treasurer, Bishop Lumley, had taken draconian measures to restore exchequer credit, placing a stop on payments, asserting personal control over all revenues, presenting a comprehensive review of the position to parliament, and seeking the king's backing for restraints on future warrants. While providing for current commitments he gradually discharged the accumulated debt for tallies

---

[53] M. A. Hicks, 'Between majorities: The "Beauchamp interregnum", 1439–49', *Hist. Res.* 72 (1999), 33–41.

[54] For the situation in Warwickshire, see Carpenter, *Locality and Polity*, 408–28.

[55] Rymer, *Foedera*, xi. 172; *CPR, 1446–52*, 78.   [56] Above, Ch. 14, sect. 4.

[57] For what follows, see Harriss, 'Marmaduke Lumley'.

dishonoured in 1446. The crisis of assignment receded, but public confidence had been shaken, and by 1449 further taxation was needed. When the Commons met they were told that Maine had been surrendered, war was imminent, and Normandy could not be defended. They marked their lack of confidence in the government by making a token grant and refusing further taxation until the session at Winchester on 16 June when war had started in all but name and fortresses in Normandy had begun to fall. The minutes of a debate among the Lords three days later show why: the Commons were demanding 'justice', specifically through commissions of the shire gentry into local corruption and lawlessness. Reluctant to face the political implications of such concessions, the Lords asked for a future grant of taxes on which loans could be raised. The Commons granted a half fifteenth spread over two years, and eventually £12,250 was borrowed for a token force to be dispatched. But no realistic grant was made for the defence of Normandy. Suffolk's regime was politically and financially bankrupt. When Lumley resigned on 16 September there was less than £500 in the treasury; he was lucky to escape the ultimate penalty at the hands of the London rebels suffered by his successor, Lord Saye and Sele.

While the shire and urban gentry were becoming disaffected, support for Suffolk among the nobility and court had been consolidated by lavish patronage. Seventy-nine grants were made to household servants in 1446–7, a quarter coming from Gloucester's lands. The leading members of the entourage—John Hampton, Robert Manfield, John Norris, Edmund Hungerford, John Wenlock, Edward Hull, Philip Wentworth, and John Say—all received four or more. But in the great distribution of Gloucester's offices and lands on the day after his death the major prizes went to the court nobility: Suffolk, Buckingham, Beaumont, Sudeley, Beauchamp, and Saye and Sele.[58] Two of these, Beauchamp and Saye and Sele, were newly ennobled, to be followed by three further creations of baronies by patent in 1448, and six in 1449, knitting together the court and the peerage. Then in June 1449 the death of the infant heiress Anne Beauchamp transferred the earldom of Warwick to Salisbury's son Richard Neville in right of his wife, Duke Henry's sister and sole heir. Neville was able to pursue his right to all the Despenser lands in the absence in France of the rival claimants, Somerset and Shrewsbury. The Nevilles were old Lancastrian supporters, but their unlooked-for establishment in Warwickshire challenged the local ascendancy of curial lords like Beauchamp, Sudeley, and the newly created earl of Wiltshire, James Butler.[59]

[58] The grants to all of these are in *CPR, 1446–52*. The grants of Gloucester's lands are mainly on pp. 42–9, 55.
[59] The peerage creations are conveniently listed in Wolffe, *Henry VI*, 215–16. For the highly complex Warwick inheritance, see the differing accounts of Carpenter, *Locality and Polity*, 439 ff., and Hicks, *Warwick the Kingmaker*, 31–48.

Gloucester's death had another immediate consequence, in leaving uncertain who was the king's heir apparent. With Henry's marriage still childless, the claims of Richard of York and his numerous sons were conspicuously ignored; instead those families who were more closely related to the Lancastrian house— Stafford, Holland, and Beaufort—were favoured by advancement.[60] York's detachment from the group of curial magnates was bound to be reinforced by his appointment as governor of Ireland in September 1447. Deprived of a second term in Normandy and disturbed by Gloucester's fall, York may well have welcomed the chance to fulfil his family's traditional role as a way of disengaging himself from English politics. Even so, the fates of the preceding earls of March from 1381 to 1425 were not auspicious and he made no attempt to leave before July 1449 when the crisis of Suffolk's regime was beginning.

From 1447 there is evidence of mounting dislocation in local society. This had broadly two aspects. First, in certain areas royal and baronial officials, protected by their lords' influence at court, prosecuted men on false indictments, distrained on their property, or used the threat of imprisonment and legal process to make them surrender lands. In Kent it was the officials of Lord Saye as constable of Dover, and those of Buckingham at Penshurst, who were later denounced by yeomen and freeholders as 'great extortioners'. In East Anglia there were similar complaints from local communities against the oppressions of Sir Thomas Tuddenham and John Heydon, stewards of the duchy of Lancaster, and their servants. On the Isle of Wight, York's steward, John Newport, so terrorized the inhabitants that they fled and left it defenceless, while at Boston Viscount Beaumont's officials provoked a riot of 500 townsmen, who sacked his manor. At a higher social level the duke of Suffolk seems to have encouraged attacks by courtiers on Fastolf's lands to silence his opposition to the surrender of Maine, himself occupying Fastolf's manor of Dedham. Victims of all ranks of society were united in demanding justice and there was a swelling chorus of seditious comment about Henry VI's unfitness to reign.[61]

Secondly, these years saw a breakdown of political restraint among the nobility in a series of local conflicts. The background to many of these is obscure, as they suddenly erupted and subsided. In May 1448 there were violent disorders in central Wales between the tenants of York and Buckingham, followed in August 1448 by clashes between the followers of York and Suffolk at Rochford in

---

[60] The Crown's dynastic policy is discussed by Griffiths, *King and Country*, 89–94.

[61] For Kent, see Harvey, *Jack Cade's Rebellion*, 30–47; for Norfolk, A. Smith, 'Litigation and politics: Sir John Fastolf's defence of his English property', in Pollard (ed.), *Property and Politics*, 59–75, and Castor, *King, Crown, and Duchy of Lancaster*, 100–27; for the Isle of Wight, *Rot. Parl.* v. 204, and for Boston, R. L. Storey, 'Lincolnshire and the Wars of the Roses', *Nott. Med. Stud.* 14 (1970), 64–85.

Essex. In May 1448 occurred the murderous confrontation near Coventry between the retainers of Sir Humphrey Stafford of Grafton and Sir Robert Harcourt, both with connections to the court. Far more serious in its consequences was the quarrel between Lord Cromwell and Sir William Taillboys, whose challenge to Cromwell's lordship in Lincolnshire had the backing of Suffolk and Beaumont. The attack on Cromwell by Taillboys' hired men as he entered the Star Chamber in November 1449 made him the avowed enemy of the regime.[62]

Both the default of justice and the surge of aristocratic disorder displayed the absence of effective royal authority and the breakdown of Suffolk's attempt to represent it. It can be argued that his rule was a courageous and responsible attempt to supply Henry VI's natural deficiency by constructing an artificial royal will based on the consensus of the court and nobility.[63] Seen in this light— as he himself did—he had endeavoured to fulfil the king's desire for peace, while making the court a centre of piety, patronage, and service and the focus for self-interested loyalty. His achievement had been vitiated by the duplicity of the French and the legacy of accumulated debt, but above all by the need to accommodate the appetites of his allies: the ambitions of the peers, and the avarice of the courtiers. These proved incompatible with the exercise of a representative royal authority, which needed to transcend sectional interests. There is much substance in this, but it cannot ultimately exculpate Suffolk for his own failings: of ineptitude and overconfidence in diplomacy, of unpreparedness for war, of his own and his allies' exploitation of the king's generosity to the detriment of the royal estate, and of indifference to the views and welfare of the political nation beyond. Ultimately his representation of royal authority operated within too restricted a circle and in too partisan a manner to survive its hour of crisis.

5. REBELLION, POPULAR AND POLITICAL, 1449–1453

When a new parliament met at Blackfriars on 6 November 1449 Rouen had already fallen, and at the end of the year Harfleur surrendered. The Commons' refusal to grant taxation in this or the next session in January reflected not merely the impossibility of recovering upper Normandy—with no army ready to fight, no ports of entry, and no one willing to lend—but their determination to punish those responsible for the collapse. When Moleyns was murdered at Portsmouth on 9 January his dying words inculpated Suffolk, and at the start of the session

---

[62] Johnson, *Duke Richard of York*, 71–2; Storey, *End of the House of Lancaster*, 57–8; R. Virgoe, 'William Tailboys and Lord Cromwell: Crime and politics in Lancastrian England', *BJRL* 55 (1973), 459–82.

[63] Watts, *Henry VI and the Politics of Kingship*, ch. 6.

on 22 January the duke sought to confront 'the odious and horrible language that runneth through your land' with a declaration of his loyalty. Only when the Commons laid a specific charge of treason was Suffolk committed to the Tower, enabling them on 7 February to 'accuse and impeach' him before the Lords of 'treasons, offences and misprisions', covering his negotiations with the French, which were detailed in a bill. The king for the moment put a stay on proceedings; he had to decide whether, like Edward III in 1376, he would permit his minister to be prosecuted or, like Richard II in 1386, would rule it illegal. If the latter, he would have to dissolve parliament, with unforeseeable repercussions. The hiatus lasted until 7 March, when the Lords, by a majority, recommended that Suffolk should come to trial. The Commons then presented a further list of 'misprisions and horrible offences' (not treasons) on Suffolk's domestic misgovernance, gathered from individuals and groups and reflecting a wide range of grievances.

Four days later (13 March) Suffolk produced his written answer (now lost), asserting that he shared responsibility for his policy with the king, the council, and even parliament. That produced a furious point-by-point rebuttal by someone in the Commons, which may never have been delivered since it survives in a single manuscript of private provenance. Rhetorical in style, and by turns sarcastic, scabrous, scornful, and venomous, it is a piece of extraordinary political polemic.[64] Essentially it was the two incontrovertible failures, the loss of Normandy and the Crown's financial bankruptcy, that the Commons sought to pin on Suffolk. But for such purely political matters—which would in modern terms constitute a vote of no confidence—impeachment was an unserviceable procedure. In constitutional terms foreign policy and governance, as Suffolk knew, were the king's responsibility; a minister could only be impeached for corrupt or treasonable acts. On these grounds the peers would probably have acquitted Suffolk, but the popular hostility towards him made it safer to follow the precedents of 1434 and 1440 and remit the charges to the king's grace. Henry quashed the charge of treason and sentenced Suffolk to five years in exile for his lesser offences.

In contrast to 1376 and 1386 the Commons had received no support from a faction among the Lords. Nor were they led by an avowed enemy of the court. Their speaker, William Tresham, was a successful lawyer and parliamentarian with attachments to the court but also to the duke of York and Lord Cromwell.[65] Tresham must have presented the Commons' demands, but it remains unclear who among them was the driving force behind Suffolk's impeachment and the programme of reform that followed. The removal of Suffolk cleared the way for

[64] Printed in Historical Manuscripts Commission, *Appendix to Third Report* (1871; repr. 1874), 279–80.

[65] Roskell, *Parliament and Politics*, ii. 137–51, and information from S. J. Payling.

a resumption bill early in the third session (29 April) at Leicester.[66] Then the news of Suffolk's capture and execution at sea by mutinous sailors, coinciding with that of the defeat of Kyriell's relief force at Formigny, brought the Crown's acceptance of the whole reform programme. The Commons' bill proposed the resumption of all royal grants from the first day of the reign except for those to the queen and the royal colleges, though before it received royal assent the king added partial exemptions in favour of the courtiers, who were allowed to keep some £3,750 worth of the £5,000 and more of Crown properties in their hands.[67]

The prologue to the resumption bill rehearsed the treasurer's statement that the Crown's debts and arrears amounted to £372,000, the current cost of the household was £24,000, and the normal revenues of the Crown only £5,000. The Commons seized on these figures to argue that the revenues resumed should be used to enable the king to live of his own. An act was introduced to provide the household with an annual income of £11,000 from the resumed lands, customs, and royal estates.[68] The Commons had thus revived the programme of financial reform which they had pressed on Henry IV—possibly at the instigation of Lord Cromwell or Bishop Lumley's under-treasurer Thomas Brown.[69] Having extracted these concessions, the Commons were ready to grant a graduated income tax on landowners similar to, but wider than, that of 1436.[70] But this, and the other measures, were aborted by the rising in Kent, the news of which abruptly ended parliament on 6 June.

Just as the voice of the 'middling men' had been asserted in parliament, so now that of the popular element made itself heard in rebellion. It was the murder of Suffolk on 1 May, with the reported threat of Lord Saye to make Kent 'a wild forest' in reprisal, that sparked the rising under Jack Cade later in the month. News of it was spread by messenger, church bells, and bills in public places. As men gathered, the parish and hundred constables mustered them at traditional locations. By 11 June a great host had congregated on Blackheath, staking out their camp in the manner of war and demanding supplies from London under menaces. Their complaints of extortion and oppression were formulated, and

---

[66] Bale's Chronicle (Six Town Chron. 125–6) states that resumption was first demanded in the Winchester session in June 1449, but other sources place it in November. See too T. Gascoigne, Loci e Libro Veritatum, ed. J. E. Thorold Rogers (Oxford, 1881), 189–90.

[67] The schedule of limited surrenders (PRO, Exch. KR Miscellanea, E 163/8/14) was probably drawn up before the start of the third session; B. P. Wolffe, The Royal Demesne in English History (London, 1971), 125–6.

[68] The copy of the Act on the parliament roll is defective; the full list and total of the allocated properties is on PRO, Exch. KR Memoranda Roll 29 Henry VI, E 159/227, Com. Rec. Mich. rot. 17 (listed in G. L. Harriss, 'The finance of the royal household, 1437–1461', D.Phil. thesis (Oxford University, 1953), app. II, table 4).

[69] Brown was York's agent at the exchequer; Johnson, Duke Richard of York, 60–1, 80.

[70] R. Virgoe, 'The parliamentary subsidy of 1450', BIHR 55 (1982), 129.

verses and songs composed.[71] After dissolving parliament at Leicester, the king reached St John's Priory at Clerkenwell on 13 June, accompanied by the retinues of the nobility. Finding Cade's camp too large and strong to attack, it was decided to send the two archbishops, with Buckingham and Beaumont, to offer a pardon if the rebels would withdraw. On meeting them Cade 'demeaned him to the lordes in such wyse and called himself and his peple peticioners answeryng to theym that his comyng to the heth was not to doo any harme but to have the desires of the comones in the parliament fulfilled'.[72] These they summarized in a bill addressed to the king, demanding a resumption, the dismissal of Suffolk's 'false affinity', the punishment of traitors, and the appointment of a noble council.[73] The delegation of lords promised redress and an answer from the king. None was sent, for in the royal camp those who urged an attack on the rebels prevailed. The royal army advanced to Blackheath on 18 June, only to find that Cade, fore-warned, had withdrawn. A body who went in pursuit were ambushed in the Weald and killed. That sparked disaffection among the lords' retinues, with some demanding the arrest of the 'traitors' whom the rebels had named. Henry VI placed Lord Saye under guard in the Tower and, as the rebels returned to Blackheath, retreated to Berkhamsted and then to Kenilworth, leaving London undefended. On 3 July Cade's men entered, along with others from Essex at Mile End. Cade tried vainly to maintain discipline but, as the London chronicler observed, 'he said he and his people were commyn to redress many points . . . but his final purpose was to robbe'.[74] In fact the looting and killing was not on the scale of 1381. The principal act of violence was judicial—the trial and execution of Lord Saye, William Crowmer, and lesser men, seized from the Tower. On 5 July the Tower garrison under Lord Scales counter-attacked, regaining control of London Bridge after an all-night battle. Next day the bishops came forward with a pardon in the queen's name, which the rebels accepted, returning home. Cade went into hiding but was soon captured and executed.

Inevitably, the rising had attracted semi-criminal riff-raff along with labour-ers, unemployed weavers, discharged soldiers, and refugees; but it had been sup-ported and probably organized by husbandmen and forty-shilling freeholders who formed a substantial element in Kentish society. As constables, hundred bailiffs, jurors, and tax collectors, they had been harried and oppressed by the network of 'extortioners' under Saye's protection—men like Slegge, Crowmer, Isle, and Est who were sheriffs, under-sheriffs, farmers of hundreds, and JPs.[75] This demand for justice at local level by the sub-gentry thus echoed that of the

---

[71] Harvey, *Jack Cade's Rebellion*, 186–8.   [72] *Six Town Chron.* 130.

[73] Probably the document printed in Harvey, *Jack Cade's Rebellion*, 191.

[74] *Chron. Lond.* 159.

[75] Detailed in Harvey, *Jack Cade's Rebellion*, ch. 2, sect. iv.

parliamentary Commons in the national context. They had risen avowedly to support the parliamentary programme of reform and to remove the 'traitors' surrounding the king, who were lampooned by name in a sophisticated parody of the religious rite for the dead Suffolk.[76] The loyalty of the 'trewe commons' to the king and common weal is voiced in the remarkable protestation which Fastolf's secretary John Payn brought from the rebels' camp at Blackheath.[77] Written in a practised and rhetorical style, it aimed to win over political opinion by claiming that the courtiers had usurped and perverted the king's power: through them 'his lands are lost, his merchandise is lost, his commons destroyed, the sea is lost, France is lost, himself so poor that he may not pay for his meat and drink'. It demanded their trial before a judicial commission.

Popular opinion thus showed itself to be politically literate, appealing to the concept of the common weal, the rule of law, and the parliamentary programme of financial reform. Merchants and gentry nonetheless derided the rebels' pretensions: the next London mayor, William Gregory, like Gower, saw them as beasts and madmen, contemptuously observing that 'they wente, as they sayde, for the comyn wele of the realme of Ingelonde . . . wenynge that they hadde wytte and wysdome for to have gydyde or put in gydyng alle Ingelonde'.[78] But others saw that they could harness and exploit this popular self-image, pointing to the duke of York as a 'king over the water', exiled for his opposition to the court, who should come and purge the realm of traitors, restore good government, and perhaps make himself king.

The aftermath of the revolt, in the late summer, saw a descent into anarchy, with widespread riotings and murders, including that of Bishop Ayscough in Wiltshire, and acts of private revenge. Any expectations of justice and reform rested with the judicial commission which sat in Kent from August to October to receive indictments of the courtiers and extortioners, and with the arrival of Richard of York from Ireland. Popular hopes that York would return as an avenging messiah had been voiced at least since the spring. Henry VI, justifiably alarmed, had probably forbidden York to return and certainly ordered his officers in North Wales to deny him passage. York felt impelled to come, fearing a campaign by the court to brand him a traitor. In public letters to the king as he progressed to London, he affirmed his loyalty and protested at the attempts to stop him.[79] Reaching London on 27 September with 5,000 men, he received

[76] 'Placebo & Dirige', printed in Robbins (ed.), *Hist. Poems*, 187–9.

[77] Printed in Harvey, *Jack Cade's Rebellion*, 188–90.

[78] J. Gairdner (ed.), *Collections of a London Citizen*, Camden Society, new ser. 17 (London 1876), 191–2.

[79] These, except for the first, are contained in M. L. Kekewich *et al.* (eds.), *The Politics of Fifteenth Century England: John Vale's Book* (Stroud, 1995), 185–90. They are discussed by M. A. Hicks, 'From megaphone to microscope: The correspondence of Richard duke of York with Henry VI in 1450 revisited', *Jnl. Med. Hist.* 25 (1999), 243–56.

Henry's assurance of his safety. The support he commanded now emboldened him to overawe the king, threaten the court, and publicly demand the arrest of the courtiers indicted in Kent. But in presuming to usurp royal justice York had overreached himself. Henry swiftly deflated his pretensions by proposing merely to set up a council of peers of which York should be a member.

Henry's answer, perhaps formulated by the new chancellor, Cardinal Kemp, was not only constitutionally correct but politically adroit. For the weakness of York's position was precisely that he did not command support among the lords. His detached eminence and submerged dynastic claim had deprived him of natural allies. When he now appealed to them to remove the low-born, upstart, and greedy courtiers, in language which echoed the articles of the rebels, it fell on deaf ears. By contrast with 1376 and 1386 there was no anti-court feeling among most of the lords, who had benefited in like measure and were strongly opposed to any resumption. York's avowed enmity to the court, on whose protection Henry VI had come to depend, made him unacceptable to the king, while the nobility would not countenance his exercise of royal authority. The summoning of a parliament for 6 November offered an escape from this impasse.

In parliament York had a natural constituency among those anxious to implement the reform programme of its predecessor. He made efforts to secure the return of his own councillors, Sir William Oldhall, Sir Walter Devereux, and Sir William Burley, along with up to two dozen other supporters.[80] Oldhall was chosen Speaker and bills were prepared for the attainder of the duke of Suffolk and the dismissal of twenty-nine evil courtiers, of whom Edmund, duke of Somerset, was the chief. This was the first recognition that Somerset, after his return from Normandy early in August, had made himself head and protector of the court affinity. For York he was doubly an enemy, as being principally culpable for the loss of his lands in Normandy.[81] York was thus riding the tigers of hatred of the court and fury at defeat; they burst forth in demonstrations in Westminster Hall, calling for justice, and in an attempted assassination of Somerset at Blackfriars on 30 November. The threat of mob violence proved fatal to York's cause; the nobility drew back from opening up political divisions by prosecuting Somerset and the court against the king's will. Henry agreed to the courtiers being suspended for a year, during which charges could be brought against them, while Somerset was temporarily confined in the Tower.

Though York had been frustrated in his personal campaign, the programme of reform suspended in June was now vigorously implemented. The Commons reintroduced the resumption bill, stiffening it by the cancellation of the king's exemptions and asking for a committee of the council to approve any future

[80] Johnson, *Duke Richard of York*, 87 nn. 56, 57.

[81] M. K. Jones, 'Somerset, York and the Wars of the Roses', *EHR* 104 (1989), 285–307.

grants. This enabled the household to meet its expenditure from the resumed revenues and over the next two years the king was able to 'live of his own'.[82] The income tax was also resuscitated. These measures of financial reform had the support of a group of 'moderate' lords, beyond the ill-famed courtiers, who now filled the principal offices: Beauchamp, Cromwell, Stourton, Sudeley, and Archbishop Kemp. But this did not place them behind York. Instead, when released from the Tower after Christmas, Somerset began to rebuild the political consensus, on the basis of Henry's confidence in him as his near relative, the support of the threatened courtiers, and the lords who mistrusted York's popularity and ambitions. A week after parliament reassembled on 20 January 1451 the king, accompanied by Somerset, Exeter, Wiltshire, and Worcester, conducted a judicial visitation of Kent, hanging thirty men while 3,000 knelt to beg Henry's mercy at Blackheath. By the time the king returned on 23 February, York's influence was in retreat. His bid for recognition as the king's heir apparent, made through a bill promoted by his councillor Thomas Young in the May session, signalled the decisive failure of his attempt to mobilize the Commons as a political force. The king dissolved parliament and imprisoned Young. York retired to his estates leaving Somerset triumphant.

The court's recovery in the first months of 1451 frustrated the local commissions set up to punish oppressions. The leading courtiers indicted in Kent in August and September 1450 secured acquittal.[83] Frustration and anger in Kent were vented in continued risings, the suppression of which bred a rooted conviction that Henry was not fit to rule. This alienation of the Kentish freeholders was to have disastrous consequences at the end of the decade.[84] In East Anglia indictments of Suffolk's agents Tuddenham and Heydon, organized by Fastolf and Paston, were likewise sidelined by Justice Prisot.

The two years from June 1449 to June 1451 brought momentous changes for political leaders and political society. Suffolk and his closest associates, Saye, Ayscough, and Moleyns, had been violently murdered. York, from being a loyal if detached heir apparent, had come to be regarded as an enemy of the court and a lurking menace to the royal dynasty. In the crisis of defeat and misgovernment the political initiative had passed first to the Commons, then to the people, and thence to the duke of York. None of these, however, could establish a legitimate authority to govern, and by 1451 the political consensus had re-formed around Somerset as the king's representative. Yet the basis for this had narrowed, for the court, though not displaced, was discredited, and York had not been disarmed. But perhaps the most significant change was the emergence of an articulate and

[82] Harriss, 'Finance of the royal household', ch. 3.
[83] Watts, *Henry VI and the Politics of Kingship*, 275 n. 60.
[84] Harvey, *Jack Cade's Rebellion*, ch. 6.

coherent demand for sound government across the whole span of political society. Government conducted in the enclaves of court and council without reference to the polity as a whole had become unacceptable.

Mutual fear and distrust now separated York from the king and court, and his isolation had disturbing parallels with Gloucester's position earlier. The nobility had no wish to destroy York; they sought to restore stability, by measures of reform to quieten popular discontent, and by loyalty to the Crown to contain York's feud with Somerset. Yet York would not and could not remain a political pariah. As Somerset's position strengthened, with his appointment in September 1451 as constable and captain of Calais (a post which York desired), York saw himself marginalized and impotent. Disturbances among the ruling families of the West Country gave him a chance to demonstrate his power. Thomas Courtenay, earl of Devon, had seen his family's local influence eroded for over a decade by Suffolk's client William, Lord Bonville. Devon had supported York in 1450–1 but the recovery of the court had ranged against him a further local enemy, James, earl of Wiltshire. What provoked him to attack Wiltshire at Lackham on 24 September 1451 is unclear, but from there he laid siege for three days to Bonville in Taunton Castle. York intervened to restore order, taking Devon and Bonville under his protection. It was a flagrant affront to Henry VI's authority, compounded when York and Devon ignored a royal summons to explain their action.[85]

York's estrangement from the court took a sinister turn when, on 23 November, his principal councillor, Oldhall, fled to sanctuary in St Martin's-le-Grand to avoid imprisonment. York read this as forewarning of a move against himself, and on 9 January at Ludlow publicly affirmed his loyalty on the sacrament. He, Devon, and Lord Cobham refused to attend a council on 17 January, and on 3 February York publicly charged Somerset with losing Normandy and preparing to surrender Calais, subverting the reforms, and intending his own destruction. He announced his intention to seize and bring his enemy to trial. York expected to rekindle hostility to the court, and summoned support from the towns and areas in the East Midlands, where his estates lay.[86] Henry gathered the nobility and blocked York's movement eastward at Northampton. Coordinating his march with Devon and Cobham, York made for London, but was refused entry and diverted towards Kent, where he encamped on Blackheath. Disappointed of popular support, due perhaps to the weather, York, Devon, and Cobham found themselves facing the retinues of the nobility in overwhelming

[85] For the background and details, see Storey, *End of the House of Lancaster*, ch. 5; M. Cherry, 'The struggle for power in mid-fifteenth century Devonshire', in Griffiths (ed.), *Patronage, the Crown and the Provinces*, 131–2.

[86] Davis (ed.), *Paston Letters*, i. 96–8; Johnson, *Duke Richard of York*, 107–9.

number. A delegation of bishops and earls, including his kin, Salisbury, and Warwick, was sent to negotiate a settlement on 2 March. York had to submit to the king and swear never again to take up arms, while his charges against Somerset were to be put to arbitration. He and his followers were promised a general pardon.

Although he professed to be acting 'for the good of England', York had turned his campaign against the courtiers into a personal vendetta. He had done so not within the council, as Gloucester had against Beaufort, but in an armed rising which bid for popular support. Having appealed past the king and peers to the political community, he was now recalled to his allegiance by the lords in an attempt to repair the shaken consensus. Neither York's act of rebellion nor Somerset's loss of Normandy were to be adjudged treasonous, and his quarrel with Somerset was to be arbitrated as a matter of personal honour. But if York had escaped the full penalty of his miscalculation, it had left him 'exposed and defenceless'. His servants and tenants were arraigned before commissions of oyer and terminer and had to plead their pardons with abject humiliation.[87] York himself remained confined to his lands with no access to the king.

Somerset had never been a courtier; his reputation and rewards had been gained as a soldier. In 1450 he had lost both, and with no inherited lands or wealth he was wholly dependent on royal favour to rebuild his position. His rule was now marked by pugnacity, proficiency, and profit.[88] Having secured the captaincy of Calais, he installed his own lieutenants, doubled the garrison, and ensured its payment. Money was also found to send Shrewsbury, England's greatest soldier, to recover Bordeaux. The military feebleness of Suffolk's regime was decisively reversed. In England the king was sent to visit disaffected areas—to Kent and the East Midlands in 1451, to the West Country and Welsh marches in 1452, to East Anglia in the winter of 1452–3—in carefully staged demonstrations of majesty and mercy to crowds of intimidated suppliants.

In the course of 1452–3 Somerset's close allies the earl of Worcester and Lord Dudley became treasurer and household treasurer, the earl of Wiltshire was given York's office of governor of Ireland, and Somerset took his office of justice of the forests south of Trent. Patronage once more flowed to the courtiers: from the end of 1451 to early in 1453 the patent rolls record some seventy grants of properties which had been resumed in 1450. Many went to Suffolk's old clique; but the chief beneficiaries were Somerset himself, the queen, and the king's

---

[87] For recent comment on York's motive and position, see Johnson, *Duke Richard of York*, 113–19; Watts, *Henry VI and the Politics of Kingship*, 279–82; Hicks, *Warwick the Kingmaker*, 80–1. York later alleged that he had been promised Somerset's committal to prison, but this seems improbable.

[88] See the assessments by Watts, *Henry VI and the Politics of Kingship*, 282–98, and Hicks, *Warwick the Kingmaker*, 75–85.

half-brothers Jasper and Edmund Tudur, created earls of Pembroke and Richmond and correspondingly endowed with estates.[89] Having thus bolstered his position with lands and allies, Somerset confidently summoned parliament to meet at Reading in March 1453. He secured a favourable House of Commons, no less than 17 per cent of whose members had household connections.[90] In the first session, a bare three weeks, the government put through its business with a brisk efficiency rare in recent years. The Commons were induced to grant a whole fif-teenth (the first since 1449) and to renew the wool subsidies at increased rates for the duration of the king's life. To echo the precedents of 1398 and 1415 was remarkable enough, but the further grant of 20,000 archers for six months' ser-vice at the expense of the counties was entirely novel.[91] The second sessions saw a systematic reversal of the anti-court legislation of 1450–1, the attainder of Oldhall, and the resumption of grants from York's followers at Dartford. Every effort was made to project the image of an active and confident monarchy. Henry thanked the Commons with his own mouth, promised them his favour, and announced that he was going to enforce peace in the localities. Meanwhile the queen's long-awaited pregnancy had been publicized by a pilgrimage to Walsingham in April 1453, when Cecily, duchess of York, had interceded for her husband, who was 'estranged from the grace and benevolent favour' of the king.[92] Somerset had, in effect, solved the problem of York by his political exile.

Somerset's authority at the centre of government, based on his ascendancy over the king and court, was not matched in the localities. Popular discontent could be overawed, but apart from Somerset's court allies the nobility discoun-tenanced his persecution of York and resented his own aggrandizement. They had supported the assertion of royal authority against York at Dartford, but over the following year and a half Somerset's representation of it was too personal and partisan to win acceptance. The earl of Devon's participation in York's rebellion had predictably lost him both his offices and his following in the West Country to Lord Bonville, but in Norfolk the duke, who had joined the king at Dartford, also found himself displaced by the revived de la Pole affinity under the queen's fol-lower Lord Scales. In June 1452 Shrewsbury, Somerset's brother-in-law and ally, was pardoned for his wife and son's forcible expulsion of Lord Berkeley from his castle and lands in the previous September, while in Warwickshire Earl Richard Neville faced not only the latent opposition of Shrewsbury and Somerset over

[89] Somerset's grants included the Isle of Wight formerly held by York and the Matthew Gurney estate in Somerset resumed in 1450; B. P. Wolffe, *The Royal Demesne in English History* (London, 1971), 102–3, 258–9.

[90] Roskell, *Commons and their Speakers*, 248.

[91] Subsequently reduced to 13,000 and commuted for an additional half fifteenth.

[92] C. Rawcliffe, 'Richard, duke of York, the king's "obeisant liegeman": A new source for the protectorates of 1454 and 1455', *Hist. Res.* 60 (1987), 237.

his wife's inheritance but an entrenched household group under the earl of Wiltshire to the south-west. It may have been this sense of a tide of political partiality that encouraged Henry Holland, duke of Exeter, to seize Ampthill Castle from Lord Cromwell in June 1452. Exeter was impecunious, he had no claim to Ampthill, and he was not favoured by Somerset, but he was aware that the ageing Cromwell's attachment to York had rendered him vulnerable. Cromwell was faced first with a fabricated charge of treason and then sustained intimidation by Exeter both in Bedfordshire and at Westminster, as he sought to regain Ampthill by process of law.[93] Each of these separate disputes should have been settled by the king's impartial authority; but cumulatively they reveal that both aggressors and defendants knew it to be ineffective. In abandoning Suffolk's practice of inclusive favour, Somerset was narrowing the basis of support among the nobility and deepening existing rivalries. In the summer of 1453 this was rendered the more dangerous as it came to involve the great northern families of Neville and Percy.

The earls of Northumberland and Salisbury, both in their fifties, had coexisted in Yorkshire peaceably if not amicably for quarter of a century. It was their younger sons, Thomas Percy, Lord Egremont, and John, Lord Neville, who began the disturbances in June, which culminated in armed confrontation at Heworth in August and Topcliffe in October. Although battle had been avoided, 'it had become a contest for regional hegemony', and this was now exported beyond the north by conflict between Salisbury's elder son, Richard Neville, earl of Warwick, and Somerset in South Wales. For on 15 June Somerset obtained the custody of George Neville's half of Glamorgan, hitherto held by Warwick along with his own half. That not only threatened Warwick's immediate control there but prefigured (as he believed) a challenge to his title to the Beauchamp lands as a whole in right of his wife. By mid-July Somerset's men had entered Glamorgan and met armed resistance from the Neville retinue, Warwick himself hastening to defend Cardiff. Warwick now reckoned Somerset as his enemy.[94] Before the dispute could develop further Henry VI, en route for the south-west, had collapsed and lay at Clarendon in a comatose condition, with Somerset in attendance.

The greater nobility's resort to violence signalled their repudiation of Somerset's attempt to represent royal authority. Retrospectively it was seen as a turning point on the road to civil war; yet in August 1453 England was not on the brink of, or even heading for, such. Somerset's ambition had threatened the

---

[93] For all these, see Cherry, 'The struggle for power in Devonshire'; Castor, *King, Crown, and Duchy of Lancaster*, ch. 5 (who emphasizes Norfolk's incompetence); Griffiths, *Reign of Henry VI*, 572–4; Carpenter, *Locality and Polity*, 437–67; S. J. Payling, 'The Ampthill dispute', *EHR* 104 (1989), 881–907.

[94] Above, Ch. 13, sect. 3, for the Neville–Percy rivalry. Also Storey, *End of the House of Lancaster*, chs. 7–9; Griffiths, *King and Country*, 321–64; Hicks, *Warwick the Kingmaker*, 75–90.

Nevilles, but they had not appealed to York, who had remained in the shadows. It was Henry's collapse, removing the source of authority in the state, that left Somerset exposed and transformed territorial rivalries into a constitutional struggle.

6. THE RULE OF YORK, 1453–1456

York's First Protectorate

If Henry's loss of his faculties might privately be read as God's judgement on the defectiveness of his rule, or even of his title, politically it nullified Somerset's pretensions to impersonate the royal will.[95] In 1422 the exercise of royal authority in the king's incapacity had been vested in the lords in council and parliament. But in 1453 these had been factionalized by the York–Somerset feud and could not exercise effective authority. To restore unity, York was accordingly recalled to the council; but when he arrived, on 12 November, he showed no desire for reconciliation and revived (via the duke of Norfolk) his charge of treason against Somerset for the loss of Normandy. Reluctantly the council bowed to York's intransigence and committed Somerset to prison. That York had been able to force the issue suggests that, following Warwick's recent clash with Somerset, he had secured the backing of the Nevilles. Political control would now rest not on the will of the lords of the council, but on the territorial power of the greatest magnates. York and the Nevilles deployed overwhelming strength; but would it provide a basis for their rule?[96]

On 30 November forty-six peers took an oath to support the council's authority, but six days later only half that number were present to accept an avowedly provisional commission to 'entend to the pollytyque rule and governance of this land'.[97] By the new year the authority of these councillors was dissolving. The opponents of York and the Nevilles began to arm: Wiltshire and Bonville in the west, Exeter and Egremont in the north, while the household esquires formed a bodyguard for the king at Windsor, and Somerset's men encamped around their imprisoned lord in the Tower of London. The Yorkist lords moved towards London with small armies. There ensued an armed stalemate in the capital for almost a month as all parties awaited the assembly of parliament on 14 February. It was against this background that Queen Margaret publicly claimed the

---

[95] C. Rawcliffe, 'The insanity of Henry VI', *The Historian*, 50 (1996), 8–12.

[96] Johnson (*Duke Richard of York*, 124–73) and Hicks (*Warwick the Kingmaker*, 91–125) have interpreted these political developments in terms of personal ambitions and power struggles, while Watts (*Henry VI and the Politics of Kingship*, 302–31) has emphasized the attempt to find a constitutional basis for magnate government.

[97] Griffiths, *King and Country*, 305–20.

regency on behalf of her incapacitated husband and newborn son. Though receiving little support, it signalled her intention of providing a rallying point for Lancastrian interests.[98]

With the meeting of parliament a political solution gradually emerged. The creation of Edward as prince of Wales on 15 March, preceded by York's explicit affirmation of allegiance, paved the way for acceptance of the duke's emerging leadership. This was given momentum by the sudden death of the chancellor, Archbishop Kemp, on 22 March. A formal delegation of lords to the prostrate king at Windsor could elicit no sign of his wishes and on 27 March the decision was taken to follow the model of the minority by appointing a protector and council. The former was charged to defend the realm from internal and external enemies; the latter to attend to the governance of the realm. After much negotiation and persuasion a body of 'neutral' lords, and even the queen's supporters Beaumont, Dudley, and Scales, agreed to join the council.[99] Behind this façade of a protectorate York's position was precarious. On his own admission he had been *persona non grata* with the king, he had irreconcilable enemies beyond the council, and he faced a hostile house of Commons. He held his office at the king's pleasure or until Prince Edward came of age. His dependence on the Nevilles was manifested politically in the appointment of Salisbury as chancellor and militarily in measures to subdue Exeter and the Percys in the north.

The Nevilles' ascendancy had provoked the Percys to join with Exeter in defiance of the Protector. As a grandson of John of Gaunt, Exeter now bid for Lancastrian loyalties in the north, forcing York to gather forces to suppress the rising in mid-June.[100] The Percys and their adherents were indicted for disturbances over the past year, while Exeter himself was imprisoned in Pontefract and forced to return Ampthill to Lord Cromwell. York had spent much of August and September 1454 trying to pacify the north, but the running fight between Nevilles and Percys continued, until early in November a pitched battle at Stamford Bridge delivered Egremont and Richard Percy into the hands of Thomas Neville, who had them arraigned and fined the ruinous sum of £11,200 in damages, for which they were committed to prison. The Neville victory quieted the north though it left the feud unresolved. If York had perforce to follow the Neville agenda in the north, in Calais he faced a challenge to his own interests. In parliament he had secured the Lords' assent for himself to replace Somerset as its captain, but Somerset's lieutenants, Lords Welles and Rivers, induced the garrison to resist his entry until the huge arrears of their wages had

[98] John Stodeley's newsletter of 19 Jan. 1454, in Gairdner (ed.), *Paston Letters*, no. 235.

[99] Griffiths, *King and Country*, 317–19, for the negotiations.

[100] T. B. Pugh, 'Richard, duke of York and the rebellion of Henry Holand, duke of Exeter, in May 1454', *Hist. Res.* 63 (1990), 248–62.

been paid. Despite raising a loan of £6,666 from the Company of the Staple and opening direct negotiations with the garrison, York had failed to win admission before the king's recovery returned the office to Somerset early in 1455.[101] However, he did wrest the lieutenantship of Ireland from the earl of Wiltshire.

In the north and at Calais, York could claim to act with the authority of his office, but to deal with the other potential centre of resistance, the royal household, he needed the authority of parliament and the council. The king's illness justified a reduction of its size and the Commons' refusal to grant further taxation dictated a reduction in its costs. Since 1452–3 these had no longer been met from the properties resumed in 1450 but increasingly from the customs. At the end of parliament the 1451 allocation was accordingly replaced by a smaller one, amounting to £6,666, to run for three years from 1 April. Then, to match this reduction of income, an ordinance by a great council on 13 November established 'a sadde and substanciall reule in the King's houshold', reducing the 'greet nombre of people' in it 'to a resonnable and a competent felisship'. This effected a reduction of almost half, to form a small, rather elderly establishment. York did not attempt to install his own men around the king, and the council accepted it as in line with the changed circumstances. In fact before it could be implemented Henry had recovered and Somerset had been reinstated.[102]

Far less success attended York's attempt to deal with Somerset himself. York vetoed a proposal to release him on bail but no formal charges were brought against him and, like Exeter, he remained in prison. York's dilemma was that, if Somerset were brought to trial, he would have to be either condemned for treason and executed or acquitted and released. The body of lords dared not consent to the first, nor York to the second. In fact York's authority as Protector was limited by the consensus of the council. Three great councils sat, each for almost a month, in May, June–July, and October–November attended by some thirty peers, half the number summoned. The continual council mustered fewer than a dozen, mainly York's supporters and bishops. Thus his rule had legality, if not fully accredited authority. It could not pretend to impartiality for it furthered his own and the Nevilles' interests, but it honoured the royal dignity and it tackled the problems of government with vigour and some success. Even so its legitimacy was denied by some at the centre and others in the localities, for whom York remained a traitor.[103]

[101] G. L. Harriss, 'The struggle for Calais: An aspect of the rivalry between Lancaster and York', *EHR* 75 (1960), 30–53.
[102] The household ordinance is in *Proc. & Ord.* vi. 220–33; the allocation of revenues in *Rot. Parl.* v. 246–7.
[103] H. R. Castor, '"Walter Blount is gone to serve traytours": The sack of Elvaston and the politics of the North Midlands in 1454', *Mid. Hist.*, 19 (1994), 21–39.

Within the limits of his commission and a deeply divided society York had, by November 1454, secured the acceptance of his authority and much of his programme by a majority of the nobility. But against the unlooked-for recovery of Henry VI in the following month, with a lucid mind and coherent speech, he had no safeguard. Henry awoke to find the antagonisms of 1453 deepened: two Lancastrian dukes in prison and the Yorkist lords controlling the key offices. He sought to restore harmony and justice. Early in February he resumed rule: the protectorate was extinguished, and the council authorized Somerset's release. On 4 March the king pronounced him guiltless and both he and York were put under bonds of 20,000 marks to accept the arbitration of their quarrel in June. The *status quo ante* was now restored: Somerset recovered the captaincy of Calais, Exeter was freed, and Salisbury was replaced as chancellor by Kemp's successor as archbishop, Thomas Bourchier. The Yorkists saw Henry as once again the instrument of Somerset and the court. They could not trust his impartiality nor look to a divided council to restrain the royal will. Their only assurance lay in controlling the royal power, but to do that by force would confirm the king's hostility and brand them as traitors. From this dilemma they sought to extricate themselves by proclaiming their loyalty to the king while demanding justice on their enemies.

The Battle of St Albans and York's Second Protectorate

After being deprived of their offices the Yorkist lords left abruptly for their estates. Somerset, fearing that the king's recovery might be short-lived, moved quickly to put his authority on a permanent basis, possibly intending to establish the queen as regent. That, rather than the arrest and prosecution of York, may have been the purpose of the great council summoned to meet at Leicester on 21 May, to which were summoned not merely lords but two selected knights from each shire, many of them royal retainers.[104] But whether anticipating proscription or enforced submission, the Yorkist lords decided to pre-empt the council by marching to London. Only as the royal party set out on 18 May did Somerset realize the danger and belatedly summon support, while the king's letters ordered the Yorkists to disperse their followers. On the morning of 22 May, Henry reached St Albans to find himself facing a Yorkist force some 3,000 strong. Although accompanied by some thirteen lords, the royal army was smaller (some 2,000) and not so well armed, for it was not expecting to fight. Indeed both sides at this point preferred negotiations. These hinged, as in 1452, on York's demand for Somerset to be delivered and stand trial. That was a direct

---

[104] *Proc. & Ord.* vi. 339–42. C. A. J. Armstrong, 'Politics and the battle of St Albans, 1455', *BIHR* 33 (1960), 1–72, evaluates the main narrative accounts.

affront to the royal dignity, for Henry had already pronounced Somerset guilt-less, though he had replaced him as constable with Buckingham. Without yielding to York's demand Buckingham played for time, hoping for the arrival of reinforcements; but even as the talks reached an impasse Warwick's men attacked the Lancastrian barricades. Veterans of the French wars on both sides fiercely engaged in a hand-to-hand struggle, until Salisbury's northerners under Sir Robert Ogle broke into Holywell Street and seized the marketplace. As the battle turned into a rout, the Yorkists pursued their quarry to the death: Somerset was hunted down and killed, Northumberland and Clifford probably targeted in the fighting. The effeminate earl of Wiltshire and the household esquires guarding Henry VI took to their heels, leaving the king hiding in a house. The fighting lasted some two to three hours, but casualties had been limited. It had been a surgical operation. On bended knee the Yorkist lords again affirmed their loyalty to the king, who 'graunted to be ruled by them'.

The battle was more than a settlement of magnate feuds. It had been fought not in the remote and lawless north or west but close to the capital, and it had resulted in the defeat and wounding of the king by those whom he had pro-claimed traitors. The shock to political society was as great as that of Cade's revolt. As in 1450, York presented himself as the agent of order, 'justice', and sound government, but this time he did not need to invoke popular support. His problem was rather to reassure and win over the appalled nobility. He offered reconciliation and stability, reaffirmed his loyalty at a solemn crown-wearing at Whitsun, and summoned a parliament for the restoration of the body politic. With their principal enemies 'brought to justice', the Yorkist lords attempted to draw a line under the past. The blame for the battle was put on a handful of courtiers alleged to have misled the king.[105] Though Exeter and Dudley were imprisoned and Wiltshire departed on pilgrimage, Buckingham and other loyal-ist lords agreed to cooperate with York, and in parliament all renewed their oaths of allegiance. The anxiety to restore political unity could not prevent bitter recriminations, nor could it heal the feuds which the deaths of Somerset, Northumberland, and Clifford had deepened. But with York and the Nevilles taking all the key military commands, and Viscount Bourchier and his brother the archbishop as treasurer and chancellor, government was again firmly under Yorkist control.

Early in the parliament committees of lords were set up to regulate the royal household, provide for the defence of Calais and Berwick, safeguard the sea, prevent the export of bullion, and restore order in Wales. In the lower house York had made sure of support: forty-seven members had previously sat in the

---

[105] M. A. Hicks, 'Propaganda and the first battle of St Albans', *Nott. Med. Stud.* 44 (2000), 167–83.

parliament of 1450–1 as against thirty in that of 1453–4. The Speaker chosen was Sir John Wenlock, whose loyalty (like that of Sir Walter Blount) had recently shifted from Queen Margaret to York.[106] The Commons quickly showed their intention to revive the reform programme of 1450. The measures passed against York's supporters in 1452–3 were annulled, and a bill of resumption closely modelled on that of 1450 was introduced. This, and the enforcement of law and order, became their prime concerns in the ensuing sessions.

In the West Country the Courtenay–Bonville quarrel reignited when the earl of Devon launched a series of attacks on his enemy's followers and property. Bonville's councillor, the lawyer Nicholas Radford, was treacherously and horrifyingly murdered, the city of Exeter was occupied, citizens and clergy ransomed, and eventually a small pitched battle was fought at Clyst.[107] These 'grevous riotes' were reported to the second session of parliament which opened on 12 November and provided the cue for York's councillor, William Burley, to lead a Commons' deputation to the Lords to ask for the duke's reappointment as Protector. With the Commons refusing to proceed to further business, the Lords accepted this, though with some hesitation. For Henry VI, though enervated by his experience at St Albans and unable to rule, was not incapacitated. So, whereas the king's collapse in 1454 had automatically vested the exercise of royal authority in the peerage, now the king himself formally commissioned a council to deal with all matters of government, only reporting to him such decisions as touched his 'honour, wurship and suertee'. The Protector's responsibility, as before, was for the defence of the realm internal and external. Thus while the Protector was appointed, and could only be removed, by the king and lords in parliament, the ruling council drew its authority from the king alone and had no fixed term. To one contemporary, at least, it appeared that a long-term solution to the problem of Henry's insufficiency had been found.[108] That was doubtless York's hope, for whereas in 1450–1 and 1455 Henry had refused to accept or sustain York's rule, now his position was to be safeguarded by the lords of parliament, and outside parliament by a permanent council. Both, it was assumed, would be responsive to Yorkist military power.

At the end of the session York went to pacify the West Country, returning for the final session of parliament on 14 January, which was to deal with the matters referred to committees in the first session. On the finance of the household the Commons had already taken the initiative with a bill for a rigorous resumption of all grants since 1422, reinstating the resumption of 1450 which 'hath not be effectuelly hadde'. From these resumed properties, and from revenues allocated

---

[106] For Wenlock's career, see Roskell, *Parliament and Politics*, ii. 229–66.

[107] Cherry, 'Struggle for power in Devonshire', 133–7.

[108] *Rot. Parl.* v. 242, 286–7, 289–90; Gascoigne, *Loci e Libro Veritatum*, 204.

to it earlier in the session, the household was provided with £6,520 for 1455–6.[109] The Protector and the Commons were of one mind in pressing the resumption. It served the interests of both, fulfilling the Commons' ideal of a household financed from the Crown revenues and York's need for it to be restricted in size and debarred from drawing on the customs. For the customs were now fully pledged to the Company of the Staple, which had agreed to finance the earl of Warwick's captaincy in Calais. Though awarded the post after Somerset's death, Warwick found himself, like York, refused admission by Somerset's lieutenants, backed by the garrison who were demanding their substantial arrears of pay. After complex negotiations these—calculated as amounting to £48,131 to the end of March—were paid by the Staplers, who were granted a lien on future customs revenues. Warwick was able to take command on 20 April. By the narrowest margin Calais passed under Yorkist control, giving Warwick a body of professional soldiers and command of the narrow seas.[110]

The household and Calais, the two principal charges, would together absorb most of the available revenue. But York also hoped to secure extraordinary taxation on the basis of the 13,000 archers furnished by parliament in 1453. The Commons' price for this seems to have been the extension of the resumption to grants of franchises, hundreds, and shire revenues, and all wardships and marriages granted since 1448, with the annulment of any regrants of resumed properties.[111] This was probably going further than York wanted and was certainly more than he could deliver. The Lords, who were directly affected and opposed to resumption in principle, brought the king to parliament to refuse assent to the bill and require York's resignation. That occurred on 25 February and led to the duke's immediate withdrawal from parliament.[112]

York's second protectorate was the last attempt to provide a political mechanism for exercising royal authority in Henry VI's default. But it could not be sustained against Henry's resumption of authority. Its closest analogy was with Henry IV's similar surrender of executive power to a council on grounds of ill health in 1406. However, the situation in 1456 had significant differences which limited its acceptability: York was not the king's heir nor (despite his professions) was he seen as a loyal supporter of the dynasty, while the council remained an unrepresentative faction of lords. York may have hoped and tried to win wider support, but never as many as thirty lay lords came to parliament and those who attended the council were mainly York's committed allies.[113] The queen

---

[109] *Rot. Parl.* v. 303, 311–12; *CPR, 1452–61*, 295–8.
[110] Harriss, 'Struggle for Calais', 43–7.   [111] *Rot. Parl.* v. 328, 330.
[112] Johnson, *Duke Richard of York*, 173; *Benet's Chron.* 216.
[113] Roskell, *Parliament and Politics*, i. 193–5. The restricted circle of those attending the council is reflected in the minutes in *Proc. & Ord.* vi. 264, 272, 275, 278–9, 285–6.

distanced herself from the protectorate, gathering support among the curial lords for a counter-stroke. The Commons' radical new resumption bill, which directly threatened the lords' franchises and profitable wardships, united them in opposition and revived their distrust of York's programme. Some—reputedly like the king himself—may have been agreeable to the continuance of a ruling council with York at its head, but essentially the cessation of the protectorship signalled the restoration of the king's authority. Once more, whoever controlled the king would exercise his governing will.

7. QUEEN MARGARET'S RULE, 1456–1459

York's dismissal revealed his predicament. His attempt to control royal authority had depended on the assent and support of the Lords. Their refusal to endorse his protectorate returned him to his position prior to the battle; yet a further resort to force would be counterproductive. Few would support it, for the trauma of recent events was too pronounced. Nor was there an obvious pretext, now that Somerset had been removed. For the moment an opportunity seemed to exist for the restoration of the rightful political order, in which an untrammelled royal authority should exercise impartial and protective rule over all subjects. Had Henry VI been able to do this, or had his death at this point vested the exercise of royal authority in a minority council, political consensus could have been restored. Otherwise, the struggle to exercise the king's authority would be resumed, though now exacerbated by blood feuds between magnate families and the precedent of armed rebellion against the Crown.

It was the latter that impelled the parties towards civil war during the following four years. York's victory had aroused the queen's fears that his submerged dynastic claim endangered her son's succession, and made her determined to represent royal authority herself. Since she could pretend to no constitutional right, this had to rest on her physical control of the king and on the support of a body of the lords. Following his dismissal, York equally had no right to exercise the royal authority, which notionally remained vested in the rump of the council in London. Hence, in the year that followed, the queen and York watched each other apprehensively, neither powerful enough to strike.

In May 1456 Queen Margaret moved to her dower estate at Tutbury and in October established the court, with the king, at Coventry and Kenilworth. In January 1457 Prince Edward was invested with his apanage of North Wales, Chester, and Cornwall and given his own council and officers, drawn from those of the queen. Increasingly he was promoted as the figurehead of the Lancastrian dynasty and the focus of loyalty. The lands and revenues of the principality and the duchy of Lancaster now provided a power base for the court in the northwest, which became the focus for the loyalty of adjacent magnates: Lord Stanley

in Lancashire and North Wales, Viscount Beaumont and Lord Welles to the east
in Leicestershire and Lincolnshire, the earl of Shrewsbury, the duke of
Buckingham, and Lord Dudley in Staffordshire and north Warwickshire, and
Lords Beauchamp and Sudeley in Worcestershire and Gloucestershire. Within
this region the authority of the Crown was thus underpinned by personal loyalty
and territorial power, strategically interposed between the Neville lands in the
north and York's estates in the Welsh marches and East Midlands.[114]

The influence of magnates favourable to the court was likewise promoted in
the north, Wales, and the West Country. Salisbury, at Middleham, faced a systematic build-up of his rivals, the new earl of Northumberland and his brother
in the east march, and the senior Neville line in Yorkshire and Durham, where
the queen's chancellor, Laurence Booth, became bishop in 1457. In the West
Country the queen won over the earl of Devon, who was pardoned for Radford's
murder and allied himself with the duke of Exeter and the earl of Wiltshire
against his rival Lord Bonville. In west Wales, Jasper, earl of Pembroke, recovered
control of Carmarthen and Aberystwyth, formerly held by Somerset.[115] Using
the king's authority and patronage, the queen had thus been able to make the
court an effective centre of power, commanding the support of a significant
number of the higher nobility: the dukes of Buckingham and Exeter, the earls of
Devon, Northumberland, Pembroke, Shrewsbury, Somerset, and Wiltshire, and
Viscount Beaumont. Many were of a new generation: all save Buckingham and
Beaumont were still under 40 in 1459 and had succeeded to their titles within the
last decade.[116]

However, there had been no hostile moves against the Yorkist lords. York and
Warwick had been summoned to great councils held at Coventry in October 1456
and April 1457, and though York may have been required to reaffirm his oath of
1452, he had been confirmed as governor of Ireland and Warwick as captain of
Calais. In October 1456 the queen replaced the Bourchiers, appointing Bishop
Waynflete as chancellor and the earl of Shrewsbury as treasurer. A residual council in London still claimed executive authority, but with decreasing effectiveness.

London's inbuilt loyalty to the Crown slowly eroded in the years 1448–60.
The corporation ceased to be a major or even significant lender to the Crown, by
comparison with the Company of the Staple or even individual merchants.[117]
Politically the Crown did not regard London as a 'safe harbour'; the king had fled
in 1450 in the face of Cade's rebels, and again left in October 1456 after anti-
Lombard riots. For their part the merchants had lost confidence in the Crown's

---

[114] For the queen's rule at Coventry, see Griffiths, *Reign of Henry VI*, 775–85.

[115] Above, Ch. 13, sect. 2; Griffiths, *King and Country*, 211–19.

[116] By then the earl of Devon (d. 1458) had been succeeded by his son.

[117] C. M. Barron, 'London and the Crown 1451–61', in Highfield and Jeffs (eds.), *The Crown and Local Communities*, 88–109 (table 1).

military and foreign policy and failure to protect trade. Their most persistent grievance was its readiness to sell licences to ship wool to Zeeland and Brabant, mainly to Italian merchants, bypassing the Calais Staple. Persistently hated as bankers and moneylenders, it was the Italians' intrusion into the Low Countries market as importers of cloth from Brabant that aroused the mercers' apprentices to attack and loot their houses in Lombard Street in April 1456. As the Italians' patrons and protectors, the Crown incurred corresponding odium, while its threats to penalize the city for the disorders generated Yorkist sympathies. London was not a Yorkist city by 1459; but the aldermanry was divided, and Warwick's buccaneering attacks on foreign shipping aroused jingoistic enthusiasm.[118]

If London's internal conflicts had encouraged the court's migration to the Midlands in 1456, it was the French devastation of Sandwich in August 1457 that brought it back in September. Popular outrage that a once victorious nation was now endangered by the divisions of the nobility forced some degree of cohabitation on the queen and the Yorkist lords under the formal authority of the king and council. The proceedings of a council in October–November 1457 'to set apart such variances as be betwixt divers lords' are unknown, but commissions were issued to array men in the coastal and inland shires, an impressive muster was held at Harringay, and it was planned to reactivate the 1453 grant of archers. Warwick was appointed to keep the sea for three years, to the anger of Exeter. A renewed attempt was made to form a government of national unity, centred on London and employing the forms of royal authority: in this Henry VI had a role as an apostle of peace. The bishops were brought in as mediators and organizers for a solemn loveday, on 24 March 1458, celebrated with a Mass and procession at St Paul's on Lady Day. The Yorkists provided financial compensation and prayers for the deaths of Somerset, Northumberland, and Clifford, with whose heirs they were reconciled, themselves being pardoned and acknowledged as true and faithful lieges. In confining itself to the settlement of personal feuds, it chose to ignore the reasons for Yorkist opposition to the Crown, seeking to bury the past rather than rewrite it. Nor did it prescribe any future political settlement. Once again this could only rest upon Henry VI's kingship, which, predictably, proved insufficient either to direct government or to ensure political harmony.[119]

---

[118] J. L. Bolton, 'The City and the Crown, 1456–61', *London Journal*, 12 (1986), 11–24; Nightingale, *Medieval Mercantile Community*, ch. 19; A Ruddock, *Italian Merchants and Shipping in Southampton, 1270–1600* (Southampton, 1951), 162–76; Griffiths, *Reign of Henry VI*, 790–7.

[119] Differing assessments of the significance of the loveday and Henry VI's role in it are made in Griffiths, *Reign of Henry VI*, 804–8; Johnson, *Duke Richard of York*, 180–4; Watts, *Henry VI and the Politics of Kingship*, 343–6; Hicks, *Warwick the Kingmaker*, 132–8.

In the immediate aftermath offices and rewards were distributed equably, and a council balancing lords and bishops from both camps met during the summer, and was reconvened for early October. But by then the queen had resolved to assert her power. At the end of that month the earl of Wiltshire was again made treasurer, with Thomas Tuddenham household treasurer, and subordinate financial offices filled by household esquires. Wiltshire began a systematic exploitation of the Crown's lands and fiscal prerogatives for the benefit of the household; he contracted with Italian merchants to ship wool on the Crown's behalf, and negotiated an annual advance of £4,000 for the household from the Company of the Staple, in return for suspending licences of exemption. These measures, with revenue from the exchequer, aimed to provide the court with direct access to a secure income.[120] Then during the winter and spring of 1458–9 it was put on a military footing: armaments were ordered, commissions of array and coastal guard were issued to its supporters, and in May individuals were summoned to Leicester for two months' service.[121] The Yorkist lords, believing themselves endangered, withdrew from London in November, Salisbury retiring to Middleham, Warwick (narrowly escaping an ambush) to Calais. Although Henry VI remained in London for the next six months, there is little evidence of any effective government at the centre. In May further riots in London forced his retirement to Coventry. There the queen summoned the Yorkist lords to a great council after midsummer, at which, according to one chronicler, they were indicted in their absence.[122]

The queen's decision to centre royal authority and resources in the court at Coventry may well have been a response to the earl of Warwick's ability to construct his own power base at Calais and to act in defiance of the Crown. Initially, Warwick's hold on Calais was uncertain, for the garrison numbered many of Somerset's men and its further enlargement by Warwick brought financial problems. With a penurious and semi-mutinous garrison Warwick turned to piracy, attacking in the course of 1458–9 Spanish, Hanseatic, and Genoese fleets. Not only was this profitable, it played to London's anti-alien phobia and jingoism. The ecstatic chronicler declared that 'all the cominalte of this lond hadde him in greet laude and chiertee . . . and soo repute and take [him] for as famous a knight as was lyving'.[123] Assured of the Staplers' support and perhaps financial backing, and enjoying popular acclaim, Warwick was also manipulating diplomacy for his own purpose. Peace negotiations had been initiated by the council in 1458 with a scheme for linking the rival parties in England into French and Burgundian marriages. Warwick's envoy Sir John Wenlock used them to strengthen Burgundy's links with Warwick, and spread rumours of further French descents on England

---

[120] Griffiths, *Reign of Henry VI*, 785–90, summarizes these financial measures.
[121] Wolffe, *Henry VI*, 315–17.   [122] *Benet's Chron.* 223.   [123] *Six Town Chron.* 147.

to discredit the queen. On every ground Queen Margaret was determined to remove Warwick from Calais; he was equally determined to stay.[124]

The disintegration of government by 1459 was a precondition of civil war, indicative of the negation of royal authority. Historians have differing views on how this had happened. Some blame the queen's implacable hostility to York, others York's dynastic ambitions and Warwick's blatant defiance of the Crown, while a third view points to the magnates' escalating feuds and their failure to sustain a council of noble unity. At the heart of the problem was an inability to agree on any substitute for Henry VI's personal rule. Kingship was the linchpin of the state; its unique authority could not be counterfeited, and once it failed political society fell apart. Only very slowly and reluctantly was this acknowledged. There was no clear progression towards conflict in 1459 and no evident *casus belli*. York and Salisbury seem to have lain low on their estates, avoiding provocation, and if the Coventry council in June did proscribe them it was three months before they responded.

8. YORK VERSUS LANCASTER, 1459–1461

The Struggle for the Throne

None of the nobility, at this point, were seeking to initiate a civil war or engineer a change of dynasty, with all the attendant risks to their lives and estates. Their principal concern was to ensure their own security within a stable political framework. As the three Yorkist leaders converged in force on the West Midlands in the late summer of 1459 they offered their loyal service to Henry VI in removing evil councillors and reforming the realm and royal estate. By 20 September Warwick had reached London with part of the Calais garrison, and Salisbury was leading a larger body of retainers southwards from Middleham, probably to meet him at Warwick.[125] Part of the king's army moved towards Nottingham to intercept Salisbury and another under Somerset to intercept Warwick. Diverted westwards, Salisbury encountered a force of the queen's Cheshire retainers under Lords Audley and Dudley, which barred his way at Bloreheath on 23 September. The Cheshire men were probably more numerous, the northerners more hardened.[126] In a half-day engagement Audley and nine of his captains perished and, though Salisbury got through, his two sons were captured. The royal army now moved southwards towards the Yorkist

---

[124] Hicks, *Warwick the Kingmaker*, 138–48.

[125] *Rot. Parl.* v. 348; Johnson, *Duke Richard of York*, 186–7; A. Goodman, *The Wars of the Roses* (London, 1981), 26–31, treats the whole campaign.

[126] J. L. Gillespie, 'Cheshiremen at Blore Heath: A swan dive', in J. Rosenthal and C. Richmond (eds.), *People, Politics and Community* (Gloucester, 1987), 77–89.

lords, who, at Worcester, solemnly affirmed their loyalty before crossing the Severn and retreating to Tewkesbury and then to Ludlow. There, heavily out-numbered, and with little support from the other nobility, they fortified a camp, as at Dartford. By then Henry VI had summoned a parliament to Coventry, from which they were excluded, and offered them a pardon if they would submit. Declaring themselves unable to trust the pardon or to come to his presence unarmed, they complained of being treated as traitors and despoiled by their enemies at court.[127] York's reluctance to fight the king, against his oath, commu-nicated itself to the army. The desertion to the king of a contingent from Calais under Andrew Trollope forced the Yorkist leaders to flee under cover of night, on 12 October. Probably deliberately they separated, York and his younger son Rutland to Ireland, Warwick, Salisbury, and York's eldest son Edward, earl of March, to Calais.

Both their forces and their strategy had been inadequate. The Lancastrian dominance of the Midlands had prevented them from converging speedily in strength. Now the Crown seized the political initiative, branding them as traitors and confiscating their lands through an act of attainder which recapitulated the stages of York's opposition since 1450. Their claim to be acting as loyal subjects, against evil counsellors and for the good of the realm, was derided and rejected.[128] The Coventry parliament was a demonstration of the court's strength and solidarity. An exceptionally large number of temporal peers—thirty-two—attended and swore to uphold Henry's kingship and Prince Edward's succession, while almost one-quarter of the Commons whose names are known were members of the royal household.[129]

In acknowledging the fact of civil war, Lancastrian rule faced the need to ensure as well as claim loyalty. One means lay ready to hand: the distribution of the lands and offices of the proscribed Yorkists among royal supporters. Some ninety-seven grants are recorded to the principal courtiers and household ser-vants, while each of the magnates around the queen received custody of the Yorkists' castles and local offices. That precluded any pardon to the Yorkists, while the revenue from their estates enhanced the Lancastrian war chest.[130] To win acceptance for the court's authority in political society at large was less easy. Many who valued unity would have echoed William Worcester's wish in January 1460 that 'God sende the Kyng victorie of hys ennemyes, and rest and pease among hys Lordes,' and had the court been able to destroy the Yorkist lords few would have lamented their fate.[131] But while they remained immune overseas

---

[127] Davies (ed.), *Eng. Chron.* 81–3.

[128] *Rot. Parl.* v. 346–9; see below for the *Somnium Vigilantis.*

[129] *Rot. Part.* v. 351. On my reckoning thirty-six of the 158 known members were household ser-vants or annuitants.   [130] Johnson, *Duke Richard of York*, 192–4.

[131] Gairdner (ed.), *Paston Letters*, no. 399.

they offered an alternative allegiance and one which was favoured in the south-east. Hence, no attempt was made to return government to the capital; rather, the whole effort was to fortify England against a Yorkist assault. On the one hand this meant strengthening the Welsh castles, the southern ports, and the midland redoubt with weapons and artillery; on the other to search out and intimidate Yorkist sympathizers by widespread commissions of oyer and terminer in the southern shires. The brutality and vindictiveness of some of these—notoriously on York's tenants at Newbury—were exploited by Yorkist propaganda and served to polarize loyalties.[132]

In Calais, Warwick was firmly enough entrenched to repulse assaults by land and sea. He had concluded a truce with Burgundy which enabled him to plunder French lands and shipping, and squeezed further 'loans' from the Staplers, now desperate to restore the flow of trade. His spies and agents in Kent kept him informed of the court's preparations and paved the way for a Yorkist return. This was planned in a meeting of York and Warwick in Dublin in March. York had been well received in Ireland, where his de facto regal authority was acknowledged, and he recruited support from the Anglo-Irish.[133] Plans were laid for a coordinated invasion of England through Kent and North Wales around midsummer 1460. Politically, the option of replacing Henry VI must have been broached, for York was now determined to assert his legitimate claim, and provisionally Warwick probably endorsed this. But the context was impossible to predict.[134]

The earls of March, Salisbury, and Warwick landed in Kent on 26 June 1460. With them was the papal legate Francesco Coppini, sent to ask support for the Council at Mantua but persuaded of the justice of the Yorkist cause. Received with open arms in Kent, the Yorkists advanced to London, where convocation was in session. As before, their professed purpose was to come to the king, whose legitimate authority they acknowledged, to remove their 'mortalle and extreme enemyes' (now named as Shrewsbury, Wiltshire, and Beaumont) and, as loyal counsellors, reform and defend the realm.[135] On 1 July the common council in London agreed to give them passage through the city and lend 3,500 marks, pro-tected by the Yorkists' oath in St Paul's before the bishops and legate not to harm Henry VI—though significantly not including his lineage. Their reception in London had transformed them from rebels to reformers and, strengthened by Kentish recruits, Warwick, March, and Faucomberg advanced swiftly towards the king, before the Lancastrian forces were fully mobilized. The court had

---

[132] Davies (ed.), *Eng. Chron.* 90; Griffiths, *Reign of Henry VI*, 857–9; Watts, *Henry VI and the Politics of Kingship*, 355–6.

[133] Above, Ch. 13, sect. 1, for York's policy in Ireland.

[134] Discussed by M. K. Jones, 'Edward IV, the earl of Warwick and the Yorkist claim to the throne', *Hist. Res.* 70 (1997), 342–52.

[135] Davies (ed.), *Eng. Chron.* 86–90, discussed more fully below.

moved from Coventry to Northampton, and the retinues of Buckingham, Beaumont, and Shrewsbury, with a local contingent under Lord Grey of Ruthin, entrenched and fortified a position in a bend of the river Nene near Delapre Abbey. Warwick enjoyed the greater numbers but had to attack a strong encampment. Battle was joined on 10 July 1460 at 2 p.m. after the bishops had conducted long and fruitless parleys. Heavy rain rendered the Lancastrian artillery useless, but it was the treachery of Lord Grey in opening up the defences to the Yorkists that precipitated the Lancastrian collapse and the deaths of their leaders. Having 'taken out' his enemies, Warwick performed obeisance to Henry VI who, 'more timorous than a woman', had remained in his tent.[136]

With the king and the Midlands under their control, the Nevilles, with the Bourchiers, took over the machinery of state and summoned a parliament in Henry VI's name. Wales was still held by Jasper Tudur, and when York eventually arrived in early September it was in the Wirral, from where he moved down the marches, reaching Gloucester on 2 October.[137] By then, and probably soon after landing, he had renounced his allegiance, and now advanced on London with the royal arms displayed and his sword borne upright. Believing that he had Warwick's tacit support, and counting on his armed strength and popular acclamation to override the allegiance which his allies had sworn to Henry VI in June, he attempted to occupy the throne in the parliament chamber. Rebuffed by Archbishop Bourchier and the other Lords, he agreed to submit his claim in writing. Having sought legal opinion and heard Henry VI's objections, the Lords accepted York's contention that his claim by blood accorded with natural law and overrode the recognition of Henry VI by statutes and oaths of allegiance. Yet they shrank from deposing Henry, agreeing that he should remain as king and recognize York as his heir, on the model of the Treaty of Troyes.[138] Not merely Henry's own innocence, but the apprehension that his debts and grants might be cancelled, underlay this compromise, which was perhaps due to Warwick. York was not wholly trusted.

The Westminster accord reduced the queen and prince to the status of rebels, stiffening Lancastrian resistance and justifying the charge that York had all along sought the crown. Queen Margaret now rebuilt her power north of the Humber, mobilizing the Percys and their followers and seeking an alliance with the Scots. She now demanded loyalty to Prince Edward rather than to Henry VI. York, eager to validate his new status, marched north in early December with Salisbury and Rutland, raising an army en route with money borrowed from London. The

[136] For the battle, Goodman, *Wars of the Roses*, 36–9; for Coppini's description of Henry VI, Griffiths, *Reign of Henry VI*, 864.

[137] In what follows I have largely followed Johnson, *Duke Richard of York*, 211–18, and Jones, 'Edward IV, the earl of Warwick and the Yorkist claim'.

[138] *Rot. Parl.* v. 375–80.

earl of March was sent to contain Pembroke in Wales. York and Salisbury reached the duke's castle at Sandal on 21 December to find themselves short of supplies and a powerful Lancastrian force close at hand. With Christmas imminent a truce was arranged until Epiphany, during which York expected reinforcements. But on 30 December a foraging party from the garrison was brought to battle at Wakefield, and York, going to its assistance, was surrounded and cut down, Salisbury being taken at Sandal and executed.[139] The news had reached London by 5 January, followed by reports of the plundering and ravaging of the northern army as it advanced via Stamford, Peterborough, and Royston to Dunstable. Warwick, with rapidly arrayed troops from Essex and Kent stiffened by Burgundian mercenaries, and with Henry VI in train, first occupied St Albans but then, on the morning of 17 January 1461, decided to redeploy his large force on Nomansland Heath a mile to the north. He was still constructing an elaborately defended position with guns and traps when the Lancastrians broke into the town about 1 p.m. and took him in the rear. The devices proved useless and in the fighting it was the disciplined retainers of the northern lords, wearing Prince Edward's livery, 'that gate the fylde'.[140] Warwick and Norfolk escaped but the aged Lord Bonville, guarding Henry VI, was taken and executed. A fortnight earlier the earl of March, with York's captains Herbert, Devereux, and Wenlock, had turned back a force advancing from Wales under the earls of Pembroke and Wiltshire at Mortimer's Cross in Herefordshire and was free to march towards London.

With a victorious army and the king once more in her possession, Queen Margaret could pretend to exercise a national authority. In fact the king was now widely recognized to be a puppet while the queen dared not force an entry into a hostile London, towards which the earl of March was approaching. She ordered a retreat to the north and March entered the city on 26 February. Deeming Henry VI to have broken the Westminster accord by his desertion to the queen, Edward of March claimed the throne by virtue of his father's indefeasible right. The taboo on Henry's deposition had finally been broken, at least among the handful of Yorkist lords and bishops at Baynard's Castle who approved his title on 3 March. Next day Edward proceeded to Westminster Hall, taking symbolic possession of the realm from the throne, and thence to the abbey to be invested with the Confessor's regalia and to receive homage. Coronation was deferred until June.[141]

[139] The sources have differing accounts of the battle; see Goodman, *Wars of the Roses*, 42–3.

[140] There are good contemporary accounts of the battle in *Registrum Abbatiae Johannis, Whetehamstede*, ed. H. T. Riley, 2 vols., Rolls ser. (1872–3) i. 390 ff., and Gregory, *Chron.* 212–14; see also Goodman, *Wars of the Roses*, 45–8.

[141] C. A. J. Armstrong, 'The inauguration ceremonies of the Yorkist kings and their title to the throne', *TRHS*, 4th ser., 30 (1948), 55–66.

Edward now had to defend his throne by arms. With Warwick and Faucomberg he marched north, recruiting as he went. The queen had abandoned the Midlands, taking her stand south-west of York at Towton near Tadcaster. She had gathered all the Lancastrian peers, some nineteen against half that number with Edward. Both armies were significantly larger than those deployed at any other battle, recognizing it to be a decisive duel between crowned kings. The advantage lay with the Lancastrians in numbers, in freshness, and in the choice of a defensive position. Having unsuccessfully contested the Yorkist crossing of the Aire at Ferrybridge on 27–8 March, the main Lancastrian army next day (Palm Sunday) positioned itself on a slight ridge on the plateau south of Towton flanked by a steep descent to the small river Cock. The Yorkists faced them across a shallow valley to the south. The battle opened with an archery duel in which the Yorkists drew advantage from the southerly wind and blinding snowstorm; that precipitated the Lancastrian advance into the mêlée where their weight of numbers pushed back the Yorkist army. The arrival of fresh troops under Norfolk, and perhaps the greater cohesion of Edward's command, at length broke the Lancastrian army, precipitating a disorderly flight in which large numbers perished. The battle had been long and bloody, with Northumberland, Clifford, and other peers killed, and Devon and Wiltshire captured and executed. Henry and Margaret, with Somerset and Exeter, were able to flee to Scotland.[142]

In that it secured Edward's throne for the following nine years, the battle of Towton was decisive, and was welcomed in the south as a delivery from Lancastrian and northern tyranny. Yet the military outcome was far from inevitable and a Lancastrian victory would have had a finality that Edward's did not, removing the dynastic challenge and providing a firm political base for a renewal of royal power, to which Sir John Fortescue might have contributed in practical rather than literary form.

A War of Arms and a War of Words

How was the war fought, in what terms was it justified, and how deeply did it divide society? The mode of warfare differed considerably from that practised by the English in France.[143] Neither the *chevauchée* of the fourteenth century nor the siege warfare of the fifteenth were relevant, nor were armies recruited by indenture for campaigns. Armies had to be mobilized quickly for imminent encounters. The retainers of both the king and the nobility formed the nucleus, and these included some captains with experience of the French wars. Lords

---

[142] A. W. Boardman, *The Battle of Towton* (Stroud, 1994) offers a more elaborate reconstruction.
[143] Goodman, *Wars of the Roses*, for what follows.

would also summon their annuitants, who would be told to bring their tenants suitably equipped. Larger forces would be raised in broadly three ways. Commissions of array for a shire were issued by the king to lords and gentry to have men ready to muster when and where ordered—these were numerous in the summer months of 1459 and 1460 and were used by the Yorkist lords in 1460–1. In the vills, men would be selected to be armed and paid wages and led by local constables. But the towns provided better-quality troops since those who performed watch and ward duties already constituted a disciplined and uniformed force under its permanent captain. The major towns would be commanded by signet letters to demonstrate their loyalty, and Coventry provided 100 men and Norwich 120. An important element (perhaps a half to two-thirds) from both town and countryside would be the archers; others would have bills, poleaxes, and glaives, and those from the towns would wear the fighting man's standard equipment of sallet (helmet), jacket, sword, buckler, and dagger. Since wages and victuals were provided for a limited period, men were not assembled until a campaign was under way; but if summoned too late they might never arrive—as perhaps happened in 1460 at Northampton. Uncertain about the response from these sources, commanders bolstered their forces by recruitment on the march. For the Yorkists, lacking authority to employ the royal summons, this was attempted unsuccessfully by York in 1452 and by Warwick in 1459, but with greater effect in 1460 and in the speedy advance north in 1461. Armies were thus composed of disparate elements, difficult to discipline and control, and overwhelmingly composed of foot. Cavalry might be used for a flank charge, and for pursuit or escape, but the main battle sequence was an archery duel followed by the mêlée. No reliable figures are available for the numbers engaged, though the relative size of the engagements seems clear: small at St Albans (1455), Ludford, Mortimer's Cross, and probably Wakefield; larger at Northampton and St Albans (1461); massive at Towton, where a contemporary estimate of 28,000 might just be within the limits of possibility.

In some situations defensive encampments were prepared, fortified by artillery: notably by York at Dartford in 1452 and again at Ludford in 1459; by the king at Northampton, and by Warwick, in intention, at St Albans (1461). The royal forces had amassed a considerable quantity of ordnance under the direction of John Judde, though guns were never effective. Arrows were still the most lethal long-distance missiles, often inflicting a mortal wound on the face. For political as well as military reasons the Yorkists targeted the nobility, the royal household, and retainers, ordering the common soldiers to be spared; the direct inverse of chivalric practice. No one was ransomed; even when captured, lords and knights were executed by their enemies; hatred and elimination were the marks of civil war. For the nobility involvement was inescapable and deadly.

If we ask why the civil war of 1459–61 was fought, and what was it about, the answer in general terms must be that it grew out of Henry VI's defective king-ship.[144] As a ruler Henry VI was unconfident, indecisive, and generally passive; his sense of insufficiency made him both over-trusting and over-suspicious, and always deeply dependent. As he showed his inability to rule, the nobility were forced to devise ways of representing his authority, with Suffolk and Somerset informally exercising a surrogate power, and York reviving the protectorship and conciliar mechanism of the minority. That these engendered division rather than unity was due partly to circumstances, partly to personalities, but essen-tially to the impossibility of representing the authority of even a semi-active king. For royal authority was constituted by the king's personal will exercised for the common good of the realm. When manipulated by a subject and directed towards individual interests, it lost legitimacy. Henry VI's acts employed the forms of royal authority and were unchallengeable, but his known pliability undermined their credibility and deprived them of political assent. The only assurance for his leading subjects lay in controlling the king's will and person, at first politically and ultimately by force of arms. That led to civil war.

Suffolk's attempt to represent royal authority enjoyed a measure of success up to 1446 because he was trusted by the king and secured a consensus among the court nobility through liberality and the pursuit of uncontroversial policies. It began to unravel with the return from France of Richard, duke of York. He was not one of the curial magnates and was neither well known nor well liked by the king. Believing himself defamed, disappointed of reappointment in France, and removed to Ireland, he came to believe that the courtiers were conspiring against him. Because York was no ordinary subject but territorially the most powerful, dynastically the most threatening, and with a family history of treason, Henry's suspicion of him was deeply ingrained and easily aroused. Hence York's prime purpose in returning from Ireland in 1450 was to seek out the king and affirm his loyalty. Over the following decade their political relationship turned on Henry's confidence in the duke's loyalty and York's trust in the king's protection and just-ice. Henry feared and mistrusted the popular support which York excited as a 'king over the water', a reformer, and even usurper. In fact York was no populist, and though he was ready to countenance the demand for reform, he sought to focus it upon the removal of the courtiers whom he labelled as traitors to the common weal. Affronted by the establishment of Somerset as the king's confidant, he came to see this as also threatening his own safety and blood. The battle of St Albans fulfilled York's demand for the removal of his enemy but at the same time destroyed the consensus among the nobility for York's representation of the king's authority; indeed he was now perceived by the queen and her supporters as a rebel and potential usurper. Yet right up to the confrontation at Ludlow his

[144] As argued by McFarlane, *England in the Fifteenth Century*, 238–40.

most insistent demand was to be treated by the king and the nobility as a loyal subject. It expressed pride in his honour, concern for his safety, and a loyalty which he increasingly regarded as conditional on his just treatment by the king.

How far did York also regard Henry VI's kingship as conditional on the good government of the realm? It has been argued that from 1450 the duke saw it as his duty to reform the realm, making a sustained appeal to public opinion in the name of the common weal.[145] In fact York's own public statements did not accuse Henry of misrule, nor propose any general reform of government, though he endorsed the parliamentary demand for resumption. It was Warwick who, in September 1459, transformed a crisis of trust between the Crown and its leading subject into a political crusade for better government. His 'articles' issued in Kent recited the misgovernment which was ruining the land: the king's impoverishment, the disorders and lack of justice, and the influence of evil counsellors. Professing a duty to the common weal and the king's estate, he and his allies required the king to reform the realm and punish the culprits. The manifesto revived the popular critique of 1450–1, making 'the provision of superior government the centrepiece of a positive appeal'.[146] Though it brought them little support before their campaign collapsed, it opened a polemical war on the limits of political obedience. Could subjects require the reform of government in the name of the common good or was their overriding duty that of obedience to the king, the basis of any commonwealth? That was the question posed in the *Somnium Vigilantis*, a sophisticated polemic which eloquently rehearsed the Yorkists' case before rejecting it. It asserted that the king alone could interpret the common weal and reform the realm. Stirring up the people was seditious, and popular favour conferred no authority. The Yorkists were betraying their estate in adopting the language of plebeian rebels and violating the king's *majestas* in requiring him to bow to the common will. The tract was directed not to a popular audience but to the king and parliament in 1459 to secure support among the Lords for the attainder of the Yorkists. The emergence of a dichotomy between subjects' obedience and royal rule for the common good bore witness to the break-up of the polity, for normally these were reciprocal obligations to ensure the stability of the commonwealth. Now, 'the married calm of the medieval polity was rent'.[147]

It was as proscribed rebels that the Yorkists exploited the demand for reform

[145] Watts, in Kekewich *et al.* (eds.), *John Vale's Book*, 3, 27; id., *Henry VI and the Politics of Kingship*, 266–82, 316. See too C. Coleman and D. Starkey (eds.), *Revolution Reassessed* (Oxford, 1986), 19–27, though note Morgan's caveat, 20 n. 33.

[146] Kekewich *et al.* (eds.), *John Vale's Book*, 27–8, and the text on pp. 208–10.

[147] J. P. Gilson, 'A defence of the proscription of the Yorkists in 1459', *EHR* 26 (1911), 512–25; M. L. Kekewich, 'The attainder of the Yorkists in 1459: Two contemporary accounts', *BIHR* 55 (1982), 25–34; McFarlane, *England in the Fifteenth Century*, 259.

in London and the Kent hinterland, where issues of misgovernment had popular resonance. Here they had a constituency which they mostly lacked among the peers. On landing in 1460 Warwick unleashed a full-scale propaganda war. Rigorous and inquisitorial Lancastrian rule furnished specific examples of tyranny, while Warwick's exploits had made him a legendary figure. A new manifesto recapitulated the misgovernment of the last decade: the king's poverty, debts, and the oppressions of his purveyors; the corruption of the law; heavy taxation; exactions of archers; the loss of lands in France; and the threat to surrender Ireland and Calais. Alongside this, the reissue of the text of the articles of the Kentish commons in 1450 made an explicit appeal to the persistent hostility of Kent to the Lancastrian court.[148] Such denunciation of Henry VI's misgovernment pointed logically to his replacement as king, and the Yorkist lords were probably prepared to be not merely rebels but revolutionaries. Yet to win admittance to London and recognition from the Church they now had to reaffirm their allegiance, and their subsequent capture of Henry at Northampton made them rebels no longer, but loyal subjects. No further appeals were made to the common weal. For York himself it was even more frustrating. Not identified with the programme for reform, and not—as was Warwick—an instinctive populist and rebel, his readiness to claim the throne as of right had now become an embarrassment to his allies.

By 1461, however, the civil war was at last being fought over the rightful title to the crown of Lancaster or York and involved irreconcilable loyalties. How did this affect different strata of political society? For the nobility, loyalty to the Crown was a compound of honour, service, and reward; the demand on their obedience was inescapable, and between 1459 and 1461 fifty-six of the total of seventy peers fought at least once and twenty-two lost their lives in or after combat.[149] The traditional partnership of king and nobility in government, based on mutual interests, fidelity, and respect, was destroyed. Future kings would have a more authoritarian and distrustful attitude towards their leading subjects, and in future the nobility would display a wariness of political commitment and give priority to family survival.[150]

Below the lords, the knights and esquires who formed the kernel of affinities both royal and seigniorial, as retainers and officers, generally found themselves inescapably committed by loyalty and self-interest. Most of the forty-eight knights and esquires attainted after Towton, and probably many of those killed,

---

[148] Texts in *Eng. Chron.* 86–90; Kekewich *et al.* (eds.), *John Vale's Book*, 210–12.

[149] C. F. Richmond, 'The nobility and the Wars of the Roses, 1459–61', *Nott. Med. Stud.* 21 (1977), 71–85; id., 'The nobility and the Wars of the Roses: The parliamentary session of January 1461', *Parlty. Hist.* 18 (1999), 261–9.

[150] McFarlane, *England in the Fifteenth Century*; Watts, *Henry VI and the Politics of Kingship*, 40–5.

were of this kind.[151] Those who merely received annuities, and had no exclusive attachment, faced less compulsion to risk their lives and inheritance by active service, and even families with traditional loyalties to the Lancastrian crown could practise neutrality. That is not to say that the gentry could easily isolate themselves from the lords' divisions. For individuals, much would depend on the prevalence and quality of lordship in their region, the proximity of the war, their own local rivalries and conflicts, and a calculation of their best interests. For a society based on hierarchy and deference, which looked to lordship as the model for and regulator of its own behaviour, aristocratic conflict was deeply unsettling. It seems to have had two divergent effects. The more obvious was to intensify local divisions by giving them national validity; but it may also have imposed restraint, as the dangers to life and livelihood, and to social stability, were foreseen. It has been suggested that the gentry were encouraged to rely on their lateral networks as a means of conflict resolution, where previously they had turned to lordship. By inducing instability, the lords had undermined their role as pillars and arbiters of local society, and both their influence locally and their status nationally were permanently diminished.[152]

Below the ranks of the gentry civil war engaged only an infinitesimal proportion of the population, yet regions, communities, and even families might be seriously divided.[153] Deference was eroded, and the onset of the crisis in 1450 was marked not only by popular rebellion, but by an articulated criticism of government. Verbal doggerel and bills complained of the perversion of law, the denial of justice, the corruption of officials, and the plunder of ordinary subjects. Preoccupied with their quarrels, neither the Crown nor the nobility seriously addressed these problems in the following decade, and in 1460 Yorkist promises of reform found fertile ground in the south-east. How many were thus attracted to fight is impossible to say, but more significant than the military participation of the populace was the widespread judgement that Henry VI had forfeited the authority to rule. The concept that a king ruled for the common good of his subjects and might be called to account had emerged from the pages of princely advice books to become a call for political action in the mouths of subjects. Their assertion in 1450 that Crown and people together constituted the common weal expressed a new conception of the polity of England.[154]

---

[151] *Rot. Parl.* v. 476–8, printed in R. Brooke, *Visits to Fields of Battle* (London, 1857), app. 1, pp. 301–7; Gregory, *Chron.* 217.

[152] Carpenter, *Locality and Polity*, 479; ead., *The Wars of the Roses* (Cambridge, 1997), 149–52, 262–3.   [153] Goodman, *Wars of the Roses*, 202–8.

[154] R. Virgoe, 'The death of William de la Pole, duke of Suffolk', *BJRL* 47 (1964–5), 502.

CHAPTER 16

Conclusion

To pass other than a negative verdict on a century that witnessed the deposition of two kings, the seizure of London twice by popular mobs, final and irreversible defeat in France, and the initiation of religious persecution might seem perverse. Yet the undoubted tensions to which these bear witness can be seen as marking the development from a feudally structured society to a politically integrated one. In these terms we may review the political, economic, and religious developments that have been discussed in this study.

Built into the political relations between the Crown and its subjects was the tension between descending and ascending theories of authority. At its most stark this was between kingship, deriving its authority from God, being answerable solely to Him, and requiring absolute obedience from subjects; and a political community judging both the exercise of royal authority and the measure of obedience to it in the name of the common good. These concepts were inherent in the nature and structure of the monarchical state and were explicitly identified as opposites in 1397–9 and 1459–61 at the time of aristocratic challenges to the Crown. More usually they tended to be accommodated to the needs of government. Thus, while the monarch's sacral and supreme authority set him apart from his nobility, investing him with the power of life and death, and over blood and inheritance, in practice he needed to secure their support and service in central government, as governors of their localities, and as companions in arms. The nobility, for their part, faced tensions between their private lordship and their role as representative of the Crown's authority, and in their competition with each other for royal favour or local control. For them the king had to be both the source of patronage and the regulator of it. Normally the partnership of Crown and nobility in government was mutually supportive; it only dissolved into stark confrontation if the nobility, distrusting the king, attempted to constrain his governing will and violate his sacrality. That they did so in the name of the common good of the realm, invoking the authority of the wider political community, revealed both the weakness of their own position and the ultimate threat to that of the king. Then indeed the unity of the state was endangered.

Whereas the king's relationship with the nobility drew on a long feudal tradition, that with the non-noble political community had acquired institutional form, in parliament, only over the preceding century. There the Commons assumed the role of petitioners for both their individual concerns and the common profit of the realm, and that of assenters to measures which touched their communities, notably legislation and taxation. By the late fourteenth century their demand for good governance was extending to the reform of the body politic and could be construed as challenging the rule of the king and lords, while their specific demands for the reform of the royal household and the resumption of royal gifts were a direct affront to the king's estate. Here the tension between the king's prerogative to rule and the Commons' representative expression of the common good was never directly resolved; or rather, was resolved through parliament's endorsement of the acts of a right-governing king. Thereby an Act of parliament bound all men to obedience. The representative assent rendered by the 'middling' people in parliament drew on their power and authority in political society. Landed gentry, merchants, and professionals like officials and lawyers encompassed a broad range of wealth, status, and experience. They exercised magistracy in rural society and civic government, and Crown and nobility depended on their inherent power and expertise as channels for their own authority. Society could not be governed by diktat from above; only by the assent and participation of this political class. This was the essential nature of Fortescue's 'regal and political rule', the 'mixed monarchy' through which England was governed until 1629.

Not surprisingly the greatest social tensions were in the sector most directly affected by demographic and economic change, agrarian society. The Black Death was a watershed which changed the ratio of land and men, producing higher wages, greater mobility, and pressure from the peasantry for the end of serfdom. The landlords' attempts to contain this through manorial discipline and the legal enforcement of wages and labour provoked social unrest culminating in the revolt of 1381. This was a revolt against lordship, demanding that labour and commodities be regulated through the market rather than the law. As, under economic pressures, this came to be effectively conceded over the next quarter-century, the labouring population became graded by wealth and occupation rather than by legal status, enjoying de facto security of tenure, and a general improvement of living standards. Through their accumulation of land or as estate officials, the wealthier peasantry formed a sub-gentry class of 'yeomen', enfranchised as forty-shilling freeholders for parliamentary elections and jury service and occupying the hundredal and lesser shire offices. Men at this level began to see themselves as part of a political community. Even among the peasantry the notion that the people's labour supported the realm and that the common good encompassed those of the lowest estate gave the revolt of 1381, and even more that of 1450, a political content. Within the villages manorial regulation and leadership now yielded to the community of the parish, organizing its moral discipline and religious life. In these respects the economic transformation had brought a new and wider political consciousness to the labouring classes as well as improved living standards.

Within the towns tensions were generated less by economic crisis than by their government. Ruled generally by a merchant oligarchy which maintained itself by varying methods of closure, it could be challenged by the crafts both over economic regulation and on occasion for control of urban government. Both merchants and crafts organized guilds to regulate their economic activities, as a means of social control and an expression of religious fraternity. Together they broadly constituted the citizenry, the freemen of the town, beyond whom the rest of its population were 'foreigners', without civic rights, including a sizeable pool of marginals and poor. Class tensions obviously existed, but few erupted into violence, either organized or not, except at times of national unrest as in 1381. Immigrant communities were generally insignificant outside London, where the Flemish and Italians were most prone to popular attacks. Towns were generally self-ordering communities whose rulers did not command the armed force required to suppress any major rebellion.

Surprisingly, it was in the religious sphere that dissent was most openly expressed, persistently sustained, and violently suppressed. Paradoxically it was the campaign by both friars and bishops, from the thirteenth century, to increase the direct participation of the laity in worship that stimulated both informed piety and criticism. The laity formed and ran religious fraternities, popularized new cults and devotions, poured their wealth into building and embellishing the friars' churches and those of their parishes, and sought salvation through large-scale endowment of masses for their souls. Criticism of these developments came more from within the Church than outside (though some laity called for disendowment of the wealthier hierarchy), indeed from its intellectual elite, in the university. Wyclif's fundamental critique of the nature of the institutional Church, its accrued doctrines, and contemporary devotional practices, led him to advocate a return to the structures and belief of the Apostolic age, and assert God's immediacy to the individual soul through the Bible. This was the most dramatic conceptual revolution of the late Middle Ages, anticipating Protestantism, but it was not translated (as was the revolt against serfdom) into structural change. The Crown had no inducement to pander to heresy; it valued the Church's support for its sacrality, while the Church needed that of the Crown against anticlericalism and dissent. Crown and Church united to persecute and demonize Lollardy as seditious and heretical, proscribe the translated Bible, and strengthen the national Church as a bastion of orthodoxy. Nonconformity became individual, localized, and lower-class, anticipating the pattern of Laudianism and Puritanism.

Alongside their religiosity, the English were renowned for their bellicose energies. In contrast to earlier centuries, these were directed not against their northern neighbours but to France. With the wealth derived from wool exports, the monarchy could indulge its aristocracy's lust for war and its own imperialist ambitions. In the fourteenth century warfare was organized to satisfy the cult and interest of chivalric society, for honour and profit. Only when war ceased was a territorial settlement proposed (in 1360) which, because it was not based on effective control, quickly fell apart. By 1400 a reaction had set in against both the pretensions of chivalry and war as an instrument of state policy. When it was again embraced by Henry V, war became a national, not merely chivalric, enterprise, directed towards the reintegration of Normandy into the English realm. It also became the vehicle for extending and diffusing the sacrality of kingship into the myth of a holy nation, God's people commissioned to fulfil His purpose. Where Richard II's own sacrality had separated him from his subjects, that of Henry V was used to sanctify a national enterprise. This was a potent, if evanescent, belief, negated by defeat but ready for later revival. The war left a legacy of enduring suspicion and contempt between French and English, propelling English policy towards isolationism. From being a continental and military power under Henry V, England was set to become an insular and naval one.

The changes during this century, as English society contracted in size but diversified in structure and became individually wealthier, produced tension between rulers and ruled and between and within its different orders. That it was able to accommodate these despite political, social, and military crises, and exhibit a high degree of stability and integration, was due partly to its maturity (for it was an old society) and partly to its flexibility. It had come to embrace a continuum of wealth, status, and authority which incorporated as twin concepts both hierarchy and the common good. This society, furnished with enduring structures of government, using a common written language, and articulating its identity in war and religion, gave shape to the English nation for the century and a half that followed.

ROYAL HOUSE OF PLANTAGENET–LANCASTER, 1360–1461

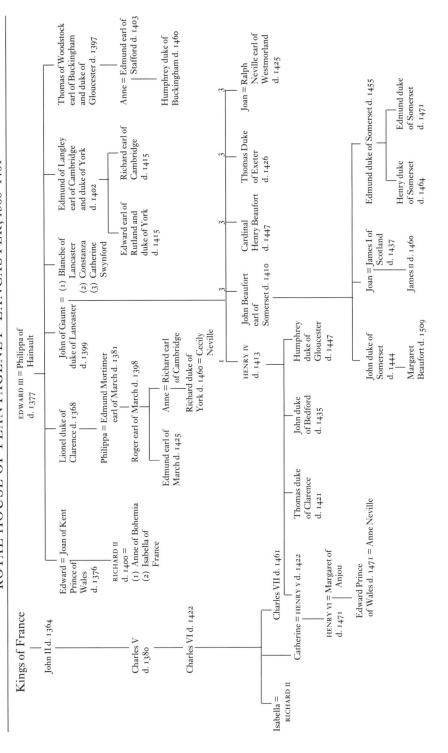

Chronology

1400   Revolt of the earls (Jan.). Death of Richard II (Feb.). Henry IV's expedition to Scotland (Aug.). Outbreak of Welsh revolt (Sept.)

1401   Act *De Heretico Comburendo*; burning of William Sawtre

1402   Battle of Homildon Hill (Aug.)

1403   Rebellion of the Percys; battle of Shrewsbury (21 July)

1404   Succession of John the Fearless (27 Apr.). Glyn Dŵr's alliance with French

1405   Rising and execution of Archbishop Scrope. French invade South Wales

1406   Capture of James I of Scotland. Illness of Henry IV. Long Parliament (Mar.–Dec.)

1407   Murder of Louis of d'Orléans in Paris (23 Nov.)

1409   Council of Pisa

1410   Administration of Henry, prince of Wales (Jan.); burning of John Badby (Mar.)

1411   Earl of Arundel's expedition to Paris (Nov.). Henry IV resumes government

1412   Treaty of Bourges (18 May); duke of Clarence's expedition to Aquitaine (Aug.)

1413   Death of Henry IV; accession of Henry V (20–1 Mar.)

1414   Oldcastle's rising (9–10 Jan.). Council of Constance opens (5 Nov.)

1415   Earl of Cambridge's conspiracy (July); Henry V's invasion of France (3 Aug.); battle of Agincourt (25 Oct.)

1416   Visit of Emperor Sigismund (1 May); naval battle of Seine and relief of Harfleur; Treaty of Canterbury (15 Aug.); tripartite conference at Calais (Sept.)

1417   Henry V's second invasion of France (Aug.); capture of Caen (24 Sept.). Ending of Schism and election of Pope Martin V

1418   Siege of Rouen commences (1 Aug.)

1419   Surrender of Rouen. Murder of John the Fearless at Montereau (10 Sept.)

1420   Treaty of Troyes (21 May); marriage of Henry V and Catherine of France (2 June)

1421   Henry V's last visit to England (1 Feb.–10 June); battle of Baugé and death of Clarence (22 Mar.). Birth of Henry VI (6 Dec.)

1422   Death of Henry V at Vincennes (1 Sept.); death of Charles VII (21 Oct.); accession of Henry VI to dual monarchy. Establishment of conciliar government with Humphrey, duke of Gloucester, as Protector

1423   Battle of Cravant (31 July)

1424   Battle of Verneuil (17 Aug.). Gloucester invades Hainault (Oct.–Apr. 1425)

1425   Confrontation of Gloucester and Bishop Beaufort (Oct.); Bedford returns to England (Dec.)

1427   Bedford and Beaufort return to France (19 Mar.)

1428   English besiege Orléans; death of earl of Salisbury (26 Oct.)

1429 Orléans relieved by Jeanne d'Arc (8 May); battle of Patay (18 June); French advance to Paris. Henry VI crowned at Westminster

1430 Henry VI goes to Normandy (23 Apr.). Jeanne d'Arc captured (24 May)

1431 Jeanne d'Arc burnt in Rouen (30 May); Henry VI crowned in Paris (16 Dec.)

1432 Henry VI returns to England (9 Feb.). Gloucester takes control of government

1433 Bedford returns to England and displaces Gloucester; Lord Cromwell's budget

1434 Bedford returns to France (1 July)

1435 Congress of Arras; Burgundy repudiates the Treaty of Troyes (21 Sept.). Death of Bedford (15 Sept.)

1436 Peasant rebellion in the Pays de Caux; English leave Paris (17 Apr.); duke of Burgundy besieges Calais

1437 Ending of Henry VI's minority

1439 Peace negotiations at Oye (July)

1440 Gloucester's further charges against Beaufort (Feb.); release of duke of Orléans (Nov.); duke of York appointed governor of Normandy

1441 Trial of Eleanor, duchess of Gloucester, for necromancy (Oct.–Nov.)

1443 Last major expedition to France under duke of Somerset (Aug.)

1444 Truce of Tours (28 May)

1445 Marriage of Henry VI to Margaret of Anjou (23 Apr.)

1447 Arrest and death of Humphrey, duke of Gloucester (23 Feb.); death of Cardinal Beaufort

1448 Delivery of Le Mans to French (16 Mar.)

1449 Seizure of Fougères (24 Mar.); Charles VII invades Normandy; fall of Rouen (Oct.)

1450 Battle of Formigny (15 Apr.). Impeachment and arrest of duke of Suffolk; his murder (2 May). Outbreak of Cade's rebellion (June–July); duke of York returns from Ireland (Sept.)

1451 French overrun Gascony

1452 Duke of York in arms at Blackheath (Mar.)

1453 Battle of Castillon (17 July) and fall of Bordeaux. Henry VI falls into coma (Aug.). Birth of Prince Edward (13 Oct.)

1454 Duke of York becomes Protector (3 Apr.). Neville–Percy confrontation in Yorkshire

1455 Henry VI recovers. Battle of St Albans (22 May) with deaths of Somerset and Northumberland. York again Protector (19 Nov.)

1456 York dismissed (25 Feb.); court moves to Coventry

1457 French raid Sandwich (28 Aug.)

1458   Loveday between Yorkist and Lancastrian lords (24 Mar.)

1459   Battle of Blore Heath (23 Sept.); Yorkists routed at Ludford and flee to Ireland
        and Calais; proscribed at 'Parliament of Devils' (Nov.)

1460   Warwick, Salisbury, and March land at Calais (26 June); battle of Northampton
        (10 July); York returns from Ireland (20 Nov.) and attempts to claim throne.
        Battle of Wakefield and deaths of York and Salisbury (30 Dec.)

1461   Queen Margaret's army advances to London; second battle of St Albans
        (17 Feb.). Earl of March's victory at battle of Mortimer's Cross (2 Feb.);
        proclaimed as Edward IV in London and Henry VI deposed (4 Mar.). Total
        defeat of Lancastrian forces at battle of Towton (24 Mar.)

Bibliography

This covers the principal books cited in each chapter. Much further work has been published in articles, both in journals and in composite volumes, and references to these will be found in the footnotes, along with citations from manuscript sources.

PRINTED SOURCES

The main chronicles of the late fourteenth century are now available with translation in Oxford Medieval Texts. They include *The Westminster Chronicle, 1381–94*, ed. L. C. Hector and B. H. Harvey (Oxford, 1982); *Knighton's Chronicle, 1337–1396*, ed. G. H. Martin (Oxford, 1995); *The St Albans Chronicle*, ed. J. Taylor and W. Childs (2003–); *Chronicle of Adam of Usk, 1377–1421*, ed. C. Given-Wilson (1997); *Gesta Henrici Quinti*, ed. F. Taylor and J. S. Roskell (Oxford, 1975); William Worcester, *Itineraries*, ed. J. H. Harvey (Oxford, 1969). Other collections are C. Given-Wilson (ed.), *Chronicles of the Revolution, 1397–1400* (Manchester, 1993), and A. Curry (ed.), *Sources for the Battle of Agincourt* (Woodbridge, 2000). For the fifteenth century, C. L. Kingsford (ed.), *Chronicles of London* (Oxford, 1905); R. Flenley (ed.), *Six Town Chronicles* (Oxford, 1911); *The Great London Chronicle* ed. A. H. Thomas and I. D. Thornley (repr. London, 1983); *An English Chronicle*, ed. J. S. Davies, Camden Society, 64 (1855); *Gregory's Chronicle*, ed. J. Gairdner, Camden Society, new ser., 17 (1876); and *The Brut, or, Chronicles of England*, pt. 2, ed. F. W. Brie, EETS, old ser., 136 (1908) are all in English. For the later fourteenth century *The Anonimalle Chronicle, 1333–1381*, ed. V. H. Galbraith (Manchester, 1927) and *Eulogium Historiarum sive Temporis*, ed. F. S Haydon, 3 vols., Rolls ser., 9, vol. iii. (London, 1863); for the early fifteenth century, *The St Albans Chronicle, 1406–1420*, ed. V. H. Galbraith (Oxford, 1937); and for the mid-century, *John Benet's Chronicle*, ed. G. L. Harriss and M. A. Harriss, in *Camden Miscellany, XXIV*, Camden Society, 4th ser., 9 (London, 1972).

Two notable contemporary tracts are *The Libelle of Englyshe Polycye*, ed. G. Warner (Oxford, 1926) and J. Fortescue, *The Governance of England*, ed. C. Plummer (Oxford, 1885). Private letter collections in English are J. Gairdner (ed.), *The Paston Letters* (Gloucester, 1986); N. Davis (ed.), *Paston Letters and Papers of the Fifteenth Century*, 2 vols. (Oxford, 1971, 1976); C. Carpenter (ed.), *The Armburgh Papers* (Woodbridge, 1998). *The Official Correspondence of Thomas Bekynton*, ed. G. Williams, 2 vols., Rolls ser. (London, 1872) is mainly diplomatic. Of central government records, there are printed *Calendars of the Patent, Close*, and *Fine Rolls* (London); a translation is projected of *Rotuli Parliamentorum*, ed. J. Strachey *et al.* (London, [1783], 1832); but the *Proceedings and Ordinances of the Privy Council of England*, ed. N. H. Nicolas, 6 vols. (London, 1834–7) has not been reprinted.

COMPOSITE VOLUMES

These mainly contain papers delivered at the annual Fifteenth Century Conference.

S. B. Chrimes, C. Ross, and R. Griffiths (eds.), *Fifteenth Century England, 1399–1509* (Manchester, 1972).

C. Ross (ed.), *Patronage, Pedigree and Power* (Gloucester, 1979).

R. A. Griffiths (ed.), *Patronage, the Crown and the Provinces* (Gloucester, 1981).

J. R. Highfield and R. Jeffs (eds.), *The Crown and Local Communities* (Gloucester, 1981).

A. J. Pollard (ed.), *Property and Politics* (Gloucester, 1984).

R. B. Dobson (ed.), *The Church, Politics and Patronage in the Fifteenth Century* (Gloucester, 1984).

M. Jones (ed.), *Gentry and Lesser Nobility* (Gloucester, 1986).

J. Rosenthal and C. Richmond (eds.), *People, Politics and Community* (Gloucester, 1987).

J. Taylor and W. Childs (eds.), *Politics and Crisis in Fourteenth Century England* (Gloucester, 1990).

M. Hicks (ed.), *Profit, Piety and the Professions* (Gloucester, 1990).

J. Kermode (ed.), *Enterprise and Individuals in Fifteenth Century England* (Stroud, 1991).

D. Clayton, R. G. Davies, and P. McNiven (eds.), *Trade, Devotion and Governance* (Stroud, 1994).

C. Barron and N. Saul (eds.), *England and the Low Countries* (Stroud, 1995).

R. H. Britnell and A. J. Pollard (eds.), *The McFarlane Legacy* (Stroud, 1995).

R. E. Archer (ed.), *Crown, Government and People in the Fifteenth Century* (Stroud, 1995).

S. D. Michalove and A. C. Reeves (eds.), *Estrangement, Enterprise and Education* (Stroud, 1998).

A. Curry and E. Matthew (eds.), *Concepts and Patterns of Service in the Late Middle Ages* (Woodbridge, 2000).

M. Hicks (ed.), *Revolution and Consumption in Late Medieval England* (Woodbridge, 2001).

Other collections

C. T. Allmand (ed.), *War, Literature and Politics* (Liverpool, 1976).

C. H. Clough (ed.), *Profession, Vocation and Culture* (Liverpool, 1982).

R. A. Griffiths and J. Sherborne, *Kings and Nobles* (Gloucester, 1986).

R. Horrox (ed.), *Fifteenth Century Attitudes* (Cambridge, 1994).

R. E. Archer and S. K. Walker (eds.), *Rulers and Ruled in Late Medieval England* (London, 1995).

I. CONCEPTS OF GOVERNANCE

W. Ullmann, *Principles of Government and Politics in the Middle Ages* (London, 1961) and R. Eccleshall, *Reason and Order in Politics* (Oxford, 1978) cover the intellectual background. S. B. Chrimes, *English Constitutional Ideas in the Fifteenth Century* (Cambridge, 1936) draws mainly on legal records.

2. THE KING AND THE COURT

M. Vale, *The Princely Court* (Oxford, 2001) is a comparative study covering north-west Europe up to 1400. C. Given-Wilson, *The Royal Household and the King's Affinity* (New Haven, 1986) covers from Edward III to Henry IV; A. R. Myers, *The Household of Edward IV* (Manchester, 1959) reaches back to Henry VI. Court life is described in C. M. Woolgar, *The Great Household in Late Medieval England* (New Haven, 1999); its astrologers in H. M. Carey, *Courting Disaster* (London, 1992); its culture in V. Scatter-good and J. Sherborne (eds.), *English Court Culture in the Late Middle Ages* (London, 1983) and J. Stratford (ed.), *The Lancastrian Court* (Donington, 2003); its military ethos in H. L. Collins, *The Order of the Garter, 1348–1461* (Oxford, 2000). For the artefacts of this period, see the exhibition catalogues: J. J. Alexander and P. Binski, *The Age of Chivalry* (London, 1987) and R. Marks and R. Williamson, *Gothic Art for England, 1400–1547* (London, 2003).

3. CENTRAL GOVERNMENT

A. L. Brown provides a good overall survey in *The Governance of Late Medieval England, 1272–1461* (London, 1989) and there is much useful material for before 1399 in T. F. Tout, *Chapters in the Administrative History of Medieval England*, 6 vols. (Manchester, 1920–33). For the chancery and its personnel, see M. Richardson, *The Medieval Chancery under Henry V*, List and Index Society (London, 1999) and other civil servants are discussed in C. H. Clough (ed.), *Profession, Vocation and Culture in Later Medieval England* (Liverpool, 1982). For the legal system, see J. H. Baker's admirable *Introduction to English Legal History* (London, 1990) and A. Musson and W. Ormrod take a fresh look at the fourteenth century in *The Evolution of English Justice* (London, 1999). A. Harding provides a general study of the courts in *The Law Courts of Medieval England* (London, 1973) and M. Hastings's *The Court of Common Pleas in the Fifteenth Century* (New York, 1947) is more detailed. The operation of the system of criminal justice is discussed in E. Powell, *Kingship, Law and Society* (Oxford, 1989) and P. C. Maddern, *Violence and the Social Order* (Oxford, 1992), though J. G. Bellamy makes a different evaluation of late medieval crime in *Crime and Public Order in England in the Later Middle Ages* (London, 1973) and *Criminal Law and Society in Late Medieval and Tudor England* (Gloucester, 1984). E. W. Ives surveys the legal profession in *The Common Lawyers of Pre-Reformation England* (Cambridge, 1983).

W. M. Ormrod usefully outlines the finances of the English state in R. Bonney (ed.), *The Rise of the Fiscal State in Europe, c.1200–1815* (Oxford, 1999). Statistics for revenues are available in A. Steel, *The Receipt of the Exchequer, 1377–1485* (Cambridge, 1954) and those for wool and cloth exports in E. M. Carus-Wilson and O. Coleman, *England's Export Trade, 1275–1547* (Oxford, 1963). Lists of the taxes levied are in M. Jurkowski, C. L. Smith, and D. Crook, *Lay Taxes in England and Wales, 1188–1688* (London, 1998).

An excellent overview of parliament in this century is provided in R. G. Davies and J. H. Denton (eds.), *The English Parliament in the Middle Ages* (Manchester, 1981), and J. G. Edwards, *The Second Century of the English Parliament* (Oxford, 1979) explores how it functioned. J. S. Roskell has been the leading historian of the English parliament with *The Commons in the Parliament of 1422* (Manchester, 1954), *The Commons and their Speakers in Medieval English Parliaments* (Manchester, 1965), and as overall editor of *The House of Commons, 1386–1421* (Stroud, 1992), which contains his valuable 'Introductory Survey'. The only study of the council covering the whole period is by J. F. Baldwin, *The King's Council during the Middle Ages* (Oxford, 1913), though now seriously out of date in some respects.

For the organization of the army and navy, C. T. Allmand's *The Hundred Years War* (Cambridge, 1988) and *Society at War* (Edinburgh, 1973) provide an excellent short introduction to late medieval warfare, and A. Curry and M. Hughes (eds.), *Arms, Armies amd Fortifications in the Hundred Years War* (Woodbridge, 1999) covers many specific topics. M. H. Keen, *The Laws of War in the Late Middle Ages* (London, 1965) is the best survey of war in legal theory, and R. W. Kaeuper, *War, Justice, and Public Order* (Oxford, 1988) considers its effect on the state. J. Sherborne, *War, Politics and Culture in Fourteenth Century England* (London, 1994) contains studies of military and naval organization, and S. Rose, *The Navy of the Lancastrian Kings*, Navy Records Society (London, 1982) is valuable for the fifteenth century. On the types of ships, see I. Friel, *The Good Ship* (London, 1995).

4. THE NOBILITY

K. B. McFarlane's innovative study on the late medieval nobility posthumously published as *The Nobility of Later Medieval England* (Oxford, 1973) had been preceded by J. M. W. Bean, *The Estates of the Percy Family, 1416–1537* (Oxford, 1958) and G. A. Holmes, *The Estates of the Higher Nobility in the Fourteenth Century* (Cambridge, 1957) and was followed by C. Given-Wilson, *The English Nobility in the Late Middle Ages* (London, 1987) and J. T. Rosenthal, *Patriarchy and Families of Privilege in Fifteenth Century England* (Philadelphia, 1991). Particular noble estates have been studied by C. Rawcliffe, *The Stafford Earls of Stafford and Dukes of Buckingham, 1394–1521* (Cambridge, 1978) and R. Somerville, *History of the Duchy of Lancaster* (London, 1953).

On the domestic culture of the nobility, A. Emery, *Greater Medieval Houses of England and Wales*, 3 vols. (Cambridge, 1997–) provides exhaustive treatment of their dwellings and C. M. Woolgar, *The Great Household in Late Medieval England* (New Haven, 1999) for their style of living, for which see also C. Dyer, *Standards of Living in the Later Middle Ages* (Cambridge, 1989). K. Mertes, *The English Noble Household, 1250–1600* (Oxford, 1988) is a broad survey but not always reliable. D. Bornstein, *Mirrors of Courtesy* (London, 1975) discusses courtesy books, and P. Coss, *The Lady in Medieval England* (Stroud, 1998) deals with the lifestyle of aristocratic women.

The chivalric ethos of the nobility is described by M. H. Keen, *Chivalry* (New Haven, 1984), and J. Barnie, *War in Medieval Society: Social Values and the Hundred Years War* (London, 1974) provides a stimulating discussion. For the Order of the Garter, see J. Vale, *Edward III and Chivalry* (Woodbridge, 1982) and H. L. Collins, *The Order of the Garter, 1348–1461* (Oxford, 2000), while M. G. A. Vale, *War and Chivalry* (London, 1981) argues for the military relevance of chivalric training.

5. AND 6. THE GENTRY AND THE LOCAL POLITY

Numerous studies of the gentry in particular counties have been made in the last twenty years. That for fifteenth-century Warwickshire by C. Carpenter, *Locality and Polity* (Cambridge, 1992) is the most detailed. For Leicestershire in the same period, E. Acheson, *A Gentry Community* (Cambridge, 1992), for Nottinghamshire, S. J. Payling, *Political Society in Lancastrian England* (Oxford, 1991), and for Derbyshire S. M. Wright, *The Derbyshire Gentry in the Fifteenth Century*, viii, (Chesterfield, Derbyshire Record Society, 1983), address the same questions, while C. F. Richmond has scrutinized the best-documented gentry family in *The Paston Family in the Fifteenth Century*, 3 vols. (Cambridge, 1990, 1996; Manchester, 2000). For the later fifteenth century, see A. J. Pollard's survey *North Eastern England during the Wars of the Roses* (Oxford, 1990). There have been fewer county studies for the fourteenth century, the most notable being N. Saul, *Knights and Esquires: The Gloucestershire Gentry in the Fourteenth Century* (Oxford, 1981) and *Scenes from Provincial Life* (Oxford, 1986). The nature and mechanism of retaining is the theme of J. M. W. Bean, *From Lord to Patron* (Pittsburgh, Pa., 1989) and of M. Hicks, *Bastard Feudalism* (London, 1995), while S. K. Walker in *The Lancastrian Affinity, 1361–1399* (Oxford, 1990) and H. Castor in *The King, the Crown, and the Duchy of Lancaster, 1399–1461* (Oxford, 2000) both examine the local context of Lancastrian lordship. The military service of the gentry is examined in M. Keen, *Origins of the English Gentleman* (Stroud, 2002) and *Nobles, Knights and Men at Arms in the Middle Ages* (London, 1996), and by P. Morgan, *War and Society in Medieval Cheshire, 1277–1403*, Chetham Society (Manchester, 1987), the same society being also studied by M. Bennett, *Community, Class and Careerism* (Cambridge, 1983).

On the houses of the gentry, the standard though dated work is by M. Wood, *The English Medieval House* (London, 1965), and the more recent publication of E. Mercer, *English Vernacular Houses* (London, 1975) should be consulted. For education and schooling, the works by N. Orme are standard: *English Schools in the Middle Ages* (London, 1973), *From Childhood to Chivalry* (London, 1984), *Education and Society in Medieval and Renaissance England* (London, 1989), and *Medieval Children* (New Haven, 2000). For literary culture J. Coleman, *English Literature in History, 1350–1400* (London, 1981) is an invaluable introduction, with particular aspects singled out in T. Turville-Petre, *The Alliterative Revival* (Cambridge, 1977), E. Salter, *Fourteenth Century English Poetry* (Oxford, 1983) and W. R. J. Barron, *English Medieval Romance* (London, 1967). For a general conspectus, see D. Wallace (ed.), *The Cambridge History of Medieval English Literature* (Cambridge, 1999). The religious attitudes of the gentry are discussed in J. T. Rosenthal, *The Purchase of Paradise* (London, 1972) and N. Saul, *Death, Art, and Memory in Medieval England* (Oxford, 2000).

For the gentry as a magistracy, see A. Musson and W. Ormrod, *The Evolution of English Justice* (London, 1999) and R. Virgoe, *East Anglian Society and the Political Community* (Norwich, 1997), and for their role as MPs, J. S. Roskell's collected biographies in *Parliament and Politics in Late Medieval England*, 3 vols. (London, 1981–3) and J. S. Roskell, L. Clark, and C. Rawcliffe (eds.), in *The History of Parliament: The House of Commons, 1386–1421*, 4 vols. (Stroud, 1992).

7. AGRARIAN SOCIETY

Agrarian society before the Black Death is surveyed by J. Hatcher and E. Miller, *Medieval England: Rural Society and Economic Change, 1086–1348* (London, 1978) and B. M. S. Campbell (ed.), *Before the Black Death: Studies in the 'Crisis' of the Early Fourteenth Century* (Manchester, 1991). The different approaches of historians are considered in J. Hatcher and M. Bailey, *Modelling the Middle Ages* (Oxford, 2001). All aspects of agrarian society are surveyed in E. Miller (ed.), *The Agrarian History of England and Wales*, iii: *1348–1500* (Cambridge, 1991) and B. M. S. Campbell examines methods of farming in *English Seigniorial Agriculture, 1250–1450* (Cambridge, 2000). Studies of the manorial economy on different estates have been made by C. Dyer, *Lords and Peasants in a Changing Society* (Cambridge, 1980), E. B. Fryde, *Peasants and Landlords in Later Medieval England* (Stroud, 1996), B. Harvey, *Westminster Abbey and its Estates in the Middle Ages* (Oxford, 1977), and R. Hilton, *The English Peasantry in the Later Middle Ages* (Oxford, 1975). The economy of the less manorialized eastern counties can be studied in M. McIntosh, *Autonomy and Community: The Royal Manor of Havering* (Cambridge, 1986), L. R. Poos, *A Rural Society after the Black Death: Essex, 1350–1525* (Cambridge, 1991), M. Bailey, *A Marginal Economy? The East Anglian Breckland in the Late Middle Ages* (Cambridge, 1989), and J. Langdon, *Horses, Oxen, and Technological Innovation* (Cambridge, 1986). Peasant family landholding is discussed by Z. Razi, *Life, Marriage and Death in a Medieval Parish* (Cambridge, 1980), R. M. Smith (ed.), *Land, Kinship, and Life Cycle* (Cambridge, 1984), P. D. A. Harvey (ed.), *The Peasant Land Market in Medieval England* (Oxford, 1984), and C. Howell, *Land, Family, and Inheritance in Transition* (Cambridge, 1983). The causes and consequences of population decline are considered in J. Hatcher, *Plague, Population and the English Economy, 1348–1500* (London, 1977), M. Ormrod and P. Lindley (eds.), *The Black Death in England* (Stamford, 1996), and R. Horrox, *The Black Death* (Manchester, 1994).

For the Peasants' Revolt, B. Dobson translates and comments on the sources in *The Peasants' Revolt of 1381* (London, 1970), and R. H. Hilton and T. H. Aston (eds.), *The English Rising of 1381* (Cambridge, 1984) contains important articles. R. H. Hilton, *Class Conflict and the Crisis of Feudalism* (London, 1985) brings together his articles, and S. Justice, *Writing and Rebellion: England in 1381* (Berkeley, 1994) discusses the literature of revolt. The Robin Hood cycle is edited by R. B. Dobson and J. Taylor, *Rymes of Robyn Hood* (London, 1976), and J. Bellamy, *Robin Hood* (London, 1985) provides a historical survey. The position of women is the theme of M. Mate, *Daughters, Wives, and Widows after the Black Death* (Woodbridge, 1998) and P. J. P. Goldberg, *Women, Work, and Life Cycle in a Medieval Economy* (Oxford, 1992).

8. TRADE, INDUSTRY, AND TOWNS

J. L. Bolton, *The Medieval English Economy, 1150–1550* (London, 1980) provides an overall survey of medieval trade. The standard work on the wool trade is T. H. Lloyd, *The English Wool Trade in the Middle Ages* (Cambridge, 1977), and the same author provides a definitive study in *England and the German Hanse, 1157–1611* (Cambridge,

1991). E. Carus-Wilson, *Medieval Merchant Venturers* (London, 1954) contains studies of the cloth trade and other commercial enterprises, and J. H. Munro, *Wool, Cloth and Gold: The Struggle for Bullion in Anglo-Burgundian Trade (1340–1478)* (Toronto, 1972) deals with relations with the Low Countries. E. Carus-Wilson and O. Coleman, *England's Export Trade, 1275–1547* (Oxford, 1963) provides the essential statistics. The role of internal trade and markets is emphasized in R. H. Britnell, *The Commercialisation of English Society* (Manchester, 1996). J. Blair and N. Ramsay (eds.), *English Medieval Industries* (London, 1991) provides authoritative studies of the techniques, while A. R. Bridbury, *Medieval English Clothmaking* (London, 1982) offers a broad evaluation of its economic role. H. Swanson, *Medieval Artisans* (Oxford, 1989) discusses their social and industrial role.

All aspects of medieval town life are covered by the contributors to D. Palliser (ed.), *The Cambridge Urban History of Britain*, i (Cambridge, 2000), and there are shorter surveys by S. Reynolds, *English Medieval Towns* (Oxford, 1977) and H. Swanson, *Medieval British Towns* (London, 1999). A number of seminal articles are collected in R. Holt and G. Rosser (eds.), *The Medieval Town* (London, 1999). The merchant class is investigated in S. Thrupp, *The Merchant Class of Medieval London* (Chicago, 1948), and J. Kermode, *Medieval Merchants: York, Beverley, and Hull* (Cambridge, 1998). Both P. Nightingale, *A Medieval Mercantile Community* (London, 1995) (on the Grocers' Company of London) and M. Kowaleski, *Local Markets and Regional Trade in Medieval Exeter* (Cambridge, 1995) cover a wider range than their titles suggest. The most important studies of individual provincial towns are R. H. Britnell, *Growth and Decline in Colchester, 1300–1525* (Cambridge, 1986), S. H. Rigby, *Medieval Grimsby: Growth and Decline* (Hull, 1993), C. Platt, *Medieval Southampton* (London, 1973), and R. S. Gottfried, *Bury St Edmunds and the Urban Crisis, 1290–1539* (Princeton, 1982). There are good studies of London's suburbs in G. Rosser, *Medieval Westminster* (Oxford, 1989) and M. Carlin, *Medieval Southwark* (London, 1996).

9. THE INSTITUTIONAL CHURCH

Both W. A. Pantin, *The English Church in the Fourteenth Century* (Cambridge, 1955) and A. Hamilton Thompson, *The English Clergy and their Organisation in the Late Middle Ages* (Oxford, 1947) provide authoritative surveys. E. F. Jacob, *Essays in the Conciliar Epoch* (Manchester, 1943) and M. Harvey, *England, Rome and the Papacy 1417–64* (Manchester, 1993) have a similar focus. K. Edwards, *The English Secular Cathedrals in the Middle Ages*, 2nd edn. (Manchester, 1967) and D. Lepine, *A Brotherhood of Canons Serving God* (Woodbridge, 1995) cover the secular foundations, while B. Dobson, *Durham Priory, 1400–1450* (Cambridge, 1973) and B. Harvey, *Living and Dying in England, 1100–1540* (Oxford, 1993) deal with the life of leading monastic houses. D. Knowles, *The Religious Orders in England*, vols. ii and iii (Cambridge, 1955, 1959) remains the standard account of English monasticism. E. Power, *Medieval English Nunneries* (Cambridge, 1922) remains indispensable for organization, with M. Olivas, *The Convent and the Community in Late Medieval England* (Woodbridge, 1998) more concerned with spiritual life.

For the universities, see A. B. Cobban, *The Medieval English Universities* (Aldershot,

1988), D. R. Leader, *A History of the University of Cambridge*, i (Cambridge, 1988), and J. I. Catto and R. Evans (eds.), *The History of the University of Oxford*, ii: *Late Medieval Oxford* (Oxford, 1992). For the students, see A. B. Emden, *Biographical Register of the University of Oxford to 1500*, 3 vols. (Oxford, 1957). On the Perpendicular style, J. H. Harvey, *The Perpendicular Style, 1330–1485* (London, 1978) and C. Wilson, *The Gothic Cathedral* (London, 1992) should be first consulted.

10. RELIGION, DEVOTION, AND DISSENT

R. N. Swanson, *Church and Society in Late Medieval England* (Oxford, 1989), id., *Religion and Devotion in Europe, 1215–1515* (Cambridge, 1995), and id., *Catholic England* (Manchester, 1993) provide an excellent introduction. E. Duffy, *The Stripping of the Altars* (New Haven, 1992) is a vivid evocation of devotional practices. A. D. Brown, *Popular Piety in Late Medieval England* (Oxford, 1995) examines religion in the Salisbury diocese, and N. Tanner *The Church in Late Medieval Norwich, 1370–1532* (Toronto, 1984) likewise in East Anglia. M. Rubin's study of the mass in *Corpus Christi* (Cambridge, 1991), D. J. F. Crouch, *Piety, Fraternity and Power* (Woodbridge, 2000), and K. Wood-Legh, *Perpetual Chantries in Britain* (Cambridge, 1965) all deal with intercession and commemoration. The English mystics are scrutinized by D. Knowles, *The English Mystical Tradition* (London, 1961) and M. Glasscoe, *English Medieval Mystics: Games of Faith* (London, 1993), and northern spirituality by J. Hughes, *Pastors and Visionaries* (Woodbridge, 1988). C. Atkinson, *Margery Kempe: Mystic and Pilgrim* (Ithaca, NY, 1983) is one among many studies of the subject.

Wyclif and Lollardy have attracted much attention. K. B. McFarlane, *John Wycliffe and the Beginnings of English Nonconformity* (London, 1952) offers the best introduction and a distinctive approach, and his *Lancastrian Kings and Lollard Knights* (Oxford, 1972) raised new questions. A. Kenny (ed.), *Wycliffe in his Times* (Oxford, 1986) contains valuable essays; G. Leff, *Heresy in the Later Middle Ages* (Manchester, 1967) expounds Wyclif's thought, and K. Ghosh, *The Wycliffite Heresy* (Cambridge, 2002) its later development. A. Hudson, *The Premature Reformation* (Oxford, 1988) is an extended investigation of Lollardy, and her *Lollards and their Books* (London, 1985) contains particular studies. Both J. A. F. Thomson, *The Later Lollards, 1414–1520* (Oxford, 1965) and M. Aston's two volumes of essays *Lollards and Reformers* (London, 1984) and *Faith and Fire* (London, 1993) connect Lollardy to the Reformation.

11. ENGLAND, FRANCE, AND CHRISTENDOM, 1360–1413

The Treaty of Brétigny and the warfare of the 1360s are well surveyed in J. Sumption, *Trial by Fire* (London, 1999). Relations with Brittany are covered in M. Jones, *Ducal Brittany, 1364–1399* (Oxford, 1970). For the Black Prince in Aquitaine, see M. Barber, *Edward, Prince of Wales and Aquitaine* (London, 1978), and for the Spanish theatre, P. E. Russell, *The English Intervention in Spain and Portugal* (Oxford, 1955). J. J. N. Palmer, *England, France and Christendom, 1377–99* (London, 1972) provides a coherent survey of English foreign relations.

12. RULING ENGLAND, 1360–1413

C. Given-Wilson, *The Royal Household and the King's Affinity* (London, 1986) covers the whole period. G. Holmes discusses the issues in *The Good Parliament* (London, 1975), and on the role of John of Gaunt, see A. Goodman, *John of Gaunt* (London, 1992). N. Saul, *Richard II* (New Haven, 1997) is now the standard work on the reign. There are collections of essays by F. R. Du Boulay and C. Barron (eds.), *The Reign of Richard II* (London, 1971), A. Goodman and J. Gillespie (eds.), *Richard II: The Art of Kingship* (Oxford, 1999), and J. Gillespie (ed.), *The Age of Richard II* (Stroud, 1997). Studies of the political role of the nobility have been made by J. S. Roskell in *The Impeachment of Michael de la Pole* (Manchester, 1984), by A. Tuck in *Richard II and the English Nobility* (London, 1973), and by A. Goodman in *The Loyal Conspiracy* (London, 1971). M. Bennett, *Richard II and the Revolution of 1399* (Stroud, 1999) deals with the end of the reign. For the reign of Henry IV, J. L. Kirby, *Henry IV of England* (London, 1970) provides a political narrative, and P. McNiven, *Heresy and Politics in the Reign of Henry IV* (Woodbridge, 1987) explores the theme of dissent. P. Strohm, *England's Empty Throne* (New Haven, 1998) also looks at challenges to Henry's title.

13. ENGLAND AND HER NEIGHBOURS

On the English in Ireland, J. F. Lydon, *The Lordship of Ireland in the Middle Ages* (Dublin, 1972) is a comprehensive introduction, and his study *The English in Medieval Ireland* (Dublin, 1984) is valuable. R. F. Frame, *English Lordship in Ireland, 1318–1361* (Oxford, 1982) provides the necessary context. The most up-to-date account of this period is by A. Cosgrove, *Late Medieval Ireland, 1370–1541* (Dublin, 1981) and in *A New History of Ireland*, ii: *1169–1534* (Oxford, 1987; 2nd impression 1993) under his editorship. For Wales, the period up to 1415 is authoritatively covered by R. R. Davies in a series of major studies: *Lordship and Society in the March of Wales, 1282–1400* (Oxford, 1978), *The Age of Conquest: Wales, 1063–1415* (Oxford, 1987), and *The Revolt of Owain Glyn Dŵr* (Oxford, 1995). For post-1415, see T. B. Pugh, *The Marcher Lordships of South Wales, 1415–1536* (Cardiff, 1963) and R. A. Griffiths, *King and Country: England and Wales in the Fifteenth Century* (London, 1991). Both R. Nicholson, *Scotland: The Later Middle Ages* (Edinburgh, 1974) and A. Grant, *Independence and Nationhood: Scotland, 1306–1469* (London, 1984) are excellent surveys. C. J. Neville, *Violence, Custom and Law* (Edinburgh, 1998) studies the border and A. Pollard, *North Eastern England* and J. Bean, *The Estates of the Percy Family* (both cited above), provide the background to the Neville-Percy feud.

14. THE ENGLISH IN FRANCE, 1413–1453

Henry V's conquests are admirably covered in C. T. Allmand, *Henry V* (London, 1992) and both M. Bennett, *Agincourt 1415* (Botley, 1991) and A. Curry (ed.), *Agincourt 1415* (Stroud, 2000) deal with the battle. R. A. Newhall's classic study *The English Conquest of Normandy, 1416–24* (New York, 1924; repr. 1971) is followed by C. T. Allmand,

Lancastrian Normandy, 1415–1450 (Oxford, 1983) and G. L. Thompson, *Paris and its People under English Rule* (Oxford, 1991). English rule in Gascony is covered in M. G. Vale, *English Gascony, 1399–1453* (Oxford, 1970). For English relations with Brittany, see G. Knowlson, *Jean V, Duc de Bretagne et l'Angleterre* (Cambridge, 1964) and with Burgundy, R. Vaughan, *John the Fearless* (London, 1966) and *Philip the Good* (London, 1970), and elsewhere by J. Ferguson, *English Diplomacy, 1422–1461* (Oxford, 1972) and J. C. Dickinson, *The Congress of Arras, 1435* (Oxford, 1955). A. Pollard, *John Talbot and the War in France, 1427–53* (London, 1983) studies the defence of Normandy.

15. RULING ENGLAND, 1413–1461

A. Pollard, *Late Medieval England, 1399–1509* (Harlow, 2000) is the most up-to-date general survey. C. T. Allmand's *Henry V* (London, 1992) and G. L. Harriss (ed.), *Henry V: The Practice of Kingship* (Oxford, 1985) deal with Henry's government, for which, see also T. B. Pugh, *Henry V and the Southampton Plot of 1415* (Southampton, 1988) and E. Powell, *Kingship, Law, and Society* (Oxford, 1989). Studies which cover the whole of Henry VI's reign are B. P. Wolffe, *Henry VI* (London, 1981), R. A. Griffiths, *The Reign of King Henry VI* (London, 1981), and J. Watts, *Henry VI and the Politics of Kingship* (Cambridge, 1996). G. L. Harriss, *Cardinal Beaufort* (Oxford, 1989) presents a leading figure of the period up to 1443, and P. A. Johnson, *Duke Richard of York, 1411–1460* (Oxford, 1988) and M. A. Hicks, *Warwick the Kingmaker* (Oxford, 1998) those at the end of the period. I. M. Harvey, *Jack Cade's Rebellion of 1450* (Oxford, 1991) and R. L. Storey, *The End of the House of Lancaster* (London, 1966) examine aspects of the break-up of the regime. M. C. Carpenter, *The Wars of the Roses* (Cambridge, 1997) analyses political causes, and A. Goodman, *The Wars of the Roses* (London, 1981) military strategy, while K. B. McFarlane, *England in the Fifteenth Century* (London, 1981) has many seminal papers.

Index

Abberbury, Sir Richard 193, 453
Abbeville (Somme) 411, 543
Abbey of the Holy Ghost 371
Abergavenny (Mon.) 521
Aberystwyth (Cards.) castle 522–3, 526, 636
Abingdon (Oxon.) 283, 293, 398
Acton, Sir Roger 394
affinity, royal 9, 28–30, 470–1, 490, 494–7, 504, 606, 638, 648
    magnate 187–97, 463, 470, 487, 490, 494, 497, 532, 570, 592, 626, 648
Agincourt (Pas-de-Calais), battle (1415) 31, 33–4, 87, 133, 176, 543–4, 550–2, 587, 591–2
d'Ailly, Pierre 431
Albany, Robert Stewart, 1ˢᵗ duke of (1398–1420) 531–3
Albany, Murdach Stewart, 2ⁿᵈ duke of (1420–25) 532–3, 590
Albergati, Nicolo, cardinal 567
Albert of Bavaria 418
Albret, lordship 408
Albret, Charles d', constable of France 430, 543
alehouses 244, 247, 249, 299
Alençon (Orne) 571
Alençon, Jean II, duke of (d. 1476) 561, 576
Alexander V, pope (1409–10) 432
Alexander de Villa Dei, *Doctrinale* 155
aliens 309
    hostility to 439, 597, 637–8, 652
    hosting of 268–9
Alington, Robert 383, 388
Aljubarotta (Spain) battle (1385) 415, 456
Alkerton, Richard 390
Alnwick (Northumberland) castle 108, 529
Alnwick, William, bishop of Lincoln (1436–49) 284, 319, 321, 397–8, 596, 600, 604
Amiens (Somme) 546
    negotiations at 421
Ampthill (Beds.) castle 102, 110, 134, 627, 629
Andrew, Richard 35
Angers (Maine-et-Loire) 550, 552, 576

d'Angle, Guichard, earl of Huntingdon (1377–80) 122
Angoulême, Jean, count of 134
Angus, George Douglas, earl of (1397–1402) 532
Anjou, Charles of, count of Maine 575, 577
Anjou, René, duke of (d. 1480) 576, 578
Anne St 369
Anne of Bohemia, queen of England (1382–94) 15, 37, 422, 465, 469–70, 477
Anne of Burgundy, duchess of Bedford (d. 1432) 40, 555, 561, 566
Anne of Woodstock, countess of Stafford (d. 1438) 103–4, 206
annuities, retaining by 19–20, 23, 28–9, 61, 189–92, 446, 479, 483, 495, 498, 500, 606, 645, 649
Anonimalle Chronicle 70
Anthony St 124
Antwerp 269
Appellants 32, 37, 73, 304, 306, 315–16, 420, 463–6, 469, 471–2, 475, 479–80, 485, 530
Appleby, Sir Edmund 152–3
Appulyerd, William 194
Aquinas, Thomas, St 4, 6, 332, 345, 368, 381
Aquitaine, duchy of 86, 88, 413–14, 419, 421, 430, 433, 505
arable cultivation 209–14, 216–22
arbitration procedure 198–9
Arblaster, Thomas 526
archdeacons, visitations by 356–8
Arden (Warw.) 139, 141, 212, 215, 224
Ardern, Robert 201
Ardres (Pas-de-Calais), royal meeting at (1396) 423
Argentan (Orne) 546, 571, 583
Aristotle, *Politics* 4, 6, 12, 345
Armagnac, Bernard, count of (1391–1418) 427, 429–30, 544–6
Armagnac family 408, 413
Armagnac, Jean IV, count of (1418–50) 575–6, 585
Armagnac supporters 545–6, 548
Armburgh family, letters 47

DATE DUE